CHAMBERS

CHILDREN'S ILLUSTRATED DICTIONARY

CHAMBERS

CHILDREN'S ILLUSTRATED DICTIONARY

Editor-in-Chief
John Grisewood

Chambers

Editor-in-Chief
John Grisewood

Senior Editor
Debra Miller

Text Editors
Nicola Barber, Richard Northcott

Text Database
Catherine Schwarz, George Davidson
Elaine Higgleton, Howard Sargeant, Anne Seaton

Text Input
Tracey McNerney, Ruth Barratt, Clive Barratt

Proof Reader
Eleanor Martlew

Designers
Siân Williams, David Anstey, Earl Neish, Smilkja Surla, Nigel Bradley

Additional Artwork Preparation
Julian Ewart, Janet Woronkowicz, Matthew Gore, Andy Archer, Narinder Sahotay

Artwork Research
Robert Perry, Bernard Nussbaum

Production Manager
Susan Latham

Production Assistant
Selby Sinton

CHAMBERS
An imprint of Larousse plc
Elsley House, 24-30 Great Titchfield Street, London W1P 7AD

First published by Chambers 1994
2 4 6 8 10 9 7 5 3

Copyright © Larousse plc 1994

The text for the dictionary entries has been abridged and adapted from the New Edition of *Chambers Pocket Dictionary* published in 1992.

A CIP catalogue record for this book is available from the British Library.

ISBN 0 550 10651 0

Printed in Italy

WELCOME TO YOUR DICTIONARY

Any good dictionary must of course be useful. At the very least it should give the correct spelling of a word, the meaning (or different meanings) of a word and the pronunciation. A dictionary can also give the part of speech to which a word belongs, it can give examples of how a word is used in context, it may explain how certain words originated. Some dictionaries warn readers of confusable words (*affect* and *effect* for example) and may even give an opinion on correct grammar and punctuation.

The Chambers Children's Illustrated Dictionary has all these features to the full. Moreover, it is a completely new and up-to-date dictionary; in some ways it is quite unlike any other children's dictionary. While we believe that this dictionary is outstandingly useful, we also think that it is thoroughly friendly and enjoyable to use, whether for browsing or purposefully consulting. But what makes it so different from other dictionaries are the superb illustrations and diagrams and the wealth of encyclopedic information it contains.

We hope that this reliable, lively, and imaginative dictionary and reference book will show how much fun learning about words and the world around us can be.

John Grisewood

HOW TO MAKE THE MOST OF YOUR DICTIONARY

Chambers Children's Illustrated Dictionary is an up-to-date dictionary combined with a basic encyclopedia. You can have fun finding out about the history and meaning of words, and enrich your vocabulary and word power. By following the 'paragraphs of knowledge' you can find out more about the world around you, its people and its places. Become a better speller, a better reader, a better writer, a better speaker, and better informed.

Chambers Children's Illustrated Dictionary is a completely new dictionary – not some revision of an old work. It is right up-to-date in its coverage of the language of today, especially the terms used in science, technology and computing. The dictionary is full of useful features which make it an exciting adventure to explore words and track down information.

Full colour topic feature boxes provide a highly visual, in-depth look at selected subjects.

Guide words give the first and last entry on each double-page spread for speedy reference.

A pronunciation guide appears regularly throughout.

Discover the history of a word's origins and the difference between confusable words, from the blue boxes.

Consult the orange 'Aside columns' for tips on how to use English well.

Coloured boxes of vocabulary lists and definitions assemble basic information on key subjects.

Carefully chosen illustrations with informative captions and labels tell you more about the word.

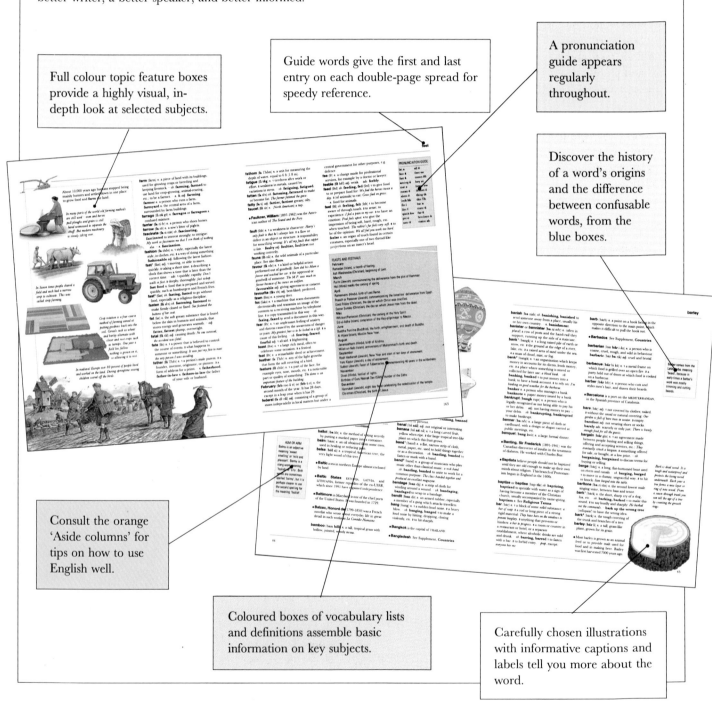

The headword printed in **bold type** shows how the word is spelt. All headwords are in alphabetical order.

Follow the 'paragraphs of knowledge' for:
- More encyclopedic information on the headword.
- Basic facts about people and places.

Cross references in SMALL CAPITAL LETTERS identify related words in the dictionary.

Irregular and alternative plural forms of nouns are given: **GOOSE, GEESE; CACTUSES or CACTI**. The plural of regular nouns are formed by adding *-s*.

Sub-headwords follow the main headword and have their own definitions.

Alternative spellings are given in **bold type**.

A repeated spelling with a little number above the headword means that there are two or more words spelt in the same way but with different meanings. They are *homographs*.

You are told how to pronounce the word. The part in black type shows where the stress falls. Where a word has more than one way of being pronounced, these are shown.

Other forms of adjectives, the comparative and superlative, are shown using the addition *-er* and *-est* where the spelling of the main word changes. So *harder* and *hardest* are not given but *cagier, cagiest* are. Some longer adjectives take *more* and *most* instead of *-er* and *-est: more successful; most successful*.

The headword's part of speech appears in abbreviated form and is printed in *italic: n., vb., adj., adv., pron., conj., prep., interj.* for noun, verb, adjective, adverb, pronoun, conjunction, preposition.

because (bi **köz**) *conj.* for the reason that: *I can't write the letter because I don't have any paper.*

●**Becket, Thomas** (1118-70) was Archbishop of CANTERBURY. He was murdered for opposing Henry the Second's attempts to control the clergy. He was made a saint in 1173.

bee (bē) *n.* a type of four-winged, stinging insect; some species live in large groups and make honey. — **a bee in your bonnet** an idea which has become an obsession.

belly (**be** li) *n.* **bellies** the part of the body containing the organs used for digesting food.

belong (bi **long**) *vb.* **belonging, belonged**
1 to be the property or right of: *This book belongs to me.* **2** to be a member of a group, etc.
belongings *n.* (*plural*) personal possessions.

bias (**bī** ås) *n.* a prejudice.
biased or **biassed** *adj.* favouring one side.

big (big) *adj.* **bigger, biggest** large or largest in size, weight, or number.

bill¹ (bil) *n.* **1** a piece of paper stating the amount of money owed for goods or services received.
2 a written plan for a proposed law.

bill² (bil) *n.* a bird's beak.

The definition is the part of the entry that tells you what the headword means.

An example sentence or phrase after a definition shows how the word is used. It is printed in *italic* type.

Idioms appear in **bold type** at the end of an entry. An idiom is a phrase with a different meaning from that of its individual words.

Other forms of verbs are shown. They are the present participle: **belonging**; and the past tense and past participle: **belonged**.

Numbered definitions each give a different meaning or use of the word. Nouns, verbs, and adjectives are grouped and numbered.

FROM ENGLISC TO ENGLISH

In AD 408 the Roman army withdrew from Britain leaving the country in the charge of the native British, a people of Celtic origin. Very soon Britain began to be invaded and settled by a new people from Scandinavia and northern Germany. We call them the Anglo-Saxons and they spoke Old English, a Germanic language and ancestor of the English we speak today. By the end of the 5th-century 'coming of the Saxons' much of what is now England had submitted to the newcomers. The British were driven into Wales and Cornwall. Who among those early Saxons could ever have imagined that 1,500 years later their speech would have become the international language of commerce, science, technology, and diplomacy? Or that it would be the main language of a vast new continent – North America – which was to remain unknown and undiscovered by Europeans for another 1,000 years and more?

So what kind of language was Old English? It was a mixture of the language of the Anglo-Saxon invaders and that of the later Viking invaders and settlers. In 890, King Alfred the Great wrote a preface to a translation of a book written by Pope Gregory. Here is what Alfred wrote in what was then called *Englisc*:

Ælfred kyning hateth gretan Waeferth biscep his
Alfred the king bids greet bishop Waeferth with his
wordum luflice ond freondlice.
words lovingly and friendly.

At a glance this looks very little like the English we know. But look closer and you will see likenesses between *kyning, gretan, biscep, wordum, luflice,* and *freondlice* with our modern *king, greet, bishop, word, lovely,* and *friendly*.

After Alfred had written this the peace of England was shattered by more Viking invasions of Danes and Norwegians and in 1066 the country was conquered by the French-speaking Normans under William. William 'the conqueror' gave all the important jobs in government, law, and the Church to Normans. For the next two hundred years two languages were spoken in England: the court spoke French, the ordinary people spoke English. Almost all writing was in Norman French or Latin.

Many thought the English of the ordinary people to be a 'rough, uncouth language'. Nevertheless poets continued to write in it. Here is an example from the 13th century:

Sumer is icumen in
Lhude sing cuccu;
Groweth sed and bloweth med
And springth the wude nu.
Sing cuccu . . .

At the end of the 14th century England's first great poet, Geoffrey Chaucer, wrote *The Canterbury Tales*. One hundred years later, William Caxton set up his printing press in London. One of the books he published was Malory's *Morte d'Arthur*. Here is an extract with the spelling modernized:

Then the king got his spear in both his hands, and ran towards Sir Mordred, crying and saying: Traitor, now is thy death-day come. And when Sir Mordred saw King Arthur, he ran until (unto) him with his sword drawn in his hand. And there King Arthur smote Sir Mordred under the shield, with a foin (thrust) of his spear, throughout the body, more than a fathom.

William the Conqueror's armies crushed any revolt by English rebels. For nearly three centuries French was the language of England's rulers; but English survived and evolved among the peasantry

Geoffrey Chaucer (*c.* 1340-1400) – his works were among the first to be written and printed in the English language. He is regarded as one of England's greatest poets.

MIXED ENGLISH

English is very adaptable and keeps up with the times. In its long history it has been enriched by words from other languages – with *cotton, sofa,* and *syrup* from Arabic; *barbecue* and *hammock* from the Caribbean; *deck* and *yacht* from Dutch, plus words from Irish, German, Hebrew, Japanese, and Spanish, and thousands of words derived from Greek (*alphabet, geography, character, philosophy*) and many more thousands from Latin (*circus, exit, index, nil*). Despite all this enrichment, English is basically a mixture of two main languages, Old English and Latin-based Norman French. Old English provided the language with basic essential words: parts of the body, names of near relations, colours, names of wild animals, and geographical features. Norman French gave English new ways of expressing more abstract ideas and emotions: *charity, grace, passion, intellect* are examples. Some 'foreign' words have duplicated Old English words – 'folk' (Old English) and 'people' (Norman French); 'wed' and 'marry'; 'freedom' and 'liberty'; 'forgive' and 'pardon' are some examples. And the English pig turned into 'pork', and sheep into 'mutton' when it was served at the Norman rulers' tables.

It is not difficult to recognize this as the English we know today. The changes to the language that have since taken place are not so great as those that happened to English from the time of Alfred to Caxton's day.

Although Caxton in his printed books helped to provide a regular way of spelling, people still spelled very much as they liked. Here is a letter that Lady Harley wrote to her son at Oxford University in 1639:

My deare Ned, I beleeue (believe) you are confident that you are more deare to me, thearefore thinke it not strange, if I am stuedious and carefull; that your peace should be kept with your God. whous favor is better than life. I longe to see you, and I hope I shall doo it shortly. I hope before this you haue reseued (received) your hate (hat) and stockens, but Burigh is sometime ngligent. Your father is thanke God well; he ride abroode. In hast I giue this ascurance that I am your affectionat mother.

The erratic spelling of those like Lady Harley was one of the reasons that Samuel Johnson brought out his great English dictionary in 1755. Since then our spelling has with a few minor changes (notably in American spelling) remained unchanged. But our pronunciations are very different. And like living human beings and the places they inhabit, our language is constantly changing and being enriched by its travels to foreign lands. English has a rich and fascinating past – the language of poets and orators (of Shakespeare and Whitman, of Lincoln and Churchill), of thinkers and scientists, of business people and teachers. It is a language which we should love and cherish. It is part of our heritage and our future. It is our duty to use it well and to look after it.

In 1474 William Caxton printed the first book in English.

SOME HELPFUL NOTES

We have decided to use the -ize ending in verbs such as *recognize, economize*. The -ise ending is equally correct and this spelling follows the entries. To spell the present participle and past participle with an *s* simply replace the *z* in *-izing, ized* with the *s*.

Many derivatives are formed by adding a word-ending (suffix) such as *-ly* or *-ness* to a headword. Such words are not defined unless you cannot work out their meaning from the headword. Indeed, many adverbs formed by adding *-ly* have been omitted.

Below the entry for the headword, there may be entries for one or more related words:
accomplish followed on separate lines by
accomplished and **accomplishment**. These are called subheads and are always defined.

Abbreviations used in the Dictionary

AD anno domini
adj. adjective
adv. adverb
BC before Christ
c. circa (Latin) about
cm centimetre
conj. conjunction
e.g. exempli gratia (Latin) for example
etc. etcetera (Latin) and so on
i.e. id est (Latin) that is
interj. interjection
kg kilogram
km kilometre
m metre
n. noun
prep. preposition
pron. pronoun
US United States
vb. verb

Where to break words

The pronunciation after each headword shows how words are broken up into syllables (a part of a word that can be pronounced on its own). *Tiger* for instance has two syllables, *ti* and *ger*. But to break a word with a hyphen so that it may be split over two lines of text does not always mean simply splitting the word into its syllables. Here are just a few guidelines:
● Break a word that is made of two nouns (a compound) at the end of the first word; so you would break *heartbeat* as *heart-beat* and *pothole* as *pot-hole*. You can probably work out where the hyphen would be best placed in these words: *armchair, brickwork, crossword, downhill, fairyland, milestone,* and *teenager*.

● Insert a hyphen after prefixes and before suffixes: *anti-climax, dis-prove, inter-national, trans-port, child-hood, hope-less, use-ful, mis-guided*.
● Insert a hyphen where a word breaks naturally: *sim-ple, car-toon, dol-drums*.
● It should be possible to pronounce correctly the first part of the word as it stands: *travel-ling, glor-ious*. A general rule is to break between two or more consonants coming together: *abs-cond, chil-dren, estab-lish, prob-lem, whist-ling*.
● Here are four examples of bad word breaks: *read-just, the-rapist, leg-end,* and *reap-pear*.

Americans accept some word breaks which are not approved by the British.

Pronunciation guide

Each headword in your dictionary is followed by a guide showing you how to pronounce the word. Below is a list of the symbols we use and the sounds they represent.

a	fat	**j**	jump	**o̊**	demon
ä	fast	**k**	cake	**p**	pen
ā	fate	**kw**	quick	**r**	red
å	among	**ks**	box	**s**	sand, mice
b	ball	**l**	lip	**t**	tip
ch	watch	**m**	milk	**th**	thing
d	dip	**n**	net	**Th**	this
e	met	**ng**	wing	**u**	but
ē	mean	**ngk**	sink	**ū**	mute
e̊	silent	**o**	got	**û**	fur
f	fish	**ō**	note	**ů**	brochure
g	goat	**ö**	all	**v**	very
h	home	**oo**	foot	**w**	win
hh	loch	**o̅o̅**	moon	**y**	yes
i	fin	**oi**	boy	**z**	zoo, bees
ī	line	**ow**	house	**zh**	vision

The syllable that is stressed in a word is shown in **bold** type. For example, in abdicate (**ab** di kāt), the first syllable is stressed.

Those symbols that are different from the letters they represent, are shown in a pronunciation guide on pages throughout your dictionary.

PRONUNCIATION GUIDE	
fat a	all ö
fate ā	foot oo
fast ä	moon o̅o̅
among å	boy oi
met e	house ow
mean ē	demon o̊
silent e̊	**thing th**
loch hh	**this Th**
fin i	but u
line ī	mute ū
quick kw	fur û
got o	brochure ů
note ō	vision zh

Aa

a or **an** the indefinite article, used before a noun: *a fossil; an elephant*.

aardvark (**ärd** värk) *n.* an African animal with a long snout, that feeds on ants.

abacus (**ab** å kŭs) *n.* a frame holding a number of wires along which small balls can be moved, used for counting.

abandon (å **ban** dŏn) *vb.* **abandoning, abandoned 1** to give up completely: *Never abandon hope*. **2** to leave a person, etc. usually intending not to return.

abate (å **bāt**) *vb.* **abating, abated** to become or make less strong or severe.

abbey (**ab** i) *n.* **abbeys 1** a group of monks or nuns living as a community. **2** the buildings occupied by such a community.

abbreviate (å **brē** vi āt) *vb.* **abbreviating, abbreviated** to shorten; to represent a long word by a shortened form: *Dr is an abbreviation of doctor.* – *n.* **abbreviation**.

abdicate (**ab** di kāt) *vb.* **abdicating, abdicated 1** to give up the right to the throne. **2** to refuse to carry out your responsibilities. – *n.* **abdication**.

abdomen (**ab** dŏ mĕn) *n.* **1** the front part of the body containing the stomach and other digestive organs. **2** the rear part of the body of insects and crabs, etc.

● **Aberdeen** is an ancient university town in north-eastern SCOTLAND. Once a rich fishing port, its wealth now comes from North Sea oil.

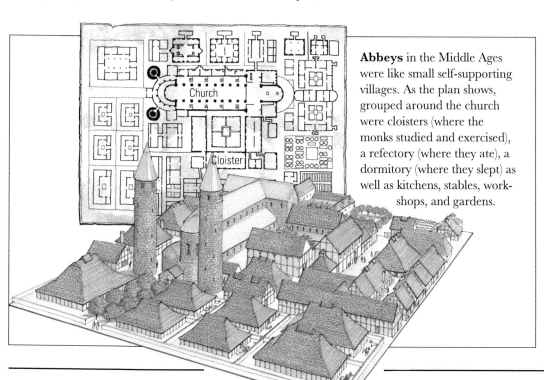

Abbeys in the Middle Ages were like small self-supporting villages. As the plan shows, grouped around the church were cloisters (where the monks studied and exercised), a refectory (where they ate), a dormitory (where they slept) as well as kitchens, stables, workshops, and gardens.

The letter *A*, like all the letters, has a long history. The earliest alphabets were taken and adapted by the Greeks. The Greek *beta*, when combined with the first letter, *aleph*, gives us the word alphabet.

The Greeks passed on their letters to the Romans who developed the alphabet we use today, although they used only capital letters. Small letters developed in the AD 700s.

An early form of the letter A, used in the Middle East over 3000 years ago.

This letter was taken by the Greeks and became alpha.

Over the years different versions of the letter A have been developed.

PRONUNCIATION GUIDE	
fat a	all ö
fate ā	foot oo
fast ä	moon o͞o
among å	boy oi
met e	house ow
mean ē	demon o̊
silent e̊	thing th
loch hh	this Th
fin i	but u
line ī	mute ū
quick kw	fur û
got o	brochure ů
note ō	vision zh

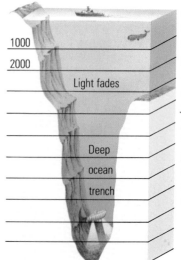

An Aboriginal shield and boomerang or wooden throwing stick. The spear and boomerang were the main weapons used by the Aboriginals as they wandered about the desert hunting or gathering food.

abhor (ab **hör**) *vb.* **abhorring, abhorred** to hate or dislike very much. – *n.* **abhorrence**.

ability (å **bil** i ti) *n.* **abilities** the power, skill, or knowledge to do something.

abject (ab jekt) *adj.* miserable or poor: *Many people in slums live in abject poverty.*

able (ā bĕl) *adj.* **1** having the necessary knowledge, power, time, etc. to do something. **2** clever, skilful. – *adv.* **ably**.

-able (-å bĕl) *suffix* forming adjectives meaning **1** that may or must be: *eatable; payable*. **2** that is suitable for: *fashionable*.

aboard (å **börd**) *adv. & prep.* on, on to, in, or into a ship, train, aircraft, etc.

abolish (å **bol** ish) *vb.* **abolishing, abolished** to stop or put an end to.

abolitionist (a bo̊ **lish** o̊n ist) *n.* a person who tries to abolish a custom or practice.

aborigine (ab o̊ **rij** i nē) *n.* **1** (usually **Aborigine**) a member of the race of people who were the original inhabitants of AUSTRALIA. (The noun **Aboriginal** is now the preferred form.) **2** a member of any race of people who were the first people to live in a country or region. – *n. & adj.* **aboriginal** or **Aboriginal**.

abort (å **bört**) *vb.* **aborting, aborted 1** to lose a baby because it is born before it has developed enough to survive outside the womb. **2** to stop a plan, etc. because of technical problems.

abortion *n.* an operation to abort a baby by removing the foetus from the womb.

about (å **bowt**) *prep.* **1** concerning; relating to: *She was worried about her puppy*. **2** here and there: *There are daisies dotted about the lawn*. **3** all around; surrounding. – *adv.* **1** nearly; approximately: *The apples weighed about a pound*. **2** nearby; close: *Is there anyone about?*

above (å **buv**) *prep.* **1** higher than; over: *The plane flew above the clouds*. **2** more or greater than in quantity or degree: *The temperature was above boiling point*.

● **Abraham** (ā brå ham) is regarded as the founder of the Jewish race. The BIBLE in the Book of Genesis tells how more than 4000 years ago God commanded Abraham to take his family to Canaan (modern ISRAEL).

abrasive (å **brā** ziv) *n.* a substance that can damage skin or rock, etc. by rubbing and scraping. – *adj.* rough; annoying.

abreast (å **brest**) *adv.* side by side and facing in the same direction: *They walked three abreast*.

abroad (å **bröd**) *adv.* in or to a foreign country.

abrupt (å **brupt**) *adj.* sudden and unexpected.

abscess (ab ses) or (ab sis) *n.* a painful swelling in a part of the body.

absence (ab sĕns) *n.* the state of being away from school or work, etc.

absent (ab sĕnt) *adj.* not in the expected place; not present. – (ab **sent**) *vb.* **absenting, absented** to keep yourself away from.

absent-minded *adj.* not noticing what you are doing or what is going on around.

absolute (ab so̊ lo͞ot) *adj.* complete; total; perfect: *He swore her to absolute secrecy*.

absolutely *adv.* completely.

absorb (åb **zörb**) *vb.* **absorbing, absorbed 1** to take or in or suck up liquid, knowledge, etc. **2** to have all of the attention of.

abstain (åb **stān**) *vb.* **abstaining, abstained** to choose not to do or take something, e.g. eating, voting.

abstract (ab strakt) *adj.* referring to something which exists only as an idea or quality.

absurd (åb **sûrd**) *adj.* ridiculous.

abundance (å bun dåns) *n.* a large amount. **abundant** *adj.* existing in large amounts.

abuse (å **būz**) *vb.* **abusing, abused 1** to use position, power, etc. wrongly. **2** to treat someone cruelly or wrongly. – (å **būs**) *n.* bad or cruel treatment of someone.

abusive *adj.* using insulting or rude language.

abysmal (å **biz** mål) *adj.* **1** extremely bad. **2** very deep; very great: *abysmal ignorance*.

abyss (å **bis**) *n.* a very large and deep hole.

An abyss usually refers to the deepest parts of the oceans, below 2000 m (6500 feet). No light penetrates these waters and the pressure is many times heavier than at the surface.

1000
2000
Light fades
Deep ocean trench

academy (å **kad** ĕ mi) *n.* **academies** a school that gives training in a particular subject.
academic (a kå **dem** ik) *adj.* to do with learning, study, education, or teaching.

accelerate (åk **sel** ĕ rāt) *vb.* **accelerating, accelerated** to increase speed.
acceleration *n.* the rate of increase of speed.
accelerator *n.* the pedal or lever that is pressed to make a vehicle move faster.

accent (**ak** sĕnt) *n.* **1** the particular way words are pronounced by people who live in a certain place. **2** emphasis put on a syllable in speaking. **3** a mark put over or under a letter to show how it is pronounced.

accept (åk **sept**) *vb.* **accepting, accepted 1** to agree to receive something offered: *I am happy to accept your gift.* **2** to agree to a suggestion: *He accepted her offer of a job.* **3** to believe to be true.
acceptable *adj.* good enough, but only just.
acceptance *n.* the act of accepting something.

access (**ak** ses) *n.* a means of approaching or entering a place. – *vb.* **accessing, accessed** to call up information on a computer.
accessible *adj.* able to be reached easily.

accessory (åk **ses** ŏ ri) *n.* **accessories** **1** something additional to, but less important than, something else. **2** an item of dress, such as a bag or tie that goes with a dress, etc.

accident (**ak** si dĕnt) *n.* **1** an unexpected event which causes damage or harm. **2** something that happens by chance.
accidental (ak si **den** tål) *adj.* not planned.

acclaim (å **klām**) *vb.* **acclaiming, acclaimed** to receive or welcome with noisy enthusiasm.

accommodate (å **kom** ŏ dāt) *vb.* **accommodating, accommodated** to provide someone with a place in which to stay.
accommodating *adj.* helpful.
accommodation *n.* a room or rooms in a house or hotel in which to live.

accompany (å **kum** på ni) *vb.* **accompanies, accompanying, accompanied 1** to come or go with; to do something with. **2** to play a musical instrument to support someone who is playing another instrument or singing.

accomplice (å **kum** plis) *n.* a person who helps another commit a crime.

accomplish (å **kum** plish) *vb.* **accomplishing, accomplished** to complete, achieve, carry out.
accomplished *adj.* clever or skilled.
accomplishment *n.* **1** a skill developed through practice. **2** the finishing of something.

accord (å **körd**) *vb.* **according, accorded** to agree: *His answer accorded with mine.*
according *adv.* **1** as said by: *According to my doctor there is no need to take any medicine.* **2** in agreement with: *All went according to plan.*
accordingly *adv.* **1** in an appropriate way: *act accordingly.* **2** therefore; for that reason.

account (å **kownt**) *n.* **1** a description or report; an explanation. **2** a deposit of money in a bank. **3** (usually in *plural*) a record of money received and spent. – *vb.* **account for; accounting, accounted** to give a reason or explanation for.

accumulate (å **kūm** ū lāt) *vb.* **accumulating, accumulated** to collect or gather something in an increasing quantity. – *n.* **accumulation.** – *adj.* **accumulative.**

accurate (**ak** ū rit) *adj.* absolutely correct.

accuse (å **kūz**) *vb.* **accusing, accused** to charge a person with having done something wrong.
accusation *n.* the act of accusing someone.

accustom (å **kus** tŏm) *vb.* **accustoming, accustomed** to make someone used to something.

ace (ās) *n.* **1** the playing card in each of the four suits with a single symbol on it. **2** in tennis, a serve that is so fast that the opposing player cannot hit the ball back.

ache (āk) *vb.* **aching, ached** to feel a dull, continuous pain.

● **Achebe, Chinua** (1930-) is a Nigerian novelist.

achieve (å **chēv**) *vb.* **achieving, achieved** to reach a goal, etc. especially through hard work.
achievement *n.* something that has been done or gained by effort.

● **Achilles** (å **kil** ēz) was a Greek hero in the siege of TROY in HOMER's poem the *Iliad.*

THE RIGHT ACCENT
When a word can be used as a verb or a noun, the **ac**cent or stress changes. You may speak with an Australian **ac**cent but ac**cent** the words in the same way. You set a good example for good con**duct**, but you con**duct** an orchestra. Other examples are object, progress, rebel, reject, and dispute.

In the Trojan War Achilles kills Hector, the Trojan leader. The Iliad *is one of the great heroic epics of ancient Greece.*

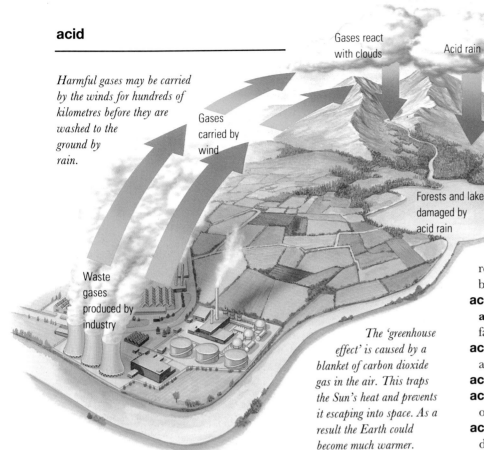

Harmful gases may be carried by the winds for hundreds of kilometres before they are washed to the ground by rain.

Gases react with clouds

Acid rain

Gases carried by wind

Acid rain and the 'greenhouse effect' are the two main threats to Earth's atmosphere. They are both caused by gases sent out by power stations, cars, and factories. Acid rain causes terrible damage to plant life.

Forests and lakes damaged by acid rain

Waste gases produced by industry

The 'greenhouse effect' is caused by a blanket of carbon dioxide gas in the air. This traps the Sun's heat and prevents it escaping into space. As a result the Earth could become much warmer.

The word acid comes from a Latin word meaning 'sour', for most acids taste sour. Some acids are dangerous, others such as citric acid in lemons are harmless. All acids turn litmus, a special kind of paper, red. Some substances are the opposite of acids. They are alkalis and turn litmus paper blue.

acid (**a** sid) *n.* **1** any of a group of substances, usually in the form of liquids, that contain hydrogen, are usually sour, and are able to dissolve metals and form salts. **2** any sour substance. – *adj.* sour to taste.
　acidic *adj.* like, or containing, acid.
　acid rain *n.* rain that contains harmful acids formed from waste gases released into the atmosphere from factories, etc.
acknowledge (ăk **no** lij) *vb.* **acknowledging, acknowledged 1** to admit or accept the truth of a fact or situation: *Jane had to acknowledge that Dan was right.* **2** to report receiving something that has been sent. **3** to express thanks for. **4** to show that you have recognized someone by greeting them.
　acknowledgement or **acknowledgment** *n.* the act of acknowledging someone.
acme (**ak** mi) *n.* the highest point of success, etc.
acne (**ak** ni) *n.* an unhealthy skin condition in which red spots form on the face.

●**Aconcagua** (a kon **kag** wa) is an extinct volcano in the ANDES in SOUTH AMERICA.

acorn (**ā** körn) *n.* the nut-like fruit of the oak tree, which has a cup-shaped outer case.
acoustic (ă **kōōs** tik) *adj.* having to do with sound or the sense of hearing.
　acoustics *n.* (*plural*) the qualities of a room such as a theatre that make it a good or bad place to listen to music or speech.
acquaint (ă **kwānt**) *vb.* **acquainting, acquainted** to make a person aware of or familiar with something.
acquire (ă **kwīr**) *vb.* **acquiring, acquired** to achieve something, especially through skill.
acquisition (ak wi **zi** shŏn) *n.* a thing obtained.
acquisitive (ă **kwi** zi tiv) *adj.* very eager to obtain and possess things.
acquit (ă **kwit**) *vb.* **acquitting, acquitted** to declare an accused person to be innocent of the crime, etc. he or she has been accused of.
acre (**ā** kĕr) *n.* a unit of measurement for land, equal to 4840 square yards.
acrobat (**ak** rŏ bat) *n.* a person in a circus, who performs balancing acts and other tricks.
　acrobatics *n.* (*plural*) acrobatic movements.
acronym (**ak** rŏ nim) *n.* a word made from the first letters or syllables of other words, for example *NATO* is an acronym of *North Atlantic Treaty Organization.*
acrophobia (ak rŏ **fō** bi ă) *n.* fear of heights.
across (ă **kros**) *prep.* **1** to, at, or on the other side of: *We saw the hotel across the lake.* **2** from one side of to the other: *She ran across the road.* **3** so as to cross: *He folded his arms across his chest.*
act (akt) *n.* **1** a thing that is done; a deed. **2** the process of doing something: *He was caught in the act of breaking the window.* **3** a major division of a play or opera, etc. **4** a law passed by a law-making body such as Parliament. – *vb.* **acting, acted 1** to behave. **2** to do something: *You need to act fast.* **3** to perform in a play or film.
　acting *n.* the profession of performing in a play or film.
action (**ak** shŏn) *n.* **1** the process of doing something: *I've put my ideas into action.* **2** something that is done.
　action replay *n.* the repeating, often in slow-motion, of a piece of film on television.

activate (**ak** ti vāt) *vb.* **activating, activated** to make something start working.

active (**ak** tiv) *adj.* moving and doing things.
activist *n.* a person who is very active, especially as a member of a political group.

activity (ak **tiv** i ti) *n.* **activities 1** the state of being active or busy. **2** (often in *plural*) things that people do, especially for pleasure.

actor (**ak** tŏr) *n.* a man or woman whose job is performing in plays or films.

actual (**ak** tū ål) *adj.* real; not imagined.
actually *adv.* really; in fact.

acupuncture (**ak** ū pungk chŭr) *n.* a method of treating illness and pain by sticking needles into the patient's skin at certain points.

acute (å **kūt**) *adj.* **1** very bad. **2** (describing the senses) keen or sharp. **3** (describing an illness) quickly becoming severe. **4** describing an angle that is less than 90°.

adage (**ad** ij) *n.* a proverb or saying.

adagio (å **däj** i ō). See **Musical terms**.

● **Adam and Eve** in the BIBLE, were the first people. They lived in the Garden of Eden.

● **Adam, Robert** (1728-92) was a famous Scottish architect.

adamant (**a** då månt) *adj.* determined; unlikely to change your mind.

adapt (å **dapt**) *vb.* **adapting, adapted** to change so as to fit new circumstances.
adaptable *adj.* good at fitting into new circumstances or situations.
adaptor *n.* a type of electrical plug used for connecting several plugs to the same socket.

add (ad) *vb.* **adding, added 1** to put together or combine two or more things. **2** to put two or more numbers together to get their total. **3** to say or write something further: *She added her signature to the end of her letter.*

adder (**ad** ĕr) *n.* the common viper, a poisonous snake with a black zigzag pattern on its back.

The adder, or common viper, is the only snake found north of the Arctic Circle.

addition (å **di** shŏn) *n.* **1** the act of adding. **2** a person or thing that is added to something else. – **in addition to** as well as; besides.
additional *adj.* extra; more than usual.

address (å **dres**) *n.* the number or name of the place where a person lives or works.

● **Adelaide** (**a** dĕ lād) is the capital of the state of South AUSTRALIA.

● **Adenauer** (**ä** dĕn ow ĕr), **Konrad** (1876-1967) was chancellor of West GERMANY (1949-1963).

adenoids (**a** dĕ noidz) *n.* (*plural*) a mass of soft flesh behind the nose.

adequate (**ad** i kwit) *adj.* enough; sufficient.

adhere (åd **hĕr**) *vb.* **adhering, adhered 1** to stick. **2** to remain loyal to a religion or belief.

adhesive (åd **hē** ziv) *adj.* sticky. – *n.* any substance used to stick things together.

adjacent (å **jā** sĕnt) *adj.* lying beside or next to: *The two friends lived in adjacent houses.*

adjective (**a** jik tiv) *n.* a word that describes a noun or pronoun, as 'dark' describes 'hair' in *She has dark hair;* and 'sad' describes 'her' in *The book made her sad.* – *adj.* **adjectival.**

adjust (å **just**) *vb.* **adjusting, adjusted** to change something slightly: *He adjusted his watch to the correct time.* – *n.* **adjustment.**

administer (åd **min** is tĕr) *vb.* **administering, administered 1** to manage, govern, or direct an organization. **2** to provide medicine.
administration *n.* the directing, managing, or governing of a company's affairs.
administrative *adj.* of or concerned with administration.

admiral (**ad** mi rål) *n.* **1** a high-ranking naval officer commanding a fleet of ships. **2** a name applied to several species of butterfly.

admire (åd **mīr**) *vb.* **admiring, admired** to regard with respect or approval. – *n.* **admiration.** – *adj.* **admiring.**
admirable (**ad** mi rå bĕl) *adj.* very good and worthy of being admired.
admirer *n.* someone who admires a particular person or thing.

admission (åd **mi** shŏn) *n.* **1** the act of allowing in or being allowed in. **2** the cost of entry.

The Red Admiral is a common butterfly species of meadows, orchards, and gardens. It is found in Europe, Asia, North Africa, and North America.

INEVITABLE ADJECTIVES
Numerous nouns are always accompanied by an inevitable cliché of an adjective:
Shame is crying
Brides are blushing
Isolation is splendid
Efforts are concerted
Questions are burning
Beliefs are cherished
Negotiations are delicate
Conclusions are inevitable

Adobe is a Spanish word for sun-dried bricks and for a house built of such bricks. The ancient Egyptians and Babylonians used sun-dried mud and straw bricks. In America adobe was a common building material used by Incas and pueblo Indians. Stone was mainly reserved for temples but even important houses were built of adobe. Spanish settlers in Mexico, Texas, and California also used the material for their new houses.

To make adobe, clay is mixed with water and straw. The mixture is placed in brick-shaped moulds. When dry, the bricks are removed from the mould and allowed to bake in the sun.

admit (åd **mit**) *vb.* **admitting, admitted 1** to agree to the truth of something, especially unwillingly. **2** to allow to enter.
admittedly *adv.* as is known to be true.
ado (å **doo**) *n.* difficulty or trouble; fuss.
adobe (å **dō** bi) *n.* sun-dried bricks made of clay and straw.
adolescent (a dŏ **les** ĕnt) *adj.* at the stage of development between child and adult, usually between the ages of 13 and 16. – *n.* a young person. – *n.* **adolescence**.
adopt (å **dopt**) *vb.* **adopting, adopted 1** to take a child of other parents into your own family, becoming its legal parent. **2** to take up a habit, position, or policy. – *adj.* **adopted**. – *n.* **adoption**.
adore (å **dör**) *vb.* **adoring, adored 1** to love deeply. **2** to worship a god, etc.
adorn (å **dörn**) *vb.* **adorning, adorned** to decorate in order to make more beautiful.

● **Adriatic** an arm of the MEDITERRANEAN SEA between ITALY and former YUGOSLAVIA.

adrift (å **drift**) *adj.* describing a boat that is not tied up; floating about without being steered.

ADORNMENT
Some words and expressions have become overworked and pretty meaningless 'fillers' or adornments: Sort of; You know; Basically; Actually; Definitely; No problem; No way.

adult (**a** dult) or (å **dult**) *adj.* fully grown; mature: *an adult person.* – *n.* **adulthood**.
advance (åd **väns**) *vb.* **advancing, advanced 1** to move forward, sometimes in a threatening way. **2** to make progress; to improve or promote. **3** to propose or suggest an idea. **4** to move to an earlier time or date than previously planned. – *n.* **1** progress; a move forward. **2** a payment made before it is due. **3** money lent to someone. – *adj.* done or given beforehand.
advantage (åd **vän** tij) *n.* something that may help someone to succeed or win. – **take advantage of** to make use of a situation in such a way as to benefit yourself.
advent (åd **vent**) *n.* **1** coming or arrival; first appearance. **2 Advent** in the CHRISTIAN calendar, the period before Christmas.
adventure (åd **ven** chŭr) *n.* an exciting and often dangerous experience.
adventurer *n.* someone eager for adventure.
adventurous *adj.* ready to take risks; daring.
adverb (ad **vûrb**) *n.* a word or group of words which describes or adds to the meaning of a verb, adjective, or another adverb, such as 'very' and 'quietly' in *They were talking very quietly.* – *adj.* **adverbial**.
adversary (ad vĕr så ri) *n.* **adversaries** an opponent in a competition; an enemy.
advertise (ad vĕr tīz) *vb.* **advertising, advertised** to draw attention to or describe goods for sale or services offered in newspapers or on the television to encourage people to buy or use them.

advertisement (åd **vûr** tiz měnt) *n.* a public notice in a newspaper or on a hoarding which advertises something; a short television film advertising something.

advice (åd **vīs**) *n.* suggestions or opinions given to someone about what he or she should do in a particular situation.

advise (åd **vīz**) *vb.* **advising, advised 1** to give advice to; to recommend. **2** to inform. − *n.* **adviser** or **advisor**.

advocate (**ad** vǒ kit) *n.* **1** See **Law**. **2** a person who supports or recommends an idea. − (**ad** vǒ kāt) *vb.* **advocating, advocated** to recommend or support an idea.

●**Aegean** the branch of the MEDITERRANEAN SEA between GREECE and TURKEY.

aerial (**ā** ri ål) *n.* a wire or rod on a radio or television set, able to send or receive signals.

aero- (**ā** rō-) **1** of air: *aerodynamics.* **2** of aircraft: *aerodrome.*

aerobics (ā **rō** biks) *n.* (*singular*) physical exercises which increase the supply of oxygen in the blood and strengthen the heart and lungs.

aeronautics (ā rō **nö** tiks) *n.* (*singular*) the science or practice of movement through the air. − *adj.* **aeronautic** or **aeronautical**.

aeroplane (**ā** rō plān) *n.* (*British*) a vehicle with wings and engines, designed for flying.

aerosol (**ā** rō sol) *n.* a substance packed under pressure, which is released from a container in the form of a fine spray.

●**Aeschylus** (**ēs** kě lǔs) (525-456 BC) was the first of three great dramatists of ancient GREECE.

●**Aesop** (**ē** sop) (6th century BC) was the author of a collection of Greek fables, using animal characters to illustrate a moral point.

affable (**af** å běl) *adj.* pleasant and friendly.

affair (å **fār**) *n.* **1** a concern, matter, event, or connected series of events: *The party was a noisy affair.* **2** (in *plural*) matters of importance and public interest: *I like to watch the news and current affairs programmes on television.* **3** (in *plural*) private business matters.

affect (å **fekt**) *vb.* **affecting, affected 1** to influence. **2** to cause someone to feel strong emotions. **3** to pretend: *He affected to walk with a limp.*

●**affect** and **effect**. Affect means 'to cause a change': *Nothing can affect our friendship.* Effect as a verb means 'to cause': *I want to effect a change.* As a noun it means a 'result': *The war had a disastrous effect on the country.*

affection (å **fek** shŏn) *n.* love or strong liking. **affectionate** *adj.* showing love.

affirm (å **fûrm**) *vb.* **affirming, affirmed** to state positively and firmly; to state as a fact.

afflict (å **flikt**) *vb.* **afflicting, afflicted** to cause physical or mental suffering.

affluent (**af** loo ěnt) *adj.* having more than enough money; rich. − *n.* **affluence**.

afford (å **förd**) *vb.* **affording, afforded 1** to have enough money or time to spend on something: *Only someone very rich could afford such a large car.* **2** to be able to do something, without risk: *I can't afford to lose my job.*

Afghan (**af** gan) *adj.* belonging to AFGHANISTAN. − *n.* **1** (also **Afghani**) a person born in AFGHANISTAN. **2** the official language of AFGHANISTAN.

●**Afghanistan**. See Supplement, **Countries**.

afraid (å **frād**) *adj.* feeling fear or frightened; worried: *The small child was afraid of the dark.*

PRONUNCIATION GUIDE	
fat a	all ö
fate ā	foot oo
fast ä	moon o͞o
among å	boy oi
met e	house ow
mean ē	demon ŏ
silent ě	thing th
loch hh	this Th
fin i	but u
line ī	mute ū
quick kw	fur û
got o	brochure ů
note ō	vision zh

Little is known about **Aesop** except that he was born a slave and that he was ugly, clownish, and witty. His fables were very popular. They include 'The Hare and the Tortoise' in which a fast-running hare and a slow, plodding tortoise run a race. The hare is so sure he will win that he stops for a rest part of the way through. Meanwhile the tortoise goes on steadily. The hare falls asleep, the tortoise plods past and wins the race. The moral is that the slow but sure are bound to succeed.

•**Africa** is the world's second largest continent. It stretches from the MEDITERRANEAN SEA in the north to the Cape of Good Hope in the south. The scorching SAHARA desert spreads over much of the northern part of the continent. Near the EQUATOR are thick rain forests. Over huge grasslands, called savanna, roam large herds of grazing animals such as ZEBRAS, GIRAFFES, and IMPALA. Other animals such as LIONS and CHEETAHS prey upon them. Africa is home to many groups of people with different languages and ways of life. Black people number seven in every ten. Many Africans are farmers. There are gold, copper, and tin mines, and industry is growing. During the 19th century most of Africa was colonized by European powers. During the 1950s and 1960s most former colonies became independent.

Most of Africa was colonized by Europeans in the 19th century; from the 1950s the colonies became independent countries. Today they are developing industries and natural resources.

African (**af** ri kản) *adj.* belonging to the continent of AFRICA, its inhabitants, etc. – *n.* a person born or living in AFRICA, or whose ancestors came from AFRICA.

Afro- (**af** rō-) African.

Afro-American *n.* an American whose ancestors came from AFRICA.

Afro-Caribbean *n.* a person from or living in the CARIBBEAN whose ancestors came originally from AFRICA.

aft (äft) *adv. & adj.* at or towards the stern.

after (**äf** tẽr) *prep.* **1** coming later in time than. **2** following in position or importance; behind. **3** about: *She asked after the patient.* **4** in pursuit of: *He ran after her.* **5** given the same name as; in imitation of: *She was called Mary after her aunt.* – *adv.* **1** later in time. **2** behind in place.

aftermath *n.* circumstances that are a result of a great and terrible event.

afterthought *n.* an idea you have after the main plan or idea has been formed.

afterwards or **afterward** *adv.* later.

again (å **gen**) or (å **gān**) *adv.* **1** once more; another time: *She decided to take the exam again.* **2** back to a previous condition or situation: *I do hope you will soon be feeling well again.*

against (å **genst**) or (å **gānst**) *prep.* **1** close to or leaning on; in contact with: *He left the ladder against the wall.* **2** in opposition to: *Burglary is against the law.* **3** in contrast to: *Her white dress stood out against the dark background.*

•**Agamemnon** (ag å **mem** non) was commander of the Greek army in the Trojan War. His quarrel with ACHILLES is the main theme of HOMER's *Iliad.*

This gold mask, once thought to be that of Agamemnon, was found in a grave at Mycenae by the German archaeologist, Heinrich Schliemann.

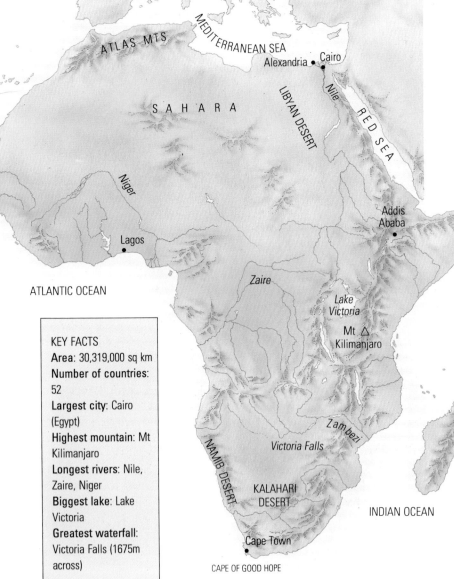

ATLAS MTS

MEDITERRANEAN SEA

Alexandria • • Cairo

SAHARA

LIBYAN DESERT

Nile

RED SEA

Niger

Lagos

ATLANTIC OCEAN

Addis Ababa •

Zaire

Lake Victoria

Mt △ Kilimanjaro

Zambezi

NAMIB DESERT

Victoria Falls

KALAHARI DESERT

INDIAN OCEAN

Cape Town •

CAPE OF GOOD HOPE

KEY FACTS
Area: 30,319,000 sq km
Number of countries: 52
Largest city: Cairo (Egypt)
Highest mountain: Mt Kilimanjaro
Longest rivers: Nile, Zaire, Niger
Biggest lake: Lake Victoria
Greatest waterfall: Victoria Falls (1675m across)

agate (**ag** åt) *n.* a type of semi-precious stone with layers of different colours.

age (āj) *n.* **1** the length of time a person or thing has existed. **2** a particular stage in life. **3** the fact of being old. **4** a period in the geological development or history marked by some particular feature: *We are studying the Bronze Age in history.* – *vb.* **ageing** or **aging**, **aged 1** to show signs of growing old. **2** to grow old. – **act** or **be your age** to behave sensibly.
  aged *adj.* **1** having a particular age. **2** (ā jid) very old.

agency (ā jěn si) *n.* **agencies** an office or business providing a particular service.

agenda (å **jen** då) *n.* a written list of subjects to be dealt with at a meeting.

agent (ā jěnt) *n.* **1** a person who represents an organization and acts on its behalf; a person who deals with someone else's business matters: *Most singers and actors have an agent to find work for them.* **2** (also **secret agent**) a spy.

aggravate (**ag** rå vāt) *vb.* **aggravating, aggravated 1** to make a bad situation or an illness, etc. worse. **2** to annoy. – *adj.* **aggravating.** – *n.* **aggravation.**

aggression (å **gre** shŏn) *n.* the act of attacking another person or country without being provoked; hostile behaviour towards someone.
  aggressive *adj.* hostile.
  aggressor *n.* in a fight or war, the person, group, or country that attacks first.

agile (a jīl) *adj.* able to move quickly and easily; nimble. – *n.* **agility** (å **jil** i ti).

●**Agincourt** (**aj** in kört) is a village in northern FRANCE where in 1415 English bowmen, led by King HENRY the Fifth, defeated the French.

agitate (**aj** i tāt) *vb.* **agitating, agitated 1** to excite or trouble a person: *The old lady was agitated because she had lost her handbag.* **2** to try to stir up public opinion for or against something: *The demonstrators were agitating for better working conditions.* – *n.* **agitation.**

agnostic (åg **nos** tik) *n.* See **Religious terms**.

ago (å **gō**) *adv.* in the past; earlier.

agony (**ag** ŏ ni) *n.* **agonies** severe bodily or mental pain.

agoraphobia (ag ŏ rå **fō** bi å) *n.* a fear of open and public places. – *n.* & *adj.* **agoraphobic.**

agree (å **grē**) *vb.* **agreeing, agreed 1** to be of the same opinion as someone else about something: *We agreed on a place to spend our*

holiday. **2** to say yes to a suggestion or instruction: *He agreed to come ice-skating with us.* **3** to be suitable or good for: *Milk doesn't agree with me.* – **agree to differ** to agree to accept each other's different opinions.
  agreeable *adj.* **1** pleasant; friendly. **2** willing to accept a suggestion.
  agreement *n.* **1** a contract or promise. **2** the state of holding the same opinion.

agriculture (**ag** ri kul chŭr) *n.* the science of cultivating the land, especially for growing crops or rearing animals. – *adj.* **agricultural.**

aground (å **grownd**) *adj.* & *adv.* describing ships that are stuck on the seabed or rocks.

ahead (å **hed**) *adv.* **1** at or in the front; forwards: *Full steam ahead!* **2** in the future: *We must plan ahead.* **3** in the lead.

aid (ād) *n.* **1** help. **2** help or support in the form of money, supplies, or services given to people who need it: *Many rich countries send aid to the poorer countries.* – *vb.* **aiding, aided** to help or support someone. – **in aid of** in support of: *They are collecting in aid of a worthy charity.*

aide (ād) *n.* an assistant or adviser.

AIDS or **Aids** (ādz) *abbreviation A*cquired *I*mmune *D*eficiency *S*yndrome, a condition transmitted by a virus which attacks the body's system of defence against disease.

ailment (āl měnt) *n.* a minor illness.

aim (ām) *vb.* **aiming, aimed 1** to point or direct a weapon, attack, or remark at someone or something. **2** to plan, intend, or try: *She was aiming to finish her homework by 8 o'clock.* – *n.* something a person intends to do.
  aimless *adj.* without any purpose.

air (ār) *n.* **1** the mixture of gases, consisting mainly of oxygen, nitrogen, and carbon dioxide, which people and animals breathe and which forms the Earth's atmosphere. **2** the space above and around the Earth, where birds and aircraft fly. **3** an appearance, look, or manner. **4** (in *plural*) behaviour put on to impress others or to show off: *She put on airs to try to impress him.* **5** a tune. – *vb.* **airing, aired 1** to let fresh air into a room. **2** to make your thoughts or opinions known publicly: *She was given the opportunity to air her opinions at the meeting.* – **by air** in an aircraft.

airborne *adj.* describing aircraft that are flying in the air, having just taken off.

air-conditioning *n.* a system used to control the temperature, dryness, or dampness of the air in a building. – *adj.* **air-conditioned.**

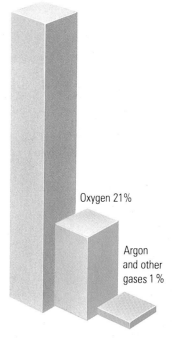

Nitrogen 78%

Oxygen 21%

Argon and other gases 1 %

Ninety-nine percent of air is composed of the colourless, tasteless, odourless gases nitrogen and oxygen. Without air all living things, apart from a few micro-organisms, could not exist. The air cloaks the Earth in a layer we call the atmosphere. The movement of air is responsible for weather.

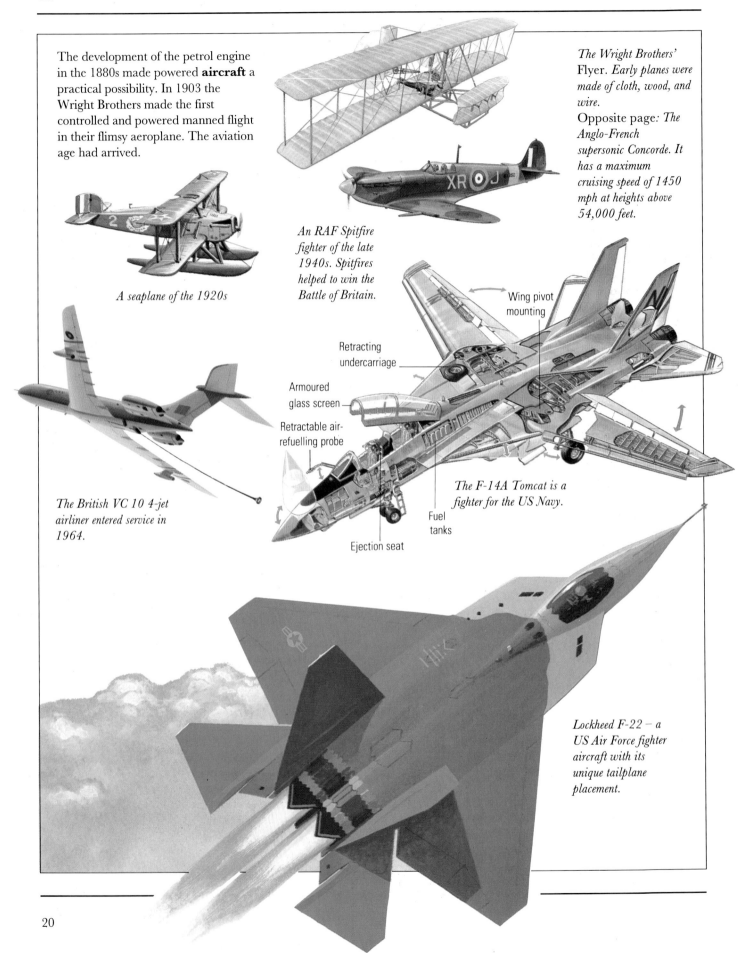

The development of the petrol engine in the 1880s made powered **aircraft** a practical possibility. In 1903 the Wright Brothers made the first controlled and powered manned flight in their flimsy aeroplane. The aviation age had arrived.

The Wright Brothers' Flyer. *Early planes were made of cloth, wood, and wire.*

Opposite page: *The Anglo-French supersonic Concorde. It has a maximum cruising speed of 1450 mph at heights above 54,000 feet.*

A seaplane of the 1920s

An RAF Spitfire fighter of the late 1940s. Spitfires helped to win the Battle of Britain.

Wing pivot mounting

Retracting undercarriage

Armoured glass screen

Retractable air-refuelling probe

The British VC 10 4-jet airliner entered service in 1964.

The F-14A Tomcat is a fighter for the US Navy.

Fuel tanks

Ejection seat

Lockheed F-22 – a US Air Force fighter aircraft with its unique tailplane placement.

aircraft *n.* any of various types of machine which can fly in the air.

air force *n.* that part of a country's defence forces which uses aircraft for fighting.

airline *n.* a company or organization which provides a regular transport service by aircraft.

airliner *n.* a large passenger aircraft.

airplane *n.* (*North American*) an aeroplane.

airship *n.* a type of aircraft that consists of a long gas-filled balloon-like structure with an engine to make it move and a room-like structure under it for passengers or cargo.

airstrip *n.* a long narrow piece of ground where aircraft can land and take off.

airtight *adj.* describing a container which air cannot get into, out of, or through.

air-traffic control *n.* the organization which manages the safe passage of aircraft.

airy *adj.* **airier, airiest** **1** with plenty of fresh, cool air. **2** not thinking about or dealing with something as seriously as you should.

aisle (īl) *n.* a passage between rows of seats in a church or theatre.

ajar (å **jär**) *adj. & adv.* partly open.

●**Ajax** in Greek legend, a hero of the Trojan war.

●**Alabama**. See Supplement, **USA**.

alarm (å **lärm**) *n.* **1** sudden fear produced by becoming aware of danger. **2** a bell or other noise which sounds to warn of danger, or on a clock to wake a person from sleep. – *vb.* **alarming, alarmed** to frighten. **alarming** *adj.* disturbing or frightening.

●**Alaska**. See Supplement, **USA**.

●**Albania**. See Supplement, **Countries**.

Albanian (ål **bā** ni ån) *adj.* of Albania, its inhabitants, or language.

albatross (**al** bå tros) *n.* a large, long-winged gull-like sea bird of the southern oceans.

album (**al** bům) *n.* a blank book for keeping photographs, stamps, etc.

alchemy (**al** kĕ mi) *n.* medieval chemistry. One of the aims of alchemy was to discover how to make gold from other metals. – *n.* **alchemist**.

●**Alcock, John** (1892-1919) was an English pilot who in 1919 made the first non-stop transatlantic flight with Arthur Brown.

alcohol (**al** kǒ hol) *n.* **1** a colourless, flammable liquid made by the fermentation of sugar, used in making drinks, etc. **2** any drink containing this liquid, such as wine or beer.

●**Alcott, Louisa May** (1832-88) was an American novelist, the author of *Little Women*.

alcove (**al** kōv) *n.* a recess in a wall.

ale (āl) *n.* a type of beer.

alert (å **lûrt**) *adj.* thinking and acting quickly; watchful and aware: *He was alert to all the dangers of his mission.* – *n.* a warning of danger: *The air-raid sirens sounded the alert.* – *vb.* **alerting, alerted** to warn someone of danger; to make someone aware of a fact.

●**Alexander the Great** (356-323 BC), king of Macedonia (a former country in southern EUROPE). He set out to conquer the world and by 323 BC ruled an empire that stretched from GREECE to INDIA.

●**Alfred the Great** (849-99) was king of WESSEX from 871. He led the Saxons to victory over the Danish invaders in 878.

alga (**al** gå) *n.* **algae** (**al** jē) or (**al** gē) (usually in *plural*) a plant which grows in water or on moist ground, with no stem, leaves, or flowers, such as seaweed.

algebra (**al** ji brå) *n.* a branch of mathematics that uses letters and other symbols to represent numbers in calculations.

●**Algeria** is a large Arab republic on the MEDITERRANEAN coast in North AFRICA. The south of the country lies in the SAHARA. This oil-rich country was ruled by FRANCE from 1848 to 1962. See also Supplement, **Countries**.

●**Algonquin** (al **gon** kwin) are a NATIVE AMERICAN people from the area around QUEBEC.

●**Alhambra** a 13th-century Moorish palace built on a hilly terrace outside Granada, SPAIN.

alibi (**al** i bī) *n.* a plea of being somewhere else when a crime was committed.

alien (**ā** li ån) *n.* a foreign-born resident of a country who has not adopted that country's nationality. – *adj.* foreign or strange.

A gold coin showing the head of Alexander the Great. Under him Greek culture spread throughout Asia. After his death his vast empire was divided among his generals.

PRONUNCIATION GUIDE	
fat a	all ö
fate ā	foot oo
fast ä	moon ōō
among å	boy oi
met e	house ow
mean ē	demon ǒ
silent ĕ	thing th
loch hh	this Th
fin i	but u
line ī	mute ū
quick kw	fur û
got o	brochure ů
note ō	vision zh

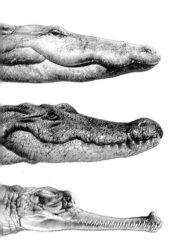

Alligators (top and below) *are clumsy on land. They look like crocodiles* (centre) *but have broader, flatter heads. When an alligator closes its mouth its teeth are hidden; a crocodile's fourth lower tooth is visible when its mouth is closed. The gharial* (bottom) *is related to the alligator.*

alight (å līt) *adj.* on fire.

align (å līn) *vb.* **aligning, aligned 1** to put in a straight line. **2** to bring into agreement with others: *The United States has aligned itself with Europe over this issue.* – *n.* **alignment**.

alike (å līk) *adj.* like one another; similar.

alive (å līv) *adj.* **1** living; having life; in existence. **2** lively; active.

alkali (al kå lī) *n.* a substance which reacts with an acid to form a salt.

all (öl) *adj.* **1** the whole amount, number, or extent of: *They picked all the apples.* **2** the greatest possible: *She ran with all speed.* **3** any whatever: *beyond all doubt* – *n.* someone's whole strength or resources: *She gave her all in the match.* – **after all** in spite of what has been said or done. – **all along** the whole time. – **all right 1** unhurt; safe. **2** adequate or satisfactory. **3** used to express agreement or approval: *"Oh, all right," she said.* – **be all for** to be very much in favour of.

all-rounder *n.* a person with many skills.

Allah (al å) or (a lä) *n.* the MUSLIM name for GOD.

allegation (al i gā shŏn) *n.* an unproved claim.

allege (å lej) *vb.* **alleging, alleged** to claim or declare to be the case without proof. – *adj.* **alleged.** – *adv.* **allegedly** (å lej id li).

allegro (å leg rō). See **Musical terms**.

allergy (a lĕr ji) *n.* **allergies** sensitivity of the body to a substance such as dust which causes a reaction such as a rash or sneezing.

allergic *adj.* having an allergy.

alleviate (å lē vi āt) *vb.* **alleviating, alleviated** to make pain or a problem less severe. – *n.* **alleviation**.

alley (a li) *n.* **alleys** (also **alleyway**) a narrow passage behind or between buildings.

alligator (a li gā tŏr) *n.* a kind of large reptile closely related to the crocodile, found in CHINA and AMERICA.

alliteration (å li tĕ rā shŏn) *n.* the repetition of the same sound at the beginning of each word in a phrase, for example 'Simple Simon sat still' or 'Peter Piper picked a peck of perfect peppercorn'.

allot (å lot) *vb.* **allotting, allotted** to give a share of or place in something.

allotment *n.* a piece of land people rent to grow vegetables on.

allow (å low) *vb.* **allowing, allowed 1** to permit someone to do something, or something to happen. **2** to take into consideration when judging or deciding; to provide: *She allowed enough food for ten people.*

allowance *n.* a sum of money, given regularly: *They have an allowance of £7 a day.*

alloy (a loi) *n.* a mixture of two or more metals. – (å loi) *vb.* **alloying, alloyed** to mix metals.

allude (å lōōd) *vb.* **alluding, alluded** to speak of indirectly or to refer to in passing. – *n.* **allusion**.

allure (å lūr) *n.* attractiveness or charm.

alluvium (å lōō vi ŭm) *n.* **alluvia** fertile soil and sand deposited by rivers or floods, especially in river valleys. – *adj.* **alluvial**.

ally (a lī) *n.* **allies** a country or person that has formally agreed to help and support another. – (å lī) *vb.* **allies, allying, allied** to join your country or yourself to another by political agreement, marriage, or friendship.

alliance *n.* an agreement by which countries ally themselves with one another.

almond (ä mŏnd) *n.* a kind of small tree related to the peach.

almost (öl mōst) *adv.* nearly but not quite.

alone (å lōn) *adj. & adv.* without anyone else; by yourself; apart from other people.

along (å long) *adv.* **1** in some direction: *I saw him walking along.* **2** in company with others: *Let's go along for the ride.* **3** into a more advanced state: *My essay is coming along nicely.* – *prep.* beside: *The bush lies along the wall.*

aloof (å lōōf) *adj.* unfriendly and distant.

aloud (å lowd) *adv.* not silently; loudly and clearly: *When I was a little boy my mother used to read aloud to me before I went to sleep.*

● **the Alps**, Europe's greatest mountain range, are centred on SWITZERLAND and stretch from FRANCE to SERBIA. Their highest point is Mont Blanc (4807 metres).

alpaca (al pak å) *n.* a South American animal, related to the llama, with silky hair.

АБВГДЕЖЗИЙКЛМНО

The Cyrillic alphabet, based on the Greek, was invented by St Cyril in the 800s when he was a missionary among the Slavic people.

ΑΒΓΔΕΖΗΘΙΚΛΜΝΞΠΟ

The Greeks took over many of the Phoenician signs, the first letter of which was aleph

حخدذرزسشصضطظعغفقكلمنهو يلا

আমাদের পোস্টমাস্টার কলিকাতার মাছকে ডাঙ্গায় তজলিলে যেরষ

The Arabic (top) *and Bengali* (above) *systems developed from the Phoenician.*

alphabet (**al** fǎ bet) *n.* the set of letters, usually in a fixed order, used in writing.
alphabetical or **alphabetic** *adj.* in the order of the letters of an alphabet. – *adv.*
alphabetically.

already (öl **red** i) *adv.* before the present time or the expected time: *He was already showing musical talent as a young child.*

also (**öl** sō) *adv.* in addition; too; besides.

altar (**öl** tǎr) *n.* a special table at the front of a Christian church, near which the priest stands.

alter (**öl** těr) *vb.* **altering, altered** to make or become different. – *n.* **alteration**.

alternate (öl **tûr** nǎt) *adj.* **1** arranged or coming one after the other by turns: *She experienced alternate periods of misery and joy.* **2** (with *plural* nouns) every other; one out of two: *He went to the gym on alternate Mondays.* – (**öl** těr nāt) *vb.*
alternating, alternated 1 to succeed or follow each other by turns. **2** to change from one thing to another by turns: *She alternated between misery and joy.*

alternative (öl **tûr** nǎ tiv) *adj.* available as a choice between two or more possibilities.

although (öl **Thō**) *conj.* in spite of the fact that; apart from the fact that; though.

altitude (**al** ti tūd) *n.* height above sea level.

alto (**al** tō) *n.* **altos 1** the lowest female singing voice. **2** the highest adult male singing voice.

altogether (öl tǒ **ge** Thěr) *adv.* **1** completely: *I am not altogether convinced.* **2** taking everything into consideration: *Altogether, I think we did very well.* **3** in total: *We made £300 altogether.*

aluminium (al ū **min** i ǔm) *n.* a light, silvery metallic element (symbol **Al**) which is not corroded by the air.

● There is more aluminium in the Earth's crust than any other metal. Most is obtained from an ore called bauxite. Alloys of aluminium are both light and strong.

always (**öl** wāz) *adv.* **1** at all times; continually. **2** in any case; if necessary: *You could always help her if she can't manage alone.*

a.m. *abbreviation* for *ante meridien* (Latin) before midday; in the morning.

amalgam (å **mal** gåm) *n.* a mixture or blend.

amateur (**am** å těr) or (**am** å chěr) *n.* **1** a person who takes part in a sport or pastime as a hobby and without being paid for it. **2** a person who is not very skilled in an activity. – *adj.* not professional.
amateurish *adj.* not very skilful.

amaze (å **māz**) *vb.* **amazing, amazed** to surprise greatly; to astonish. – *adj.* **amazed**: *I was amazed to see her there.* – *n.* **amazement**. – *adj.* **amazing**.

● **Amazon** a great river in SOUTH AMERICA and the second longest river in the world (6437 km) after the NILE.

Amateur comes from a Latin word for 'love' and originally meant 'a person who does something for the love of it rather than being paid for it'. Sometimes the word is used to suggest a lack of talent as in an *amateurish performance.*

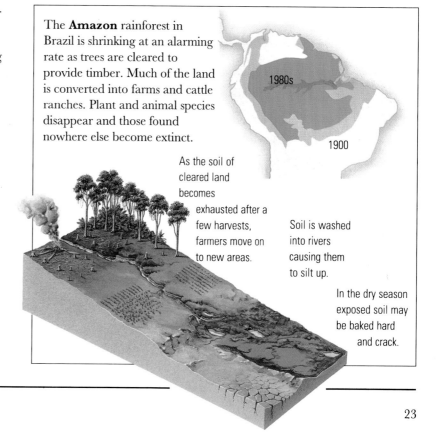

The **Amazon** rainforest in Brazil is shrinking at an alarming rate as trees are cleared to provide timber. Much of the land is converted into farms and cattle ranches. Plant and animal species disappear and those found nowhere else become extinct.

As the soil of cleared land becomes exhausted after a few harvests, farmers move on to new areas.

Soil is washed into rivers causing them to silt up.

In the dry season exposed soil may be baked hard and crack.

1980s

1900

A piece of polished amber containing the body of an insect, preserved almost intact.

---

ambassador (ǎm **bas** ǎ dǒr) *n.* a diplomat of the highest rank appointed by his or her government to represent their country abroad.

amber (**am** bẽr) *n.* a hard, clear, yellow or brownish fossil resin used in jewellery.

ambidextrous (am bi **deks** trũs) *adj.* able to use both hands equally well.

ambiguous (ǎm **big** ū ǔs) *adj.* having more than one possible meaning; not clear.

ambition (ǎm **bi** shǒn) *n.* **1** a strong desire for success, fame, or power. **2** a thing someone desires to do or achieve.

ambitious *adj.* **1** having a strong desire for success. **2** requiring hard work and skill: *He set an ambitious programme of work to be completed during the term.*

amble (**am** bẽl) *vb.* **ambling, ambled** to walk without hurrying.

ambulance (**am** bū lǎns) *n,* a specially equipped vehicle for carrying sick or injured people to hospital.

ambush (**am** boosh) *n.* the act of lying in wait to attack someone by surprise.

amen (ä **men**) *interj.* an expression used to show agreement, said especially at the end of a prayer.

amend (ǎ **mend**) *vb.* **amending, amended** to correct, improve, or make minor changes to something. – *n.* **amendment**.

amenity (ǎ **mē** ni ti) *n.* **amenities** a facility for the public to use: *The city has excellent amenities, including a sports centre and an entertainment complex.*

● **America** is often used for the UNITED STATES. The original word, Americas, includes NORTH AMERICA, CENTRAL AMERICA, and the CARIBBEAN islands. The Americas were named after the Italian explorer Amerigo VESPUCCI.

American (ǎ **mer** i kǎn) *adj.* of the UNITED STATES of America or the continent of America, the people who live or were born there, and the languages they speak. – *n.* a person born or living in the United States of America, or the continent of America. **American Indian.** See **Native American**. **Americanism** *n.* a word, phrase, or custom that is characteristic of Americans.

● **American War of Independence** fought between BRITAIN and its 13 American colonies from 1775 to 1783. The colonies won their independence and became the UNITED STATES of America. A basic cause of the war was that the British taxed the colonies but would not allow the colonies any representation in the British parliament. See George WASHINGTON and DECLARATION OF INDEPENDENCE.

The American colonists declared that 'taxation without representation is tyranny'. The **American War of Independence** began in 1775. At first the British were successful. Native North Americans fought alongside the rebels. After six years struggle the British surrendered at Yorktown, Virginia.

The map shows the main battles of the War.

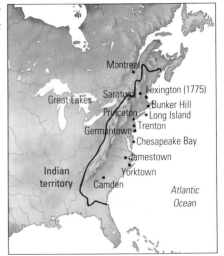

Battle of Bunker Hill (1775). The Americans defended the hill (Breed's Hill) from two British attacks but fled at the third.

amethyst (**am** i thist) *n.* a type of purple or violet quartz used as a gemstone.

amicable (**am** i cǎ běl) *adj.* friendly.

ammonia (ǎ **mō** ni ǎ) *n.* a strong-smelling gas used in making fertilizers, glue, etc.

ammonite (**am** ǒ nīt) *n.* a coil-shaped fossilized shell.

ammunition (a mū **ni** shǒn) *n.* bullets, shells, or bombs made to be fired from a weapon.

amnesia (ǎm **nē** zhyǎ) *n.* loss of memory.

amnesty (**am** něs ti) *n.* **amnesties** a general pardon, especially for people guilty of political crimes.

amoeba (ǎ **mē** bǎ) *n.* **amoebae** (ǎ **mē** bē) or (ǎ **mē** bī), or **amoebas** a microscopic, single-celled organism which usually lives in water.

among (ǎ **mung**) or **amongst** (ǎ **mungst**) *prep.* **1** in the middle of a number of people or things: *She was among friends.* **2** between: *They divided the cake among them.*

amorphous (ǎ **mör** fǔs) *adj.* shapeless.

amount (ǎ **mownt**) *n.* a quantity; a total or extent: *She earns a large amount of money.* – *vb.* **amounting, amounted** to be equal or add up to in size or number, etc.

ampersand (**am** pěr sand) *n.* the sign **&**, meaning 'and'.

amphibian (ǎm **fi** bi ǎn) *n.* a creature, such as a frog or toad, that spends part of its life on land and part in water.

● Amphibians were one of the earliest groups of animals on Earth. Most amphibians lay their eggs in water in a protective layer of jelly. The young hatch into tadpoles and develop into adults through METAMORPHOSIS.

amphibious *adj.* living on land and in water.

amphitheatre (**am** fi thē ǎ těr) *n.* a round building without a roof, with tiers of seats round a central open area, used as a theatre.

ample (**am** pěl) *adj.* more than enough; plenty.

amplify (**am** pli fī) *vb.* **amplifies, amplifying, amplified 1** to make a sound or electrical signal stronger. **2** to add detail to a story: *Later, he amplified upon his reasons for leaving.*

amputate (**am** pū tāt) *vb.* **amputating, amputated** to cut off, especially part or all of a limb. – *n.* **amputation.**

● Amsterdam is the biggest city in the NETHERLANDS. With VENICE, it is one of the most beautiful canal cities in EUROPE.

● Amundsen (ä mun sĕn), **Roald** (1872-1928) was a Norwegian explorer, and in 1911 the first to reach the SOUTH POLE.

amuse (ǎ **mūz**) *vb.* **amusing, amused** to make someone laugh; to keep someone entertained and interested. – *adj.* **amused:** *I was amused by the clowns' performance.* – *adv.* **amusedly** (ǎ **mūz** id li). – *adj.* **amusing.** **amusement** *n.* **1** the state of being amused. **2** something that amuses.

an. See **a.**

anachronism (ǎ **nak** rǒ ni zěm) *n.* the representation of something in a historical period in which it did not exist.

anaconda (a nǎ **kon** dǎ) *n.* a very large South American snake which can reach 9 metres in length. It kills its prey by squeezing it to death.

The anaconda lives on the banks of slow-moving rivers in South America. Like many snakes, anacondas can unhinge their jaws to swallow prey larger than themselves.

anaemia (ǎ **nē** mi ǎ) *n.* a condition in which there are not enough red cells in the blood, causing tiredness and paleness.

anaesthetic (an ěs **thet** ik) *n.* a drug or gas that causes either total unconsciousness (**general anaesthetic**) or lack of feeling in part of the body (**local anaesthetic**), so that surgery may be performed without pain.

anagram (**an** ǎ gram) *n.* a word, phrase, or sentence formed from the letters of another. 'Despair' is an anagram of 'praised'.

analogy (ǎ **nal** ǒ ji) *n.* **analogies** a similarity.

analyse (**an** ǎ līz) *vb.* **analysing, analysed** to examine the content of something in detail. **analysis** *n.* **analyses** a detailed examination of the structure and content of something.

anarchy (**an** ǎr ki) *n.* confusion and lack of order, especially political; the failure of law and government. – *adj.* **anarchic** (an **är** kik).

anatomy (ǎ **nat** ǒ mi) *n.* **anatomies 1** the science of the structure of the human or animal body, or plants, especially studied through dissection. **2** the structure of an animal or plant. – *adj.* **anatomical** (an ǎ **tom** i kǎl).

PRONUNCIATION GUIDE

fat a	all ö
fate ā	foot oo
fast ä	moon ōō
among å	boy oi
met e	house ow
mean ē	demon ǒ
silent ě	thing th
loch hh	this Th
fin i	but u
line ī	mute ū
quick kw	fur û
got o	brochure ǔ
note ō	vision zh

Anchor comes from a Greek word meaning 'hook'. The earliest anchors were made of cast iron with a wooden cross-piece or 'stock'. This type of anchor was replaced in the 19th century by one with a movable metal stock. This was known as the Admiralty anchor. Soon various stockless anchors came into use.

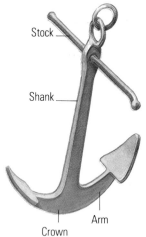

Stock —
Shank —
Arm
Crown

TYPES OF ANGLE

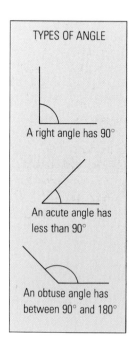

A right angle has 90°

An acute angle has less than 90°

An obtuse angle has between 90° and 180°

ancestor (**an** sis tŏr) *n.* a person who was a member of your family a long time ago, and from whom you are descended.
 ancestral (an **ses** trăl) *adj.* of your ancestors.
anchor (**ang** kŏr) *n.* a heavy piece of metal with hooks which dig into the seabed, attached by a cable to a ship to stop it floating away.
ancient (**ān** shĕnt) *adj.* **1** dating from very long ago; very old. **2** dating from before the end of the ROMAN EMPIRE in AD 476.
and (and) or (ănd) *conj.* **1** used to show addition: *Two and two equals four.* **2** used to show a result or reason: *On ice it is easy to fall and bang your head.* **3** used to show repetition or duration: *It rained and rained.* **4** used to show progression: *The balloon got bigger and bigger.*

●**Andersen, Hans Christian** (1805-75) was a Danish writer of fairytales which include *The Little Mermaid* and *The Ugly Duckling.*

●**Anderson, Elizabeth Garrett** (1836-1917) was the first woman to practise medicine in Britain.

●**Andes** (**an** dēz) the longest mountain range in the world, which runs the whole length (7000 km) of the west side of SOUTH AMERICA.

●**Andorra** (an **dö** rä). See Supplement, **Countries**.

●**Andrew, Saint** (1st century) was one of the twelve apostles of JESUS in the NEW TESTAMENT. He is patron saint of SCOTLAND. His feast day is 30 November.

anecdote (**an** ik dōt) *n.* a short, interesting, and usually amusing account of an incident.
anemometer (an ĕ **mo** mi tĕr) *n.* an instrument for measuring wind speed.
angel (**ān** jĕl) *n.* a messenger of God, represented in human form with wings.
anger (**ang** gĕr) *n.* a feeling of great or violent displeasure. *– vb.* **angering, angered** to make angry; to displease.
 angry *adj.* **angrier, angriest** feeling or showing anger. *– adv.* **angrily**.
angle¹ (**ang** gĕl) *n.* **1** the space between two straight lines or surfaces that meet. **2** a corner. *– vb.* **angling, angled** to place at an angle.
angle² (**ang** gĕl) *vb.* **angling, angled** to use a rod and line to try to catch fish. *– n.* **angler**.

Anglican (**ang** gli kăn) *adj.* of or relating to the CHURCH OF ENGLAND. *– n.* a member of an Anglican Church.
Anglo-Saxon (ang glō **sak** sŏn) *n.* **1** a member of any of the Germanic tribes which settled in ENGLAND and parts of SCOTLAND in the 5th century. **2** Old English, the ENGLISH language before about 1150. *– adj.* of the Anglo-Saxons or the Old English language.

SPELL IN ANGLO-SAXON	
king *cyning*	south *suth*
penny *pennig*	ship *scip*
green *grene*	sheep *sceap*
hot *hat*	milk *milc*
cold *cald*	cup *cuppe*
hill *hill*	cow *cu*
kiss *cyssan*	mouse *mus*

A helmet showing skilled Anglo-Saxon metalwork.

●**Angola** (ang gō lä). See Supplement, **Countries**.

angry. See **anger**.
anguish (**ang** gwish) *n.* great pain or suffering, especially of the mind.
angular (**ang** gū lăr) *adj.* **1** thin and bony. **2** having an angle or angles.
animal (**an** i măl) *n.* a living being that is not a plant and which can feel things and move when it wants.
animosity (an i **mos** i ti) *n.* **animosities** a strong dislike or hatred.

●**Ankara** (**ang** kă rä) is the capital of TURKEY.

ankle (**ang** kĕl) *n.* the joint connecting the leg and the foot.

●**Anne, Queen** (1665-1714) was queen of GREAT BRITAIN from 1702. She was the last STUART monarch.

annex (ă **neks**) *vb.* **annexing, annexed** to take possession of land or territory, especially by conquest or occupation. *– n.* **annexation**.
 annexe or **annex** (**an** eks) *n.* a building added on to, or used as an addition to, another.

annihilate (å **nī** hi lāt) *vb.* **annihilating, annihilated** to destroy completely. – *n.* **annihilation**.

anniversary (a ni **vûr** så ri) *n.* **anniversaries** **1** the date on which an event took place in a previous year. **2** the celebration of this event on the same date each year.

announce (å **nowns**) *vb.* **announcing, announced** to make known publicly: *He announced his retirement.* – *n.* **announcement**. **announcer** *n.* a person who introduces programmes on radio or television.

annoy (å **noi**) *vb.* **annoying, annoyed** to anger or distress: *His lack of concern annoys me.*

annual (**an** ū ål) *adj.* happening every year: *They have an annual trip to the sea in July.*

anomaly (å **nom** å li) *n.* **anomalies** something which is different from what is usual. **anomalous** *adj.* different from the usual.

anonymous (å **non** i mûs) *adj.* done or written by a person whose name is not known.

anorexia (a nǒ **rek** si å) or **anorexia nervosa** (a nǒ **rek** si å nûr **vō** så) *n.* an illness in which the sufferer refuses to eat, and loses a lot of weight. – *n.* & *adj.* **anorexic**.

another (å **nu** Thĕr) *adj.* & *pron.* **1** one more: *Would you like another cake?* **2** one more of the same kind. **3** one of a different kind: *another country.*

answer (**an** sĕr) *n.* **1** something said or done in response to a question or letter, etc. **2** the solution to a problem. – *vb.* **answering, answered 1** to make a reply or answer: *She answered my question immediately.* **2** to respond to a doorbell or the telephone: *He couldn't answer the door because he was in the bath.* **answerable** *adj.* responsible for. **answering machine** *n.* a machine which records telephone messages when you are absent.

ant (ant) *n.* a small, often wingless insect, which lives in organized colonies.

Worker ants with aphids

Ants are 'social' insects and live together in colonies. In an ant colony there are different chambers which the ants use to lay eggs and bring up the young.

Worker ants with larvae

Wood ant

Adult ants emerging from pupae

Queen ant lays eggs

anteater *n.* a South African animal with a long snout, which mainly eats termites.

antagonist (an **tag** ǒ nist) *n.* an opponent or enemy. – *adj.* **antagonistic**. **antagonize** or **antagonise** *vb.* **antagonizing, antagonized** to make someone feel anger.

Antarctic (ant **ärk** tik) *n.* the area round the SOUTH POLE.

● **Antarctica** (an **tär** ti kå) is the continent around the SOUTH POLE. Very little can grow there as average temperatures are below freezing.

Amundsen Sea

PACIFIC OCEAN

Weddell Sea

ATLANTIC OCEAN

South Pole

INDIAN OCEAN

In 1911 the Norwegian, Roald Amundsen, was the first person to reach the South Pole. He was closely followed by Captain Scott.

antelope (**an** ti lōp) *n.* **antelope** any of several types of deer-like animal with horns.

● Antelope are found in large herds in AFRICA and sometimes in ASIA. They can run very fast and are very graceful animals. Types of antelope include the impala, the gnu, and the tiny dikdik.

antenna (an **ten** å) *n.* **antennae** (an **ten** ē) one of a pair of feelers on the head of some insects or crabs, used for touching.

anthem (**an** thĕm) *n.* a song of praise.

anthology (an **thol** ǒ ji) *n.* **anthologies** a collection of poems or other writing.

● **Anthony, Susan B.** (1820-1906) campaigned for the ending of slavery in the UNITED STATES and also for the right of American women to vote.

WHAT'S THE ANSWER? Answer is an Anglo-Saxon word. The second half has the same root as 'swear'. The first part 'an' means 'against', so the whole word means 'to swear against'.

The main difference between horns and antlers is that horns are permanent, whereas antlers are shed each year. As a rule only male antelope have antlers which may be used in combat as they compete for females during the mating season.

anthropology (an thrŏ **pol** ŏ ji) *n.* the study of human beings, especially their society, customs, and beliefs. – *n.* **anthropologist**.

anti- (**an** ti-) **1** opposed to; against: *anti-aircraft*. **2** opposite to: *anticlockwise*.

antibiotic (an ti bī **ot** ik) *n.* any substance such as a medicine which is used to kill the bacteria that cause disease.

antibody (**an** ti bo di) *n.* **antibodies** a substance produced by the blood to fight harmful bacteria.

anticipate (an **ti** si pāt) *vb.* **anticipating, anticipated 1** to see what will be needed or wanted in the future and do what is necessary in advance: *We anticipated her arrival by preparing the spare room.* **2** to expect: *We anticipate a large crowd.* – *n.* **anticipation**.

anticlockwise (an ti **clok** wīz) *adv. & adj.* in the opposite direction to that in which the hands of a clock move.

antics (**an** tiks) *n.* (*plural*) silly behaviour.

anticyclone (an ti **sī** klōn) *n.* See **Weather terms**.

antidote (**an** ti dōt) *n.* **1** a medicine given to stop the harmful effects of a poison. **2** anything that prevents something bad.

• **Antigua and Barbuda** (an **tē** gå ån bär **boo** då). See Supplement, **Countries**.

antiquated (**an** ti kwā tid) *adj.* out of date.

antique (an **tēk**) *n.* a piece of furniture or china, etc. which is old and usually valuable.

antiseptic (an ti **sep** tik) *n. & adj.* a substance, or describing a substance, that kills germs and so prevents infection or disease: *My brother uses antiseptic mouthwash every morning.*

antler (**ant** lěr) *n.* either of the two branched horns on the head of a stag.

antonym (**an** tŏ nim) *n.* a word opposite in meaning to another word: *'Wide' and 'narrow' are antonyms.*

anus (**ā** nŭs) *n.* the opening at the end of the food canal, between the buttocks.

anvil (**an** vil) *n.* a heavy iron block on which metal objects can be hammered into shape.

anxious (**angk** shŭs) *adj.* **1** worried or fearful about what will or may happen: *I was anxious about their safety when they didn't come home.* **2** causing worry or fear: *It was an anxious moment when she fell.* – *n.* **anxiety** (ang **zī** ě ti).

any (**e** ni) *adj.* **1** one, no matter which: *I can't find any answer.* **2** some, no matter which: *Have you*

any apples? **3** a very small amount of: *I won't tolerate any nonsense.* **4** whichever or whatever: *Any child could tell you.* – *pron.* any one or any amount: *I haven't got any at all.*

anybody *pron.* any person, no matter which: *Anybody could do it.*

anyhow *adv.* **1** in spite of what has been said or done. **2** carelessly; in an untidy state.

anything *pron.* a thing of any kind; a thing, no matter which: *I can't think of anything to say.*

anyway *adv.* **1** nevertheless; in spite of what has been said or done: *I don't agree, but I'll do it anyway.* **2** in any way or manner.

Anzac (**an** zak) *n.* a soldier in the *A*ustralian and *N*ew *Z*ealand *A*rmy *C*orps during the First WORLD WAR.

aorta (ā **ör** tå) *n.* the main artery in the body, carrying blood from the heart.

• **Apaches** (å **pach** ēz) a NATIVE AMERICAN tribe of the south-western UNITED STATES. They resisted American settlers, and a long series of wars under such chiefs as Cochise and Geronimo finally ended in 1886. Today thousands of Apaches live on reservations.

apart (å **pärt**) *adv.* **1** in or into pieces: *It fell apart in my hands.* **2** separated by a certain distance or time: *They've lived apart for two months.* **3** to or on one side: *The house is set apart from the rest.*

apathy (**a** på thi) *n.* lack of interest or enthusiasm. – *adj.* **apathetic** (a på **thet** ik).

ape (āp) *n.* an animal related to monkeys, with little or no tail. – *vb.* **aping, aped** to imitate.

There are four kinds of **ape**. The gorilla and chimpanzee are African; orang-utan live in Borneo and Sumatra; gibbons live in south-east Asia. Apes have highly developed hands with 'opposable' thumbs. They enjoy swinging from branches. Apes have large brains.

Gorilla

Chimpanzee

●**Apennines** (**a** pĕ nīnz) a mountain range in ITALY.

aperture (**a** pĕr chŭr) *n*. a small opening.

apex (**ā** peks) *n*. **apexes** or **apices** (**ā** pi sēz) the highest point or tip.

aphid (**ā** fid) or **aphis** (**ā** fis) *n*. **aphids** or **aphides** (**ā** fi dēz) a small insect which feeds by sucking the juices from plants.

Aphrodite (a frŏ **dī** ti). See **Myths and Legends**.

apiary (**ā** pi å ri) *n*. **apiaries** a place where bees are kept.

Apollo. See **Myths and Legends**.

apology (å **pol** ŏ ji) *n*. **apologies** an expression of regret for a mistake or wrongdoing.
apologetic *adj*. showing regret for a fault, etc.
apologize or **apologise** *vb*. **apologizing, apologized** to say you are sorry.

apostle (å **po** sĕl) *n*. a person sent out to preach about JESUS CHRIST in the early CHRISTIAN church, especially one of his twelve original disciples.

apostrophe (å **po** strŏ fi) *n*. the mark ('), used to show the omission of a letter or letters, for example *I'm* for *I am*, and to show possession, for example *Anne's book*.

appal (å **pöl**) *vb*. **appalling, appalled** to shock or horrify.
appalling *adj*. **1** causing feelings of shock or horror. **2** (*colloquial*) extremely bad: *The weather was appalling; it rained all weekend*.

●**Appalachians** (a på **lā** chi ånz) heavily forested mountains forming the great eastern range that runs from Newfoundland, CANADA to Alabama in the UNITED STATES.

apparatus (a på **rā** tŭs) or (a på **ra** tŭs) *n*. **apparatuses** or **apparatus** the equipment needed for a particular purpose.

apparent (å **par** ĕnt) or (å **pār** ĕnt) *adj*. **1** easy to see or understand: *His reason for leaving was apparent*. **2** seeming to be real: *It was an apparent mistake, but I couldn't be sure*.

appeal (å **pēl**) *vb*. **appealing, appealed 1** to make an urgent or formal request: *She appealed for calm*. **2** to be pleasing, interesting, or attractive: *His sense of humour appeals to me*.
appealing *adj*. pleasing, attractive.

appear (å **pēr**) *vb*. **appearing, appeared 1** to become visible or come into sight: *The bird suddenly appeared above the rooftops*. **2** to seem: *They appear to be very happy*.
appearance *n*. **1** an act or instance of appearing. **2** how a person or thing looks.

appendicitis (å pen di **sī** tis) *n*. inflammation of the appendix.

appendix (å **pen** diks) *n*. **appendices** (å **pen** di sēz) **1** a section containing extra information at the end of a book. **2** a small, tube-like sac attached to the lower end of the large intestine.

appetite (**a** pi tīt) *n*. a desire, especially for food.
appetizing *adj*. increasing the appetite, especially by looking or smelling delicious.

applaud (å **plöd**) *vb*. **applauding, applauded** to show approval by clapping. – *n*. **applause**.

apple (**a** pĕl) *n*. a firm, round, edible fruit with a green, red, or yellow skin and white flesh.

Just four of over 1800 named varieties of apple: 1. Granny Smith. 2. Cox's Orange Pippin. 3. McIntosh. 4. Red Delicious.

appliance (å **plī** åns) *n*. a machine, instrument, or tool used for a particular job.

application (a pli **kā** shŏn) *n*. **1** a formal request. **2** in computers, a program designed to perform a particular function.

apply (å **plī**) *vb*. **applies, applying, applied 1** to make a formal request, e.g. for a job. **2** to put or spread on a surface.

Gibbon

Orang-utan

appoint (å **point**) *vb.* **appointing, appointed**
1 to give a person a job or position. **2** to fix or
agree on a date, time, or place.
   appointment *n.* **1** an arrangement to meet
someone. **2** the act of giving someone a job.

appreciate (å **prē** shi āt) *vb.* **appreciating,**
appreciated 1 to be grateful or thankful for:
They appreciated all our hard work. **2** to be aware
of the value or quality, etc. of: *I appreciate your*
friendship. **3** to understand or be aware of: *We*
appreciate your concern in this matter.
   appreciation *n.* gratitude or thanks.
   appreciative *adj.* expressing appreciation.

apprehension (a pri **hen** shŏn) *n.* fear or
anxiety about the future.
   apprehensive *adj.* anxious.

approach (å **prōch**) *vb.* **approaching,**
approached 1 to come near or nearer in
space or time: *The children got excited as the*
holidays approached. **2** to suggest or propose
something to: *The company approached him with*
an offer of work. – *n.* **1** the act of coming near.
2 a way to, or means of reaching, a place: *The*
approach to the castle was very steep. **3** a request
for help or support; a suggestion or proposal.
   approachable *adj.* **1** friendly and ready to
listen and help. **2** that can be reached.

approve (å **prōōv**) *vb.* **approving, approved**
1 to agree to or permit: *They approved our*
annual budget. **2** to be pleased with or think well
of: *I approve of your choice of colour.*
   approval *n.* **1** a favourable opinion. **2** official
permission.

approximate (å **proks** i måt) *adj.* almost exact
or accurate.

apricot (**ā** pri kot) *n.* a small, round, pale-
orange fruit with a soft furry skin.

April (**ā** pril) *n.* the fourth month of the year.
April has 30 days.

apron (**ā** prŏn) *n.* a piece of cloth, etc. worn
over the front of your clothes to protect them.

apse (aps) *n.* the domed east end of a church.

apt (apt) *adj.* **1** suitable: *This is an apt moment to*
pause. **2** likely: *You're apt to get lost in the dark.*

aqualung (**a** kwå lung) *n.* an apparatus
consisting of air cyclinders worn by divers on
their backs, with tubes leading to the mouth,
allowing them to breathe under water.

aquarium (å **kwā** ri ům) *n.* **aquariums** or
aquaria (å **kwā** ri å) a glass tank, or a
building containing several such tanks (in a
zoo, for example), for keeping fish and other
water animals.

Apricots grow on a small
tree belonging to the plum
family. They are sweet
and peach-like to taste
and can be eaten fresh,
canned, or dried. People
once thought that apricots
came from America, but
in fact they originate
from China.

The most
famous
aqueducts were built by the Romans. Between 312 BC
and AD 226 they built 11 aqueducts to supply Rome.

Aquarius (å **kwā** ri ůs) *n.* See **zodiac**.

aqueduct (**a** kwi dukt) *n.* a canal, etc. especially
in the form of a tall bridge across a valley.

● **Aquinas** (å **kwī** nås), **Saint Thomas** (1225-
74) was an Italian Dominican friar.

Arab (**a** råb) *n.* **1** one of the people living in the
MIDDLE EAST and North AFRICA. **2** a breed of
horse famous for its grace and speed.
   Arabic *n.* the language of the Arabs.
   Arabic numeral *n.* any of the numbers 0, 1,
2, 3, 4, 5, 6, 7, 8, or 9, brought to EUROPE
from INDIA by the Arabs.

arable (**a** rå běl) *adj.* describing land that is
suitable or used for growing crops.

arachnid (å **rak** nid) *n.* any of a class of eight-
legged insect-like creatures, such as spiders.

arbitrary (**är** bi trå ri) *adj.* based on personal or
random choice, not rules.

arbitrate (**är** bi trāt) *vb.* **arbitrating,**
arbitrated to act as a judge in a quarrel or
disagreement. – *n.* **arbitrator**.

arc (ärk) *n.* a part of the line which forms a circle or other curve. – *vb.* **arcing, arced** to form an arc.

arcade (är **kād**) *n.* a row of arches supported by columns; a covered passage, usually lined with shops: *Burlington Arcade in the West End of London is a famous shopping centre.*

arch (ärch) *n.* **1** a curved structure forming an opening, a support, or an ornament. **2** the raised part of the sole of the foot, between the heel and the toes.

Keystone

Most arches span openings and support weight. They are made of wedge-shaped stone or brick blocks called voussoirs. The centre stone at the top of the arch is called the keystone. Pressure from each side of the arch supports the arch.

Piers

Lancet arch   Shouldered arch

Trefoil arch   Four-centre arch   Ogee arch

arch- (ärch-) or (ärk-), or **archi-** (är ki-) chief; most important: *archangel*; *archduke*.

archaeology (är ki **ol** ŏ ji) *n.* the study of the history and culture of ancient civilizations through studying tools or pots, etc., dug up from the ground. – *adj.* **archaeological** (är ki ŏ **loj** i kål). – *n.* **archaeologist**.

archaeopteryx (är ki **op** tĕ riks) *n.* an ancient fossil bird with sharp teeth.

archaic (är **kā** ik) *adj.* ancient.

archer (**ärch** ĕr) *n.* a person who shoots with a bow and arrows.

archery *n.* the sport of shooting with a bow.

● **Archimedes** (är ki **mē** dēz) (*c.*287-212 BC) was a Greek mathematician and inventor who discovered the principle of buoyancy and the lever.

archipelago (är ki **pel** å gō) *n.* **archipelagos** **1** a group of islands. **2** an area of sea with many islands.

Pottery

At first **archaeological** sites were ransacked for the treasures they contained, but by the early 1800s archaeologists had begun to uncover sites carefully, noting everything they found and where they found it. Today carbon dating (dating by measuring one type of carbon that objects contain) and dendrochronology (dating by tree rings) help tell archaeologists when objects were made.

The skull of an early human-like creature.

WORDS USED IN ARCHAEOLOGY

artefact any object made by humans.
barrow an earth-covered dolmen.
Bronze Age from about 3000 to 1800 BC.
cromlech a ring of standing stones.
dolmen a burial chamber consisting of several upright stones.
flint the most favoured stone of prehistoric people.
henge a sacred circle of stones.

Iron Age began about 1400 BC.
megaliths stone monuments
menhir a single upright stone.
quern two circular stones used to grind corn.
sarcophagus a stone coffin.
sherd a fragment of pottery.
Stone Age the name given to the time when people used only stone for tool making. It includes the Palaeolithic (old stone age), the Mesolithic (middle stone age), and Neolithic (new stone age).

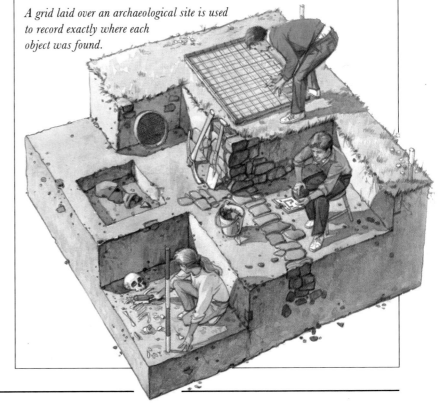
A grid laid over an archaeological site is used to record exactly where each object was found.

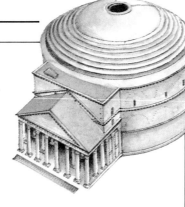

Architecture is the art and the science of designing buildings. Some of the greatest architecture of the past was made by the Egyptians, Greeks, Romans, Indians, Chinese, and the Aztecs and Incas. Modern architects design airports, factories, office blocks – even whole towns.

The Pantheon, or Temple of All Gods, Rome, is the greatest Roman example of the use of concrete.

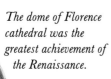

The dome of Florence cathedral was the greatest achievement of the Renaissance.

The Taj Mahal in India was begun in 1632. It is perhaps the most famous building in the world.

The Lloyds Building, London, an impressive example of modern architecture.

Sears Tower, Chicago (443 m), World Trade center (411m) and Empire State Building, New York (381m).

architect (är ki tekt) *n.* a person qualified to design buildings and other large structures. **architecture** *n.* **1** the art of designing and constructing buildings. **2** a particular style of building: – *adj.* **architectural.**

archive (är kīv) *n.* (usually in *plural*) a collection of old public documents or records, etc.

Arctic (ärk tik) *n.* the area round the NORTH POLE consisting of mostly frozen sea surrounded by land.

ardent (är děnt) *adj.* enthusiastic; passionate. – *n.* **ardour.**

arduous (är dū ůs) *adj.* difficult to do.

are. See **be.**

area (ā ri å) *n.* **1** the extent or size of a flat surface: *The area of this field is 30m².* **2** a region or part: *This area of the country is famous for its wine.* **3** any space set aside for a particular purpose: *This is the dining area of the house.*

arena (å rē nå) *n.* an area surrounded by seats, for public shows or sports contests, etc.

Ares (ā rēz). See **Myths and Legends.**

●**Argentina** is the second largest country in SOUTH AMERICA. It was ruled by SPAIN until 1810. Buenos Aires is the capital and also the country's main port. See also Supplement, **Countries.**

argue (är gū) *vb.* **arguing, argued 1** to exchange views with someone, especially angrily: *They argued about who should do the washing up.* **2** to suggest reasons for or against something: *He argued against eating in that restaurant because it is too expensive.*

argument (är gū měnt) *n.* **1** a quarrel. **2** a reason for or against something.

arid (a rid) *adj.* dry; having very little water.

Aries (ā rēz) *n.* See **zodiac.**

arise (å rīz) *vb.* **arising, arose** (å rōz), **arisen** (å riz ěn) **1** to come into being: *The question arose as we were speaking.* **2** to result or be caused: *His decision to go arose from our meeting.* **3** to get up or stand up.

aristocracy (a ri **stok** rå si) *n.* **aristocracies 1** the highest social class, usually owning land and having titles. **2** government by this class. **aristocrat** (**a** ris tǒ krat) *n.* a member of the aristocracy. – *adj.* **aristocratic.**

●**Aristotle** (a ris **to** těl) (384-322 BC) was a Greek philosopher who believed happiness comes from human reason.

arithmetic (å **rith** mě tik) *n.* the science of adding, subtracting, multiplying, and dividing numbers.

● **Arizona**. See Supplement, **USA**.

ark (ärk) *n.* **1** in the BIBLE, the vessel built by NOAH in which his family and animals survived the Flood. **2 Ark** a chest in a synagogue in which the law scrolls are kept.

● **Arkansas** (**är** kån sö). See Supplement, **USA**.

● **Arkwright, Richard** (1732-92) was the English inventor of the cotton spinning frame which helped pioneer the modern factory system.

arm[1] (ärm) *n.* **1** either of the two upper limbs of the body, from the shoulders to the hands. **2** anything shaped like this: *an arm of the sea.* **3** the sleeve of a garment. **4** the part of a chair, etc. that supports an arm.

arm[2] (ärm) *n.* (usually in *plural*) a weapon.

armada (är **mä** då) *n.* a fleet of ships.

● In 1588 Spain sent a great fleet of armed ships, the Spanish Armada, to invade ENGLAND. CATHOLIC SPAIN wanted to crusade against England, which was a PROTESTANT country. The Spanish were heavily defeated by the faster English ships.

The defeat of the Spanish Armada in 1588.

armadillo (är må **di** lō) *n.* **armadillos** a small South American burrowing animal covered with a hard bony shell.

● **Armenia** (är **mē** ni å). See Supplement, **Countries**.

armistice (**är** mi stis) *n.* a stopping of hostilities.

armour (**är** mŏr) *n.* **1** a metal suit or covering formerly worn as a protection against injury in battle. **2** metal covering to protect ships or tanks, etc. against damage from weapons. **3** a protective covering on some animals and plants.

armoured *adj.* protected by armour.

● **Armstrong, Neil** (1930-) was an American astronaut. On 21 July 1969 he became the first person to set foot on the Moon.

army (**är** mi) *n.* **armies 1** a large number of people armed and organized for fighting on land. **2** a large number: *an army of children.*

aroma (å **rō** må) *n.* a distinctive, usually pleasant smell that a substance gives off.

aromatic (a rō **ma** tik) *adj.* having a strong, but sweet or pleasant smell.

arose. See **arise**.

around (å **rownd**) *adv.* **1** on every side: *The children gathered around to listen to the story.* **2** here and there; in different directions or to different places: *They drove around for several hours.* – *prep.* **1** on all sides of: *She wore a bracelet around her wrist.* **2** at or to different points. **3** somewhere in or near: *Their house is around here.*

arouse (å **rowz**) *vb.* **arousing, aroused 1** to cause an emotion or reaction, etc. **2** to cause to become active; to stir.

arrange (å **rānj**) *vb.* **arranging, arranged 1** to put into the proper order: *I arranged the words alphabetically.* **2** to plan in advance: *We arranged to meet at the station.*

arrangement *n.* **1** (usually in *plural*) a plan or preparation for some future event. **2** the act of putting things into a proper order or pattern. **3** an agreement.

arrest (å **rest**) *vb.* **arresting, arrested 1** to take a person into custody: *The police arrested the thief.* **2** to stop or slow the development of a disease, etc.: *The doctor tried to arrest the spread of the illness.* – *n.* See **Law**.

Armadillo is Spanish for 'little armed one', an apt description for a creature whose body is encased in a kind of armour.

— Helmet

Visor —

— Breast plate

— Gauntlet

— Leg harness

— Sword

In the Middle Ages knights – and their horses – rode to battle encased in up to sixty pieces of plate armour. The invention of firearms made armour obsolete.

Prehistoric people made arrowheads of stone or bone for hunting and for warfare. Together with spears, arrows have been used in all parts of the world throughout history. Illustrated are an arrow for a medieval long bow and a 'bolt' used on the more powerful crossbow.

arrive (å rīv) *vb.* **arriving, arrived 1** to reach a place or destination: *She arrived home much earlier than expected.* **2** to come to a conclusion or decision, etc.: *He arrived at that conclusion after reading many books on the subject.*

    arrival *n.* **1** the act of arriving: *Her arrival was greeted with loud cheers.* **2** a person or thing that has arrived, especially a newborn baby: *The doting parents proudly presented their new arrival.*

arrogant (**a** rŏ gånt) *adj.* having too high an opinion of your own importance. – *n.* **arrogance.**

arrow (**a** rō) *n.* a thin, straight stick with a point at one end and which is fired from a bow.

    arsenal (**är** sě nål) *n.* a factory or store for weapons or explosives.

arsenic (**är** sě nik) *n.* a powerful poison.

arson (**är** sǒn) *n.* the crime of deliberately setting fire to a building, etc. – *n.* **arsonist.**

art (ärt) *n.* **1** the creation of works of beauty. **2** (in *plural*) the different branches of creative activity, e.g. music, painting, and literature. **3** a skill: *He has an art for dealing with people.*

    artful *adj.* **1** cunning. **2** skilful.

    artless *adj.* simple and natural in manner.

artefact (**är** ti fakt) *n.* an object made by humans, for example a tool, especially with historical or archaeological interest.

Artemis (**är** ti mis). See **Myths and Legends.**

artery (**är** tě ri) *n.* **arteries** a tube that carries blood from the heart through the body.

arthritis (är **thrī** tis) *n.* inflammation of a joint or joints, causing pain and great difficulty in moving. – *n.* & *adj.* **arthritic** (är **thri** tik).

arthropod (**är** thrō pod) *n.* a creature with a body in segments, limbs connected by joints, and its skeleton on the outside, such as a spider.

Artery is a Greek word meaning 'air carrier'. Because there is little blood in the arteries of dead bodies, ancient Greek doctors who dissected them thought arteries carried air around the body.

• **Arthur, King** was a legendary British ruler of the AD 500s. He was leader of the Knights of the Round Table.

artichoke (**är** ti chōk) *n.* the name of two vegetables: Jerusalem (an edible tuber); and globe (a thistle-like plant).

article (**är** ti kěl) *n.* **1** a thing or object: *How many articles did you buy?* **2** a usually short written composition in a newspaper or magazine: *Did you read his article on sharks in the last issue?* **3** in grammar, 'the' (the **definite article**) or 'a' or 'an' (the **indefinite article**), or any equivalent word in other languages.

articulate (är **tik** ū lāt) *vb.* **articulating, articulated** to pronounce words or speak clearly and distinctly.

artificial (är ti **fi** shål) *adj.* **1** made by humans; not occurring naturally. **2** made in imitation of a natural product.

    artificial intelligence *n.* a branch of computer science which studies ways of making computers learn, understand, and make judgements like people do.

artillery (är **til** ě ri) *n.* **artilleries** large guns for use on land.

Artillery includes mounted guns and rocket launchers that are too heavy to be classed as small arms. Most artillery is mobile, such as anti-aircraft artillery mounted on tanks.

artist (**är** tist) *n.* a person who produces works of art, especially paintings.

    artistic *adj.* **1** liking or skilled in painting or music, etc. **2** made or done with skill and good taste. – *adv.* **artistically.**

    artistry *n.* artistic skill and imagination.

as (az) or (åz) *conj.* **1** when; while; during: *She played as I sang.* **2** because; since: *I couldn't carry it as it was so heavy.* **3** in the manner which: *Behave as you like.* **4** that which; what: *Do as you're told.* **5** although: *Try as he might, he still couldn't reach.* – *prep.* in the role of: *Speaking as her friend, I think you're mistaken.* – *adv.* to whatever extent or amount. – *pron.* **1** that, who, or which also: *She is a singer, as is her brother.* **2** for the reason that: *Come early so as to avoid the rush.* **3** a fact that: *He'll be late, as you know.* – **as it were** in a way; to some extent. – **as well** also.

asbestos (as **bes** tŏs) *n.* a mineral made up of fibres that can be woven into fireproof cloth.

ascend (å **send**) *vb.* **ascending, ascended** to climb, go, or rise up. – **ascend the throne** to become king or queen.

ascent (å **sent**) *n.* **1** the act of climbing, going up, or rising. **2** an upward slope.

ascertain (a sěr **tān**) *vb.* **ascertaining, ascertained** to find out; to discover the truth.

ASCII (**as** ki) *abbreviation.* See **Computer terms**.

Asgard (**as** gärd). See **Myths and Legends**.

ash[1] (ash) *n.* the dust that remains after something is burned.

Ash Wednesday *n.* the first day of Lent.

ash[2] (ash) *n.* a forest tree with silver-grey bark; the hard, pale wood from this tree.

ashamed (å **shāmd**) *adj.* **1** feeling shame or embarrassment: *He was ashamed of his unjust behaviour.* **2** hesitant or reluctant through shame or a fear of being wrong: *She was ashamed to show us her messy room.*

●**Asia** (**ā** zhå) is the biggest continent. It stretches from the Arctic in the north to the equator in the south. It covers nearly a third of the Earth's land surface. The world's highest mountains, the HIMALAYAS, are in Asia, and so is the lowest point on the land surface, the shores of the Dead Sea. The river valleys of CHINA are among the most heavily populated places in the world. Most Asians are farmers and the chief crops are wheat and rice. JAPAN is the only truly industrialized nation. There is a huge variety of animal life from elephants to pandas. Asia was the birthplace of civilization and many cultures have flourished there, including that of MESOPOTAMIA, CHINA, and the Indus Valley.

Asian (**ā** shån) or (**ā** zhån) *n.* **1** a person born and living in ASIA. **2** a person of Asian descent. – *adj.* of ASIA, its people, languages, etc.

Asiatic (ā shi **at** ik) or (ā zi **at** ik) *adj.* Asian.

aside (å **sīd**) *adv.* **1** on or to one side: *He pushed me aside as he ran along the corridor.* **2** apart: *Do you write anything else aside from poetry?*

ask (äsk) *vb.* **asking, asked** **1** to put a question to someone or call for an answer to a question: *He asked the girl what she thought about it.* **2** to inquire about: *Let's ask the way.* **3** to make a request; to seek: *The little boy asked for an ice cream.* **4** to invite: *Philip asked us to come to tea.* **5** to expect: *They ask too much of her.* – **ask after** to ask for news of a person or thing.

askew (å **skū**) *adj. & adv.* not properly straight.

asleep (å **slēp**) *adj. & adv.* in or into a sleeping state: *fall asleep.*

asp (asp) *n.* a small poisonous snake.

aspect (**a** spekt) *n.* **1** a particular or distinct part of a problem or subject, etc.: *Which aspect of the matter shall we discuss first?* **2** appearance or look: *The old castle has a spooky aspect.*

KEY FACTS
Area: 44,418,500 sq km
Number of countries: 49
Largest country: China
Largest city: Tokyo
Highest mountain: Mount Everest
Longest river: Chang Jiang (Yangtze)

Asia stretches from Turkey in the west to the Pacific Ocean in the east.

asphalt (**as** falt) *n.* a black, tar-like substance used as a surface for roads or roofs, etc.

aspire (å **spīr**) *vb.* **aspiring, aspired** to have a strong desire to achieve something, e.g. an ambition: *She aspires to greatness.* – *n.* **aspiration** (a spi **rā** shŏn). – *adj.* **aspiring.**

aspirin (**as** prin) *n.* a drug widely used for relieving pain and fever.

The North African wild ass is probably the ancestor of the domestic donkey. The legs are often striped and the ears long. Wild asses live in semi-desert areas.

ass (as) *n.* a donkey, especially a wild one.

assassin (å **sa** sin) *n.* a person who murders someone, especially for political reasons.
  assassinate *vb.* **assassinating, assassinated** to murder. – *n.* **assassination**.

assault (å **sölt**) *n.* a violent attack. – *vb.* **assaulting, assaulted** to make an assault.

assegai or **assagai** (a **sė** gī) *n.* a thin, light, iron-tipped wooden spear used in AFRICA.

assemble (å **sem** bėl) *vb.* **assembling, assembled 1** to gather or collect together: *The class assembled in the playground.* **2** to put together the parts of a machine, etc.: *She assembled the parts of the model car kit.*
  assembly *n.* **assemblies** a group of people gathered together, especially for a meeting.

assert (å **sûrt**) *vb.* **asserting, asserted 1** to state firmly. **2** to insist on or defend your rights or opinions, etc. – *n.* **assertion**.
  assertive *adj.* expressing your opinions in a strong and confident manner.

assess (å **ses**) *vb.* **assessing, assessed 1** to judge the quality or importance of something. **2** to estimate the cost or value of something.

asset (a **set**) *n.* **1** a valuable skill, quality, or person. **2** (in *plural*) the total value of the possessions of a person or company.

assign (å **sīn**) *vb.* **assigning, assigned** to give a task, etc. to someone or appoint someone to a position or task: *The teacher assigned her to the post of class monitor.*

assist (å **sist**) *vb.* **assisting, assisted 1** to help. **2** to take part in a ceremony, etc.

associate (å **sō** shi āt) *vb.* **associating, associated 1** to connect in the mind: *I always associate lambs with spring.* **2** to mix socially: *We don't associate with him.*
  association *n.* **1** an organization or club. **2** a partnership. **3** a connection in the mind.

assorted (å **sör** tid) *adj.* mixed; containing various different kinds: *That stall sells assorted fruit and vegetables from all over the world.*
  assortment *n.* a mixed collection.

assume (å **sōōm**) or (å **sūm**) *vb.* **assuming, assumed 1** to accept something, though without proof; to take for granted: *I assumed he was free to help, but in fact he wasn't.* **2** to take upon yourself a responsibility: *He assumed the role of judge.*

assumption (å **sum** shǒn) *n.* something accepted as true without proof.

assure (å **shōōr**) *vb.* **assuring, assured 1** to state positively and confidently. **2** to convince someone: *I assured her of my innocence.*
  assurance *n.* **1** a promise, guarantee, or statement that a thing is true. **2** confidence.

asterisk (a **stė** risk) *n.* a star-shaped mark (*) used in printing and writing, to mark a reference to a note or an omission.

astern (å **stûrn**) *adv.* & *adj.* **1** in or towards the stern of a boat. **2** backwards. **3** behind.

asteroid (a **stė** roid) *n.* any of the small planets moving around the Sun.

Asteroids, or 'minor planets', mainly travel between the orbits of Mars and Jupiter. The largest, Ceres, is under 1000 km in diameter.

asthma (as **må**) *n.* an illness, usually caused by an allergy, which makes breathing difficult.

astonish (å **ston** ish) *vb.* **astonishing, astonished** to surprise greatly.

astound (å **stownd**) *vb.* **astounding, astounded** to amaze greatly or shock.

astray (å **strā**) *adj.* & *adv.* out of the right or expected way. – **go astray** to get lost.

astride (å **strīd**) *adv.* with a leg on each side.

astro- (a **strō**-) of stars or space.

astrology (å **strol** ǒ ji) *n.* the study of the movements of the stars and planets and their influence on people's lives. – *n.* **astrologer**.

astronaut (a **strǒ** nöt) *n.* a person trained for space travel.

Astronomy is the oldest of all the sciences. Early astronomers divided the year into months, weeks, and days based on the movements of the Sun, Earth, and Moon. Until the 1540s people believed that the Earth was the centre of the universe.

A Mesopotamian 'star map' of 2000 BC

Halley's Comet as depicted on the Bayeux Tapestry. Edmund Halley (1656 -1742) showed that the comet named after him appears at regular intervals.

The Hubble Space Telescope is above the Earth's atmosphere and so can send back pictures of distant objects.

The telescope that Galileo constructed in 1609. He challenged many accepted theories about the universe.

A terrestrial telescope at Mount Palomar Observatory, California. Its reflecting mirror is five metres in diameter.

 Hektor

 Davida

astronomy (å **stron** ŏ mi) *n.* the scientific study of the stars and planets, etc. – *n.* **astronomer**.

astronomical (a strŏ **nom** i kål) or **astronomic** *adj.* describing numbers or amounts, etc. that are very large.

astute (å **stūt**) *adj.* able to judge quickly.

asylum (å **sī** lŭm) *n.* **1** a place of safety or protection. **2** a mental hospital.

at (at) *prep.* expressing **1** position or location: *We're staying at home.* **2** direction: *Look at the book.* **3** position in time: *We always eat at one o'clock.* **4** state or occupation: *Over there you can see the children at play.* **5** time during which: *He often works at night.* **6** cost: *The shop sells these clothes at a high price.*

●**Ataturk** (**a** tå **tûrk**), **Kemal** (1881-1938) was a statesman, creator of the modern Turkish state.

atheism (**ā** thi i zěm) *n.* See **Religious terms**.

●**Athens** is the capital of GREECE and in about 400 BC was the centre of civilization.

athlete (**ath** lēt) *n.* a person who is good at sport, especially track and field events.
athletic (åth **let** ik) *adj.* describing someone who is physically fit and strong.

athletics *n.* (*singular*) track and field events such as running and shot-putting, etc.

Atlantic (åt **lan** tik) *n.* the Atlantic Ocean separates EUROPE and AFRICA from AMERICA. It is the second largest ocean after the PACIFIC.

atlas (**at** lås) *n.* **atlases** a book of maps.

atmosphere (**at** mŏ sfēr) *n.* **1** the gases surrounding a planet. **2** the air in a particular place. **3** the mood of a place.

atoll (**a** tol) *n.* a ring-shaped coral reef surrounding a lagoon.

atom (**a** tŏm) *n.* **1** the smallest particle of an element that can take part in a chemical reaction. **2** this particle as a source of nuclear energy. **3** a small amount.
atomic *adj.* using nuclear energy.

atrocity (å **tro** si ti) *n.* **atrocities** wicked or cruel behaviour.

attach (å **tach**) *vb.* **attaching, attached** **1** to fasten. **2** to associate yourself with. – *adj.* **attached**.

Atoms are made up of a system of tiny particles. An atom has a nucleus which contains protons (with a positive charge) and neutrons (no charge), and has electrons (negative charge) spinning around it.

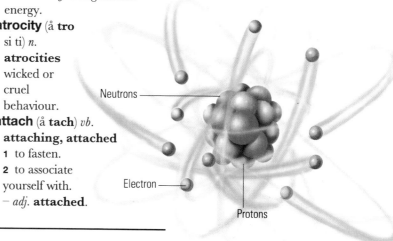

Neutrons

Electron

Protons

attack (å **tak**) *vb.* **attacking, attacked 1** to make a sudden or violent attempt to hurt, damage, or capture: *The hungry fox attacked the chickens.* **2** to criticize strongly in speech or writing: *The article attacked his decisions.* **3** to begin to do something with enthusiasm or determination. – *n.* **1** an act of attacking. **2** a sudden spell of illness: *Mark is suffering from an attack of 'flu.*

attain (å **tān**) *vb.* **attaining, attained 1** to complete successfully or accomplish. **2** to reach. – *adj.* **attainable.** – *n.* **attainment.**

attempt (å **tempt**) *vb.* **attempting, attempted 1** to try: *We attempted to follow his instructions, but they were very confusing.* **2** to try to climb or master a mountain or problem, etc.: *They unsuccessfully attempted Everest.* – *n.* an endeavour to achieve something.

attend (å **tend**) *vb.* **attending, attended 1** to be present at: *Tom attended the party.* **2** to go regularly: *She attends the local school.* **3** to give attention to or take action about: *Can you attend to this matter immediately.*
attendance *n.* the act of attending.

attention (å **ten** shǒn) *n.* **1** the act of concentrating: **2** special care.

attentive (å **ten** tiv) *adj.* **1** concentrating: *Try to be attentive during the class.* **2** polite: *They were attentive to the needs of their guests.*

attic (**a** tik) *n.* a space or room at the top of a house under the roof.

● **Attila** (å **ti** lå) (406-53) was king of the HUNS. He inflicted devastation on the ROMAN EMPIRE.

attire (å **tīr**) *n.* clothing, especially formal.

attitude (**a** ti tūd) *n.* a way of thinking or behaving.

attorney (å **tûr** ni) *n.* **attorneys 1** a person able to act for another in legal or business matters. **2** (*US*) a lawyer.

attract (å **trakt**) *vb.* **attracting, attracted 1** to cause to come close or stay close: *Light attracts moths.* **2** to be attractive to.
attractive *adj.* **1** appealing: *This is an attractive use of colour.* **2** good-looking.

attribute (å **trib** ūt) *vb.* **attributing, attributed** to think of something as being written, made, said, or caused by: *That remark was attributed to the artist.* – (**a** tri būt) *n.* a quality, characteristic, or feature.

aubergine (**ō** běr zhēn) *n.* a tropical plant which produces a dark purple fruit.

● **Auckland** (**ōk** lånd) is the largest city in NEW ZEALAND and the country's chief seaport.

auction (**ōk** shǒn) *n.* a public sale in which each item is sold to the person who offers the most money. – *vb.* **auctioning, auctioned** to sell in this way.

audacious (ö **dā** shǔs) *adj.* bold and daring.

audible (**ö** di běl) *adj.* loud enough to be heard.

audience (**ö** di ěns) *n.* **1** a group of people watching a performance. **2** a formal interview with an important person.

audio (**ö** di ō) *adj.* of sound, hearing, or the recording and broadcasting of sound.

audition (**ö** di shǒn) *n.* a short performance to test the ability of an actor, singer, or musician.

auditorium (ö di **tör** i ǔm) *n.* **auditoriums** or **auditoria** the part of a theatre or hall, etc. where the audience sits.

● **Audubon** (**ö** dǔ bon), **John** (1785-1851) was an American wildlife painter, notably of birds.

August (**ö** gǔst) *n.* the eighth month of the year. August has 31 days.

august (ö **gust**) *adj.* noble; imposing.

auk (ök) *n.* a sea bird with a heavy body, short wings, and black and white feathers.

Auks are found only in the northern hemisphere. Like penguins, they stand erect and dive underwater to catch fish. They spend most of their lives at sea, visiting land only to breed.

aunt (änt) *n.* the sister of your father or mother, or the wife of your uncle.

● **Austen** (**os** tin), **Jane** (1775-1817) was one of England's greatest novelists. *Emma* and *Pride and Prejudice* are the best known of her six works.

austere (ö **stēr**) *adj.* serious; severe; stern.
austerity (ö **ste** ri ti) *n.* **1** strictness or harshness. **2** extreme simplicity of dress, etc.

Australasian (o strå **lā** zhǎn) *adj.* of or relating to AUSTRALIA, NEW ZEALAND, and the Pacific islands.

Attorney is based on a French word for 'turn' and it applies to someone to whom people can turn for help in legal matters.

●**Australia** is a huge island and the world's smallest continent, the last to be discovered by Europeans. Its first inhabitants were the ABORIGINES. Much of Australia is a dry flat desert and most of the population (16 million) live around the coasts. Cattle and sheep farming, and mining are all important. See also Supplement, **Countries**.

KEY FACTS
Capital: Canberra
Longest river: Darling
Largest reef: Great Barrier Reef

All marsupials – except for the American opossum – live in Australia. The only food of koalas is eucalyptus leaves.

Australian (o **strā** li ån) *adj.* of or relating to AUSTRALIA. – *n.* a person born or living in AUSTRALIA.

●**Austria** is now a small central-European country. Under the HABSBURG rulers until 1918, it was one of the largest and most powerful nations. Its capital is VIENNA. See also Supplement, **Countries**.

authentic (ö **then** tik) *adj.* **1** genuine. **2** reliable.
author (ö thồr) *n.* the writer of a book or play.
authority (ö **tho** ri ti) *n.* **authorities 1** the power or right to control or judge others. **2** (often in *plural*) the person or people who have power, especially political or administrative. **3** an expert: *She's an authority on the feeding habits of starfish.*
authorize (ö thồr īz) or **authorise** *vb.* **authorizing, authorized** to give someone the power or right to do something: *Anthony authorized him to collect the money.* – *n.* **authorization**.
auto- (ö tō-) of or by yourself or itself.
autobiography (ö tō bī **og** rå fi) *n.* **autobiographies** the story of a person's life written by that person. – *n.* **autobiographer**. – *adj.* **autobiographical.**

autocross (ö tō kros) *n.* motor-racing on a rough grass track.
autograph (ö tồ gräf) *n.* a person's signature, especially a famous person's, usually kept as a souvenir.
automatic (ö tồ **ma** tik) *adj.* **1** describing a machine that works by itself. **2** unconscious.
automation (ö tồ **mā** shồn) *n.* the use of automatic machines and equipment to control production in manufacturing.
automobile (ö tồ mō bēl) *n.* (*US*) a car.
autonomy (ö **to** nồ mi) *n.* **autonomies** the power or right of a country or state, etc. to govern itself.
autopsy (ö top si) *n.* **autopsies** an examination of a dead body to find out the cause of death.
autumn (ö tŭm) *n.* the season of the year, between summer and winter, when leaves change colour and fall. – *adj.* **autumnal**.
available (å **vāl** å bĕl) *adj.* able or ready to be obtained or used. – *n.* **availability**.
avalanche (a vå länsh) *n.* a sudden, huge fall of snow and ice down a mountain.

●**Avalon** (**a** vå lon) is the place in legend where King ARTHUR was taken after his death.

avarice (**a** vå ris) *n.* greed for wealth etc.
avenge (å venj) *vb.* **avenging, avenged** to punish someone in return for harm they have done to someone else. – *n.* **avenger**.
avenue (**a** vẽ nū) *n.* a broad road or street, often with trees along the sides.

Much of Australia is dry flat desert. Most of its people live along the coasts in four main cities.

average (**a** vĕ rij) *n.* **1** the usual amount or number. **2** the result obtained by adding together a group of numbers and dividing the total by the number of numbers in the group; for example the average of 1 and 3 is (1+3)÷2, i.e. 2. – *adj.* **1** ordinary: *It's just an average day.* **2** estimated by taking an average: *What's the average number of visitors?* **3** mediocre: *Her singing is better than average.*

averse (å vûrs) *adj.* reluctant or opposed: *He is not averse to helping.*

aversion (å vûr shŏn) *n.* a strong dislike.

avert (å vûrt) *vb.* **averting, averted** to turn away: *The Sun was so strong he averted his eyes.*

aviary (ā vi å ri) *n.* **aviaries** a large, enclosed area in which birds are kept.

aviation (ā vi ā shŏn) *n.* the science or practice of flying in aircraft.

avid (**a** vid) *adj.* enthusiastic: *He's an avid reader of science fiction.*

avocado (a vŏ kä dō) *n.* **avocados** (also **avocado pear**) a pear-shaped green fruit with a large stone, and creamy, light green flesh.

avocet (**a** vŏ set) *n.* a wading bird with long legs, black and white feathers, and a long beak.

avoid (å **void**) *vb.* **avoiding, avoided** to keep away from a place, person, or action, etc.: *Sam avoided her gaze by looking the other way.*

await (å **wāt**) *vb.* **awaiting, awaited** to wait for: *He awaits for her reply.*

awake (å **wāk**) *vb.* **awaking, awoke** (å **wōk**), **awoken** to stop or to cause to stop sleeping. – *adj.* **1** not sleeping. **2** alert or aware.

awaken (å **wā** kĕn) *vb.* **awakening, awakened** to awake.

award (å **wörd**) *vb.* **awarding, awarded** to give someone something especially as a payment or prize. – *n.* a payment or prize.

aware (å **wār**) *adj.* knowing about or conscious of something: *I am aware of your contribution.*

away (å **wā**) *adv.* **1** showing distance or movement from a particular place, position, person, or time: *They walked away from the building.* **2** in or to another or usual place: *We put the books away.* **3** gradually into nothing: *The music faded away.* – *adj.* distant: *She is far away.*

awe (ö) *n.* admiration, fear, and wonder.

awful (ö fŭl) *adj.* (*colloquial*) **1** very bad. **2** very great: *It's an awful shame.*
awfully *adv.* **1** very badly: *He behaves awfully to his mother.* **2** very: *awfully hot.*

awhile (å **wīl**) *adv.* for a short time.

awkward (ök wård) *adj.* **1** clumsy and ungraceful. **2** embarrassed or embarrassing.

awoke, awoken. See **awake.**

axe or (*US*) **ax** (aks) *n.* a tool with a long handle and a heavy metal blade, for cutting down trees or chopping wood, etc.

axiom (**ak** si ŏm) *n.* a fact or principle which is generally accepted as true.

axle (**ak** sĕl) *n.* a rod on which a wheel or pair of wheels turns.

axolotl (**ak** sŏ lo tĕl) *n.* a newt-like salamander which lives in Mexican lakes.

● **Ayers** (ā ĕrz) **Rock** is the world's largest rock, in AUSTRALIA. Its base is about 9 km round.

● **Azerbaijan** (az ĕr bī **jän**). See Supplement, **Countries.**

Aztec (**az** tek) *n.* a member of a Mexican Indian people whose great empire was overthrown by the Spanish in the 16th century. – *adj.* of the Aztecs, their language, and culture.

azure (**a** zhŭr) or (**ā** zhŭr) *adj.* deep sky-blue.

The **Aztec** empire was a great native American civilization when Spanish soldiers discovered it. Within two years of the Spanish commander Hernando Cortes landing in Mexico in 1519 he had completely destroyed the empire. The invaders demolished the magnificent city of Tenochtitlan and built Mexico city on its site.

Quetzalcoatl, the plumed serpent, was one of the chief Aztec gods.

An Aztec pyramid with stairways leading to a temple at the top. Here the Aztecs sacrificed human beings to the gods.

Bb

babble (ba běl) *vb.* **babbling, babbled** to talk quickly in a way that is hard to understand.

baboon (bå **boon**) *n.* a large African monkey.

● **Babur** (1483-1530) was the first Mogul emperor. He invaded India in about 1525.

baby (bā bi) *n.* **babies** a newborn or very young child or animal.

baby-sit *vb.* **baby-sitting, baby-sat** to look after children while their parents are out.

● **Babylonia** in southern Mesopotamia, was one of the great civilizations of the ancient world. The Hanging Gardens of Babylon, the capital, were one of the SEVEN WONDERS OF THE WORLD.

Babylon: The Ishtar Gate.

● **Bach, Johann Sebastian** (1685-1750) was the most famous member of a German family of composers.

bachelor (bach ě lŏr) *n.* an unmarried man.

back (bak) *n.* **1** the rear part of the human body from the neck to the bottom of the backbone. **2** the upper part of an animal's body. **3** the part of an object that is opposite to or furthest from the front: *They sat at the back of the room.* – *adj.* situated behind or at the back: *He walked out through the back door.* – *adv.* **1** to or towards the rear; away from the front: *They moved back to let him pass.* **2** in or into an original position: *Please put the bowl back in the cupboard when you've used it.* – *vb.* **backing, backed 1** to help or support, usually with money: *Tim's father backed their project.* **2** to move backwards. – *vb.* **back up 1** to assist. **2** to copy information kept on a computer on to another disk.

backbone *n.* **1** the spine. **2** the main support.

background *n.* the space behind the main figures of a picture.

backwards (bak wårdz) *adv.* **1** towards the back or rear. **2** with your back facing the direction you are going. **3** in reverse order.

bacon (bā kŏn) *n.* meat from the back and sides of a pig, usually salted or smoked.

bacteria (bak tēr i å) *n.* (*plural*) a group of microscopic single-celled organisms.

● Bacteria are found in large numbers everywhere. There are thousands of different kinds. Most are quite harmless, although some, known as germs, can cause diseases. Antibiotic drugs, such as penicillin, can kill these germs. The French chemist, Louis PASTEUR, studied bacteria and found that they made food go bad.

bad (bad) *adj.* **worse** (wûrs), **worst** (wûrst) **1** not good. **2** naughty. **3** not skilled or clever: *I'm not athletic; I've always been bad at games.* **4** harmful: *Smoking is bad for you.* – *n.* unpleasant things.

badge (baj) *n.* a small emblem or button.

badger (baj ĕr) *n.* an animal with a grey coat and black and white stripes on its head, which lives underground and is active at night.

European Badgers live in woods in underground setts which they clean regularly by removing old bedding. American badgers live on the prairies.

badminton (bad min tŏn) *n.* a game for two or four people played with rackets and a shuttlecock which is hit across a high net.

baffle (ba fĕl) *vb.* **baffling, baffled 1** to confuse or puzzle. **2** to hinder: *They baffled our attempts to find out the truth.* – *adj.* **baffling**.

bag (bag) *n.* a container made of cloth, plastic, paper, etc., for carrying things.

baggy *adj.* **baggier, baggiest** hanging loose.

baggage (bag ij) *n.* a traveller's luggage.

● **Baghdad** is the capital of IRAQ, on the river Tigris. It was founded in AD 762.

● **Bahamas**. See Supplement, **Countries**.

● **Bahrain**. See Supplement, **Countries**.

● **Baikal, Lake** in Siberia, is the world's deepest freshwater lake.

bail[1] (bāl) *n.* money given to a law court to obtain a person's release, as a guarantee that he or she will return to court for trial. – *vb.* **bail out**, **bailing**, **bailed** to provide bail for.

bail[2] or **bale** (bāl) *vb.* **bailing, bailed** to remove water from a boat with a bucket.

● **Baird, John Logie** (1888-1946) was a Scottish pioneer of a mechanical form of television which he demonstrated in 1926.

bairn (bārn) *n.* a Scottish word for a child.

bait (bāt) *n.* **1** food put on a hook or in a trap to attract fish or animals. **2** anything intended to tempt. – *vb.* **baiting, baited 1** to put food on a hook or in a trap. **2** to annoy or tease.

bake (bāk) *vb.* **baking, baked** to cook cakes, bread, vegetables, etc. using dry heat in an oven. – *n.* **baker**.

bakery *n.* **bakeries** a place where bread and cakes are made or sold.

baking powder *n.* a powder containing sodium bicarbonate, used to make cakes rise.

balalaika (ba lå lī kå) *n.* a Russian musical instrument with a triangular body, a neck like a guitar, and usually three strings.

balance (ba låns) *n.* **1** an instrument for weighing, usually with two dishes hanging from a bar supported in the middle. **2** a state of stability in which the weight of a body is evenly distributed. **3** an amount left over. – *vb.* **balancing, balanced** to be in or put into a

state of balance: *Can you balance a basketball on one finger?* – **in the balance** not decided.
balanced *adj.* **1** in a state of balance. **2** fair; considering all sides of an argument.

●**Balboa, Vasco Nuñez de** (1475-1519) was a Spanish adventurer and explorer who was the first European to discover the PACIFIC, in 1513.

balcony (**bal** kŏ ni) *n.* **balconies** a platform surrounded by a wall or railing, projecting from the wall of a building.
bald (böld) *adj.* **1** describing a person who has little or no hair on the head. **2** describing birds or animals without feathers or fur.
Balder. See **Myths and Legends**.

●**Baldwin, James** (1924-87) was an American writer whose works include *Go Tell It on the Mountain*.

bale (bāl) *n.* a large bundle of cloth or hay, etc.
balk or **baulk** (bölk) *vb.* **balking, balked** to hesitate or refuse to go on.
Balkan (**böl** kån) *adj.* **1** of the peninsula in south eastern Europe, surrounded by the Adriatic, Aegean, and Black seas. **2** of its peoples or countries.
ball¹ (böl) *n.* **1** a round or roundish object used in some sports. **2** anything round or nearly round in shape: *a snowball*.
ball-bearing *n.* an arrangement of small steel balls between the moving parts of some machines, to help reduce friction.
ball² (böl) *n.* a formal social meeting for dancing.
ballroom *n.* a large hall where balls are held.
ballad (**ba** låd) *n.* a slow, usually romantic, song.
ballast (**ba** låst) *n.* heavy material used to keep a ship without cargo steady.
ballerina (ba lĕ **rē** nå) *n.* a female ballet-dancer.
ballet (**ba** lā) *n.* a classical style of dancing and mime, using set steps and body movements. – *n.* **ballet-dancer.**

●Classical ballet follows strict rules and traditions. There are standard positions for the legs, arms, and hands. The person who arranges the dance movements is the choreographer. Modern ballet includes freer, less traditional dance steps.

Classical **ballet** as we know it today began in France during the reign of Louis the Fourteenth (1638-1715). The king's dancing master, Pierre Beauchamp, worked out the five basic positions of the feet. These positions are the starting and finishing points of all steps. In ballet, dancers use their bodies to mime the story.

First position

Second position

Third position

In all five positions the shoulders are kept down; the elbows are rounded to create a flowing line through the arms to the fingertips.

Fourth position

Fifth position

Satin ballet shoes are delicate; they last at most a week!

BALLET TERMS

barre the exercise bar used in classwork.
choreography the art of dance composition.
corps de ballet the main body of dancers.
jeté a leap from one foot to another.

pas any dance step.
pirouette a spin on one foot.
pointes on the points of the toes.
positions five positions of the feet on which ballet is based.

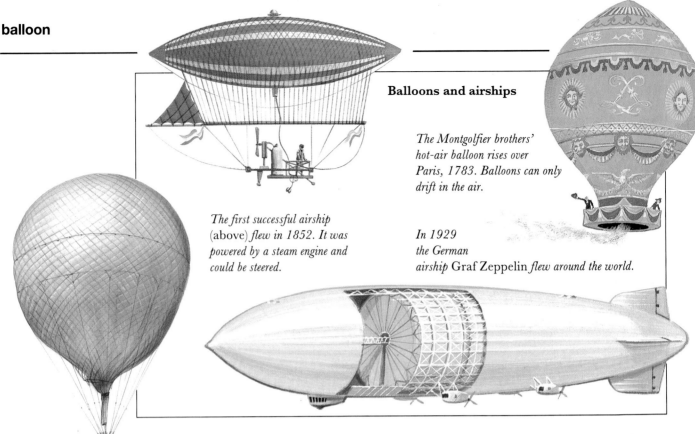

Balloons and airships

The Montgolfier brothers' hot-air balloon rises over Paris, 1783. Balloons can only drift in the air.

The first successful airship (above) flew in 1852. It was powered by a steam engine and could be steered.

In 1929 the German airship Graf Zeppelin *flew around the world.*

Hot-air balloons were used for reconnaissance in war during the 19th century.

ALM OR ARM
Balmy is an adjective meaning 'sweet smelling' or 'mild and pleasant'. Barmy is a slang word meaning 'foolish' or 'silly'. Both words are sometimes spelled 'balmy', but it is perhaps clearer to use the second spelling for the meaning 'foolish'.

balloon (bå **loon**) *n.* **1** a small rubber bag filled with air or other gas, often used as a toy. **2** a large bag, made of light material and filled with a light gas or hot air, designed to float in the air carrying people in a basket underneath. – *n.* **ballooning**. – *n.* **balloonist**.

ballot (**ba** lŏt) *n.* the method of voting secretly by putting a marked paper into a container.

balm (bäm) *n.* an oil obtained from some trees, used in healing or reducing pain.

balsa (**böl** så) *n.* a tropical American tree; the very light wood of this tree.

● **Baltic** a sea in northern Europe almost enclosed by land.

● **Baltic States**: ESTONIA, LATVIA, and LITHUANIA, former republics of the ex-USSR, which since 1991 have regained independence.

● **Baltimore** in Maryland is one of the chief ports of the United States. It was founded in 1729.

● **Balzac, Honoré de** (1799-1850) was a French novelist who wrote about everyday life in great detail in such works as *La Comédie Humaine*.

bamboo (bam **boo**) *n.* a tall, tropical grass with hollow, jointed, woody stems.

ban (ban) *n.* an official order that something may not be done: *There is a ban here on using hosepipes in the summer.* – *vb.* **banning, banned** to forbid or prevent.

banal (bå **näl**) *adj.* not original or interesting.

banana (bå **nä** nå) *n.* **1** a long curved fruit, yellow when ripe. **2** the large tropical tree-like plant on which this fruit grows.

band¹ (band) *n.* a flat, narrow strip of cloth, metal, paper, etc. used to hold things together or as a decoration. – *vb.* **banding, banded** to fasten or mark with a band.

band² (band) *n.* a group of musicians who play music other than classical music: *a rock band.* – *vb.* **banding, banded** to unite to work for a common purpose: *The class banded together and produced an excellent magazine.*

bandage (**ban** dij) *n.* a strip of cloth for winding around a wound. – *vb.* **bandaging, bandaged** to wrap in a bandage.

bandit (**ban** dit) *n.* an armed robber, especially a member of a gang which attacks travellers.

bang (bang) *n.* **1** a sudden loud noise. **2** a heavy blow. – *vb.* **banging, banged 1** to make a loud noise by hitting, dropping, closing violently, etc. **2** to hit sharply.

● **Bangkok** is the capital of THAILAND.

● **Bangladesh**. See Supplement, **Countries**.

banish (**ba** nish) *vb.* **banishing, banished** to send someone away from a place, usually his or her own country. – *n.* **banishment**.

banister or **bannister** (**ba** ni stěr) *n.* (often in *plural*) a row of posts and the hand-rail they support, running up the side of a staircase.

bank¹ (bangk) *n.* **1** a long raised pile of earth or snow, etc. **2** the ground at the edge of a river, lake, etc. **3** a raised area of sand under the sea. **4** a mass of cloud, mist, or fog.

bank² (bangk) *n.* **1** an organization which keeps money in accounts for its clients, lends money, etc. **2** a place where something is stored or collected for later use: *a blood bank.* – *vb.* **banking, banked 1** to put money into a bank; to have a bank account. **2** to rely on: *I'm banking on good weather for the barbecue.*
banker *n.* a person who manages a bank.
banknote *n.* paper money issued by a bank.

bankrupt (**bangk** rupt) *n.* a person who is legally recognized as not being able to pay his or her debts. – *adj.* not having money to pay your debts. – *vb.* **bankrupting, bankrupted** to make bankrupt.

banner (**ba** něr) *n.* a large piece of cloth or cardboard, with a design or slogan carried at public meetings, etc.

banquet (**bang** kwit) *n.* a large formal dinner.

● **Banting, Sir Frederick** (1891-1941) was the Canadian discoverer of insulin in the treatment of diabetes. He worked with Charles Best.

● **Baptists** believe people should not be baptized until they are old enough to make up their own minds about religion. This branch of Protestantism began in England in the 1600s.

baptize or **baptise** (bap **tīz**) *vb.* **baptizing, baptized** to sprinkle with water as a sign of having become a member of the Christian church, usually accompanied by name-giving.
baptism *n.* See **Religious Terms**.

bar (bär) *n.* **1** a block of some solid substance: *a bar of soap.* **2** a rod or long piece of a strong rigid material: *They have bars on the windows to prevent burglary.* **3** anything that prevents or hinders: *a bar to progress.* **4** a room or counter in a restaurant or hotel, or a separate establishment, where alcoholic drinks are sold and drunk. – *vb.* **barring, barred 1** to fasten with a bar. **2** to forbid entry. – *prep.* except: *everyone bar me.*

barb (bärb) *n.* a point on a hook facing in the opposite direction to the main point, which makes it difficult to pull the hook out.

● **Barbados**. See Supplement, **Countries**.

barbarian (bär **bār** i ån) *n.* a person who is coarse, cruel, rough, and wild in behaviour.
barbaric (bär **ba** rik) *adj.* cruel and brutal.

barbecue (**bär** bi kū) *n.* **1** a metal frame on which food is grilled over an open fire. **2** a party held out of doors at which food is cooked on a barbecue.

barber (**bär** běr) *n.* a person who cuts and styles men's hair, and shaves their beards.

● **Barcelona** is a port on the MEDITERRANEAN, in the Spanish province of Catalonia.

bare (bār) *adj.* **1** not covered by clothes; naked. **2** without the usual or natural covering: *Our garden is full of bare trees in winter.* **3** empty.
barefoot *adj.* not wearing shoes or socks.
barely *adv.* scarcely or only just: *There is barely enough food for all the guests.*

bargain (**bär** gin) *n.* **1** an agreement made between people buying and selling things, offering and accepting services, etc.: *They eventually struck a bargain.* **2** something offered for sale, or bought, at a low price. – *vb.* **bargaining, bargained** to discuss terms for buying or selling.

barge (bärj) *n.* a long, flat-bottomed boat used on rivers and canals. – *vb.* **barging, barged 1** to move in a clumsy, ungraceful way. **2** to hit or knock: *Sam barged into the table.*

baritone (**ba** ri tōn) *n.* the second lowest male singing voice, between bass and tenor.

bark¹ (bärk) *n.* the short, sharp cry of a dog, fox, etc. – *vb.* **barking, barked 1** to make this sound. **2** to say loudly and sharply: *He barked out the commands.* – **bark up the wrong tree** (*colloquial*) to have the wrong idea.

bark² (bärk) *n.* the tough covering of the trunk and branches of a tree.

barley (**bär** li) *n.* a tall, grass-like plant, grown for its grain.

● Most barley is grown as an animal feed or to provide malt used for food and in making beer. Barley was first harvested 7000 years ago.

Barber comes from the Latin *barba*, meaning 'beard', because in early times a barber's work was mostly trimming and cutting beards.

Bark is dead wood. It is tough and waterproof and protects the living wood underneath. Each year a tree forms a new layer or ring of new wood. From a sawn-through trunk you can tell the age of a tree by counting the growth rings.

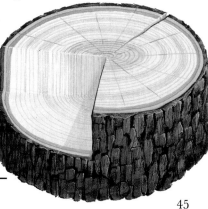

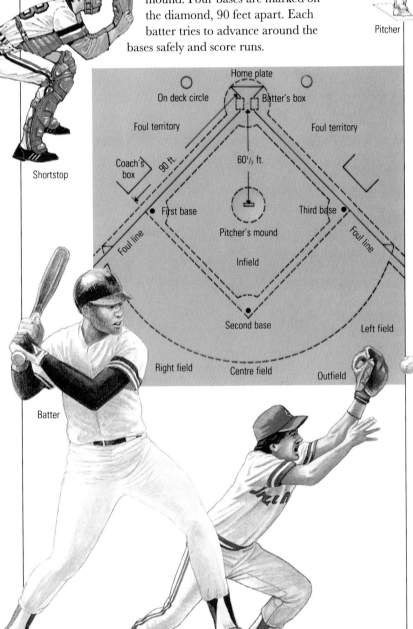

Baseball is the American national game. It evolved from the 18th-century English game of rounders. It began in 1845 when Alexander Cartwright organized the Knickerbocker Club in New York and established the rules. He said the game would consist of nine innings and that each team would have nine players. It is played on a large field on which is marked a square known as the 'diamond'. At the base of the square is the home plate where the batter stands; in the centre of the square is the pitcher's mound. Four bases are marked on the diamond, 90 feet apart. Each batter tries to advance around the bases safely and score runs.

Pitcher

Shortstop

Home plate

On deck circle

Batter's box

Foul territory

Foul territory

Coach's box

90 ft.

60½ ft.

First base

Third base

Pitcher's mound

Foul line

Foul line

Infield

Second base

Left field

Right field

Centre field

Outfield

Batter

bar mitzvah (bär **mits** vå) *n.* See **Religious Terms**.

barn (bärn) *n.* a building in which grain or hay, etc. is stored, or for cattle, etc.

● **Barnum, Phineas** and **Bailey, J. A.** were the creators of the Barnum and Bailey Circus, in 1881.

barometer (bå **rom** i těr) *n.* an instrument which measures the pressure of the atmosphere, used to predict likely changes in the weather.

barrack (**ba** råk) *n.* (usually in *plural*) a building or buildings for housing soldiers.

barrel (**ba** rěl) *n.* **1** a large round container, with a flat top and bottom and curving out in the middle, usually made of planks of wood held together with metal bands. **2** the long, hollow, tube-shaped part of a gun or pen.

barren (**ba** rěn) *adj.* not able to produce crops or fruit, etc.: *Barren land surrounds the house.*

barricade (**ba** ri kād) *n.* a barrier made of anything which can be piled up quickly. It is often used to block a street. – *vb.* **barricading, barricaded**.

barrier (**ba** ri ěr) *n.* **1** a fence, gate, bar, etc. put up to defend, block, protect, separate, etc. **2** any thing that separates people, etc.: *They can't communicate because of a language barrier.*

barrow (**ba** rō) *n.* a small one-wheeled cart used to carry tools, earth, etc.

barter (**bär** těr) *vb.* **bartering, bartered** to trade or exchange goods or services without using money.

base (bās) *n.* **1** the lowest part or bottom; the part which supports something or on which something stands. **2** the origin, root, or foundation of something. **3** the headquarters or centre of activity or operations. **4** in baseball, one of several fixed points which players run between. – *vb.* **basing, based 1** to make or use as the base: *This book is based on a true story.* **2** to give as a headquarters or centre of operations: *The troops were based in France.*

baseball *n.* **1** a game played with a bat and ball by two teams of nine people, in which the person batting may score a point, or run, by running round a pitch marked with four bases. **2** the ball used in this game.

basement (bās měnt) *n.* the lowest floor of a building, usually below ground level.

bashful (**bash** fůl) *adj.* lacking confidence; shy.

basic (bā sik) *adj.* **1** of, or forming, the base or basis. **2** of or at a very simple or low level: *I'm surprised you made such a basic mistake.* – *n.* **1** (usually in *plural*) the essential parts or simplest principles: *This is too confusing; let's get back to basics.* **2** BASIC. See **Computer Terms**.
basically *adv.* mostly, essentially; described in simple or general terms.

basin (bā sin) *n.* **1** a wide, open dish, especially for holding water. **2** a bowl or sink in a bathroom, etc. for washing yourself in. **3** a valley or area of land drained by a river, or streams running into a river.

basis (bā sis) *n.* **bases** (bā sēz) a principle on which an idea or theory is based.

bask (bäsk) *vb.* **basking, basked 1** to lie in warmth or sunshine. **2** to enjoy and take great pleasure: *Beth is basking in his approval.*

basket (bäs kit) *n.* a container made of strips of wood or cane, woven together.
basketball *n.* **1** a game in which two teams of five players score by throwing a ball into a net on a high post at each end of the court. **2** the ball used in this game.

● This popular American game is played on a rectangular court. The ball can be advanced by bouncing it along or by passing it to a teammate. A player cannot take more than one step while holding the ball.

Basque (bäsk) *n.* **1** a member of a people living in the western Pyrenees, in Spain and France. **2** the language spoken by these people.

bass¹ (bās) *n.* the lowest male singing voice; a singer with such a voice.
bass drum *n.* a large drum that produces a very low sound.

bass² (bas) *n.* **bass** a type of fish.

bassoon (bå sōōn) *n.* a woodwind instrument.

baste (bāst) *vb.* **basting, basted** to pour hot fat or butter over roasting meat, etc.

● **Bastille** is the name of a fortress prison in Paris. The storming of the *Bastille* by the mob on 14 July 1789 marked the start of the FRENCH REVOLUTION.

bat¹ (bat) *n.* a shaped piece of wood, with a flat or curved surface, for hitting the ball in cricket, baseball, table-tennis, etc. – *vb.* **batting, batted 1** to take a turn at hitting a ball with a bat in cricket, baseball, etc. **2** to hit with a bat.

Pipistrelle

Long eared bat

Greater Horseshoe bat

bat² (bat) *n.* a mouse-like animal with wings.

batch (bach) *n.* a number of things or people prepared, dealt with, etc. at the same time.

bath (bäth) *n.* a large open container for water, in which to wash the whole body: *The bath is made out of enamel.* – *vb.* **bathing, bathed** to wash in a bath.

bathe (bāTh) *vb.* **bathing, bathed 1** to swim in the sea, etc. for pleasure. **2** (*US*) to have a bath. **3** to wash part of the body with a liquid, etc. to clean it or to lessen pain.

baton (ba tǒn) *n.* **1** a thin stick used by an orchestra conductor. **2** a short stick passed from one runner to another in a relay race.

battalion (bå tal yǒn) *n.* an army unit made up of several smaller units (companies), and forming part of a larger unit (a brigade).

batter¹ (ba tėr) *vb.* **battering, battered** to strike or hit hard and often, or continuously: *We could hear the wind battering against the door.*

batter² (ba tėr) *n.* eggs, flour, and usually either milk or water, beaten together.

battery (ba tė ri) *n.* **batteries 1** a small container holding chemicals which produce or store electricity, or a container of two or more such cells. **2** a long line of small cages in which hens, etc. are kept.

battle (ba tėl) *n.* **1** a fight between opposing armies or people. **2** a competition between opposing groups or people: *a battle of wits.*

battlement (ba tėl mėnt) *n.* a low wall around the top of a castle, etc.

bauxite (bŏk sīt) *n.* a substance like clay, the main source of aluminium.

bay¹ (bā) *n.* a wide inward bend of a coastline.

bay² (bā) *n.* **1** a small area of a room set back into a wall. **2** an area for parking, or loading and unloading, vehicles.

bay³ (bā) *adj.* describing a horse that is reddish-brown in colour. – *n.* a bay-coloured horse.

● **Bayeux Tapestry** a long strip of 11th-century embroidery depicting the NORMAN invasion of ENGLAND and kept at Bayeux in FRANCE.

Bats fly like birds but are mammals. Most bats are nocturnal. They produce high-pitched shrieks and use the echoes bouncing back from objects to tell where those objects are.

PRONUNCIATION GUIDE	
fat **a**	all **ŏ**
fate **ā**	foot **oo**
fast **ä**	moon **ōō**
among **å**	boy **oi**
met **e**	house **ow**
mean **ē**	demon **ǒ**
silent **ė**	thing **th**
loch **hh**	this **Th**
fin **i**	but **u**
line **ī**	mute **ū**
quick **kw**	fur **û**
got **o**	brochure **ů**
note **ō**	vision **zh**

bazaar (bå **zär**) *n.* **1** a market place in Eastern countries. **2** a sale of goods, etc.

be (bē) *vb.* **am, are, is; being; was, were; been 1** to exist or live: *I think, therefore I am.* **2** to occur: *Lunch is in an hour.* **3** to occupy a position in space: *Sue is at home.* **4** used to link a subject and what is said about it: *She is a doctor.* **being** *n.* **1** life. **2** any living person or thing.

beach (bēch) *n.* the sandy or stony shore of a sea.

beacon (**bē** kǒn) *n.* a warning or guiding device for ships, etc., such as a lighthouse.

bead (bēd) *n.* a small, usually round, ball of glass, stone, etc. strung with others in a necklace, etc.

beak (bēk) *n.* the hard part of a bird's mouth.

beaker (**bēk** ěr) *n.* a large drinking-glass, or a large often plastic cup without a handle.

beam (bēm) *n.* **1** a long, straight, thick piece of wood, used in a building. **2** a ray of light. **3** a narrow wooden bar on which gymnasts perform balancing exercises. – *vb.* **beaming, beamed 1** to smile broadly with pleasure. **2** to send out rays of light, radio waves, etc.

bean (bēn) *n.* any of several kinds of climbing plant which produce edible seeds in long thin pods. – **full of beans** (*colloquial*) full of energy.

bear[1] (bār) *vb.* **bearing, bore** (bör), **borne** (börn) **1** to carry, bring, or take: *They came bearing gifts.* **2** to support a weight. **3** to produce: *This tree bears fruit every year.* **4** to put up with.
bearable *adj.* able to be put up with.
bearing *n.* **1** the way a person stands, walks, etc. **2** a relation or effect: *Your remarks have no bearing on the situation.*

bear[2] (bār) *n.* a large, heavily built, four-legged animal with thick fur.

beard (bērd) *n.* the hair that grows on a man's chin and neck. – *adj.* **bearded**.

beast (bēst) *n.* **1** any large, especially four-footed, wild animal. **2** (*colloquial*) a difficult or unpleasant person or thing.

beat (bēt) *vb.* **beating, beat, beaten 1** to hit violently and repeatedly, especially to harm. **2** to strike repeatedly, e.g. to remove dust or make a sound. **3** to knock repeatedly: *The waves beat against the shore.* **4** to do something better, sooner, or quicker than: *Nick beat me in the race.* **5** to mix or stir thoroughly: *Beat the eggs with a whisk.* **6** to move in a regular pattern of strokes, etc.: *Your heart beats quickly after exercise.* – *n.* **1** a regular stroke, or its sound: *the beat of a heart.* **2** the main accent in music.

● **the Beatles** an English rock group of the 1960s and early 1970s.

Beaufort scale (**bō** fôrt skāl) *n.* an international scale of wind speeds, from 0 for calm to 12 for hurricane, devised by Sir Francis *Beaufort* (1774–1857).

beautiful (**bū** ti fǔl) *adj.* with an appearance or qualities which please the senses; pleasing.

beautify (**bū** ti fī) *vb.* **beautifies, beautifying, beautified** to make beautiful.

beauty (**bū** ti) *n.* **beauties 1** a quality pleasing to the senses, especially the eye or ear. **2** a benefit: *The beauty of the plan is its simplicity.*

beaver (**bē** věr) *n.* a large, rat-like animal, with thick, soft fur, strong front teeth, and a large flat tail, which builds dams in rivers and streams. – *vb.* **beaver away, beavering, beavered** to work very hard.

became. See **become**.

because (bi **köz**) *conj.* for the reason that: *I can't write the letter because I don't have any paper.*

Bears are carnivores (flesh-eating animals), but they also love honey! The largest bear is the brown bear of Alaska; the smallest is the sun bear of south-east Asia. The polar bear's white fur makes it less noticeable against the ice and snow.

Grizzly bear

Black bear

Polar bear

Brown bear

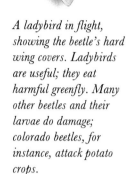

●**Becket, Thomas** (1118-70) was Archbishop of CANTERBURY. He was murdered for opposing Henry the Second's attempts to control the clergy. He was made a saint in 1173.

become (bi **kum**) *vb.* **becoming, became** (bi **kām**), **become 1** to come or grow to be: *He became an excellent juggler after years of practice.* **2** to happen to: *What became of him?*

●**Becquerel, Antoine Henri** (1852-1908) was a French physicist who discovered the radioactive properties of uranium.

bed (bed) *n.* **1** a piece of furniture for sleeping on. **2** the bottom of a river, lake, or sea. **3** an area of ground in a garden, for growing plants: *flower-bed.*
   bedding *n.* **1** mattresses, blankets, etc. **2** straw, etc. for animals to sleep on.
   bedrock *n.* **1** the solid rock forming the lowest layer under soil and rock fragments. **2** the basic principle or idea on which something rests.

Bedouin (**be** doo in) *n.* **Bedouin** or **Bedouins** a member of a wandering Arab tribe that lives in the deserts of the MIDDLE EAST.

bee (bē) *n.* a type of four-winged, stinging insect; some species live in large groups and make honey. – **a bee in your bonnet** an idea which has become an obsession.

Most bees live alone; they are solitary.

Bumble bee

beeline *n.* a straight line between two places.
beech (bēch) *n.* a kind of forest tree with smooth silvery bark and small nuts.
beef (bēf) *n.* the meat of a bull, cow, or ox.
been. See **be.**
beer (bēr) *n.* a type of alcoholic drink made from malt, barley, sugar, hops, and water.

●**Beethoven** (**bāt** hō věn), **Ludwig van** (1770-1827) was a German composer of some of the greatest music, which includes nine symphonies and six concertos. He began to go deaf at the age of 30, but continued composing.

beetle (bē těl) *n.* an insect with a pair of hard front wings that fold over its back.
beetroot (bēt root) *n.* a type of plant with a round, red root which is cooked as a vegetable.
before (bi **för**) *prep.* **1** earlier than: *I hope to arrive before noon.* **2** in front of: *He stood before the table.* – *conj.* **1** earlier than the time when: *Do it before you forget.* **2** rather than; in preference to: *I'd die before I'd surrender.* – *adv.* previously; in the past: *Haven't we met before?*
beg (beg) *vb.* **begging, begged 1** to ask for money, food, etc. **2** to ask earnestly or humbly.
began. See **begin.**
begin (bi **gin**) *vb.* **beginning, began** (bi **gan**), **begun** (bi **gun**) to start. – *n.* **beginning.**
begun. See **begin.**
behave (bi **hāv**) *vb.* **behaving, behaved 1** to act in a stated way: *She trained her puppy to behave well.* **2** to act in a suitable, polite, or orderly way: *Behave yourself at the party.*
behaviour (bi **hāv** yǒr) *n.* way of behaving; manners: *good behaviour.*
behind (bi **hīnd**) *prep.* **1** at or towards the back of or the far side of. **2** later or slower than; after in time: *Our project is behind schedule.* **3** supporting: *We're all behind you.* **4** being the cause of: *The reasons behind his decision are not clear.* – *adv.* **1** in or to the back or far side of. **2** remaining: *Did you leave something behind?* **3** following: *The children ran behind the car.* – *adj.* late: *They are behind with their payments.*

Queen bee

Worker bees

beige (bāzh) *adj.* a pale pinkish-yellow colour.

●**Beijing** (**Peking**) is the capital of CHINA.

●**Beirut** is a port and capital of the LEBANON. In recent years it has been torn apart by civil war.

A ladybird in flight, showing the beetle's hard wing covers. Ladybirds are useful; they eat harmful greenfly. Many other beetles and their larvae do damage; colorado beetles, for instance, attack potato crops.

Beehive

Honeybees are social insects and live in colonies. They build a nest or hive. In every hive there is one queen and a few male drones who fertilize the queen. Thousands of female workers make honey by gathering plant nectar and storing it in wax cells. They also look after the queen and the larvae.

How a bell is cast
Bells are made by pouring molten metal between a solid core mould and an outer mould in the shape of the bell.

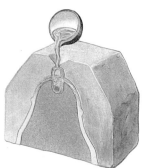

Below: *The Liberty Bell* see **Liberty Bell**.

● **Belarus**. See Supplement, **Countries**.

belated (bi **lāt** id) *adj.* happening or coming late.

● **Belfast** is the capital of NORTHERN IRELAND.

● **Belgium**. See Supplement, **Countries**.

belief (bi **lēf**) *n.* **1** a principle or idea accepted as true, especially without proof: *belief in the afterlife.* **2** trust or confidence: *She has a strong belief in his ability.* **3** a person's religious faith.
believe (bi **lēv**) *vb.* **believing, believed 1** to accept as true. **2** to think, assume, or suppose: *I believe this is the person you're looking for.* **3** to have religious faith.

● **Belize**. See Supplement, **Countries**.

bell (bel) *n.* **1** a deep, hollow, usually metal, object, rounded at one end and wide and open at the other, with a small hammer inside, which gives a ringing sound when struck. **2** any other device which makes a ringing sound.

● **Bell, Alexander Graham** (1847-1922) was the Scottish-American inventor of the telephone. The first words transmitted by telephone were by Bell to his assistant: "Mr Watson, come here; I want you."

● **Bellini, Giovanni** (1430-1516) was a leading painter of the Italian RENAISSANCE.

bellow (be lō) *vb.* **bellowing, bellowed** to make a loud, deep cry like that of a bull.

● **Bellow, Saul** (1915-) is a Canadian-born novelist living in the United States, whose works include *Herzog.*

bellows (be lōz) *n.* (*singular* or *plural*) a device consisting of or containing a bag-like part which is squeezed to create a current of air.
belly (be li) *n.* **bellies** the part of the body containing the organs used for digesting food. **bellybutton** *n.* (*colloquial*) the navel.
belong (bi long) *vb.* **belonging, belonged 1** to be the property or right of: *This book belongs to me.* **2** to be a member of a group, etc.: *He belongs to the local youth club.* **3** to have a proper place: *The papers belong in this drawer.*
belongings *n.* (*plural*) personal possessions.

below (bi **lō**) *prep.* lower in position, rank, amount, etc.: *The water is below its usual level.* – *adv.* at, to, or in a lower place, point, or level.
belt (belt) *n.* **1** a long, narrow piece of leather or cloth worn around the waist to keep clothing in place or for decoration. **2** a strap passed across the body, to secure a person in a seat: *Fasten your seatbelt!*

● **Ben Nevis** in Scotland, is the highest mountain in the British Isles at 1343 m (4406 ft).

bench (bench) *n.* **1** a long wooden or stone seat. **2** a work-table for a carpenter, scientist, etc.
bend (bend) *vb.* **bending, bent 1** to make or become angled or curved. **2** to move or stretch in a curve: *This road bends to the left.* **3** to move the body to form a curve: *He bent down to pick something up.* – *n.* a curve or bent part.
beneath (bi **nēth**) *prep.* **1** under; below. **2** not worthy of. – *adv.* below, underneath.
Benedictine *n.* (ben i **dik** tin) a member of the Christian community that follows the teachings of St Benedict (480–543).
beneficial (ben i **fi** shål) *adj.* having good results.
benefit (**ben** i fit) *n.* **1** something good gained. **2** advantage: *He ran the club for the children's benefit.* **3** (often in *plural*) a payment made by a company insurance scheme, etc., usually to someone who is ill or out of work. – *vb.* **benefiting, benefited** to gain an advantage.

● **Benin**. See Supplement, **Countries**.

bent. See **bend**.

● **Benz, Karl** (1844-1929) was a German engineer who made the first petrol-powered car, in 1885.

bequeath (bi **kwēTh**) *vb.* **bequeathing, bequeathed** to leave belongings in a will.

● **Bering Sea** the part of the PACIFIC Ocean between Alaska and Siberia, named after the Danish explorer, V. J. *Bering* (1681-1741).

● **Berlin** is the capital of Germany.

● **Berlin, Irving** (1888-1989) was an American composer of musicals. His most famous song is *White Christmas.*

●**Berlioz, Hector** (1803-69) was a French composer.

●**Bermuda** is a British colony in the western ATLANTIC Ocean, 922 km from the UNITED STATES.

●**Bernstein, Leonard** (1918-90) was an American composer. He wrote *West Side Story*.

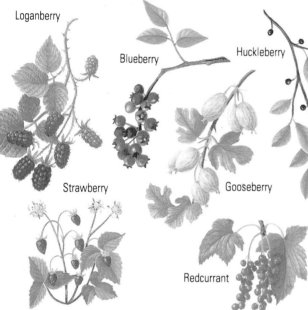

Loganberry

Blueberry

Huckleberry

Strawberry

Gooseberry

Redcurrant

berry (be ri) *n.* **berries** a small, round, juicy fruit without a stone, various kinds of which are used as food, such as the strawberry.

berth (bûrth) *n.* a sleeping-place in a ship or train.

beside (bi sīd) *prep.* **1** next to, by the side of, or near. **2** compared with. **3** not relevant to: *Your remark is beside the point.*

besides (bi sīdz) *prep.* in addition to; as well as.

besiege (bi sēj) *vb.* **besieging, besieged** to surround a town, etc. with an army in order to force it to surrender.

●**Bessemer, Sir Henry** (1813-98) was the inventor of a steel-making process.

best (best) *adj.* **1** most excellent, suitable, or desirable: *This is the best book I've ever read.* **2** most successful, clever, etc.: *He is best at playing football.* – *adv.* **1** most successfully, etc.: *He wanted to do best in the exam.* **2** more than all others: *I like her best.* – *n.* the most excellent or suitable person or thing, most desirable quality, etc.: *He is the best of the bunch.*

bet (bet) *vb.* **betting, bet** or **betted 1** to risk money, etc. by guessing at the outcome or result of a future event, winning extra money, etc. if the guess is right and losing your money if it is wrong. **2** (*colloquial*) to feel sure or confident that: *I bet she'll be late.* – *n.* a sum of money betted. – *n.* **betting**.

●**Bethlehem** is a small town in ISRAEL; birthplace of JESUS and home of King DAVID.

betray (bi trā) *vb.* **betraying, betrayed 1** to hand over a friend, your nation, etc. to the enemy. **2** to break a promise: *He betrayed my trust.* – *n.* **betrayal**.

better (bet ẽr) *adj.* **1** good to a greater extent; more suitable, desirable, etc.: *Muriel is a better swimmer than I am.* **2** more successful, etc. at. **3** recovered from illness: *I had a headache yesterday, but I feel better today.* – *adv.* to a greater degree: *Carol likes cats better than dogs.* – **all the better for** very much better as a result of.

between (bi twēn) *prep.* **1** in, to, through, or across the space dividing two people, places, times, etc.: *There is a park between the two roads.* **2** to and from: *There is a regular bus service between Leeds and Bradford.* **3** acting together: *They bought the car between them.* **4** shared out among: *Divide the money between them.*

beware (bi wār) *vb.* to be careful; to be on your guard: *Beware of the dog!*

bewilder (bi wil dẽr) *vb.* **bewildering, bewildered** to confuse or puzzle: *Arithmetic bewilders some people.* – *adj.* **bewildering**.

beyond (bi yond) *prep.* **1** on the far side of: *We could see the sea beyond the hills.* **2** farther on than something in time or place: *I can't plan anything beyond July.* **3** out of the range, reach, power, understanding, possibility, etc. of: *It's beyond me.* – *adv.* farther away; to or on the far side of.

●**Bhutan**. See Supplement, **Countries**.

bi- (bī-) *prefix* **1** having or involving two: *bifocal.* **2** happening twice in every one, or once in every two: *bi-monthly.* **3** on or from both sides: *bilateral.*

bias (bī ås) *n.* **1** a prejudice. **2** a tendency or principal quality of a person's character. – *vb.* **biasing, biased** or **biassing, biassed** to influence or prejudice.
biased or **biassed** *adj.* favouring one side.

PRONUNCIATION GUIDE	
fat a	all ö
fate ā	foot oo
fast ä	moon ōō
among å	boy oi
met e	house ow
mean ē	demon ỏ
silent ẻ	thing th
loch hh	this Th
fin i	but u
line ī	mute ū
quick kw	fur û
got o	brochure ů
note ō	vision zh

Bible (**bī** bel) *n.* the sacred writings of the Christian Church, consisting of the Old and New Testaments.
biblical or **Biblical** (**bib** li kål) *adj.* of, like, or according to the Bible.

biceps (**bī** seps) *n.* **biceps** a muscle with two heads or attachments, such as the muscle in the arm which bends the elbow.

bicker (**bik** er) *vb.* **bickering, bickered** to argue or quarrel, usually about unimportant things: *The children were bickering about who should walk the dog.* – *n.* **bickering.**

bicycle (**bī** si kel) *n.* a vehicle consisting of a metal frame with two wheels, one behind the other, and a seat, which is driven by the rider turning pedals with his or her feet. – *vb.* **bicycling, bicycled** to ride a bicycle. – *n.* **bicyclist.**

bid (bid) *vb.* **bidding, bid** to offer an amount of money when trying to buy something, especially at an auction: *He bid against two other people.* – *n.* **1** an offer of a price, especially at an auction. **2** an attempt to obtain: *They made a bid for freedom.* – *n.* **bidder.**

biennial (bī **en** i ål) *adj.* **1** happening once in every two years. **2** lasting two years. – *n.* a plant which takes two years to flower.

big (big) *adj.* **bigger, biggest 1** large or largest in size, weight, or number: *She had hurt her big toe.* **2** significant, important: *This was his big day.* **3** older or adult: *She is my big sister.*

bigot (**big** ot) *n.* a person who refuses to tolerate the opinions of other people. – *adj.* **bigoted.** – *n.* **bigotry.**

bike (bīk) *n.* (*colloquial*) a bicycle or motorcycle.

bile (bīl) *n.* a yellowish or greenish thick bitter liquid produced by the liver to help digestion.

bill[1] (bil) *n.* **1** a piece of paper stating the amount of money owed for goods or services received. **2** a written plan for a proposed law: *A bill must be approved in Parliament before it can become law.*

● **Bill of Rights** the first ten amendments to the United States CONSTITUTION, dealing with human rights.

bill[2] (bil) *n.* a bird's beak.

billabong (**bil** å bong) *n.* (*Australian*) a pool of water left when a river has become dry.

billiards (**bil** yårdz) *n.* (*singular*) a game played on a cloth-covered table with pockets at the sides and corners, into which balls must be struck with long thin sticks called 'cues'.

billion (**bil** yon) *n.* **1** in Britain and Europe, a million million. **2** in the United States, and increasingly in Britain and Europe, a thousand million. – *n.* & *adj.* **billionth.**

billow (**bil** ō) *n.* an upward-moving mass of water, smoke, mist, etc. – *vb.* **billowing, billowed** to move in great waves or clouds.

billy goat (**bil** i gōt) *n.* a male goat.

bin (bin) *n.* a large container often used for rubbish, or for storing some kinds of food.

binary (**bī** nå ri) *adj.* **1** consisting of two. **2** relating to the binary system.
binary system *n.* the system of calculating which uses only the numbers 0 and 1.

bind (bīnd) *vb.* **binding, bound** (bownd) **1** to tie or fasten tightly. **2** to be obliged or to promise to do something: *I am bound to secrecy.* **3** to fasten together the pages of a book.

binoculars (bi **nok** ū lårz) *n.* (*plural*) an instrument with lenses for making distant objects look nearer.

biodegradable (bī ō di **grad** å bel) *adj.* able to be broken down by bacteria and other living things, and so decay naturally.

biography (bī **og** rå fi) *n.* **biographies** a written account of another person's life.

biology (bī **ol** ō ji) *n.* the science and study of living things. – *adj.* **biological** (bī ō **loj** i kål). – *n.* **biologist.**

biosphere (**bī** ō sfēr) *n.* the parts of the Earth's atmosphere where living things exist.

birch (bûrch) *n.* a small tree with pointed leaves and smooth bark, valued for its wood.

bird (bûrd) *n.* a two-legged, egg-laying creature with feathers, a beak, and two wings. – **kill two birds with one stone** (*colloquial*) to achieve two things with a single action.

birth (bûrth) *n.* **1** the act or process of being born. **2** family history or origin: *He was of humble birth.* **3** beginning, origins.
birth control *n.* the prevention of pregnancy by the use of contraceptives.
birthday *n.* the anniversary of the day on which a person was born.

biscuit (**bis** kit) *n.* a crisp, flat cake.

bishop (**bi** shop) *n.* **1** a senior priest in the Christian Church. **2** a piece in the game of chess, which may only be moved diagonally.

● **Bismarck, Otto von** (1815-98) was a German statesman, known as the Iron Chancellor.

Biscuit comes from Medieval Latin *bis coctus,* which means 'twice cooked'.

Birds have hollow bones for lightness and strong breast muscles for working wings. While all birds lay eggs, some, such as the penguin, do not fly. Birds' beaks and claws have many different shapes for different purposes.

Broad wings help the vulture to soar high, while the albatross on long wings can glide for hours. The swallow's wings are built for speed, enabling it to catch insects in flight.

Toucan

Hummingbirds

Bluejay

Vulture

Swallow

Albatross

Eye

Crown

Beak

Flight feathers

Breast

Rump

Toucans, hummingbirds, and birds of paradise come from tropical rain forests.

Crossbill

Bird of Paradise

Vane

Barbs

Pheasant

Ostrich egg compared with that of a hummingbird.

Ostrich egg

Hummingbird egg

Blackbird

Shaft

American bull bison –
'buffalo' – fighting
during the mating season.
Huge herds of bison once
roamed the plains but
Europeans killed such
great numbers that by
1889 there were only
500 left. Today bison
are a protected species
living in reserves.

bison (bī sŏn) *n.* **bison** a type of shaggy wild cattle with large heads, short horns, and humps on their backs.

bit¹ (bit) *n.* a small piece. – **a bit** (*colloquial*) **1** a short time or distance: *She shouted to him to wait a bit.* **2** a little; slightly; rather: *I feel a bit of a fool.* **3** a lot: *Lifting this weight takes a bit of doing.*

bit². See **bite**.

bit³ (bit) *n.* See **Horse Terms**.

bit⁴ (bit) *n.* See **Computer Terms**.

bitch (bich) *n.* a female of the dog family.

bite (bīt) *vb.* **biting, bit** (bit), **bitten 1** to grasp, tear, or cut with the teeth. **2** (of insects and snakes) to make a hole in a person's skin and inject venom or suck blood. – *n.* a wound caused by biting.

bitter (bit ĕr) *adj.* **1** having a sharp, acid, and often unpleasant taste. **2** feeling or causing sadness, pain, and resentment: *The divorce left them both with bitter memories.* **3** showing a lot of dislike, hatred, or opposition: *The war was a bitter struggle.* – *n.* **bitterness**.

bivalve (bī valv) *n.* any of several kinds of shellfish, e.g. an oyster, with a shell made up of two parts held together by a type of hinge.

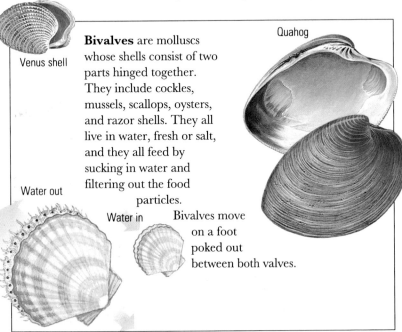

Venus shell

Water out

Water in

Quahog

Bivalves are molluscs whose shells consist of two parts hinged together. They include cockles, mussels, scallops, oysters, and razor shells. They all live in water, fresh or salt, and they all feed by sucking in water and filtering out the food particles.

Bivalves move on a foot poked out between both valves.

bizarre (bi zär) *adj.* odd or very strange.

black (blak) *adj.* **1** of the colour of coal, the night sky, etc. **2** without light. **3** (also **Black**) of dark-skinned people, especially of African, West Indian, or Australian Aboriginal origin. – *n.* **1** the colour of coal, the night sky, etc. **2** (also **Black**) a person of African, West Indian, or Australian Aboriginal origin. – *vb.* **blacking, blacked** to make black. – **in the black** with money on the credit side of an account.

black belt *n.* a belt showing the wearer has reached the highest possible level of skill in judo, karate, etc.

blackbird *n.* a small European bird, the male of which is black with a yellow beak.

black hole *n.* an area in space which pulls matter into itself, thought to exist where a star has collapsed.

blacksmith *n.* a person who makes and repairs by hand things made of iron, such as horseshoes.

● **Black Sea** an inland sea between RUSSIA, the UKRAINE, TURKEY, BULGARIA, and ROMANIA.

bladder (blad ĕr) *n.* **1** the bag-like organ in the body in which urine collects. **2** a small, air-filled pouch in certain plants, e.g. seaweed.

blade (blād) *n.* **1** the cutting part of a knife, sword, etc. **2** the wide flat part of an oar, etc.

● **Blake, William** (1757-1827) was an English poet and artist, author of *Songs of Innocence*.

blame (blām) *vb.* **blaming, blamed** to consider a person or thing as responsible for something that has gone wrong. – *n.* responsibility for something that has gone wrong: *Who took the blame for the crash?*

blameless *adj.* innocent; free from blame.

bland (bland) *adj.* almost without taste; uninteresting: *We complained because the vegetables were overcooked and bland.*

blank (blangk) *adj.* **1** describing paper, magnetic tape, video tape, etc. with nothing printed or recorded on it. **2** not filled in; empty: *She helped* *him to fill in the blank form.* **3** showing no expression or interest: *She gave him a blank look.* – **draw a blank** to fail.

blanket (**blangk** it) *n.* a thick, warm covering, usually made of wool, used to cover beds.

blare (blār) *vb.* **blaring, blared 1** to make a sound like a trumpet. **2** to sound or say loudly and harshly. – *n.* a loud, harsh sound: *The blare of her radio annoyed the neighbours.*

blast (bläst) *n.* **1** an explosion. **2** a strong, sudden gust of air. **3** a sudden loud sound of a car horn. – *vb.* **blasting, blasted 1** to blow up a tunnel, rock, etc. with explosives. **2** to make a loud or explosive noise: *The radio was blasting out loud music.* – *vb.* **blast off** (of a spacecraft) to be launched.

blaze (blāz) *n.* **1** a bright, strong fire or flame. **2** a brilliant display: *The show opened in a blaze of publicity.* – *vb.* **blazing, blazed** to burn or shine brightly.

blazing *adj.* burning brightly.

bleach (blēch) *vb.* **bleaching, bleached** to make something become white or lose its colour, through exposure to the sun or by chemicals. – *n.* a chemical used to bleach clothes, etc.

bleak (blēk) *adj.* **1** exposed and desolate; cold and not welcoming. **2** offering little or no hope: *The prospects for a recovery are bleak.*

bleat (blēt) *vb.* **bleating, bleated** to make a noise like a sheep, goat, or calf.

bleed (blēd) *vb.* **bleeding, bled** (bled) to lose or let out blood.

bleep (blēp) *n.* a short, high burst of sound, usually made by an electronic machine.

blemish (**blem** ish) *n.* a stain, mark, or fault. – *vb.* **blemishing, blemished** to stain or spoil the beauty of.

blend (blend) *vb.* **blending, blended 1** to mix different things together. **2** to shade gradually into: *The sea blended into the sky.* – *n.* a mixture.

● **Blériot, Louis** (1872-1936) was a French pilot who, on 25 July 1909, became the first person to cross the English Channel by air.

bless (bles) *vb.* **blessing, blessed** or **blest 1** to ask God to show favour to or protect. **2** to praise, to give honour or glory to.

blessing *n.* **1** a wish or prayer for happiness or success. **2** a cause of happiness; a benefit or advantage. **3** approval or good wishes. **4** a short prayer said before or after a meal.

● **Bligh, William** (1754-1817) was a British naval officer whose crew mutinied during the famous voyage of the *Bounty.* Bligh survived an epic journey of 6300 km in an open boat.

blew. See **blow[1]**.

blight (blīt) *n.* **1** a disease that causes plants to wither and die. **2** a person or thing that causes decay or destruction, or spoils things.

blind (blīnd) *adj.* **1** not able to see. **2** unable or unwilling to understand or appreciate: *She was blind to his faults.* **3** unthinking, without reason or purpose: *He felt an overwhelming blind hatred.* – *n.* a screen to stop light coming through a window. – *vb.* **blinding, blinded 1** to make blind. **2** to make unreasonable or foolish: *She was blinded by anger.* – *n. & adj.* **blinding.** – *n.* **blindness.** – **turn a blind eye to** to pretend not to notice.

blindfold *n.* a piece of cloth used to cover the eyes to prevent a person from seeing.

blink (blingk) *vb.* **blinking, blinked 1** to open and shut the eyes very quickly. **2** to flash a light on and off. – *n.* an act of blinking.

blip (blip) *n.* **1** a sudden, sharp sound produced by a machine. **2** a spot of light on a screen showing the position of an object.

blister (**blis** těr) *n.* a thin bubble on the skin containing liquid, caused by something rubbing or burning the skin. – *vb.* **blistering, blistered** to come up in blisters.

blizzard (**bli** zǎrd) *n.* a lot of snow falling and being blown by the wind.

bloat (blōt) *vb.* **bloating, bloated** to swell or puff out: *I felt bloated after such a huge meal.*

blob (blob) *n.* **1** a small, soft, round mass of something: *He took a blob of jam.* **2** a small drop of liquid.

FINEST BLENDS
When parts of two words are put together to make a new word it is called blending. 'Motel' is a blend of motor car and hotel; 'Eurovision' is a blend of European and television; and 'smog' is a blend of smoke and fog.

Blériot on his historic cross-Channel flight. He took off from Calais and 37 minutes later he touched down at Dover.

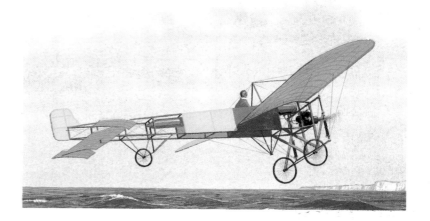

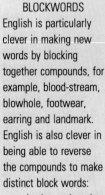

bloc (blok) *n.* a group of countries that have a common interest, purpose, or policy.

block (blok) *n.* **1** a mass of solid wood, stone, ice, etc., usually with flat sides. **2** a piece of wood or stone on which to chop and cut food. **3** a large building containing offices or flats. – *vb.* **blocking, blocked** to make progress difficult or impossible; to obstruct.

blockade *n.* the closing off of a port or region by surrounding it with soldiers or ships to stop people and goods from passing in and out. – *vb.* **blockading, blockaded**.

blond (of a woman, usually **blonde**) (blond) *adj.* having pale yellow hair and light-coloured or pale skin.

blonde *n.* a woman with pale yellow hair.

blood (blud) *n.* the red liquid pumped through the body by the heart.

blood donor *n.* a person who gives blood for use by a person who is ill, in operations, etc.

blood group or **type** *n.* any one of the four types into which human blood is classified, A, B, AB, and O.

bloodhound *n.* a large dog with a very good sense of smell, used for tracking.

bloodstream *n.* the blood flowing through the body.

bloom (bloom) *n.* a flower, especially on a plant valued for its flowers. – *vb.* **blooming, bloomed 1** to be in flower. **2** to be healthy.

blooming *adj.* **1** flowering. **2** bright; beautiful. **3** very healthy; flourishing.

blossom (blo som) *n.* **1** a flower or mass of flowers, especially on a fruit tree. **2** the state of flowering: *in blossom.* – *vb.* **blossoming, blossomed 1** to develop flowers. **2** to grow well or develop into: *She has blossomed into an accomplished dancer.*

Cherry

Blossom of fruit trees. The aim of all plants is to produce seeds and so maintain the species. To do this they produce flowers, which are the plant's reproductive organs.

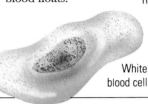

Blood is made up of four different substances: red cells which carry oxygen around the body; white cells which fight harmful bacteria; platelets which help the blood to clot when we bleed; and plasma, the liquid in which blood floats.

Red blood cell

Platelets

White blood cell

blot (blot) *n.* **1** a spot or stain, especially of ink. **2** a stain on a person's good reputation.

blouse (blowz) *n.* a woman's shirt.

blow¹ (blō) *vb.* **blowing, blew** (bloo), **blown 1** to be moving, especially rapidly: *The wind blew hard.* **2** to move or be moved by a current of air, wind, etc.: *The wind blew the fence down.* **3** to send air from the mouth; to form or shape by blowing air from the mouth: *Let's blow bubbles!* – *vb.* **blow up 1** to explode. **2** to fill up or swell up with air or gas. **3** to make a photograph bigger.

blowhole *n.* **1** a hole in ice through which animals such as seals can breathe. **2** a hole on top of a whale's head through which it blows air and water.

blow² (blō) *n.* **1** a stroke or knock with the hand or a weapon. **2** a sudden shock or misfortune. – **come to blows** to end up fighting.

blown. See **blow¹**.

blubber (blub ĕr) *n.* the fat of sea animals such as the whale. – *vb.* **blubbering, blubbered** (*colloquial*) to weep noisily.

blue (bloo) *adj.* **1** describing the colour of a clear, cloudless sky. **2** sad or depressed. – *n.* **1** the colour of a clear, cloudless sky. **2** blue

Apple

paint, dye, or material. – **once in a blue moon** hardly ever.

blueberry *n.* **blueberries** a dark blue berry from a bush common in North America.

bluebird *n.* a small blue-backed North American songbird.

Blue Peter *n.* a blue flag with a white square, flown on a ship which is about to sail.

blues *n.* **1** a feeling of sadness. **2** slow, sad jazz music of black American origin.

bluff[1] (bluf) *vb.* **bluffing, bluffed** to try to deceive someone by pretending to be stronger, cleverer, etc. than you really are.

bluff[2] (bluf) *n.* a steep cliff or bank of ground.

blunder (blun děr) *vb.* **blundering, blundered 1** to make a stupid, clumsy, and usually serious mistake. **2** to move about awkwardly and clumsily. – *n.* a stupid, clumsy, and usually serious mistake.

blunt (blunt) *adj.* **1** having no point or sharp edge. **2** honest and direct in a rough way.

blur (blûr) *n.* **1** a thing not clearly seen or heard. **2** a smear – *vb.* **blurring, blurred** to make or become less clear.

blush (blush) *n.* **1** a red or pink glow on the skin of the face, caused by shame or embarrassment. **2** a pink, rosy glow. – *vb.* **blushing, blushed 1** to become red or pink in the face because of shame or embarrassment. **2** to feel ashamed or embarrassed: *I blush when I think of my past mistakes.* – *adj.* **blushing**.

boa (bō ǎ) *n.* (also **boa constrictor**) a large South American snake that kills by winding itself round its prey and crushing it.

● **Boadicea**. See **Boudicca**.

boar (bōr) *n.* **1** (also **wild boar**) a wild pig. **2** a male pig kept for breeding.

board (bōrd) *n.* **1** a long flat strip of wood or other material. **2** a flat piece of wood or card used for a specific purpose: *notice board; chessboard*. **3** an official group of people controlling or managing an organization.

boast (bōst) *vb.* **boasting, boasted** to talk with too much pride about your own abilities, achievements, etc.

boat (bōt) *n.* a small vessel for travelling over water. – *vb.* **boating, boated** to sail in a boat for pleasure. – **in the same boat** in the same difficult circumstances.

Boats are usually small, open craft. The first real boat was a canoe hollowed out of a tree trunk. Small oval-shaped boats called coracles, from Wales and Ireland, were made by stretching hide over a wickerwork frame. Similar was the kayak, a sealskin covered canoe used by the Inuit. Until the invention of the steam engine, boats were propelled by oars, paddles, poles, or by sails.

An Egyptian sailing vessel

An Inuit kayak

A coracle of 6000 BC

SOME TYPES OF BOAT

dinghy a small open boat propelled by oars or sail.

gondola a flat bottomed boat used in Venice.

punt a long flat-bottomed boat propelled by a pole.

sampan a flat-bottomed oriental boat with oars.

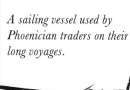

A sailing vessel used by Phoenician traders on their long voyages.

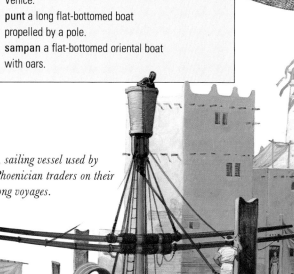

The bobcat is active mainly at night. It uses its keen eyesight and hearing to track down the small animals it eats.

In the 14th century a bonfire was a *bone fire*, an open-air burning of bones, which was a common event in those days.

bob (bob) *vb.* **bobbing, bobbed** to move up and down quickly.

bobbin (**bob** in) *n.* a small cylindrical object on which thread is wound, used in sewing.

bobcat (**bob** kat) *n.* a wild cat of North America with brown fur marked with darker spots and lines. It eats rodents, snakes and sometimes livestock and poultry.

bobsleigh (**bob** slā) or **bobsled** (**bob** sled) *n.* a sledge with metal runners.

body (**bo** di) *n.* **bodies 1** the whole physical structure of a person or animal. **2** the physical structure of a person or animal excluding the head and limbs. **3** a corpse. **4** the main or central part of anything. **5** a group of people. **bodily** *adj.* of the body: *the bodily functions.* – *adv.* concerning the whole body: *She picked the child up bodily.*

body building *n.* physical exercise which makes the muscles bigger and stronger.

bodyguard *n.* a person or group of people who guard an important person.

bodywork *n.* the outer painted structure of a motor car, etc.

Boer (bör) *n.* a descendant of the early Dutch settlers in SOUTH AFRICA. – *adj.* of or relating to the Boers.

bog (bog) *n.* an area of very wet, spongy ground. – *vb.* **bog down, bogging, bogged** to prevent from progressing: *She gets bogged down by details.*

bogey or **bogy** (**bō** gi) *n.* a mischievous spirit.

boggle (**bog** êl) *vb.* **boggled boggled** to be amazed at or unable to understand or imagine: *The mind boggles at how many grains of sand there are on the shore.*

●**Bogotá** is the capital of Colombia.

bogus (**bō** gůs) *adj.* false; not genuine.

●**Bohr, Niels** (1885-1962) a Danish physicist.

boil[1] (boil) *vb.* **boiling, boiled 1** (of liquids) to start to bubble and turn from liquid to gas when heated. **2** to contain a liquid which is boiling: *The kettle is boiling.* **3** to cook by boiling. **boiler** *n.* an apparatus for heating a building's hot water supply. **boiling-point** *n.* the temperature at which a liquid, especially water, boils.

boil[2] (boil) *n.* a painful red pus-filled swelling on the skin.

boisterous (**boi** stě růs) *adj.* very lively, noisy.

bold (bōld) *adj.* **1** daring or brave: *He made a bold attempt to rescue his friend.* **2** striking and clearly marked: *A zebra has bold markings.* **3** printed in thick, black letters, for example, **bold**.

bole (bōl) *n.* the trunk of a tree.

●**Bolívar, Simón** (1783-1830) was a South American hero who freed PERU, BOLIVIA, COLOMBIA, ECUADOR, and VENEZUELA from Spanish rule.

●**Bolivia**. See Supplement, **Countries**.

Bolshevik (**bol** she vik) *n.* a Russian communist or any communist. – *adj.* **1** of the Bolsheviks. **2** communist. – *n.* **Bolshevism**.

bolt (bōlt) *n.* **1** a bar to fasten a door or gate. **2** a small, thick, round bar of metal, with a screw thread, used with a nut to fasten things together. **3** a flash of lightning. **4** a sudden

A **bog** contains peat (decayed plant life) which is acidic. The acid prevents things from decaying, even if they have been buried in a bog for many years.

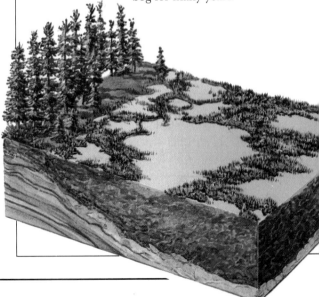

movement, especially to escape: *The thieving cat made a bolt for it.* – *vb.* **bolting, bolted 1** to fasten a door or window with a bolt. **2** to eat very quickly. **3** to run away suddenly and quickly: *The horse bolted, shedding its rider.*

bomb (bom) *n.* **1** a hollow case or other device containing explosive substances. **2** the atomic bomb or any nuclear bomb. – *vb.* **bombing, bombed** to attack with a bomb.
bomber *n.* an aircraft built for bombing.
bombshell *n.* a piece of surprising news.

bombard (bom **bärd**) *vb.* **bombarding, bombarded 1** to attack with large, heavy guns or bombs. **2** to direct questions or abuse at someone very quickly and without stopping.

● **Bombay** is a city on the west coast of INDIA.

bonanza (bŏ **nan** ză) *n.* a usually unexpected and sudden source of good luck or wealth.

● **Bonaparte, Napoleon**. See **Napoleon**.

bond (bond) *n.* **1** (usually in *plural*) something which restrains or imprisons a person: *The prisoner broke his bonds.* **2** something that joins people together: *They were united by a bond of friendship.* – *vb.* **bonding, bonded 1** to join or tie together. **2** to stick together.

bondage (bon dij) *n.* **1** slavery. **2** the state of being confined or imprisoned.

The face of a man who died over 2000 years ago. His body was found in the Tollund bog in Denmark in May 1950. The peat has preserved his hair and skin just as it was when he was put to death by hanging. (The noose is still visible around his neck.) He may have been sacrificed for ritual purposes or hanged for some crime.

Wooden figures found in a bog near Roos Carr, England. The acid in the peat has preserved them perfectly.

bone (bōn) *n.* **1** any of the pieces of hard tissue that form the skeleton. **2** (in *plural*) the basic or essential part: *They need to understand the bare bones of the subject.* – *vb.* **boning, boned 1** to take bones out of meat, etc. **2** to make a piece of clothing stiff by adding pieces of bone or some other hard substance.
bone-dry *adj.* completely dry.
bony *adj.* **bonier, boniest 1** of or like bone. **2** thin.

bonfire (bon fīr) *n.* a large, outdoor fire, often burned to celebrate something.

● **Bonn** was the capital of West Germany until Germany reunited and took Berlin as its capital.

bonnet (bon it) *n.* (*British*) the hinged cover over a car's engine.

bonus (bō nŭs) *n.* an extra sum of money given on top of what is due.

book (book) *n.* **1** a number of printed pages bound together along one edge and protected by covers. **2** a number of sheets of blank paper bound together. – *vb.* **booking, booked** to reserve a ticket in advance. – *n.* **booking**.

● The first books were written on rolls of papyrus in ancient Egypt. The Romans also used parchment rolls, made from sheepskin. In the Middle Ages books were handwritten and beautifully decorated by monks. The first printed book was GUTENBERG's Bible in 1452.

boom[1] (boom) *n.* a loud, deep, resounding sound, like that made by a large drum or gun.
boom[2] (boom) *n.* a sudden increase or growth in business and prosperity. – *vb.* **booming, boomed** to prosper rapidly.

boomerang (boom ĕ rang) *n.* a piece of flat, curved wood used by Australian Aborigines for hunting, often so balanced that, when thrown to a distance, it returns to the thrower.

● **Boone, Daniel** (1734-1820) was an American explorer and frontiersman.

boost (boost) *vb.* **boosting, boosted 1** to improve or encourage: *Her good exam results boosted her spirits.* **2** to make greater or increase: *Increased sales have boosted profits.* – *n.* **1** a piece of help or encouragement. **2** a rise or increase.

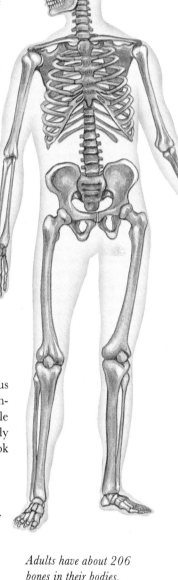

Adults have about 206 bones in their bodies. Each arm has 32, each leg 31, the skull 29, the spine 26, and the chest 25. The smallest bone, the stapes, is in the ear. It is only 2 mm long.

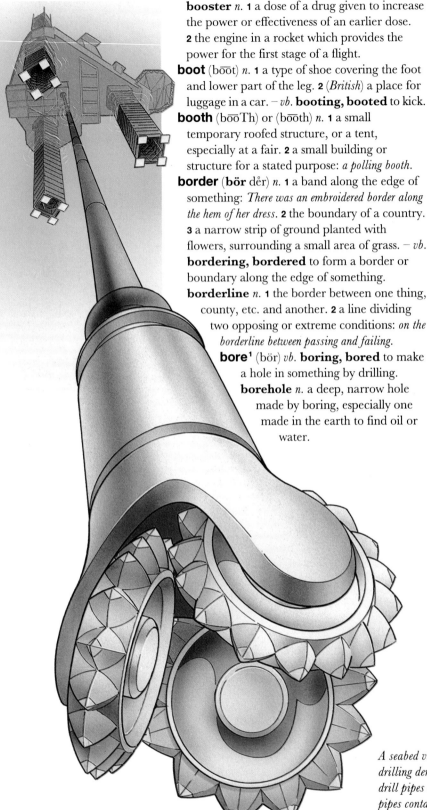

booster *n.* **1** a dose of a drug given to increase the power or effectiveness of an earlier dose. **2** the engine in a rocket which provides the power for the first stage of a flight.

boot (boot) *n.* **1** a type of shoe covering the foot and lower part of the leg. **2** (*British*) a place for luggage in a car. – *vb.* **booting, booted** to kick.

booth (booTh) or (booth) *n.* **1** a small temporary roofed structure, or a tent, especially at a fair. **2** a small building or structure for a stated purpose: *a polling booth*.

border (bör dẽr) *n.* **1** a band along the edge of something: *There was an embroidered border along the hem of her dress.* **2** the boundary of a country. **3** a narrow strip of ground planted with flowers, surrounding a small area of grass. – *vb.* **bordering, bordered** to form a border or boundary along the edge of something.

borderline *n.* **1** the border between one thing, county, etc. and another. **2** a line dividing two opposing or extreme conditions: *on the borderline between passing and failing*.

bore¹ (bör) *vb.* **boring, bored** to make a hole in something by drilling.
borehole *n.* a deep, narrow hole made by boring, especially one made in the earth to find oil or water.

bore² (bör) *vb.* **boring, bored** to make someone feel uninterested, by being dull and unimaginative. – *n.* a dull, uninteresting, tedious person or thing. – *adj.* **bored**. – *adj.* **boring**.
boredom *n.* the state of being bored.

bore³. See **bear¹**.

boric acid (bö rik a sid) *n.* an acid, usually in the form of a white powder, used as a mild antiseptic and in glass-making.

born (börn) *adj.* **1** brought into being by birth. **2** having a natural ability: *She is a born leader.* – **in all your born days** (*colloquial*) in all your lifetime or experience. – **not born yesterday** not a fool.

borough (bur ů) *n.* **1** in Britain, a town or urban area which sends a member to Parliament. **2** a division of a large town especially of London or New York.

borrow (bo rō) *vb.* **borrowing, borrowed** to take something temporarily, usually with permission and with the intention of returning it. – **live on borrowed time** to live longer than expected.

borzoi (bör zoi) *n.* a large dog originally used for hunting. It has a narrow head and a long, soft coat.

● **Bosnia-Hercegovina**. See Supplement, **Countries**.

bosom (boo zŏm) *n.* **1** a woman's chest or breasts. **2** a loving or protective centre.
bosom friend *n.* a very close friend.

● **Bosporus** a strip of water joining the Black Sea and the Sea of Marmara, dividing EUROPE from ASIA.

boss (bos) *n.* (*colloquial*) a person who employs or who is in charge of others.
bossy *adj.* **bossier, bossiest** (*colloquial*) liking to give orders and commands to others. – *adv.* **bossily**. – *n.* **bossiness**.

● **Boston** is the capital of Massachusetts, USA.

A seabed view of a rotary drill bit used to bore for oil. The drilling derrick is a tower that supports the drill pipes. The drill pipes are lengthened by adding extra sections. The drill pipes contain several channels. Mud pumped at high pressure down one channel cools and lubricates the boring bit and forces drilled rock up through the outer pipe channel.

●**Boston Tea Party** On 16 December 1773 a band of American colonists boarded a British ship in Boston harbour and dumped overboard its cargo of tea in protest at the high taxes collected by the British government. This was an event leading to the AMERICAN WAR OF INDEPENDENCE.

botany (**bot** å ni) *n.* the scientific study of plants. – *adj.* **botanic** (bồ **tan** ik) or **botanical**. – *n.* **botanist**.

● There are over 300,000 different kinds of plant, from microscopic algae to giant Redwood trees. In 1753 Carolus LINNAEUS, a Swedish botanist, invented the first real system for naming plants.

●**Botany Bay** is near Sydney, AUSTRALIA, and is where Captain COOK landed in 1770.

both (bōth) *adj. & pron.* the two: *Both girls owned bicycles.* – *adv.* as well: *She both works and runs a family.*

bother (**bo** Thẻr) *vb.* **bothering, bothered 1** to annoy, worry, or trouble: *The flies bothered them.* **2** to take the time or trouble: *Don't bother about the washing up.* **3** to worry: *She was bothered about her exams.* – *n.* a minor trouble or worry.

●**Botswana**. See Supplement, **Countries**.

●**Botticelli, Sandro** (1445-1510) was a leading painter from Florence, Italy.

bottle (**bo** tẻl) *n.* a hollow, usually glass or plastic container with a narrow neck, for holding liquids. – *vb.* **bottling, bottled 1** to put into or store in bottles. **2** to hide feelings: *She had bottled up her sadness for many years.*

bottom (**bo** tồm) *n.* **1** the lowest position or part; the point farthest away from the top, most important, or most successful part: *He was bottom of the class.* **2** the part of the body on which a person sits. – *adj.* lowest or last.

●**Boudicca, Queen** (*died about* AD 61) was a British heroine who led a revolt against the Romans.

bough (bow) *n.* a branch of a tree.
bought. See **buy**.
boulder (bōl dẻr) *n.* a large rock or stone, rounded and worn smooth by the weather.

American colonists disguised as Native North Americans throwing a cargo of tea overboard into Boston harbour. They said that 'taxation without representation is tyranny'.

boulevard (**bōōl** ẻ värd) *n.* a broad street lined with trees.

bounce (bowns) *vb.* **bouncing, bounced 1** to spring or jump back from a solid surface. **2** to move or spring suddenly: *She bounced about the room.* – *n.* the act of springing back from a solid surface.

bound[1] (bownd) *adj.* **1** tied with a rope, etc. **2** restricted to or by: *housebound; snowbound.* **3** certain: *It was bound to happen.*

bound[2] (bownd) *adj.* going to or towards: *southbound.*

bound[3] (bownd) *n.* a jump or leap upwards. – *vb.* **bounding, bounded** to spring or leap.

boundary (**bownd** å ri) *n.* **boundaries** a line marking the farthest limit of an area, etc.

bouquet (boo **kā**) *n.* **1** a bunch of flowers arranged in an artistic way, given as a gift, etc. **2** the delicate smell of wine.

bout (bowt) *n.* **1** a period of illness: *He has had a bout of flu.* **2** a boxing or wrestling match.

bovine (**bō** vīn) *adj.* of or like cattle.

bow[1] (bow) *vb.* **bowing, bowed 1** to bend the head or the upper part of the body forwards and downwards, usually as a sign of greeting or respect, or to acknowledge applause. **2** to accept or submit to, especially unwillingly: *I must bow to the inevitable.* – *n.* an act of bowing.

bow[2] (bō) *n.* **1** a knot with a double loop. **2** a weapon made of a piece of curved wood, bent by a string attached to each end, for shooting arrows. **3** a long thin piece of wood with horsehair stretched along its length, for playing the violin, cello, etc.

bow[3] (bow) *n.* the front part of a ship or boat.

bowel (**bow** ẻl) *n.* the organs for digesting food next after the stomach; the intestines.

bowl[1] (bōl) *n.* **1** a round, deep dish for mixing or serving food, for holding liquids or flowers, etc. **2** the round, hollow part of an object, such as a spoon or pipe.

PRONUNCIATION GUIDE	
fat **a**	all **ö**
fate **ā**	foot **oo**
fast **ä**	moon **ōō**
among **å**	boy **oi**
met **e**	house **ow**
mean **ē**	demon **ồ**
silent **ẻ**	thing **th**
loch **hh**	this **Th**
fin **i**	but **u**
line **ī**	mute **ū**
quick **kw**	fur **û**
got **o**	brochure **ủ**
note **ō**	vision **zh**

bowl² (bōl) *vb.* **bowling, bowled** to throw a ball towards the person batting, in cricket, etc. – *vb.* **bowl over** (*colloquial*) to impress greatly. **bowling** *n.* a game played indoors in which a ball is rolled at a group of skittles in order to knock them down.

box¹ (boks) *n.* **1** a usually square or rectangular container made from wood, cardboard, plastic, etc. and with a lid, for holding things. **2** a separate compartment for a particular purpose, for example, for a group of people in a theatre, or for a horse in a stable. – *vb.* **boxing, boxed 1** to put into or provide with a box. **2** to stop from moving, confine or enclose: *Their car was boxed in so that they could not get out.*

box² (boks) *vb.* **boxing, boxed** to fight with hands protected by thick leather gloves, especially as a sport. – *n.* **boxing**. **boxer** *n.* **1** a person who boxes. **2** a medium-sized breed of dog with a short, smooth coat.

boy (boi) *n.* a male child. – *n.* **boyhood**.

boycott (**boi** kot) *vb.* **boycotting, boycotted** to refuse to have any business or social dealings with a company or a country because you disapprove of something it is doing.

● **Boyle, Robert** (1627-91) was an Irish chemist who formulated a law on the physical properties of gases.

brace (brās) *n.* **1** a device, usually made from metal, which supports or holds two things together. **2** (*British*; in *plural*) straps worn over the shoulders, for holding trousers up. **3** a wire device worn on the teeth to straighten them. – *vb.* **bracing, braced 1** to make tight or stronger, usually by supporting in some way. **2** to prepare yourself for a blow or a shock.

bracelet (**brās** lit) *n.* a band or chain worn as a piece of jewellery round the arm or wrist.

bracken *n.* a type of fern.

bracket (**brak** it) *n.* **1** either one of a pair of symbols, [ ], ( ), or < >, used to group together or enclose words, figures, etc. **2** a group or category falling within a certain range: *That bike is out of my price bracket.* **3** an L-shaped piece of metal or strong plastic, used for attaching shelves to walls. – *vb.* **bracketing, bracketed** to enclose or group together words, etc. in brackets.

● **Brahms, Johannes** (1833-97) was a German composer.

braid (brād) *n.* **1** a band or tape, often made from threads twisted together, used as a decoration on uniforms. **2** a length of hair consisting of several lengths which have been twisted together. – *vb.* **braiding, braided** to twist several lengths of hair, etc. together.

Braille (brāl) *n.* a system of printing using raised dots, which blind people can feel with their fingers and so read what is printed. It was invented by a blind French teacher, Louis *Braille*, in the 1800s.

A B C D E
F G H I J
K L M N O
P Q R S T
U V W X Y
Z and for of the
with fraction numeral poetry apostrophe
hyphen dash comma semicolon colon

brain (brān) *n.* the soft grey organ inside the head which controls thought, sight, etc. **brainteaser** *n.* a difficult exercise or puzzle.

brake (brāk) *n.* **1** a device on a vehicle for making it slow down or stop. **2** anything which makes something stop or prevents progress: *There was a brake on public spending.* – *vb.* **braking, braked** to use a brake.

bramble (**bram** bĕl) *n.* a common wild prickly bush which produces blackberries.

bran (bran) *n.* the outer covering of grain separated from flour.

branch (bränch) *n.* **1** a shoot or stem growing out like an arm from the main body of a tree. **2** a main division of a railway line, river, road, or mountain range: *The train travelled along a branch line on the railway.* – *vb.* **branching, branched** to divide from the main part.

Captain Boycott was a British landlord in Ireland who, in the 1880s, charged his tenants rents that were much too high. As a result the tenants *boycotted* him.

Bracken is the world's commonest fern but unlike most ferns has creeping underground stems which can grow more than a metre in a year. In this way bracken spreads rapidly.

brand (brand) *n.* **1** a maker's name or trademark. **2** a variety or type: *Her brand of humour doesn't appeal to everybody.* **3** (also **branding-iron**) an iron used for burning identifying marks on cattle, etc.

brass (bräs) *n.* **1** a hard yellowish metal, a mixture of copper and zinc. **2** wind instruments made of brass, such as the trumpet; the brass instruments in an orchestra.

brave (brāv) *adj.* without fear of danger or pain. – *n.* **bravery**.

brawl (bröl) *n.* a noisy quarrel or fight.

bray (brā) *n.* the loud, harsh sound made by a donkey. – *vb.* **braying, brayed**.

● **Brazil**. See Supplement, **Countries**.

bread (bred) *n.* a food made from flour, water, and yeast, baked in an oven.

breadth (bredth) *n.* the measurement from one side to the other.

break (brāk) *vb.* **breaking, broke** (brōk), **broken 1** to become divided into two or more parts by force: *Jim dropped the cup and broke it.* **2** to be damaged, so as to no longer work and be in need of repair: *The lawnmower broke while she was cutting the grass.* **3** to do something not allowed: *David broke all the rules.* **4** to stop work, etc. for a short period of time: *At 4 o'clock we always break for tea.* **5** to do better than: *Dan broke the school's high jump record.* **6** to become lower in tone, especially of the voice of a boy becoming an adult. – *n.* **1** an act of breaking. **2** a brief pause in work, lessons, etc. – *vb.* **break away** to escape from control. – *vb.* **break down 1** to use force to knock down a door, etc. **2** to stop working properly. – *vb.* **break in 1** to enter a building by force, especially to steal things inside. **2** to train a horse to carry a saddle and a rider. – *vb.* **break off 1** to remove or be removed by breaking. **2** to come to an end suddenly.

breakfast (**brek** fǎst) *n.* the first meal of the day.

breast (brest) *n.* **1** either of the two fleshy parts on the front of a woman's body which produce milk. **2** the front part of the body between the neck and stomach.

breath (breth) *n.* **1** the air drawn into and sent out from the lungs. **2** an act of breathing air in. **Breathalyzer** or **Breathalyser** *n.* a piece of equipment used to test the amount of alcohol on a driver's breath.

breathless *adj.* **1** having difficulty in breathing normally, either from illness or from hurrying, etc. **2** very eager or excited.

breathe (brēTh) *vb.* **breathing, breathed** to draw air into, and force it out of, the lungs. – *n.* **breathing**.

bred. See **breed**.

breed (brēd) *vb.* **breeding, bred** (bred) **1** to produce young, usually of animals. **2** to keep animals or plants for the purpose of producing more, or developing new types. – *n.* **1** a group of animals within a species which all share some characteristics. **2** a kind or type.

breeze (brēz) *n.* a gentle wind.

brew (brōō) *vb.* **brewing, brewed 1** to make beer, etc. by mixing, boiling, and fermenting. **2** to make tea or coffee by mixing the leaves, grains, etc. with boiling water. **3** to get stronger and threaten: *There's a storm brewing.*
brewery *n.* **breweries** a place where beer, etc. is brewed.

briar or **brier** (brī ěr) *n.* any prickly bush.

bribe (brīb) *n.* a gift, usually money, offered to someone to persuade him or her to do something. – *vb.* **bribing, bribed** to give or promise money, etc. to a person to persuade him or her to do something. – *n.* **bribery**.

brick (brik) *n.* **1** a rectangular block of baked clay used for building. **2** a child's usually plastic or wooden, rectangular, cylindrical, etc. toy for building. **3** something in the shape of a brick: *He was so hot he bought a brick of ice-cream.*
bricklayer *n.* a person who builds with bricks. – *n.* **bricklaying**.

Bricks are generally laid in horizontal layers known as courses. *The patterns in which they are laid are called* bonds.

Running bond

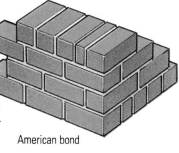

English bond

American bond

Bricks are made of clay. The clay is mined and crushed into small particles. Water is added to make a stiff mud, together with other chemicals. Most bricks are shaped and cut by machine then oven dried and 'fired' at a very high temperature in kilns. Some specially shaped bricks are hand made in moulds, air dried and then fired.

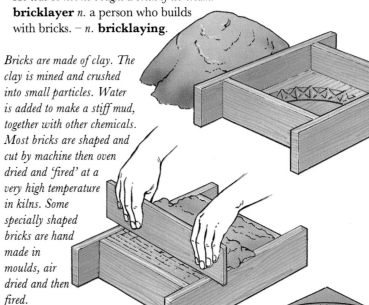

bride (brīd) *n.* a woman who has just been, or is about to be, married.

bridegroom *n.* a man who has just been, or is about to be, married.

bridge[1] (brij) *n.* **1** a structure joining the two sides of a road, railway, or river to allow people, vehicles, etc. to cross. **2** anything joining or connecting two separate things. **3** the narrow raised platform from which the captain of a ship directs its course. **4** a small piece of wood on a violin, guitar, etc. which keeps the strings stretched tight. **5** the hard, bony, upper part of the nose. – *vb.* **bridging, bridged 1** to build a bridge over. **2** to make a connection, close a gap.

bridge[2] (brij) *n.* a card game for four people.

bridle (brī děl). See **Horse terms**.

There are three basic types of **bridge**: *Beam*, in which a beam of steel is supported on each bank; *arch*, formed of one or several arches; *suspension*, in which the main part is a beam supported by steel cables suspended from towers. The longest single-span bridge is the Humber Suspension bridge across the estuary of the River Humber, England.

Beam

Suspension

Arch

Forth bridge, Scotland

brief (brēf) *adj.* lasting only a short time; short or small; concise. – *n.* **1** (in *plural*) a woman's or man's underpants without legs. **2** instructions given for a job or task. – *vb.* **briefing, briefed** to prepare a person by giving instructions in advance: *Rachel briefed him on the procedure.*

bright (brīt) *adj.* **1** giving out or shining with much light. **2** describing a colour that is strong, light, and clear. **3** lively and cheerful. **4** clever and quick at learning. – *adv.* **brightly**: *a fire burning brightly.* – *n.* **brightness**.

brighten (brī těn) *vb.* **brightening, brightened 1** to make or become bright or brighter. **2** to make or become happier.

brilliant (bril yånt) *adj.* **1** very bright and sparkling. **2** of outstanding intelligence or talent. **3** (*colloquial*) excellent. – *n.* **brilliance**.

brim (brim) *n.* **1** the top edge or lip of a cup, glass, bowl, etc. **2** the projecting edge of a hat.

bring (bring) *vb.* **bringing, brought** (bröt) **1** to take something or someone to a stated place or person. **2** to cause or result in: *War brings misery.* **3** to cause to be in a certain state: *Can you bring him to his senses?* – *vb.* **bring about** to cause to happen. – *vb.* **bring forward** to move to an earlier date or time. – *vb.* **bring out 1** to make clear, emphasize. **2** to publish. **3** to cause to be covered with a rash, etc.: *Cats bring me out in spots.* – *vb.* **bring up** to care for and educate a child: *She was brought up by her grandparents when her parents went to work abroad.*

brink (bringk) *n.* **1** the edge or border of a steep, dangerous place or of a river. **2** the point immediately before the start of something dangerous, unknown, exciting, etc: *We are on the brink of new discoveries.*

brisk (brisk) *adj.* **1** lively, active, or quick: *We all went for a brisk walk.* **2** pleasantly cold and fresh: *It was a brisk day.* – *n.* **briskness**.

bristle (bri sěl) *n.* a short, stiff hair on or from an animal's back, etc.

British (brit ish) *adj.* of GREAT BRITAIN or its people.

● **British Columbia**. See **Canada**.

● **British Isles** made up of two large nations, the United Kingdom of GREAT BRITAIN and NORTHERN IRELAND (comprising ENGLAND, Northern Ireland, SCOTLAND, and WALES) and the Republic of IRELAND, and two small British dependencies, the Isle of Man and the Channel Islands.

brittle (**bri** tĕl) *adj.* hard but easily broken.

broad (bröd) *adj.* **1** large in extent from one side to the other. **2** wide and open; spacious. **3** general, not detailed: *They undertook a broad inquiry.* **4** clear: *It happened in broad daylight.*
broaden *vb.* **broadening, broadened** to make or become broad or broader.
broadly *adv.* widely; generally: *Broadly speaking it's a good idea.*

broadcast (**bröd** käst) *vb.* **broadcasting, broadcast 1** to send out a programme by radio or TV. **2** to make something widely known. – *n.* a TV or radio programme. – *n.* **broadcaster.** – *n.* **broadcasting.**

● **Broadway** is a street in New York where most of the main theatres are found.

broccoli (**brok** ŏ li) *n.* a variety of cauliflower with green or purple flower-like heads.
broil (broil) *vb.* **broiling, broiled** (especially *North American*) to grill food.
broke¹ . See **break**.
broke² (brōk) *adj.* (*colloquial*) without money.
broken (**brō** kĕn) *adj.* **1** smashed, fractured: *Robert has a broken leg.* **2** interrupted: *They had a broken sleep because of the noise.* **3** not working properly: *The TV is broken.*
bronchitis (brong **kī** tis) *n.* an infection of the two large air tubes, the bronchi, in the lungs, causing coughing, difficulty in breathing, etc.
bronco (**brong** kō) *n.* **broncos** a wild or half-tamed horse from the western United States.

● **Brontë** All the Brontë sisters were famous writers: Charlotte (1816-55), author of *Jane Eyre*, Emily (1818-48) who wrote *Wuthering Heights*, and Anne (1820-49).

bronze (bronz) *n.* a mixture of copper and tin. – *adj.* **1** made of bronze. **2** of the colour of bronze.
the Bronze Age *n.* the period in history when tools, weapons, etc. were made out of bronze, between about 3000 and 1000 BC.
bronze medal *n.* a medal given to the person who comes third in a race or contest.
brooch (brōch) *n.* **brooches** a decoration or piece of jewellery, fastened to clothes by a pin.
brood (brōod) *n.* a number of young animals, especially birds, born or hatched at the same time. – *vb.* **brooding, brooded** (of birds) to sit on eggs until the young are born.

In many parts of the world a period called the Copper Age was followed by the **Bronze Age** when people learned how to strengthen copper by adding tin, so producing an *alloy*.

A 7th-century BC bronze axehead (left) and a bucket.

The Chinese bronze vessel (right) was used for preparing sacrificial food for the dead.

Outside a copper mine near Salzburg, Austria, in about 1200 BC. Mined copper ore was carried out to be crushed and washed out from the rock. The concentrated ore was smelted in furnaces. The molten metal could then be cast in moulds. The oldest known moulds were open moulds (left).

brook (brook) *n.* a small stream.

broom (brōōm) *n.* a brush with a long handle for sweeping the floor.

broth (broth) *n.* a thin, clear soup made by boiling meat, fish, or vegetables.

brother (bru Thẻr) *n.* **1** a boy or man with the same parents as another person or people. **2** (plural **brethren**) a man who is a member of a religious group, especially a monk. **brother-in-law** *n.* **brothers-in-law 1** the brother of your husband or wife. **2** the husband of your sister.

brought. See **bring**.

brow (brow) *n.* **1** (usually in *plural*) an eyebrow. **2** the forehead. **3** the top of a hill or road.

brown (brown) *adj.* having a colour similar to that of bark, coffee, etc. – *n.* any of various dark colours similar to bark, coffee, etc. – *vb.* **browning, browned** to make or become brown by cooking or burning in the sun, etc.

●**Brown, John** (1800-59) was the leader of an anti-slave movement in the United States. He is remembered in the song *John Brown's Body*.

browse (browz) *vb.* **browsing, browsed** to look through a book, reading only bits.

●**Bruce, Robert the** (1274-1329) was king of Scotland. He defeated the English army at Bannockburn in 1314.

●**Brueghel** (broi gẻl) is the name of a family of Flemish painters of the 1500s and 1600s.

bruise (brōōz) *n.* an injury caused by a blow, turning the skin a darker colour but not breaking it. – *vb.* **bruising, bruised** to cause a bruise on.

●**Brunei**. See Supplement, **Countries**.

●**Brunel, Isambard Kingdom** (1806-59) was a British engineer who built bridges, railways, and ships.

brush (brush) *n.* **brushes 1** a tool with lengths of stiff bristles, etc., for tidying the hair, painting, etc. **2** a fox's tail. – *vb.* **brushing, brushed 1** to rub with a brush to remove dirt, dust, etc. **2** to remove or apply with a brush: *He brushed away the crumbs.* **3** to touch lightly in passing: *She brushed against the table.*

Brussels sprout (bru sẻlz **sprowt**) *n.* (usually in *plural*) a small, round, cabbage-like vegetable.

brutal (brōō tål) *adj.* very cruel, severe, or violent. – *n.* **brutality** (broo **tal** i ti), **brutalities**.

bubble (bu bẻl) *n.* **1** a thin film of liquid forming a ball round air or gas, especially one which floats in liquid: *The children love playing with soap bubbles.* **2** a ball of air or gas which has formed in a solid: *We found lots of air bubbles in the glass.* – *vb.* **bubbling, bubbled 1** to form bubbles. **2** to make the sound of bubbling liquid: *The water bubbled away in the pan.*

●**Buchan, John** (1875-1940) was a Scottish statesman and writer of adventure stories.

buck¹ (buk) *n.* the male of some animals, especially the rabbit, hare, or deer. – *vb.* **bucking, bucked** (of a horse) to make a series of rapid jumps into the air, with the back arched and legs held stiff.

buck² (buk) *n.* (*US colloquial*) a dollar.

bucket (**buk** it) *n.* a round, open-topped container for holding or carrying liquids, etc.

buckle (bu kẻl) *n.* a flat piece of metal attached to one end of a strap or belt, with a pin in the middle which goes through a hole in the other end of the strap or belt to fasten it.

bud (bud) *n.* a small swelling on the stem of a tree or plant which will grow into leaves or a flower; a partly opened flower: *rosebuds*.

●**Budapest** is the capital of HUNGARY.

A bud is an undeveloped shoot of a plant. If the covering of the bud is peeled back, the tightly packed leaves or flowers can be seen inside.

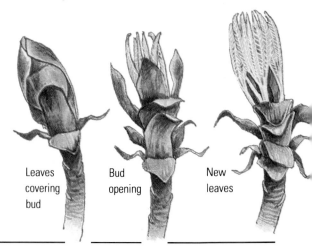

Leaves covering bud

Bud opening

New leaves

Buddhism The name Buddha means 'enlightened one'. He taught that a good cause will bring about a good consequence; bad cause, bad consequences. The ultimate goal is *nirvana*, a state of mind of complete peace. For Buddhists the wheel of life *(right)* is a symbol that life is an endless recurrence of cycles.

(Left) *Buddha in a characteristic pose, with legs folded and with a restful expression.*

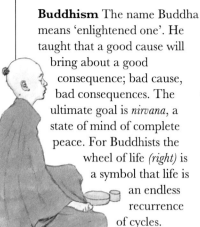

Saffron-robed Buddhist monks (above). They devote their time to prayer and meditation to achieve perfection.

Buddhism (**bood** i zěm) *n.* the religion founded by the *Buddha*, Gautama, in the 500s BC, which teaches spiritual purity and freedom from human concerns. – *n.* & *adj.* **Buddhist**.

budge (buj) *vb.* **budging, budged** to move or cause to move: *I could not budge the heavy load.*

budgerigar (**buj** ě ri gär) *n.* a type of small parrot native to Australia, often kept as a pet.

budget (**buj** it) *n.* **1** a plan showing how money coming in will be spent. **2 the Budget** a government plan telling people how much money it intends to raise in taxes and how it intends to spend it. – *vb.* **budgeting, budgeted** to calculate so as not to spend more money than you earn.

●**Buenos Aires** is the capital of ARGENTINA.

buff (buf) *n.* **1** a dull yellow colour. **2** a soft, undyed leather. **3** (*colloquial*) a person who knows a lot about a certain subject: *Eleanor is an opera buff.*

buffalo (**buf** ǎ lō) *n.* **buffalo** or **buffaloes 1** a kind of large wild cow with long curved horns, several varieties of which are found in Asia and Africa. **2** the American bison.

●**Buffalo Bill** (1846-1917) was an American showman who travelled Europe with his Wild West Show. His real name was William Cody.

buffet[1] (**boof** ā) *n.* **1** a cold meal set out on tables from which people help themselves. **2** a sideboard for holding china, glasses, etc.

buffet[2] (**buf** it) *vb.* **buffeting, buffeted** to strike or knock about.

bug (bug) *n.* **1** any insect with a flat body and a mouth which can suck blood; an insect thought of as dirty and living in dirty houses, etc. **2** any germ or virus causing infection or illness: *She caught a stomach bug.* **3** (*colloquial*) a small, hidden microphone. **4** See **Computer Terms**.

bugle (**bū** gěl) *n.* a brass instrument like a small trumpet – *n.* **bugler**.

build (bild) *vb.* **building, built 1** to make or construct from parts: *Birds build nests from twigs and moss.* **2** to develop gradually: *The politician is building a good following.* – *n.* physical form, especially of the human body: *a slim build.*

  builder *n.* a person who builds, or organizes the building of, houses, etc.

  building *n.* a structure with walls and a roof.

bulb (bulb) *n.* **1** the onion-shaped part of the stem of certain plants from which the roots grow: *Tulips grow from bulbs.* **2** (also **light-bulb**) a pear-shaped glass and metal device from which electric light is produced.

●**Bulgaria**. See Supplement, **Countries**.

bulge (bulj) *n.* a swelling, especially where you would expect to see something flat.

bulk (bulk) *n.* **1** large size; large body, shape, or person. **2** the greater or main part of.

bull (bool) *n.* the uncastrated male of the cattle family; also the male elephant, whale, and other large animals. – **a bull in a china shop** a person who acts in a rough and careless way and is likely to break things.

  bulldog *n.* a small, fierce, heavily built dog with a large head.

BUILDING TERMS

aqueduct a bridge that carries water across a river or valley.

barrage an artificial dam in a river.

cement a powdery substance that sets hard after being mixed with water.

foundation the underground structure supporting a building.

macadam a road surface made with small stones rolled in cement.

slate a rock that splits easily, used in roofing.

bullfrog *n.* a large frog with a loud croak, found in the UNITED STATES.

bull's-eye *n.* the small circular centre of a target used in shooting, darts, etc.

bulldozer (**bool** dō zĕr) *n.* a powerful tractor with a vertical blade at the front, for clearing the ground or making it level.

bullet (**bool** it) *n.* a small metal cylinder with a pointed end, for firing from guns.

bulletin (**bool** i tin) *n.* **1** a short official statement of news issued as soon as the news is known. **2** a short leaflet produced regularly.

bully (**bool** i) *n.* **bullies** a person who hurts or frightens weaker or smaller people. – *vb.*
bullies, bullying, bullied to act like a bully.

bulrush (**bool** rush) *n.* a tall strong grass-like water plant.

bumblebee (**bum** bĕl bē) *n.* a large, hairy bee.

bump (bump) *vb.* **bumping, bumped 1** to knock or hit something. **2** to hurt or damage by hitting. **3** to collide. – *n.* **1** a knock, jolt, or collision. **2** a dull sound caused by a knock or collision. **3** a lump or swelling on the body, especially one caused by a blow.
bumpy *adj.* **bumpier, bumpiest** having a lot of bumps: *a bumpy road.*

bun (bun) *n.* a small, round, sweetened roll.

bunch (bunch) *n.* **1** a number of things fastened or growing together. **2** (in *plural*) long hair divided into two pieces and tied separately at each side or the back of the head. **3** (*colloquial*) a group or collection of people or things. – *vb.*
bunching, bunched to group together in a bunch: *The puppies bunched together to keep warm.*

bundle (**bun** dĕl) *n.* a number of things loosely tied together; a loose parcel.

bungalow (**bung** gå lō) *n.* a single-storey house.

bunk (bungk) *n.* a narrow bed attached to the wall in a cabin in a ship or caravan, etc.

● **Bunyan, John** (1628-88) was an English preacher and author of *The Pilgrim's Progress*. He began writing while in prison for 12 years.

buoy (boi) *n.* a brightly coloured floating object fastened to the bottom of the sea by an anchor, to warn ships of rocks, etc.

burden (**bûr** dĕn) *n.* **1** something to be carried; a load. **2** a duty which is difficult, time-consuming, costly, etc.

bureau (**bū** rō) *n.* **bureaux** or **bureaus 1** a desk for writing at, with drawers. **2** (*US*) a chest of drawers. **3** an office or department: *Get the information from the appropriate bureau.*

burglar (**bûr** glår) *n.* a person who enters a building illegally to steal.

● **Burke, Robert** and **Wills, William** were leaders of an expedition which set out in 1860 to cross Australia from north to south.

● **Burkina Faso**. See Supplement, **Countries**.

burial (**ber** i ål) *n.* the burying of a dead body.

● **Burma**. See **Myanmar**.

burn (bûrn) *vb.* **burning, burned** or **burnt**
1 to be or set on fire. **2** to damage or destroy by fire. – *n.* an injury caused by fire, acid, etc.
burning *adj.* **1** on fire. **2** feeling extremely hot. **3** very strong, important, or intense.

● **Burns, Robert** (1759-96) was a Scottish lyric poet who wrote in the Scottish dialect.

burnt. See **burn**.

burrow (**bu** rō) *n.* a hole or tunnel dug by rabbits and other small animals for shelter.
– *vb.* **burrowing, burrowed 1** to make a hole or tunnel in or under something. **2** to search: *Tom burrowed into his pockets.*

burst (bûrst) *vb.* **bursting, burst 1** to break open or into pieces, usually suddenly and violently: *The balloon burst.* **2** to make your way suddenly or violently: *They burst into the room.* **3** to be full of a strong emotion: *Duncan is bursting with anger.* **4** to do something suddenly and noisily: *Jack burst out laughing.* – *n.* **1** an instance of bursting or breaking open. **2** a sudden brief period of: *With a burst of speed the car disappeared over the brow of the hill.*

● **Burundi**. See Supplement, **Countries**.

bury (**be** ri) *vb.* **buries, burying, buried 1** to place a dead body in a grave, the sea, etc. **2** to hide in the ground: *The dog is burying a bone.*

bus (bus) *n.* a large road vehicle which carries passengers to and from established stopping points, along a fixed route and for payment.

bush (boosh) *n.* **1** a thick, woody plant with many branches, smaller than a tree. **2** wild, uncultivated country, covered with shrubs, especially in Australia.

PRONUNCIATION GUIDE

fat **a**	all **ö**
fate **ā**	foot **oo**
fast **ä**	moon **ōō**
among **å**	boy **oi**
met **e**	house **ow**
mean **ē**	demon **ŏ**
silent **ĕ**	thing **th**
loch **hh**	this **Th**
fin **i**	but **u**
line **ī**	mute **ū**
quick **kw**	fur **û**
got **o**	brochure **ů**
note **ō**	vision **zh**

Bungalow comes from a Hindi word *bangla* meaning 'belonging to Bengal', where thatched one-storey houses are common.

bush-baby *n.* **bush-babies** a small, furry, African animal with big eyes and a long tail.

business (**biz** nis) *n.* **1** the buying and selling of goods and services. **2** a shop, firm, commercial company, etc. **3** your usual occupation, trade, or profession. **4** the things that are your proper or rightful concern: *Mind your own business.*

bust (bust) *n.* **1** the upper front part of a woman's body. **2** a sculpture of a person's head, shoulders, and chest.

bustle (**bu** sĕl) *vb.* **bustling, bustled 1** to busy yourself noisily and energetically. **2** to make someone hurry, work hard, etc.: *He bustled her out of the room.* − *n.* hurried, noisy activity.

busy (**bi** zi) *adj.* **busier, busiest 1** fully occupied, with a lot of work to do: *Terry was too busy to talk to me.* **2** full of activity: *a busy street.*

but (but) *conj.* **1** opposite to what is expected: *She fell down but didn't hurt herself.* **2** in contrast: *You've been to Spain but I haven't.* **3** other than: *You can't do anything but wait.* − *prep.* except: *all but him.* − *adv.* only: *I can but try.*

butcher (**booch** ĕr) *n.* a person or shop that sells meat. − *vb.* **butchering, butchered** to kill and prepare an animal for sale as food.

butt (but) *vb.* **butting, butted** to push or hit hard with the head like a goat. − *n.* a blow with the head or horns. − *vb.* **butt in** to interrupt.

butter (**but** ĕr) *n.* a pale yellow solid fat made from cream or milk, which is spread on bread, etc. and used in cooking. − *vb.* **buttering, buttered** to put butter on. − *adj.* **buttered**.

butterfly (**but** ĕr flī) *n.* **butterflies** a type of insect with large, delicate, and usually brightly coloured wings.

In the jungles of south-east Asia and New Guinea there are vast numbers of butterflies including many varieties of birdwings (below and right). They come in all shapes and sizes, and an amazing range of beautiful patterns and dazzling colours. Males sometimes congregate in hundreds to drink from muddy river banks.

The Life Of A Butterfly
The female lays her eggs (1), the caterpillar hatches (2), eats and when fully grown spins a belt of silk and binds itself to a twig (3). It sheds its skin and becomes a pupa. Inside, the caterpillar turns into a butterfly (4). This process is called 'metamorphosis'.

At rest, most butterflies fold their wings over their bodies, (above) while moths hold their wings spread out flat (below).

The largest butterfly is the Queen Alexandra's birdwing; the smallest is the Western pygmy blue.

In 330 Constantine the Great transferred the capital of the Roman Empire from Rome to his new city (Constantinople), built on the Greek port of **Byzantium**. When the Roman empire finally collapsed in 476 Constantinople became the capital of what is called the Byzantine empire. During the Emperor Justinian's reign (527-565) the empire expanded and prospered. It became a centre of learning and art and evolved its own form of Christianity in the Orthodox Church. It was overthrown by the Turks in 1453, a date which marks the end of the Middle Ages.

Elaborate gold and enamel religious works of art were greatly prized.

Hagia Sophia – 'Church of Holy Wisdom' – was built by Justinian as a Christian church but was turned into a mosque.

The Byzantine navy had a secret weapon called 'Greek Fire'. It was a mixture of quicklime, petroleum, and sulphur which burst into flames on contact with water.

Constantinople

Mediterranean Sea

Boundary of the
Byzantine Empire by 565

Egypt

button (**but** ŏn) *n.* **1** a small usually round piece of metal, plastic, etc. sewn on to clothes, which fastens them. **2** a small round disc pressed to operate a door or bell, etc. – *vb.* **buttoning, buttoned** to fasten using buttons.

buttress (**but** rĕs) *n.* a support built on to the outside of a wall.

buy (bī) *vb.* **buying, bought** (bŏt) to get something by paying for it. – *n.* a thing bought: *That bike was a good buy.*

　buyer *n.* a person who buys, a customer.

buzz (buz) *vb.* **buzzing, buzzed 1** to make a continuous humming or rapidly vibrating sound like a bee. **2** to be filled with activity or excitement: *The factory is buzzing with activity.* – *n.*

buzzard (**buz** ård) *n.* a large eagle-like bird of prey.

by (bī) *prep.* **1** next to, beside, near; past: *We drove by the house.* **2** through, along, or across: *The door was locked so we entered by the window.* **3** used to show the person or thing that does something: *John was bitten by a dog.* **4** used to show method or means: *Dan likes to travel by air.* **5** not later than: *You must be home by 10pm.* **6** used in stating rates of payment, etc.: *The workers are paid by the hour.* – *adv.* **1** near: *Louise lives close by.* **2** past: *Drive by without stopping.* – **by and by** after a short time.

bypass *n.* **1** a road which avoids a busy area or town. **2** a tube inserted into a blood vessel to provide an alternative route for the blood flow, either temporarily during an operation or permanently to get round a blockage in the blood vessel.

by-product *n.* **1** a substance or product obtained or formed during the making of something else. **2** an unexpected, extra result.

bystander *n.* a person who watches but does not take part in what is happening.

● **Byrd** (bûrd), **Richard** (1888-1957) was an American pilot and polar explorer.

● **Byron, Lord** (1788-1824) was an English poet. He left England in 1816 and lived in Switzerland, Italy, and Greece until his death.

byte (bīt) *n.* a group of eight binary digits forming a unit of memory in a computer.

● **Byzantium** was an ancient Greek city on the Bosporus. It was rebuilt in AD 330 by Constantine and named Constantinople. Today it is in TURKEY and is called Istanbul.

Cc

The letter *C*, like all the letters, has a long history. The earliest alphabets were taken and adapted by the Greeks. The Greek *beta*, when combined with the first letter, *aleph*, gives us the word alphabet.

The Greeks passed on their letters to the Romans who developed the alphabet we use today, although they used only capital letters. Small letters developed in the AD 700s.

7

An early form of the letter C, used in the Middle East over 3000 years ago.

Γ

This letter was taken by the Greeks and became gamma.

c

Over the years different versions of the letter C have been developed.

cab (kab) *n.* **1** a taxi. **2** the driver's compartment in a lorry, railway engine, etc.

cabbage (**kab** ij) *n.* a vegetable with green or red edible leaves forming a large round head.

cabin (**ka** bin) *n.* **1** a small house, especially made of wood. **2** on a ship, a sleeping compartment. **3** the section of a plane for pilot and crew.

cabinet (**ka** bin it) *n.* **1** a piece of furniture with shelves and doors, for storing or displaying things: *Nina put the cup in the china cabinet.* **2** the group of ministers in charge of the various departments of government.

cable (**kā** běl) *n.* **1** a strong thick rope made of hemp or metal wire, used e.g. on ships. **2** an enclosed set of wires carrying telephone signals or electricity.

cable television *n.* television programmes transmitted by cable, rather than broadcast over radio waves.

● **Cabot, John** (1450-99) was an Italian navigator who discovered the mainland of NORTH AMERICA on behalf of Henry the Seventh of England in 1497.

cackle (**ka** kĕl) *n.* **1** the sound that a hen or goose makes. **2** a laugh like this.

cactus (**kak** tŭs) *n.* **cacti** (**kak** tī) or **cactuses** any of many prickly desert plants whose thick stems store water.

cadaver (kǎ **dav** ĕr) *n.* a dead human body.

cadet (kǎ **det**) *n.* a student at a military, naval, or police training school.

● **Caesar, Julius** (100-44 BC) was a Roman general, statesman, and author. He is most famous for his part in turning the ROMAN REPUBLIC into an empire ruled by one man. A group of enemies stabbed him to death in the forum at Rome.

cage (kāj) *n.* **1** a container with bars, etc., in which to keep captive birds or animals. **2** any structure or framework shaped like a cage: *The human heart is protected by the rib cage.* – *vb.* **caging, caged** to put in a cage.

● **Cairo** (**kī** rō), on the banks of the river NILE, is the capital of EGYPT and one of the biggest cities in AFRICA. Nearby are the PYRAMIDS and the statue of the sphinx.

● **Cajun** people are descended from French-speaking settlers in Louisiana, USA.

cake (kāk) *n.* **1** a food made by baking a mixture of flour, fat, eggs, sugar, etc. **2** a solid block of soap, etc. – *vb.* **caking, caked** to dry as a thick hard crust; to cover in a thick crust.

● **Calamity Jane** (1852-1903) real name Martha Jane Canary, was an American pioneer and expert at shooting.

calcium (**kal** si ŭm) *n.* an element (symbol **Ca**), a soft silvery metal, compounds of which are found in the ground and in such foods as milk and cheese.

There are dozens of different cacti, but they all have one thing in common: they grow in hot desert climates. This is because they can store water in their fleshy stems. They are covered with prickly spines which protect their store of water from desert animals.

calculate (**kal** kū lāt) *vb.* **calculating,**
calculated 1 to work out or find out by
mathematical means. **2** to make plans that
depend on some possibility: *The ski shop has*
not calculated on a winter without snow.
calculation *n.* the act of calculating.
calculator *n.* a small electronic machine for
doing mathematical calculations.

● **Calcutta** is the capital of the state of West
Bengal in INDIA and is India's chief port. It was
the capital of British India until 1912 when
Delhi replaced it.

calendar (**kal** ĕn dǎr) *n.* a table in the form of a
booklet or chart that shows the months and
days of the year. Calendars were first
used in ancient Babylon. The one
we use today is the Gregorian
calendar, introduced by Pope
Gregory in 1582.

calf[1] (käf) *n.* **calves** the
young of a cow, and of
several other animals, e.g.
the elephant.

calf[2] (käf) *n.* **calves** the
thick fleshy back part of the
leg below the knee.

● **Calgary** is a city in Alberta,
CANADA.

Calculate comes from a
Latin word meaning
'pebble', because small
stones were once used
for counting.

This stone shows the
Aztec 20-day month.
They had 18 months
plus a final five, unlucky
days.

● **California**. See Supplement, **USA**.

caliph or **khalif** (**kā** lif) or (**ka** lif) *n.* a Muslim
civil and religious leader.

call (köl) *vb.* **calling, called 1** to shout or speak
loudly in order to attract attention or in
announcing something: *The teacher called out the*
winners' names; to ask someone to come: *Call the*
children! **2** to telephone: *We called her from the*
airport. **3** to waken: *Call me at eight.* **4** to make a
visit: *We called at the grocer's.* **5** to give a name
to. **6** (of a bird, etc.) to make its typical or
characteristic sound. – *n.* **1** a shout or cry.
2 the cry of a bird or animal. **3** a brief visit.
4 a telephone conversation: *I'll give you a call*
tomorrow. – *vb.* **call back** to visit again; to
telephone again. – *vb.* **call for 1** to require:
Editing dictionaries calls for concentration. **2** to
collect; to fetch: *Mustafa called for his laundry.*
calligraphy (kǎ **lig** rǎ fi) *n.* handwriting as an
art. – *n.* **calligrapher**.

callus or **callous** (**ka** lǔs) *n.* an area of hard
thick skin, often on the hand or foot, caused by
constant pressure or rubbing.

calm (käm) *adj.* **1** relaxed and in control; not
anxious, upset, angry, etc.: *Colin's voice was*
calm despite the shock. **2** (of weather, etc.) still,
quiet, peaceful; not rough or stormy. – *vb.*
calming, calmed to make or become
calmer. – *n.* **calmness**.

calorie (**ka** lŏ ri) *n.* a unit of the energy-
producing value of various types of food: *Meg's*
diet allows her 1000 calories a day.

Calvinism (**kal** vin i zĕm) *n.* the teachings of
the 16th-century Christian reformer John
Calvin (1509-64). – *n.* **Calvinist**.

● **Cambodia**. See Supplement, **Countries**.

● **Cambridge 1** a university town in eastern
ENGLAND. **2** a city in Massuchusetts, USA, home
of Harvard University and the Massachusetts
Instituté of Technology.

came. See **come**.

camel (**ka** mĕl) *n.* an animal with a long neck
and either one hump (the **dromedary**) or
two (the **Bactrian camel**), that stores fat in its
hump(s) as a source of energy, can survive long
periods in the desert without food or water,
and is used for carrying loads or for riding.

Calligraphy looks like particularly
beautiful handwriting, written very
carefully. It is done using a pen or
brush. Special documents such as
scrolls or certificates may be written
by a calligrapher.

Viewfinder Shutter-speed dial

Lens

Light Mirror

To take a picture, the camera's shutter opens and light passes through a lens into a small aperture – the iris. There it is focused onto a light-sensitive film by a second set of lenses. The image formed is upside down.

camera (**ka** mĕ rå) *n.* **1** an apparatus for taking still photographs or making moving films, with a lens through which light passes to form an image on film that is sensitive to light. **2** a similar apparatus used in television that receives the image of a scene and converts it into electrical signals.

●**Cameroon**. See Supplement, **Countries**.

camomile (**ka** mŏ mīl) *n.* a plant with white or yellow sweet-smelling flowers.

camouflage (**ka** mŏ fläzh) *n.* **1** colouring used on military equipment, vehicles, or buildings, or for soldiers' uniforms, that imitates the colours of nature and so makes them difficult for an enemy to see. **2** colouring on an animal that blends with the animal's natural surroundings and makes it difficult to see: *A polar bear has natural camouflage because its fur is the same colour as snow.* – *vb.* **camouflaging, camouflaged** to disguise or conceal with some kind of camouflage.

camp (kamp) *n.* **1** a piece of ground where people live in tents for a while. **2** a permanent site where troops are housed or trained. – *vb.* **camping, camped** to stay in a tent, cooking meals in the open, etc. – *n.* **camping.** **camper** *n.* a person who camps. **campsite** *n.* a piece of land for camping on.

campaign (kam **pān**) *n.* **1** an organized series of actions to gain a particular result. **2** the operations of an army while fighting in a particular area. – *vb.* **campaigning, campaigned** to take part in a campaign.

campus (**kam** půs) *n.* the grounds of a college or university.

can¹ (kan) *vb.* (*auxiliary*) **1** to be able to: *Can you lift that?* **2** to know how to: *Can he swim yet?* **3** to feel able to: *How can you believe that?* **4** used to express surprise: *Can it really be that late?* **5** to have permission to: *Can I take an apple?* **6** used when asking for help, etc.: *Can you give me the time, please?*

can² (kan) *n.* a sealed metal container.

●**Canada** is the second largest country in the world. The distance from the PACIFIC Ocean to the ATLANTIC is farther than from NORTH AMERICA to EUROPE. Most Canadians live in a narrow belt along the UNITED STATES border. The north of the country is covered by forests and lakes. The great central plains are given over to pasture and raising cattle. The west of the country is mountainous. Most Canadians speak English but Quebec is French-speaking. The federal parliament is in Ottawa. The Canadian dollar is the currency. See also Supplement, **Countries**.

Canadian (kå **nā** di ån) *n.* a person who comes from Canada. – *adj.* belonging to Canada.

PRONUNCIATION GUIDE	
fat **a**	all **ö**
fate **ā**	foot **oo**
fast **ä**	moon **ōō**
among **å**	boy **oi**
met **e**	house **ow**
mean **ē**	demon **ŏ**
silent **ė**	thing **th**
loch **hh**	this **Th**
fin **i**	but **u**
line **ī**	mute **ū**
quick **kw**	fur **û**
got **o**	brochure **ů**
note **ō**	vision **zh**

Canada is often called 'the land of the future'. The country's enormous mineral and oil reserves have hardly been touched.

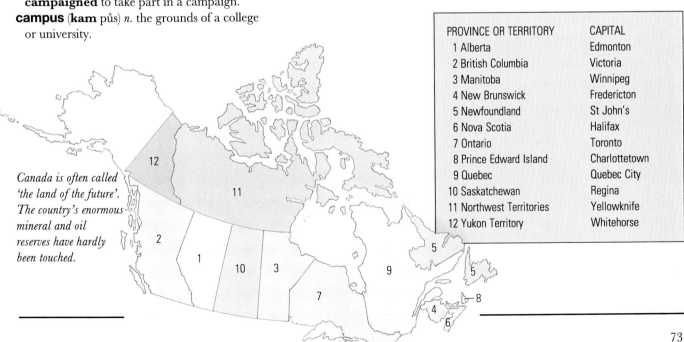

PROVINCE OR TERRITORY	CAPITAL
1 Alberta	Edmonton
2 British Columbia	Victoria
3 Manitoba	Winnipeg
4 New Brunswick	Fredericton
5 Newfoundland	St John's
6 Nova Scotia	Halifax
7 Ontario	Toronto
8 Prince Edward Island	Charlottetown
9 Quebec	Quebec City
10 Saskatchewan	Regina
11 Northwest Territories	Yellowknife
12 Yukon Territory	Whitehorse

Until the 1500s **canals** could be built only across flat country. With the invention of the canal lock they could also be built across high ground. The Erie Canal *(below)* in New York State was completed in 1825, with a total of 83 locks and a series of aqueducts.

The gates open allowing the ship into the lock, then close again.

Water pours into the lock through openings in the upper gates.

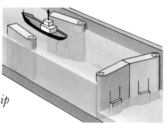

When the water level in the lock is the same as that beyond the gates, they are opened and the ship can pass through.

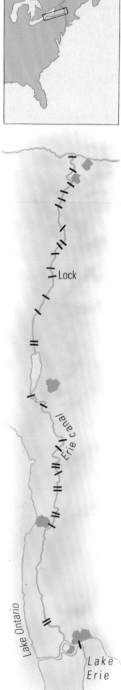

Lock

Erie canal

Lake Ontario

Lake Erie

canal (kả **nal**) *n.* an artificial channel or waterway for ships, barges, etc., or for bringing water into a particular area.

●**Canaletto** (ka nả **let** ō), **Antonio** (1695-1768) was a Venetian painter.

canary (kả **nār** i) *n.* **canaries** a small yellow singing bird of the finch family.

●**Canberra** is the capital of AUSTRALIA.

cancel (kan sẻl) *vb.* **cancelling, cancelled** **1** to stop something already arranged from taking place: *The game was cancelled because of the snow.* **2** to stop something in progress from continuing. **3** to tell a supplier you no longer want something.

cancer (kan sẻr) *n.* a serious illness in which there are one or more diseased areas (tumours) in the body consisting of new cells growing in an uncontrolled way.

Cancer (kan sẻr) *n.* See **zodiac**.

candid (kan did) *adj.* saying honestly and openly what you think; outspoken.

candidate (kan di dảt) *n.* **1** a person who is competing with others for a job, prize, parliamentary seat, etc. **2** a person taking an examination.

candle (kan dẻl) *n.* a stick of hard wax with a wick inside that is burnt to provide light.

The wicks of hand-made candles are dipped over and over again into a vat of melted wax. Candles can also be made in a mould.

candy (kan di) *n.* **candies** a sweet. – *vb.* **candies, candying, candied** to coat with sugar: *The sweet maker candied the plums.*

cane (kān) *n.* the hollow stem of plants of the grass or reed families, e.g. bamboo. **2** a walking-stick.

canine (kā nīn) *adj.* relating to dogs.

cannabis (ka nả bis) *n.* **1** a drug obtained from the Indian hemp plant. **2** the hemp plant itself.

cannon (ka nỏn) *n.* **cannon** or **cannons** a large gun on wheels.

cannot (kan ỏt) *vb.* *(auxiliary)* can not.

canny (ka ni) *adj.* **cannier, canniest** shrewd.

canoe (kả **nōō**) *n.* a light narrow boat moved by one or more paddles. – *vb.* **canoeing, canoed** to travel by canoe. – *n.* **canoeing**. – *n.* **canoeist**.

canopy (ka nỏ pi) *n.* **canopies** a covering hung or held up over something or someone for shelter or ornament.

canter (kan tẻr) *n.* a horse-riding pace between trotting and galloping.

●**Canterbury** **1** a cathedral and university city in Kent, England. The Archbishop of Canterbury is the senior bishop in the CHURCH OF ENGLAND. **2** the largest province of South Island, NEW ZEALAND.

cantilever (kan ti lē vẻr) *n.* a beam or other support projecting from a wall to support a balcony or staircase, etc.

● **Canute** or **Cnut** (kå **nūt**) (994-1035) was a Danish king of England.

canvas (**kan** vås) *n.* a thick cloth used for sails, tents, etc. and for painting pictures on.

canvass (**kan** vås) *vb.* **canvassing, canvassed** to ask for votes or support for a person or proposal: *We all canvassed for Mrs Singh in the election.*

canyon (**kan** yŏn) *n.* a deep river valley with steep sides; a gorge.

cap (kap) *n.* **1** a hat with a peak, of any of various types, some worn as part of a uniform or as an indication of occupation: *Nurses wear caps.* **2** a lid, cover, or top, e.g. for a bottle or pen. **3** a little metal or paper case containing a small amount of gunpowder, that explodes when struck. **4** a protective covering fitted over a damaged or decayed tooth. – *vb.* **capping, capped** to put a cap on, or cover the top or end of, with a cap.

capable (**kā** på bĕl) *adj.* **1** having the ability or the personality for: *He was capable of much better work.* **2** clever; able; efficient.

capacity (kå **pas** i ti) *n.* **capacities 1** the amount that something can hold. **2** ability; power: *Don has a vast capacity for learning.* **3** function; role: *We are here in our capacity as peace-makers.*

cape[1] (kāp) *n.* a short cloak.

cape[2] (kāp) *n.* a part of the coast that projects into the sea: *the Cape of Good Hope.*

● **Cape Horn** is the southernmost tip of SOUTH AMERICA.

● **Cape Town** is the capital of Cape Province. It is SOUTH AFRICA's law-making capital.

● **Cape Verde Islands**. See Supplement, **Countries**.

capital (**ka** pi tål) *n.* **1** the chief city of a country, usually where the government is based: *Edinburgh is the capital of Scotland.* **2** a capital letter used at the beginning of a sentence or a name, as in *My name is John.* – *adj.* **1** chief. **2** (of a letter of the alphabet) in its large form, as used at the beginnings of names and sentences.

capitalism *n.* an economic system based on private ownership of business and industry with free competition and profit-making.

● **Capitol** the building in Washington D.C. where the United States CONGRESS meets. It stands on Capitol Hill.

capitulate (kå **pi** tū lāt) *vb.* **capitulating, capitulated** to surrender and stop fighting.

Capricorn (**kap** ri körn) *n.* See **zodiac**.

capsize (kap **sīz**) *vb.* **capsizing, capsized** (of a boat) to tip over completely.

capsule (**kap** sūl) *n.* **1** a small container holding a dose of medicine, that is swallowed whole and dissolves to release its contents. **2** (also **space capsule**) a part of a spacecraft designed to separate and travel independently.

The United States Capitol contains the chamber of the Senate in the north wing and that of the House of Representatives in the south wing. On top of the dome stands a six-metre bronze statue of Freedom.

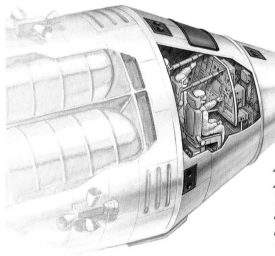

captain (**kap** tin) *n.* **1** a leader, chief: *Linda was captain of the college hockey team.* **2** the commander of a ship or a company of troops.

caption (**kap** shŏn) *n.* the words that accompany a photograph or cartoon, etc.

captive (**kap** tiv) *n.* a person or animal that has been caught or taken prisoner. – *adj.* kept prisoner; unable to get away: *The captive tiger was kept in a cage.* – *n.* **captivity**.

capture (**kap** chŭr) *vb.* **capturing, captured 1** to catch. **2** to gain possession of: *The nature film captured Isobel's interest.* – *n.* the capturing of someone or something.

A cross-section of an Apollo space capsule. The American Apollo Space Program was launched as part of the 'space race' between the USA and the former Soviet Union.

The first commercial three-wheeled, petrol-driven **car** was produced by the German Karl Benz in 1885. Other makes soon followed, but it was Henry Ford in the United States who introduced the first successful way of producing cars quickly and cheaply.

Karl Benz's Motorwagen – the world's first car to use an internal combustion engine.

An 1898 Renault, the world's first fully enclosed car.

An Italian racing car – the Ferrari 312T3

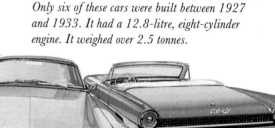

A motorcar for millionaires, the Bugatti Royale. Only six of these cars were built between 1927 and 1933. It had a 12.8-litre, eight-cylinder engine. It weighed over 2.5 tonnes.

Chrysler Imperial

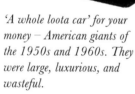

'A whole loota car' for your money – American giants of the 1950s and 1960s. They were large, luxurious, and wasteful.

Cadillac

Ford Galaxie Convertible

PARTS OF A CAR

accelerator a pedal that regulates engine speed by controlling fuel flow.

crankshaft is turned by the connecting rods from the pistons. The up-and-down motion of the pistons is converted into rotary motion.

disc brakes are operated by friction pads pressing against a metal disc that turns with the wheel.

fanbelt drives the cooling fan from a pulley on the crankshaft.

spark plug a device that generates a spark to ignite the petrol/air mixture in the cylinder.

suspension a system of (usually) springs that supports a car's body.

Cars are quite complicated machines made up of thousands of parts. They are driven by internal combustion engines which burn a mixture of air and petrol in cylinders.

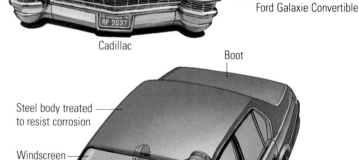

Boot

Steel body treated to resist corrosion

Windscreen

Driveshaft to rear wheel

Five speed manual gearbox

Bonnet

car (kär) *n.* a motor vehicle, usually with four wheels, for carrying a small number of people.

carapace (**ka** rå pās) *n.* the thick shell of certain creatures such as the tortoise.

● **Caravaggio** (ka rå **vaj** i ō) (1573-1610) was the Italian painter of *The Death of the Virgin.*

caravan (**ka** rå van) *n.* **1** a vehicle equipped for living in, towed by a car. **2** a group of travellers usually with camels, crossing the desert.

carbohydrate (kär bō **hī** drāt) *n.* a group of compounds of carbon with hydrogen and oxygen, especially the sugars and starches which form the main source of energy in food.

carbon (**kär** bŏn) *n.* an element (symbol **C**) found in diamonds, graphite, and charcoal, and present in all organic matter.

carbon dioxide *n.* a gas (CO_2) present in the air, breathed out by humans and animals, and used by plants in PHOTOSYNTHESIS.

carburettor (**kär** bū re tŏr) *n.* a device that mixes petrol with air and controls the amount of this mixture that is taken into an engine.

carcase or **carcass** (**kär** kås) *n.* the dead body of an animal.

card (kärd) *n.* **1** a thick, stiff kind of paper. **2** a playing card. **3** a small rectangular piece of card or plastic, showing your identity, job, membership of an organization, etc. **4** a small plastic rectangle issued by a bank, used when making payments, as a guarantee for a cheque or for operating a cash machine. **5** a postcard.

cardboard (**kärd** bŏrd) *n.* a stiff material made from pulped waste paper, used for making boxes, card, etc.

cardiac (**kär** di ak) *adj.* relating to the heart: *cardiac arrest.*

● **Cardiff** (**Caerdedd** in Welsh) is the capital of WALES.

cardinal (**kär** di nål) *n.* **1** a leading clergyman in the Roman Catholic Church, who elects the pope and advises him. **2** a North American songbird of which the male is bright red.

cardinal number *n.* a number expressing quantity, such as one, two, or three, as distinct from a number expressing order (an **ordinal number**), such as first, second, or third.

cardinal point *n.* any of the four main points of the compass – north, south, east, and west.

care (kār) *n.* **1** attention: *Bill took great care with his pruning.* **2** caution; gentleness; regard for safety. **3** looking after someone or something, or the state of being looked after. **4** worry or anxiety: *She didn't have a care in the world. – vb.*

caring, cared 1 to mind or be upset by something: *I don't care if we have to leave the party early.* **2** to be interested in: *We all care about our welfare services.* **3** to have a wish for: *Would you care to join us? – vb.* **care for 1** to look after someone: *Sue is caring for her grandmother.* **2** to be fond of someone.

caring *adj.* showing concern for others.

career (kå **rēr**) *n.* **1** your professional life; your progress in your job; **2** a job, occupation, or profession: *Janet has chosen a career in journalism. – vb.* **careering, careered** to rush with your head bent forward: *Jim careered around the corner on his bike.*

caress (kå res) *vb.* **caressing, caressed** to touch gently and lovingly. – *n.* a gentle touch.

cargo (**kär** gō) *n.* **cargoes** the goods carried by a ship, aircraft, or other vehicle.

Caribbean (ka ri **bē** ån) *adj.* relating or belonging to the West Indies.

caribou (**ka** ri bōō) *n.* **caribous** or **caribou** a type of reindeer found in NORTH AMERICA.

caricature (**ka** ri kå choor) *n.* a drawing of someone with their most distinctive features exaggerated for comic effect.

caries (**kā** ri ēz) *n.* the gradual decay of teeth.

● **Carnegie** (**kär** nĕ gi), **Andrew** (1835-1919) was a Scottish-born industrialist who made a fortune in the UNITED STATES as a steel manufacturer. He was a great philanthropist.

carnival (**kär** ni vål) *n.* a period of public festivity with street processions, colourful costumes, and singing and dancing.

carnivore (**kär** ni vŏr) *n.* any of a group of animals with teeth specialized for eating flesh. – *adj.* **carnivorous** (kår **niv** ŏ růs).

● All carnivores have powerful jaws for chopping up their food, curved claws for tearing, and long sharp teeth for killing their victims. All have good eyesight, smell, and hearing, and are fast and intelligent. Some hunt in packs (wild dogs and hyenas) and others hunt alone (leopards and jaguars).

carol (**ka** rŏl) *n.* a religious song, especially one sung by Christians at CHRISTMAS.

PRONUNCIATION GUIDE	
fat a	all ö
fate ā	foot oo
fast ä	moon ōō
among å	boy oi
met e	house ow
mean ē	demon ŏ
silent ĕ	thing th
loch hh	this Th
fin i	but u
line ī	mute ū
quick kw	fur û
got o	brochure ů
note ō	vision zh

A medieval carpenter at work. The design of many of the tools used then – and indeed in Roman times – have altered surprisingly little.

carp (kärp) *n.* a large fish of lakes and rivers.

carpenter (**kär** pĕn tĕr) *n.* a person skilled in wood, e.g. in building houses, or in making and repairing fine furniture. – *n.* **carpentry**.

carpet (**kär** pit) *n.* a covering for floors, made of heavy, usually woven and tufted, fabric.

carriage (**ka** rij) *n.* **1** a four-wheeled horse-drawn passenger vehicle. **2** a railway coach. **3** the process or cost of transporting goods.

carrion (**ka** ri ŏn) *n.* rotting flesh of dead animals.

● **Carroll, Lewis** (1832-98), real name Charles Dodgson, was a mathematician and writer of children's stories, such as *Alice's Adventures in Wonderland* and *Through the Looking Glass*.

carrot (**ka** rŏt) *n.* a long and pointed orange-coloured root vegetable.

carry (**ka** ri) *vb.* **carries, carrying, carried 1** to hold something in your hands, have in a pocket, bag, etc., or support its weight on your body, while moving from one place to another: *Nana carried the shopping from the store to the car.* **2** to bring, take, or convey. **3** to have on your person: *Mark always carries a pen.* **4** to bear responsibilities, etc. **5** to be able to be heard a distance away: *The sound of the traffic carried across the valley.* – **get carried away** (*colloquial*) to become over-enthusiastic.

● **Carson** (**kär** sŏn), **Kit** (1809-68) was an American pioneer.

cart (kärt) *n.* **1** a two- or four-wheeled, horse-drawn vehicle. **2** a light vehicle pushed or pulled by hand.

● **Cartier** (**kär** ti ā), **Jacques** (1491-1557) was a French explorer of CANADA.

cartilage (**kär** ti lij) *n.* a tough flexible substance found in the body round the ends of the bones at joints and between the vertebrae.

carton (**kär** tŏn) *n.* a plastic or cardboard container in which food of various types is packaged for sale: *Jack drank a carton of milk.*

cartoon (**kär** tōōn) *n.* a humorous drawing in a newspaper, etc., often ridiculing someone or something; (also **animated cartoon**) a film made by photographing a series of drawings, giving the impression of movement.

cartoonist *n.* an artist who draws cartoons.

● Perhaps the most famous cartoon animator was WALT DISNEY. His cartoon characters, Mickey Mouse and Donald Duck, are popular worldwide.

cartridge (**kär** trij) *n.* **1** a small case containing the explosive charge and bullet for a gun. **2** a plastic case containing film, for loading directly into a camera.

carve (kärv) *vb.* **carving, carved 1** to cut wood, stone, etc. into a shape: *Artists carve statues from wood.* **2** to cut meat into slices. – *n.* **carving**.

cascade (kas **kād**) *n.* a waterfall or series of waterfalls.

case¹ (kās) *n.* **1** a box, container, or cover, for storage, protection, carrying, etc.: *My camera has a leather case.* **2** a suitcase.

case² (kās) *n.* **1** a particular occasion, situation, or set of circumstances. **2** an example, instance,

— Moat

Castles were built to be safe from attack, with high, thick walls and a deep moat to prevent the enemy from getting in. Defending soldiers could fight off attacks and sit out long sieges by invading armies. Many castles were built on hills. After guns were invented in the 1300s castles were not much good as fortresses.

or occurrence. **3** a person receiving some sort of treatment or care. **4** a matter requiring investigation: *The police are looking into the case.* **5** a matter to be decided in a law court. **6** the argument for or against something with the relevant facts fully presented. – **as the case may be** according to how things turn out.

cash (kash) *n.* coins or paper money, as distinct from cheques and credit cards. – *vb.* **cashing, cashed** to obtain or give cash in return for a cheque, etc.

cash flow *n.* the amount of money coming into, and going out of, a business, etc.

cashier (kash **ēr**) *n.* the person in a business firm, etc. who deals with the cash.

cashmere (**kash** mēr) *n.* very fine soft wool from a long-haired Asian goat.

cask (käsk) *n.* a barrel for holding liquids.

casket (**käs** kit) *n.* **1** a small case for holding jewels, etc. **2** (*North American*) a coffin.

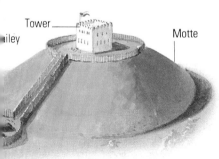

An 11th-century motte-and-bailey castle. The wooden tower stands on a mound (motte).

Tower
iley
Motte

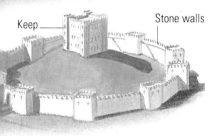

A 12th-century stone-walled castle with a central tower or keep.

Keep
Stone walls

A heavily fortified castle under siege. All kinds of siege machinery were needed. They included powerful catapults that hurled stones, giant siege towers, and scaling ladders.

● **Caspian Sea** the world's largest inland body of water. Most of it lies within the former USSR.

● **Cassandra** a female prophet in Greek legend who always predicted disaster.

casserole (**ka** sě rōl) *n.* a dish with a lid, in which food is cooked. – *vb.* **casseroling, casseroled** to cook in a casserole.

cassette (kå **set**) *n.* **1** a small sealed plastic case containing magnetic recording tape, for use in a cassette-recorder or video equipment. **2** a case containing a film, to load into a camera.

cast (käst) *vb.* **casting, cast 1** to throw: *Janet cast her fishing-line into the stream.* **2** to turn, direct, shed, or cause to fall or arise: *cast doubt on*; *cast a shadow*; *cast a spell.* **3** to release from a secured state: *The boat was cast adrift.* **4** (of animals) to shed skin, horns, etc. **5** to give an actor a part in a play or film. **6** to shape metal, plastic, plaster, etc. by pouring it in a molten or liquid state into a mould. – *n.* **1** an act of throwing dice, a fishing-line, etc. **2** an object shaped by pouring molten metal, plastic, plaster, etc. into a mould. **3** (also **plaster cast**) a covering of plaster around a broken limb, etc. to support it while it heals. **4** the set of actors or performers in a play, opera, etc.

castaway *n.* a person who has been shipwrecked.

castanets (kas tå **nets**) *n.* (*plural*) a Spanish musical instrument consisting of two small hollow pieces of wood or plastic attached to each other by string, held in the palm, and clicked together rhythmically with the fingers.

castle (**kä** sěl) *n.* **1** a large fortified building with battlements and towers. **2** (also **rook**) a chess piece that can be moved any number of squares forwards, backwards, or sideways.

castrate (kå **strāt**) *vb.* **castrating, castrated** to remove the testicles of a male animal.

● **Castro, Fidel** (1927-) has been the revolutionary leader of Cuba's Communist regime since 1959.

casual (**kazh** ū ål) *adj.* **1** happening by chance, without plan: *We made a casual visit to Gran's house without telephoning her first.* **2** careless; without serious purpose: *Alice has a very casual attitude to work.* **3** (of clothes) informal.

casualty (**kazh** ū ål ti) *n.* **casualties** a person who is killed or hurt in an accident or war.

Castanet comes from a Spanish word which originally meant 'chestnut', because the shape of a castanet resembles a chestnut.

A feline family painting. In the back row are a lion and tiger. In the front row from left: a tabby cat, a wild cat, a lynx, a black panther, and a snow leopard.

cat (kat) *n.* any member of a family of four-legged furry carnivores with claws and whiskers. They include lions and tigers and the small animal belonging to this family, kept as a pet. – **let the cat out of the bag** (*colloquial*) to give away a secret unintentionally.

cat's eye *n.* a small glass reflecting device, set into the road surface to guide drivers.

catalogue (**kat** å log) *n.* **1** a list of items arranged in a systematic order, especially alphabetically. **2** a booklet, etc. containing a list of goods for sale. – *vb.* **cataloguing, catalogued** to make a list of books, etc.

catalyst (**ka** tå list) *n.* a substance that causes or speeds up a chemical reaction without going through a chemical change itself.

catamaran (ka tå må **ran**) *n.* a sailing-boat with two hulls lying parallel to each other, joined across the top by the deck.

cataract (**kat** å rakt) *n.* **1** a condition of the eye in which the lens becomes clouded, causing blindness. **2** a huge, spectacular waterfall.

catarrh (kå **tär**) *n.* inflammation of the lining of the nose, causing a lot of thick mucus.

catastrophe (kå **ta** strô fi) *n.* a great disaster, causing destruction, loss of life, etc.: *The plane crash was the area's worst catastrophe for ten years.* – *adj.* **catastrophic** (ka tå **strof** ik).

catch (kach) *vb.* **catching, caught** (köt) **1** to stop a moving object and hold it: *Bill caught the falling apple.* **2** to manage to trap, especially after a hunt or chase: *Hank caught the foal after chasing it around the field.* **3** to be in time to get, reach, see, etc.: *I must catch the last post.*

The Charlotte Dundas, *a catamaran built in 1801, had a boiler in one hull, an engine in the other, and a paddlewheel between.*

4 to overtake or draw level with. **5** to discover so as to prevent, or to encourage, the development of: *The disease can be cured if caught early.* **6** to surprise someone doing something wrong or embarrassing: *Dad caught me stealing some biscuits.* **7** to become infected with: *Wrap up well so you don't catch cold.* **8** to get accidentally attached or held: *My dress caught on a nail.* – *n.* **1** an act of catching. **2** a small device for keeping a lid, door, etc. closed. **catching** *adj.* infectious.

category (**kat** ě gŏ ri) *n.* **categories** a set of things classed together because of some quality or qualities they all have in common: *History books are grouped in the same category.*

cater (**kā** těr) *vb.* **catering, catered** to supply food, accommodation, or entertainment for: *The hotel caters for wedding receptions.*

caterpillar (**ka** těr pi lår) *n.* the many-legged worm-like larva of a butterfly or moth.

cathedral (kå **thē** drål) *n.* the principal church of a diocese in which a bishop has his *cathedra* (Latin for 'chair').

●**Catherine the Great** (1729-96) deposed her husband, Tsar Peter the Third, and became empress of RUSSIA in 1762.

catholic (**kath** ŏ lik) *adj.* relating to the ROMAN CATHOLIC Church. – *n.* **Catholic** a member of the ROMAN CATHOLIC Church.

cattle (**ka** těl) *n.* (*plural*) cows, bulls, oxen.

caught. See **catch**.

cauliflower (**ko** li flow ěr) *n.* a variety of cabbage with an edible white flower.

cause (köz) *n.* **1** something which produces an effect; the person or thing through which something happens: *The wind was the cause of the damage.* **2** a reason or justification. **3** an ideal, aim, etc., that people support and work for: *Training dogs for the blind is a good cause.* – *vb.* **causing, caused** to bring about.

caution (**kö** shǒn) *n.* **1** care in avoiding danger.

Cathedrals were built in many styles and with great splendour to the glory of God.

2 a warning. **3** a scolding for an offence, with a warning not to repeat it. – *vb.* **cautioning, cautioned** to warn: *Dad cautioned me not to touch the electric cable.*

cautious (**kö** shůs) *adj.* careful; wary.

cavalier (ka vå **lēr**) *n.* a supporter of King Charles the First during the 17th-century English CIVIL WAR. – *adj.* thoughtless, offhand.

cave (kāv) *n.* a large natural hollow in a cliff or hillside, or underground. – *vb.* **cave in, caving, caved** to collapse inwards: *The walls caved in under the pressure.*

● **Cavell, Edith** (1865-1915) was an English nurse in Brussels during the First WORLD WAR. She was shot by the Germans for helping Allied soldiers to escape.

cavity (**kav** i ti) *n.* **cavities 1** a hollow or hole. **2** a hole in a tooth, caused by decay.

● **Caxton, William** (1421-91) was the man who introduced the printing press to ENGLAND.

cease (sēs) *vb.* **ceasing, ceased** to end. **ceaseless** *adj.* continuous.

cedar (**sē** dår) *n.* a tall evergreen tree with spreading branches and needle-like leaves.

cede (sēd) *vb.* **ceding, ceded** to hand over or give up formally.

ceiling (**sē** ling) *n.* the inner roof of a room.

celebrate (**se** li brāt) *vb.* **celebrating, celebrated 1** to mark a success or other happy occasion, such as a birthday, with festivities. **2** to conduct a religious ceremony. – *n.* **celebration.**

celebrity (si **leb** ri ti) *n.* **celebrities** a famous person.

celery (**sel** ě ri) *n.* a vegetable with crisp stalks.

cell (sel) *n.* **1** a small room for an inmate in a prison or monastery. **2** the smallest unit of living matter. **3** a battery.

cellar (**se** lår) *n.* a room, usually underground, for storing wine, etc.

● **Cellini** (chi **lē** ni), **Benvenuto** (1500-71) was a sculptor and goldsmith from Florence, ITALY.

cello (**che** lō) *n.* **cellos** a stringed musical instrument similar to a violin but much larger.

cellular (**sel** ū lår) *adj.* composed of cells.

cellulose (**sel** ū lōs) *n.* the substance of which the cell walls of plants chiefly consist.

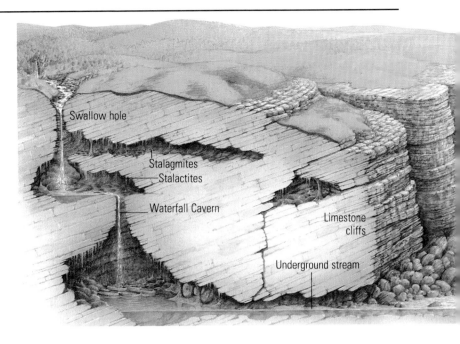

Swallow hole

Stalagmites
Stalactites

Waterfall Cavern

Limestone cliffs

Underground stream

Celsius (**sel** si ůs) *adj.* according to the scale on a centigrade thermometer.

● Invented by the Swedish scientist, Anders *Celsius* (1701-44), this scale is very simple. It is divided into 100 degrees. Zero degrees is the temperature at which water freezes, 100 degrees is boiling point.

Celt (kelt) *n.* a member of one of the ancient peoples that inhabited most parts of EUROPE in pre-Roman and Roman times, or of the peoples descended from them, e.g. in SCOTLAND, WALES, and IRELAND. **Celtic** *adj.* relating to the Celts.

cement (si **ment**) *n.* a grey powder consisting of clay and lime, to which sand and water are added to produce mortar or concrete. – *vb.* **cementing, cemented** to stick together with cement; to cover with cement.

cemetery (se **mě** tri) *n.* **cemeteries** a burial ground for the dead.

cent (sent) *n.* a coin worth a hundredth of the currency unit of several countries, for example the dollar.

centaur (**sen** tör) *n.* See **Myths and Legends.**

centigrade (**sen** ti grād) *adj.* **1** (of a scale) divided into 100 degrees. **2** same as **Celsius.**

centimetre (**sen** ti mē těr) *n.* the 100th part of a metre.

centipede (**sen** ti pēd) *n.* a small insect-like creature with a long body of many sections, each section having a pair of legs.

Most caves are formed in limestone and are the result of the rock being dissolved or worn away by water mixed with carbon dioxide over thousands of years. Scientists who study caves are known as speleologists.

PRONUNCIATION GUIDE	
fat **a**	all **ö**
fate **ā**	foot **oo**
fast **ä**	moon **ōo**
among **å**	boy **oi**
met **e**	house **ow**
mean **ē**	demon **ǒ**
silent **ê**	thing **th**
loch **hh**	this **Th**
fin **i**	but **u**
line **ī**	mute **ū**
quick **kw**	fur **û**
got **o**	brochure **ů**
note **ō**	vision **zh**

central (**sen** trål) *adj.* **1** at, or forming, the centre of something; near the centre of a city, etc.; easy to reach: *The coach station is in a central part of the city.* **2** principal: *Lady Dashwood is the central character in the novel.*

● **Central African Republic**. See Supplement, **Countries**.

● **Central America** is the name for the neck of land between MEXICO and COLOMBIA that joins North and SOUTH AMERICA. It consists of the independent republics of COSTA RICA, EL SALVADOR, GUATEMALA, HONDURAS, NICARAGUA, PANAMA, and BELIZE. Most people of Central America are of NATIVE AMERICAN or Spanish origin.

centre (**sen** těr) *n.* **1** a part at the middle of something: *He loves chocolates with soft centres.* **2** a point inside a circle or sphere that is an equal distance from all points on the circumference or surface. **3** a central area. **4** a place where a particular activity is concentrated: *We play squash at the sports centre.* **5** a person or thing that acts as a focus of interest. – *adj.* at the centre; central. – *vb.* **centring, centred 1** to place in or at the centre. **2** to focus your thoughts.
centre of gravity *n.* the point on a body at which it balances.
centri- (**sen** tri-) centre, middle.
centrifugal (sen tri **fū** gål) *adj.* describing the force that appears to keep a circling body away from the centre it is revolving around.
century (**sen** tū ri) *n.* **centuries 1** a period of 100 years: *From 1849 to 1949 is a century.* **2** in the game of cricket, 100 runs. **3** in ancient Rome, a company of (originally) one hundred foot soldiers.
ceramics (sě **ram** iks) *n.* (*singular*) the art of making pottery.
cereal (**sěr** i ål) *n.* **1** any plant that produces an edible grain: *Wheat, oats, and rice are cereals.* **2** a breakfast food prepared from grain. – *adj.*

relating to edible grains.
ceremonial (se rě **mō** ni ål) *adj.* used for, or involving, a ceremony: *The clan have a ceremonial handshake.*
ceremony (**se** rě mō ni) *n.* **ceremonies** a ritual or formal act performed to mark a particular occasion. – **stand on ceremony** to insist on behaving formally.
certain (**sûr** tǎn) *adj.* **1** definite or known beyond doubt; absolutely sure. **2** particular, and, though known, not named or specified: *I met a certain friend of yours.*
certainly *adv.* without any doubt; definitely.
certainty *n.* **certainties** something that cannot be doubted or is bound to happen.
certificate (sěr **tif** i kåt) *n.* an official document that formally states particular facts (*a marriage certificate*), an achievement or qualification (*a First-Aid certificate*).
certify (**sûr** ti fī) *vb.* **certifies, certifying, certified** to declare or confirm officially.

● **Cervantes** (sěr **van** tēz), **Miguel de** (1547-1616) was a Spanish writer best known for his novel, *Don Quixote de la Mancha*, the story of an elderly knight who lives in a fantasy world of giants and castles.

● **Cézanne, Paul** (1839-1906) was a French painter noted for his solid shapes and use of tones of colour.

● **Chad**. See Supplement, **Countries**.

● **Chadwick, Sir James** (1891-1974) was an English physicist and discoverer of the neutron.

● **Chagall** (sha **gal**), Marc (1887-1985) was a Russian-born painter, best known for his stage sets, tapestries, and stained glass windows.

chain (chān) *n.* **1** a series of connected links or rings, usually of metal. They are used to fasten, hold, support, or to transmit motion. **2** a series of things connected: *a chain of events.* **3** a number of shops, hotels, etc. under common ownership: *a chain store.* **4** in chemistry, a number of atoms linked in a series to form a molecule, etc. – *vb.* **chaining, chained** to fasten with a chain.
chainsaw *n.* a large, power-driven saw, the blade of which is a fast-revolving chain made of metal teeth.

Cereal and serial sound the same, but a cereal is a plant which produces grain, while a serial is a story told in episodes.

Cereals belong to the grass family. Rice is the main food crop for over half the world's population.

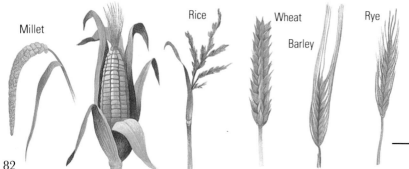

Millet Maize Rice Wheat Barley Rye

For hundreds of years only the most important people sat on **chairs**. During the Renaissance people began to improve their homes with beautiful furniture. In the 18th century Britain produced many great furniture designers.

Rocking chair

One of George Hepplewhite's many chair back designs

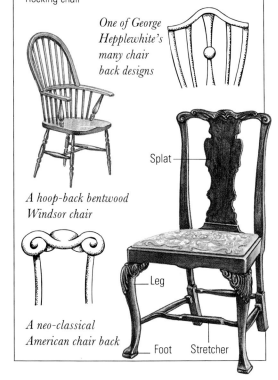

A hoop-back bentwood Windsor chair

Splat

A neo-classical American chair back

Leg

Foot | Stretcher

chair (chār) *n.* **1** a seat for one person, with a back-support and usually four legs. **2** a person in charge of a meeting, a **chairperson**. – *vb.* **chairing, chaired** to control a meeting.

chalet (**sha** lā) *n.* a style of house typical of snowy Alpine regions, built of wood, with window-shutters and a heavy, sloping roof.

chalk (chök) *n.* **1** a soft white rock composed of calcium carbonate from fossilized sea shells. **2** a stick of this substance used for writing.

challenge (**cha** linj) *vb.* **challenging, challenged 1** to call on someone to take part in a fight or contest: *Matthew challenged him to a duel.* **2** to test, especially in a stimulating way: *We set a task that challenges you.* – *n.* an invitation to a contest. – *n.* **challenger**.

chamber (**chām** běr) *n.* **1** a hall for the meeting of an assembly, especially a legislative body. **2** one of the parts which make up many commonwealth parliaments.

chameleon (kå **mēl** yŏn) *n.* a type of lizard that changes colour to match its surroundings.

champion (**cham** pi ŏn) *n.* **1** in games, competitions, etc., a competitor that has defeated all others. **2** the supporter or defender of a person or cause: *Mrs Pankhurst was the champion of women's right to vote.* – *vb.* **championing, championed** to strongly support or defend a person or cause.

chance (chäns) *n.* **1** the way that things happen unplanned and unforeseen. **2** a possibility or probability: *There is a chance it may snow.* **3** a possible or probable success: *I don't stand a chance.* **4** an opportunity: *This is your big chance to meet the president.* **5** a risk: *It looks like raining, but I'll take a chance.* – *vb.* **chancing, chanced 1** to risk. **2** to do or happen by chance. **chancy** *adj.* **chancier, chanciest** risky.

chancellor (**chän** sě lŏr) *n.* the head of the government in certain European countries.

change (chānj) *vb.* **changing, changed 1** to make or become different; to alter: *Jan changed her hairstyle.* **2** to give, leave, or substitute one thing for another: *Can I change this hat for a different colour.* **3** to exchange, usually your position, with another person, etc.: *Do you mind if we change places?* **4** to remove clothes, etc. and replace them with clean or different ones. **5** to make into or become something different: *In the film, the good doctor changed into a wicked monster.* **6** to obtain or supply another kind of money for: *Can you change these dollars into pounds?* **7** on a journey, to leave one vehicle and get into another: *You must change trains at Newport.* – *n.* **1** the process of changing or an instance of it. **2** a variation from your regular habit, etc.: *Let's eat out for a change.* **3** money returned from the amount given in payment. **changeable** *adj.* liable to change often.

channel (**cha** něl) *n.* **1** a natural or artificial water course, such as the bed of a stream or an irrigation channel. **2** a narrow stretch of water joining two seas. **3** a set of frequencies on which television or radio programmes are transmitted.

The chameleon is a remarkable lizard. It can change colour to suit its surroundings or mood; it can move its eyes independently of each other; and it has a tongue which shoots out at lightning speed to a length greater than its body.

Of the 80 films that Chaplin made, probably the best known are The Kid *(1921),* City Lights *(1931), and* The Great Dictator *(1940), his first 'talkie' in which he satirized the German Nazi dictator, Adolf Hitler.*

The Egyptians, Assyrians (below), Greeks and Romans (right) all built chariots.

● **Channel Islands** British dependencies in the English Channel. The four main islands are Jersey, Guernsey, Alderney, and Sark.

chant (chänt) *vb.* **chanting, chanted** to recite in a singing voice; to keep repeating, especially loudly and rhythmically: *The football crowd chanted, "Scotland". – n.* a type of singing used in religious services.

Chanukkah (hä nŭ kå). Same as **Hanukkah**.

chaos (kā os) *n.* complete confusion; utter disorder. – *adj.* **chaotic**. – *adv.* **chaotically**.

chapel (cha pĕl) *n.* a small church.

chaplain (chap lin) *n.* a clergyman or -woman attached to a school, hospital, etc.

● **Chaplin, Charles** (1889-1977) was an English-American film star. His famous role as a baggy-trousered tramp endeared him to millions.

chapter (chap tĕr) *n.* a main part of a book: *The book I'm reading has 17 chapters.*

character (ka råk tĕr) *n.* **1** the combination of qualities that makes up a person's nature or personality; the qualities that typify anything. **2** strong, admirable qualities such as determination, courage, and honesty. **3** interesting qualities: *We've bought a house with character.* **4** a person in a story or play. – **out of character** not typical of a person's nature. **characterize** or **characterise** *vb.*

characterizing, characterized 1 to describe, give the chief qualities of. **2** to be a distinctive and typical feature of.

characteristic *adj.* **1** typical: *It's characteristic of him to be so kind.* **2** distinctive. – *adv.* **characteristically**.

charcoal (chär kōl) *n.* a form of carbon, produced by partially burning wood, used for drawing and as a fuel.

charge (chärj) *vb.* **charging, charged 1** to ask for as the price of something; to ask someone for an amount as payment. **2** to record as a debt against: *Charge the breakages to me.* **3** to accuse officially: *The driver was charged with manslaughter.* **4** to rush at in attack: *The bull charged at the dog.* **5** to give a task to: *He was charged with looking after the books.* **6** (of a battery, etc.) to store up, or cause to store up, electricity. – *n.* **1** a price, cost, or fee. **2** control, care, responsibility: *The police arrived and took charge.* **3** something of which you are accused: *She was arrested on a charge of armed robbery.*

chariot (cha ri ŏt) *n.* a two-wheeled vehicle pulled by horses, used in ancient times in war or for racing. – *n.* **charioteer**.

The hippodrome (meaning 'horse course') was an arena for chariot racing in ancient Rome.

Entrance

Emperor's box

charitable (**cha** ri tå bĕl) *adj.* kind and understanding in your attitude to others.

charity (**cha** ri ti) *n.* **charities** assistance given to those in need; an organization established to provide such assistance.

● **Charlemagne** (**shär** lĕ mān) (747-814) was king of the Franks and extended his territory into GERMANY and ITALY. The administration of his empire was centralized, but Charlemagne tried hard to maintain the customs and traditions of the lands he conquered. He was a patron of learning.

● **Charles, Prince of Wales** (1948-) is the eldest son and heir of ELIZABETH the Second.

● **Charles the First** (1600-49) was king of ENGLAND and SCOTLAND. He defied parliament and ruled so badly that in 1642 the country was split by CIVIL WAR. Charles was convicted of treason and beheaded.

charm (chärm) *n.* **1** the power of delighting, attracting, or fascinating. **2** (in *plural*) delightful qualities possessed by a person, place, or thing. **3** an object believed to have magical powers.
charming *adj.* delightful; pleasing; attractive.

chart (chärt) *n.* **1** a map, especially one designed to aid navigation by sea or air, or one on which weather developments are shown. **2** information presented as a diagram.

charter (**chär** tĕr) *n.* **1** a document guaranteeing certain rights and privileges issued by a ruler or government. **2** the hire of aircraft or ships for private use. − *vb.*
chartering, chartered to hire an aircraft.

chase (chās) *vb.* **chasing, chased 1** to go after in an attempt to catch: *The dog chased after the rabbit.* **2** to force away, out, etc.: *Edna chased the pigeons off her herb garden.* **3** to rush; to hurry.

chasm (**ka** zĕm) *n.* a deep crack in the ground, found, for example close to a cliff edge.

chat (chat) *vb.* **chatting, chatted** to talk in a friendly, informal way. − *n.* informal, familiar talk; a friendly conversation.
chat show *n.* a television or radio programme in which well-known people are interviewed informally.

chatter (**cha** tĕr) *vb.* **chattering, chattered 1** to talk rapidly and unceasingly, usually about trivial matters. **2** (of the teeth) to keep knocking together because of cold or fear.

● **Chaucer** (**chö** sĕr), **Geoffrey** (1345-1400) was one of the first people to write in English, rather than Latin. He wrote *The Canterbury Tales.*

Geoffrey Chaucer on horseback, from a manuscript of his works.

THE COOK (from *The Canterbury Tales*)

A Cook they hadde with hem for the nones
They had a Cook with them who stood alone
To boille the chicknes with the marybones
For boiling chicken with a marrow-bone
And poudre-marchant tart and galyngale
Sharp flavouring-powder and a spice for savour
Wel koude he knowe a draughte of London ale,
He could distinguish London ale by flavour,
He coude roooste, and sethe, and broille, and frye,
And he could roast and seethe and broil and fry,
Maken mortreux, and wel bake a pye.
Make good thick soup and bake a tasty pie
Geoffrey Chaucer (*with a translation by Nevill Coghill*)

---

chauvinism (**shō** vin i zĕm) *n.* an unreasonable belief in the superiority of your own nation, sex, etc. − *n.* **chauvinist.** − *adj.* **chauvinistic.**

cheap (chēp) *adj.* **1** low in price; less than the usual price; good value for money. **2** low in price but of poor quality: *She bought lots of cheap plastic jewellery.* − *n.* **cheapness.**

cheat (chēt) *vb.* **cheating, cheated 1** to trick, deceive, swindle. **2** to act dishonestly so as to gain an advantage: *Martin cheats at cards.* − *n.* **1** a person who cheats. **2** a dishonest trick.

check (chek) *vb.* **checking, checked 1** to make sure something is as it should be or someone is doing what they should be, by inspecting or investigating it. **2** to prevent, stop: *He nearly swore, but checked himself.* **3** (*US*) to mark with a tick. **4** to get luggage accepted for air transport: *Our bags were checked through to Singapore.* − *n.* **1** an inspection or investigation made to find out about something or to ensure that something is as it should be. **2** a stoppage in, or control on, progress or development. **3** a pattern of squares: *The dress is in cotton with a purple check.* − *n.* **checker.**
check-up *n.* a thorough examination, especially a medical one.

cheek (chēk) *n.* **1** either side of the face below the eye. **2** rude speech or behaviour.

PRONUNCIATION GUIDE	
fat a	all ö
fate ā	foot oo
fast ä	moon o͞o
among å	boy oi
met e	house ow
mean ē	demon ŏ
silent ĕ	thing th
loch hh	this Th
fin i	but u
line ī	mute ū
quick kw	fur û
got o	brochure ŭ
note ō	vision zh

Unlike other cats that stalk their prey slowly and pounce, cheetahs chase their prey.

cheer (chēr) *n.* a shout of approval or encouragement. – *vb.* **cheering, cheered** to give approval or encouragement by shouting: *They came to cheer her on.* – *vb.* **cheer up** to make or become more cheerful.
cheerful *adj.* **1** happy; optimistic. **2** in a good mood; willing – *n.* **cheerfulness.**
cheese (chēz) *n.* a soft or hard food made from milk.

cheetah (chē tå) *n.* a large long-legged spotted animal of the cat family found in AFRICA and ASIA, the fastest-running of all mammals. Cheetahs have a top speed of nearly 100 km/h.
chef (shef) *n.* the chief cook in a restaurant, etc.

● **Chekhov** (**chek** of), **Anton** (1860-1904) was a Russian playwright. His works include *Uncle Vanya, Three Sisters,* and *The Cherry Orchard.*

chemical (**kem** i kål) *adj.* relating to, or made using, chemistry or chemicals. – *n.* a substance produced by or used in chemistry.
chemist (**kem** ist) *n.* **1** a scientist specializing in chemistry. **2** a person qualified to dispense medicines; a pharmacist.
chemistry (**kem** i stri) *n.* the science of elements and compounds and how they work together.

● The true science of chemistry began in the 1600s when chemists discovered the elements, simple substances which make up all other substances.

cheque (chek) *n.* a printed form on which to fill in instructions to a bank to pay a certain person, etc. a certain amount of money.
chequer or, in North America, **checker** (**chek** ẻr) *n.* **1** a pattern of squares alternating in colour as on a chessboard. **2** (*North American*) one of the pieces used in the game of draughts.

● **Chernobyl** is a city in the UKRAINE where, in April 1986, explosions at a nuclear power station caused a serious escape of radioactivity.

● **Cherokees** are a NATIVE AMERICAN people who now live in Oklahoma.

cherry (**che** ri) *n.* **cherries** a small round red, yellow, or dark purple fruit with a stone.
chess (ches) *n.* a board game for two people each with 16 playing pieces, the most important pieces being the kings. The object of the game is to trap your opponent's king.

chest (chest) *n.* **1** the part of the body between the neck and the waist that contains the heart and lungs, or the front part of this. **2** a big, strong, box with a hinged lid used for storage or transport.
chestnut (**ches** nut) *n.* either of two shiny reddish-brown nuts – the edible **sweet chestnut** and the **horse chestnut** (also known as a 'conker').

● **Chevrolet** (**shev** rồ lā), **Louis** (1879-1941) an American racing driver and car manufacturer.

chew (choo) *vb.* **chewing, chewed** to use the teeth to crush food before swallowing.

● **Cheyenne** (shī **an**) are a tribe of NATIVE AMERICANS of Montana and Oklahoma.

chic (shēk) *adj.* elegant or fashionable.

● **Chicago** is a city in Illinois, USA on Lake Michigan. Its O'Hare airport is the busiest in the world. The first skyscraper was built there in 1884.

chick (chik) *n.* a baby bird.
chicken (**chik** ẻn) *n.* the farmyard fowl bred for its eggs and flesh; its flesh used as food.
chickenpox *n.* a mild infectious disease, especially of childhood, with itchy spots.
chief (chēf) *n.* **1** the head of a clan, etc. **2** a leader; the person in charge of any group, organization, etc. – *adj.* most important.
chiefly *adv.* mainly; especially; above all.
chieftain (**chēf** tån) *n.* the head of a tribe or clan; a leader or commander.

Domestic chickens are descended from the Asian jungle fowl. The males have a fleshy comb and wattles at the sides of the beak.

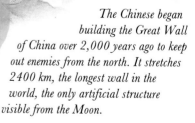

child (chīld) *n.* **children** (**chil** drĕn) **1** a boy
or girl who is not an adult. **2** someone's son
or daughter: *Simon is my friend's only child.*
childhood *n.* the state or time of being a
child: *Grandad loves to talk about his childhood.*
childish *adj.* silly; immature.

● **Chile**. See Supplement, **Countries**.

chill (chil) *n.* **1** a feeling of coldness: *There's a
wintry chill in the air.* **2** a feverish cold. **3** a
feeling, especially sudden, of depression or
fear. – *vb.* **chilling, chilled** to make or
become cold: *Mark chilled the wine.*
chilly *adj.* rather cold. – *n.* **chilliness**.
chime (chīm) *n.* a set of tuned bells; the sound
made by them.
chimney (**chim** ni) *n.* **chimneys** a narrow
shaft through which smoke from a fire escapes.
chimpanzee (chim păn **zē**) *n.* an African ape.

● Chimpanzees can walk upright although they
often use their hands to help push themselves
along the ground. They live in family groups
and are very fond of their young. They are
playful and intelligent animals.

chin (chin) *n.* the part of your face below your
mouth. – **keep your chin up** (*colloquial*) to
stay cheerful in spite of misfortune.

● **China** is the nation with the biggest population
(one billion). The HIMALAYAS and deserts cut
China off from its Asian neighbours. Most
people live in the east along the great rivers,
Chang Jiang and HUANG HO. China has an
ancient civilization. For most of its history it
was an empire. In 1949 it became a
communist republic. Its capital is Beijing and
its principal language is Mandarin Chinese.
See also Supplement, **Countries**.

china (**chī** nǎ) *n.* plates, cups, etc. made from a
fine pottery. – *adj.* made of china.
chinchilla (chin **chi** lǎ) *n.* a small South
American, squirrel-like
rodent.
Chinese (chī **nēz**) *n.*
Chinese a native of
CHINA; the language of the
main ethnic group of
CHINA. – *adj.* of CHINA, its
people, etc.

*The giant panda is found
in the bamboo forests of
western China. It is
becoming dangerously rare.*

The earliest Chinese civilization grew up on
the banks of **China**'s great rivers. The
farmers relied on the rivers for water to grow
crops and for transport. The first dynasty
(ruling family) we know of was called the
Shang (*c.*1500 BC). They grew crops, kept
animals, and wove silk. The Chou
dynasty (*c.*1027 BC) used iron for weapons
and tools. The Chi'n dynasty (*c.*221 BC)
united a vast empire but was soon
succeeded by the Han dynasty which ruled
until AD 220.

*The bronze model
of a horse and
chariot was
made in the
AD 100s.
Chinese art
also included
carving,
painting, and
fine porcelain.*

*The Chinese language is
written in picture-signs, or
characters. There are more
than 40,000 characters, but a
Chinese person can manage
with 5,000. While Chinese
writing is the same through the
country, the spoken language
varies from area to area with
hundreds of dialects. The most
common is Mandarin.*

*The Chinese began
building the Great Wall
of China over 2,000 years ago to keep
out enemies from the north. It stretches
2400 km, the longest wall in the
world, the only artificial structure
visible from the Moon.*

A microchip contains thousands of electronic components all mounted in a single block of plastic. Microchips can perform at almost the speed of light, more than a million operations per second.

chipmunk (**chip** mungk) *n.* a black-and-white-striped American squirrel with a bushy tail.

chiropodist (ki **rop** ỏ dist) *n.* a person who treats disorders of the feet, e.g. corns.

chirp (chûrp) *vb.* **chirping, chirped** a short high sound made by birds, grasshoppers, etc.

chisel (**chi** zẻl) *n.* a tool with a strong metal blade, used for shaping wood or stone.

● **Chisholm, Shirley** (1924-) was the first black woman to be elected to the United States House of Representatives, the lower house in Congress.

chlorine (**klö** rēn) *n.* an element (symbol **Cl**), a poisonous strong-smelling yellowish-green gas used in bleaches and disinfectants.

chlorophyll (**klo** rỏ fil) *n.* the green colouring matter in plants that absorbs the energy from the Sun.

chocolate (**chok** låt) *n.* the roasted and ground seeds of the cacao, a tropical American tree, used in the form of a powder, paste, or solid block.

choice (chois) *n.* **1** the act or process of choosing: *I've made my choice in this matter.* **2** the right, power, or opportunity to choose: *I'd rather not go but I have no choice.* **3** something or someone chosen: *It was a good choice.* – *adj.* of specially good quality: *These are choice tomatoes.*

choir (kwīr) *n.* a group of singers.

chink (chingk) *n.* a small slit or crack: *Light shone through the chink in the door.*

chip (chip) *vb.* **chipping, chipped 1** to knock or strike small pieces off a hard object or material; to be broken off in small pieces. **2** to shape by chipping: *The artist chipped a design into the stone.* – *n.* **1** a small piece chipped off: *a chip of marble.* **2** a place from which a piece has been chipped off: *There was a big chip in the rim.* **3** (*British*) a strip of fried potato. **4** a plastic counter used as a money token in gambling. **5** (also **microchip** or **silicon chip**) a very small piece of silicon, on which a large amount of information can be stored electronically.

choke (chōk) *vb.* **choking, choked** to be prevented, wholly or partially, from breathing: *Hans choked on a piece of food.*

cholesterol (kỏ **les** tẻ rol) *n.* a fatty substance found in body tissues and in animal fats. It is thought to cause fatty deposits in the blood vessels that narrow and harden them.

choose (chōōz) *vb.* **choosing, chose** (chōz), **chosen** (**chō** zẻn) to select one or more things or persons from a larger number: *Which would you choose – raspberries or blackberries?*

chop (chop) *vb.* **chopping, chopped** to cut with a vigorous downwards or sideways slicing action, with an axe, knife, etc. – *n.* **1** a slice of pork, lamb, or mutton containing a bone, especially a rib. **2** a chopping action or stroke.

● **Chopin** (**sho** pan), **Frédéric** (1810-49) was a Polish-born composer famous for his piano works.

chore (chör) *n.* a boring task.

choreography (ko ri **og** rå fi) *n.* the arrangement of the sequence and pattern of movements in dancing. – *n.* **choreographer**.

chorus (**kö** růs) *n.* **1** a set of lines in a song, sung after each verse. **2** a large choir.

chose, chosen. See **choose**.

christen (**kri** sẻn) *vb.* **christening, christened** to give a person, especially a baby, a name, as part of the religious ceremony of receiving him or her into the Christian Church. – *n.* **christening**.

Christian (**kris** chẳn) *n.* a person who believes in, and follows the teachings of, JESUS CHRIST. **Christianity** (kris ti **an** i ti) *n.* the religion based on the teachings of JESUS CHRIST.

● Christianity is one of the world's great religions. Christians believe that JESUS CHRIST is the son of God. They read of his teachings, life, and death by crucifixion in the NEW TESTAMENT of the Bible.

Christmas (**kris** mås) *n.* the annual Christian festival commemorating the birth of JESUS CHRIST, held on 25 December.

chronicle (**kron** i kẻl) *n.* a record of events in the order in which they happened.

chrysalis (**kris** å lis) *n.* the pupa of a butterfly.

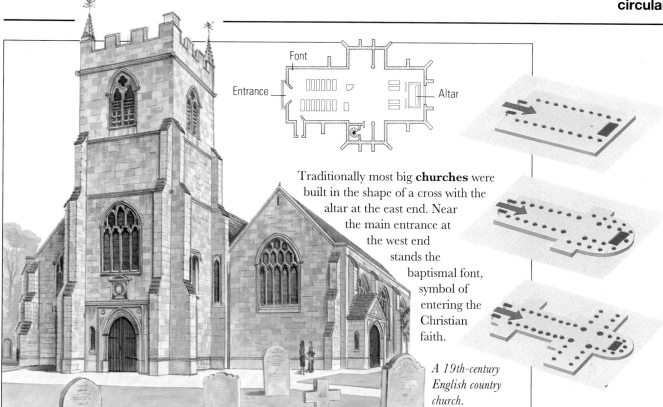

Font

Entrance

Altar

Traditionally most big **churches** were built in the shape of a cross with the altar at the east end. Near the main entrance at the west end stands the baptismal font, symbol of entering the Christian faith.

A 19th-century English country church.

Throughout the ages churches have been built in many different styles; but all serve the same purpose, as places for prayer and the performing of religious services and as places that house all kinds of religious objects.

church (chûrch) *n.* **1** a building for public Christian worship. **2 Church** the profession of the clergy: *He chose to enter the Church.*

● **Church of England** the official state Church in England, which has the Sovereign as its head.

● **Church of Scotland** the largest Presbyterian Church in Scotland.

● **Churchill, Winston** (1874-1965) was a British statesman. As prime minister (1940-45) he led his country in the Second WORLD WAR.

churn (chûrn) *n.* a container in which milk is shaken about to make butter.

chutney (**chut** ni) *n.* an Indian pickle.

● **Cid, El** (1040-99) was a Spanish national hero in Spain's struggle against the Moors.

cider (sī děr) *n.* an alcoholic drink made from apples.

cinder (sin děr) *n.* a piece of burnt coal or wood.

● **Cinderella** is the name of a character in a fairy tale by Perrault, and a symbol of a person whose merits and charms go unnoticed.

cinema (si ně må) *n.* **1** a theatre in which motion pictures are shown. **2** the art or business of making films.

● The art of making motion pictures came from an invention called the kinetoscope, built by an American, Thomas Edison, in 1891. At about the same time the French Lumière brothers invented a similar machine and, in 1896, gave the world's first public film show, in Paris.

cinnamon (si nå mŏn) *n.* a spice obtained from the bark of an Asian tree.

cipher (sī fěr) *n.* a secret code.

circle (sûr kěl) *n.* **1** a line evenly and continuously curved so as to form a round figure, with every point on it an equal distance from the centre. **2** anything in the form of a circle: *We sat around the reader in a circle.* **3** the upper floor of seats in a theatre, etc. **4** a group of people associated in some way: *I met his circle of friends.* – *vb.* **circling, circled** to move in a circle; to draw a circle round.

circuit (sûr kit) *n.* **1** a complete course, journey, or route round something: *They tracked the boat's circuit around the lake.* **2** a race track, etc.

circular (sûr kū lår) *adj.* having the form of a circle; round.

circulate (sûr kū lāt) *vb.* **circulating,
circulated 1** to move round freely, especially
in a fixed route: *There is too much traffic
circulating through the town centre.* **2** to spread; to
pass round: *Please circulate the report.*

circulation *n.* **1** the act of circulating. **2** the
flow of blood around the body. **3** the number
of copies sold of a newspaper, etc.

circum- (sûr kŭm-) round about.

circumcise (sûr kŭm sīz) *vb.* **circumcising,
circumcised** to cut away the foreskin of the
penis, as a religious rite or medical necessity.
– *n.* **circumcision**.

circumference (sir **kum** fě rěns) *n.* the outer
line or edge of a circle.

circumstance (sûr kŭm stǎns) *n.* a fact,
occurrence, or condition, relating to an act or
event: *He died in mysterious circumstances.*

circus (sûr kŭs) *n.* a travelling company of
performers including acrobats, clowns, etc.

cistern (sis těrn) *n.* a tank storing water.

citadel (sit å del) *n.* a fortress dominating the
centre of a city.

citizen (si ti zěn) *n.* an inhabitant of a city.

citrus (sit rŭs) *n.* any tree of the group that
includes the lemon and orange.

city (si ti) *n.* **cities** any large town, usually with
a cathedral.

civil (si vil) *adj.* **1** relating to the community and
citizens of a country: *We heard about the civil
disturbances.* **2** relating to ordinary citizens; not
military, legal, or religious. **3** polite.

civil engineer *n.* someone who designs and
builds roads, bridges, tunnels, etc.

civil rights *n.* (*plural*) the personal rights of
any citizen, especially to freedom and equality
regardless of race, religion, sex, or sexuality.

civil war *n.* a war between citizens of the
same state.

● **Civil War, American** (1861-5) was fought
between the government (Union) and the
southern states (Confederacy). The main
quarrel was over slavery. After the confederate
army was defeated slaves were freed.

● **Civil War, English** (1642-9) was fought
between the Royalists under CHARLES the First
and the Parliamentarians or Roundheads.
The war was over the king's right to raise
taxes. The Royalists lost the war and the king
was captured, put on trial, and executed.
Parliament ruled without a king until 1660.

The American Civil War
When Abraham Lincoln was
elected president in 1860, the
South feared that he would abolish
slavery and the southern economy
would suffer as a result. Eleven
southern states seceded and formed
the Confederate States of
America. The war started
on 12 April 1861. The cost
of the war was appalling
– more than 600,000
Americans died. But the
Union was preserved.

States of the Union
Confederate States

*The major battles of the
American Civil War
were fought in the east
and south-east of the
United States.*

*The rapid fire
gun, the
Gatling Gun,
developed in 1861
by the American
inventor Richard
Gatling.*

Ulysses S. Grant (left)
*(1822-1885) was the
commander of the Union
forces. He was tough and
determined.*
Robert E. Lee (right)
*(1807-70) led the forces
of the South.*

The English Civil War

King Charles I believed in 'divine right', claiming his right to rule came directly from God. He quarrelled with parliament over taxes and his right to imprison those who opposed him. In 1629 he dissolved parliament and for 11 years tried to rule alone. The first major battle of the war took place at Edgehill in 1642.

A musketeer of the New Model Army which defeated the Royalists.

Oliver Cromwell who led the Roundheads to victory over the King.

Charles was tried for treason and executed.

The Confederates won the first big battle of the war at Bull Run, Virginia in 1861.

civilian (si **vil** yån) *n.* anyone who is not in the armed forces or the police.

civilize or **civilise** (**si** vil īz) *vb.* **civilizing, civilized** to educate and enlighten. **civilization** *n.* **1** the state of being civilized; the act of civilizing. **2** a stage of development in human society that is socially, politically, culturally, and technologically advanced.

claim (klām) *vb.* **claiming, claimed 1** to state something firmly, insisting on its truth: *John claimed he had seen a ghost.* **2** to declare to be, to have done, etc. **3** to demand as a right: *We claimed on our insurance.* – *n.* **1** a statement you insist is true. **2** a demand for something that you believe you have a right to.

clammy (**klam** i) *adj.* **clammier, clammiest** moist or damp: *Nick has clammy hands.*

clamp (klamp) *n.* **1** a tool with adjustable jaws for gripping things firmly; a fastening device, used in woodwork, etc. **2** a heavy metal device that can be fitted to the wheels of a car to prevent it being moved. – *vb.* **clamping, clamped** to hold with a clamp.

clan (klan) *n.* a group of families, in Scotland, generally with the same surname.

clap (klap) *vb.* **clapping, clapped** to strike the palms of your hands together with a loud noise; to applaud. – *n.* **1** an act of clapping. **2** the sudden loud noise made by thunder.

clarify (**kla** ri fī) *vb.* **clarifies, clarifying, clarified** to make easier to understand.

clarinet (kla ri **net**) *n.* a woodwind instrument with keys and a single reed. – *n.* **clarinettist**.

clarity (**kla** ri ti) *n.* clearness.

clash (klash) *n.* **1** a loud noise, like pieces of metal striking each other. **2** a serious disagreement; a quarrel or argument. – *vb.* **clashing, clashed 1** to strike against each other noisily. **2** to fight; to disagree violently. **3** (of two or more events that you ought to or would like to attend) to be planned for the same time.

clasp (kläsp) *n.* **1** a fastening on jewellery, a bag, etc. **2** a firm grip, or act of gripping. – *vb.* **clasping, clasped 1** to take hold of firmly. **2** to fasten or secure with a clasp.

class (kläs) *n.* **1** a lesson; a number of pupils taught together. **2** a category or type: *Standard class railway tickets are cheaper than first.* – *vb.* **classing, classed** to put into a category.

classic (**klas** ik) *adj.* of the highest quality; established as the best. – *n.* an established work of literature: *The* Iliad *is a Greek classic.*

Scottish clans carried on bitter feuds – the Macdonalds and Campbells, for instance, were long-standing enemies. Each clan was distinguished by its tartan.

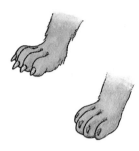

Nails and claws are made of hard skin, like animals' horns. When they are broad and flat they are called nails, but if they are sharp and pointed they are called claws. A close look at an animal's claws will tell you about its way of life. Cats and birds of prey have very sharp claws. They are hooked for holding on to and tearing prey.

CLICHE CORNER
Clichés are words or phrases that have been used too often and so have become tired, trite, and hackneyed. Here are some clichés using 'twinned' words:
by leaps and bounds
to pick and choose
tooth and nail
trials and tribulations
hammer and tongs
slow but sure
fast and furious

classical (klas i kål) *adj.* **1** of ancient Greek and Roman literature, art, etc. **2** showing the influence of ancient Greece and Rome in architecture, etc. **3** having an established formal style: *He prefers classical music.*

classify (klas i fī) *vb.* **classifies, classifying, classified** to put into a particular group.

clause (klöz) *n.* part of a sentence that has its own subject, verb, object, etc.

claustrophobia (klö strå fō bi å) *n.* fear of being in confined spaces. – *adj.* **claustrophobic.**

claw (klö) *n.* one of the sharply-pointed hooked nails of an animal or bird; the foot of an animal or bird with claws: *The cat family has sharp claws.*

clay (klā) *n.* soft sticky earth that can be formed into pottery, bricks, etc. and baked hard.

clean (klēn) *adj.* **1** free from dirt: *Denise changed from her dirty sports gear into clean clothes.* **2** not containing anything harmful to health; pure: *clean water.* **3** unused; unmarked: *Write on a clean sheet of paper.* **4** neat and even: *It was a clean cut.* **5** clear of legal offences: *She has a clean driving licence.* **6** (of nuclear installations, etc.) not producing a harmful level of radioactivity. – *vb.* **cleaning, cleaned 1** to make free from dirt. **2** to dust, polish floors and furniture, etc.

cleanly *adv.* **1** smoothly and easily. **2** fairly.

clear (klēr) *adj.* **1** easy to see through. **2** (of weather, etc.) not misty or cloudy. **3** easy to see, hear, or understand: *Your simple explanation makes it clear.* **4** bright; sharp: *What a clear photograph!* **5** (of vision) able to see well. **6** free of obstruction: *The road ahead is clear.* **7** well away from: *Stay well clear of the rocks.* **8** free from guilt, etc.: *My conscience is clear.* – *adv.* **1** in a clear manner. **2** completely: *They got clear away.* **3** out of the way of: *Keep or steer clear of trouble!* – *vb.* **clearing, cleared 1** to make or become clear, free of obstruction, etc. **2** to move out of the way. **3** to prove to be innocent.

clearing *n.* an area in a forest, etc. that has been cleared of trees, etc.

clearly *adv.* obviously: *Clearly he's wrong.*

clench (klench) *vb.* **clenching, clenched** to close tightly: *John clenched his fist in anger.*

●**Cleopatra** (klē ō pat rå) (69-30 BC), Queen of Egypt, is famous for her love affairs with Julius CAESAR and later with Mark Antony. When Antony was defeated in battle he stabbed himself to death; Cleopatra then died from a poisonous snake bite.

clergy (klûr ji) *n.* **clergies** (*plural* or, sometimes, *singular*) ministers and rabbis.

clerical *adj.* **1** relating to clerks, office workers, or office work. **2** relating to the clergy.

clerk (klärk) *n.* a person in an office or bank who deals with letters, accounts, files, etc.

●**Cleveland**, Ohio, in the UNITED STATES, is a major port on Lake ERIE.

clever (kle vẻr) *adj.* good or quick at learning and understanding: *Mary is clever at maths.*

cliché (klē shā) *n.* a phrase that has become stale through repetition.

click (klik) *n.* a short sharp sound like that of two parts of a mechanism locking into place.

client (klī ểnt) *n.* a person using the professional services of a lawyer, bank manager, etc.

cliff (klif) *n.* a high steep rock face.

climate (klī måt) *n.* the average weather conditions of a particular part of the world.

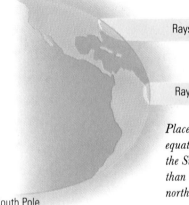

North Pole

Rays hit Earth at an angle

Rays hit Earth directly

South Pole

Places near the equator get more of the Sun's rays than those farther north or south.

climax (klī maks) *n.* the high point of a series of events or of an experience.

climb (klīm) *vb.* **climbing, climbed** to go towards the top of a hill, ladder, etc.: *Ann climbed the big tree.* – *n.* an act of climbing.

cling (kling) *vb.* **clinging, clung** (klung) to hold tightly; to stick: *Mud clings to your boots.*

clinic (klin ik) *n.* a department of a hospital where outpatients receive treatment or advice.

●**Clinton, William Jefferson** (1946-) was elected president of the UNITED STATES in 1992. He was governor of Arkansas from 1978-80 and from 1982-92.

clip (klip) *vb.* **clipping, clipped** to cut or trim hair, wool, etc. – *n.* **1** an act of clipping.

clipper (**klip** ẽr) *n.* a fast sailing ship with large sails in the 1800s.

cloak (klōk) *n.* a loose outdoor garment, usually sleeveless. – *vb.* **cloaking, cloaked** to cover up or conceal: *The affair was cloaked in mystery.*

The first mechanical clocks appeared around 1300 in Europe. The pendulum clock was developed in 1656. Today electric clocks are remarkably accurate timepieces.

A ship's chronometer of the 1700s, with a slowly unwinding spring.

This clock's pendulum controls its speed.

clock (klok) *n.* an instrument for measuring and showing time by means of pointers on a dial or displayed figures. – **against the clock** very fast, because of lack of time. – **round the clock** throughout the day and night.

clockwise *adj. & adv.* in the same direction as the moving hands of a clock.

clockwork *n.* a mechanism like that of a clock, working by means of gears and a spring. – *adj.* operated by clockwork.

clod (klod) *n.* a lump of earth or clay, etc.

clog (klog) *n.* a shoe carved from wood. – *vb.* **clogging, clogged** to block.

cloister (**kloi** stẽr) *n.* a covered walk built against the wall of a church, college, etc.

close¹ (klōs) *adj.* **1** near in space or time; at a short distance: *at close range.* **2** near in relationship, friendship: *She is very close to her mother.* **3** almost touching. **4** dense or compact; with little space between. **5** (of a contest) with little difference between entrants. **6** stuffy.

close² (klōz) *vb.* **closing, closed 1** to shut: *Please close the window.* **2** to finish; to come or bring to an end: *The meeting closed with the national anthem.* **3** to catch up: *The police were closing on him.* – *n.* an end or conclusion. – *vb.*

close down 1 (of a business) to close permanently. **2** (of a television or radio station)

to stop broadcasting at the end of the day. – *vb.* **close in** to come nearer and surround.

closed *adj.* shut; blocked.

clot (klot) *n.* a soft mass, especially of solidified liquid matter such as blood. – *vb.* **clotting, clotted** to form into clots.

cloth (kloth) *n.* woven or knitted material.

● Fabric from as far back as 6000 BC has been found. Once the secret of weaving had been discovered, it spread around the world. Only a few people, such as the African Bushmen, do not weave their cloth.

clothe (klōTh) *vb.* **clothing, clothed** to cover or provide with clothes.

clothes (klōThz) *n.* (*plural*) things people wear to cover the body for warmth or decoration.

clothing (**klō** Thing) *n.* clothes.

cloud (klowd) *n.* **1** a grey or white mass floating in the sky, made of particles of water or ice. **2** a mass of dust, smoke, or moving insects in the air. – *vb.* **clouding, clouded** to become overcast with clouds. – *adj.* **cloudless.** – **on cloud nine** (*colloquial*) extremely happy.

cloudburst *n.* a sudden downpour of rain.

cloudy *adj.* **cloudier, cloudiest 1** full of clouds; overcast. **2** (of a liquid) not clear; milky.

Clouds form when water vapour condenses into droplets. Three main types of cloud are Cirrus (streaky), Cumulus (fluffy) and Stratus (layer). Heights are indicated by: Cirro (very high), Alto (high), Strato (low), and Nimbo (rain cloud).

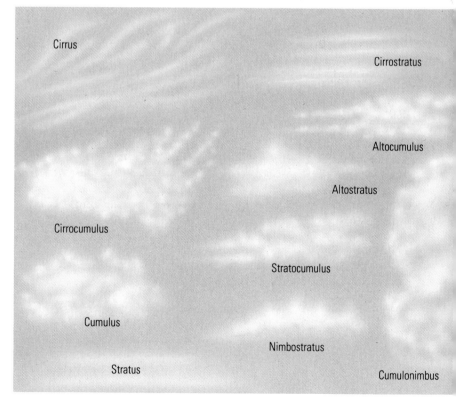

clove (klōv) *n.* the strong-smelling dried flower-bud of a tropical tree, used as a spice.

clover (klō věr) *n.* a plant grown as cattle fodder, with leaves divided into usually three parts and pink, purple, or white flowers.

clown (klown) *n.* a comic performer in a circus or pantomime, usually wearing ridiculous clothes and make-up. – *vb.* **clowning, clowned** to behave ridiculously: *Tim was clowning about with a plant pot on his head.*

club (klub) *n.* **1** a stick, usually thicker at one end, used as a weapon. **2** a stick with a specially shaped head, for playing golf. **3** a society or association; the place where such a group meets. **4** a playing-card of the suit **clubs,** bearing a black cloverleaf-shaped symbol. – *vb.* **clubbing, clubbed 1** to beat or strike with a club. **2** to contribute money for a special purpose: *The class clubbed together and bought the teacher a present.*

clue (klōō) *n.* a fact which helps to solve a problem, crime, or mystery.

clump (klump) *n.* **1** a group of trees, plants, or people standing close together. **2** a dull heavy sound: *Hugh jumped off the wall with a clump.* – *vb.* **clumping, clumped 1** to walk with a heavy tread. **2** to form into clumps.

clumsy (klum zi) *adj.* **clumsier, clumsiest** unskilful with the hands or awkward.

clung. See **cling.**

cluster (klus těr) *n.* **1** a small group or gathering. **2** a number of flowers growing together on one stem.

clutch (kluch) *vb.* **clutching, clutched** to grasp tightly: *Sheila clutched her little brother's hand.* – *n.* **1** (usually in *plural*) control or power: *He is in his boss's clutches.* **2** a pedal in a motor vehicle that you press to change gear.

clutter (klu těr) *n.* an untidy accumulation of things. – *vb.* **cluttering, cluttered** to overcrowd or make untidy.

coach (kōch) *n.* **1** a railway carriage. **2** a bus designed for long-distance travel. **3** a trainer or instructor in a sport, or a private tutor. – *vb.* **coaching, coached** to train in a sport, or teach privately.

coal (kōl) *n.* a hard black mineral made of carbon formed by decayed and compressed plants, mined and used as a fuel.
coalmine *n.* a place where coal is taken out of the ground.

coarse (körs) *adj.* **1** rough or open in texture. **2** crude; not refined. – *n.* **coarseness.**

Coal is found in seams or layers under the ground. It is called a fossil fuel because it was made from dead plants millions of years ago. The dead plants in swamps first became peat and under great pressure turned into coal. The hardest coal is known as anthracite.

Coal forests

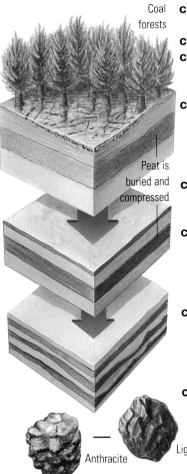

Peat is buried and compressed

Anthracite   Lignite

● **coarse** and **course** sound the same, but coarse means 'rough', while a course is a 'race track' or a 'series of lessons'.

coast (kōst) *n.* the edge of the land, alongside the sea; the seaside or seashore. – *adj.* **coastal.** **coastline** *n.* the shape of the coast.

coat (kōt) *n.* **1** an outer garment with long sleeves; a jacket. **2** the hair, fur, or wool of an animal. **3** a covering or application of paint, dust, sugar, etc. – *vb.* **coating, coated** to cover with a layer of something. – *n.* **coating.**

coax (kōks) *vb.* **coaxing, coaxed** to persuade using flattery, promises, kind words, etc.

cob (kob) *n.* **1** a strong horse with short legs. **2** a male swan. **3** a hazelnut. **4** a corncob.

cobweb (kob web) *n.* a web made by a spider.

Nature at its most fascinating – a spider spins a beautifully constructed web. It lays out a line of silk as it moves about, anchoring it at intervals in much the same way as a mountaineer with a safety line.

cock (kok) *n.* a male bird.

● **Cockerell, Christopher** (1910-) is the English inventor of the HOVERCRAFT.

Cockney or **cockney** (kok ni) *n.* **cockneys 1** a native of London, especially of the East End. **2** the dialect used by Cockneys.

cockroach (kok rōch) *n.* a large black or brown beetle-like insect.

cocoa (**kō** kō) *n.* a powder made from the roasted and ground seeds of the cacao tree.

coconut (**kō** kŏ nut) *n.* the large oval fruit of the **coconut palm.** It has a hard hairy brown shell filled with solid edible white flesh and a clear, sweet liquid (**coconut milk**).

cocoon (kŏ **kōōn**) *n.* the silky casing spun round itself by an insect larva, inside which it undergoes transformation into its adult form.

cod (kod) *n.* **cod** a large edible white fish.

code (kōd) *n.* **1** a system of words, letters, or symbols, used in place of those really intended, for secrecy or brevity. **2** in computing, a set of programming instructions. **3** a set of principles of behaviour.

● Codes using letters of the alphabet can usually be broken by experts because they know that some letters of the alphabet occur more often than others. In English *e, t, a,* and *o* are the commonest letters.

● **Cody, William**. See **Buffalo Bill**

coelacanth (**sē** lå kanth) *n.* a primitive fish believed extinct till a live specimen was found in 1938.

coffee (**kof** i) *n.* a tropical shrub whose roasted and ground seeds (beans) are used to make a drink.

coffer (**kof** ẽr) *n.* a large chest.

coffin (**kof** in) *n.* a box in which to bury or cremate a corpse.

cog (kog) *n.* one of a series of teeth on the edge of a wheel which turns a wheel with another series of teeth.

coherent (kō **hēr** ẽnt) *adj.* **1** logically and clearly developed; consistent: *His argument was coherent.* **2** speaking intelligibly. – *n.* **coherence**.

coil (koil) *vb.* **coiling, coiled** to wind round and round in loops to forms rings or a spiral: *After watering the garden Tom coiled up the hosepipe.* – *n.* something looped into a spiral.

coin (koin) *n.* a small stamped piece of metal used as money.

coinage *n.* the official currency of a country.

coincide (kō in **sīd**) *vb.* **coinciding, coincided** **1** to happen at the same time. **2** to agree: *Your ideas coincide with mine.*

coincidence (kō **in** si dêns) *n.* the combination of events happening by chance: *It was a coincidence that Terry was wearing the same tie as Duncan.*

coke (kōk) *n.* the solid fuel left after gases have been extracted from coal.

cold (kōld) *adj.* **1** having a low temperature; not hot or warm. **2** unfriendly: *He is always cold to me.* – *n.* **1** lack of heat or warmth; cold weather. **2** an illness of the nose and throat, with running nose, sneezing, coughing, etc.: *She caught a cold.* – *n.* **coldness**.

cold-blooded *adj.* (of fish, reptiles, etc.) having a body temperature that varies with that of the environment.

● **Coleridge, Samuel Taylor** (1772-1834) was an English Romantic poet. He wrote *The Ancient Mariner.*

coliseum (ko li **sē** ŭm) *n.* a large stadium or amphitheatre for entertainment.

collaborate (kŏ **lab** ŏ rāt) *vb.* **collaborating, collaborated** to work together with others on something: *Both classes collaborated on the science project.* – *n.* **collaboration**.

collage (ko **läzh**) *n.* a design or picture made by pasting pieces of paper or cloth, or parts of photographs, etc. to a background surface.

collapse (kŏ **laps**) *vb.* **collapsing, collapsed** **1** to fall, give way, or cave in: *The bridge collapsed in the storm.* **2** to drop exhausted or

The Colosseum in Rome was a giant sports stadium holding over 50,000 people. It was started in AD 72. A sheet or awning could be put over the spectators to protect them from the Sun or bad weather. The arena (floor) was used for gladiatorial combats and could be flooded for sea battles.

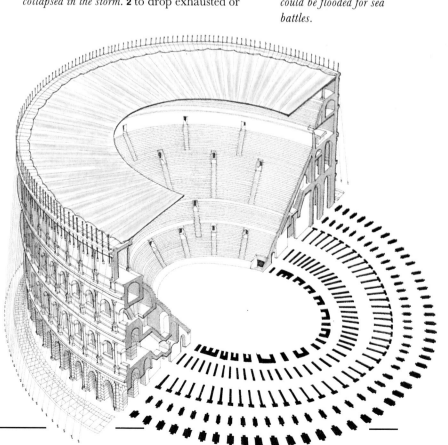

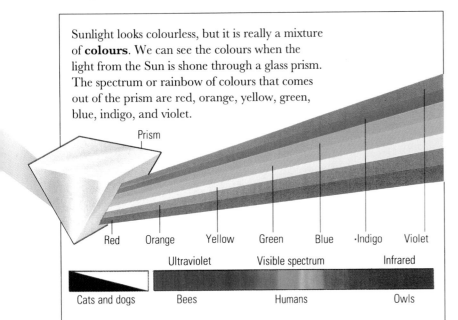

Sunlight looks colourless, but it is really a mixture of **colours**. We can see the colours when the light from the Sun is shone through a glass prism. The spectrum or rainbow of colours that comes out of the prism are red, orange, yellow, green, blue, indigo, and violet.

Prism

Red   Orange   Yellow   Green   Blue   ·Indigo   Violet

Ultraviolet   Visible spectrum   Infrared

Cats and dogs   Bees   Humans   Owls

Not all animals can see light from the same part of the spectrum.

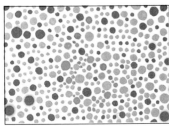

People who are colour-blind cannot tell some colours apart. If your colour vision is normal you should be able to see the number 6.

The three 'primary colours' when mixing light are red, green, and blue. Added together these primary colours make white light; but they can be mixed in such a way as to give virtually any other colour.

The 'primary colours' of paint or the primary pigment colours are red, yellow, and blue, or more accurately, magenta, yellow, and cyan. All three added together make brown, or they can be mixed in such a way as to make all other colours.

helpless: *The hikers collapsed in the heat.* **3** to break down emotionally. **4** to fold up compactly for storage or space-saving: *The camp bed collapses into a small space.*

collar (**ko** lår) *n.* **1** a band or flap round the neck of a garment; the neck of a garment: *There is a mark on your shirt collar.* **2** a band worn round the neck by a dog, etc.
  collarbone *n.* either of two bones linking the shoulder-blades to the breastbone.
colleague (**ko** lēg) *n.* a fellow worker.
collect (kŏ **lekt**) *vb.* **collecting, collected 1** to bring or come together; to gather; to accumulate: *The boys collected nuts from the trees.* **2** to build up an assortment of things of a particular type: *collect stamps.* **3** to call for; to fetch; to pick up: *We'll collect you after the show.*
  collection *n.* an accumulated assortment of things of a particular type: *He has a remarkable postcard collection.*
college (**ko** lij) *n.* a place (not a university) providing further education.
collide (kŏ **līd**) *vb.* **colliding, collided** to crash into: *The motorbike collided into the wall.*
collie (**ko** li) *n.* a long-haired kind of sheepdog.
colliery *n.* **collieries** a coalmine with its buildings.
collision (kŏ **li** zhŏn) *n.* a crash.
colloquial (kŏ **lō** kwi ål) *adj.* words used in conversation rather than in formal speech.

● **Colombia**. See Supplement, **Countries**.

colon[1] (**kō** lon) *n.* a punctuation mark (:), used to introduce a list or an example.
colon[2] (**kō** lon) *n.* the large intestine.
colonel (**kûr** nĕl) *n.* an army officer, in charge of a regiment, below a brigadier in rank.
colonize or **colonise** (**ko** lŏ nīz) *vb.* **colonizing, colonized** to establish a colony.
colony (**ko** lŏ ni) *n.* **colonies 1** a settlement abroad controlled by the founding country; the settlers living there. **2** a group of animals, birds, etc. of one type living together.

● **Colorado**. See Supplement, **USA**.

colossal (kŏ **los** ål) *adj.* huge; vast.
colour (**ku** lŏr) *n.* **1** red, blue, green, etc. **2** a property that surfaces have when light falls on them and is reflected or absorbed: *The colour of a clear sky is blue.* **3** a colouring substance, especially paint. – *vb.* **colouring, coloured**

1 to put colour on; to paint or dye. **2** to influence: *Don't allow your feelings to colour your judgement.* – **off colour** (*colloquial*) unwell.
colour-blind *adj.* unable to distinguish certain colours. – *n.* **colour-blindness**.
colourful *adj.* **1** full of bright colour. **2** lively.
primary colour *n.* in the light spectrum, any of the colours red, green, or blue; in pigments, any of the colours red, blue, and yellow.
colt (kōlt) *n.* See **Horse terms**.

● **Columbus, Christopher** (1451-1506) was a Genoese sailor and explorer who discovered AMERICA for SPAIN in 1492 while seeking a westward route to the Spice Islands of the Indies.

column (ko lŭm) *n.* **1** in architecture, a usually cylindrical pillar with a base and capital. **2** something similarly shaped: *A column of smoke rose from the chimney.* **3** a vertical row of numbers: *He added up the column of figures.* **4** a vertical strip of print on a newspaper page; a regular section in a newspaper.
columnist (ko lŭm nist) *n.* a person writing a regular section of a newspaper.

● **Comanche** (kǒ **man** chē), a NATIVE AMERICAN tribe, now in Oklahoma, were skilled horseriders and buffalo hunters.

comb (kōm) *n.* **1** a rigid toothed object for tidying and arranging hair. **2** the fleshy crest on the head of some cock birds.
combat (**kom** bat) *n.* fighting; a struggle. – *vb.* **combating, combated** to fight against.
combine (kǒm **bīn**) *vb.* **combining, combined** to join together; to unite: *Trudi combined the blue and yellow to make green.*
combination *n.* two or more things, people, etc. combined; the resulting mixture or union: *He and his brother make a good combination.*
combine harvester *n.* an agricultural vehicle equipped both to reap and thresh a crop.
combustion (kǒm **bus** chǒn) *n.* the process of catching fire and burning: *An internal combustion engine runs by burning petrol.*
come (kum) *vb.* **coming, came** (kām), **come 1** to move in the direction of the speaker or hearer. **2** to reach a place; to arrive. **3** to form an opinion, etc.: *She came to the conclusion it was a good idea.* **4** to meet with: *I hope they don't come to any harm.* **5** to extend to or reach a level or standard. **6** to total: *That comes to £20.* **7** to

On the first of his four voyages Columbus discovered the Bahamas and went on to explore Cuba.

The Niña, the Pinta, and the Santa Maria set sail for the New World in August 1492.

have as a source or place of origin: *Where does he come from?* **8** to happen: *How did he come to hurt himself?* **9** to turn out: *His wish came true.*
– *vb.* **come along 1** to progress; to improve. **2** to hurry up. – *vb.* **come back** to be recalled to mind: *It's all coming back to me now.* – *vb.* **come through** to survive.
comedian (kǒ **mē** di ǎn) *n.* an entertainer who tells jokes, performs comic sketches, etc.
comedy (**ko** mi di) *n.* **comedies** an amusing play or film with a happy ending.
comet (**ko** mit) *n.* a heavenly body with a tail-like trail, travelling around the Sun.

● The tail of a comet always points away from the Sun. The head is a frozen ball of ice, dust, and chunks of rock. The most famous comet is Halley's comet, seen by WILLIAM the Conqueror, which returns to Earth every 76 or 77 years. It is due to return in 2062.

A comet tail is so fine that a rocket can pass through it unharmed. Comets are believed to be left-over particles from the beginning of the solar system.

> COME, COME
> A phrasal verb is a verb combined with an adverb or with a preposition: come about; come across; come along; come back; come down; come from; come in; come into; come off; come out; come round; come through; come together; come up; come under.

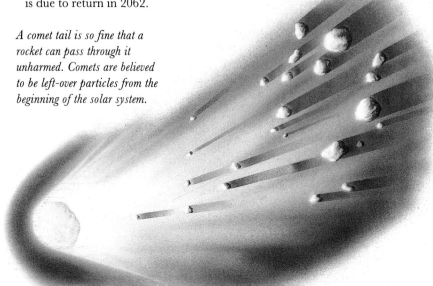

The Commonwealth of Independent States (CIS) was formed in 1991 as an attempt to preserve a loosely unified association of independent ex-Soviet republics, following the break-up of the Soviet Union. At over 17 million square kilometres, Russia is the world's biggest country by area.

comfort (**kum** fŏrt) *n.* **1** a pleasant feeling of physical and mental contentedness or wellbeing. **2** a person or thing that provides such relief or consolation: *My dog is a great comfort when I'm left on my own.* – *vb.* **comforting, comforted** to console.

comfortable (**kum** fŏr tå bėl) *adj.* **1** in a state of physical wellbeing; at ease. **2** providing comfort: *This is a comfortable bed.*

comic (**ko** mik) *adj.* amusing; funny. – *n.* **1** a comedian. **2** a magazine containing stories told through a series of pictures. **comical** *adj.* funny; amusing; humorous.

comma (**ko** må) *n.* a punctuation mark (,) indicating a break in a sentence.

command (kŏ **mand**) *vb.* **commanding, commanded** **1** to order formally. **2** to have authority over. – *n.* **1** an order. **2** control; charge: *He is second in command.* **3** knowledge of: *Her command of the Italian language is second to none.* **4** an instruction to a computer.

commence (kŏ **mens**) *vb.* **commencing, commenced** to begin.

comment (**ko** ment) *n.* **1** a remark or observation, especially a critical one. **2** talk or discussion: *The teacher made some kind comments about our homework.* – *vb.* **commenting, commented** to make observations.

commerce (**ko** mûrs) *n.* the buying and selling of goods and services; trade, banking etc.

commercial (kŏ **mûr** shål) *adj.* relating to commerce, business, or trade. – *n.* a radio or television advertisement.

commit (kŏ **mit**) *vb.* **committing, committed** **1** to carry out or perform a crime, error, etc. **2** to promise to do something.

committee (kŏ **mit** ē) *n.* (*singular* or *plural*) a group of people selected from a larger body, e.g. a club, to do certain work on its behalf.

commodity (kŏ **mod** i ti) *n.* **commodities** something that is bought and sold, especially raw materials.

common (**ko** mŏn) *adj.* **1** happening often; frequent; familiar: *Lochs are common in Scotland.* **2** shared by two or more people, things, etc.: *characteristics common to both animals.* **common sense** *n.* practical good sense: *It's common sense to wash a wound.*

commonplace (**ko** mŏn plās) *adj.* ordinary.

commonwealth (**ko** mŏn welth) *n.* an association of states that have joined together for their common good.

● **Commonwealth** an association of over 50 countries, some large like AUSTRALIA, CANADA, INDIA, and NIGERIA, others tiny like the island of Nauru. The Commonwealth stands for friendship and co-operation between its peoples, once part of the British Empire. Queen ELIZABETH is head of the Commonwealth.

● **Commonwealth of Independent States** is formed mainly of what was the Union of Soviet Socialist Republics. There were 15 republics, which are now separate countries.

COMMONWEALTH OF INDEPENDENT STATES

State	Capital
ARMENIA	Yerevan
AZERBAIJAN	Baku
BELARUS	Minsk
ESTONIA	Tallinn
GEORGIA	Tbilisi
KAZAKHSTAN	Almaty
KYRGYZSTAN	Bishkek
LATVIA	Riga
LITHUANIA	Vilnius
MOLDOVA	Chisinau
RUSSIA	Moscow
TAJIKISTAN	Dushanbe
TURK-MENISTAN	Ashgabot
UKRAINE	Kiev
UZBEKISTAN	Tashkent

commotion (ko̊ **mō** sho̊n) *n.* a disturbance; an upheaval: *The scuffle caused a commotion.*

communicate (ko̊ **mūn** i kāt) *vb.* **communicating, communicated** to make something known; to exchange information. **communication** *n.* **1** the exchanging or giving of ideas and information, etc. **2** (in *plural*) the systems involved in sending information, etc. especially by electronic means or radio waves.

communism (**ko** mū ni ze̊m) *n.* a political doctrine which believes private property should be abolished, and land, factories, etc. owned and controlled by the people. – *n. & adj.* **communist**.

community (ko̊ **mūn** i ti) *n.* **communities** the group of people living in a particular locality: *There is a large black community in Bradford.*

commute (ko̊ **mūt**) *vb.* **commuting, commuted** to travel regularly between home and work. – *n.* **commuter**.

● **Comoros**. See Supplement, **Countries**.

compact (ko̊m **pakt**) *adj.* **1** firm and dense in form or texture. **2** small, but with all essentials neatly contained; taking up little space: *My computer is very compact.* – *vb.* **compacting, compacted** to compress.

compact disc *n.* a plastic disc containing digitally stored information or music, played on a special machine (**compact-disc player**) using a laser beam.

Pits –
measuring only
0.5 micrometres wide –
in the surface of a compact
disc carry information
which is read by a laser
beam. The pulses of
information are changed
back into the original sound.

Pits containing digital information

Lenses and mirrors reflect a laser beam off the disc's surface.

companion (ko̊m **pan** yo̊n) *n.* a friend.

company (**kum** på ni) *n.* **companies 1** the presence of another person or other people; guests or visitors. **2** a business organization.

comparative (ko̊m **pa** rå tiv) *adj.* **1** as compared with others: *This show is a comparative success.* **2** as observed by comparing one another: *We discussed their comparative strengths.* – *n.* a comparative adjective or adverb, as in *This book is* **smaller** *than that book* and *Peg runs* **faster** *than Rana.*

compare (ko̊m **pār**) *vb.* **comparing, compared** to examine things of the same kind to see what differences there are: *Mary compared Mark's handwriting with Sam's.*

comparison (ko̊m **pa** ri so̊n) *n.* an act of, or a reasonable basis for, comparing: *There can be no comparison between them.*

compartment (ko̊m **pärt** me̊nt) *n.* a separated section: *The drawer has a secret compartment.*

compass (**kum** på̊s) *n.* **1** an instrument for direction-finding containing a dial marked with 32 points, with a magnetic needle that always points to magnetic north. **2** (often in *plural*) an instrument consisting of two hinged legs, for drawing circles, etc.

compatible (kom **pat** i be̊l) *adj.* See **Computer terms**.

compel (ko̊m **pel**) *vb.* **compelling, compelled** to force: *The storm compelled us to take shelter.* **compelling** *adj.* irresistibly fascinating.

compensate (ko̊m **pe̊n** sāt) *vb.* **compensating, compensated 1** to pay someone for an injury, etc. **2** to make up for a loss, disadvantage, etc. **compensation** *n.* a sum of money given to make up for loss or injury.

compete (ko̊m **pēt**) *vb.* **competing, competed 1** to take part in a contest.

competent (kom **pe̊** te̊nt) *adj.* **1** efficient. **2** having sufficient skill to do something.

competition (kom pe̊ **ti** sho̊n) *n.* **1** an event in which people compete to find out who is best at something. **2** rivals, e.g. in business.

competitive (ko̊m **pet** i tiv) *adj.* **1** involving rivalry. **2** enjoying rivalry; aggressive; ambitious: *Jackie is highly competitive. She wants to be a success.* – *n.* **competitiveness**.

competitor (ko̊m **pet** i to̊r) *n.* a person, team, firm, or product that competes; a rival.

complacent (ko̊m **plā** se̊nt) *adj.* self-satisfied.

Companion comes from Latin words meaning 'with' and 'bread', so producing a word meaning 'one who eats bread with another'.

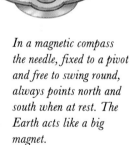

In a magnetic compass the needle, fixed to a pivot and free to swing round, always points north and south when at rest. The Earth acts like a big magnet.

complain (kŏm **plān**) *vb.* **complaining, complained 1** to express that you are not satisfied or pleased: *Dad complained when the plane was late.* **2** to say that you are suffering from: *Tina complained of having toothache.*

complement (**kom** pli mĕnt) *n.* something that completes, perfects, or goes well with: *The music is a complement to the mood of the movie.*

complete (kŏm **plēt**) *adj.* **1** whole; finished; with nothing missing: *The jigsaw is complete.* **2** thorough; absolute; total. – *vb.* **completing, completed** to finish. – *n.* **completion.**

complex (**kom** pleks) *adj.* **1** composed of many interrelated parts: *A motor car is a complex machine.* **2** complicated: *a complex problem.*

complexion (kŏm **plek** shŏn) *n.* the colour of the skin, especially of the face.

complicate (**kom** pli kāt) *vb.* **complicating, complicated** to make complex.

compliment (**kom** pli mĕnt) *n.* an expression of admiration or approval. – (**kom** pli ment) *vb.* **complimenting, complimented** to congratulate; to pay a compliment to. **complimentary** *adj.* **1** admiring or approving. **2** given free: *complimentary tickets.*

compose (kŏm **pōz**) *vb.* **composing, composed 1** to create music; to write a poem, letter, article, etc. **2** to make up or constitute: *The school is composed of several classes.* **composed** *adj.* calm; controlled. **composer** *n.* someone who composes music.

composition (kom pŏ **zi** shŏn) *n.* **1** something composed, especially a musical or literary work. **2** what something consists of.

compound (**kom** pownd) *n.* **1** in chemistry, a substance made up of the atoms of two or more elements. **2** something made up of two or more parts: *Flies have compound eyes.*

comprehend (kom pri **hend**) *vb.* **comprehending, comprehended** to understand.

comprehensible (kom pri **hen** si bĕl) *adj.* capable of being understood.

comprehensive (kom pri **hen** siv) *adj.* **1** covering or including everything or a great deal. **2** (of a school) providing teaching for children of all abilities between the ages of 11 and 18. – *n.* a comprehensive school.

compress (kŏm **pres**) *vb.* **compressing, compressed** to press together or squeeze.

comprise (kŏm **prīz**) *vb.* **comprising, comprised** to contain, include, or consist of: *The magazine comprises text and pictures.*

compromise (**kom** prŏ mīz) *n.* something agreed on after each side has given up claims or demands.

compulsory (kŏm **pul** sŏ ri) *adj.* required by the rules, law, etc.; obligatory.

computer (kŏm **pūt** ĕr) *n.* an electronic machine that can quickly process, store, analyse, and retrieve data.

concave (kon **kāv**) *adj.* a surface that curves inwards: *The inside of a cup is concave.*

conceal (kŏn **sēl**) *vb.* **concealing, concealed** to hide: *The ugly fuse box is concealed by a curtain.*

concede (kŏn **sēd**) *vb.* **conceding, conceded** to admit to be true or correct.

concentrate (kon **sĕn** trāt) *vb.* **concentrating, concentrated 1** to give all your attention and energy to something. **2** to bring or come together in one place: *Coalmines are concentrated in the north of the country.* **3** to make a liquid stronger by removing water or other diluting substance from it. **concentration** *n.* intensive mental effort: *It takes all Mary's concentration to play bridge.*

concept (**kon** sept) *n.* an abstract or general idea.

conception (kŏn **sep** shŏn) *n.* **1** the idea you have of something. **2** the fertilization in the womb of a female egg by the male sperm.

concern (kŏn **sûrn**) *vb.* **concerning, concerned 1** to have to do with; to be about: *It concerns your son.* **2** to worry, bother, or interest: *Matt's illness concerns his wife a lot.* – *n.* a cause of worry; a subject of interest. **concerned** *adj.* worried. **concerning** *prep.* about; regarding.

concert (**kon** sĕrt) *n.* a musical performance given before an audience by singers or players.

concerto (kŏn **cher** tō) *n.* **concertos** a musical composition for one or more solo instruments and orchestra.

concise (kŏn **sīz**) *adj.* brief, but covering essential points. – *n.* **conciseness.**

conclude (kŏn **klōōd**) *vb.* **concluding, concluded 1** to come or bring to an end. **2** to reach an opinion after thinking about it: *Joe concluded his Dad was right after all.*

conclusion (kŏn **klōō** zhŏn) *n.* **1** an end. **2** an opinion based on reasoning: *My advice helped him come to a conclusion.*

conclusive (kŏn **klōō** siv) *adj.* decisive: *The evidence is conclusive, she is innocent.*

concourse (**kon** kŏrs) *n.* a large open area for people, in a railway station, airport, etc.

| PRONUNCIATION GUIDE |
fat a	all ŏ
fate ā	foot oo
fast ä	moon ōō
among å	boy oi
met e	house ow
mean ē	demon ŏ
silent ĕ	thing th
loch hh	this Th
fin i	but u
line ī	mute ū
quick kw	fur û
got o	brochure ŭ
note ō	vision zh

Computers are used all around us – when we buy goods from a supermarket, draw money out of a bank, or book a holiday computers help. Small personal computers are used in schools, homes, factories, and offices. The main ability of computers is to do a lot of basic tasks quickly and accurately. The 'computer revolution' began in the 1940s with room-sized machines, the ancestors of our laptop personal computers.

Mainframe computer

Charles Babbage (1792-1871) spent much of his life developing calculating machines. He is respected as a computing pioneer born before his time.

Laptop computer

Pocket calculator

Early computers – mainframes – such as the American ENIAC (Electronic Numerical Integrator And Computer) of 1946 needed whole rooms to contain them. In the 1970s electronic equipment was miniaturized.

The output from a computer can be a visual display on a screen or printed paper.

Printer

Disk

Disk drive

Screen

The four basic parts of a computer: input, processing, memory, and output. It also needs a program – instructions telling the processing unit how to do different tasks.

The machinery and electronics (keyboard, disk drives, printer) are the hardware. Software progams stored on disks tell the computer what to do.

Keyboard

Mouse   Across

A mouse is a simple hand-controller. By moving the mouse you direct the cursor about the screen.

INPUT   PROGRAM

PROCESSING   MEMORY

OUTPUT

Down

COMPUTER TERMS
ASCII short for American Standard Code for Information Interchange, a system of codes to represent letters and numbers.
backup a copy of a file.
BASIC Beginner's All-purpose Symbolic Instruction Code, a programming language.
bit Binary DigIT: 0 or 1.
bug a program error.
compatible (of) a computer or program able to work with another computer.
data information given to, stored in, and operated on a computer.
disk a flat metal disc on which data is stored.
drive part of a computer that transfers information to disks and reads from them.
file a collection of data.
program a sequence of instructions.
RAM Random Access Memory. What is stored on this is lost when the computer is turned off.
ROM Read Only Memory, the computer's permanent memory.
software a program for use in a computer.

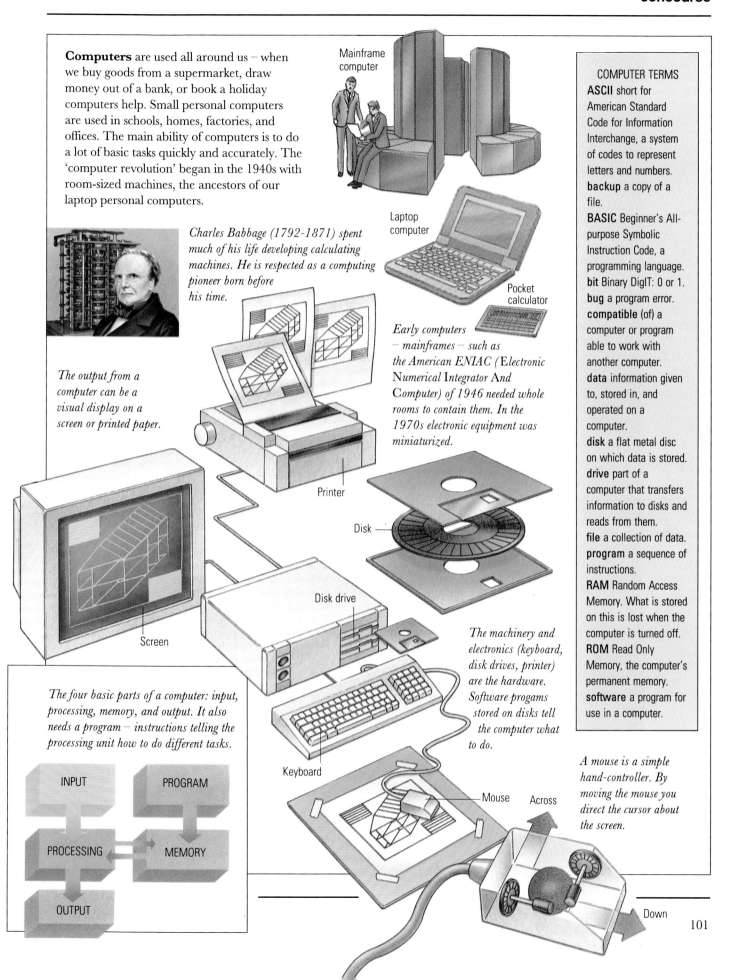

The 20th century has seen widespread use of reinforced concrete in building. One example is the Habitat scheme (above) designed in 1967.

To make the sections of the Habitat scheme, concrete was poured around reinforcing mesh in moulds, and left to dry and harden.

concrete (**kon** krēt) *n.* a building material made by mixing cement, sand, gravel, and water. – *adj.* **1** made of concrete. **2** able to be felt, touched, seen, etc.: *concrete objects.*

condemn (kŏn **dem**) *vb.* **condemning, condemned 1** to say that something is wrong or evil. **2** to find guilty; to convict.

condense (kŏn **dens**) *vb.* **condensing, condensed 1** to compress; to make denser: *This story has been condensed from a novel.* **2** to turn from gas or vapour to liquid or solid: *Steam condenses to water as it cools.*
  condensation *n.* condensed water vapour.

condition (kŏn **di** shŏn) *n.* **1** a particular state. **2** a state of health, or suitability for use: *He is overweight and out of condition.* **3** a disorder: *He has a heart condition.* **4** (in *plural*) circumstances: *You shouldn't have to suffer poor working conditions.* **5** a qualification.

condom (**kon** dŏm) *n.* a thin rubber sheath worn on the penis as a contraceptive, and to prevent the spread of disease.

condor (**kon** dŏr) *n.* a large South American vulture: *Condors eat the meat of dead animals.*

The Andean condor is the world's largest flying bird. It can reach heights of over 4000 metres, gliding upwards in rising air currents.

conduct (kŏn **dukt**) *vb.* **conducting, conducted 1** to lead or guide. **2** to direct an orchestra or choir. **3** to transmit heat or electricity: *Metal conducts heat.* – (**kon** dukt) *n.* behaviour: *Try to be on your best conduct.*

conductor (kŏn **duk** tŏr) *n.* **1** the director of a choir or orchestra. **2** a material, etc. that conducts heat or electricity, e.g. copper wires.

cone (kōn) *n.* **1** in geometry, a solid figure that has a round base and ends in a point. **2** the oval fruit of a coniferous tree, made up of overlapping woody scales.

confer (kŏn **fûr**) *vb.* **conferring, conferred 1** to consult together. **2** to give an honour: *The Queen conferred a medal on the brave policewoman.*

conference (**kon** fĕ rĕns) *n.* a formal meeting.

confess (kŏn **fes**) *vb.* **confessing, confessed 1** to own up to a fault, wrongdoing, etc. **2** to tell your sins to a priest.
  confession *n.* the admission of a sin, fault, etc.

confide (kŏn **fīd**) *vb.* **confiding, confided** to speak about personal matters to someone you trust: *Hamish always confides in his mother.*

confidence (**kon** fi dĕns) *n.* **1** trust in a person or thing. **2** faith in your own ability.
  confident *adj.* sure: *I'm confident of success.*

confidential (kon fi **den** shăl) *adj.* secret: *The Prime Minister gets all confidential information.*

confine (kŏn **fīn**) *vb.* **confining, confined 1** to restrict; to limit. **2** to keep prisoner.
  confined *adj.* narrow; restricted.

confirm (kŏn **fûrm**) *vb.* **confirming, confirmed 1** to prove correct. **2** to support or prove: *The actress refused to confirm or deny the rumour.* **3** to accept someone into full membership of the Christian Church.

confiscate (**kon** fis kāt) *vb.* **confiscating, confiscated** to take away something from someone, as a penalty. – *n.* **confiscation.**

conflict (**kon** flikt) *n.* **1** disagreement; fierce argument; a quarrel. **2** a fight, battle, or war. – (kŏn **flikt**) *vb.* **conflicting, conflicted** to be incompatible or in opposition: *The demands of a career often conflict with those of family life.*

confluence (**kon** floo ĕns) *n.* the place where one river flows into another.

conform (kŏn **fôrm**) *vb.* **conforming, conformed** to obey rules, etc.

confront (kŏn **frunt**) *vb.* **confronting, confronted 1** to face defiantly or accusingly:

He confronted his tormentors. **2** to deal firmly with: *Let's confront the problem.*

● **Confucianism** (kǒn **fū** shån izm) is the teachings of the Chinese philosopher *Confucius* (551-479 BC), with emphasis on morality, consideration for others, obedience, and good education.

confuse (kǒn **fūz**) *vb.* **confusing, confused 1** to put into a muddle or mess. **2** to fail to distinguish: *Jan confuses 'conker' with 'conquer'.*

confusion (kǒn **fū** zhǒn) *n.* disorder; muddle.

congested (kǒn **jest** id) *adj.* **1** crowded. **2** (of the nose) blocked with mucus. – *n.* **congestion.**

● **Congo.** See Supplement, **Countries.**

congratulate (kǒn **grat** ū lāt) *vb.* **congratulating, congratulated** to express your pleasure at someone's success. – *n.* **congratulation.** – *adj.* **congratulatory.**

congregate (kong gri gāt) *vb.* **congregating, congregated** to come together in a crowd. **congregation** *n.* a gathering or assembly of people, especially for worship in church.

congress (kong gres) **1** a large meeting gathered to discuss something. **2 Congress** a name used for the law-making body in some countries, especially the Congress of the UNITED STATES. – *adj.* **congressional.**

conifer (ko ni fěr) or (kō ni fěr) *n.* a tree that bears cones, such as pines and larches.

conjure (kun jǔr) *vb.* **conjuring, conjured** to perform tricks that deceive the eye, by skilful use of the hands. **conjurer** or **conjuror** *n.* an entertainer who conjures.

connect (kǒ **nekt**) *vb.* **connecting, connected 1** to join; to link: *Connect the plug to the wire.* **2** to associate or involve: *They are connected with advertising.* **connection** or **connexion** *n.* **1** a link: *There is a strong connection between smoking and heart disease.* **2** a relationship. **3** an influential contact.

● **Connecticut** (kǒ **ne** ti kǔt). See Supplement, **USA.**

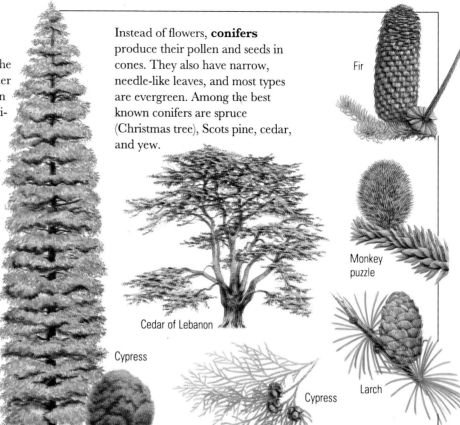

Instead of flowers, **conifers** produce their pollen and seeds in cones. They also have narrow, needle-like leaves, and most types are evergreen. Among the best known conifers are spruce (Christmas tree), Scots pine, cedar, and yew.

Fir

Monkey puzzle

Cedar of Lebanon

Cypress

Cypress

Larch

conquer (kong kěr) *vb.* **conquering, conquered 1** to gain possession over territory by force: *In 1066 the Normans conquered England.* **2** to defeat. – *n.* **conqueror.**

conquest (kong kwest) *n.* **1** the act of conquering. **2** a conquered territory.

● **Conrad, Joseph** (1857-1924) was a Polish novelist who wrote in English after a career at sea. His works include *Lord Jim.*

conscience (kon shěns) *n.* a feeling about what is right and wrong that guides your behaviour: *I have a clear conscience.*

conscientious (kon shi en shǔs) *adj.* careful; thorough; painstaking.

conscious (kon shǔs) *adj.* **1** awake and aware of your surroundings. **2** deliberate: *She made a conscious effort to be polite.*

consecutive (kǒn **sek** ū tiv) *adj.* following one after the other.

consent (kǒn **sent**) *vb.* **consenting, consented** to agree. – *n.* permission.

consequence (kon si kwěns) *n.* something that follows from an action.

PRONUNCIATION GUIDE	
fat a	all ö
fate ā	foot oo
fast ä	moon ōo
among å	boy oi
met e	house ow
mean ē	demon ǒ
silent ě	thing th
loch hh	this Th
fin i	but u
line ī	mute ū
quick kw	fur û
got o	brochure ů
note ō	vision zh

Over the last 30 years we have become aware of the damage we do to the environment. International agreements now exist to protect endangered species and to preserve their habitats. The map shows countries with agreements to protect United Nations World Heritage Sites and Wetlands of International Importance.

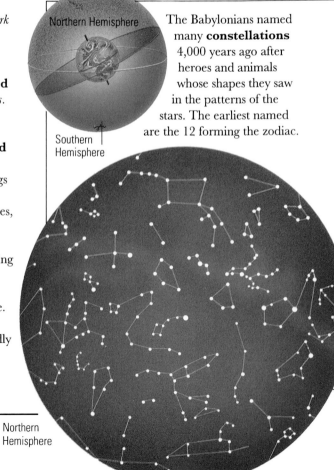

World Heritage Sites Protected

Wetlands of International Importance Protected

Wetlands and World Heritage Sites Protected

conservation (kon sĕr **vā** shŏn) *n.* the preservation and protection of wildlife, etc.

conservative (kŏn **sûrv** å tiv) *adj.* **1** favouring what is established or traditional; disliking change. **2** restrained; not flamboyant. **3 Conservative** relating to the Conservative Party, the right-wing political party in the United Kingdom, supporting private ownership of industry.

conserve (kŏn **sûrv**) *vb.* **conserving, conserved** to keep safe from damage or loss.

consider (kŏn **sid** ĕr) *vb.* **considering, considered** to think about carefully; to look at thoughtfully.

considerable (kŏn **sid** ĕr å bĕl) *adj.* large; great: *There is still a considerable amount of work to do.* – *adv.* **considerably**.

considerate (kŏn **sid** ĕr åt) *adj.* careful and thoughtful to others.

consist (kŏn **sist**) *vb.* **consisting, consisted** to be made up of: *A week consists of seven days.*

consistent (kŏn **sis** tĕnt) *adj.* unchanging, reliable, regular, steady. – *n.* **consistency**.

console¹ (kŏn **sōl**) *vb.* **consoling, consoled** to comfort, in distress grief.
consolation *n.* a person or thing that brings you comfort.

console² (**kon** sōl) *n.* a panel of dials, switches, etc. for operating an electronic machine.

consonant (**kon** sŏ nånt) *n.* a letter representing a sound you make by obstructing the passage of the breath in any of several ways; not a vowel.

conspicuous (kŏn **spik** ū ůs) *adj.* noticeable.

conspire (kŏn **spīr**) *vb.* **conspiring, conspired** to plot secretly together especially for an unlawful purpose.

constable (**kun** stå bĕl) or (**kon** stå bĕl) *n.* a policeman or policewoman.

●**Constable, John** (1776-1837) was an English landscape painter. His works include *The Haywain* and *Salisbury Cathedral*.

constant (**kon** stånt) *adj.* **1** never stopping. **2** unchanging: *Her temperature is now constant.*

●**Constantinople**, formerly Istanbul, TURKEY, was named after the emperor Constantine in AD 330 and was capital of the Byzantine Empire.

constellation (kon stĕ **lā** shŏn) *n.* a group of stars having a name.

Northern Hemisphere

Southern Hemisphere

The Babylonians named many **constellations** 4,000 years ago after heroes and animals whose shapes they saw in the patterns of the stars. The earliest named are the 12 forming the zodiac.

Northern Hemisphere

constitute (**kon** sti tūt) *vb.* **constituting, constituted** to go together to make: *Children constituted the main part of the audience.*

constitution (kon sti **tū** shǒn) *n.* **1** a set of rules governing an organization. **2** the way in which something is made up. – *adj.* **constitutional**.

● The United States Constitution, the supreme law of the land, was written in 1787 at a convention held in Philadelphia. The 55 delegates attending became known as the Founding Fathers. It sets out a federal system of government. It states that the UNITED STATES is a republic with a president elected by the people. There is also a CONGRESS that makes laws, and a SUPREME COURT.

constrict (kǒn **strikt**) *vb.* **constricting, constricted** to enclose tightly, especially too tightly. – *n.* **constriction**.

construct (kǒn **strukt**) *vb.* **constructing, constructed 1** to build. **2** to form, compose. **construction** *n.* **1** the process of building. **2** a building. – *adj.* **constructional**. **constructive** *adj.* useful in a positive way: *The talks were most constructive.*

consult (kǒn **sult**) *vb.* **consulting, consulted 1** to ask the advice of: *She consulted a lawyer.* **2** to refer to a map, book, etc. **consultant** *n.* **1** a person who gives professional advice. **2** a senior hospital doctor.

consume (kǒn **sūm**) *vb.* **consuming, consumed 1** to eat or drink. **2** to use up. **3** to destroy: *The fire consumed the office block.*

consumption (kǒn **sump** shǒn) *n.* the amount consumed: *Mopeds have a low petrol consumption.*

contact (**kon** takt) *n.* **1** touching physically. **2** a means of communication. – (**kon** takt) or (kǒn **takt**) *vb.* **contacting, contacted** to get in touch with.

contain (kǒn **tān**) *vb.* **containing, contained 1** to hold or have: *The art gallery contains fine paintings.* **2** to control or prevent the spread of: *The fire-fighters managed to contain the blaze.* **container** *n.* a box, tin, carton, etc.

contaminate (kǒn **tam** i nāt) *vb.* **contaminating, contaminated** to make impure; to pollute or infect; to make radioactive. – *n.* **contamination**.

contemporary (kǒn **tem** pǒ rǎ ri) *adj.* **1** belonging to the same period or time; of the same age. **2** modern; present day: *He particularly likes contemporary art.*

contempt (kǒn **tempt**) *n.* scorn; a low opinion.

content[1] (kǒn **tent**) *adj.* satisfied; happy; uncomplaining. – *n.* **contentment**. **contented** *adj.* peacefully happy or satisfied.

content[2] (**kon** tent) *n.* **1** the subject matter of a book, speech, etc. **2** (in *plural*) the things contained in something: *Doug emptied out the contents of his pockets.*

contest (**kon** test) *n.* a competition; a struggle. – *vb.* (kǒn **test**) **contesting, contested 1** to enter a competition. **2** to dispute a decision. **contestant** *n.* a competitor.

NOT DISCONTENTED
If you say that you are 'not discontented' what you really mean is that you are contented. In the same way we might say 'not bad' when we mean 'good' or 'not unlike' when we mean 'like'. This is a not uncommon verbal device known as litotes (līt ǒ tēz), a means of understating what we wish to say.

Southern
Hemisphere

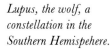

Lupus, the wolf, a constellation in the Southern Hemispehere.

The flag of Australia shows the Southern Cross constellation and the Commonwealth Star. New Zealand's flag displays four stars of the Southern Cross.

Australia

New Zealand

Southern Cross
Constellation

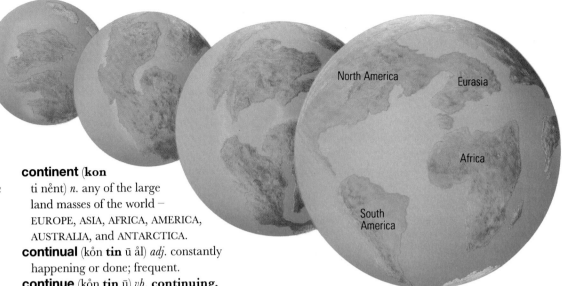

North America
Eurasia
Africa
South America

For a long time scientists have seen that the shapes of Europe, America, and Africa looked as if they could fit together like pieces in a jigsaw. Then in 1912 the idea was put forward of continental drift in which it was suggested that America was once joined to Africa. The illustration shows how over millions of years the single continent we call Pangea broke up to produce the jigsaw of continents we know today.

continent (kon ti něnt) *n.* any of the large land masses of the world – EUROPE, ASIA, AFRICA, AMERICA, AUSTRALIA, and ANTARCTICA.

continual (kǒn **tin** ū ǎl) *adj.* constantly happening or done; frequent.

continue (kǒn **tin** ū) *vb.* **continuing, continued 1** to go on; not to stop: *They continued working all night.* **2** to start again after a break: *We'll continue the lesson later.*

continuous (kǒn **tin** ū ǔs) *adj.* never ceasing; unbroken; uninterrupted: *The noise was continuous, it did not stop for a moment.*

contour (kon tōōr) *n.* **1** (usually in *plural*) the distinctive outline of something **2** (also **contour line**) a line on a map joining points of the same height or depth.

contraceptive (kon trǎ **sep** tiv) *n.* a drug or device that prevents pregnancy.

contract (kon trakt) *n.* a legal agreement setting out terms. – (kǒn **trakt**) *vb.* **contracting, contracted 1** to shrink. **2** (of muscles) to make or become shorter, so as to bend a joint.

contraction *n.* a shortened form of a word or phrase: *'Aren't' is a contraction of 'are not'.*

contradict (kon trǎ **dikt**) *vb.* **contradicting, contradicted 1** to say the opposite of or deny a statement, etc. made by someone else. **2** to disagree or be inconsistent with: *Her two accounts contradict each other.* – *n.* **contradiction.** – *adj.* **contradictory.**

contralto (kǒn **trǎl** tō) *n.* **contraltos** the female singing voice that is lowest in pitch.

contrary *adj.* (**kon** trǎ ri) opposite; quite different; opposed: *My Mum and I have contrary views on bringing up children.*

contrast (kon träst) *n.* **1** difference between things or people that are being compared: *It snowed yesterday – today is warm by contrast.* **2** a

person or thing that is strikingly different from another. – (kǒn **träst**) *vb.* **contrasting, contrasted 1** to compare so as to reveal differences. **2** to show a contrast.

contribute (kǒn **trib** ūt) or (**kon** tri būt) *vb.* **contributing, contributed** to give for some joint purpose: *We contribute money to charity.* – *n.* **contributor.**

contribution *n.* something contributed, e.g. money, or an article for a magazine.

control (kǒn **trōl**) *n.* **1** authority or charge; power to influence or guide: *in control; take control; under control; out of control.* **2** a method of limiting: *The government has imposed strict controls on spending.* **3** (in *plural*) the levers, switches, etc. by which a machine, etc. is operated. – *vb.* **controlling, controlled 1** to have control over: *Please control your dog.* **2** to regulate.

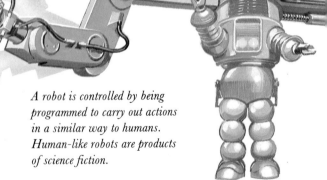

A robot is controlled by being programmed to carry out actions in a similar way to humans. Human-like robots are products of science fiction.

controversy (**kon** trổ vûr si) or (kổn **trov** ẻr si) *n.* **controversies** a disagreement which has existed for a long time. – *adj.* **controversial** (kon trổ **vûr** shẳl).

conundrum (kổ **nun** drủm) *n.* a problem.

conurbation (kon ûr **bā** shổn) *n.* a wide spread built-up area.

convalescent (kon vẳ le sẻnt) *n.* a person recovering from an illness. – *n.* **convalescence**.

convenient (kổn **vēn** i ẻnt) *adj.* fitting in with your plans, etc.: *It will be convenient if you can start work tomorrow morning.*

convent (**kon** vẻnt) *n.* a building where a community of nuns live.

convention (kổn **ven** shổn) *n.* **1** a large conference. **2** a custom.
conventional *adj.* **1** traditional; customary. **2** (of weapons or war) non-nuclear.

conversation (kon vẻr **sā** shổn) *n.* informal talk between people.

converse¹ (kổn **vûrs**) *vb.* **conversing, conversed** to talk informally.

converse² (**kon** vûrs) or (kổn **vûrs**) *adj.* reverse; opposite. – *n.* opposite.

convert (kổn **vûrt**) *vb.* **converting, converted 1** to change in form or function: *We converted the garage into a stable.* **2** to win over to another religion, opinion, etc.

convex (kon **veks**) *adj.* outward-curving, like the surface of the eye.

convey (kổn **vā**) *vb.* **conveying, conveyed 1** to carry; to transport. **2** to communicate: *It is difficult to convey exactly what I mean.*

convict (kổn **vikt**) *vb.* **convicting, convicted** to prove someone guilty of a crime: *The court convicted her of theft.* – (**kon** vikt) *n.* a person serving a prison sentence.

convince (kổn **vins**) *vb.* **convincing, convinced** to persuade: *Peter convinced me that he was telling the truth.* – *adj.* **convincing**.

cook (kook) *vb.* **cooking, cooked** to prepare food by heating.

●**Cook, James** (1728-79) explored the coasts of New Zealand and Australia and was the first to cross the ANTARCTIC CIRCLE.

cool (kool) *adj.* **1** neither very cold nor very warm. **2** lacking enthusiasm; unfriendly: *She gave me a cool response.* – *vb.* **cooling, cooled** to make or become cool. – *n.* **coolness**. – *vb.* **cool off** to calm down.

co-operate (kō op ẻ rāt) *vb.* **co-operating, co-operated** to work or act together. – *n.* **co-operation**.

cope (kōp) *vb.* **coping, coped** to deal with problems, etc. successfully.

●**Copenhagen** is a port and capital of DENMARK.

●**Copernicus** (kổ **pûr** ni kửs), **Nicolaus** (1473-1543) was a Polish scientist. He showed that the Earth is not the centre of the universe and that the Earth itself rotates.

copious (**kō** pi ổs) *adj.* plentiful.

●**Copland** (**kōp** lẳnd), **Aaron** (1900-90) was an American composer who used folk music and jazz in his compositions.

copper (**ko** pẻr) *n.* an element (symbol **Cu**), a brownish-red metal. – *adj.* of the brownish-red colour of copper.

●Copper was one of the first metals to be used. Pure copper is soft, but if mixed with other metals it makes alloys, like brass and bronze, which are better for making tools. It conducts electricity easily and so is used to make electric wires.

coppice (**ko** pis) *n.* a small wood.

Copper comes from the Latin name for Cyprus, *Cyprium*, where copper was first found.

When he reached New Zealand Captain Cook met warlike Maoris with tattooed faces who paddled out to him in their elaborately carved canoes.

One kind of coral island is the atoll, a ringed reef that encloses a central lagoon. The original volcanic island sinks and more coral and sand build up on top of the reef.

copy (**ko** pi) *n.* **copies 1** an imitation or reproduction. **2** one of the many specimens of a book, or of a particular issue of a magazine, newspaper, etc. – *vb.* **copies, copying, copied 1** to imitate: *Jack copies everything his brother does.* **2** to make a copy of.

coral (**ko** răl) *n.* a hard pink, red, or white material made up of the skeletons of tiny sea creatures, and much used in jewellery.

cord (körd) *n.* **1** thin rope or thick string. **2** the cable of an electrical appliance.

corduroy (**kör** dŭ roi) *n.* **1** a thick ribbed cotton fabric. **2** (in *plural*) trousers made of corduroy.

core (kör) *n.* **1** the centre of an apple, etc., containing the seeds. **2** the essential part: *You must try to understand the core of the subject.* **3** the inner part of the Earth. **4** a computer memory.

corgi (**kör** gi) *n.* a small Welsh breed of dog.

cork (körk) *n.* **1** the light outer bark of a Mediterranean tree, the cork oak. **2** a piece of this used as a stopper for a bottle, etc.

corkscrew *n.* a tool with a spiral spike for pulling corks out of bottles.

corn[1] (körn) *n.* cereal plants, especially wheat, oats, or barley, and in North America maize.

corn[2] *n.* (körn) a small patch of hardened skin, especially on a toe.

cornea (**kör** ni ă) *n.* the transparent covering of the eyeball.

corner (**kör** nĕr) *n.* a point or place where lines or surface-edges meet; the inside or outside of the angle so formed.

corolla (**kŏ rol** ă) *n.* the grouping of petals on a flower.

coronation (ko rŏ **nā** shŏn) *n.* the ceremony of crowning a king or queen.

corps (kör) *n.* **corps** (körz) **1** a military section: *the intelligence corps.* **2** people engaged in particular work: *the diplomatic corps.*

corpse (körps) *n.* a dead human being.

corpuscle (**kör** pus ĕl) *n.* a blood cell.

correct (kŏ **rekt**) *vb.* **correcting, corrected 1** to set or put right; to remove errors from. **2** to mark the errors in. **3** to adjust or make better. – *adj.* **1** free from error; accurate. **2** right; proper; appropriate. – *n.* **correctness**.

correction *n.* **1** the act of correcting. **2** an alteration that corrects something.

correspond (ko rĕs **pond**) *vb.* **corresponding, corresponded 1** to be similar or equivalent: *The increase in wages was followed by a corresponding increase in prices.* **2** to exchange letters.

correspondent *n.* **1** a person with whom you exchange letters. **2** a person employed by a newspaper to write reports: *a political correspondent; a sports correspondent.*

corridor (**ko** ri dör) *n.* a passageway, especially one off which rooms open.

corrode (kŏ **rōd**) *vb.* **corroding, corroded** to eat away a material little by little; to rust.

corrosion (kŏ **rō** zhŏn) *n.* the process of corroding. – *adj.* **corrosive**.

corrupt (kŏ **rupt**) *vb.* **corrupting, corrupted 1** to change for the worse, especially morally. **2** to spoil, deform, or make impure. **3** to bribe. **4** to decay or deteriorate. – *adj.* morally evil.

● **Cortés** (**kör** tez), **Hernando** (1485-1547) was a Spanish soldier who conquered the AZTEC Empire in MEXICO.

Hernando Cortés was the best known of the Spanish conquistadors. He was welcomed by Montezuma, the Aztec ruler, and showered with gifts. In return, Cortés plundered the Aztec empire and captured Montezuma.

cosmic (**koz** mik) *adj.* belonging or relating to the universe. – *adv.* **cosmically**.

cosmonaut (**koz** mŏ nöt) *n.* a Russian astronaut.

cost (kost) *vb.* **costing, cost 1** to be obtainable at a certain price: *This car costs a lot of money.* **2** to involve the loss or sacrifice of: *His foolish behaviour at work cost him his job.* – *n.* **1** what something costs. **2** loss or sacrifice. – **at all costs** no matter what the effort may be.

● **Costa Rica**. See Supplement, **Countries**.

costly (**kost** li) *adj.* **costlier, costliest 1** expensive. **2** involving big losses or sacrifices.

Egyptian   Minoan

1640s
England

1920s

Roman

Viking

Costumes in
the ancient world,
like the Roman toga, were based
on the tunic. In Europe in the
Middle Ages the rich alone could
afford fine materials. In the
Renaissance the rich had a taste for
sumptuous fabrics and exaggerated styles.   19th Century

1960s

costume (**kos** tūm) *n.* clothing, especially of a
particular historical period or country.
cot (kot) *n.* a bed with high sides for a child.

●**Côte d'Ivoire** (**Ivory Coast**). See Supplement, **Countries**.

cottage (**ko** tij) *n.* a small house, especially an
old stone one, in a village or the countryside.
cotton (**ko** tŏn) *n.* **1** the soft downy fibres that
cover the seeds of the cotton plant. **2** the plant
itself. **3** thread or cloth made from the fibres.

●The Cotton Belt of the UNITED STATES produces over 15% of the world's cotton. The cotton gin, invented by Eli WHITNEY in 1793
increased production greatly.

couch (kowch) *n.* a sofa or settee.
cougar (**koo** går) *n.* (especially *US*) a puma.

*Cougar is one of the
names of the North
American mountain
lion.*

cough (kof) *vb.* **coughing, coughed** to force
out air, mucus, etc. from the throat or lungs
with a rough sharp noise. – *n.* an act or sound
of coughing.
could (kood) *vb.* (*auxiliary*) **1** *past tense* of **can**: *I
found I could lift it.* **2** used to express a possibility
or a possible course: *You could try telephoning her.*
3 used in making requests: *Could you help me?*
– **could be** (*colloquial*) that may be the case.
council (**kown** sĕl) *n.* a group of people who
advise, administer, discuss, or legislate.
councillor *n.* a member of a council.
counsel (**kown** sĕl) *n.* **1** advice. **2** a lawyer or
group of lawyers that gives legal advice and
fights cases in court. – *vb.* **counselling,
counselled** to advise.
count[1] (kownt) *vb.* **counting, counted 1** to say
numbers in order: *Can you count to 100?* **2** to
find the total amount of, by adding up item by
item: *Please count the sheep in the field.* **3** to
include: *There are five mouths to feed if you count
the dog!* – *n.* **1** an act of counting. **2** the number
counted. – *adj.* **countable**. – **count me in**
I'm willing to be included.
countdown *n.* a count backwards, having
zero as the moment for action, used especially
in launching a rocket.
count[2] (kownt) *n.* a European nobleman.
counter[1] (**kown** tĕr) *n.* **1** the long flat-topped
fitting in a shop, bank, etc. over which goods
are sold, food is served, or business done. **2** a
small disc used in various board games.

Counter in the first
sense was once used to
describe a table on
which money was
counted; it then was
used for any narrow
table. A counter is also
an object for counting
in certain games.
Counter in the second
sense comes from a
French word meaning
'against'.

PRONUNCIATION GUIDE

fat **a**	all **ö**
fate **ā**	foot **oo**
fast **ä**	moon **o͞o**
among **å**	boy **oi**
met **e**	house **ow**
mean **ē**	demon **ȯ**
silent **ė**	thing **th**
loch **hh**	this **Th**
fin **i**	but **u**
line **ī**	mute **ū**
quick **kw**	fur **û**
got **o**	brochure **ü**
note **ō**	vision **zh**

Squash courts are enclosed within four walls and have an entrance in the back. The game originates from Harrow School, England where boys practised hitting a ball about in a courtyard while waiting to get into a rackets court. A rackets ball is hard but the boys practised with a soft or 'squash' ball.

counter² (**kown** tĕr) *adv.* in the opposite direction to: *Results ran counter to expectations.*

counter- (**kown** tĕr-) *prefix* **1** against: *counter-attack.* **2** rivalry: *counter-attraction.*

counter-clockwise (kown tĕr **klok** wīz) *adj. & adv.* anticlockwise.

counterfeit (**kown** tĕr fit) *adj.* **1** made in imitation of a genuine article, especially with a dishonest purpose. **2** not genuine; insincere. – *vb.* **counterfeiting, counterfeited** to copy for a dishonest purpose; to forge.

countess (**kown** tis) *n.* the wife of a count.

country (**kun** tri) *n.* **countries 1** the land of any of the nations of the world. **2** your native land: *Scotland is my country.* **3** open land, with moors, woods, hills, fields, etc.
  country-and-western *n.* folk music or songs of a style popular among white people of the southern UNITED STATES.
  countryside *n.* land away from towns.

county (**kown** ti) *n.* **counties** any of the geographical divisions of local government within ENGLAND, WALES, and IRELAND.

couple (**ku** pĕl) *n.* **1** a man and wife, or other pair of people romantically attached. **2** two of a kind: *a couple of pears.*

courage (**ku** rij) *n.* **1** bravery; lack of fear. **2** cheerfulness in coping with setbacks.

courageous (kŭ **rā** jŭs) *adj.* having courage.

courier (**koo** ri ĕr) *n.* **1** a guide who looks after parties of tourists. **2** a messenger.

course (körs) *n.* **1** the path that anything moves in. **2** a direction taken or planned: *The rocket went off course.* **3** the normal progress of something: *the course of history.* **4** a series of lessons, etc. **5** a prescribed treatment, e.g. medicine to be taken, over a period. **6** any of the successive parts of a meal: *Curry was the main course.* **7** the ground over which a game is played or a race run. – **of course 1** as expected. **2** without doubt. **3** admittedly.

court (kört) *n.* **1** the judge, law officials, and members of the jury gathered to hear and decide on a legal case. **2** the place (**courtroom**) or building used for such a hearing. **3** an area marked out for a particular game: *a squash court.* – *vb.* **courting, courted 1** to try to win the favour of. **2** to risk or invite: *He courts danger with his rash behaviour.* – **the ball is in your court** you must make the next move. – **go to court** to take legal action.
  courtyard *n.* an open space surrounded by buildings or walls.

courteous (**kûr** ti ŭs) *adj.* polite; considerate.

courtesy (**kûr** tė si) *n.* **courtesies 1** polite and thoughtful behaviour: *Jack treats everyone with the same courtesy.* **2** a courteous act.

cousin (**ku** zin) *n.* a son or daughter of your uncle or aunt.
  second cousin *n.* a son or daughter of your parent's cousin.

cover (**ku** vĕr) *vb.* **covering, covered 1** to form a layer over: *The blossom covered the lawn with a pink layer.* **2** to protect or conceal by putting something over: *Sheila covered her head with a blanket.* **3** to extend over: *Forests cover huge areas of Canada.* **4** to sprinkle, mark all over, etc. **5** to deal with a subject: *The book covers the French Revolution.* – *n.* **1** something that covers; a lid, top, protective casing, etc. **2** the covering of something: *She has filled her garden with plants that give good ground cover.* **3** the binding of a book, magazine, etc. **4** shelter, protection: *Take cover!* **5** insurance. – *vb.* **cover for** to take over the duties of an absent colleague, etc. – *n. & adj.* **covering.** – *vb.* **cover up** to conceal a mistake, etc. – **under cover** in secret.

The markings on a tennis court are always the same regardless of its surface. Lines are painted on hard courts, but chalk lines mark grass courts. In doubles matches the playing area is enlarged by including the alleys. Serves in double games must still land in the service courts.

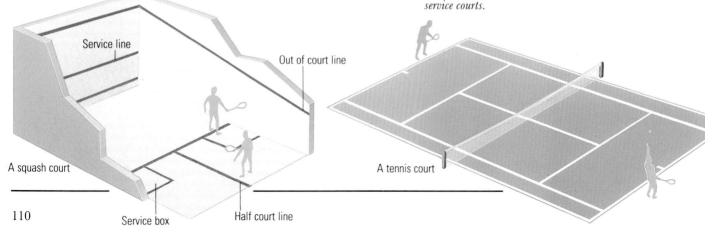

Service line

Out of court line

A squash court

Service box

Half court line

A tennis court

cow (kow) *n.* **1** the female of cattle. **2** the female of other large animals, e.g. the elephant, whale, seal, and moose. – **till the cows come home** (*colloquial*) for a very long time.
cowboy *n.* in the western UNITED STATES, a man in charge of cattle, especially as a character in films of the WILD WEST.

● The great days of cowboys lasted from the 1860s to 1900. Cattle were grazed on the vast grasslands and herded to the railroad stations. On the range the cowboy was his own boss. He travelled light, owning nothing more than his horse, saddle, and bedroll. Cowboys rarely carried pistols.

coward (**kow** ård) *n.* someone easily frightened, or lacking courage to face danger. – *n.* **cowardice** (**kow** år dis) – *adj.* **cowardly**.
coy (koi) *adj.* shy. – *n.* **coyness**.
coyote (koi ō ti) or (kī ō ti) *n.* **coyote** or **coyotes** a small North American wolf.
crab (krab) *n.* an edible shellfish with a wide flat shell and five pairs of legs, the front pair taking the form of pincers. See CRUSTACEANS.
crack (krak) *vb.* **cracking, cracked 1** to fracture partially without falling to pieces: *Although the jug was cracked we still used it.* **2** to split, making a sudden sharp noise: *Ned cracked a nut with his teeth.* **3** to strike sharply: *The cowgirl cracked her whip.* **4** to force open a safe. **5** to solve a code or problem. – *n.* **1** a sudden sharp sound. **2** a partial fracture. **3** a narrow opening. – *vb.* **crack down on** to take firm action against.
  cracker *n.* **1** a thin crisp unsweetened biscuit. **2** a small noisy firework.
-cracy (-krå si) *suffix* rule or domination by a particular group, etc.: *democracy*.
cradle (**krā** děl) *n.* **1** a cot for a small baby. **2** a place of origin; the home of something: *The city of Ur is the cradle of civilization.*
craft (kräft) *n.* **1** a skill or occupation, especially one requiring the use of the hands: *They practised crafts such as weaving and pottery.* **2** a boat or ship, or an air or space vehicle.
  crafty *adj.* **craftier, craftiest** clever, shrewd.
cram (kram) *vb.* **cramming, crammed 1** to stuff full: *He crammed all he could get into the case.* **2** to study intensively for an examination.
cramp (kramp) *n.* a painful involuntary contraction of a muscle. – *vb.* **cramping, cramped** to restrict tiresomely.
  cramped *adj.* too small.

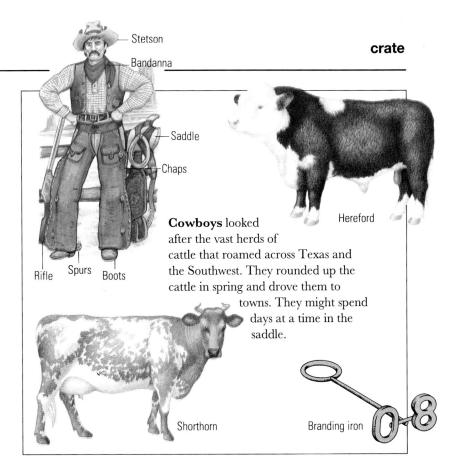

Stetson
Bandanna
Saddle
Chaps
Rifle Spurs Boots
Hereford
Shorthorn
Branding iron

Cowboys looked after the vast herds of cattle that roamed across Texas and the Southwest. They rounded up the cattle in spring and drove them to towns. They might spend days at a time in the saddle.

crane (krān) *n.* **1** a machine for lifting heavy weights, having a long arm from which lifting gear is suspended. **2** any of various large, long-legged, long-necked birds.

● A crane's long arm is called a 'jib'. Modern cranes have a powerful motor which winches the hook, raises and lowers the jib, and turns the cab around.

cranefly *n.* **craneflies** a long-legged two-winged insect, the daddy-long-legs.
cranium (**krā** ni ům) *n.* **crania** or **craniums** the dome of the skull, enclosing the brain.
crash (krash) *vb.* **crashing, crashed 1** to fall or strike with a banging or smashing noise. **2** to collide: *The plane crashed into the mountain.* **3** (of a business or the stock exchange) to collapse. **4** (of a computer or program) to fail completely. – *n.* **1** a violent impact or breakage. **2** a deafening noise: *The music was interrupted by the crash of cymbals.* **3** a traffic or aircraft accident. **4** the failure of a computer.
  crash helmet *n.* a protective helmet worn by motor-cyclists.
crass (kras) *adj.* stupid; insensitive.
crate (krāt) *n.* a strong box made of slats, for carrying goods: *a milk crate.*

Cranes can be fixed in one place, like the tower cranes erected on building sites.

Craters on the Moon
Most of the craters on the Moon were formed when smaller bodies crashed into its surface and blasted out a crater ten times their own width.

In the blast, rocky material was thrown out for hundreds of kilometres.

The violent impact produced shock waves causing mountains to be formed in the centre of the crater.

Over time dust settles in the crater.

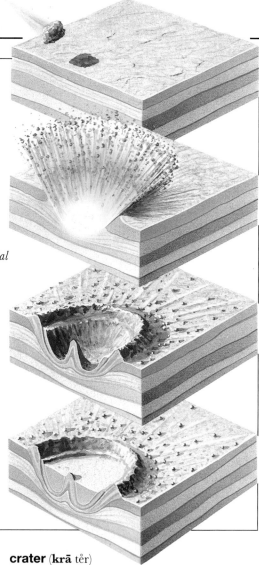

crater (**krā** těr) *n.* **1** the bowl-shaped mouth of a volcano. **2** a hole left in the ground where a bomb or mine has exploded.

crave (krāv) *vb.* **craving, craved** to desire overwhelmingly: *An addict craves for drugs.*

crawl (kröl) *vb.* **crawling, crawled 1** (of insects, worms, etc.) to move along the ground. **2** to move along on hands and knees. **3** to progress very slowly: *Rush hour traffic crawls along.* **4** to be covered with crawling insects: *The kitchen is crawling with cockroaches.* – *n.* **1** a crawling motion. **2** a very slow pace.

craze (krāz) *n.* a fashion or something that is popular for a short time; a fad.
crazy *adj.* **crazier, craziest 1** mad; insane. **2** madly enthusiastic: *Joan is crazy about swimming.* – *adv.* **crazily**. – *n.* **craziness**.

creak (krēk) *n.* the squeaking noise made by an unoiled hinge or loose floorboard. – *vb.* **creaking, creaked** to make this noise.

cream (krēm) *n.* **1** the yellowish-white fatty substance on top of milk, from which butter and cheese are made. **2** any of many cosmetic preparations similar to cream in texture.

crease (krēs) *n.* a line made by folding, pressing, or crushing.

create (krē **āt**) *vb.* **creating, created 1** to form from nothing. **2** to bring into existence: *We need to create a system if we want to do this properly.*
creation *n.* **1** the act of creating. **2** something created, such as a play or a painting.
creative *adj.* having the ability to make something new; imaginative. – *n.* **creativity**.
creator *n.* a person who creates.

creature (**krē** chǔr) *n.* any living thing.

● **Crécy** is a village in northern FRANCE where, in 1346, an English army defeated the French.

credit (**kre** dit) *n.* **1** faith placed in something. **2** a cause of honour: *To her credit, she didn't say anything.* **3** acknowledgement, recognition, or praise: *Give him credit for trying.* **4** trust given to someone promising to pay later for goods already supplied: *They often buy goods on credit.* – *vb.* **crediting, credited 1** to believe; to place faith in. **2** to attribute a quality or achievement to: *I credited you with more sense.*

creed (krēd) *n.* a statement of the main points of personal or religious beliefs.

creek (krēk) *n.* a narrow coastal inlet.

creep (krēp) *vb.* **creeping, crept 1** to move slowly and silently. **2** to move with the body close to the ground; to crawl. **3** (of plants) to grow along the ground, up a wall, etc.
creepy *adj.* **creepier, creepiest** (*colloquial*) frightening.

cremate (kri **māt**) *vb.* **cremating, cremated** to burn a corpse to ashes. – *n.* **cremation**.

crept. See **creep**.

crescent (**kre** sĕnt) *n.* the Moon in its first quarter, the new Moon.

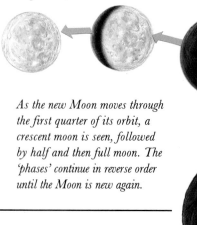

As the new Moon moves through the first quarter of its orbit, a crescent moon is seen, followed by half and then full moon. The 'phases' continue in reverse order until the Moon is new again.

cress (kres) *n.* plants whose sharp-tasting leaves are used in salads, etc.

crest (krest) *n.* **1** a comb or vertical tuft of feathers on the head of certain birds. **2** the topmost ridge of a mountain. – *adj.* **crested**.

● **Crete** is a Greek island in the MEDITERRANEAN where the Minoan civilization flourished 5000 years ago.

crew (kroo) *n.* a team of people operating a ship, aircraft, train, bus, etc.

crib (krib) *n.* a baby's cot or cradle. – *vb.* **cribbing, cribbed** to copy or plagiarize.

cricket¹ (**kri** kit) *n.* an outdoor game played with a ball, bats, and wickets, between two sides of eleven players. – *n.* **cricketer**.

There are about 2,500 species of cricket, most of which live in tropical regions. Their long thin antennae distinguish them from grasshoppers.

cricket² (**kri** kit) *n.* a grasshopper-like insect, the male of which makes a chirping noise by rubbing its forewings together.

crime (krīm) *n.* an illegal act; an act punishable by law; an act gravely wrong morally.

criminal (**kri** mi nål) *n.* a person guilty of a crime. – *adj.* against the law: *criminal activities.*

crimson (**krim** zŏn) *n.* & *adj.* purplish red.

crisis (**krī** sis) *n.* **crises** (**krī** sēz) **1** a crucial or decisive moment. **2** a serious time.

crisp (krisp) *adj.* **1** dry and brittle: *Crisp biscuits break into crumbs.* **2** (of vegetables or fruit) firm and fresh. **3** (of weather) fresh; bracing. – *adj.* **crispy, crispier, crispiest**.

criterion (krī **tēr** i ŏn) *n.* **criteria** a standard or principle on which to base a judgement.

critic (**kri** tik) *n.* **1** a person whose job it is to review literature, art, drama, or music. **2** a person who finds fault with something. **critical** *adj.* **1** always finding fault. **2** relating to a critic or criticism: *It was a good critical review.*

3 relating to a crisis; decisive; crucial.

criticism *n.* **1** fault-finding. **2** reasoned assessment, especially of art, music, etc.

criticize or **criticise** *vb.* **criticizing, criticized** to find fault, express disapproval.

croak (krōk) *n.* the throaty noise made by a frog.

● **Croatia**. See Supplement, **Countries**.

crochet (**krō** shā) *n.* decorative work consisting of intertwined loops, made with wool or thread and a hooked needle. – *vb.* **crocheting, crocheted** to work in crochet.

crockery (**kro** kĕ ri) *n.* plates, cups, etc.

● **Crockett, Davy** (1786-1836) was an American frontiersman whose bravery and good humour are legendary. He is famous too for his rifle, *Betsy*, and his raccoonskin cap.

crocodile (**kro** kŏ dīl) *n.* a large, thick-scaled, long-tailed tropical reptile with huge jaws.

crocus (**krō** kŭs) *n.* **crocuses** a spring-flowering plant that grows from a bulb.

● **Cromwell, Oliver** (1599-1658) helped lead Parliament's army to victory in the English CIVIL WAR and later became Lord Protector. He brutally crushed the Irish Catholics.

crook (krook) *n.* **1** a bend or curve: *He carried it in the crook of his arm.* **2** a thief or swindler. **crooked** (**kroo** kid) *adj.* bent, curved.

crop (krop) *n.* **1** a cereal or other plant grown as food; the season's yield from such a plant: *Sugar beet is an important crop in Belgium.* **2** a batch: *This year's crop of graduates is one of the best ever.* **3** a horse rider's short whip. – *vb.* **cropping, cropped 1** to trim; to harvest. **2** to grow a plant for its produce.

Crop rotation is a system of planting different crops grown in rotation on the same land. On three fields, for example, the rotation might be maize, oats, and clover. This allows the soil to rest and be restored so that it can remain in use and give high yields.

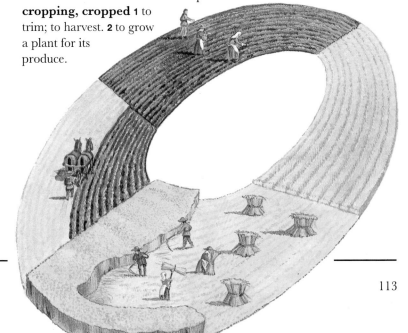

Over the years the basic design of the cross has been elaborated and embellished in many ways. Here are a few different types of cross.

Greek

St Andrew's

Celtic

St Anthony's

Latin

Maltese

croquet (**krō** kā) *n.* a game played on a lawn, in which mallets are used to drive wooden balls through wire hoops.

cross (kros) *n.* 1 a mark, structure, or symbol composed of two lines, one crossing the other in the form + or ×; the mark × indicating a mistake or cancellation, as distinct from a tick. 2 an intermingling between breeds or species; the resulting hybrid: *Our dog is a cross between a spaniel and a poodle.* – *vb.* **crossing, crossed** 1 to move, pass, or get across. 2 to place one across the other: *He crossed his legs.* 3 to meet; to intersect. 4 to delete or cancel by drawing a line through: *Paul crossed out the message on the letter.* 5 to interbreed: *They tried to cross a sheep with a goat.* – *adj.* angry; in a bad temper.

cross-examine *vb.* **cross-examining, cross-examined** to question, especially a witness, so as to develop or throw doubt on his or her statement. – *n.* **cross-examination**.

crouch (krowch) *vb.* **crouching, crouched** to bend low or squat with legs close to the chest and with hands on the ground.

crow (krō) *n.* 1 a large black bird or any of several related large birds including the rook, raven, jackdaw, and magpie. 2 the shrill cry of a cock. – *vb.* **crowing, crowed** or **crew** (krōō) 1 to cry shrilly. 2 to triumph gleefully; to gloat: *The winning team crowed over the dejected losers.* – **as the crow flies** in a straight line.

crowbar *n.* a heavy iron bar with a bent, flattened end, used as a lever.

crowd (krowd) *n.* 1 a large number of people gathered together: *There was a large crowd waiting at the airport.* 2 the spectators or audience at an event: *The football crowd cheered as the team came on to the pitch.* – *vb.* **crowding, crowded** to move in a large, tightly-packed group. – *adj.* **crowded**.

crown (krown) *n.* 1 the circular, usually jewelled, gold headdress of kings and queens. 2 the part of a tooth projecting from the gum. – *vb.* **crowning, crowned** 1 to place a crown ceremonially on the head of; to make king or queen. 2 to make perfect: *Her efforts were crowned with success.* 3 to put an artificial crown on a tooth.

crowning *adj.* greatest: *her crowning moment.*

crucial (**krōō** shăl) *adj.* 1 decisive; critical. 2 very important: *This is the crucial set in the tennis match.*

crucifix (**krōō** si fiks) *n.* a representation of Christ on the cross.

crude (krōōd) *adj.* 1 in its natural, unrefined state: *crude oil.* 2 vulgar; tasteless.

cruel (**krōō** ĕl) *adj.* deliberately and pitilessly causing pain or suffering. – *adv.* **cruelly.** – *n.* **cruelty, cruelties.**

● **Crufts** is an annual dog show held in Britain.

cruise (krōōz) *vb.* **cruising, cruised** 1 to sail about for pleasure, calling at different places. 2 (of a vehicle or aircraft) to go at a steady, comfortable speed.

crumb (krum) *n.* a tiny piece of cake, etc.

crumble (**krum** bĕl) *vb.* **crumbling, crumbled** to break into crumbs or powdery fragments: *The fragile pots crumbled in her hands.*

crumple (**krum** pĕl) *vb.* **crumpling, crumpled** 1 to make or become creased or crushed: *She crumpled the letter in her hand.* 2 to collapse.

crunch (krunch) *vb.* **crunching, crunched** to crush or grind noisily between the teeth or under the foot: *She crunched a carrot.*

crusade (krōō **sād**) *n.* 1 a CHRISTIAN military expedition in medieval times to regain the Holy Land of Palestine from the MUSLIMS. 2 a campaign in aid of a cause: *Our school started a no-smoking crusade.* – *vb.* **crusading, crusaded** to campaign. – *n.* **crusader**.

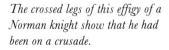

Palestine, Holy Land of the Bible, was overrun by Muslims in 638. In 1095 the Pope called on Christian warriors to recover the Holy Land from the 'infidels'. The numerous expeditions – until the end of the 13th century – were known as **crusades**, from the Spanish word *cruzada* – 'marked with the cross'.

The crossed legs of this effigy of a Norman knight show that he had been on a crusade.

Diamond

Graphite

crush (krush) *vb.* **crushing, crushed 1** to break, damage, or distort by compressing violently. **2** to crumple or crease. **3** to defeat or subdue. – *n.* **1** violent compression. **2** a dense crowd. **3** a drink made from fruit juice.

crust (krust) *n.* **1** the hard-baked outer surface of a loaf of bread; a piece of this. **2** the outer surface of the Earth.

crustacean (kru **stā** shǎn) *n.* a large group of mainly aquatic creatures with hard shells, e.g. crabs, lobsters, crayfish, shrimps, etc.

● Crustaceans are a large group of about 10,000 creatures. They are invertebrates (animals without backbones). Many have pincers on their front legs.

crux (kruks) *n.* **cruxes** a crucial point.

cry (krī) *vb.* **cries, crying, cried 1** to shed tears; to weep: *The baby cried when she fell over and hurt herself.* **2** to shout or shriek, in pain or fear, or to get attention or help. **3** (of an animal or bird) to utter its characteristic noise. – *n.* **cries 1** a shout or shriek. **2** an excited utterance or exclamation. **3** an appeal or demand: *Her act was a cry for help.* **4** the characteristic sound of an animal or bird: *We heard the cry of a gull.* – *vb.* **cry off** to cancel an engagement.

crypt (kript) *n.* an underground chamber beneath a church, used for burials.

cryptic (**krip** tik) *adj.* puzzling, mysterious.

crystal (**kris** tǎl) *n.* (also **rock crystal**) a mineral, a colourless transparent quartz. – *adj.* like crystal in brilliance and clarity.

● Snowflakes, salt grains, and diamonds are all crystals. In a crystal the molecules are arranged in a regular pattern: for example, all snowflakes are six-sided crystals.

crystallize or **crystallise** *vb.* **crystallizing, crystallized 1** to form into crystals. **2** (of plans, ideas, etc.) to make or become clear.

cub (kub) *n.* a young fox, bear, lion, or wolf.

● **Cuba.** See Supplement, **Countries**.

cube (kūb) *n.* **1** a solid figure having six equal square faces. **2** in maths, the product of a number multiplied by itself twice.

cubicle (**kū** bi kěl) *n.* a small compartment for sleeping or undressing in, screened for privacy.

cuckoo (koo kōo) *n.* a bird known for its distinctive two-note call, that lays its eggs in the nests of other, smaller birds.

cucumber (**kū** kum běr) *n.* a long green vegetable with juicy white flesh, used in salads. – **cool as a cucumber** (*colloquial*) calm.

cud (kud) *n.* the half-digested food that a cow or other ruminant brings back into the mouth from the stomach to chew again. – **chew the cud** (*colloquial*) to ponder.

cuddle (**ku** děl) *vb.* **cuddling, cuddled** to hug or embrace affectionately. – *n.* a hug.

cue[1] (kū) *n.* the final words of an actor's speech that serve as a prompt for another to say or do something.

cue[2] (kū) *n.* a stick tapering to a point, used to strike the ball in billiards, snooker, and pool.

cuff (kuf) *n.* **1** the lower end of a sleeve, usually at the wrist. **2** (*North American*) the turned-up part of a trouser leg.

culprit (**kul** prit) *n.* a person guilty of a misdeed.

cultivate (**kul** ti vāt) *vb.* **cultivating, cultivated 1** to prepare and use land or soil for crops. **2** to develop or improve: *She tried to cultivate a taste for literature.*

culture (**kul** chǔr) *n.* **1** the customs, ideas, art, etc. of a particular civilization or social group. **2** appreciation of art, music, etc. **3** a crop of bacteria grown for study. – *adj.* **cultural**. **cultured** *adj.* well-educated.

The scientific study of crystals is called crystallography. Scientists measure the angles between crystal faces and analyse the surface arrangements.

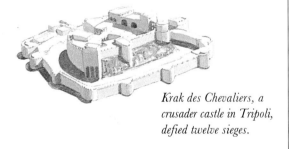

Krak des Chevaliers, a crusader castle in Tripoli, defied twelve sieges.

Richard I 'the Lionheart' was an ardent crusader but failed to recapture Jerusalem.

cumbersome (**kum** běr sǒm) *adj.* awkward.

cunning (**ku** ning) *adj.* clever, sly, crafty, or artful.

cup (kup) *n.* **1** a small round container with a handle, from which to drink. **2** an ornamental, usually silver, vessel awarded as a prize in sports competitions, etc.

cupboard (**ku** bǒrd) *n.* a piece of furniture, or a recess, fitted with doors, shelves, etc., for storing food, etc.

curb (kûrb) *n.* **1** something that restrains or controls. **2** (*North American*) a kerb. – *vb.* **curbing, curbed** to restrain or control: *The owner tried to curb the power of the unions.*

One of the earliest coins, from Anatolia, and a spade-shaped early Chinese coin. (Bottom) A 7th century Chinese banknote.

CURIOUS CURRENCY WORDS

Many strange words appear on coins and banknotes. Here is the meaning of a few:

Latin words

REGINA	Queen
REX	King

Countries

CUMHURIYETI	Turkey
DANSKE	Denmark
DEUTSCHLAND	Germany
ESPAÑA	Spain
HELVETIA	Switzerland
ISLAND	Iceland
MAGYAR	Hungary
NORGE	Norway
ÖSTERREICH	Austria
SUOMI	Finland
SVERIGE	Sweden

---

cure (kūr) *vb.* **curing, cured 1** to restore to health; to heal; to get rid of an illness, harmful habit, etc. **2** to preserve meat, fish, etc. by salting, smoking, etc. – *n.* something that cures or remedies: *Many people rely on herbal medicines as cures.* – *adj.* **curable**.

●**Curie, Marie** (1867-1934) was a Polish-born scientist who, with her husband, Pierre, was one of the earliest workers in the science of RADIOACTIVITY.

curio (kūr i ō) *n.* **curios** an article valued for its rarity or unusualness.

curiosity (kū ri **os** i ti) *n.* eagerness to know.

curious (**kūr** i ůs) *adj.* **1** strange; odd: *A curious thing happened last night.* **2** eager or interested: *I am curious to see what happens.* **3** inquisitive.

curl (kûrl) *vb.* **curling, curled 1** to twist or roll into coils or ringlets: *Norma curled her hair in the lastest fashion.* **2** to move in, or form into, a spiral, coil, or curve. – *n.* a ringlet of hair. – *vb.* **curl up** to sit or lie with the legs tucked up.

curlew (**kûr** lū) *n.* a long-legged wading bird with a long curved beak and loud cry.

currant (**ku** rånt) *n.* **1** a small dried seedless grape used in cooking. **2** any of several small soft berries: *blackcurrants, redcurrants.*

currency (**ku** rěn si) *n.* **currencies** the money, or coins and notes, in use in a country: *The currency of the US and Canada is dollars and cents.*

current *adj.* **1** generally accepted: *Salt is bad for you according to the current view.* **2** belonging to the present: *Who is your current boyfriend?* – *n.* **1** a continuous flow of water or air. **2** the flow of electricity through a circuit or wire.

currently *adv.* at the present time.

curriculum (ků **rik** ū lům) *n.* **curricula** a course of study at school or university.

curriculum vitae (ků **rik** ū lům vē tī) *n.* **curricula vitae** a written summary of personal details and the main events of your education and career, sent when applying for certain jobs. It is often referred to as a C.V.

curry (**ku** ri) *n.* **curries** a dish, originally Indian, of meat or vegetables cooked with hot spices.

curse (kûrs) *n.* **1** a word used in swearing; a blasphemous expression of anger; an oath. **2** an evil; a cause of harm: *the curse of drugs.* – *vb.* **cursing, cursed**.

cursor (**kûr** sǒr) *n.* a flashing marker on a computer screen indicating the current position of the operator.

curt (kûrt) *adj.* rudely brief; abrupt.

curtail (kûr **tāl**) *vb.* **curtailing, curtailed** to restrict: *The plans for a new town were curtailed.*

curtain (**kûr** tin) *n.* a hanging cloth over a window or open space for privacy or to exclude light. A curtain is also hung in front of a stage to screen it from the auditorium.

curve (kûrv) *n.* **1** a line no part of which is straight, or a surface no part of which is flat: *There is a curve in the road.* **2** any smoothly arched line or shape, like part of a circle or sphere. – *vb.* **curving, curved** to form a curve; to bend or move in a curve.

cushion (**koo** shŏn) *n.* a pillow or a stuffed fabric case used for making a seat comfortable, for kneeling on, etc.: *The sofa has huge, soft cushions.* – *vb.* **cushioning, cushioned** to reduce the unpleasant or violent effect of: *The soft, muddy ground cushioned her fall.*

●**Custer, George** (1839-76) was an American army officer ordered to resettle CHEYENNE and SIOUX Indians in reservations. He was killed at a SIOUX village at Little Bighorn River in an attack led by Chief SITTING BULL.

custody (**ku** stŏ di) *n.* **1** protective care; the right to be guardian of a child, awarded to someone by a court of law. **2** imprisonment.

custom (**kus** tŏm) *n.* **1** a traditional activity or practice: *Morris dancing is an old English custom.* **2** a personal habit.
  customary *adj.* usual. – *adv.* **customarily.**
customer (**kus** tŏ mẽr) *n.* a person who buys goods from a shop.
customs (**kus** tŏmz) *n.* the place at a port, airport, etc. where baggage is inspected for goods on which duty must be paid.
cut (kut) *vb.* **cutting, cut 1** to slit, pierce, slice, or sever with a sharp-edged instrument; to be so slit, pierced, etc. **2** to divide by cutting. **3** to trim hair, nails, etc.; to reap corn or detach flowers. **4** to make or form by cutting. **5** to shape the pieces of a garment: *He always wears badly cut clothes.* **6** to injure or wound with a sharp edge or instrument. **7** to reduce: *The working week was cut to 35 hours.* – *n.* **1** an act of cutting. **2** a slit, incision, or injury made by cutting. **3** a reduction. **4** a deleted passage in a play, etc. – *vb.* **cut back** to reduce spending, etc. – *vb.* **cut down 1** to fell a tree. **2** to reduce: *He tried to cut down on spending.*
  cutting *n.* an extract, article, or picture cut from a newspaper, etc. – *adj.* hurtful; sarcastic.
cutlery (**kut** lĕ ri) *n.* knives, forks, and spoons.

●**Cutty Sark** a British clipper launched in 1869 and now kept at GREENWICH, London. She served in the English-Chinese tea trade in the 1870s and later in the Australian wool trade.

cwm (koom) *n.* in Wales, a valley.
cycle (**sī** kĕl) *n.* **1** a constantly repeating series of events that happen over and over again: *the cycle of the seasons.* **2** a bicycle or motor cycle. – *vb.* **cycling, cycled** to ride a bicycle.

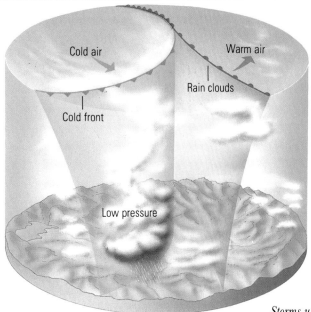

cyclone (**sī** klōn) *n.* **1** a system of winds blowing spirally inward towards a centre of low pressure; a depression. **2** a violent wind storm.
cygnet (**sig** nĕt) *n.* a young swan.
cylinder (**si** lin dẽr) *n.* **1** a solid or hollow object shaped like a tube. **2** a container of this shape. **3** in an internal-combustion engine, the chamber inside which the piston moves.
cymbal (**sim** bǎl) *n.* a plate-like brass musical instrument, either beaten with a drumstick, or used as one of a pair that are struck together.
cynic (**si** nik) *n.* a person who believes the worst about people. – *adj.* **cynical.** – *n.* **cynicism.**
cypress (**sī** prĕs) *n.* a slim coniferous tree.
Cypriot (**sip** ri ŏt) *n.* a native of CYPRUS, a MEDITERRANEAN island. – *adj.* of or belonging to CYPRUS, its people, etc.

●**Cyprus.** See Supplement, **Countries.**

cystic fibrosis (**sis** tik fĩ brō sis) *n.* an inherited disease of children causing the formation of cysts and excess mucus in the body, which interfere with breathing and digestion.
czar and **czarina.** See **tsar.**
Czech (chek) *n.* **1** a native of the CZECH REPUBLIC of Bohemia and Moldavia. **2** the official language of the CZECH REPUBLIC.

●**Czech Republic.** See Supplement, **Countries.**

Storms usually occur with cyclones. The cold air along a cold front forces the warmer air to rise along a warm front. Clouds develop and as the air rises and cools, the water vapour it carries condenses, and rain begins to fall.

PRONUNCIATION GUIDE	
fat a	all ŏ
fate ā	foot oo
fast ä	moon o͞o
among å	boy oi
met e	house ow
mean ē	demon ŏ
silent ĕ	thing th
loch hh	this Th
fin i	but u
line ī	mute ū
quick kw	fur û
got o	brochure ǔ
note ō	vision zh

D d

dab (dab) *vb.* **dabbing, dabbed** to touch lightly, etc.: *I dabbed at the stain with a damp cloth.* – *n.* a small amount of something.

dabble (**da** bĕl) *vb.* **dabbling, dabbled** to do or study something without serious effort: *He dabbles in eastern religions.* – *n.* **dabbler.**

dachshund (**dak** sŭnd) or (**dash** ŭnd) *n.* a breed of small dog with a long body and short legs.

daddy (**da** di) *n.* **daddies** (*colloquial*) a father.

daffodil (**daf** ŏ dil) *n.* a plant which grows from a bulb, with a yellow trumpet-shaped flower.

dagger (**da** gĕr) *n.* a knife or short sword with a pointed end, used for stabbing.

Dáil (doil) or **Dáil Éireann** (ā rǎn) *n.* the lower and more important house of the parliament of the Republic of IRELAND.

daily (**dā** li) *adj.* happening, appearing, etc. every day, or every weekday. – *adv.* every day. – *n.* **dailies** a newspaper published every day.

● **Daimler** (dām lĕr), **Gottlieb** (1834-1900) was a German inventor who built the first motorcycle.

dainty (**dān** ti) *adj.* **daintier, daintiest** small, pretty, and usually delicate. – *adv.* **daintily.** – *n.* **daintiness.**

dairy (**dār** i) *n.* **dairies** **1** a place where milk, butter, cheese, etc. are sold. **2** the building on a farm where butter and cheese are made.

dais (**dā** is) or (dās) *n.* a raised platform in a hall, e.g. for speakers at a meeting.

daisy (**dā** zi) *n.* **daisies** a common small flower with a yellow centre and usually white petals.

dale (dāl) *n.* a valley.

● **Dallas** is a major oil city in Texas; President Kennedy was assassinated there in 1963.

Dalmatian (dal **mā** shǎn) *n.* a large short-haired dog, white with dark spots.

dam (dam) *n.* a wall built across a river, etc. to hold back the water. – *vb.* **damming, dammed** to hold back with a dam.

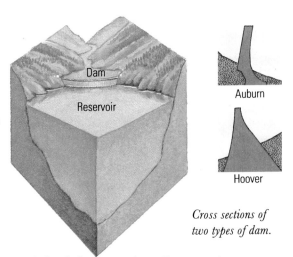

Cross sections of two types of dam.

A dam built across a river valley causes the water behind it to flood the valley and form a reservoir to store water.

damage (**da** mij) *n.* **1** harm or injury, or loss caused by injury. **2** (in *plural*) payment due for loss or injury caused by another person, organization, etc. – *vb.* **damaging, damaged** to cause harm to. – *adj.* **damaged.**

● **Damascus** (dǎ **mas** kǔs) is the capital of SYRIA and the world's oldest continuously inhabited city.

damp (damp) *adj.* slightly wet. – *n.* slight wetness, e.g. in walls or the air, especially if cold and unpleasant. – *n.* **dampness.**

dampen *vb.* **dampening, dampened** to make slightly wet.

dance (däns) *vb.* **dancing, danced** **1** to make a repeated series of rhythmic steps or movements, usually in time to music. **2** to perform a particular series of such steps or movements: *Can you dance the tango?* – *n.* **1** a series of fixed steps, usually made in time to music. **2** a social gathering at which people dance. – *n.* **dancer**. – *n.* **dancing**.

Tap dancing – popular in the 1930s

Dancers depicted on a wall of ancient Egypt.

Terpsichore, one of the nine Muses, presided over dancing.

Throughout history people the world over have **danced** – for pleasure, to act out stories, to prepare for battle, or as part of religious rituals.

dandelion (**dan** dě lī ǒn) *n.* a common wild plant with indented leaves, yellow flowers and round fluffy seed-heads.

dandruff (**dan** drǔf) *n.* small pieces of dead skin on the head under the hair.

Dane (dān) *n.* **1** a person born in DENMARK. **2** any of the VIKINGS from SCANDINAVIA who invaded Britain in the 9th to 11th centuries.

danger (**dān** jěr) *n.* **1** a situation or state in which someone or something may suffer harm, an injury, or a loss: *Danger is all around us.* **2** something that may cause harm or injury. **dangerous** *adj.* likely to cause harm or injury.

dangle (**dang** gěl) *vb.* **dangling, dangled** to hang loosely.

Danish (**dān** ish) *adj.* of DENMARK or its inhabitants. – *n.* the language spoken in DENMARK.

dank (dangk) *adj.* unpleasantly wet and cold.

● **Dante** (**dan** tā), **Alighieri** (1265-1321) is ITALY's greatest poet, the author of the *Divine Comedy*.

● **Danube** (**dan** ūb) the second longest river in EUROPE. Only the VOLGA is longer.

dappled (**da** pěld) *adj.* marked with rounded patches of a different, usually darker, colour.

dare (dār) *vb.* **daring, dared** **1** to be brave enough to do something frightening, difficult, or dangerous: *Dare I tell him?* **2** to challenge someone to do something dangerous, etc.: *I dare you to climb that tree.* – *n.* a challenge to do something dangerous, etc.
daring *adj.* bold or courageous.

dark (därk) *adj.* **1** without light. **2** (of a colour) not light or pale; closer to black than white. **3** (of a person or the colour of skin or hair) not light or fair. – *n.* **1** the absence of light: *Can you see in the dark?* **2** the time of day when night begins and there is no more light: *Don't go out after dark.* – *n.* **darkness**. – **in the dark** not knowing or aware.
the Dark Ages *n.* (*plural*) in European history, the period of time from about the 5th to the 11th centuries when Goths, Vandals, and Huns swept down from the north and destroyed many fine buildings and works of art of the ROMAN EMPIRE.
darken *vb.* **darkening, darkened** to make or become dark or darker.

dart (därt) *n.* **1** a narrow, pointed weapon that can be thrown or fired. **2** a small sharp-pointed missile used in the game of darts. **3** a sudden, quick movement. – *vb.* **darting, darted** to move suddenly and quickly: *The rat darted across the room.* – *adj.* **darting**.

Darwinism (**där** win i zěm) *n.* the theory of the development of the various species of plants and animals by evolution, proposed by Charles *Darwin* (1809-82) in his book *Origin of Species*.

dash (dash) *vb.* **dashing, dashed** **1** to run quickly; to rush: *Quick! Dash for cover.* **2** to destroy or put an end to hopes, etc.: *Hopes of a quiet evening were quickly dashed.* – *n.* **1** a quick run or sudden rush. **2** a small amount of something added, especially a liquid. **3** a short line (–) used in writing to show a break in a sentence, etc.
dashing *adj.* smart, stylish.

PRONUNCIATION GUIDE	
fat a	all ö
fate ā	foot oo
fast ä	moon ōō
among å	boy oi
met e	house ow
mean ē	demon ŏ
silent ě	thing th
loch hh	this Th
fin i	but u
line ī	mute ū
quick kw	fur û
got o	brochure ǔ
note ō	vision zh

King David, the first king of a united Israel, with his son, the future King Solomon. As a boy David had been a shepherd and the slayer of the Philistine warrior Goliath. He was also a musician who wrote many of the psalms in the Bible.

data (dā tå) *n.* (originally *plural* but now usually treated as *singular*. See also **datum**) **1** facts or information. **2** See **Computer terms**.

database *n.* a large amount of information stored in a computer.

date¹ (dāt) *n.* **1** the day of the month, and/or the year, in which something happened, is happening, or is going to happen. **2** a statement on a letter, etc. giving the day, the month, and the year when it was written, sent, etc. **3** (*colloquial*) a planned meeting or social outing. **4** (*North American; colloquial*) a person whom you are meeting. – *vb.* **dating, dated 1** to put a date on: *This cheque hasn't been dated.* **2** to find or decide on the date of.

dated *adj.* old-fashioned.

date² (dāt) *n.* the fruit of the date-palm, brown, sticky, and sweet-tasting when dried.

daughter (dö tẻr) *n.* a female child considered in relation to her parents.

daughter-in-law *n.* **daughters-in-law** a son's wife.

daunt (dönt) *vb.* **daunting, daunted** to frighten or discourage. – *adj.* **daunting**.

● **David** (1018-993 BC) was the second king of ISRAEL. He united the people of ISRAEL and made Jerusalem their capital.

● **David, Saint** is the patron saint of WALES. His feast day is 1 March.

● **Davy, Humphry** (1778-1829) was an English chemist and inventor of the miner's lamp.

dawdle (dö dẻl) *vb.* **dawdling, dawdled** to waste time, especially by moving or doing something very slowly. – *n.* **dawdler**.

dawn (dön) *n.* **1** the time of day when light first appears as the Sun rises. **2** the beginning of a new period of time, etc. – *vb.* **dawn on, dawning, dawned** to be realized by: *It suddenly dawned on me that she was right.*

day (dā) *n.* **1** the period of twenty-four hours from one midnight to the next. **2** the period of time from sunrise to sunset. **3** the period of time in any twenty-four hours normally spent doing something, especially working. – **day by day** as each day passes.

daydream *n.* pleasant thoughts which take your attention away from what you are doing.

daze (dāz) *vb.* **dazing, dazed** to make someone feel confused or unable to think clearly: *She wasn't injured by the fall, just slightly dazed.*

dazzle (da zẻl) *vb.* **dazzling, dazzled 1** to cause to be unable to see properly, with or because of a strong light. **2** to impress greatly by beauty, charm, skill, etc. – *adj.* **dazzling**.

dead (ded) *adj.* **1** no longer living. **2** with nothing living or growing in or on it: *Mars is almost certainly a dead planet.* **3** not, or no longer, functioning: *The radio's gone dead.* **4** no longer in use: *Latin is a dead language.* – *n.* (*plural*) dead

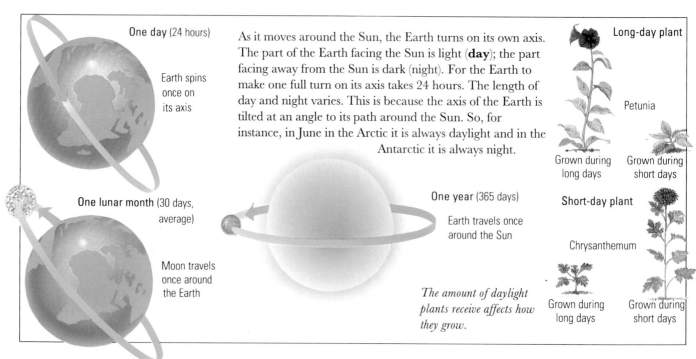

One day (24 hours)

Earth spins once on its axis

One lunar month (30 days, average)

Moon travels once around the Earth

As it moves around the Sun, the Earth turns on its own axis. The part of the Earth facing the Sun is light (**day**); the part facing away from the Sun is dark (night). For the Earth to make one full turn on its axis takes 24 hours. The length of day and night varies. This is because the axis of the Earth is tilted at an angle to its path around the Sun. So, for instance, in June in the Arctic it is always daylight and in the Antarctic it is always night.

One year (365 days)

Earth travels once around the Sun

The amount of daylight plants receive affects how they grow.

Long-day plant

Petunia

Grown during long days

Grown during short days

Short-day plant

Chrysanthemum

Grown during long days

Grown during short days

people: *Don't speak ill of the dead.* – **the dead of night** or **winter** the quietest or coldest part of the night or winter.

dead heat *n.* in a race, competition, etc., the result when two or more competitors produce equally good performances.

deadline *n.* a time by which something must be done, produced, or finished.

deadlock *n.* a situation in which no further progress towards an agreement is possible.

deadly *adj.* **deadlier, deadliest 1** causing or likely to cause death. **2** (*colloquial*) very dull or uninteresting. – *adv.* very; absolutely.

●**Dead Sea** a salt-water lake on the ISRAEL-JORDAN border.

deaf (def) *adj.* **1** unable to hear at all or to hear well. **2** not willing to listen to: *He was deaf to all protests.* – *n.* (*plural*) deaf people. – **turn a deaf ear to** to ignore.

deafen *vb.* **deafening, deafened** to make deaf or temporarily unable to hear.

Sign language is used by deaf people to communicate. As well as finger spelling, based on the shapes of letters, there are about 1,500 other signs.

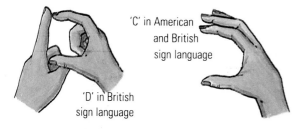

'C' in American and British sign language

'D' in British sign language

deal (dēl) *n.* **1** a bargain, agreement, or arrangement, especially in business or politics. **2** treatment: *Passengers in economy class got a raw deal.* **3** the process of sharing out cards among the players in a card game. – *vb.* **dealing, dealt** (delt) **1** to buy and sell: *They deal in oriental carpets.* **2** to divide the cards among the players in a card game: *You're supposed to deal out the entire pack.* – *n.* **dealer.** – **deal someone a blow** to hit or strike someone.

dealings *n.* (*plural*) business contacts.

dealt. See **deal.**

dean (dēn) *n.* **1** a senior clergyman in a cathedral. **2** a senior official in some universities.

dear (dēr) *adj.* **1** high in price; charging high prices. **2** used in addressing someone at the start of a letter. **3** loved: *They are dear friends.*

dearth (dûrth) *n.* a lack.

death (deth) *n.* **1** the time, act, or manner of dying, or the state of being dead. **2** something which causes you to die: *Smoking will be the death of him.* – **at death's door** almost dead. **the death penalty** *n.* punishment by death.

●**Death Valley**, California, was named by gold seekers, many of whom died crossing the valley during the 1849 gold rush.

debate (di **bāt**) *n.* **1** a formal discussion, often in front of an audience, in which two or more people put forward opposing views on a particular subject. **2** any general discussion on a subject, not necessarily in one place or at one time. – *vb.* **debating, debated** to hold or take part in a debate about something.

debatable or **debateable** *adj.* uncertain.

debris or **débris** (**de** brē) *n.* what remains of something crushed, smashed, destroyed, etc.

debt (det) *n.* **1** something which is owed. **2** the state of owing something: *in debt.*

decade (**de** kād) *n.* a period of ten years.

decadence (**de** kå děns) *n.* a falling to low standards in morals, art, etc. – *adj.* **decadent.**

decapitate (di **kap** i tāt) *vb.* **decapitating, decapitated** to cut off the head of.

decay (di **kā**) *vb.* **decaying, decayed 1** to make or become rotten, ruined, weaker in health or power, etc. **2** (of radioactive substances) to lose radioactivity. – *n.* the state or process of decaying.

deceased (di **sēst**) *adj.* dead.

deceit (di **sēt**) *n.* dishonesty.

deceitful *adj.* deceiving.

deceive (di **sēv**) *vb.* **deceiving, deceived** to convince that something is true when it is not.

December (di **sem** ber) *n.* the twelfth month of the year. December has 31 days.

decent (**dē** sent) *adj.* **1** suitable; modest, not vulgar or immoral. **2** kind, tolerant, or likeable.

decency *n.* **decencies** decent behaviour.

The Dead Sea is 395 metres below sea level, the lowest place on the Earth's surface. Nothing can live in the Dead Sea for it is six times more salty than ordinary sea water. The water is so dense that even non-swimmers can float on it.

PRONUNCIATION GUIDE	
fat a	all ŏ
fate ā	foot oo
fast ä	moon ōō
among å	boy oi
met e	house ow
mean ē	demon ŏ
silent ě	thing th
loch hh	this Th
fin i	but u
line ī	mute ū
quick kw	fur û
got o	brochure ů
note ō	vision zh

deception (di **sep** shŏn) *n.* **1** an act of deceiving. **2** something which deceives or misleads. **deceptive** *adj.* deceiving; misleading.

decibel (**de** si bel) *n.* a unit used to measure the loudness of a sound.

decide (di **sīd**) *vb.* **deciding, decided 1** to make a choice or judgement about something; to make someone decide: *We've decided against a camping holiday.* **2** to make the final result of something certain: *a deciding factor.*

deciduous (di **sid** ū ŭs) *adj.* (of trees or shrubs) that have leaves that fall off in autumn. Losing their leaves in autumn helps deciduous trees to conserve water through winter. The chlorophyll that makes the leaves green breaks down and hidden colours are seen.

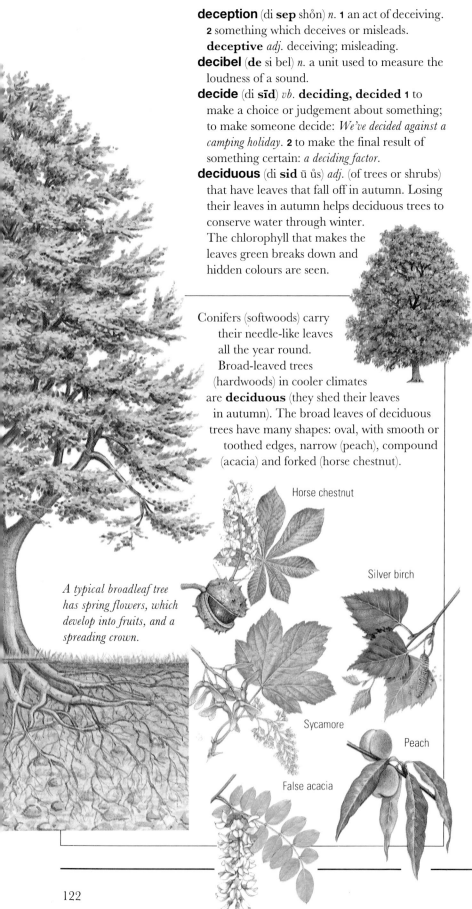

Conifers (softwoods) carry their needle-like leaves all the year round. Broad-leaved trees (hardwoods) in cooler climates are **deciduous** (they shed their leaves in autumn). The broad leaves of deciduous trees have many shapes: oval, with smooth or toothed edges, narrow (peach), compound (acacia) and forked (horse chestnut).

A typical broadleaf tree has spring flowers, which develop into fruits, and a spreading crown.

Horse chestnut

Silver birch

Sycamore

Peach

False acacia

decimal (**de** si mål) *adj.* based on ten.

decipher (di **sī** fĕr) *vb.* **deciphering, deciphered 1** to translate a code or an unfamiliar or strange form of writing into ordinary, understandable language: *She learned to decipher Egyptian hieroglyphics.* **2** to work out the meaning of: *She deciphered his handwriting.*

decision (di **si** zhŏn) *n.* **1** the act of deciding. **2** something decided. **decisive** *adj.* **1** putting an end to doubt. **2** willing and able to make decisions with firmness. – *n.* **decisiveness**.

deck (dek) *n.* **1** a platform extending from one side of a ship to the other, and forming a floor. **2** (especially *US*) a pack of playing cards.

declare (di **klār**) *vb.* **declaring, declared 1** to announce publicly: *War was declared in 1939.* **2** to say firmly. – *n.* **declaration**.

●**Declaration of Independence** a document adopted on 4 July 1776, declaring the 13 American colonies independent of Britain.

decline (di **klīn**) *vb.* **declining, declined 1** to refuse an invitation, etc., especially politely. **2** to become less in quality or quantity.

decompose (dē kŏm **pōz**) *vb.* **decomposing, decomposed** to decay or rot.

decorate (**de** kŏ rāt) *vb.* **decorating, decorated 1** to beautify with ornaments, etc.: *Every room was decorated with holly.* **2** to put paint or wallpaper on. **3** to award a medal to. **decoration** *n.* something used to decorate.

The Purple Heart is the oldest US military decoration. George Washington issued the first three in 1782 and the medal still bears his profile. This award is for being killed or wounded in action.

decorative (**de** kŏ rå tiv) *adj.* ornamental.

decrease (dē **krēs**) *vb.* **decreasing, decreased** to make or become less. – (**dē** krēs) *n.* a lessening or loss.

decree (di **krē**) *n.* a formal order or ruling made by someone in high authority.

dedicate (**de** di kāt) *vb.* **dedicating, dedicated** to give yourself or your time, money, etc. wholly or chiefly to: *To play tennis* *really well, you have to dedicate all your time to it.*

dedicated *adj.* **1** working very hard at or spending a great deal of time and energy on something. **2** (of computers, etc.) designed to carry out one particular function.

deduce (di **dūs**) *vb.* **deducing, deduced** to think out or judge on the basis of what you know or assume to be fact.

deduct (di **dukt**) *vb.* **deducting, deducted** to take away a number or an amount. – *n.* **deduction**.

deed (dēd) *n.* something someone has done; a notable achievement.

deep (dēp) *adj.* **1** reaching far down from the top or surface: *The water's not very deep here.* **2** going or being far in from the outside surface or edge. **3** coming from or going far down; long and full: *Take a deep breath.* **4** (of a colour) strong and relatively dark. **5** low in pitch: *He's got a deep voice.* **6** obscure; hard to understand: *Parts of this novel are very deep.* – *adv.* **1** deeply. **2** far down or in. **3** late on in, or well into, a period of time. – *n.* the ocean.

deepen *vb.* **deepening, deepened** to make or become deeper, greater, more intense, etc.

deeply *adv.* very greatly.

the Deep South *n.* the south-east part of the UNITED STATES, roughly the states of South Carolina, Georgia, Louisiana, Mississippi, and Alabama.

deer (dēr) *n.* **deer** a large, four-footed, hoofed animal, the male of which often has antlers.

●Deer chew the cud and have cloven hooves (divided in half). They eat leaves, fruit, grass, and bark. The world's largest deer is the North American moose.

defeat (di **fēt**) *vb.* **defeating, defeated 1** to beat, win a victory over, e.g. in a war, competition, game, or argument. **2** to cause plans, etc. to fail: *Locking the door but leaving the key in defeats the whole object.* – *n.* the act of defeating or state of being defeated.

defect (dē fekt) *n.* a flaw, fault, or imperfection. – (di **fekt**) *vb.* **defecting, defected** to leave your country, political party, or group, especially to support or join an opposing one.

defective *adj.* imperfect; having defects.

defence (di **fens**) *n.* **1** the act of defending against attack. **2** the method, means,

equipment, or (often in *plural*) fortifications used to protect against attack. **3** the armed forces of a country. **4** in a law-court, the person on trial and the lawyer acting for him or her.

defend (di **fend**) *vb.* **defending, defended 1** to guard or protect against attack. **2** to be the lawyer acting on behalf of the accused person in a trial. – *n.* **defender**.

defensive (di **fen** siv) *adj.* **1** defending or ready to defend. **2** attempting to justify your actions when criticized or when expecting criticism: *You'll never improve if you're always so defensive.*

defer¹ (di **fûr**) *vb.* **deferring, deferred** to leave until a later time. – *n.* **deferment**.

defer² (di **fûr**) *vb.* **deferring, deferred** to give in to the wishes, opinions, or orders of: *I'll defer to your superior expertise.*

Red deer

Moose

Fallow deer

Muntjac

Reindeer

defiance (di **fī** åns) *n.* open disobedience; challenging or opposition. – *adj.* **defiant**.

deficient (di **fi** shėnt) *adj.* not having all that is needed: *Your diet is deficient in protein.*

define (di **fīn**) *vb.* **defining, defined** to give the exact meaning of a word, etc.

definite (**de** fi nit) *adj.* **1** not liable to change. **2** sure; certain. **3** clear and precise.

definition (de fi **ni** shŏn) *n.* a statement of the meaning of a word or phrase.

definitive (di **fin** i tiv) *adj.* final and settling a matter once and for all. – *adv.* **definitively**.

deflate (di **flāt**) *vb.* **deflating, deflated 1** to make or grow smaller by the release of gas. **2** to take away the hopes, etc. of.

Unlike their relations, cattle and antelope, deer have antlers rather than permanent horns. Female deer, except reindeer or caribou, do not grow antlers. Deer are naturally wild, but some of them, such as reindeer or caribou, have been domesticated.

●**Defoe** (di fō), **Daniel** (1660-1731) was the English author of *Robinson Crusoe*.

deft (deft) *adj.* skilful, quick, and neat.

defy (di fī) *vb.* **defies, defying, defied** to resist or disobey boldly and openly.

●**de Gaulle** (dĕ göl), **Charles** (1890-1970) was a French general, statesman, and president (1958-69).

degree (di grē) *n.* **1** an amount or extent. **2** (*symbol* °) a unit of temperature. **3** (*symbol* °) a unit by which angles are measured, one 360th part of a complete revolution. **4** an award or title given by a university or college.

deity (dā i ti) *n.* **deities** a god or goddess.

dejected (di **jek** tid) *adj.* sad; miserable.

●**Delaware**. See Supplement, **USA**.

delay (di lā) *vb.* **delaying, delayed 1** to slow down or cause to be late: *The train was delayed when a tree fell on to the track.* **2** to put off to a later time. **3** to be slow in doing something; to linger. – *n.* **1** the act of delaying or state of being delayed. **2** the amount of time by which someone or something is delayed.

delegate (**de** li gāt) *vb.* **delegating, delegated 1** to give some of your work, power, etc. to someone else. **2** to name someone as a representative, as the one to do a job, etc. – (**de** li gắt) *n.* someone chosen to be the representative for another person or group of people at a conference or meeting.

delete (di lēt) *vb.* **deleting, deleted** to rub out or remove, especially from something written.

●**Delhi** (**del** i) is the capital of INDIA.

deliberate (di **lib** ĕ rắt) *adj.* **1** done on purpose. **2** slow and careful. – (di **lib** ĕ rāt) *vb.* **deliberating, deliberated** to think about carefully: *The jury deliberated on their verdict.*

delicacy (**de** li kắ si) *n.* **delicacies 1** the state or quality of being delicate. **2** something considered particularly delicious to eat.

delicate (**de** li kắt) *adj.* **1** easily damaged or broken. **2** not strong or healthy. **3** small, neat, and careful: *She danced with delicate movements.* **4** requiring tact: *Richard handled the delicate situation with his usual skill.*

delicious (di **li** shŭs) *adj.* very pleasant, especially to taste or smell.

delight (di **līt**) *vb.* **delighting, delighted 1** to please greatly. **2** to take great pleasure from: *He delights in teasing everybody.* – *n.* **1** great pleasure. **2** something or someone that gives great pleasure. – *adj.* **delighted**.

deliver (di **li** vĕr) *vb.* **delivering, delivered** to carry goods, letters, etc. to a person or place.

●**Delphi** is an ancient Greek city, site of the oracle of Apollo.

delta (**del** tǎ) *n.* a roughly triangular area of land at the mouth of a river whose main stream has split into several channels.

deluge (**del** ūj) *n.* **1** a flood. **2** a very heavy fall of rain.

demand (di **mänd**) *vb.* **demanding, demanded 1** to ask or ask for firmly, forcefully, or urgently. **2** to require or need: *This wound demands urgent medical attention.* – *n.* **1** a forceful request or order. **2** people's desire or ability to buy or obtain goods, etc.: *There is a constant demand for gloves and scarves in winter.*

demi- (**de** mi-) half or partly: *A demigod is part human and part god.*

PRONUNCIATION GUIDE	
fat a	all ö
fate ā	foot oo
fast ä	moon ōō
among å	boy oi
met e	house ow
mean ē	demon ŏ
silent ĕ	thing th
lo**ch hh**	this **Th**
fin i	but u
line ī	mute ū
qui**ck kw**	fur û
got o	brochure ŭ
note ō	vision zh

A delta may form where a river flowing slowly across a plain into the sea deposits sand and soil. Mudbanks build up and the river flows through them in channels. This blocked-up river mouth is called a delta because its shape is often like the Greek letter delta △.

Democracy in ancient Greece was supposed to be government of the people, by the people, for the people – yet this did not apply to women or slaves. Voting took place in the open air and politicians took it in turn to address the people.

democracy (di **mok** rå si) *n.* **democracies** a form of government in which the people govern themselves or elect representatives to govern them.
   democrat (**de** mŏ krat) *n.* **1** a person who believes in democracy. **2 Democrat** a supporter of the Democratic Party, one of the two chief political parties in the UNITED STATES. – *adj.* **democratic**.
demolish (di **mo** lish) *vb.* **demolishing, demolished** to pull or tear down a building.
   demolition *n.* the act of demolishing.
demon (**dē** mŏn) *n.* an evil spirit.
demonstrate (**de** mŏn strāt) *vb.*
   demonstrating, demonstrated 1 to show or prove by reasoning or providing evidence. **2** to show how something is done, operates, etc. **3** to show your support, opposition, etc. by protesting or marching in public. – *n.* **demonstration**. – *n.* **demonstrator**.
   demonstrative (di **mon** strå tiv) *adj.* showing feelings openly.
den (den) *n.* a wild animal's home.
denial (di **nī** ål) *n.* an act of refusing something to someone.
denim (**de** nim) *n.* tough cotton cloth used for making jeans, etc., usually blue.

● **Denmark**. See Supplement, **Countries**.

denomination (dĕ no mi **nā** shŏn) *n.* **1** a religious group with its own particular beliefs and practices. **2** a particular unit of value of a postage stamp, coin, or banknote, etc.
denote (di **nōt**) *vb.* **denoting, denoted 1** to mean; to be the name of or sign for. **2** to be a sign, mark, or indication of. – *n.* **denotation**.
denounce (di **nowns**) *vb.* **denouncing, denounced** to condemn an action, idea, etc.
dense (dens) *adj.* **1** closely packed or crowded together. **2** thick.
   density *n.* **densities 1** the state of being dense. **2** the number or quantity of something in a given unit of area or volume.
dent (dent) *n.* a hollow in the surface of something, made by pressure or a blow: *After the accident there was a huge dent in the front of my car.* – *vb.* **denting, dented** to make a dent in.
dental (**den** tål) *adj.* concerned with teeth.
dentist (**den** tist) *n.* a person qualified to repair or remove decayed teeth, fit false teeth, etc.
   dentistry *n.* the branch of medicine which specializes in the care and repair of the teeth.
deny (di **nī**) *vb.* **denies, denying, denied 1** to declare something not to be true. **2** to refuse to give or allow: *They were denied the right to a fair trial.* – **deny yourself** to do without.
deodorant (dē **ō** dŏ rånt) *n.* a substance that prevents or conceals body odour.
depart (di **pärt**) *vb.* **departing, departed 1** to leave: *The plane for Paris will depart from gate 10.* **2** to stop following a usual course of action.
   departure *n.* going away or leaving.
department (di **pärt** mĕnt) *n.* a section of any business or organization, with responsibility for one particular part of the organization's work.
depend (di **pend**) *vb.* **depending, depended 1** to be able to trust: *You can depend on her to arrive on time.* **2** to be decided by or vary according to: *He may come; it depends on how he's feeling.*
   dependable *adj.* trustworthy or reliable.
   dependant *n.* a person who is kept or supported financially by another.
   dependent *adj.* **1** relying on for financial or other support. **2** decided or influenced by.
depict (di **pikt**) *vb.* **depicting, depicted 1** to paint or draw. **2** to describe. – *n.* **depiction**.
deplore (di **plör**) *vb.* **deploring, deplored** to feel or express great disapproval of.
   deplorable *adj.* very bad or regrettable.

DEPENDENT CLAUSE
A main clause is one that can stand alone as a sentence and make sense: *The cat was sittting on the mat.* A dependent clause is one that cannot stand alone and makes incomplete sense: *when I looked through the window.* The whole sentence should read: *When I looked through the window, the cat was sitting on the mat.*

Denim takes its name from Nîmes, France, where the cloth was first made in the 1600s.

An area of low air pressure is called a depression. As the air rises, its moisture condenses, clouds form, and it rains.

Depression

deport (di **pört**) vb. **deporting**, **deported** to exile; to send out of the country.

deposit (di **po** zit) vb. **depositing**, **deposited** 1 to put or leave: *The washing was deposited in the middle of the table.* 2 to put money in a bank, etc. – n. 1 a sum of money deposited in a bank, etc. 2 solid matter that has settled at the bottom of a liquid.

depot (**de** pō) n. 1 a warehouse. 2 a place where buses, trains, and certain types of vehicles are kept and repaired.

depress (di **pres**) vb. **depressing**, **depressed** to make sad and gloomy. – adj. **depressing**.

depressed adj. 1 sad and gloomy. 2 suffering from high unemployment and low standards of living: *This has become a depressed area.*

depression n. 1 a feeling of sadness. 2 a period of low business and industrial activity accompanied by a rise in unemployment. 3 an area of low pressure in the atmosphere.

deprive (di **prīv**) vb. **depriving**, **deprived** to take or keep from; to prevent from using or enjoying: *The prisoners were deprived of their basic human rights.*

deprived adj. lacking in food, housing, etc.

depth (depth) n. 1 deepness; the distance from the top downwards. 2 (of feelings) intensity or strength. 3 extensiveness: *I'm always amazed at the depth of his knowledge.* 4 somewhere far from the surface or edge of: *The ship sank to the depths of the ocean.* 5 (of sound) lowness of pitch. – **in depth** deeply and thoroughly.

deputy (**de** pū ti) n. **deputies** a person appointed to act on behalf of or as an assistant to someone: *the deputy sheriff.*

derive (di **rīv**) vb. **deriving**, **derived** 1 to obtain: *He derives a lot of pleasure from his work.* 2 to come from, or be traced back to, a source: *Many English words are derived from French.*

derivation n. the act of deriving or the state or process of being derived.

dermatology (dûr mà **tol** ŏ ji) n. the branch of medicine concerned with the study of the skin.

derrick (**de** rik) n. 1 a type of crane with a movable arm. 2 a framework built over an oil-well, used for raising and lowering the drill.

Derrick gets its name from gallows on which criminals were hanged in London. The name of the hangman was Derrick, after whom the gallows were named.

● **Descartes** (dā **kärt**), **René** (1596-1650) was a French philosopher. The basis of his thinking was, 'I think, therefore I am'.

descend (di **send**) vb. **descending**, **descended** 1 to go or move down from a higher to a lower place or position. 2 to lead or slope downwards.

descendant n. a person or animal that is the child, grandchild, etc. of another.

descent (di **sent**) n. 1 the act or process of coming or going down. 2 a slope downwards.

describe (di **skrīb**) vb. **describing**, **described** to say what someone or something is like: *Can you describe how you felt?*

description (di **skrip** shŏn) n. a statement of what someone or something is like.

descriptive (di **skrip** tiv) adj. describing, especially describing well or vividly.

desert[1] (di **zûrt**) vb. **deserting**, **deserted** to leave a place or person, intending not to return: *She deserted her child.*

deserted adj. empty or abandoned.

desert[2] (**de** zĕrt) n. an area of land where there is little water or rainfall.

Some of the main deserts of the world. The driest is the Atacama in South America, the largest is the Sahara in Africa.

Sahara	9,065,000 sq km
Great Australian	3,885,000 sq km
Libyan	1,295,000 sq km
Gobi	777,000 sq km
Rub'al Khali	647,500 sq km
Kalahari	310,000 sq km
Kara Kum	284,900 sq km
Atacama	64,750 sq km

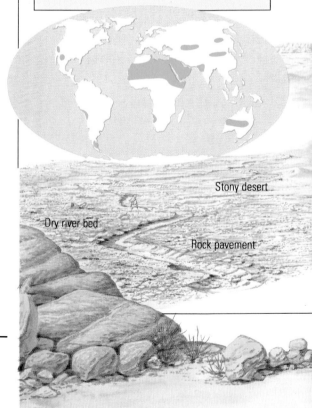

Dry river bed

Stony desert

Rock pavement

deserve (di **zûrv**) vb. **deserving, deserved** to have earned or be worthy of something good or something bad: *She deserves a medal.*

desiccate (de si kāt) vb. **desiccating, desiccated** to dry something, especially food in order to preserve it. – adj. **desiccated**.

design (di **zīn**) vb. **designing, designed 1** to prepare a plan, drawing, or model of something before it is made. **2** to plan, intend, or develop for a particular purpose: *This pen has been designed especially for left-handed people.* – n. **1** a plan, drawing, or model showing how something is to be made. **2** the art or job of making such drawings, plans, etc. **3** the way in which something has been made.
designer n. a person whose job it is to make designs, plans, patterns, drawings, etc.

designate (**dez** ig nāt) vb. **designating, designated** to appoint to a job or post.

desire (di **zīr**) n. a longing for something. – vb. **desiring, desired** to long for.
desirable adj. pleasing; worth having.

desk (desk) n. a table, often with drawers, used for writing, reading, etc.

desolate (de sǒ lǎt) adj. **1** (of a place) deserted, barren, and lonely. **2** very sad: *Life is pretty desolate now that my friends have moved.*

despair (di **spār**) vb. **despairing, despaired** to be without or lose hope: *I despair of finding my cat now that she's been gone so long.*

desperate (**des** pěr åt) adj. **1** willing to take risks fearlessly because of hopelessness and despair: *He's desperate and will try anything.* **2** very serious, difficult, dangerous, and almost hopeless: *With winter approaching the plight of the refugees is desperate.* **3** in great or urgent need: *They are desperate for money; please give what you can.* – n. **desperation**.

despise (di **spīz**) vb. **despising, despised** to look down on with contempt. – adj. **despicable**.

despite (di **spīt**) prep. in spite of.

despondent (di **spon** děnt) adj. sad.

despot (**des** pot) n. a person who has total power, especially one who uses such power in a cruel or oppressive way. – adj. **despotic**.

dessert (di **zûrt**) n. sweet food served after the main course of a meal.

destination (de sti **nā** shǒn) n. the place to which someone or something is going or being sent.

destined (**des** tind) adj. intended for a particular purpose: *He was destined to be a politician.*

destiny (**des** ti ni) n. **destinies** a person's purpose or future as arranged by fate.

destitute (**des** ti tūt) adj. extremely poor.

destroy (di **stroi**) vb. **destroying, destroyed** to damage something beyond repair: *The bomb destroyed a row of shops.*
destroyer n. **1** a person or thing that destroys. **2** a type of small, fast warship.

destruction (di **struk** shǒn) n. **1** the act of destroying. **2** something that destroys.
destructible adj. able to be destroyed.
destructive adj. causing destruction or serious damage: *Toys don't last five minutes with him, he's so destructive.*

Deserts are not necessarily hot. The polar regions are deserts. Most deserts are rocky, not sandy. Sand only covers 11 percent of the Sahara.

Sand dunes

Salt pan

Oasis

Sandy desert

Camels are ideally suited for the job of making long journeys across deserts. They are powerful and swift and can go for days without eating or drinking, living off the fat stored in their humps.

detach (di **tach**) *vb.* **detaching, detached** to unfasten or separate: *The trailer can be detached quite easily.* – *adj.* **detachable**.

detail (**dē** tāl) *n.* **1** a small feature, fact, or item. **2** something considered unimportant.

detain (di **tān**) *vb.* **detaining, detained 1** to stop, hold back, keep waiting, or delay: *I'm sorry I'm late – I was detained in a meeting.* **2** (of the police, etc.) to keep someone in a cell, prison, or elsewhere, especially before trial.

detect (di **tekt**) *vb.* **detecting, detected** to see or notice: *Do I detect a touch of envy in your voice?* **detective** *n.* a police officer whose job is to solve crime by gathering evidence.

deter (di **tûr**) *vb.* **deterring, deterred** to discourage someone from doing something because of fear of unpleasant consequences.

detergent (di **tûr** jĕnt) *n.* a chemical substance used for cleaning.

deteriorate (di **tēr** i ŏ rāt) *vb.* **deteriorating, deteriorated** to grow worse: *His condition deteriorated during the night.* – *n.* **deterioration**.

determine (di **tûr** min) *vb.* **determining, determined 1** to fix or find out exactly: *Careful questioning determined who was in the area on the night of the crime.* **2** to decide: *I determined not to let them see how nervous I felt.* **determination** *n.* firmness or strength of will. **determined** *adj.* **1** having firmly decided: *He was determined to win.* **2** having a strong will.

detest (di **test**) *vb.* **detesting, detested** to hate.

detour (**dē** tōōr) *n.* a route away from and longer than a planned or more direct route.

● **Detroit** is the largest city in Michigan, USA, and 'Automobile Capital' of America.

Deutschmark (**doich** märk) *n.* (*symbol* **DM**) the standard unit of currency in GERMANY.

● **de Valera, Eamon** (1882-1975) was an Irish patriot, prime minister, and president.

devastate (**de** vå stāt) *vb.* **devastating, devastated** to cause great destruction in or to: *The country has been devastated by years of civil war.* – *adj.* **devastated**. – *n.* **devastation**.

develop (di **vel** ŏp) *vb.* **developing, developed 1** to make or become more mature, more advanced, more detailed, etc.: *Within a few years this place has developed from a fishing village into a major resort.* **2** to begin to

have: *I'm developing an interest in politics.* **3** to make the picture on a photographic film become visible by a chemical process.

development *n.* **1** the act of developing or the process of being developed: *We observed each stage of their development from caterpillar to adult moth.* **2** a new stage, event, or situation.

deviate (**dē** vi āt) *vb.* **deviating, deviated** to depart from what is considered correct.

device (di **vīs**) *n.* something made for a special purpose, such as a tool or instrument.

devil (**de** vil) *n.* any evil or wicked spirit.

devious (**dē** vi ŭs) *adj.* not honest; cunning.

devise (di **vīz**) *vb.* **devising, devised** to invent, make up, or put together a plan, etc.

devote (**dē** vōt) *vb.* **devoting, devoted** to give up wholly to or use entirely for: *He devoted all his free time to training.*

devour (di **vowr**) *vb.* **devouring, devoured** to eat up greedily. – *adj.* **devouring**.

devout (di **vowt**) *adj.* **1** sincerely religious. **2** deeply-felt; earnest.

dew (**dū**) *n.* tiny drops of moisture coming from the air as it cools at night.

diabetes (dī å **bē** tēz) *n.* a disease in which the body fails to absorb sugar and starch properly from the blood due to a deficiency of insulin. **diabetic** (dī å **bet** ik) *n.* a person suffering from diabetes.

● **Diaghilev, Sergei** (1872-1929) was a Russian impresario and founder of *Ballets Russes*, a Russian ballet company in Paris.

Among the great dancers in Diaghilev's Ballets Russes were such geniuses as Vaslav Nijinsky and Tamara Karsavina seen here in Fokine's The Spirit of the Rose.

PRONUNCIATION GUIDE

fat **a**	all **ö**
fate **ā**	foot **oo**
fast **ä**	moon **ōō**
among **å**	boy **oi**
met **e**	house **ow**
mean **ē**	demon **ŏ**
silent **ĕ**	thing **th**
loch **hh**	this **Th**
fin **i**	but **u**
line **ī**	mute **ū**
quick **kw**	fur **û**
got **o**	brochure **ŭ**
note **ō**	vision **zh**

diagnosis (dī ǎg **nō** sis) *n.* **diagnoses** the identification of a disease from looking at the patient's symptoms.

diagonal (dī **ag** ŏ nǎl) *adj.* sloping or slanting.

diagram (dī å gram) *n.* a simple line drawing, showing how a machine, etc. works.

A **diagram** is a sketch or plan which explains rather than represents the actual appearance of something. A diagram of a diamond will show the structure of the crystal rather than its wonderful sparkle; and to illustrate how an aircraft moves, a crude-looking childish drawing will do.

dial (dī ǎl) *n.* a disc or plate on a clock, radio, meter, etc., with numbers or other measurements marked on it and a movable pointer, used to indicate speed, time, etc.

dialect (dī å lekt) *n.* a form of a language spoken in a particular region.

dialogue (dī å log) *n.* **1** the words spoken by the characters in a play, book, etc. **2** a discussion of ideas, especially between two groups.

dialysis (dī **al** i sis) *n.* **dialyses** the removal by filtering out of harmful wastes from the blood of people suffering from kidney failure.

diameter (dī **am** i tĕr) *n.* a straight line drawn from one side of a circle to the other side and passing through its centre; the length of the line.

diamond (dī å mǒnd) *n.* **1** a usually colourless transparent precious stone, a crystallized form of carbon, the hardest of all minerals. It is also used in industrial cutting tools. **2** a shape or figure with four equal straight sides and angles which are not right angles. **3** (in *plural*) one of the four suits of playing cards with red symbols of this shape. **4** a baseball pitch.

diaper (dī å pĕr) *n.* (*US*) a baby's nappy.

diaphragm (dī å fram) *n.* the wall of muscle which separates the chest from the abdomen.

diary (dī å ri) *n.* **diaries** a written record of daily events in a person's life.

●**Dias** (dē ås), **Bartolomeu** (1450-1500) was a Portuguese explorer and the first European to round the Cape of Good Hope.

dice (dīs) *n.* **dice** a small cube with a different number of spots, from 1 to 6, on each of its sides, used in games of chance.

●**Dickens, Charles** (1812-70) was an English novelist whose works include *David Copperfield*, *Oliver Twist*, and *Great Expectations*.

●**Dickinson, Emily** (1830-86) was an American poet. Her themes were love, nature, and God.

dictate (dik **tāt**) *vb.* **dictating, dictated 1** to say or read out something for someone else to write down. **2** to give orders to or try to impose your wishes on someone: *I will not be dictated to!*

dictionary (dik shǒn å ri) *n.* **dictionaries** a book containing the words of a language arranged alphabetically with their meanings or translations into another language.

did. See **do**.

●**Diderot** (dē dĕ rō), **Denis** (1713-84) was a French philosopher.

didn't did not.

die (dī) *vb.* **dies, dying, died 1** to stop living, cease to be alive: *Shakespeare died in 1616.* **2** to cease to exist, come to an end, or fade away: *The fight for equality will never die.* **3** to stop working suddenly and unexpectedly: *The motor*

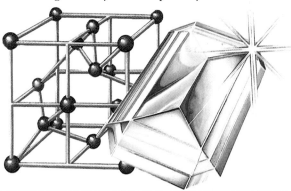

Diamonds are crystals. They are harder than anything else in the world. They are made of pure carbon. The atoms in a diamond are arranged in a dense latticework. This is why diamonds are so hard.

Lambeosaurus

Parasaurolophus

The Archaeopteryx ('ancient wing') was about the size of a crow. It had small, sharp teeth and bony fingers half way down its wings.

The word **dinosaur** means 'terrible lizard'. Dinosaurs lived between 65 and 225 million years ago. They included the largest and most ferocious animals ever to have lived on Earth. About 65 million years ago the dinosaurs suddenly and mysteriously died out. Most of what we know about dinosaurs comes from bones and tracks that have been preserved as fossils in rocks. The first dinosaur discoveries were made in England. In 1822 Mary Mantell, a doctor's wife, noticed some fossil teeth in a pile of road-menders' stones. They belonged to what became named as iguanodon.

Hadrosaurids ('big reptiles') had a broad beak like a duck's, so many people called them duckbilled dinosaurs.

The skull of a Camarasaurus, a member of the sauropod group.

Deinonychus had three strong, clasping fingers on its hands. Each finger was armed with a heavy claw (shown here).

The sauropod group of dinosaurs were the largest animals that have ever lived on land. Most of these huge creatures looked like enormous elephants with long necks and tails. Although they looked terrifying, they were harmless plant-eating creatures.

Stegosaurus was a plant-eater. It developed bony plates along its back to help protect itself from large flesh-eaters such as Allosaurus. It had a tiny brain for its size.

just died. – **be dying for** (*colloquial*) to have a strong desire or need for something. – *vb.* **die away** to become steadily weaker and finally stop: *The applause began before the last notes of music had died away.*

dying *adj.* **1** occurring immediately before death: *His comrades recorded his dying words.* **2** disappearing: *Real craftsmen are a dying breed.*

diet (**dī** ĕt) *n.* **1** the sort of food normally eaten by a person or animal. **2** a limited variety or quantity of food that a person is allowed to eat, especially in order to lose weight or because of illness. – *vb.* **dieting, dieted** to limit your food to what is allowed by a prescribed diet.

differ (**di** fĕr) *vb.* **differing, differed 1** to be different, unlike, or of more than one kind: *Earth differs from the other planets in having an atmosphere which can sustain life.* **2** to disagree: *We differ on several issues.*

difference (**di** fĕ rĕns) *n.* **1** what makes one thing or person unlike another: *What is the difference between these two soap bars?* **2** the amount by which one quantity or number is greater or less than another. **3** a quarrel.

different *adj.* **1** not the same: *Our house is different from all the others.* **2** separate; distinct; various: *They all like different things.*

difficult (**di** fi kŭlt) *adj.* **1** requiring great skill, intelligence, or effort. **2** not easy to please.

difficulty *n.* **difficulties 1** the state or quality of being difficult. **2** a difficult thing to do or understand. **3** (usually in *plural*) trouble or embarrassment, especially financial.

diffident (**di** fi dĕnt) *adj.* lacking in confidence; shy. – *n.* **diffidence**.

dig (dig) *vb.* **digging, dug** (dug) **1** to turn up or move earth, etc., especially with a spade. **2** to make a hole, etc. by digging. **3** to poke: *The springs in this chair keep digging into me.* – *n.* a place where archaeologists are digging to uncover ancient ruins, etc.

digest (dī **jest**) or (di **jest**) *vb.* **digesting, digested** to break down food in the stomach, etc. into a form which the body can use.

digestion *n.* the act of digesting food.

digit (**di** jit) *n.* any of the ten figures 0 to 9.

digital *adj.* **1** showing quantity, time, etc. by means of numbers rather than by a pointer on a scale, dial, etc. **2** processing information which is in the form of a series of digits, generally in binary form: *a digital computer.*

dignity (**dig** ni ti) *n.* **1** seriousness and formality.

2 goodness and nobility of character.

dilapidated (di **lap** i dā tid) *adj.* falling to pieces because of neglect or age.

dilemma (di **lem** å) *n.* a situation in which you must choose between two courses of action, both equally undesirable.

diligent (**di** li jĕnt) *adj.* hard-working; done with care and serious effort. – *n.* **diligence**.

dilute (dī **lōōt**) or (di **lōōt**) *vb.* **diluting, diluted** to make a liquid thinner or weaker by mixing with water or another liquid.

dim (dim) *adj.* **dimmer, dimmest 1** not bright or distinct. **2** lacking enough light to see clearly. **3** faint; not clearly remembered: *I have a dim memory of what happened.* – *vb.* **dimming, dimmed** to make or become dim. – *n.* **dimness**. – **take a dim view of** (*colloquial*) to disapprove of.

dime (dīm) *n.* a coin of the UNITED STATES and CANADA worth ten cents.

dimension (dī **men** shŏn) *n.* a measurement of length, breadth, height, etc.

diminish (di **min** ish) *vb.* **diminishing, diminished** to become less or smaller.

diminutive (di **min** ū tiv) *adj.* very small.

dimple (**dim** pĕl) *n.* a small hollow, especially in the skin of the cheeks or chin.

din (din) *n.* a continuous and unpleasant noise.

dine (dīn) *vb.* **dining, dined 1** to eat dinner. **2** (upon) to eat for your dinner.

dinghy (**ding** gi) *n.* **dinghies 1** a small open boat propelled by oars, sails, or an outboard motor. **2** a small collapsible rubber boat, especially one kept for use in emergencies.

dingo (**ding** gō) *n.* **dingoes** a species of wild dog found in AUSTRALIA.

dinner (**di** nĕr) *n.* the main meal of the day, usually eaten in the evening.

dinosaur (**dī** nŏ sör) *n.* any animal of the large number of species of extinct reptiles of the order *Dinosauria*.

diocese (**dī** ŏ sis) *n.* the district over which a bishop has authority.

dip (dip) *vb.* **dipping, dipped 1** to put into a liquid for a short time. **2** to go down briefly and then up again. **3** to slope downwards. **4** to put your hand, etc. into a dish, container, etc. and take out some of the contents: *He dipped into the tin for another biscuit.* – *n.* **1** an act of dipping. **2** a downward slope, especially in a road. **3** a short swim or bathe.

Pteranodon (*'winged and toothless'*) had a turkey-sized body, but its wingspan measured up to seven metres

diphthong (**dif** thong) or (**dip** thong) *n.* two vowel sounds pronounced as one syllable, as the sound represented by *ou* in *sounds*.

diploma (di **plō** må) *n.* a document certifying that you have passed a certain examination or completed a course of study.

diplomat (**dip** lò mat) *n.* a government official or representative engaged in diplomacy.
diplomacy (di **plō** må si) *n.* the art or profession of making agreements, treaties, etc. between countries.

direct (di **rekt**) or (dī **rekt**) *adj.* **1** straight; following the quickest and shortest path from beginning to end or to a destination. **2** (of a person's manner, etc.) open, straightforward. – *vb.* **directing, directed 1** to point, aim, or turn in a particular direction. **2** to show the way: *Tim directed me to the farm.* **3** to order or instruct.
directly *adv.* **1** in a direct manner. **2** by a direct path. **3** at once; immediately.

direction (di **rek** shŏn) or (dī **rek** shŏn) *n.* **1** the place or point towards which you are moving or facing. **2** (usually in *plural*) instructions on how to operate a piece of equipment, etc.

director (di **rek** tŏr) or (dī **rek** tŏr) *n.* **1** any of the most senior managers of a business firm. **2** the person directing a play, film, etc. – *n.* **directorship**.

PRONUNCIATION GUIDE	
fat **a**	all **ö**
fate **ā**	foot **oo**
fast **ä**	moon **ōō**
among **å**	boy **oi**
met **e**	house **ow**
mean **ē**	demon **ŏ**
silent **ê**	thing **th**
loch **hh**	this **Th**
fin **i**	but **u**
line **ī**	mute **ū**
quick **kw**	fur **û**
got **o**	brochure **ŭ**
note **ō**	vision **zh**

SOME RECENT DISASTERS

1979 March. Water pump breaks down releasing radioactive steam at Three Mile Island, Penn, USA.
1980s. Great areas of Africa, notably Ethiopia, suffer prolonged drought, crop failure and famine.
1984 December. Toxic gas leaked from a pesticide plant at Bhopal, India. Possibly 10,000 deaths.
1986 April. Nuclear reactor explodes at Chernobyl, Ukraine. 100,000 may die from radiation-induced cancer, a further 30,000 fatalities are possible worldwide.
1987 *Herald of Free Enterprise*, British ferry capsized off Zeebrugge, Belgium. 188 casualties.
1988 July. In Cornwall 20 tonnes of aluminium sulphate are flushed down rivers after an accident at a water treatment works. 60,000 fish are killed. Local people suffer vomiting, ulcers and memory loss.
1988 21 December. American Pan Am Boeing 747 explodes in Lockerbie, Scotland. 270 deaths.
1991 February. Iraqi forces set alight 600 oil wells causing serious contamination of agricultural land and water supplies.
1991 July. *Kirki*, Greek tanker breaks up off Western Australia spilling millions of litres of crude oil, causing marine pollution of a conservation zone.

directory (di **rek** tŏ ri) or (dī **rek** tŏ ri) *n.* **directories** a book with a list of names and addresses, usually arranged alphabetically.

dirt (dûrt) *n.* **1** any unclean substance, e.g. mud or dust. **2** soil; earth.
dirty *adj.* **dirtier, dirtiest 1** marked with dirt. **2** which involves you becoming marked with dirt: *Unblocking the drains is a dirty job.* – *vb.* **dirties, dirtying, dirtied** to make dirty.

dis- (dis-) *prefix* turns the main word into the opposite, usually negative, e.g. *disconnect, discontinue, dislike, disloyal, disobey.*

disadvantage (dis åd **vän** tij) *n.* **1** a difficulty, drawback, or weakness. **2** an unfavourable situation. – *vb.* **disadvantaging, disadvantaged** to put at a disadvantage.

disagree (dis å **grē**) *vb.* **disagreeing, disagreed 1** to have a different opinion: *I disagree with him.* **2** to be opposed to: *I disagree with capital punishment.* **3** to conflict with each other: *The two theories disagree.*
disagreement *n.* a quarrel.

disappear (dis å **pēr**) *vb.* **1** to go out of sight; to vanish. **2** to cease to exist. – *n.* **disappearance**.

disappoint (dis å **point**) *vb.* to fail to fulfil the hopes or expectations of.
disappointment *n.* **1** the state of being disappointed. **2** something that disappoints.

disapprove (dis å **prōōv**) *vb.* to have a low opinion of: *She disapproves of late nights.* – *n.* **disapproval**. – *adj.* **disapproving**.

disaster (di **zä** stěr) *n.* **1** an event causing great damage, injury, or loss of life. **2** a total failure: *The meal was a disaster.* – *adj.* **disastrous**.

disc (disk) *n.* **1** any flat thin circular object. **2** a compact disc. **3** a layer of cartilage between vertebrae. **4** in computing, a disk.
disc jockey *n.* **disc jockeys** a person who presents a programme of recorded pop music.

discard (dis **kärd**) *vb.* **discarding, discarded** to get rid of as useless or unwanted.

discern (di **sûrn**) *vb.* **discerning, discerned** to notice; to judge.
discerning *adj.* having good judgement.

discharge (dis **chärj**) *vb.* **discharging, discharged 1** to allow to leave; to send away or dismiss, especially from employment: *Two officers have been discharged from the police force.* **2** to perform or carry out: *He has always discharged his duties satisfactorily.* **3** to flow out. – (**dis** chärj) *n.* the act of discharging.

disciple (di **sī** pěl) *n.* a person who follows the teachings of another.

discipline (**di** si plin) *n.* **1** strict training intended to produce ordered and controlled behaviour; the ordered behaviour resulting from this. **2** punishment designed to create obedience. – *vb.* **disciplining, disciplined** to train to behave in an ordered way.

disclose (dis **klōz**) *vb.* **disclosing, disclosed** to make known. – *n.* **disclosure**.

disco (**dis** kō) *n.* **discos** a discotheque.

discomfit (dis **kum** fit) *vb.* **discomfiting, discomfited** to cause to feel embarrassed.

discomfort (dis **kum** fȯrt) *n.* slight physical pain. – *vb.* **discomforting**.

discord (**dis** kȯrd) *n.* disagreement; conflict.

discotheque (**dis** kȯ tek) *n.* a night-club with dancing to recorded pop music.

discount (**dis** kownt) *n.* an amount deducted from the normal price. – *vb.* **discounting, discounted 1** (dis **kownt**) to disregard as unlikely, untrue, or irrelevant. **2** (**dis** kownt) to make a deduction from a price. – **at a discount** for less than the usual price.

discourage (dis **ku** rij) *vb.* **discouraging, discouraged 1** to deprive of confidence, hope, or the will to continue: *When I failed my driving test for the third time, I felt completely discouraged.* **2** to try to prevent someone from doing something: *We were always discouraged from eating sweets.* – *n.* **discouragement**.

discover (di **skuv** ȇr) *vb.* **discovering, discovered 1** to be the first person to find. **2** to find by chance, especially for the first time. **discovery** *n.* **discoveries 1** the act of discovering. **2** a person or thing discovered.

discriminate (dis **krim** i nāt) *vb.* **discriminating, discriminated 1** to recognize a difference: *They are both brilliant tennis players, so it's hard to discriminate between them.* **2** to give different treatment to different people or groups in identical circumstances, usually without justification: *This law discriminates against dog owners.* **discrimination** *n.* unjustifiably different treatment given to different people or groups.

discus (**dis** kůs) *n.* a heavy disc thrown in athletic competitions.

discuss (di **skus**) *vb.* **discussing, discussed** to talk about. – *n.* **discussion**.

disdain (dis **dān**) *n.* dislike arising out of lack of respect; contempt.

disease (di **zēz**) *n.* illness or lack of health caused by infection rather than by an accident.

disgrace (dis **grās**) *n.* shame or loss of favour or respect, or something likely to cause this: *You have brought disgrace to our family name.* – *vb.* **disgracing, disgraced** to bring shame upon. – *adj.* **disgraceful**.

disguise (dis **gīz**) *vb.* **disguising, disguised 1** to hide the identity of someone or something by a change of appearance: *The robbers disguised themselves as security guards.* **2** to conceal the true nature of: *It was a mistake, and there's no disguising the fact.*

disgust (dis **gust**) *vb.* **disgusting, disgusted** to sicken; to provoke intense dislike. – *adj.* **disgusted**. – *adv.* **disgusting**.

dish (dish) *n.* any shallow, usually roundish container in which food is served or cooked.

dishearten (dis **här** tȇn) *vb.* **disheartening, disheartened** to dampen the courage of.

dishevelled (di **shev** ȇld) *adj.* untidy; in a mess.

dishonest (dis **on** ist) *adj.* likely to deceive or cheat; insincere. – *n.* **dishonesty**.

dishonour (dis **on** ȯr) *n.* shame; loss of honour. – *vb.* **dishonouring, dishonoured** to bring dishonour on. – *adj.* **dishonourable**.

Most discuses are made of wood but have rounded metal rims. Women's discuses are lighter and smaller than men's.

Women's discus

Men's discus

An ancient Greek statue of a discus thrower. Discus throwing was a popular event in the Greek Olympic Games. Competitors get extra force by spinning several times before releasing the discus. The athlete who achieves the greatest distance after 6 throws is the winner.

disillusioned (dis i lōō zhŏnd) *adj.* sad at having discovered the unpleasant truth: *I'm disillusioned with show business.*

disinfect (dis in **fekt**) *vb.* **disinfecting, disinfected** to clean with a substance that kills germs.

disintegrate (dis **in** ti grāt) *vb.* **disintegrating, disintegrated** to shatter.

disinterested (dis **in** três tid) *adj.* unbiased; objective: *We chose him as a judge because we knew he'd give a disinterested opinion.*

● **disinterested** and **uninterested**. The first word means 'free from bias'; the second word means 'bored', 'having no interest in'.

disk (disk) *n.* in computing **1** (also **floppy disk**) a flat plastic disc, coated with a magnetic substance, on to which data can be copied. **2** (also **hard disk**) a stack of flat metal disks on which data is stored inside a computer.

dislocate (dis lŏ **kāt**) *vb.* **dislocating, dislocated** to put a bone out of joint.

dismal (**diz** mål) *adj.* not cheerful.

dismantle (dis **man** tĕl) *vb.* **dismantling, dismantled** to take to pieces.

dismay (dis **mā**) *n.* a mixture of sadness and deep disappointment or discouragement. – *vb.* **dismaying, dismayed** to fill with dismay.

dismiss (dis **mis**) *vb.* **dismissing, dismissed** **1** to refuse to consider or accept. **2** to put out of employment: *Adrian was dismissed from his job for doing careless work.* – *n.* **dismissal**.

● **Disney, Walt** (1901-66) was an American cartoon film maker, creator of Mickey Mouse.

disorder (dis **ör** dĕr) *n.* **1** confusion or disturbance. **2** a disease or illness.

dispatch (dis **pach**) *vb.* **dispatching, dispatched** to send to a place for a particular reason. – *n.* a report carried by a government official, or sent to a newspaper by a journalist.

dispel (di **spel**) *vb.* **dispelling, dispelled** to drive away or banish.

dispense (di **spens**) *vb.* **dispensing, dispensed** **1** to give out: *The courts dispense justice.* **2** to prepare and distribute medicine.

disperse (di **spûrs**) *vb.* **dispersing, dispersed** **1** to spread out over a wide area: *Elephant herds are dispersed throughout the region.* **2** to break up and leave: *After the match the crowd dispersed.* – *n.* **dispersal** or **dispersion**.

The disposal of the millions of tonnes of waste from mines, factories, and homes is a growing problem. Most of the waste is buried in landfill sites, the base of which is lined to prevent harmful liquids leaking into nearby water. At the end of each day the rubbish is levelled and covered with topsoil.

Pollutants leach into water table

display (di **splā**) *vb.* **displaying, displayed** **1** to put on view. **2** to show or betray: *You displayed great courage.* – *n.* the act of displaying: *There's going to be a firework display.*

dispose (di **spōz**) *vb.* **disposing, disposed** to get rid of; to deal with or settle: *Let's dispose of the paperwork.*

dispute (di **spūt**) *vb.* **disputing, disputed** **1** to question or deny the validity of. **2** to quarrel over possession of: *The area beyond the river is disputed territory.* – *n.* an argument.

disregard (dis ri **gärd**) *vb.* **disregarding, disregarded** to pay no attention to; to dismiss as unworthy of consideration. – *n.* dismissive lack of attention or concern: *You've shown complete disregard for other people's feelings.*

disrupt (dis **rupt**) *vb.* **disrupting, disrupted** to disturb the order or peaceful progress of. – *n.* **disruption**. – *adj.* **disruptive**.

dissect (di **sekt**) or (dī **sekt**) *vb.* **dissecting, dissected** to cut open for scientific or medical examination: *In biology today I dissected a frog.* – *n.* **dissection**.

dissent (di **sent**) *n.* disagreement, especially open or hostile.

dissident (**di** si dĕnt) *n.* a person who disagrees publicly, especially with a government.

dissolve (di **zolv**) *vb.* **dissolving, dissolved** **1** to break up and merge with a liquid: *Sugar dissolves easily in milk.* **2** to bring an assembly to a close: *Parliament was dissolved.*

distance (**di** ståns) *n.* **1** the separation between points in space or time; the extent of this separation. **2** any faraway point or place. – *vb.* **distancing, distanced** to put at a distance: *He distanced himself from government policy.*

distant *adj.* **1** far away or far apart in space or time. **2** not closely related. **3** unfriendly.

distil (di **stil**) *vb.* **distilling, distilled 1** to purify a liquid by converting it to a vapour, then cooling the vapour to liquid form again. **2** to produce alcoholic spirit in this way.

distinct (di **stingkt**) *adj.* **1** easily seen, heard, or recognized. **2** noticeably different.

distinctive *adj.* easily recognized because very individual. – *n.* **distinctiveness**.

distinguish (di **sting** gwish) *vb.* **distinguishing, distinguished 1** to mark or recognize as different: *Males are distinguished from females by their darker plumage.* **2** to see the difference between. **3** to identify: *I could barely distinguish the figure in the dim light.*

distinguished *adj.* **1** famous and well respected. **2** with a dignified appearance.

distort (di **stört**) *vb.* **distorting, distorted 1** to twist out of shape. **2** to change the meaning or tone of by inaccurate retelling: *That's a distorted version of the story.* – *n.* **distortion**.

distract (di **strakt**) *vb.* **distracting, distracted** to divert the attention of: *Don't distract him from his work.*

distracted *adj.* anxious and confused.

distraction *n.* **1** something that diverts the attention, especially an amusement. **2** anxiety; anger: *That noise is driving me to distraction.*

distress (di **stres**) *n.* **1** mental or emotional pain. **2** financial difficulty. **3** great danger; peril: *We're getting radio signals from a yacht in distress.* – *vb.* **distressing, distressed** to upset.

distribute (di **strib** ūt) *vb.* **distributing, distributed 1** to give out: *The leaflet was distributed to every household.* **2** to supply or deliver goods, etc. – *n.* **distribution**.

district (**dis** trikt) *n.* a region.

disturb (di **stûrb**) *vb.* **disturbing, disturbed 1** to interrupt. **2** to inconvenience. **3** to upset the order of. – *adj.* **disturbing**.

disturbance *n.* **1** an outburst of noisy or violent behaviour. **2** an act of disturbing.

disturbed *adj.* emotionally upset.

ditch (dich) *n.* a narrow channel dug in the ground, especially for drainage.

ditto (**di** tō) *n.* **dittos** the same thing; that which has just been said.

dive (dīv) *vb.* **diving, dived 1** to leap head first into water. **2** to fall steeply through the air. **3** to throw yourself to the side or to the ground: *He dived for the ball.* – *n.* an act of diving.

diver *n.* a person who works underwater.

diverse (dī **vûrs**) *adj.* various; assorted.

diversion (dī **vûr** shǒn) *n.* a detour from a usual route.

divert (dī **vûrt**) *vb.* **diverting, diverted 1** to cause to change direction: *Our flight was diverted from London to Manchester.* **2** to draw away, especially attention: *The news from abroad has diverted public attention from the troubles at home.*

divide (di **vīd**) *vb.* **dividing, divided 1** to split up or separate into parts: *Divide into groups of three.* **2** to share: *How are we going to divide this cake between us?* **3** to determine how many times one number is contained in another.

divine (di **vīn**) *adj.* of, from, or relating to a god.

division (di **vi** zhǒn) *n.* **1** the act of dividing; the state of being divided. **2** something that divides or separates; a gap or barrier. **3** the process of determining how many times one number is contained in another. – *adj.* **divisional**.

divorce (di **vörs**) *n.* **1** the legal ending of a marriage. **2** a complete separation.

Diwali (di **wä** li) *n.* the HINDU or SIKH festival of light, held in October or November.

Dixie (**dik** si) *n.* (also **Dixieland**) the southern states of the UNITED STATES, especially with reference to the American CIVIL WAR.

dizzy (**di** zi) *adj.* **dizzier, dizziest** experiencing or causing a spinning sensation and loss of balance: *When I got off the roundabout I felt quite dizzy.* – *adv.* **dizzily**. – *n.* **dizziness**.

● **Djibouti** (ji **boo** ti). See Supplement, **Countries**.

The deep-sea pressure suit, like a spacesuit, has joints in the limbs and a porthole face mask. Air, or a special mixture of gases for deep diving, is contained in tanks. The diver can communicate with surface workers by microphones and headphones. Divers in such suits can descend to 600 metres.

Three stylish dives often used in competitions. Divers sometimes add fancy mid-air movements.

do (dōō) *vb.* **does** (duz), **doing, did** (did), **done** (dun) **1** to carry out, perform, or commit. **2** to finish or complete. **3** to be enough or suitable: *That will do.* **4** to be in a particular state: *Business is doing well.* **5** to provide as a service: *Do they do lunches here? – vb.* (*auxiliary*) **1** used in questions and negative statements or commands: *Do you smoke? I don't like wine. Don't do that!* **2** used to avoid repetition of a verb: *She eats as much as I do.* **3** used for emphasis: *She does know you've arrived. – n.* **dos** or **do's** (*colloquial*) **1** a party or other gathering: *The office Christmas do is next Tuesday.* **2** something done as a rule or custom: *dos and don'ts. – vb.* **do away with 1** to murder. **2** to abolish. – *vb.* **do up** (*colloquial*) **1** to repair, clean, or improve the decoration of: *We did up the house just before selling it.* **2** to fasten; to tie or wrap up.

docile (**dō** sīl) *adj.* willing to obey.

dock (dok) *n.* a harbour where ships are loaded, unloaded, and repaired; (in *plural*) the area surrounding this. – *vb.* **docking, docked 1** to bring or come into a dock. **2** to cause space vehicles to link up in space.

doctor (dok tôr) *n.* a person trained and qualified to practise medicine.

doctrine (**dok** trin) *n.* a set of religious or political beliefs. – *adj.* **doctrinal** (dok **trīn** ål).

document (**do** kū měnt) *n.* any piece of official writing, such as a certificate. – (**do** kū ment) *vb.* **documenting, documented** to provide written evidence to support or prove.

dodge (doj) *vb.* **dodging, dodged 1** to avoid by moving quickly away, especially sideways: *He dodged through the traffic.* **2** to escape or avoid by cleverness or deceit: *Wendy dodged the visit to her great aunt's by saying she felt ill.*

dodo (**dō** dō) *n.* **dodos** or **dodoes** a large grey flightless bird of Mauritius, extinct since the 17th century. – **as dead as a dodo** completely out-of-date or forgotten about.

doe (dō) *n.* **does** or **doe** an adult female rabbit, hare, or small deer, e.g. the fallow deer.

doesn't does not.

dog (dog) *n.* **1** any of a family of four-legged mammals that includes the wolf and the fox; especially a domesticated species of this family. **2** the male of any such animal.

DOG TERMS

bat ear an erect ear.

bitch a female dog.

dam the female parent

dewclaws a rudimentary pad and claw on the inside of the legs.

dock to shorten the tail by cutting.

drop ear with the ends of the ears drooping forwards.

sire the male parent.

whelp to give birth to puppies.

Dogs can be grouped according to the kind of work they do. There are sporting dogs such as pointers, setters, and retrievers which scent out game and retrieve it; hounds which are trained for hunting; working and herding dogs such as police dogs, rescue dogs, and sheepdogs; terriers, bred to drive game out of holes in the ground; and toy dogs kept as pets or to keep guard.

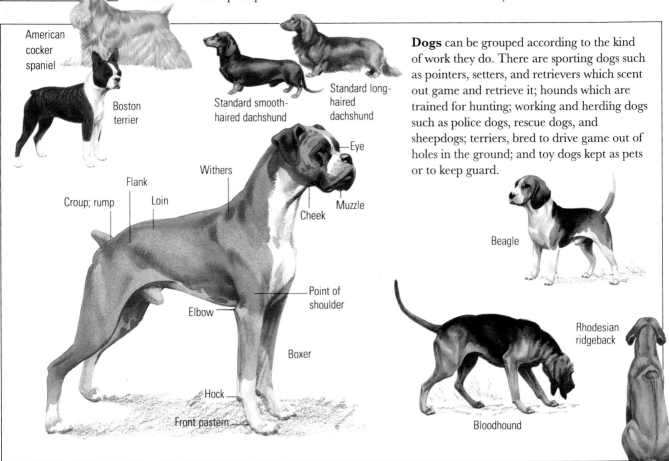

American cocker spaniel

Boston terrier

Standard smooth-haired dachshund

Standard long-haired dachshund

Croup; rump

Flank

Loin

Withers

Eye

Muzzle

Cheek

Point of shoulder

Elbow

Boxer

Hock

Front pastern

Beagle

Bloodhound

Rhodesian ridgeback

● Prehistoric people tamed dogs to help them hunt wild animals. Today there are more than 100 breeds of dog. The Saint Bernard is the largest; the Yorkshire terrier is one of the smallest. Dogs live for about 12 years.

dogfish *n.* any of various kinds of small shark.

dogged (**dog** id) *adj.* determined.

Dogstar *n.* Sirius, the brightest star in the sky, part of the Greater Dog constellation.

doggerel (**dog** ĕ rĕl) *n.* badly written poetry.

dogma (**dog** mă) *n.* a belief or principle laid down by an authority as unquestionably true.

dogmatic (dog **mat** ik) *adj.* (of a person) stating opinions very forcefully; intolerant.

dole (dōl) *n.* (*British*; *colloquial*) unemployment benefit.

doll (dol) *n.* a toy in the form of a model of a human being, especially a baby.

dollar (**do** lăr) *n.* (*symbol* **$**) the standard unit of currency in the UNITED STATES, CANADA, AUSTRALIA, NEW ZEALAND and other countries, divided into 100 cents.

dolphin (**dol** fin) *n.* a highly intelligent smooth-skinned marine mammal of the whale family.

dome (dōm) *n.* a roof in the shape of a hemisphere.

Domesday Book (**dōōmz** dā book) *n.* a survey of all lands in ENGLAND, commissioned by WILLIAM the Conqueror in 1086.

domestic (dŏ **mes** tik) *adj.* **1** of or relating to the home, the family, or private life. **2** (of animals) not wild.

domesticate *vb.* **domesticating, domesticated** to train an animal for life in the company of people.

dominant (**do** mi nănt) *adj.* most important, evident, or active; foremost.

dominate (**do** mi nāt) *vb.* **dominating, dominated 1** to have command or influence over: *Don't let him dominate you.* **2** to be the most important or evident person or thing in: *Election news dominates all the front pages.*

● **Dominica** (dŏ **min** i kă). See Supplement, **Countries**.

● **Dominican Republic**. See Supplement, **Countries**.

dominion (dŏ **min** yŏn) *n.* **1** rule; power; influence. **2** a territory or country governed by a single ruler or government.

domino (**do** mi nō) *n.* **dominoes** a small rectangular tile, marked with a varying number of dots (or left blank), used to play the game of **dominoes**.

donate (dŏ **nāt**) *vb.* **donating, donated** to give, especially to charity. – *n.* **donation**.

● **Donatello** (don ă **tel** ō) (*c.*1386-1466) was a sculptor from Florence, ITALY noted for his 'realism'.

● **Don Juan** (don **jōō** ăn) in legend was a Spanish nobleman famous for seducing women.

donkey (**dong** ki) *n.* **donkeys** an animal of the horse family, smaller than a horse and with longer ears. Also known as an ass.

donkey-work *n.* **1** heavy manual work. **2** preparation; groundwork.

● **Donne** (dun), **John** (?1572-1631) was an English churchman and poet.

● **Don Quixote** (don kē **hō** tē) is a novel by the Spanish writer CERVANTES which describes the adventures of a crazy old knight.

The inverted bowl shape of domes is found on many religious buildings such as mosques and churches. The Taj Mahal in India and the Mosque of Omar in Jerusalem carry one as does St Peter's, Rome and St Paul's Cathedral, London, shown here.

Dollar is from a German word *taler*, the name of a silver coin made in 1518 from metal found at Joachims*thal*, Bohemia.

A cutaway showing the structure of a dome.

don't (dōnt) do not.

doodle (dōō dĕl) *vb.* **doodling, doodled** to scribble aimlessly. – *n.* a meaningless scribble.

doom (dōōm) *n.* unavoidable death, ruin, or other unpleasant fate.

door (dör) *n.* a movable barrier opening and closing an entrance, e.g. to a room.

dormant (dör mȧnt) *adj.* inactive; hibernating.

dormitory (dör mi tri) *n.* **dormitories** a large bedroom for several people, in a school, etc.

dormouse (dör mows) *n.* **dormice** (dör mīs) a small animal, like a mouse with a squirrel's tail, that lives in a forest. It is active at night.

dose (dōs) *n.* a quantity of medicine taken at one time.

● **Dostoyevsky** (dos toi **ef** ski), **Fyodor** (1821-81) was the Russian author of *Crime and Punishment*.

dot (dot) *n.* a small round mark; a spot; a point. – *vb.* **dotting, dotted 1** to put a dot on. **2** to scatter. – **on the dot** exactly.

double (du bȅl) *adj.* **1** made up of two similar parts; paired; in pairs. **2** of twice the usual weight, size, etc.: *A double portion of dessert, please.* **3** for two people: *We booked a room with a double bed.* **4** with two different uses or aspects: *Everything he says has a double meaning.* – *adv.* **1** twice. **2** with one half over the other: *Towels should be folded double.* – *vb.* **doubling, doubled 1** to make or become twice as large in size, number, etc. **2** to have a second use or function: *This milk bottle doubles as a vase.* **3** to act as a substitute. – **at the double** quickly. **double-cross** *vb.* **double-crossing, double-crossed** to betray. **double dutch** *n.* (*colloquial*) nonsense.

doubt (dowt) *vb.* **doubting, doubted 1** to feel uncertain about; to be suspicious, or show mistrust, of. **2** to be inclined to disbelieve. – *n.* **1** uncertainty, suspicion, or mistrust. **2** an inclination to disbelieve; a reservation. – **no doubt** surely; probably.

doubtful *adj.* **1** feeling doubt. **2** uncertain; able to be doubted. **3** likely not to be the case.

dough (dō) *n.* a mixture of flour, water, and other ingredients, the basis of bread etc.

● **Douglas** (dug lȧs), **Donald W.** (1892-1981) was a United States aircraft designer and founder of what is now the McDonnell Douglas Corporation.

dour (dōōr) *adj.* stern; sullen.

dove (duv) *n.* a bird of the pigeon family.

down[1] (down) *adv.* **1** towards or in a low or lower position, level, or state; on or to the ground. **2** from a greater to a lesser size, amount, or level: *We saw a scaled down model of the building.* **3** in writing; on paper: *Please take down notes.* **4** as a deposit: *Henry put down £50 for the bike.* **5** from earlier to later times: *This story has been handed down through generations.* – *prep.* **1** in a lower position on. **2** along; at a further position on, by, or through: *Our good friends live down the road.* **3** from the top to, or towards, the bottom. – *adj.* **1** sad; in low spirits: *Tina felt very down because she didn't want the holiday to end.* **2** going towards or reaching a lower position: *a down pipe.* **3** made as a deposit: *a down payment.* **4** (of a computer, etc.) not working properly. – **down under** (*colloquial*) in or to Australia or New Zealand.

down and out *n.* & *adj.* (a person who is) homeless and penniless.

downfall *n.* the cause of failure or ruin.

downhearted *adj.* dejected; discouraged.

downstream *adj.* & *adv.* farther along a river towards the sea; flowing with the current.

down-to-earth *adj.* sensible and practical.

downtown *n.* *adj.* & *adv.* to, at, etc. the lower part of the city, or the city centre.

down[2] (down) *n.* soft fine feathers or hair.

● **Downing Street** the office of the British prime minister in London.

● **Doyle, Arthur Conan** (1859-1930) was a Scottish novelist, creator of Sherlock HOLMES.

doze (dōz) *vb.* **dozing, dozed** to sleep lightly. – *n.* a brief period of light sleeping.

dozen (du zĕn) *n.* **dozen** or **dozens** a set of twelve.

drab (drab) *adj.* **drabber, drabbest 1** dull; dreary. **2** of a dull greenish-brown colour.

● **Dracula** (dra kū lȧ), **Count** was a Transylvanian vampire in a novel of the same name by Bram Stoker.

drag (drag) *vb.* **dragging, dragged 1** to pull along slowly and with force. **2** to move along scraping the ground. **3** to search a lake with a hook. – *n.* **1** an act of dragging; a dragging effect. **2** (*colloquial*) a tedious person or thing.

Dragonflies are found near fresh water in all parts of the world. They are useful to people because they feed on harmful pests such as mosquitoes. They are swift, skilful fliers and superb hunters. Dragonflies have long, narrow, red, blue, green, or black bodies and two pairs of transparent, veined wings.

dragon (**dra** gǒn) *n.* a large mythical fire-breathing reptile-like creature with wings.
dragonfly *n.* **dragonflies** an insect with a long thin body and two sets of wings.
drain (drān) *vb.* **draining, drained 1** to cause or allow liquid to escape; to empty a container in this way: *Dave drained off the fat from the gravy.* **2** (of liquid, etc.) to escape; to flow away. – *n.* a pipe for carrying away liquid.
drainage *n.* the process or system of draining.
drake (drāk) *n.* a male duck.

● **Drake, Francis** (*c.*1543-96) was an English sailor and adventurer who helped defeat the Spanish ARMADA in 1588.

drama (**drä** må) *n.* **1** a play; any work performed by actors. **2** plays in general. **3** a situation full of excitement and emotion.

● Tragedy and comedy are the main kinds of drama. The oldest plays we know were written down in Greece over 2400 years ago. Early dramas took place in the open. In the Middle Ages actors performed plays on carts in the streets. People began building covered theatres 500 years ago.

dramatic (drå **mat** ik) *adj.* **1** of or relating to plays, the theatre, or acting. **2** exciting; sudden and striking; drastic. – *adv.* **dramatically**.
dramatist *n.* a writer of plays.
drank. See **drink**.
drape (drāp) *vb.* **draping, draped** to hang cloth loosely over something.
drastic (dras tik) *adj.* extreme; severe.
draught (dräft) *n.* a current of air, especially indoors.
draughts *n.* (*singular*) a game for two people played with 24 discs on a chequered board.
draw (drö) *vb.* **drawing, drew** (drōō), **drawn 1** to make a picture of something or someone, especially with a pencil. **2** to pull out, take out, or extract: *They had to draw water from a well.* **3** to move: *Please draw nearer.* **4** to take from a fund or source: *During the match we needed to*

draw on extra reserves of energy. **5** to attract: *Don't show off and draw attention to yourself.* **6** to end a game, etc. with neither side winning. **7** to suck air; (of a chimney) to cause air to flow through a fire, allowing burning. – *n.* **1** a result in which neither side is the winner; a tie. **2** a person or thing with the potential to attract many people.
drawback *n.* a disadvantage.
drawbridge *n.* a bridge that can be lifted to prevent access across.
drawing *n.* any picture drawn in pencil.
-drawn pulled by: *horse-drawn*.
drawer (drör) *n.* a sliding lidless storage box fitted as part of a piece of furniture.
dread (dred) *vb.* **dreading, dreaded** & *n.* (to look ahead with) great fear or apprehension.

Outlines with shading

Pen and ink drawing

You can use many media to **draw** – crayons, pencils, chalk, brushes. Remember that straight lines seem to converge at one place, called a vanishing point; and circles, the top of a tower, for instance, will look oval at various eye-levels.

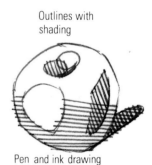

Light source

Soft pencil shading

dreadlocks *n.* (*plural*) thin braids of hair tied tightly, especially worn by RASTAFARIANS.

dream (drēm) *n.* **1** a series of thoughts and images occurring during sleep. **2** a distant ambition, especially unattainable. − *vb.* **dreaming, dreamt** (dremt) or **dreamed 1** to have thoughts and visions during sleep. **2** to have a distant ambition or hope: *She dreams of becoming a ballerina.* **3** to imagine: *I never dreamt I could win the high jump.* − *n.* **dreamer**.

dreary (drēr i) *adj.* **drearier, dreariest 1** dull and depressing. **2** uninteresting. − *adv.* **drearily**. − *n.* **dreariness**.

dredge (drej) *vb.* **dredging, dredged** to clear the bottom of or deepen the sea or a river by bringing up mud and waste. − *n.* a machine for dredging.

dregs (dregz) *n.* (*plural*) solid particles in a liquid that settle at the bottom.

drench (drench) *vb.* **drenching, drenched** to make soaking wet.

dress (dres) *vb.* **dressing, dressed 1** to put clothes on: *We have to dress in a school uniform.* **2** to treat and bandage wounds: *The nurse cleaned and dressed the cut.* − *n.* a woman's garment with top and skirt in one piece. **dressing** *n.* **1** any sauce added to food, especially salad. **2** a covering for a wound.

dressage (dres äzh) *n.* See **Horse terms**.

drew. See **draw**.

drey (drā) *n.* a squirrel's nest.

• **Dreyfus** (drā fûs), **Alfred** (*c.*1859-1935) was a French Jewish officer falsely jailed for spying.

dribble (dri bĕl) *vb.* **dribbling, dribbled 1** to fall or flow in drops. **2** to allow saliva to run slowly down from the mouth.

drift (drift) *n.* **1** a pile or mass formed by the wind or a current: *a snow drift.* **2** a general movement or tendency to move. − *vb.* **drifting, drifted 1** to float or be blown along. **2** to move aimlessly from one place to another.

drill (dril) *n.* **1** a tool for boring holes. **2** a training exercise, or a session of it. − *vb.* **drilling, drilled 1** to make a hole with a drill. **2** to exercise or teach through repeated practice.

drink (dringk) *vb.* **drinking, drank** (drangk), **drunk** (drungk) **1** to swallow a liquid. **2** to drink alcohol: *The problem is, he drinks.* **3** to drink a toast to. − *n.* **1** a liquid suitable for drinking. **2** a glass of alcohol of any kind. − *adj.* **drinkable**. − *n.* **drinker**.

drip (drip) *vb.* **dripping, dripped 1** to fall in drops. **2** to release a liquid in drops: *That tap's dripping.* − *n.* the action or noise of dripping.

drive (drīv) *vb.* **driving, drove** (drōv), **driven** (dri vĕn) **1** to control the movement of a vehicle. **2** to travel in a vehicle: *We drive to work.* **3** to produce motion in; to cause to function: *The pump is driven by electricity.* − *n.* **1** a trip in a vehicle, especially for pleasure. **2** a path for vehicles. **3** energy and enthusiasm.

drizzle (dri zĕl) *n.* fine light rain. − *vb.* **drizzling, drizzled** to rain lightly.

dromedary (dro mĕ dā ri) *n.* **dromedaries** a camel with a single hump.

droop (drōop) *vb.* **drooping, drooped 1** to hang loosely. **2** to be weak with tiredness.

drop (drop) *vb.* **dropping, dropped 1** to fall or allow to fall: *Drop your weapons!* **2** to decline, lower, or weaken: *The temperature dropped.* **3** to stop discussing: *Let's drop the subject.* **4** to set down from a vehicle; to deliver or hand in: *Could you drop this parcel off at the post office.* − *n.* **1** a small mass of liquid, especially falling. **2** a descent; a fall. **3** a vertical distance.

drought (drowt) *n.* lack of rainfall over a long period.

drove. See **drive**.

drown (drown) *vb.* **drowning, drowned 1** to kill or die by suffocating in a liquid. **2** to apply an excessive amount of liquid to; to soak or flood: *They drown everything in tomato sauce.*

drug (drug) *n.* **1** any substance used in the treatment of disease. **2** any substance taken for its effect on the mind.

drum (drum) *n.* a percussion instrument consisting of a hollow frame with a skin or other membrane stretched tightly across its

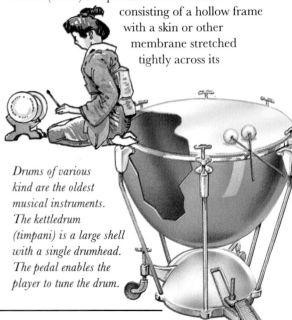

Drums of various kind are the oldest musical instruments. The kettledrum (timpani) is a large shell with a single drumhead. The pedal enables the player to tune the drum.

The two main types of **duck** are dabbling ducks and diving ducks. Dabbling ducks feed on the surface of the water. Diving ducks go underwater for food. They live at sea and include eider ducks and sawbills.

male

Shoveler

female

female

Eider male

Goosander

female

Red-breasted merganser

male

Goldeneye

male

male

female

Pintail male

opening. – *vb.* **drumming, drummed 1** to beat a drum. **2** to make continuous tapping or thumping sounds: *She drummed her fingers nervously on the table.* – *n.* **drummer**.

drunk (drungk) *vb.* See **drink**. – *adj.* lacking control in movement, speech, etc. through having drunk too much alcohol.

dry (drī) *adj.* **drier, driest 1** free from moisture or wetness. **2** with little or no rainfall. **3** from which all the water has evaporated or been taken: *The carrots have boiled dry.* **4** thirsty. – *vb.* **dries, drying, dried 1** to make or become dry. **2** to preserve something by removing all moisture, fruit for instance.

dual (dū ål) *adj.* consisting of or representing two separate parts: *a dual carriageway.*

dubious (dū bi ůs) *adj.* feeling doubt; unsure: *I'm a bit dubious about taking the car.*

●**Dublin** is the capital of the Republic of IRELAND. It lies on the River Liffey.

duchess (du chis) *n.* the wife of a duke.

duck[1] (duk) *n.* **1** any of a family of water birds with short legs, webbed feet, and a broad flat beak. **2** the female of such a bird, as opposed to the male *drake.* – **be like water off a duck's back** (*colloquial*) to have no effect at all.
  duck-billed platypus *n.* an Australian egg-laying amphibious mammal with thick fur, a broad tail, and a duck-like beak.

duckling *n.* a young duck.

duck[2] (duk) *vb.* **ducking, ducked 1** to lower the head or body suddenly, so as to avoid a blow. **2** to push briefly under water.

duct (dukt) *n.* **1** any tube in the body carrying liquids, such as tears. **2** a pipe or channel carrying liquids, protecting electric cables, etc.

due (dū) *adj.* **1** owed; payable: *Your subscription to this magazine is now due.* **2** expected according to timetable or pre-arrangement: *When is her baby due?* – *adv.* directly: *It's due north of here.*

duel (dū êl) *n.* in former times, a pre-arranged fight between two people.

duet (dū et) *n.* a piece of music for two singers or players; a pair of musical performers.

dug (dug). See **dig**.

duke (dūk) *n.* a nobleman of the highest rank outside the royal family. – *n.* **dukedom**.

dull (dul) *adj.* **1** (of colour or light) lacking brightness or clearness. **2** (of sounds) deep and low; muffled. **3** (of weather) cloudy; overcast. **4** (of pain) not sharp. **5** uninteresting.

●**Dumas** (dōō mä), **Alexandre** (1802-70) was the French author of *The Three Musketeers.*

dumb (dum) *adj.* not able to speak.
  dumbfound *vb.* **dumbfounding, dumbfounded** to astonish into silence.

dummy (du mi) *n.* **dummies** a life-size model of the human body, e.g. for displaying clothes.

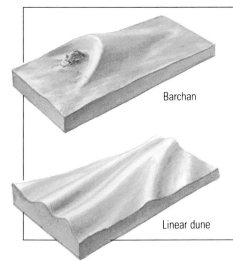

Barchan

Linear dune

Desert sand **dunes** are shaped by the wind. A 'barchan' has a crescent-shaped front and a long tail. 'Linear' dunes are created in strong steady winds which cut troughs in the desert floor.

dump (dump) *vb.* **dumping, dumped 1** to put down heavily or carelessly: *Don't just dump your bag in the hall.* **2** to dispose of rubbish, especially improperly: *An old armchair had been dumped by the roadside.* **3** to transfer data from a computer's memory to a disk or printed page. – *n.* a place where rubbish may be dumped.

●**Duncan, Isadora** (1878-1927) was an American dancer whose style was controversial.

dune (dūn) *n.* a low ridge of sand.
dungeon (dun jǒn) *n.* a prison cell, especially underground.

●**Dunlop, John** (1840-1921) was the Scottish inventor of the pneumatic tyre.

duplicate (dū pli kåt) *adj.* identical to another: *duplicate keys.* – *n.* an exact copy, e.g. of a key or a document. – (dū pli kāt) *vb.* **duplicating, duplicated 1** to make an exact copy of. **2** to repeat. – *n.* **duplication.** – *n.* **duplicator.**
durable (dūr å běl) *adj.* sturdy; long-lasting.
duration (dūr ā shǒn) *n.* the length of time that something lasts or continues.

●**Dürer** (dū rěr), **Albrecht** (1471-1528) was a German artist, famous for his engravings.

during (dūr ing) *prep.* **1** throughout the time of: *The shop is out of bounds during school hours.* **2** in the course of: *The phone rang during the night.*
dusk (dusk) *n.* twilight, the period of half darkness before night.
dust (dust) *n.* **1** earth, sand, or household dirt in the form of a fine powder. **2** any substance in powder form: *When the explorers tried to lift the mummy, it turned to dust.* – *vb.* **dusting, dusted 1** to remove dust from furniture, etc. **2** to sprinkle with a substance in powder form: *Dust the cake with icing sugar.*
dusty *adj.* **dustier, dustiest** covered with, or containing, dust.
Dutch (duch) *n.* **1** the language of the NETHERLANDS. **2** the people of the NETHERLANDS. – *adj.* of the NETHERLANDS, its people, or their language.
duty (dū ti) *n.* **duties 1** something you are obliged to do; a moral or legal responsibility: *I feel it's my duty to warn you that he is a dangerous influence.* **2** a task to be performed, especially in connection with a job: *My duties include answering the phone.* **3** tax on goods.
duvet (doo vā) *n.* a thick quilt filled with feathers or artificial fibres, for use on a bed.
dwell (dwel) *vb.* **dwelling, dwelt** or **dwelled** to reside. – *n.* **dweller.** – *vb.* **dwell on** or **upon** to think or speak about at length.
dwelling *n.* a place of residence; a house.
dwindle (dwin děl) *vb.* **dwindling, dwindled** to shrink in size, number, or intensity.

●**Dyaks** (dī aks) are people who live on the island of Borneo. Until quite recently they practised head-hunting and cannibalism. They use elaborately carved masks in their rituals.

dye (dī) *vb.* **dyeing, dyed** to colour or stain permanently. – *n.* any colouring substance.
dying (dī ing) *vb.* present participle of **die.** – *adj.* **1** expressed immediately before death: *It was his dying wish.* **2** final: *They scored in the dying seconds of the match.*
dyke or **dike** (dīk) *n.* a wall or bank built to prevent flooding or keep back the sea.
dynamic (dī **nam** ik) or (di **nam** ik) *adj.* full of energy, enthusiasm, and new ideas.
dynamite (dī nå mīt) *n.* an explosive. – *vb.* **dynamiting, dynamited** to blow up using dynamite.
dynamo (dī nå mō) *n.* **dynamos** a device that converts mechanical movement into electrical energy.
dynasty (di nås ti) *n.* **dynasties** a succession of rulers from the same family.
dyslexia (dis **lek** si å) *n.* difficulty in reading and spelling, unrelated to intelligence; 'word-blindness'. – *adj.* & *n.* **dyslexic.**
dyspepsia (dis **pep** si å) *n.* indigestion.

E e

each (ēch) *adj.* & *pron.* every one of two or more people, animals, or things considered separately: *Each girl took an apple.*

eager (ē gĕr) *adj.* showing enthusiasm; keen.

eagle (ē gĕl) *n.* any of various kinds of large birds of prey.

● Eagles soar into the sky on broad wings then swoop to seize their prey in powerful talons. They eat by tearing off flesh with their strong hooked beaks. The bald eagle is the national emblem of the UNITED STATES. It is not really bald, but has white feathers on its head.

ear (ēr) *n.* one of the two parts of the body on either side of the head with which we hear.

eardrum *n.* the small thin piece of skin inside the ear, which transmits vibrations made by sound waves to the inner ear.

earring *n.* a piece of jewellery worn on the ear.

earl (ûrl) *n.* a British nobleman.

early (ûr lĭ) *adv.* & *adj.* **earlier, earliest** **1** happening or existing near the beginning of a period of time: *They discovered traces of an early Roman settlement.* **2** happening or arriving sooner than usual, or sooner than expected or intended: *I was early, and the performance had not yet begun.*

earn (ûrn) *vb.* **earning, earned 1** to gain money by working. **2** to deserve: *She felt that she had earned a rest.*

earnings *n.* (*plural*) money earned.

earnest (ûr nist) *adj.* serious.

● **Earp** (ûrp), **Wyatt** (1848-1929) was a UNITED STATES lawman in the days of the WILD WEST.

Imperial eagle

Golden eagle

Bald eagle

Eagles belong to the same family as hawks and vultures. They all have strong curved talons. Two species, the bald eagle and the golden eagle, breed in North America. The bald eagle is found nowhere else in the world.

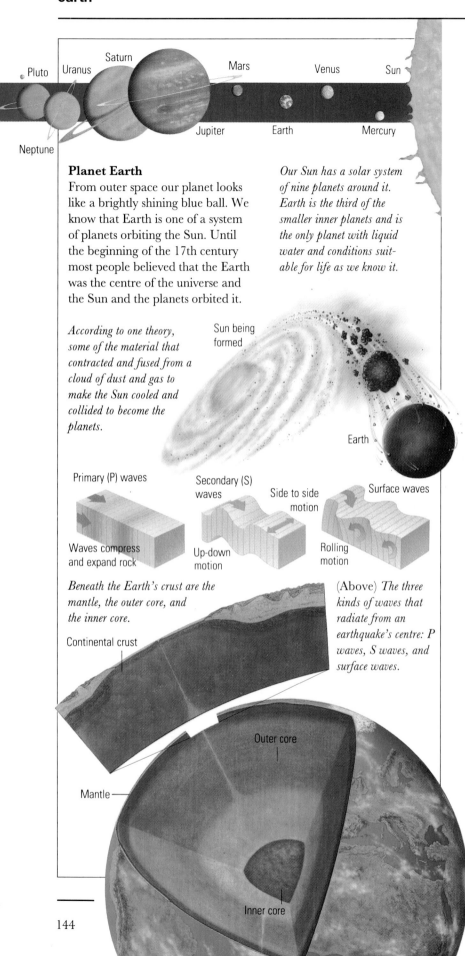

Pluto · Uranus · Saturn · Mars · Venus · Sun · Neptune · Jupiter · Earth · Mercury

Planet Earth

From outer space our planet looks like a brightly shining blue ball. We know that Earth is one of a system of planets orbiting the Sun. Until the beginning of the 17th century most people believed that the Earth was the centre of the universe and the Sun and the planets orbited it.

Our Sun has a solar system of nine planets around it. Earth is the third of the smaller inner planets and is the only planet with liquid water and conditions suitable for life as we know it.

According to one theory, some of the material that contracted and fused from a cloud of dust and gas to make the Sun cooled and collided to become the planets.

Sun being formed

Earth

Primary (P) waves

Secondary (S) waves

Side to side motion

Surface waves

Waves compress and expand rock

Up-down motion

Rolling motion

Beneath the Earth's crust are the mantle, the outer core, and the inner core.

(Above) The three kinds of waves that radiate from an earthquake's centre: P waves, S waves, and surface waves.

Continental crust

Mantle

Outer core

Inner core

earth (ûrth) *n.* **1 Earth** the planet on which we live, the third planet in order of distance from the Sun. **2** the soil in which plants grow. – **cost the earth** (*colloquial*) to be very expensive.

earthquake *n.* a shaking of the Earth's surface.

earthworm *n.* the common worm.

earwig (ēr wig) *n.* an insect with pincers at the end of its body.

ease (ēz) *n.* **1** freedom from pain or anxiety. **2** absence of difficulty: *She completed the course with ease.* – *vb.* **easing, eased 1** to free from pain or anxiety: *The drugs eased the pain of his wound.* **2** to move something heavy or awkward gently or gradually in or out of position.

easel (ē zěl) *n.* a stand for supporting a picture.

east (ēst) *n.* the direction from which the Sun rises, or any part of the Earth lying in that direction. – *adj.* **1** in the east; on the side which is on or nearest the east. **2** coming from the direction of the east: *An east wind was blowing.* – *adv.* towards the east. – **the East** the countries of ASIA, east of EUROPE.

eastern *adj.* of the east.

eastward *adv.* (also **eastwards**) & *adj.* towards the east.

Easter (ēs těr) *n.* See **Religious terms**.

easy (ēz i) *adj.* **easier, easiest 1** not difficult: *The test was easy.* **2** not stiff or formal; leisurely: *They walked at an easy pace.* – *n.* **easiness**.

easily *adv.* **1** without difficulty. **2** clearly; beyond doubt: *She was easily the best runner.*

eat (ēt) *vb.* **eating, ate** (et) or (āt), **eaten 1** to bite, chew, and swallow food. **2** to destroy something by chemical action: *The rust had eaten away the bodywork of the car.*

eatable *adj.* fit to be eaten.

● **eatable** and **edible**. The first word suggests that something is not only fit to eat but nice to eat, while the second word means simply that something is fit to eat without doing harm.

ebb (eb) *vb.* **ebbing, ebbed** (of the tide) to move away from the land.

ebony (e bǒ ni) *n.* a type of hard, almost black wood. – *adj.* made from this wood.

eccentric (ik **sen** trik) *adj.* odd; unusual. – *n.* an eccentric person.

echo (e kō) *n.* **echoes** the repeating of a sound caused by the sound waves striking a surface and coming back. – *vb.* **echoes, echoing, echoed** to send back an echo of a sound.

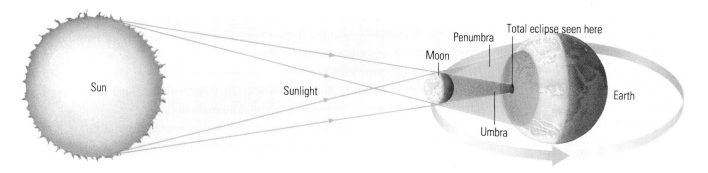

Sun

Sunlight

Moon

Penumbra

Total eclipse seen here

Umbra

Earth

eclipse (i **klips**) *n.* when one planet or heavenly body is partly or totally hidden by another. For example a **solar eclipse** happens when the Moon comes between the Sun and the Earth, and a **lunar eclipse** happens when the Earth's shadow falls across the Moon. – *vb.* **eclipsing, eclipsed**.

ecology (i **kol** ỏ ji) *n.* (the study of) the relationship between living things and their surroundings. – *adj.* **ecological** (ē kỏ **loj** i kảl).

● Ecology shows us that most plants and animals can live only in a special set of surroundings, such as a pond, field, or forest. All the animals living there eat the plants or one another. These plants and animals are linked in what is called a food web. If some kinds die out, those that eat them lose their food and may die too. That is why it is important not to upset the balance of nature by polluting the atmosphere and rivers.

economy (i **kon** ỏ mi) *n.* **economies 1** the system used by a country to organize its money and resources. **2** careful management of money or other resources to avoid waste and cut down on spending. – *adj.* of the cheapest kind.

ecu (e kū) *n.* the *E*uropean *c*urrency *u*nit.

●**Ecuador**. See Supplement, **Countries**.

eczema (**ek** si mả) *n.* a skin disorder.

-ed *suffix* **1** used to form past tenses: *walked*. **2** used to form adjectives from nouns: *bearded*.

eddy (**e** di) *n.* **eddies** a current of water running back against the current, forming a small whirlpool. – *vb.* **eddies, eddying, eddied** to move in this way.

●**Eddy, Mary Baker** (1821-1910) was an American religious leader and the founder of the Christian Science movement.

edge (ej) *n.* **1** the part farthest from the middle of something; a border or boundary. **2** the area beside a cliff or steep drop. **3** the cutting side of something sharp such as a knife. – *vb.* **edging, edged 1** to form or make a border to: *She edged the dress with lace*. **2** to move little by little: *She edged towards the cake*.

edgy *adj.* **edgier, edgiest** (*colloquial*) easily annoyed; nervous or tense.

edible (**ed** ả **bẻl**) *adj.* fit to be eaten.

edifice (**e** di fis) *n.* a large impressive building.

●**Edinburgh** is the capital of SCOTLAND. It stands on a sea inlet, the Firth of Forth. Edinburgh castle is perched on an extinct volcano in the city centre. The elegant New Town was built in the 18th century.

●**Edison, Thomas Alva** (1847-1931) was an American inventor, notably of the phonograph and the electric light bulb.

In a solar eclipse (eclipse of the Sun), the Moon passes between the Sun and Earth and casts its shadow across the Earth. An eclipse is total only if seen from within the Moon's central shadow or umbra.

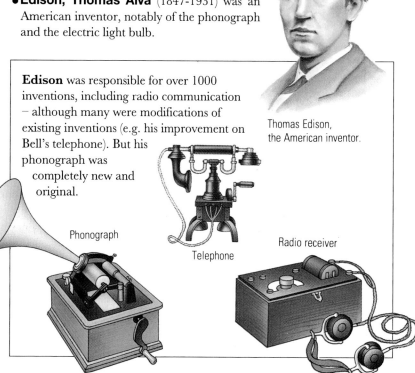

Edison was responsible for over 1000 inventions, including radio communication – although many were modifications of existing inventions (e.g. his improvement on Bell's telephone). But his phonograph was completely new and original.

Thomas Edison, the American inventor.

Phonograph

Telephone

Radio receiver

145

Electricity comes from a Greek word for amber. This is because amber, when rubbed, can be given an electric charge and made to attract small pieces of paper or cloth.

edit (**e** dit) *vb.* **editing, edited** to prepare a book, newspaper, programme, film, etc. for publication or broadcasting, especially by making corrections or alterations.
edition (i **di** shŏn) *n.* a number of copies of a book, etc. printed at one time.
editor *n.* a person who edits.

●**Edmonton** is the capital of Alberta, CANADA.

educate (**e** dū kāt) *vb.* **educating, educated** to train and teach; to provide school instruction for. – *adj.* **educative**.
educated *adj.* having received an education.
education *n.* the process of teaching at school, college, and university. – *adj.* **educational**.

●**Edward** was the name of nine kings of ENGLAND. The first, Edward the Confessor (reigned 1042-66), founded Westminster Abbey; the last, Edward the Eighth, gave up his throne in 1936 to marry a divorced American woman.

Edwardian (ed **wörd** i ăn) *adj.* of, or characteristic of, Britain in the years 1901-10, the reign of King *Edward* the Seventh.
eel (ēl) *n.* any of several kinds of fish with a long smooth snake-like body and very small fins.
eerie (**ēr** i) *adj.* **eerier, eeriest** strange and frightening. – *adv.* **eerily**. – *n.* **eeriness**.
efface (i **fās**) *vb.* **effacing, effaced** to rub or wipe out.
effect (i **fekt**) *n.* **1** a result: *The effect of the explosion was to make the house fall down.* **2** an impression given or produced: *She has had a good effect on him.* **3** operation; working state: *They put their plans into effect.* – *vb.* **effecting, effected** to cause to happen. – **for effect** in order to make an impression on others. – **in effect** in reality.
effective *adj.* **1** having power to produce a desired result. **2** in, or coming into, operation: *The new law is effective from 1 April.*
efficient (i **fi** shĕnt) *adj.* capable of producing good results with competence. – *n.* **efficiency**.
effluent (**e** floo ĕnt) *n.* industrial waste or sewage that is released into a river or the sea.
effort (**e** fŏrt) *n.* **1** something that requires hard mental or physical work. **2** an attempt to do something: *She made an effort to win the race.*
effortless *adj.* done without apparent effort.

egg¹ (eg) *n.* **1** the reproductive cell produced by a female animal from which the young one develops. **2** a reproductive cell produced in a hard shell by female birds, reptiles, and certain animals. **3** a hen's egg, used as food. – **put all your eggs into one basket** to depend entirely on one plan.

●Eggs only grow if they are fertilized by male cells. In mammals the fertilized eggs grow inside the mother's body. Birds, reptiles, and fish lay eggs that contain food for the developing young.

egg² (eg): **egg on** *vb.* **egging, egged** to urge or encourage.
ego (**ē** gō) *n.* **egos** personal pride.
egocentric *adj.* interested in yourself only.
egotism *n.* the habit of having a high opinion of yourself. – *n.* **egotist**.

●**Egypt** More than 5000 years ago the people of ancient Egypt built a great civilization on the banks of the river NILE whose annual flooding made Egypt's soil fertile. Food was plentiful, and rich families lived in fine houses. The kings, or pharaohs, built huge temples and PYRAMIDS as tombs. See also Supplement, **Countries**.

For most of their history, the ancient **Egyptians** were united under one ruler – the pharaoh (king), who was worshipped as a god. The Egyptians believed in an afterlife and built elaborate tombs in pyramids or in caves.

(Top) *A shaduf is used to raise water for irrigation.* (Right) *Important places in Egyptian history.*

Alexandria

Giza

River Nile

Luxor

Abu Simbel

Egyptian (i **jip** shån) *adj.* of or belonging to Egypt. – *n.* a citizen of Egypt.

eider (ī dĕr) or **eider duck** *n.* a large sea duck.
eiderdown *n.* a quilt usually filled with the down or soft feathers of the eider.

● **Eiffel Tower** made of wrought iron, it soars 300 metres above Paris. It was built by Gustave *Eiffel* for an exhibition in 1889.

eight (āt) *n.* the number or figure 8. – *n.*, *adj.*, & *adv.* **eighth** (ātth).
eighteen (ā tēn) *n.* the number or figure 18. – *n.*, *adj.*, & *adv.* **eighteenth**.
eighty (ā ti) *n.* the number or figure 80. – *n.*, *adj.*, & *adv.* **eightieth**.

● **Einstein, Albert** (1879-1955) was a German-born scientist who made the greatest scientific advances since NEWTON 200 years earlier. His theory of RELATIVITY revolutionized the way we look at the world.

eisteddfod (ī **sted** fŏd) (in Welsh (ī **steTh** vŏd)) *n.* **eisteddfods** or **eisteddfodau** (ī **sted** fŏ dī) (in Welsh (ī **steTh** vŏ dī)) an annual Welsh arts festival.

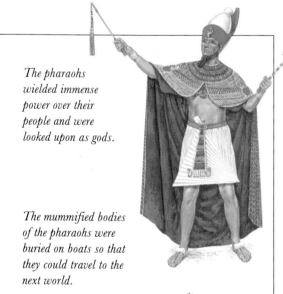

The pharaohs wielded immense power over their people and were looked upon as gods.

The mummified bodies of the pharaohs were buried on boats so that they could travel to the next world.

either (ē Thĕr) or (ī Thĕr) *adj.* **1** any one of two: *Either chair is comfortable.* **2** each of two; both: *She had a garden with a fence on either side.* – *pron.* any one of two things, people, etc. – *adv.* also: *I found him rather unpleasant, and I didn't like his wife either.* – **either ... or** introducing two choices or possibilities: *Either he goes or I do.*

eject (i **jekt**) *vb.* **ejecting, ejected** to throw out with force. – *n.* **ejection**.

eke (ēk): **eke out** *vb.* **eking, eked** to make something last longer by adding something else to it or by careful use.

elaborate (i **lab** ŏ råt) *adj.* **1** complicated in design: *She was knitting an elaborate jumper.* **2** carefully planned or worked out: *He had worked out an elaborate plan.* – (i **lab** ŏ rāt) *vb.* **elaborating, elaborated** to add detail: *She elaborated on her idea.* – *n.* **elaboration**.

eland (ē lånd) *n.* **elands** or **eland** a large African antelope with spiral horns.

elapse (i **laps**) *vb.* **elapsing, elapsed** (of time) to pass.

elastic (i **las** tik) *adj.* able to return to its original shape or size after being pulled or pressed out of shape. – *n.* stretchable cord or fabric woven with strips of rubber.

elbow (**el** bō) *n.* the joint where the human arm bends.

elder[1] (**el** dĕr) *adj.* older: *My elder sister is clever.* – *n.* a person who is older.
elderly *adj.* rather old.

elder[2] (**el** dĕr) *n.* a small tree with white flowers and purple-black or red berries.

eldest (**el** dĕst) *adj.* oldest. – *n.* a person who is the oldest of three or more.

elect (i **lekt**) *vb.* **electing, elected** **1** to choose by vote: *The president was elected with a majority vote.* **2** to choose to do something: *She elected to stay at home.*
election *n.* the process of choosing people for an official position by taking a vote.

electric (i **lek** trik) *adj.* produced by, worked by, or generating electricity.
electrical *adj.* related to or operated by electricity.
electrician *n.* a person whose job is to install and repair electrical equipment.
electricity *n.* the energy that is used to make heat and light, etc. The electricity we use flows through wires as electric current.

electrode (i **lek** trōd) *n.* either of the two points by which electric current enters or leaves a battery or other electrical apparatus.

Democratic elections began to develop in Athens in the 5th century BC. All male citizens had a say in government. They used metal discs to cast their vote.

electromagnet (i lek trō **mag** nit) *n.* a piece of soft metal, usually iron, made magnetic by the passage of an electric current through a coil of wire wrapped around the metal. – *adj.* **electromagnetic** (i lek trō mag **net** ik).

electron (i **lek** tron) *n.* a particle, present in all atoms, which has a negative electric charge.

electronic (i lek **tron** ik) *adj.* operated by means of very small electrical circuits which handle very low levels of electric current. **electronics** *n.* (*singular*) the study of the behaviour of electronic circuits.

● Electronics deals with the way in which electrons flow through certain crystals, gases, or a vacuum. Electronic devices such as transistors and silicon chips are used in computers, television, and radio. Without electronics, space travel would be impossible.

elegant (e li gånt) *adj.* having good taste in dress or style. – *n.* **elegance**.

element (e li měnt) *n.* **1** a part of anything which combines with other features to make a whole. **2** any one of 105 known substances that cannot be split into simpler substances. **elementary** *adj.* dealing with basic facts.

elephant (e li fånt) *n.* **elephants** or **elephant** the largest living land animal, with thick greyish skin, a nose in the form of a long hanging trunk, and two curved tusks.

There are two species of elephant: the Indian elephant (above) and the much larger African elephant (below). Both the male and female African elephant have tusks; in the Indian elephant, the female seldom has tusks. The Indian elephant can be trained to move heavy loads.

elevate (e li vāt) *vb.* **elevating, elevated** to raise or lift: *The car was elevated on blocks.* **elevation** *n.* **1** the act of raising to a higher position. **2** the height of a place above sea level.

eleven (i **lev** ěn) *n.* the number or figure 11. – *n., adj., & adv.* **eleventh**. – **at the eleventh hour** at the last possible moment.

eligible (e li jå běl) *adj.* **1** suitable, or deserving to be chosen: *She is an eligible candidate for the job.* **2** having a right: *They are eligible for compensation.* – *n.* **eligibility**.

eliminate (i **lim** i nāt) *vb.* **eliminating, eliminated** to get rid of or exclude: *The team was eliminated from the competition.*

● **Eliot, T. S.** (1888-1965) was an American-born British poet and playwright.

● **Elizabeth the First** (1533-1603) became queen of England in 1558. In her reign the English defeated the Spanish ARMADA, Francis DRAKE sailed round the world, and William SHAKESPEARE was writing his plays.

● **Elizabeth the Second** (1926-) is queen of the UNITED KINGDOM and head of the COMMONWEALTH.

Elizabethan (i liz å **bē** thån) *adj.* of, or relating to, the reign of Queen ELIZABETH THE FIRST.

elk (elk) *n.* **elks** or **elk** the largest of all deer, found in northern EUROPE and ASIA, and in NORTH AMERICA, where it is called the moose.

ellipse (i **lips**) *n.* a regular oval shape.

elliptical (i **lip** tik ål) or **elliptic** *adj.* having the shape of an ellipse.

elm (elm) *n.* any of various tall trees with broad leaves and clusters of small flowers.

elongate (ē long gāt) *vb.* **elongating, elongated** to lengthen or stretch out.

eloquence (e lǒ kwěns) *n.* the power of using words well. – *adj.* **eloquent**.

● **El Salvador**. See Supplement, **Countries**.

else (els) *adj. & adv.* different from or in addition to something already mentioned: *Would you like something else?* – **or else** or if not; otherwise: *Hurry up, or else you'll be late.*

elude (i lōōd) *vb.* **eluding, eluded 1** to escape or avoid by quickness or cleverness: *The burglar eluded the police for many days.* **2** to baffle: *The meaning of his words eluded her.*

elusive (i **loo** siv) *adj.* difficult to find or catch.

em- (em-) *prefix.* See **en-**.

emancipate (i **man** si pāt) *vb.* **emancipating, emancipated** to set free from slavery, or from some other harmful restrictions. – *adj.* **emancipated**. – *n.* **emancipation**.

embalm (im **bäm**) *vb.* **embalming, embalmed** to preserve a dead body from decay by treatment with chemicals or drugs.

embankment (im **bangk** mênt) *n.* a bank or wall of earth made to carry a road or railway, or to rise on either side of a road or railway.

embark (im **bärk**) *vb.* **embarking, embarked 1** to go, or put, on board ship: *They embarked the goods on the ship.* **2** to begin: *They embarked upon their voyage.*

embarrass (im **ba** rås) *vb.* **embarrassing, embarrassed** to cause someone to feel anxious, self-conscious, or ashamed: *His flattery embarrassed her.* – *adj.* **embarrassed**. – *adj.* **embarrassing**. – *n.* **embarrassment**.

embassy (em **bå** si) *n.* **embassies** the official residence of an ambassador.

embellish (im **bel** ish) *vb.* **embellishing, embellished 1** to make a story more interesting by adding details which may not be true. **2** to make beautiful with decoration. – *adj.* **embellished**. – *n.* **embellishment**.

ember (em **bêr**) *n.* (usually in *plural*) a piece of smouldering coal or wood in a dying fire.

embezzle (im **be** zêl) *vb.* **embezzling, embezzled** to steal money with which you have been entrusted. – *n.* **embezzler**.

emblem (em **blêm**) *n.* an object chosen to represent an idea or a country: *The bald eagle is the emblem of the United States.*

embrace (im **brās**) *vb.* **embracing, embraced 1** to hold closely in the arms, affectionately or as a greeting. **2** to accept enthusiastically: *She embraced Catholicism and became a devout believer.* – *n.* a loving hug.

embroider (im **broi** dêr) *vb.* **embroidering, embroidered** to decorate cloth with sewn designs. – *n.* **embroidery**.

embryo (em **bri** ō) *n.* **embryos** a human or animal in the earliest stages of development before birth.

emend (i **mend**) *vb.* **emending, emended** to correct.

emerald (e **mê** råld) *n.* **1** a bright-green precious stone. **2** a bright green colour.

emerge (i **mûrj**) *vb.* **emerging, emerged 1** to come out from hiding or into view. **2** to become known or apparent. – *n.* **emergence**.

emergency (i **mûrj** ên si) *n.* **emergencies** an unexpected and serious happening which calls for immediate action.

●**Emerson, Ralph Waldo** (1803-82) was an American philosopher, writer, and poet.

emigrant (e mi grånt) *n.* a person who leaves their native country and settles in another.

emigrate (e mi grāt) *vb.* **emigrating, emigrated** to leave your native country and settle in another. – *n.* **emigration**.

eminent (e mi nênt) *adj.* famous and admired. **eminently** *adv.* very: *an eminently sensible plan.*

emir (e **mēr**) *n.* a title given to various MUSLIM rulers in the MIDDLE EAST or West AFRICA.

emit (i **mit**) *vb.* **emitting, emitted** to give out light, heat, a sound, a smell, etc.

emotion (i **mō** shôn) *n.* a strong feeling. **emotional** *adj.* **1** of the emotions. **2** tending to express emotions easily or excessively.

emphasis (em få sis) *n.* **emphases** importance or extra stress to show that something has a special meaning. – *vb.* **emphasize** or **emphasise emphasizing, emphasized**. **emphatic** (em **fa** tik) *adj.* expressed with or expressing emphasis. – *adv.* **emphatically**.

empire (em pīr) *n.* a group of nations or states under the control of a single ruler or country.

Canada

Australia

New Zealand

South Africa

Many countries try to find some object that uniquely represents them as an emblem on their flags, crests, etc. Examples are the maple leaf in the national arms of Canada, sprays of wattle around the Australian arms, four stars of the Southern Cross for New Zealand, and a trekker's wagon on the arms of South Africa.

Endangered species
Throughout time, animals and plants have died out naturally. Most of the animals and plants in danger of becoming extinct today are threatened by humans. Overhunting, overfishing, the destruction of habitats, and the pollution of the air and seas are taking their toll.

Bald eagle

Pampas deer

Bareheaded rock fowl

Tasmanian wolf

Giant panda

Monkey-eating eagle

employ (im **ploi**) *vb.* **employing, employed**
1 to give paid work to. **2** to occupy the time or attention of: *She was busily employed in writing letters.* – *adj.* **employable**.
  employee *n.* a person who works for another.
  employer *n.* a person or company that employs workers.
  employment *n.* an occupation.
empty (**emp** ti) *adj.* **emptier, emptiest**
having nothing inside; not occupied, inhabited, or furnished. – *vb.* **empties, emptying, emptied** to make or become empty. – *adv.* **emptily**. – *n.* **emptiness**.
emu (**ē mū**) *n.* a large Australian flightless bird.
en- (en-) *prefix* meaning to put into or on: *enrage, enclose.* Before b, p, and m, en- becomes **em-**.
enamel (i **nam** ĕl) *n.* **1** a hardened coloured

glass-like substance applied as a decorative or protective covering to metal or glass. **2** the hard white covering of the teeth.
enchant (in **chänt**) *vb.* **enchanting, enchanted** to charm or delight.
  enchanting *adj.* charming; delightful.
encircle (in **sûr** kĕl) *vb.* **encircling, encircled** to surround, form a circle round.
enclose (in **klōz**) *vb.* **enclosing, enclosed**
1 to put inside a letter or its envelope. **2** to shut in or surround. – *adj.* **enclosed**.
encompass (in **kum** pås) *vb.* **encompassing, encompassed** to include, especially to contain a wide range or coverage of.
encounter (in **kown** tĕr) *vb.* **encountering, encountered** to meet, especially unexpectedly: *They encountered many difficulties.* – *n.* **1** a chance meeting. **2** a fight or battle.
encourage (in **ku** rij) *vb.* **encouraging, encouraged 1** to give support, confidence, or hope to. **2** to urge: *She encouraged him to go to college.* – *n.* **encouragement**.
encyclopedia or **encyclopaedia**
(in sī klō **pē** di å) *n.* a reference work containing information on every branch of knowledge, or on one particular branch, usually arranged in alphabetical order.
end (end) *n.* **1** the point farthest from the beginning, or either of the points farthest from the middle, where something stops.
2 a finish or conclusion: *The speech came to an end.* **3** an object or purpose: *The ends justify the means.* – *vb.* **ending, ended** to finish.
endanger (in **dān** jĕr) *vb.* **endangering, endangered** to put in danger.
  endangered species *n.* a species of animal threatened with extinction.
endeavour (in **dev** ŏr) *vb.* **endeavouring, endeavoured** to try very hard to do something. – *n.* a determined attempt or effort.
endure (in **dūr**) *vb.* **enduring, endured** to bear patiently, put up with. – *adj.* **endurable**.
  endurance *n.* the capacity for toleration.
enemy (e **nĕ** mi) *n.* **enemies** a hostile person, nation, or force. – *adj.* hostile; belonging to a hostile nation or force.
energetic (en ĕr **jet** ik) *adj.* having or displaying energy. – *adv.* **energetically**.
energy (e **nûr** ji) *n.* **energies** vigorous activity; liveliness or vitality; the power to do work.

● Energy can exist in different forms: as stored energy (potential energy), as energy of motion

In the explosion of an atomic bomb vast quantities of energy are released. The splitting of an atom's nucleus is called nuclear fission.

(kinetic energy), chemical energy (as when fuel burns), electrical energy (produced by generators) and nuclear energy, etc.

engage (in **gāj**) *vb.* **engaging, engaged 1** to take on as a worker. **2** to involve or occupy: *She engaged him in conversation.*
  engaged *adj.* **1** bound by a promise to marry. **2** busy; occupied.
  engagement *n.* **1** a firm agreement between two people to marry. **2** an appointment.
  engaging *adj.* charming or attractive.

engine (**en** jin) *n.* **1** a piece of machinery which turns any type of energy into movement. **2** a railway locomotive.

engineer (en ji **nēr**) *n.* **1** a person who designs, makes, or works with machinery. **2** a person who designs or constructs roads, bridges, etc.

Steam locomotives are now rare. In the 1700s steam engines powered factory engines that made the Industrial Revolution possible.

● **England** is the largest country in the UNITED KINGDOM. Sea surrounds most of it. Green fields spread over the plains and low hills that cover most of the country. England gets its names from the ANGLO-SAXONS who settled on the island 1500 years ago.

English (**ing** glish) *adj.* **1** of England or its people. **2** of or using the English language. – *n.* the main language of GREAT BRITAIN, NORTH AMERICA, and many other countries.

engrave (in **grāv**) *vb.* **engraving, engraved** to carve letters or designs on stone, wood, metal, etc. – *n.* **engraver**.

enigma (i **nig** må) *n.* a puzzle or riddle.– *adj.* **enigmatic** (e nig **mat** ik).

enjoy (in **joi**) *vb.* **enjoying, enjoyed 1** to find pleasure in. **2** to have the benefit of something good: *The room enjoys sunlight all day.* – *adj.* **enjoyable**. – *n.* **enjoyment**.

enlarge (in **lärj**) *vb.* **enlarging, enlarged** to make larger.

enlist (in **list**) *vb.* **enlisting, enlisted 1** to join one of the armed forces. **2** to obtain support and help. – *n.* **enlistment**.

enormous (i **nör** mŭs) *adj.* huge.

enough (i **nuf**) *adj.* in the number or quantity needed: *Is there enough food to eat?* – *adv.* to the necessary degree or extent. – *pron.* the amount needed: *I've eaten enough, thank you.*

enquire, enquiry. See **inquire**.

enrage (in **rāj**) *vb.* **enraging, enraged** to make very angry. – *adj.* **enraged**.

enrich (in **rich**) *vb.* **enriching, enriched** to improve in quality, value, flavour, etc.

enrol (in **rōl**) *vb.* **enrolling, enrolled** to add the name of a person to a list, for example to join a club. – *n.* **enrolment**.

ensign (**en** sīn) *n.* a flag flown by a ship.

ensure (in **shōōr**) *vb.* **ensuring, ensured** to make certain: *Please ensure you switch off the lights.*

enter (**en** tềr) *vb.* **entering, entered 1** to come in or go in. **2** to register for a competition.

enterprise (**en** tềr prīz) *n.* **1** a project or undertaking. **2** boldness and initiative: *He showed great enterprise by setting up a new business.* – *adj.* **enterprising**.

PRONUNCIATION GUIDE	
fat **a**	all **ö**
fate **ā**	foot **oo**
fast **ä**	moon **ōō**
among **å**	boy **oi**
met **e**	house **ow**
mean **ē**	demon **ŏ**
silent **ê**	thing **th**
loch **hh**	this **Th**
fin **i**	but **u**
line **ī**	mute **ū**
quick **kw**	fur **û**
got **o**	brochure **ů**
note **ō**	vision **zh**

EPONYMS

Names of places

Amerigo Vespucci
America

Simon Bolivar
Bolivia

Sir George Everest
Mount Everest

Abel Tasman
Tasmania

The Sciences

André Ampère
ampere

Alexander Bell
decibel

Anders Celsius
Celsius

James Watt
Watt

Clothing

Amelia Bloomer
bloomers

Jules Leotard
leotard

Levi Strauss
Levis ®

Duke of Wellington
wellingtons

An assortment

George Gallup
gallup poll

Joseph Guillotin
guillotine

William Hoover
hoover ®

Candido Jacuzzi
jacuzzi ®

Julius Caesar
July

Adolphe Saxe
saxophone

Fruits and Flowers

Michel Begon
begonia

Adam Buddle
buddleia

Alexander Garden
gardenia

Maria Smith
Granny Smith
(apple)

entertain (en tĕr **tān**) *vb.* **entertaining, entertained 1** to provide amusement. **2** to give hospitality to a guest.

entertainer *n.* a person who provides amusement, especially professionally.

entertainment *n.* something that entertains, for example a theatrical show.

enthuse (in **thūz**) *vb.* **enthusing, enthused** to be enthusiastic.

enthusiasm (in **thū** zi a zĕm) *n.* lively or passionate interest or eagerness.

enthusiast *n.* a person filled with enthusiasm; a fan. – *adj.* **enthusiastic**. – *adv.* **enthusiastically**.

entice (in **tīs**) *vb.* **enticing, enticed** to tempt or persuade someone to do something.

entire (in **tīr**) *adj.* whole, complete.

entitle (in **tī** tĕl) *vb.* **entitling, entitled** to give someone a right to have, or to do, something: *They are entitled to claim some money back.*

entrance[1] (en **trăns**) *n.* a way in, e.g. a door.

entrance[2] (in **trăns**) *vb.* **entrancing, entranced** to grip the attention and imagination of. – *adj.* **entrancing**.

entry (en trī) *n.* **1** the act of coming or going in. **2** a place of entering, such as a door. **3** an item written on a list.

enumerate (i **nūm** ĕ rāt) *vb.* **enumerating, enumerated** to list one by one.

envelop (in **vel** ŏp) *vb.* **enveloping, enveloped** to cover, wrap, surround, or conceal. – *n.* **envelopment**.

envelope (en vĕ lōp) or (on vĕ lōp) *n.* a thin flat paper packet or cover, especially for a letter.

envious (en vi ŭs) *adj.* feeling or showing envy.

environment (in **vīr** ŏn mĕnt) *n.* **1** the surroundings or conditions within which something or someone exists: *The sunny room was a pleasant environment in which to work.* **2** the natural conditions necessary for the healthy existence of all plants, animals, and people: *Many people are concerned about the effects of global warming on the environment.* – *adj.* **environmental** (in vī rŏn **men** tăl).

envisage (in **viz** ij) *vb.* **envisaging, envisaged** to picture in the mind and to consider to be likely in the future.

envoy (en voi) *n.* **1** a diplomat. **2** a messenger.

envy (en vi) *n.* bitter or resentful feelings of desire for another person's better fortune, success, or possessions. – *vb.* **envies, envying, envied** to feel envy towards a person: *I envy her because of her success.*

ephemeral (i fem ĕ răl) *adj.* lasting for only a very short time.

epic (**e** pik) *n.* **1** a long poem that tells a story about heroic acts, the history of nations, etc. **2** a long adventure story or film.

epidemic (e pi **dem** ik) *n.* a sudden and widespread outbreak of a disease.

epigram (**e** pi gram) *n.* a witty or sarcastic saying, or a short poem with such an ending.

episcopal (i **pis** kŏ păl) *adj.* relating to or governed by bishops.

episode (**e** pi sōd) *n.* **1** one of several events or distinct periods making up a longer sequence. **2** one of the separate parts in which a radio or television serial is broadcast.

epistle (i **pis** ĕl) *n.* a letter, especially a long one (in the NEW TESTAMENT).

epitaph (**e** pi tăf) *n.* an inscription on a gravestone.

epitome (i **pit** ŏ mi) *n.* a person or thing that is a perfect or typical example of something: *She was the epitome of good behaviour.*

epoch (**ē** pok) *n.* **1** a particular period of history. **2** a division of a geological period.

eponym (**e** pŏ nim) *n.* a person after whom something is named.

equal (**ē** kwăl) *adj.* **1** the same in size, amount, or value. **2** having or entitled to the same rights. – *n.* a person or thing of the same age, rank, ability, worth, etc. – *vb.* **equalling, equalled** to be the same in amount, value, or size; to be as good as; to match. – *n.* **equality** (i **kwol** i ti) **equalities**.

equalize or **equalise** *vb.* **equalizing, equalized** to make or become equal.

equation *n.* **1** a mathematical formula which states that two quantities or groups are equal. **2** a scientific formula expressing the reaction of chemical compounds.

equator (i **kwāt** ŏr) *n.* an imaginary line passing round the Earth at an equal distance from the NORTH and SOUTH POLES.

equatorial (e kwă **tör** i ăl) *adj.* of the equator.

● **Equatorial Guinea**. See Supplement, **Countries**.

equestrian (i **kwes** tri ăn) *adj.* of horses.

equilateral (ē kwi **lat** ĕ răl) or (e kwi **lat** ĕ răl) *adj.* having all sides of equal length.

equilibrium (ē kwi **lib** ri ŭm) or (e kwi **lib** ri ŭm) *n.* a state in which weights, forces, etc. are equally balanced.

equinox (ē kwi noks) or (e kwi noks) *n.* either of the two occasions on which the Sun crosses the equator, making night and day equal in length. The **vernal** or **spring equinox** occurs around 21 March and the **autumnal equinox** around 23 September.

equip (i kwip) *vb.* **equipping, equipped** to provide with the necessary tools, supplies, abilities, etc. – *n.* **equipment**.

equivalent (i kwiv å lĕnt) *adj.* equal in value, power, meaning, etc.: *They looked for a vase of an equivalent value to replace the broken one.* – *n.*

era (ēr å) *n.* **1** a distinct period in history marked by an important event. **2** in geology, a main division of time.

eradicate (i rad i kāt) *vb.* **eradicating, eradicated** to get rid of completely.

erase (i rāz) *vb.* **erasing, erased** to rub out; to remove all trace of something.

erect (i rekt) *adj.* upright; not bent or leaning. – *vb.* **erecting, erected** to put up or to build.

● **Erie, Lake** is one of the GREAT LAKES between CANADA and the UNITED STATES.

● **Eritrea**. See Supplement, **Countries**.

erode (i rōd) *vb.* **eroding, eroded** to wear away or be destroyed gradually.

Eros (ē ros). See **Myths and Legends**.

erosion (i rō zhŏn) *n.* the wearing away of rock or soil by the action of wind, water, or ice.

err (ûr) *vb.* **erring, erred** to make a mistake.

errand (e rånd) *n.* a short journey made to get or do something, especially for someone else.

erratic (i rat ik) *adj.* irregular; having no fixed pattern or course. – *adv.* **erratically**.

error (e rŏr) *n.* a mistake or inaccuracy.

erupt (i rupt) *vb.* **erupting, erupted 1** (of a volcano) to throw out lava, ash, and gases. **2** to break out suddenly and violently: *His anger erupted suddenly.* – *n.* **eruption**.

escalate (es kå lāt) *vb.* **escalating, escalated** to increase rapidly: *Prices have escalated since the war began.* – *n.* **escalation**.

escape (i skāp) *vb.* **escaping, escaped 1** to gain freedom: *They escaped from prison.* **2** to manage to avoid: *He escaped punishment.* – *n.* **1** an act of escaping. **2** the avoiding of danger or harm: *That was a narrow escape.*

escort (es kört) *n.* people or vehicles that accompany others for protection, guidance, or as a mark of honour. – (i skört) *vb.* **escorting, escorted** to accompany.

Eskimo (es ki mō) *n.* **Eskimos** or **Eskimo**. See **Inuit**.

especial (i spe shål) *adj.* special. – *adv.* **especially**.

Esperanto (e spĕ ran tō) *n.* a language invented in 1887 for international use.

espionage (e spi ŏ näzh) *n.* spying.

essay (e sā) *n.* a short formal piece of writing, usually dealing with a single subject.

essence (e sĕns) *n.* **1** the basic quality of something that determines its nature or character. **2** a concentrated liquid obtained from a plant, and often used to flavour food: *He added a drop of almond essence to the cake.*

> **LESS -ESS**
> -ess is a suffix which is often added to words to denote a feminine person or animal. Because these words sound demeaning and pejorative, many are quite rightly rarely used, for example authoress, conductress, poetess, sculptress. A few -ess words, such as actress, hostess, waitress, lioness remain, and the feminine of titles, such as baroness, duchess, goddess, are still used.

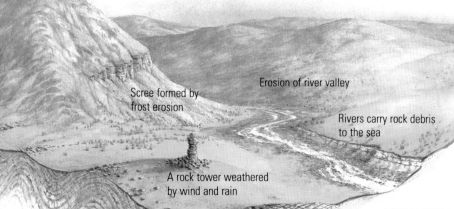

Rain containing carbon dioxide from the air will dissolve limestone.

Erosion and weathering both help to shape the Earth. The action of wind, rain, ice, and snow physically breaks down rocks into smaller particles such as sand. Once broken down, the bits are transported elsewhere by ice, wind, water, or gravity. This is erosion.

Scree formed by frost erosion

Erosion of river valley

A rock tower weathered by wind and rain

Rivers carry rock debris to the sea

In deserts, sand-laden wind can sculpt rocks into weird shapes.

essential (i **sen** shål) *adj.* absolutely necessary. – *n.* a basic piece of equipment or information: *They took only the bare essentials for the journey.* **essentially** *adv.* basically; most importantly.

establish (i **stab** lish) *vb.* **establishing, established 1** to set something up, a university or a business, for example. **2** to show or prove: *They established the cause of death.* **establishment** *n.* **1** the act of establishing something. **2** a business organization, such as a shop or public or government institution.

estate (i **stāt**) *n.* **1** a large piece of land owned by a person or group of people. **2** an area of land on which development has taken place, for example, houses (a **housing estate**) or factories (an **industrial** or **trading estate**).

esteem (i **stēm**) *vb.* **esteeming, esteemed** to value or respect.

estimate (e sti māt) *vb.* **estimating, estimated** to calculate size, amount, value, etc. roughly or without measuring. – (e sti måt) *n.* a rough assessment of size, etc.

● **Estonia** (e **stō** ni å) was a republic of the former USSR but since 1991 has been independent. See also Supplement, **Countries**.

estuary (es tū å ri) *n.* **estuaries** the wide lower part of a river which flows into the sea.

etch (ech) *vb.* **etching, etched** to make designs on metal or glass by cutting lines with acid. **etching** *n.* a print made from an etched plate.

eternal (i **tûr** nål) *adj.* without beginning or end; everlasting and unchanging.

eternity (i **tûr** ni ti) *n.* **eternities** time regarded as having no end.

ether (**ē** thêr) *n.* a colourless sweet-smelling liquid, used as an anaesthetic.

ethical (**eth** i kěl) *adj.* **1** of or concerning morals, justice, or duty. **2** morally right.

● **Ethiopia**. See Supplement, **Countries**.

ethnic (**eth** nik) *adj.* having a common race or culture: *The Kurds form an ethnic group.*

etiquette (e ti ket) *n.* conventions of correct or polite social behaviour.

● **Etna** is an active volcano in Sicily.

● **Etruscans** were the original people to live in Tuscany, ITALY. The Romans defeated them in about 200 BC.

The flag of the EU has 12 gold stars

More of **Europe**'s land can be farmed than of other continent's and it is rich in coal, iron, and other raw materials. The people of Europe are made up of many different nationalities. Each has its own language and customs. The largest European country is Russia; the smallest is the Vatican in Rome.

Reykjavik

Edinburg
Belfast ●
Dublin ●
London
Pari

PYRENEES

Lisbon Madrid

KEY FACTS
Number of countries: 47
Area: 10,531,623 sq km.
Highest point: Mount Elbrus (5633 m)
Longest river: Volga (3700 km)
Biggest lake: Caspian Sea
Biggest island: Great Britain

etymology (e ti **mol** ȯ ji) *n.* **etymologies** the study of the origin and development of words.

eucalyptus (ū kå **lip** tůs) *n.* **eucalyptuses** or **eucalypti** (ū kå **lip** tī) a tall evergreen tree, native to AUSTRALIA.

● **Euclid** was a Greek mathematician who lived and worked around 300 BC.

euphemism (**ū** fě mi zěm) *n.* the use of a mild or inoffensive term in place of one considered offensive or unpleasantly direct, for example *pass on* instead of *die*.

● **Euphrates** (ū **frā** tēz) is a river that flows through TURKEY into the river Tigris. The MESOPOTAMIAN civilization once flourished around it.

● **Euripides** (ūr **ip** i dēz) was a Greek dramatist (5th century BC).

● **Europe** is the sixth biggest continent but is second in population size. Most of Europe has a mild climate and fertile soil. There are some high mountains including the ALPS and URAL

MOUNTAINS. Europeans have settled in other parts taking their customs and knowledge with them. Much of Europe's wealth comes from its factories, farms, and mines.

European (ū rō **pē** ån) *adj.* of, or relating to, Europe. – *n.* a native or inhabitant of Europe.

● **European Union** a group of western European nations that work together to form a political and economic union. Its members are BELGIUM, DENMARK, FRANCE, IRELAND, ITALY, GERMANY, GREECE, LUXEMBOURG, the NETHERLANDS, PORTUGAL, SPAIN, and the UNITED KINGDOM.

evacuate (i **vak** ū āt) *vb.* **evacuating, evacuated** to leave a place, especially because of danger. – *n.* **evacuation.**
evacuee *n.* an evacuated person.
evade (i **vād**) *vb.* **evading, evaded** to escape or avoid by trickery or skill.
evaporate (i **vap** ȯ rāt) *vb.* **evaporating, evaporated** to change from a solid or liquid into gas. – *n.* **evaporation.**
eve (ēv) *n.* the day before a notable event.

● **Eve** was the first woman in the BIBLE.

even (ē vẽn) *adj.* **1** smooth and flat; level. **2** constant or regular: *They were travelling at an even 50 km per hour.* **3** (of a number) divisible by 2, with nothing left over: *8 is an even number.* **4** equal: *The scores were even.* – *adv.* **1** used with a comparative *adj.* or *adv.* to emphasize a comparison with something else: *He's good, but she's even better.* **2** used with an expression stronger than a previous one: *He looked sad, even depressed.* **3** used to introduce a surprising piece of information: *Even John was there!*
evening (**ēv** ning) *n.* the last part of the day, from late afternoon until bedtime.
event (i **vent**) *n.* **1** something that happens; an incident, especially an important one. **2** an item in a programme of sports, etc.
eventual (i **ven** choo ål) *adj.* happening gradually, or at the end of a period of time.
ever (e vẽr) *adv.* at any time: *Have you ever seen anyone so beautiful?*
evergreen *adj.* having leaves all the year round. – *n.* an evergreen tree or shrub.

● **Everest**, in the HIMALAYAS, is the world's highest peak (8848 metres above sea level).

● **Everglades** a huge swamp that covers 10,000 sq km of southern Florida, USA. The animal life includes SNAKES, TURTLES, ALLIGATORS, and many kinds of MAMMALS and BIRDS.

every (ev ri) *adj.* **1** each single, omitting none: *Every child must be vaccinated against smallpox.* **2** the greatest or best possible: *We're making every effort to avoid war.* – *adv.* at the end of each stated period of time, distance, etc.: *every fourth week; every six centimetres.*
everybody *pron.* every person.
everyday *adj.* **1** used on ordinary days, rather than on special occasions: *She wore a plain, everyday dress.* **2** common or usual.
everyone *pron.* every person.
everything *pron.* **1** all things; all. **2** the most important thing: *Fitness is everything in sport.*
everywhere *adv.* in or to every place.
evidence (e vi dẽns) *n.* **1** information that gives grounds for belief and which points to, reveals, or suggests something. **2** See **Law.**
evident *adj.* clear to see or understand.
evil (ē vil) *adj.* bad, wicked, or offensive; harmful. – *n.* a source of wickedness or harm.

CHANGES OF MEANING

Etymologists study word origins and also how words can change their meaning. For instance:
acre once meant simply 'a field'.
clown once meant 'a countryman'.
cunning used to mean 'knowing or clever'.
gallon once meant 'a bucket or container'.
knave once meant 'a servant'.
nice once meant 'hard to please' or 'fussy'.
silly once meant 'blessed or holy'
paradise once meant 'royal park.
villain once meant 'peasant'.
yard was once 'a wand or stick'.

Millions of years

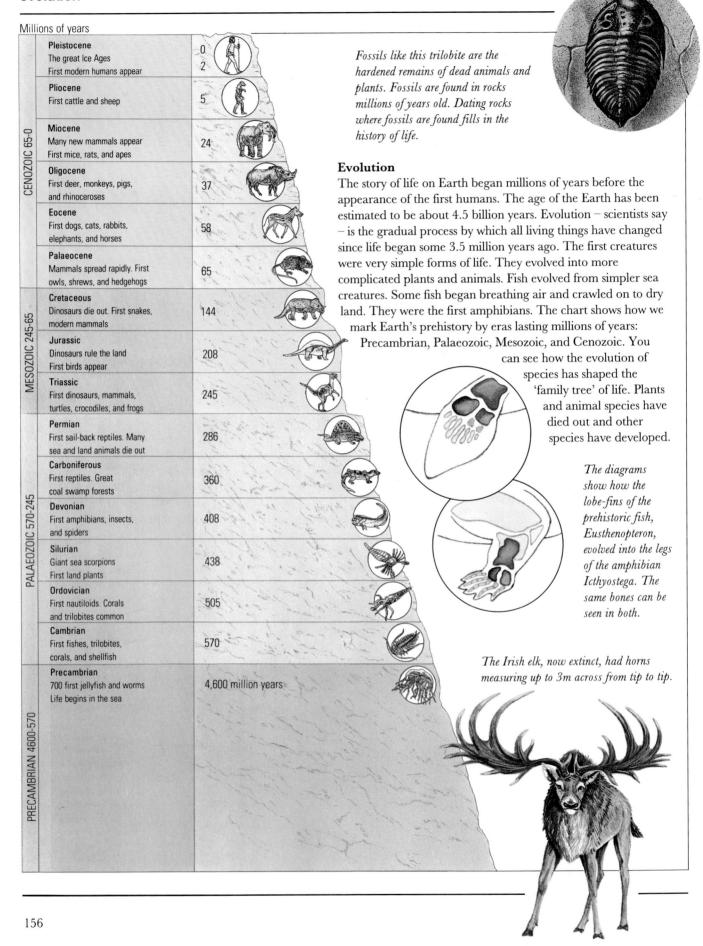

Era	Period	Millions of years
CENOZOIC 65-0	**Pleistocene** — The great Ice Ages. First modern humans appear	0 / 2
	Pliocene — First cattle and sheep	5
	Miocene — Many new mammals appear. First mice, rats, and apes	24
	Oligocene — First deer, monkeys, pigs, and rhinoceroses	37
	Eocene — First dogs, cats, rabbits, elephants, and horses	58
	Palaeocene — Mammals spread rapidly. First owls, shrews, and hedgehogs	65
MESOZOIC 245-65	**Cretaceous** — Dinosaurs die out. First snakes, modern mammals	144
	Jurassic — Dinosaurs rule the land. First birds appear	208
	Triassic — First dinosaurs, mammals, turtles, crocodiles, and frogs	245
PALAEOZOIC 570-245	**Permian** — First sail-back reptiles. Many sea and land animals die out	286
	Carboniferous — First reptiles. Great coal swamp forests	360
	Devonian — First amphibians, insects, and spiders	408
	Silurian — Giant sea scorpions. First land plants	438
	Ordovician — First nautiloids. Corals and trilobites common	505
	Cambrian — First fishes, trilobites, corals, and shellfish	570
PRECAMBRIAN 4600-570	**Precambrian** — 700 first jellyfish and worms. Life begins in the sea	4,600 million years

Fossils like this trilobite are the hardened remains of dead animals and plants. Fossils are found in rocks millions of years old. Dating rocks where fossils are found fills in the history of life.

Evolution

The story of life on Earth began millions of years before the appearance of the first humans. The age of the Earth has been estimated to be about 4.5 billion years. Evolution – scientists say – is the gradual process by which all living things have changed since life began some 3.5 million years ago. The first creatures were very simple forms of life. They evolved into more complicated plants and animals. Fish evolved from simpler sea creatures. Some fish began breathing air and crawled on to dry land. They were the first amphibians. The chart shows how we mark Earth's prehistory by eras lasting millions of years: Precambrian, Palaeozoic, Mesozoic, and Cenozoic. You can see how the evolution of species has shaped the 'family tree' of life. Plants and animal species have died out and other species have developed.

The diagrams show how the lobe-fins of the prehistoric fish, Eusthenopteron, evolved into the legs of the amphibian Icthyostega. The same bones can be seen in both.

The Irish elk, now extinct, had horns measuring up to 3m across from tip to tip.

evolution (ē vŏ lōō shŏn) or (e vŏ lōō shŏn) *n.* **1** the process of gradual development. **2** the gradual development of present-day plants and animals, including humans, from earlier, more primitive forms of life. – *adj.* **evolutionary.**

evolve (i **volv**) *vb.* **evolving, evolved** to develop or produce gradually.

ewe (ū) *n.* a female sheep.

ex- (eks-) *prefix* **1** former: *ex-wife.* **2** outside: *Their telephone number is ex-directory.*

exact (ig **zakt**) *adj.* absolutely accurate or correct: *She gave him the exact amount.*

exaggerate (ig **zaj** ě rāt) *vb.* **exaggerating, exaggerated** to describe someone or something as being greater in extent, etc. than is really the case. – *n.* **exaggeration.**

examination (ig za mi **nā** shŏn) *n.* a set of tasks, often written, designed to test knowledge or ability.

examine (ig **zam** in) *vb.* **examining, examined** to inspect, consider, or look into closely: *They examined her ideas.* – *n.* **examiner.**

example (ig **zäm** pěl) *n.* **1** something or someone that is a typical specimen. **2** something that illustrates a fact or rule.

excavate (eks **kǎ** vāt) *vb.* **excavating, excavated** to dig up or uncover historical remains. – *n.* **excavation.** – *n.* **excavator.**

exceed (ik **sēd**) *vb.* **exceeding, exceeded** to be greater than; to go beyond.

excel (ik **sel**) *vb.* **excelling, excelled** to be exceptionally good; to be better than.

excellence (ek **sě** lěns) *n.* great worth; very high or exceptional quality. – *adj.* **excellent.**

except (ik **sept**) *prep.* leaving out; not including: *I like all fruit except apples.* **exceptional** *adj.* remarkable or outstanding.

excess (ek **ses**) *n.* an amount greater than is usual, necessary, or wise: *an excess of ice cream will make you feel sick.* **excessive** *adj.* beyond what is usual.

exchange (iks **chānj**) *vb.* **exchanging, exchanged** to give in return for something else: *The two leaders exchanged gifts.* – *n.* **1** the giving and taking of one thing for another. **2** a place where things are traded, or international financial deals carried out.

excite (ik **sīt**) *vb.* **exciting, excited** to arouse feelings of happiness and nervousness: *She was excited about her birthday party.* – *adj.* **excited.** – *n.* **excitement** the state of being excited.

exclaim (ik **sklām**) *vb.* **exclaiming, exclaimed** to call out suddenly.

exclamation (eks clǎ **mā** shŏn) *n.* a word or expression uttered suddenly and loudly. **exclamation mark** *n.* the punctuation mark (!) used after an exclamation: *It's a ghastly tie!*

exclude (ik **sklōōd**) *vb.* **excluding, excluded** to prevent from sharing or taking part; to omit: *They voted to exclude him from the club.*

exclusion (ik **sklōō** zhŏn) *n.* the act of excluding, or the state of being excluded.

exclusive (ik **sklōō** siv) *adj.* **1** limited to only one place, group, or person: *These gardens are exclusive to the residents of the surrounding houses.* **2** not including: *The rent is exclusive of bills.*

excursion (ik **skûr** shŏn) *n.* a short trip.

excuse (ik **skūz**) *vb.* **excusing, excused 1** to pardon or forgive. **2** to offer an explanation of a wrongdoing. **3** to free from a duty: *He excused her from doing the washing-up.* – (ik **skūs**) *n.* an explanation for a wrongdoing, offered as an apology or justification.

execute (**ek** si kūt) *vb.* **executing, executed 1** to put to death by order of the law. **2** to perform: *She executed a perfect pirouette.* **execution** *n.* the act of putting to death.

executive (ig **zek** ū tiv) *adj.* in an organization, concerned with administration.

exercise (**ek** sěr sīz) *n.* **1** physical training for health or pleasure. **2** an activity intended to develop a skill: *He practised finger exercises on the piano.* **3** a task designed to test ability: *She gave him a simple exercise to test his spelling.* – *vb.* **exercising, exercised 1** to keep fit and healthy by training. **2** to use, bring into use: *He exercised his right to vote.*

exert (ig **zûrt**) *vb.* **exerting, exerted 1** to bring into action forcefully: *She exerted her authority.* **2** to force yourself to make a strenuous effort. – *n.* **exertion.**

exhale (eks **hāl**) *vb.* **exhaling, exhaled** to breathe out. – *n.* **exhalation** (eks hǎ **lā** shŏn).

exhaust (ig **zöst**) *vb.* **exhausting, exhausted 1** to make very tired. **2** to use up completely: *They had exhausted their supplies.* **3** to say all that can be said about a subject. – *n.* the parts of an engine through which the waste gases escape. – *adj.* **exhausted.** – *adj.* **exhausting.** – *n.* **exhaustion.**

exhibit (ig **zib** it) *vb.* **exhibiting, exhibited 1** to present or display for public appreciation. **2** to show or display a quality, feelings, etc. – *n.* an object displayed publicly, e.g. in a museum. **exhibition** *n.* a display, for example of works of art, to the public.

Early explorers relied on three basic navigational aids: the astrolabe and backstaff were used to calculate a ship's latitude (how far north or south of the equator). The compass showed in which direction the ship was sailing.

Astrolabe

Backstaff

Compass

Marco Polo 1271-5
Vespucci 1499
Magellan 1519-22
Columbus 1492

The Norwegian, Roald Amundsen, arrived at the South Pole using dogs to pull the sledges.

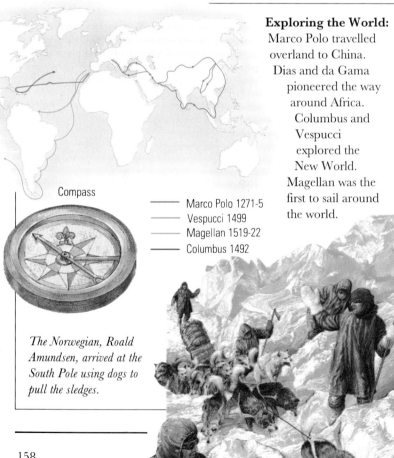

exhilarate (ig **zil** å rāt) *vb.* **exhilarating, exhilarated** to fill with a lively cheerfulness. – *n.* **exhilaration**.

exile (**ek** sīl) *n.* enforced absence from someone's home country or town, especially for a long time, often as a punishment. – *vb.* **exiling, exiled** to send into exile.

exist (ig **zist**) *vb.* **existing, existed** to be, especially to be present in the real world rather than in story or imagination.
existence *n.* the state of existing.

exit (**eg** zit) *n.* a way out of a building, etc.

exotic (ig **zot** ik) *adj.* **1** introduced from a foreign, especially distant and tropical, country: *exotic plants*. **2** interestingly different.

expand (ik **spand**) *vb.* **expanding, expanded** to make or become greater in size, extent, or importance. – *adj.* **expandable**.

expanse (ik **spans**) *n.* a wide area or space.

expansive (ik **span** siv) *adj.* **1** ready or eager to talk; open. **2** wide-ranging.

expect (ik **spekt**) *vb.* **expecting, expected** **1** to think something is likely to happen or come. **2** to require, or regard as normal. **3** (*colloquial*) to suppose: *I expect you're right.*

Exploring the World: Marco Polo travelled overland to China. Dias and da Gama pioneered the way around Africa. Columbus and Vespucci explored the New World. Magellan was the first to sail around the world.

expectation *n.* **1** the state of expecting. **2** (often in *plural*) something expected.

expedition (ek spě **di** shŏn) *n.* an organized trip with a purpose, or the group making it: *a climbing expedition*.

expel (ik **spel**) *vb.* **expelling, expelled** to force out: *She was expelled from school for misconduct.*

expense (ik **spens**) *n.* the act of spending money, or money spent. – **at the expense of** causing damage to the pride, health etc.

expensive (ik **spen** siv) *adj.* costing a large amount of money.

experience (ik **spēr** i ĕns) *n.* **1** practice in an activity. **2** knowledge or skill gained through practice. – *vb.* **experiencing, experienced** **1** to have practical acquaintance of. **2** to feel or undergo: *They experienced hunger.*

experienced *adj.* having knowledge or skill: *Ralph is an experienced musician.*

experiment (ik **spe** ri měnt) *n.* **1** a trial carried out in order to test a theory, a machine's performance, etc. or to discover something unknown. **2** an attempt at something original. – (ik **spe** ri ment) *vb.* **experimenting, experimented** to make such a trial.

expert (**ek** spûrt) *n.* a person who knows a lot about a particular subject. – *adj.* skilled.

expertise (ek spěr **tēz**) *n.* special skill or knowledge.

expire (ik **spīr**) *vb.* **expiring, expired** to come to an end, cease to be valid. – *n.* **expiry**.

explain (ik **splān**) *vb.* **explaining, explained** **1** to make clear or easy to understand. **2** to give, or be, a reason for.

explanation *n.* **1** the act or process of explaining. **2** a statement or fact that explains. – *adj.* **explanatory** (ik **splan** å tŏ ri).

explicit (ik **spli** sit) *adj.* stated or shown clearly: *explicit instructions.*

explode (ik **splōd**) *vb.* **exploding, exploded** **1** to burst or shatter violently; to blow up. **2** to suddenly show a strong or violent emotion.

exploit (**ek** sploit) *n.* (usually in *plural*) an act or feat, especially a bold or daring one. – (ik **sploit**) *vb.* **exploiting, exploited** **1** to take unfair advantage of so as to achieve your own aims. **2** to make good use of: *exploit oil resources.* – *n.* **exploitation**.

explore (ik **splör**) *vb.* **exploring, explored** **1** to search or travel through a place for the purpose of discovery. **2** to examine carefully: *We must explore every possibility.* – *n.*

exploration. – *n.* **explorer.**

explosion (ik **splō** zhŏn) *n.* a blowing up, or the noise caused by this.

export (ik **spört**) *vb.* **exporting, exported** to send or take goods, etc. to another country, especially for sale. – (**ek** spört) *n.* **1** the act or business of exporting. **2** something exported.

expose (ik **spōz**) *vb.* **exposing, exposed 1** to remove cover, protection, or shelter from: *Out on the hills we were exposed to the wind.* **2** to discover or make known a crime, etc.

exposure (ik **spō** zhŭr) *n.* the act of exposing or the state of being exposed.

When you look at something, the light rays reflected from the object are focused upside down on the retina, but the brain interprets this as the right way up.

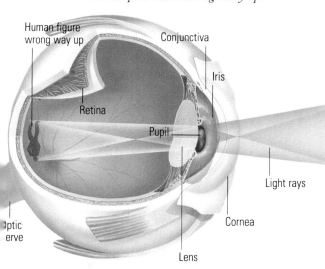

Human figure wrong way up
Conjunctiva
Iris
Retina
Pupil
Light rays
Optic nerve
Cornea
Lens

express (ik **spres**) *vb.* **expressing, expressed 1** to put into words. **2** to show or reveal.

expression *n.* **1** the act of expressing. **2** a look on the face that displays feelings. **3** a word or phrase: *a popular expression.*

expressive *adj.* showing meaning or feeling in a clear or lively way. – *n.* **expressiveness.**

extant (ek **stant**) *adj.* still existing.

extend (ik **stend**) *vb.* **extending, extended 1** to make longer or larger. **2** to stick out: *The jetty extended into the water.* – *adj.* **extendable** or **extendible.**

extension (ik **sten** shŏn) *n.* an added part, making the original larger or longer.

extensive (ik **sten** siv) *adj.* large in area.

extent (ik **stent**) *n.* **1** the area over which something extends. **2** amount; degree: *What was the extent of the damage?*

exterior (ik **stēr** i ŏr) *adj.* on, from, or for use on the outside. – *n.* an outside part or surface.

exterminate (ik **stûr** mi nāt) *vb.* **exterminating, exterminated** to get rid of.

external (ik **stûr** nål) *adj.* from, or on, the outside.

extinct (ik **stingkt**) *adj.* **1** no longer in existence: *The dodo is an extinct bird.* **2** (of a volcano) no longer active. – *n.* **extinction.**

extinguish (ik **sting** gwish) *vb.* **extinguishing, extinguished** to put out a fire.

extra (**ek** strå) *adj.* additional; more than is usual, necessary, or expected.

extra- (**ek** strå-) *prefix* outside or beyond: *We do extra-curricular activities after school.*

extract (ik **strakt**) *vb.* **extracting, extracted** to pull out, especially by force: *He was forced to have the painful tooth extracted.* – (**ek** strakt) *n.* a passage selected from a book, etc.: *The author read an extract from his new novel.*

extraordinary (ik **strör** di nå ri) *adj.* unusual.

extravagant (ik **stra** vå gånt) *adj.* spending or costing too much. – *n.* **extravagance.**

extreme (ik **strēm**) *adj.* **1** very high in degree or intensity: *The explorers suffered from the extreme cold.* **2** farthest, in any direction, especially out from the centre: *She stood on the extreme left.* **3** very violent or strong; not moderate; severe: *The situation called for extreme measures.*

extrovert (**ek** strŏ vûrt) *n. & adj.* (a person who is) sociable and outgoing. – *adj.* **extroverted.**

eye (ī) *n.* **1** the organ of sight in humans and animals. **2** (often in *plural*) sight; vision: *Surgeons need good eyes.* **3** attention, gaze, or observation: *Keep your eyes on the ball.* **4** the ability to appreciate and judge: *He has an eye for beauty.* – *vb.* **eyeing** or **eying, eyed** to look at carefully: *She eyed the stranger with suspicion.*

eyebrow *n.* the arch of hair above each eye.

eyelash *n.* any of the short hairs that grow on the edge of the eyelid.

eyelid *n.* either of the two folds of skin that can be moved to cover or open the eye.

eye-opener *n.* something which makes you suddenly understand.

eyesight *n.* the ability to see.

eyesore *n.* an ugly thing, especially a building.

eyewitness *n.* a person who sees something happen, especially a crime.

eyelet (ī lĕt) *n.* a small hole through which a lace, etc. is passed.

PRONUNCIATION GUIDE

fat **a**	all **ö**
fate **ā**	foot **oo**
fast **ä**	moon **ōō**
among **å**	boy **oi**
met **e**	house **ow**
mean **ē**	demon **ŏ**
silent **ĕ**	thing **th**
loch **hh**	this **Th**
fin **i**	but **u**
line **ī**	mute **ū**
quick **kw**	fur **û**
got **o**	brochure **ů**
note **ō**	vision **zh**

Ff

fable (**fā** bĕl) *n.* **1** a story with a moral, usually with animals as characters. **2** a lie; a false story.

fabric (**fab** rik) *n.* woven or knitted cloth.

fabulous (**fab** ū lŭs) *adj.* marvellous.

façade or **facade** (få **säd**) *n.* the front of a building.

face (fās) *n.* **1** the front part of the head, from forehead to chin. **2** facial expression: *The basset has such a sad face.* **3** a surface or side, of a mountain, gem, geometrical figure, etc. – *vb.* **facing, faced 1** to be opposite to; to look at or look in some direction. **2** to confront, brave, or accept problems, difficulties, etc.: *Diana faced the sad news bravely.* – **face to face** facing or confronting each other. – *vb.* **face up to** to accept an unpleasant fact, etc.

facial (**fā** shǎl) *adj.* of the face: *What a strange facial expression!*

facility (få **sil** i ti) *n.* **facilities 1** skill or ability with little effort. **2** a building, service, or piece of equipment for a particular activity: *The council provides a home-help facility for the elderly.*

fact (fakt) *n.* a thing known to be true or to exist.

factor (**fak** tŏr) *n.* something that helps bring about a result.

factory (**fak** tŏr i) *n.* **factories** a building where things are made by machines: *He works in a car factory.*

factual (**fak** choo ǎl) *adj* concerned with facts.

faculty (**fak** ǔl ti) *n.* **faculties 1** any of the mental or physical powers. **2** a particular talent or aptitude for something. **3** a section of a university: *Arts faculty.*

fad (fad) *n.* a short-lived fashion.

fade (fād) *vb.* **fading, faded** to lose strength, freshness, or colour.

Fahrenheit (**fā** rĕn hīt) *n.* a scale of temperature on which water boils at 212° and freezes at 32°.

fail (fāl) *vb.* **failing, failed 1** not to succeed; to be unsuccessful in. **2** to judge not good enough to pass a test, etc. **3** not to bother doing something: *Al failed to go to the lecture.*

failure *n.* **1** lack of success. **2** a stoppage in functioning.

faint (fānt) *adj.* **1** pale; dim; indistinct. **2** physically weak and dizzy. **3** feeble; unenthusiastic. – *vb.* **fainting, fainted** to lose consciousness: *The soldier fainted in the heat.*

fair¹ (fār) *adj.* **1** just; not using dishonest methods or discrimination. **2** having light-coloured hair or skin. **3** quite good. **4** sizeable: *The garden is a fair size.* **5** fine: *Fair weather has set in.* – *adv.* in a fair way. – *n.* **fairness**.

fair² (fār) *n.* (also **funfair**) an entertainment of sideshows, amusements, rides, etc.

fairy (**fār** i) *n.* **fairies** an imaginary small creature with magical powers.

fairy tale *n.* a story about fairies, magic, etc.

Winged fairies – illustrated in a children's book.

faith (fāth) *n.* **1** trust. **2** strong belief, e.g. in God. **faithful** *adj.* loyal and true; accurate.

fake (fāk) *n.* a person, thing, or act that is not genuine: *That banknote is a fake.* – *adj.* not genuine; false. – *vb.* **faking, faked** to pretend to feel an emotion or have an illness.

falcon (fŏl kėn) *n.* a bird of prey.

fall (fŏl) *vb.* **falling, fell** (fel), **fallen 1** to descend or drop, especially accidentally. **2** to drop to the ground after losing balance: *The horse tripped over the fence and fell.* **3** (of rain, snow, etc.) to come down. **4** to become less: *The temperature fell suddenly.* – *n.* **1** an act or way of falling: *a spectacular fall.* **2** something, or an amount, that falls. **3** a drop in quality, quantity, value, temperature, etc. – *vb.* **fall apart 1** to break in pieces. **2** to fail; to collapse.

false (fŏls) *adj.* **1** untrue; mistaken. **2** artificial.

falter (fŏl tėr) *vb.* **faltering, faltered 1** to move unsteadily. **2** to say hesitantly.

fame (fām) *n.* the condition of being famous.

familiar (fă **mil** i år) *adj.* **1** well known or recognizable: *I don't know his name but his face is familiar.* **2** frequently met with: *Cycling in the park is a familiar sight.*

family (**fam** li) *n.* **families 1** a group consisting of parents and their children. **2** a group of related people; relatives. **3** a related group of races, languages, plants, animals, etc.: *Cats and tigers belong to the same family.*

famine (**fa** min) *n.* a severe shortage of food.

famous (**fā** mŭs) *adj.* well known.

fan¹ (fan) *n.* **1** a hand-held object made of paper, silk, etc., for creating a current of air to cool the face. **2** an electric machine with revolving blades, for producing a current of air.

fan² (fan) *n.* an enthusiastic supporter or devoted admirer: *She's a keen fan of that band.*

fanatic (fă **nat** ik) *n.* someone with an excessive enthusiasm for something. – *adj.* **fanatical.** – *n.* **fanaticism.**

fancy (**fan** si) *n.* **fancies 1** your imagination. **2** an idea or whim. **3** a sudden liking: *Pat took a fancy to the pony.* – *adj.* elaborate. – *vb.* **fancies, fancying, fancied 1** to think or believe. **2** to have a desire for.

fang (fang) *n.* **1** a long pointed tooth. **2** the tooth of a poisonous snake.

fantastic (făn **tas** tik) *adj.* **1** (*colloquial*) splendid; amazing. **2** weird. – *adv.* **fantastically.**

fantasy (**fan** tă si) *n.* **fantasies** a longed-for but unlikely happening.

far (făr) *adv.* **farther, farthest** or **further**

Falcons, together with hawks, are day-flying birds of prey, and are found all over the world. Falcons are fast-fliers and swoop down on their victims from above, hitting them with their claws. They use their large, hooked beaks for tearing flesh. The peregrine falcon is one of the fastest fliers in the world. In a dive, it can reach 280 km/h.

Peregrine falcon

male

female

Lesser kestrel

Hobby

Kestrel

The kestrel is a small falcon.

male

female

The merlin, sometimes known as the pigeon hawk, is the smallest of the falcons.

(**fûr** Thėr), **furthest** (**fûr** Thist) **1** at, to, or from, a great distance: *We have cycled far from the city centre.* **2** to or by a great extent: *Jim's far nicer than his sister.* **3** at or to a distant time. – *adj.* **1** distant; remote: *He travelled to the far west of Canada.* **2** the more distant: *Sarah sat at the far side of the room.* – **as far as I'm concerned** in my opinion. – **far and wide** extensively.

Far East *n.* the countries of East and South-East ASIA. – *adj.* **Far-Eastern.**

far-fetched *adj.* unlikely.

far-reaching *adj.* having widespread effects.

far-sighted *adj.* wise; forward-looking.

●**Faraday, Michael** (1791-1867) was an English scientist best known for his experiments with ELECTRICITY.

farce (färs) *n.* a comedy with a series of ridiculously unlikely turns of events.

fare (fār) *n.* the price paid by a passenger to travel on a bus, train, etc.

Fan is simply an abbreviation of fanatic, someone who is madly keen on an idea.

Plough

Winnowing rice

About 10,000 years ago humans stopped being mainly hunters and settled down in one place to grow food and **farm** the land.

In many parts of the world old farming methods are still used – oxen and horses pull ploughs and grain is still hand winnowed to separate the chaff. But modern machinery is slowly taking over.

Ploughing with oxen

Picking tea

Tractor

In Saxon times people shared a field and each had a narrow strip to cultivate. This was called strip farming.

Crop rotation is a four-course method of farming aimed at putting goodness back into the soil. Cereals such as wheat and barley alternate with clover and root crops such as turnips. One year a field lies fallow – nothing is grown on it, so allowing it to rest.

In medieval Europe over 80 percent of people lived and worked on the land. During springtime sowing children scared off the birds.

farm (färm) *n.* a piece of land with its buildings, used for growing crops or breeding and keeping livestock. – *vb.* **farming, farmed** to use land for crop-growing, animal-rearing, etc.; to be a farmer. – *n.* & *adj.* **farming**.
farmer *n.* a person who runs a farm.
farmyard *n.* the central area of a farm, surrounded by farm buildings.
farrago (fă **rä** gō) *n.* **farragos** or **farragoes** a confused mixture.
farrier (**fa** ri ểr) *n.* a person who shoes horses.
farrow (**fa** rō) *n.* a sow's litter of piglets.
fascinate (**fa** si nāt) *vb.* **fascinating, fascinated** to interest strongly; to intrigue: *My work so fascinates me that I can think of nothing else.* – *n.* **fascination**.
fashion (**fa** shŏn) *n.* **1** style, especially the latest style, in clothes, etc. **2** a way of doing something.
fashionable *adj.* following the latest fashion.
fast[1] (fäst) *adj.* **1** moving, or able to move, quickly. **2** taking a short time. **3** describing a clock that shows a time that is later than the correct time. – *adv.* **1** quickly; rapidly: *Don't walk so fast.* **2** deeply; thoroughly: *fast asleep.*
fast food *n.* food that is prepared and served quickly, such as hamburgers and French fries.
fast[2] (fäst) *vb.* **fasting, fasted** to go without food, especially as a religious discipline.
fasten (**fa** sĕn) *vb.* **fastening, fastened** to make firmly closed or fixed: *Sue fastened the buttons of her coat.*
fat (fat) *n.* the soft greasy substance that is found below the skin in humans and animals, that stores energy and generates warmth. – *adj.* **fatter, fattest** plump; overweight.
fatal (**fā** tǎl) *adj.* causing death: *No one survived; the accident was fatal.*
fate (fāt) *n.* **1** a power that is believed to control the course of events. **2** what happens to someone or something: *It was just my fate to meet the very person I was avoiding.*
father (**fa** Thĕr) *n.* **1** a person's male parent. **2** a founder, inventor, originator, or pioneer. **3** a form of address for a priest. – *n.* **fatherhood**.
father-in-law *n.* **fathers-in-law** the father of your wife or husband.

fathom (**fa** Thŏm) *n.* a unit for measuring the depth of water, equal to 6 ft (1.8 m).

fatigue (fă **tēg**) *n.* **1** tiredness after work or effort. **2** weakness in metals, caused by variations in stress. – *vb.* **fatiguing, fatigued**.

fatten (**fa** tĕn) *vb.* **fattening, fattened** to make or become fat: *The farmer fattened the geese.*

fatty (**fa** ti) *adj.* **fattier, fattiest** greasy; oily.

faucet (**fö** sit) *n.* (*North American*) a tap.

●**Faulkner, William** (1897-1962) was the American author of *The Sound and the Fury.*

fault (fölt) *n.* **1** a weakness in character: *Harry's only fault is that he's always late.* **2** a flaw or defect in an object or structure. **3** responsibility for something wrong: *It's all my fault that supper is late.* – **faulty** *adj.* **faultier, faultiest** not working correctly.

fauna (**fö** nå) *n.* the wild animals of a particular place. See also **flora**.

favour (**fā** vŏr) *n.* **1** a kind or helpful action performed out of goodwill: *Sam did his Mum a favour and washed her car.* **2** the approval or goodwill of someone: *The M.P. was much in favour because of his views on welfare.*

favourable *adj.* giving agreement or consent.

favourite (**fāv** rit) *adj.* best-liked; preferred.

fawn (fön) *n.* a young deer.

fax (faks) *n.* **1** a machine that scans documents electronically and transmits an image of the contents to a receiving machine by telephone line. **2** a copy transmitted in this way. – *vb.* **faxing, faxed** to send a document in this way.

fear (fēr) *n.* **1** an unpleasant feeling of anxiety and distress caused by the awareness of danger or pain: *My greatest fear is to be locked in a lift.* **2** a cause of this feeling. – *vb.* **fearing, feared**.

fearful *adj.* **1** afraid. **2** frightening.

feast (fēst) *n.* **1** a large rich meal, often to celebrate some occasion. **2** a festival.

feat (fēt) *n.* a remarkable deed or achievement.

feather (**fe** Thĕr) *n.* any of the light growths that form the soft covering of a bird.

feature (**fē** chŭr) *n.* **1** a part of the face, for example eyes, nose, mouth, etc. **2** a noticeable part or quality of something: *The dome is an important feature of the building.*

February (**feb** roo å ri) or (**feb** ū ri) *n.* the second month of the year. It has 28 days, except in a leap year when it has 29.

federal (**fe** dĕ rål) *adj.* consisting of a group of states independent in local matters but under a central government for other purposes, e.g. defence.

fee (fē) *n.* a charge made for professional services, for example by a doctor or lawyer.

feeble (**fē** bĕl) *adj.* weak. – *adv.* **feebly**.

feed (fēd) *vb.* **feeding, fed** (fed) **1** to give food to or prepare food for: *We feed the horses twice a day.* **2** (of animals) to eat: *Cows feed on grass.* – *n.* food for animals.

feel (fēl) *vb.* **feeling, felt** (felt) **1** to become aware of through touch. **2** to sense; to experience: *I feel a pain in my ear.* **3** to have an emotion: *Fred feels upset.* **4** to give the impression of being soft, hard, rough, etc. when touched: *The rabbit's fur feels very soft.* **5** to be of the opinion: *We all feel you work too hard.*

feeler *n.* an organ of touch found in certain creatures, especially one of two thread-like projections on an insect's head.

PRONUNCIATION GUIDE	
fat **a**	all **ö**
fate **ā**	foot **oo**
fast **ä**	moon **o͞o**
among **å**	boy **oi**
met **e**	house **ow**
mean **ē**	demon **ŏ**
silent **ĕ**	thing **th**
loch **hh**	this **Th**
fin **i**	but **u**
line **ī**	mute **ū**
quick **kw**	fur **û**
got **o**	brochure **ů**
note **ō**	vision **zh**

FEASTS AND FESTIVALS

February
Ramadan (Islam), a month of fasting.
Ash Wednesday (Christian), beginning of Lent.

March
Purim (Jewish), commemorating the deliverance from the plot of Hamman.
Holi (Hindu) marks the coming of spring.

April
Ramanavami (Hindu), birth of Lord Rama.
Pesach or Passover (Jewish), commemorating the Israelites' deliverance from Egypt.
Good Friday (Christian), the day on which Jesus was crucified.
Easter Sunday (Christian), the day on which Jesus rose from the dead.

May
Whitsun/Pentecost (Christian), the coming of the Holy Spirit.
Id-al-Adha (Islam), major four-day festival.

June
Buddha Purnima (Buddhist), the birth, enlightenment, and death of Buddha.
Al Hijara (Islam), Muslim New Year.

August
Janamashtami (Hindu), birth of Krishna.
Milad-un-Nabi (Islam), anniversary of Muhammad's birth and death.

September
Rosh Hashanah (Jewish), New Year and start of ten days of atonement.
Yom Kippur (Jewish), the Day of Atonement.
Sukkoth (Jewish), Feast of Tabernacles, commemorating 40 years in the wilderness.

November
Diwali (Hindu), festival of lights.
Birthday of Guru Nanak Dev (Sikh), founder of the Sikhs.

December
Hanukkah (Jewish), eight day feast celebrating the rededication of the temple.
Christmas (Christian), the birth of Jesus.

Ferret comes from a Latin word *fur* meaning 'thief', probably because the animal invades the burrows of other creatures.

Fencing was one of the original sports included in the modern Olympic Games. Fencers use one of three types of weapon – the foil, which has no cutting edge; the epeé, which has a stiff blade; and the sabre, which has two cutting edges and a point.

feet. See **foot**.

feign (fān) *vb.* **feigning, feigned** to pretend to have or be: *Suzie feigned illness.* – *adj.* **feigned**.

feline (fē līn) *adj.* like a cat.

fell¹. See **fall**.

fell² (fel) *vb.* **felling, felled** to cut down a tree.

fellow (fe lō) *n.* **1** a man or boy: *Come along, old fellow.* **2** a companion or equal.

felt¹. See **feel**.

felt² (felt) *n.* a fabric formed by pressing together wool fibres, etc.

female (fē māl) *adj.* of the sex that gives birth to children, produces eggs, etc. – *n.* a female animal or plant.

feminine (fe mi nin) *adj.* womanly or belonging to a woman. – *n.* **femininity**.

feminism (fe mi ni zěm) *n.* a movement supporting the attitude that women's rights and opportunities should be equal to those of men. – *n.* **feminist**.

femur (fē mǔr) *n.* the thigh bone.

fen (fen) *n.* low marshy land.

fence (fens) *n.* a barrier of wood and/or wire, for enclosing or protecting land. – *vb.* **fencing, fenced 1** to enclose or separate with a fence: *The farmer fenced in her cows.* **2** to fight with swords (**fencing**). – *n.* **fencer**.

fender (fen děr) *n.* **1** (*North American*) the wing of a car. **2** a low guard around a fireplace to keep ash, etc. within the hearth.

fermentation (fûr men tā shǒn) *n.* a chemical change that takes place in a substance through the action of micro-organisms, as in the conversion of sugar into alcohol.

●**Fermi** (fûr mi), **Enrico** (1901-54) was an Italian-born scientist who built the first nuclear reactor in the UNITED STATES, in 1942.

Competitions begin with fencers on guard

fern (fûrn) *n.* a flowerless plant that reproduces by spores rather than seeds.

ferocious (fě rō shǔs) *adj.* fierce; cruel; savage. – *n.* **ferocity** (fě ros i ti) or **ferociousness**.

●**Ferranti, Sebastian** (1864-1930) was an English electrical engineer, known best for generating ELECTRICITY.

ferret (fe rit) *n.* a small albino type of polecat, used for driving rabbits and rats from their holes.

ferry (fe ri) *n.* **ferries** a boat that carries passengers and often cars across a river or strip of water. – *vb.* **ferries, ferrying, ferried**.

fertile (fûr tīl) *adj.* **1** of land that can produce abundant crops. **2** capable of producing young fruit, etc. – *n.* **fertility** (fûr til i ti).
  fertilize or **fertilise** *vb.* **fertilizing, fertilized 1** to make fertile: *Bees fertilize flowers.* **2** to add nutrients to soil.
  fertilizer or **fertiliser** *n.* a substance dug into soil to make it more fertile.

fervent (fûr věnt) *adj.* enthusiastic; earnest. – *n.* **fervour**.

fester (fes těr) *vb.* **festering, festered** to become infected.

festival (fes ti vǎl) *n.* **1** a day or time of celebration. **2** a saint's day.

festive (fes tiv) *adj.* of, or suitable for, a celebration; lively and cheerful.
  festivity *n.* **festivities** celebration.

fetch (fech) *vb.* **fetching, fetched** to go and get, and bring back: *Please fetch Gran's glasses.*

fête or **fete** (fāt) *n.* an outdoor entertainment with competitions, stalls, etc., usually to raise money for a charitable purpose.

fetlock (fet lok) *n.* (the tuft of hair on) the projection on a horse's leg just above the hoof.

fetus. See **foetus**.

feud (fūd) *n.* a long and bitter quarrel.

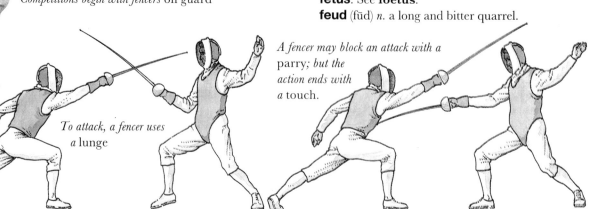

To attack, a fencer uses a lunge

A fencer may block an attack with a parry; but the action ends with a touch.

Under the **feudal** system the king owned all the land but granted certain powerful lords land in return for their promising to help him fight his enemies. The lords in turn granted land to lesser lords called knights, who promised to fight for them in return. Below the knights came yeomen, or farmers, who were free men. At the lowest level were the peasants, known as villeins or serfs, who worked for the lord.

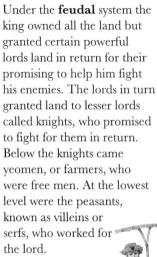

The feudal system created a society with the most powerful people at the top and the mass of the people at the bottom.

King John's great seal which was attached to the Magna Carta in 1215. The charter, which the English barons compelled the king to sign, made the king answerable to the law and promised a fair trial and justice to everyone.

feudal (fū dål) *adj.* of the social system of medieval EUROPE, in which tenants were obliged to serve under their lord in battle, and were in return protected by him. – *n.* **feudalism**.

fever (fē věr) *n.* an illness causing an abnormally high body temperature.

few (fū) *adj.* not many; hardly any. – *pron.* hardly any things, people, etc. – **a few** a small number; some. – **as few as** no more than.

fiancé or **fiancée** (fi on sā) *n.* a man or woman to whom you are engaged to be married.

● **Fianna Fail** (fē å nå foil) was founded by Eamon DE VALERA in 1926 as a strongly nationalistic and republican political party in Ireland.

fiasco (fi as kō) *n.* **fiascos** a complete failure: *The show was a fiasco: the actors forgot their lines.*

fibre (fī běr) *n.* **1** a fine thread of a natural or artificial substance. **2** the indigestible parts of edible plants that help to move food quickly through the body. **3** strength of character.

fibre glass *n.* a material made of fine threadlike pieces of glass used for insulation in boat building, etc.

fibre optics *n.* (*singular*) the use of threads of glass to carry information in the form of light.

fibula (fib ū lå) *n.* **fibulae** (fib ū lě) or **fibulas** the narrower of the two bones in the lower leg.

fickle (fik ěl) *adj.* changeable, especially in affections.

fiction (fik shŏn) *n.* **1** literature concerning imaginary characters or events. **2** a pretence; a lie. – *adj.* **fictitious**. – *adj.* **fictional**.

fiddle (fi děl) *n.* (*colloquial*) **1** a violin. **2** a fraud. – *vb.* **fiddling, fiddled** to tinker, toy, or meddle: *Please stop fiddling with your hair.* **fiddly** *adj.* **fiddlier, fiddliest** awkward to do.

fidget (fi jit) *vb.* **fidgeting, fidgeted** to move restlessly; to feel nervous.

field (fēld) *n.* **1** a piece of land enclosed for growing crops or for using as pasture for animals. **2** an area marked off as a ground for a sport, etc. **3** an area of knowledge or study: *My teacher's particular field is economics.*

field event *n.* in athletics, a contest involving jumping, throwing, etc., as distinct from a track event.

field hockey *n.* (*North American*) ordinary hockey as distinct from ice hockey.

fiend (fēnd) *n.* a devil; an evil spirit.

fierce (fērs) *adj.* violent and aggressive.

fiery (fīr i) *adj.* **fierier, fieriest 1** like fire. **2** easily enraged; passionate; spirited.

fifteen (fif tēn) *n.* **1** the number or figure 15. **2** a set of 15 things or people: *The school rugby 15 won all their matches.* – *n.*, *adj.*, & *adv.* **fifteenth**.

fifty (fif ti) *n.* **fifties** the number or figure 50. – *n.*, *adj.*, & *adv.* **fiftieth**.

fig (fig) *n.* a soft fruit full of tiny seeds; the tree bearing it.

Turkey and California are two of the world's main fig-producing areas. Because figs are too delicate to keep easily, much of the crop is canned or dried.

fight (fīt) *vb.* **fighting, fought** (föt) **1** to attack or engage in combat with fists or weapons, etc. **2** to struggle: *Pete fought to keep up with the rest of the group.* **3** to campaign: *We must fight for equal rights.* **4** to quarrel: *Don't let's fight over such a silly thing.* – *n.* **1** a battle; a violent struggle; a quarrel. **2** a contest.

figure (fig ůr) or (fig ūr) *n.* **1** an indistinctly seen person: *There were three figures in the distance.* **2** the shape of the body. **3** a symbol representing a number; a numeral. **4** a well-known person: *a public figure.* **5** a diagram. – *vb.* **figuring, figured 1** to play a part in a story, incident, etc.: *The witches figure in Macbeth.* **2** (*North American*) to think; to reckon. – *vb.* **figure out** to work out; to understand.

● **Fiji**. See Supplement, **Countries**.

filament (fi lå měnt) *n.* a fine thread or fibre, especially in a light bulb.

file[1] (fīl) *n.* a tool with a rough surface for smoothing or rubbing away wood, etc.

file[2] (fīl) *n.* **1** a folder or box in which to keep loose papers. **2** a collection of papers kept in this way. **3** See **Computer terms**. – *vb.* **filing, filed** to put papers, etc. into a file.

fill (fil) *vb.* **filling, filled 1** to make full: *Polly filled the kettle.* **2** to take up the space in: *People filled the office.* **3** to become full. **4** to put material into a hole, etc. to level the surface. **filling-station** *n.* a place where you can get petrol for your car.

film (film) *n.* **1** a strip of thin flexible plastic or other substance, coated so as to be sensitive to light and exposed inside a camera to produce still or moving pictures. **2** a motion picture. **3** a fine skin or coating: *A film of dirt covered the car.* – *vb.* **filming, filmed** to use a camera to take moving pictures.

filter (fil těr) *n.* a device that allows liquid, gas, smoke, etc. through but traps solid matter. – *vb.* **filtering, filtered** to pass through a filter.

filth (filth) *n.* repulsive dirt.
filthy *adj.* **filthier, filthiest** extremely dirty.

fin (fin) *n.* a thin wing-like projection on a fish's body, with which it balances and steers itself.

final (fī nål) *adj.* **1** occurring at the end; last. **2** definite; not to be altered: *That is my final decision.* – *n.* the last round of a competition.

finance (fī nans) or (fi **nans**) *n.* **1** money affairs; their study or management. **2** (in *plural*) your financial state: *I must put my finances in order before I can buy a house.* – (fi **nans**) or (fi **nans**) *vb.* **financing, financed** to provide funds for: *The house was financed by the bank.*

male

female

Finches are found throughout the world. They eat seeds, insects, and leaves and live in wooded areas. Most species have attractive songs. The sexes usually differ.

Bullfinch

finch (finch) *n.* a small songbird with a short sturdy beak adapted for crushing seeds.

find (fīnd) *vb.* **finding, found** (fownd) **1** to discover through search, enquiry, or chance: *I found the dog's bone in my bed.* **2** to seek out and provide: *I'll find you a plumber.* **3** to realize or discover: *Jim found it difficult to ask for the money loan.* – *vb.* **find out** to discover.

fine[1] (fīn) *adj.* **1** of high quality; excellent. **2** (of weather) bright; not rainy. **3** well; healthy. **4** pure; refined. **5** thin; delicate.

fine[2] (fīn) *n.* an amount of money to be paid as a penalty. – *vb.* **fining, fined**.

● **Fine Gael** (fi ně **gāl**) is an Irish political party founded by W.T. Cosgrave in 1923.

finger (fing gěr) *n.* one of the five jointed parts of the hand; any of the four of these except the thumb.
fingerprint *n.* a mark, unique to each individual, left on a surface by a fingertip, useful as a means of identification.

finish (**fi** nish) *vb.* **finishing, finished 1** to come to an end; to stop: *Have you finished talking?* **2** to complete or perfect: *Isobel has nearly finished the crossword.* **3** to give a particular treatment to the surface of cloth, etc. – *n.* **1** the end. **2** the last part of a race, etc.

● **Finland**. See Supplement, **Countries**.

Finn (fin) *n.* a native or citizen of FINLAND. **Finnish** *adj.* of, belonging to, or relating to FINLAND. – *n.* the language of FINLAND.

fiord. See **fjord**.

fir (fûr) *n.* an evergreen tree with cones and thin needle-like leaves.

fire (fīr) *n.* **1** flames coming from something that is burning. **2** a destructive burning: *Thick black smoke rose from the warehouse fire.* **3** a pile of burning fuel, used for warmth or cooking. – *vb.* **firing, fired 1** to send off a bullet or other missile from a gun, etc. **2** to launch a rocket. **3** (*colloquial*) to dismiss from employment. **4** to bake pottery in a kiln. – **catch fire** to begin to burn.

fire alarm *n.* a bell or other device activated to warn people of fire.

firearm *n.* a gun, pistol, revolver, or rifle.

fire engine *n.* a vehicle carrying fire-fighting equipment.

fire-fighter *n.* a person who puts out large fires. – *n.* **fire-fighting**.

fireplace *n.* a recess for a fire in a room.

fireproof *adj.* resistant to fire and fierce heat.

firework *n.* a device containing explosive chemicals that are ignited to produce bangs and spectacular flashes.

firm¹ (fûrm) *adj.* strong; steady; solid; not soft.

firm² (fûrm) *n.* a business company.

first (fûrst) *adj.* **1** earliest in time or order: *King Alfred was the first king of England.* **2** foremost in importance: *Jill won first prize in the competition.* – *adv.* **1** before anything or anyone else: *Barbara arrived first, and Chris followed soon after.* **2** foremost: *Kay jumped in feet first.* **3** before doing anything else: *First make sure of the facts.* – **at first** at the beginning.

first aid *n.* immediate emergency treatment given to an ill or injured person.

first-class *adj.* of the highest grade or quality: *They stayed in a first-class hotel.*

First Lady *n.* **First Ladies** (*US*) the wife of the American President.

firstly *adv.* first; to begin with.

Fire was possibly human beings' earliest discovery – and probably made by accident. Fire meant that people could be warm in cold winter months. With fire meat and vegetables could be cooked so they became more tasty and tender. Fire could also scare off wild animals at night.

Using a bow drill was one way of making sparks.

When certain stones, such as flints, are rubbed together they send out sparks. If this is done near tinder-dry wood, a fire can be kindled.

firth (fûrth) *n.* in Scotland, a river estuary.

fish (fish) *n.* **fish** or **fishes** a cold-blooded creature with fins that lives in water and breathes through gills. – *vb.* **fishing, fished** to try to catch fish.

● Some fish, such as salmon, protect their eggs by building nests. Male sea horses have a pouch into which the female lays her eggs. The male carries them until they hatch.

fishy *adj.* **fishier, fishiest 1** of or like a fish. **2** (*colloquial*) odd; suspicious.

fission (**fi** shŏn) *n.* (usually **nuclear fission**) the splitting of the nucleus of an atom, with a release of energy.

fist (fist) *n.* a clenched hand.

fit¹ (fit) *vb.* **fitting, fitted 1** to be, or be made, the right shape or size for: *My shoes fit well.* **2** to be small or few enough to go into: *Sally managed to fit all her luggage into the car.* **3** to be suitable or appropriate for: *This punishment fits the crime.* – *adj.* **fitter, fittest** healthy.

fit² (fit) *n.* **1** a sudden loss of consciousness with uncontrolled movements. **2** a sudden burst: *Tim burst into a fit of giggles.*

● **Fitzgerald, F. Scott** (1896–1940) was an American writer. His novels include *Tender is the Night* and *The Great Gatsby*.

five (fīv) *n.* the number or figure 5. – *adj.* 5 in number. – *n.*, *adj.*, & *adv.* **fifth** (fifth) or (fiftth).

fix (fiks) *vb.* **fixing, fixed 1** to attach firmly. **2** to mend or repair. **3** to direct; to concentrate: *Roland fixed his eyes on her.* **4** to arrange a time. **fixed** *adj.* **1** fastened; immovable. **2** unvarying: *You can't budge her, she has fixed ideas on this.*

fixture (**fiks** chŭr) *n.* **1** a permanently fixed piece of furniture or equipment. **2** an event in a sports calendar.

fjord or **fiord** (**fē** örd) *n.* a long narrow inlet in a high rocky coast, especially in NORWAY.

flaccid (**flak** sid) or (**fla** sid) *adj.* limp and soft.

flag (flag) *n.* a usually rectangular piece of cloth with a distinctive design, flown from a pole to represent a country, party, etc., or used for signalling. – *vb.* **flagging, flagged** to signal. – **with flags flying** triumphantly.

flagon (**fla** gŏn) *n.* a large bottle or jug.

flair (flār) *n.* a natural talent for something.

flake (flāk) *n.* a small flat particle: *snowflakes*. – *adj.* **flaky, flakier, flakiest**.

flamboyant (flam **boi** ånt) *adj.* dashing and colourful. – *n.* **flamboyance**.

flame (flām) *n.* the flickering mass of burning gases coming from something that is on fire.

flamingo (flå ming gō) *n.* **flamingos** a large long-legged wading bird with a curved beak and pink plumage.

flammable (**fla** må běl) *adj.* liable to catch fire.

flank (flangk) *n.* the side of an animal or human body, between ribs and hip. – *vb.* **flanking, flanked** to be or move at the side of.

flap (flap) *vb.* **flapping, flapped** to wave up and down or backwards and forwards: *A bird flaps its wings.* – *n.* **1** a broad piece of something attached along one edge and hanging loosely: *pocket flaps*. **2** a hinged section on an aircraft wing adjusted to control speed.

flare (flār) *vb.* **flaring, flared 1** to burn with sudden brightness. **2** to widen towards the edge or bottom: *flared trousers*.

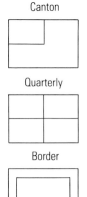
Canton

Quarterly

Border

Triangle

Flags are divided into various geometrical patterns consisting of horizontal or vertical stripes, rectangles, triangles, etc. all of which have special names.

Flags are symbols of many things. They represent nations (the tricolore), international organizations (UN, EU), business companies, trade unions, and individual people. They can also be used for signalling (at sea) and act as warnings. The study of flags and their meanings is called *vexillology*.

During the French Revolution of 1789 the flag of the monarchy (left) was replaced by the Bastille flag and then by the French national colours.

The first US flag – the Continental Colours of 1776 – shows 13 red and white stripes.

Japan's naval ensign adds rays to the Sun disc shown on the national flag.

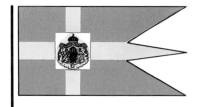

The Swedish royal flag is based on the national flag.

The Red Cross was founded in Switzerland. Its flag is a reversed version of the Swiss national flag.

FLAG TERMS
canton upper rectangular corner of a flag, often used for a special design (e.g. the stars in the American national flag).
device an emblem or symbol.
field the background colour.
hoist to raise a flag.
pennant a triangular flag.
standard the personal flag of a ruler.

flash (flash) *n.* **1** a sudden brief blaze of light. **2** an instant: *I'll be back in a flash.* **3** a brief but intense occurrence: *Laura had a sudden flash of inspiration.* – *vb.* **flashing, flashed 1** to shine briefly. **2** to move or pass quickly: *The train flashed past.* – **a flash in the pan** (*colloquial*) an impressive but untypical success.
flashlight *n.* (*North American*) a torch.
flask (fläsk) *n.* **1** a narrow-necked bottle used in chemical experiments, etc. **2** a vacuum flask.
flat (flat) *adj.* **flatter, flattest 1** level; horizontal; even. **2** without hollows. **3** not bent or crumpled. **4** toneless and expressionless. – *adv.* **1** stretched out rather than curled up, etc. **2** into a flat compact shape: *This deckchair folds flat for storage.* – *n.* a set of rooms for living in, especially all on one floor.
flatfish *n.* a flat-bodied fish with both eyes on one side, that lies on the sea bed.
flatten *vb.* **flattening, flattened** to make or become flat or flatter.
flatter (fla těr) *vb.* **flattering, flattered** to compliment excessively or insincerely.
flattery *n.* **flatteries** excessive praise.

●**Flaubert** (flō bār), **Gustave** (1821-80) was a French novelist, author of *Madame Bovary*.

flaunt (flönt) *vb.* **flaunting, flaunted** to display or parade, in the hope of being admired.
flautist (flö tist) *n.* a flute-player.
flavour (flā vŏr) *n.* the taste of any particular food or drink: *strawberry flavour.*
flaw (flö) *n.* a fault. – *adj.* **flawed**.
flax (flaks) *n.* a blue-flowered plant whose stem yields a fibre used for making linen, and whose seeds are used to make linseed oil.
flea (flē) *n.* a tiny wingless jumping insect that lives on the bodies of animals and human beings and sucks its hosts' blood. It carries germs from one host to another.
flea market *n.* (*colloquial*) a street market selling second-hand goods.
fleck (flek) *n.* a spot or speck. – *adj.* **flecked**.
fled. See **flee**.
fledgeling (flej ling) *n.* a young bird learning to fly.
flee (flē) *vb.* **fleeing, fled** (fled) to run away; to escape danger.
fleece (flēs) *n.* a sheep's woolly coat.
fleet (flēt) *n.* a number of ships under one command.
fleeting (flē ting) *adj.* short-lived; brief.

●**Fleming, Alexander** (1881-1955) was a Scottish doctor who discovered penicillin.

flesh (flesh) *n.* **1** the body's soft tissues covering the bones under the skin. **2** the pulp of a fruit or vegetable – **in the flesh** in person.
flew. See **fly²**.
flex¹ (fleks) *vb.* **flexing, flexed** to bend a limb.
flex² (fleks) *n.* flexible insulated electric cable.
flexible (flek så bĕl) *adj.* **1** bending easily: *Ballet dancers have to be very flexible.* **2** adaptable to suit circumstances. – *n.* **flexibility**.
flicker (fli kĕr) *vb.* **flickering, flickered 1** to shine unsteadily: *The oil lamp flickered.* **2** to move lightly to and fro: *The shadows flickered across the lawn.* – *n.* an unsteady light.
flight (flīt) *n.* **1** the action or power of flying: *We watched the bird's flight across the meadow.* **2** a journey made by or in an aircraft. **3** a set of steps or stairs leading straight up or down.
flightless *adj.* (of birds) unable to fly.

flimsy (flim zi) *adj.* **flimsier, flimsiest 1** (of clothing, etc.) light and thin. **2** (of a structure) without strength; frail.
fling (fling) *vb.* **flinging, flung** (flung) to throw violently or vigorously: *Margaret flung her shoes in the corner.* – *n.* **1** a lively reel: *the Highland fling.* **2** a try; a go.
flint (flint) *n.* a hard quartz found in limestone.
flip (flip) *vb.* **flipping, flipped** to toss a coin, etc. so that it turns over in mid air.
flippant (fli pånt) *adj.* not serious about grave matters; frivolous. – *n.* **flippancy**.
flipper (fli pěr) *n.* a limb on a whale, seal, penguin, etc., used for swimming.

In 1928 Fleming noticed that a spot of green mould stopped the growth of some bacteria he was cultivating. This led to the development of the life-saving antibiotic, penicillin.

Ostrich

Emu

Rhea

Adelie penguin

Kiwi

Five birds with something very unusual in common: they cannot fly. Ostrich, the largest of all birds. Adelie penguin, stands erect and can swim. Emu, from Australia. Kiwi, nocturnal from New Zealand. Rhea, from South America.

There are over 200 varieties of poppy.

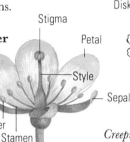

Inside a **flower** are male parts, called stamens, and female parts, stigma. The stamens contain grains of pollen which fertilize the stigma from which a fruit forms.

Parts of a typical flower
All the specialized structures of a flower can be seen in this cross section.

Two of six basic flower arrangements

Disk floret   Ray floret   Spike

Stigma
Petal
Style
Sepal
Anther
Stamen

Composite flower head

Creeping thistle: each seed has a parachute of long hairs.

Field scabious occurs widely throughout Europe.

flirt (flûrt) *vb.* **flirting, flirted 1** to behave romantically towards someone without serious intentions. **2** to consider briefly: *Flo flirted with the idea of becoming a vet.* – *n.* someone who flirts. – *adj.* **flirtatious**.

flit (flit) *vb.* **flitting, flitted** to dart lightly from place to place. – *n.* an act of flitting.

float (flōt) *vb.* **floating, floated 1** to rest or move on the surface of a liquid. **2** to drift about or hover in the air.

flock (flok) *n.* a group of creatures, especially birds or sheep. – *vb.* **flocking, flocked** to gather or move in a crowd.

floe (flō) *n.* a floating ice sheet.

flog (flog) *vb.* **flogging, flogged** to beat; to whip.

flood (flud) *n.* **1** an overflow of water over dry land: *The flood happened when the river burst its banks.* **2** any overwhelming flow or quantity: *There was a flood of replies to the ad.* – *vb.* **flooding, flooded 1** to overflow or submerge land. **2** to fill too full.

floor (flör) *n.* **1** the lower interior surface of a room or vehicle. **2** all the rooms on the same level in a building: *Jim's office is on the first floor.* **3** the bed of the sea, etc.

flop (flop) *vb.* **flopping, flopped** to fall, drop, move, or sit limply and heavily. – *n.* **1** a flopping movement or sound. **2** (*colloquial*) a failure. – *adv.* **floppily**. – *n.* **floppiness**. – *adj.* **floppy, floppier, floppiest**.

floppy disk *n.* a flexible magnetic disk for storing data for use in a computer.

flora (flör å) *n.* the plants of a particular place or time. See also **fauna**.

●**Florence** (*Firenze* in Italian) is a city in central ITALY which in the 1300s was the artistic centre of EUROPE under the MEDICI family.

●**Florida**. See Supplement, **USA**.

florist (**flo** rist) *n.* a person who grows or sells flowers.

flotsam (**flot** såm) *n.* goods lost by shipwreck and found floating on the sea.

flounder¹ (**flown** děr) *vb.* **floundering, floundered 1** to thrash about helplessly, as when caught in a bog. **2** to have difficulties in speaking or acting clearly.

flounder² (**flown** děr) *n.* a type of flatfish.

flour (**flow** ěr) *n.* powder from ground grain, especially wheat, used for baking, etc.

flourish (**flu** rish) *vb.* **flourishing, flourished 1** to be strong and healthy; to grow well. **2** to do well; to prosper: *Despite the recession, Anthony's business is flourishing.*

flout (flowt) *vb.* **flouting, flouted** to defy an order, etc. openly.

flow (flō) *vb.* **flowing, flowed 1** to move along freely like water. **2** to keep moving steadily. **3** (of words or ideas) to come readily to mind or in speech or writing. **4** (of blood or electricity) to circulate. – *n.* **1** the act of flowing. **2** a continuous stream or outpouring.

flower (**flow** ěr) *n.* the usually brightly coloured part of a plant or tree from which the fruit or seed grows. – *vb.* **flowering, flowered** to produce flowers; to bloom.

flown. See **fly²**.

flue (flōō) *n.* an outlet for smoke or gas.

fluent (flōō ĕnt) *adj.* **1** speaking or writing in an easy flowing style. **2** spoken or written with ease: *Jean speaks fluent German.* – *n.* **fluency**.

fluff (fluf) *n.* small bits of soft woolly material. – *n.* **fluffiness**. – *adj.* **fluffy, fluffier, fluffiest**.

fluid (flōō id) *n.* a substance, such as liquid or gas, that can flow freely. – *adj.* **1** able to flow.

flung. See **fling**.

flurry (flu ri) *n.* **flurries 1** a brief shower of rain, snow, etc. **2** (*colloquial*) a commotion.

flush¹ (flush) *vb.* **flushing, flushed 1** to blush or go red. **2** to clean out with a rush of water. – *n.* a rosiness, especially of the face; a blush.

flush² (flush) *adj.* **1** level with an adjacent surface. **2** (*colloquial*) having plenty of money.

flute (flōōt) *n.* a woodwind instrument that is held horizontally out to the side of the head.

flutter (flu tĕr) *vb.* **fluttering, fluttered 1** to fly with a rapid wing movement or drift with a twirling motion. **2** to move about in a restless, aimless way. – *n.* agitation; excitement.

fly¹ (flī) *n.* **flies** a two-winged insect or any of various other flying insects: *mayfly; butterfly.*

fly² (flī) *vb.* **flies, flying, flew** (flōō), **flown** (flōn) **1** (of a bird, bat, or insect) to move through the air on wings; (of an aircraft or spacecraft) to travel through the air or through space. **2** to operate and control an aircraft, etc.

flying (flī ing) *n.* the activity of piloting, or travelling in, an aircraft.

flying fox *n.* a fruit-eating bat.

flying saucer *n.* any of a number of unidentified circular flying objects reported in the sky from time to time.

foal (fōl) *n.* the young of a horse or of a related animal. – *vb.* **foaling, foaled**.

foam (fōm) *n.* **1** a mass of tiny bubbles forming on the surface of liquids. **2** a substance composed of tiny bubbles.

focus (fō kŭs) *n.* **focuses 1** the point at which rays of light or sound waves meet or, from which they seem to diverge. **2** the point where an object must stand to appear as a clear image in a lens or mirror. **3** the adjustment of the eye or the lens of an instrument, etc., to obtain a clear image. **4** a centre of interest or attention. – *vb.* **focusing, focused 1** to bring or be brought into focus; to meet at a focus. **2** to adjust the focus of your eye or an instrument. **3** to concentrate: *Tim focused his attention on the game.*

fodder (fo dĕr) *n.* food, especially hay and straw, for cattle and other farm animals.

foetus (fē tŭs) *n.* a young creature growing in an egg or womb.

fog (fog) *n.* a thick cloud of condensed watery vapour suspended in the air reducing visibility; thick mist. – *vb.* **fogging, fogged** to obscure. – *adj.* **foggy, foggier, foggiest**.

foil¹ (foil) *vb.* **foiling, foiled** to prevent or frustrate a person or attempt.

foil² (foil) *n.* metal beaten into thin sheets.

foil³ (foil) *n.* a long slender sword with its point protected by a button.

fold¹ (fōld) *vb.* **folding, folded 1** to double over so that one part lies on top of another: *Fold the paper in two.* **2** to bring in close to the body: *The bird folded its wings.* **3** to stir an ingredient gently into a mixture. – *n.* **1** a doubling of one layer over another. **2** a crease.

folder *n.* a cardboard or plastic cover in which to keep loose papers.

fold² (fōld) *n.* an enclosure for sheep or cattle.

-fold (-fōld) *suffix* multiplied by a stated number: *The company's profits increased threefold.*

foliage (fō li ij) *n.* the leaves on a tree or plant.

folk (fōk) *n.* (*plural*) people. – *adj.* of popular origin: *Steve loves listening to folk music.*

folklore *n.* the customs, beliefs, stories, traditions, etc. of particular peoples.

follow (fo lō) *vb.* **following, followed 1** to go or come after: *Tuesday follows Monday.* **2** to result; to be a consequence. **3** to go along a road, etc.: *They followed the river.* **4** to watch someone or something as they move: *Her eyes followed him up the street.* **5** to obey.

following *n.* a body of supporters. – *adj.* coming after; next: *We need to deal with the following points.* – *prep.* after.

folly (fo li) *n.* **follies** foolishness.

fond (fond) *adj.* having a liking for; loving. – *n.* **fondness**.

fondle (fon dĕl) *vb.* **fondling, fondled** to stroke.

●**Fonteyn** (fon tān), **Dame Margot** (1919-91) was a British ballerina.

food (fōōd) *n.* a substance taken in, or absorbed, by a living thing, that provides energy or helps growth.

food chain *n.* a series of living organisms, each of which is fed on by the next in the series.

ENGLISH FOLK AND FRENCH PEOPLE
From 1066 until the late 14th century Norman French was the language of the court, the law, and parliament. The peasantry's English absorbed words, especially words to do with law, titles and parliament; justice, jury, felony, govern, prince, duke, and baron are all Norman. Many borrowed words settled alongside the native English words helping to make our language rich in synonyms, such as:
folk people
brotherly fraternal
forgive pardon
give donate.

Focus is the Latin word for 'fireplace', the central point in a room. It was also a 'burning point' when a lens was used for focusing the rays of the sun to burn something.

fool (fool) *n.* a person lacking common sense or intelligence. – *vb.* **fooling, fooled 1** to mislead; to deceive: *You tried to fool me into believing you could sing.* **2** to behave stupidly: *Stop fooling around and do your homework!*
foolish *adj.* unwise; senseless. – *n.* **foolishness**.

foot (foot) *n.* **feet** (fēt) **1** the part of the leg on which a human being or animal stands or walks. **2** the bottom or lower part of something: *We met at the foot of the hill.* **3** a measure of length equal to 12 inches (30.48 cm). – **have your feet on the ground** to have plenty of common sense.

football *n.* **1** any of several team games played with a large ball that players try to kick or head into the opposing team's goal or carry across their opponents' goal line. **2 American football** a game played by two teams of eleven players wearing heavily padded and protective clothing, with an oval ball. **3** the ball used in the game.

footing *n.* **1** the stability of your feet on the ground: *I slipped and lost my footing.* **2** basis or status. **3** relationship: *on a friendly footing.*

footprint *n.* the mark of a foot or shoe.

footwear *n.* shoes, boots, socks, etc.

for (för) *prep.* **1** intended to be given or sent to: *This present is for Patrick.* **2** towards: *We are heading for home.* **3** throughout a time or distance: *I've known him for two years.* **4** in order to have, etc.: *Let's meet for a chat.* **5** at a cost of: *I bought a ticket for £5.* **6** to the benefit of: *What can I do for you?* **7** on account of: *This town is famous for its school.* **8** suitable to the needs of: *She writes books for children.*

forbade or **forbad**. See **forbid**.

forbid (för bid) *vb.* **forbidding, forbade** (för **bad**) or (för **bād**) or **forbad, forbidden 1** to order someone not to do something. **2** to prohibit: *I forbid you to watch T.V.*

force (förs) *n.* **1** strength; power; impact. **2** strength: *I was convinced by the force of her argument.* **3** in physics, a power causing movement, alteration, etc.: *the force of gravity.* **4** any organized body: *a workforce; the police force.* – *vb.* **forcing, forced 1** to make or compel: *Tim was forced to leave the country when his visa ran out.* **2** to obtain by effort, strength, threats, etc.: *He forced an admission from them.*
forceful *adj.* powerful.

ford (förd) *n.* a shallow crossing-place in a river.

●**Ford, Henry** (1863-1947) was an American car manufacturer who introduced mass-production methods to make cheap cars.

fore- (för-) *prefix* **1** before: *forewarn.* **2** in front: *foreground.*

forearm (för ärm) *n.* the lower part of the arm between wrist and elbow.

forecast (för käst) *vb.* **forecasting, forecast** or **forecasted** to predict; to gauge or estimate weather, statistics, etc., in advance. – *n.* a warning, prediction, or advance estimate.

forefather (för fä Ther) *n.* an ancestor.

forefinger (för fing gẻr) *n.* the finger next to the thumb; the index finger.

forefront (för frunt) *n.* the very front.

foreground (för grownd) *n.* the part of a view or picture nearest to the viewer.

forehead (fo rid) or (för hed) *n.* the part of the face between the eyebrows and hairline.

foreign (fo rin) *adj.* of, from, or relating to, another country.
foreigner *n.* a person from another country.

foremost (för mōst) *adj.* leading; best.

foresee (för sē) *vb.* **foreseeing, foresaw** (för sö), **foreseen** to see or know in advance.

foresight (för sīt) *n.* the ability to foresee: *Debra had great foresight in leaving when she did.*

forest (fo rist) *n.* a dense growth of trees extending over a large area.
forestry *n.* the management of forests.

(Below) A mixed forest of aspens and larch in the Nevada Rockies. *(Right)* A South American rainforest. The crowns of the trees merge to form a canopy of leafy vegetation, the home of many frogs, lizards, birds, mammals, and insects.

foretell (fŏr **tel**) *vb.* **foretelling, foretold** (fŏr **tōld**) to predict.

forever (fŏr **ev** ĕr) *adv.* always; eternally.

forfeit (**fŏr** fit) *n.* something that you must hand over as a penalty.

forgave. See **forgive.**

forge (fŏrj) *n.* a furnace for heating metals; a workshop where metal is shaped into horseshoes, tools, etc. – *vb.* **forging, forged 1** to shape metal by heating and hammering. **2** to make an imitation of a signature, banknote, etc. for a dishonest purpose.

forget (fŏr **get**) *vb.* **forgetting, forgot** (fŏr **got**), **forgotten 1** to be unable to remember: *Fiona forgot her own room number.* **2** to stop being aware of: *Mike forgot his headache in the excitement.* **3** to leave behind accidentally: *Rachel forgot her umbrella on the train.*

forgetful *adj.* tending to forget.

forgive (fŏr **giv**) *vb.* **forgiving, forgave** (fŏr **gāv**), **forgiven** to stop being angry with someone who has done something wrong.

forgiveness *n.* the act of forgiving.

forgiving *adj.* patient and tolerant.

forgot, forgotten. See **forget.**

fork (fŏrk) *n.* **1** an eating or cooking implement with prongs, for spearing and lifting food. **2** a pronged digging or lifting tool. **3** the division of a road, etc. into branches: *Take the right fork.* – *vb.* **forking, forked** to divide into two branches: *The road forks at that point.*

form (fŏrm) *n.* **1** shape; figure or outward appearance. **2** kind, type, variety: *Karate is a form of martial art.* **3** a document with spaces for inserting information. **4** a school class. – *vb.* **forming, formed 1** to organize or set up: *Let's form a committee.* **2** to take shape. **3** to make a shape. – **in good form** in good health.

formal (**fŏr** măl) *adj.* **1** involving etiquette, ceremony, or conventional procedure generally: *You must wear formal dress to the ball.* **2** stiffly polite rather than relaxed and friendly.

format (**fŏr** mat) *n.* **1** the size and shape of something, especially a book or magazine. **2** an arrangement of data to suit the input system of a computer. – *vb.* **formatting, formatted.**

formation (fŏr **mā** shŏn) *n.* **1** the process of forming or establishing. **2** a particular pattern.

former (**fŏr** mĕr) *adj.* **1** belonging to an earlier time. **2** previous; earlier.

formerly *adv.* previously; in the past.

formidable (fŏr **mid** ă bĕl) *adj.* impressive.

formula (**fŏr** mū lă) *n.* **formulas** or **formulae** (**fŏr** mū lē) **1** the make-up of a chemical compound expressed in symbols: *H_2O is the formula for water.* **2** a mathematical rule expressed in figures and letters.

fort (fŏrt) *n.* a fortified military building.

forth (fŏrth) *adv.* forwards: *Her beads swung back and forth.* – **and so forth** and so on.

forthcoming *adj.* **1** happening soon. **2** describing a person who is willing to talk.

fortify (**fŏr** ti fī) *vb.* **fortifies, fortifying, fortified** to strengthen a building, city, etc. in preparation for an attack.

● **Fort Knox** (noks) in Louisville, Kentucky, is where the United States Treasury Department's gold is stored.

fortnight (**fŏrt** nīt) *n.* a period of 14 days.

fortress (**fŏr** trĕs) *n.* a large fort or castle.

fortunate (**fŏr** chŭ năt) *adj.* lucky.

fortune (**fŏr** chŭn) *n.* **1** luck. **2** your destiny. **3** a large sum of money.

● **Fort Worth** is an industrial city in Texas.

forty (**fŏr** ti) *n.* **forties** the number or figure 40. – *n., adj., & adv.* **fortieth.**

forties *n.* (*plural*) **1** the period of time between your fortieth and fiftieth birthdays. **2** the period of time between the fortieth and fiftieth years of a century.

Format is the size and shape of a book. In a portrait format the book is taller than it is wide; in a landscape, it is wider than it is tall.

Portrait

Landscape

Fortnight is a shortening of 'fourteen nights', going back to the Middle Ages when time was reckoned by nights, not days.

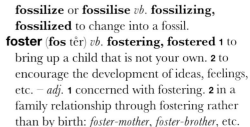

In the centre of all Roman towns was the forum around which were grouped all the important buildings – government offices and temples, and a market place.

The word fossil comes from a Latin word meaning 'dug up'. Most fossils are found in sedimentary rocks – limestone and shale – which have been formed in the sea. So fossils of sea creatures are more common than those of land creatures.

forum (**fŏr** ŭm) *n.* a public square in ancient Rome where public business was conducted and law courts held.

forward (**fŏr** wård) *adv.* **1** (also **forwards**) in the direction in front or ahead of you. **2** (also **forwards**) progressing from first to last. **3** on or onward; to a later time: *Don't forget to put the clocks forward.* **4** to an earlier time: *They decided to bring the wedding forward a month.* **5** into view or public attention: *Please put forward your suggestions.* – *adj.* **1** in the direction in front or ahead of you. **2** at the front. **3** advanced in development: *How far forward are the plans?* **4** concerning the future: *It's always wise to do a little forward planning.* – *n.* a player in football, hockey, etc. whose task is to score rather than defend the goal.

fossil (**fo** sil) *n.* the remains of, or the impression left by, an animal or vegetable in rock. – *adj.* formed naturally when organic matter decomposes: *Coal and oil are fossil fuels.*

fossilize or **fossilise** *vb.* **fossilizing, fossilized** to change into a fossil.

foster (**fos** těr) *vb.* **fostering, fostered 1** to bring up a child that is not your own. **2** to encourage the development of ideas, feelings, etc. – *adj.* **1** concerned with fostering. **2** in a family relationship through fostering rather than by birth: *foster-mother, foster-brother,* etc.

● **Foster, Stephen** (1826-64) wrote some of the best-known songs in America, including *Oh! Susanna* and *Swanee River.*

fought. See **fight**.

foul (fowl) *adj.* **1** disgusting: *What a foul smell.* **2** filthy. **3** contaminated: *The factory was surrounded by foul air.* – *n.* in sport, a breaking of the rules.

found[1]. See **find**.

found[2] (fownd) *vb.* **founding, founded** to start or establish: *The city was founded in 1193.*
  foundation *n.* **1** (usually in *plural*) See **Building terms. 2** the basis of a theory.

foundry (**fown** dri) *n.* **foundries** a place where metal or glass is melted and cast.

fountain (**fown** tin) *n.* **1** a structure producing a jet of water for drinking or for ornamental effect. **2** a spring of water.

four (fŏr) *n.* the number or figure 4. – *n., adj.,* & *adv.* **fourth.**
  fourth dimension *n.* time, as opposed to the dimensions of length, breadth, and height.

fourteen (fŏr **tēn**) *n.* the number or figure 14. – *n., adj.,* & *adv.* **fourteenth.**

fowl (fowl) *n.* **fowls** or **fowl** a farmyard bird.

fox (foks) *n.* a dog-like wild animal with a bushy tail, especially the reddish-brown variety found in EUROPE and NORTH AMERICA.
  foxglove *n.* a tall wild plant with hanging purple or white thimble-shaped flowers.

A sea animal such as an ammonite dies, sinks to the seabed and is covered in protective sediment.

The material around the shell hardens into rock and the shell itself may be replaced with lime. Over millions of years what was once seabed may be thrown up into a mountain range. The dug up fossil may not be the original animal preserved, but scientists can tell a great deal from it.

foyer (**foi** ā) *n.* the entrance hall of a hotel, etc.

fraction (**frak** shŏn) *n.* **1** a quantity that is not a whole number, e.g. 0.25 or ³/₇. **2** a small part. – *adj.* **fractional**.

fracture (**frak** chůr) *n.* a break in anything hard, especially bone. – *vb.* **fracturing, fractured** to break.

fragile (**fra** jīl) *adj.* easily broken or damaged. – *n.* **fragility** (fră **jil** i ti).

fragment (**frag** měnt) *n.* **1** a small piece of something that has broken. **2** something incomplete.

fragrant (**frā** grănt) *adj.* sweet smelling. **fragrance** *n.* a scent or odour.

frail (frāl) *adj.* **1** easily broken or destroyed; delicate; fragile. **2** in poor health.

frame (frām) *n.* **1** a structure round which something is built or to which other parts are added. **2** a structure that surrounds and supports: *Jill chose a red picture frame.* – *vb.* **framing, framed 1** to put a frame round. **2** (*colloquial*) to dishonestly direct suspicion for a crime, etc. at someone innocent. **3** to put together: *frame your ideas.* **framework** *n.* a basic supporting structure.

franc (frangk) *n.* the standard unit of currency in FRANCE, BELGIUM, SWITZERLAND, and several other French-speaking countries.

● **France** is the largest country in western EUROPE. Originally inhabited by Celts it was conquered by Franks in the AD 400s. For many centuries the French and English were enemies and fought many wars. Today France is a rich country with many farms and factories. The capital and biggest city is Paris. The French have a distinctive art and culture. France is a republic and a member of the EUROPEAN COMMUNITY. See also Supplement, **Countries**.

franchise (**fran** chīz) *n.* the right to vote.

● **Francis of Assisi, Saint** (1181-1226) was an Italian saint and founder of the Franciscan order of friars.

Frank (frangk) *n.* a member of a Germanic people that invaded Gaul in the late 5th century AD.

frank (frangk) *adj.* open and honest.

Frankenstein (**frang** kěn stīn) *n.* a name for a creation or creature that destroys its creator.

● *Frankenstein* was the title of Mary Shelley's novel (written in 1818) and the name of the person in the book who created a human monster.

● **Franklin, Benjamin** (1706-90) was an American statesman, inventor, and scientist. He invented the lightning conductor.

frantic (**fran** tik) *adj.* **1** desperate, with fear or anxiety. **2** rushed: *We made a frantic attempt to meet the deadline.* – *adv.* **frantically**.

fraternal (fră **tûr** nǎl) *adj.* of, or relating to, a brother; brotherly.

fraud (fröd) *n.* **1** an act of deliberate deception. **2** someone who pretends to be something that he or she is not.

fray (frā) *vb.* **fraying, frayed** (of cloth or rope) to wear away so that the threads come loose.

freak (frēk) *n.* a person, animal, or event that is abnormal: *A three-headed dog would be a freak.*

freckle (**fre** kěl) *n.* a small brown mark on the skin.

● **Frederick the Great** (1712-86) was king of Prussia and a brilliant general.

free (frē) *adj.* **freer, freest 1** allowed to move as you please; not shut in; not tied or fastened. **2** allowed to do as you please; not controlled: *Hungary is now a free nation.* **3** costing nothing: *We got a free ride to the airport.* **4** not busy: *I'll be free after lunch.* – *adv.* **1** without payment: *We travelled free of charge.* **2** without restriction: *The horses were allowed to wander free.* – *vb.* **freeing, freed** to make free; to release.

freedom *n.* **1** the condition of being free to act, move, etc. without restriction. **2** liberty or independence.

free enterprise *n.* business done without government interference or control.

free-range *adj.* describing hens that move about freely and are not kept in a battery.

freebie (**frē** bi) *n.* (*colloquial*) something given or provided without charge.

freeze (frēz) *vb.* **freezing, froze** (frōz), **frozen 1** to turn into ice or solidify as a result of cold. **2** to cover or become covered with ice: *The pond freezes over every winter.* **3** to become blocked up or stop operating because of frost or ice. **4** to preserve by refrigeration at below freezing-point.

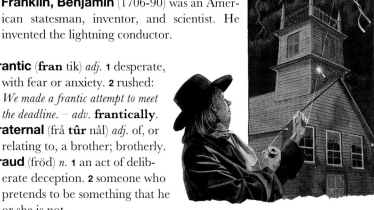

In 1752 the American scientist Benjamin Franklin proved that lightning is electric by flying a kite in a thunderstorm. Attached to the kite was a metal key. When lightning struck the kite, a spark flashed as electricity passed down the string to the key.

freezer *n.* a refrigerated cabinet or compartment in which to preserve food at below freezing-point.

freight (frāt) *n.* **1** transport of goods by rail, road, sea, or air. **2** goods transported this way.

French (french) *adj.* **1** belonging to FRANCE or its inhabitants. **2** relating to the French language. – *n.* **1** the Romance language spoken in FRANCE, parts of BELGIUM and SWITZERLAND, and elsewhere. **2** the people of FRANCE.

French Canadian *n.* & *adj.* (of) a native of the French-speaking part of CANADA.

French dressing *n.* a salad dressing made from oil, spices, and lemon juice or vinegar.

French windows *n.* (*plural*) a pair of glass doors that open on to a garden, balcony, etc.

frenzy (fren zi) *n.* **frenzies** wild agitation or excitement; frantic activity. – *adj.* **frenzied**.

frequency (frē kwen si) *n.* **frequencies 1** the condition of happening often; a repeated occurrence. **2** in radio, the particular rate of waves per second at which a signal is sent out.

frequent (frē kwênt) *adj.* recurring at short intervals: *We are frequent visitors to the galleries.*

fresco (fres kō) *n.* **frescos** a picture painted on a wall, usually while the plaster is still damp.

fresh (fresh) *adj.* **1** newly made, gathered, etc.: *These mushrooms were fresh this morning.* **2** another; different; clean: *Start on a fresh sheet of paper.* **3** new; additional: *We received fresh supplies.* **4** bright and alert. **5** (of water) not salt. – *n.* **freshness**.

freshen *vb.* **freshening, freshened** to make fresh or fresher.

freshwater *adj.* found in rivers and lakes, not in the sea.

fret¹ (fret) *vb.* **fretting, fretted** to worry, especially unnecessarily; to show anxiety.

fret² (fret) *n.* a narrow metal ridge across the neck of a stringed musical instrument.

fretsaw (fret sö) *n.* a narrow-bladed saw for cutting designs in wood or metal.

●**Freud** (froid), **Sigmund** (1856-1939) was a Viennese doctor who became known as the 'father of modern psychiatry'.

friction (frik shŏn) *n.* **1** the rubbing of one thing against another. **2** the resistance met with by an object that is moving against another or through liquid or gas. **3** quarrelling; conflict.

●Smooth objects cause much less friction than rough ones. When we want things to slow down we add friction, for example putting on the brakes of a car.

Friday (frī dā) *n.* the sixth day of the week.

fridge (frij) *n.* (*colloquial*) a refrigerator.

friend (frend) *n.* **1** someone you know and like. **2** someone who gives support or help: *Edward is a true friend of the poor.*

friendly *adj.* **friendlier, friendliest 1** kind; behaving as a friend. **2** on close or affectionate terms. – *n.* **friendliness**.

-friendly made easy for the person for whom it is intended: *This computer is user-friendly.*

friendship *n.* the relationship between friends.

In 1789 a group of women marched to the palace of Versailles and seized the royal family.

The French Revolution was sparked off on 14 July 1789 when an angry Paris mob stormed the fortress prison of the Bastille. France had to live through years of upheaval until order was restored in 1795 and a republic established.

Anyone who was considered an enemy of the Revolution was beheaded on the guillotine.

fright (frīt) *n.* sudden fear; a shock.

frighten *vb.* **frightening, frightened 1** to make afraid. **2** to scare away.

frightened *adj.* afraid.

frightful *adj.* ghastly; frightening; bad.

frill (fril) *n.* **1** a pleated strip of cloth attached along one edge to a garment, etc. as a decoration. **2** something extra serving no very useful purpose. – *adj.* **frilly, frillier, frilliest.**

fringe (frinj) *n.* **1** a border of loose threads on a carpet, tablecloth, garment, etc. **2** hair cut to hang down over the forehead. **3** the part farthest from the main area or centre.

fritter (**fri** tĕr) *vb.* **frittering, frittered** to waste.

frivolous (**fri** vŏ lŭs) *adj.* silly; not sufficiently serious. – *n.* **frivolity** (fri **vol** i ti), **frivolities.**

frock (frok) *n.* a woman's or girl's dress.

frog (frog) *n.* a small amphibious animal with webbed feet and long powerful hind legs.

frogspawn *n.* a mass of frog's eggs encased in protective jelly.

frolic (**fro** lik) *vb.* **frolicking, frolicked** to frisk or run about playfully. – *adj.* **frolicsome.**

from (from) *prep.* indicating **1** a starting-point in place or time: *It was a long journey from London to Glasgow.* **2** a lower limit: *You can get tickets from £12 upwards.* **3** movement out of: *Philippa took a letter from the drawer.* **4** distance away: *The hotel is 16 miles from Dover.* **5** a viewpoint: *I can see the house from here.* **6** removal: *They took it away from her.* **7** point of attachment: *The hat was hanging from a nail.* **8** source or origin: *The covers are made from an old curtain.*

front (frunt) *n.* **1** the side or part of anything that is farthest forward or nearest to the viewer; the most important side or part, for example the side of a building where the main door is. **2** the part of a vehicle or vessel that faces the direction in which it moves: *Ian prefers to sit at the front of the bus.* **3** in war, the area where the soldiers are nearest to the enemy. **4** See **Weather terms.** – *vb.* **fronting, fronted** (of a building) to have its front facing or beside a road, etc. – *adj.* situated, etc. at the front.

frontier (**frun** tēr) *n.* **1** a boundary between countries. **2** (in *plural*) limits: *the frontiers of knowledge.*

frost (frost) *n.* frozen water vapour forming a white powdery deposit on surfaces.

frostbite *n.* the destruction of bodily tissues by freezing. – *adj.* **frostbitten.**

frosty *adj.* **frostier, frostiest 1** cold enough for frost to form. **2** unfriendly. – *adv.* **frostily.**

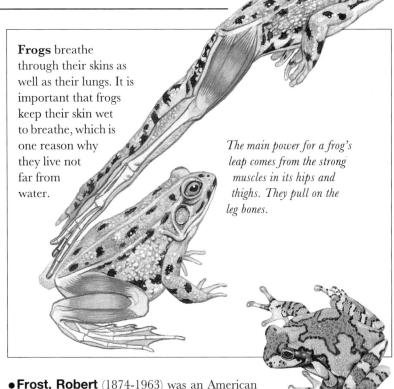

Frogs breathe through their skins as well as their lungs. It is important that frogs keep their skin wet to breathe, which is one reason why they live not far from water.

The main power for a frog's leap comes from the strong muscles in its hips and thighs. They pull on the leg bones.

Common tree frog. Tree frogs are usually less than 5 cm long.

●**Frost, Robert** (1874-1963) was an American poet, author of *A Boy's Will.*

froth (froth) *n.* a mass of tiny bubbles forming on the surface of a liquid.

frown (frown) *vb.* **frowning, frowned** to wrinkle the forehead and draw the eyebrows together in worry, disapproval, deep thought, etc. – *n.* a disapproving expression.

froze, frozen. See **freeze.**

frugal (**fr o o** gǎl) *adj.* thrifty.

fruit (froot) *n.* the seed-carrying product of a plant, especially if it has edible flesh, is sweet, and is used especially as a dessert: *Apples and bananas are fruit.*

fruitless *adj.* useless; done in vain.

frustrate (fru **strāt**) *vb.* **frustrating, frustrated 1** to prevent someone from doing or getting something; to foil a plan, attempt, etc. **2** to make someone feel disappointed, useless, etc. – *n.* **frustration.**

frustrated *adj.* **1** disappointed. **2** unfulfilled in your ambitions for yourself.

fry[1] (frī) *vb.* **fries, frying, fried** to cook in hot oil or fat.

fry[2] (frī) *n.* (*plural*) newly spawned fish.

●**Fry, Elizabeth** (1780-1845) was a QUAKER and an active reformer of English prisons.

fudge (fuj) *n.* a soft toffee.

PRONUNCIATION GUIDE	
fat **a**	all **ŏ**
fate **ā**	foot **oo**
fast **ä**	moon **o͞o**
among **å**	boy **oi**
met **e**	house **ow**
mean **ē**	demon **ŏ**
silent **ĕ**	thing **th**
loch **hh**	this **Th**
fin **i**	but **u**
line **ī**	mute **ū**
quick **kw**	fur **û**
got **o**	brochure **ŭ**
note **ō**	vision **zh**

fuel (**fū** ĕl) *n.* something that can be burned as a source of heat or power.

● The most important fuels are COAL, OIL, and natural GAS. These are formed underground from the remains of prehistoric plants or animals. They are known as fossil fuels.

fulcrum (**ful** krŭm) or (**fool** krŭm) *n.* **fulcrums** the point on which a lever is supported, turns, or balances.

fulfil (fool **fil**) *vb.* **fulfilling, fulfilled 1** to carry out or perform: *Sarah fulfilled her promises.* **2** to satisfy requirements. **3** to achieve: *Jack fulfilled his ambition by winning.* – *n.* **fulfilment**.

full (fool) *adj.* **1** holding, containing, or having as much as possible: *The bucket is full of water.* **2** complete: *We always do a full day's work.* **3** detailed: *I'd like a full report.* **4** occupied: *My hands are full.* **5** rich and varied: *Andrew has led a full life.* **6** (of the Moon) at the stage when it is a complete disc. – *adv.* **1** completely; at maximum capacity: *Is the heater full on?* **2** exactly; directly: *The ball hit him full on the nose.* – **full well** perfectly well. – **in full** **1** completely. **2** in detail.

full stop *n.* a punctuation mark (.) showing the end of a sentence.

fully *adv.* **1** to the greatest possible extent. **2** completely: *Ben has finished his studies and is now fully qualified.* **3** in detail: *We'll deal with it more fully next week.*

● **Fulton, Robert** (1765-1815) was an American inventor who built a submarine and developed a steamboat.

fumble (**fum** bĕl) *vb.* **fumbling, fumbled** to handle things, or grope, clumsily.

fume (fūm) *n.* smoke or vapour, especially if strong-smelling or poisonous. – *vb.* **fuming, fumed 1** to be furious. **2** to give off fumes.

fun (fun) *n.* **1** enjoyment. **2** a source of amusement or entertainment. – **in fun** as a joke. – **make fun of** to laugh at unkindly.

function (**fungk** shŏn) *n.* **1** the special purpose or task of a machine, person, bodily part, etc.: *It is the machine's function to photocopy.* **2** an organized event such as a party, reception, meeting, etc. **3** in computing, a series of tasks that a computer is programmed to perform at the touch of a single key. – *vb.* **functioning, functioned** to work; to operate.

Puffballs are fungi which range in size from a golf ball to a football. If a puffball is squeezed, spores (reproductive cells) escape in what looks like a smokelike puff.

All species of chanterelles have funnel-shaped fruitbodies growing on the ground. The group includes some of the most highly prized edible mushrooms.

fund (fund) *n.* a sum of money for a special purpose. – *vb.* **funding, funded** to provide money for: *The council will fund the project.*

fundamental (fun dă **men** tăl) *adj.* basic: *These are the fundamental rules of physics.*

funeral (**fū** nĕ răl) *n.* the ceremonial burial or cremation of a dead person.

fungus (**fung** gŭs) *n.* **funguses** or **fungi** (**fung** gē), (**fung** gī) or (**fun** jī) any of a group of plants, including mushrooms and toadstools, that reproduce by spores, not seeds.

funnel (**fu** nĕl) *n.* **1** a tube with a cone-shaped

Unlike higher plants, **fungi** lack chlorophyll and so cannot make their food (photosynthesize). Instead some live off dead matter such as rotting leaves and wood, while others are parasites and feed off living plants and animals. Moulds are simple, shapeless fungi. Larger fungi grow into toadstools mushrooms, and truffles.

Fly agaric

opening through which liquid, etc. can be poured into a narrow-necked container. **2** a chimney on a steamship or steam engine through which smoke escapes.

funny (**fu** ni) *adj.* **funnier, funniest 1** amusing; causing laughter. **2** strange. – *adv.* **funnily**.

funny bone *n.* a place in the elbow joint where the nerve passes close to the skin.

fur (fûr) *n.* the thick fine soft coat of a hairy animal. – *vb.* **furring, furred** to coat or become coated with a fur-like deposit.

furious (**fūr** i ůs) *adj.* **1** violently angry. **2** raging.

furnace (**fûr** nis) *n.* an enclosed chamber in which heat is produced, for heating water, etc.

furnish (**fûr** nish) *vb.* **furnishing, furnished 1** to provide with furniture: *Wendy has furnished her new office.* **2** to supply or equip someone with what he or she requires.

furniture (**fûr** ni chůr) *n.* movable household equipment, such as tables, chairs, beds, etc.

furrow (**fu** rō) *n.* a groove or trench cut into the earth by a plough.

further (**fûr** Thěr) *adj.* **1** more distant or remote: *We crossed to the further side of the stream.* **2** more extended: *There will be a further delay.* **3** additional: *The police could find no further clues.* – *adv.* **1** at or to a greater distance or more distant point. **2** to or at a more advanced point: *His idea was further developed.* – *vb.* **furthering, furthered** to help the progress of.

furthermore *adv.* in addition; moreover.

furthest (**fûr** Thist) *adj.* most distant or remote. – *adv.* **1** at or to the greatest distance or most distant point. **2** at or to the most advanced point; to the greatest extent or degree.

furtive (**fûr** tiv) *adj.* secretive; sly; cautious: *a furtive look.*

fury (**fūr** i) *n.* **furies** violent anger.

fuse (fūz) *n.* a safety device in an electrical plug, containing a wire that melts and so breaks the circuit when the current becomes too strong; the wire itself. – *vb.* **fusing, fused** (of an electrical circuit or appliance) to stop working because of the melting of a fuse. – **blow a fuse** (*colloquial*) to fly into a temper.

fuselage (**fū** ze läzh) *n.* the main body of an aircraft, carrying crew and passengers.

fusion (**fū** zhon) *n.* **1** the process of melting together. **2** the combining of atomic nuclei with the resulting release of energy.

fuss (fus) *n.* agitation and excitement, especially over something trivial. – *vb.* **fussing, fussed** to worry needlessly. – **make a fuss** to complain. – **make a fuss of** (*colloquial*) to pay a lot of attention to someone.

fussy *adj.* **fussier, fussiest** too concerned with details. – *adv.* **fussily**. – *n.* **fussiness**.

futile (**fū** tīl) *adj.* foolish, vain, or pointless.

futon (**fōō** ton) or (**fū** ton) *n.* a cloth-filled mattress designed to be used on the floor and rolled up when not in use.

future (**fū** chůr) *n.* the time to come; events that are still to occur. – *adj.* yet to happen – **in future** from now on.

fuzz (fuz) *n.* a mass of fine fibres or hair.

A chest-of-drawers with elements of ancient Greek and Roman design.

A plain, undecorated American rocking chair.

G g

gable (gā bĕl) *n.* the triangular parts of the side walls of a house between the sloping parts of the roof.

● **Gabon**. See Supplement, **Countries**.

gadget (ga jit) *n.* any small device or tool.
Gaelic (gā lik) or (ga lik) *n.* any of the closely related Celtic languages spoken in the Scottish Highlands, Ireland, or formerly the Isle of Man.
gag (gag) *vb.* **gagging, gagged 1** to silence someone by putting something in or over their mouth. **2** to deprive of free speech.

● **Gagarin** (gå ga rin), **Yuri** (1934-68) was a Russian cosmonaut. He made the first human space flight, in 1961. He died in a plane crash.

gaggle (ga gĕl) *n.* a flock of geese.
gain (gān) *vb.* **gaining, gained 1** to get, obtain, or earn. **2** to benefit: *She gained from the experience.* **3** to experience an increase in: *The car gained speed.* **4** (of a clock) to go too fast: *My watch gains five minutes every hour.* − *n.* an increase.

● **Gainsborough, Thomas** (1727-88) was an English landscape and portrait painter.

gait (gāt) *n.* a way of walking.
galaxy (ga lăk si) *n.* **galaxies** a group of stars and planets held together by the force of gravity.

● Our Sun is just one of about 100,000 million stars that belong to the MILKY WAY galaxy. And our galaxy is just one of billions. The nearest is called *Andromeda*.

gale (gāl) *n.* a very strong wind.

● **Galileo** (ga li lā ō) (1564-1642) was an Italian scientist who perfected the design of the telescope and established the *Copernican* theory of the universe in which the Sun is the centre.

gallant (ga lănt) *adj.* brave.
galleon (ga li ŏn) *n.* a large three-masted Spanish ship used for war or trade from the 15th to the 18th century.

Galleons had square sails on two front masts and three-cornered lateen sails on one or two rear masts. This meant that galleons could sail into the wind.

gallery (**ga** lě ri) *n.* **galleries** a room or building used to display works of art.

galley (**ga** li) *n.* **galleys 1** a long ship propelled by sails and oars. **2** the kitchen on a ship.

gallon (**ga** lŏn) *n.* a measure of liquid equal to eight pints or, in the United Kingdom, 4.546 litres (an **imperial gallon**), and in the United States, 3.785 litres.

gallop (**ga** lŏp) *n.* the fastest pace at which a horse moves, with all four legs leaving the ground together. – *vb.* **galloping, galloped** (of a horse) to move at a gallop.

gallows (**ga** lōz) *n.* (*singular*) a wooden frame on which criminals are put to death by hanging.

● **Galvani, Luigi** (1737-98) was an Italian scientist who researched ELECTRICITY.

● **Gambia.** See Supplement, **Countries**.

gamble (**gam** běl) *vb.* **gambling, gambled 1** to bet money on the result of a card game, horse-race, etc. **2** to take a chance or risk: *They gambled on the weather being fine.* – *n.* **1** an act of gambling; a bet. **2** a risk, or a situation involving risk: *We were forced to take a gamble.*

game (**gām**) *n.* **1** an amusement or pastime. **2** a competitive activity with rules, involving some form of skill. **3** certain birds and animals that are killed for sport.

gander (**gan** děr) *n.* a male goose.

● **Gandhi, Indira** (1917-84) was an Indian prime minister.

● **Gandhi, Mohandas** (1869-1948), known as Mahatma, was an Indian statesman who led pacific opposition to British rule.

gang (gang) *n.* **1** a group of criminals, thieves, etc. **2** a group of friends.

gangster *n.* a member of a gang of criminals.

● **Ganges** (**gan** jēz) the greatest river in India.

gannet (**ga** nit) *n.* a large white sea bird.

gantry (**gan** tri) *n.* **gantries** a large metal supporting framework.

gaol (jāl) *n.* a prison.

gap (gap) *n.* **1** a break or open space: *The dog escaped through a gap in the fence.* **2** a break in time; an interval: *After a gap of three years.*

Rose

In the ancient world the Egyptian Royal **Gardens** were famous, while the terraced gardens at Babylon became one of the wonders of the world as the 'Hanging Gardens'. Many Roman villas had sumptuous gardens. In the Middle Ages monasteries were noted for their herb and cloister gardens. In the 1700s English landscape gardeners placed natural-looking lawns around big houses.

Informal garden border

Formal herb garden

gape (gāp) *vb.* **gaping, gaped** to stare with the mouth open, especially in surprise or wonder. – *n.* an open-mouthed stare. – *adj.* **gaping**.

garage (**ga** räzh), (**ga** rij), or (gå **räzh**) *n.* **1** a building in which cars, etc. are kept. **2** a place where cars, etc. are bought, sold, and repaired, often also selling petrol, etc.

garbage (**gär** bij) *n.* (*US*) domestic waste.

garda (**gär** då) *n.* **gardai** (**gär** dē) (a member of) the police force in the Irish Republic.

garden (**gär** děn) *n.* a piece of ground attached to a house, on which flowers, vegetables, trees, etc. are grown. – *adj.* (of a plant) cultivated, not wild. – *vb.* **gardening, gardened** to work at the care of a garden and its plants, usually as a hobby. – *n.* **gardener**.

gargle (**gär** gěl) *vb.* **gargling, gargled** to blow air from the lungs through a liquid held in the mouth without swallowing the liquid.

gargoyle (**gär** goil) *n.* an ugly carved open-mouthed head or figure acting as a rainwater spout, especially on a church.

● **Garibaldi** (ga ri **böl** di), **Giuseppe** (1807-82) was an Italian patriot who helped to create the modern, united state of ITALY.

The gargoyles on Notre Dame cathedral in Paris are probably the best known of all those on Gothic cathedrals.

garish (**gär** ish) *adj.* unpleasantly bright.

garlic (**gär** lik) *n.* a plant of the onion family, whose strong-tasting bulb is used as a flavouring in cooking. – *adj.* **garlicky**.

garment (**gär** mėnt) *n.* an article of clothing.

garnet (**gär** nit) *n.* any of various hard minerals, especially a red variety used as a gemstone.

garnish (**gär** nish) *vb.* **garnishing, garnished** to decorate food.

garret (**ga** rėt) *n.* an attic room.

garrison (**ga** ri sȯn) *n.* a group of soldiers stationed in a town or fortress.

garter (**gär** tėr) *n.* a band of tight material, worn on the leg to hold up a stocking or sock.

● **Garvey, Marcus** (1887-1940) was a Jamaican who founded the Universal Negro Improvement Association in the UNITED STATES.

gas (gas) *n.* **1** any freely moving substance which is neither solid nor liquid. **2** (*US*) petrol.

gash (gash) *n.* a deep open cut or wound.

gasp (gäsp) *vb.* **gasping, gasped** to take a sharp breath in, through surprise, sudden pain, etc. – *n.* a sharp intake of breath.

gastric (**gas** trik) *adj.* of the stomach.

gate (gāt) *n.* **1** a hinged barrier, moved to open or close an entrance in a wall, fence, etc. **2** any of the numbered exits at an airport through which passengers can board or leave an aircraft.
   gateway *n.* an entrance with a gate across it.

gather (**ga** Thėr) *vb.* **gathering, gathered 1** to come together in one place: *Huge crowds gathered in the marketplace.* **2** to collect, pick, or harvest. **3** to increase in speed or force: *The car gathered speed.* **4** to learn or understand: *I gather that you passed your exam.*
   gathering *n.* a meeting or assembly.

gaucho (**gow** chō) *n.* a modern cowboy of the South American plains.

gaudy (**gö** di) *adj.* **gaudier, gaudiest** coarsely and brightly coloured or decorated.

gauge (gāj) *vb.* **gauging, gauged 1** to estimate or guess a measurement, size, etc. **2** to judge: *She gauged the seriousness of the situation immediately.* – *n.* a measuring instrument.

● **Gauguin** (**gō** gan), **Paul** (1848-1903) was a French POST-IMPRESSIONIST painter.

gaunt (gönt) *adj.* thin or thin-faced through hunger or illness. – *n.* **gauntness**.

● **Gautama** (**gow** tå må) was the name of the BUDDHA.

gauze (göz) *n.* **1** thin transparent cloth, especially cotton used to dress wounds. **2** thin wire mesh. – *adj.* **gauzy, gauzier, gauziest**.

gave. See **give**.

gay (gā) *adj.* **1** happily carefree. **2** bright and attractive. – *n.* a homosexual man.

gaze (gāz) *vb.* **gazing, gazed** to stare fixedly for a long time. – *n.* a fixed stare.

gazelle (gå **zel**) *n.* **gazelles** or **gazelle** a small graceful antelope of AFRICA and ASIA.

gear (gēr) *n.* one of a set of small wheels with interlocking teeth, which combine to change the speed or direction of motion in a machine. – *vb.* **gearing, geared** to design to suit a particular need: *The course is geared to linguists.*

● Gear wheels turn at different speeds in proportion to the number of teeth they possess. A small wheel will turn twice as fast as a large one if it has half the number of teeth.

Geiger counter (**gī** gėr **kown** tėr) *n.* an instrument for measuring radioactivity.

gel. See **jell**.

gelatine (je lå **tēn**) or **gelatin** (je lå **tin**) *n.* a clear jelly-like substance made by boiling animal bones and hides, used in foods, glues, and photographic materials.

gem (jem) *n.* (also **gemstone**) a precious stone cut and polished for use in jewellery.

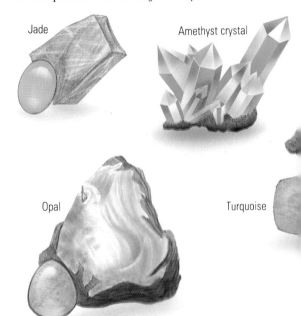

Jade

Amethyst crystal

Opal

Turquoise

Gemini (je mi nī) *n.* See **zodiac**.

gender (jen děr) *n.* the condition of being male or female; sex.

gene (jēn) *n.* a basic component in cells responsible for passing characteristics from parents to children, such as the colour of eyes, hair, etc.

general (je ně rål) *adj.* **1** involving or applying to all or most parts, people, or things; widespread; not specific, limited, or localized: *The general opinion was that he should resign.* **2** not detailed or definite; rough; vague: *She gave the police a general description of the burglars.* **3** not specialized: *His general knowledge is very wide.* – *n.* a senior army officer.

generalize or **generalise** *vb.* **generalizing, generalized** to speak in general terms or form general opinions, leaving out details. – *n.* **generalization**.

generate (je ně rāt) *vb.* **generating, generated** to produce or create.

generation *n.* **1** the act of producing, for example electricity. **2** all people born and living at about the same time, considered as a group: *He is one of the younger generation.*

generator *n.* a machine which produces one form of energy from another, such as electricity from wind or wave power.

generosity (ge ně **ro** si ti) *n.* a generous act.

generous (je ně růs) *adj.* **1** willing to give money or gifts unselfishly; large and given unselfishly: *He gave a generous donation to the charity.* **2** large: *She cut generous portions of cake.*

genesis (je ně sis) *n.* **geneses** (je ně sēz) **1** a beginning or origin. **2 Genesis** the first book in the OLD TESTAMENT.

genetics (jě **net** iks) *n.* (*singular*) the study of the transmission of hereditary characteristics.

● **Genghis Khan** (jen gis kän) (1162-1227) was a Mongol chief who conquered a mighty empire.

genie (jē ni) *n.* **genies** or **genii** (jē ni ī) in fairy stories, a spirit with the power to grant wishes.

genitals (je ni tålz) *n.* (*plural*; also **genitalia** (je ni **tā** li å)) the external reproductive organs.

genius (jē ni ůs) *n.* **geniuses** a person of outstanding creative or intellectual ability.

gentile (jen tīl) *n.* a person who is not Jewish.

gentle (jen těl) *adj.* **1** moderate and mild-mannered: *She was a gentle woman who never raised her voice.* **2** light and soft; not harsh. – *n.* **gentleness**. – *adv.* **gently**.

genuine (jen ū in) *adj.* **1** authentic, not artificial or fake. **2** honest; sincere.

geography (jē **og** rå fi) *n.* the scientific study of the Earth's surface, especially physical features, climate, and population. – *n.* **geographer**.

● Ptolemy of Alexandria, who lived about AD 150, was the most famous ancient geographer. His map of the then known world is remarkably accurate.

geology (jē **ol** ǒ ji) *n.* the scientific study of the Earth's structure, especially its history as shown in the formation of rocks. – *adj.* **geological** (jē ǒ **loj** i kål). – *n.* **geologist**.

Geology: There are three kinds of rock: igneous, formed from molten rock from deep inside the Earth; sedimentary, which is hardened layers of sediment; and metamorphic, which is either igneous or sedimentary rock changed by heat or pressure inside the Earth.

Obsidian Granite Slate Marble Coal Limestone Sandstone

Obsidian and granite are igneous rocks; marble and slate are metamorphic rocks; coal, limestone, and sandstone are sedimentary rocks.

Areas of volcanic activity are rich in minerals that have crystallized after being forced to the surface under pressure.

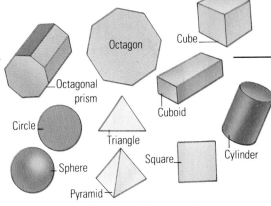

Octagon

Cube

Octagonal prism

Circle

Triangle

Cuboid

Square

Cylinder

Sphere

Pyramid

In geometry two-dimensional figures are plane figures; *three-dimensional shapes are* solids.

geometry (jē **om** ě tri) *n.* the branch of mathematics dealing with lines, angles, shapes, and their relationships.

●**George** is the name of six British kings. George the First (1660-1727) was a German ruler who inherited the British throne from his great-grandfather, James the First. George the Third (1738-1820) lost what became the UNITED STATES. George the Sixth (1895-1952) was the father of ELIZABETH THE SECOND.

●**George, Saint** is the patron saint of ENGLAND. His feast day is on 23 April.

●**Georgia**. See Supplement, **Countries**.

●**Georgia**. See Supplement, **USA**.

geranium (jě **rān** i ům) *n.* a house or garden plant with fragrant leaves and bright flowers.

gerbil (**jûr** bil) *n.* a mouse-like desert animal with long hind legs, native to AFRICA and ASIA.

geriatric (je ri **a** trik) *adj.* dealing with the old.

germ (jûrm) *n.* any microscopic plant or creature, especially one causing disease.

German (**jûr** mǎn) *n.* **1** a native of GERMANY. **2** the official language of GERMANY, AUSTRIA, and parts of SWITZERLAND. – *adj.* of GERMANY, its people, or their language.

●**Germany** After the Second WORLD WAR Germany was divided into two nations: West Germany and East Germany (a communist country). The two Germanys reunited under a federal government in 1990. Germany lies in the middle of EUROPE and has the largest population of any European nation. Germany's mines and factories have helped to make it one of the world's richest countries. Its capital is Berlin. See also Supplement, **Countries**.

●**Geronimo** (jě **ron** i mō) (1829-1909) was a warrior and leader of the APACHE Indians.

●**Gershwin** (**gûr** shwin), **George** (1898-1937) was the American composer of such works as *Rhapsody in Blue*.

gesture (**jes** chǔr) *n.* a movement of a part of the body as an expression of feelings, especially when speaking. – *vb.* **gesturing, gestured** to move a part of the body to express feelings.

get (get) *vb.* **getting, got** (got) (or *US* **gotten** (**go** těn)) **1** to receive or obtain: *I'm getting a new car*. **2** to have or possess: *I've got a new car*. **3** to go, move, travel, or arrive: *I got to Paris on Friday*. **4** to fetch, take, or bring: *I'll get it down from the shelf*. **5** to put into a particular state or condition: *She got him into trouble*. **6** to become: *He began to get angry*. **7** (*colloquial*) to understand: *I don't get the joke*.

●**Getty, John Paul** (1892-1976) was born into an American oil family and became the richest man in the world.

●**Gettysburg, Battle of** took place between 1 and 3 July 1863 and was an important Union victory over the invading Confederate army in the American CIVIL WAR.

geyser (**gē** zěr) *n.* an underground spring that spouts out hot water and steam.

●**Ghana**. See Supplement, **Countries**.

ghastly (**gäst** li) *adj.* **ghastlier, ghastliest** extremely frightening; hideous; horrific.

ghost (gōst) *n.* **1** the spirit of a dead person when visible in some form to a living person. **2** a suggestion, hint, or trace. – *adj.* **ghostly**.

giant (**jī** ǎnt) *n.* in fairy stories, a huge, strong, often cruel creature of human form.

gibbon (**gi** bǒn) *n.* a small tailless tree-dwelling ape with very long arms, native to ASIA.

giblets (**jib** lěts) *n.* (*plural*) the heart, liver, and other edible internal organs of fowl.

●**Gibraltar** is a tiny British colony, a rocky peninsula, on the south coast of SPAIN.

giddy (**gi** di) *adj.* **giddier, giddiest** **1** suffering an unbalancing spinning sensation because of tiredness or illness. **2** frivolous.

gift (gift) *n.* **1** something given; a present. **2** a natural ability: *He has a gift for music.*
gifted *adj.* having a great natural ability.

gigantic (jī **gan** tik) *adj.* huge; enormous.

giggle (**gi** gĕl) *vb.* **giggling, giggled** to laugh quietly in short bursts or in a nervous or silly way. – *n.* such a laugh.

gild (gild) *vb.* **gilding, gilded** or **gilt** to cover with a thin coating of gold.

gill (gil) *n.* the breathing organ of many sea animals, especially the slit on either side of a fish's head.

gin¹ (jin) *n.* an alcoholic spirit made from grain flavoured with juniper berries.

gin² (jin) *n.* a wire noose laid as an animal trap.

ginger (**jin** jĕr) *n.* **1** a hot-tasting root of a plant used in medicine and as a spice in cooking. **2** a reddish-brown colour.
gingerbread *n.* cake flavoured with ginger.

gingerly (**jin** jĕr li) *adv.* & *adj.* with caution.

gingham (**ging** ăm) *n.* striped or checked cotton cloth.

●**Giotto** (**jo** tō) (1266-1337) was a painter from Florence, ITALY, noted especially for his FRESCOS.

gipsy (**jip** si). See **gypsy**.

giraffe (ji **räf**) *n.* a tall African mammal with a very long neck, long legs, and a ginger-coloured coat with regular brown patches.

girder (**gûr** dĕr) *n.* a large beam of wood, iron, or steel used to support a floor, wall, road, etc.

girl (gûrl) *n.* a female child.

girth (gûrth) *n.* distance around something.

give (giv) *vb.* **giving, gave** (gāv), **given** (**gi** vĕn) **1** to transfer ownership or possession of something: *She gave him my watch.* **2** to provide or produce: *Cows give milk.* **3** to perform an action, service, etc.: *She gave a lecture on beetles.* **4** to pay: *I gave 20 pence for it.* **5** to break: *The chair gave under his weight.* – *vb.* **give in** to admit defeat. – *vb.* **give out 1** to distribute. **2** to emit. **3** to break down or come to an end: *Their resistance gave out.* – *vb.* **give over 1** to transfer. **2** to set aside: *The morning was given over to games.* – *vb.* **give up 1** to admit defeat; to stop making an effort: *She gave up trying to talk sense to him.*

2 to renounce a habit: *He has given up smoking.*

gizzard (**gi** zărd) *n.* a bird's second stomach, with muscles that break down hard food.

glacier (**gla** si ĕr) or (**glā** si ĕr) *n.* an enormous slow-moving mass of ice, formed from an accumulation of snow.

glad (glad) *adj.* **gladder, gladdest** happy or pleased: *I'll be glad to go back to school.*

gladiator (**gla** di ā tŏr) *n.* in ancient Rome, a man trained to fight against other men or animals in an arena.

glamour (**gla** mŏr) *n.* great attractiveness, especially created on a person by make-up, clothes, etc. – *adj.* **glamorous**.

glance (gläns) *vb.* **glancing, glanced** to look very quickly or indirectly. – *n.* a brief look, often indirect.

gland (gland) *n.* an organ that produces chemical substances that are used by, or excreted from, the body, e.g. sweat glands.

Glamour once meant 'magic' or 'spell', but by the 19th century had come to mean 'magic beauty'.

The results of the action of **glaciers** millions of years ago can be seen today. Valleys contained huge glaciers, creeping slowly downhill. The glacier's scouring action wore away the sides and floor of its valley.

Lakes may form in the armchair-shaped cirques made by glaciers.

Pyramidal peak

Cirque

Crevasses

Movement of glacier

Sometimes a glacier carries rocks a long distance away. These are known as erratics.

In traditional **glass**-blowing a gob of molten glass at the end of a tube was blown to produce a bubble that could be shaped before it cooled.

To make stained glass artists fitted pieces of coloured glass together with lead to make designs or pictures.

Glass is made from melting sand, limestone, and soda ash. Lead replaces limestone to give crystal its sparkle.

GLASS-MAKING METHODS

blowing Today blowing is done by machines, e.g. to make bottles and light bulbs.

pressing Glass is pushed into a mould and then cooled, e.g. to make ovenware.

casting Molten glass is poured into moulds to make, e.g., lenses for telescopes.

rolling Rollers squeeze molten glass into sheets.

floating A way of making sheet glass, done by floating molten glass across a bath of molten tin.

glare (glār) *vb.* **glaring, glared** to stare angrily. – *n.* **1** an angry stare. **2** dazzling light. **glaring** *adj.* **1** unpleasantly bright. **2** obvious.

● **Glasgow** is SCOTLAND's largest city.

glasnost (glas nost) *n.* openness and willingness to provide information on the part of governments (especially Soviet).

glass (gläs) *n.* **1** a hard, brittle, usually transparent substance made by melting together and then rapidly cooling a mixture of compounds. **2** an article made from this substance, especially a drinking cup. **3** (in *plural*) spectacles. – *adj.* made of glass.

glaze (glāz) *vb.* **glazing, glazed 1** to fit glass panes into a window, door, etc. **2** to give a hard shiny transparent coating to pottery. **3** to become dull and expressionless: *His eyes glazed over with boredom.*

gleam (glēm) *n.* **1** a gentle glow. **2** a brief flash of light. **3** a brief appearance or sign: *There was a gleam of excitement in his eyes.* – *vb.* **gleaming, gleamed** to glow gently.

glee (glē) *n.* great delight; joy.

glen (glen) *n.* a long narrow valley, especially in Scotland.

● **Glendower, Owen** (*c.*1350-*c.*1416) was a Welsh chieftain who fought the English.

● **Glenn, John** (1921-) was the first American to orbit the Earth, on 20 February 1962.

glide (glīd) *vb.* **gliding, glided 1** to move smoothly: *They glided along the ice.* **2** (of birds) to sail through the air without beating the wings. **3** (of an aircraft) to fly without engine power. **glider** *n.* a small aircraft with no engine, kept in flight by rising currents of warm air.

glimmer (gli měr) *vb.* **glimmering, glimmered** to glow faintly. – *n.* **1** a faint glow. **2** a hint or trace: *a glimmer of hope.*

glimpse (glimps) *n.* a very brief look. – *vb.* **glimpsing, glimpsed** to see for only a moment.

glisten (gli sěn) *vb.* **glistening, glistened** (usually of something wet, icy, etc.) to give off faint flashes of light.

glitter (gli těr) *vb.* **glittering, glittered** to shine with bright flashes of light; to sparkle.

gloat (glōt) *vb.* **gloating, gloated** to feel or show smug satisfaction, for example about your own success: *He gloated over his exam results.* – *n.* an act of gloating.

globe (glōb) *n.* **1** the Earth. **2** a sphere with a map of the world on it.

gloom (gloom) *n.* **1** near-darkness. **2** sadness or despair. – *adv.* **gloomily.** – *adj.* **gloomy, gloomier, gloomiest.**

glorify (glö ri fī) *vb.* **glorifies, glorifying, glorified** to exaggerate the beauty, importance, etc. of: *The film glorified war.*

glorious (glö ri ŭs) *adj.* splendidly beautiful.

glory (glö ri) *n.* **glories 1** great honour and prestige. **2** great beauty or splendour.

gloss[1] (glos) *n.* **1** shiny brightness on a surface. **2** a superficial attractiveness. – *vb.* **glossing, glossed** to give a shiny finish to. **glossy** *adj.* **glossier, glossiest** smooth and shiny. – *adv.* **glossily.** – *n.* **glossiness.**

gloss[2] (glos) *n.* a short explanation of a difficult word or phrase in a text. **glossary** *n.* **glossaries** a list of glosses, often at the end of a book.

glove (gluv) *n.* a covering for the hand, usually with separate fingers.

glow (glō) *vb.* **glowing, glowed 1** to give out a steady heat or light without flames. **2** to shine brightly, as if very hot: *Her cheeks were glowing with health.* – *n.* **1** a steady flameless heat or light. **2** intensity of a pleasant feeling.

glower (glow ẽr) *vb.* **glowering, glowered** to stare angrily. – *n.* an angry stare; a scowl.

glucose (glōō kōz) *n.* a sugar present in plant and animal tissue.

glue (glōō) *n.* any adhesive. – *vb.* **glueing** or **gluing, glued** to join with glue.

glum (glum) *adj.* **glummer, glummest** in low spirits; sullen.

glut (glut) *n.* an excessive supply of goods, etc.

glutton (glu tǒn) *n.* **1** a person who eats too much. **2** a person whose behaviour suggests an eagerness for something unpleasant: *He's a glutton for punishment.* – *adj.* **gluttonous**. **gluttony** *n.* the practice of eating too much.

gnarled (närld) *adj.* twisted; with knots and lumps, usually as a result of age: *The branches of the oak tree were gnarled with age.*

gnat (nat) *n.* any of various small biting and often bloodsucking flies.

gnaw (nö) *vb.* **gnawing, gnawed 1** to bite with a scraping action, causing a gradual wearing away. **2** to persistently cause physical or mental pain: *Jealousy gnawed at her for many years.*

gnome (nōm) *n.* a small fairy-tale creature who lives underground, often guarding treasure.

gnu (nōō) or (nū) *n.* **gnus** or **gnu** a type of large African antelope.

go (gō) *vb.* **goes, going, went** (went), **gone** (gon) **1** to walk, move, or travel. **2** to lead or extend: *There is a path going across the field.* **3** to visit or attend, once or regularly: *I go to school.* **4** to be destroyed or taken away; to disappear: *The peaceful atmosphere has gone.* **5** to proceed: *The scheme is going well.* **6** to be used up: *All his money goes on sweets.* **7** to belong: *Where does this go?* **8** to apply: *The same goes for you.* **9** (of colours, etc.) to match or blend. – *n.* **goes 1** a turn: *It's my go.* **2** an attempt: *Have a go.* – *vb.* **go against** to be contrary to; to be decided unfavourably for: *The court case went against him.* – *vb.* **go ahead** to proceed. – *vb.* **go along with** to agree with and support. – *vb.* **go off 1** to explode. **2** to become rotten. – *vb.* **go out** to become extinguished. – *vb.* **go through with** to carry out to the end.

go-ahead (*colloquial*) *adj.* ambitious. – *n.* permission to start.

go-kart *n.* a low racing vehicle consisting of a frame with wheels, engine, and steering gear.

goal (gōl) *n.* **1** the set of posts through which the ball is struck to score points in various games. **2** an act of scoring in this way. **3** an aim.

goat (gōt) *n.* a horned and bearded animal of the sheep family.

gobble (go bĕl) *vb.* **gobbling, gobbled 1** to eat hurriedly and noisily. **2** (of turkeys) to make a loud swallowing noise in the throat.

goblin (gob lin) *n.* in folk-tales, an evil spirit.

god (god) *n.* **1 God** in the CHRISTIAN, JEWISH, and MUSLIM religions, the creator and ruler of the universe. **2** in other religions, a super-human masculine being with power over nature and humans, an object of worship. **godchild** *n.* **godchildren** a child for whom a godparent is responsible. **goddess** *n.* a superhuman feminine being. **godparent** *n.* a person with responsibility for the religious education of another, especially a child.

● **Goethe** (gût ě), **Johann Wolfgang von** (1749-1832) was a German poet and play-wright as well as a scientist and statesman.

goggles (go gĕlz) *n.* (*plural*) protective spectacles with edges fitting closely against the face.

Alpine ibex are amazingly nimble and sure footed.

The various breeds of domestic **goat** are descended from the Persian wild goat.

Cretan wild goat

Apennine mountain goat

Feral goat

The chamois is unusual in having horns that are hooked at the end.

Pure gold bars. A country's wealth is measured by the quantity of gold it has. The USA stores its vast stock of gold in Fort Knox, Kentucky.

gold (gōld) *n.* **1** an element (symbol **Au**), a soft yellow precious metal used for making jewellery, coins, etc. **2** articles made from it. – *adj.* **1** made of gold. **2** gold-coloured.

golden *adj.* **1** gold-coloured. **2** made of or containing gold. **3** excellent; extremely valuable: *She was given a golden opportunity.* **4** (of an anniversary) 50th.

golden eagle *n.* a large northern mountain eagle with golden-brown plumage.

goldfinch *n.* a small European songbird.

goldfish *n.* **goldfishes** or **goldfish** a small deep-orange freshwater fish, often kept in aquariums.

gold medal *n.* a medal awarded to the winner of a sporting contest, etc.

● **Golden Gate** a strait leading from the PACIFIC OCEAN into San Francisco Bay, spanned by a suspension bridge.

golf (golf) *n.* a game played on a large outdoor course, the object being to hit a small ball into each of a series of holes using a set of long-handled clubs, taking as few strokes as possible.

● **Goliath** (gǒ lī̇ åth) was a giant in the BIBLE who was killed by David with a stone from his sling.

gondola (gon dǒ lå) *n.* a long narrow flat-bottomed boat with pointed upturned ends, used on the canals of Venice.

gone (gon). See **go**. – *adj.* **1** departed. **2** lost.

gong (gong) *n.* a hanging metal plate which sounds when struck.

good (good) *adj.* **better** (be těr), **best** (best) **1** pleasant: *They had good weather.* **2** competent; talented: *She is good at sports.* **3** morally correct; virtuous. **4** beneficial: *The medicine is good for you.* **5** bringing happiness or pleasure: *He brought good news.* **6** well-behaved. – *n.* **1** moral correctness; virtue. **2** benefit; advantage: *It will do you good.* – *interjection* an expression of approval or satisfaction. – **as good as** almost; virtually. – **for good** for ever; permanently. **Good Friday** *n.* See **Feasts and Festivals**.

goodness *n.* **1** being good; kindness. **2** nourishing quality.

goose (gōos) *n.* **geese** (gēs) **1** a long-necked, web-footed bird like a large duck. **2** the female, as opposed to the gander, the male.

gopher (gō fěr) *n.* any of various burrowing animals of NORTH and CENTRAL AMERICA.

● **Gorbachev** (gör bå chef), **Mikhail** (1931-) is a Russian statesman who introduced many reforms.

GOLF TERMS
birdie 1 stroke under par
bogey 1 stroke over par
drive the first shot off the tee
driver a No 1 wood
eagle 2 shots under par
handicap a stroke or shot allowance given to a player so that he or she can play on equal terms with a superior player
par the number of shots it should take an expert to complete a hole or round.

Some people think that the forerunner to the game of **golf** was played by the Chinese 2,000 years ago. Others claim the Romans were the first to knock balls into holes. The game we know probably developed in Scotland where the game's first written rules were drawn up in 1744.

Everything that a golfer needs can be put in a golf bag. Bags are often carried by hired caddies.

Some golf balls comprise long strips of rubber wound around a core. The dimples on the casing help the ball to fly smoothly.

A golf course has 9 or 18 holes in areas called greens. The golfer hits the ball into each hole in turn. The aim is to finish each hole in the fewest number of strokes.

gore[1] (gör) *n.* blood from a wound.

gore[2] (gör) *vb.* **goring, gored** to pierce with a horn or tusk.

gorge (görj) *n.* a deep narrow valley, usually containing a river. – *vb.* **gorging, gorged** to eat or swallow greedily.

gorgeous (**gör** jůs) *adj.* attractive; magnificent.

gorilla (gŏ **ril** ǎ) *n.* the largest of all apes, native to West Africa.

gosling (**goz** ling) *n.* a young goose.

gospel (**gos** pĕl) *n.* **1** the life and teachings of Christ. **2 Gospel** any of the NEW TESTAMENT books attributed to Matthew, Mark, Luke, and John.

gossip (**go** sip) *n.* **1** talk or writing about the private affairs of others, often spiteful and untrue. **2** a person who engages in or spreads such talk. **3** casual and friendly chat. – *vb.* **gossiping, gossiped 1** to take part in, or pass on, malicious gossip. **2** to chat. – *adj.* **gossipy**.

got. See **get**.

Goth (goth) *n.* a member of a Germanic people who invaded parts of the ROMAN EMPIRE.

gotten (**go** tĕn) (*US*). See **get**.

gouge (gowj) *n.* **1** a chisel with a rounded hollow blade, used for cutting grooves or holes in wood. **2** a groove or hole made using this. – *vb.* **gouging, gouged** to cut or press out.

goulash (**goo** lash) *n.* a thick meat stew from HUNGARY.

gourd (gōōrd) *n.* a hard-skinned fleshy fruit related to the cucumber.

govern (**gu** vĕrn) *vb.* **governing, governed** to control and direct the affairs of a country, state, or organization. – *adj.* **governing**.

government (**gu** vĕr mĕnt) *n.* a body of people, usually elected, with the power to control the affairs of a country or state.

governor *n.* **1** the elected head of a state in the UNITED STATES. **2** the head of an institution, for example a prison. **3** a member of a governing body of a school, hospital, etc.

gown (gown) *n.* **1** a woman's long formal dress. **2** an official robe worn by clergy, lawyers, etc.

● **Goya, Francisco de** (1746-1828) was a Spanish painter whose works criticized society.

grab (grab) *vb.* **grabbing, grabbed** to seize suddenly and often with violence: *The thief grabbed the woman's handbag.* – *n.* **1** an act of taking suddenly or greedily. **2** a mechanical device with scooping jaws, used for excavation.

grace (grās) *n.* **1** elegance and beauty of form or movement. **2** decency; politeness: *He had the grace to offer.* **3** a short prayer of thanks to God said before or after a meal.

graceful *adj.* having or showing elegance and beauty of form or movement.

gracious (**grā** shůs) *adj.* kind and polite.

grade (grād) *n.* **1** a stage or level on a scale of quality, rank, size, etc. **2** a mark given for an exam or an essay. **3** (especially *US*) a particular class or year in school. – *vb.* **grading, graded 1** to arrange in different levels. **2** to award a mark indicating grade to.

gradient (**grā** di ĕnt) *n.* the steepness of a slope.

gradual (**gra** joo ǎl) *adj.* changing or happening slowly, by degrees.

graduate (**gra** joo āt) *vb.* **graduating, graduated 1** to receive an academic degree from a college or university. **2** to move up from a lower to a higher level, often in stages. – (**gra** joo ǎt) *n.* a person with a higher-education degree.

graffiti (grǎ **fēt** i) *n.* (*plural*) words or drawings, scratched or painted on walls in public places.

graft (gräft) *n.* **1** a living plant shoot inserted into another to form a new growth. **2** a healthy piece of skin or bone, or an organ, used to replace an unhealthy piece of the body. – *vb.* **grafting, grafted** to attach a graft.

● **Graham, Martha** (1894-1991) was an American pioneer of modern dance.

grain (grān) *n.* **1** a single seed of a cereal plant. **2** cereal plants or their seeds as a whole. **3** a very small amount: *There was a grain of truth in his story.* **4** the direction or arrangement of the lines of fibre in wood, paper, or leather.

gram or **gramme** (gram) *n.* the basic unit of weight in the metric system, one thousandth of a kilogram, equal to 0.035 ounces.

grammar (**gra** mǎr) *n.* the branch of language study dealing with the rules by which words are formed and combined into sentences.

grammatical (grǎ **mat** i kǎl) *adj.* correct according to the rules of grammar.

granary (**gra** nǎ ri) *n.* **granaries** a building where grain is stored.

grand (grand) *adj.* large or impressive in size, appearance, or style.

Many gourds have attractive names such as Aladdin's turban, Warted gourd, Nest-egg gourd, and Luffa.

The Grand Canyon in Arizona is the deepest gorge on Earth. It is about 350 km long, up to 20 km across and as much as 2 km deep. The Colorado river runs through the canyon.

● **Grand Canyon** carved by the Colorado River in Arizona, is a wonder of nature.

grandchild (granchīld), **grandchildren**, **granddaughter**, **grandson** *n.* a child, daughter, or son, of your son or daughter. **grandfather**, **grandmother**, **grandparent** *n.* the father or mother of your father or mother.

grandeur (**gran** jĕr) *n.* impressive beauty.

granite (**gra** nit) *n.* a hard grey or red rock, often used for building.

grant (gränt) *vb.* **granting, granted** to give, allow, or fulfil: *The judge granted him a pardon.* – *n.* an amount of money from a public fund for a specific purpose: *a home improvement grant.* **granted** I admit that it is true.

● **Grant, Ulysses** (1822-85) was a Union general in the American CIVIL WAR.

Granth (grunt) *n.* (also **Granth Sahib** (grunt **sä** ib)) the sacred scripture of the Sikh religion.

grape (grāp) *n.* a green or dark-purple berry growing in clusters on vines, eaten as a fruit, pressed to make wine, and dried to make currants, raisins, and sultanas. **grapevine** *n.* **1** a vine on which grapes grow. **2** (*colloquial*) the network through which gossip is spread.

graph (gräf) *n.* a diagram which shows changes or comparisons in value or quantity, by means of printed dots, lines, or blocks.

grapple (**gra** pĕl) *vb.* **grappling, grappled** to grasp and struggle or fight.

grasp (gräsp) *vb.* **grasping, grasped 1** to take a firm hold of; to clutch. **2** to understand: *She was unable to grasp the problem.* – *n.* **1** a grip or hold. **2** ability to understand: *The lecture on nuclear physics was beyond their grasp.* **grasping** *adj.* greedy, especially for wealth.

grass (gräs) *n.* **1** any of numerous wild plants with green blade-like leaves, covering the ground in fields, lawns, etc., and eaten by various animals. **2** (*slang*) a person who betrays others, especially to the police. **grasshopper** *n.* a jumping insect that makes a chirping noise by rubbing its long back legs against its wings. **grass snake** *n.* a small harmless European snake with a brownish-green body.

grate¹ (grāt) *n.* a framework of iron bars for holding coal, etc. in a fireplace.

grate² (grāt) *vb.* **grating, grated** to cut into shreds by rubbing against a rough surface.

grateful (**grāt** fŭl) *adj.* showing thanks.

Grape cultivation is one of the oldest human arts. Grapes are grown in vineyards, mostly in warm, temperate lands such as the Mediterranean zone, California, and Australia.

There are many varieties of grape such as the Cabernet, Sauvignon, Chardonnay, and Pinot Noir.

Different wines are put into bottles of different shapes: Bordeaux, Burgundy, and Chianti, for example.

gratify (**gra** ti fī) *vb.* **gratifies, gratifying, gratified** to please, satisfy, or indulge, for example a desire. – *n.* **gratification**.

gratitude (**gra** ti tūd) *n.* thankfulness.

grave¹ (grāv) *n.* a hole dug in the ground for burying a dead body in.

grave² (grāv) *adj.* giving cause for great concern: *The girl was in grave danger.*

gravel (**gra** věl) *n.* a mixture of small stones and coarse sand, used for the surface of paths.

gravity¹ (**gra** vi ti) *n.* the natural force which causes objects to be drawn towards each other, especially the force which attracts things towards the Earth, causing them to fall towards or stay on the ground.

gravity² (**gra** vi ti) *n.* seriousness.

gravy (**grā** vi) *n.* **gravies** a sauce made from the juices released by meat as it is cooking.

gray (grā) (especially *US*). Same as **grey**.

graze (grāz) *vb.* **grazing, grazed** (of animals) to eat grass.

grease (grēs) *n.* **1** animal fat softened by melting. **2** any thick oily substance, especially to lubricate the moving parts of machinery. **greasy** *adj.* **greasier, greasiest** containing, or covered in, grease. – *n.* **greasiness**.

great (grāt) *adj.* **1** very large in size, quantity, intensity, or extent. **2** very enjoyable; excellent or splendid. **3** most important. **4** enthusiastic; keen: *She is a great reader.*

the Great Bear *n.* Ursa Major, a constellation of stars in the northern hemisphere, whose seven brightest stars form the Plough.

Great Britain *n.* the largest island in EUROPE, containing ENGLAND, WALES, and SCOTLAND, and forming, together with NORTHERN IRELAND, the UNITED KINGDOM.

Great Dane *n.* a large smooth-haired dog.

● **Great Barrier Reef** off the north-east coast of AUSTRALIA, is the world's largest reef.

● **Great Lakes** a chain of five lakes between CANADA and the UNITED STATES: Superior, Michigan, Huron, Erie, and Ontario.

● **Great Wall of China** the world's longest defensive wall stretching for 2400 km. It was built over 2000 years ago.

great- (grāt-) *in compounds* indicating a family relationship that is one generation more remote than that of the base word: *great-grandmother.*

● **Greece**. See Supplement, **Countries**.

● **Greece, ancient** was a great civilization which started about 2500 years ago. In the city of Athens the Greeks established a new form of government, democracy. They developed arts and sciences and built fine buildings. The Greeks loved athletic sports, dance, and drama. Modern civilization owes much to the ideas of ancient Greece.

Many fine examples of Greek 'red figured' and 'black figured' painted pottery have survived.

A silver four drachma ancient Greek coin, the 'owl' piece, symbolizing the owl-eyed goddess, Athena.

A bronze head of Aphrodite (left), the goddess of love, beauty, and fertility.

The building of the Parthenon in Athens, completed in 432 BC. It was one of the finest of all Greek temples.

greed (grēd) *n.* an excessive desire for something.
greedy *adj.* **greedier, greediest** filled with greed. – *adv.* **greedily**.

Greek (grēk) *n.* **1** the official language of GREECE. **2** a native or inhabitant of GREECE. – *adj.* of GREECE, its people, or their language.

green (grēn) *adj.* **1** of the colour between yellow and blue in the visible spectrum, the colour of the leaves of most plants. **2** covered with grass, bushes, etc.: *The green areas of the city are very precious*. **3** showing concern for, or designed to be harmless to, the environment. **4** extremely jealous or envious: *He was green with envy when he saw my new bike.* – *n.* any shade of the colour of the leaves of most plants.
greenhouse *n.* a building with walls and a roof made of glass, used for growing plants which need special protection or conditions.
greenhouse effect *n.* the effect of masses of carbon dioxide and other gases in the atmosphere, preventing the escape of the Sun's heat reflected by the Earth's surface, causing warming of the Earth's atmosphere.

● **Greene, Graham** (1904-91) was an English novelist whose works include *Our Man in Havana*.

● **Greenland** is a large island in the north ATLANTIC belonging to Denmark.

● **Greenwich** (**gre** nij) near London, is where the 0° line of longitude runs and is used for calculating time all over the world.

greet (grēt) *vb.* **greeting, greeted** to address or welcome, especially in a friendly way.

● **Gregory, Saint** (540-604), known as Gregory the Great, was the pope who sent Augustine to convert the English to CHRISTIANITY.

gremlin (**grem** lin) *n.* an imaginary mischievous creature blamed for faults in machinery or electronic equipment.

● **Grenada**. See Supplement, **Countries**.

grew. See **grow**.

grey (grā) *adj.* of a colour between black and white, the colour of ash and slate.

greyhound (**grā** hownd) *n.* a tall thin breed of dog capable of great speed.

grid (grid) *n.* **1** a pattern of lines that cross each other to form squares. **2** a network of cables and pipes for supplying power to a large area.

griddle (**gri** dĕl) *n.* (also **girdle** (**gûr** dĕl)) a flat iron plate which is heated for baking or frying.

grief (grēf) *n.* great sorrow and unhappiness.

● **Grieg** (grēg), **Edvard** (1843-1907) was the Norwegian composer of *Peer Gynt*.

grieve (grēv) *vb.* **grieving, grieved** to feel grief, especially at a death.

grill (gril) *vb.* **grilling, grilled** to cook under radiated heat. – *n.* a device on a cooker which radiates heat downwards.

grim (grim) *adj.* **grimmer, grimmest** stern and unsmiling.

grimace (**gri** mås) *n.* an ugly twisting of the face, expressing pain or disgust.

grime (grīm) *n.* thick dirt.

● **Grimm** was the name of two German brothers who collected fairy tales in the 19th century.

grin (grin) *vb.* **grinning, grinned** to smile broadly, showing the teeth. – *n.* a broad smile.

grind (grīnd) *vb.* **grinding, ground** (grownd) to crush into small particles or powder between two hard surfaces.

grip (grip) *vb.* **gripping, gripped 1** to take or keep a firm hold of. **2** to capture the imagination or attention of. – *n.* **1** a firm hold. **2** a part that can be gripped.
gripping *adj.* holding the attention.

grisly (**griz** li) *adj.* **grislier, grisliest** horrible.

grit (grit) *n.* **1** small hard particles of stone, etc. **2** (*colloquial*) courage and determination. – *vb.* **gritting, gritted 1** to spread grit on icy roads. **2** to clench the teeth to overcome pain: *She gritted her teeth while the doctor pulled the thorn out.*

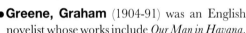

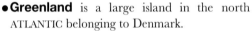

Greenwich in London is at 0 degrees longitude. A place half way round the world from Greenwich is at 180 degrees longitude.

Far right: The racing greyhound is the fastest breed of dog and can achieve speeds of over 57 km/h. Greyhounds are depicted on ancient Egyptian wall paintings hunting gazelles. Today, many greyhounds compete on oval race tracks where they chase a mechanical hare.

grizzly bear (**griz** li bār) *n.* a large fierce greyish-brown North American bear.

groan (grōn) *vb.* **groaning, groaned** to make a long deep sound in the back of the throat, expressing pain, distress, disapproval, etc. – *n.* the sound of groaning.

grocer (**grō** sẽr) *n.* a person selling food and general goods.

groom (grōōm) *n.* **1** a person who looks after horses and cleans stables. **2** a bridegroom. – *vb.* **grooming, groomed 1** to clean, brush, and generally smarten animals, especially horses. **2** to train or prepare for a specific purpose or job: *Peter was being groomed to take over the firm.*

groove (grōōv) *n.* a long narrow channel.

grope (grōp) *vb.* **groping, groped** to search by feeling about with the hands e.g. in the dark.

gross (grōs) *adj.* **1** total, with no deductions: *What is your gross income?* **2** very great; glaring: *He is guilty of gross negligence.* – *n.* **gross** twelve dozen, 144.

grotesque (grō **tesk**) *adj.* very unnatural or strange-looking, so as to cause fear or laughter.

grotto (**gro** tō) *n.* **grottos** or **grottoes** a cave.

ground[1] (grownd) *n.* **1** the solid surface of the Earth; soil; land. **2** (in *plural*) an area of land attached to or surrounding a building: *They strolled around the grounds.* **3** the range of subjects under discussion: *The book covers a lot of ground.* **4** (usually in *plural*) a reason or justification: *He had grounds for complaint.* – *vb.* **grounding, grounded 1** to base an argument, complaint, etc. **2** to hit the seabed or shore and remain stuck. – *adj.* on the ground: *ground forces.*

ground control *n.* the people or equipment on the ground that direct and monitor the flight of an aircraft or spacecraft.

ground[2]. See **grind**.

group (grōōp) *n.* **1** a number of people or things gathered or classed together. **2** a band of musicians, especially playing pop music. – *vb.* **grouping, grouped** to form a group.

grouse (grows) *n.* **grouse** or **grouses** a small plump brown game bird.

grow (grō) *vb.* **growing, grew** (grōō), **grown 1** to develop into a larger, more mature form. **2** (of hair, nails, etc.) to increase in length. **3** to cultivate plants. – *vb.* **grow up** to become, or be in the process of becoming, an adult.

grown *adj.* fully developed and mature.

growth *n.* **1** the process or rate of growing. **2** an increase in economic activity or profitability: *Tourism is a growth industry.*

growl (growl) *vb.* **growling, growled** (of animals) to make a deep rough sound in the throat, showing hostility.

grub (grub) *n.* the worm-like larva of an insect, especially a beetle.

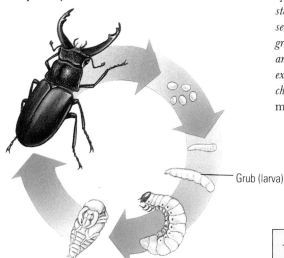

Grub (larva)

The grub is an early stage in the development of the beetle. Drastic changes in appearance at various stages of growth can be seen in several animal groups – insects (as here) and in amphibians (for example frogs). This change of form is called metamorphosis.

grudge (gruj) *vb.* **grudging, grudged** to feel a sense of unfairness or resentment at. – *n.* a long-standing feeling of resentment: *He will always bear this grudge.* – *adj.* **grudging**.

gruelling (**grōō** ẽl ing) *adj.* exhausting.

gruesome (**grōō** sõm) *adj.* inspiring horror.

gruff (gruf) *adj.* (of a voice) deep; unfriendly.

grumble (**grum** bẽl) *vb.* **grumbling, grumbled 1** to complain in a bad-tempered way. **2** to make a low rumbling sound. – *n.* **1** a complaint. **2** a rumbling sound.

grumpy (**grum** pi) *adj.* **grumpier, grumpiest** bad-tempered. – *adv.* **grumpily**.

grunt (grunt) *vb.* **grunting, grunted** (of animals, especially pigs) to make a low rough sound in the back of the throat. – *n.* the sound of grunting.

guarantee (ga rån **tē**) *n.* a formal promise, especially by a manufacturer to repair or replace an article found to be faulty within a stated period of time. – *vb.* **guaranteeing, guaranteed 1** to promise. **2** to ensure.

guard (gärd) *vb.* **guarding, guarded 1** to protect from danger or attack, or from escaping. **2** to take precautions to prevent: *You must guard against catching a cold.* – *n.* a person or group whose job is to provide protection from danger or attack, or to prevent escape. **guarded** *adj.* cautious.

guardian (**gär** di ån) *n.* a person legally responsible for the care of another.

The groom in bridegroom has nothing to do with horses. The original word was *gome* meaning 'man'. The word *grome* crept in by mistake.

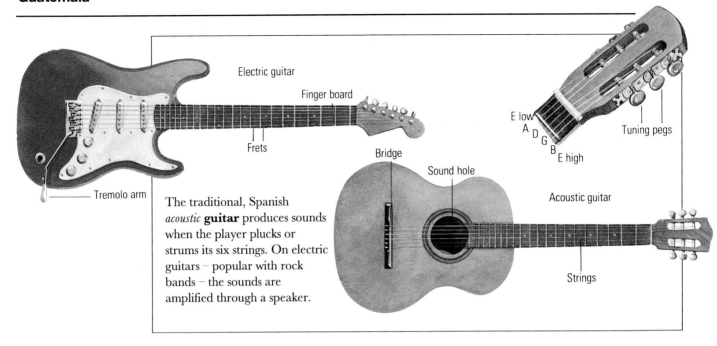

Electric guitar

Finger board

Frets

Tremolo arm

The traditional, Spanish *acoustic* **guitar** produces sounds when the player plucks or strums its six strings. On electric guitars – popular with rock bands – the sounds are amplified through a speaker.

Bridge

Sound hole

E low
A
D
G
B
E high

Tuning pegs

Acoustic guitar

Strings

A guerrilla (sometimes spelled guerilla) is a member of an irregular army, whereas gorilla is the name of a particular species of great ape.

● **Guatemala**. See Supplement, **Countries**.

guerrilla or **guerilla** (gĕ **ril** å) *n.* a member of a small, unofficial army that makes surprise attacks, e.g. against government troops.

guess (ges) *vb.* **guessing, guessed** to make an estimate or form an opinion, based on little or no information. – *n.* an estimate.

guest (gest) *n.* **1** a person who receives hospitality in the home of another. **2** a person staying at a hotel, etc.

guide (gīd) *vb.* **guiding, guided 1** to lead, direct, or show the way to. **2** to advise or influence: *Be guided by your parents.* – *n.* **1** a person who leads the way, e.g. for tourists or mountain climbers. **2** a book containing information on a particular subject.
guide dog *n.* a dog specially trained to guide a blind person safely.

guillotine (gi lŏ tēn) *n.* an instrument for beheading, consisting of a large heavy blade sliding rapidly down between two upright posts. – *vb.* **guillotining, guillotined**.

guilt (gilt) *n.* **1** shame or regret because you know you have done wrong. **2** the state of having done wrong or having broken a law.
guilty *adj.* **guiltier, guiltiest 1** judged to be responsible for a crime or wrongdoing. **2** feeling or showing guilt: *a guilty look.*

● **Guinea**. See Supplement, **Countries**.

● **Guinea-Bissau**. See Supplement, **Countries**.

guitar (gi **tär**) *n.* a musical instrument with six strings that are plucked or strummed. – *n.* **guitarist**.

gulag (**g$\overline{oo}$** lag) *n.* a network of labour camps that existed in the former SOVIET UNION.

gulf (gulf) *n.* a stretch of sea with land on most sides.
Gulf Stream *n.* (also **North Atlantic Drift**) a warm ocean current flowing from the Gulf of MEXICO towards north-east EUROPE.

gull (gul) *n.* any of various species of sea bird.

gullet (**gu** lit) *n.* the tube by which food passes from the mouth to the stomach.

gullible (**gu** lå bĕl) *adj.* easily tricked or fooled.

gully (**gu** li) *n.* **gullies** (or **gulley, gulleys**) a channel worn by running water.

gulp (gulp) *vb.* **gulping, gulped 1** to swallow food or drink eagerly or in large mouthfuls. **2** to make a swallowing motion, for example because of fear. – *n.* a swallowing motion.

gum[1] (gum) *n.* the firm flesh around the roots of the teeth.

gum[2] (gum) *n.* **1** a sticky substance from the trunks and stems of certain trees and plants. **2** this or any similar substance used as glue.

gun (gun) *n.* **1** any weapon which fires bullets or shells from a metal tube. **2** any instrument which forces something out under pressure: *He used a spray gun to paint the car.*
gunpowder *n.* an explosive mixture of saltpetre, sulphur, and charcoal.

gurgle (**gûr** gĕl) *vb.* **gurgling, gurgled** to make a bubbling noise. – *n.*

guru (**g͞oo** r͞oo) *n.* a SIKH spiritual leader.

gush (gush) *vb.* **gushing, gushed** to cause liquid to flood out suddenly and violently.

● **Gustavus Adolphus** (1594-1632) known as the 'Lion of the North', was king of SWEDEN.

gut (gut) *n.* the intestines; the insides of a person or animal.

● **Gutenberg** (**g͞oo** tĕn bûrg), **Johann** (1400-68) was the German inventor of printing with movable type.

gutter (**gu** tĕr) *n.* a channel for carrying away rainwater, fixed to the edge of a roof or built between a pavement and a road.

guy[1] (gī) *n.* **1** (*colloquial*) a man or boy. **2** a crude model of Guy Fawkes, burnt on a bonfire on Guy Fawkes Day.

Guy Fawkes Day *n.* 5 November, the anniversary of the discovery of the Gunpowder Plot, a plot to blow up Parliament in 1605 of which Guy Fawkes was the leader, celebrated with firework displays.

guy[2] (gī) *n.* a rope or wire used to hold something, especially a tent, firm or steady.

● **Guyana**. See Supplement, **Countries**.

gymkhana (jim **kä** nå) *n.* a local public event consisting of competitions in horse-riding.

gymnasium (jim **nā** zi ům) *n.* **gymnasiums** or **gymnasia** a building or room with equipment for physical exercise.

gymnast (**jim** nast) *n.* a person skilled in gymnastics.

gymnastics *n.* (*singular*) physical exercises designed to strengthen the body and improve agility.

gynaecology (gī nĕ **kol** ŏ ji) *n.* the branch of medicine dealing with diseases and disorders of the female body especially the reproductive system. – *n.* **gynaecologist**.

gypsy (**jip** si) *n.* **gypsies** a member of a dark-skinned travelling people, originally from north-west INDIA.

gyrate (jī **rāt**) *vb.* **gyrating, gyrated** to move with a spiralling motion. – *n.* **gyration**.

gyroscope (**jī** rŏ skōp) *n.* an apparatus consisting of a circular frame containing a disc which spins rapidly around a free-moving axis. The axis keeps the same position regardless of any movement of the frame. Gyroscopes are used in ships' compasses, etc.

One of the biggest revolutions in communications in Europe came in the 1400s when **Gutenberg** discovered how to print with movable metal type. Books could now be produced more quickly and more efficiently.

Block printing – carved in reverse out of wood

Gutenberg's metal type – movable and reusable

H h

habit (**ha** bit) *n.* **1** a regular activity or tendency which is hard to give up. **2** a long loose garment worn by monks and nuns.

habitat (**ha** bi tat) *n.* the natural home of an animal or plant.

●**Habsburg** was the name of a family that held the title of Holy Roman Emperor almost continuously between 1273 and 1806; they were emperors of AUSTRIA between 1806 and 1918.

hacienda (ha si **en** då) *n.* in Spanish-speaking countries, a large estate with a house on it.

hacker *n.* a person who gains access to computer files, without permission.

had. See **have**.

haddock (**ha** dŏk) *n.* **haddock** a small, North Atlantic sea fish used as food.

hadn't had not.

●**Hadrian** (AD 76-138) was a Roman emperor. A wall in northern ENGLAND was named after him.

haggard (**ha** gård) *adj.* looking tired and ill because of pain or worry.

haggle (**ha** gĕl) *vb.* **haggling, haggled** to bargain over or argue about a price.

hail¹ (hāl) *n.* frozen rain falling as ice. **hailstone** *n.* a single lump of hail.

hail² (hāl) *vb.* **hailing, hailed** to call out to in order to attract attention: *Hail that taxi!*

hair (hār) *n.* **1** a thread-like strand that grows from the skin of animals and humans. **2** a mass of these strands, especially on a person's head. **hair-raising** *adj.* extremely frightening. **hairy** *adj.* **hairier, hairiest** covered in hair.

●**Haiti**. See Supplement, **Countries**.

hake (hāk) *n.* **hake** or **hakes** a sea fish like cod.

half (häf) *n.* **halves** (hävz) **1** one of two equal parts which together form a whole. **2** the fraction equal to one divided by two. – *adj.* forming or equal to half. – *adv.* **1** to the extent or amount of one half: *The job is only half finished.* **2** almost: *I'm half dead with exhaustion.*

half-brother or **half-sister** *n.* a brother or sister with whom you have only one parent in common.

half-hearted *adj.* not eager.

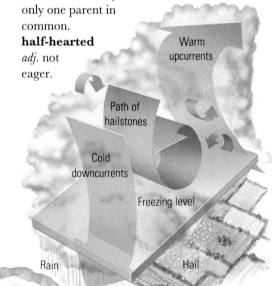

Hail is formed when raindrops in a storm cloud are repeatedly lifted by air currents and frozen high in the cloud. When heavy enough, the hailstones fall out of the cloud.

half mast *n.* the position halfway up a flagpole, where flags are flown as a mark of respect for a dead person.

half-time *n.* an interval between the two halves of a match.

halibut (**ha** li bŭt) *n.* **halibut** a kind of large, flat, sea fish used for food.

hall (höl) *n.* **1** a room or passage just inside the entrance to a house, usually allowing access to other rooms and the stairs. **2** a building or large room, used for concerts, meetings, etc.

Hallowe'en (ha lō **ēn**) *n.* the evening of 31 October.

halo (**hā** lō) *n.* **halos** or **haloes** a ring of light around the head of a saint in paintings, etc.

● **Hals, Frans** (*c.*1580-1666) was a Dutch portrait painter. He is best known for the *Laughing Cavalier.*

halt (hölt) *n.* a short or temporary stop. – *vb.* **halting, halted** to stop or cause to stop.

halter (**höl** tẽr) *n.* a rope or strap for holding and leading a horse by its head.

halve (häv) *vb.* **halving, halved 1** to divide into two equal parts. **2** to reduce by half: *Over the last year we have halved our costs.*

ham¹ (ham) *n.* the top part of the back leg of a pig, salted and smoked and used as food.

ham² (ham) *n.* (*colloquial*) **1** a bad actor. **2** an amateur radio operator.

hamlet (**ham** lit) *n.* a small village.

hammer (**ha** mẽr) *n.* a tool with a heavy metal head on the end of a handle, used for driving nails into wood. – *vb.* **hammering, hammered 1** to hit with a hammer. **2** to strike loudly and repeatedly: *He hammered on the door.*

● **Hammerstein, Oscar** (1895-1960) wrote the lyrics for musical shows. He is best known for his collaboration with Richard RODGERS on such shows as *The Sound of Music.*

hammock (**ha** mŏk) *n.* a piece of canvas hung at each end and used as a bed, e.g. in a ship.

hamper¹ (**ham** pẽr) *vb.* **hampering, hampered** to hinder the movement of.

hamper² (**ham** pẽr) *n.* a large basket.

hamster (**ham** stẽr) *n.* a small rodent with a short tail and pouches in its mouth for storing food, often kept as a pet.

hand (hand) *n.* **1** the part of the body at the end of each arm, with a thumb, four fingers, and a palm. **2** help; assistance: *Let me give you a hand.* **3** a needle or pointer on a clock, watch, or gauge. **4** (*colloquial*) applause: *Give him a big hand.* **5** See **Horse terms**. – *vb.* **handing, handed** to deliver or give using the hands. – **at hand** nearby; about to happen: *Help is at hand!* – **by hand** delivered by messenger, not by post. – **from hand to mouth** with only enough money and food for immediate needs. – *vb.* **hand down** to pass a tradition, etc. on to the next generation. – **in hand** under control.

handbag *n.* a small bag used mainly by women for carrying money and small items.

handout *n.* money or food given to people who need it.

hands-on *adj.* involving practical experience rather than just information or theory: *Adam got some hands-on experience of nursing by working in a hospital over summer.*

● **Handel, George Frederick** (1685-1759) was a German composer who wrote the *Messiah.*

handicraft (**han** di kräft) *n.* an activity which requires skilful use of the hands, for example pottery or model-making.

handkerchief (**hang** kẽr chif) *n.* **handkerchiefs** a small, square of cloth or soft paper used for wiping your nose.

handle (**han** dẽl) *n.* the part of an object by which it is held so that it may be used or operated. – *vb.* **handling, handled 1** to touch, hold, move, or operate with the hands. **2** to deal with or manage, especially successfully or in the correct way: *You handled a difficult situation very well.* – *n.* **handling.** – **fly off the handle** (*colloquial*) to become extremely angry very suddenly.

handlebars *n.* (*plural*) a curved metal bar for steering a bicycle or motorcycle.

handsome (**han** sŏm) *adj.* **1** good-looking. **2** generous: *He made a handsome donation.*

handy (**han** di) *adj.* **handier, handiest 1** conveniently placed and easy to use. **2** clever with your hands: *He's handy with an axe.*

hang (hang) *vb.* **hanging, hung** (hung) (except for sense **2** which has **hanged** for its past tenses) **1** to fasten or be fastened from above. **2** to suspend by a rope around the neck until dead: *The prisoner hanged himself.* **3** to droop: *He hung his head in shame.*

hanger *n.* a metal, wooden, or plastic frame on which clothes are hung up.

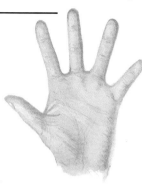

Parts of the body were once used as measuring units. A finger's breadth was a digit and two digits made an inch. From thumb to little finger (stretched) was a span. A yard was measured from the nose to the fingertip of an outstretched arm.

HANGING, DANGLING & GENERALLY MISPLACED
'Gazing out of the window, the boys were playing' or 'Sleeping in my bed, the burglar startled me'. These are examples of 'hanging' participles not relating to the correct subject. The boys are not gazing out of the window, and the burglar is not sleeping in my bed. Correct sentences would be: 'Gazing out of the window, I saw the boys were playing', and 'Sleeping in my bed, I was startled by the burglar'.

Carthage in North Africa was a city founded by the Phoenicians. It fought three great wars against Rome to decide who should rule the Mediterranean world. In the second Punic (the Roman word for Phoenician) war Hannibal crossed the Alps with 50,000 men and many elephants (right) to avoid a sea battle.

hang-glider *n.* a large, light, metal frame with cloth stretched across it, which flies using air currents, with a harness hanging below it for the pilot. – *n.* **hang-gliding.**

hang-up *n.* (*colloquial*) an emotional problem.

hangar (**hang** år) *n.* a large shed in which aircraft are kept.

● **Hannibal** (247-183 BC) was a general from CARTHAGE who led his army over the ALPS to invade ROME.

● **Hanukkah** is a Jewish festival, usually in December, that lasts eight days.

haphazard (hap **haz** ård) *adj.* random; done by chance.

happen (**ha** pěn) *vb.* **happening, happened 1** to take place or occur. **2** to have the good or bad luck to: *I happened to meet him on the way.*

happy (**ha** pi) *adj.* **happier, happiest 1** feeling or showing pleasure or contentment: *a happy smile.* **2** willing: *I'd be happy to go to the concert with you.* – *n.* **happiness.**

happily *adv.* **1** in a happy way. **2** luckily.

happy medium *n.* a reasonable middle course between two extreme positions.

harangue (hå **rang**) *n.* a loud, forceful speech to persuade people to do something. – *vb.* **haranguing, harangued** to give such a speech.

harass (**ha** rås) *vb.* **harassing, harassed** to annoy or trouble a person constantly or frequently. – *adj.* **harassed.** – *n.* **harassment.**

harbour (**här** bŏr) *n.* a place of shelter for ships. – *vb.* **harbouring, harboured** to give shelter or protection to someone, for example a criminal.

hard (härd) *adj.* **1** firm or solid: *The rock was hard beneath her feet.* **2** difficult to do, understand, solve, or explain: *He found his French homework hard to do.* **3** harsh; cruel: *He was a hard taskmaster.* **4** causing or suffering hardship: *They were hard times.* – *adv.* **1** with great effort or energy: *I told him to work hard.* **2** with difficulty; as a result of great effort: *It was a hard-won victory.* – *n.* **hardness.** – **hard at it** working hard. – **hard done by** (*colloquial*) unfairly treated.

hardback *n.* a book with a hard cover.

hard copy *n.* information from a computer printed on paper.

hard disk or **disc** *n.* a metal disk with a magnetic coating, used for storing information in a computer.

harden *vb.* **hardening, hardened 1** to make or become hard or harder. **2** to become less sympathetic: *He hardened his heart to her tears.*

hardened *adj.* toughened through experience: *He is a hardened criminal.*

hardship *n.* severe suffering and pain.

hardware *n.* **1** metal goods such as pots, cutlery, tools, etc. **2** the mechanical and electronic equipment used in computing.

hardwood *n.* wood from a slow-growing deciduous tree, such as the oak or ash.

hardly (**härd** li) *adv.* only with difficulty; scarcely: *She could hardly keep her eyes open.*

hardy (**här** di) *adj.* **hardier, hardiest** tough; strong; able to bear difficult conditions. – *n.* **hardiness.**

● **Hardy, Thomas** (1840-1928) was an English novelist whose works include *Tess of the d'Urbervilles.*

hare (här) *n.* an animal like a rabbit but slightly larger, with longer legs and ears, and which can run very fast.

Unlike rabbits, hares do not burrow. They are also bigger and have longer ears than rabbits. In winter the coat of the mountain hare may turn white, as does the fur of the North American snowshoe rabbit (which is a hare).

harm (härm) *n.* physical or mental injury or damage. – *vb.* **harming, harmed**.

harmony (här mŏ ni) *n.* **harmonies 1** in music, a pleasing combination of two or more notes produced at the same time. **2** agreement in opinions and feelings: *The friends worked together in harmony.*

harmonize or **harmonise** *vb.* **harmonizing, harmonized** to add notes to a simple tune to form harmonies.

harness (här nis) *n.* **1** a set of leather straps used to attach a cart to a horse, and to control the horse's movements. **2** a similar set of straps for attaching to a person's body, for example to hold a child who is just learning to walk. – *vb.* **harnessing, harnessed 1** to put a harness on a horse, person, etc. **2** to control and make use of natural resources, especially to produce power: *Windmills harness the power of the wind to make electricity.*

● **Harold the Second** (1022-66) was the last ANGLO-SAXON king of ENGLAND. He was killed at the Battle of HASTINGS.

harp (härp) *n.* a large, three-sided musical instrument with a series of strings stretched vertically across it, played by plucking the strings with the fingers. – *n.* **harpist**.

harpoon (här pōōn) *n.* a spear with barbs, fastened to a rope, used for catching whales.

harpsichord (härp si körd) *n.* a keyboard instrument in which the strings are plucked mechanically when the player presses the keys.

harsh (härsh) *adj.* **1** grating; unpleasant to the senses: *The gate made a harsh grating noise as it was opened.* **2** strict, cruel, or severe.

harvest (här vist) *n.* **1** the gathering in of ripened crops. **2** the crops gathered. – *vb.* **harvesting, harvested**.

has. See **have**.

haste (hāst) *n.* great urgency of movement.

hasten (hā sĕn) *vb.* **hastening, hastened** to move or do something quickly.

hasty *adj.* **hastier, hastiest** hurried.

● **Hastings, Battle of** In 1066 near a town called Hastings on the Sussex coast, the Normans under William

the Conqueror defeated HAROLD the Second and became rulers of ENGLAND.

hat (hat) *n.* a covering for the head, usually worn out of doors.

hatch[1] (hach) *n.* **1** a door covering an opening in a ship's deck. **2** a door in an aircraft or spacecraft.

hatch[2] (hach) *vb.* **hatching, hatched 1** to break out of an egg: *The chicks hatched out in the nest.* **2** to plan or devise a plot in secret: *They hatched up a scheme to rob the bank.*

hatchet (hach it) *n.* a small axe.

hate (hāt) *vb.* **hating, hated** to dislike very much. – *n.* great dislike.

hatred (hāt rid) *n.* extreme dislike.

haughty (hö ti) *adj.* **haughtier, haughtiest** very proud; arrogant. – *adv.* **haughtily**.

haul (höl) *vb.* **hauling, hauled** to pull with great effort or difficulty. – *n.* **1** the distance to be travelled: *It's only a short haul.* **2** an amount gained at any one time, for example of fish caught in a single net.

haunt (hönt) *vb.* **haunting, haunted 1** (of a ghost) to visit a place regularly. **2** (of unpleasant thoughts) to keep coming back to a person's mind: *I was haunted by the memory of his leaving.* – *n.* (*colloquial*) a favourite place visited frequently. – *adj.* **haunted**.

● **Havana** is the capital of CUBA.

At the Battle of Hastings in 1066 the English fought on foot with axes and spears – no match for the Normans who fought on horseback.

have (hav) *vb.* **has, having, had** **1** to possess.
2 to receive, obtain, or take: *Have a drink!* **3** to
think of or hold in the mind: *I've had an idea.*
4 to experience, enjoy, or suffer: *I have a
headache.* **5** to be in a certain state: *The book has
a page missing.* **6** to take part in or hold: *Let's
have a party.* **7** to be required to: *I had to run fast.*
– *vb.* (*auxiliary*) used with past participles of
verbs to show that an action has been
completed: *I have seen the film.*
haven (hā věn) *n.* a place of safety or rest.
havoc (ha vǒk) *n.* great destruction.

● **Hawaii** (hå wī i). See Supplement, **USA**.

hawk¹ (hök) *n.* a bird of prey with short,
rounded wings, and which is believed to have
very good eyesight: *Watch him like a hawk.*
hawk² (hök) *vb.* **hawking, hawked** to
carry goods round trying to sell them.
hawthorn (hö thörn) *n.* a thorny tree or
shrub with pink or white flowers and red
berries.

● **Hawthorne, Nathaniel** (1804-64) was an
American novelist and author of *The Scarlet
Letter.*

hay (hā) *n.* grass which has been cut and dried,
used as food for cattle.
hay fever *n.* an allergic reaction to pollen,
which causes sneezing and sore eyes.

● **Haydn** (hī děn), **Franz** (1732-1809) was an
Austrian composer – the 'father of the symphony'.

hazard (ha zǎrd) *n.* something which is likely to
cause harm or danger. – *vb.* **hazarding,
hazarded** to put forward a guess.
hazardous *adj.* dangerous.
haze (hāz) *n.* a thin mist, cloud of dust, or
smoke which makes it difficult to see.
hazy *adj.* **hazier, haziest** **1** misty. **2** vague:
She was hazy about the details of the plan.
hazel (hā zěl) *n.* a small tree or shrub on which
nuts grow; its wood.
he (hē) *pron.* a male person or animal already
referred to.
head (hed) *n.* **1** the top or front part of a body,
containing the eyes, nose, mouth, brain, and
ears. **2** the head thought of as the centre of
intelligence, imagination, ability, etc.: *Use your
head!* **3** the person with the most authority in an

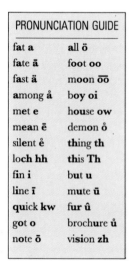

Scientists have listed
nearly 300 different
kinds of **hawk**.
Falcons form
one group.
Hawking or
falconry is an
ancient sport dating
back to ancient China
and very popular in the
Middle Ages. It is the
art of training these
birds of prey to hunt
game. The trainer
(falconer) hoods the bird
to calm it and attaches
leg straps (*jesses*).

A 16th-century falconer

PRONUNCIATION GUIDE

fat **a**	all **ö**
fate **ā**	foot **oo**
fast **ä**	moon **ōō**
among **å**	boy **oi**
met **e**	house **ow**
mean **ē**	demon **ŏ**
silent **ě**	thing **th**
loch **hh**	this **Th**
fin **i**	but **u**
line **ī**	mute **ū**
quick **kw**	fur **û**
got **o**	brochure **ů**
note **ō**	vision **zh**

organization, country, etc.: *He is head of the civil
service.* **4** the top or upper part of something,
e.g. a table or bed. **5** the top part of a plant
which produces leaves or flowers. **6** the side of
a coin bearing the head of a monarch, etc.:
Heads or tails? – *vb.* **heading, headed** **1** to be
at the front of or top of: *We headed the queue.*
2 to be in charge of. **3** to move in a certain
direction: *They headed for the door.* – **keep
your head** to remain calm in a crisis.
headgear *n.* anything worn on the head.
headline *n.* a title of a newspaper article,
written above the article in large letters.
headquarters *n.* the centre of an
organization from which activities are
controlled.
headstrong *adj.* (of people) difficult to
persuade; determined; obstinate.
headwind *n.* a wind which is blowing towards
someone.
heal (hēl) *vb.* **healing, healed** to make or
become healthy or normal again.
health (helth) *n.* the state of being physically
and mentally fit and free from illness.
healthy *adj.* **healthier, healthiest** **1** having
or showing good health. **2** in a good state: *The
country has a healthy economy.*
heap (hēp) *n.* **1** a collection of things in an
untidy pile or mass. **2** (usually in *plural*;
colloquial) a large amount or number.

hear (hēr) *vb.* **hearing, heard** (hûrd) **1** to perceive sounds with the ear; to listen to. **2** to be told about or informed of: *I have heard about his problems.* **3** to be contacted by letter or telephone: *I heard from my Swedish friend last week.* – *n.* **hearer.** – *vb.* **hear out** to allow someone to say what they want to say.

hearing *n.* **1** the sense by which sound is perceived. **2** the distance within which something can be heard. **3** an opportunity to state a case: *They gave him a fair hearing.*

hearsay *n.* rumour; gossip.

hearse (hûrs) *n.* a car used for carrying a coffin.

● **Hearst** (hûrst), **William Randolph** (1863-1951) was an American newspaper publisher.

heart (härt) *n.* **1** the hollow, muscular organ inside the chest, which pumps blood around the body. **2** the central or most important part: *This is the heart of the problem.* **3** a playing card with a red symbol of such a shape on it.

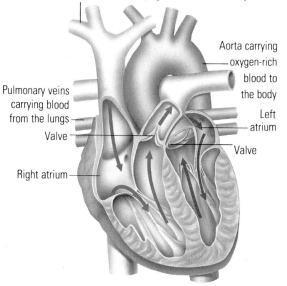

Superior vena cava carrying blood from the body

Aorta carrying oxygen-rich blood to the body

Pulmonary veins carrying blood from the lungs

Valve

Left atrium

Valve

Right atrium

An adult heart weighs about 300 g and beats over 100,000 times a day.

● In an adult person the heart works at between 70 and 80 beats a minute. The blood carries OXYGEN from the LUNGS and energy from the food we eat. Arteries carry this rich red blood to feed the body. Veins carry away 'tired blood' to the heart to be recharged with OXYGEN.

– **break someone's heart** to cause someone great sorrow. – **by heart** by or from memory.

heart attack *n.* a sudden failure of the heart to work properly.

heartbeat *n.* the sound of the heart pumping blood.

heartless *adj.* cruel; very unkind.

heat (hēt) *n.* **1** the state of being hot; the high temperature produced by something. **2** warmth of feeling, especially anger or excitement: *She regretted what she had said in the heat of the argument.* **3** in a sports competition, a preliminary race or contest which eliminates competitors. – *vb.* **heating, heated** to make or become hot or warm.

● Heat is a form of energy. It travels in three ways: by conduction (a conductor such as a metal iron allows heat to pass through it); by convection (molecules in the air carrying heat from a radiator); by radiation (the Sun's heat travels in the form of electromagnetic waves).

heatwave *n.* a period of very hot weather.

heath (hēth) *n.* an area of open, common, flat land with poor soil, often covered with bushes.

heathen (hē Thĕn) *n.* a person who does not follow one of the established religions. – *adj.*

heather (he Thĕr) *n.* a low shrub which grows especially on open land with poor soil.

heave (hēv) *vb.* **heaving, heaved** to lift or pull with great effort.

heaven (he vĕn) *n.* **1** the place believed to be the abode of God, angels, and the righteous after death. **2** (usually in *plural*) the sky: *The heavens opened and we got soaked.*

heavenly *adj.* **1** (*colloquial*) very pleasant; beautiful. **2** of or from heaven or the sky.

The heart is a pump which powers our blood or circulatory system, which is a network of blood vessels. Arteries take blood rich in food and oxygen from the heart to all parts of the body. Blood which has used up all its oxygen is carried back to the heart by veins.

heavy (**he** vi) *adj.* **heavier, heaviest 1** having great weight. **2** great in size, amount, force, power, etc.: *There was heavy traffic in the city.* **3** severe, intense, or excessive: *They experienced heavy fighting.* – *n.* **heaviness.** – **heavy going** difficult or slow progress.

Hebrew (**he** broō) *n.* the ancient language of the Hebrews, revived and spoken in a modern form by Jews in ISRAEL. – *adj.* of the Hebrew language or people.

● **Hebrews** The Jewish people were once known as Hebrews or Israelites. There were twelve tribes descended from ABRAHAM. Their greatest leader was MOSES.

hectare (**hek** tār) or (**hek** tär) *n.* a metric unit of land measurement (10,000 square metres).

hectic (**hek** tik) *adj.* busy and excited.

● **Hector** in Greek mythology, was a prince of TROY, killed by ACHILLES.

hedge (hej) *n.* a fence or boundary formed by bushes and shrubs planted close together. – *vb.* **hedging, hedged 1** to avoid making a decision or giving a clear answer. **2** to enclose an area of land with a hedge. **3** to protect yourself from possible loss or criticism in a bet or argument, by backing both sides: *I hedged my bets and agreed with no one.*

hedgehog *n.* a small brown insect-eating animal with a thick coat covered with spines.

heel (hēl) *n.* **1** the rounded back part of the foot. **2** the part of a sock, shoe, etc. that covers the heel. – **kick your heels** to be kept waiting for some time. – **dig your heels in** to behave stubbornly.

heifer (**he** fẽr) *n.* a young cow.

height (hīt) *n.* **1** the distance from the bottom of something to the top. **2** a distance above the ground from a recognized point, especially above sea-level.

heighten *vb.* **heightening, heightened** to make or become higher, greater, or stronger.

heir (ār) *n.* a person who by law receives wealth, a title, etc. when the owner or holder dies.

held. See **hold**.

● **Helen** of TROY, in Greek mythology, was the wife of Menelaus, king of Sparta, but ran away with PARIS, prince of TROY. Menelaus followed with a great army, starting the Trojan War.

Helicopter is a modern word made of two Greek ones: *helikos* meaning 'screw' and *pteron* meaning 'wing'

A helicopter has spinning rotor blades which provide both 'lift' and 'thrust'. The blade has the same aerofoil shape as a plane's fixed wing. As it spins, air flows over the blade, producing lift.

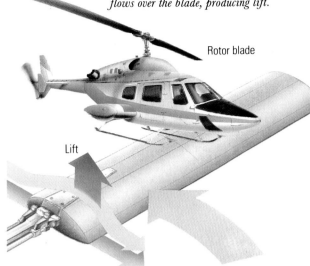

Rotor blade

Lift

helicopter (**he** li kop tẽr) *n.* an aircraft, lifted and propelled by rotating blades, which takes off and lands vertically.

helium (**hē** li ủm) *n.* a light gas (symbol **He**) which does not burn, used in airships.

hell (hel) *n.* believed to be the place of punishment for the wicked after death.

he'll he will.

helm (helm) *n.* the wheel or tiller by which a ship is steered. – **at the helm** in control.

helmet (**hel** mit) *n.* a hard, protective covering for the head.

help (help) *vb.* **helping, helped 1** to assist; to contribute towards making difficulties, pain, etc. less severe; to improve a situation. **2** to prevent or control: *I can't help the bad weather.* – *n.* **1** a person or thing that helps. **2** a remedy or relief. – *n.* **helper.**

helpful *adj.* giving help; useful.

helpless *adj.* weak and defenceless.

hem (hem) *n.* a bottom edge of a piece of clothing, folded over and sewn down. – *vb.* **hemming, hemmed** to make a hem on.

● **Hemingway, Ernest** (1899-1961) was an American author whose works include *A Farewell to Arms* and *For Whom the Bell Tolls.*

hemisphere (**he** mi sfẽr) *n.* **1** one half of a sphere. **2** one half of the Earth's sphere divided into the **Northern hemisphere** and the **Southern hemisphere.**

hemp (hemp) *n.* a plant producing coarse fibre.

hen (hen) *n.* a female bird.

hence (hens) *adv.* **1** for this reason: *She suffers from vertigo, hence her unwillingness to climb up the tower.* **2** from this time: *a few days hence.*

henge (henj) *n.* a circular, prehistoric monument consisting of large upright stones.

●**Henry** is the name of eight English kings. Henry the First was the son of WILLIAM THE CONQUEROR; Henry the Second quarrelled with Thomas BECKET; Henry the Fifth was a brilliant soldier; Henry the Eighth married six times and broke away from the pope.

●**Henry the Navigator** (1394-1460) was a Portuguese prince who set up a navigation school and pioneered exploration.

heptagon (**hep** tå gon) *n.* a shape with seven sides. − *adj.* **heptagonal** (hep **tag** ổ nål).

her (hûr) *pron.* & *adj.* (of or belonging to) a female person or animal, or a thing thought of as female, e.g. a ship.

herald (**he** råld) *vb.* **heralding, heralded** to be a sign of the approach of; to proclaim: *Dark clouds in the sky heralded a storm.*

herb (hûrb) *n.* a plant used to flavour food or to make medicines. Sage, thyme, parsley, garlic, rosemary, basil, and fennel are just a few used in cooking. In the days before modern medicine, herbs were used to treat many illnesses.

herbivore (**hûr** bi vör) *n.* an animal which eats only plants, and not other animals.

herd (hûrd) *n.* a large group of animals, especially cattle, which live and feed together.

here (hēr) *adv.* at, in, or to this place: *Put the dish down here.* − *n.* this place. − *interjection* calling for someone's attention. − **neither here nor there** of no importance.

hereditary (hễ **red** i tå ri) *adj.* able to be passed on from parents to children.

heredity (hễ **red** i ti) *n.* **heredities** the passing on of physical and mental characteristics from parents to children.

hermit (**hûr** mit) *n.* a person who lives alone, especially for religious reasons.

hermit crab *n.* a small crab that lives in another sea-creature's discarded shell.

hero (**hēr** ō) *n.* **heroes** **1** a person who is admired for bravery and courage. **2** the main male character in a story, play, etc.

heroic (hễ **rō** ik) *adj.* very brave.

heroism (**he** rō i zễm) *n.* great bravery.

●**Herod the Great** (74-4 BC) was a ruler in Judea who, according to the NEW TESTAMENT, ordered all the male infants in the town of BETHLEHEM to be slaughtered.

The rear parts of a hermit crab are not protected by a shell, so for protection it backs into the disused shell of a sea snail.

Stonehenge − a prehistoric circle of standing stones on Salisbury Plain, England − is the most dramatic and most famous of such early monuments. It was probably built as a place of worship to the Sun and Moon sometime after 1800 BC. The illustration shows how the massive stone blocks were dragged to the site on wooden rollers.

heroine (**he** rō in) *n.* **1** a woman admired for her bravery and courage. **2** the main female character in a play, story, etc.

heron (**he** rŏn) *n.* a large wading bird, with long legs and a long neck.

herring (**he** ring) *n.* **herring** or **herrings** a small sea fish, valued as food.

hers (hûrz) *pron.* someone or something belonging to her.

herself (hûr **self**) *pron.* **1** the reflexive form of **her** and **she**: *She made herself a dress.* **2** used for emphasis: *She did it herself.* **3** (also **by herself**) alone; without help.

hesitate (**he** zi tāt) *vb.* **hesitating, hesitated** to stop briefly, especially because of uncertainty. − *n.* **hesitation**.

heterosexual (he tĕ rō **sek** shoo ål) *adj.* sexually attracted to people of the opposite sex.

hexagon (**hek** så gŏn) *n.* a shape with six sides. − *adj.* **hexagonal** (hek **sag** ŏ nål).

heyday (**hā** dā) *n.* a time of great success.

hibernate (**hī** bĕr nāt) *vb.* **hibernating, hibernated** (of certain animals) to pass the winter in a sleep-like state. − *n.* **hibernation**.

● Before hibernating, animals eat as much food as they can find and then seek a warm, safe place to sleep through the winter.

hiccup or **hiccough** (**hi** kup) *n.* **1** the sound caused by a sudden breathing in of air caused by a spasm in the diaphragm. **2** (*colloquial*) a minor problem or interruption: *The tape machine broke down causing a slight hiccup in the proceedings.* − *vb.* **hiccuping, hiccuped** or **hiccoughing, hiccoughed**.

hide¹ (hīd) *vb.* **hiding, hid** (hid), **hidden** (**hi** dĕn) **1** to put a person or thing in a place where they cannot be easily found. **2** to keep information or feelings secret: *She could not hide her pleasure at the news.* **hidden** *adj.* difficult to see or find.

hide² (hīd) *n.* the skin of an animal.

hideous (**hi** di ŭs) *adj.* extremely ugly.

hieroglyph (**hīr** ŏ glif) *n.* a picture or symbol used to represent a word, syllable, or sound, especially in the ancient Egyptian language. **hieroglyphic** *adj.* relating to hieroglyphs.

hi-fi (**hī** fī) *n.* equipment which reproduces sound accurately.

high (hī) *adj.* **1** reaching up to or situated at a great distance from the bottom: *The city is full of high buildings.* **2** of a particular height: *The tree is about three metres high.* **3** great; intense: *There was a high wind.* − *adv.* at or to a height; in or into a raised position.

highbrow *adj.* (of art, literature, etc.) intellectual.

high explosive *n.* a very powerful explosive, such as dynamite.

high fidelity *n.* the reproduction of sound with great accuracy.

highlight *n.* **1** the best or most memorable part of something: *The highlight of our evening at the circus was the trapeze act.* **2** a lighter patch in someone's hair, usually made artificially. − *vb.* **highlighting, highlighted** to draw attention to or emphasize: *She uses make-up to highlight the blueness of her eyes.*

highly *adv.* **1** very: *It is highly likely that she will pass.* **2** with approval: *He speaks highly of her.*

high-powered *adj.* very powerful; efficient.

high tide *n.* the time when the tide is farthest up the shore.

highway *n.* (especially *US*) a public road.

highwayman *n.* **highwaymen** (*historical*) a robber, usually on horseback, who attacked and robbed people travelling on public roads.

hijack (**hī** jak) *vb.* **hijacking, hijacked** to take control of a vehicle while it is moving and force it to go to a place chosen by the hijacker. − *n.* **hijacker**. − *n.* **hijacking**.

hike (hīk) *n.* a long walk, usually in the country, often carrying equipment on your back. − *vb.* **hiking, hiked** to go on a hike. − *n.* **hiker**.

hilarious (hi **lār** i ŭs) *adj.* very funny.

hill (hil) *n.* an area of high land, smaller than a mountain.

hilt (hilt) *n.* the handle of a sword or dagger.

● **Hilton, Conrad** (1887-1979) was an American hotel owner, 'king of the innkeepers'.

him (him) *pron.* a male person or animal. **himself** *pron.* **1** the reflexive form of **him** and **he**: *He taught himself to dance.* **2** used for emphasis: *He did it himself.* **3** (also **by himself**) alone; without help.

Early Egyptian hieroglyphs represented different objects. Later ones stood for sounds, rather than things.

ah   i   *   w   b   p   f   m

n   r   h   ḥ   ch   ch or sh   s   z or s

sh   q   k   g   t   th   d   dj

* vowel sound does not exist in English

●**Himalayas** This mountain range is the highest in the world and separates INDIA from CHINA. Many of ASIA's greatest rivers rise here.

hind¹ (hīnd) *adj.* at the back: *The dog sat up on its hind legs.*

hind² (hīnd) *n.* a female deer.

hinder (**hin** děr) *vb.* **hindering, hindered** to delay or keep back; to prevent progress.

Hindu (**hin** dōō) *n.* a person who practises Hinduism. – *adj.* of Hindus or Hinduism. **Hinduism** *n.* the main religion of INDIA, which includes worship of many gods, a belief in reincarnation, and the arrangement of people in society in different levels or castes.

hinge (hinj) *n.* the movable joint by means of which a door is fastened to a door-frame, and on which the door turns when it opens or closes. – *vb.* **hinging, hinged 1** to hang or turn on. **2** to depend on: *The success of the plan hinged on his ability to pass unnoticed in the crowd.* – *adj.* **hinged**.

hint (hint) *n.* a statement or piece of advice that passes on information without giving it openly or directly: *She gave him a hint to help him answer the question.* – *vb.* **hinting, hinted** to suggest, especially slightly or indirectly.

hip (hip) *n.* the upper, fleshy part of the thigh just below the waist.

Hippocratic oath (**hi** pō cra tik **ōth**) *n.* an oath taken by doctors by which they agree to observe a code about rules of behaviour. It is named after *Hippocrates*, a Greek physician of the 5th century BC.

hippodrome (**hi** pǒ drōm) *n.* in ancient Rome, an open-air racecourse for horses and chariots.

hippopotamus (hi pǒ **pot** å mǔs) *n.* **hippopotamuses** a large African mammal with very thick, wrinkled skin and short legs, living in or near rivers and lakes.

●Hippopotamus means 'river horse'. In fact the hippo is related to the pig. Of all land animals only the elephant is bigger.

hire (hīr) *vb.* **hiring, hired 1** to use something temporarily which belongs to someone else in exchange for money. **2** to employ someone to do some work for you. – *n.* an act of hiring.

●**Hiroshima** (hi **rosh** i må) or (hi rǒ **shē** må) is a Japanese city on which the first atomic bomb was dropped on 6 August 1945.

HISTORY HIGHLIGHTS	
BC	
c. 2600	Pyramids built in Egypt
400	Age of Pericles begins in Athens
4	Probable birth of Jesus at Bethlehem
AD	
476	End of Western Roman Empire
800	Charlemagne crowned Holy Roman Emperor
1066	Norman invasion of England
1096	Start of first Crusade
1260	Kublai Khan becomes ruler of China
1341-51	Bubonic plague (Black Death) ravages Europe
1453	Turks capture Constantinople: end of Eastern Roman Empire
1492	Christopher Columbus lands in the New World
1588	English fleet defeats the Spanish Armada
1620	Mayflower sails to America with Pilgrim Fathers
1642-6	English Civil War
1775	American War of Independence begins
1789	French Revolution
1815	Napoleon finally defeated at Waterloo
1854	Crimean War begins
1861	American Civil War begins
1914	Outbreak of First World War
1917	Russian Revolution
1939	Second World War begins
1945	Atomic bombs dropped on Hiroshima and Nagasaki
1947	India becomes independent
1949	Mao ZeDong establishes Communist China
1969	First person lands on the Moon
1980	AIDS virus first recognized
1991	USSR is officially dissolved. Civil War in Yugoslavia

hirsute (**hûr** sūt) *adj.* hairy; shaggy.

his (hiz) *adj.* of or belonging to a male person or animal. – *pron.* something belonging to him.

Hispanic (hi **span** ik) *adj.* of SPAIN, the Spanish, or other Spanish-speaking countries and peoples, e.g. Mexican.

hiss (his) *n.* a sharp sound like that of a long *s.* – *vb.* **hissing, hissed** (of snakes, geese, people, etc.) to make a hiss.

historian (hi **stör** i ån) *n.* a person who studies or writes about history.

historic (hi **sto** rik) *adj.* famous in history. **historical** *adj.* of or about people or events from history: *She writes historical novels.*

history (**hi** stǒ ri) *n.* **histories 1** the study of events that happened in the past. **2** a record or account of past events and developments: *He wrote a history of the computer.*

hit (hit) *vb.* **hitting, hit 1** to strike a person or thing with a blow, missile, etc. **2** to knock against something, especially hard or violently: *She hit her head on the door.* **3** to drive a ball with a stroke of a bat. – *n.* **1** a blow, stroke, or shot. **2** (*colloquial*) something which is popular or successful: *The musical was an immediate hit.*

hitch (hich) *vb.* **hitching, hitched 1** to fasten with a piece of rope. **2** (*colloquial*) to hitchhike: *They hitched a ride.* – *n.* a minor, temporary difficulty: *The concert went without a hitch.*

hitchhike (hich hīk) *vb.* **hitchhiking, hitchhiked** to travel by means of free rides in other people's vehicles. – *n.* **hitchhiker**.

● **Hitler, Adolf** (1889-1945) was the *Führer*, or leader of Nazi Germany during the Second WORLD WAR. Millions of people died in Nazi death camps.

● **HIV** *abbreviation* human immunodeficiency virus, any of several types of virus which cause AIDS.

hive (hīv) *n.* a box for housing bees. – *vb.* **hive off**; **hiving, hived** to separate a company from a larger group.

hoard (hörd) *n.* a store of money, food, treasure, usually hidden away for use in the future. – *vb.* **hoarding, hoarded** to store food, money etc. for use in the future. – *n.* **hoarder**.

hoarding (hör ding) *n.* a large, wooden surface on which to display posters etc.

hoarse (hörs) *adj.* (of the voice) rough and croaking, especially because of a sore throat or too much shouting.

hoax (hōks) *n.* a trick played to deceive people, done either humorously or spitefully. – *vb.* **hoaxing, hoaxed** to trick. – *n.* **hoaxer**.

hobble (ho bel) *vb.* **hobbling, hobbled** to walk with difficulty taking unsteady steps.

hobby (ho bi) *n.* **hobbies** an activity or occupation done in spare time for relaxation.

Hobson's choice (hob sonz chois) *n.* the choice of taking what is offered, or nothing.

hock¹ (hok) *n.* a German white wine from the RHINE valley.

hock² (hok) *n.* a joint in the hind leg of a horse.

hockey (ho ki) *n.* **1** a game for two teams of eleven players in which each team tries to score goals, played with long clubs which are bent at one end and a small, hard ball. **2** (*US*) same as **ice hockey**.

Hoard and horde: the first word means a store or stockpile, while a horde is a large group of people or insects.

● **Hockney, David** (1937-) is an English painter.

hoe (hō) *n.* a long-handled tool with a metal blade at one end, used for loosening soil, removing weeds, etc. – *vb.* **hoeing, hoed**.

hog (hog) *n.* **1** a castrated male pig. **2** (*US*) a pig. – *vb.* **hogging, hogged** (*colloquial*) to use or occupy selfishly: *My sister hogs the bathroom!*

● **Hogarth** (hō gärth), **William** (1697-1764) was an English satirical painter.

Hogmanay (hog mà nā) *n.* New Year's Eve.

hoist (hoist) *vb.* **hoisting, hoisted 1** to lift or heave up something heavy using ropes and pulleys. **2** See **Flag terms**.

● **Holbein** (hol bīn), **Hans** (1497-1543) was a German painter who worked in England.

hold¹ (hōld) *vb.* **holding, held** (held) **1** to have or keep in your hand, or in something else stated. **2** to support, keep, or stay in a particular state: *Despite all his pulling the knot held firm.* **3** to detain: *She was held in prison for three months.* **4** to contain or be able to contain: *The bottle holds three litres.* **5** to cause to take place; to conduct: *Let's hold a meeting.* **6** to have or possess: *She holds the world record.* – *n.* power; influence: *She has a hold over him.* – *n.* **holder**. – **get hold of** (*colloquial*) **1** to manage to speak to someone: *He's impossible to get hold of at weekends.* **2** to get, buy, or obtain: *I can't get hold of that colour of paint anywhere.* – *vb.* **hold down** to manage to keep: *He cannot hold down a job.* – **hold forth** to give opinions about something, usually loudly and at great length. – *vb.* **hold off** to delay, not begin: *I hope the rain holds off.* – *vb.* **hold on 1** to keep: *I'm holding on to the receipt in case I want to get my money back.* **2** (*colloquial*) (especially when telephoning) to wait: *Can you hold on a minute?* – *vb.* **hold out 1** to continue to stand firm, resist difficulties: *We can hold out against the enemy until they surrender.* **2** to continue to demand or fight for something: *I held out for more money.* – *vb.* **hold with** to approve of.

hold² (hōld) *n.* the place where cargo is stored in ships and aircraft.

hole (hōl) *n.* **1** an opening or gap in or through something: *There was a hole in the wall.* **2** an animal's burrow. **3** (*colloquial*) an unpleasant or gloomy place. – *vb.* **holing, holed 1** to make a

Otto I, who became king of Germany in 936, wanted to revive the old Roman Empire. In 962 he had the pope crown him Emperor Augustus, of the **Holy Roman Empire**, founding a line of emperors which lasted until 1806. By 1100 the Empire stretched from the Baltic, nearly to the Mediterranean.

Otto I, also known as Otto the Great, the first Holy Roman Emperor

hole in. **2** to hit a ball into a hole. – **pick holes in** to find fault with.

holiday (**ho** li dā) *n.* (often in *plural*) a period of time taken as a break from work or school often spent away from home. – *vb.* **holidaying, holidayed** to spend a holiday.

● **Holiday, Billie** (1915-59) was an American JAZZ singer.

● **Holland**. See **Netherlands**.

hollow (**ho** lō) *adj.* **1** containing an empty space; not solid. **2** sunken: *The old man had hollow cheeks.* **3** (of sounds) echoing as if made in a hollow place. **4** worthless; insincere: *He made hollow promises that he knew he would not keep.* – *n.* a small valley or depression in the land. – *vb.* **hollowing, hollowed** to make a hole in.

holly (**ho** li) *n.* **hollies** a tree or shrub with dark, shiny evergreen leaves.

hollyhock (**ho** li hok) *n.* a tall flowering plant.

● **Hollywood** is a district of Los Angeles, USA, centre of the cinema industry.

● **Holmes** (hōmz), **Sherlock** is the detective who appears with his friend Dr Watson in the stories

of Arthur Conan DOYLE (1859-1930).

holocaust (**ho** lǒ köst) *n.* large-scale destruction and loss of life.

hologram (**ho** lǒ gram) *n.* a kind of photograph, created by lasers which shows objects in three dimensions.

holster (**hōl** stěr) *n.* a leather case for a pistol.

holy (**hō** li) *adj.* **holier, holiest** belonging to or associated with God or gods; sacred. – *n.* **holiness**.

● **Holy Roman Empire** is the name of the German empire founded by Otto the First in 962 and which continued in name until 1806.

home (hōm) *n.* **1** the place where someone lives. **2** the country or area someone originally comes from. **3** a place where people who need care or rest live, e.g. orphans or old people. – *adj.* of your home, country, or family. – **at home** feeling at ease or familiar with a place. – **bring home to** to make quite obvious to. **homesick** *adj.* sad and depressed at being away from home. – *n.* **homesickness**.

homeopathy (hō mē **o** påth i) *n.* a way of healing a patient by giving them small doses of drugs which normally make them ill.

Around the fire, poets of ancient Greece, such as Homer, told stories of the capture of cities and warriors dying bravely.

SOME HOMOPHONES	
beer	bier
here	hear
lie	lye
meet	meat
scull	skull
sum	some
there	their
wait	weight
ware	wear

PRONUNCIATION GUIDE	
fat **a**	all **ö**
fate **ā**	foot **oo**
fast **ä**	moon **ōō**
among **å**	boy **oi**
met **e**	house **ow**
mean **ē**	demon **ô**
silent **ĕ**	thing **th**
loch **hh**	this **Th**
fin **i**	but **u**
line **ī**	mute **ū**
quick **kw**	fur **û**
got **o**	brochure **ů**
note **ō**	vision **zh**

● **Homer** (hō mĕr) was a Greek poet who lived around 800 BC. He wrote two great poems, the *Iliad* and the *Odyssey*.

homonym (ho mŏ nim) *n.* a word having the same sound and spelling as another word, but a different meaning, for example *kind* (helpful) and *kind* (sort).

homophone (ho mŏ fōn) *n.* a word which has the same sound as another word but has a different spelling and meaning, for example *bear* and *bare*.

homosexual (hō mō **sek** shoo ål) *n.* a person who is sexually attracted to people of the same sex.

● **Honduras**. See Supplement, **Countries**.

honest (o nĕst) *adj.* truthful; trustworthy.
honestly *adv.* **1** in an honest way. **2** truly.
honesty *n.* the state of being honest.
honey (hu ni) *n.* **honeys** the edible, thick, sweet substance made by bees.
honeycomb *n.* the structure formed by the rows of wax cells in which bees store honey.
honeymoon *n.* a holiday taken by a newly married couple.
honeysuckle (hu ni su kĕl) *n.* a climbing garden shrub with sweet-smelling flowers.

● **Hong Kong** is a tiny British colony off the coast of CHINA. It will be returned to the Chinese government in 1997.

honour (o nŏr) *n.* **1** great respect or public regard. **2** a pleasure or privilege: *It was an honour to accompany him.* – *vb.* **honouring, honoured 1** to respect greatly. **2** to give someone an award, title, or honour as a mark of respect for their ability or an achievement.
honourable *adj.* worthy of honour.

hood (hood) *n.* **1** a usually loose covering for the whole head, often attached to a coat at the collar. **2** a folding, usually removable, roof or cover on a car, cooker, push-chair, etc.

hoof (hōōf) *n.* **hoofs** or **hooves** the horny part at the end of the feet of horses, cows, etc.

hook (hook) *n.* a small piece of plastic, wood, or metal shaped like a J, used for catching and holding things. – *vb.* **hooking, hooked** to catch with or fasten with a hook.

hooligan (hōōli gån) *n.* a violent or badly-behaved young person. – *n.* **hooliganism**.

hoop (hōōp) *n.* a ring of metal used round barrels, or a large wooden ring used as a toy.

hoot (hōōt) *n.* **1** the call of an owl. **2** the sound of a car horn, siren, steam whistle, etc. – *vb.* **hooting, hooted** to make a hoot.

hop[1] (hop) *vb.* **hopping, hopped 1** (of people) to jump on one leg. **2** (of small birds, animals, and insects) to jump on both or all legs. – *n.* a short jump. – **hopping mad** (*colloquial*) very angry indeed.

hop[2] (hop) *n.* a tall climbing plant; the dried fruit of which is used to flavour beer.

hope (hōp) *n.* **1** a desire for something, with some confidence of obtaining it. **2** a person, thing, or event upon which someone is relying for help: *She is the only hope that I have left.* – *vb.* **hoping, hoped** to wish or desire that something may happen.
hopefully *adv.* **1** in a hopeful way. **2** (*colloquial*) it is to be hoped: *Hopefully, they won't be late.*
hopeless *adj.* **1** not likely to be successful. **2** (*colloquial*) not good: *I'm hopeless at drawing.*

● **Hopi** (hō pi) a NATIVE AMERICAN tribe of the south western UNITED STATES.

horde (hörd) *n.* a crowd or large group.

horizon (hŏ **rī** zŏn) *n.* the line at which the Earth and the sky seem to meet.

horizontal (ho ri **zon** tål) *adj.* at right angles to vertical; parallel to the horizon; level or flat.

hormone (**hör** mōn) *n.* a chemical substance produced by some part of a plant or animal body, which has a specific effect on that body.

horn (hörn) *n.* **1** either of a pair of hard, bony objects which grow on the heads of cows, sheep, etc.; a deer's antlers. **2** the bone-like substance of which horns are made. **3** (also **French horn**) a coiled brass wind instrument. **4** an apparatus for making a warning sound, especially on a vehicle.

● Horn is a kind of hard skin. Finger and toe nails are made of horn. So are the feathers and beaks of birds.

hornet (**hör** nit) *n.* a large wasp.

horoscope (**ho** rŏ skōp) *n.* a description of a person's future based on the position of the stars and planets at the time of their birth.

horrible (**ho** rå bĕl) *adj.* **1** causing horror or fear. **2** (*colloquial*) unpleasant. – *adv.* **horribly**.

horror (**ho** rŏr) *n.* great fear or disgust.

horse (hörs) *n.* a large, four-legged animal with a long mane and tail, ridden for pleasure and used to pull carts, etc.

horseshoe *n.* a piece of curved iron nailed to a horse's hoof to protect the foot.

hose (hōz) *n.* (also **hosepipe**) a flexible tube for directing water, e.g. for watering plants.

Percheron, a draught horse from France

The **horse** was one of the first animals to be tamed, valued for its speed and strength. The horse we know today developed over millions of years from a creature the size of a fox with short legs and four-toed feet. It was called Eohippus or 'dawn horse'.

Thoroughbred   Arab   Morgan

American Saddlebred

Camargue   Lusitano   Lipizzaner

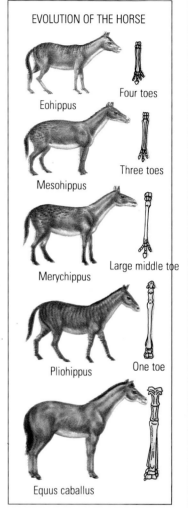

EVOLUTION OF THE HORSE

Eohippus — Four toes

Mesohippus — Three toes

Merychippus — Large middle toe

Pliohippus — One toe

Equus caballus

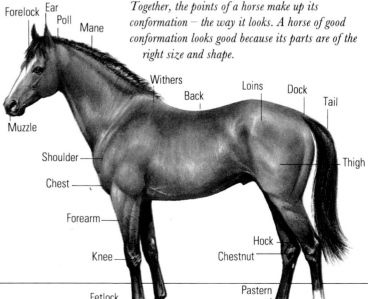

The different parts of a horse are called points. Together, the points of a horse make up its conformation – the way it looks. A horse of good conformation looks good because its parts are of the right size and shape.

Forelock Ear Poll Mane

Withers Back Loins Dock Tail

Muzzle

Shoulder Thigh

Chest

Forearm

Hock Chestnut

Knee

Fetlock Pastern

Hoof Heel

HORSE TERMS

aids the signals given by a rider to tell a horse or pony what to do.

bit the metal or rubber device attached to the bridle and placed in the horse's mouth.

bridle the part of the saddlery placed over the horse's head.

colt a young, male ungelded horse.

dressage a horse's performance of set manoeuvres.

eventing a (usually) three-day competition: dressage, cross-country, and show jumping.

filly a female foal.

gait the pace of a horse: walk, trot, canter, gallop.

hand a unit of measurement of a horse's height.

mare an adult female horse.

near side the left side of a horse

off side the right side of a horse.

stallion an adult male horse.

hospice (ho spis) *n.* a home which cares for people suffering from incurable diseases.

hospitable (ho **spit** å běl) *adj.* showing kindness to guests or strangers.

hospital (ho spi tål) *n.* a place where people who are physically or mentally ill receive medical or surgical care and nursing.

hospitality (hos pi **tal** i ty) *n.* a friendly welcome for guests or strangers.

host¹ (hōst) *n.* **1** a person who receives and entertains guests or strangers in their own home. **2** a person who introduces performers, etc. on a television or radio show. – *vb.* **hosting, hosted** to act as a host.

host² (hōst) *n.* a very large number.

hostage (ho stij) *n.* a person who is held prisoner as a guarantee that the conditions of an agreement will be carried out.

hostel (ho stěl) *n.* **1** a building which provides overnight accommodation as a charity, especially for the homeless. **2** a youth hostel.

hostile (ho stīl) *adj.* unfriendly; aggressive. **hostility** (hǒ **stil** i ti) *n.* **hostilities** (in *plural*) acts of war; battles.

hot (hot) *adj.* **hotter, hottest 1** having or producing a great deal of heat. **2** having a higher temperature than is normal or desirable. **3** (of food) spicy; causing a burning sensation on the tongue. **4** strongly favoured: *He is a hot favourite.* – **hot and bothered** (*colloquial*) unable to think clearly.

hot dog *n.* a hot sausage in a soft bread roll.

hothouse *n.* a greenhouse which is kept warm for growing tender or tropical plants in.

hotel (hō **tel**) *n.* a large house or building where travellers or people on holiday receive food and lodging in return for payment.

● **Houdini** (hōō **dē** ni), **Harry** (1874-1926) was an American 'escapologist' – someone who could escape from seemingly impossible combinations of chains and locks.

hound (hownd) *n.* a hunting-dog: *wolfhound; foxhound.* – *vb.* **hounding, hounded** to chase or bother relentlessly.

hour (**ow** ěr) *n.* **1** 60 minutes. There are 24 hours in a day. **2** a point in time: *They woke at an early hour.* **3** the time allowed or fixed for some activity: *I work strictly office hours.* **hourly** *adj.* happening or done every hour. – *adv.* every hour.

house (hows) *n.* **1** a building in which people,

PRONUNCIATION GUIDE	
fat **a**	all **ö**
fate **ā**	foot **oo**
fast **ä**	moon **ōō**
among **å**	boy **oi**
met **e**	house **ow**
mean **ē**	demon **ǒ**
silent **ě**	thing **th**
loch **hh**	this **Th**
fin **i**	but **u**
line **ī**	mute **ū**
quick **kw**	fur **û**
got **o**	brochure **ů**
note **ō**	vision **zh**

especially a single family, live. **2** a building used for a particular purpose: *We visited the opera house.* **3** a business firm: *She works for a publishing house.* **4** a family, especially an important or noble one: *Mary Queen of Scots was a member of the House of Stuart.* – (howz) *vb.* **housing, housed 1** to provide with a house or similar shelter. **2** to store. – **like a house on fire** (*colloquial*) very well: *From their very first meeting they got on like a house on fire.*

houseboat *n.* a boat which is built to be lived in, and is usually moored in the same place.

household *n.* the people who live together in a house and make up a family.

House of Commons *n.* in GREAT BRITAIN and CANADA, the lower, elected assembly in parliament.

House of Lords *n.* in GREAT BRITAIN, the upper assembly in parliament, made up of peers and bishops.

House of Representatives *n.* in the UNITED STATES, the lower house or chamber of CONGRESS.

housing *n.* houses as a group.

Chinese thatch house of 2000 BC

People in prehistoric times lived in caves. The first **houses** were shelters made of mud and branches. Later people learned to make bricks from clay, quarry stone and use timber. And so until quite recent times the style of houses has been influenced by building materials available locally, including straw and reeds (for thatch), flints, and clay (for adobe). Weather, too, has influenced house styles.

An Indonesian house built on stilts

●**Houston** (**hū** stòn) is the largest city in Texas, USA and a major centre for space research.

hovel (**ho** vềl) *n*. a small, dirty, dismal dwelling.

hover (**ho** vêr) *vb*. **hovering, hovered 1** to remain in the air without moving in any direction: *The bird hovered above its prey*. **2** to move around while still remaining near a person or thing: *His mother hovered around, distracting him from his homework*.

hovercraft *n*. a vehicle which can move over land or water, supported by a cushion of air.

how (how) *adv*. **1** in what way; by what means: *How did it happen?* **2** to what extent: *How old is he?* **3** in what condition, especially of health: *How is she feeling now?* **4** to what extent is something good or successful: *How was your holiday?* – *conj*. (*colloquial*) that: *He told me how he'd done it alone*. – *n*. a manner or means of doing something: *She tried to explain the how and why of it all*. – **how about** would you like?: *How about another cake?* – **how come** (*colloquial*) for what reason?

however (how **ev** ểr) *adv*. and *conj*.

An American timber house

English Tudor house (1500s)

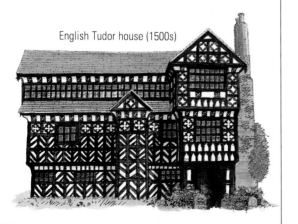

1 nevertheless: *I tried my best; however, I did not pass the test*. **2** by whatever means: *However hard you push, it won't open*.

howl (howl) *n*. a long, loud, sad cry, for example made by a dog. – *vb*. **howling, howled**.

●**Huang Ho** or **Yellow River**, is the second longest river in China (4845 km/3010 miles).

hub (hub) *n*. the central part of a wheel.

huddle (**hu** dềl) *vb*. **huddling, huddled 1** to heap or crowd together closely. **2** to sit curled up. – *n*. **1** a confused mass or crowd. **2** a secret or private conference: *They went into a huddle*.

●**Hudson, Henry** (*c*.1550-1611) was an English explorer after whom the Hudson river in New York state is named.

hue (hū) *n*. a colour or shade.

hug (hug) *vb*. **hugging, hugged 1** to hold tightly in your arms, especially to show affection. **2** to keep close to: *The ship hugged the shore*. – *n*. a tight grasp with the arms.

huge (hūj) *adj*. very large.

●**Hughes** (hūz), **Langston** (1902-67) was a black American poet.

●**Hugo** (**hū** gō), **Victor** (1802-1885) was a French writer, author of *Les Misérables*.

Huguenot (**hū** gề nō) *n*. (*historical*) a French Protestant.

hull[1] (hul) *n*. the frame or body of a ship.

hull[2] (hul) *n*. the outer covering of certain fruit and vegetables, especially the pod of beans and peas.

hum (hum) *vb*. **humming, hummed** to make a sound as though you are saying m-m-m-m without opening your mouth.

human (**hū** mản) *adj*. **1** of or belonging to people. **2** having the better qualities of people. – *n*. a person.

humankind *n*. human beings as a race.

humane (hū **mān**) *adj*. kind; sympathetic.

humanity (hū **man** i ti) *n*. **humanity 1** the human race. **2** the qualities of humans, especially in being kind or showing mercy.

humble (**hum** bềl) *adj*. modest; not vain.

●**Humboldt** (**hum** bōlt), **Baron Alexander von** (1767-1835) was a German explorer.

HUMBLE PIE
Humble comes from the Latin, meaning 'lowly' or 'mean'. But the phrase 'to eat humble pie' has quite a different origin. It comes from 'umbles', the cheaply-bought inner parts of an animal.

humbug (**hum** bug) *n.* nonsense; rubbish: *His speech was humbug.*

humdrum (**hum** drum) *adj.* dull; ordinary.

humerus (**hū** mě rŭs) *n.* **humeri** (**hū** mě rī) the bone in the upper part of the arm.

humid (**hū** mid) *adj.* damp; moist.

humiliate (**hū mil** i āt) *vb.* **humiliating, humiliated** to make someone feel ashamed or look foolish in front of another person. – *adj.* **humiliating**. – *n.* **humiliation**.

●**hummingbird** the smallest bird in the world, hardly larger than a bumble bee. It can beat its wings up to 70 times a second which allows it to hover in mid air. This also causes the distinctive humming sound.

Hummingbirds, like bees, collect nectar from flowers.

humorous (**hū** mǒ rŭs) *adj.* funny; amusing.

humour (**hū** mǒr) *n.* the ability to amuse or be amused: *His sense of humour makes me laugh.* – *vb.* **humouring, humoured** to please someone by doing what he or she wishes: *They humoured the baby by singing to him.*

hump (hump) *n.* a small, rounded lump, e.g. on the back of a camel.

humus (**hu** mus) *n.* a substance like earth found in soil, made from decayed plants, leaves, and animal matter, etc. which helps to keep soil fertile.

Hun (hun) *n.* (*historical*) a member of a powerful and warlike people who invaded EUROPE in the 4th and 5th centuries.

hunch (hunch) *n.* an idea or belief based on feelings or suspicions rather than on clear evidence. – *vb.* **hunching, hunched** to sit with your body curled up or bent.

hunchback *n.* a person with a large rounded lump on their back, usually caused by a problem with the spine. – *adj.* **hunchbacked**.

hundred (**hun** drěd) *n.* **hundreds** or (after another number) **hundred 1** the number which is ten times ten; 100. **2** (usually in *plural*; *colloquial*) very many: *There were hundreds of people.* – *n.* & *adj.* **hundredth**.

hung (hung) *vb.* see **hang**.

Hungarian *n.* a person who comes from Hungary; the language of Hungary. – *adj.* belonging or relating to Hungary.

●**Hungary**. See Supplement, **Countries**.

hunger (**hung** gěr) *n.* the desire or need for food. – *vb.* **hungering, hungered** to have a strong desire for something.

hungry (**hung** gri) *adj.* **hungrier, hungriest** wanting or needing food. – *adv.* **hungrily**.

hunk (hungk) *n.* a large slice of bread, etc.

hunt (hunt) *vb.* **hunting, hunted 1** to chase and kill animals for food or for sport. **2** to search for: *They are hunting for a new house in this area.* – *n.* a group of people meeting together on horses to hunt foxes.

hunter *n.* a person or animal that hunts.

hurdle (**hûr** děl) *n.* **1** one of a series of light frames to be jumped in a hurdles race: *He won the 500 metres hurdles.* **2** a problem or difficulty: *The first hurdle for any author is to find a publisher willing to publish their books.* – *vb.* **hurdling, hurdled** to jump hurdles in a race. – *n.* **hurdling**.

hurdler *n.* a person or horse that runs hurdle races.

hurl (hûrl) *vb.* **hurling, hurled** to throw violently: *He hurled a stone at the window.*

hurling (**hûr** ling) or **hurley** (**hûr** li) *n.* a traditional Irish game resembling hockey, played by two teams with 15 players each.

hurricane (**hu** ri kăn) *n.* a violent storm especially one with winds blowing at over 120 km per hour.

hurry (**hu** ri) *vb.* **hurries, hurrying, hurried** to move or act quickly: *She hurried to finish her homework* – *n.* great haste or speed; eagerness: *In our hurry to leave we forgot the picnic.* – *vb.* **hurry up** to move more quickly than before.

hurried *adj.* forced to act quickly, especially too quickly.

hurt (hûrt) *vb.* **hurting, hurt 1** to injure or cause physical pain to. **2** to upset or cause emotional pain to: *She hurt my feelings with her harsh words.* – *adj.* **1** injured. **2** upset.

hurtful *adj.* causing emotional pain: *Her hurtful remarks were totally unnecessary.*

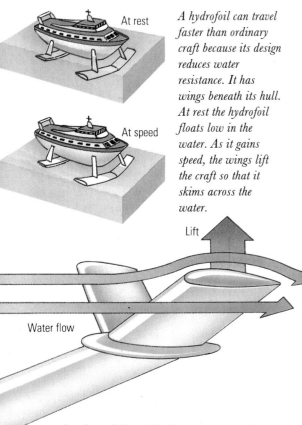

A hydrofoil can travel faster than ordinary craft because its design reduces water resistance. It has wings beneath its hull. At rest the hydrofoil floats low in the water. As it gains speed, the wings lift the craft so that it skims across the water.

husband (**huz** bånd) *n.* a man to whom a woman is married.

hush (hush) *interjection* be quiet; be still. – *n.* silence, especially after noise. – *vb.* **hush up**; **hushing, hushed** to keep secret.

husky¹ (**hus** ki) *adj.* **huskier, huskiest** (of a voice) rough and dry in sound. – *adv.* **huskily**. – *n.* **huskiness**.

husky² (**hus** ki) *n.* **huskies** a large, strong dog used to pull sledges across snow.

hut (hut) *n.* a small house or shelter.

hutch (huch) *n.* a box with a wire front in which small animals, e.g. rabbits, are kept.

hyacinth (**hī** å sinth) *n.* a plant which grows from a bulb and has sweet-smelling flowers.

hybrid (**hī** brid) *n.* an animal or plant produced by crossing different species or varieties. – *adj.* produced by combining elements from different species, varieties, etc.

hydrant (**hī** drånt) *n.* a pipe connected to the main water supply in a street.

hydraulic (hī **drö** lik) *adj.* worked by the pressure of water or some other liquid carried in pipes: *Many lorries have hydraulic brakes.*

hydroelectricity (hī drō i lek **tris** i ti) *n.* electricity produced by means of water-power. – *adj.* **hydroelectric**.

hydrofoil (**hī** drō foil) *n.* a boat fitted with a wing-shaped device which lifts it out of the water as its speed accelerates.

hydrogen (**hī** drŏ jĕn) *n.* a gas (symbol **H**), the lightest element known, which produces water when combined with oxygen.

hyena (hī **ē** nå) *n.* a dog-like animal with a shrill cry that lives in AFRICA and ASIA.

hygiene (**hī** jēn) *n.* the practice or study of staying healthy and preventing the spread of disease, especially by keeping yourself and your surroundings clean. – *adj.* **hygienic**.

hymn (him) *n.* a song of praise especially to God.

hyper- (**hī** pĕr) *prefix* over, beyond, more than: *hyperactive, hyperinflation, hypermarket.*

hyperactive (hī pĕr **ak** tiv) *adj.* (especially of a child) more active than is normal.

hyperbole (hī **pûr** bŏl li) *n.* the use of exaggeration to produce an effect.

hyphen (**hī** fĕn) *n.* a punctuation mark (-) used to join up two words, e.g. bare-headed, or two parts of a word split over the end of one line and the beginning of the following one.
hyphenate *vb.* **hyphenating, hyphenated** to join two words or parts of words with a hyphen. – *n.* **hyphenation**.

hypnosis (hip **nō** sis) *n.* **hypnoses** (hip **nō** sēz) a sleep-like state in which someone is totally relaxed and acts only on the suggestion of another person.
hypnotize or **hypnotise** (hip nŏ tīz) *vb.* **hypnotizing, hypnotized** to put someone in a state of hypnosis.

hypochondria (hī pō **kon** dri å) *n.* a fear of becoming ill.

hypocrite (**hi** pŏ krit) *n.* a person who pretends to have feelings or beliefs they do not actually hold, or who hides their true character. – *adj.* **hypocritical**. – *n.* **hypocrisy** (hi **pok** rĕ si).

hypodermic syringe (hī pō **dûr** mik sĕ **rinj**) *n.* a syringe with a fine hollow needle, used for injecting drugs under the skin.

hypothermia (hī pō **thûr** mi å) *n.* an illness caused by exposure to cold in which the body temperature falls below normal.

hysterectomy (his tĕ **rek** tŏ mi) *n.* **hysterectomies** the surgical removal of a woman's womb.

hysteria (hi **stēr** i å) *n.* a wild or uncontrolled emotional state, often expressed by uncontrolled laughing or crying. – *adj.* **hysterical** (hi **ste** ri kål).

The spotted hyena is a powerful and aggressive animal. It hunts in packs at night.

Husband is from a Norse word meaning 'someone who has a household'.

I i

I (ī) *pron.* used by the speaker or writer to refer to himself or herself.

Iberian (ī **bēr** i ån) *adj.* of the Iberian Peninsula (now divided into SPAIN and PORTUGAL), its inhabitants, languages, culture, and history.

ibex (ī beks) *n.* **ibex, ibexes**, or **ibices** (ī bi sēz) a wild mountain goat with large, backward-curving horns.

Ibis. See **Myths and Legends**.

ibis (ī bis) *n.* **ibis** or **ibises** a wading bird with a long, slender, downward-curving beak.

● **Ibsen, Henrik** (1828-1906) was a Norwegian dramatist whose work includes *Peer Gynt*.

ice (īs) *n.* **1** frozen water. **2** a sheet of this, for example lying on the surface of water or a road. **3** ice cream or water ice.

ice age *n.* a period of time during which large areas of the Earth's surface are covered with ice.

iceberg *n.* a huge mass of ice floating in the sea, most of which lies beneath the water.

icecap *n.* a permanent covering of ice, for example at the North or South Poles.

ice hockey *n.* a form of hockey played on ice by skaters, and with a puck instead of a ball.

ice skate *n.* a skate with a metal blade for use on ice.

icing *n.* a mixture of sugar, egg whites, water, and flavouring, used to coat cakes.

icy *adj.* **icier, iciest** very cold.

● **Iceland**. See Supplement, **Countries**.

Icelandic (īs **lan** dik) *adj.* of ICELAND or its language. – *n.* the Icelandic language.

icicle (ī si kěl) *n.* a long hanging spike of ice, formed by water freezing as it drops.

● **Idaho**. See Supplement, **USA**.

Sea level

Water increases in volume and so decreases in density as it freezes to a solid. This is why **icebergs** float, with about seven-eighths of their volume below the surface. Some Antarctic icebergs are more than 100 km long.

Under the Antarctic ice sheet (above left) there is land. The Arctic (above right) is mostly a mass of pack ice covering an ocean.

idea (ī **dē** å) *n.* **1** a thought, image, or concept formed by the mind. **2** a plan or intention: *The idea is that you should become a doctor.* **3** a main aim or feature: *The idea of the game is to win as many cards as possible.*

ideal (ī **dē** ål) *adj.* perfect; best possible: *Flying is the ideal way of travelling quickly.* − *n.* the highest standard of behaviour, etc.

identical (ī **den** ti kål) *adj.* being exactly alike in every respect: *They wore identical ties.*

identify (ī **den** ti fī) *vb.* **identifies, identifying, identified 1** to recognize someone or something as being a particular person or thing; to establish the identity of. **2** to associate one person or thing with another. **identification** *n.* something which allows a person or thing to be identified.

identity (ī **den** ti ti) *n.* **identities** who or what a person or thing is: *The winner's identity is not yet known.*

idiot (**i** di ŏt) *n.* (*colloquial*) a foolish or stupid person. − *adj.* **idiotic** (i di **ot** ik).

idle (**ī** děl) *adj.* **1** not being used. **2** not wanting to work; lazy. − *n.* **idleness.** − *adv.* **idly.**

idol (**ī** dŏl) *n.* an image, especially of a god, used as an object of worship.

if (if) *conj.* **1** in the event that; supposing that: *If what you say is true, we'll have to go.* **2** although; even though. **3** whenever: *I like to visit John if I can.* **4** whether: *I merely asked if I could help you.*

igloo (**i** glōō) *n.* a dome-shaped INUIT house built with blocks of snow and ice.

igneous (**ig** ni ůs) *adj.* formed by molten rock from the Earth's core becoming hard.

ignite (ig **nīt**) *vb.* **igniting, ignited** to set fire to; to catch fire: *You must ignite the gas first.*

ignition (ig **ni** shŏn) *n.* the system (e.g. an electric spark) used to ignite the fuel in an internal combustion engine.

ignorant (**ig** nŏ rant) *adj.* knowing very little; uneducated. − *n.* **ignorance.**

ignore (ig **nör**) *vb.* **ignoring, ignored** to take no notice of deliberately.

iguana (i **gwä** nå) *or* (i gū **ä** nå) *n.* **iguanas** a large grey-green tree-dwelling lizard.

● **Iliad** This epic poem by HOMER tells the story of the war between the Greeks and Trojans (the people of TROY or Ilium).

ill (il) *adj.* **worse** (wûrs), **worst** (wûrst) **1** not in good health; sick. **2** bad or harmful: *ill effects.* **illness** *n.* a disease.

ill- (il-) *prefix* meaning badly: *ill-informed; ill-timed; ill-treat.*

illegal (i **lē** gål) *adj.* against the law.

illegible (i **lej** å běl) *adj.* difficult to read.

● **Illinois**. See Supplement, **USA**.

illogical (i **loj** i kål) *adj.* not based on careful thinking or reason.

illuminate (i **lōōm** i nāt) *vb.* **illuminating, illuminated 1** to light up or make bright. **2** to make clearer and more easily understood: *Your clear explanation is illuminating.*

illusion (i **lōō** zhŏn) *n.* a false impression, idea, belief, or understanding: *His fake gold jewellery gave an illusion of wealth.*

illustrate (i **lů** strāt) *vb.* **illustrating, illustrated** to provide a book, text, etc. with pictures and diagrams. − *adj.* **illustrated.** − *n.* **illustrator.** **illustration** *n.* a picture or diagram in a book, etc. that explains or decorates it.

im- (im-) *prefix.* See **in-.**

I'm I am.

image (**i** mij) *n.* a likeness of a person or thing, especially a portrait or statue.

imagine (i **maj** in) *vb.* **imagining, imagined 1** to form a mental picture: *Can you imagine what it would be like to be a movie star?* **2** to suppose or guess: *I can't imagine where she's got to.* **imaginary** *adj.* not real. **imagination** *n.* the ability to form mental images of things, etc. you have not seen. **imaginative** *adj.* having a lively imagination.

imitate (**i** mi tāt) *vb.* **imitating, imitated** to copy the behaviour, appearance, etc. of. **imitation** *n.* **1** an act of imitating. **2** a copy.

immature (i må **tūr**) *adj.* not fully grown or developed. − *n.* **immaturity.**

immediate (i **mēd** i åt) *adj.* **1** happening or done at once and without delay. **2** nearest or next in space, time, or relationship: *They invited only their immediate family.* **immediately** *adv.* at once.

immense (i **mens**) *adj.* very large.

immigrate (**i** mi grāt) *vb.* **immigrating, immigrated** to move into a foreign country. − *n.* **immigration.**

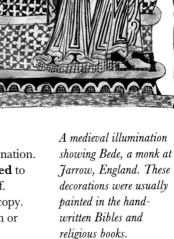

A medieval illumination showing Bede, a monk at Jarrow, England. These decorations were usually painted in the hand-written Bibles and religious books.

When threatened a group of impala leap in the air in all directions in order to confuse the predator.

immigrant *n.* a person who immigrates. (He or she is an **emigrant** from the country they have left.)

imminent (**i** mi nėnt) *adj.* likely to happen soon.

immobile (i **mō** bīl) *adj.* motionless.

immoral (i **mör** ål) *adj.* morally wrong or bad.

immortal (i **mör** tål) *adj.* living forever and never dying. – *n.* **immortality** (i mör **tal** i ti).

immune (i **mūn**) *adj.* protected by inoculation from, or having a natural resistance to, a particular disease. – *n.* **immunity**.

impact (**im** pakt) *n.* **1** a collision. **2** a strong impression: *The book had a powerful impact on Jo.*

impair (im **pār**) *vb.* **impairing, impaired** to damage or weaken, especially in quality or strength: *Smoking impairs health.*

impala (im **pä** lå) *n.* **impalas** a graceful African antelope with curving horns.

impartial (im **pär** shål) *adj.* not favouring one person, etc. more than another; fair.

impatient (im **pā** shėnt) *adj.* **1** unwilling to wait; intolerant. **2** restlessly eager. – *n.* **impatience**.

impeach (im **pēch**) *vb.* **impeaching, impeached** to charge with a serious crime, especially treason.

impede (im **pēd**) *vb.* **impeding, impeded** to get in the way; to hinder.

imperfect (im **pûr** fikt) *adj.* having faults; spoilt.

imperial (im **pēr** i ål) *adj.* of or suitable for an empire, emperor, or empress.

impertinent (im **pûr** ti nėnt) *adj.* rude.

implement (**im** pli mėnt) *n.* a tool or utensil; a piece of equipment.

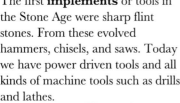

The first **implements** or tools in the Stone Age were sharp flint stones. From these evolved hammers, chisels, and saws. Today we have power driven tools and all kinds of machine tools such as drills and lathes.

A Viking ironing board with a smoothing stone.

From the open-fire spit to the microwave oven.

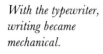

With the typewriter, writing became mechanical.

– (**im** pli ment) *vb.* **implementing, implemented** to carry out or perform. – *n.* **implementation**.

imply (im **plī**) *vb.* **implies, implying, implied** to suggest or express indirectly.

impolite (im pŏ **līt**) *adj.* not polite; rude.

import (im **pört**) *vb.* **importing, imported** to bring goods, etc. in from another country. – (**im** pört) *n.* something imported.

important (im **pör** tånt) *adj.* **1** having great value, influence, or effect. **2** of great significance or value to: *Her happiness is important to me.* – *n.* **importance**.

impose (im **pōz**) *vb.* **imposing, imposed** to force yourself, your opinions etc. on. **imposing** *adj.* impressive.

impossible (im **pos** å bėl) *adj.* **1** that cannot be done or cannot happen. **2** that cannot be true; difficult to believe. – *adv.* **impossibly**.

impracticable (im **prak** ti kå bėl) *adj.* not able to be done, put into practice, or used.

impractical (im **prak** ti kål) *adj.* lacking common sense.

impregnable (im **preg** nå bėl) *adj.* not able to be seized, defeated, or taken by force.

impress (im **pres**) *vb.* **impressing, impressed** to produce a strong, lasting, and usually favourable impression on someone.

impression *n.* **1** an idea or effect produced in the mind or made on the senses: *Philip made a good impression with her friends because he's such fun to be with.* **2** a vague or uncertain idea or belief: *I had an impression that something was wrong, but I couldn't be sure.* **3** the number of copies of a book, newspaper, etc. printed at one time.

Impressionism *n.* a 19th-century movement in painting which aimed to represent nature, especially the play of light on objects, exactly as seen by the artist, without regard for the classical rules of composition, colouring, etc. – *n.* & *adj.* **Impressionist**.

impressive *adj.* making a strong impression: *The Vatican is an impressive building.*

imprison (im **pri** zŏn) *vb.* **imprisoning, imprisoned** to put in prison. – *n.* **imprisonment**.

improbable (im **pro** bå bėl) *adj.* **1** unlikely to happen. **2** hard to believe. – *adv.* **improbably.**

impromptu (im **promp** tū) *adj.* & *adv.* made or done without preparation.

improve (im **prōōv**) *vb.* **improving, improved** to make or become better, of higher quality or value; to make progress.

improvise (**im** prŏ vīz) *vb.* **improvising, improvised** to compose, recite, or perform music, verse, etc. without preparing it in advance. – *n.* **improvisation**.

impulse (**im** puls) *n.* **1** a sudden push forwards: *The impulse of the huge wave knocked down the wall.* **2** a sudden desire or urge to do something: *Abigail bought the dress on impulse.* – *adj.* **impulsive**.

in (in) *prep.* **1** used to express the position or inclusion of a person or thing: *Rory was in the classroom.* **2** into: *Get in the car.* **3** after: *Come back in an hour.* **4** during: *In winter some animals hibernate.* **5** used to express arrangement or shape: *List them in alphabetical order.* **6** by the means of; using: *The opera was sung in Italian.* – *adv.* **1** indoors: *The cat came in when I called him.* **2** at home or work: *I won't be in tomorrow.* **3** so as to be added: *Beat in the eggs.*

in-patient *n.* a patient temporarily living in hospital while receiving treatment there.

in- (in-) *prefix* (also **il-** before words beginning with **l**; **im-** before **b**, **m**, and **p**; and **ir-** before **r**) **1** not; non-; lack of: *inactive, inhospitable; irrelevant.* **2** towards; within: *imprison.*

inanimate (in **an** i måt) *adj.* without life; not living: *Rocks are inanimate objects.*

inarticulate (in är **tik** ū låt) *adj.* unable to express yourself clearly or to speak distinctly.

inaugurate (in **ög** ū rāt) *vb.* **inaugurating, inaugurated** to place in office with a formal ceremony: *Every four years an American president is inaugurated.* – *n.* **inauguration**.

●**Inca** The Inca civilization was centred on modern PERU and lasted from about AD 1200 until its eventual destruction by the Spanish conquistadors.

incense¹ (**in** sens) *n.* a spice or other substance which gives off a pleasant smell when burned.

incense² (in **sens**) *vb.* **incensing, incensed** to make very angry.

incentive (in **sen** tiv) *n.* something that encourages action, work, etc., such as extra money paid to workers to increase production.

incessant (in **ses** ånt) *adj.* continual.

inch (inch) *n.* a measure of length equal to one twelfth of a foot (2.54 centimetres).

incident (**in** si děnt) *n.* an event or occurrence.

incidental (in si **den** tål) *adj.* of minor importance: *They were merely incidental expenses.*

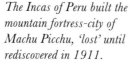

Inca headdress was often elaborate

The Incas of Peru built the mountain fortress-city of Machu Picchu, 'lost' until rediscovered in 1911.

Inca rule, at its height, extended from Ecuador to southern Chile. Inca society, headed by a godlike emperor, was ruthlessly efficient. The people were divided into groups of ten with an overseer; a local chief was appointed over 100 people. Higher officials were responsible for 1000 or 10,000 people. The Incas constructed elaborate irrigation systems and had an extensive road system.

In battle, Inca soldiers used slings, bolas which were stones linked by lengths of string, spears and clubs.

The Incas used hand-held, stone hammers to shape their building stone.

incidentally *adv.* by the way.

incinerate (in **sin** ě rāt) *vb.* **incinerating, incinerated** to burn to ashes.

incinerator *n.* a furnace for burning rubbish.

incline (in **klīn**) *vb.* **inclining, inclined** to slope from a horizontal or vertical line.

include (in **klōōd**) *vb.* **including, included 1** to take in as part of a whole. **2** to contain.

An Indian maharajah or ruler.

The Indian emperor Asoka erected many stone pillars to remind people of his power.

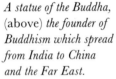

A statue of the Buddha, (above) the founder of Buddhism which spread from India to China and the Far East.

The earliest **Indian** civilization was that of the Indus valley (*c.*2500-1600 BC). From about 1500 BC Aryans (or Indo-Europeans) from Russia overran the north and settled down with the native Indians, the Dravidians. The whole subcontinent was first unified under the Mauryan emperors (321-184 BC). Much later the Mogul Muslim empire was established in the north. It lasted until 1858.

Under the old caste system society was divided into four classes. The highest were the Brahman, the priests, scholars, and rulers. Such people as street traders were of the lowest caste.

The Golden Temple in the sacred city of Amritsar in India is the holiest place of Sikh devotion.

income (**in** kum) *n.* money received as payment for work, etc.

incompetent (in **kom** pě tĕnt) *adj.* lacking the necessary ability. – *n.* **incompetence**.

inconvenience (in kŏn **vēn** i ĕns) *n.* something which causes trouble or difficulty.

incorporate (in **kör** pŏ rāt) *vb.* **incorporating, incorporated 1** to contain as part of a whole. **2** to include or be included as part of a whole: *Ivor incorporated my ideas in his story.* – *n.* **incorporation**.

increase (in **krēs**) *vb.* **increasing, increased** to make or become greater in size, intensity, or number. – (**in** krēs) *n.* growth.

incredible (in **kred** å bĕl) *adj.* difficult to believe; amazing. – *adv.* **incredibly**.

incubate (**ing** kū bāt) *vb.* **incubating, incubated** to hatch eggs by sitting on them to keep them warm.

indeed (in **dēd**) *adv.* **1** without any question: *It was indeed brave of Rory to put out the fire.* **2** used for emphasis: *It's very wet indeed.*

indefinite (in **def** i nit) *adj.* without exact limits.

indefinite article *n.* either of the words **a** or **an**, describing no particular person or thing.

independent (in di **pen** dĕnt) *adj.* **1** not under the control or authority of others, especially of a country or state. **2** not relying on others for money, care, or help. – *n.* **independence**.

index (**in** deks) *n.* **indexes** an alphabetical list of names, subjects, etc. dealt with in a book. It is usually at the end of the book, and gives the page numbers on which each item appears.

● **India** is a part of ASIA and has more people than any other country except CHINA. To the north are the HIMALAYAS. Although India's industries are growing, most Indians are farmers and grow rice, wheat, cotton, and tea. Bombay and Calcutta are among the world's biggest cities and New Delhi is the capital. Modern India, the world's biggest democracy, became a republic in 1947 after 200 years of British rule. See also Supplement, **Countries**.

Indian (**in** di ån) *n.* **1** a person born in INDIA. **2** the former name of any of the various native peoples of America (excluding the INUIT), now called NATIVE AMERICANS. – *adj.* relating to INDIA or the Indian subcontinent, its inhabitants, languages, and culture.

● **Indiana**. See Supplement, **USA**.

indicate (**in** di kāt) *vb.* **indicating, indicated** to point out or show.

indication *n.* a sign.

indifferent (in **dif** ĕ rĕnt) *adj.* showing no interest: *Jon was totally indifferent to my problem.*

indigenous (in **dij** ĕ nŭs) *adj.* belonging naturally to a country or area; native.

indignant (in **dig** nånt) *adj.* showing anger or a sense of ill-treatment.

individual (in di **vi** joo ål) *adj.* **1** relating to a single person or thing. **2** particular to one person; showing or having a particular person's unique qualities or characteristics. – *n.* a particular person, animal, or thing.

●**Indonesia**. See Supplement, **Countries**.

indoor (in **dör**) *adj.* used, done, happening, etc. inside a building: *an indoor garden.*
indoors *adv.* in or into a building: *Stay indoors.*

induce (in **dūs**) *vb.* **inducing, induced 1** to persuade or cause to do. **2** to cause to happen.

●**Indus** This river flows through INDIA and PAKISTAN. Along its banks one of the world's first civilizations grew up.

industry (in **dus** tri) *n.* **industries 1** the business of producing goods. **2** a branch of manufacturing and trade: *the coal industry.* **3** hard work or effort: *Bees work with great industry.*
industrial *adj.* of, relating to, or concerned with industry.
industrialize or **industrialise** *vb.*
industrializing, industrialized to become industrially developed. – *n.* **industrialization.**
industrious *adj.* busy and hard-working.

●**Industrial Revolution** This is the name given to the breakthrough in the use of machine tools in EUROPE (especially ENGLAND) from 1750 to 1850. The main inventions were steam power and textile machinery. The results were factories, railways, and industrial towns.

inedible (in **ed** å běl) *adj.* not fit to eat.

inept (in **ept**) *adj.* awkward; done without skill.

inequality (in i **kwol** i ti) *n.* **inequalities** a lack of equality, fairness, or evenness.

inevitable (in **ev** i tå běl) *adj.* that cannot be avoided; certain to happen.

infamous (in **få** mŭs) *adj.* notoriously bad.

infant (in **fånt**) *n.* a very young child.

infantry (in **fån** tri) *n.* **infantries** soldiers who are trained to fight on foot.

infect (in **fekt**) *vb.* **infecting, infected** to give a person germs or the disease they cause.
infection *n.* a disease caused by germs.
infectious *adj.* describing a disease that is capable of being transmitted by air, water, etc.: *Measles is an infectious disease.*

inferior (in **fēr** i ŏr) *adj.* poorer in quality; lower in value, rank, or status: *Izzy is so good at swimming she makes the rest of us feel inferior.*

infest (in **fest**) *vb.* **infesting, infested** (of something harmful, e.g. vermin) to be present in large numbers.

infinite (in **fi** nit) *adj.* having no boundaries or limits in size, extent, time, or space.

infinitive (in **fin** i tiv) *n.* a verb form which expresses an action but does not refer to a particular subject or time, in English often used with *to*: *Tell him to go.*

inflammable (in **flam** å běl) *adj.* easily set on fire: *Petrol is highly inflammable.*

inflammation (in **flå må** shŏn) *n.* a place in the body showing redness and swelling.

The Spinning Jenny, the first multi-reel spinning machine, was made by James Hargreaves in 1764.

The first steam engine – built by Thomas Newcomen in 1712 – was used to pump water out of mines. Steam power was to cause a revolution in industry.

Workers – mainly poorly paid women and girls – in an early 19th-century flax mill.

inflate (in **flāt**) *vb.* **inflating, inflated 1** to expand with air or gas. **2** to increase prices.
inflation *n.* **1** the process of inflating or being inflated. **2** a general increase in the level of prices. – *adj.* **inflationary**.
influence (in floo ĕns) *n.* **1** the power that one person or thing has to affect another. **2** a person or thing that has such a power: *Try to be a good influence on him.* – *vb.* **influencing, influenced** to have an effect on.
influential (in floo **en** shăl) *adj.* having influence.
influenza (in floo **en** ză) *n.* an infectious illness caused by a virus, whose symptoms include headache, fever, and muscle pains.
inform (in **förm**) *vb.* **informing, informed 1** to give knowledge or information: *Ivan informed us that he was leaving school.* **2** to give information about someone to the police.
information *n.* knowledge gained or given; facts; news.
informative *adj.* giving useful or interesting information.
informal (in **för** măl) *adj.* without ceremony; relaxed. – *n.* **informality** (in för **mal** i ti).
ingenious (in **jēn** i ŭs) *adj.* showing or having skill and originality.
ingenuity (in jĕ **nū** i ti) *n.* inventive cleverness, skill, or originality.
ingot (**ing** got) *n.* a brick-shaped mass of metal, especially of gold or silver.
ingredient (in **grē** di ĕnt) *n.* one of several things that goes into a mixture, especially in cooking: *Flour is an essential ingredient of bread.*
inhabit (in **hab** it) *vb.* **inhabiting, inhabited** to live or dwell in a place.
inhabitant *n.* a person or animal that lives permanently in a place.
inhale (in **hāl**) *vb.* **inhaling, inhaled** to breathe in air, gas, etc.
inherit (in **he** rit) *vb.* **inheriting, inherited 1** to receive property, etc. from a member of your family on his or her death. **2** to receive characteristics from your parents and ancestors: *Anita has inherited her father's blue eyes.*
inheritance *n.* something inherited.
inhuman (in **hū** măn) *adj.* cruel and unfeeling.
initial (i **ni** shăl) *adj.* of or at the beginning. – *n.* the first letter of a word or name: *George Bernard Shaw's initials are G. B. S.*
initiative (i **ni** shă tiv) *n.* the ability or skill to take decisions.
inject (in **jekt**) *vb.* **injecting, injected** to introduce a liquid, such as medicine, into the body using a hypodermic syringe. – *n.* **injection**.
injure (in **jŭr**) *vb.* **injuring, injured** to harm or damage: *Dan injured his knee in football.*
injury *n.* **injuries** physical harm or damage.
injustice (in **jus** tis) *n.* **1** unfairness or lack of justice. **2** an unjust act.
ink (ingk) *n.* a coloured liquid used in writing, printing, and drawing.
inland (in **lănd**) *adj.* of or in that part of a country which is not beside the sea. – *adv.* away from the sea: *The wind blew inland.*
inlet (in let) *n.* a narrow length of water running inland from a sea coast.
inn (in) *n.* a public house or small hotel.
inner (in ĕr) *adj.* situated close to the centre.
innocent (i nŏ sĕnt) *adj.* **1** pure. **2** not guilty of a crime. **3** trusting and naive. – *n.* **innocence**.
inoculate (i **nok** ū lāt) *vb.* **inoculating, inoculated** to give a mild form of a disease to create immunity against that disease, usually by injection. – *n.* **inoculation**.

The eight-spotted forester moth of North America.

inorganic (in ör **gan** ik) *adj.* not made of or found in living animal or plant material.
input (**in** poot) *n.* the information put into a computer.
inquire or **enquire** (in **kwīr**) *vb.* **inquiring, inquired** or **enquiring, enquired** to ask for information about.
inquiring *adj.* eager to discover things.
inquiry or **enquiry** *n.* **inquiries** or **enquiries 1** a request for information. **2** an investigation.
inquisitive (in **kwiz** i tiv) *adj.* eager for information. – *n.* **inquisitiveness**.
insane (in **sān**) *adj.* not of sound mind.
insanity (in **san** i ti) *n.* the state of being insane.
insanitary (in **san** i tă ri) *adj.* so dirty as to be dangerous to health.

PRONUNCIATION GUIDE

fat a | all ö
fate ā | foot oo
fast ä | moon oō
among å | boy oi
met e | house ow
mean ē | demon ŏ
silent ĕ | thing th
loch hh | this Th
fin i | but u
line ī | mute ū
quick kw | fur û
got o | brochure ů
note ō | vision zh

Of all forms of life, the most varied are the **insects**. More than 900,000 species are known but the number of individual insects is beyond count. They are highly adaptable and have conquered all environments.

The male goliath beetle of Africa, the world's heaviest insect, can weigh over 100 gm. Silverfish are primitive wingless insects.

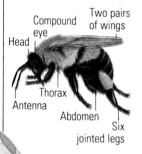

Head — Compound eye — Two pairs of wings — Thorax — Antenna — Abdomen — Six jointed legs

Most insects (like the bee) have four wings, but flies have only two. Insects breathe through tiny holes called 'spiracles' along the sides of their body.

A lacewing – a member of a large and varied group of carnivorous insects.

A praying mantis – the female may eat the male while mating!

Male stag beetles wrestling with their antlers (enlarged jaws) when competing for a female.

Ants (bottom) are social insects, living in colonies.

insect (**in** sekt) *n.* any of many kinds of small invertebrates with a body consisting of a head, thorax, and abdomen, three pairs of legs, and usually one or two pairs of wings.

insecticide (in **sek** ti sīd) *n.* a substance for killing insects.

insert (in **sûrt**) *vb.* **inserting, inserted** to put, place, or fit something inside something else: *Insert the coin into the slot machine.*

inside (in **sīd**) *n.* the inner side, surface, or part of something: *The inside of the chest was painted blue.* – *adj.* being on, near, towards, or from the inside: *Jake put his wallet away safely in an inside pocket.*

insignia (in **sig** ni å) *n.* **insignia** or **insignias** badges or emblems of office.

insincere (in sin **sēr**) *adj.* not genuine; false; hypocritical. – *n.* **insincerity** (in sin **se** ri ti).

insist (in **sist**) *vb.* **insisting, insisted** to demand firmly: *You must insist upon your rights.*

insolent (**in** sŏ lĕnt) *adj.* rude. – *n.* **insolence**.

insomnia (in **som** ni å) *n.* a continual inability to sleep. – *n.* & *adj.* **insomniac**.

inspect (in **spekt**) *vb.* **inspecting, inspected** to look at or examine closely. – *n.* **inspection**.

inspire (in **spīr**) *vb.* **inspiring, inspired 1** to stimulate a person to activity, especially artistic or creative activity. **2** to fill a person with a feeling of confidence and encouragement. **inspiration** (in spi **rā** shŏn) *n.* **1** a supposed power which stimulates the mind, especially to artistic activity or creativity. **2** a brilliant or inspired idea. – *adj.* **inspirational**.

install (in **stöl**) *vb.* **installing, installed** to put equipment, machinery, etc. in place.

instalment (in **stöl** mĕnt) *n.* **1** one of a series of payments of a debt: *We're paying for the car in 12 instalments.* **2** one of several parts published or broadcast at regular intervals.

instance (**in** ståns) *n.* an example.

instant (**in** stånt) *adj.* **1** immediate: *He was an instant success.* **2** (of food, etc.) very quickly prepared: *Tim prefers to drink instant coffee.* – *n.* a very brief period of time. – *adj.* **instantaneous**. **instantly** *adv.* at once; immediately.

instead (in **sted**) *adv.* as an alternative.

instinct (**in** stingkt) *n.* **1** a natural, involuntary, and usually unconscious reaction, response, or impulse: *Birds build nests by instinct.* **2** intuition. **instinctive** *adj.* prompted by instinct.

institute (**in** sti tūt) *n.* an organization which promotes research, education, or any other particular cause.

The Colorado beetle, originally from North America, is a notorious potato pest.

United States Air Force

Royal Air Force

Insignia are emblems, badges, or signs identifying an organization, rank, or honour. In the British army, for instance, a corporal wears two chevron stripes on both arms and a sergeant three stripes as insignia of rank.

instruct (in **strukt**) *vb.* **instructing, instructed 1** to teach. **2** to direct or order: *She instructed her solicitors to sue the manufacturers.*
instruction *n.* **1** (often in *plural*) a direction, order, or command. **2** (in *plural*) detailed guidelines, e.g. on how to operate a machine.
instructor *n.* a teacher.

instrument (in stroo měnt) *n.* **1** a tool. **2** (also **musical instrument**) any of several devices which can be made to produce music.

insulate (in sū lāt) *vb.* **insulating, insulated** to prevent the passing of heat, sound, electricity, etc. from a wire, etc. by covering it with some special material.

insult (in **sult**) *vb.* **insulting, insulted** to behave or speak rudely or offensively to. – (**in** sult) *n.* a rude remark or action.

insure (in **shoor**) *vb.* **insuring, insured** to arrange for the payment of a sum of money in case of the loss or theft of property, or injury to someone, by paying regular amounts of money to an insurance company. – *n.* **insurance**.

intact (in **takt**) *adj.* whole; not broken.

integrate (in ti grāt) *vb.* **integrating, integrated 1** to fit parts together to form a whole. **2** to mix freely with other groups in society, etc. – *n.* **integration**.

integrity (in **teg** ri ti) *n.* honesty.

intellect (in **tě** lekt) *n.* the ability to think.
intellectual *adj.* having a highly developed ability to think and understand. – *n.* a person with great mental ability.

intelligence (in **tel** i jěns) *n.* the ability to learn.
intelligent *adj.* clever.

intend (in **tend**) *vb.* **intending, intended** to plan or have in mind as a purpose.

intense (in **tens**) *adj.* **1** very great or extreme. **2** very deeply felt: *intense joy.* – *n.* **intensity**.

intensive (in **ten** siv) *adj.* **1** done with or requiring considerable amounts of thought, effort, time, etc.: *This is a labour-intensive task.* **2** thorough; concentrated.

intent (in **tent**) *n.* something which is aimed at; a purpose: *It is his intent to run for election.*

intention (in **ten** shŏn) *n.* that which you plan or intend to do; an aim or purpose.
intentional *adj.* said, done, etc. on purpose.

inter (in **tûr**) *vb.* **interring, interred** to bury.

inter- (**in** tĕr-) *prefix* between or among.

intercept (in tĕr **sept**) *vb.* **intercepting, intercepted** to stop or catch, for example a person, missile, etc. on the way from one place to another. – *n.* **interception**.

Insulate comes from the Latin word *insula* meaning 'island', expressing the idea of 'to isolate, to detach'.

Clarinet

There are four kinds of musical **instrument**: woodwind such as clarinets and flutes; brass such as trombones and trumpets; strings such as violins, harps, and guitars; and percussion which include drums, gongs, and tambourines.

Violin

Cymbal

French horn

intercom (in **tĕr** kom) *n.* a system consisting of microphones and loudspeakers which allow communication within a building, ship, etc.

interest (**in** trĕst) *n.* **1** curiosity: *Ian has an interest in frogs.* **2** the power to attract a person's attention and curiosity: *The T.V. programme lacked any interest.* **3** a hobby or pastime. **4** money paid as a charge for borrowing money. – *vb.* **interesting, interested 1** to attract the attention and curiosity of: *The new film interests me.* **2** to cause someone to take a part in some activity: *Can I interest you in signing our petition?*
interesting *adj.* holding the attention.

interface (**in** tĕr fās) *n.* a device, such as an electrical circuit, which allows two pieces of equipment to be linked and operated together.

interfere (in tĕr **fēr**) *vb.* **interfering, interfered 1** to involve yourself in matters which do not concern you. **2** to hinder the progress of. – *adj.* **interfering**.

interior (in **tēr** i ŏr) *adj.* of the inside; inner: *interior decoration.* – *n.* **1** the inside. **2** the part of a country that is farthest from the coast.

interjection (in tĕr **jek** shŏn) *n.* a word, phrase, or sound used as an exclamation to express surprise, sudden disappointment, pain, etc.

intermediate (in tĕr **mēd** i ăt) *adj.* in the middle; placed between two points, stages, or extremes in place or time.

internal (in **tûr** nål) *adj.* of, on, in, or suitable for the inside; inner: *the internal organs of the body.* – *adv.* **internally.**

international (in tĕr **na** shŏ nål) *adj.* of or involving two or more nations. – *n.* a sports match between two national teams.

interplanetary (in tĕr **plan** i tå ri) *adj.* happening or existing between planets.

interpret (in **tûr** prit) *vb.* **interpreting, interpreted 1** to explain the meaning of a foreign word, dream, etc. **2** to bring out your idea of the meaning: *How would you interpret this piece of music?* – *n.* **interpretation.**
interpreter *n.* a person who translates speech in a foreign language as the words are spoken.

interrogate (in **te** rŏ gāt) *vb.* **interrogating, interrogated** to question or examine closely. – *n.* **interrogation.** – *n.* **interrogator.**

interrupt (in tĕ **rupt**) *vb.* **interrupting, interrupted 1** to break into a conversation by asking a question or making a comment: *I was interrupted by the lecturer.* **2** to make a break in the continuous activity of an event.
interruption *n.* **1** the act of interrupting. **2** something that interrupts, such as a question.

intersect (in tĕr **sekt**) *vb.* **intersecting, intersected** to divide by passing or cutting through or across. – *n.* **intersection.**

interval (in tĕr vål) *n.* **1** a period of time between two events. **2** a space or distance between two things. **3** (*British*) a short break between the acts of a play or opera.

interview (in tĕr vū) *n.* **1** a meeting at which an employer meets and judges a prospective employee. – *vb.* **interviewing, interviewed** to hold an interview with.

intestine (in **tes** tin) or (in **tes** tēn) *n.* the tubes through which food passes after it has left the stomach.

intimate (in ti måt) *adj.* **1** sharing a close and affectionate friendship. **2** very private or personal: *We told her our most intimate wishes.*

intimidate (in **tim** i dāt) *vb.* **intimidating, intimidated** to frighten someone into doing what you want. – *adj.* **intimidating.**

into (**in** too) *prep.* **1** towards the inside or middle of: *The customers went into the shop.* **2** against; into contact or collision with: *The bull smashed into the fence.* **3** expressing a change of state or condition: *Tim changed into a suit for the wedding.*

intolerant (in **tol** ĕ rånt) *adj.* unwilling to accept ideas, etc. different from your own. – *n.* **intolerance.**

intrepid (in **tre** pid) *adj.* bold and daring.

intricate (**in** tri kåt) *adj.* full of complicated details or parts: *Jo is using an intricate knitting pattern.*

intrigue (**in** trēg) *n.* a secret plot or plan. – (in **trēg**) *vb.* **intriguing, intrigued** to excite the curiosity or interest: *This problem intrigues me.* – *adj.* **intriguing.**

introduce (in trŏ **dūs**) *vb.* **introducing, introduced 1** to make a person known by name to another: *Tamsin introduced me to her dad.* **2** to announce or present a radio or television programme to an audience. **3** to bring something new into a place, situation, etc. for the first time: *Can you remember when the metric system was introduced?*
introduction *n.* **1** the act of introducing. **2** a section at the beginning of a book which explains briefly what it is about.

intrude (in **trood**) *vb.* **intruding, intruded** to force or impose yourself where you are unwanted and unwelcome. – *n.* **intruder.**

Inuit (**in** oo it) *n.* **Inuit** or **Inuits** a member of any of several native peoples living in GREENLAND, CANADA and North Alaska. (**Eskimo** is the established English name but the people themselves prefer **Inuit.**)

invade (in **vād**) *vb.* **invading, invaded 1** to enter a country by force. **2** to interfere with a person's privacy, etc. – *n.* **invader.**

invalid¹ (**in** vå lid) *n.* a person who is constantly ill or who is disabled.

invalid² (in **val** id) *adj.* having no legal force: *This document is invalid.*

invaluable (in **val** ū å bĕl) *adj.* whose value is too great to be measured.

invasion (in **vā** zhŏn) *n.* an act of invading.

INTO AND IN TO
Two separate words are needed when *in* is an adverb belonging to the verb that comes before it, and *to* is part of an infinitive verb that comes after it: *The players went in to shelter from the rain.* Into as one word is a preposition: *He crashed the car into the wall.*

The biggest invasion in history – the allied landings in Normandy, northern France, in June 1944. Over 350,000 troops were put ashore.

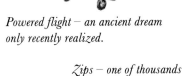

Powered flight – an ancient dream only recently realized.

The wheel – driving force of many other inventions.

Zips – one of thousands of revolutionary ordinary inventions like safety pins and safety razors!

Human civilization is largely a story of discovery and **invention**. Many important inventions have come from the work of one person, others have been the result of many people working patiently together as a team.

A potter's wheel.

The computer, the modern successor to Charles Babbage's mechanical 'Analytical Engine' of 1823.

Hans Lippershey's telescope of 1608.

SOME GREAT INVENTIONS

BC
7000 Pottery
3000 Wheel (Asia)
3000 Plough (Mesopotamia)

AD
105 Paper from pulp (China)
1440 Printing press (Germany)
1590 Microscope (Netherlands)
1593 Thermometer (Italy)
1608 Telescope (Netherlands)
1650 Air Pump (Germany)
1712 Steam engine (England)
1793 Cotton gin (US)
1800 Lathe (England)
1804 Steam locomotive (England)
1822 Camera (France)
1837 Telegraph (US)
1858 Refrigerator (France)
1866 Dynamite (Sweden)
1876 Telephone (Scotland)
1885 Motor car engine (Germany)
1895 Radio (Italy)
1903 Aeroplane (US)
1925 Television (Scotland)
1940 Penicillin (England)
1946 Electronic computer (US)
1948 Transistor (US)
1955 Hovercraft (England)
1960 Laser (US)
1979 Compact disc (Japan)
1984 Apple Mac (US)

invent (in **vent**) *vb.* **inventing, invented 1** to make or use for the first time: *Samuel Morse invented the telegraph.* **2** to think or make up an excuse, false story, etc. – *n.* **inventor**.
invention *n.* **1** something invented, especially a device, machine, etc. **2** (*colloquial*) a lie.
inventory (in **věn** tŏ ri) *n.* **inventories** a list of the articles, goods, etc. found in a particular place, such as of goods for sale in a shop.
invertebrate (in **vûr** tĕ brăt) *n.* an animal without a backbone such as an insect, a worm, or snail.
invest (in **vest**) *vb.* **investing, invested 1** to put money into a business in order to make a profit. **2** to devote time, effort, energy, etc. to something, usually for future gain: *Mark invested a lot of time in planning the outing.* – *n.* **investor**.
investigate (in **ves** ti găt) *vb.* **investigating, investigated** to carry out a thorough and often official inquiry: *The police investigated the cause of the break-in.* – *n.* **investigation**.
invincible (in **vin** să bĕl) *adj.* that cannot be defeated; unconquerable.
invisible (in **viz** ă bĕl) *adj.* **1** not able to be seen. **2** unseen. – *n.* **invisibility**. – *adv.* **invisibly**.
invite (in **vīt**) *vb.* **inviting, invited** to ask someone to come to your house, to a party, etc.: *Irma invited all her friends to the barbecue.*
invitation (in vi **tā** shŏn) *n.* a request to a person to come or go to a party, meal, etc.

invoice (in vois) *n.* a list delivered with goods giving details of price, quantity, etc.
involuntary (in **vol** ŭn tă ri) *adj.* describing an action, movement, muscle action, etc. that is done without being controlled by the will; unintentional. – *adv.* **involuntarily**.
involve (in **volv**) *vb.* **involving, involved 1** to require as a necessary part: *Ballet involves hours of practice.* **2** to cause someone to take part in: *David involved me in his little scheme.* **3** to make yourself emotionally concerned in: *Andrea involved herself in her mother's problems.*
iodine (ī ŏ dēn) *n.* a non-metallic element (symbol **I**), found in seaweed.
ion (ī ŏn) *n.* an electrically charged atom.

● **Iowa**. See Supplement, **USA**.

● **Iran**. See Supplement, **Countries**.

● **Iraq**. See Supplement, **Countries**.

irate (ī **rāt**) *adj.* very angry.

● **Ireland** is the second largest island of the British Isles. Much of its economy is based on farming and fishing. NORTHERN IRELAND is part of the UNITED KINGDOM. Its capital city is Belfast. Southern Ireland is the Republic of Ireland. Its capital is Dublin. See also Supplement, **Countries**.

iridescent (i ri **des** ěnt) *adj.* having many bright rainbow-like colours which seem to shimmer. – *n.* **iridescence**.

iris (ī ris) *n.* **1** the coloured, central membrane in the eye. It controls the size of the pupil. **2** a tall flower with long, sword-shaped leaves.

Irish (ī rish) *adj.* of IRELAND, its inhabitants, history, culture, or Celtic language. – *n.* **Irishman, Irishmen**. – *n.* **Irishwoman, Irishwomen**.

iron (ī ŏrn) *n.* **1** a heavy grey metallic element (symbol **Fe**). It is used for making tools and in engineering. It is a good conductor of heat. **2** a flat-bottomed household tool used for smoothing the creases out of and pressing clothes. – *adj.* **1** made of iron: *The iron railings are rusting.* **2** like iron, especially in being very strong and inflexible: *Ivan has an iron will.* – *vb.* **ironing, ironed** to smooth the creases out of clothes with an iron.

Iron Age *n.* the period in history following on from the BRONZE AGE when people made weapons and tools out of iron, (about 1000 BC).

irony (ī rŏ ni) *n.* **ironies** a form of humour, or a way of mocking by saying the opposite of what is clearly true: *"How very clever of you to be so late!" he said, full of irony.*
ironic (ī **ron** ik) *adj.* (also **ironical**) containing irony. – *adv.* **ironically**.

irrational (i **ra** shŏn ǎl) *adj.* not able to think logically and clearly.

irregular (i **reg** ū lǎr) *adj.* **1** not happening at regular intervals. **2** not smooth or balanced: *This rocky surface is very irregular.* **3** not conforming to rules or routine: *Her eating habits are irregular – some days she eats nothing.* – *n.* **irregularity** (i reg ū **lar** i ti), **irregularities**.

irresistible (i ri **zist** ǎ běl) *adj.* too tempting to be resisted: *The delicious ice cream was irresistible.*

irresponsible (i ri **spon** sǎ běl) *adj.* **1** reckless; careless. **2** not reliable or trustworthy. – *n.* **irresponsibility**. – *adv.* **irresponsibly**.

irrigate (**i** ri gāt) *vb.* **irrigating, irrigated** to supply land with water through canals, ditches, etc. – *n.* **irrigation**.

irritate (**i** ri tāt) *vb.* **irritating, irritated 1** to make angry or annoyed. **2** to make part of the body sore. – *adj.* **irritating**. – *n.* **irritation**.

is. See **be**.

-ish (-ish) *suffix* forming adjectives meaning **1** slightly; having a trace of: *reddish; autumnish.* **2** like: *childish.* **3** having as a nationality: *Swedish.* **4** about; roughly: *fiftyish.*

Isis (ī sis). See **Myths and Legends**.

Islam (iz **läm**) *n.* the MUSLIM religion, based on the worship of one god (Allah) and the teachings of MUHAMMAD. – *adj.* **Islamic**.

● Islam is the main religion in North AFRICA and parts of south-east ASIA. It was first preached by the prophet MUHAMMAD who was born in Mecca in AD 570. The followers of Islam are called MUSLIMS. Their holy book is the KORAN and their place of worship is a mosque.

island (ī lǎnd) *n.* a piece of land completely surrounded by water.
islander *n.* a person who lives on an island.

isle (īl) *n.* a small island.

-ism (-i zěm) *suffix* forming nouns meaning **1** a formal set of ideas etc.: *feminism.* **2** a quality: *heroism.* **3** an activity or practice: *criticism.* **4** discrimination on the grounds of: *ageism.*

iso- (ī sō-) same; equal.

isolate (ī sŏ lāt) *vb.* **isolating, isolated** to separate from others. – *adj.* **isolated**. – *n.* **isolation**.

isosceles (ī sos ě lēz) *n.* a triangle having two sides of equal length.

● **Israel**. See Supplement, **Countries**.

Israeli (iz **rāl** i) *adj.* of the modern state of Israel or its inhabitants. – *n.* a person born in Israel.

issue (**i** shoo) *n.* **1** the giving out, publishing, or making available of something: *I bought the first issue of the magazine.* **2** a subject for discussion: *Unemployment is the main issue of the debate.* – *vb.* **issuing, issued 1** to give or send out, distribute, publish, or make available. **2** to supply: *The troops were issued with weapons.*

-ist (-ist) *suffix* **1** a believer in some formal system of ideas, principles, or beliefs: *feminist.* **2** a person who carries out some activity or practises some art: *novelist.*

● **Istanbul**. See **Constantinople**.

it (it) *pron.* **1** the thing, animal, baby, or group already mentioned: *We watched the movie and enjoyed it very much.* **2** the person in question: *Who is it?* **3** used as the subject with impersonal verbs and when describing the weather or distance or telling the time: *What time is it? It's raining.* **4** used to refer to a general situation: *How's it going?*

IRISH WORDS AND TERMS
The form of Gaelic spoken in parts of Ireland has given a number of words to the English language. They include:
blarney, brat, brogue, galore, leprechaun, shamrock and smithereens. Also *banshee* a female spirit that wails when a death is about to occur; *Garda*, the police force of Southern Ireland; *machree* a term of endearment meaning 'my heart'; and *shillelagh* a club-like weapon. The Prime Minister of the Republic of Ireland is *Taoiseach*.

Sloping italic *type is a streamlined version of the Small Roman hand developed by Italian scholars in the 1300s. It is based on lettering from books of the 700s.*

abcdef

Perhaps best known of Italian food are pizza and, in all its different guises, pasta.

A street scene in 15th-century Florence, one of the great centres of Renaissance learning and art. But it was trade that made Florence grow.

Italian (i **tal** yǎn) *adj.* of ITALY, its inhabitants, culture, history, or its language. – *n.* **1** a person born or living in ITALY. **2** the Romance language spoken in ITALY.

italic (i **tal** ik) *n.* (usually in *plural*) a typeface, first used in ITALY, with characters which slope upwards to the right, e.g. *italic.*

Throughout history, **Italy** has played an enormously powerful part in the culture and development of Europe. The Romans ruled and gave their civilization and administration to a vast area of the world. The Latin language is the ancestor of all Europe's Romance languages. The Renaissance flowered in Italy. For a long time the whole Christian Church was governed from there. In the arts, science, and industry Italy's contribution has been great.

Pisa's cathedral and Leaning Tower.

● **Italy** is a peninsula in southern EUROPE and is noted for its impressive ruins of the ROMAN EMPIRE, for the VATICAN, and for its medieval cities such as FLORENCE and VENICE. It was the birthplace of the RENAISSANCE. The northern cities are highly industrialized and there is much rich farmland. The southern part is relatively underdeveloped. See also Supplement, **Countries**.

itch (ich) *n.* an unpleasant irritation on the surface of the skin which makes you want to scratch. – *vb.* **itching, itched 1** to have an itch and want to scratch. **2** to feel a strong or restless desire – *n.* **itchiness**. – *adj.* **itchy, itchier, itchiest**.

-ite (-īt) *suffix* forming nouns denoting **1** a place or national group: *Israelite*. **2** a follower of: *Jacobite*. **3** a fossil: *ammonite*. **4** a mineral: *graphite*. **5** a salt of a certain formula: *nitrite*.

item (ī těm) *n.* **1** a separate unit, especially one on a list. **2** a separate piece of information.

itinerary (ī **tin** ě rǎ ri) *n.* **itineraries** a plan of a route for a journey.

-itis (-ī tis) *suffix* in the names of diseases, inflammation of: *appendicitis*.

its (its) *adj.* belonging to it: *The dog scratched its ear.* – *pron.* the one or ones belonging to it. **itself** *pron.* **1** the reflexive form of **it** meaning its own self: *The cat licked itself.* **2** used for emphasis: *It's the book itself that interests me, not the contents.* **3** (also **by itself**) without help.

● **its** and **it's**. The first word means 'belonging to it': *The dog is eating its bone.* It's is an abbreviation of *it is*: *It's time to go.*

● **Ivan** the name of several rulers of Russia including Ivan III 'the Great' (1404-1505) and Ivan IV 'the Terrible' (1530-84), the first Russian ruler to use the title *tsar*.

-ive (-iv) *suffix* having a quality, performing an action, etc.: *creative*; *detective*.

ivory (ī vǒ ri) *n.* the bony, creamy-white substance which forms the tusks of elephants, hippopotamuses, and walruses.

Ivory Coast. See **Côte d'Ivoire**.

ivy (ī vi) *n.* **ivies** an evergreen climbing shrub with dark leaves with five points.

-ize or **-ise** (-īz) *suffix* forming verbs meaning **1** to make or become: *equalize*. **2** to treat or react to: *criticize*.

J j

jab (jab) *vb.* **jabbing, jabbed** to poke or prod. – *n.* **1** a poke or prod. **2** (*colloquial*) an injection.

jack (jak) *n.* **1** a device for raising heavy objects off the ground. **2** in cards, (also **knave**) the card bearing a picture of a page. **3** the male of certain animals, e.g. the donkey. – *vb.* **jacking, jacked**.

jackal (**jak** öl) *n.* a dog-like animal of AFRICA and ASIA, that feeds on the remains of creatures killed by other animals.

jackdaw (**jak** dö) *n.* a bird of the crow family.

jacket (**jak** it) *n.* **1** a short coat, especially a long-sleeved hip-length one. **2** something worn over the top half of the body: *Don't forget your life-jacket*. **3** a cover for a hardback book.

jackknife (**jak** nīf) *n.* a large pocket knife with a folding blade. – *vb.* **jackknifing, jackknifed** (of an articulated vehicle) to go out of control in such a way that the trailer swings round against the cab.

jackpot (**jak** pot) *n.* the maximum win to be made in a lottery, card game, etc.

Jacobean (ja kổ **bē** ån) *adj.* relating or belonging to the reign of James the First of England (the Sixth of Scotland) (1603-25).

Jacuzzi (jå **kōō** zi) *n.* ® a large bath with underwater jets that massage the body.

jade (jād) *n.* a hard, usually green stone.

jagged (**jag** id) *adj.* having a rough or sharp uneven edge.

jaguar (**jag** ū år) *n.* a large spotted South American animal of the cat family.

jail or **gaol** (jāl) *n.* prison. – *vb.* **jailing, jailed** or **gaoling, gaoled** to imprison.

jam¹ (jam) *n.* a thick sticky food made from fruit boiled with sugar, used as a spread on bread.

jam² (jam) *vb.* **jamming, jammed 1** to fill a street so full that movement comes to a stop. **2** to push or shove; to cram, press, or pack: *A huge crowd jammed into the stadium.* **3** to stick or wedge. **4** to stick and stop working: *Paper has jammed in the photocopier.* **5** to put on with sudden force: *Mum jammed on the brakes to avoid the dog.* – *n.* **1** a mass of vehicles so tightly crowded together that movement comes to a stop: *traffic jams*. **2** a stoppage of machinery, etc.

● **Jamaica**. See Supplement, **Countries**.

jamboree (jam bổ **rē**) *n.* a large rally of Scouts.

● **James** is the name of six kings of Scotland and two of Great Britain. James the Sixth of Scotland (a descendant of Henry the Seventh of England) became James the First of England in 1603. In this way the two crowns united.

● **James, Henry** (1843-1916) was an American novelist whose works include *The Ambassadors*, *The Turn of the Screw*, and *The Portrait of a Lady*.

January (**jan** ū å ri) or (**jan** ū ri) *n.* the first month of the year. January has 31 days.

A finely carved Chinese jade pot of the 1700s. It was made to hold brushes used in Chinese writing, an art form that has been described as 'dancing on paper'.

Tokugawa Ieyasu who in 1603 became the shogun or military commander of Japan.

A bullet-shaped high-speed electric train – symbol of Japan's technical efficiency.

Hokkaido

The four main islands of Japan. There is evidence of people living there from around 30,000 BC.

Honshu

A beautifully carved netsuke or toggle.

Shikoku

Kyushu

A Chinese-style Buddhist temple. But Shinto, 'the way of the gods', was Japan's main religion.

Japan is the richest country in Asia. It is made up of four large and many small islands. Mountains cover most of Japan; the highest is a beautiful volcano called Fujiyama. Most Japanese live in cities and work in factories. Japan was defeated in the Second World War, but afterwards became the 'workshop of the world'. The capital is Tokyo. See also Supplement, **Countries**.

Japanese (ja på **nēz**) *adj.* of JAPAN, its people or language. – *n.* **1** a native of JAPAN. **2** the language of JAPAN.

jar¹ (jär) *n.* a wide-mouthed cylindrical container, usually of glass.

jar² (jär) *vb.* **jarring, jarred 1** to have a harsh effect. **2** to jolt or vibrate. **3** to clash or conflict: *These buildings jar with the environment.*

jargon (jär gǒn) *n.* the specialized vocabulary of a particular trade or profession.

jasmine (**jaz** min) *n.* a shrub with sweet-smelling yellow, white, or red flowers.

jaundice (**jön** dis) *n.* a condition in which there is an excess of bile in the blood, a pigment of which turns the skin yellow.

javelin (**jav** ê lin) *n.* a light spear for throwing.

jaw (jö) *n.* either of the two hinged parts of the skull in which the teeth are set.

jay (jā) *n.* a noisy bird of the crow family.

jazz (jaz) *n.* popular music of black American origin, with strong, catchy rhythms, performed with much improvization.

● Jazz was played by blacks of New Orleans in the late 1800s. There have since been many styles but all have strong rhythms and emphasize improvization. Famous jazz performers include Louis Armstrong, Duke Ellington, Charlie Parker, and Billie HOLIDAY.

jealous (**je** lǔs) *adj.* **1** envious of someone else, his or her possessions, talents, etc. **2** suspicious and resentful of possible rivals; possessive. **jealousy** *n.* **jealousies** envy.

jeans (jēnz) *n.* (*plural*) denim trousers.

jeep (jēp) *n.* a light military vehicle capable of travelling over rough country.

jeer (jēr) *vb.* **jeering, jeered** to mock; to laugh unkindly: *Joan jeered at his accent.*

● **Jefferson, Thomas** (1743-1826) was the chief author of the American DECLARATION OF INDEPENDENCE and later president of the UNITED STATES.

Jekyll and Hyde (**je** kêl ånd **hīd**) *n.* a person with apparently two distinct personalities, one good, the other evil.

jell or **gel** (jel) *vb.* **jelling, jelled** or **gelling, gelled** to become firm; to set.

jelly (**je** li) *n.* **jellies** a wobbly, transparent, fruit-flavoured dessert set with gelatine. **jellyfish** *n.* **jellyfish** or **jellyfishes** a sea creature with a translucent jelly-like body.

● **Jenner, Edward** (1749-1823) was an English doctor who discovered vaccination by showing that injections of cowpox virus produce immunity against SMALLPOX.

jeopardy (**je** pår di) *n.* danger of harm or loss. **jeopardize** or **jeopardise** *vb.* **jeopardizing, jeopardized** to put at risk of harm or loss.

jerboa (jûr **bō** å) *n.* a small rat-like animal of AFRICA and ASIA, with long hind legs.

● **Jericho** is a village in JORDAN on the site of a biblical city captured by the Israelites.

jerk (jûrk) *n.* **1** a quick tug or pull. **2** a sudden movement. – *vb.* **jerking, jerked 1** to pull with sharply. **2** to move with sharp suddenness.

jersey (**jûr** zi) *n.* **jerseys** a knitted garment worn on the upper part of the body; a pullover.

● **Jerusalem** is the capital of ISRAEL and a holy city of the JEWS, CHRISTIANS, and MUSLIMS.

jest (jest) *n.* a joke or prank. – **in jest** as a joke.

jester (**jes** těr) *n.* a colourfully dressed professional clown employed by a king or noble to amuse the court.

Jesuit (**je** zū it) *n.* a member of the Society of Jesus, a Roman Catholic order founded by Ignatius Loyola in 1534.

● **Jesus Christ** (*c.*6 BC–*c.*AD 30) was the founder of CHRISTIANITY. He was born in BETHLEHEM and was brought up as a Jew. His life and teachings are contained in the New Testament of the BIBLE. He was betrayed, condemned to death, and crucified. CHRISTIANS believe he is the son of GOD and that he rose from the dead.

jet (jet) *n.* **1** a strong fast stream of liquid or gas, forced under pressure from a narrow opening. **2** (also **jet aircraft**) an aircraft powered by a jet engine. – *vb.* **jetting, jetted 1** to travel by jet aircraft. **2** to come out in a jet; to spurt.

jet engine *n.* an engine using jet propulsion for forward thrust.

jetsam (**jet** såm) *n.* goods jettisoned from a ship and washed up on the shore.

jettison (**je** ti sǒn) *vb.* **jettisoning, jettisoned 1** to throw cargo overboard to lighten a ship, aircraft, etc. in an emergency. **2** to abandon.

jetty (**je** ti) *n.* **jetties 1** a stone or wooden landing-stage. **2** a stone barrier built out into the sea to protect a harbour from currents.

Jew (jōō) *n.* **1** a member of the HEBREW race. **2** someone whose religion is JUDAISM.

Jewish *adj.* relating or belonging to the Jews or to JUDAISM.

jewel (**jōō** ěl) *n.* a precious stone.

jeweller *n.* a person who deals in, makes, or repairs jewellery.

jewellery or (especially *US*) **jewelry** *n.* articles worn for personal decoration, such as bracelets, necklaces, brooches, rings, etc.

jib (jib) *n.* the projecting arm of a crane from which the lifting gear hangs. – *vb.* **jibbing, jibbed** (of a horse) to refuse a jump.

jig (jig) *n.* a lively country dance or folk dance.

jigsaw (**jig** sö) *n.* **1** (also **jigsaw puzzle**) a picture mounted on wood or cardboard, and sawn into pieces. The pieces are put together again to rebuild the picture. **2** a fine-bladed saw.

jihad (ji **had**) *n.* a holy war for ISLAM.

jingle (**jing** gěl) *n.* **1** a short sharp ringing sound, as of coins or keys. **2** a simple rhyming verse or song. – *vb.* **jingling, jingled** to make a ringing sound.

● **Joan of Arc** (1412-31) was a French national heroine who led a force against the English in the Hundred Years War. She was burned for witchcraft by the English.

job (job) *n.* **1** a person's regular paid employment. **2** a piece of work. **3** a completed task: *Mary made a good job of the pruning.* **4** a function or responsibility: *It is Kay's job to make sure everyone sits in the right place.*

The jerboa or desert rat (above left) looks like a miniature kangaroo. It can hop up to three metres in each bound.

Joan of Arc was convinced that the 'voices' she heard were from heaven telling her to rescue France from the English. She commanded the French army.

An eagle-shaped brooch made by an Ostrogoth in Spain (AD 400s)

Jewellery has been made since prehistoric times, when the bones and teeth of animals were used. Today jewellery is mostly made of gems and precious metals.

A jewel bearing the inscription 'Alfred had me made'. It was probably one of a set of book pointers that Alfred, King of Wessex, ordered to be made.

The crown used at the coronation of King Stephen of Hungary on Christmas Day AD 1000.

This gold ring is a fine example of Viking craftsmanship.

jockey (**jo** ki) *n.* **jockeys** a rider, especially professional, in horse races.

jodhpurs (**jod** pĕrz) *n.* (*plural*) trousers that are tight-fitting from knee to calf, worn for riding.

jog (jog) *vb.* **jogging, jogged 1** to prompt the memory. **2** to run at a gentle, steady pace, for exercise. – *n.* **jogger**. – *n.* **jogging**.

●**Johannesburg** (jō **ha** nĕz bûrg) the largest city in SOUTH AFRICA.

●**John the Baptist** was a preacher and cousin of JESUS whom he baptized. He was beheaded by King HEROD.

●**Johnson, Amy** (1903-41) was an English pilot who made many solo flights.

●**Johnson, Samuel** (1709-84) was an English writer famous for his wit and his *Dictionary*.

join (join) *vb.* **joining, joined 1** to connect, attach, link, or unite. **2** to become a member: *Philippa joined the film society.* **3** to meet: *Roads join at a crossroad.* **4** to come together with: *We joined them for supper.* – *n.* a seam or joint. – *vb.* **join in** to take part.

joint (joint) *n.* **1** the place where two or more pieces join. **2** a part of the skeleton, such as the knee or elbow, where two bones meet. – *adj.* owned, done, etc. in common; shared: *We have a joint account at the bank.*

joist (joist) *n.* a beam supporting a floor.

joke (jōk) *n.* a humorous story: *Steve is always cracking jokes.* – *vb.* **joking, joked** to make jokes; to speak in jest, not in earnest. – *adv.* **jokingly**. – **beyond a joke** (*colloquial*) not funny; intolerable. – **joking apart** to be serious, seriously. – **take a joke** to be able to laugh at a joke played on you.

joker *n.* **1** an extra card in a pack, usually bearing a picture of a jester, used in certain games. **2** a cheerful person, always full of jokes.

●**Jolliet** (**zho** li ā), **Louis** (1645-1700) was a French-Canadian explorer of NORTH AMERICA.

jolly (**jo** li) *adj.* **jollier, jolliest 1** cheerful. **2** happy; enjoyable. – *n.* **jolliness**.
Jolly Roger *n.* a pirate ship's flag.

jolt (jōlt) *vb.* **jolting, jolted 1** to move along jerkily. **2** to jog or jar: *The bus jolted to a halt.* – *n.* **1** a jarring shake. **2** an emotional shock.

●**Jordan**. See Supplement, **Countries**.

jostle (**jo** sĕl) *vb.* **jostling, jostled** to push and shove: *The people jostled to get on the train.*

jot (jot) *n.* the least bit: *I've not a jot of sympathy.* – *vb.* **jotting, jotted** to write down hastily: *Please jot down your address.*

journal (**jûr** nål) *n.* **1** a magazine. **2** a diary in which to recount daily activities.
journalism *n.* the profession of writing for newspapers, television, etc. – *n.* **journalist**. – *adj.* **journalistic**.

journey (**jûr** ni) *n.* **journeys 1** a process of travelling from one place to another. **2** the distance covered by a journey. – *vb.* **journeying, journeyed** to make a journey.

joust (jowst) *n.* a contest between two knights on horseback, armed with lances. – *vb.* **jousting, jousted** to take part in a joust.

jovial (**jō** vi ål) *adj.* merry; cheerful.

jowl (jowl) *n.* loose flesh under the chin.

joy (joi) *n.* **1** a feeling of happiness. **2** a cause of this: *The puppy was a great joy to Liz.*
joyful *adj.* happy; full of joy.
joyride *n.* a reckless drive in a stolen vehicle.

●**Joyce, James** (1882-1941) was an Irish novelist whose works include *Ulysses* and *Dubliners*.

jubilee (**jōō** bi lē) *n.* a special anniversary, especially the 25th, 50th, or 60th (respectively a **silver**, **golden**, and **diamond jubilee**).

Judaism (**jōō** dā i zĕm) *n.* the religion of the JEWS, having its basis in the OLD TESTAMENT and the TALMUD.

●Observances in Judaism include the Sabbath as a day of rest, and the holy days of YOM KIPPUR, PASSOVER, and PENTECOST.

judge (juj) *n.* **1** a public officer who hears and decides cases in a law court. **2** a person appointed to decide the winner of a contest: *At the dog show the judge gave our poodle second place.* – *vb.* **judging, judged 1** to try a case in a law court as judge. **2** to decide the winner of a contest.
judgement or **judgment** *n.* **1** the decision of a judge in a court of law. **2** the ability to make wise or sensible decisions; good sense.

judo (**jōō** dō) *n.* a Japanese form of wrestling.

jug (jug) *n.* a container for liquids with a handle and a shaped lip for pouring.

PRONUNCIATION GUIDE

fat **a**	all **ŏ**
fate **ā**	foot **oo**
fast **ä**	moon **ōō**
among **å**	boy **oi**
met **e**	house **ow**
mean **ē**	demon **ŏ**
silent **ĕ**	thing **th**
loch **hh**	this **Th**
fin **i**	but **u**
line **ī**	mute **ū**
quick **kw**	fur **û**
got **o**	brochure **ů**
note **ō**	vision **zh**

Jubilee is of Hebrew origin and refers to a year of celebrations every 50 years. The word comes from *jobel*, a ram's horn, for jubilee year was proclaimed by blowing a horn.

juggernaut (**ju** gĕr nöt) *n.* a very large lorry.

juggle (**ju** gĕl) *vb.* **juggling, juggled** to keep several objects in the air at one time by skilful throwing and catching. – *n.* **juggler.**

juice (jōōs) *n.* **1** liquid from fruit or vegetables: *carrot juice.* **2** the body's natural fluids: *Digestive juices break down food in the stomach.*

juicy *adj.* **juicier, juiciest 1** full of juice; rich and succulent. **2** (*colloquial*) describing gossip that is intriguing or spicy.

● **Julius Caesar**. See **Caesar**.

July (joo lī) *n.* the seventh month of the year. July has 31 days.

jumble (**jum** bĕl) *vb.* **jumbling, jumbled** to mix; to throw together untidily. – *n.* a confused mass: *She left a jumble of clothes in the bedroom.*

jumbo (**jum** bō) (*colloquial*) *adj.* extra-large.

jump (jump) *vb.* **jumping, jumped 1** to spring off the ground, pushing off with the feet; to leap: *Joy jumped and touched the joists.* **2** to get over or across by jumping: *Jim jumped over the fence.* **3** to make a startled movement: *Jack jumped when the alarm went off.* **4** to omit: *Let's jump the next chapter.* – *n.* **1** an act of jumping. **2** an obstacle to be jumped. **3** a startled movement. – *vb.* **jump at** to accept eagerly: *Rory jumped at the chance to go swimming.*

jumper (**jum** pĕr) *n.* a sweater or jersey.

junction (**jungk** shŏn) *n.* **1** a place where roads or railway lines meet; an intersection. **2** a point of exit from, and access to, a motorway.

June (jōōn) *n.* the sixth month of the year. June has 30 days.

jungle (**jung** gĕl) *n.* dense tropical forest.

junior (**jōō** ni ŏr) *adj.* **1** low, or lower, in rank, class, etc. **2** younger than. – *n.* **1** a person of low, or lower, rank in a profession, organization, etc. **2** a pupil in a junior school. **3** a person younger than the one in question: *She's three years his junior.*

juniper (**jōō** ni pĕr) *n.* an evergreen shrub with prickly leaves and purple berries used as a medicine.

junk¹ (jungk) *n.* (*colloquial*) rubbish. – *adj.* cheap and worthless.

junk food *n.* food with little nutritional value.

junk² (jungk) *n.* a Far-Eastern flat-bottomed square-sailed boat.

Juno. See **Myths and Legends**.

● **Jupiter¹** is the largest planet in the solar system.

Jupiter². See **Myths and Legends**.

jury (**jōōr** i) *n.* **juries** a group of usually 12 people sworn to give an honest verdict on the evidence presented to a law court on a particular case.

just¹ (just) *adj.* fair; reasonable; based on justice: *The judge's decision was just.*

just² (just) *adv.* **1** exactly; precisely. **2** a short time before: *He had just gone.* **3** at this or that very moment: *I was just leaving.* **4** and no more: *There was only just enough.* **5** barely; narrowly: *The knife just missed his ear.* **6** only; merely; simply: *Pam sent just a brief note.* – **just in case** as a precaution.

justice (**jus** tis) *n.* **1** the quality of being just; fairness. **2** the quality of being reasonable. **3** administration of the law: *a miscarriage of justice.* **4** (*US*) a judge.

justify (**jus** ti fī) *vb.* **justifies, justifying, justified** to prove or show that something is right, just, or reasonable. – *n.* **justification.**

jut (jut) *vb.* **jutting, jutted** to project.

juvenile (**jōō** vĕn īl) *adj.* of young people.

Jupiter is so huge that a thousand Earths could fit on it. It spins faster than any of the other planets; a day on Jupiter lasts 10 hours. Jupiter consists of 90 percent hydrogen and 10 percent helium. Jupiter's main features are its ring and its Great Red Spot, probably a swirling mass of gases in a never-ending storm.

Callisto

Ganymede

Io

Europa

Jupiter's core is hotter than the surface of the Sun. Its clouds exposed to space are bitterly cold.

Io is a sulphur-covered world of constantly erupting volcanoes.

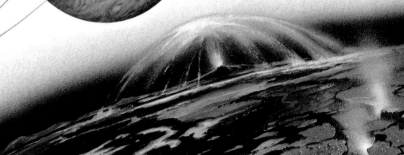

K k

K *abbreviation* in computing, a unit of memory equal to 1024 BYTES or words.

kaleidoscope (kå **lī** dǒ skōp) *n.* a tube inside which fragments of coloured glass, etc. are reflected in mirrors, so as to form changing symmetrical patterns as the tube is turned.

kangaroo (kang gå **rōō**) *n.* an Australian MARSUPIAL animal with large powerful hind legs adapted for leaping long distances. The female carries her young in a pouch on her abdomen.

● **Kansas**. See Supplement, **USA**.

karaoke (ka ri **ō** ki) *n.* the originally Japanese form of entertainment in which amateur performers sing pop songs to the accompaniment of pre-recorded music.

karate (kå **rä** ti) *n.* an originally Japanese system of unarmed self-defence.

kayak (**kī** ak) *n.* **1** a canoe covered with seal skin, used by the INUIT. **2** a similar fibreglass craft used in the sport of canoeing.

● **Kazakhstan**. See Supplement, **Countries**.

● **Keats** (kēts), **John** (1795-1821) was an English ROMANTIC poet.

keel (kēl) *n.* the timber or metal bar extending along the base of a ship, from which the hull is built up.

keen (kēn) *adj.* **1** eager; willing. **2** enthusiastic about; fond of: *Kate is keen on hockey.* **3** (of competition, rivalry, etc.) fierce.

keep¹ (kēp) *vb.* **keeping, kept** (kept) **1** to have; to possess. **2** to save. **3** to store: *I always keep stamps in my desk.* **4** to remain in a certain state, position, place, etc.: *Please keep quiet.* **5** to continue or be frequently doing something: *Keep smiling.* **6** to own an animal, etc. for use or pleasure: *Mark keeps hens at the bottom of his garden.* – *vb.* **keep back 1** not to reveal information, etc. **2** to suppress laughter, tears.

keep² (kēp) *n.* the central tower in a castle.

keg (keg) *n.* a small barrel.

● **Keller, Helen** (1880-1968) was an American author and social reformer who, despite being both blind and deaf, was taught to read BRAILLE and to talk.

The keep or donjon *was a massive tower and the strongest point in a castle. It stood in a courtyard called a* bailey. *The keep contained garrison quarters, a well-head, a Great Hall, and the lord's sleeping quarters.*

●**Kennedy** one of the most famous families in UNITED STATES history. It has provided the country with a president (John F. Kennedy), three senators, an attorney general, and an ambassador to GREAT BRITAIN.

kennel (**ke** nêl) *n.* a small shelter for a dog.

●**Kentucky**. See Supplement, **USA**.

●**Kenya**. See Supplement, **Countries**.

kept. See **keep**[1].

kerb (kûrb) *n.* the row of stones forming the edge of a pavement.

kernel (**kûr** nêl) *n.* a seed within a husk, the edible part of a nut, or the stone of a fruit.

kerosene (**ke** rŏ sēn) *n.* paraffin oil distilled from petroleum.

kestrel (**kes** trêl) *n.* a small type of falcon.

ketchup (**kech** up) *n.* a thick sauce made from tomatoes, vinegar, spices, etc.

kettle (**ke** têl) *n.* a kitchen vessel with a spout, lid, and handle, for boiling water in.
  kettledrum *n.* a large drum, shaped like a cauldron and mounted on a tripod.

key (kē) *n.* **1** a piece of shaped metal designed to turn a lock, wind a clock, grip and turn a nut, etc. **2** one of a series of buttons or levers pressed to sound the notes on a musical instrument, or to print or display a character on a computer, calculator, etc. **3** something that provides an answer or solution: *Understanding science is the key to solving this problem.* **4** a table explaining signs and symbols used on a map, etc. – *vb.* **keying, keyed** to enter data into a computer by operating keys.
  keyboard *n.* the set of keys on a piano, etc. or the bank of keys for operating a computer, etc.

khaki (**kä** ki) *n.* a brownish-green colour.

kibbutz (ki **boots**) *n.* **kibbutzim** (ki boo **tsēm**) in ISRAEL, a farm owned and run jointly by the people who work on it.

kick (kik) *vb.* **kicking, kicked 1** to hit or propel with the foot: *The cow kicked my leg.* **2** to swing or jerk the leg vigorously. **3** to get rid of a habit, etc. – *n.* **1** a blow with the foot. **2** a swing of the leg: *high kicks.* **3** (*colloquial*) a thrill of excitement. – *n.* **kicker.** – *vb.* **kick off 1** to start a football game by kicking the ball away from the centre. **2** to begin a discussion, etc.

kid[1] (kid) *n.* **1** (*colloquial*) a young person. **2** a young goat.

kid[2] (kid) *vb.* **kidding, kidded** (*colloquial*) **1** to pretend. **2** to fool or deceive, especially for fun.

kidnap (**kid** nap) *vb.* **kidnapping, kidnapped** to seize someone illegally, usually demanding a ransom for his or her release.

kidney (**kid** ni) *n.* **kidneys** one of a pair of abdominal organs that filter waste from the blood and pass it out of the body as urine.

●**Kilimanjaro** (ki li man **jä** rō) in TANZANIA, is an extinct VOLCANO and the highest mountain in AFRICA.

kill (kil) *vb.* **killing, killed 1** to cause the death of: *The frost killed the seedlings.* **2** (*colloquial*) to cause pain to: *My feet are killing me.* **3** (*colloquial*) to put an end to: *You certainly know how to kill a conversation.* – *n.* **killer.**
  killjoy *n.* someone who spoils others' pleasure.

kiln (kiln) *n.* an oven for baking pottery or bricks, or for drying grain.

kilo- (**ki** lō-) one thousand.

kilogram or **kilogramme** (**ki** lŏ gram) *n.* a unit of weight equal to 1000 grams.

kilometre (**ki** lŏ mē têr) or (ki **lom** i têr) *n.* a unit of distance equal to 1000 metres.

kilowatt (**ki** lŏ wot) *n.* a unit of electrical power.

kilt (kilt) *n.* a tartan knee-length skirt, worn by men as part of Scottish Highland dress.

kimono (ki **mō** nō) *n.* **kimonos** a long loose wide-sleeved Japanese garment.

kin (kin) *n.* your relations.

kind[1] (kīnd) *n.* **1** a group, class, sort, or type: *Foxes and wolves are kinds of dog.* **2** nature or character: *They differ in kind.* – **a kind of** something like a: *It's a kind of magazine.*

kind[2] (kīnd) *adj.* friendly, helpful, generous. – *n.* **kindness.**

kindergarten (**kin** dêr gär tên) *n.* a school for children aged between four and six.

king (king) *n.* **1** a male ruler of a nation. **2** a person, creature, or thing considered supreme in strength, etc.: *The lion is the king of beasts.* **3** in cards, the one bearing a picture of a king.

PRONUNCIATION GUIDE

fat **a**	all **ö**
fate **ā**	foot **oo**
fast **ä**	moon **ōō**
among **å**	boy **oi**
met **e**	house **ow**
mean **ē**	demon **ŏ**
silent **ê**	thing **th**
loch **hh**	this **Th**
fin **i**	but **u**
line **ī**	mute **ū**
quick **kw**	fur **û**
got **o**	brochure **ů**
note **ō**	vision **zh**

An 18th-century kiln or furnace (above) and an African kiln of about 400 BC (below). The process of placing objects in a kiln is known as 'firing'.

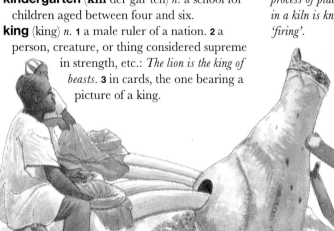

kingdom *n.* **1** a country ruled by a king or queen. **2** any of the three divisions of the natural world: *the animal, plant, or mineral kingdoms.*

● **King, Martin Luther** (1929-68) was an American civil rights leader who worked for racial justice. He was awarded the NOBEL peace prize in 1964. He was assassinated in Memphis.

kingfisher (**king** fish ẽr) *n.* a bird with brilliant blue and orange plumage that dives for fish.

● **Kipling, Rudyard** (1865-1936) was an English writer of adventure stories and poems including *The Jungle Books* and *Just So Stories.*

● **Kiribati**. See Supplement, **Countries**.

kirk (kûrk) *n.* (*Scottish*) a church.

kiss (kis) *vb.* **kissing, kissed** to touch with the lips, as a greeting or sign of affection.

kit (kit) *n.* **1** a set of instruments, equipment, etc. needed for a purpose: *The tool kit is under the stairs.* **2** a set of clothing and personal equipment for a soldier, footballer, etc. **3** a set of parts ready for assembling: *model train kit.*

kitchen (**ki** chẽn) *n.* a room where food is prepared and cooked.

kite (kīt) *n.* **1** a long-tailed BIRD OF PREY of the hawk family. **2** a light frame covered in light material, with a long holding string attached to it, for flying in the air for fun.

kitten (**ki** tẽn) *n.* a young cat.

kiwi (**kē** wē) *n.* a flightless, long-beaked bird from NEW ZEALAND.

knack (nak) *n.* the ability to do something with ease: *She has the knack of mending machines.*

knead (nēd) *vb.* **kneading, kneaded** to press and squeeze dough with your hands.

knee (nē) *n.* **1** the middle joint of the leg between your ankle and hip; the same joint in an animal. **2** the lap: *Lucy sat with her small son on her knee.*

kneel (nēl) *vb.* **kneeling, knelt** (nelt) **or kneeled** to go down on one or both knees.

knelt. See **kneel**.

knew. See **know**.

knife (nīf) *n.* **knives** (nīvz) a cutting instrument or weapon, in the form of a blade fitted into a handle. – *vb.* **knifing, knifed** to stab with a knife.

knight (nīt) *n.* **1** in the MIDDLE AGES, a soldier, usually on a horse, serving a FEUDAL lord. **2** in chess, a piece shaped like a horse's head.

knit (nit) *vb.* **knitting, knitted** or **knit** to make a fabric or garment by looping wool or cotton around a pair of special needles.

knives see **knife**.

knob (nob) *n.* **1** a handle, especially rounded, on a door or drawer. **2** a button on mechanical or electrical equipment, pressed or turned to operate it.

knock (nok) *vb.* **knocking, knocked 1** to tap with the knuckles or some object: *I kept knocking the door but there was no reply.* **2** to strike and so push, especially accidentally: *Kate knocked the cup off the table.* **3** to strike, bump, or bang against: *The gate knocked against the wall.* – *n.* **1** an act of knocking. **2** a tap. – *vb.* **knock down 1** to strike someone to the ground. **2** to demolish a building. – **knocking on** (*colloquial*) nearly: *Ernest must be knocking on 60 by now.* – **knock on the head** (*colloquial*) to put an end to. – **knock sideways** (*colloquial*) to come as a severe shock.

knoll (nōl) *n.* a small round hill.

● **Knossos** (**no** sŏs) or (**kno** sŏs) is a ruined city in CRETE with remains of the MINOAN civilization (1700-1450 BC).

In the Middle Ages in Europe both **knights** and their strong horses wore heavy plate armour. A knight's armour weighed up to 30 kg, so heavy that he would have to be winched onto his horse.

knot (not) *n.* **1** a join or tie in string, etc. made by looping the ends around each other and pulling tight. **2** a bond. **3** a tangle in hair, string, etc. **4** a hard mass in a tree trunk where a branch has grown out from it. – *vb.* **knotting, knotted** to tie in a knot.

know (nō) *vb.* **knowing, knew** (nū), **known 1** to be aware of; to be certain; to have an understanding of: *I know there was a stranger in the garden, but I don't know where he went.* **2** to be familiar with: *I know her well.* **3** to recognize or identify: *I know your face from somewhere.* **4** to think of as: *They knew him as a kindly man.* – **in the know** (*colloquial*) having information not known to most. – **know a thing or two** (*colloquial*) to be pretty shrewd. – *vb.* **know backwards** (*colloquial*) to know thoroughly. **knowing** *adj.* shrewd; clever. **know-how** *n.* (*colloquial*) skill; ability.

knowledge (**no** lij) *n.* **1** the fact of knowing; awareness: *The knowledge that the house is insured makes me feel safer.* **2** the information you have acquired through learning or experience. **knowledgeable** *adj.* well-informed. **known**. See **know**.

Knights jousting in a tournament. They used blunt swords and lances but even so many were killed or wounded.

A knight's shield carried his coat-of-arms so that he could be recognized in battle.

●**Knox** (noks), **John** (1514-72) was a Scottish religious reformer who established the presbyterian Church of Scotland.

knuckle (**nu** kĕl) *n.* a joint of a finger.

koala (kō **ä** lå) *n.* (also **koala bear**) an Australian tree-climbing MARSUPIAL animal that looks like a small bear. It has thick grey fur and large ears, and feeds on eucalyptus leaves.

●**Kohl** (kōl), **Dr Helmut** (1930-) is Chancellor of GERMANY.

●**Koran** (kō **rän**) *n.* the holy book of ISLAM, believed by MUSLIMS to be composed of the revelations of ALLAH to MUHAMMAD.

●**Korea** (kŏ **rē** å), **North**. See Supplement, **Countries**.

●**Korea**, **South**. See Supplement, **Countries**.

●**Korean War** (1950-53) began when North Korea, a Communist country, attacked South Korea. Nearly 3 million people died, including 50,000 Americans.

kosher (**kō** shĕr) *adj.* in agreement with Jewish law.

●**Krakatoa** (kra kå **tō** å) is an island VOLCANO in INDONESIA which erupted violently in 1883.

kremlin (**krem** lin) *n.* the citadel of a Russian town, especially that of Moscow.

●**Kublai Khan** (**kōō** blī kän) (1214-94) was a Mongol ruler, grandson of GENGHIS KHAN.

●**Ku Klux Klan** (kōō kluks **klan**) This secret organization was formed after the American CIVIL WAR (1861-5) by white southerners, using violence against blacks, Jews, and Catholics.

●**Kuwait** (koo **wāt**). See Supplement, **Countries**.

●**Kwanzaa** (kwan **zä**) is an African-American festival held in late December.

●**Kyrgyzstan** (**kûr** gi stan). See Supplement, **Countries**.

Clove hitch

Reef knot

Bowline

Sheepshank

Two half hitches

Stone Age hunters used knots to tie arrowheads to shafts. Today everyone needs to tie a knot at some time or other.

A KNOCKOUT
Until about the end of the 14th century – the time of Chaucer – the *k* was still pronounced in words such as knee, knife, knight, and know. In the same way the *g* was pronounced in gnat and gnaw. What we have is a ghost spelling of a former pronunciation. Yet how did the *h* get into ghost when the Old English word was *gast*?

L l

label (lā bĕl) *n.* a small written note attached to a parcel, object, etc. giving details of its contents, manufacturer, owner, etc.

laboratory (lǎ **bo** rǎ tǒ ri) *n.* **laboratories** a room or building specially equipped for scientific experiments and research.

labour (lā bǒr) *n.* **1** physical or mental work, especially when hard. **2** workers as a group: *They were hired as skilled labour.* **3** the process of giving birth to a baby: *She had an easy labour.* **4 Labour** in the United Kingdom, the Labour Party. – *vb.* **labouring, laboured 1** to work hard or with difficulty. **2** to move with difficulty: *The car laboured slowly up the hill.*

Labrador (**lab** rǎ dör) *n.* a breed of large dog.

● **Labrador** is a region of north-eastern CANADA.

labyrinth (**la** bi rinth) *n.* a complicated network of passages; a maze.

lace (lās) *n.* **1** a delicate material made from fine thread woven into net-like patterns. **2** a string drawn through holes, used for fastening shoes, etc. – *vb.* **lacing, laced** to fasten with a lace.

lack (lak) *n.* something missing or in short supply. – *vb.* **lacking, lacked** to be without or to have too little of. – *adj.* **lacking.**

lacquer (**la** kĕr) *n.* a clear substance used to form a protective, shiny covering on wood, etc.

lad (lad) *n.* a boy or a youth.

ladder (**la** dĕr) *n.* a piece of equipment consisting of a set of horizontal rungs or steps between two long vertical supports, used for climbing up or down.

ladle (lā dĕl) *n.* a large spoon with a long handle and deep bowl, for serving liquid.

lady (lā di) *n.* **ladies** a woman.
ladybird *n.* a small beetle with black spots.

● **Lafayette** (la fī **et**), **Marquis de** (1757-1834) was a French soldier who fought for the American colonists in the WAR OF INDEPENDENCE. He was also a leader in the FRENCH REVOLUTION.

lagoon (lǎ **goon**) *n.* a shallow stretch of water separated from the sea by rocks, etc.

laid (lād) See **lay¹**.

lain. See **lie²**.

lair (lār) *n.* a wild animal's den.

lake (lāk) *n.* an area of water surrounded by land.

● The world's largest lake is the salty Caspian Sea, 438,695 sq km (169,390 sq miles). The largest freshwater lake is Lake Superior, one of the GREAT LAKES.

Lakes may contain fresh water or salt water. The Caspian, a salt lake between south-eastern Europe and Asia is the world's largest and is regarded as an inland sea. Freshwater lakes are constantly fed and drained by rivers.

The five Great Lakes lie on the border of Canada and the United States.

The huge Caspian Sea at its deepest is about 1000 m. It is 1225 km long but is known to be shrinking.

lamb (lam) *n.* a young sheep. – *vb.* **lambing, lambed** to give birth to a lamb.

lame (lām) *adj.* not able to walk properly.

lament (lå **ment**) *vb.* **lamenting, lamented** to feel or express regret or sadness.

lamp (lamp) *n.* an appliance for producing a steady light, using electricity, oil, or gas.

lance (läns) *n.* a long spear with a hard, pointed head at one end, used by horse riders.

● **Lancelot**, in legend, was one of ARTHUR's knights and lover of Queen Guinevere.

land (land) *n.* **1** the part of the Earth's surface not covered by water. **2** the ground or soil, especially in terms of its use or quality: *This region contains much good farmland.* – *vb.* **landing, landed 1** to come to rest on the ground or water after flight. **2** to bring on to land from a ship.
  landing *n.* **1** the process of coming to shore or to ground. **2** the level part of a staircase between flights of steps, or at the very top.
  landmark *n.* **1** a conspicuous or well-known object on land. **2** an event of great importance: *It was a landmark in the history of computing.*
  landscape *n.* the area and features of land that can be seen from a single point.
  landslide *n.* a fall of land or rock down the side of a hill or cliff.

lane (lān) *n.* **1** a narrow road or street. **2** a division of a road for a single line of traffic.

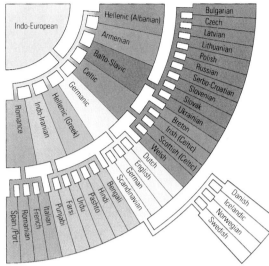

A barrier lake is where a river valley has become naturally blocked as a result of a landfall, for example, or debris left by a glacier.

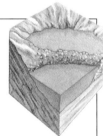

A volcanic lake is where the crater of an extinct volcano fills up. Lakes may also form where hollow lava flows have collapsed.

Rift valley lakes occur along major faults or fissure lines such as the long, narrow lochs in the Great Glen fault in Scotland.

language (**lang** wij) *n.* **1** human speech. **2** the speech of a particular nation or group of people. **3** any other way of communication: *She expressed herself using sign language.* **4** a system of symbols, used to write computer programs.

lank (lank) *adj.* (of hair) straight and limp.
  lanky *adj.* **lankier, lankiest** thin, tall, and awkward.

lantern (**lan** tĕrn) *n.* a clear case for holding a light, and shielding the flame from the wind.

● **Laos**. See Supplement, **Countries**.

lap[1] (lap) *vb.* **lapping, lapped 1** to drink liquid by scooping it up with the tongue. **2** (of water) to wash against a shore with a light splashing sound. – *vb.* **lap up 1** to drink by lapping, especially eagerly or greedily. **2** to listen eagerly: *He lapped up our praise.*

lap[2] (lap) *n.* the front part of the body, from waist to knees, when a person is sitting.
  laptop *adj.* (of a computer) small enough to be used on your lap.

lap[3] (lap) *n.* one circuit of a racetrack. – *vb.* **lapping, lapped** to get ahead of a competitor in a race by one or more laps.

lapel (lå **pel**) *n.* the part of a coat joined to the collar and folded back across the chest.

● **Lapland** is a region in the north of SCANDINAVIA, the home of the LAPPS.

Lapp (lap) *n.* **1** (also **Laplander** (**lap** land ĕr)) a member of a nomadic people living in SCANDINAVIA. **2** the language spoken by this people. – *adj.* of this people, their language, etc.

From the Indo-European parent have developed eight families or groups of languages, shown on this family tree. English, for example, belongs to the Germanic family, which also includes German, Dutch, and the Scandinavian languages. The Romance family includes Italian, French, Spanish, Portuguese, and Romanian.

PRONUNCIATION GUIDE	
fat **a**	all **ŏ**
fate **ā**	foot **oo**
fast **ä**	moon **ōō**
among **å**	boy **oi**
met **e**	house **ow**
mean **ē**	demon **ŏ**
silent **ĕ**	thing **th**
loch **hh**	this **Th**
fin **i**	but **u**
line **ī**	mute **ū**
quick **kw**	fur **û**
got **o**	brochure **ů**
note **ō**	vision **zh**

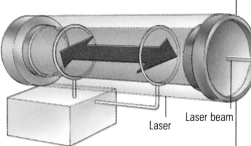

A **laser** beam is intense pure light, with waves that are all the same length. Light from an ordinary torch is a mixture of different wavelengths and contains all the colours of the spectrum. That is why the light spreads out as it shines from the torch.

Laser beam

Laser

Ordinary light – a mixture of wavelengths and therefore colours.

A laser has three main parts: the material that produces the beam, a power source, and a reflective resonator (usually mirrors).

Laser light – an intense beam of pure light.

Laser light can be used to perform delicate operations on the eye by producing minute welds.

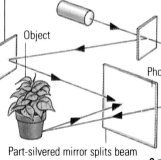

Object

Photographic plate

Part-silvered mirror splits beam

In a hologram or 'solid' picture a laser beam is split. The interference between the two beams makes a 3-D picture.

lapse (laps) *n.* **1** a slight mistake or failure in virtue, attention, or memory: *A lapse in concentration led him to lose the game.* **2** a passing away of time: *There was a lapse of two years.* – *vb.* **lapsing, lapsed** to fail to behave properly.

large (lärj) *adj.* great in size or amount.
  largely *adv.* mainly; to a great extent: *I was largely to blame for the accident.*

lark (lärk) *n.* any of several kinds of song-birds, which flies high into the air as it sings.

larva (lär vå) *n.* **larvae** (lär vē) a developing insect in a state which is different from the adult, for example a caterpillar. – *adj.* **larval.**

larynx (la ringks) *n.* a hollow organ in the throat, forming the upper end of the windpipe and containing the vocal cords.

laser (lā zěr) *n.* a device that produces a narrow and very intense beam of single-coloured light.

● The word laser comes from *L*ight *A*mplification by *S*timulated *E*mission of *R*adiation. Lasers do not generate light, they make it stronger. Lasers can be used in shops to read bar codes. Some lasers are used to perform delicate operations on the human eye.

lash (lash) *n.* **1** (usually in *plural*) an eyelash. **2** a stroke or blow with a whip. – *vb.* **lashing, lashed** to hit or beat with a lash.

lass (las) *n.* a girl or young woman.

lasso (lå soo) *n.* **lassos** or **lassoes** a long rope with a loop which tightens when the rope is pulled, used for catching animals.

last¹ (läst) *adj.* **1** coming at the end of a series: *This is the last race today.* **2** most recent: *I saw her last week.* **3** least likely or suitable: *He was the last person to expect help from.* – *adv.* **1** after all others: *He came last in the race.* **2** most recently. – *n.* the person or thing that is last.

last² (läst) *vb.* **lasting, lasted 1** to continue to exist; to remain in being. **2** to be enough for the needs of: *We have enough water to last us two days.* **3** to remain in good condition: *This bread will only last one more day.*

latch (lach) *n.* a door catch consisting of a bar which is lowered or raised from its notch by a lever or string.

late (lāt) *adj.* **1** coming or arriving after the expected or usual time. **2** far on in the day or night: *It was late afternoon.* **3** having died, especially recently: *He paid tribute to the late prime minister.* – *adv.* **1** after the expected or usual time: *We arrived late because of the heavy traffic.* **2** far on in the day, night, or season.
  lately *adv.* in the recent past; not long ago.
  later *adj. & adv.* at some time after.
  latest *adj.* most recent.

lateral (la tě rål) *adj.* at, to, or from the side.

lathe (lāTh) *n.* a machine for shaping wood or metal.

lather (lä Thěr) *n.* a foam made by mixing water and soap. – *vb.* **lathering, lathered.**

Latin (la tin) *n.* the language spoken in Ancient Rome and its empire. – *adj.* **1** of, relating to, or in the Latin language. **2** (of a language) derived from Latin.

- With the fall of the ROMAN EMPIRE in AD 476 and the breakdown of communication, local variations of spoken Latin developed. These evolved into the Romance languages: Italian, Provençal, French, Catalan, Spanish, Portuguese, and Romanian. Latin words form a large part of the vocabulary of many European languages.

Latin America *n.* the countries of Central and South America, where the official language is either Spanish or Portuguese. – *n.* & *adj.* **Latin American**.

latitude (**la** ti tūd) *n.* **1** a distance north or south of the Equator,

Lines of latitude and longitude are marked on maps so that you can pinpoint specific places.

Latitude 90°N
45°N
0°
35°S
90°S

measured in degrees. **2** scope for freedom of action or choice.

latter (**la** tẽr) *adj.* **1** nearer to the end: *We only discovered the beach in the latter part of the holiday.* **2** being the second of two people, things, etc. mentioned. **3** recent; modern. – *n.* the second of two people, things, etc. mentioned: *We had hoped to see both Tom and Philip, but the latter had already left.*

latterly *adv.* **1** recently. **2** towards the end.

- **Latvia**. See Supplement, **Countries**.

laugh (läf) *vb.* **laughing, laughed** to make sounds with the voice as a sign of happiness or amusement. – *n.* an act or sound of laughing. – *vb.* **laugh at** to make fun of or ridicule.

laughable *adj.* deserving to be laughed at; not very good. – *adv.* **laughably**.

laughter *n.* the act or sound of laughing.

launch¹ (lönch) *vb.* **launching, launched 1** to slide a boat or ship into the water, especially for the first time. **2** to send a spacecraft, missile, etc. into the air. **3** to introduce a new product on to the market: *The book was launched with a big advertising campaign.* – *n.* an act of launching.

launching-pad or **launch pad** *n.* a platform from which a spacecraft is launched.

launch² (lönch) *n.* a large motorboat.

laundry (lön dri) *n.* **laundries** a place where clothes and linen are washed, especially in return for payment.

laurel (lö rẽl) *n.* a small evergreen tree with smooth, dark, shiny leaves.

lava (lä vå) *n.* the molten rock and liquid which flows from a volcano.

lavender (**la** vẽn dẽr) *n.* a plant or shrub with sweet-smelling pale bluish-purple flowers.

- **Lavoisier** (la **vwa** zi ā), **Antoine** (1743-94) was a French chemist who discovered the composition of air and devised a system of chemical names.

law (lö) *n.* **1** a collection of rules which govern what people can and cannot do, and by which people live or a country or state is governed. **2** a rule in science based on practice or observation, which says that under certain conditions certain things will always happen.

lawful *adj.* allowed by or according to law.

lawless *adj.* ignoring or breaking the law.

lawyer (lö yẽr) *n.* a person whose work it is to know about the law, and give legal advice.

lawn (lön) *n.* an area of smooth, mown grass.

lawn-mower *n.* a machine for cutting lawns.

- **Lawrence, D. H.** (1885-1930) was an English novelist and poet who wrote *Sons and Lovers* and *Lady Chatterly's Lover*.

lax (laks) *adj.* slack; not careful or strict.

lay¹ (lā) *vb.* **laying, laid 1** to place or put on a surface. **2** to design or prepare: *He laid plans for his escape.* **3** to put plates and cutlery on a table ready for a meal. **4** to produce eggs. – *vb.* **lay aside** to discard or abandon.

layer *n.* a thickness or covering, especially one of several on a surface.

layout *n.* an arrangement or plan of how land, buildings, pages, etc. are to be set out.

- **lay** and **lie**. The verb to lie means 'to rest' or 'to be horizontal'. The verb to lay means 'to put down or to place'. A confusion arises because the past tense of lie is lay: *It is a warm day, I shall lie in the sun. Yesterday, I lay in bed thinking.* Now here are examples of the verb to lay: *After you finish reading, lay the book down. I'm sure I laid my pen on the desk yesterday.* Laid here is the past tense of lay. There is another verb to lie meaning 'not to tell the truth'. Its past tense is lied: *Tom has never lied to me; he is truthful.*

The Supreme Court is the highest court in the USA. The president appoints judges, subject to Senate consent, to decide whether laws are constitutional.

TERMS USED IN LAW

advocate a lawyer employed by a party in a law case to represent them in court.

appeal a request to a higher court to change a decision given by a lower one.

arrest the taking into custody by the police of a person suspected of a crime.

bail money offered by an arrested person in order to be allowed free until the trial. If the person does not appear at the trial, the bail is forfeited.

evidence written or spoken information that help the court to find out the facts of a case.

statute law made by a legislature (law-making body), such as parliament.

trial the hearing of a legal dispute in court.

verdict the decision of the judge (or the jury) after hearing the evidence in a trial in court.

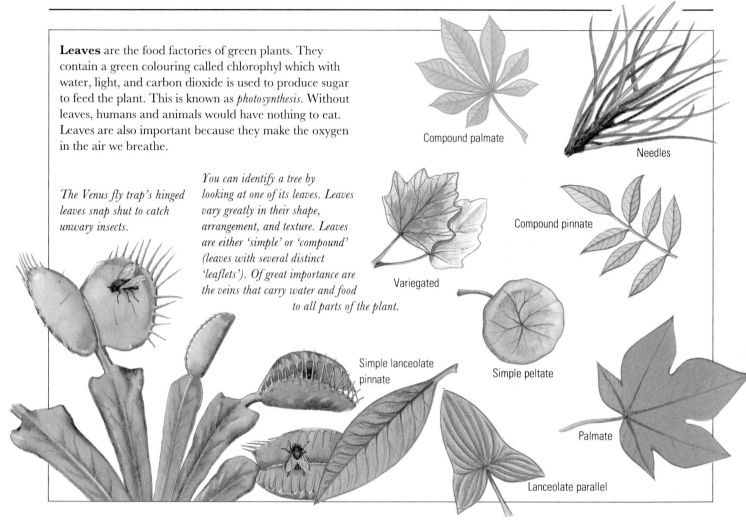

Leaves are the food factories of green plants. They contain a green colouring called chlorophyl which with water, light, and carbon dioxide is used to produce sugar to feed the plant. This is known as *photosynthesis*. Without leaves, humans and animals would have nothing to eat. Leaves are also important because they make the oxygen in the air we breathe.

The Venus fly trap's hinged leaves snap shut to catch unwary insects.

You can identify a tree by looking at one of its leaves. Leaves vary greatly in their shape, arrangement, and texture. Leaves are either 'simple' or 'compound' (leaves with several distinct 'leaflets'). Of great importance are the veins that carry water and food to all parts of the plant.

Compound palmate

Needles

Compound pinnate

Variegated

Simple peltate

Simple lanceolate pinnate

Palmate

Lanceolate parallel

PRONUNCIATION GUIDE	
fat **a**	all **ö**
fate **ā**	foot **oo**
fast **ä**	moon **o͞o**
among **å**	boy **oi**
met **e**	house **ow**
mean **ē**	demon **o̊**
silent **e̊**	thing **th**
loch **hh**	this **Th**
fin **i**	but **u**
line **ī**	mute **ū**
quick **kw**	fur **û**
got **o**	brochure **ů**
note **ō**	vision **zh**

lay². See **lie²**.

lazy (lā zi) *adj.* **lazier, laziest** not wanting to take exercise, work hard, etc.; idle. – *adv.* **lazily**. – *n.* **laziness**.

lead¹ (lēd) *vb.* **leading, led** (led) **1** to guide by going in front. **2** to cause to feel or think in a certain way: *His encouraging words led her to try harder.* **3** to experience: *He leads a miserable existence.* **4** to go: *All roads lead to Rome.* **5** to have as an end or consequence: *This decision will lead to problems.* **6** to be the most important person in a particular field: *They lead the world in engineering.* – *n.* **1** the guidance given by leading; an example: *Follow the first singer's lead.* **2** the amount by which a person is in front of others in a race or contest. **3** a strap or chain for holding a dog. **4** a wire taking electricity from a source to an appliance. – *vb.* **lead off** to begin. **leader** *n.* someone who leads or guides others. **leading** *adj.* acting as leader; guiding.

lead² (led) *n.* a soft, heavy, bluish-grey metallic element (symbol **Pb**) used in alloys.

leaf (lēf) *n.* **leaves** a thin, flat, usually green part growing usually from the stem of a plant. – *vb.* **leafing, leafed** to turn the pages of a book quickly: *She leafed through the book.*

league (lēg) *n.* an organization of nations, etc.

leak (lēk) *n.* **1** an unwanted crack or hole which allows liquid or gas to pass in or out of a container. **2** liquid or gas which has escaped through such a crack or hole. – *vb.* **leaking, leaked 1** to allow liquid or gas to pass in or out through a crack or hole: *Our roof leaks in the rain.* **2** to make known secret information without authorization: *The story was leaked to a newspaper journalist.*

lean¹ (lēn) *vb.* **leaning, leant** (lent) or **leaned 1** to slope or be placed in a sloping position; to bend: *She leaned over the cot.* **2** to rest or be rested against something for support: *He leaned the ladder against the shed.* **leaning** *n.* a liking or preference.

lean² (lēn) *adj.* **1** (of a person or animal) thin. **2** (of meat) not containing much fat.

leap (lēp) *vb.* **leaping, leapt** (lept) or **leaped** to jump suddenly or with force, high in the air or over a long distance. – *n.* an act of leaping or jumping.

leap year *n.* a year of 366 days, 29 February being the extra day.

●Leap years are necessary because the calendar year (365 days) is slightly shorter than the solar year. Century years are leap years only when they can be evenly divided by 400.

●**Lear** (lēr), **Edward** (1812-88) was an English artist and writer of limericks and nonsense verse such as *The Owl and the Pussy Cat*.

learn (lûrn) *vb.* **learning, learnt** or **learned** 1 to gain knowledge or a skill through experience, study, or by being taught. 2 to be informed of: *He learned of the problem too late*.
learned (lûr nid) *adj.* having great learning, especially through years of study; scholarly.
learning *n.* knowledge gained through study.

lease (lēs) *n.* a contract by which the owner of a house or land agrees to let another person use it for a stated period of time in return for rent. – *vb.* **leasing, leased**.

least (lēst) *adj. & adv.* smallest; slightest. – *pron.* the smallest amount. – **at least 1** at all events; anyway. 2 not less than.

leather (le Ther) *n.* the skin of an animal made smooth by tanning.

leave¹ (lēv) *vb.* **leaving, left** (left) 1 to go away from; to move out of. 2 to go without taking: *I left all my luggage behind*. 3 to allow to remain in a particular condition: *Leave the window open*.

leave² (lēv) *n.* permission to do something: *He gave her leave to visit her mother.* – **on leave** officially absent from work.

●**Lebanon**. See Supplement, **Countries**.

lecture (lek chŭr) *n.* a formal talk on a particular subject given to an audience, for example at university. – *vb.* **lecturing, lectured** to give a lecture.
lecturer *n.* a person who lectures.

led. See **lead**¹.

ledge (lej) *n.* a narrow horizontal shelf.

leek (lēk) *n.* a long thin vegetable with broad, flat, dark green leaves and a white base, closely related to the onion.

left¹ (left). See **leave**¹.

leftover *n.* (in *plural*) pieces of food that have not been eaten up at a meal.

left² (left) *adj.* the opposite side to right. – *adv.* on or towards the left side. – *n.* the left side, part, direction, etc.
left-handed *adj.* 1 having the left hand stronger and more skilful than the right. 2 for use by left-handed people.
left-wing *adj.* of, relating to, or supporting the political Left. – *n.* **left-winger**.

leg (leg) *n.* 1 one of the limbs on which animals, birds, and people walk and stand. 2 a long narrow support of a table, chair, etc. 3 one stage in a journey, competition, or race: *She got through to the final leg of the competition.* – **on its last legs** near to being no longer usable.

legal (lē gǎl) *adj.* 1 lawful; allowed by the law. 2 of or relating to the law.
legalize or **legalise** (lē gǎ līz) *vb.* **legalizing, legalized** to make legal or lawful.

legend (le jĕnd) *n.* a traditional story which may or may not be true.

legible (le jǎ bĕl) *adj.* (of handwriting) clear enough to be read. – *n.* **legibility**.

legion (lē jŏn) *n.* a unit in the ancient Roman army, containing between three thousand and six thousand soldiers. – *adj.* great in number: *Books on this subject are legion*.

legislate (le jis lāt) *vb.* **legislating, legislated** to make laws. – *n.* **legislator**.
legislation *n.* 1 the act of legislating. 2 a group of laws.

In every Roman legion a bearer carried a standard into battle. It was a great disgrace for a legion to lose its standard.

●**Leif Ericsson** (970-?) was a Viking explorer who in about 1000 landed in an area he called Vinland, possibly Maryland, USA.

leisure (le zhŭr) *n.* time when someone does not have to work. – **at your leisure** at a convenient time.

An old Icelandic saga describes how Leif Ericsson sailed to where the land was green with trees and sweet 'grapes'. He named the place Vinland (wineland).

A concave lens is thinner in the middle than at the edges. It makes things look smaller.

A convex lens is thicker in the middle than at the edges. It makes things look bigger.

lemon (**le** mŏn) *n.* an oval-shaped citrus fruit with pale yellow skin and sour-tasting flesh.

lend (lend) *vb.* **lending, lent 1** to give someone the use of something on the understanding that it is to be returned. **2** to allow someone the use of money, especially in return for interest paid on it. – *n.* **lender.** – **lend a hand** to help.

length (length) *n.* **1** the distance from one end of an object to the other. **2** a period of time. **3** trouble or effort; action taken: *She went to great lengths to organize his party.*
lengthen *vb.* **lengthening, lengthened** to make or become longer.

lenient (**le** ni ĕnt) *adj.* punishing only lightly.

● **Lenin, Vladimir** (1870-1924) was a revolutionary and from 1917 was the first leader of the Soviet Union.

● **Leningrad**. See **Saint Petersburg**.

lens (lenz) *n.* a piece of glass or clear plastic curved on one or both sides, used to concentrate or separate light rays in cameras, spectacles, etc.

Lent (lent) *n.* in the CHRISTIAN religion, the time from Ash Wednesday to EASTER Sunday.

lentil (**len** til) *n.* a small orange, brown, or green seed from a pod-bearing plant, eaten as food.

Leo (**le** ō) *n.* See **zodiac**.

● **Leonardo da Vinci** (lē ŏ **när** dō då **vin** chi) (1452-1519) was an Italian painter and very versatile inventor. He designed forts and canals (with locks), a helicopter, and a machine gun.

leopard (**le** pård) *n.* a large animal of the cat family, with a yellowish-brown coat and black spots, found in Africa and Asia.

leotard (**le** ŏ tärd) *n.* a tight-fitting garment, worn for dancing and exercise.

leprechaun (**lep** rĕ kön) *n.* a small mischievous elf in Irish folklore.

lesbian (**lez** bi ån) *n.* a woman who is sexually attracted to other women.

● **Lesotho**. See Supplement, **Countries**.

-less *suffix* meaning 'without', e.g. homeless.

less (les) *adj.* smaller in size, amount, duration, etc.: *There is less milk in these new bottles.* – *adv.* not so much; to a smaller extent: *I am eating less than before.* – *prep.* without; minus.

In 1917 armed workers and Bolshevik-led soldiers attacked the Winter Palace.

Lenin was the leading figure in the Russian Revolution. When uprisings broke out in war-exhausted Russia in 1917, Lenin led the Bolshevik party which overturned the government and took control.

● **less** and **fewer**. As a rough guide, use 'less' for a quantity and 'fewer' for a number of things: *The less ground we clear the fewer flowers can be grown.*

lessen *vb.* **lessening, lessened** to make or become less.

lesser *adj.* smaller than another in size, quantity, or importance.

lesson (**le** sŏn) *n.* a period of teaching in a particular subject: *I enjoyed my art lesson today.*

let (let) *vb.* **letting, let 1** to allow or permit: *She let him in to the house.* **2** to rent out rooms, a building, or land in return for payment. **3** used to give orders, requests, warnings, permission, etc.: *Let him go!* – *vb.* **let down 1** to lower. **2** to disappoint. **3** to allow the air to escape from.

lethal (**le** thål) *adj.* enough to cause death.

letter (**le** tĕr) *n.* **1** a written symbol, usually part of an alphabet, used to express a speech sound. **2** a written or printed message usually sent by post in an envelope.

lettuce (**le** tis) *n.* a green plant with large edible leaves used as a salad vegetable.

level (**le** vĕl) *n.* **1** a height, value, or extent: *She measured the level of the liquid in the jar.* **2** position, status, or importance: *The discussions were at government level.* – *adj.* **1** having a flat, smooth, even surface. **2** having the same height as something else: *The table is level with the bed.* – *vb.* **levelling, levelled** to make flat or smooth.

lever (lē věr) *n.* **1** a simple device for lifting and moving heavy loads, being a rigid bar resting on a fixed point, one end being raised by pushing down on the other. **2** a handle for operating a machine. – *vb.* **levering, levered** to move or open using a lever.
leverage *n.* the mechanical power gained by using a lever.

leveret (le vě rět) *n.* a young hare.

lexicon (lek si kǒn) *n.* a dictionary.

liable (lī å běl) *adj.* **1** legally bound or responsible: *He is liable for the damage to my car.* **2** likely to do, have, or suffer: *She is liable to behave badly.*

liaise (lē āz) *vb.* **liaising, liaised** to establish a close working relationship with other people.

liar (lī år) *n.* a person who tells lies.

liberal (li bě rål) *adj.* **1** given or giving generously, freely, or abundantly: *He gave her a liberal helping of cream.* **2** tolerant of different opinions. – *n.* **1** an open-minded person.
liberalize or **liberalise** *vb.* **liberalizing, liberalized** to make or become more liberal.

liberate (li bě rāt) *vb.* **liberating, liberated** to set free.

● **Liberia**. See Supplement, **Countries**.

liberty (li běr ti) *n.* **liberties 1** freedom from captivity or from slavery. **2** freedom to do, think, and speak as you please.

● **Liberty Bell** This bell hung in the Pennsylvania State House in Philadelphia and was rung when the DECLARATION OF INDEPENDENCE was adopted on 8 July 1776. It now hangs in the Liberty Bell Pavilion in Philadelphia.

Libra (lib rå) *n.* See **zodiac**.

library (lī brå ri) *n.* **libraries 1** a collection of books, either for public or private use. **2** the building which houses such a collection.
librarian (lī brār i ån) *n.* a person who is employed in or in charge of a library.

● **Library of Congress** in Washington D.C., the world's largest library. It contains more than 80 million items in 470 languages.

● **Libya**. See Supplement, **Countries**.

licence or (*US*) **license** (lī sěns) *n.* a document giving official permission to own a dog, TV, etc.

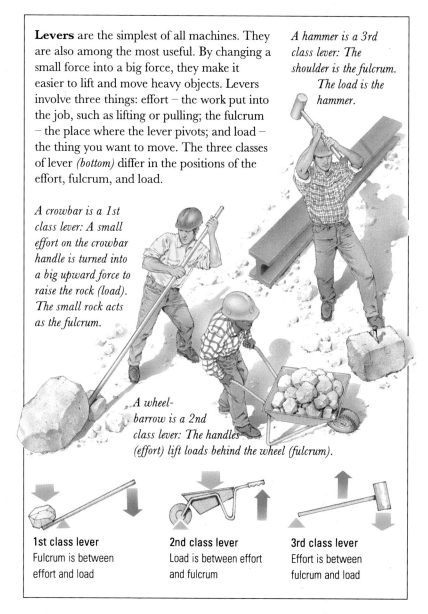

Levers are the simplest of all machines. They are also among the most useful. By changing a small force into a big force, they make it easier to lift and move heavy objects. Levers involve three things: effort – the work put into the job, such as lifting or pulling; the fulcrum – the place where the lever pivots; and load – the thing you want to move. The three classes of lever *(bottom)* differ in the positions of the effort, fulcrum, and load.

A crowbar is a 1st class lever: A small effort on the crowbar handle is turned into a big upward force to raise the rock (load). The small rock acts as the fulcrum.

A wheelbarrow is a 2nd class lever: The handles (effort) lift loads behind the wheel (fulcrum).

A hammer is a 3rd class lever: The shoulder is the fulcrum. The load is the hammer.

1st class lever
Fulcrum is between effort and load

2nd class lever
Load is between effort and fulcrum

3rd class lever
Effort is between fulcrum and load

license (lī sěns) *vb.* **licensing, licensed** to give a licence or permit for something.

lichen (lī kěn) or (li chěn) *n.* any of a large group of simple plants formed from fungi and algae, which grow in patches on stones, trees, and soil.

lick (lik) *vb.* **licking, licked 1** to pass the tongue over to moisten, taste, or clean. **2** to flicker over or around: *The flames licked around the coals in the fire.* – *n.* an act of licking with the tongue.

licorice (li kǒ ris) (*US*). See **liquorice**.

lid (lid) *n.* a cover for a pot, box, etc.

lie¹ (lī) *n.* a false statement made with the intention of deceiving. – *vb.* **lies, lying, lied** to say things which are not true.

Library comes from a Latin word meaning a 'bookseller's shop'. The French still use the word *librairie* in the same way.

lie² (lī) *vb.* **lying, lay** (lā), **lain** (lān) **1** to be in or move into a flat position on a supporting surface. **2** to be or remain in a particular state: *Many animals lie dormant throughout the winter.* **3** to be situated; to stretch or be spread out to view: *The harbour lay before us.* – *n.* the way or direction in which something is lying. – **lie in wait for** to wait in ambush for.

●**Liechtenstein**. See Supplement, **Countries**.

lieutenant (lef **ten** ȧnt) *n.* **1** a deputy acting for a superior. **2** a junior officer in the army.

life (līf) *n.* **lives** (līvz) **1** the state of being able to grow, develop, and change which distinguishes living animals and plants from dead ones and from matter such as rocks, etc. **2** the period between birth and death. **3** the length of time a thing exists or is able to function: *These batteries have a long life.* **4** living things as a group: *She studies marine life.* – **a matter of life and death** an extremely important matter.

lifebelt *n.* a ring or belt which floats in water, used to support people in danger of drowning.

lifeguard *n.* an expert swimmer employed at a swimming-pool or beach to rescue people in danger of drowning.

lift (lift) *vb.* **lifting, lifted 1** to raise to a higher position. **2** (of cloud, fog, etc.) to clear. **3** to remove a barrier or restriction: *As soon as they reached an agreement the ban was lifted.* – *n.* **1** an act of lifting. **2** (*British*) a compartment which moves up and down in a vertical shaft between the floors of a building transporting people and goods. – *vb.* **lift off** (of a spacecraft) to rise from the ground.

ligament (**li** gȧ mėnt) *n.* a band of tough tissue that joins bones and cartilages together.

light¹ (līt) *n.* **1** the natural power from the Sun, lamps, candles etc. which makes sight possible and things visible. **2** any source of light, such as the Sun, a lamp, a candle, etc. **3** daylight; dawn: *They got up at first light.* **4** (usually in *plural*) a traffic light: *Turn left at the lights.* – *adj.* **1** having light; not dark. **2** (of a colour) pale; closer to white than black. – *vb.* **lighting, lit** (lit) or **lighted 1** to bring light to. **2** to cause to begin to burn: *She lit the fire.* – *n.* **lightness**.
lighten *vb.* **lightening, lightened** to make or become brighter, less dark.
lighthouse *n.* a building on the coast with a flashing light to warn of rocks.
light-year *n.* the distance light travels in a year, 9,460,700,000,000 km.

Glass

Perspex

Cardboard

Without **light** from the Sun, all life on Earth would come to an end. Green plants need sunlight to make food, and humans and all the other animals on Earth depend on plants for food. Light is a form of energy. It radiates freely though space and does not involve the movement of any material such as air. In empty space, light travels at about 300 million metres per second. The light from the Sun takes eight minutes to reach Earth.

Clear glass is transparent – *you can see objects through it. Perspex is* translucent – *you can see light through it. Cardboard is* opaque – *no light passes through it.*

The position of light on the electromagnetic spectrum. On either side, are ultraviolet and infrared rays.

When light rays pass from one substance to another (for example from air to water), they are bent. This bending distorts the image (in the example below, the straws) seen by the eye. This is called refraction.

Light waves vibrate in all directions. In polarized light the direction of the waves is limited.

Long wavelengths
Short Wavelengths
Radio waves
Television waves
Radar waves
Microwaves
Infrared rays
Visible light
Ultraviolet rays
X-rays
Gamma rays
Cosmic rays
Unpolarized light
Polarized light
Refraction

light² (līt) *adj.* **1** of little weight; easy to lift or carry. **2** low in amount: *It is only light rain.* **3** easy to do: *She is only capable of light work.* **4** not serious or profound, but for amusement only: *She took some light reading for the holiday.* – *adv.* **1** in a light manner. **2** with little luggage: *We like to travel light.* – *n.* **lightness**. – **get off lightly** to escape without severe punishment.

lighten *vb.* **lightening, lightened 1** to make less heavy. **2** to make or become happier or more cheerful.

light-hearted *adj.* **1** (of a person) happy and free from worry. **2** not serious; cheerful.

lightning (līt ning) *n.* a flash of light caused by electricity between clouds or between a cloud and the Earth, especially during a storm. – *adj.* very quick and sudden.

like¹ (līk) *adj.* **1** similar; resembling: *She is very like her mother.* **2** typical of: *It's just like him to forget.* **3** in the correct state or mood for: *I feel like a drink.* – *prep.* in the same manner as; to the same extent as: *He can run like a deer.*

likelihood *n.* probability.

likely *adj.* probable: *It's likely that he will be late.* – *adv.* probably. – *n.* **likeliness**.

liken *vb.* **likening, likened** to think or speak of something as being similar to something else: *Jill likened his voice to a growl.*

likeness *n.* a similarity.

likewise *adv.* in the same or a similar manner.

like² (līk) *vb.* **liking, liked 1** to find pleasant or agreeable: *He's nice; I like him.* **2** to be fond of; to prefer: *She likes her tea without sugar.*

likeable or **likable** *adj.* easy to like; lovable.

liking *n.* a taste: *I have a liking for chocolates.*

lilac (lī låk) *n.* a small tree or shrub which has bunches of white or pale pinkish-purple, sweet-smelling flowers.

The lily family is large: as well as true lilies, it includes the hyacinth, bluebell, tulip, onion, and asparagus!

Wood lily

lily (li li) *n.* **lilies** a plant grown from a bulb, with white or coloured trumpet-shaped flowers growing at the end of a tall stem.

limb (lim) *n.* **1** an arm, leg, or wing. **2** a main branch on a tree. – *adj.* **limbed**.

lime¹ (līm) *n.* a white substance, calcium oxide, produced by heating limestone and used for making cement and fertilizer.

limestone *n.* a rock made mainly of calcium.

lime² (līm) *n.* **1** a small, round, sour-tasting, green citrus fruit. **2** the colour of this fruit. **3** a tree with heart-shaped leaves.

limerick (li mě rik) *n.* a humorous poem of five lines with the first, second, and fifth lines, and the third and fourth lines, rhyming.

limit (li mit) *n.* **1** a point or amount beyond which something does not or may not pass: *Drivers must take care not to exceed the speed limit.* **2** (often in *plural*) the boundary or edge of an area. – *vb.* **limiting, limited** to restrict.

limited *adj.* **1** having a limit or limits. **2** not great: *She has only a limited understanding.*

limp¹ (limp) *vb.* **limping, limped** to walk with an awkward or uneven step, because one leg is weak or injured. – *n. & adj.* **limping**.

limp² (limp) *adj.* not stiff or firm; hanging loosely. – *n.* **limpness**.

● **Lincoln, Abraham** (1809-65) was an American statesman who led the Union during the CIVIL WAR and became the 16th President. He was assassinated.

● **Lindbergh, Charles** (1902-74) was an American pilot who made the first solo flight across the Atlantic, in 1927.

line¹ (līn) *n.* **1** a long narrow mark, streak, or stripe. **2** a length of thread, rope, wire, etc., especially for a particular purpose: *He bought a new fishing-line.* **3** (often in *plural*) an outline or shape, especially as part of the design: *They admired the clean lines of the car.* **4** a row of words.

line² (līn) *vb.* **lining, lined** to cover the inside of something with another material.

lining *n.* a piece of material, etc. used to line boxes, etc.

linear (li ni år) *adj.* like a line.

linen (li něn) *n.* cloth made from flax.

liner (lī něr) *n.* a large passenger ship or aircraft.

linger (ling gěr) *vb.* **lingering, lingered** to be slow to do something; to delay.

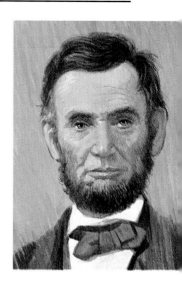

The Civil War which Lincoln hoped would be over in a few months dragged on for four years and cost the lives of half a million men.

Lindbergh took off from Roosevelt Field in New York in a plane called Spirit of St Louis. *Thirty-three hours and 3,600 miles later he landed in Paris to a hero's welcome.*

Evergreen oak
Quercus ilex

Pedunculate oak
Quercus robur

Red oak
Quercus borealis

Linnaeus used his two-word (binomial) naming system to name many common plants and trees. The first name is the plant's genus; the second the species. The three trees shown are of the genus Quercus *(oak).*

link (lingk) *n.* **1** a ring of a chain. **2** a connection between two people or things. **3** a means of communication or travel: *A new rail link will connect London and Paris.* – *vb.* **linking, linked**.

●**Linnaeus, Carolus** (1707-78) was a Swedish botanist who established a method of classifying living things.

linnet (**li** nit) *n.* a small brown song-bird.
linseed (**lin** sēd) *n.* the seed of flax.
lintel (**lin** tĕl) *n.* a horizontal wooden or stone beam placed over a doorway or window.
lion (**lī** ŏn) *n.* a large flesh-eating animal of the cat family, with a tawny yellow coat.
lioness *n.* a female lion.

lisp (lisp) *vb.* **lisping, lisped** to pronounce the sounds *s* and *z* as *th*. – *n.* the act of lisping.
list (list) *n.* a series of names, numbers, prices, etc. written down or said one after the other.
listen (**li** sĕn) *vb.* **listening, listened** to give attention so as to hear something.

●**Lister, Joseph** (1827-1912) was an English surgeon who first used antiseptics.

●**Liszt, Franz** (1811-86) was a Hungarian pianist and composer.

lit. See **light¹**.
literal (**li** tĕ rǎl) *adj.* following the exact meaning of words or a text: *a literal translation.*

Lions of the African plains live in groups (prides) of up to 30 animals. The females do most of the hunting.

lip (lip) *n.* **1** either of the folds of flesh which form the edge of the mouth. **2** the edge or rim of something, especially a container for liquid.
liquefy (**li** kwi fī) *vb.* **liquefies, liquefying, liquefied** to make or become liquid.
liquid (**li** kwid) *n.* a fluid or watery substance. – *adj.* (of a substance) able to flow and change shape; in a state between solid and gas: *liquid nitrogen.*
liquorice (**li** kŏ ris) *n.* a Mediterranean plant with sweet roots used in confectionery.

●**Lisbon** is the capital of PORTUGAL.

literate (**li** tĕ rǎt) *adj.* **1** able to read and write. **2** competent and experienced in: *He is computer-literate.*
literature (**li** trǎ chŭr) *n.* written material of high quality, valued for its language and content, such as novels, poems, and plays.

●**Lithuania**. See Supplement, **Countries**.

litmus (**lit** mŭs) *n.* a substance obtained from certain lichens, which is turned red by acids and blue by alkalis.
litmus paper *n.* paper treated with litmus, used to test liquids for acidity and alkalinity.
litre (**lē** tĕr) *n.* a metric unit of capacity equal to one cubic decimetre, or about 1.75 pints.

litter (**li** tĕr) *n.* **1** a mess of paper and rubbish in a public place. **2** straw and hay used as bedding for animals. **3** a number of animals born to the same mother at the same time: *The sow had a litter of five piglets.* – *vb.* **littering, littered** (of objects) to lie untidily around.

little (**li** tĕl) *adj.* small in size, extent, or amount: *She was little for her age.* – *n.* anything small in size, amount, or extent: *I can do a little to help out.* – *adv.* **1** to a small degree or extent: *Run around a little to keep warm.* **2** not much or at all: *Little did he understand the importance of her words.*

liturgy (**li** tûr ji) *n.* **liturgies** the standard form of service in a church.

live[1] (liv) *vb.* **living, lived 1** to have life; to be alive. **2** to last: *The memory of the accident lives on.* **3** to have as your home: *She lives next door.* – *vb.* **live up to** to behave in a manner worthy of: *It's hard to live up to her expectations.*

live[2] (līv) *adj.* **1** having life; not dead. **2** (of a radio or television broadcast) as the event takes place and not from a recording.
livestock *n.* farm animals.

livelihood (**līv** li hood) *n.* a job that provides income to live on.

lively (**līv** li) *adj.* **livelier, liveliest** active and full of energy and high spirits. – *n.* **liveliness**.

liver (**li** vĕr) *n.* a large organ in the body which carries out several important functions, such as cleaning the blood.

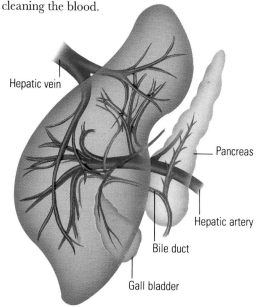

Hepatic vein

Pancreas

Hepatic artery

Bile duct

Gall bladder

The liver is a large gland that produces the digestive juices that burn up the fat you eat. It also makes proteins used in the blood. It stores vitamins and minerals until needed.

● The liver is often called the body's laboratory. It manufactures bile, a digestive fluid, urea, a waste product, and various blood proteins. It stores glycogen which is used to make glucose when needed.

● **Liverpool** is a big seaport on the river Mersey in north-west ENGLAND. It has two universities and two cathedrals.

living (**li** ving) *adj.* having life; alive. – *n.* livelihood or means of earning money.

● **Livingstone, David** (1813-73) was a Scottish missionary doctor who explored AFRICA.

lizard (**li** zărd) *n.* a reptile with a long body and tail, four legs, and a scaly skin.

llama (**lä** må) *n.* a domesticated South American mammal of the camel family.

load (lōd) *n.* **1** something that is carried; a burden. **2** (in *plural*; *colloquial*) a large amount: *He's got loads of money.* – *vb.* **loading, loaded 1** to put a load of something on or in a vehicle, washing-machine, etc. **2** to put film, audio, or video tape into a camera, tape, or video recorder. **3** to put a disk into a computer.

loaf (lōf) *n.* **loaves** (lōvz) a large piece of bread.

loan (lōn) *n.* anything lent, but especially a sum of money. – *vb.* **loaning, loaned** to lend.

loathe (lōTh) *vb.* **loathing, loathed** to feel dislike or disgust for.

lobby (**lo** bi) *n.* **lobbies 1** a small entrance-hall, passage, or waiting-room from which several rooms open. **2** a group of people who try to influence the government, politicians, etc. in favour of a particular cause.

lobe (lōb) *n.* the broad, lower part of the ear.

lobster (**lob** stĕr) *n.* a large edible shellfish with large claws, which goes red when boiled. Lobsters are CRUSTACEANS.

local (**lō** kål) *adj.* **1** of or belonging to your home area or neighbourhood. **2** affecting a small area or part only: *a local anaesthetic.*

locate (lō **kāt**) *vb.* **locating, located** to find the exact position of.
location *n.* **1** a position or situation. **2** a place outside the studio for filming: *The film was made on location in Spain.*

loch (lohh) *n.* (*Scottish*) a lake.

Lizards vary greatly. The Komodo dragon of Indonesia (above) is the largest living lizard. It can grow up to 3 metres long. It hunts for food such as deer, pigs, and monkeys. The thorny devil of Australia (top) has grooved skin that channels rain or dew towards its mouth.

Locking cylinder

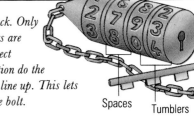

Simple wooden **locks** were developed in ancient Egypt. The Yale lock was invented in 1861. It contains a series of pins and drivers, which are all raised only when the correct key is inserted. Combination locks have no key. They are worked by a dial.

When the door is locked springs push a row of pins into the metal cylinder so it cannot be turned.

The notches on the key push the pins free of the cylinder so the key can turn the cylinder.

Correct key

Wrong key

A combination lock. Only when the tumblers are turned to the correct number combination do the slots inside them line up. This lets you withdraw the bolt.

Spaces   Tumblers

Correct numbers

Scrambled numbers

Locusts have huge appetites and in swarms they do immense damage to crops. For much of the time, locusts lead solitary lives but from time to time they swarm in hundreds of millions.

lock¹ (lok) *n.* **1** a small device for fastening doors, lids, etc., which has a bolt which usually needs a key to move it. **2** a closed part of a canal or river where the water level may be controlled, allowing boats to pass between higher and lower sections of the canal or river. – *vb.* **locking, locked** to fasten a door, box, bag, etc. with a lock. – *adj.* **lockable**.

locker *n.* a small, lockable cupboard used, for example for sports equipment.

lock² (lok) *n.* curl of hair.

locomotive (lō kō mō tiv) *n.* a railway engine for pulling trains.

locust (lō kůst) *n.* any of several kinds of large insect related to the grasshopper, which travel about in swarms and eat and destroy crops.

lodge (loj) *n.* **1** a small house at the gate to the grounds of a large house. **2** a porter's room in a university or college. **3** the home of a beaver or otter. – *vb.* **lodging, lodged 1** to live in rented accommodation. **2** to become firmly fixed: *He had a piece of bone lodged in his throat.*

lodger *n.* a person who rents accommodation in someone else's home.

lodging *n.* (usually in *plural*) a room or rooms rented in someone else's home.

loft (loft) *n.* a room or space under a roof.

lofty *adj.* **loftier, loftiest 1** of great or imposing height: *They looked at the lofty ceiling of the cathedral.* **2** of high or noble character: *She has lofty ideals.* – *adv.* **loftily**. – *n.* **loftiness**.

log (log) *n.* **1** part of a tree trunk or thick bare branch, especially when used as firewood. **2** a detailed record of events occurring during a ship's voyage. – *vb.* **log in** or **on** to gain access

to a computer system by keying in a personal code. – *vb.* **log out** or **off** to leave a computer system by keying in a closing command.

logo (lō gō) or (lo gō) *n.* **logos** a small design used as the symbol of an organization.

logic (lo jik) *n.* the science of reasoning correctly.

loiter (loi těr) *vb.* **loitering, loitered** to stand around or pass your time doing nothing in particular. – *n.* **loiterer**.

● **London** is the capital of the UNITED KINGDOM and stands on the river Thames. It is a great commercial city and contains the historic Houses of Parliament, Westminster Abbey, and the Tower of London.

● **London, Jack** (1876-1916) was an American novelist who wrote over 50 books.

lone (lōn) *adj.* alone; isolated.

lonely (lōn li) *adj.* **lonelier, loneliest 1** (of a person) sad because without companions or friends; solitary: *He leads a lonely existence.* **2** (of a place) isolated. – *n.* **loneliness**.

long¹ (long) *adj.* **1** measuring a great distance from one end to the other: *We live at the end of a long road.* **2** measuring a stated amount in space or time: *My ruler is 30cm long.* **3** having a large number of items: *She wrote a long shopping list.* **4** lasting for an extended period of time: *The ballet was very long.* – *adv.* **1** for or during a long period of time: *The battle happened long ago.* **2** throughout the whole time: *She cried all night long.* – **as long as 1** provided that. **2** while; during the time that. – **before long** soon.

long² (long) *vb.* **longing, longed** to want very much. – *adv.* **longingly.**
longing *n.* a great desire: *a longing for chocolate.*

● **Longfellow, Henry** (1807-82) was an American poet who wrote *The Song of Hiawatha.*

longitude (**lon** ji tūd) or (**long** gi tūd) *n.* a distance measured in degrees east or west of 0°, the imaginary line passing from north to south through Greenwich.

look (look) *vb.* **looking, looked 1** to turn the eyes in a certain direction so as to see. **2** to consider, examine, or give attention to. **3** to seem to be or appear: *She looked unhappy.* **4** to search for. **5** to investigate: *She looked into the matter for him.* – *n.* **1** an act of looking; a glance or view: *Let's have a good look.* **2** the general appearance of a thing or person: *I don't like the look of those dark clouds.* – *vb.* **look after** to take care of. – *vb.* **look ahead** to consider what will happen in the future. – *vb.* **look forward to** to wait for with pleasure. – *vb.* **look out** to keep watch. – *vb.* **look up to** to respect.
lookout *n.* a careful watch.

loom¹ (lōōm) *n.* a machine for weaving thread.

loom² (lōōm) *vb.* **looming, loomed** to appear in some enlarged or threatening form: *A large ship loomed up in the mist.*

loop (lōōp) *n.* **1** the oval-shaped coil formed in a piece of rope, chain, etc. as it crosses over itself. **2** a U-shaped bend in a river. – *vb.*
looping, looped to form into a loop.

loose (lōōs) *adj.* **1** no longer tied or held in confinement; free: *The dog broke loose from his grasp.* **2** not tight or close-fitting: *He likes wearing loose T-shirts.* **3** not held together; not fastened or firmly fixed in place; not packeted. – **at a loose end** with nothing to do.
loosen *vb.* **loosening, loosened 1** to become loose or looser. **2** to become less tense or stiff.

loot (lōōt) *n.* stolen goods, especially those stolen during a battle or riot. – *vb.* **looting, looted.**

lop (lop) *vb.* **lopping, lopped** to cut the ends off something: *They lopped the branches off the tree.*

● **Lorca, Federico García** (1899-1936) was a Spanish poet killed in the Spanish Civil War.

lord (lörd) *n.* (*British*) a male member of the nobility. – **live like a lord** to live in luxury. – *vb.* **lording, lorded: lord it over** (*colloquial*) to act like a lord, especially in being

haughty, proud, and domineering. – **the (House of) Lords** the upper, non-elected chamber of the British parliament.
the Lord's Prayer *n.* the prayer that Christ taught his disciples.

lore (lör) *n.* the whole body of knowledge, especially traditional knowledge, on a subject.

In 1801 the French inventor Joseph-Marie Jacquard designed the first automatic loom. It used punched-cards which enabled it to weave patterned fabrics.

● **Los Angeles** in California, is the second largest city in the UNITED STATES. It lies on the Pacific Ocean. It contains Disneyland and HOLLYWOOD.

lorry (**lo** ri) *n.* **lorries** a large heavily built road vehicle for transporting heavy loads.

lose (lōōz) *vb.* **losing, lost** (lost) **1** to stop having; to fail to keep, especially through carelessness. **2** to suffer the loss of someone through death. **3** to leave accidentally or be unable to find: *I lost my way in the fog.* **4** to fail to win a game, battle, etc. – *vb.* **lose out 1** to suffer loss or be at a disadvantage. **2** to fail to get something you desire.
loser *n.* **1** a person who loses. **2** (*colloquial*) a person who seems likely to always fail.
losing *adj.* failing; never likely to be successful.

loss (los) *n.* **1** the act of losing something. **2** the thing, amount, etc. that is lost.

PRONUNCIATION GUIDE	
fat a	all ö
fate ā	foot oo
fast ä	moon ōō
among å	boy oi
met e	house ow
mean ē	demon ô
silent ė	thing th
loch hh	this Th
fin i	but u
line ī	mute ū
quick kw	fur û
got o	brochure ů
note ō	vision zh

Path of sound waves

Wires bringing signals to coil

Cone vibrates

Permanent magnet　Coil

Most loudspeakers consist of a cone attached to an electromagnet. The cone is made of a special paper. The electric signals are fed to the coil of the electromagnet, and the coil vibrates as the electrical signals change. The vibrations move the cone, which vibrates the air and so creates sound waves.

Lunch is not a shortening of 'luncheon'. In fact the second word is a lengthening of the first. The word was based on the English dialect word *nuncheon*, meaning 'drink taken at noon'.

lost (lost) *past participle* of **lose**. – *adj.* **1** missing; no longer to be found. **2** unable to find the way: *We were lost in the woods*.

lost cause *n.* an aim or ideal which will never be achieved.

lot (lot) *n.* **1** (*colloquial*; often in *plural*) a great number or amount: *He collected lots of nuts from under the tree*. **2** an item for sale by auction. **3** (especially *US*) an area of land: *a parking lot*.

lotion (lō shŏn) *n.* a liquid that is put on the skin to protect or clean it.

loud (lowd) *adj.* **1** making a great sound; noisy. **2** capable of making a great sound: *His car has a loud horn*. – **out loud** aloud; loudly.

loudspeaker *n.* a device which converts electrical signals into sound in radios, etc.

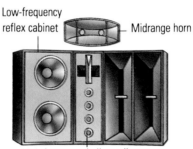

Low-frequency reflex cabinet　Midrange horn

High-frequency bullet radiators

● **Louis** was the name of eighteen kings of FRANCE. Louis the Fourteenth (1638-1715) ruled for 72 years and built the palace of VERSAILLES. Louis the Sixteenth (1754-93) was beheaded in the FRENCH REVOLUTION.

● **Louisiana**. See Supplement, **USA**.

lounge (lownj) *vb.* **lounging, lounged** to lie or recline comfortably. – *n.* a sitting-room.

● **Lourdes** is a town in south-west FRANCE where the Virgin Mary appeared in 1858 to a peasant girl called Bernadette Soubirous. It is now a centre of pilgrimage.

louse (lows) *n.* **lice** (līs) a wingless insect with a flat body and short legs, which sucks the blood of the animal or person it is living on.

lout (lowt) *n.* a bad-mannered, aggressive man.

● **Louvre** a museum and art gallery in Paris.

love (luv) *n.* **1** a feeling of great affection for, and devotion to, another person. **2** a strong liking for something: *a love for music*. **3** in tennis, no score. – *vb.* **loving, loved 1** to feel great affection for. **2** to enjoy very much; to like.

lovable or **loveable** *adj.* worthy of or inspiring love or affection.

lovely *adj.* **lovelier, loveliest** very beautiful; attractive; delightful. – *n.* **loveliness**.

low¹ (lō) *adj.* **1** not reaching up to a high level; not tall: *They sat on a low wall*. **2** situated close to the ground, sea-level, or the horizon: *The sun was low in the sky*. **3** of less than average amount: *This cheese is low in fat*. **4** making little sound; soft: *She spoke in a low voice*. **5** (of notes) produced with slow vibrations and having a deep pitch: *The double bass is one of the lowest instruments in the orchestra*. – *adv.* **1** in or to a low position, state, or manner. **2** in a small quantity. **3** quietly. – *n.* **lowness**.

the Low Countries *n.* (*plural*) the NETHERLANDS, BELGIUM, and LUXEMBOURG.

lower *adj.* not as high as something else in position, status, height, value, etc. – *adv.* in or to a lower position. – *vb.* **lowering, lowered 1** to make or become lower in amount, sound, etc.: *Please lower the volume*. **2** to pull or let down: *He lowered the window blinds*.

low tide or **water** *n.* the time the tide or water is at its lowest level.

low² (lō) *vb.* **lowing, lowed** (of cattle) to make a low, gentle, mooing sound.

loyal (loi ål) *adj.* faithful and true to someone.

loyalist *n.* a loyal supporter.

loyalty *n.* **loyalties** being loyal.

lozenge (lo zinj) *n.* a small sweet or tablet.

lubricate (lōō bri kāt) *vb.* **lubricating, lubricated** to cover with oil, grease, or some other such substance, to make smooth or slippery. – *n.* **lubrication**.

lucid (lōō sid) *adj.* easily understood; expressed clearly: *He gave a lucid account of the events leading up to the accident*. – *n.* **lucidity**.

luck (luk) *n.* **1** chance, especially when thought of as bringing good fortune. **2** events in life which cannot be controlled and seem to happen by chance: *He's had his share of bad luck*.

lucky *adj.* **luckier, luckiest 1** having good luck. **2** bringing good luck: *My lucky charm*. – *adv.* **luckily**. – *n.* **luckiness**.

ludicrous (lōō di krůs) *adj.* ridiculous.

lug (lug) *vb.* **lugging, lugged** to pull or drag.

luggage (lu gij) *n.* suitcases and bags.

● **Luke, Saint** is the author of the third gospel and the Acts of the Apostles in the NEW TESTAMENT.

lukewarm (lŏŏk **wörm**) *adj.* **1** moderately warm. **2** not enthusiastic; indifferent.

lull (lul) *vb.* **lulling, lulled** to make or become calm or quiet. − *n.* a period of calm and quiet.

lullaby (**lu** lǎ bī) *n.* **lullabies** a soothing song to lull children to sleep.

lumbago (lum **bā** gō) *n.* rheumatic pain in the lower part of the back.

lumber¹ (**lum** běr) *n.* **1** useless and disused pieces of furniture which have been stored away. **2** (especially *US*) timber.
  lumberjack *n.* a person employed to fell, saw up, and move trees.

lumber² (**lum** běr) *vb.* **lumbering, lumbered** to move about clumsily: *Elephants lumbered by.*

lump (lump) *n.* **1** a small, solid, shapeless mass. **2** a swelling on the surface of something. − *vb.* **lumping, lumped** to form into a lump.

lunacy (**lōō** nǎ si) *n.* **lunacies** great foolishness.

lunar (**lōō** nǎr) *adj.* like or caused by the moon.

lunatic (**lōō** nǎ tik) *adj.* foolish, or eccentric. − *n.*

lunch (lunch) *n.* a meal eaten in the middle of the day between breakfast and dinner.

lung (lung) *n.* an organ for breathing.

lunge (lunj) *n.* a sudden plunge forwards. − *vb.* **lunging, lunged**.

lure (lōŏr) *vb.* **luring, lured** to attract or entice by offering some reward: *The escaped tiger was lured back into its cage with a piece of meat.* − *n.* a person or thing which tempts or attracts.

lurk (lûrk) *vb.* **lurking, lurked** to lie in wait, especially in ambush.

lush (lush) *adj.* green and growing abundantly.

lustre (**lus** těr) *n.* the shiny appearance of a surface in reflected light.

lute (lōōt) *n.* an ancient guitar-like instrument with a pear-shaped body and a long neck.

● **Luther, Martin** (1483-1546) was a German priest who quarrelled with the Roman Catholic Church and started the Protestant REFORMATION.

● **Luxembourg**. See Supplement, **Countries**.

luxurious (lug **zūr** i ǔs) or (luk **zhŏŏr** i ǔs) *adj.* enjoying or providing luxury.

luxury (**luk** shǔ ri) *n.* **luxuries 1** expensive, rich, extremely comfortable surroundings and

possessions. **2** something pleasant, often expensive, but not necessary. − *adj.* relating to or providing luxury: *We stayed in a luxury hotel.*

-ly (-li) *suffix* used to form adverbs: *cleverly.*

lymph (limf) *n.* a colourless liquid containing white blood cells, found in animal tissue.

lynx (lingks) *n.* an animal of the cat family, with long legs, a short tail, and tufted ears.

● **Lyons** is a large city in eastern FRANCE.

lyre (līr) *n.* a U-shaped, harp-like instrument.
  lyre-bird *n.* an Australian pheasant-like bird, the male of which has lyre-shaped tail feathers.

lyric (**li** rik) *adj.* having the form of a song. − *n.* (usually in *plural*) the words of a song.

Saint Luke's Gospel contains the parable of the Good Samaritan in which a person from Samaria, a country despised by the Jews, comes to the aid of a traveller who had been beaten up by robbers.

Martin Luther pinning up the list of 95 arguments, setting out what he thought was wrong with the Church.

Mm

macabre (må **käb** ĕr) *adj.* strange and ghastly: *She related the macabre story of his death.*

macaroon (ma kå **rōōn**) *n.* a sweet biscuit.

● **MacArthur, Douglas** (1880-1964) was an American general who distinguished himself in the Second WORLD WAR and the Korean War.

macaw (må **kö**) *n.* a large, long-tailed, brightly coloured tropical American parrot.

● **Macdonald, Sir John** (1815-91) was the first prime minister of CANADA.

● **Macedonia**. See Supplement, **Countries**.

● **Machiavelli** (ma kē å **ve** li), **Niccolò** (1469-1527) was an Italian statesman whose name became a byword for devious plotting.

machine (må **shēn**) *n.* any device with moving parts, designed to perform a particular task.

● There are six kinds of simple machine used to help people do things: the wheel and axle, lever, pulley, screw, wedge, and inclined plane. The wheel, for instance, enables loads to be moved more easily by reducing the friction between the load and the ground.

machine code or **language** *n.* a code used for writing instructions in a form which a computer can understand.

machine-gun *n.* any of various portable guns that fire a continuous stream of bullets.

machinery *n.* **1** machines in general. **2** the working or moving parts of a machine.

machinist *n.* a person who operates a machine.

Machines change energy from one form into another more useful form; they make jobs easier. Until the Industrial Revolution in the 1700s, there were very few machines. Steam engines became common in the 1700s. In the 1800s came other forms of energy such as the internal combustion engine and the electric motor making possible motor cars, aircraft, and many types of electrical machines.

The small electric motor in a drill is powerful. Its turning force is increased as it is slowed down by the gearing mechanism.

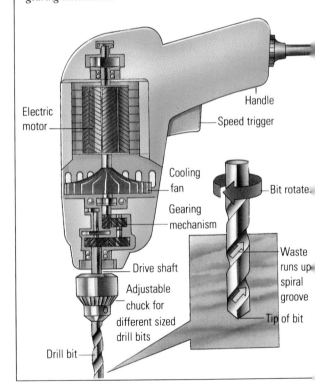

Electric motor
Handle
Speed trigger
Cooling fan
Gearing mechanism
Bit rotate
Drive shaft
Adjustable chuck for different sized drill bits
Waste runs up spiral groove
Tip of bit
Drill bit

mad (mad) *adj.* **madder, maddest 1** insane. **2** foolish or senseless: *You must be mad to go out in this weather without an umbrella.* **3** very angry: *She was mad with me for being late.* – *n.* **madness. madden** *vb.* **maddening, maddened** to make angry, to enrage. – *adj.* **maddening**.

●**Madagascar**. See Supplement, **Countries**.

●**Madras** is an Indian east coast seaport.

●**Madrid** is the capital of SPAIN. It is the seat of the country's parliament (Cortes) and home of the Prado museum.

Pulleys change the direction of a force. A lifting tackle has several pulleys and makes lifting easier. Pulling the rope a long distance lifts the load a shorter distance.

A forklift truck is a hydraulic machine. It uses liquid pressure to transmit power because liquid cannot be compressed. Inside a hydraulic jack, a large movement of the smaller piston causes a small change of the large piston.

Effort

Distance moved by load = 1

Load

Large piston

Oil Force

Small piston

magazine (ma gă zēn) *n.* a weekly or monthly paperback publication.

●**Magellan** (må **ge** lån), **Ferdinand** (1480-1521) was a Portuguese mariner and explorer.

maggot (**ma** gŏt) *n.* the worm-like larva of various flies, especially the housefly.

magic (**ma** jik) *n.* **1** in stories, the power of supernatural forces to affect people, objects, and events. **2** the art of performing entertaining illusions and conjuring tricks. **3** the quality of being wonderful, charming, or delightful: *The magic of the music crept over him.* – *adj.* **1** of or used in sorcery or conjuring. **2** (*colloquial*) excellent. – **like magic 1** mysteriously. **2** suddenly. **3** excellently.
magical *adj.* **1** relating to the art or practice of magic. **2** fascinating; wonderful; charming.
magician *n.* **1** a performer of illusions. **2** in stories, a person with supernatural powers.

magistrate (**ma** ji strāt) *n.* a judge in a lower court of law dealing with minor offences.

magma (**mag** må) *n.* molten rock beneath the Earth's crust.

●**Magna Carta** an agreement signed in 1215 by King John of ENGLAND. It gave rights to the barons and made the king answerable to the law.

magnesium (mag **nē** zi ŭm) *n.* an element (symbol **Mg**), a light silvery-white metal that burns with a dazzling white flame.

magnet (**mag** nit) *n.* a piece of metal, especially iron, with the power to attract and repel iron, and the tendency to point in a north-south direction when freely suspended.
magnetic (mag **net** ik) *adj.* **1** having the powers of or operating by means of a magnet or magnetism. **2** charming or attractive.
magnetic north *n.* the direction in which a compass's magnetic needle always points, slightly east or west of true north.
magnetic tape *n.* a thin plastic tape coated with magnetic material, on which sound, television images, can be recorded etc.

magnificent (mag **ni** fi sĕnt) *adj.* impressive. – *n.* **magnificence**. – *adv.* **magnificently**.

magnify (**mag** ni fī) *vb.* **magnifies, magnifying, magnified** to cause to appear larger, for example by using a microscope.

magnolia (mag **nō** li å) *n.* a tree or shrub with large sweet-smelling white or pink flowers.

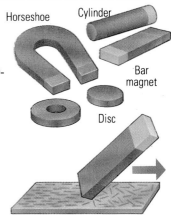

Horseshoe

Cylinder

Bar magnet

Disc

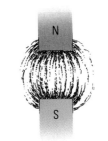

The pushing and pulling forces around a magnet are invisible. But if you scatter iron filings on a piece of paper and place a magnet under the paper some of the lines of force become clear.

The Magyars were a race of people who came originally from the steppes (plains) of Russia. Under their leader, Prince Arpad, they occupied what we now call Hungary in the 9th century. This illustration is from a manuscript showing their arrival in Hungary.

Malaria was once believed to have been caused by 'bad air' given off in marshy places. It was therefore named in Italy *mal'aria*, meaning 'bad air'.

Magyar (**mag** yär) *n.* **1** a member of the predominant race of people in HUNGARY. **2** the Hungarian language. – *adj.* of the Magyars or their language.

mahogany (må **hog** å ni) *n.* **mahoganies** a tropical American tree; any of various related African and Asian trees.

maid (mād) *n.* a female servant.

mail (māl) *n.* **1** the postal system. **2** letters, parcels, etc. sent by post. – *vb.* **mailing, mailed** to send by post.

main (mān) *adj.* most important; chief. – *n.* (in *plural*) the network of pipes or cables by which power, water, etc. is distributed.
mainframe *n.* a large powerful computer.
mainly *adv.* for the most part; largely.

● **Maine**. See Supplement, **USA**.

maintain (mān **tān**) *vb.* **maintaining, maintained 1** to keep in existence: *She maintains the tradition of giving generously to charity.* **2** to keep in good condition: *It is difficult to maintain such a large house.* **3** to pay the expenses of: *She is maintained financially by her parents.* **4** to assert: *He maintained that my argument was incorrect.*

maintenance (**mān** tĕ nåns) *n.* **1** the process of keeping something in good condition. **2** money paid by one person to support another.

maize (māz) *n.* a tall cereal plant widely grown for its edible yellow grain.

majesty (**ma** jĕs ti) *n.* **majesties** impressive dignity; splendour. – *adj.* **majestic**.

major (**mā** jŏr) *adj.* **1** great in number, size, importance, etc.: *This is our major area of* concern. **2** (of a musical key or scale) having two full tones between the first and third notes. – *n.* **1** an army officer. **2** (*US*) a student's main subject of study. – *vb.* **majoring, majored** to specialize in a particular subject of study.

majority (må **jo** ri ti) *n.* **majorities** the greater number; the largest group.

● **Major, John** (1943-) became the prime minister of the UNITED KINGDOM in 1990.

make (māk) *vb.* **making, made 1** to create, manufacture, or produce by mixing, combining, or shaping materials: *Let's make a cake.* **2** to cause to be or become; to bring about: *She added more ingredients to make the cake bigger.* **3** to force: *He made her jump off the wall.* **4** to cause to appear: *Long hair makes her look younger.* **5** to gain, earn, or acquire: *He has made a fortune.* **6** to add up to or amount to: *4 and 4 makes 8.* **7** to carry out or produce: *He made a good speech.* – *n.* a manufacturer's brand: *What make of car did you buy?* – **make believe** to pretend. – *vb.* **make out** to see.

mal- *prefix* meaning bad or not: *maladjusted, malformed, maltreat.*

malaria (må **lār** i å) *n.* an infectious disease producing bouts of fever, caused by the bite of a certain type of mosquito. – *adj.* **malarial**.

● **Malawi**. See Supplement, **Countries**.

Malay (må **lā**) *n.* **1** a member of a race of people that inhabit MALAYSIA, SINGAPORE, and INDONESIA. **2** their language. – *adj.* of the Malays or their language.

● **Malaysia**. See Supplement, **Countries**.

● **Maldives**. See Supplement, **Countries**.

male (māl) *adj.* **1** of the sex which has a sperm-producing or similar organ, not of the sex which gives birth to young. **2** of or characteristic of men; masculine. – *n.* a male person, animal, or plant. – *n.* **maleness**.

● **Mali**. See Supplement, **Countries**.

malice (**ma** lis) *n.* the desire to hurt others.

malignant (må **lig** nånt) *adj.* **1** feeling or showing hatred; malicious or malevolent. **2** a medical term describing cancerous tumours.

malleable (**ma** li å běl) *adj.* **1** able to be shaped easily, without breaking: *Bronze is a very malleable metal.* **2** easily influenced.

mallet (**ma** lit) *n.* a hammer with a wooden head.

malt (mölt) *n.* prepared barley or other grain, used to make beer or whisky.

● **Malta**. See Supplement, **Countries**.

Maltese (möl **tēz**) *n.* a native or inhabitant of the Mediterranean island of Malta. – *adj.* of Malta.

mammal (**ma** mål) *n.* any warm-blooded animal the female of which gives birth to live young and produces milk to feed them.

mammoth (**ma** môth) *n.* a large hairy prehistoric animal that looked like an elephant. – *adj.* huge.

man (man) *n.* **men 1** an adult male human being. **2** human beings as a whole.

mankind *n.* the human race as a whole.

manslaughter *n.* the crime of killing someone without intending to do so.

manacle (**ma** nå kěl) *n.* a handcuff.

manage (**ma** nij) *vb.* **managing, managed 1** to be in overall control or charge of: *I manage my own affairs.* **2** to succeed in doing or producing something: *We just managed to arrive at the theatre in time.* – *adj.* **manageable**.

management *n.* the managers of a company.

manager *n.* a person in overall charge.

mane (mān) *n.* the long hair growing from the neck of horses, lions, and other animals.

● **Manet** (**ma** nā), **Edouard** (1832-83) was a French Impressionist painter.

manganese (**mang** gå nēz) *n.* an element (symbol **Mn**), a brittle greyish-white metal, used in making steel, glass, and bronze.

● **Manhattan** is an island at the mouth of the Hudson River and a New York borough.

mania (**mā** ni å) *n.* **1** a form of mental illness characterized by over-active, over-excited behaviour, and sometimes violence. **2** a craze: *My children have a mania for skateboarding.*

manifest (**ma** ni fest) *vb.* **manifesting, manifested** to show or display clearly: *She manifested her intelligence even as a small child.* – *n.* **manifestation**.

manifesto (ma ni **fes** tō) *n.* **manifestos** or **manifestoes** a statement of policy.

manipulate (må **nip** ū lāt) *vb.* **manipulating, manipulated 1** to handle, especially skilfully. **2** to control or influence cleverly, especially to your own advantage. – *n.* **manipulation**.

● **Manitoba** is a province of CANADA.

manner (**ma** něr) *n.* **1** way; fashion: *She dresses in a sloppy manner.* **2** behaviour towards others: *She has a good manner with children.*

A kid suckling a goat. Mammals are the most highly developed of the many different forms of animal. All mammals give birth to live young (not hatched from an egg) and the young feed on milk from the mother's body. Mammals usually have four limbs.

mannerism *n.* an individual characteristic, for example a gesture or facial expression.

manoeuvre (må **noo** věr) *n.* **1** a movement performed with considerable skill: *Parking the car can be a difficult manoeuvre.* **2** (in *plural*) military exercises, especially on a large scale. – *vb.* **manoeuvring, manoeuvred 1** to move something accurately and with skill. **2** to use ingenuity, and perhaps deceit, in handling something or someone: *He manoeuvred her into a position where she could not win the game.*

manor (**ma** nôr) *n.* **1** in medieval EUROPE, an area of land under the control of a lord. **2** a large house on a country estate.

● **Mansfield, Katherine** (1888-1923) was a New Zealand short-story writer.

mansion (**man** shŏn) *n.* a large house.

manual (**man** ū ål) *adj.* **1** of the hand or hands. **2** using the body, rather than the mind; physical: *He is a manual worker.* – *n.* a book of instructions, e.g. for repairing a car.

PRONUNCIATION GUIDE	
fat **a**	all **ŏ**
fate **ā**	foot **oo**
fast **ä**	moon **ōō**
among **å**	boy **oi**
met **e**	house **ow**
mean **ē**	demon **ŏ**
silent **ě**	thing **th**
loch **hh**	this **Th**
fin **i**	but **u**
line **ī**	mute **ū**
quick **kw**	fur **û**
got **o**	brochure **ů**
note **ō**	vision **zh**

manufacture (ma nū **fak** chŭr) *vb.*
manufacturing, manufactured to make from raw materials, especially in large quantities using machinery. – *n.* the practice or process of manufacturing. – *n.*
manufacturer. – *adj.* & *n.* **manufacturing**.

manure (mă **nūr**) *n.* any substance, especially animal dung, used on soil as a fertilizer.

manuscript (ma nū skript) *n.* an author's handwritten or typed version of a book.

Manx (mangks) *adj.* of the Isle of Man.
Manx cat *n.* a breed of tailless cat.

many (me ni) *adj.* great in number; numerous.
– *pron.* a great number of people or things.

●**Mao Zedong** (1893-1976) was a Chinese communist statesman and president of the People's Republic of China until 1959.

A conical projection

Maori (**mow** ri) *n.* **Maori** or **Maoris 1** a member of the aboriginal Polynesian people of New Zealand. **2** the language of this people.
– *adj.* of this people or its language.

map (map) *n.* a diagram of the Earth's surface, showing geographical and other features, for example the position of towns and roads.

maple (**mā** pĕl) *n.* a broad-leaved tree whose seeds float by means of wing-like growths.

●**Marat, Jean** (1743-93) was a French revolutionary. He was stabbed to death in his bath by Charlotte Corday.

Mercator projection

Polar zenithal projection

A projection is the way in which map-makers show the curved surface of the Earth on a flat map.

Different types of **map**. A relief map shows the surface of the land, the hills, rivers, forests, etc. Maps of the sea-bed are important for plotting a ship's course, and in the search for minerals. Star maps help navigation. Perhaps the most commonly used are road maps.

Relief map

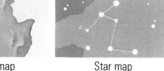

Star map

Sea map

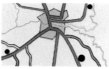

Road map

marathon (ma rǎ thǒn) *n.* a long-distance running race, usually 42km (26 miles).

●The marathon is named after a Greek soldier's run from the town of Marathon to Athens in 490 BC to bring news of a Greek victory over the Persians.

marble (**mär** bĕl) *n.* **1** hard streaky-looking limestone rock that can be highly polished, used in building and sculpture. **2** a small hard glass ball used in children's games.

March (märch) *n.* the third month of the year, following February. March has 31 days.

march (märch) *vb.* **marching, marched 1** (of soldiers etc.) to walk in a formal manner, usually at a brisk pace and in step with others. **2** to walk in a purposeful way. – *n.* **1** an act of marching. **2** a procession of people often taking part in an organized protest.

An early Marconi wireless set, with a speaker and headphones. In modern radios the glass valves have been replaced by tiny transistors.

●**Marconi** (mär **kō** ni), **Guglielmo** (1874-1937) was an Italian scientist, the inventor of radio.

mare (mār) *n.* an adult female horse.

margarine (**mär** jǎ rēn), (**mär** gǎ rēn), (mär jǎ **rēn**) or (mär gǎ **rēn**) *n.* a butter-like substance made from vegetable oils and often milk.

margin (**mär** jin) *n.* **1** the blank space around a page of writing or print. **2** any edge or border.
marginal *adj.* small and unimportant.

●**Marie Antoinette** (1755-93) was the wife of Louis the Sixteenth of FRANCE. Her frivolity contributed to the FRENCH REVOLUTION during which she was guillotined.

marine (mǎ **rēn**) *adj.* concerned with or found in the sea: *marine animals.* – *n.* a soldier trained to serve on land or at sea.

marionette (ma ri ŏ **net**) *n.* a puppet with jointed limbs moved by strings.

maritime (**ma** ri tīm) *adj.* of the sea or ships.

mark (märk) *n.* **1** a visible blemish, for example a scratch or stain. **2** a number or letter used to grade a student's, competitor's, etc. work. **3** a symbol: *She wrote a question mark against his name.* – *vb.* **marking, marked 1** to become spoiled by a blemish. **2** to award a grade to. **marked** *adj.* obvious or noticeable.

● **Mark, Saint** was writer of one of the gospels in the NEW TESTAMENT.

market (**mär** kit) *n.* **1** a gathering of people to buy and sell various goods. **2** the building or other public location in which this takes place. **3** a particular region or section of the population to which goods may be sold: *These records are aimed at the teenage market.* – *vb.* **marketing, marketed** to offer for sale.

● **Marlborough** is a province of New Zealand.

● **Marlowe, Christopher** (1564-93) was an English poet and playwright.

marmalade (**mär** må lād) *n.* a bitter jam made from any citrus fruit, especially oranges.

marmoset (**mär** mŏ zet) *n.* any of various small South American monkeys.

maroon[1] (må **rōōn**) *n.* & *adj.* (of) a dark brownish- or purplish-red colour.

maroon[2] (må **rōōn**) *vb.* **marooning, marooned** to leave in isolation in a deserted place: *Robinson Crusoe was marooned.*

marriage (**ma** rij) *n.* **1** the relationship of being husband and wife. **2** the act of becoming husband and wife; a wedding.

marrow (**ma** rō) *n.* **1** (also **bone marrow**) the soft tissue in the hollow centre of bones. **2** a large oblong rounded vegetable with thick green skin and soft white flesh.

marry (**ma** ri) *vb.* **marries, marrying, married** to take as a husband or wife.

Mars[1]. See **Myths and Legends**.

● **Mars**[2] is also called the 'Red Planet'. It is about half the size of Earth and has two moons.

● **Marseilles** is an important French port on the Mediterranean.

marsh (märsh) *n.* an area of low-lying wet land.

marsupial (mär **sōō** pi ål) *n.* any member of a class of mammals, including kangaroos and koala, whose young are born undeveloped and are carried in an external pouch on the mother's body until fully developed.

martial (**mär** shål) *adj.* of or relating to war. **martial art** *n.* any of various self-defence techniques of Far Eastern origin.

martin (**mär** tin) *n.* a small bird of the swallow family, with a square or slightly forked tail.

martyr (**mär** tẽr) *n.* a person who chooses to die rather than give up his or her beliefs.

marvel (**mär** vẽl) *n.* a wonderful person or thing. **marvellous** *adj.* wonderful or astonishing.

● **Marx Brothers** This American comedy team was made up of Chico (1891-1961), Groucho (1890-1977), Harpo (1893-1964), and Zeppo (1901-79).

Marxism (**märks** i zẽm) *n.* the theories of Karl *Marx* (1818-83), German economist and philosopher, stating that communism will eventually replace capitalism. – *n.* & *adj.* **Marxist**.

● **Maryland**. See Supplement, **USA**.

● **Mary, Queen of Scots** (1542-87) was heir to ELIZABETH the First of England who had her executed for treason.

Two Viking probes visited Mars in 1976. The probe in the picture is viewing the enormous volcanic mountain of Olympus Mons. The planet's atmosphere is only about a hundredth part as thick as Earth's. On the left of the picture is Phobos, one of the two tiny moons of Mars.

marzipan (**mär** zi pan) *n.* a sweet paste of crushed almonds and sugar.

mascot (**mas** kȯt) *n.* a person, animal, or thing thought to bring good luck.

masculine (**mas** kū lin) *adj.* male or manly.

mash (mash) *vb.* **mashing, mashed** to beat or crush into a pulpy mass: *Mash the potatoes!*

mask (mäsk) *n.* any covering for the face, worn for amusement, for protection, or as a disguise. – *vb.* **masking, masked** to disguise.

In ancient Greece plays were acted in huge open-air theatres. Men wearing stylized masks (depicting comedy or tragedy, etc.) played all the parts.

mason (**mā** sȯn) *n.* (also **stonemason**) a person trained in working with stone.

mass¹ (mas) *n.* **1** a large quantity gathered together; a lump. **2** (*colloquial*; often *plural*) a large quantity or number: *There was masses of food left over.* **3** a measure of the quantity of matter in a body. – *adj.* involving a large number of people: *They held a mass meeting.*

mass² (mas) *n.* in the Roman Catholic and Orthodox Churches, the Holy Communion service.

●**Massachusetts**. See Supplement, **USA**.

massacre (**ma** så kėr) *n.* a cruel killing of large numbers of people or animals.

massage (**ma** säzh) *n.* a technique of easing pain or stiffness in the body, especially the muscles, by rubbing, kneading, and tapping with the hands; a body treatment using this technique. – *vb.* **massaging, massaged**.

massive (**ma** siv) *adj.* very big, and heavy.

mast (mäst) *n.* any upright wooden or metal supporting pole, especially one carrying the sails of a ship, or a radio or television aerial.

master (**mäs** tėr) *n.* a male person, who has authority over someone or something. – *vb.* **mastering, mastered** to become skilled in: *He has mastered Dutch.*

mastiff (**ma** stif) *n.* a large powerful breed of dog, formerly used for hunting.

mastodon (**ma** stȯ don) *n.* a prehistoric elephant-like mammal.

mat (mat) *n.* a flat piece of carpet, used as a decorative or protective floor-covering, or for wiping shoes on to remove dirt. – *vb.* **matting, matted** to become tangled into a dense mass. – *adj.* **matted**.

matador (**ma** tå dör) *n.* the principal toreador in a bullfight, the person who kills the bull.

match¹ (mach) *n.* a small piece of wood coated on the tip with a substance that produces a flame when rubbed on a rough surface.

match² (mach) *n.* **1** a contest or game. **2** a person or thing that has similar qualities to, or combines well with, another. – *vb.* **matching, matched 1** to combine well. **2** to be equal to: *I can't match that offer.*

matching *adj.* similar; part of the same set.

mate (māt) *n.* **1** an animal's breeding partner. **2** (*colloquial*) a friend. – *vb.* **mating, mated** to bring animals together for breeding.

material (må **tēr** i ål) *n.* **1** any substance out of which something is made. **2** cloth; fabric.

materialism *n.* excessive interest in money, etc.

maternal (må **tûr** nål) *adj.* **1** of or like a mother. **2** related on the mother's side of the family.

mathematics (ma thi **mat** iks) *n.* (*singular*) the science dealing with measurements, numbers, quantities, and shapes.

●**Matisse** (ma **tēs**), **Henri** (1869-1954) was a French painter and sculptor.

matrimony (**ma** tri mȯ ni) *n.* being married.

matt (mat) *adj* a dull surface without gloss.

matter (**ma** tėr) *n.* **1** the substance from which all physical things are made; material. **2** material of a particular kind: *She took plenty of reading matter on holiday.* – *vb.* **mattering, mattered** to be important or significant: *Does the extra cost matter to you?*

●**Matthew, Saint** was one of Jesus' apostles and author of the first gospel in the New Testament.

mattress (**ma** trĕs) *n.* a large flat fabric-covered pad, used on a bed for sleeping on.

mature (må **choōr**) *adj.* **1** fully grown or developed. **2** behaving with adult good sense: *He behaves in a mature way for a 12-year-old.* – *vb.* **maturing, matured** to make or become fully developed. – *n.* **maturity**.

maul (möl) *vb.* **mauling, mauled** to attack savagely: *The gamekeeper was mauled by a lion.*

●**Mauna Loa** on the island of Hawaii, is the world's largest active volcano.

●**Mauritania**. See Supplement, **Countries**.

●**Mauritius**. See Supplement, **Countries**.

mauve (möv) *n.* & *adj.* (of) a pale purple colour.

maximum (**mak** si mŭm) *adj.* greatest possible. – *n.* the greatest possible number or quantity.

May (mā) *n.* the fifth month of the year, following April. May has 31 days.
mayfly *n.* a short-lived insect with transparent wings, appearing briefly in spring.

may (mā) *vb.* **might** (mīt) expressing:
1 permission: *You may go now.* **2** possibility: *I may well leave.* **3** ability: *May I help you?* **4** used to introduce the first of a pair of statements, with the sense of 'although': *You may be rich, but you're not happy.*

maybe (**mā** bē) *adv.* it is possible; perhaps.

●**Mayflower** This was the ship which, in 1620, carried the PILGRIMS from Plymouth in ENGLAND to Massachusetts in AMERICA.

The Mayflower *was a small sailing ship about 27 metres long. Its Puritan Pilgrim passengers were looking for religious freedom in the New World.*

mayor (**mā** ŏr) or (mār) *n.* the head of a town or city. – *adj.* **mayoral**.

maze (māz) *n.* a confusing network of paths or passages; any confusingly complicated system.

me (mē) *pron.* used by a speaker or writer to refer to himself or herself.

●**Mead, Margaret** (1901-78) was an American anthropologist who studied Native Americans and people of the Pacific Islands.

meadow (**me** dō) *n.* a field of grass.

meagre (**mē** gěr) *adj.* inadequate; scanty.

meal (mēl) *n.* **1** an occasion on which food is eaten. **2** food eaten on one occasion.

mean[1] (mēn) *vb.* **meaning, meant** (ment) **1** to intend: *He didn't mean any harm.* **2** to be sincere about: *He means what he says.*
meaning *n.* the sense in which a statement, action, or word is intended to be understood.

mean[2] (mēn) *adj.* **1** not generous. **2** unkind.

mean[3] (mēn) *n.* **1** a midway position between two extremes. **2** a mathematical average.

meander (mi **an** děr) *vb.* **meandering, meandered** (of a river) to bend and curve.

means (mēnz) *n.* **1** (*singular* or *plural*) the instrument or method used to achieve some object. **2** (*plural*) wealth; resources.

meanwhile (**mēn** whīl) *adv.* at the same time.

measles (**mē** zělz) *n.* (*singular*) an infectious disease, common in children.

measure (**me** zhůr) *n.* **1** size, volume, etc. determined by comparison with an instrument graded in standard units. **2** a standard unit of size; a system of such units; a standard amount: *We use a metric measure;* **3** (usually in *plural*) an action; a step: *It was necessary to take drastic measures.* – *vb.* **measuring, measured** to determine the size, volume, etc. of something: *She used a ruler to measure the table.*

meat (mēt) *n.* the flesh of animals, usually not including fish, used as food.

●**Mecca** in Saudi Arabia is the Holy City of the MUSLIMS and MUHAMMAD's birthplace.

mechanic (mi **kan** ik) *n.* a skilled worker who repairs or maintains machinery.

The pyramid builders of Egypt over 5,000 years ago used parts of the body to measure. The cubit was the length from fingers to elbow.

USEFUL MEASURES
Imperial
2 teaspoons = 1 dessertspoon.
2 dessertspoons = 1 tablespoon.
16 tablespoons = 1 cup.
2 cups = 1 pint.
1 pint = 20 fluid oz.
American
1 American pint = 16 fluid oz.
1 American cup = 8 fluid oz.
Metric equivalents
1 teaspoon = 5 ml.
1 pint = 0.5 litres app.
1 lb = 0.5 kg app.

mechanical *adj.* **1** of or concerning machines. **2** done without much thought: *mechanical work.*

mechanism (**me** kå ni zěm) *n.* a working part of a machine, or its system of working parts.

medal (**me** dål) *n.* a flat piece of metal decorated with a design or inscription and offered as an award for merit or bravery.

medallist *n.* a person awarded a medal.

meddle (**me** dål) *vb.* **meddling, meddled** to interfere: *Stop meddling in my personal affairs!*

media. See **medium**.

mediaeval or **medieval** (me di **ē** vål) *adj.* of or relating to the Middle Ages.

medical (**me** di kål) *adj.* of doctors or the science or practice of medicine. – *n.* a medical examination to determine physical health.

●**Medici** (**mě dē** chi) was the name of the ruling family of Florence, ITALY.

Florence, city of the powerful Medici family, and one of the great centres of the Italian Renaissance.

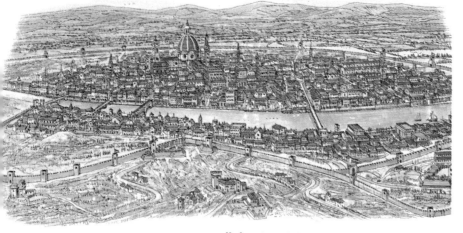

medicine (**med** sin) *n.* **1** a substance that you swallow or drink, used to treat or prevent disease or illness. **2** the science or practice of treating or preventing illness.

mediocre (mē di **ō** kěr) *adj.* rather inferior.

meditate (**me** di tāt) *vb.* **meditating, meditated** to spend time in deep thought.

medium (**mē** di ům) *n.* **media** or **mediums** **1** something by or through which an effect is produced. **2** (usually in *plural*; also **mass medium**) a means by which news, information, etc. is communicated to the public, usually television, radio, and the press collectively. – *adj.* midway; average: *She fits a medium size in skirts.*

meet (mēt) *vb.* **meeting, met** (met) **1** to come together by chance or arrangement: *They met at a party.* **2** to be present at the arrival of: *She met him off the train.*

meeting *n.* an assembly or gathering.

megabyte (**me** gå bīt) *n.* in computing, a unit of storage capacity equal to 1,048,576 bytes.

megalith (**me** gå lith) *n.* a very large stone.

melancholy (**me** lån kǒ li) *adj.* sad.

melanin (**me** lå nin) *n.* the black or dark brown colouring found in the skin, hair, and eyes.

●**Melbourne** in Victoria state, is AUSTRALIA's second largest city.

mellow (**me** lō) *adj.* **1** (of character) calm and relaxed with age or experience. **2** (of sound, colour, light, etc.) soft, rich, and pure.

melody (**me** lǒ di) *n.* **melodies** the sequence of single notes that form a tune.

melon (**me** lǒn) *n.* a large edible fruit with a thick skin, sweet juicy flesh, and many seeds.

melt (melt) *vb.* **melting, melted** to become soft through the action of heat; to dissolve.

●**Melville, Herman** (1819-91) was an American writer, author of *Moby Dick.*

member (**mem** běr) *n.* **1** a person belonging to a group or organization. **2** an arm or leg.

membrane (**mem** brān) *n.* a thin film of skin covering, connecting, or lining organs or cells in plants or animals.

memorable (**me** mǒ rå běl) *adj.* worth remembering; easily remembered.

memorial (mě **mör** i ål) *n.* a thing that honours or commemorates a person or an event, for example a statue.

memorize or **memorise** (**me** mǒ rīz) *vb.* **memorizing, memorized** to learn thoroughly; to learn by heart.

memory (**me** mǒ ri) *n.* **memories 1** the power of the mind to remember: *I can recite the whole poem from memory.* **2** the part of a computer in which information is stored.

menace (**me** nås) *n.* a source of danger: *Drug addiction is a menace for society today.* – *vb.* **menacing, menaced** to threaten.

mend (mend) *vb.* **mending, mended** to repair.

●**Mendel, Gregor** (1822-84) was an Austrian monk, founder of the science of GENETICS.

menopause (**me** nǒ pöz) *n.* the time in a woman's life when she stops menstruating, usually between the ages of 45 and 50.

A menorah stood in the first Temple at Jerusalem and is still used today. Its branches symbolize the seven days of creation recorded in the Bible.

menorah (mĕ **nör** å) *n.* a candlestick with seven branches used in Jewish worship.

menstruate (**mens** trōō āt) *vb.* **menstruating, menstruated** to discharge blood monthly from the womb. – *n.* **menstruation**.

mental (**men** tål) *adj.* relating to or done using the mind or intelligence: *mental arithmetic*.

mention (**men** shŏn) *vb.* **mentioning, mentioned** to speak of or make reference to. – *n.* a remark, usually a brief reference to.

menu (**me** nū) *n.* **1** a list of dishes available in a restaurant. **2** a list of computer functions displayed on a screen.

●**Menzies, Sir Robert** (1894-1978) was an Australian statesman and prime minister.

merchant (**mûr** chånt) *n.* a trader. – *adj.* used for trade: *He is captain of a merchant ship*.

●**Mercury** is the smallest planet in the solar system and the closest to the Sun.

mercury (**mûr** kūr i) *n.* an element (symbol **Hg**), a heavy poisonous silvery-white metal that is liquid at ordinary temperatures, used in thermometers and in dentistry.

mercy (**mûr** si) *n.* **mercies 1** kindness or forgiveness shown when punishment is possible or justified. **2** a piece of good luck; a welcome happening: *Let's be grateful for small mercies*. **mercifully** *adv.* luckily; thankfully.

merge (**mûrj**) *vb.* **merging, merged** to blend, combine, or join with something else: *The two companies merged under a new name*.

meridian (mĕ **rid** i ån) *n.* a line of longitude.

meringue (mĕ **rang**) *n.* a cake made from a crisp cooked mixture of sugar and egg-whites.

merit (**me** rit) *n.* **1** worth or excellence. **2** (often in *plural*) a good point or quality. – *vb.* **meriting, merited** to deserve; to be worthy of or entitled to.

mermaid (**mûr** mād) *n.* a mythical sea creature with a woman's head and upper body, and a fish's tail.

merry (**me** ri) *adj.* **merrier, merriest** cheerful and lively. – *adv.* **merrily**. – *n.* **merriment**.

mesh (mesh) *n.* netting made of fine wire or thread.

mesmerize or **mesmerise** (**mez** mĕ rīz) *vb.* **mesmerizing, mesmerized** to grip the attention of.

Mesmerize, meaning 'to fascinate' is named after one of the earliest people to practise hypnotism, the Austrian physicist Friedrich *Mesmer* (1734-1815).

Mesopotamia, now mostly in Iraq, was a region between the Tigris and Euphrates rivers which was the centre of many early civilizations, including the earliest, the Sumerian.

The Chaldean king, Nebuchadnezzar (604-561 BC), rebuilt the Mesopotamian city of Babylon in such fabulous splendour that it came to be regarded as one of the wonders of the world.

A Sumerian princess wearing an elaborate headdress, earrings, and necklaces, made of gold and silver, decorated with blue lapis-lazuli and red carnelian gem stones.

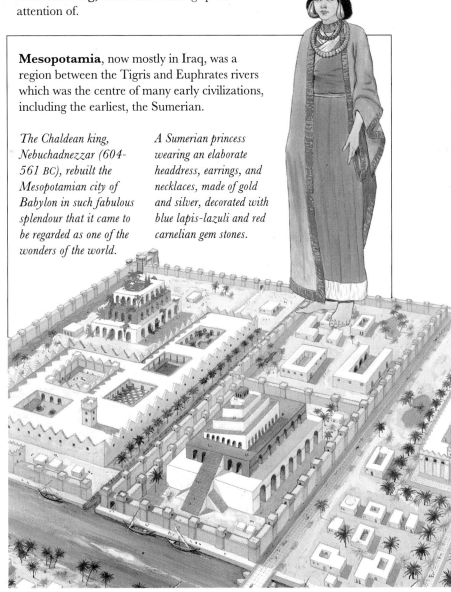

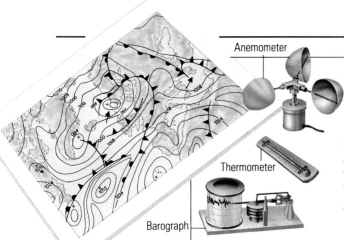

One of the main jobs of a **meteorologist** is weather forecasting. Meteorologists use a number of instruments. An anemometer records wind speed; a barograph records atmospheric pressure.

Anemometer

Thermometer

Barograph

Specially equipped weather ships are anchored far from shipping lanes to record conditions at sea.

Balloons called 'radio-sondes' carry instruments that measure the air pressure, temperature, and humidity.

Weather maps record conditions at a particular time using standard symbols. Isobars are lines connecting places where air pressure is the same. The closer the isobars, the stronger the winds. The chart also show warm (rounded symbols) and cold (triangular symbols) fronts.

The Old Woman meterorite weighs 2758 kg. It was discovered in California in 1976. It is composed of iron and nickel and may have formed part of a planet that disintegrated 4 billion years ago!

mess (mes) *n.* **1** an untidy or dirty state; a state of disorder. **2** a communal dining room, especially in the armed forces. – *vb.* **messing, messed** to put into an untidy, dirty, or damaged state: *The children messed up their bedroom.* – *adv.* **messily.** – *adj.* **messy, messier, messiest.**.

message (me sij) *n.* a spoken or written words sent from one person to another.

messenger (me sĕn jĕr) *n.* a person who carries messages between people.

Messiah (mĕ sī å) *n.* **1** in Christianity, JESUS CHRIST. **2** in Judaism, the king of the Jews still to be sent by God to free them.

metabolism (mĕ **tab** ŏ li zĕm) *n.* the system of chemical processes in a living body, from which energy, growth, and waste matter are produced.

metal (me tål) *n.* any of a group of elements that can conduct heat and electricity, can be worked into different shapes, and typically have a shiny appearance, e.g. iron and copper.

metallurgy (me **tal** ûr ji) *n.* the scientific study of the nature and properties of metals. – *n.* **metallurgist.**

metamorphosis (me tå **mörf** ŏ sis) or (me·tå mör **fō** sis) *n.* **metamorphoses 1** a complete change of form, appearance, or character. **2** in biology, the change of physical form that occurs during the development into adulthood of some creatures, for example butterflies.

metaphor (me tå fŏr) *n.* an expression in which the person, action, or thing referred to is described as if it really were what it resembles: *He has a heart of gold.*

meteor (mē ti ŏr) *n.* any of countless small bodies travelling through space, which enter the Earth's atmosphere.

meteorite *n.* a meteor fallen to Earth as a lump of rock or metal.

meteorology (mē ti ŏ **rol** ŏ ji) *n.* the study of the Earth's atmosphere and patterns of weather – *n.* **meteorologist.**

meter (mē tĕr) *n.* an instrument for measuring and recording quantities of gas, etc.

method (me thŏd) *n.* a system.

methodical (mi **thod** i kål) *adj.* efficient and orderly; done in an orderly way.

Methodism (me thŏ di zĕm) *n.* the beliefs and practices of a branch of the PROTESTANT Church founded by followers of John WESLEY (1703-88). – *n.* & *adj.* **Methodist.**

metre¹ (mē tĕr) *n.* the principal unit of length in the metric system, equal to 39.37 inches.

metre² (mē tĕr) *n.* **1** in poetry, the arrangement of words and syllables in a rhythmic pattern.

metric (me trik) *adj.* based on the metre.

metropolis (mĕ **trop** ŏ lis) *n.* **metropolises** a large city, especially a capital or cultural centre.

metropolitan (me trŏ **pol** i tån) *adj.* typical of, or situated in, a large city.

● **Mexico** is the southern neighbour of the UNITED STATES. Its capital, Mexico City, is one of the world's biggest cities. Mexico's official language is Spanish. The country was Spain's first colony in the Americas. Spanish conquistadores from 1519 conquered the powerful AZTEC empire. Spanish rule lasted until 1821. See also Supplement, **Countries.**

● **Miami** is Florida's second largest city. Miami Beach is one of the most popular tourist spots in the UNITED STATES.

● **Michelangelo** (mī kĕ **lanj** ĕ lō) (1475-1564) was an Italian sculptor, and painter of the ceiling of the Sistine chapel in Rome.

● **Michigan**. See Supplement, **USA.**

micro- (mī krō-) very small: *microchip*.

microbe (mī krōb) *n.* any tiny organism invisible to the naked eye, e.g. a germ.

microchip (mī krō chip) *n.* (also **chip**) a tiny piece of silicon carrying several electrical circuits, used in computers, etc.

● **Micronesia**. See Supplement, **Countries**.

microphone (mī krō fōn) *n.* an instrument which picks up sounds to be recorded or broadcast.

microscope (mī krō skōp) *n.* an instrument with a system of lenses for viewing objects too small to be seen with the naked eye.

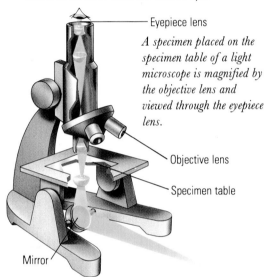

Eyepiece lens

A specimen placed on the specimen table of a light microscope is magnified by the objective lens and viewed through the eyepiece lens.

Objective lens

Specimen table

Mirror

microscopic (mī krō **sko** pik) *adj.* too small to be seen without the aid of a microscope.

microwave (mī krō wāv) *n.* an electromagnetic wave of very short wavelength, used in cooking and radar.

mid (mid) *adj.* being the part at or in the middle: *She stopped me in mid sentence.*

midday *n.* twelve o'clock.

midnight *n.* twelve o'clock at night.

midsummer *n.* the period of time in the middle of summer, around 21 June.

the Midwest *n.* the central northern states of the UNITED STATES. – *adj.* **Midwestern**.

middle (mī dĕl) *adj.* **1** at a point between two ends or extremes, and especially the same distance from each. **2** moderate, not extreme: *He steered a middle course.* – *n.* the middle point, part, or position. – **in the middle of** during.

the Middle Ages *n.* (*plural*) the period in Europe between the 12th and 15th centuries.

During the **Middle Ages** in Europe people lived under the feudal system. Religion was a powerful force because the church had great authority. Monasteries were islands of learning in a sea of ignorance and superstition. Gradually universities were founded and trade expanded.

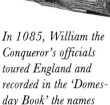

In 1085, William the Conqueror's officials toured England and recorded in the 'Domesday Book' the names of all landowners.

William quickly crushed any revolt by English rebels, thus consolidating his rule over the land.

In the Middle Ages merchants bought spices and silks from the East in exchange for wool and cloth.

A European medieval town on market day was a bustling, noisy place. A dancing bear entertains the crowds.

Few people could read or write. In monasteries monks preserved ancient learning, copying books by hand.

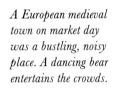

the Middle East *n.* all the countries between, but not including, Tunisia and Pakistan.

midge (mij) *n.* small insect; a gnat.

midwife (**mid** wīf) *n.* **midwives** (**mid** wīvz) a nurse trained to supervise childbirth.

might[1] (mīt) *vb.* **1** past tense of **may**: *He asked if he might be of assistance.* **2** used to express possibility: *He might win if he tries hard.* **3** used to request permission: *Might I speak to you?*

might[2] (mīt) *n.* power or strength.

    mighty *adj.* **mightier, mightiest 1** having great strength or power. **2** very large. – *adv.* **mightily**. – *n.* **mightiness**.

migraine (**mē** grān) or (**mī** grān) *n.* a painfully severe headache.

migrant (**mī** grånt) *n.* a person or animal that migrates.

migrate (mī **grāt**) *vb.* **migrating, migrated 1** (of animals, especially birds) to travel from one region to another at certain times of the year. **2** to settle in another country. – *n.* **migration**.

mild (mīld) *adj.* **1** gentle in temperament or behaviour. **2** not sharp or strong in flavour or effect. **3** (of climate) rather warm.

mildew (**mil** dū) *n.* mould.

mile (mīl) *n.* a unit of distance equal to 1760 yards (1.6km).

mileage (**mīl** ij) *n.* the number of miles travelled.

    milestone *n.* a very important event: *The promotion was a milestone in her career.*

militant (**mi** li tånt) *adj.* ready to take strong or violent action; aggressively active.

military (**mi** li tå ri) *adj.* by or for the armed forces. – *n.* the armed forces.

milk (milk) *n.* a whitish liquid produced by female mammals as food for their young; this liquid produced by a cow or goat and used by humans as food. – *vb.* **milking, milked** to take milk from an animal. – *n.* **milkiness**.

the Milky Way *n.* **1** the line of faint white light in the sky at night, formed by millions of distant stars. **2** the Galaxy.

mill (mil) *n.* **1** a building containing a large machine that grinds grain into flour. **2** any of various smaller machines or devices for grinding: *a peppermill.*

millennium (mi **len** i ům) *n.* **millennia** a period of a thousand years. – *adj.* **millennial**.

    ● **Miller, Arthur** (1915-) is an American playwright, author of *Death of a Salesman.*

milli- (**mi** li-) a thousandth part: *millisecond.*

milligram (**mi** li gram) *n.* (also **milligramme**) a unit of weight, one thousandth of a gram.

millimetre (**mi** li mē tèr) *n.* a unit of length, equal to one thousandth of a metre.

million (**mil** yŏn) *n.* **millions** the number 1,000,000.

    millionaire *n.* a person whose wealth amounts to a million pounds, dollars, etc.

millipede (**mi** li pēd) *n.* a small worm-like creature with numerous pairs of legs.

● **Milne, A. A.** (1882-1956) was a British children's writer, author of *Winnie-the-Pooh.*

● **Milton, John** (1608-74) was an English poet, author of the epic *Paradise Lost.*

mime (mīm) *vb.* **miming, mimed** to act using only movements and gestures.

mimic (**mi** mik) *vb.* **mimicking, mimicked** to imitate, especially for comic effect; to copy.

The 11th-century minaret at the Jami Mosque in Simnan, Iran.

minaret (mi nå **ret**) *n.* a tower on a mosque, from which Muslims are called to prayer.

mind (mīnd) *n.* **1** the power of thinking and understanding; the place where thoughts, memory, and feelings exist; the intelligence. **2** attention: *His mind wanders easily.* **3** wish; inclination: *She has changed her mind.* – *vb.* **minding, minded 1** to look after, care for, or keep safe: *She minds the children when I am out.* **2** to be upset: *Do you mind if I don't come?*

mine[1] (mīn) *pron.* something or someone belonging to, or connected with, me; those belonging to me: *That book is mine.*

mine[2] (mīn) *n.* **1** a place from which coal, minerals, metal ores, or precious stones are dug up. **2** an exploding device, designed to destroy enemy ships, troops, etc. – *n.* **mining**. **miner** *n.* a person who works in a mine.

mineral (**mi** nè rål) *n.* any solid substance such as iron ore, salt, etc. that forms naturally in the rocks in the Earth. – *adj.* containing minerals.

PRONUNCIATION GUIDE

fat **a**	all **ö**
fate **ā**	foot **oo**
fast **ä**	moon **oo**
among **å**	boy **oi**
met **e**	house **ow**
mean **ē**	demon **ò**
silent **ė**	thing **th**
loch **hh**	this **Th**
fin **i**	but **u**
line **ī**	mute **ū**
quick **kw**	fur **û**
got **o**	brochure **ů**
note **ō**	vision **zh**

● Some minerals, such as gold and platinum, are made up of only one ELEMENT. Others, such as salt, consist of two or more elements. Some minerals are metallic, such as copper, while others are non-metallic, like sulphur.

mingle (**ming** gĕl) *vb.* **mingling, mingled** to become blended or mixed; to associate with.

mini (**mi** ni) (*colloquial*) *n.* a small or short one of its kind, especially a miniskirt. – *adj.* small or short of its kind; miniature.

miniature (**mi** nå chŭr) *n.* a small copy or model of anything. – *adj.* small-scale.

minimum (**mi** ni mŭm) *n.* the lowest possible number, quantity, or degree, or the lowest reached or allowed: *I keep the housework to a minimum.* – *adj.* lowest reached or allowed: *Five pounds is the minimum amount you can invest.*

minister (**mi** ni stĕr) *n.* **1** a senior politician with responsibilities in a government department. **2** a member of the clergy.

● **Minnesota**. See Supplement, **USA**.

minnow (**mi** nō) *n.* a small freshwater fish.

Minoan (mi **nō** ån) *adj.* relating to the Bronze Age civilization of CRETE and other Aegean islands, approximately 3000-1100 BC.

minor (**mī** nŏr) *adj.* **1** not as great in importance or size; insignificant: *She has only minor injuries.* **2** below the age of legal adulthood. – *n.*

mint¹ (mint) *n.* any of various herbs of regions with purplish-green leaves used as a flavouring.

mint² (mint) *n.* a place where coins are produced under government authority.

minus (**mī** nŭs) *prep.* (*colloquial*) without. – *n.* (also **minus sign**) a sign (-) indicating that a following quantity is to be subtracted. – *adj.* negative or less than zero.

minute¹ (**mi** nit) *n.* **1** a sixtieth part of an hour; sixty seconds. **2** (*colloquial*) a short while: *Wait a minute!* **3** (usually in *plural*) the official written record of what is said at a formal meeting.

minute² (**mī** nūt) *adj.* very small; tiny.

● **Minutemen** were colonial volunteers during the American War of Independence. They were prepared to fight 'at a minute's notice'.

miracle (**mi** rå kĕl) *n.* an act or event breaking the laws of nature, and therefore thought to be caused by a supernatural force.

miraculous (mi **rak** ū lŭs) *adj.* **1** of the nature of a miracle. **2** (*colloquial*) amazing: *She had a miraculous escape from the car crash.*

mirage (**mi** räzh) *n.* an optical illusion, especially of a distant mass of water.

mirror (**mi** rŏr) *n.* a glass surface coated with an alloy of mercury and other metals so as to reflect light and produce reflections. – *vb.* **mirroring, mirrored** to reflect.

mis- (mis-) *prefix* **1** wrong or wrongly: *misclassify*. **2** negative; lack: *mistrust*.

The Apple mint (above) *is one of several mint plants used as a flavouring in cooking, or in making mint tea.*

The first European civilization we know about started on the island of Crete about 4,500 years ago. It is called **Minoan** after the legendary king, Minos. The Minoans built several cities linked by paved roads.

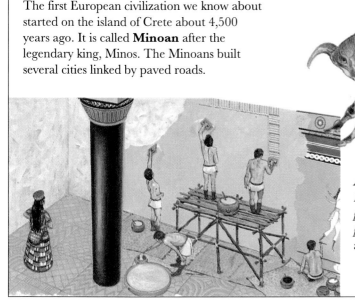

A state room at the royal palace at Knossos being decorated (left). *Wall paintings show the dangerous but popular sport of bull-leaping* (shown above).

The royal palace at Knossos as it may have looked in Minoan times. The royal apartments lay around a central courtyard, with public rooms upstairs.

*Throughout the ages
people have attributed
magical properties to
mistletoe. It is
particularly familiar
through the Christmas
tradition of kissing under
a sprig of the plant.*

mischief (**mis** chif) *n.* behaviour that annoys or irritates but causes no serious harm.
mischievous *adj.* playfully troublesome.

miser (**mī** zěr) *n.* a person who lives in poor conditions in order to store up wealth; any ungenerous person. – *adj.* **miserly.**

miserable (**mi** zěr å běl) *adj.* very unhappy: *She has had a miserable life.*

misery (**mi** zě ri) *n.* **miseries 1** great unhappiness. **2** poverty or squalor.

mislay (mis **lā**) *vb.* **mislaying, mislaid** to lose something, usually temporarily by not remembering where it was put.

mislead (mis **lēd**) *vb.* **misleading, misled** (mis **led**) to cause to take an undesirable course of action; to cause to have a false impression or belief. – *adj.* **misleading.**

misprint (**mis** print) *n.* a mistake in printing.

miss (mis) *vb.* **missing, missed 1** to fail to hit or catch something: *He missed the ball when I threw it.* **2** to fail to arrive in time for: *I missed my plane.* **3** to fail to take advantage of: *You have missed your chance.* **4** to regret the absence of: *I miss my parents terribly.* **5** to refrain from going to a place or an event: *I'll have to miss the next class.* – *n.* a failure to hit or catch something.
missing *adj.* absent; lost; not able to be found.

missile (**mi** sīl) *n.* any weapon or object that is thrown or fired.

mission (**mi** shŏn) *n.* a purpose for which a person or group of people is sent: *The medical team were sent on a dangerous mission.*

● **Mississippi.** See Supplement, **USA.**

● **Missouri.** See Supplement, **USA.**

misspell (mis **spel**) *vb.* **misspelling, misspelt** or **misspelled** to spell incorrectly.

mist (mist) *n.* a cloud of condensed water vapour in the air near the ground; thin fog.
misty *adj.* **mistier, mistiest** covered with mist. – *adv.* **mistily.** – *n.* **mistiness.**

mistake (mi **stāk**) *vb.* **mistaking, mistook** (mi **stook**), **mistaken 1** to identify incorrectly; to wrongly assume or understand: *She mistook my silence for disapproval.* to make the wrong choice of: *He mistook his road in the fog.* – *n.* an error.

mistletoe (**mi** sěl tō) *n.* an evergreen shrub that grows as a parasite on trees and produces clusters of white berries in winter.

mistreat (mis **trēt**) *vb.* **mistreating, mistreated** to treat cruelly or without care.

misunderstand (mis un děr **stand**) *vb.* **misunderstanding, misunderstood** (mis un děr **stood**) to fail to understand properly.
misunderstanding *n.* **1** a failure to understand properly. **2** a disagreement.

mix (miks) *vb.* **mixing, mixed 1** to put together or combine to form one mass: *She was mixing the ingredients for a cake.* **2** to do at the same time; to combine: *Let's not mix business with pleasure.* – *n.* a collection of people or things mixed together. – *vb.* **mix up** to confuse: *I always mix him up with his brother.*
mixed *adj.* consisting of different kinds: *I have mixed feelings about my new job.*
mixture *n.* **1** a blend of ingredients prepared for a particular purpose: *The doctor gave her some cough mixture.* **2** a combination: *I felt a mixture of sadness and relief.*

moan (mōn) *n.* a low prolonged sound expressing sadness, grief, or pain. – *vb.* **moaning, moaned 1** to utter or produce a moan. **2** (*colloquial*) to complain, especially without good reason. – *n.* **moaner.**

moat (mōt) *n.* water-filled trench round a castle.

mob (mob) *n.* a large disorderly crowd.

mobile (**mō** bīl) *adj.* able to move or be moved easily; not fixed: *The mobile library visits once a week.* – *n.* a hanging decoration moved around by air currents. – *n.* **mobility** (mō **bil** i ti).

moccasin (**mo** kå sin) *n.* a deerskin shoe.

mock (mok) *vb.* **mocking, mocked** to speak or behave with contempt towards: *She mocked his efforts to climb the tree.* – *adj.* false; sham: *mock leather.* – *adj.* **mocking.**
mockingbird *n.* a grey American bird that copies the calls of other birds.

mode (mōd) *n.* a way of doing.

model (**mo** děl) *n.* **1** a small-scale representation or replica: *He built a model of the ship out of matchsticks.* **2** one of several types or designs of manufactured article: *He bought the latest model in the Renault range.* **3** a person who displays clothes to potential buyers by wearing them. – *vb.* **modelling, modelled 1** to display clothes by wearing them. **2** to work as a model for an artist or photographer. **3** to shape into a particular form: *She modelled the clay to look like a human head.* – *adj.* built as a replica: *He loves to play with his model railway.*

moderate (**mo** dě råt) *adj.* **1** not extreme; not strong or violent. **2** average: *Alex is of moderate intelligence.* – *adj.* **moderately.**

modern (**mo** děrn) *adj.* **1** belonging to the present or to recent times; not old or ancient. **2** involving or using the very latest available techniques, styles, etc.: *The light railway is the latest in modern transport.*
modernize or **modernise** *vb.* **modernizing, modernized** to bring up to modern standards. – *n.* **modernization**.

modest (**mo** dist) *adj.* not having or showing pride; humble: *He is very modest about his achievements.* – *n.* **modesty**.

modify (**mo** di fī) *vb.* **modifies, modifying, modified** to change the form slightly. – *n.* **modification**.

module (**mo** dūl) *n.* **1** a separate unit that combines with others to form a larger unit, structure, or system: *The building was made out of mass-produced modules.* **2** a separate self-contained part of a space vehicle used for a particular purpose: *The lunar module was used to land on the Moon's surface.* – *adj.* **modular**.

● **Mogul** (**mō** gŭl) a member of the ruling dynasty in INDIA from the 16th to the 19th century.

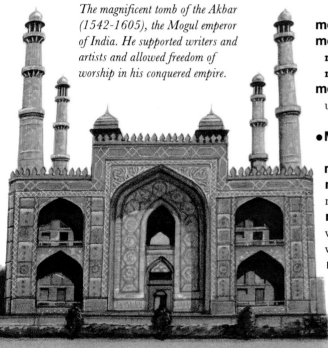

The magnificent tomb of the Akbar (1542-1605), the Mogul emperor of India. He supported writers and artists and allowed freedom of worship in his conquered empire.

● **Mohammed**. See **Muhammad**.

mohair (**mō** hār) *n.* the long soft hair of the angora goat; a yarn or fabric made of this.

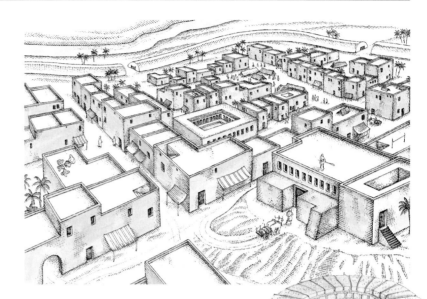

● **Mohenjo Daro** was an important city built in the Indus Valley in PAKISTAN between 2500 and 1800 BC.

● **Mohicans** were a confederacy of Algonquin-speaking Native Americans from New York State who fought with the Mohawks.

moist (moist) *adj.* damp; slightly wet.
moisten (**moi** sěn) *vb.* **moistening, moistened** to make or become damp.
moisture *n.* liquid in tiny drops in the air.
molar (**mō** lår) *n.* any of the large back teeth, used for chewing and grinding.

● **Moldova**. See Supplement, **Countries**.

mole[1] (mōl) *n.* a raised dark spot on the skin.
mole[2] (mōl) *n.* a small burrowing insect-eating mammal with tiny eyes and soft dark fur.
molecule (**mo** li kūl) *n.* the smallest unit into which a chemical compound can be divided without losing its basic nature.
molecular (mǒ **lek** ū lår) *adj.* of or relating to molecules.
mollusc (**mo** lŭsk) *n.* any of numerous limbless invertebrate creatures with a soft body and a hard shell, including snails.
molten (**mōl** těn) *adj.* in a melted state.
moment (**mō** měnt) *n.* **1** a short while: *The operation took only a moment.* **2** a particular point in time: *At that moment, she appeared.*
momentary *adj.* lasting for only a moment.
momentum (mō **men** tǔm) *n.* the amount or force of motion in a moving object.

An artist's impression of the ancient city (top) of Mohenjo Daro as it may have looked at the height of power and prosperity. Like modern American cities, it was built on a grid pattern! Some of the houses had brick-lined shafts (above) in their courtyards. The shafts may have been used as wells or for storage.

●**Mona Lisa** This is perhaps the world's most famous painting. It hangs in the Louvre, Paris and was painted by LEONARDO DA VINCI. The subject is a smiling woman.

monarch (**mo** nårk) *n.* a king or queen.

monastery (**mo** nås tě ri) *n.* **monasteries** the home of a community of monks or nuns.

Monday (**mun** di) *n.* the second day of the week; the day between Sunday and Tuesday.

●**Monet** (**mon** ā), **Claude** (1840-1926) was a French Impressionist painter: *The Water Lily Pond.*

money (**mu** ni) *n.* **1** coins or banknotes used as a means of buying things. **2** wealth in general.

●**Mongolia.** See Supplement, **Countries**.

mongoose (**mong** gōōs) *n.* **mongooses** a long-tailed weasel-sized mammal of Africa and Asia that preys on snakes and rats.

A mongoose can pounce so quickly that a cobra has no time to strike with its fangs.

mongrel (**mung** grěl) *n.* a dog of mixed breeding.

monitor (**mo** ni tǒr) *n.* **1** any instrument or person that checks, records, or controls. **2** a small screen in a television studio showing the picture being broadcast.

monk (mungk) *n.* a member of a religious community of men. – *adj.* **monkish**.

monkey (**mung** ki) *n.* **monkeys** a long-tailed, furry animal related to apes.

●There are about 400 different kinds of monkey. Most live in tropical forests in AFRICA, ASIA, and SOUTH AMERICA.

monologue (**mo** nǒ log) *n.* a long speech by one person in a conversation or a film or play.

monopoly (mǒ **nop** ǒ li) *n.* **monopolies** the only supplier of a commodity or service.

monotonous (mǒ **not** ǒ nǔs) *adj.* lacking in variety; unchanging. – *n.* **monotony**.

monsoon (mon **sōōn**) *n.* in southern ASIA, a wind that blows from the south-west in summer, bringing rain, and from the north-east in winter.

monster (**mon** stěr) *n.* any large and frightening imaginary creature.

monstrous (**mon** strǔs) *adj.* **1** huge. **2** outrageous; absurd: *She wore a monstrous outfit.*

●**Montana.** See Supplement, **USA**.

●**Montenegro** with Serbia forms Yugoslavia. See Supplement, **Countries**.

●**Montezuma** (mon tě **zōōm** å) (1466-1520) was the last AZTEC emperor of MEXICO. He surrendered to the Spanish conquistador, Cortes.

month (munth) *n.* any of the twelve named divisions of the year, varying in length between 28 and 31 days.

monthly *adj.* happening, published, etc. once a month. – *adv.* once a month.

●**Montreal** (mon tri **öl**) is an island city in Quebec, CANADA. It is the largest French-speaking city outside of FRANCE.

Monkeys are mammals that look rather like people. Monkeys and apes are called primates. American monkeys use their tail as an extra hand, to grasp tree branches. African and Asian monkeys cannot do this.

Mandrill – from Africa

Colobus monkey from Africa

Spider monkey – from South America

Woolly monkey from South America

monument (mo nū měnt) *n.* something, for example a statue, built to preserve the memory of a person or event.

This monument, called the Tempietto, was built in Rome at the time of the Renaissance to mark the probable spot where Jesus's apostle Peter was crucified. It is built in the classical Greek style.

monumental (mo nū **men** tål) *adj.* like a monument, especially huge and impressive.

mood (mo͞od) *n.* a state of mind at a particular time: *I'm not in the mood for dancing.* – *adj.* **moody, moodier, moodiest**.

Moon (mo͞on) *n.* **1** the heavenly body that moves once around the Earth each month, often visible as a circle or crescent in the sky at night. **2 moon** any similar smaller body circling another planet.

● On 21 July 1969 *Apollo 11* astronauts Neil Armstrong and Edwin Aldrin became the first people to walk on the surface of the Moon.

moonlight *n.* sunlight reflected by the moon.

Moor (mo͞or) *n.* a member of an Arab people of north-west Africa, whose ancestors ruled parts of Spain between the 8th and 15th centuries.

moor (mo͞or) *n.* an open area usually covered with coarse grass and heather.

moose (mo͞os) *n.* **moose** a large North American deer.

mop (mop) *n.* a tool for washing or wiping floors, consisting of a large sponge or a set of thick threads on a long handle.

moral (mo rål) *adj.* **1** of or relating to the principles of good and evil, or right and wrong. **2** conforming to what is considered by society to be good: *She lived a moral life.*

morale (mo͝ **räl**) *n.* level of confidence or optimism: *Morale in the winning team was high.*

more (mōr) *adj.* a greater number or quantity of: *I've got more pudding than you.* – *adv.* **1** used to form the comparative of many adjectives and adverbs, especially those of two or more syllables: *She is more graceful than her partner.* **2** to a greater degree; with a greater frequency: *I visit my aunt more than my uncle.* – *pron.* a greater, or additional, number or quantity of people or things: *Please can I have some more?*

Mormon (**mör** mŏn) *n.* a member of the Church of Jesus Christ of Latter-Day Saints, established in the UNITED STATES in 1830.

morning (**mör** ning) *n.* the part of the day from sunrise to midday.

● **Morocco**. See Supplement, **Countries**.

● **Morrison, Toni** (1931-) is an American novelist: *The Song of Soloman*. She won the Nobel Prize for Literature in 1993.

PRONUNCIATION GUIDE	
fat **a**	all **ŏ**
fate **ā**	foot **oo**
fast **ä**	moon **o͞o**
among **å**	boy **oi**
met **e**	house **ow**
mean **ē**	demon **o͝**
silent **ė**	thing **th**
loch **hh**	this **Th**
fin **i**	but **u**
line **ī**	mute **ū**
quick **kw**	fur **û**
got **o**	brochure **ů**
note **ō**	vision **zh**

Moon rocks brought back by the Apollo project can be dated back to 4.5 billion years – soon after the Moon was created.

The side of the Moon which faces Earth has huge plains called 'maria'. The far side is covered with craters and mountain ranges. Because the Moon has no air or atmosphere, there is nothing to protect it from the heat of the Sun in the day and the cold at night.

A mosaic from Pompeii in southern Italy depicting Alexander the Great leading a charge.

Morse code (mörs **kōd**) *n.* a code used for sending messages, each letter of a word being represented as a series of short or long radio sounds or flashes of light. It was invented by Samuel *Morse* (1791-1872).

morsel (**mör** sêl) *n.* a small piece of food.

mortal (**mör** tål) *adj.* **1** certain to die at some future time: *All humans are mortal.* **2** causing death: *He struck his opponent a mortal blow.*

mortar (**mör** tår) *n.* a mixture of sand, water, and cement or lime, used to bond bricks.

mortgage (**mör** gij) *n.* a loan from a building society or bank in order to buy a house, etc.

mosaic (mō **zā** ik) *n.* a design formed by fitting together pieces of coloured stone or glass.

● **Moscow** is the capital of RUSSIA. Its citizens are called Muscovites.

● **Moses** in the BIBLE, was a Jewish leader, lawgiver, and prophet.

● **Moses, Grandma** (1860-1961) was an American artist.

Moslem. See Muslim.

mosque (mosk) *n.* a Muslim place of worship.

mosquito (mồs **kē** tō) *n.* **mosquitos** or **mosquitoes** a small long-legged insect. The females suck blood from animals and people, and pass on diseases, such as malaria.

moss (mos) *n.* any variety of small flowerless plant growing as a thick mass on rocks or tree trunks in damp conditions.

most (mōst) *adj.* the greatest part, amount, or number of: *They had a competition to see who could eat the most biscuits.* – *adv.* **1** used to form the superlative of many adjectives and adverbs, especially those of more than two syllables: *This is the most beautiful garden I have ever seen.* **2** to the greatest degree; with the greatest frequency: *I like chocolate ice cream the most.* – *pron.* the greatest number or quantity, or the majority of people or things: *Many people saw the show: most enjoyed it.* – **at most** certainly not more than. – **for the most part** mostly.

motel (mō **tel**) *n.* a hotel near a road, intended for motorists.

moth (moth) *n.* a butterfly-like insect with a wide body and dull colouring, that usually flies at night.

mother (**mu** Thêr) *n.* a female parent. – *vb.* **mothering, mothered** to treat with care and protection. – *n.* **motherhood.**
mother-in-law *n.* **mothers-in-law** the mother of someone's husband or wife.

motion (**mō** shồn) *n.* **1** the act of moving and changing position: *The hammock swung with the ship's motion.* **2** a single body movement; a gesture. **3** a proposal for formal discussion at a meeting. – *vb.* **motioning, motioned** to give a signal or direction: *She motioned to him to approach.* – *adj.* **motionless.**
motion picture *n.* (especially *US*) a film.

motive (**mō** tiv) *n.* a reason for action.

motor (**mō** tồr) *n.* any device for converting energy into movement. – *adj.* of or relating to cars or other road vehicles: *the motor show.*
motorbike *n.* (*colloquial*) a motorcycle.
motorcycle *n.* any two-wheeled road vehicle powered by a petrol engine. – *n.* **motorcyclist.**
motorist *n.* a person who drives a car.
motorway *n.* a road for fast-moving traffic, usually with three lanes on each carriageway.

motto (**mo** tō) *n.* **mottos** or **mottoes** a phrase adopted as a principle of behaviour: *'Never give up' was his motto.*

mould[1] (mōld) *n.* a growth of fungus on substances in damp conditions.

mould[2] (mōld) *n.* a hollow shaped container into which a liquid substance is poured to take on the container's shape when it cools and sets: *I made a jelly in a star-shaped mould.* – *vb.* **moulding, moulded 1** to shape using a mould. **2** to form with the hands.

moult (mōlt) *vb.* **moulting, moulted** (of animals) to shed old feathers, hair, or skin.

A trail bike – a motorbike made specially for riding over rough ground.

Hand controls
Saddle
Mudguard
Front forks
Exhaust
Engine
Strong metal frame
Drive chain to back wheel
Rear shock absorber
Shock absorbers to cushion bumps
Knobbly-pattern tyre grips sand and mud

mount (mownt) *vb.* **mounting, mounted 1** to go up: *We mounted the stairs.* **2** to get up on to, for example a horse. **3** to increase in level or intensity: *The tension mounted as the match progressed.* **4** to put in a frame or on a background for display: *The picture was mounted on grey card.*

mountain (**mown** tin) *n.* a very high steep hill.

●The greatest mountain ranges are the Alps of Europe, the Rockies and the Andes of America, and the Himalayas of Asia. The Himalayas have many of the World's highest peaks, including Mount Everest, the biggest.

mountainous *adj.* having many mountains.

●**Mount Rushmore** in the Black Hills of South Dakota, has carved into it the faces of four United States presidents.

mourn (mörn) *vb.* **mourning, mourned** to feel or show deep sorrow at the death or loss of a person or thing. – *n.* **mourner**.

mourning *n.* grief felt or shown over a death.

mouse (mows) *n.* **mice** (mīs) **1** a small furry long-tailed rodent. **2** a hand-held device connected by wire to a computer, used to control certain functions.

moustache (mŭ **stäsh**) *n.* a line of unshaved hair above a man's upper lip.

mouth (mowth) *n.* **mouths** (mowThz) **1** an opening in the head through which food is taken in and speech or sounds emitted. **2** an opening, for example of a cave or a bottle.

move (mōōv) *vb.* **moving, moved 1** to change position or go from one place to another. **2** to make progress of any kind: *They are moving towards a solution.* **3** to change your place of living or working: *We are about to move house.* **4** to affect the feelings or emotions of: *He was deeply moved by their singing.* – *n.* **1** an act of moving the body: *They watched his every move.* **2** an act of moving a piece in a board game.

movable or **moveable** *adj.* portable.

movement *n.* **1** changing position or going from one point to another. **2** an organization of people who share the same beliefs.

moving *adj.* **1** having an effect on the emotions; touching; stirring: *The music at her wedding was very moving.* **2** in motion; not still.

mow (mō) *vb.* **mowing, mowed** or **mown** to cut grass or a crop by hand or with a machine.

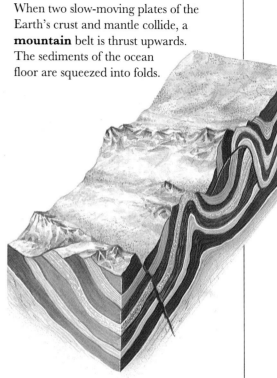

When two slow-moving plates of the Earth's crust and mantle collide, a **mountain** belt is thrust upwards. The sediments of the ocean floor are squeezed into folds.

Young mountains, such as the Himalayas (top) *are high and rugged. Old mountains are smoother and lower.*

●**Mozambique**. See Supplement, **Countries**.

●**Mozart, Wolfgang Amadeus** (1756-91) was an Austrian prodigy who became one of the greatest composers of operas and symphonies.

much (much) *adj. & pron.* **more** (mōr), **most** (mōst) (of) a great amount or quantity of something: *I haven't much time. Much has been said of his abilities.* – *adv.* **1** by a great deal: *She is much prettier.* **2** to a great degree: *I don't like her much.*

muck (muk) *n.* (*colloquial*) dirt.

mucus (**mū** kŭs) *n.* thick sticky liquid secreted by glands in the nose, etc.

mud (mud) *n.* soft wet earth. *adj.* **muddy, muddier, muddiest**.

muddle (**mu** dĕl) *vb.* **muddling, muddled 1** to put into a disordered, mixed-up state. **2** to confuse someone or be confused: *She had muddled up the front and back door keys.* – *n.* a state of disorder. – *adj.* **muddled**.

muezzin (mōō **ez** in) *n.* the MUSLIM official who calls worshippers to prayer.

muffle (**mu** fĕl) *vb.* **muffling, muffled 1** to make quieter. **2** to wrap up against the cold.

Two hundred years after his death, Mozart's music is played and listened to by people all over the world. He died in poverty in his 36th year.

MUSICAL TERMS

adagio at a slow pace.

allegro fast and lively.

andante at a moderate speed.

beat the pulse of a piece of music.

chord a group of notes played at the same time.

forte loud.

fortissimo very loud.

largo slow.

movement the separate sections into which a long piece of music is divided.

octave from one note to another note of the same name.

opus a single work by a composer.

pianissimo very soft.

presto at a fast pace.

symphony a large work for an orchestra, usually in three or four movements.

tempo the pace or speed of a piece of music.

Biceps, the muscle in the upper arm, contracts when you bend your arm. The other muscle, the triceps, relaxes.

Biceps contracted

Triceps relaxed

Biceps relaxed

Triceps contracted

272

mug¹ (mug) *n.* a drinking-cup with a handle, used without a saucer.

mug² (mug) *vb.* **mugging, mugged** to attack and rob violently. – *n.* **mugger**.

● **Muhammad** (mǔ **ham** åd) (AD 570-632) was an Arab prophet and the founder of ISLAM. Sayings revealed to him by ALLAH (God) are in the KORAN.

mulberry (mul bě ri) *n.* **mulberries** a deciduous tree with purple edible berries.

mule (mūl) *n.* the offspring of a donkey and a horse, used as a working animal.

multi- (mul ti-) *prefix* many: *multicoloured*.

multiple (mul ti pěl) *adj.* involving or affecting many parts: *multiple injuries*.

multiply (mul ti plī) *vb.* **multiplies, multiplying, multiplied** 1 to add a number to itself a given number of times. For example, 12 multiplied by 10 equals 120. 2 to increase in number: *The rabbits quickly multiplied*.

multitude (mul ti tūd) *n.* 1 a great number. 2 a huge crowd of people. – *adj.* **multitudinous**.

mumble (mum běl) *vb.* **mumbling, mumbled** to speak unclearly.

mummy¹ (mu mi) *n.* **mummies** a child's word for mother.

mummy² (mu mi) *n.* **mummies** a human or animal corpse preserved with spices.

mumps (mumps) *n.* a disease causing painful swelling of the salivary glands near the ears.

munch (munch) *vb.* **munching, munched** to chew, especially noisily.

mural (mū rǎl) *n.* a picture painted directly on to a wall.

murder (mûr děr) *n.* the act of unlawfully and intentionally killing a person. – *vb.* **murdering, murdered** – *n.* **murderer**.

murky *adj.* **murkier, murkiest** gloomy; (of water) dark and dirty. – *n.* **murkiness**.

murmur (mûr mŭr) *n.* a quiet continuous sound, for example of running water or low voices. – *vb.* **murmuring, murmured** to speak softly and indistinctly.

muscle (mu sěl) *n.* tissue in the body responsible for the movement of joints, etc.

muscular (mus kū lǎr) *adj.* 1 relating to or consisting of muscle. 2 strong.

museum (mū zē ǔm) *n.* a place where objects of artistic, scientific, or historic interest are displayed to the public.

mushroom (mush room) *n.* any of several types of fast-growing fungus with an umbrella-shaped cap, many of which are edible.

music (mū zik) *n.* the art of making sound in a rhythmically organized harmonious form.

musical *adj.* 1 of or producing music. 2 pleasant to hear; melodious.

musician (mū zi shǎn) *n.* a person skilled in performing or composing music.

Muslim (mooz lim) or **Moslem** (moz lěm) or (mooz lěm) *n.* a follower of Islam.

mussel (mu sěl) *n.* a small edible shellfish.

must (must) *vb.* expressing 1 need: *I must earn some extra money*. 2 duty or obligation: *You must help him*. 3 certainty: *You must be Charles*.

muster (mus těr) *vb.* **mustering, mustered** to gather soldiers together, for duty etc.

mustang (mus tang) *n.* a wild horse native to the plains of the western UNITED STATES.

mustard (mus tård) *n.* a strong-tasting paste made from crushed mustard seeds.

mute (mūt) *adj.* not able to speak; dumb.

mutiny (mū ti ni) *n.* **mutinies** an act of rebellion against established authority.

mutter (mu těr) *vb.* **muttering, muttered** to speak in a quiet voice often when complaining.

mutton (mu tǒn) *n.* the flesh of an adult SHEEP.

mutual (mū choo ǎl) *adj.* felt by each of two or more people about others: *mutual admiration*.

muzzle (mu zěl) *n.* 1 the jaws and nose of an animal. 2 an arrangement of straps fitted round an animal's jaws to prevent it biting.

my (mī) *adj.* of or belonging to me.

myself *pron.* 1 the form of *me* used when the speaker or writer is the object of an action he or she performs: *I did myself a favour.* used to emphasize *I* or *me*. 3 (also **by myself**) alone.

● **Myanmar**. See Supplement, **Countries**.

mysterious (mi stēr i ǔs) *adj.* difficult or impossible to understand or explain.

mystery (mi stě ri) *n.* **mysteries** an event that cannot be, or has not been, explained.

mystify (mi sti fī) *vb.* **mystifies, mystifying, mystified** to puzzle or bewilder.

myth (mith) *n.* 1 an ancient story dealing with gods and heroes. 2 a false notion.

mythical *adj.* 1 relating to myth. 2 imaginary.

mythology (mi thol ǒ ji) *n.* **mythologies** a collection of myths.

myxomatosis (mik sǒ mǎ tō sis) *n.* an infectious, usually fatal disease in rabbits.

MYTHS & LEGENDS

GREEK & ROMAN MYTHOLOGY
(Roman names shown in brackets)

Aphrodite (Venus) goddess of love and beauty.

Apollo son of Zeus and twin of Artemis. God of poetry, music, and archery.

Ares (Mars) god of war, son of Zeus.

Artemis (Diana) Moon goddess, twin of Apollo.

Athena (Minerva) goddess of wisdom, arts and crafts, and war.

Atlas one of the Titans who made war on Zeus and as a punishment was made to carry the world on his shoulders.

Centaur a creature with a man's head, arms, and trunk joined to the four-legged body of a horse.

Cronus one of the Titans.

Demeter (Ceres) the corn goddess.

Dionysus (Bacchus) god of wine.

Eros (Cupid) god of love and son of Aphrodite.

Graces these three daughters of Zeus bestowed beauty, charm, and happiness: Aglaia (brilliance), Thalia (charm), and Euphrosyne (joy).

Hades (Pluto) ruler of the Underworld which is also known as Hades, the world beneath the Earth's surface where the souls of the dead live.

Hephaestus (Vulcan) the heavenly blacksmith.

Hera (Juno) queen of heaven.

Heracles (Hercules) son of Zeus, famous for his great strength.

Hermes (Mercury) the messenger of the gods.

Muses nine daughters of Zeus, they presided over the arts and sciences.

Orpheus a skilled musician who could even move inanimate things with his lyre.

Pan (Faunus) god of forests and flocks.

Perseus son of Zeus.

Pluto ruler of Hades.

Poseidon (Neptune) god of the sea.

Satyrs forest gods or demons attendant upon Bacchus.

Titans children of Uranus and Gaia, of immense size and strength, they overthrew Uranus and set up Cronos as king. He was overthrown by Zeus.

Uranus oldest of the Greek gods.

Zeus (Jupiter) lord of the Heavens and bringer of thunder and lightning.

The Greek supreme god, Zeus, asks Demeter, the corn goddess, why the crops have failed. "My daughter, Persephone, has disappeared. I cannot rest until I find her," she replies.

NORSE MYTHOLOGY

Asgard the home of the gods.

Balder god of summer sun, and son of Odin and Frigga.

Frey god of fertility and crops.

Freyja goddess of love, marriage, and the dead. Her chariot was drawn by two cats.

Frigga wife of Odin.

Odin the supreme god.

Thor the god of thunder.

Valhalla the hall in Asgard where the souls of heroes killed in battle were welcomed by Odin.

Valkyries Odin's nine hand-maidens.

Odin, the king of the Norse gods *(far right)*.

Freyja, Odin's first wife.

EGYPTIAN MYTHOLOGY

Horus son of Osiris and Isis, represented as a winged sun-disc.

Isis the principal goddess of Egypt and wife of Osiris.

Osiris chief god of the underworld.

Ra the sun-god, ancestor of the pharaohs. Represented with a falcon's head.

Set jealous brother of Osiris. He came to be regarded as the embodiment of evil.

Isis

Anubis

Ra

Osiris

Horus

Nn

nadir (**nā** dēr) or (**na** dēr) *n.* the absolute depth of despair or degradation, etc.

naff (naf) *adj.* (*slang*) **1** stupid; foolish. **2** tasteless.

nag (nag) *vb.* **nagging, nagged 1** to keep finding fault with someone. **2** to keep urging someone to do something: *Naomi nagged me into dancing with her.* – *n.* a person who nags.

nail (nāl) *n.* **1** the small horny covering at the tip of a finger or toe. **2** a metal spike hammered into something, for example to join two objects together. – *vb.* **nailing, nailed**.

naked (**nā** kid) *adj.* **1** wearing no clothes. **2** without fur, feathers, or foliage. **3** blank; empty. **4** (of the eye) unaided by a telescope or microscope: *I could see the star with a naked eye.*

name (nām) *n.* **1** a word or words by which an individual person, place, or thing is called and referred to. **2** reputation: *She's got a bad name for reliability.* **3** a famous person, firm, etc.: *What are the big names in fashion?* – *vb.* **naming, named 1** to give a name to. **2** to mention or identify by name: *Name three Belgian poets.* **3** to choose or appoint: *Nick was named as leader.* – **make a name for yourself** to become famous.

●**Namibia**. See Supplement, **Countries**.

nanny (**na** ni) *n.* **nannies** a children's nurse.
nanny goat *n.* an adult female goat.

●**Nansen, Fridtjof** (1861-1930) was a Norwegian explorer who made the first crossing of Greenland.

nap (nap) *n.* a short sleep. – *vb.* **napping, napped** to have a nap.

napkin (**nap** kin) *n.* (also **table napkin**) a piece of cloth or paper for wiping your mouth and fingers at mealtimes.

●**Naples** is a port in southern ITALY. It is dominated by Vesuvius, an active volcano.

●**Napoleon** (1769-1821) was a Corsican soldier who became emperor of FRANCE in 1804 and conquered ITALY, SPAIN, EGYPT, the NETHERLANDS, and most of central EUROPE. He was eventually defeated by the Prussians and British in 1815 at Waterloo.

narcotic (när **kot** ik) *n.* a drug that deadens pain, produces a temporary sense of well-being, and can be addictive.

narrate (nå **rāt**) *vb.* **narrating, narrated** to tell a story. – *n.* **narration**. – *n.* **narrator**.

narrow (**na** rō) *adj.* **1** of little breadth; not wide. **2** (of interests or experience) restricted; limited. **3** close; only just achieved, etc.: *The Republicans won a narrow victory.* – *vb.* **narrowing, narrowed** to make or become narrow: *The road suddenly narrowed.* – *n.* **narrowness**.
narrowly *adv.* **1** only just; barely. **2** with close attention: *The witch eyed him narrowly.*
narwhal (**när** wål) *n.* an arctic whale, the male of which has a long spiral tusk.

As well as being a brilliant general Napoleon was a skilful statesman who restored order to France.

nasal (**nā** sål) *adj.* relating to the nose.

nasty (**näs** ti) *adj.* **nastier, nastiest**
1 unpleasant; disgusting. 2 malicious; ill-natured: *My cat's got a nasty temper.* – *adv.* **nastily.** – *n.* **nastiness.**

nation (**nā** shŏn) *n.* 1 the people living in, and together forming, a single state. 2 a group of people with a common history, language, etc.

national (**na** shŏn ål) *adj.* 1 belonging to a particular nation: *The sari is a national dress of India.* 2 concerning the whole nation.
nationalism *n.* pride in the history, culture, successes, etc. of your own nation. – *n.* **nationalist.** – *adj.* **nationalistic.**
nationality (na shŏn **al** i ti) *n.* **nationalities** the national group to which you belong: *Picasso's nationality was Spanish.*
national park *n.* an area of countryside, usually important for its natural beauty, wildlife, etc., under the care of the nation.

● In the UNITED STATES the first national park, Yellowstone National Park, was established in 1872. It is famous for its springs and geysers such as 'Old Faithful'.

native (**nā** tiv) *adj.* 1 being or belonging to the place of your birth. 2 born a citizen of a particular place: *Ann is a native Italian.* 3 originating in a particular place: *Elephants are native to Africa and India.*

● **Native Americans** were the first people to live in America. They are sometimes called Indians because Christopher COLUMBUS thought he had arrived in India in 1492.

natural (**na** chů rål) *adj.* 1 normal; unsurprising. 2 instinctive; not learnt; innate: *Kindness was natural to her.* 3 (of manner, etc.) simple, easy and direct; not artificial. 4 relating to nature: *We are surrounded by areas of natural beauty.* 5 (of materials) derived from plants and animals.
natural gas *n.* a gas mixture, mainly methane, found under the ground or sea-bed.
naturalist *n.* a person who studies wildlife.
naturally *adv.* of course; not surprisingly.

nature (**nā** chůr) *n.* 1 the physical world not made by people; the forces that have formed it and control it. 2 what something is, or consists of. 3 an essential character; attitude, or outlook: *Philip is quiet and retiring by nature.* 4 a kind, type, etc.: *What nature of fish is this?*

naughty (**nö** ti) *adj.* **naughtier, naughtiest** mischievous; disobedient.

nausea (**nö** si å) *n.* an inclination to vomit.

nautical (**nö** ti kål) *adj.* relating to ships or sailors. – *adv.* **nautically.**

● **Navajos** (**na** vå hōz) make up the largest NATIVE AMERICAN tribe. Originally from what is now Canada, many now live on reservations in Arizona, New Mexico, and Utah.

nave (nāv) *n.* the main central part of a church.

navel (**nā** věl) *n.* the small hollow in the belly at the point where the umbilical cord was cut.

navigate (**na** vi gāt) *vb.* **navigating, navigated** to direct and steer the course of a ship, aircraft, or other vehicle. – *n.* **navigator.**
navigation *n.* 1 the act or skill of navigating.

navy (**nā** vi) *n.* **navies** the warships of a state; the organization to which they belong, one of the three armed services.

● **Nazareth** is a town in ISRAEL where JESUS spent much of his life.

Neanderthal (ni **an** děr täl) *adj.* denoting a primitive type of person of the early Stone Age.

Among Plains Indians tribal lore was passed from one generation to the next in long evening sessions around the fire.

Native Americans came to America from Asia over 20,000 years ago and developed many different lifestyles. The Spaniards who conquered Central America in the 1500s were amazed at the civilizations of the Incas and Aztecs. To the north most people lived as hunters and farmers in small villages.

The Anasazi of what is now the southwestern United States lived in villages called pueblos. The houses were joined together to form a single large building.

Hiawatha was a Mohawk Indian leader. The Indian in the poem The Song of Hiawatha *by Henry Wadsworth Longfellow was not based on the real Hiawatha.*

near

PRONUNCIATION GUIDE

fat **a**	all **ö**
fate **ā**	foot **oo**
fast **ä**	moon **ōō**
among **å**	boy **oi**
met **e**	house **ow**
mean **ē**	demon **ŏ**
silent **ė**	thing **th**
loch **hh**	this **Th**
fin **i**	but **u**
line **ī**	mute **ū**
quick **kw**	fur **û**
got **o**	brochure **ů**
note **ō**	vision **zh**

The 'empty' space between stars contains hydrogen atoms and tiny grains of solid material. In some regions of a galaxy the grains are found close together, forming dark clouds of dust and gas. Such regions are called nebulae.

near (nēr) *prep.* **1** at a short distance from. **2** close to in amount, etc.: *She was near tears at the end of the sad film.* – *adv.* close: *The ball came near to hitting her.* – *adj.* close: *The passengers had a near escape.* – *vb.* **nearing, neared** to approach. – *n.* **nearness.**

nearby *adj. & adv.* a short distance away.

nearly *adv.* almost but not quite.

nearside *n.* the side of a horse or vehicle nearer the kerb.

near-sighted *adj.* (*US*) short-sighted.

neat (nēt) *adj.* **1** tidy; clean; orderly. **2** elegantly or cleverly simple: *That was a neat explanation.* **3** skilful or efficient: *Neat work!* – *n.* **neatness.**

● **Nebraska**. See Suppliment, **USA**.

nebula (**ne** bū lå) *n.* **nebulae** (**ne** bū lē) or **nebulas** the bright mass of a star cluster.

necessary (**ne** sě så ri) *adj.* **1** needed; essential; indispensable: *Food is necessary for life.* **2** inevitable; unavoidable: *a necessary evil.* – *adv.* **necessarily** (**ne** sě så ri li) or (ne sě **se** ri li).

necessity (ně **se** si ti) *n.* **necessity** **1** something necessary or essential: *They took food and other necessities on their expedition.* **2** circumstances that make something necessary or unavoidable: *She did it from necessity rather than choice.*

neck (nek) *n.* **1** the part of the body between the head and the shoulders. **2** the part of a garment at the neck.

necklace *n.* a string of beads or other ornaments worn around the neck.

need (nēd) *vb.* **needing, needed** **1** to require. **2** to be required or obliged: *Do you need to shout?* – *n.* something you require.

needless *adj.* unnecessary. – *adv.* **needlessly.**

needle (**nē** děl) *n.* **1** a thin pointed steel sewing instrument with an eye for the thread. **2** a longer, thicker implement of metal, wood, etc. for knitting, crocheting, etc. **3** the pointed end of a hypodermic syringe. **4** the moving pointer on a compass or other instrument.

needlework *n.* sewing and embroidery.

needy (**nē** di) *adj.* **needier, neediest** poverty-stricken; destitute.

negative (**ne** gå tiv) *adj.* **1** meaning or saying 'no'; expressing denial, refusal, or prohibition. **2** unenthusiastic or pessimistic: *His feelings for the scheme are entirely negative.* **3** in mathematics, less than zero. **4** in medicine, showing that something has not happened or is not present: *The result of the cancer test was negative.* **5** (of film) having the light and shade of the actual image reversed, or complementary colours in place of actual ones. – *n.* denial.

neglect (ni glekt) *vb.* **neglecting, neglected** **1** not to give proper care and attention to. **2** to leave duties, etc. undone. – *n.* lack of proper care and attention.

negotiate (ni gō shi āt) *vb.* **negotiating, negotiated** to discuss together so as to reach a satisfactory arrangement. – *n.* **negotiation.**

Negro (**nē** grō) *n.* **Negroes** (sometimes *offensive*) a person belonging to the black-skinned race originally from AFRICA. – *adj.* of, belonging to, or relating to this race.

● **Nehru, Jawaharlal** (1889-1964) was an Indian statesman who fought for Indian independence and was India's first prime minister.

neigh (nā) *vb.* **neighing, neighed** to make the loud sound of a horse.

neighbour (**nā** bǒr) *n.* a person living near or next door to another.

neighbourhood *n.* a district or locality.

neighbouring *adj.* nearby: *Joe lives in a neighbouring town.*

neighbourly *adj.* friendly.

neither (**nī** Thĕr) or (**nē** Thĕr) *adj. & pron.* not the one nor the other: *Neither proposal is acceptable.* – *conj.* (introducing the first of two or more alternatives; usually paired with **nor**) not: *I neither know nor care.* – *adv.* nor; also not: *If you won't, neither shall I.*

● **Nelson, Horatio** (1758-1805) was a British admiral at a time when Britain was at war with France. His most famous battle was his last, at Trafalgar on 21 October 1805.

neo- (**nē** ō-) new, or a new form of; modern: *Their office is in a neo-Georgian building.*

● **Nepal**. See Supplement, **Countries**.

nephew (**ne** fū) *n.* the son of your brother or sister, or of your brother- or sister-in-law.

Neptune[1]. See **Myths and Legends**.

Neptune[2] is a large planet, far out in the solar system. It circles the Sun in 165 years.

● **Nero** (AD 37-68) was a Roman emperor, famous for his cruelty to CHRISTIANS. He may have started the fire that nearly destroyed Rome.

nerve (nûrv) *n.* **1** one of the cords, consisting of a bundle of fibres, that carry instructions for movement and information on sensation between the brain or spinal cord and other parts of the body. **2** courage. **3** (in *plural*) nervousness; tension or stress: *Calm your nerves.*

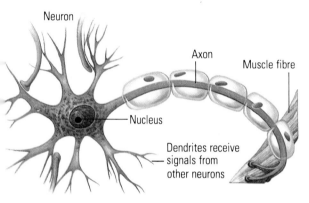

A muscle nerve cell or neuron, the nerve's control centre. The axon is a tubelike extension that carries messages.

nervous (**nûr** vŭs) *adj.* **1** timid; easily agitated. **2** apprehensive; uneasy. – *n.* **nervousness**.
nervous system *n.* the network of communication including the brain, nerves, and spinal cord.

-ness (-nĕs) *suffix* used to form nouns indicating a state, condition, or degree: *slowness; darkness.*

nest (nest) *n.* a structure built by birds or other creatures, e.g. rats, wasps, etc., in which to lay eggs or give birth to and look after young.

net¹ (net) *n.* **1** a material made of thread, cord, etc. knotted or woven so as to form regularly shaped meshes. **2** a piece of this in any of various shapes appropriate to different uses: *a fishing-net; a tennis-net.*
network *n.* **1** any system resembling a mass of criss-crossing lines: *a network of streets.* **2** any co-ordinated system involving large numbers of people, branches, etc.: *a telecommunications network.* **3** in computers, a system of linked terminals capable of passing information to one another. – *vb.* **networking, networked** **1** to broadcast on a network. **2** (of computer users) to pass information to one another's machines.

net² (net) *adj.* (also *British* **nett**) profit remaining after all expenses have been paid.

● **Netherlands**. See Supplement, **Countries**.

nettle (**ne** tĕl) *n.* a plant covered with hairs that sting if touched.
neuter (**nū** tĕr) *adj.* neither male nor female.
neutral (**nū** trăl) *adj.* **1** not taking sides in a quarrel or war. **2** not belonging or relating to either side: *neutral ground.*
neutron (**nū** tron) *n.* one of the electrically uncharged particles in the nucleus of an atom.

● **Nevada**. See Supplement, **USA**.

never (**ne** vĕr) *adv.* **1** not ever; at no time. **2** not: *I never realized that.*
nevertheless *adv.* in spite of that.
new (nū) *adj.* **1** recently made, bought, built, opened, etc. **2** recently discovered: *They appear to have found a new planet.* **3** just invented, etc.: *The doctor is performing the operation using new techniques.* – *adv.* only just: *He held the newborn baby in his arms.* – *n.* **newness**.
New Testament *n.* the part of the BIBLE concerned with the life and teachings of JESUS.
New Year's Day *n.* 1 January.
New Year's Eve *n.* 31 December.

● **New Brunswick** is a province of CANADA.

● **New England** is a region in the north-eastern corner of the United States. It is made up of six states: Maine, New Hampshire, Vermont, Massachusetts, Rhode Island, and Connecticut.

● **Newfoundland** is a province of CANADA.

● **New Hampshire**. See Supplement, **USA**.

● **New Jersey**. See Supplement, **USA**.

● **New Mexico**. See Supplement, **USA**.

● **New Orleans** on the Mississippi in Louisiana, is one of the United States' liveliest cities. There is a strong French influence and the blacks of New Orleans developed jazz there. The city's greatest event is the annual Mardi Gras carnival.

news (nūz) *n.* (*singular*) information about recent events, especially as reported in newspapers or on radio or television.
newspaper *n.* a daily or weekly publication containing news, advertisements, articles, etc.

The tiny hairs on a nettle leaf are like hollow needles. If they pierce the skin and break off, poison enters the wound from a small reservoir at the base of the hair.

newt (nūt) *n.* a small amphibious animal with a long body and tail and short legs.

● **Newton, Sir Isaac** (1642-1727) was an English scientist and mathematician. He was the first to explain the force of gravity and his experiments showed that white light is a mixture of all the colours of the rainbow. He built the first reflecting telescope.

In a darkened room Isaac Newton put a glass prism in a beam of sunlight shining through a tiny hole in the wall. He noticed that the white light was split into the colours of the rainbow: red, orange, yellow, green, blue, indigo, violet.

● **New York City** at the mouth of the Hudson River, is the largest city in the United States. The island of Manhattan is the heart of the city and has many of its most famous sights; its towering skyscrapers, Broadway, Fifth Avenue, and Wall Street. Its five boroughs are Brooklyn, the Bronx, Manhattan, Queens, and Staten Island.

● **New York State**. See Supplement, **USA**.

● **New Zealand** is a country east of Australia in the south Pacific, consisting of two main islands. North Island is mountainous and has hot springs. The Canterbury Plain on South Island is famous for sheep pasture. Much of New Zealand's wealth depends on farming. About eight per cent of the population are MAORIS, the original inhabitants. The capital of New Zealand is Wellington.

next (nekst) *adj.* **1** following in time or order: *The next day was bright and sunny.* **2** following this one: *Let's visit the museum next week.* **3** adjoining; neighbouring: *They sat in the next compartment.* – *adv.* **1** immediately after that or this: *What happened next?* **2** on the next occasion: *When I next saw her she was driving her car.* **3** following, in order of degree: *the next longest river after the Amazon.* – **next door** in the neighbouring house.
next of kin *n.* your closest relative.

● **Niagara Falls** one of the most spectacular sights in North America. They stand on the border between CANADA and the UNITED STATES.

The Niagara Falls is made up of two waterfalls: the American Falls in the United States, and the Horseshoe Falls in Canada.

nibble (ni běl) *vb.* **nibbling, nibbled** to take very small bites of: *The rabbit nibbled the lettuce.*

● **Nicaragua**. See Supplement, **Countries**.

nice (nīs) *adj.* **1** pleasant. **2** good; satisfactory.

nicety (nī sě ti) *n.* **niceties** a small detail.
niche (nēsh) *n.* a recess in a wall, suitable for a lamp or ornament, etc.
nick (nik) *n.* a small cut. – *vb.* **nicking, nicked 1** to make a small cut in. **2** (*slang*) to steal.
nickel (ni kěl) *n.* **1** an element (symbol **Ni**), a silvery metal used especially in alloys. **2** in the USA and CANADA, a coin worth five cents.
nickname (nik nām) *n.* a name, additional to the real one, given to a person or place in fun, affection, or contempt.
niece (nēs) *n.* the daughter of your sister or brother, or of your sister- or brother-in-law.

● **Niger**. See Supplement, **Countries**.

● **Nigeria**. See Supplement, **Countries**.

night (nīt) *n.* the time of darkness between sunset and sunrise.
nightfall *n.* the beginning of night; dusk.
nightly *adj.* & *adv.* happening every night.
nightingale (nīt ing gāl) *n.* a small bird with a melodious song, heard especially at night.

● **Nightingale, Florence** (1820-1910) was the founder of modern nursing. Against much opposition she organized sanitary barrack hospitals in the Crimean War (1854–56), so saving thousands of lives. She was called the 'lady of the lamp'.

nightmare (nīt mār) *n.* a frightening dream.
nil (nil) *n.* in games, etc., a score of zero.

● **Nile** the world's longest river. It flows 6671 km from near the equator in AFRICA to the Mediterranean Sea.

nimble (nim běl) *adj.* quick and agile. – *n.* **nimbleness.** – *adv.* **nimbly.**
nine (nīn) *n.* the number or figure 9. – *n., adj.,* & *adv.* **ninth.** – **dressed up to the nines** (*colloquial*) wearing your best clothes.
nineteen (nīn tēn) *n.* the number or figure 19. – *n., adj.,* & *adv.* **nineteenth.**
ninety (nīn ti) *n.* **nineties** the number or figure 90. – *n., adj.,* & *adv.* **ninetieth.**
nip (nip) *vb.* **nipping, nipped 1** to pinch or squeeze sharply. **2** to give a sharp little bite to: *The parrot nipped my ear.* – *n.* a pinch.
nippy *adj.* **nippier, nippiest** (*colloquial*) **1** cold; chilly. **2** quick-moving; nimble.

nipple (**ni** pĕl) *n.* the pointed projection on a breast, in the female the outlet of the ducts from which the young suck milk.

nitrogen (**nī** trŏ jĕn) *n.* an element (symbol **N**), a gas making up four-fifths of the air. It is colourless and has no taste or smell. All plants and animals need nitrogen.

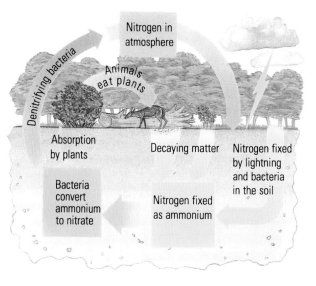

The nitrogen cycle: nitrogen passes from air to soil, to plants, to animals which eat plants, and eventually back into the air.

no¹ *interjection* used as a negative reply, expressing denial, refusal, or disagreement.

no² (nō) *adj.* **1** not any. **2** certainly not a; far from a: *He's no fool.* **3** hardly any: *I'll do it in no time.* **4** not allowed: *No smoking!*
nobody (**nō** bŏ di) *pron.* no person; no one.
nowhere *adv.* in or to no place; not anywhere.

Nobel prize (nō **bel prīz**) *n.* any of the prizes, awarded annually for work in physics, chemistry, medicine, literature, and the promotion of peace, instituted by Alfred *Nobel* (1833-96), Swedish discoverer of dynamite.

noble (**nō** bĕl) *adj.* **1** honourable. **2** generous. **3** of high birth or rank. **4** grand, splendid, or imposing in appearance. – *n.* a person of noble rank. – *n.* **nobleness**. – *adv.* **nobly**.

nocturnal (nok **tûr** nål) *adj.* **1** (of animals) active at night. **2** of or belonging to the night.

nod (nod) *vb.* **nodding, nodded 1** to make a brief bow with the head, in agreement, greeting, etc. **2** to become drowsy. – **the Land of Nod** the imaginary country to which sleepers go.

Noh or **No** (nō) *n.* traditional Japanese drama, developed from religious dance.

noise (noiz) *n.* **1** a sound: *I can hear no noise in the church.* **2** a harsh, disagreeable sound; a din. – *adj.* **noiseless**. – *n.* **noiselessness**.
noisy *adj.* **noisier, noisiest** making a lot of noise: *The noisy children screamed and shouted.* – *adv.* **noisily**. – *n.* **noisiness**.

nomad (**nō** mad) *n.* a member of a people without a permanent home, who travel from place to place seeking food and pasture. – *adj.* **nomadic**.

nominate (**no** mi nāt) *vb.* **nominating, nominated** to suggest someone formally as a candidate for election, for a job, etc. – *n.* **nomination**.

nominee (no mi **nē**) *n.* a person who is nominated as a candidate, or for a job, etc.

non- (non-) *prefix* **1** not; the opposite of: *non-existent.* **2** not belonging to the category of: *Jan prefers to read non-fiction.* **3** not having the skill or desire to be: *Abigail prefers to sit in a carriage for non-smokers.*

nonchalant (**non** shå lånt) *adj.* coolly unconcerned. – *n.* **nonchalance**.

none (nun) *pron.* (with *singular* or *plural* verb) **1** not any. **2** no one: *None were as kind as she.*

nonsense (**non** sĕns) *n.* **1** words or ideas that do not make sense. **2** silly behaviour. – *interjection* you're quite wrong.

non-starter (non **stärt** ĕr) *n.* a person, thing, idea, etc. that has no chance of success.

noodle (**nōō** dĕl) *n.* (usually in *plural*) a thin strip of pasta, usually made with egg.

noon (nōōn) *n.* midday; twelve o'clock.

noose (nōōs) *n.* a loop made in the end of a rope with a sliding knot.

nor (nör) *conj.* (used to introduce alternatives after **neither**) *She neither knows nor cares.*

Nordic (**nör** dik) *adj.* of or belonging to Scandinavia or its inhabitants.

norm (nörm) *n.* an accepted way of behaving, etc.: *Adam followed all the social norms.*

normal (**nör** mål) *adj.* usual; typical; not extraordinary. – *n.* what is average or usual. – *n.* **normality** (nör **mal** i tï). **normally** *adv.* usually: *We normally close on Fridays.*

Norman (**nör** mån) *n.* a person from Normandy, especially one of the Scandinavian settlers of France who conquered England in 1066. – *adj.* of or belonging to the Normans.

Nomads are found mainly in Africa and Asia, the Arab Bedouin being the best known.

PRONUNCIATION GUIDE	
fat **a**	all **ŏ**
fate **ā**	foot **oo**
fast **ä**	moon **ōō**
among **å**	boy **oi**
met **e**	house **ow**
mean **ē**	demon **ŏ**
silent **ĕ**	thing **th**
loch **hh**	this **Th**
fin **i**	but **u**
line **ī**	mute **ū**
quick **kw**	fur **û**
got **o**	brochure **ů**
note **ō**	vision **zh**

Odin, the chief of the Norse gods. He owned two ravens, Thought and Memory. He sent them out daily to report on what was going on in the world.

Norse (nörs) *adj.* of or belonging to ancient or medieval Scandinavia. – *n.* (*plural*) the Scandinavians, especially the Norwegians.

north (nörth) *n.* the direction to your left when you face the rising sun, or any part of the Earth, a country, town, etc. lying in that direction. – *adj.* **1** in the north. **2** coming from the direction of the north: *a north wind*.

northerly *adj.* **1** (of a wind, etc.) coming from the north. **2** looking, lying, etc. towards the north. – *adv.* to or towards the north.

northern *adj.* of the north.

northerner *n.* a person who lives in or comes from the north.

the North Pole *n.* the point on the Earth's surface representing the northern end of its axis.

northward *adv. & adj.* towards the north.

● **North America** includes CANADA, the UNITED STATES, MEXICO, Central America and the West Indian Islands of the Caribbean Sea. It stretches from cold, Arctic lands to hot deserts and sub-tropical swamps. High mountains include the Rocky Mountains. The Great Lakes are the world's largest freshwater lakes. Famous natural wonders include Niagara Falls and the Grand Canyon. There are both huge cities and areas with very few people. Most people in North America speak English, Spanish, or French.

● **North Carolina**. See Supplement, **USA**.

● **North Dakota**. See Supplement, **USA**.

● **Northern Ireland** was created in 1920 to remain part of the UNITED KINGDOM after the independence of the rest of IRELAND. It is made up of six, predominantly Protestant, counties of the nine counties of the province of Ulster. The capital is Belfast.

● **North Korea**. See Supplement, **Countries**.

● **North Sea** the part of the ATLANTIC Ocean separating GREAT BRITAIN from SCANDINAVIA. It is rich in fish and the sea bed holds oil and gas.

● **Norway** is a long narrow country with many mountains and forests. The coast is pierced with steep inlets called fjords. Fishing and oil from the NORTH SEA make Norway a rich kingdom. Its capital is Oslo.

Norwegian (nör wē jån) *adj.* of or belonging to Norway, its inhabitants, or their language. – *n.* a native of NORWAY; its language.

nose (nōz) *n.* **1** the projecting organ above the mouth, with which you smell and breathe; an animal's snout or muzzle. **2** the sense of smell. – *vb.* **nosing, nosed 1** to move carefully forward: *She nosed the car out of the yard.* **2** to pry: *They nosed around the room looking for evidence.*

nose cone *n.* the cone-shaped cap on the front of a rocket, etc.

nostalgia (no **stal** jå) *n.* a yearning for the past. – *adj.* **nostalgic**. – *adv.* **nostalgically**.

nostril (**nos** tril) *n.* either of the two openings in the nose, through which you breathe, etc.

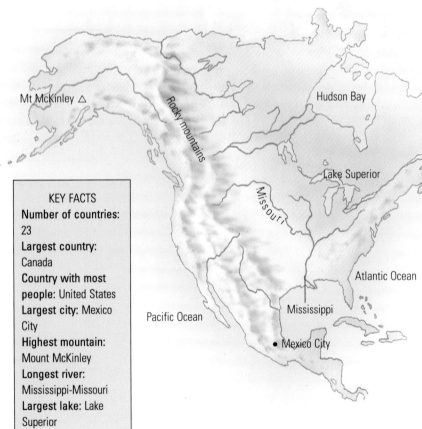

KEY FACTS
Number of countries: 23
Largest country: Canada
Country with most people: United States
Largest city: Mexico City
Highest mountain: Mount McKinley
Longest river: Mississippi-Missouri
Largest lake: Lake Superior

Mt McKinley △

Rocky mountains

Hudson Bay

Missouri

Lake Superior

Pacific Ocean

Atlantic Ocean

Mississippi

● Mexico City

The continent of North America stretches north from tropical Panama to the icy Arctic Ocean, and east from the Pacific Ocean to the Atlantic Ocean.

not (not) *adv.* (often shortened to **-n't**) **1** used to make a sentence negative: *It's not fair* or *It isn't fair.* **2** used with verbs of opinion, intention, etc. to make the clause or infinitive following the verb negative: *I don't think he's right* (= I think he is not right). **3** used in place of a negative clause or predicate: *I might be late, but I hope not.* **4** absolutely no: *Not a sound could be heard.* – **not at all** don't mention it.

notable (nō tå běl) *adj.* worth noting; significant. – *adv.* **notably**.

notch (noch) *n.* a small V-shaped cut.

note (nōt) *n.* **1** a brief record made for later reference: *Oliver took a note of the number.* **2** a short informal letter: *He sent me a note to say when he was arriving.* **3** a banknote. **4** attention; notice: *Take note of the warning.* **5** a single musical sound.
notecase *n.* a case for banknotes; a wallet.
noted *adj.* well known: *She is noted for her style.*

nothing (nu thing) *n.* **1** no thing; not anything. **2** very little; something of no importance or not very impressive. **3** the number 0. – **be nothing to do with 1** to be unconnected with. **2** to be no concern of. – **come to nothing** to fail. – **have nothing to do with 1** to avoid. **2** to be unconnected with. **3** to be no concern of.

notice (nō tis) *n.* **1** an announcement displayed or delivered publicly. **2** attention: *Your fine result was brought to my notice.* **3** a warning given before leaving, or dismissing someone from, a job: *Natasha is going to Russia and has given in her notice.* – *vb.* **noticing, noticed** to observe: *I couldn't help noticing your new motorbike.* – **at short notice** with little warning.
noticeable *adj.* easily seen. – *adv.* **noticeably**.

notify (nō ti fī) *vb.* **notifies, notifying, notified** to inform or warn.

notion (nō shŏn) *n.* **1** an impression, idea, or understanding. **2** a belief. **3** an inclination or fancy. **4** (in *plural*; *US*) pins, needles, etc.

notorious (nŏ tör i ůs) *adj.* well-known for a bad reason. – *n.* **notoriety** (nō tŏ **rī** ě ti).

nought (nöt) *n.* the figure 0; zero.

noun (nown) *n.* a word used as the name of a person, animal, thing, place, or quality.

nourish (nu rish) *vb.* **nourishing, nourished** to supply with food needed for survival and growth. – *adj.* **nourishing**.
nourishment *n.* food.

● **Nova Scotia** is a province of CANADA.

novel¹ (**no** věl) *n.* a long, written story.
novelist *n.* the writer of a novel.

The novels of Charles Dickens were often illustrated and first appeared as serials in magazines. This scene is from David Copperfield.

novel² (**no** věl) *adj.* new; original: *a novel idea.*

novelty (**no** věl ti) *n.* **novelties** something new and strange.

November (nō **vem** běr) *n.* the eleventh month of the year. November has 30 days.

novice (**no** vis) *n.* **1** a beginner. **2** a person who has recently joined a religious community.

now (now) *adv.* **1** at the present time or moment. **2** immediately: *You'd better go now.* **3** in these circumstances; as things are: *I planned to, but now I can't.* **4** up to the present: *She has now been teaching for 13 years.* – **as of now** from this time onward. – **for now** for the time being. – **just now** a moment ago.

nowadays (**now** å dāz) *adv.* in these present times: *Few people wear hats nowadays.*

nowhere. See **no²**.

nozzle (**no** zěl) *n.* a fitting attached as an outlet to the end of a hose, etc.

nuclear (**nū** kli år) *adj.* **1** of or relating to atoms or their nuclei: *Sarah is studying nuclear physics.* **2** relating to atomic energy or weapons.
nuclear reactor *n.* an apparatus for producing nuclear energy.

nucleus (**nū** kli ůs) *n.* **nuclei** (**nū** kli ī) **1** the positively charged central part of an atom. **2** the central part of a plant or animal cell.

nude (nūd) *adj.* wearing no clothes; naked.

nudge (nuj) *vb.* **nudging, nudged 1** to poke gently with the elbow, to get attention, etc. **2** to push slightly. – *n.* a gentle prod.

nugget (**nu** git) *n.* a lump, especially of gold.

Nostalgia comes from the Greek *nostos* 'return home' and *algos* 'pain'. Together they produce the meaning 'homesickness'.

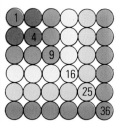

Square number
progression

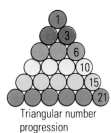

Triangular number
progression

*Some sequences of
numbers can be shown
as patterns. A number
multiplied by itself is
called a square* (top).
*A triangular
arrangement gives the
progression 1, 3, 6,
10, 15, 21 and so on.*

The **numbers** 1, 2, 3, 4, etc. we use so often
in everyday life are called natural numbers
because they were thought to be natural, in
existence, and correspond to something in
reality such as two eyes, four legs, etc.

Chinese

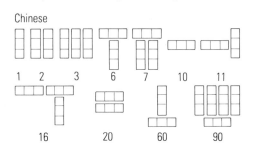

| 1 | 2 | 3 | | 6 | 7 | | 10 | 11 |

| 16 | | 20 | | 60 | | 90 |

Roman

I   II   III   IV   V   VI   VII   VIII   IX   X

1   2   3   4   5   6   7   8   9   10

XI   XV   XX   L   XC   C   CX   CL   D   M

11   15   20   50   90   100   110   150   500   1000

*Over the centuries different peoples had devised
various ways of writing numbers. Our modern
Arabic numbers were originally developed in India.*

١	٢	٣	٤	٥	٦	٧	٨	٩	٠		Arabic
1	ζ	ζ	Ψ	૫	Ⴑ	7	8	9			Spanish AD 976
1	૨	3	૪	५	૬	૮	8	9	०		W. Europe 1360
1	૨	૨	૪	5	6	7	8	9	०		Italy 1400
1	2	3	4	5	6	7	8	9	10	0	Modern
1	2	3	4	5	6	7	8	9	10	0	Computer

*This diagram shows how
our modern numerals
were derived from ancient
Arabic.*

nuisance (**nū** såns) *n.* an annoying or
troublesome person, thing, or circumstance.

numb (num) *adj.* **1** deprived completely, or
partly, of the ability to feel: *My fingers are numb
with cold.* **2** too stunned to feel emotion: *I am
numb with shock.*

number (**num** běr) *n.* **1** the means or system by
which groups of individual things are counted.
2 a numeral or set of numerals. **3** a numeral or
set of numerals identifying something or
someone: *What is your telephone number?* **4** a
single issue of a magazine, etc.

● Our modern numbers are derived from Arabic
numerals. Unlike many of the ancient systems,
we have a zero to represent nothing. By using the
digits 0 to 9 we can construct any number we can

think of. The word digit comes from the Latin
word *digitus* meaning 'finger'.

numeral (**nū** mě rål) *n.* a symbol used to
express a number: *5 and V are numerals for five.*

numerical (nū **me** ri kål) *adj.* relating to, or
consisting of, numbers.

numerous (**nū** mě růs) *adj.* many; a large
number: *The box contains numerous types of rings.*

numismatics (nū miz **mat** iks) *n.* (*singular*) the
study, or collecting, of coins and medals.

nun (nun) *n.* a woman who lives in a convent in
obedience to certain vows.

nurse (nûrs) *n.* a person who is trained to look
after sick or injured people, especially in
hospital. – *vb.* **nursing, nursed** to look after
sick or injured people. – *n.* **nursing**.
nursing home *n.* a small hospital or home,
for example for old people.

nursery (**nûr** sě ri) *n.* **nurseries** a place where
children are looked after while their parents
are at work, etc.

nut (nut) *n.* **1** a fruit consisting of a kernel
contained in a hard shell; the kernel itself. **2** a
small usually hexagonal piece of metal with a
hole through it, for screwing on to a bolt.

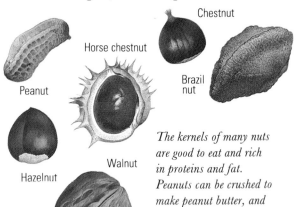

Chestnut

Horse chestnut

Brazil
nut

Peanut

Hazelnut

Walnut

*The kernels of many nuts
are good to eat and rich
in proteins and fat.
Peanuts can be crushed to
make peanut butter, and
flour ground from
chestnuts is used to bake
bread.*

nutmeg (**nut** meg) *n.* the hard seed of the fruit
of an Indian tree, used grated as a spice.

nutrition (nū **tri** shǒn) *n.* **1** the process of
nourishment. **2** food. – *adj.* **nutritional**.
nutritious *adj.* nourishing.

nuzzle (**nu** zěl) *vb.* **nuzzling, nuzzled** (usually
of animals) to rub with the nose.

nylon (**nī** lon) *n.* a synthetic material from
which a wide variety of products are made,
including clothing, ropes, and brushes.

O o

oak (ōk) *n.* **1** a large, acorn-bearing tree of the beech family, with lobed leaves. **2** its hard wood.

● **Oakley, Annie** (1860-1926) was an American markswoman and entertainer. Her story inspired Irving Berlin's musical *Annie, Get Your Gun.*

oar (ōr) *n.* a long pole with a broad, flat blade used for rowing a boat.

oasis (ō ā sis) *n.* **oases** (ō ā sēz) a fertile area in a desert where water is found and plants grow.

Where water fills an aquifer (a rock which holds water), and where the aquifer breaks the surface, an oasis will form. If the water is trapped between two layers of rock wells can be drilled.

oat (ōt) *n.* a cereal plant grown for its seeds.

oath (ōth) *n.* **1** a solemn promise to tell the truth, be loyal, etc. **2** a swearword.

obedience (ǒ bēd i ěns) *n.* the act or practice of obeying. – *adj.* **obedient.**

obey (ǒ bā) *vb.* **obeying, obeyed** to do what you are told to do by someone.

obituary (ǒ bi choo å ri) *n.* **obituaries** an announcement of a person's death.

object¹ (**ob** jikt) *n.* **1** a thing that can be seen or touched. **2** an aim or purpose. **3** in grammar, the noun, etc. affected by the action of the verb or a preposition.

object² (ǒb **jekt**) *vb.* **objecting, objected 1** to express dislike or disapproval: *I object to these high prices.* **2** to give as a reason for opposing: *I object that he is never on time.* – *n.* **objector.**

  objection *n.* an expression of disapproval.
  objectionable *adj.* unpleasant.

objective (ǒb **jek** tiv) *n.* a thing aimed at or wished for; a goal. – *n.* **objectivity.**

oblige (ǒ **blīj**) *vb.* **obliging, obliged** to bind morally, legally, or by physical force: *All citizens are obliged to do community work.*
  obliging *adj.* willing to help other people.

oblique (ǒ **blēk**) *adj.* sloping; not vertical or horizontal. – *n.* an oblique line (/).

obliterate (ǒ **blit** ě rāt) *vb.* **obliterating, obliterated** to destroy completely. – *n.* **obliteration.**

oblong (**ob** long) *adj.* forming or being a rectangle which is longer than it is broad.

oboe (ō bō) *n.* a wind instrument.

obscure (ǒb **skūr**) *adj.* **1** dark; dim. **2** not clear; hidden; difficult to see. **3** not well known.

observation (ob zěr **vā** shǒn) *n.* **1** the act of noticing or watching; the state of being observed or watched. **2** perception: *Test her powers of observation.* **3** a remark or comment.

observatory (ǒb **zûrv** å tǒ ri) *n.* **observatories** a place specially equipped for observing and studying the stars and weather.

observe (ǒb **zûrv**) *vb.* **observing, observed 1** to notice. **2** to watch carefully.
  observer *n.* **1** a person who observes. **2** a person who goes to meetings, etc. to watch and listen but not take part.

The letter *O*, like all the letters, has a long history. The earliest alphabets were taken and adapted by the Greeks. The Greek *beta*, when combined with the first letter, *aleph*, gives us the word alphabet.

  The Greeks passed on their letters to the Romans who developed the alphabet we use today, although they used only capital letters. Small letters developed in the AD 700s.

An early form of the letter O, used in the Middle East over 3000 years ago.

This letter was taken by the Greeks and became omicron.

Over the years different versions of the letter O have been developed.

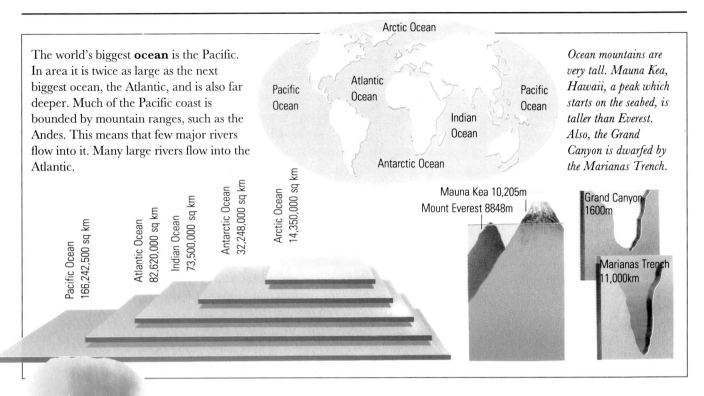

The world's biggest **ocean** is the Pacific. In area it is twice as large as the next biggest ocean, the Atlantic, and is also far deeper. Much of the Pacific coast is bounded by mountain ranges, such as the Andes. This means that few major rivers flow into it. Many large rivers flow into the Atlantic.

Ocean mountains are very tall. Mauna Kea, Hawaii, a peak which starts on the seabed, is taller than Everest. Also, the Grand Canyon is dwarfed by the Marianas Trench.

Arctic Ocean
Atlantic Ocean
Pacific Ocean
Pacific Ocean
Indian Ocean
Antarctic Ocean

Pacific Ocean 166,242,500 sq km
Atlantic Ocean 82,620,000 sq km
Indian Ocean 73,500,000 sq km
Antarctic Ocean 32,248,000 sq km
Arctic Ocean 14,350,000 sq km

Mauna Kea 10,205m
Mount Everest 8848m

Grand Canyon 1600m
Marianas Trench 11,000km

In parts of the oceans there are holes – 'smokers' – in the sea floor where hot liquids and gases leak into the water from the hot rocks beneath.

obsolete (ob sŏ lēt) *adj.* out of date.

obstacle (ob stå kĕl) *n.* a person or thing that stands in a person's way or prevents progress: *The fallen branch was an obstacle on the road.*

obstinate (ob sti nåt) *adj.* refusing to change your opinion; stubborn.

obstruct (ŏb strukt) *vb.* **obstructing, obstructed 1** to block or close. **2** to prevent or hinder the movement of.
obstruction *n.* **1** a thing that obstructs or blocks: *Your motorbike is causing an obstruction at the entrance.* **2** the act of obstructing.

obtain (ŏb tān) *vb.* **obtaining, obtained** to get, to come into possession of, often by effort: *Mark managed to obtain tickets for the game.*

obtuse (ŏb tūs) *adj.* (of an angle) between 90° and 180°.

obverse (ob vûrs) *n.* the side of a coin with the head or main design on it.

obvious (ob vi ŭs) *adj.* easily seen or understood; evident. – *adv.* **obviously.**

occasion (ŏ kā zhŏn) *n.* **1** a particular event or happening. **2** a special event or celebration. – **on occasion** from time to time.
occasional *adj.* happening infrequently.

Occident (ok si dĕnt) *n.* the countries in the West, especially Europe and America, as opposed to the **Orient.**

occupant (o kū pånt) *n.* a person who occupies a place: *The occupant of the house is away.*

occupation (o kū pā shŏn) *n.* **1** a person's job or profession. **2** an activity that occupies a person's attention, free time, etc.

occupy (o kū pī) *vb.* **occupies, occupying, occupied 1** to have possession of or live in a house, etc. **2** to be in or fill time, space, etc. **3** to take possession of by force: *The Iraqis occupied Kuwait in 1991.*
occupier *n.* a person who lives in a building.

occur (ŏ kûr) *vb.* **occurring, occurred 1** to happen or take place. **2** to come into the mind: *It occurred to her that she could do better.*
occurrence *n.* an event: *Falling meteorites are a rare occurrence.*

ocean (ō shǎn) *n.* any one of the five great areas of sea water that cover most of the Earth's surface: the Atlantic, Indian, Pacific, Arctic, and Antarctic Oceans. – *adj.* **oceanic** (ō shi **an** ik).

ocelot (o sĕ lot) *n.* a wild cat, found in the forests of Central America.

●**O'Connor, Flannery** (1925-64) was an American novelist and short-story writer.

octagon (ok tå gon) *n.* a flat figure with eight sides. – *adj.* **octagonal** (ok **tag** ŏ nål).

octave (ok tāv) *n.* the series of notes between the first note and the eighth note on a major or minor scale.

October (ok **tō** bĕr) *n.* the tenth month of the year. October has 31 days.

octopus (ok tŏ pŭs) *n.* **octopuses** a sea creature with a soft body and eight tentacles.

odd (od) *adj.* **1** left over when others are put into groups or pairs. **2** not matching: *He's wearing odd socks.* **3** unusual; strange.

oddity *n.* **oddities** a strange person or thing.

odds *n.* (*plural*) the chance or probability, expressed as a ratio, that something will or will not happen: *The odds are 10 to 1 in favour of our winning the game.*

odour (ō dŏr) *n.* a usually distinctive smell: *I love the odour of new-mown hay.*

●**Odyssey** an epic poem by the Greek poet HOMER. It is the story of the journeys of Ulysses (Odysseus) after the Trojan Wars.

of (ov) *prep.* **1** used to show origin, cause, or authorship: *people of Paris; die of hunger; poems of Whitman.* **2** belonging to; connected with. **3** used to define a component, ingredient, characteristic, etc.: *built of bricks; an area of marsh; a heart of gold.* **4** about: *tales of Rome.*

off (of) *adv.* **1** away; at or to a distance: *The new school is a couple of miles off.* **2** in or into a position which is not attached; loose; separate: *The handle came off.* **3** ahead in time: *Easter is a week off.* **4** no longer operating: *Turn the radio off.* **5** stopped or cancelled: *The match was rained off.* **6** in or into a state of sleep: *He dozed off.* **7** away from work or duties: *Take an hour off.* **8** away from a course: *Turn off into a side street.* – *adj.* **1** most distant; farthest away. **2** not good; not up to standard: *He's having an off day.* – *prep.* **1** from; away from: *Please take your feet off the table!* **2** removed from; no longer attached to. **3** opening out of; leading from: *Olga lives in a side street off the main road.* – **off and on** occasionally.

offhand or **offhanded** *adj.* casual or careless.

offspring *n.* **offspring 1** a person's child. **2** the young of an animal.

offence or (*US*) **offense** (ŏ fens) *n.* **1** the breaking of a rule; a crime. **2** any cause of anger, annoyance, or displeasure.

offend (ŏ fend) *vb.* **offending, offended** to cause someone to feel hurt or angry; to insult. – *adj.* **offended**. – *n.* **offender**. – *adj.* **offending**.

offensive (ŏ fen siv) *adj.* **1** giving or likely to give offence; insulting. **2** unpleasant, disgusting, repulsive, especially to the senses: *The mess in the kitchen after the party was quite offensive.* – *n.* **1** an aggressive action or attitude: *Go on the offensive.* **2** an attack. – *n.* **offensiveness**.

offer (o fĕr) *vb.* **offering, offered 1** to put forward a gift, payment, suggestion, etc. to be accepted, refused, or considered. **2** to provide: *We camped on the hill offering the best view.* **3** to state willingness to do something: *Jane offered to wash the car.* – *n.* **1** an act of offering. **2** that which is offered, especially an amount of money offered to buy something.

offering *n.* anything offered, especially a gift.

office (o fis) *n.* the room or building in which the business of a firm is done.

officer *n.* **1** a person in a position of authority and responsibility in the armed forces. **2** a person with a position of authority in an organization. **3** a policeman or policewoman.

official (ŏ fi shăl) *adj.* **1** of or relating to an office or position of authority. **2** given or authorized by a person in authority: *an official report.* – *n.* a person who is in a position of authority.

often (o fĕn) *adv.* **1** many times; frequently. **2** in many cases. – **every so often** sometimes.

ogre (ō gĕr) or **ogress** (ō gris) *n.* in fairy stories, a frightening, cruel, ugly giant.

●**Ohio**. See Supplement, **USA**.

oil (oil) *n.* **1** a usually thick liquid which will not mix with water and which burns easily, obtained from plants, animals, and minerals, and used as a fuel, lubricant, food, etc. **2** petroleum. – *vb.* **oiling, oiled** to apply oil to, lubricate. – *adj.* **oiled**.

oil-rig *n.* a structure, plus all the equipment, machinery, etc., used for drilling oil.

oil slick *n.* a patch of oil, especially one forming a film on water.

oil-tanker *n.* a large ship for carrying oil.

oil well *n.* a well bored in the ground or sea bed to obtain petroleum.

Each of the octopus's arms has two rows of suckers which help it to seize its prey.

The derrick on an oil platform is a tall metal tower that houses the drilling equipment. The drill bit at the end of the drill pipe cuts through rock with metal teeth.

SOME -OLOGIES

Term	Study of
anthropology	*mankind*
astrology	*heavens*
cardiology	*heart*
chronology	*dates*
cosmology	*universe*
dendrology	*trees*
entomology	*insects*
etymology	*word origins*
genealogy	*ancestry*
hydrology	*water*
meteorology	*weather*
odontology	*teeth*
ornithology	*birds*
pathology	*diseases*
rhinology	*noses*
speleology	*caves*
topology	*shapes*
vexillology	*flags*

A Greek athlete competes in the long-jump. Notice that he carries a weight in each hand.

oily *adj.* **oilier, oiliest** of, containing, or like oil; covered with oil.

ointment (**oint** měnt) *n.* a substance rubbed on the skin to heal injuries or as a cosmetic.

● **Oklahoma**. See Supplement, **USA**.

old (ōld) *adj.* advanced in age; having existed for a long time. **2** having a stated age: *Fiona is five years old.* **3** relating to the end period of a long life: *old age.* **4** worn out or shabby through long use: *old shoes.* **5** no longer in use; out of date. **6** belonging to the past. **7** former or earlier: *Their old house didn't have a garden.* – *n.* **1** an earlier time: *men of old.* **2** (*plural*) old people.

old-fashioned *adj.* **1** in a style common some time ago; out of date. **2** in favour of acting according to the moral views of the past.

Old Testament *n.* the first part of the Christian Bible, containing the Hebrew scriptures.

old wives' tale *n.* an ancient belief or theory considered foolish and unscientific.

the Old World *n.* the Eastern hemisphere, comprising Europe, Asia, and Africa.

olive (**o** liv) *n.* **1** an evergreen Mediterranean tree. **2** the small, oval fruit of this tree, eaten as a food or pressed to extract its oil. – *adj.* dull yellowish-green in colour.

Olympian (ŏ **lim** pi ăn) *n.* in mythology, any of the 12 ancient Greek gods thought to live on Mount Olympus in Greece.

Olympic (ŏ **lim** pik) *adj.* **1** of the Olympic Games. **2** of ancient Olympia.

Olympic Games *n.* (*plural*) **1** the games celebrated every four years in Olympia in ancient Greece, including athletic, musical, and literary competitions. **2** a modern international sports competition held every four years.

● This is the world's oldest athletics competition. The first Olympic Games were held at Olympia in GREECE in 776 BC. The modern Games have been held every four years since 1896, each time in a different country. The winners are awarded medals but no prize money.

● **Oman**. See Supplement, **Countries**.

ombudsman (**om** boodz măn) *n.* **ombudsmen** an official appointed to investigate complaints by the public.

omelette or (especially *US*) **omelet** (**om** lět) *n.* a dish of beaten eggs fried in a pan.

omen (ō měn) *n.* a sign of a future event.

omission (ō mi shŏn) *n.* something that has been left out or neglected.

omit (ō **mit**) *vb.* **omitting, omitted** to leave out, either by mistake or on purpose: *James omitted his address on the form.*

Most olives come from countries around the Mediterranean. The oil we get from pressing olives is good for our health and is used for cooking.

on (on) *prep.* **1** touching, supported by, attached to: *There's a sheet on the bed.* **2** carried with: *I've got no money on me.* **3** very near to or along the side of: *I live in a house on the shore.* **4** at or during a certain time: *We'll see you on Sunday.* **5** within the limits of: *a picture on page nine.* **6** about: *Emma is reading a book on Jane Austen.* **7** through contact with; as a result of: *Jill cut herself on the broken bottle.* **8** in the state or process of: *The house is on fire!* – *adv.* **1** (especially of clothes) covering: *When we are born we have no clothes on.* **2** ahead, forwards: *Go on home. I'll see you later on.* **3** continuously; without interruption: *He keeps on about his toothache.* **4** in or into operation: *Put the radio on.* – *adj.* **1** working, broadcasting, or performing: *You're on in two minutes.* **2** taking place: *Which films are on this week?* – **on and on** continuously. – **on time** at the right time.

ongoing *adj.* continuing; in progress.

on line *adj.* (of computers) directly controlled by the central processing unit.

onlooker *n.* a person who watches and does not take part; an observer. – *n.* **onlooking**.

onset *n.* **1** a beginning, especially of something unpleasant. **2** an attack.

onward *adj.* moving forward in place or time: *We changed at Heathrow for the onward journey.*

once (wuns) *adv.* **1** a single time; on one occasion. **2** at some time in the past: *Once upon a time...* – *conj.* as soon as: *Once she's arrived we can eat.* – *n.* one time or occasion. – **all at once 1** suddenly. **2** all at the same time.

one (wun) *adj.* **1** being a single unit, number, or thing. **2** being a particular person or thing, especially as distinct from others of the same kind: *Lift one leg and then the other.* **3** being a particular but unspecified instance or example: *We'll visit him one day soon.* **4** being the only such: *Olive is the one woman who can beat her.* – *n.* the number or figure 1, the lowest cardinal number. – *pron.* **1** (often referring to a noun already mentioned) an individual person, thing, or example: *Buy the blue one.* **2** anybody: *One can't do better than that.* – **at one with** in agreement. – **one and all** everyone.

one-sided *adj.* (of a competition) with one person or side having a great advantage over the other.

one-way *adj.* of a road or street in which traffic can move in one direction only.

● **O'Neill, Eugene** (1888-1953) was one of America's greatest playwrights whose works include *Mourning Becomes Electra* and *The Iceman Cometh.*

onion (un yŏn) *n.* a vegetable with an edible bulb which has a strong taste and smell.

only (ōn li) *adj.* **1** without any others of the same type: *This is the only horse in this class.* **2** having no brothers or sisters: *He's an only child.* **3** (*colloquial*) best: *Flying is the only way to travel.* – *adv.* **1** not more than; just. **2** alone; solely. **3** not longer ago than; not until: *I spoke to her only a minute ago.* – *conj.* but; however: *Come if you want to, only don't complain if you're bored.* – **if only** I wish: *If only you could be on time.*

onomatopoeia (o nō ma tŏ pē å) *n.* the use of a word which imitates the sound represented, such as *boo, hiss,* and *squelch.*

onslaught (**on** slöt) *n.* a fierce attack.

● **Ontario**. See **Canada**.

onus (ō nůs) *n.* **onuses** a burden.

ooze (ōōz) *vb.* **oozing, oozed** to flow or leak out gently or slowly: *Mud oozed from the pipes.*

opal (ō pål) *n.* a blue-white precious stone, which has iridescent reflections in it.

opaque (ō **pāk**) *adj.* not able to be seen through; not transparent. – *n.* **opaqueness**.

open (ō pěn) *adj.* **1** allowing things or people to go in or out; not blocked, closed, or locked. **2** (of a container) not sealed; with the inside visible. **3** not enclosed or restricted: *They sailed on the open sea.* **4** (of a shop, etc.) receiving customers; ready for business. **5** ready to consider new ideas; unprejudiced: *He's very fair, he has an open mind.* – *vb.* **opening, opened 1** to make or become open or more open. **2** to unfasten or to allow access. **3** to start or begin working: *The shop opens at nine.* **4** to declare open with an official ceremony: *The mayor opened the new hospital.* – *n.* **openness**. – *vb.* **open up 1** to open the door. **2** to make more accessible or available: *roads opening up the more remote areas.*

open air *n.* unenclosed space outdoors. – *adj.* (**open-air**) in the open air; outside.

opener *n.* **1** a device for opening something: *bottle-opener.* **2** the first item on a programme.

opening *n.* **1** a hole, gap. **2** the act of making or becoming open. **3** a beginning. **4** an opportunity or chance. – *adj.* of or forming an opening; first: *It's opening night at the opera.*

openly *adv.* without trying to hide anything.

The bulb of an onion is made up of tightly packed layers of leaves containing a special kind of oil. Vapour from the oil makes your eyes water.

opera (o pě rå) *n.* a dramatic work set to music, in which the singers are usually accompanied by an orchestra.

● Opera started in ITALY in the late 1500s, and rapidly became a popular form of entertainment. Some of the greatest operas have come from Austria (Mozart), Germany (Wagner), and Italy itself (Verdi, Rossini).

fat **a**	all **ö**
fate **ā**	foot **oo**
fast **ä**	moon **ōō**
among **å**	boy **oi**
met **e**	house **ow**
mean **ē**	demon **ŏ**
silent **ě**	thing **th**
lo**ch** **hh**	this **Th**
fin **i**	but **u**
line **ī**	mute **ū**
quick **kw**	fur **û**
got **o**	brochure **ů**
note **ō**	vision **zh**

operate (o pĕ rāt) *vb.* **operating, operated**
1 to function or work: *The engine is operating well.* **2** to manage a business, etc.: *Jenny operates a computer business.* **3** to perform surgery.
operating theatre *n.* the specially equipped room in a hospital where surgery is performed.
operation (o pĕ **rā** shŏn) *n.* **1** an act or process of working or operating: *The operation of the video-recorder is complicated.* **2** the state of working or being active: *The factory is not yet in operation.* **3** an activity; something done. **4** an act of surgery to treat a part of the body.
operational *adj.* able or ready to work: *Only two computers out of ten are operational.*
operator (o pĕ rā tŏr) *n.* a person who operates a machine or apparatus.
opinion (ŏ **pin** yŏn) *n.* **1** a belief or judgement which seems likely to be true, but which is not based on proof. **2** a judgement given by an expert: *Olga asked her doctor's medical opinion.*
opossum (ŏ **pos** ŭm) *n.* a small, tree-dwelling, American or Australian marsupial.

● **Oppenheimer, J. Robert** (1904-67) was an American physicist who helped develop the atomic bomb and later opposed development of the hydrogen bomb.

opponent (ŏ **pō** nĕnt) *n.* a person who belongs to the opposing side in a contest, etc.
opportunity (o pŏr **tūn** i ti) *n.* **opportunities** an occasion offering a possibility; a chance: *By joining the sports club you'll have the opportunity to meet new people.*
oppose (ŏ **pōz**) *vb.* **opposing, opposed 1** to resist or fight against by force or argument. **2** to object; to disagree: *I oppose corporal punishment.* – *n.* **opposer.** – *adj.* **opposing.**
opposite (o pŏ zit) *adj.* **1** being on the other side of, or at the other end of, a real or imaginary line or space. **2** facing in a directly different direction: *opposite sides of the coin.* **3** completely or diametrically different: *We have opposite ideas about how to bring up dogs.* – *adv.* in or into an opposite position: *I live opposite.* – *prep.* across from and facing.
opposition (o pŏ zi shŏn) *n.* the act of resisting or fighting against someone or something by force or argument.
oppress (ŏ **pres**) *vb.* **oppressing, oppressed 1** to govern with cruelty and injustice. **2** to weigh heavily upon: *Margaret was oppressed by her worries.* – *n.* **oppressor.**

oppression *n.* the state of suffering injustice.
oppressive *adj.* **1** cruel, tyrannical, and unjust. **2** (of the weather) hot and sultry.
opt (opt) *vb.* **opting, opted** to make a choice: *Owen opted to study law instead of medicine.* – *vb.*
opt out to choose or decide not to take part in something.
optician (op ti shăn) *n.* a person who makes and sells glasses and contact lenses.
optimism (**op** ti mi zĕm) *n.* a tendency to take a bright, hopeful view of things and expect the best possible outcome. – *n.* **optimist.** – *adj.* **optimistic.** – *adv.* **optimistically.**
option (**op** shŏn) *n.* an act of choosing: *You have two options – to speak or to remain silent.*
optional *adj.* not compulsory.
or (ör) *conj.* used to introduce: **1** alternatives: *red or pink or blue.* **2** a synonym or explanation: *a puppy or young dog.* **3** an afterthought: *She's laughing – or is she crying?* **4** the second part of an indirect question: *Ask her whether she thinks he'll come or not.* **5** because if not: *Run or you'll be late.* **6** and not: *never joins in or helps.* – **or else 1** otherwise. **2** (*colloquial*) expressing a threat or warning: *Give it to me or else!*
-or (-ŏr) *suffix* used to form words meaning the person or thing performing the action: *actor.*

● **-or** and **-our.** In the United States most *-our* words are spelled *-or*, but there are exceptions. The word *glamour* is spelled *-our* in both countries. In Britain the following words are spelled *-or*: *error, horror, languor, liquor, pallor, squalor, stupor, tenor, terror,* and *tremor.*

oracle (o rå kĕl) *n.* a holy place in ancient Greece or Rome where a god was believed to give advice through a priest or priestess.
oral (ō rål) *adj.* **1** spoken or verbal; not written. **2** of or used in the mouth: *oral hygiene.*
orange (o rinj) *n.* a round, juicy citrus fruit with a thick reddish-yellow skin. Orange trees are evergreens and grow in warm climates. – *adj.* orange-coloured or orange-flavoured.

Ripe fruit

Unripe fruit

Oranges grow on a tree with dark leaves. The fruit develops from the ovaries of white, fragrant flowers. The delicious juice of the orange is rich in vitamin C.

orang-utan (o̊ **rang** oo tan) or **orang-outang** (o̊ **rang** oo tang) *n.* a large ape with shaggy reddish-brown hair and long strong arms, found in the forests of Borneo and Sumatra.

●The name orang-utan comes from the Malay words meaning 'man of the woods'. Human beings are orang-utans' main enemies.

orator (o rå to̊r) *n.* a person who is skilled in persuading people through public speech.

orb (örb) *n.* anything in the shape of a globe, such as a star, the Sun, or a planet.

orbit (ör bit) *n.* the curved path in which a moon or spacecraft moves around a planet or star. – *vb.* **orbiting, orbited**.

orchard (ör chård) *n.* a garden or piece of land where fruit trees are grown.

orchestra (ör kis trå) *n.* a group of musicians who play a variety of different instruments together, led by a conductor.

orchid (ör kid) *n.* any of several types of plant which usually have brightly-coloured flowers.

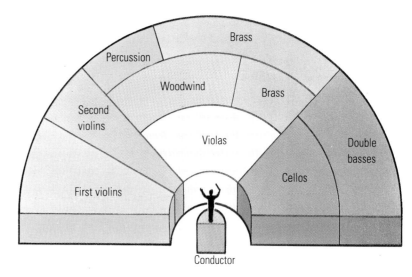

The musicians in an orchestra are arranged like this in a half-circle in front of the conductor. This arrangement produces the best blend of sound.

There are over 15,000 kinds of orchid. Most grow in warm, rainy forests.

— Early-purple orchid

The lower petal of the bee orchid resembles a bee which attracts a male insect to mate with it.

ordain (ör **dān**) *vb.* **ordaining, ordained** to make someone a priest, vicar, etc.

ordeal (ör dēl) *n.* a difficult or testing experience: *Jim described his ordeal in rescuing the horses from the fire.*

order (ör děr) *n.* **1** a state in which everything is in its proper place; tidiness. **2** an arrangement of objects according to importance, value, position, etc.: *The words in this dictionary appear in alphabetical order.* **3** a command, instruction, or direction. **4** a state of peace and harmony in society. **5** an instruction to a supplier, waiter, etc. to provide something. – *vb.* **ordering, ordered 1** to give a command to. **2** to instruct a waiter, etc. to supply something: *Can you order a hamburger and fries for me?* – *adj.* **ordered**. – **in order 1** in accordance with the rules. **2** suitable or appropriate: *Such behaviour just isn't in order.* **3** in the correct sequence. – **in order to** so as to be able to.

orderly *adj.* **1** in good order; well-arranged. **2** well-behaved; quiet. – *n.* **orderliness**.

ordinary (ör di nå ri) *adj.* usual; normal; unexceptional; familiar. – *adv.* **ordinarily**. – **out of the ordinary** unusual; strange.

ore (ör) *n.* a rock or mineral from which a metal or other valuable substance can be removed.

●**Oregon**. See Supplement, **USA**.

organ (ör gån) *n.* **1** a part of a body or plant which has a special function, for example a kidney or leaf. **2** a usually large musical instrument with a keyboard and pedals, in which sound is produced by air being forced through pipes of different lengths.

The word orchestra once meant 'dancing place' for in ancient Greek theatres dancers and musicians performed on a space between the audience and stage. When the Italians invented opera their theatres were arranged with the musicians in the same way. And so people began to use the word orchestra to describe the group of musicians.

organic (ör **gan** ik) *adj.* **1** of, relating to, or produced by a bodily organ or organs. **2** (of food, crops, etc.) produced without being treated with chemicals. – *adv.* **organically**.

organist *n.* a person who plays the organ.

organism (ör gå ni zêm) *n.* a living animal or plant.

organize or **organise** (ör gå nīz) *vb.* **organizing, organized 1** to give an orderly structure to: *Organize the books into a neat pile.* **2** to arrange, provide, or prepare: *Organize a meal.* – *adj.* **organized**.

organization or **organisation** *n.* **1** a group of people formed into a society, union, or especially business. **2** the act of organizing.

organizer or **organiser** *n.* someone or something that organizes.

orient (ö ri ênt) *n.* **the Orient** the countries in eastern Asia, as opposed to the **Occident**.

oriental *adj.* relating to the Orient; eastern.

orienteering (ö ri ên **tēr** ing) *n.* a sport in which contestants race over an unfamiliar, cross-country course, finding their way to check points using a map and compass.

origami (o ri **gä** mi) *n.* the originally Japanese art of folding paper into shapes and figures.

origin (o ri jin) *n.* a beginning or starting-point.

original *adj.* **1** existing from the beginning; earliest; first: *Who was the car's original owner?* **2** (of an idea) never thought of before; fresh or new. **3** (of a person) creative or inventive. – *n.* the first example of something which is copied, reproduced, or translated to produce others. – *n.* **originality**.

originate *vb.* **originating, originated** to bring or come into being; to start.

ornament (ör nå mênt) *n.* a small, usually decorative object.

ornate (ör **nāt**) *adj.* highly decorated.

ornithology (ör ni **thol** ô ji) *n.* the scientific study of birds. – *n.* **ornithologist**.

orphan (ör fån) *n.* a child who has lost both parents. – *vb.* **orphaning, orphaned**.

orphanage *n.* a home for orphans.

orthodox (ör thô doks) *adj.* believing in or conforming with generally accepted opinions.

Orthodox Church *n.* the eastern CHRISTIAN Church, separated from the western Church in the eleventh century, found especially in the Balkans and Russia.

orthopaedics (ör thô **pēd** iks) *n.* (*singular*) the branch of medicine concerned with curing diseases and correcting injuries of the bones.

Goldsmiths and silversmiths are renowned for producing marvellously ornate ornaments.

●**Orwell, George** (1903-50) was an English writer whose novels include *1984* and *Animal Farm*. His real name was Eric Arthur Blair.

-ory (-ô ri) *suffix* forming nouns meaning a place for: *dormitory*; *laboratory*.

●**Osaka** (ō sä kå) is JAPAN's second largest city.

oscillate (o si lāt) *vb.* **oscillating, oscillated** to swing backwards and forwards like a pendulum.

●**Oslo** is the capital of NORWAY.

osprey (os pri) *n.* **ospreys** a bird of prey.

Frightened ostriches do not hide their heads in the sand, as people used to think! Ostriches can live for 50 years or more.

ostrich (o strich) *n.* the largest living bird, able to run quickly but not fly.

other (**u** Thêr) *adj.* **1** remaining from a group when one or some have been specified already: *Close the other eye.* **2** different from the ones already mentioned: *He knows many other people.* **3** far or opposite: *He's on the other side of the garden.* – *pron.* another person or thing.

otherwise *conj.* or else; if not: *I already have the book, otherwise I'd have to borrow yours.* – *adv.* **1** in other respects: *He is good at languages but otherwise not very bright.* **2** in a different way: *Muriel couldn't act otherwise than as she did.*

●**Ottawa** is the capital of CANADA in the province of Ontario.

otter (**o** tĕr) *n.* a small fish-eating river animal with smooth dark fur, a slim body, and webbed feet with claws.

Ottoman (**o** tŏ mån) *adj.* of the Ottomans or the Ottoman Empire, which lasted from the 13th century until the end of the First WORLD WAR, and which was centred in what is now TURKEY.

ought (öt) *vb.* (*auxiliary*) used to express **1** duty or obligation: *You ought to help if you can.* **2** advisability: *You ought to see a doctor.* **3** expectation: *She ought to be here soon.* **4** shortcoming or failure: *He ought to have been here hours ago.*

ounce (owns) *n.* **1** a unit of weight equal to one sixteenth of a pound. **2** a fluid ounce.

our (owr) *adj.* of, belonging to, or done by us: *Have you met our children?*

ours *pron.* the one or ones belonging to us: *Those parcels are ours, not yours.*

ourselves *pron.* **1** the reflexive form of **us** and **we**: *We helped ourselves to cakes.* **2** used for emphasis: *We ourselves know nothing about that.*

-ous (-ůs) *suffix* forming adjectives meaning having the character, quality, or nature of: *marvellous; venomous.*

out (owt) *adv. & adj.* **1** away from the inside; not in or at a place: *Go out into the garden.* **2** not in your home or place of work: *I called but you were out.* **3** to or at an end; to or into a state of being completely finished, exhausted, extinct, etc.: *The milk has run out.* **4** aloud: *She cried out.* **5** in all directions from a central point: *Share out the sweets.* **6** (of a person batting in sport) no longer able to bat, for example because of having the ball caught by an opponent: *The star player was bowled out.* **7** removed; dislocated: *He has to have a tooth out.* **8** (of a flower) in bloom. **9** (of a tide) at the lowest level of water. – *vb.* **outing, outed** to become publicly known: *Murder will out.*

out- (owt-) **1** external; separate; from outside: *outpatient; outhouse.* **2** away from the inside, especially as a result: *output; outpouring.* **3** going away or out of; outward: *outdoor; outboard.*

outback (**owt** bak) *n.* isolated, remote areas of a country, especially Australia.

outboard (**owt** börd) *adj.* (of a motor or engine) portable and designed to be attached to the outside of a boat's stern.

outbreak (**owt** brāk) *n.* a sudden occurrence, usually of something unpleasant.

outburst (**owt** bûrst) *n.* **1** a sudden, violent expression of strong emotion, especially anger. **2** a sudden period of great activity.

outcry (**owt** krī) *n.* **outcries** a noisy protest: *The new tax caused a public outcry.*

outdoor (owt **dör**) *adj.* done or taking place in the open air: *Outdoor sport is healthy.*

outdoors *adv.* in or into the open air.

outer (**owt** ĕr) *adj.* **1** external; belonging to or for the outside. **2** further from the centre or middle: *The castle has an outer wall.*

The first **Ottomans** were nomadic Turkish tribes that migrated to the Middle East from Asia. The name comes from *Osman* or *Othman* who was the first sultan or ruler of the empire.

An Ottoman sipahi *or* cavalryman *(above). In return for military service he received a land grant from the government.*

A janissary (right), an elite soldier.

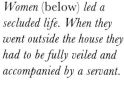

Women (below) led a secluded life. When they went outside the house they had to be fully veiled and accompanied by a servant.

The empire reached its greatest extent under Suleiman the Magnificent. Only his failure to capture Vienna in 1529 prevented an invasion of western Europe.

outer space *n.* space beyond the Earth's atmosphere.

outfit (**owt** fit) *n.* a set of clothes worn for a particular occasion. **2** (*colloquial*) a group of people working as a team.

outgoing (owt **gō** ing) *adj.* **1** friendly. **2** leaving: *The outgoing flight is full.*

outing (**owt** ing) *n.* a short pleasure trip.

outlandish (owt **lan** dish) *adj.* (of appearance, manner, habit, etc.) very strange; odd.

outlaw (**owt** lö) *n.* a criminal who is a fugitive from, or deprived of the protection of, the law. – *vb.* **outlawing, outlawed 1** to make someone an outlaw. **2** to forbid officially.

outlay (**owt** lā) *n.* money spent on something.

outlet (**owt** let) *n.* **1** a way or passage out, especially for water or steam. **2** a way of releasing or using energy, talents, etc.: *Sport is an outlet for her frustrations.*

outline (**owt** līn) *n.* **1** a line forming or marking the outer edge of an object. **2** a drawing with only the outer lines and no shading. **3** the main points without the details. – *vb.* **outlining, outlined 1** to draw the outline of. **2** to give a brief description of the main features of.

outlook (**owt** look) *n.* **1** a view from a particular place. **2** a person's mental attitude or point of view. **3** a prospect for the future: *The trade outlook for next year looks good.*

outlying (**owt** lī ing) *adj.* distant.

outpost (**owt** pōst) *n.* a remote settlement.

output (**owt** poot) *n.* **1** the amount produced. **2** information in either printed or coded form after it has been processed by a computer. – *vb.* **outputting, outputted** to produce information, power, etc. as output.

outrage (**owt** rāj) *n.* an act of great cruelty or violence. – *vb.* **outraging, outraged** to insult, shock, or anger greatly.

outrageous *adj.* **1** extravagant. **2** greatly offensive to accepted standards of decency, etc.

outright (owt **rīt**) *adv.* **1** completely: *She paid for it outright.* **2** immediately; at once: *The rabbit was killed outright.* **3** openly; honestly: *Ask outright.* – (**owt** rīt) *adj.* **1** complete: *I felt an outright fool.* **2** clear: *the outright winner.*

outset (**owt** set) *n.* a beginning or start.

outside (owt **sīd**) *n.* **1** the outer surface; the external parts. **2** everything that is not within the bounds or scope of something: *We must view the problem from the outside.* **3** the farthest limit. – (**owt** sīd) *adj.* **1** of, on, or near the outside. **2** not forming part of your regular job, etc.: *Riding is Lucy's outside interest.* **3** unlikely: *Ray has only an outside chance of winning.* – (owt **sīd**) *adv.* outdoors. – *prep.* **1** on or to the outside of. **2** beyond the limits of: *We live outside the city.*

outskirts (owt **skûrts**) *n.* (*plural*) the outer parts or area, especially of a town or city.

outspoken (owt **spō** kĕn) *adj.* saying exactly what you think; frank.

outstanding (owt **stand** ing) *adj.* **1** excellent; superior; remarkable: *He's an outstanding rider.* **2** not yet paid, done, etc.: *outstanding debts.*

outward (**owt** wård) *adj.* **1** on or towards the outside. **2** (of a journey) away from a place. **outwards** *adv.* (also **outward**) towards the outside; in an outward direction.

oval (**ō** văl) *adj.* shaped like an egg.

ovary (**ō** vă ri) *n.* **ovaries** either of the two female reproductive organs which produce eggs and hormones.

ovation (ō **vā** shăn) *n.* warm applause.

oven (**u** vĕn) *n.* an enclosed compartment for baking or roasting food, or drying clay, etc.

over (**ō** vĕr) *adv.* **1** above and across. **2** outwards and downwards: *Try to knock it over.* **3** across a space; to or on the other side: *Fly over from Australia.* **4** from one person, side, or condition to another: *We'll win them over.* **5** through, from beginning to end, usually with concentration: *Think it over thoroughly.* **6** again; in repetition: *Do it twice over.* **7** remaining: *There were two left over.* – *prep.* **1** in or to a position which is above or higher in place, importance, authority, value, number, etc. **2** above and from one side to another: *They flew over the sea.* **3** so as to cover: *His hair was flopping over his eyes.* **4** out and down from: *It fell over the edge.* **5** throughout the extent of: *Read over that page again.* **6** during: *Visit him sometime over the weekend.* **7** more than: *It happened over a year ago.* **8** concerning; about.

over- (**ō** vĕr-) *prefix* **1** excessively: *overconfident.* **2** above; in a higher position or authority: *overlord.* **3** across the surface; covering: *overcoat.* **4** down; away from an upright position: *overturn; overhang.*

overboard (**ō** vĕr börd) *adv.* over the side of a ship or boat into the water.

overcast (**ō** vĕr **käst**) *adv.* cloudy.

overcome (ō vĕr **kum**) *vb.* **overcoming, overcame** (ō vĕr **kām**), **overcome 1** to defeat; to succeed in a struggle against; to deal successfully with. **2** to affect strongly; to overwhelm: *The children were overcome with sleep.*

Ned Kelly, the outlaw, and his gang of bushrangers (bandits) roamed Australia staging holdups and raiding banks. He often wore home-made armour.

overdue (ō vẻr **dū**) *adj.* (of bills, work, etc.) not yet paid, delivered, etc. although the date for doing this has passed: *My rent is a week overdue.*

overgrown (ō vẻr **grōn**) *adj.* **1** (of a garden, etc.) dense with plants. **2** grown too large.

overhaul (ō vẻr **hȯl**) *vb.* **overhauling, overhauled** to examine carefully and repair.

overhead (ō vẻr **hed**) *adv. & adj.* directly above.

overlap (ō vẻr **lap**) *vb.* **overlapping, overlapped** (of two parts) to have one part partly covering the other.

overlook (ō vẻr **look**) *vb.* **overlooking, overlooked 1** to give a view of from a higher position. **2** to fail to see or notice. **3** to allow a mistake, crime, etc. to go unpunished.

overpower (ō vẻr **pow** ẻr) *vb.* **overpowering, overpowered 1** to defeat by greater strength. **2** to weaken or reduce to helplessness.

overseas (ō vẻr **sēz**) *adv.* abroad.

oversee (ō vẻr **sē**) *vb.* **overseeing, oversaw** (ō vẻr **sö**), **overseen** to supervise.

oversight (ō vẻr **sīt**) *n.* a mistake made through a failure to notice something.

overtake (ō vẻr **tāk**) *vb.* **overtaking, overtook** (ō vẻr **took**), **overtaken 1** (especially *British*) to catch up with and go past a car, a person, etc. moving in the same direction. **2** to draw level with and begin to do better than.

overtime (ō vẻr **tīm**) *n.* time spent working at a job beyond regular hours.

overture (ō vẻr **tūr**) *n.* an orchestral introduction to an opera or ballet.

overwhelm (ō vẻr **welm**) *vb.* **overwhelming, overwhelmed 1** to overpower; to defeat by superior force or numbers. **2** to supply or offer something in great amounts to: *We were overwhelmed with offers of help.* – *adj.* **overwhelming**.

ovum (**ō** vǔm) *n.* **ova** (**ō** vǎ) an egg-cell which, when fertilized, can develop into a new individual.

owe (ō) *vb.* **owing, owed 1** to have to pay money to someone: *Owen owes Olive £5.* **2** to feel required to give: *You owe me an explanation.*

owing *adj.* still to be paid; due. – **owing to** because of; on account of.

owl (owl) *n.* a bird of prey with a large broad head, flat face, large eyes, a short hooked beak, and a hooting cry, active at night.

owlet *n.* a young owl.

own (ōn) *adj.* belonging to or for oneself or itself: *my own sister.* – *pron.* one or something belonging to yourself or itself: *have a room of your own.* – *vb.* **owning, owned 1** to have as a possession: *I own the house.* **2** to admit or confess: *He owned up to the robbery.* – **on your own 1** alone. **2** without help: *Ann built the stable on her own.*

owner *n.* a person who owns something. – *n.* **ownership**.

ox (oks) *n.* **oxen** a bull used for pulling loads.

Oxbridge (**oks** brij) *n. & adj.* (*British*) (of or from) the universities of *Ox*ford and Cam*bridge* considered together.

● **Oxford** is a university city in central southern England. It is also an important industrial city.

oxide (**ok** sīd) *n.* a compound of oxygen and another element.

oxygen (**ok** si jẻn) *n.* a colourless, odourless gas (symbol **O**) which forms part of the air and water and which is essential to life.

● Humans and other land animals absorb this life-supporting gas from the air they breathe. Fish absorb dissolved oxygen from the water. Substances burn by combining with oxygen.

oxymoron (ok si **mö** ron) *n.* a figure of speech in which contradictory terms are used together: *the wisest fool in Christendom.*

oyster (**oi** stẻr) *n.* an edible shellfish which sometimes produces a pearl.

ozone (**ō** zōn) *n.* a type of oxygen with a powerful smell, used in bleaching, sterilizing water, and purifying air.

ozone-friendly *adj.* not containing chemicals thought to harm the ozone layer.

ozone layer *n.* the layer of ozone, high above the Earth's surface, that protects the Earth from harmful radiation from the Sun.

A plant (above) damaged by radiation. Harmful radiation from the Sun is normally filtered before it reaches Earth by a layer of ozone in the stratosphere. Near the South Pole a 'hole' has appeared caused by pollution.

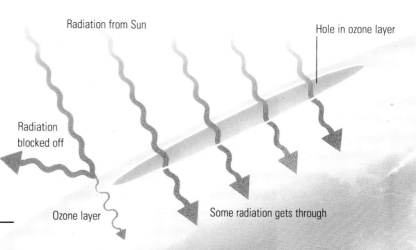

Radiation from Sun

Hole in ozone layer

Radiation blocked off

Ozone layer

Some radiation gets through

Pp

The letter *P*, like all the letters, has a long history. The earliest alphabets were taken and adapted by the Greeks. The Greek *beta*, when combined with the first letter, *aleph*, gives us the word alphabet.

The Greeks passed on their letters to the Romans who developed the alphabet we use today, although they used only capital letters. Small letters developed in the AD 700s.

ꟼ

An early form of the letter P, used in the Middle East over 3000 years ago.

Γ

This letter was taken by the Greeks and became pi.

P

Over the years different versions of the letter P have been developed.

pace (pās) *n.* **1** a single step. **2** the distance covered by one step. **3** rate of movement or progress: *He can't stand the pace.* – *vb.* **pacing, paced** to keep walking about in an anxious or impatient manner: *She paced the floor nervously.*

pacemaker *n.* an electronic device fitted next to the heart to regularize its beat.

Pacific (på **sif** ik) *adj.* of, belonging or relating to, the **Pacific Ocean**.

pacifist (**pa** si fist) *n.* someone who opposes war. – *n.* **pacifism**.

pack (pak) *n.* **1** things tied into a bundle for carrying; a rucksack. **2** a complete set of playing cards. **3** a troop of animals hunting together, for example dogs or wolves. – *vb.* **packing, packed 1** to put goods, clothes, etc. in boxes, suitcases, etc. for transport or travel. **2** to cram: *The hall was packed with people.* – *vb.* **pack up 1** to stop work, etc. **2** to put away in the proper place.

package (**pak** ij) *n.* something wrapped and secured with string, sticky tape, etc.; a parcel.

packet (**pak** it) *n.* a paper, cardboard, or plastic bag or container, with its contents: *She bought a packet of sweets from the shop.*

pact (pakt) *n.* an agreement reached between two or more opposing parties, states, etc.

pad (pad) *n.* **1** a thick soft piece of material used to cushion, protect, shape, or clean. **2** a leg-guard for a batsman or wicket keeper in cricket. **3** a quantity of sheets of paper fixed together into a block. **4** (also **launch pad**) a rocket-launching platform. **5** the fleshy underside of an animal's paw. – *vb.* **padding, padded** to fill with layers of soft material.

paddle[1] (**pa** dĕl) *vb.* **paddling, paddled** to walk about barefoot in shallow water.

paddle[2] (**pa** dĕl) *n.* a short light oar with a blade at one or both ends, used to move and steer a canoe, etc. – *vb.* **paddling, paddled** to move a canoe, etc. with paddles.

paddle wheel *n.* a large engine-driven wheel at the side or back of a ship which moves the ship through the water as it turns.

paddock (**pa** dŏk) *n.* a small field for a horse.

paddy (**pa** di) *n.* **paddies** (also **paddy field**) a field in which rice is grown.

padlock (**pad** lok) *n.* a detachable lock with a U-shaped bar that can be passed through a ring or chain and locked in position.

pagan (**pā** găn) *adj.* of or following a religion in which a number of gods are worshipped.

page (pāj) *n.* one side of one of the sheets of paper in a book, magazine, etc.

pageant (**pa** jănt) *n.* a series of dramatic scenes, usually depicting historical events; any colourful spectacle. – *n.* **pageantry**.

pagoda (på **gō** då) *n.* an oriental temple, in the form of a tall tower with each storey having its own projecting roof.

The roof of each storey of a pagoda curves upwards. In China pagodas usually have an odd number of storeys and are octagonal; in Japan they usually have only five storeys and are square.

paid. See **pay**.

pail (pāl) *n.* **1** a bucket. **2** the amount contained in a bucket.

pain (pān) *n.* **1** physical or emotional suffering. **2** (in *plural*) trouble taken or efforts made in doing something: *He took great pains with his appearance.*
painful *adj.* causing pain: *a painful injury.*
painstaking *adj.* conscientious and thorough.

●**Paine, Thomas** (1737-1809) was an English-born American writer (*The Rights of Man*) who supported the FRENCH REVOLUTION and fought in the American War of Independence.

paint (pānt) *n.* coloured liquid used to decorate buildings or create pictures. – *vb.* **painting, painted 1** to apply a coat of paint to walls, woodwork, etc. **2** to make pictures using paint.
painter *n.* **1** a person who decorates houses. **2** an artist who paints pictures.
painting *n.* **1** the art of creating pictures in paint. **2** a painted picture.

Prehistoric art: early artists painted animals, like this bison, deep inside their caves.

●Stone Age hunters may have used painting as magic. They drew wounded beasts on their cave walls, perhaps with the idea that such pictures would help them kill real animals on their next hunt. In the Middle Ages most artists worked for the Church. Their paintings showed scenes from the Bible to help people who could not read to understand the teachings of the Bible. Later in Europe, princes and rich merchants paid artists to paint pictures to decorate their homes. More recently artists have experimented with new ideas. Modern painters such as PICASSO, have produced pictures that concentrate on basic shapes and patterns and therefore appear more abstract.

●**Painted Desert** is a 20,000 sq. km area of plateau country in Arizona. It is noted for its brilliant-coloured rocks.

pair (pār) *n.* **1** a set of two identical or corresponding things, e.g. shoes or gloves, intended for use together. **2** something consisting of two joined, corresponding parts: *a pair of scissors*, etc. – **in pairs** in twos.

●**Pakistan.** See Supplement, **Countries.**

pal (pal) *n.* (*colloquial*) a friend.
palace (**pa** lås) *n.* the official residence of a sovereign, bishop, archbishop, or president.
palate (**pa** låt) *n.* the roof of the mouth.
pale (pāl) *adj.* **1** (of a person, face, etc.) having less colour than normal, for example from illness or fear. **2** (of a colour) closer to white than black; light: *I like the colour pale green.*
palette (**pa** lět) *n.* a hand-held board with a thumb hole, on which an artist mixes colours.
palindrome (**pa** lin drōm) *n.* a word or phrase that reads the same backwards and forwards, e.g. *eye, Hannah*, or *Able was I ere I saw Elba.*
palisade (**pa** li sād) *n.* a tall fence of pointed wooden stakes fixed edge to edge.

●**Palladio, Andrea** (1508-80) was an Italian architect.

palm¹ (päm) *n.* the inner surface of the hand between the wrist and the fingers.
palm² (päm) *n.* a tree usually with a single trunk and a cluster of long blade-like leaves.
palomino (pa lō **mē** nō) *n.* **palominos** a cream horse with a white tail and mane.
palpitate (**pal** pi tāt) *vb.* **palpitating, palpitated** (of the heart) to beat rapidly. – *n.* **palpitation.**
pamper (**pam** pěr) *vb.* **pampering, pampered** to spoil.
pamphlet (**pam** flět) *n.* a booklet or leaflet.
pan (pan) *n.* a metal pot used for cooking.
panama (pa nåma) *n.* (also **panama hat**) a lightweight hat for men, made from the plaited leaves of a palm-like Central American tree.

●**Panama.** See Supplement, **Countries.**

The coconut palm (right) *can grow as high as 30m. Dates are the fruit of the date palm. Most palms grow in warm climates.*

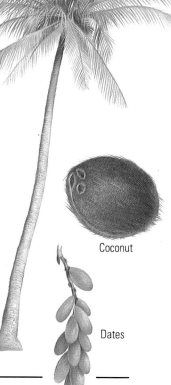

Coconut

Dates

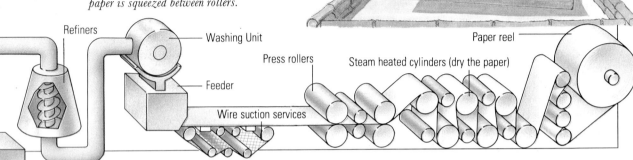

Before **paper** was invented, people wrote on clay tablets or animal skins. The Egyptians wrote on a kind of paper made from papyrus reed (from which we get the name paper).

Paper-making was invented during the Chinese Han dynasty (202 BC-AD 220). Frames of hemp pulp were allowed to dry in the sun.

Modern paper-making: A barking drum debarks specially treated logs to make pulp, which is made into a thin slurry with water. The slurry passes onto an endless web of wire mesh; the water is sucked out and the web of paper is squeezed between rollers.

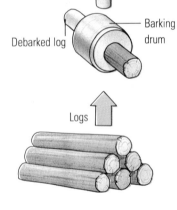

Refiners · Washing Unit · Press rollers · Steam heated cylinders (dry the paper) · Paper reel · Feeder · Wire suction services · Chipper · Barking drum · Debarked log · Logs

● **Panama Canal** This canal crosses Panama and is used by ships as a short cut from the PACIFIC to the ATLANTIC OCEAN. Completed in 1914, it is 81.6 km long.

pancake (**pan** kāk) *n.* a round of thin batter cooked on both sides in a frying-pan.

pancreas (**pang** kri ås) *n.* a gland lying behind the stomach, that helps with digestion.

panda (**pan** då) *n.* (also **giant panda**) a large black and white bear-like animal of TIBET and CHINA.

pandemonium (pan dě **mō** ni ům) *n.* noise, chaos, and confusion.

pander (**pan** děr) *vb.* **pandering, pandered** to indulge or gratify someone: *She pandered to his taste for sweet things.*

pane (pān) *n.* a sheet of glass in a window, etc.

panel (**pa** něl) *n.* **1** a rectangular wooden board forming a section of a wall or door. **2** any of the metal sections forming the bodywork of a vehicle. **3** a board bearing the instruments and dials for controlling an aircraft, etc. **4** a team of people selected to judge a contest, etc.

pang (pang) *n.* a painfully acute feeling of hunger, remorse, etc.: *She felt a pang of regret.*

panic (**pa** nik) *n.* a sudden overpowering fear. *– vb.* **panicking, panicked** to feel panic.

panorama (pa nő **rä** må) *n.* an open and all-round view, for example of a landscape. *– adj.* **panoramic**.

● **Pankhurst, Emmeline** (1858-1928) was an English suffragette who helped to obtain the vote for British women.

pansy (**pan** zi) *n.* **pansies** a small garden plant with broad-petalled flowers of many colours.

pant (pant) *vb.* **panting, panted** to breathe in gasps as a result of exertion.

panther (**pan** thěr) *n.* **1** the name usually given to a black leopard. **2** (*North American*) a puma.

pantomime (**pan** tŏ mīm) *n.* a Christmas entertainment, usually based on a popular fairy tale, with songs, comedy acts, etc.

pants (pants) *n.* (*plural*) **1** an undergarment worn over the bottom, with holes for the legs. **2** (*North American*) trousers.

papal (**pā** pål) *adj.* of, or relating to, the pope.

paper (**pā** pěr) *n.* **1** a material manufactured in thin sheets from wood, rags, etc., used for writing and printing on, wrapping things, etc. a newspaper. **3** a set of questions on a certain subject for a written examination. **4** (in *plural*) personal documents, for example your passport. *– vb.* **papering, papered** to decorate with wallpaper.

paper clip *n.* a metal clip formed from bent wire, for holding papers together.

papier-mâché (pa pi ā **ma** shā) *n.* a light material consisting of pulped paper mixed with glue and sometimes other substances, and moulded into shape while wet.

PRONUNCIATION GUIDE	
fat **a**	all **ö**
fate **ā**	foot **oo**
fast **ä**	moon **ōo**
among **å**	boy **oi**
met **e**	house **ow**
mean **ē**	demon **ŏ**
silent **ě**	thing **th**
loch **hh**	this **Th**
fin **i**	but **u**
line **ī**	mute **ū**
quick **kw**	fur **û**
got **o**	brochure **ů**
note **ō**	vision **zh**

papoose (på **pōōs**) *n.* a Native American baby.

● **Papua-New Guinea**. See Supplement, **Countries**.

papyrus (på **pī** rŭs) *n.* **papyri** (på **pī** rī) or **papyruses** a tall water plant native to North Africa used by the ancient Egyptians, Greeks, and Romans to make a paper-like material.

parable (**pa** rå bĕl) *n.* a story whose purpose is to make a moral or religious lesson.

parachute (**pa** rå shōōt) *n.* an umbrella-like apparatus that slows the fall of a person dropped from an aircraft. – *vb.* **parachuting, parachuted** to drop by parachute. – *n.* **parachutist**.

parade (på **rād**) *n.* a ceremonial procession of people, vehicles, etc.

paradox (**pa** rå doks) *n.* a statement that seems to contradict itself, for example *'More haste, less speed'*. – *adj.* **paradoxical**.

paraffin (**pa** rå fin) *n.* a fuel oil obtained from petroleum or coal and used in aircraft, etc.

paragraph (**pa** rå gräf) *n.* a section of a piece of writing, starting on a fresh line, and dealing with a distinct point or idea.

● **Paraguay**. See Supplement, **Countries**.

parakeet (**pa** rå kēt) *n.* a small parrot.

parallel (**pa** rå lel) *adj.* **1** (of lines) being at every point the same distance apart. **2** similar; exactly equivalent; corresponding. – *adv.* alongside and at an unvarying distance from: *The railway runs parallel to the road.* – *vb.* **paralleling, paralleled** to equal; to correspond to or be equivalent to. **parallelogram** *n.* a four-sided shape with opposite sides parallel to each other.

paralyse (**pa** rå līz) *vb.* **paralysing, paralysed 1** to affect the body, or part of the body, so that it cannot move or feel. **2** to disrupt: *The strike has paralysed the whole country.* **paralysis** (på **ral** i sis) *n.* loss of the power of motion or of sensation in any part of the body.

paramedic (pa rå **med** ik) *n.* a person who does medical work but who is not a doctor, surgeon, or nurse.

paramount (**pa** rå mownt) *adj.* supreme.

parapet (**pa** rå pit) *n.* a low wall along the edge of a bridge, balcony, etc.

paraphrase (**pa** rå frāz) *vb.* **paraphrasing, paraphrased** to express in other words.

parasite (**pa** rå sīt) *n.* an animal or plant that lives on, and obtains its nourishment from, another.

parasol (**pa** rå sol) *n.* a sunshade.

paratroops (**pa** rå trōōps) *n.* (*plural*) troops trained to parachute into enemy territory. **paratrooper** *n.* a member of the paratroops.

parcel (**pär** sĕl) *n.* something wrapped in paper, etc. and secured with string or sticky tape. – *vb.* **parcelling, parcelled 1** to wrap up in a parcel. **2** to divide into portions and share out: *She parcelled out the rations amongst the group.*

parch (pärch) *vb.* **parching, parched** to dry up; to deprive soil, plants, etc. of water.

parchment (pärch mĕnt) *n.* a material formerly used for binding books and for writing on, made from goat-, calf-, or sheepskin.

pardon (pär dŏn) *vb.* **pardoning, pardoned 1** to forgive or excuse someone for a fault or offence. **2** to cancel the punishment of. – *n.* **1** forgiveness. **2** the cancellation of a punishment. – *adj.* **pardonable**.

parent (**pā** rĕnt) *n.* a father or mother. – *adj.* **parental** (på **ren** tål). – *n.* **parenthood**.

parenthesis (på **ren** thĕ sis) *n.* **parentheses** (på **ren** thĕ sēz) **1** a word or phrase inserted into a sentence as a comment, usually marked off by brackets or dashes, for example: *She declined – for she hated coffee – and asked instead for tea.* **2** (in *plural*) a pair of round brackets used to enclose such a comment.

● **Paris[1]** is the capital of FRANCE through which flows the river Seine. It contains many famous landmarks: the Eiffel Tower, the cathedral of Notre Dame, the Arc de Triomphe, and the Louvre museum (once a palace). Paris is a cultural centre with a university, theatres, and art galleries. It is also a major industrial area.

● **Paris[2]** was a Trojan prince whose abduction of HELEN of Sparta caused the Trojan War.

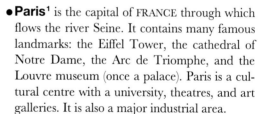
Mistletoe

Dodder

Mistletoe is really a semi-parasite; it takes some food from its host but also makes its own by photosynthesis. The dodder is a true parasite, depending solely on its host.

Paris's most famous landmark: the 300-metre tall Eiffel Tower built by Gustave Eiffel in 1889 for the Paris Exposition.

The much endangered parrot family includes these colourful macaws from South America. Their hooked beaks can open a brazil nut with ease – and cut off a finger just as easily!

PARLIAMENTS BY OTHER NAMES

Althing	Iceland
Congress	USA
Cortes	Spain
Dáil	Ireland
Diet	Japan
Eduskunta	Finland
Folketing	Denmark
Knesset	Israel
Majlis	Iran
Riksdag	Sweden
States General	Netherlands
Storting	Norway

parish (**pa** rish) *n.* a district or area served by its own church and priest or minister.

park (pärk) *n.* **1** an area in a town with grass and trees, reserved for the public. **2** an area of land kept as a nature reserve: *We visited the wild-life park.* – *vb.* **parking, parked** to manoeuvre into position and leave a vehicle temporarily.
parking-lot *n.* (*North American*) a car park.
parking-meter *n.* a coin-operated meter in the street beside which a car may be parked for a limited period.

●**Parker, Charlie** (1920-55) was an American jazz saxophonist and composer.

●**Parker, Dorothy** (1893-1967) was an American poet and satirical short-story writer.

parliament (**pär** lå mėnt) *n.* the law-making assembly of some nations; **Parliament** in Britain, the House of Commons and House of Lords.
parliamentary (pär lå **men** tå ri) *adj.* of, relating to, or issued by, a parliament.

●**Parnell, Charles Stewart** (1846-91) was an Irish nationalist leader and an MP.

parody (**pa** rŏ di) *n.* **parodies** a comic or satirical imitation of a work, or the style, of a particular writer, composer, etc.
parole (på **rōl**) *n.* the release of a prisoner before the end of his or her sentence, on promise of good behaviour: *on parole.*
parrot (**pa** rŏt) *n.* a tropical, especially South American, bird with a hooked beak and colourful plumage.
parsley (**pärs** li) *n.* a plant with curled feathery leaves used as a flavouring in cooking.
parsnip (**pär** snip) *n.* a root vegetable.
part (pärt) *n.* **1** a portion, piece, or bit; some but not all of something. **2** a section of a book; any of the episodes of a story broadcast as a serial. **3** a performer's role in a play, opera, etc.: *He played the part of Macduff in Shakespeare's* Macbeth. – *vb.* **parting, parted** to separate: *She parted the curtains and peeped out.*
parting *n.* **1** the act of taking leave or separating. **2** a line of exposed scalp dividing hair brushed in opposite directions.
partly *adv.* to a certain extent; not completely.

●**Parthenon** a temple on the Acropolis in ATHENS, built in the 5th century BC.

partial (**pär** shål) *adj.* **1** incomplete; in part only. **2** favouring one side or person unfairly; biased.
participate (pär **tis** i pāt) *vb.* **participating, participated** to take part or be involved. – *n.* **participant**. – *n.* **participation**.
participle (**pär** ti si pėl) *n.* a word formed from a verb and used as an adjective or to form different tenses of a verb. The **present participle** in English is formed with **-ing** (*We heard cheering news*; *I was going*). The **past participle** is formed with **-ed, -t,** or **-en** (*The biscuits were broken*; *The cakes will be burnt*).
particle (**pär** ti kėl) *n.* a tiny unit of matter such as a molecule, atom, or electron; a tiny piece.
particular (pär **tik** ū lår) *adj.* **1** specific; single; individually known or referred to: *She was looking for a particular colour.* **2** especial: *He took particular care.* **3** difficult to satisfy; fastidious: *My mother is very particular about hygiene.* – *n.* (in *plural*) personal details: *He took down her particulars.* – **in particular** especially.
particularly *adv.* **1** more than usually: *The food was particularly good.* **2** specifically; especially: *She particularly hates board games.*
partition (pär **ti** shŏn) *n.* a screen or thin wall dividing a room.

partner (pärt nẻr) *n.* **1** one of two or more people jointly owning or running a business. **2** the person you are dancing with; the person who is on the same side as you in a game of, for example tennis. – *vb.* **partnering, partnered** to act as a partner to.
partnership *n.* a business jointly owned or run by two or more people.

partridge (pär trij) *n.* a grey-and-brown game bird.

party (pär ti) *n.* **parties 1** a social event often with invited guests, for enjoyment or celebration. **2** a group of people involved in a certain activity together: *They came across a party of French tourists in the church.* **3** a national organization of people united by a common political aim: *I voted for the Labour Party.*

pass (päs) *vb.* **passing, passed 1** to come alongside and move beyond: *I passed her on the stairs.* **2** to run, flow, move: *Blood passes through our veins.* **3** to achieve the required standard in a test: *I passed my driving test first time.* **4** (of time) to go by; to use up time in some activity: *The three hours allowed for the exam passed slowly.* **5** to hand around or transfer; to circulate: *Pass the sugar round, please.* **6** in sport, to throw or kick the ball to another player in your team. – *n.* **1** a route through a gap in a mountain range. **2** an official card or document permitting someone to enter somewhere, etc. – *vb.* **pass away** to die. – *vb.* **pass out** to faint.
passable *adj.* **1** barely adequate: *He gave a passable imitation of the sound made by a chimpanzee.* **2** (of a road, etc.) able to be travelled along: *This road is not passable in the winter because of the snow.* – *adv.* **passably**.
passing *adj.* lasting only briefly; casual.

passage (pa sij) *n.* **1** (also **passageway**) a route through; a corridor, narrow street, or channel. **2** a section of a book or of music.

passenger (pa sẻn jẻr) *n.* a traveller in a vehicle driven by someone else.

passion (pa shỏn) *n.* **1** a violent emotion, for example hate, anger, or envy. **2** great enthusiasm: *He has a passion for old churches.*
passionate *adj.* strongly emotional; keen.

Passover (pås ō vẻr) *n.* an eight-day Jewish festival held in the spring, celebrating the sparing of the first-born Israelite children, and the freeing of the Israelites from Egypt.

passport (päs pört) *n.* an official document issued by the government, giving proof of the holder's identity and nationality.

past (päst) *adj.* **1** of a time before the present; of an earlier time. **2** over; finished: *The days when I could run that fast are past.* – *prep.* **1** up to and beyond: *She went past me.* **2** after in time or age: *It's ten past three.* – *adv.* so as to pass by: *Go past.* – *n.* the time before the present.

paste (päst) *n.* a stiff moist mixture usually of powder and water, for example a mixture of flour and water used as a glue.

pastel (pas tẻl) *n.* a chalk-like crayon. – *adj.* (of colours) delicately pale.

● **Pasteur, Louis** (1822-95) was a French scientist who founded the science of microbiology.

pasteurize or **pasteurise** (päs chẻ rīz) *vb.* **pasteurizing, pasteurized** to kill bacteria in milk, beer, etc. by a special heating process. – *n.* **pasteurization**.

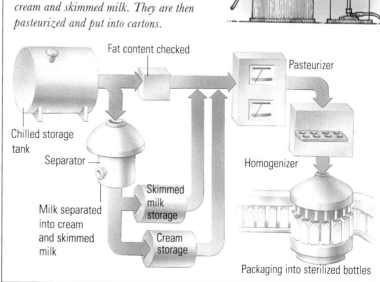

Louis **Pasteur** gave his name to the process he invented for killing germs in liquids such as milk and wine – *pasteurization*.

In pasteuriztion special equipment heats milk for a few minutes to kill off dangerous bacteria which could cause tuberculosis. The machine shown has a separator which separates milk into cream and skimmed milk. They are then pasteurized and put into cartons.

Pasteur showed, using a swan-necked flask (below), that food went bad because of airborne germs.

Fat content checked
Pasteurizer
Chilled storage tank
Separator
Homogenizer
Milk separated into cream and skimmed milk
Skimmed milk storage
Cream storage
Packaging into sterilized bottles

pastime (päs tīm) *n.* a hobby.

pastor (päs tŏr) *n.* a member of the clergy.

pastry (pā stri) *n.* **pastries** dough made with flour, fat, and water, used for pie-crusts.

pasture (päs chŭr) *n.* an area of grassland suitable for the grazing of cattle, etc.

pat (pat) *vb.* **patting, patted** to strike lightly or affectionately with the palm of your hand.

Saint Patrick, the patron saint of Ireland, was born in Britain but died in Ireland in 461 at the age of 76.

PATRON SAINTS		
St Andrew	Scotland	30 Nov.
St Anthony	Lost articles	13 June
St Cecilia	Music	22 Nov.
St Christopher	Travellers	25 July
St David	Wales	1 March
St Denis	France	9 Oct.
St George	England	23 April
St Luke	Doctors	18 Oct.
St Peter	Fishermen	29 June
St Valentine	Sweethearts	14 Feb.

patch (pach) *n.* **1** a piece of material sewn or glued on to cover a hole or reinforce a worn part. **2** a plot of earth: *She planted carrots in her vegetable patch.* – *vb.* **patching, patched** to mend a hole or garment by sewing patches on. **patchwork** *n.* needlework done by sewing together pieces of patterned fabric.

patella (på tel å) *n.* **patellae** (på tel ē) or **patellas** the knee-cap.

patent (pā tĕnt) or (pa tĕnt) *n.* an official licence from the government granting a company the right to be the only manufacturers allowed to make and sell a particular article. – *vb.* **patenting, patented**.

paternal (på tûr nål) *adj.* of, or like, a father.

path (päth) *n.* (also **pathway**) a track for walking.

pathetic (på thet ik) *adj.* moving to pity; touching or pitiful. – *adv.* **pathetically**.

patience (pā shĕns) *n.* **1** the ability to endure delay, trouble, pain, or hardship calmly. **2** a solo card game. **patient** *adj.* having or showing patience. – *n.* a person who is being treated by, or is registered with, a doctor, dentist, etc. – *adv.* **patiently**.

patriarch (pā tri ärk) or (pa tri ärk) *n.* the male head of a family or tribe.

●**Patrick, Saint** (5th century) is the patron saint of IRELAND. His feast day is 17 March.

patriot (pa tri ŏt) or (pā tri ŏt) *n.* someone who loves and serves his or her country devotedly.

patrol (på trōl) *vb.* **patrolling, patrolled** to make a regular systematic tour of an area to see that there is no trouble. – *n.* a group of people performing this duty.

patron (pā trŏn) *n.* **1** a person who gives financial support, for example to an artist or charity. **2** a regular customer of a shop, etc. **patron saint** *n.* the guardian saint of a country, profession, craft, etc. See also **saints**.

patter (pa tĕr) *vb.* **pattering, pattered** (of rain, footsteps, etc.) to make a light rapid tapping noise.

pattern (pa tĕrn) *n.* **1** a model, guide, or set of instructions for making something. **2** a decorative design, on wallpaper or fabric, etc. **patterned** *adj.* having a decorative design.

●**Paul, Saint** (died AD 64) was a Christian missionary and the main author of Epistles in the NEW TESTAMENT. His feast day is 29 June.

●**Pauling, Linus** (1901-) is an American chemist noted for his opposition to nuclear tests.

paunch (pönch) *n.* a protruding belly.

pauper (pö pĕr) *n.* a poor person.

pause (pöz) *n.* usually a short break in some activity, etc. – *vb.* **pausing, paused**.

pave (pāv) *vb.* **paving, paved** to surface a street, path, etc. with stone slabs, cobbles, etc.

pavement (pāv mĕnt) *n.* a raised paved footpath edging a road, etc.

pavilion (på vil i ŏn) *n.* **1** a building in a sports ground in which players change their clothes and store equipment. **2** a temporary building in which to display exhibits at a trade fair, etc.

paw (pö) *n.* the foot of a four-legged mammal.

pawn¹ (pön) *vb.* **pawning, pawned** to deposit an article of value with a pawnbroker as a pledge for a sum of money borrowed. **pawnbroker** *n.* a person who lends money in exchange for pawned articles.

pawn² (pön) *n.* a chess piece of lowest value.

pay (pā) *vb.* **paying, paid 1** to give money to someone in exchange for goods, services, etc. **2** to settle a bill, debt, etc. **3** to give wages or salary to an employee. **4** to make a profit, or make as profit: *This business doesn't pay.* – *n.* money given or received for work, etc.; wages; salary. – *n.* **payer**. – *vb.* **pay up** to pay what is due, especially reluctantly.

payment *n.* **1** a sum of money paid. **2** the act of paying or process of being paid.

pea (pē) *n.* the round green seed of a climbing plant, growing in pods and eaten as a vegetable.

peace (pēs) *n.* **1** freedom from war; a treaty or agreement ending a war. **2** quietness or calm; freedom from mental agitation; serenity: *At last she had found peace of mind.*

peaceful *adj.* calm and quiet; serene.

peace offering *n.* something offered to end a quarrel or as an apology.

peach (pēch) *n.* a round fruit with velvety yellowish-pink skin, juicy yellow flesh, and a large stone.

peacock (**pē** kok) *n.* a bird of the pheasant family, the male of which has magnificent tail feathers that it can spread out like a fan.

peahen *n.* a female peacock.

A peacock attracts its mates by spreading out its spectacular tail. It looks very proud of itself – 'as proud as a peacock'!

peak (pēk) *n.* **1** a pointed summit; the top of a mountain or hill. **2** a time of maximum use, for example in consumer use: *Much electricity is consumed at peak periods.* **3** the front part of a cap that sticks out over the face. – *vb.* **peaking, peaked** to reach the height of power or popularity: *The peak of his fame was in the 1960s.*

Peanuts, sometimes known as groundnuts, grow underground. They are covered by red, papery skin and contained in wrinkled yellowish pods.

peal (pēl) *n.* **1** the ringing of a bell or set of bells, each with a different note. **2** a burst of noise: *They heard peals of laughter.*

peanut (**pē** nut) *n.* an edible nut that ripens underground in a pod-like shell.

pear (pār) *n.* a fruit with white juicy flesh.

pearl (pûrl) *n.* a bead of hard bluish-white material formed by an oyster inside its shell, prized as a gem; an imitation of this. – *adj.* like a pearl in colour or shape.

● **Pearl Harbor** was a United States naval base in Hawaii which was attacked by the Japanese on 7 December 1941, thus bringing America into the Second WORLD WAR.

● **Peary, Robert** (1856-1920) was an American explorer who claimed to have been the first to reach the NORTH POLE in 1909.

peasant (**pe** zănt) *n.* in poor agricultural societies, a farm worker or small farmer.

peat (pēt) *n.* a material consisting of partly-rotted vegetable matter found in bogs and hilly areas, and used dried as a fuel.

pebble (**pe** běl) *n.* a small stone worn round and smooth by water.

peck (pek) *vb.* **pecking, pecked 1** to strike, nip, or pick up with the beak: *The hen pecked the corn* **2** to kiss quickly: *He pecked her on the cheek.*

PRONUNCIATION GUIDE	
fat **a**	all **ö**
fate **ā**	foot **oo**
fast **ä**	moon **ōō**
among **å**	boy **oi**
met **e**	house **ow**
mean **ē**	demon **ŏ**
silent **ė**	thing **th**
loch **hh**	this **Th**
fin **i**	but **u**
line **ī**	mute **ū**
quick **kw**	fur **û**
got **o**	brochure **ů**
note **ō**	vision **zh**

peckish *adj.* (*colloquial*) rather hungry.

peculiar (pi **kū** li år) *adj.* **1** strange; odd. **2** belonging exclusively or typically to: *This habit is peculiar to snails.*

peculiarity (pi kū li **a** ri ti) *n.* **peculiarities** a distinctive feature, characteristic, or trait.

pedal (**pe** dål) *n.* a lever operated by the foot, for example on a machine, vehicle, or musical instrument. – *vb.* **pedalling, pedalled** to operate by means of a pedal.

Bicycle pedals are linked to the back wheel with a chain. Pushing the pedals turns the back wheel, which moves the bicycle forwards.

peddle (**pe** děl) *vb.* **peddling, peddled** to go from place to place selling small goods.

pedestal (**pe** di stål) *n.* the base on which a statue or column is mounted.

pedestrian (på **des** tri ån) *n.* a person travelling on foot, especially in a street.

pedigree (**pe** di grē) *n.* a person or animal's line of descent; a family tree. – *adj.* (of an animal) pure-bred.

peel (pēl) *vb.* **peeling, peeled 1** to strip the skin or rind off a fruit or vegetable. **2** (of skin, paint, etc.) to flake off in patches. – *n.* the rind of fruit.

peep¹ (pēp) *vb.* **peeping, peeped 1** to look quickly. **2** to emerge briefly or partially: *The sun peeped from behind the clouds.*

peep² (pēp) *n.* the faint high-pitched cry of a baby bird; a cheep.

peer¹ (per) *n.* **1** a member of the nobility, in Britain, a duke, marquess, earl, viscount, or baron. **2** someone who is your equal in age, rank, etc.

peerage *n.* the title or rank of a peer.

peer² (pēr) *vb.* **peering, peered** to look hard at something.

peg (peg) *n.* **1** a coat hook fixed to a wall, etc. **2** a wooden or plastic clip for fastening washed clothes to a line to dry; a clothes peg. – **off the peg** (of clothes) ready to wear; ready-made.

pejorative (pi **jo** rå tiv) *adj.* (of an expression) critical and disapproving, uncomplimentary.

Pekinese (pē ki **nēz**) or **Pekingese** (pē ki **nēz**) or (pē king **ēz**) *n.* a small, short-legged, silky-coated dog, originally a Chinese breed.

● **Peking**. See **Beijing**.

pelican (**pe** li kån) *n.* **pelican** or **pelicans** a large water bird with a pouched beak for holding fish.

pellet (**pe** lit) *n.* a small ball of material, for example paper, lead etc.

pell-mell (pel **mel**) *adv.* in confused haste.

pelt¹ (pelt) *vb.* **pelting, pelted 1** to throw violently: *He was pelted with stones.* **2** (of rain, hail, etc.) to fall fast and heavily.

pelt² (pelt) *n.* the skin of a dead animal, especially with the fur still on it.

pelvis (**pel** vis) *n.* the bony structure into which the base of the spine fits, enclosing the bowels, organs of reproduction, etc. – *adj.* **pelvic**.

pen¹ (pen) *n.* a small enclosure for animals. – *vb.* **penning, penned** to enclose in a pen.

pen² (pen) *n.* a writing instrument that uses ink.

penknife *n.* a pocket knife.

penalty (**pe** nål ti) *n.* **penalties** a punishment or disadvantage for wrongdoing, breaking a contract or rule, etc.

pencil (**pen** sil) *n.* an instrument used for writing and drawing, consisting of a wooden part containing a stick of graphite or other material.

pendant (**pen** dånt) *n.* an ornament suspended from a neck chain, necklace, bracelet, etc.

pendulum (**pen** dū lům) *n.* any weight hung from a fixed point so as to swing freely, for example the swinging weight that regulates the movement of a clock.

● Each swing of a pendulum takes the same amount of time, no matter whether the swing is big or small. This makes pendulums useful for keeping time in clocks.

A pendulum at the top of its swing has potential energy stored in it. Gravity makes it swing, work is done, and potential energy becomes kinetic energy.

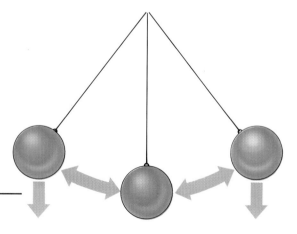

penetrate (pe nĕ trāt) *vb.* **penetrating, penetrated** to find a way in; to enter, especially with difficulty. – *n.* **penetrability**.
penetrating *adj.* **1** (of a voice) loud and clear; strident; carrying. **2** (of a mind) acute; discerning: *Her penetrating mind grasped the problem immediately.*
penguin (**peng** gwin) *n.* a black and white sea bird of the Antarctic and Southern Hemisphere, with webbed feet and wings adapted as flippers for swimming.

Rockhopper
Adelie
King
Emperor penguin

Penguins are swimming birds. They cannot fly. There are 18 different types of penguin.

penicillin (pe ni **sil** in) *n.* an antibiotic taken from moulds, used to treat infection.
peninsula (pĕ **nin** sū lå) *n.* a piece of land almost surrounded by water: *Italy is a peninsula.*
penis (**pē** nis) *n.* the male organ used for sexual intercourse.

●**Penn, William** (1644-1718) was an English QUAKER leader, founder of Pennsylvania.

pennant (pe nånt) *n.* a small triangular flag, used on ships for identification or for signalling.

●**Pennsylvania**. See Supplement, **USA**.

penny (pe ni) *n.* **pennies** in Britain, a bronze coin equal to a hundredth part of a pound.
pension (**pen** shŏn) *n.* a regular payment made to someone who has retired from work, etc. – *vb.* **pensioning, pensioned** to grant a pension to.
pensioner *n.* a person who receives a pension.
pentagon (**pen** tå gon) *n.* **1** a shape with five sides and five angles. **2 Pentagon** the five-sided building in Washington DC that is the headquarters of the United States Department of Defense. – *adj.* **pentagonal** (pen **tag** ŏ nål).

Pentecost (**pen** ti kost) *n.* **1** in the Christian Church, a festival on Whit Sunday, commemorating the descent of the Holy Spirit on the apostles. **2** in the Jewish faith, Shabuoth or the Feast of Weeks, a harvest festival.
penthouse (**pent** hows) *n.* a luxurious flat built on to the roof of a tall building.
penultimate (pĕ **nul** ti måt) *adj.* next to last.
peony (**pē** ŏ ni) *n.* **peonies** a garden plant or small shrub with large globular flowers.
people (**pē** pĕl) *n.* **1** (*plural*) men, women, and children in general. **2** a nation or race: *They are a warlike people.*
pepper (pe pĕr) *n.* **1** a hot-tasting seasoning prepared from the dried and crushed berries of a tropical climbing plant. **2** the red, yellow, or green fruit of the capsicum.
peppermint *n.* a mint plant with a strong-tasting oil, used in flavouring sweets, etc.

●**Pepys** (pēps), **Samuel** (1633-1703) was an English government official who wrote a famous diary which gives a lively idea of London of his day.

per (pûr) *prep.* for each: *60 km per hour.*
perceive (pĕr **sēv**) *vb.* **perceiving, perceived 1** to observe or notice: *I have perceived a change.* **2** to understand, interpret, or view: *It depends on how you perceive your role.* – *adj.* **perceivable**.
per cent (pĕr **sent**) *adv.* (symbol **%**) in every 100: *Only 40 per cent of people voted.*
percentage *n.* an amount, number, or rate stated as a proportion of 100.
perch¹ (pûrch) *n.* a branch or other narrow support above ground for a bird to rest on. – *vb.* **perching, perched**.

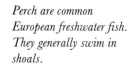

perch² (pûrch) *n.* **perch** or **perches** any of several edible, spiny-finned fish.
percolate (**pûr** kŏ lāt) *vb.* **percolating, percolated** to ooze, trickle, or filter.
percussion (pĕr **ku** shŏn) *n.* musical instruments played by striking, for example drums, cymbals, etc. – *adj.* **percussive**.
perfect (**pûr** fikt) *adj.* **1** faultless; flawless; excellent; absolutely satisfactory. **2** (*colloquial*) absolute; utter: *She is talking perfect nonsense.* – (pĕr **fekt**) *vb.* **perfecting, perfected** to improve to a high standard.

Perch are common European freshwater fish. They generally swim in shoals.

PRONUNCIATION GUIDE

fat a	all ö
fate ā	foot oo
fast ä	moon o͞o
among å	boy oi
met e	house ow
mean ē	demon ŏ
silent ĕ	thing th
loch hh	this Th
fin i	but u
line ī	mute ū
quick kw	fur û
got o	brochure ŭ
note ō	vision zh

In its simplest form, a periscope is two mirrors at 45° angles near the top and bottom of a tube.

perfection *n.* **1** the state of being perfect. **2** the process of making something complete, etc.

perforate (**pûr** fŏ rāt) *vb.* **perforating, perforated** to make a hole or holes in.

perforation *n.* **1** a hole made in something. **2** a row of small holes made in paper, for example a sheet of stamps, for ease of tearing.

perform (pĕr **fŏrm**) *vb.* **performing, performed 1** to carry out a task, job, action, etc.; to do or accomplish. **2** to act, sing, play, dance, etc. – *n.* **performer**.

performance *n.* **1** the performing of a play, dance, piece of music, etc. before an audience; a dramatic or artistic presentation or entertainment. **2** the act or process of performing a task, etc.

perfume (**pûr** fūm) *n.* **1** a sweet smell; a scent or fragrance. **2** a fragrant liquid. – *vb.* **perfuming, perfumed** to give a sweet smell to; to apply perfume to. – *n.* **perfumery**.

perhaps (pĕr **haps**) *adv.* possibly; maybe.

peril (**pe** ril) *n.* grave danger. – *adj.* **perilous**.

perimeter (pĕ **rim** i tĕr) *n.* the edge or boundary of an enclosed area or shape.

period (**pēr** i ŏd) *n.* **1** a length of time. **2** a certain phase or stage in history, etc. **3** a woman's time of menstruation. – *adj.* dating from, or designed in the style of, the historical period in question: *They wore period costume for the play.*

periodic (pēr i **od** ik) *adj.* happening at regular intervals; occasional.

periodical *n.* a magazine published weekly, monthly, quarterly, etc.

periscope (**pe** ri skōp) *n.* an optical instrument consisting of a tube containing mirrors which allow you to see things around corners, used especially in submarines for looking above the surface of the water.

perish (**pe** rish) *vb.* **perishing, perished 1** to die. **2** (of materials) to decay or rot.

perishable *adj.* (of food) liable to rot quickly.

perk (pûrk) *vb.* **perking, perked** to become or make more lively and cheerful.

permafrost (**pûr** må frost) *n.* land that is permanently frozen, in polar areas.

permanent (**pûr** må nĕnt) *adj.* lasting for ever.

permission (pĕr **mi** shŏn) *n.* consent: *She has my permission to go to the party.*

permit (pĕr **mit**) *vb.* **permitting, permitted** to consent to or give permission for; to give someone leave or authorization. – (**pûr** mit) *n.* a document authorizing something.

perpendicular (pûr pĕn **dik** ū lår) *adj.* **1** vertical; upright. **2** at right angles to: *The wall is perpendicular to the floor.*

perpetrate (**pûr** pĕ trāt) *vb.* **perpetrating, perpetrated** to commit a crime, error, etc.

perpetuate (pĕr **pe** choo āt) *vb.* **perpetuating, perpetuated 1** to cause to last or continue: *These arguments only perpetuate this feud.* **2** to preserve the memory of someone.

persecute (**pûr** si kūt) *vb.* **persecuting, persecuted** to ill-treat, oppress, or torment, especially because of religious or political beliefs. – *n.* **persecution**. – *n.* **persecutor**.

persevere (pûr si **vēr**) *vb.* **persevering, persevered** to keep on trying. – *n.* **perseverance**.

Persian (**pûr** zhån) *adj.* of Persia (modern IRAN), its people, or language. – *n.* **1** a native or citizen of Persia. **2** the language of Persia.

persist (pĕr **sist**) *vb.* **persisting, persisted 1** to continue in spite of discouragement, etc.: *They persisted with their walk despite the bad weather.* **2** (of rain, etc.) to continue steadily.

persistent *adj.* **1** continuing with determination in spite of discouragement. **2** constant; endless. – *n.* **persistence**.

person (**pûr** sŏn) *n.* **persons** (*formal*) or **people 1** an individual human being. **2** someone's body: *The police found drugs concealed on his person.* **3** in grammar, one of the three classes into which pronouns and verb forms fall. The **first person** describes the speaker (*I* or *we*), the **second person** the person addressed (*you*) and the **third person** the person(s) or thing(s) spoken of (*she, he, it,* or *they*). – **in person** actually present yourself.

In the Arctic winter all moisture in the soil freezes. In summer the top layer may thaw. The subsoil remains permanently frozen.

The Trans-Alaska oil pipeline (below) was built on supports to prevent it thawing the permafrost.

Persia (now known as Iran, from the words 'Aryan') ruled over a vast and flourishing empire from the 6th to 4th centuries BC. Under Darius I (*reigned* 521-486) Susa was its administrative centre and Persepolis its magnificent centre of state. Darius built roads to link all parts of his empire and encouraged trade by introducing a standard currency.

Darius I organized the empire into 20 provinces called satraps.

The palace steps at Persepolis show people bringing gifts for the king.

A Persian foot soldier.

The Parthians were a nomadic people who moved into Persia about 1000 BC. They were famous for their way of fighting on horseback. They would gallop away from the enemy, as if fleeing, then turn in the saddle and shoot arrows.

---

personal (**pûr** son ål) *adj.* **1** coming from someone as an individual, not from a group or organization: *This is my personal opinion.* **2** done or attended to by the individual person in question, not by a substitute: *I will give it my personal attention.* **3** relating to someone's private concerns: *The media published details of her personal life.*

personal pronoun *n.* in grammar, any of the pronouns representing a person or thing, for example *I, you, he, him, she, it, they, us.*

personal stereo *n.* a small cassette player with earphones, that is worn by the listener.

personality (pûr son **al** i ti) *n.* **personalities**
1 a person's nature; the qualities that give someone's character individuality. **2** a well-known person; a celebrity.

personnel (pûr sò **nel**) *n.* (*plural*) the people employed in a business or other organization.

perspective (pèr **spek** tiv) *n.* **1** the representation of objects in drawing and painting which gives a sense of depth by making them smaller the more distant they are. **2** a balanced view of a situation: *It is important to get things into perspective.*

perspire (pèr **spīr**) *vb.* **perspiring, perspired** to sweat.

perspiration *n.* the salty moisture produced by the sweat glands of the skin.

persuade (pèr **swād**) *vb.* **persuading, persuaded 1** to urge successfully: *We persuaded her to come for a walk.* **2** to convince: *We*

persuaded him of the necessity to take out insurance.

persuasion *n.* the act of urging, coaxing, or persuading.

persuasive *adj.* having the power to persuade; convincing. – *n.* **persuasiveness**.

●**Perth 1** a city in SCOTLAND. **2** the capital of Western AUSTRALIA.

pertinent (**pûr** ti nènt) *adj.* relating to; concerned with; relevant. – *n.* **pertinence.**

perturb (pèr **tûrb**) *vb.* **perturbing, perturbed** to make anxious or agitated. – *adj.* **perturbed.**

●**Peru**. See Supplement, **Countries**.

pessimism (**pe** si mi zèm) *n.* the tendency to emphasize the gloomiest aspects of anything, and to expect the worst to happen. – *n.* **pessimist.** – *adj.* **pessimistic.**

pest (pest) *n.* **1** an insect or animal harmful to plants, food, or livestock. **2** a person or thing that is a constant nuisance.

pester (**pes** tèr) *vb.* **pestering, pestered** to annoy constantly: *Stop pestering me with questions.*

pet (pet) *n.* **1** a tame animal or bird kept as a companion. **2** someone's favourite. – *adj.* **1** kept as a pet. **2** of or for pets. **3** favourite.

petal (**pe** tål) *n.* any of the group of coloured parts forming the head of a flower.

peter (**pē** tèr): **peter out** *vb.* **petering, petered** to dwindle away to nothing.

Insect pests (for example locusts or colorado beetles) are devastating. Chemicals can destroy such pests, but biological control – finding a natural predator, for instance – does less harm to other living things.

Peter's ambition was to make Russia a great European power. He had enormous energy and was constantly at work making laws, drilling troops, planning towns, and building ships.

Pharaoh comes from the word *peraa* which means 'great house'. This was the palace in which the pharaoh lived. Egyptians believed that each pharaoh was the same god in the shape of a different man.

● **Peter, Saint** (*died* AD 67) was the leader of JESUS's apostles in the NEW TESTAMENT and is regarded by Roman CATHOLICS as the first pope. His feast day is 29 June.

● **Peter the Great** (1672-1725) was the tsar of Russia who built St Petersburg.

petition (pě **ti** shŏn) *n.* a formal written request to an authority to take some action, signed by a large number of people. – *vb.* **petitioning, petitioned** to make an appeal or request to. – *n.* **petitioner**.

petrel (**pet** rĕl) *n.* any of several sea birds that live far from land, especially the storm petrel.

petrify (**pe** tri fī) *vb.* **petrifies, petrifying, petrified 1** to terrify; to paralyse with fright: *Snakes petrify Sam.* **2** to change into stone; to become fossilized.

petrol (**pet** rŏl) *n.* a flammable liquid obtained from petroleum, used as fuel for motor vehicles.

petroleum (pě **trō** li ŭm) *n.* a dark-coloured mineral oil, found in rocks and refined into products such as petrol and paraffin.

petty (**pe** ti) *adj.* **pettier, pettiest 1** of minor importance; trivial. **2** childishly spiteful.
petty cash *n.* money kept for small expenses.

petulant (**pe** tū lănt) *adj.* bad-tempered. – *n.* **petulance**.

pew (pū) *n.* one of the long benches with backs used as seating in a church.

pewter (**pū** tĕr) *n.* a metal, an alloy of tin and lead.

phantom (**fan** tŏm) *n.* a ghost. – *adj.* imaginary.

pharaoh (**fār** ō) *n.* a king of ancient EGYPT.

pharmacist (**fär** mǎ sist) *n.* a person trained to prepare and dispense drugs and medicines.

phase (fāz) *n.* a stage or period in growth or development. – *vb.* **phasing, phased** to organize or carry out in stages.

pheasant (**fe** zǎnt) *n.* **pheasant** or **pheasants** any of various species of game bird.

phenomenon (fi **nom** i nŏn) *n.* **phenomena** something that happens or exists, especially something unusual or scientifically explainable.

phial (**fī** ăl) *n.* a little medicine bottle.

● **Phidias** (500-432 BC) was a Greek sculptor and architect of the PARTHENON in Athens.

● **Philadelphia** in Pennsylvania, is known as the 'birthplace of the nation'. The DECLARATION OF INDEPENDENCE was signed there, and it was the capital of the UNITED STATES from 1790 to 1800.

philanthropy (fi **lan** thrŏ pi) *n.* love for your fellow human beings, especially in the form of generosity to the poor. – *adj.* **philanthropic** (fi lǎn **throp** ik). – *n.* **philanthropist**.

philately (fi **lat** ě li) *n.* the study and collecting of postage stamps. – *n.* **philatelist**.

● **Philippines**. See Supplement, **Countries**.

philology (fi **lol** ŏ ji) *n.* the study of language, its history, and development; the study of related languages. – *n.* **philologist**.

philosophy (fi **los** ŏ fi) *n.* **philosophies 1** the search for truth and knowledge concerning the universe. **2** any particular or set of beliefs.
philosopher *n.* a person who studies philosophy.

phobia (**fō** bi ǎ) *n.* a fear or hatred of something: *She has a phobia about spiders.*

SOME COMMON PHOBIAS	
Phobia	A fear of
acrophobia	heights
agoraphobia	open spaces
arachnaphobia	spiders
aerophobia	flying
bibliophobia	books
claustrophobia	confined spaces
hippophobia	horses
hydrophobia	water
ornithophobia	birds
pyrophobia	fire
xenophobia	strangers
zoophobia	animals

Phoenician (fě **ni** shŏn) *adj.* of ancient Phoenicia on the coast of Syria, its people, colonies, language, and arts. – *n.* **1** one of the Phoenician people. **2** their language.

phoenix (**fē** niks) *n.* in Arabian legend, a bird that every 500 years sets itself on fire and is reborn from its ashes.

phone (fōn) *n.* a telephone. – *vb.* **phoning, phoned** to telephone.

phonetics (fŏ **net** iks) *n.* (*singular*) the study of speech sounds.

phosphorus (fos fŏ rŭs) *n.* a poisonous, non-metallic element (symbol **P**).

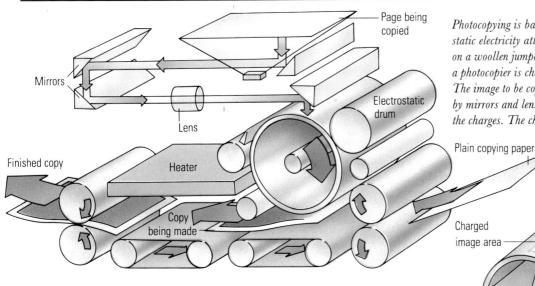

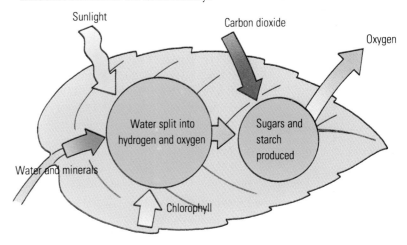

Photocopying is based on the principle that static electricity attracts objects. (Rub a balloon on a woollen jumper!) The electrostatic drum in a photocopier is charged with static electricity. The image to be copied is beamed onto the drum by mirrors and lenses, and it alters the pattern of the charges. The charged parts attract the toner (granules of ink).

This is transferred to a blank sheet of paper and fixed in place by heat.

In a photocopier, powdered pigment called toner sticks to paper in a pattern that corresponds to electrical charges on a rotating drum.

photocopy (fō tō ko pi) *n.* **photocopies** a copy of a document, drawing, etc. made on a photocopier. – *vb.* **photocopies, photocopying, photocopied** to make a photographic copy of.
photocopier *n.* a machine that makes photocopies.

photograph (fō tŏ gräf) *n.* an image recorded by camera using the action of light on special film. – *vb.* **photographing, photographed** to take a photograph of a person or thing.
photographer (fŏ **tog** rå fĕr) *n.* a person who takes photographs, especially professionally.
photography *n.* the art or process of taking photographs.

photosynthesis (fō tō **sin** thĕ sis) *n.* the manufacture by plants of substances essential for life from carbon dioxide and water, using the energy from sunlight.

phrase (frāz) *n.* a set of words expressing a single idea, forming part of a sentence.

phrenology (frĕ **nol** ŏ ji) *n.* the practice of examining the shape of a person's skull, supposedly to find out about their character.

physical (**fi** zi kål) *adj.* **1** of the body rather than the mind; bodily: *He has great physical strength.* **2** relating to objects that can be seen or felt: *Things that we can see are part of the physical world.*

physician (fi **zi** shån) *n.* a doctor.

physics (**fi** ziks) *n.* (*singular*) the science that includes the study of heat, light, sound, electricity, mechanics, and magnetism. – *n.* **physicist**.

physique (fi **zēk**) *n.* the structure of the body with regard to size, shape, etc.

pi (pī) *n.* The Greek letter (π) used in mathematics as a symbol representing the ratio of the circumference of a circle to its diameter, in numerical terms it equals 3.142.

piano (pi **an** ō) *n.* **pianos** a large musical instrument with a keyboard. When the keys are pressed down they operate a set of hammers that strike tuned wires to produce the sound. – *n.* **pianist** (**pē** å nist).

●**Picasso, Pablo** (1881-1973) was a Spanish painter whose abstract style has greatly influenced artists of the 20th century.

Photosynthesis means 'building with light'. It is a remarkable and complex process in which plants combine water from the soil with carbon dioxide from the air to make food in the form of glucose sugar. The process takes place only in light and with the help of chlorophyll (the green colouring matter in plants).

Piccard's bathyscaphe, Trieste *in which he dived 12,000 m in the Mariana Trench in the Pacific Ocean. It needed powerful lights to probe the inky blackness. Cameras filmed creatures that live at such depths and which had never before been seen alive.*

● **Piccard, Auguste** (1884-1962) was a Swiss inventor who explored the atmosphere and the ocean depths. In his bathyscaphe in 1960 he went deeper into the ocean than anyone before.

piccolo (**pi** cǒ lō) *n.* **piccolos** a small musical wind instrument similar to the flute.

pick[1] (pik) *vb.* **picking, picked 1** to choose or select. **2** to gather flowers from a plant, fruit from a tree, etc. – *n.* **1** (*singular* or *plural*) the best of a group: *He is the pick of the bunch.* **2** your own preferred selection: *Take your pick.* – *n.* **picker**. – *vb.* **pick at** to eat only small quantities of food. – *vb.* **pick out 1** to select from a group. **2** to recognize or distinguish amongst a group or crowd. – *vb.* **pick up 1** to lift or raise. **2** to learn or acquire a habit, skill, language, etc. over a time. **3** to give a lift to or take someone or something where required.

pick[2] (pik) *n.* a tool with a long metal head for breaking ground, rock, ice, etc.

picket (**pi** kit) *n.* **1** a group of strikers stationed outside their place of work to persuade other employees not to go in. **2** a stake fixed in the ground.

● **Pickford, Mary** (1893-1979) was a star of silent films, known as 'America's Sweetheart'.

pickle (**pi** kěl) *n.* **1** a preserve of vegetables, for example onions or beetroot, in vinegar and salt water or a tart sauce. **2** (*colloquial*) a mess; a quandary: *She's in a real pickle.*

pickpocket (**pik** po kit) *n.* a thief who steals from people's pockets.

picnic (**pik** nik) *n.* a meal eaten out in the open air. – *vb.* **picnicking, picnicked**.

picture (**pik** chǔr) *n.* **1** a representation of someone or something on a flat surface; a drawing, painting, or photograph. **2** a view; a mental image: *The report gave him a clear picture of the battle.* – *vb.* **picturing, pictured 1** to imagine or visualize; to describe vividly. **2** to represent in a picture or photograph.

picturesque (pik chǔ **resk**) *adj.* (of places or buildings) charming to look at.

pie (pī) *n.* a food consisting of a filling with a covering of pastry: *Apple pie or mince pie?*

pie chart *n.* a diagram in which quantities are represented as parts of a circle.

piebald (**pī** böld) *adj.* having patches of black and white. – *n.* a piebald horse.

piece (pēs) *n.* **1** a portion of some material or something; a bit or a section: *She cut herself a piece of cake.* **2** a musical, artistic, literary, or dramatic work: *He has written several pieces of fine music.* **3** a coin: *She took out a 50 pence piece.*

pier (pēr) *n.* a structure built of stone, wood, or iron, projecting into water for use as a landing-stage or breakwater.

pierce (pērs) *vb.* **piercing, pierced 1** to puncture; to make a hole with something sharp. **2** to penetrate: *The wind pierced through her thin clothing.* – *adj.* **piercing**.

A pig's feet are called trotters. Its nose is called a snout. Above are four breeds of pig.

pig (pig) *n.* a plump short-legged farm animal with a blunt snout and curly tail. It is raised for its meat (pork, ham, or bacon).

piglet *n.* a baby pig.

pigsty *n.* **pigsties** a pen, etc. for pigs.

pigeon (**pi** jǒn) *n.* a bird of the dove family.

pigment (**pig** měnt) *n.* any substance that gives something its colour.

pile[1] (pīl) *n.* a number of things lying on top of each other; a quantity of something in a heap or mound. – *vb.* **piling, piled**.

pile² (pīl) *n.* the raised cropped threads that give a soft thick surface to carpet, velvet, etc.

pilfer (pil fĕr) *vb.* **pilfering, pilfered** to steal in small quantities. – *n.* **pilferer**.

pilgrim (pil grim) *n.* a person who makes a journey to a holy place.

pilgrimage *n.* a journey to a shrine or other holy place, or to a place celebrated or made special by its associations.

The Pilgrim Fathers left England to escape persecution for their Protestant faith. Their disciplined lives and modest ways deeply influenced American life.

● **Pilgrim Fathers** members of a sect of PURITANS called Separatists who on 6 September 1620 sailed from Plymouth in the *Mayflower* on a perilous nine-week journey. They landed at what is now Plymouth Rock, Massachusetts. Here they founded a colony. The following year they gathered in their first harvest. This event is celebrated in the United States as THANKSGIVING DAY.

pill (pil) *n.* a small tablet of medicine.

pillar (pi lår) *n.* a vertical post serving as a support; a column.

pillar box *n.* a public letter box.

pillion (pil yŏn) *n.* a seat for a passenger on a motorcycle or horse, behind the rider.

pillow (pi lō) *n.* a cushion for the head, especially a large rectangular one on a bed.

pillowcase *n.* (also **pillowslip**) a washable cover for a pillow.

pilot (pī lŏt) *n.* **1** a person who flies an aircraft. **2** a person employed to conduct or steer ships into and out of harbour. – *adj.* (of a scheme) serving as a first test; experimental.

pimple (pim pĕl) *n.* a small swelling on the skin; a spot. – *adj.* **pimply, pimplier, pimpliest**.

pin (pin) *n.* **1** a short stainless steel implement with a sharp point and small round head, for fastening, attaching, etc., used especially in dressmaking. **2** any of the legs on an electric plug. – *vb.* **pinning, pinned 1** to secure with a pin. **2** to hold fast or trap.

pinafore (pin å för) *n.* an apron.

pincers (pin sĕrz) *n.* (*plural*) **1** a hinged tool with claw-like jaws for gripping things. **2** the hinged end of a crab's or lobster's claw.

pinch (pinch) *vb.* **pinching, pinched 1** to squeeze or nip flesh between thumb and finger; to squeeze painfully. **2** (*colloquial*) to steal. – *n.* **1** an act of pinching; a nip or squeeze. **2** a quantity of salt that can be held between thumb and finger; a small amount. – **at a pinch** if absolutely necessary.

pine¹ (pīn) *n.* a cone-bearing evergreen tree with dark green needle-like leaves.

pine² (pīn) *vb.* **pining, pined** to long or yearn: *The kitten was pining for its mother.*

pineapple (pīn a pĕl) *n.* a large tropical fruit with juicy yellow flesh and a prickly skin.

pink (pingk) *n.* **1** a colour between red and white. **2** a type of plant with fragrant red, pink, or multiple-coloured flowers, including the carnation and sweet william. – *adj.* of the colour pink. – *adj.* **pinkish**.

pint (pīnt) *n.* a unit of liquid measure equal to one-eighth of a gallon or about 0.568 of a litre.

pioneer (pī ŏ nĕr) *n.* an explorer of unknown lands; someone who does something that no one has done before in a particular field or discipline: *The Wright Brothers were pioneers in the history of flight.* – *vb.* **pioneering, pioneered** to explore and open up a route, etc.

pious (pī ŭs) *adj.* religiously devout.

pip¹ (pip) *n.* the small seed of a fruit such as an apple, pear, orange, or grape.

pip² (pip) *n.* (usually in *plural*) one of a series of short high-pitched time signals on the radio.

pipe (pīp) *n.* **1** a hollow tube for water, gas, oil, etc. to flow along. **2** a little bowl with a hollow stem for smoking tobacco, etc. **3** a wind instrument consisting of a simple wooden or metal tube. – *vb.* **piping, piped 1** to move gas, water, oil, etc. through pipes. **2** to play on a pipe or on the bagpipes. – *vb.* **pipe down** (*colloquial*) to stop talking; to be quiet.

Pineapples are so named because they look like pine cones. The plants grow to a height of just over a metre, bearing long, rough-edged, and sharp-pointed leaves, from the centre of which grow the flower stem. This develops into the fruit.

pipeline *n.* a series of connected pipes laid underground to convey gas, water, oil, etc. – **in the pipeline** (*colloquial*) in preparation.

pipistrelle (pi pi **strel**) *n.* a reddish-brown bat.

piranha (pi **rän** ǎ) *n.* a small fierce carnivorous freshwater fish found in South America.

pirate (**pī** rǎt) *n.* someone who attacks and robs ships at sea. – *n.* **piracy** (**pī** rǎ si) or (**pi** rǎ si).

● **Pisa** is a city in ITALY, famous for its leaning tower.

Pisces (**pī** sēz) *n.* See **zodiac**.

pistil (**pis** til) *n.* the female, seed-producing part of a flower.

pistol (**pis** tŏl) *n.* a small gun held in the hand.

piston (**pis** tŏn) *n.* in engines, a disc or solid metal cylinder that slides up and down within a hollow cylinder.

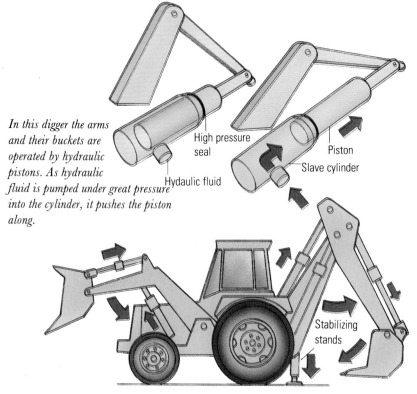

In this digger the arms and their buckets are operated by hydraulic pistons. As hydraulic fluid is pumped under great pressure into the cylinder, it pushes the piston along.

High pressure seal

Hydaulic fluid

Piston

Slave cylinder

Stabilizing stands

pit (pit) *n.* **1** a big deep hole in the ground. **2** a coalmine. – *vb.* **pitting, pitted 1** to set or match in competition or opposition: *He was pitted against a tough opponent.* **2** marked by scars and holes: *The surface of the Moon is pitted with craters.*

pit bull terrier *n.* a large breed of bull terrier originally developed for dogfighting.

pitch¹ (pich) *vb.* **pitching, pitched 1** to set up a tent or camp. **2** to throw or fling violently. **3** to fall heavily forward. **4** (of a ship) to move around violently. – *n.* **1** the field or area of play in any of several sports. **2** a degree of intensity; a level: *The noise had reached such a pitch that she couldn't hear him.* **3** the angle of steepness of a slope: *The roof had a steep pitch.* **4** in music, the highness or lowness of a note.

pitchfork *n.* a long-handled fork with two or three sharp prongs, for tossing hay.

pitch² (pich) *n.* a thick black substance obtained from tar, used for waterproofing ships, etc.

pitcher (**pich** ěr) *n.* a jug with handles.

pitfall (**pit** fŏl) *n.* a hidden danger.

pitiful (**pi** ti fŭl) *adj.* **1** arousing pity; wretched or pathetic: *The wet kitten was a pitiful sight.* **2** sadly inadequate or ineffective: *He cannot support his family on his pitiful wage.*

● **Pittsburgh** in Pennsylvania, is known as the 'steel capital' of the UNITED STATES.

pity (**pi** ti) *n.* a feeling of sorrow for the troubles and sufferings of others; compassion. – *vb.* **pities, pitying, pitied** to feel or show pity for. – *adj.* **pitying**. – **take pity on** to feel or show pity for, especially in a practical way.

pivot (**pi** vŏt) *n.* the central point round which something turns, swivels, or revolves. – *vb.* **pivoting, pivoted** to turn, swivel, or revolve.

place (plās) *n.* **1** an area, region, district, etc.; a country, city, town, village, building, room, etc. **2** a seat or space at table. **3** something or someone's usual position: *Put it back in its place!* **4** a point reached, for example in a conversation or a book: *The end of the chapter is a good place to stop.* **5** a position within an order, for example of competitors in a contest: *He finished in third place.* – *vb.* **placing, placed 1** to put. **2** to submit: *Let's place an order.* – **all over the place** in disorder or confusion.

placid (**pla** sid) *adj.* calm; tranquil.

plagiarize or **plagiarise** (**plā** jǎ rīz) *vb.* **plagiarizing, plagiarized** to steal ideas from someone else's work, and use them as if they were your own. – *n.* **plagiarism**.

plague (plāg) *n.* **1** any of several highly infectious diseases which tend to occur on a large scale. **2** an overwhelming invasion by something unwelcome: *The crops were destroyed by a plague of locusts.* – *vb.* **plaguing, plagued**.

plaice (plās) *n.* **plaice** an edible brown flatfish.

In the 1300s, a form of **plague** called the Black Death killed a quarter of the people of Europe. Plague is given to people by fleas from infected rats.

At night carts were loaded with corpses to be taken away for burial.

Artists depicted death in such forms as a skeleton on horse-back.

● **Plaid Cymru** (plīd **kum** ri) is the name of the Welsh National Party.

plain (plān) *adj.* **1** all of one colour; unpatterned; undecorated. **2** simple; unsophisticated; without improvement: *We eat very plain food.* **3** obvious; clear; straightforward; direct: *Let me speak in plain language.* – *n.* a large level expanse of land.

● **Plains Indians**, who traditionally lived on the grasslands of North America, were until the 1600s mainly nomadic hunters and gatherers. They hunted buffalo on foot. When the Spanish introduced horses, the Plains Indians could follow buffalo with ease. Later Plains Indians fought many battles with the United States army who were protecting settlers heading west across traditional American Indian hunting grounds.

plait (plat) *vb.* **plaiting, plaited** to arrange hair by interweaving three or more lengths. – *n.* a length of interwoven hair or other material.

plan (plan) *n.* **1** a thought-out arrangement or method for doing something. **2** a drawing or diagram of a floor of a house, the streets of a town, etc. done as though from above. – *vb.* **planning, planned** to devise a scheme for; to prepare; to make plans: *It is important to plan ahead.*

plane[1] (plān) *n.* an aeroplane.

plane[2] (plān) *n.* **1** a level surface. **2** a level or standard: *She is on a higher intellectual plane.* – *vb.* **planing, planed** (of a boat) to skim over the surface of the water.

plane[3] (plān) *n.* a carpenter's tool for smoothing wood.

plane[4] (plān) *n.* (also **plane tree**) a tree with large leaves and flaking bark.

planet (**pla** nit) *n.* **1** any of the nine heavenly bodies – Mercury, Venus, Mars, Earth, Jupiter, Saturn, Uranus, Neptune and Pluto – that revolve round the Sun. **2** any similar body revolving round any star. – *adj.* **planetary**.

planetarium (pla ni **tār** i ům) *n.* **planetaria** or **planetariums** a building housing an apparatus that shows the motion of the planets by projecting images on to a domed ceiling.

plank (plangk) *n.* a long flat piece of timber.

plankton (**plangk** tŏn) *n.* tiny plants and animals that drift in seas.

The Native Americans depended on huge herds of buffalo (bison) for food, clothing, shelter, and fuel. When the bison were reduced to near extinction by the white settlers, the Native Americans succumbed. The remains of the Plains nations were forced on to reservations, often on poor land.

plant (plänt) *n.* **1** any member of the vegetable kingdom, any living thing that grows from the ground, having a stem, root, and leaves. **2** a factory, its buildings and equipment. – *vb.* **planting, planted** to put seeds or plants into the ground to grow.

●**Plantagenet** was the name given to a line of English kings from Henry the Second, who came to the throne in 1154, to Richard the Third, who was crowned in 1483.

Four varieties of tulip (below). *The red flower is a common tulip; the other three are new cross-bred varieties.*

plantation (plän **tā** shŏn) *n.* an estate growing crops such as tea, coffee, rubber, and cotton on a large scale.

plasma (**plaz** må) *n.* the liquid content of blood, in which the blood cells are suspended.

plaster (**plås** tẽr) *n.* **1** a material consisting of lime, sand, and water, that is applied to walls when soft, and dries to form a hard smooth surface. **2** (also **sticking-plaster**) a piece of sticky tape, usually with a dressing attached, for protecting a wound.

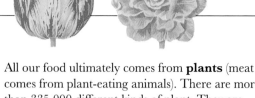

All our food ultimately comes from **plants** (meat comes from plant-eating animals). There are more than 335,000 different kinds of plant. They are placed in different groups such as algae, mosses, and flowering plants. Plants include the biggest living things, the giant redwood trees of California.

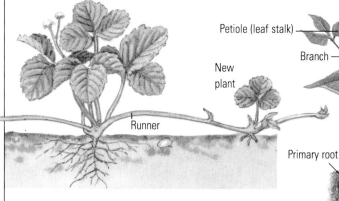

Terminal bud

Stem

Petiole (leaf stalk)

Branch

New plant

Runner

Primary root

Strawberries (above) *send out side shoots called runners. Where they touch the ground, roots form. New leaves grow and the runner dies away.*

plastic (**plas** tik) *n.* any of many synthetic materials that can be moulded to any shape when soft. – *adj.* made of plastic.

plastic surgery *n.* surgery to repair or replace damaged flesh, or to improve the appearance, especially of the face.

plate (plāt) *n.* **1** a shallow dish for serving food on or eating food off. **2** a sheet of metal, glass, or other rigid material used in building.

plateau (pla tō) or (pla **tō**) *n.* **plateaux** (pla tōz) or (pla **tōz**) or **plateaus** an area of high land, more or less uniformly level.

platform (**plat** fŏrm) *n.* **1** a raised floor for speakers, performers, etc. **2** the raised walkway alongside the track at a railway station, giving access to trains. **3** a floating structure moored to the sea bed, for oil-drilling, etc.

platinum (**pla** ti nŭm) *n.* an element (symbol **Pt**), a heavy silvery-white precious metal.

●**Plato** (429-347 BC) was a Greek philosopher. He believed the things we see around us are only poor copies of perfect things in an ideal world.

Platonic (plå **ton** ik) *adj.* of, or relating to, *Plato*, the Greek philosopher.

platypus (**pla** ti pŭs) *n.* **platypuses** (also **duck-billed platypus**) a furry Australian egg-laying water mammal, with a ducklike beak and webbed feet.

play (plā) *vb.* **playing, played** **1** (especially of children) to amuse with games and toys. **2** to fiddle or meddle with; to behave irresponsibly towards someone: *He was playing with my emotions.* **3** to take part in a game or sport. **4** to make a joke against someone: *My sister played a trick on me.* **5** to act a role in a play, etc.; to perform in. **6** to perform music on an instrument. **7** to turn on a radio, tape-recording, etc. – *n.* **1** recreation; playing games: *The children were at play.* **2** a dramatic piece for the stage.

player *n.* **1** a participant in a game or sport. **2** a performer on a musical instrument.

playing card *n.* one of a pack of 52 cards used in card games.

playwright *n.* an author of plays.

plead (plēd) *vb.* **pleading, pleaded** or (*Scottish* or *US*) **pled** (pled) **1** to appeal earnestly: *The captives pleaded for their freedom.* **2** (of an accused person) to state in a court of law that you are guilty or not guilty. **3** to argue in defence of: *She pleaded his case.* – *adj.* **pleading**.

pleasant (**ple** zǎnt) *adj.* **1** giving pleasure; enjoyable; agreeable. **2** (of a person) friendly.

please (**plēz**) *vb.* **pleasing, pleased** to give satisfaction, pleasure, or enjoyment. – *adv.* used politely to accompany a request, order, etc.: *Pass the salt, please.* – *adj.* **pleasing**. **pleased** *adj.* happy; satisfied; glad; delighted.

pleasure (**ple** zhǔr) *n.* **1** a feeling of enjoyment or satisfaction: *I take pleasure in my surroundings.* **2** an activity you enjoy. – *adj.* used for or done for pleasure: *We went on a pleasure trip.*

pleat (**plēt**) *n.* a fold sewn or pressed into cloth, etc. – *vb.* **pleating, pleated** to make pleats in.

plectrum (**plek** trǔm) *n.* a small flat implement used for plucking the strings of a guitar.

pledge (**plej**) *n.* **1** a solemn promise. **2** a token or symbol: *I give you this ring as a pledge of my love.*

plentiful (**plen** ti fǔl) *adj.* in good supply.

plenty (**plen** ti) *pron.* **1** enough, or more than enough. **2** a lot: *Plenty of folk would agree.* – *n.* wealth or sufficiency: *We live in times of plenty.*

pleurisy (**plōōr** i si) *n.* an illness in which the lungs become inflamed.

The platypus and the spiny anteater are the only members of the most primitive order of living mammals the monotremata *(egg-laying mammals). They are found only in Australia.*

pliers (**plī** ěrz) *n.* (*plural*) a hinged tool with jaws for gripping, bending, or cutting wire, etc.

Plimsoll line (**plim** sǒl līn) *n.* a line painted round a ship's hull showing how far down into the water it may safely sit when loaded.

plod (**plod**) *vb.* **plodding, plodded 1** to walk slowly with a heavy tread. **2** to work slowly, methodically, and thoroughly. – *n.* **plodder**.

plot[1] (**plot**) *n.* **1** a secret plan; a conspiracy. **2** the story of a play, film, novel, etc. – *vb.* **plotting, plotted 1** to plan secretly: *The rebels plotted to kill the dictator.* **2** to mark the course of a ship or plane. – *n.* **plotter**.

plot[2] (**plot**) *n.* a piece of ground.

plough (**plow**) *n.* **1** a farm tool with blades used for turning up the soil in ridges and furrows. **2 Plough** (also **Great Bear**) a constellation of seven stars. – *vb.* **ploughing, ploughed** to turn over soil with a plough.

plover (**plu** věr) *n.* any of various seashore birds, most with long wings.

pluck (**pluk**) *vb.* **plucking, plucked 1** to pull the feathers off a bird before cooking. **2** to pick flowers or fruit from a plant or tree. **3** to remove by pulling: *She plucked out her grey hairs.* **4** to play the strings of a violin, guitar, etc. using the fingers or a plectrum. **5** to summon up courage. – *n.* courage.

plug (**plug**) *n.* **1** a piece of rubber, plastic, etc. shaped to fit a hole as a stopper, for example in a bath or sink. **2** the device with metal pins that is fitted to the end of the flex of an electrical appliance which is pushed into a socket to connect with the power supply. – *vb.* **plugging, plugged 1** to stop or block up a hole, etc. with something. **2** (*colloquial*) to give favourable publicity to a product, etc.

plum (**plum**) *n.* an oval red, purple, green, or yellow fruit with soft juicy flesh and a stone.

plumage (**plōō** mij) *n.* a bird's feathers.

plumber (**plum** ěr) *n.* a person who fits and repairs water pipes, heating systems, baths, etc.

plump (**plump**) *adj.* full, rounded, chubby.

plunder (**plun** děr) *vb.* **plundering, plundered** to steal valuable goods, or loot a place, especially during a war; to rob or ransack. – *n.* **plunderer**.

plunge (**plunj**) *vb.* **plunging, plunged 1** to dive, throw yourself or fall: *He plunged into the pool.* **2** to involve yourself rapidly and enthusiastically. – *n.* a dive. **plunger** *n.* a rubber cup at the end of a long handle, used to clear blocked drains.

plural (**plōōr** ǎl) *n.* the form of a noun, pronoun, or verb used for two or more people or things, etc. For example the plural of *house* is *houses* and the plural of *mouse* is *mice*.

plus (**plus**) *prep.* **1** with the addition of: *2 plus 5 equals 7.* **2** in combination with: *Bad luck, plus his own obstinacy, brought about his downfall.* – *n.* **pluses** (also **plus sign**) the symbol (+) meaning addition or positive value.

Pluto[1]. See **Myths and Legends**.

● **Pluto**[2] is a planet. It is farther away from the Sun than any of the other planets.

plutonium (ploo **tōn** i ŭm) *n.* a radioactive metallic element (symbol **Pu**).

ply¹ (plī) *n.* **plies** thickness of yarn, rope, or wood, measured by the number of strands or layers that compose it.

ply² (plī) *vb.* **plies, plying, plied** to keep supplying someone: *He plied them with drinks.*

p.m. *abbreviation* for *post meridien* (Latin), after midday; in the afternoon.

pneumatic (nū **mat** ik) *adj.* containing or inflated with air: *pneumatic tyres.*

pneumonia (nū **mōn** i ǎ) *n.* a serious illness which affects the lungs.

poach¹ (pōch) *vb.* **poaching, poached 1** to cook in gently boiling water. **2** to simmer.

poach² (pōch) *vb.* **poaching, poached** to catch fish, etc. illegally on someone else's property. – *n.* **poacher**. – *n.* **poaching**.

pocket (**po** kit) *n.* an extra piece sewn into or on to a garment to form an enclosed section for carrying things in. – *adj.* designed, or small enough, to be carried in a pocket; smaller than standard: *He got out his pocket calculator.* – *vb.* **pocketing, pocketed** (*colloquial*) to steal.

pod (pod) *n.* the long seedcase of a pea, etc.

●**Poe, Edgar Allan** (1809-49) was an American writer of dark and mysterious poems and novels.

poem (**pō** im) *n.* a piece of writing in verse, sometimes with rhymes.

poet (**pō** it) *n.* a writer of poems.

poetry (**pō** ě tri) *n.* **1** the art of composing poems. **2** poems collectively.

●Almost all poetry uses metre (rhythm), and much of it uses rhyme. Other techniques are *alliteration* (words beginning with the same letter) and *assonance* (words with the same vowel sounds). The main kinds of poetry are lyric (dealing with personal emotion), dramatic (as in plays), and narrative (as in ballads and epics).

point (point) *n.* **1** a sharp end or tip: *She sharpened the point of her pencil.* **2** a dot, for example inserted before a decimal fraction, as in *2.1.* **3** a punctuation mark, especially a full stop. **4** a position, place, or location: *He was posted at the look-out point.* **5** a stage, temperature, etc.: *The water reached boiling-point.* **6** aim or intention: *That is the point of this procedure.* **7** a unit or mark in scoring: *You have scored 11 points.* **8** any of the 32 directions marked on a compass. – *vb.* **pointing, pointed 1** to aim: *He pointed the camera at her.* **2** to extend a finger towards someone or something, so as to direct attention there; (of a sign, etc.) to indicate a certain direction. **3** to face in a certain direction: *She lay with toes pointing upward.*

point of view *n.* **points of view** someone's own way of seeing something.

poise (poiz) *n.* self-confidence, calm.

poised *adj.* calm and dignified.

poison (**poi** zŏn) *n.* a substance that causes illness or death when swallowed or absorbed into the body. – *vb.* **poisoning, poisoned** to harm or kill with poison; to pollute: *The river is poisoned by waste from the factory.*

poisonous *adj.* **1** liable to cause injury or death if swallowed or absorbed. **2** producing, or able to inject, a poison: *Watch out for poisonous snakes!*

The little golden poison-arrow frog is the deadliest of animals.

Spiders are killers. They have sharp curved fangs for stabbing their prey. Poison is squirted through a tube in the fang into the prey's body.

Poison tube
Poison gland
Small teeth
Curved fang

The blue-ringed octopus lives in the seas around Australia. Its coloured rings warn that its bite is deadly.

POET'S CORNER
Some of the terms used in poetry:
ballad a poem describing an historical or legendary event.
epic a long narrative poem about heroic or legendary people.
foot a unit of two or more syllables forming part of a poem's metre.
limerick a kind of nonsense verse in five lines.
meter the pattern and rhythm of poetry.
ode a medium-length poem, usually in praise of something.
sonnet a 14-lined poem.

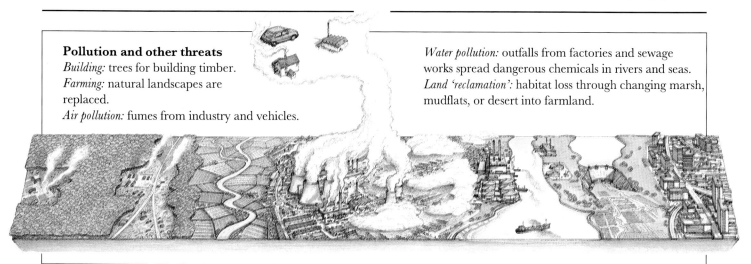

Pollution and other threats
Building: trees for building timber.
Farming: natural landscapes are
replaced.
Air pollution: fumes from industry and vehicles.

Water pollution: outfalls from factories and sewage
works spread dangerous chemicals in rivers and seas.
Land 'reclamation': habitat loss through changing marsh,
mudflats, or desert into farmland.

poke (pōk) *vb.* **poking, poked 1** to thrust,
prod, or jab: *He poked the fire.* **2** to project: *Her
big toe poked through a hole in her sock.* – *n.* a prod
poker *n.* a metal rod for stirring a fire.
poker (pō kẻr) *n.* a card game in which players
bet on the cards dealt to them.

●**Poland**. See Supplement, **Countries**.

polar (pō lảr) *adj.* relating to the Earth's North
or South Pole or the regions round them.
polar bear *n.* a white bear found in the Arctic.
pole¹ (pōl) *n.* **1** either end of the Earth's axis: *We
flew over the North Pole.* **2** either end of a
magnet, the one having a repelling, the other
an attracting, force.
pole² (pōl) *n.* a rod, especially fixed in the
ground as a support.
polecat (pōl kat) *n.* **1** a dark-brown animal of
the weasel family. **2** (*US*) a skunk.
police (pỏ lēs) *n.* (*plural*) the body of men and
women employed by the government of a
country to keep order, enforce the law, etc.
policeman, policemen or **policewoman,
policewomen** *n.* a member of a police force.
policy¹ (po li si) *n.* **policies** a plan of action,
decided on by a body or individual: *It's not our
policy to give out information.*
policy² (po li si) *n.* **policies** (also **insurance
policy**) a document confirming an insurance
agreement. – *n.* **policy-holder**.
polio (pō li ō) *n.* a viral disease of the brain and
spinal cord. Polio is an abbreviation of
poliomyelitis.
Polish (pō lish) *adj.* of, or relating to, POLAND,
its culture, or people. – *n.* the language of
POLAND.

polish (pol ish) *vb.* **polishing, polished 1** to
make or become smooth and glossy by
rubbing. **2** to improve or perfect: *She polished up
her French for her interview.* – *n.* a substance used
for polishing surfaces.
polite (pỏ līt) *adj.* well-mannered; courteous.
politic (po li tik) *adj.* prudent; wise; shrewd.
political (pỏ lit i kảl) *adj.* relating to politics.
politician (po li ti shản) *n.* someone engaged
in politics.
politics *n.* (*singular*) the science of government.
poll (pōl) *n.* **1** (in *plural*) a political election:
victory at the polls. **2** the votes cast at an election.
pollen (po lẻn) *n.* the fine powder produced by
flowers in order to fertilize other flowers.
pollinate (po lẻ nāt) *vb.* **pollinating,
pollinated** to carry pollen between flowers.
pollute (pỏ lūt) *vb.* **polluting, polluted** to
make a substance dirty or dangerous with
harmful substances; to make impure: *The river
has been polluted by chemicals from the factory.* – *n.
& adj.* **pollutant**. – *n.* **pollution**.
polo (pō lō) *n.* a ball game played on horseback
using long-handled hammers to hit the ball.

●**Polo, Marco** (1254-1324) was a Venetian
merchant who spent 24 years at the court of
Kublai Khan in CHINA.

poly- (po li-) *prefix* many or much.

●**Polynesia**, meaning 'many islands', is one of
the three divisions of the islands in the Pacific.
The other two are Melanesia and Micronesia.

polysyllable (po li si lả bẻl) *n.* a word of three
or more syllables.

PRONUNCIATION GUIDE	
fat a	all ö
fate ā	foot oo
fast ä	moon o͞o
among å	boy oi
met e	house ow
mean ē .	demon ỏ
silent ẻ	thing th
loch hh	this Th
fin i	but u
line ī	mute ū
quick kw	fur û
got o	brochure ủ
note ō	vision zh

polythene (**po** li thēn) *n.* a light tough plastic.

polyunsaturated (po li un **sa** chǔ rā tid) *adj.* (of especially fish or vegetable oils and fats) free of cholesterol, therefore not liable to cause fatty deposits in the blood vessels.

polyvinyl chloride (po li **vī** nil **klör** īd) *n.* a plastic used for coating electric wires and as a clothing material; PVC.

pomegranate (**po** mi gra nåt) *n.* a round seedy fruit with red juicy flesh.

pommy (**po** mi) *n.* **pommies** (*Australian* & *New Zealand colloquial*) a British person.

pomp (pomp) *n.* ceremonial grandeur.

● **Pompeii** was a Roman town near Naples, ITALY, that was buried in volcanic ash from Vesuvius in AD 79.

On 24 August, AD 79 a cloud appeared over the Roman town of Pompeii. Moments later a massive explosion blew the top off the nearby volcano, Mt Vesuvius. The town was buried under 67 m of ash and 2,000 people died of suffocation from the fumes. Pompeii was forgotten until it was rediscovered in the 18th century.

pompous (**pom** pǔs) *adj.* self-important.

pond (pond) *n.* a small area of water.

ponder (**pon** děr) *vb.* **pondering, pondered** to consider or contemplate.

ponderous (**pon** dě rǔs) *adj.* laborious.

pony (**pō** ni) *n.* **ponies** a small breed of horse.

pony-trekking *n.* cross-country pony-riding in groups.

● **Pony Express** a system of delivering mail by horseback in the United States during the 1860s. It used a relay of 80 riders and 400 horses.

poodle (**poo** děl) *n.* a breed of dog with a curly coat that is traditionally clipped.

pool[1] (pool) *n.* **1** a small area of still water: *We played in the rock pools.* **2** a swimming-pool.

pool[2] (pool) *n.* **1** a collection of money, vehicles, etc. shared by several people. **2** a game like billiards. – *vb.* **pooling, pooled** to put money, etc. into a common supply for general use.

poor (poor) or (pör) *adj.* **1** not having enough money to live comfortably. **2** not well supplied with: *Japan is a country poor in minerals.*

poorly *adv.* not well; badly.

pop[1] (pop) *n.* **1** a sharp, explosive noise, like that of a cork coming out of a bottle. **2** (*colloquial*) sweet non-alcoholic fizzy drinks. – *vb.* **popping, popped 1** to make a popping noise. **2** to spring out; to protrude: *His eyes popped with surprise.* **3** to do something quickly: *I'll just pop next door.*

popcorn *n.* maize grains heated till they puff up and burst open.

pop[2] (pop) *n.* (also **pop music**) modern music, usually with a strong beat, often played with guitars, keyboards, etc.

pope or **Pope** (pōp) *n.* the bishop of Rome, the head of the Roman Catholic Church. He is accepted by Roman Catholics as the representative of JESUS CHRIST on Earth. He lives in the Vatican City.

poplar (**pop** lår) *n.* a tall slender tree.

poppy (**po** pi) *n.* **poppies** a plant with large scarlet flowers and a hairy wiry stem.

popular (**po** pū lår) *adj.* liked or enjoyed by most people: *Tennis is a pastime still popular with the young.* – *n.* **popularity** (po pū lar i ti).

populate (**po** pū lāt) *vb.* **populating, populated** (of people or animals) to inhabit.

population *n.* **1** all the people living in a particular country, area, etc. **2** the number of people living in a particular area, etc.: *The city has a population of two million.*

porcelain (**pör** sě lin) *n.* a fine white pottery.

porch (pörch) *n.* a structure forming a covered entrance to the doorway of a building.

porcupine (**pör** kū pīn) *n.* a large rodent covered with long spines.

A North African crested porcupine. The porcupine can rattle its quills to warn off enemies.

pore[1] (pör) *n.* a tiny opening in skin or in a plant surface, through which fluids can pass.

pore[2] (pör) *vb.* **poring, pored** to study books, etc. with intense concentration: *Martin pored over his history books to prepare for the exam.*

pork (pörk) *n.* the flesh of a pig used as food.

porpoise (**pör** pǒs) *n.* a sea mammal, like a dolphin, but with a blunt snout.

porridge (**po** rij) *n.* a dish of oatmeal boiled in water or milk.

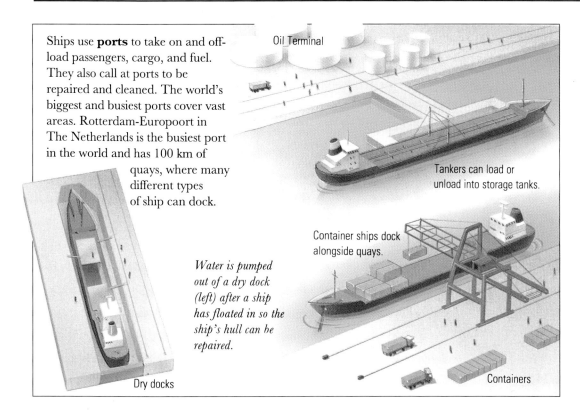

Ships use **ports** to take on and off-load passengers, cargo, and fuel. They also call at ports to be repaired and cleaned. The world's biggest and busiest ports cover vast areas. Rotterdam-Europoort in The Netherlands is the busiest port in the world and has 100 km of quays, where many different types of ship can dock.

Water is pumped out of a dry dock (left) after a ship has floated in so the ship's hull can be repaired.

Oil Terminal

Tankers can load or unload into storage tanks.

Container ships dock alongside quays.

Containers

Dry docks

Oil is carried around the world by sea. At an oil terminal tankers can load or unload into storage tanks.

Container ships dock alongside quays where special cranes load or unload their cargo containers.

port¹ (pört) *n.* a town with a harbour.

port² (pört) *n.* the left side of a ship or aircraft.

portable (pör tå bĕl) *adj.* designed to be easily carried or moved. – *n.* a portable radio, television, typewriter, etc. – *n.* **portability**.

porter¹ (pör tĕr) *n.* a doorman or caretaker at a college, office, or factory.

porter² (pör tĕr) *n.* a person employed to carry luggage or parcels.

●**Porter, Cole** (1891-1964) was an American light music composer. His songs include *Night and Day*.

porthole (pört hōl) *n.* a round opening in a ship's side.

portico (pör ti kō) *n.* **porticos** or **porticoes** a porch or covered way alongside a building, supported by pillars.

portion (pör shŏn) *n.* a piece or part of a whole; a share: *Divide the cake into 12 equal portions.*

portrait (pör trit) *n.* a drawing, photograph, etc. of a person, especially of the face only.

portray (pör trā) *vb.* **portraying, portrayed** to describe or depict; to act the part of a character in a play, film, etc. – *n.* **portrayal**.

●**Portugal**. See Supplement, **Countries**.

Portuguese (pör chŭ gēz) *adj.* of, or belonging to, PORTUGAL or its inhabitants. – *n.* **1** a native or citizen of PORTUGAL. **2** the language of PORTUGAL, also spoken in BRAZIL, ANGOLA, and MOZAMBIQUE.

pose (pōz) *n.* **1** a position or attitude of the body: *She adopted a relaxed pose.* **2** an artificial way of behaving, often purely for effect: *His punk style is just a pose.* – *vb.* **posing, posed 1** to take up a position for a photograph, portrait, etc. **2** to pretend to be: *He posed as a journalist to get into the conference.* **3** to ask or put forward a question. **4** to cause a problem, etc.

position (pŏ **zi** shŏn) *n.* **1** a place where something or someone is: *The house is in a fine position overlooking the bay.* **2** a way of sitting, standing, lying, or facing: *She propped the book in an upright position.* **3** someone's opinion or viewpoint. **4** a job or post: *She holds a senior position at the bank.* **5** the place of a competitor in a contest: *He is lying in fourth position.* – *vb.* **positioning, positioned** to place.

positive (po zi tiv) *adj.* **1** sure; definite: *I have positive proof of her guilt.* **2** expressing agreement or approval: *We received a positive response.*

possess (pŏ **zes**) *vb.* **possessing, possessed** to own; to have as a feature or quality: *He possesses a quick mind.*

possession *n.* **1** the condition of possessing something; ownership: *A precious antique has come into my possession.* **2** (in *plural*) something owned; someone's property or belongings.

possessive *adj.* **1** unwilling to share things that you own: *He is very possessive about his car.* **2** in grammar, describing the form of a noun, pronoun, or adjective that shows possession, for example *Jack's, its,* or *her.*

possible (**po** si bĕl) *adj.* **1** achievable; able to be done: *This feat is not possible.* **2** imaginable; conceivable: *It's possible that he's still there.*

possibility *n.* **possibilities 1** something that is possible. **2** (in *plural*) promise or potential: *This idea has possibilities.*

post¹ (pōst) *n.* a strong pole fixed upright in the ground, as a support or a marker: *She was the first past the post.*

post² (pōst) *n.* a position or job: *He has got a teaching post in Kenya.*

post³ (pōst) *n.* **1** the official system for the delivery of mail. **2** letters and parcels delivered by this system; mail. – *vb.* **posting, posted** to put mail into a postbox; to send by post.

postage *n.* the charge for sending a letter, etc.

postal *adj.* of or relating to the post office.

postcard *n.* a card for writing messages on, often with a picture on one side.

postcode *n.* a combination of letters and numbers added to addresses and used to sort mail for delivery.

postman, postmen or **postwoman, postwomen** *n.* a man or woman whose job is to deliver mail.

postmark *n.* a mark stamped on mail by the post office, cancelling the stamp and showing the date and place of posting.

post office *n.* the local office where you can buy stamps and various types of licence, etc.

● In early times messages were carried by riders on horseback. Fresh messengers and horses waited at 'posts', usually inns along the road. Later post coaches were used.

post- (pōst-) *prefix* after: *postwar.*

poster (**pōs** tĕr) *n.* **1** a large advertisement for public display. **2** a large printed picture.

● **Post-Impressionism** was the work of French painters that followed IMPRESSIONISM between 1885 and 1905. Artists experimented freely with expression, form, and design instead of representing nature realistically. The movement included such artists as CEZANNE, GAUGIN, VAN GOGH, and DEGAS.

post meridiem (pōst mĕ **rid** i ĕm) after noon. Usually abbreviated to p.m.

post-mortem (pōst **mor** tĕm) *n.* a medical examination of a dead person.

postpone (pōst **pōn**) *vb.* **postponing, postponed** to put off till later.

posture (**pos** chŭr) *n.* the way you hold your body in standing, sitting, or walking.

pot (pot) *n.* any of various deep round domestic containers used for cooking or serving food, or for storage.

potter *n.* a person who makes pottery.

pottery *n.* **potteries** pots, dishes, etc. made from baked clay.

● There are two main kinds of pottery: porcelain, made with white clay that lets the light through; and stoneware, made from various colours of clay. Stoneware is usually thicker and does not let light through. Firing pots in kilns makes the pots rock hard and hardens the glaze.

A pottery head made by the Nok people of Nigeria between 400 BC and AD 200.

Muslim artists of the 8th century concentrated on intricate designs, as can be seen in this Persian bowl.

Pottery was a key invention which followed when humans adapted to a settled way of life. The earliest known pottery, shaped by hand, dates from about 8,000 BC.

A Roman amphora (right), used to hold wine or olive oil.

A potter shaping a vessel on a wheel. For thousands of years potters have made pots by hand.

potassium (pǒ **tas** i ǔm) *n.* an element (symbol **K**), a soft silvery-white metal.

potato (pǒ **tā** tō) *n.* **potatoes** a white vegetable with a dark skin that grows underground.

potential (pǒ **ten** shǎl) *adj.* possible or likely, though as yet not tested or actual: *He is a potential world champion.* – *n.* the ability to achieve something that a person or thing has; powers or resources not yet developed or made use of: *She has not yet fulfilled her potential.*

pothole (**pot** hōl) *n.* **1** a cave. **2** a hole worn in a road surface.

● **Potter, Beatrix** (1866-1943) was an English author and illustrator of children's animal story books including *The Tale of Peter Rabbit.*

pouch (powch) *n.* **1** a purse or small bag. **2** in marsupials such as the kangaroo, a pocket of skin on the belly in which the young are carried. **3** a fleshy fold in the cheek of hamsters and other rodents, for storing undigested food.

poultry (**pōl** tri) *n.* farmyard birds such as hens.

pounce (powns) *vb.* **pouncing, pounced** to leap on; to grab eagerly.

pound[1] (pownd) *n.* **1** (also **pound sterling**; *symbol* £) the currency of the United Kingdom, divided into 100 pence. **2** (*abbreviation* **lb**) a measure of weight equal to 16 ounces or 453 grams.

pound[2] (pownd) *n.* an enclosure where stray animals or illegally parked cars are taken and kept for collection.

pound[3] (pownd) *vb.* **pounding, pounded** to beat or bang vigorously.

pour (pör) *vb.* **pouring, poured 1** to flow in a downward stream. **2** to empty liquid out of a jug, teapot, etc. **3** to rain heavily.

poverty (**po** věr ti) *n.* the state of being poor.

powder (**pow** děr) *n.* any substance in the form of fine dust-like particles. – *vb.* **powdering, powdered** to sprinkle or cover with powder.

power (**pow** ěr) *n.* **1** control and influence exercised over others. **2** strength, vigour, force, or effectiveness. **3** an ability or skill: *Animals do not have the power of speech.* **4** any of the forms of energy, for example *nuclear power, electrical power*; any of these as the driving force of a machine, etc. – *adj.* using mechanical or electrical power; motor-driven: *The shop has a full range of power tools.* – *vb.* **powering, powered** to supply with power: *nuclear-powered warships.*

The potato was introduced to Europe from South America in the 1500s. A potato plant has pink or white flowers. Tubers (the parts of the plant we eat) form underground on the stems.

powerful *adj.* having great power, strength, authority, or influence.

power station *n.* an electricity generating station.

practical (**prak** ti kǎl) *adj.* **1** concerned with action instead of theory: *He can put his knowledge to practical use.* **2** (of a person) sensible and efficient in deciding and acting.

practical joke *n.* a trick played on someone.

practically *adv.* **1** almost. **2** in a practical way.

practice (**prak** tis) *n.* **1** the process of carrying something out: *She put her ideas into practice.* **2** repeated exercise to improve an ability in an art, sport, etc.

practise (**prak** tis) *vb.* **practising, practised** to do exercises repeatedly in an art, sport, etc. so as to improve your performance.

pragmatic (prag **mat** ik) *adj.* concerned with what is practicable and convenient.

● **Prague** is the capital of the CZECH REPUBLIC.

prairie (**prār** i) *n.* in North America, a treeless grass-covered plain.

prairie dog *n.* a North American rodent that lives in burrows and barks like a dog.

praise (prāz) *vb.* **praising, praised 1** to express admiration or approval of. **2** to worship or glorify with hymns, etc.

prank (prangk) *n.* a trick; a practical joke.

prawn (prön) *n.* a shellfish like a large shrimp.

pray (prā) *vb.* **praying, prayed** to address God, making earnest requests or giving thanks.

prayer *n.* **1** an address to God, making a request or giving thanks: *She says her prayers every day.* **2** an earnest hope or desire.

pre- (prē-) *prefix* before in **1** time, for example *pre-war,* **2** position, for example *prefix.*

preach (prēch) *vb.* **preaching, preached** to deliver a sermon as part of a religious service.

precarious (pri **kār** i ǔs) *adj.* unsafe; insecure.

precaution (pri **kö** shǒn) *n.* a measure taken to avoid a risk or danger: *She wore a coat as a precaution against the cold.* – *adj.* **precautionary**.

Prairie dogs sometimes place sentries on guard at the entrances to their burrows.

PRONUNCIATION GUIDE

fat **a**	all **ö**
fate **ā**	foot **oo**
fast **ä**	moon **o͞o**
among **å**	boy **oi**
met **e**	house **ow**
mean **ē**	demon **ỏ**
silent **ė**	thing **th**
loch **hh**	this **Th**
fin **i**	but **u**
line **ī**	mute **ū**
quick **kw**	fur **û**
got **o**	brochure **ů**
note **ō**	vision **zh**

precede (pri **sēd**) *vb.* **preceding, preceded** to go before, in time, order, position, rank, or importance.

    precedence *n.* the greatest importance; priority: *Safety takes precedence over all else.*

    precedent *n.* a previous incident, legal case, etc. that serves as a basis for a decision in a present one.

precinct (**prē** singkt) *n.* **1** (also in *plural*) the enclosed grounds of a large building, etc.: *The library lies within the university precincts.* **2** a traffic-free zone in a town, etc.: *We walked through the pedestrian precinct.* **3** (*US*) any of the districts into which a city is divided for administrative or policing purposes.

precious (**pre** shůs) *adj.* **1** valuable. **2** dear; treasured: *Her memories are precious to her.*

precipice (**pre** si pis) *n.* a sheer cliff.

précis (**prā** sē) *n.* **précis** (**prā** sēz) a summary of a piece of writing: *My précis contains the main points.*

precise (pri **sīs**) *adj.* **1** exact: *I can't see at this precise moment.* **2** clear; detailed: *He gave her precise instructions.*

    precisely *adv.* exactly.

    precision (pri **si** zhỏn) *n.* accuracy.

predator (**pre** då tỏr) *n.* a bird or animal that kills and feeds on others.

predecessor (**prē** di se sỏr) *n.* **1** the person who had your job before you. **2** an ancestor.

predicament (pri **dik** å měnt) *n.* a difficulty that someone finds themselves in; a dilemma.

predict (pri **dikt**) *vb.* **predicting, predicted** to foretell or forecast.

    prediction *n.* something foretold.

preen (prēn) *vb.* **preening, preened** (of a bird) to clean and smooth its feathers with its beak.

preface (**pre** fås) *n.* an explanatory statement at the beginning of a book. – *vb.* **prefacing, prefaced** to introduce with some preliminary matter or remark: *She prefaced her speech by welcoming her guests.*

prefer (pri **fûr**) *vb.* **preferring, preferred** to like better: *I prefer tea to coffee.*

    preferable (**pref** ěr å běl) *adj.* more desirable, suitable, or advisable; better.

    preference (**pref** ěr ěns) *n.* **1** the preferring of one thing, etc. to another: *She chose pink in preference to purple.* **2** favourable consideration: *I will give preference to experienced applicants.*

prefix (**prē** fiks) *n.* a group of letters such as *un-*, *re-*, *non-*, *de-* added to the beginning of a word to create a new word.

pregnant (**preg** nånt) *adj.* carrying an unborn child or young in the womb. – *n.* **pregnancy, pregnancies**.

prehistoric (prē hi **sto** rik) *adj.* belonging or relating to the time before there were written historical records. – *n.* **prehistory**.

The tiger is a skilled predator. It stalks its prey by creeping slowly towards it until it is near enough to pounce. The tiger makes sure that the wind is blowing its own scent away from the other animal.

prejudice (**pre** joo dis) *n.* a biased opinion or unreasonable dislike of something or someone: *He was a victim of racial prejudice.* – *vb.* **prejudicing, prejudiced** to cause someone to feel unreasonable dislike; to bias.

preliminary (pri **lim** in å ri) *adj.* occurring at the beginning; introductory or preparatory.

premier (**prem** i ẻr) *adj.* first in rank; most important; leading: *Rotterdam is Europe's premier port.* – *n.* a prime minister.

première (**prem** i er) *n.* the first public performance of a play or showing of a film.

premium (**prē** mi ûm) *n.* **1** an amount paid regularly to an insurance company. **2** an extra sum added to wages or to interest.

prepare (pri **pār**) *vb.* **preparing, prepared** to make or get ready for something.

preparation (pre på **rā** shŏn) *n.* the process of preparing or being prepared.

preparatory (pri **pa** rå tŏ ri) *adj.* serving to prepare for something; introductory.

prepared *adj.* willing: *He is not prepared to lend any more money.*

preposition (pre pŏ **zi** shŏn) *n.* a word such as *to, from, into, against,* that describes the position, movement, etc. of things or people in relation to one another.

prescribe (pri **skrīb**) *vb.* **prescribing, prescribed** to advise as a remedy.

prescription (pri **skrip** shŏn) *n.* instructions from a doctor for preparing a medicine, etc.

presence (**pre** zẻns) *n.* **1** the state, or circumstance, of being in a place. **2** someone's physical bearing: *The actress has great presence.*

present *adj.* **1** being here; being at the place or occasion in question. **2** existing now: *This is the present situation.* – *n.* the present time. **2** a verb in the present tense. – **at present** now.

presently *adv.* **1** soon; shortly. **2** (especially *US*) at the present time; now.

present[1] (pri **zent**) *vb.* **presenting, presented 1** to give formally or ceremonially: *He presented her with a medal.* **2** to introduce a person, especially to someone distinguished.

present[2] (**pre** zẻnt) *n.* something given; a gift.

present[3] (**pre** zẻnt). See **presence**.

preserve (pri **zûrv**) *vb.* **preserving, preserved 1** to save from loss, damage, decay, or deterioration. **2** to treat food, for example by freezing, smoking, drying, pickling, or boiling in sugar, so that it will last.

preservative *n.* a substance used to treat food to prevent it decaying.

preside (pri **zīd**) *vb.* **presiding, presided** to take the chair at a meeting; to be in charge.

president (**pre** zi dẻnt) *n.* **1** the elected head of state in a republic. **2** the head of an organization. – *adj.* **presidential** (pre zi **den** shål).

presidency *n.* **presidencies** the rank or period of office of a president.

The faces of four American presidents are carved into Mt Rushmore. They are George Washington, Thomas Jefferson, Abraham Lincoln, and Theodore Roosevelt.

●**Presley, Elvis** (1935-77) was an American singer whose new type of music had world-wide impact, for which he was dubbed 'King of Rock 'n' Roll'.

press (pres) *vb.* **pressing, pressed 1** to push steadily; to hold firmly against something; to flatten: *He pressed his nose against the glass.* **2** to iron clothes, etc. **3** to persuade; to ask insistently: *He is pressing for a pay rise.* – *n.* **1** any apparatus for pressing, flattening, squeezing, etc.: *a trouser press.* **2** a printing-press. **3** newspapers in general.

pressed *adj.* under pressure; in a hurry.

pressing *adj.* urgent: *I have a pressing meeting.*

pressure (**pre** shŭr) *n.* **1** the force produced by pushing on something. **2** forceful persuasion: *They put pressure on her to resign.* **3** tension, strain: *He found the pressures of family life too much.*

prestige (pre **stēzh**) *n.* fame or reputation due to rank or success.

presume (pri **zūm**) *vb.* **presuming, presumed** to suppose something to be the case: *We presumed he was right.*

Water pressure increases the deeper you go in the ocean. At 3,785 metres, where the wreck of the Titanic *lies, water pressure is 350 times that at the surface.*

Scuba diver 130m

Nuclear sub 700m

Wreck of Titanic 3,785m

Trieste bathyscaphe dived to 11,000m

pretence (pri **tens**) *n.* an act put on deliberately to mislead: *His anger was mere pretence.*

pretend (pri **tend**) *vb.* **pretending, pretended** to make believe; to give the impression that something is the case when it is not: *He pretended to be asleep.*

pretentious (pri **ten** shŭs) *adj.* pompous and self-important; showy; ostentatious.

pretext (**prē** tekst) *n.* a false excuse.

● **Pretoria** is the administrative capital of SOUTH AFRICA. Parliament is in Cape Town.

pretty (**pri** ti) *adj.* **prettier, prettiest** charming to look at. – *adv.* fairly; rather: *I am pretty tired.*

prevail (pri **vāl**) *vb.* **prevailing, prevailed 1** to win through. **2** to be widespread or generally accepted: *They accepted the prevailing opinion.*

prevent (pri **vent**) *vb.* **preventing, prevented** to stop someone from doing something, or something from happening: *The roadblock prevented us from passing.* – *adj.* **preventable** or **preventible**. – *n.* **prevention**.

preview (**prē** vū) *n.* a showing of a film, play, exhibition, etc., before it is shown to the general public.

previous (**prē** vi ŭs) *adj.* earlier: *They had met on a previous occasion.*

prey (prā) *n.* a creature that is hunted and killed for food: *The owl was in search of prey.* – *vb.* **preying, preyed** to hunt for food.

This anaconda is killing its prey by squeezing it to death. Like pythons and boas, anacondas are constrictors.

prickle (**pri** kĕl) *n.* a sharp point or thorn on a plant or creature.

prickly *adj.* **pricklier, prickliest 1** having prickles. **2** (*colloquial*) irritable; over-sensitive.

pride (prīd) *n.* **1** a feeling of pleasure and satisfaction at your own or someone else's accomplishments, etc. **2** self-respect; personal dignity. **3** a group of lions. – *vb.* **priding, prided** to congratulate yourself on: *He prided himself on his youthful figure.*

priest (prēst) *n.* in some Christian churches, an ordained minister. – *adj.* **priestly**.

prim (prim) *adj.* **primmer, primmest** formal and prudish; easily shocked by anything rude,

primaeval or **primeval** (prī **mē** văl) *adj.* the early period of the history of the Earth.

primary (**prī** mă ri) *adj.* **1** first or most important; principal: *Money is our primary concern.* **2** earliest in order or development: *She is still at the primary stage.* – *n.* **primaries** (also **primary election**) in the United States, a preliminary election, in which voters choose candidates for political office.

primarily (**prī** mă ri li) or (prī **me** ri li) *adv.* chiefly; mainly.

primary colour *n.* one of the colours from which all others can be produced by mixing. The primary colours of light are red, green, and blue; those of paint are red, yellow, and blue.

primate (**prī** māt) *n.* **1** (also (**prī** măt)) an archbishop. **2** a member of the highest order of mammals, including monkeys, apes, humans.

prime (prīm) *adj.* chief; fundamental.

● **Priam** in Greek mythology, was king of TROY.

price (prīs) *n.* **1** the amount, usually in money, for which a thing is sold or offered. **2** what must be given up in order to gain something: *Loss of freedom is the price of celebrity.* – **at a price** at great expense.

priceless *adj.* too valuable to have a price.

prick (prik) *vb.* **pricking, pricked** to pierce slightly with a fine point.

prime minister *n.* the chief minister of a government.

prime number *n.* a number that is exactly divisible only by itself and one, e.g. 3.

primitive (**prim** i tiv) *adj.* **1** belonging to earliest times, or the earliest stages of development: *primitive man.* **2** simple, rough, or crude: *They were living in primitive conditions.*

primrose (**prim** rōz) *n.* a small wild plant with pale yellow flowers that appear in spring.

prince (prins) *n.* a male member of a royal family, especially the son of a king and queen.

Prince of Wales *n.* the title given to the eldest son of the British sovereign.

princess *n.* the wife or daughter of a prince.

Edward, Prince of Wales, was known as the Black Prince from the colour of his armour. A brilliant general, he died before his father, King Edward II.

●**Prince Edward Island (P.E.I.)** is Canada's smallest province. Charlotte-town is the capital.

principal (**prin** si pål) *adj.* first in rank or importance; chief; main. – *n.* the head of an educational institution.

principle (**prin** si pål) *n.* a general truth or scientific law, especially one that explains the way a machine works.

print (print) *vb.* **printing, printed 1** to reproduce text or pictures on paper in large quantities, using a printing-press or other mechanical means. **2** to write in separate letters instead of joined-up writing. – *n.* **1** a mark made on a surface by the pressure of something in contact with it: *She could see her footprints in the sand.* **2** a photograph made from a negative.

●The chief methods of printing are letterpress (from a raised surface), lithography (from flat plates), and photogravure (from designs cut into the plate).

printer *n.* a person or business engaged in printing books, newspapers, etc.

printing *n.* the art or business of producing books, etc. in print.

printing press *n.* a machine for printing books, newspapers, etc.

print-out *n.* information from a computer printed out on paper.

prior (**prī** ôr) *adj.* **1** (of an engagement) already arranged for the time in question; previous. **2** more urgent or pressing: *Her ill daughter has a prior claim to her time.*

priority *n.* something that must be attended to before anything else.

prise (prīz) *vb.* **prising, prised** to lever something open: *Pat prised open the lid.*

prism (**pri** zěm) *n.* a transparent solid with triangular ends that separates a beam of white light into the colours of the spectrum.

prison (**pri** zǒn) *n.* a building where criminals are confined.

prisoner *n.* a person who is held in captivity.

private (**prī** vǎt) *adj.* **1** not open to the general public: *You may not enter the private rooms.* **2** kept secret from others; confidential: *This is a private matter.* **3** relating to your personal, as distinct from your professional, life: *His private affairs were widely reported in the papers.* – **in private** not in public; in secret. – *n.* **privacy**.

privatize or **privatise** *vb.* **privatizing, privatized** to transfer a state-owned business to private ownership. – *n.* **privatization**.

privilege (**pri** vi lij) *n.* a special right or advantage granted to an individual or a selected few.

privileged *adj.* enjoying the advantages of wealth and class.

To print in colour four different inks on four cylindrical printing plates are used. The four inks are yellow, magenta (red), cyan (blue), and black. Each colour is printed in turn one after the other. Mixed together these four colours can give the effect of all other colours.

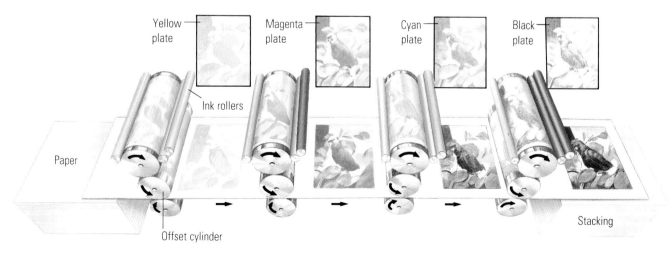

Yellow plate — Magenta plate — Cyan plate — Black plate — Ink rollers — Paper — Offset cylinder — Stacking

Pioneer-Venus 2 *acted as a carrier to four smaller probes on the way to Venus in 1978. As it approached Venus, Pioneer launched its four probes towards different parts of the planet.*

prize (prīz) *n.* **1** something won in a competition, game, etc. **2** a reward given in recognition of excellence: *She won the school music prize.* – *adj.* valued highly by a person. – *vb.* **prizing, prized** to value highly.

pro- (prō-) *prefix* in favour of; admiring or supporting: *He is very pro-French.*

probable (pro bå běl) *adj.* likely to happen: *A draw seems the probable outcome.*
  probability *n.* **probabilities** a likelihood.
  probably *adv.* almost certainly.

probation (prŏ **bā** shŏn) *n.* **1** the system under which someone convicted of a crime is allowed to go free under the supervision of a probation officer: *He was put on probation for six months.* **2** a period during which a new employee is observed on the job, before he or she is given the job permanently. – *adj.* **probationary**.

probe (prōb) *n.* **1** a long slender usually metal instrument used by doctors to examine a wound. **2** (also **space probe**) an unmanned spacecraft that records and transmits data back to Earth. – *vb.* **probing, probed 1** to examine with a probe. **2** to investigate closely.

problem (**prob** lěm) *n.* **1** a person, situation, or matter that is difficult to understand or deal with. **2** a puzzle or mathematical question.

proboscis (prŏ **bo** sis), (prŏ **bos** kis), or (prŏ **bō** sis) *n.* a flexible, elongated nose or snout, for example the trunk of an elephant.

procedure (prō **sē** jŭr) *n.* an established routine. – *adj.* **procedural**.

proceed (prŏ **sēd**) *vb.* **proceeding, proceeded 1** to make your way; to move: *They proceeded slowly along the road.* **2** to go on; to continue after stopping: *She proceeded with her work after the interruption.*

proceeds (**prō** sēdz) *n.* (*plural*) money made by an event, sale, etc.

process (**prō** ses) *n.* a series of operations or stages resulting in development or transformation. – *vb.* **processing, processed** to put through the required stages; to deal with appropriately: *The office is processing my request.*

procession (prŏ **se** shŏn) *n.* a line of people or vehicles proceeding in orderly formation.

proclaim *vb.* **proclaiming, proclaimed** to announce publicly.

procrastinate (prō **kras** ti nāt) *vb.* **procrastinating, procrastinated** to keep putting off doing something. – *n.* **procrastination**. – *n.* **procrastinator**.

prod (prod) *vb.* **prodding, prodded** to poke, jab, or nudge. – *n.* a poke, jab, or nudge.

prodigal (pro di gål) *adj.* extravagant or wasteful.

prodigy (**pro** di ji) *n.* **prodigies** a person, especially a child, of extraordinary brilliance or talent.

produce (prŏ **dūs**) *vb.* **producing, produced 1** to bring out or present to view. **2** to make or manufacture. **3** to direct a play, a radio or television programme for presentation. – (**pro** dūs) *n.* what is produced, especially from land or livestock: *The shop sells farm produce.*

product (**pro** dukt) *n.* **1** something made to be sold for example through manufacture or agriculture. **2** a result: *This book is the product of hours of thought.* **3** in mathematics, the number got by multiplying: *The product of 2 and 4 is 8.*

production (prŏ **duk** shŏn) *n.* **1** the process of manufacturing or growing something: *The car goes into production next year.* **2** a particular presentation of a play, opera, ballet, etc.
  productive *adj.* yielding a lot; fertile; fruitful.

profession (prŏ **fe** shŏn) *n.* an occupation, especially one that requires extensive training, e.g. medicine, law, teaching, engineering.
  professional *adj.* **1** earning your living in the performance, practice, or teaching of something that is a pastime for others: *She is a professional tennis player.* **2** belonging to a trained profession. – *n.* someone who is trained in a certain field.
  professor *n.* a teacher in a university.

profile (**prō** fil) *n.* **1** a side view of something, especially a face or head. **2** a brief outline or sketch of a person.

profit (**pro** fit) *n.* money gained from selling something for more than was paid for it. – *vb.* **profiting, profited** to benefit.

A production line assembly using computer-controlled robots to do the routine jobs.

profitable *adj.* **1** (of a business, etc.) making a profit. **2** useful; fruitful. − *n.* **profitability**.

profound (prŏ **fownd**) *adj.* deep; intense: *She fell into a profound sleep.*

programme (**prō** gram) *n.* **1** a leaflet giving information about a theatre performance, entertainment, ceremony, etc. **2** a plan or schedule: *What's the programme for this morning?* **3** a scheduled radio or television presentation. **4** **program** a set of coded instructions to a computer. − *vb.*

programming, programmed to set a computer to perform a set of tasks.

progress (**prō** gres) *n.* **1** movement while travelling in any direction; course: *They watched her erratic progress.* **2** movement towards a destination, goal, or state of completion: *The trial has made slow progress.* **3** advances or development: *Scientists are making progress in the treatment of cancer.* − (prō **gres**) *vb.*

progressing, progressed to advance or develop; to improve.

progressive *adj.* advanced in outlook; using, or favouring, new methods.

prohibit (prō **hib** it) *vb.* **prohibiting, prohibited** to forbid, especially by law.

prohibition (prō i **bi** shŏn) *n.* a law or decree prohibiting something.

project (**pro** jekt) *n.* **1** a plan, scheme, or proposal. **2** a research or study assignment. − (prŏ **jekt**) *vb.* **projecting, projected** to jut out: *The headland projects into the bay.*

projection *n.* **1** something that protrudes from a surface. **2** the showing of a film or transparencies on a screen. **3** a forecast based on present trends and other known data. **4** on maps, the representation of part of the Earth's sphere on a flat surface.

projector *n.* a machine for projecting films or transparencies on to a screen.

projectile (prō **jek** tīl) *n.* an object that is thrown with force: *Arrows are projectiles.*

●**Prokofiev, Sergei** (1891-1953) was a Russian composer: *Peter and the Wolf.*

prolific (prō **lif** ik) *adj.* abundant and plentiful.

prolong (prō **long**) *vb.* **prolonging, prolonged** to make longer; to extend.

prominent (**pro** mi nĕnt) *adj.* **1** jutting out; protruding; bulging: *He has a prominent chin.* **2** leading; notable: *She is a prominent politician.* − *n.* **prominence**.

promise (**pro** mis) *vb.* **promising, promised** **1** to give an undertaking to do or not do something. **2** to look likely to do something: *The young pianist promises to have a great future.*

promising *adj.* showing promise; talented.

promontory (**pro** mŏn tŏ ri) *n.* **promontories** a part of a coastline that projects into the sea.

promote (prŏ **mōt**) *vb.* **promoting, promoted** **1** to raise to a more senior position: *He has been promoted to lieutenant.* **2** to contribute to; to work for the cause of: *Exercise promotes health.* − *n.* **promotion**. − *adj.* **promotional**.

prompt (prompt) *adj.* immediate; quick; punctual: *They were prompt to offer help.* − *adv.* punctually: *They met at 2.15 prompt.*

prone (prōn) *adj.* **1** lying flat. **2** liable to suffer from: *She is prone to illness.*

prong (prong) *n.* a point or spike, especially one of those making up the head of a fork.

pronoun (**prō** nown) *n.* a word such as *she, him, they, it* used in place of a noun.

pronounce (prŏ **nowns**) *vb.* **pronouncing, pronounced** **1** to say a word. **2** to declare officially or formally: *He pronounced her innocent.*

pronounced *adj.* noticeable; distinct.

pronunciation (prŏ nun si **ā** shŏn) *n.* the usual way of pronouncing words, sounds, etc.

proof (prōōf) *n.* conclusive evidence that something is true or a fact. − *adj.* designed to withstand or be free from: *The roof is proof against storms.*

prop (prop) *n.* **1** a stick used to support things: *She raised the washing line with a clothes prop.* **2** a person or thing that you depend on for help or emotional support. − *vb.* **propping, propped** to support or hold upright with a prop.

propaganda (pro pă **gan** dă) *n.* information presented so as to influence public feeling.

Political propaganda in China. Large posters of Party leaders formed the backdrop to speeches at a meeting of the Communist party in Shanghai in 1948. Propaganda posters are used to great effect for such things as road safety campaigns and health warnings.

Most boats with engines are pushed through the water by one or more **propellers.** As the propeller spins, its blades screw their way through the water, pushing it backwards. This thrusts the boat forwards.

The first ships with engines used paddle-wheels (above) to propel them. As the wheels turned, the paddles pushed against the water, driving the ships forwards. A boat with propellers is sucked forwards as the propeller's blades work like underwater sails or wings.

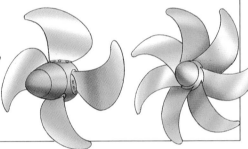

A propeller's blades are curved and angled to bite into the water. A submarine's propeller (right) may have seven blades to give extra thrust at low speeds.

propel (prŏ **pel**) *vb.* **propelling, propelled** to drive or push forward.

propeller *n.* a device consisting of a shaft with blades that is turned by the engine to propel a ship or an aircraft.

proper (**pro** pĕr) *adj.* **1** real; genuine: *We need a proper holiday.* **2** right; correct: *You must learn the proper grip.*

properly *adv.* **1** suitably; appropriately; correctly. **2** with strict accuracy: *Spiders can't properly be called insects.*

proper noun *n.* the name of a particular person, place, or thing.

property (**pro** pĕr ti) *n.* **properties** **1** something that someone owns: *That book is my property.* **2** a piece of land. **3** a quality.

prophecy (**pro** fĕ si) *n.* **prophecies** the foretelling of what will happen in the future.

prophet (**pro** fit) *n.* a person who predicts what may happen in the future.

proportion (prŏ **pör** shŏn) *n.* **1** a part of a total: *She has offended a large proportion of the population.* **2** the size of one element or group in relation to the whole or total: *Only a small proportion of lawyers are women.* **3** the correct balance between parts or elements: *The hands are out of proportion with the head.*

propose (prŏ **pōz**) *vb.* **proposing, proposed** **1** to offer a plan, etc. for consideration; to suggest. **2** to intend: *I don't propose to sell.* **3** to make an offer of marriage.

proposal *n.* **1** something proposed or suggested; a plan. **2** an offer of marriage.

proprietor (prŏ **prī** ĕ tŏr) *n.* an owner, especially of a shop, hotel, business, etc.

propulsion (prŏ **pul** shŏn) *n.* the process of driving forward; a force that propels: *A squid swims by jet propulsion.* – *adj.* **propulsive**.

prose (prōz) *n.* ordinary written or spoken language as distinct from verse or poetry.

prosecute (**pro** si kūt) *vb.* **prosecuting, prosecuted** to bring a criminal action against someone.

prospect (**pro** spekt) *n.* **1** something likely to happen: *She was sad at the prospect of losing her job.* **2** (in *plural*) an outlook for the future; chances of success, etc.

prosper (**pro** spĕr) *vb.* **prospering, prospered** to do well, especially financially.

prosperity *n.* success; wealth: *The factory has brought prosperity to the town.*

prosperous *adj.* wealthy and successful.

protect (prŏ **tekt**) *vb.* **protecting, protected** to shield from danger; to guard against injury.

protection *n.* the action of protecting or condition of being protected; shelter, refuge.

protective *adj.* giving protection; tending to protect: *She feels protective towards her children.*

protein (**prō** tēn) *n.* any of a group of organic compounds essential to the make-up of all living cells.

protest (prŏ **test**) *vb.* **protesting, protested** **1** to express an objection, opposition, or disagreement. **2** to declare in response to an accusation: *He protested his innocence.* – (**prō** test) *n.* **1** a declaration of disapproval; an objection. **2** an organized public demonstration.

Protestant (**pro** ti stănt) *n.* a member of any of the Christian Churches that rejected the authority of the pope and separated from the Roman Catholic Church in the 16th century. – *n.* **Protestantism**.

proton (**prō** ton) *n.* an atomic particle with a positive electrical charge.

prototype (**prō** tō tīp) *n.* a first working version, for example of a vehicle or aircraft.

protrude (prŏ trōͦd) *vb.* **protruding, protruded** to project; to stick out: *Eric has protruding ears!* – *n.* **protrusion**.

●**Proust, Marcel** (1871-1922) was a French novelist: *Remembrance of Things Past*.

proud (prowd) *adj.* **1** feeling pride at your own or another's accomplishments, your possessions, etc. **2** arrogant; conceited: *She is too proud to talk to us.* **3** honoured; delighted.

prove (prōͦv) *vb.* **proving, proved 1** to show to be true, correct, or a fact. **2** to be found to be, when tried; to turn out to be.

proverb (**pro** vûrb) *n.* a saying that gives advice or expresses a supposed truth about life: 'Look before you leap'.

provide (prŏ **vīd**) *vb.* **providing, provided** to supply. – *n.* **provider**.
provided or **providing that** *conj.* on the condition or understanding that.

province (**pro** vins) *n.* an administrative division of a country.

provincial (prŏ **vin** shǎl) *adj.* **1** belonging to or relating to a province. **2** relating to the parts of a country away from the capital: *He has a provincial accent.* – *n.* **provincialism**.

provision (prŏ **vi** zhŏn) *n.* **1** something provided or made available; facilities: *There is provision for disabled pupils.* **2** preparations; measures taken in advance: *We must make provision for the future.* **3** (in *plural*) food.
provisional *adj.* liable to be altered.

provoke (prŏ **vōk**) *vb.* **provoking, provoked 1** to annoy or infuriate, especially deliberately. **2** to cause or stir up: *The interview provoked a storm of protest.*

prow (prow) *n.* the front part of a ship.

prowl (prowl) *vb.* **prowling, prowled** to move about stealthily. – *n.* **prowler**.

proximity (prok **sim** i ti) *n.* nearness; closeness.

prudent (**prōͦ** děnt) *adj.* wise or careful; frugal; shrewd. – *n.* **prudence**.

prune¹ (prōͦn) *vb.* **pruning, pruned** to cut off branches from a shrub to improve its growth.

prune² (prōͦn) *n.* a dried plum.

pry (prī) *vb.* **pries, prying, pried** to investigate the personal affairs of others.

psalm (säm) *n.* a sacred song from the Book of Psalms in the Old Testament of the Bible.

pseudo- (**sū** dō-) or **pseud-** *prefix* false.

pseudonym (**sū** dō nim) *n.* a false name used by an author.

psychiatry (sī **kī** å tri) *n.* the study of the treatment of mental illness. – *adj.* **psychiatric** (sī ki **a** trik). – *n.* **psychiatrist**.

psychology (sī **kol** ŏ ji) *n.* the study of the human mind and the reasons for human behaviour. – *n.* **psychologist**.
psychological (sī kŏ **loj** i kål) *adj.* relating to the mind.

psychopath (**sī** kō path) *n.* a person with a personality disorder who is liable to behave violently without feeling any guilt.

pterodactyl (te rō **dak** til) *n.* an extinct flying reptile with a bird-like skull and leathery wings.

●**Ptolemy** (**tol** ě mi) (AD 100-168) was a Greek astronomer who proposed that the Earth was the centre of the universe.

puberty (**pū** běr ti) *n.* the stage in life during which the reproductive organs develop.

public (**pub** lik) *adj.* **1** of, or concerning, all the people of a country or community: *The government is concerned about public health.* **2** provided for the use of the community: *The town has two public parks.* **3** made, done, held, etc. openly, for all to see and hear: *He made a public announcement.* – *n.* (*singular* or *plural*) the people or community. – **in public** in the presence of other people.
publication *n.* the process of publishing a book, magazine, newspaper, etc.
publicity *n.* advertising or other activity designed to rouse public interest in something.
publicize or **publicise** *vb.* **publicizing, publicized** to advertise.

publish (**pub** lish) *vb.* **publishing, published** to prepare, produce, and distribute printed material, computer software, etc. for sale.
publisher *n.* a person or company engaged in the business of publishing books, etc.

Pterodactyls (meaning 'winged fingers') belonged to the group pterosaurs or 'winged lizards'. Most pterodactyls had long wings, little or no tail, and a toothless beak. Some were as small as a sparrow; others bigger than an eagle.

FAMOUS PSEUDONYMS	
Pseudonym	*Real Name*
Mark Twain	*Samuel Langhorne Clemens*
George Eliot	*Mary Ann Evans*
George Sand	*Aurore Dupin*
Lewis Carroll	*Charles Lutwidge Dodgson*
Voltaire	*François-Marie Arouet*

●**Puccini, Giacomo** (1858-1924) was the Italian composer whose operas include *La Bohème* and *Tosca*.

pudding (**poo** ding) *n.* any sweet food served as dessert.

puddle (**pu** děl) *n.* a small pool, especially of rainwater on the road.

●**Puerto Rico**, an island in the Caribbean, is a self-governing part of the United States.

puff (puf) *n.* **1** a small cloud of smoke, dust, or steam emitted from something. **2** (*colloquial*) breath: *I am quite out of puff.* – *vb.* **puffing, puffed 1** to breathe with difficulty. **2** (of smoke, steam, etc.) to emerge in small gusts.

puffin (**pu** fin) *n.* a black and white sea bird.

pug (pug) *n.* a small dog with a flattened snout.

●**Pulitzer Prizes** are awarded each year for outstanding achievements in American journalism, literature, and music. They are named after the Hungarian-born newspaper magnate Joseph Pulitzer (1847-1911).

pull (pool) *vb.* **pulling, pulled 1** to grip strongly and draw or force towards yourself; to tug or drag. **2** to draw a trailer, etc.: *The car was pulling a caravan.* – *n.* **1** an act of pulling. **2** attraction; attracting force: *He feels the pull of his homeland.* – *vb.* **pull in 1** (of a train) to halt at a station. **2** (of a vehicle or driver) to move to the side of the road. – *vb.* **pull out 1** to extract. **2** to withdraw from a competition, etc.

pulley (**poo** li) *n.* **pulleys** a device for lifting and lowering weights, consisting of a wheel with a rope or belt.

pullover (**pool** ō věr) *n.* a knitted garment pulled on over the head; a sweater or jumper.

pulmonary (**pool** mǒn ǎ ri) *adj.* of the lungs.

pulp (pulp) *n.* **1** the soft part of a fruit or vegetable. **2** a soft wet mass of mashed food or other material: *Paper is made from wood pulp.*

pulpit (**pool** pit) *n.* a platform in a church, from which the preacher delivers the sermon.

pulse[1] (puls) *n.* **1** the rhythmical beat of blood being pumped through the body, noticeable where an artery nears the skin surface, for example at the wrist. **2** a regular throbbing beat in music. – *vb.* **pulsing, pulsed** to throb.

pulse[2] (puls) *n.* the edible seeds of plants such as beans, peas, and lentils.

puma (**pū** mǎ) *n.* one of the big cats of America; the cougar.

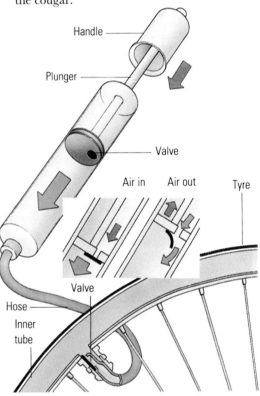

Most pumpkins are orange and they grow at ground level on a trailing plant. In the US, pumpkin pie is a traditional dish on Thanksgiving Day. At Hallowe'en (the evening before All Saints' Day on 31st October) children carve Jack-o'-lanterns (hollowed out pumpkins).

How a bicycle pump works. A valve allows the air to flow only one way.

pump (pump) *n.* any of various devices for forcing liquids or gases into or out of something, etc. – *vb.* **pumping, pumped**.

pumpkin (**pump** kin) *n.* a large round thick-skinned yellow fruit used as a vegetable.

pun (pun) *n.* a form of joke consisting of a play on words, especially one where an association is created between words of similar sound but different meaning, for example *A pun is a punishable offence.* – *vb.* **punning, punned**.

punch¹ (punch) *vb.* **punching, punched** to hit with your fist. – *n.* a blow with the fist.

punch² (punch) *n.* a tool for cutting holes in leather, paper, etc. – *vb.* **punching, punched** to pierce: *The inspector punched our tickets.*

punctual (**pungk** choo ål) *adj.* happening at the arranged time; not late. – *n.* **punctuality** (pungk choo **al** i ti).

punctuate (**pungk** choo āt) *vb.* **punctuating, punctuated** to put punctuation marks into a piece of writing.

punctuation mark *n.* any of the set of marks such as the full stop, comma, question mark, colon, etc. used in written matter.

puncture (**pungk** chẻr) *n.* a small hole pierced in something with a sharp point: *We were late because we had a puncture in one of our tyres.* – *vb.* **puncturing, punctured** to make a hole in something.

punish (**pun** ish) *vb.* **punishing, punished** to cause someone who has done something wrong to suffer for their offence.

punishable *adj.* (of offences) liable to be punished, especially by law.

punishment *n.* the act of punishing or process of being punished: *A fine is a punishment.*

● **Punjabi** (poon **jä** bi) *n.* & *adj.* (of) a language spoken in the Punjab in north-west INDIA.

punk (pungk) *n.* a follower of punk rock, and punk styles such as spiky brightly-coloured hair and black torn clothes.

punk rock *n.* loud aggressive rock music popular in the 1970s and 1980s.

pupa (**pū** på) *n.* **pupae** (**pū** pē) or **pupas** the form an insect takes during the stage when it is changing from larva to adult.

pupil¹ (**pū** pil) *n.* someone who is being taught; a schoolchild or student.

pupil² (**pū** pil) *n.* the circular opening in the middle of the eye through which the light passes to the retina.

puppet (**pu** pit) *n.* a doll that can be made to move by strings or sticks attached to its limbs, or by fitting over the hand.

puppy (**pu** pi) *n.* **puppies** a young dog.

● **Purcell, Henry** (1659-95) was an English composer of songs and church music.

purchase (**pûr** chås) *vb.* **purchasing,** **purchased** to obtain in return for payment; to buy. – *n.* something that has been bought. – *n.* **purchaser**.

purdah (**pûr** då) *n.* the separation of women from public view in some Muslim and Hindu societies.

pure (pūr) *adj.* **1** consisting of itself only; unmixed with anything else: *My ring is pure gold.* **2** unpolluted; wholesome: *She tasted the pure water.* **3** virtuous; free from sin or guilt. – *n.* **pureness**. – **pure and simple** and nothing else: *It's jealousy pure and simple.*

pure-bred *adj.* (of animals) of unmixed breed.

purge (pûrj) *vb.* **purging, purged** to get rid of impure or unwanted elements from anything.

purify (**pū** ri fï) *vb.* **purifies, purifying, purified** to make pure; to remove all harmful substances. – *n.* **purification**. – *n.* **purifier**.

Water from reservoirs goes to the water works to be purified. The water is filtered through beds of sand to remove dirt and bacteria particles. Chlorine may be added to kill germs. Fluoride is sometimes added to water to help strengthen teeth.

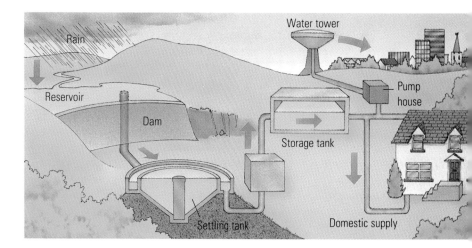

puritan (**pū** ri tån) *n.* **1 Puritan** a supporter of the 16th- to 17th-century Protestant movement in England and America that tried to rid church worship of ritual. **2** a person of strict moral principles. – *adj.* **puritanical** (pū ri **tan** i kål).

purity (**pū** ri ti) *n.* the state of being pure.

purple (**pûr** pẻl) *n.* a colour that is a mixture of blue and red. – *adj.* of this colour.

purpose (**pûr** pòs) *n.* **1** the function for which something is intended: *I don't know the purpose of this.* **2** an intention, aim, or goal. – **on purpose** intentionally; deliberately.

purr (pûr) *vb.* **purring, purred** (of a cat) to make a soft, vibrating sound when happy.

purse (pûrs) *n.* **1** a small container carried in the pocket or handbag, for keeping cash, etc. in. **2** (*North American*) a woman's handbag.

PRONUNCIATION GUIDE	
fat **a**	all **ö**
fate **ā**	foot **oo**
fast **ä**	moon **ōō**
among **å**	boy **oi**
met **e**	house **ow**
mean **ē**	demon **ỏ**
silent **ê**	thing **th**
loch **hh**	this **Th**
fin **i**	but **u**
line **ī**	mute **ū**
quick **kw**	fur **û**
got **o**	brochure **ů**
note **ō**	vision **zh**

Building a pyramid in the Egyptian desert. Labourers drag blocks on wooden sledges up the huge ramp built alongside the unfinished pyramid. In the foreground, men are smoothing and squaring blocks.

Pythagoras is perhaps most famous for formulating his theory the Pythagorean Theorem *which states that in a right-angled triangle the square on the hypotenuse equals the sum of the squares on the other two sides.*

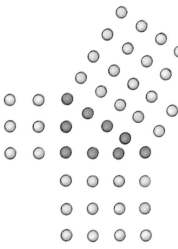

pursue (pŭr **sū**) *vb.* **pursuing, pursued** to follow in order to overtake, capture, etc.

pursuit (pŭr **sūt**) *n.* **1** the act of pursuing or chasing: *They followed in hot pursuit.* **2** an occupation or hobby.

pus (pus) *n.* the thick yellowish liquid that forms in infected wounds.

push (poosh) *vb.* **pushing, pushed** to force away from yourself; to press, thrust, or shove. – *n.* **1** an act of pushing; a thrust or shove. **2** determination, drive. – **at a push** if forced.

pushover *n.* (*colloquial*) **1** someone easily got the better of. **2** a task easily accomplished.

put (poot) *vb.* **putting, put 1** to place in, or move to, a position or situation. **2** to cause to be: *My joke put him in a good mood.* **3** to apply: *I put pressure on them to go.* – *vb.* **put across** to communicate ideas, etc. to others. – *vb.* **put aside** to save money for future use. – *vb.* **put back 1** to replace. **2** to postpone: *We put the meeting back a month.* **3** to adjust a clock to an earlier time. – *vb.* **put forward 1** to offer a proposal or suggestion. **2** to propose someone's name for a post, etc.; to nominate. **3** to advance the time or date of: *We put the wedding forward a month.* – *vb.* **put off 1** to postpone; to cancel. **2** to cause to lose concentration; to distract. **3** to cause to lose enthusiasm for something: *Her accident put me off climbing.* – *vb.* **put on 1** to switch on an electrical device, etc. **2** to present a play, show, etc. – *vb.* **put out 1** to extinguish a light or fire. **2** to inconvenience. **3** to offend or annoy. – *vb.* **put together** to join up the parts of. – *vb.* **put**

up 1 to build; to erect. **2** to raise prices. – *vb.* **put upon** to take unfair advantage.

putt (put) *vb.* **putting, putted** in golf, to send the ball gently forward towards the hole.

putty (**pu** ti) *n.* a paste used to fix glass in window frames, fill holes in wood, etc.

puzzle (**pu** zĕl) *vb.* **puzzling, puzzled 1** to perplex, bewilder, or baffle. **2** to wonder or worry. – *n.* **1** a baffling problem. **2** a game or toy designed to test knowledge or memory.

pyjamas or (*US*) **pajamas** (på **jä** måz) *n.* (*plural*) a sleeping-suit consisting of a loose jacket or top, and trousers.

pylon (**pī** lon) *n.* a tall steel structure for supporting electric power cables.

pyramid (**pi** rå mid) *n.* **1** any of the huge ancient Egyptian royal tombs built on a square base, with four sloping triangular sides meeting at the top. **2** a solid of this shape, with a square or triangular base.

● **Pyrenees** a mountain range forming the border between FRANCE and SPAIN.

Pyrrhic victory (**pi** rik **vik** tŏ ri) *n.* a victory won at so great a cost in lives, etc. that it can hardly be regarded as a triumph at all.

● **Pythagoras** was a Greek mathematician of the 6th century BC who laid the foundations of geometry.

python (**pī** thŏn) *n.* any of several large non-poisonous snakes, including the boa constrictor, that kill their prey by crushing.

Qq

●**Qatar**. See Supplement, **Countries**.

quack (kwak) *n.* the cry of a duck. – *vb.* **quacking, quacked** to make this cry.

quad (kwod) *n.* (*colloquial*) a quadrangle.

quadr- (kwodr-) or **quadri-** (kwod ri-) four.

quadrangle (**kwod** rang gĕl) *n.* a square, rectangle, or other four-sided figure.

quadrant (**kwod** rånt) *n.* **1** a quarter of the circumference of a circle. **2** an instrument used for measuring altitude.

quadrilateral (kwod ri lat ĕ rål) *n.* a four-sided two-dimensional figure.

quadruped (**kwod** roo ped) *n.* a four-footed animal: *Horses are quadrupeds; humans are bipeds.*

quadruple (**kwod** roo pĕl) or (kwo **droo** pĕl) *vb.* **quadrupling, quadrupled** to multiply by four or increase fourfold.

quagmire (**kwag** mīr) or (**kwog** mīr) *n.* a bog.

quail[1] (kwāl) *vb.* **quailing, quailed** to lose courage or feel fear; to flinch.

quail[2] (kwāl) *n.* a bird of the partridge family.

quaint (kwānt) *adj.* pleasingly old-fashioned.

quake (kwāk) *vb.* **quaking, quaked** (of people) to shake or tremble with fear, etc.

Quaker (**kwā** kĕr) *n.* a member of a Christian sect, the Religious Society of Friends, founded by George Fox in the 17th century.

qualify (**kwo** li fī) *vb.* **qualifies, qualifying, qualified 1** to complete a training, pass an examination, etc., that gives you professional status: *Julia qualified as a vet after studying for several years.* **2** to make suitable for a task, job, etc.: *Quentin is hardly qualified to judge.* **qualification** *n.* a skill or ability that fits you for some job, etc.

quality (**kwo** li ti) *n.* **qualities 1** standard of goodness. **2** high standard: *Margaret Atwood writes novels of quality.* – *adj.* of high quality.

qualm (kwäm) *n.* **1** a sudden feeling of apprehension. **2** a pang of conscience: *Have you any qualms about disqualifying her?*

quantity (**kwon** ti ti) *n.* **quantities 1** the property things have that makes them measurable or countable; size or amount. **2** an amount that can be counted or measured; a specified amount: *There was a tiny quantity of milk in the jug.* **3** largeness of amount; bulk.

quantum (**kwon** tŭm) *n.* **quanta** in physics, an indivisible unit of any form of physical energy. **quantum leap** or **jump** *n.* a sudden transition; a spectacular advance.

quarantine (**kwo** rån tēn) *n.* the isolation of people or animals to prevent the spread of any infectious disease.

quarrel (**kwo** rĕl) *n.* **1** an angry disagreement or argument. **2** a cause of such disagreement; a complaint: *I've no quarrel with the management.* – *vb.* **quarrelling, quarrelled 1** to argue or dispute angrily. **2** to disagree and fall out. **quarrelsome** *adj.* inclined to quarrel.

quarry[1] (**kwo** ri) *n.* **quarries** an open excavation for the purpose of extracting stone or slate for building.

quarry[2] (**kwo** ri) *n.* **quarries** a prey.

The common quail of Europe, Asia, and North Africa is 18 cm long, and mottled brown in colour. American quail such as the bobwhite and the crested quail are more colourful and slightly larger.

Quartz is found nearly everywhere. Sand is mostly made of quartz. In its pure form it has no colour and is as clear as glass. Quartz forms six-sided crystals.

KEY QUESTION
What does *qwerty* stand for? It is simply an ACRONYM for the first six letters on a normal computer or typewriter keyboard and it is used to describe such keyboards.

Mary, queen of Scots, on her way to her execution at Fotheringhay Castle in 1587. She was said to have plotted against Elizabeth I, queen of England.

quarter (kwör tĕr) *n.* **1** one of four equal parts into which an object or quantity may be divided; the fraction ¹/₄, one divided by four. **2** any of the three-month divisions of the year. **3** (*US*) a coin worth 25 cents. – *vb.* **quartering, quartered** to divide into quarters. – *adj.* being one of four equal parts.

quartet or **quartette** (kwör tet) *n.* a group of four singers or instrumental players.

quartz (kwörts) *n.* a common rock-forming mineral, silicon dioxide.

quasar (kwā zär) *n.* a highly luminous star-like source of radio waves, outside our galaxy.

quaver (kwā vĕr) *vb.* **quavering, quavered** (of someone's voice) to be unsteady; to shake or tremble. – *n.* **1** a very short musical note. **2** a tremble in the voice. – *adj.* **quavery**.

quay (kē) *n.* a wharf for the loading and unloading of ships.

● **Quebec** is the largest province in CANADA. The largest city is Montreal, the second biggest French-speaking city in the world.

queen (kwēn) *n.* **1** a woman who rules a country, having inherited her position by birth. **2** the wife of a king. **3** a large female ant, bee, or wasp that lays eggs. **4** the most powerful chess piece.

● **Queensland**. See **Australia**.

queer (kwēr) *adj.* odd, strange, or unusual.

quench (kwench) *vb.* **quenching, quenched** to get rid of thirst by drinking.

query (kwēr i) *n.* **queries** a question, often one that raises a doubt. – *vb.* **queries, querying, queried** to raise a doubt about.

quest (kwest) *n.* a search or hunt.

question (kwes chŏn) *n.* **1** an utterance which requests information or an answer; the form of words in which this is expressed: *Can you put your question in writing, please?* **2** a doubt or query: *Their behaviour raises questions about their loyalty.* **3** an uncertainty: *There is no question about the cause of the fire.* – *vb.* **questioning, questioned 1** to ask someone questions; to interrogate. **2** to raise doubts about; to query: *I'd question whether it's possible.*

question mark *n.* the punctuation mark (?) placed after a question.

queue (kū) *n.* a line or file of people or vehicles waiting for something. – *vb.* **queuing, queued**.

quick (kwik) *adj.* **1** taking little time; speedy: *The train journey to Newport is very quick.* **2** lasting briefly: *a quick glance.* **3** not delayed; immediate: *a quick response.* **4** intelligent; alert; sharp: *quick-witted.* – *adv.* rapidly.

quiet (kwī ĕt) *adj.* **1** making little or no noise; soft. **2** (of a place, etc.) peaceful; tranquil; without noise or bustle. **3** silent; saying nothing: *Katie kept quiet about it.* – *n.* absence of, or freedom from, noise. – *adv.* **quietly**. – *n.* **quietness**. – **on the quiet** secretly.

quill (kwil) *n.* a pen made from a bird's feather.

quilt (kwilt) *n.* a thick, padded bedcover.

quince (kwins) *n.* the acid fruit of an Asian tree.

quinine (kwi nēn) *n.* a bitter-tasting drug, used to treat malaria.

quintuplet (kwin tŭp lĕt) *n.* one of five children born to a mother at one birth.

quip (kwip) *n.* a witty remark.

quirk (kwûrk) *n.* an odd habit or mannerism.

quit (kwit) *vb.* **quitting, quitted** or **quit 1** to leave a place, etc. **2** to leave, give up a job.

quite (kwīt) *adv.* **1** completely; entirely: *I don't quite understand; it's not quite clear.* **2** to a high degree: *The work is quite exceptional.* **3** rather; fairly; to some degree: *She's quite promising.*

quiver (kwi vĕr) *vb.* **quivering, quivered** to shake or tremble slightly; to shiver. – *n.*

quixotic (kwik sot ik) *adj.* absurdly chivalrous.

quiz (kwiz) *n.* **quizzes** any series of questions as a test of knowledge. – *vb.* **quizzing, quizzed**.

quota (kwō tå) *n.* someone's allocated share: *I've done my quota of work.*

quote (kwōt) *vb.* **quoting, quoted** to repeat the exact words of: *The teacher liked to quote Milton to the class.*

quotation *n.* **1** something quoted. **2** an estimated price for a job.

quotation marks *n.* (*plural*) the punctuation marks (" " or ' ') used to show the beginning and end of a quotation, or on either side of a word or phrase on which attention is focused.

R r

rabbi (**ra** bī) *n.* **1** a Jewish religious leader. **2** a Jewish scholar or teacher of the law. – *adj.*

rabbit (**ra** bit) *n.* a small, long-eared, burrowing animal with a fluffy white tail.

rabble (**ra** běl) *n.* a noisy, disorderly crowd.

rabies (**rā** bēz) *n.* a fatal disease of the nervous system which is caught by being bitten by an infected animal.

The raccoon belongs to the same family as the panda. Most of the seven species are about the size of a cat.

raccoon or **racoon** (rå **kōōn**) *n.* a small furry North American animal, with a black striped tail and face.

race¹ (rās) *n.* **1** a contest of speed between runners, horses, cars, etc. **2** (in *plural*) a series of such contests over a fixed course, especially for horses or dogs. **3** any contest or rivalry, especially to be the first to do or get something: *the arms race.* – *vb.* **racing, raced** **1** to take part in a race. **2** to run or move quickly. – *n.* **racing**.

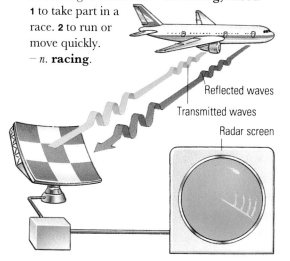

Reflected waves

Transmitted waves

Radar screen

race² (rās) *n.* **1** a major division of human beings having particular physical characteristics, such as size, hair type, or skin colour. **2** a nation, or other group of people.

● **Rachmaninov** (rak **man** in of), **Sergei** (1873-1943) was a Russian pianist and composer.

racial (**rā** shǎl) *adj.* **1** of, or relating to, a particular race. **2** based on race.

racialism or **racism** *n.* a belief that a particular race is superior to others. – *n. & adj.* **racialist** or **racist**.

racket or **racquet** (**rak** it) *n.* a wooden or metal oval frame with catgut or nylon strings stretched across it, used for playing tennis, etc.

radar (**rā** där) *n.* a device for detecting the direction, speed, and distance of an aircraft, ship, etc. by bouncing radio waves off it.

radiate (**rā** di āt) *vb.* **radiating, radiated** **1** to send out rays of light, heat, electromagnetic radiation, etc. **2** (of light, heat, electromagnetic radiation, etc.) to be emitted in rays: *Light radiates from the stars.* **3** to spread out from a central point as radii: *In Paris, roads radiate from the Arc de Triomphe in all directions.*

radiation *n.* the sending out of energy in the form of electromagnetic waves or particles, such as X-rays.

Radar sends out high-frequency radio waves and picks up the signals reflected by an object. The reflected signals displayed as 'blips' on a screen show the distance and direction of an object.

The letter *R*, like all the letters, has a long history. The earliest alphabets were taken and adapted by the Greeks. The Greek *beta*, when combined with the first letter, *aleph*, gives us the word alphabet.

The Greeks passed on their letters to the Romans who developed the alphabet we use today, although they used only capital letters. Small letters developed in the AD 700s.

An early form of the letter R, used in the Middle East over 3000 years ago.

This letter was taken by the Greeks and became rho.

Over the years different versions of the letter R have been developed.

radiator (rā di ā tŏr) *n.* **1** an apparatus for heating a room, consisting of a series of pipes through which hot water (or hot oil) is circulated. **2** an apparatus for cooling an internal combustion engine.

radical (rad i kål) *adj.* **1** of or relating to the basic nature of something; fundamental; far-reaching: *radical changes.* **2** in favour of extreme political and social reforms. – *n.* a person who holds radical political views. – *n.* **radicalism.** – *adv.* **radically.**

radio (rā di ō) *n.* **radios 1** the sending and receiving of messages, etc. without connecting wires, using electromagnetic waves. **2** an electrical apparatus which receives, transmits, or broadcasts signals using electromagnetic waves. – *adj.* **1** of, for, transmitting, or transmitted by radio. **2** controlled by radio. – *vb.* **radios, radioing, radioed** to send a message by radio.

radio telescope *n.* a telescope that can pick up radio waves generated by stars, planets, etc.

radioactivity (rā di ō ak **tiv** i ti) *n.* the spontaneous disintegrating of the atomic nuclei of some elements, for example uranium, resulting in the giving off of radiation.

radish (**rad** ish) *n.* a plant with pungent-tasting, red-skinned white roots.

radius (**rā** di ůs) *n.* **radii** (**rā** di ī) or **radiuses** a straight line running from the centre of a circle to a point on its circumference.

● **Raeburn** (rā bûrn), **Henry** (1756-1823) was a Scottish portrait painter.

raft (räft) *n.* a flat structure of logs, timber, etc. that floats on water.

rafter (**räf** tĕr) *n.* any of several sloping beams supporting a roof.

rag (rag) *n.* a scrap of cloth, especially a piece which has been worn or torn off old clothes.

ragged (**ra** gid) *adj.* **1** (of clothes) old, worn, and tattered: *Rana was wearing a ragged skirt.* **2** with a rough and irregular edge; jagged. – *adv.* **raggedly.** – *n.* **raggedness.**

rage (rāj) *n.* violent anger. – *vb.* **raging, raged 1** to be violently angry. **2** (of the wind, sea, a battle, etc.) to be stormy: *The hurricane raged all night.* – *adj.* **raging.**

raid (rād) *n.* a sudden unexpected attack.

rail (rāl) *n.* **1** a usually horizontal bar supported by vertical posts, forming a fence or barrier. **2** a horizontal bar used to hang things on. **3** either of a pair of lengths of steel forming a track for the wheels of a train.

railing *n.* (usually in *plural*) a fence or barrier.

railroad *n.* (*US*) a railway.

railway *n.* **1** a track or set of tracks formed by two parallel steel rails fixed to sleepers, for trains to run on. **2** a system of such tracks, plus all the trains, buildings, and people required.

rain (rān) *n.* water falling from the clouds in drops. – *vb.* **raining, rained 1** (of rain) to fall. **2** to fall like rain: *The bullets rained down on them.*

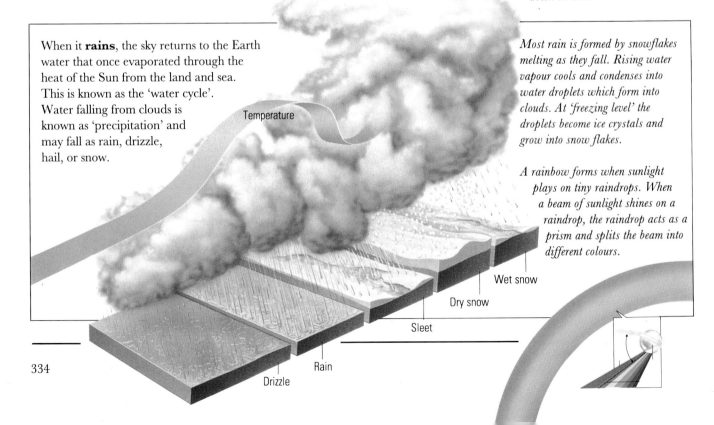

When it **rains**, the sky returns to the Earth water that once evaporated through the heat of the Sun from the land and sea. This is known as the 'water cycle'. Water falling from clouds is known as 'precipitation' and may fall as rain, drizzle, hail, or snow.

Most rain is formed by snowflakes melting as they fall. Rising water vapour cools and condenses into water droplets which form into clouds. At 'freezing level' the droplets become ice crystals and grow into snow flakes.

A rainbow forms when sunlight plays on tiny raindrops. When a beam of sunlight shines on a raindrop, the raindrop acts as a prism and splits the beam into different colours.

Temperature

Wet snow

Dry snow

Sleet

Rain

Drizzle

rainbow *n.* an arch of colours in the sky (red, orange, yellow, green, blue, indigo, and violet), caused by light from the sun's rays being reflected and refracted through rain.

rainforest *n.* a tropical forest, with broad-leaved, evergreen trees and heavy rainfall.

rainy *adj.* **rainier, rainiest**.

raise (rāz) *vb.* **raising, raised 1** to move or lift to a high position or level: *All who agree, raise your hand.* **2** to put in an upright or standing position. **3** to build. **4** to increase the value, amount, or strength of: *Please don't raise your voice.* **5** to collect or gather together: *We raised £200 for Dogs for the Blind.* **6** to bring up or rear: *raise a family.* – *n.* **1** an act of raising or lifting. **2** (*colloquial*, especially *US*) an increase in salary. – *adj.* **raised**. – *n.* **raising**.

raisin (**rā** zin) *n.* a dried grape.

rake (rāk) *n.* a long-handled tool with a comb-like part at one end, used for smoothing or breaking up earth, gathering leaves together, etc. – *vb.* **raking, raked 1** to collect, gather, or remove with, or as if with, a rake: *In autumn you must rake the leaves.* **2** to search carefully: *Laura raked through the files to find the papers she needed.*

● **Raleigh, Sir Walter** (1552-1618) was an English soldier, explorer, and poet. He introduced tobacco and potatoes from America to England.

rally (**ra** li) *vb.* **rallies, rallying, rallied 1** to come or bring together again after being dispersed: *The colonel rallied his troops after the battle.* **2** to come or bring together for some common cause or action: *We rallied behind our team when they were in trouble.* – *n.* **rallies 1** a reassembling of forces to make a new effort. **2** a mass meeting of people with a common cause. **3** in tennis, a long series of strokes between players before one finally wins the point.

ram (ram) *n.* **1** a male sheep. **2** the **Ram** the constellation and sign of the zodiac Aries. **3** a battering-ram. – *vb.* **ramming, rammed** to force down or into position by pushing hard.

Ramadan or **Ramadhan** (**ra** må dän) *n.* the ninth month of the Muslim year, during which Muslims fast between sunrise and sunset.

ramble (**ram** běl) *vb.* **rambling, rambled 1** to go for a long walk or walks, especially in the countryside, for pleasure. **2** to speak or write in an aimless or confused way: *Rebecca rambled on about her boring boyfriend.* – *n.* a walk for pleasure. – *n.* & *adj.* **rambling**.

rambler *n.* **1** a climbing plant, especially a rose. **2** a person who goes walking for pleasure.

● **Rameses** or **Ramses** is the name of any of 12 pharaohs of ancient EGYPT to about 1090 BC. The most famous was Rameses the Second who built the rock temple at Abu Simbel.

ramp (ramp) *n.* a sloping surface between two different levels, especially one that can be used instead of steps.

ramshackle (**ram** sha kěl) *adj.* (especially of buildings) badly made and likely to fall down.

ran. See **run**.

ranch (ränch) *n.* a large farm, especially one in North America, for rearing cattle or horses.

random (**ran** dŏm) *adj.* lacking a plan, system, or order; irregular; haphazard.

rang. See **ring²**.

range (rānj) *n.* **1** an area between limits within which things may move, function, etc.; the limits forming this area: *The range of local radio stations is 50 miles.* **2** a number of items, products, etc. forming a distinct series: *This is a new range of ties, in a wide range of colours.* **3** a group of mountains forming a distinct series or row. – *vb.* **ranging, ranged 1** to put in a row or rows. **2** to put someone into a specified group: *He ranged himself among her enemies.* **3** to vary or change between specified limits: *The horses range from big Clydesdales to tiny Shetland ponies.* **4** to roam: *Sheep range over the hills.*

ranger *n.* a person who looks after a forest.

rank¹ (rangk) *n.* **1** a line or row of people or things. **2** a line of soldiers standing side by side. **3** a position of seniority within an organization, the armed forces, etc.

rank² (rangk) *adj.* **1** coarsely overgrown and untidy. **2** offensively strong in smell or taste.

ransack (**ran** sak) *vb.* **ransacking, ransacked** to search thoroughly: *Rioters ransacked the Church.*

ransom (**ran** sŏm) *n.* money paid in return for the release of a kidnapped person.

The temple of Rameses II was carved out of solid rock on the banks of the Nile. It was moved to a higher position in 1964 when the Aswan High Dam was built.

rap (rap) *n.* **1** the sound made by a quick sharp tap or blow. **2** (*slang*) blame or punishment: *She had to take the rap.* – *vb.* **rapping, rapped** to strike sharply: *Robert rapped on the window.*

rape¹ (rāp) *n.* the crime of forcing someone, to have sex against their will. – *n.* **rapist**.

rape² (rāp) *n.* a plant with brilliant yellow flowers, grown for its seeds.

●**Raphael** (1483-1520) was one of the greatest artists of the Italian RENAISSANCE. His real name was Raffaello Sanzio.

rapid (ra pid) *adj.* moving or happening quickly. – *n.* **rapidity** or **rapidness**.

A 17th-century rapier. Rapiers were long and narrow, two-edged and pointed. Swords of various shapes and sizes were for centuries important battle-field weapons. Later men fought duels with swords.

rapier (rā pi ěr) *n.* a long thin two-edged sword.

rare (rār) *adj.* not done, found, or occurring very often: *Rhinos are becoming rare.*

rash¹ (rash) *adj.* reckless; hasty: *a rash move.*

rash² (rash) *n.* a redness on the skin.

rasher (ra shěr) *n.* a thin slice of bacon or ham.

rasp (räsp) *n.* **1** a coarse, rough file. **2** a harsh, rough, grating sound. – *adj.* **rasping**.

raspberry (räz bě ri) *n.* **raspberries** an edible red berry that grows on a shrub.

Rastafarian (ras tå får i ån) *n.* a follower of an originally West Indian sect, which regards blacks as the chosen people and reveres Haile Selassie, former emperor of Ethiopia, as the Messiah. – *adj.* of Rastafarians.

rat (rat) *n.* **1** a rodent like a large long-tailed mouse. **2** (*colloquial*) a person who is disloyal towards his or her friends, party, etc.

rat race *n.* (*colloquial*) the fierce, unending competition for success in business, etc.

rate (rāt) *n.* **1** the number of times something happens, etc. within a given period of time; *at the rate of 20 miles an hour.* **2** a price or charge, often measured per unit: *What is the rate of pay for the job?* **3** class or rank: *second-rate.* – *vb.* **rating, rated 1** to give a value to: *Roy is rated an excellent teacher.* **2** to be worthy of; to deserve: *Do you think he rates a pay rise?*

rather (rä Thěr) *adv.* **1** more readily; from preference: *I'd rather stay at home than go out.* **2** more truly or properly: *They are my parents, or rather my mother and stepfather.* **3** to a certain extent; somewhat: *They married rather late in life.*

A thornback ray. Like their relations the sharks, rays have skeletons made of cartilage rather than bone.

ratio (rā shi ō) *n.* **ratios** the number or degree of one class of things in relation to another class of things: *The ratio of dogs to cats is 5 to 3.*

ration (ra shǒn) *n.* a fixed allowance of food, clothing, petrol, etc. during a time of shortage. – *vb.* **rationing, rationed** to share out, especially something which is in short supply.

rational (ra shǒ nål) *adj.* **1** of or based on reason or logic. **2** able to think, form opinions, make judgements, etc. – *adv.* **rationally**.

rattle (ra těl) *vb.* **rattling, rattled 1** to make a series of short sharp hard sounds in quick succession: *The dog rattled the cat flap asking to come in.* **2** to cause crockery, etc. to make such a noise. **3** to move along rapidly, often with a rattling noise. – *n.* **1** a series of short sharp hard sounds in quick succession. **2** a baby's toy filled with small pellets which rattle when shaken.

rattlesnake *n.* a poisonous American snake with loose rings on the tail which rattle.

rave (rāv) *vb.* **raving, raved 1** to talk wildly as if mad or delirious. **2** to talk enthusiastically about: *Rose raved about her new pony.*

raven (rā věn) *n.* a large blue-black bird of the crow family. – *adj.* glossy blue-black.

ravine (rå věn) *n.* a deep steep-sided gorge.

raw (rö) *adj.* **1** not cooked: *Lions eat raw meat.* **2** not processed, purified, or refined. **3** not trained or experienced: *raw recruits.* – **in the raw** in a natural state; naked.

raw deal *n.* harsh, unfair treatment.

raw material *n.* any material, usually in its natural state, out of which something is made.

ray¹ (rā) *n.* a narrow beam of light or radioactive particles.

ray² (rā) *n.* a fish with a broad flat body, and eyes on the top of its head.

A rattlesnake rattles its tail as a warning that it is about to strike. Twenty-nine species of rattlesnake live in the Americas.

razor (**rā** zŏr) *n.* a sharp-edged instrument used for shaving.

reach (rēch) *vb.* **reaching, reached 1** to arrive at; to get as far as: *We reached the hotel by nightfall.* **2** to be able to touch or get hold of: *If I stand on tiptoe, I can reach the ceiling.* **3** to project or extend: *The curtains reach the floor.* **4** to make contact or communicate with. – *n.* the distance you can stretch your arm, etc.

One of the important 'little inventions' – the safety razor invented in 1880 by King C. Gillette.

react (rē **akt**) *vb.* **reacting, reacted 1** to respond to something which has been done or said, etc. **2** to undergo a chemical reaction.

reaction *n.* **1** a reacting or response to something: *The American Revolution was a reaction to British misrule.* **2** a complete change of opinions, feelings, etc. to the opposite of what they were: *The idea was popular at first but then a reaction set in.* **3** a process of change occuring in the atoms and molecules of substances when different substances are put together.

reactionary *adj.* (of a person) opposed to change or progress.

read (rēd) *vb.* **reading, read** (red) **1** to look at and understand printed or written words. **2** to speak aloud words which are printed or written. **3** to interpret or understand the meaning of: *Can you read a map?* **4** (of writing) to be, or not be, coherent, fluent, and logical: *This essay reads well but that one reads badly.* – (red) *adj.* educated through reading: *John is very well read.* – **read between the lines** to

understand a meaning which is implied.

readable *adj.* **1** legible. **2** interesting to read.

reading *n.* **1** the action of a person who looks at and understands what is written or printed. **2** the ability to read: *His reading is poor.* **3** an event at which a play, poetry, etc. is read to an audience. **4** information, figures, etc. shown by an instrument or meter.

read-out *n.* information received from a computer, either on paper or on a screen.

ready (**re** di) *adj.* **readier, readiest 1** prepared and available for action or use. **2** willing: *Rob is always ready to help.* **3** prompt; quick: *ready to find fault.* **4** likely or about to do: *The plant is just ready to flower.* – *adv.* **readily.** – *n.* **readiness**.

real (**rē** ǎl) *adj.* **1** which actually exists; not imaginary. **2** not imitation; genuine: *real leather.* **3** actual; true: *What was the real reason?* **4** important, or serious: *a real problem.*

realism (**rē** ǎl i zêm) *n.* **1** in art and literature, a style that presents things as they really are. **2** an acceptance of things as they are. – *n.* **realist.** – *adj.* **realistic.** – *adv.* **realistically**.

reality (rē **al** i ti) *n.* **realities 1** the fact of being real. **2** the real nature of something.

really *adv.* **1** actually; in fact: *Do you really mean that?* **2** very: *It was a really lovely day.*

realize or **realise** (**rē** ǎ līz) *vb.* **realizing, realized 1** to come to know or understand: *I now realize how lucky I am.* **2** to make real; to make come true: *Anna realized her ambition of becoming a doctor.* – *n.* **realization**.

realm (relm) *n.* **1** a kingdom. **2** a field of interest, study, or activity: *the realm of music.*

rear[1] (rēr) *n.* the back part; the area at the back: *We like to sit at the rear of the classroom.* – *adj.* at the back: *Look behind you through the rear window.*

rear[2] (rēr) *vb.* **rearing, reared** to feed, care for, and educate: *They reared three children.*

reason (**rē** zǒn) *n.* **1** a justification or motive for an action, belief, etc. **2** an underlying explanation or cause: *What is the reason for her rude behaviour?* **3** the power of the mind to think – *vb.* **reasoning, reasoned 1** to use the mind to form opinions, reach conclusions, etc.: *He reasoned that there were several solutions to the problem.* **2** to try to persuade by argument.

reasonable *adj.* **1** sensible; showing reason or good judgement. **2** fair; not excessive.

PRONUNCIATION GUIDE	
fat **a**	all **ŏ**
fate **ā**	foot **oo**
fast **ä**	moon **o͞o**
among **å**	boy **oi**
met **e**	house **ow**
mean **ē**	demon **ŏ**
silent **ĕ**	thing **th**
loch **hh**	this **Th**
fin **i**	but **u**
line **ī**	mute **ū**
quick **kw**	fur **û**
got **o**	brochure **ů**
note **ō**	vision **zh**

rebel (**re** běl) *n.* **1** a person who opposes or fights against people in authority or oppressive conditions. **2** a person who does not accept the rules of normal behaviour, dress, etc. – *adj.* rebelling. – (ri **bel**) *vb.* **rebelling, rebelled** to resist authority or oppressive conditions openly and with force: *In the French Revolution the ordinary people rebelled.*
> **rebellion** *n.* an act of rebelling; a revolt.
> **rebellious** *adj.* rebelling or likely to rebel.

receipt (ri **sēt**) *n.* a written note saying that money or goods have been received.

receive (ri **sēv**) *vb.* **receiving, received 1** to get, be given, or accept: *Thank you for your postcard which I received yesterday.* **2** to experience or suffer: *receive injuries.*

recent (**rē** sěnt) *adj.* happening, done, having appeared, etc. not long ago: *recent history.*

recess (ri **ses**) or (**rē** ses) *n.* **1** an open space or alcove set in a wall. **2** a temporary break from work, especially of a law-court.
> **recession** *n.* a temporary decline in economic activity, trade, and prosperity.

recipe (**re** si pi) *n.* a list of ingredients for, and set of instructions on how to prepare food.

recite (ri **sīt**) *vb.* **reciting, recited** to repeat aloud from memory: *Robert recited his poem.*
> **reckless** (**rek** lěs) *adj.* very careless; acting or done without any thought of the consequences.

reckon (**re** kǒn) *vb.* **reckoning, reckoned 1** to calculate, compute, or estimate: *The shop assistant reckoned the bill.* **2** to think or suppose.

recognize or **recognise** (**re** kǒg nīz) *vb.* **recognizing, recognized 1** to identify a person or thing known or experienced before: *I'd recognize Isobel anywhere.* **2** to admit or be aware of: *I recognize my mistakes.* **3** to show approval of and gratitude for: *The school recognized her courage.* – *adj.* **recognizable.**
> **recognition** (re kǒg ni shǒn) *n.* the act or state of recognizing.

recommend (re kǒ **mend**) *vb.* **recommending, recommended 1** to advise. **2** to suggest as being suitable to be accepted, chosen, etc.: *I recommend this novel.* – *n.* **recommendation.**

reconcile (re kǒn **sīl**) *vb.* **reconciling, reconciled 1** to make friendly again, for example after a quarrel. **2** to harmonize. **3** to resign yourself to a situation, fact, etc. – *n.* **reconciliation** (re kǒn si li **ā** shǒn).

record (**re** kǒrd) *n.* **1** a formal written report of facts, events, or information. **2** a disc on which sound is recorded. **3** (in races, games, or almost any activity) a performance which has never yet been beaten. – (ri **kǒrd**) *vb.* **recording, recorded 1** to set down in writing or some other permanent form. **2** to register sound, music, speech, etc. on a record or tape.

A video recorder stores signals for both sounds and pictures on magnetic tape. This tape is stored in a plastic cassette.

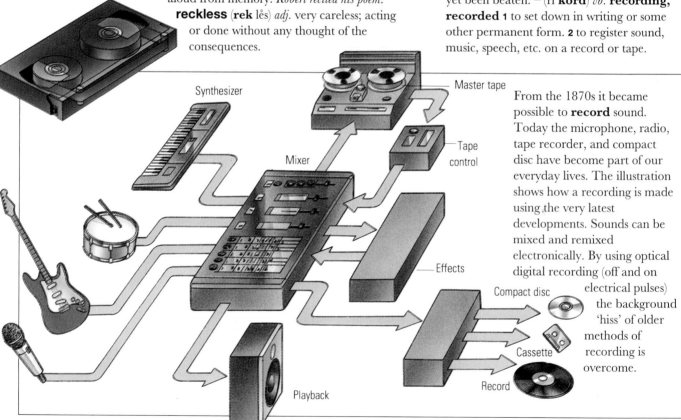

Synthesizer
Mixer
Master tape
Tape control
Effects
Compact disc
Cassette
Record
Playback

From the 1870s it became possible to **record** sound. Today the microphone, radio, tape recorder, and compact disc have become part of our everyday lives. The illustration shows how a recording is made using the very latest developments. Sounds can be mixed and remixed electronically. By using optical digital recording (off and on electrical pulses) the background 'hiss' of older methods of recording is overcome.

recount (ri **kownt**) *vb.* **recounting, recounted** to tell a story, etc. in detail.

recover (ri **ku** vẽr) *vb.* **recovering, recovered** **1** to get or find again: *They recovered the lost kitten.* **2** to get well again. – *adj.* **recoverable.**

recovery *n.* **recoveries** state of having recovered: *Bill made a quick recovery from his flu.*

recreation (re krē **ā** shŏn) *n.* a pleasant and often refreshing activity done in your spare time: *My favourite recreation is swimming.*

recruit (ri **krūt**) *n.* a newly enlisted member of the army, air force, navy, etc.

rectangle (**rek** tang gẽl) *n.* a four-sided figure with opposite sides which are equal and four right angles. – *adj.* **rectangular.**

recur (ri **kur**) *vb.* **recurring, recurred** to happen or come round again or at intervals: *Your cough may recur.* – *n.* **recurrence.**

red (red) *adj.* **redder, reddest 1** of the colour of blood. **2** (of hair or fur) a colour between a golden brown and a deep reddish-brown. – *n.* – **see red** (*colloquial*) to become angry.

Red Cross *n.* an international organization which brings medical relief to the victims of wars and natural disasters.

red flag *n.* **1** a red banner used as a symbol of revolution. **2** a flag used to warn of danger.

red tape *n.* (*derogatory*) unnecessary rules and regulations which result in delay.

redwood *n.* a large Californian conifer.

● **Red Sea**. This sea divides Arabia from northeast AFRICA. It is linked to the Mediterranean by the SUEZ CANAL.

reduce (ri **dūs**) *vb.* **reducing, reduced 1** to make or become less, smaller, etc. **2** to lower the price of.

reduction (ri **duk** shŏn) *n.* **1** an act of reducing; the state of being reduced. **2** the amount by which something is reduced: *a reduction of £5.*

redundant (ri **dun** dånt) *adj.* **1** (of workers) no longer needed and therefore dismissed. **2** not needed; superfluous. – *n.* **redundancy.**

reed (rēd) *n.* a tall stiff grass of wet places.

reef (rēf) *n.* a ridge of rocks, sand, etc. just above or below the surface of the sea.

reel (rēl) *n.* **1** a cylindrical object on which thread, film, fishing-lines, etc. can be wound. **2** a lively Scottish, Irish, or American dance.

– *vb.* **reeling, reeled 1** to wind on a reel. **2** to stagger or sway. **3** to whirl or appear to move: *The room began to reel and then she fainted.*

refer (ri **fur**) *vb.* **referring, referred 1** to talk or write about; to mention: *refer to your problems.* **2** to relate, concern, or apply to: *Does this refer to me?* **3** to look for information.

referee (refẽ **rē**) *n.* an umpire or judge, for example of a game or in a dispute.

reference (**ref** ĕ rẽns) *n.* **1** a mention of something; an illusion: *The judge made reference to the accused's past good conduct.* **2** a direction in a book to another passage or book where information can be found: *a reference book.*

referendum (re fẽ **ren** dům) *n.* **referendums** or **referenda** the act of giving the people the chance to vote on some important matter.

refine (ri **fīn**) *vb.* **refining, refined** to make pure by removing dirt, waste substances, etc.

reflect (ri **flekt**) *vb.* **reflecting, reflected 1** to send back light, heat, sound, etc.: *White clothes reflect the sun's rays.* **2** (of a mirror, etc.) to give an image of. **3** to consider carefully.

reflection *n.* (also **reflexion**) **1** the act of reflecting. **2** the sound, heat, light, etc. reflected. **3** a reflected image: *Rona saw her reflection in the mirror.* **4** careful consideration.

reform (ri **fŏrm**) *vb.* **reforming, reformed 1** to improve or remove faults from a person, behaviour, etc. **2** to give up bad habits, improve your behaviour, etc. – *n.* a correction or improvement, especially in some social or political system: *The abolition of slavery was an important reform.* – *n.* **reformer.**

reformation (re fŏr **mā** shŏn) *n.* **1** the act of reforming or state of being reformed; improvement. **2 Reformation** the 16th-century religious movement which led to the development of the various Protestant churches in Europe.

The Reformation: In England between 1536 and 1540 the monasteries were dissolved (closed) by Henry VIII, who had broken all ties with the pope. He decided that the great wealth of the monasteries should go to the Crown. The money helped to pay for wars with France.

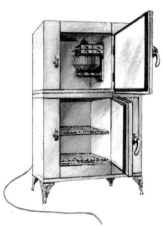

A refrigerator of about 1930 with a compartment for ice and shelves for food.

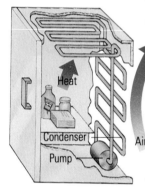

An electric refrigerator: a fluid called a refrigerant evaporates into a gas inside the coils in the freezing compartment, absorbing heat and lowering the temperature. A pump compresses the gas and turns it back into a liquid. It releases the heat absorbed from the freezer compartment to the room outside the refrigerator.

refract (ri **frakt**) *vb.* **refracting, refracted** to deflect or bend a ray of light, sound, etc. at a different angle when that ray enters it from another medium. – *n.* **refraction**.

refrain (ri **frān**) *vb.* **refraining, refrained** to avoid: *Please refrain from smoking.*

refresh (ri **fresh**) *vb.* **refreshing, refreshed** to give renewed strength and enthusiasm to.

refrigerate (ri **frij** ė rāt) *vb.* **refrigerating, refrigerated** to make or keep food very cold to prevent it from going bad. – **refrigerator**.

refuge (re fūj) *n.* shelter or protection from danger: *The girls found refuge in a cave.*

refugee (refū **jē**) *n.* a person who seeks shelter, especially from persecution.

refund (ri **fund**) *vb.* **refunding, refunded** to pay money, etc. back to someone. – (**rē** fund) *n.* **1** the paying back of money, etc. **2** the money, etc. paid back. – *adj.* **refundable**.

refuse¹ (ri **fūz**) *vb.* **refusing, refused** to say you won't do what you have been asked to do. **refusal** *n.* an act of refusing.

refuse² (**ref** ūs) *n.* rubbish.

regal (**rē** gǎl) *adj.* of, or like, a king or queen.

regard (ri **gärd**) *vb.* **regarding, regarded 1** to consider someone or something in a specified way: *The author regards this as her finest book.* **2** to pay attention to; to take notice of. **3** to look at attentively or steadily. – *n.* **1** thought or attention. **2** care or consideration; sympathy. **3** respect and affection: *held in high regard.*

regarding *prep.* about; concerning.

reggae (**re** gā) *n.* popular West Indian music.

regime (rā **jēm**) *n.* a system of government.

●**Regina** is the capital of Saskatchewan, Canada.

region (**rē** jŏn) *n.* an area or a country with particular geographical, social, etc. characteristics: *the Arctic region.*

register (**re** ji stėr) *n.* **1** a book containing a written list or record of names, events, etc. **2** a machine, especially one in a shop (**cash register**) which lists sales and in which money is kept. – *vb.* **registering, registered 1** to enter an event, name, etc. in an official register. **2** to enrol formally. – *adj.* **registered**.

regret (ri **gret**) *vb.* **regretting, regretted** to feel sorry, distressed, disappointed about: *I regret missing your visit.* – *n.* a feeling of sorrow.

regrettable *adj.* unwelcome; unfortunate.

regular (**re** gū lår) *adj.* usual; normal; customary: *It's past Roy's regular bedtime.*

regulate (**re** gū lāt) *vb.* **regulating, regulated** to control or adjust a piece of machinery, the heat or sound available, etc. as required: *Please can you regulate the tuning of the radio.*

regulation *n.* a rule or instruction.

rehearse (ri **hûrs**) *vb.* **rehearsing, rehearsed** to practise a play, piece of music, etc. – *n.* **rehearsal**.

reign (rān) *n.* the time during which a king or queen rules. – *vb.* **reigning, reigned 1** to be a monarch. **2** to dominate: *Silence reigns.*

rein (rān) *n.* (usually in *plural*) one of two straps attached to a bridle for guiding a horse.

reindeer (**rān** dēr) *n.* **reindeer** or **reindeers** a large deer found in Arctic regions.

reinforce (rē in **förs**) *vb.* **reinforcing, reinforced** to make stronger.

reject (ri **jekt**) *vb.* **rejecting, rejected 1** to refuse to accept, agree to, admit, believe, etc.: *Robin rejected my friendship.* **2** to throw away or discard. – (**rē** jekt) *n.* a person or thing that is rejected. – *n.* **rejection**.

relapse (ri **laps**) *vb.* **relapsing, relapsed** to return to a former bad state or condition.

relate (ri **lāt**) *vb.* **relating, related 1** to tell a story. **2** to form a connection or relationship between facts, events, etc.: *He related his unhappiness to the fact that he never married.*

related *adj.* **1** of the same family. **2** connected.

The reindeer is the only deer in which the female carries antlers. Reindeer are related to caribou but unlike the caribou, reindeer of Arctic Europe and Asia are domesticated.

relation *n.* **1** a connection between one person or thing and another. **2** a person who belongs to the same family through birth or marriage; a relative. **3** reference; respect: *in relation to.* **4** (in *plural*) the social, political, or personal contact between people, countries, etc.

relative (**re** lå tiv) *n.* a person who is related to someone else by birth or marriage. – *adj.* **1** compared with something else; comparative: *the relative speeds of a car and train.* **2** existing only in relation to something else: *'Hot' and 'cold' are relative terms.* – *adv.* **relatively.**

relativity *n.* **1** the state of being relative. **2** (also **special theory of relativity**) EINSTEIN's theory (published in 1905) that the mass of a body varies with its speed, based on the premises that all motion is relative and that the speed of light relative to an observer is constant.

relax (ri **laks**) *vb.* **relaxing, relaxed 1** to make or become less tense, nervous, or worried. **2** to rest completely from work or effort. **3** to make or become less strict: *The school must relax the rules.* – *adj.* **relaxed.** – *adj.* **relaxing.**

relaxation *n.* **1** the act of relaxing. **2** a relaxing activity: *Golf is a popular relaxation.*

relay (**re** lā) *n.* a set of people that relieves others doing some task, etc. – *vb.* **relaying, relayed** to receive and pass on news, etc.

release (ri **lēs**) *vb.* **releasing, released 1** to free a prisoner, etc. from captivity: *He released the rabbit from its hutch.* **2** to relieve someone suffering from something unpleasant, a duty, etc. **3** to loosen your grip and stop holding.

relentless (ri **lent** lĕs) *adj.* something which never stops: *The traffic noise was relentless.*

relevant (**re** lĕ vånt) *adj.* connected with the matter being discussed, etc. – *n.* **relevance.**

reliable (ri **lī** å bĕl) *adj.* able to be trusted: *a reliable bus service.* – *n.* **reliability.**

relief (ri **lēf**) *n.* **1** the lessening or removal of pain, worry, oppression, or distress. **2** help, often in the form of money, food, clothing, and medicine, given to people in need.

relief map *n.* a map which shows the variations in the height of the land.

relieve (ri **lēv**) *vb.* **relieving, relieved 1** to lessen or stop a person's pain, worry, boredom, etc.: *Aspirin can relieve a headache.* **2** to take a burden from: *Relieve her of the heavy bag.*

religion (ri **lij** ŏn) *n.* **1** a belief in, or the worship of, a god or gods. **2** a particular system of belief or worship, such as Christianity or Judaism.

religious *adj.* **1** of, or relating to, religion. **2** pious; devout.

relish (**rel** ish) *vb.* **relishing, relished** to enjoy greatly; to look forward to with great pleasure. – *n.* **1** pleasure. **2** a spicy sauce or pickle.

reluctance (ri **luk** tåns) *n.* lack of enthusiasm. **reluctant** *adj.* unwilling; not wanting.

rely (ri **lī**) *vb.* **relies, relying, relied 1** to depend on or need: *I rely on you to give me a lift tomorrow.* **2** to trust someone to do something.

remain (ri **mān**) *vb.* **remaining, remained 1** to be left when something else, another part, etc. has been lost, used up, etc. **2** to stay in the same place; not to leave: *Ron remained in the room after the others had left.*

remainder *n.* the number or part that is left after the rest has gone, been taken away, etc.

remains *n.* (*plural*) what is left after part has been taken away, eaten, destroyed, etc.

remark (ri **märk**) *vb.* **remarking, remarked** to notice and comment on. – *n.* a comment.

remarkable *adj.* worth mentioning; unusual.

RELIGIOUS TERMS

agnostic someone who belives that nothing can be known about the existence of God.

atheism the belief that there is no god.

baptism a Christian rite of immersion, or being sprinkled with water to signify purification.

bar mitzvah a Jewish ceremony in which usually a 13-year-old boy formally accepts full religious responsibilities. A similar ceremony for a girl is a **bas mitzvah**.

circumcision the cutting away of the foreskin, a practice especially important to the Jews.

Easter an annual Christian festival commemorating the resurrection of Jesus.

hegira Muhammad's escape from Mecca to Medina in AD 622. It was taken as the beginning of the history of Muslim people.

Koran the Holy Book of Islam.

kosher the term signifying that food is fit to be eaten according to Jewish ritual.

Rosh Hashanah the Jewish New Year.

Sabbath a day of the week set aside for rest and religious observance: for Jews it is Saturday.

Trinity a Christian term for God as existing in the form of three divine persons: the Father, Son, and Holy Spirit.

yoga a Hindu philosophy involving union with the Absolute Being.

Yom Kippur a Jewish fast day.

All the major religions have special symbols or signs. The yin and yang of Taoism, for instance, are two opposing forces of nature which need to be balanced for harmony.

Christian cross

Islam's crescent moon and star

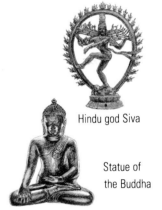

Hindu god Siva

Statue of the Buddha

Taoist symbol of yin and yang

Judaism's star of David

Symbol of Sikhism

PRONUNCIATION GUIDE

fat **a**		all **ö**	
fate **ā**		foot **oo**	
fast **ä**		moon **ōō**	
among **å**		boy **oi**	
met **e**		house **ow**	
mean **ē**		demon **ô**	
silent **ě**		thing **th**	
loch **hh**		this **Th**	
fin **i**		but **u**	
line **ī**		mute **ū**	
quick **kw**		fur **û**	
got **o**		brochure **ů**	
note **ō**		vision **zh**	

● **Rembrandt** (1606-69) perhaps the greatest of the Dutch painters, is noted for his portraits and his use of shade and light.

remedy (rem ě di) *n.* **remedies 1** any drug or treatment which cures or controls a disease. **2** anything which solves a problem.

remember (ri mem běr) *vb.* **remembering, remembered 1** to bring to mind something or someone that had been forgotten. **2** to keep a fact, idea, etc. in your mind: *In America, remember to drive on the right.*

remind (ri mīnd) *vb.* **reminding, reminded** to help someone to remember something: *Rachel reminded us that it was her birthday.* **reminder** *n.* something that makes a person remember something or someone.

remote (ri mōt) *adj.* **1** far away or distant in time or place. **2** very small or slight: *They have only a remote chance of winning.* – *n.* **remoteness**.

remove (ri mōōv) *vb.* **removing, removed 1** to move a person, thing, etc. to a different place. **2** to take off: *Jack removed his overcoat.*

renaissance (ri nā såns) *n.* **1** a rebirth or revival. **2 Renaissance** the revival of arts, literature, and classical scholarship, and the beginnings of modern science, in Europe in the 14th to 16th centuries.

render (ren děr) *vb.* **rendering, rendered 1** to cause to become. **2** to give or provide help, a service, etc.

rendezvous (ron di vōō) *n.* **rendezvous** (**ron** di vōōz) an appointment to meet.

renew (ri nū) *vb.* **renewing, renewed 1** to make fresh or like new again. **2** to begin again; to repeat. **3** to make a licence, lease, loan, etc. valid for a further period of time. – *adj.* **renewable**. – *n.* **renewal**.

● **Renoir** (**ren** wär), **Pierre** (1841-1919) was a French painter of the Impressionist school.

rent (rent) *n.* money paid to the owner of a property by a tenant in return for the use or occupation of that property. – *vb.* **renting, rented** to pay rent for a building, etc.

repair (ri pār) *vb.* **repairing, repaired** to restore something damaged or broken to good working condition; to mend: *Eleanor repaired the watch herself.* – *n.* an act of repairing.

repeal (ri pēl) *vb.* **repealing, repealed** to make a law, etc. no longer valid: *Capital punishment was repealed long ago.*

repeat (ri pēt) *vb.* **repeating, repeated** to say, do, etc. again: *He repeated his accusation in front of the teacher.* – *n.* an act of repeating.

repel (ri pel) *vb.* **repelling, repelled 1** to force or drive back or away. **2** to cause a feeling of disgust or loathing: *Spiders repel some people.*

repent (ri pent) *vb.* **repenting, repented** to feel great sorrow or regret for something you have done. – *n.* **repentance**.

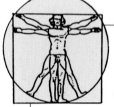

From the 1300s Europeans began to rediscover the learning of ancient Greece and Rome. This **Renaissance** ('rebirth') was an exciting time of thought and discovery. Artists such as Leonardo Da Vinci and Michelangelo produced great paintings and sculpture. Scientists such as Galileo and Copernicus had new ideas about the universe. Explorers such as Columbus discovered new lands.

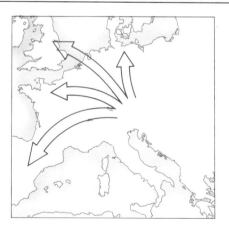

A merchant and his wife in Renaissance Italy. In the background is a French chateau built in the Italian style.

Italy in the late 1300s was the birthplace of the Renaissance. The invention of printing in the 1450s helped the spread of the Renaissance all over Europe.

A future idea anticipated: This sketch of a flying machine is by Leonardo da Vinci, who was both an artist and a scientist.

repetition (re pĕ **ti** shŏn) *n.* the act of repeating or being repeated.

> **repetitious** (re pĕ **ti** shŭs) or **repetitive** (rĕ **pet** i tiv) *adj.* having too much repetition: *Hanna's work is dull and repetitive.*

replace (ri **plās**) *vb.* **replacing, replaced 1** to put something back in a previous or proper position: *Robert never replaces the tools properly.* **2** to take the place of or be a substitute for: *Word processors have largely replaced typewriters.* **3** to use or substitute one person or thing in place of another: *Replace the broken lock with a new one.* – *adj.* **replaceable.**

> **replacement** *n.* **1** the act of replacing. **2** a person or thing that replaces another.

replica (**re** pli kă) *n.* an exact copy.

reply (ri **plī**) *vb.* **replies, replying, replied** to say or do something in answer: *I have already replied to your question.* – *n.* **replies** something said, written, or done in answer or response.

report (ri **pört**) *n.* **1** a detailed statement, description, or account, especially after investigation. **2** (*British*) a statement of a pupil's work and behaviour at school. – *vb.*

> **reporting, reported 1** to bring back as an answer, news, or account. **2** to give an official account or description of. **3** to make a complaint about someone, especially to a person in authority. – *adv.* **reportedly.**

repose (ri **pōz**) *n.* a state of rest.

represent (rep rĕ **zent**) *vb.* **representing,**

> **represented 1** to serve as a symbol or sign for; to stand for or correspond to: *Letters represent sounds. A thesis represents years of hard work.* **2** to speak or act on behalf of.
> **representative** *adj.* **1** representing. **2** being a good example of something; typical. – *n.* a person who represents someone or something else, especially a person who represents, or sells the goods of, a business, or a person who represents a constituency in Parliament.
> **the House of Representatives** *n.* the lower house of the United States Congress.

reproduce (rē prŏ **dūs**) or (re prŏ **dūs**) *vb.*

> **reproducing, reproduced 1** to make or produce a copy or imitation of; to duplicate. **2** to produce offspring of the same kind as itself: *an organism which can reproduce itself.*
> **reproduction** *n.* a copy or imitation.

reptile (**rep** tĭl) *n.* any of the group of cold-blooded vertebrates which have a body covered with scales or bony plates, for example snakes, lizards, crocodiles, and dinosaurs.

republic (ri **pub** lik) *n.* a form of government in which there is no monarch, and in which power is held by the people or their elected representatives, especially one in which the head of state is an elected president.

> **republican** *adj.* **1** of, like, or for a republic. **2 Republican** of the Republican Party in the UNITED STATES.
> **Republican Party** *n.* one of the two major political parties in the UNITED STATES.

reputable (**re** pū tă bĕl) *adj.* well thought of.

reputation (re pū **tā** shŏn) *n.* the generally held opinion about a person with regard to their abilities, character, etc.

request (ri **kwest**) *n.* **1** the act of asking for something. **2** something asked for: *Our request is for money for the refugees.* – *vb.* **requesting, requested** to ask for, especially politely.

require (ri **kwīr**) *vb.* **requiring, required 1** to need; to wish to have: *All living things require oxygen.* **2** to have as a necessary condition for success, etc.: *You require a brain to think.*

> **requirement** *n.* something that is needed, asked for, essential, ordered, etc.

rescue (**res** kū) *vb.* **rescuing, rescued** to free from danger, evil, trouble, captivity, etc.

research (ri **sûrch**) *n.* a detailed and careful investigation into some area of study. – *vb.*

> **researching, researched.** – *n.* **researcher.**

resemble (ri **zem** bĕl) *vb.* **resembling, resembled** to be or look like or similar to.

resent (ri **zent**) *vb.* **resenting, resented** to feel anger or bitterness towards.

reserve (ri **zûrv**) *vb.* **reserving, reserved** to order in advance: *We reserved seats for the theatre.* – *n.* **1** something which is set aside for later use. **2** an area of land set aside for a particular purpose, for example for the protection of animals, or (especially in AUSTRALIA) for the original native inhabitants: *a nature reserve.*

> **reservation** *n.* **1** a booking. **2** (usually in *plural*) a doubt or objection which prevents you being able to accept something.

Republic comes from two Latin words, *res* meaning 'affair or thing' and *publica* meaning 'public'. The word was originally *respublica*, but the *s* was dropped in French, which is the source of the English word.

A simple, single-celled organism such as an amoeba reproduces by splitting into two by the process of cell division or mitosis.

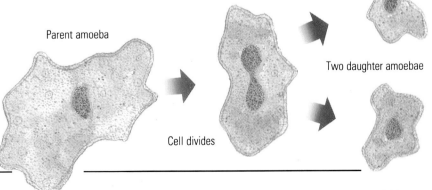

Parent amoeba

Cell divides

Two daughter amoebae

Georg Simon Ohm (1789-1854) was a German physicist who found that the electrical resistance of a conductor (the material through which an electric current flows) depends on its thickness, its length, and the material it is made from. The unit of resistance, the ohm, is named after him.

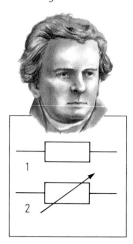

Symbols used to show fixed resistance (1) and variable resistance (2). In electronics a resistor is a circuit component that has resistance. The resistance in a variable resitor can be altered. It is used as a volume control in radios, for instance.

reservoir (**re** zĕr vwär) *n.* a place, usually an artificial lake, where water is stored.

reside (ri **zīd**) *vb.* **residing, resided** to live or have your home in, especially permanently.

residence (**re** zi dĕns) *n.* **1** a house or dwelling. **2** the act of living in a place.

 resident *n.* a person who lives in a place.

resign (ri **zīn**) *vb.* **resigning, resigned 1** to give up a job, etc. **2** to bring yourself to accept something with patience: *Patrick resigned himself to the fact that he couldn't go to the match.*

 resignation (re zig **nā** shŏn) *n.* **1** the act of resigning. **2** showing calm acceptance.

resin (**re** zin) *n.* a sticky substance produced by certain trees, for example firs and pines.

resist (ri **zist**) *vb.* **resisting, resisted 1** to oppose; to fight against someone or something; to refuse to give in to or comply with. **2** to remain undamaged by: *a metal which resists corrosion.* – *adj.* **resistible**.

 resistance *n.* **1** the act of resisting. **2** the ability to be unaffected by something, especially disease. **3** the force that one object exerts on the movement of another, causing it to slow down or stop. **4** the opposition to the passage of heat, electricity, etc. through a substance.

resolution (re zŏ **loo** shŏn) *n.* **1** the act of making a firm decision. **2** a formal expression of opinion, will, etc.: *The committee passed a resolution to ban smoking.*

resolve (ri **zolv**) *vb.* **resolving, resolved 1** to take a firm decision to. **2** to pass a resolution, especially formally. **3** to find an answer to a problem, etc. – *n.* determination.

resort (ri **zört**) *vb.* **resorting, resorted** to turn to as a way of solving a problem, etc. when other methods have failed: *Pam resorted to acupuncture when the medicine did her no good.* – *n.* a place visited by many people on holiday.

resound (ri **zownd**) *vb.* **resounding, resounded** (of sounds) to ring or echo. **resounding** *adj.* **1** echoing and ringing. **2** clear and decisive: *The team won a resounding victory.*

resource (ri **zörs**) or (ri **sörs**) *n.* **1** a person or thing which gives help, support, etc. when needed. **2** (usually in *plural*) a means of support, for example money and property. **3** (usually in *plural*) a country's or business's natural source of wealth: *natural resources.*

respect (ri **spekt**) *n.* **1** admiration; good opinion: *The headmistress is held in great respect.* **2** consideration of or attention to: *The rioters*

showed no respect for the law. **3** (in *plural*) a greeting or expression of admiration, esteem, and honour. – *vb.* **respecting, respected 1** to show or feel admiration for. **2** to show consideration, or thoughtfulness to.

 respecting *prep.* about; concerning.

 respective *adj.* belonging to or relating to each person or thing mentioned; separate.

respiration (re spi **rā** shŏn) *n.* breathing.

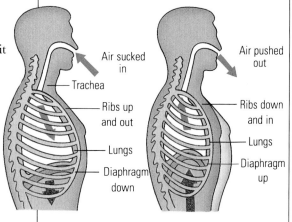

Land vertebrates have lungs for breathing or **respiration**. Breathe in and your diaphragm contracts, increasing the space inside your chest. Air flows in to fill the space. Breathe out and your diaphragm relaxes, reducing the space inside your chest. The air rushes out.

Air sucked in – Trachea – Ribs up and out – Lungs – Diaphragm down

Air pushed out – Ribs down and in – Lungs – Diaphragm up

respond (ri **spond**) *vb.* **responding, responded 1** to answer or reply. **2** to act or behave in reply or response: *I smiled at her, but she didn't respond.* **3** to react favourably or well.

responsible (ri **spon** să bĕl) *adj.* **1** having control over and being accountable for; having as a job: *Ellen is responsible for ordering new books.* **2** having to answer or account for something to: *You are responsible to the headmistress.* **3** having many important duties, especially the taking of important decisions: *Alison has a very responsible job.* – *adv.* **responsibly.** – *n.* **responsibility, responsibilities**.

rest[1] (rest) *n.* **1** a short period of relaxation or freedom from work, activity, worry, etc. **2** sleep; repose. **3** calm; tranquillity. **4** a state of not moving or working. – *vb.* **resting, rested**

1 to stop working or moving. **2** to relax, especially by sleeping. **3** to set, place, or lie on or against something.

rest[2] (rest): **the rest** the remainder: *Six of the group went today, the rest will go later.*

restaurant (**res** tå ront) *n.* a place where meals may be bought and eaten.

restore (ri **stör**) *vb.* **restoring, restored 1** to return a building, painting, etc. to its original condition by repairing, cleaning, etc. **2** to bring back, a normal, healthy state: *The teacher restored discipline.* **3** to return something lost.

restrain (ri **strān**) *vb.* **restraining, restrained** to prevent someone from doing something.

restrict (ri **strikt**) *vb.* **restricting, restricted 1** to keep within certain limits. **2** to limit or regulate the use of: *In droughts we have to restrict the use of hosepipes.*

result (ri **zult**) *n.* **1** an outcome or consequence of something: *The flood was the result of the storm.* **2** a number or quantity obtained by calculation, etc. **3** (in *plural*) a list of final scores in a series of football matches, etc. **4** (in *plural*) marks a student has obtained in an examination. – *vb.* **resulting, resulted** to be a consequence of some action, etc.: *Carelessness results in mistakes.*

resume (ri **zūm**) *vb.* **resuming, resumed** to begin again after an interruption.

résumé (**re** zūm ā) or (**rā** zūm ā) *n.* **1** a summary. **2** (*US*) a curriculum vitae.

retail (**rē** tāl) *n.* the sale of goods to customers who will not resell them. – *adj.* of, relating to, or concerned with such sale of goods. – *vb.* **retailing, retailed** (**rē** tāl) to sell goods in small quantities to customers. – *n.* **retailer.**

retain (ri **tān**) *vb.* **retaining, retained 1** to continue to have, contain, hold, use, etc: *the sea retains heat longer than the land.* **2** to remember. **3** to hold back or keep in place.

retina (**re** ti nå) *n.* **retinas** or **retinae** (**re** ti nē) the light-sensitive lining at the back of the eye which receives the image from the lens.

retire (ri **tīr**) *vb.* **retiring, retired 1** to stop working permanently, usually on reaching an age at which a pension can be received. **2** to go away to rest, especially to go to bed. **retirement** *n.* the state of being retired. **retiring** *adj.* shy and reserved.

retreat (ri **trēt**) *vb.* **retreating, retreated** to withdraw; to move back or away from a position or battle: *The troops retreated after the enemy attack.* – *n.* the act of retreating.

retrieve (ri **trēv**) *vb.* **retrieving, retrieved 1** to get or bring back again; to recover. **2** to rescue or save: *John retrieved the situation.* **3** to recover information from storage in a computer memory. – *adj.* **retrievable.**

return (ri **tûrn**) *vb.* **returning, returned 1** to come or go back again to a former place, state, or owner. **2** to give, send, put back, etc. in a former position: *Ruby returned the books she had borrowed.* **3** to come back to in thought or speech: *We'll return to the topic later.* **4** to answer or reply: *I'm returning your telephone call.* **5** (of a jury) to give a verdict. – *n.* **1** an act of coming back from a place, state, etc. **2** an act of returning something to a former place, etc. **3** profit from work, a business, or investment, etc. – *adj.* **returnable.**

reunion (ri **ū** ni ôn) *n.* a meeting of people who have not met for some time.

reveal (ri **vēl**) *vb.* **revealing, revealed 1** to make known a secret, etc. **2** to show: *Sam revealed his operation scar.* – *adj.* **revealing.**

revenge (ri **venj**) *n.* injury, harm, or wrong done in return for injury, harm, or wrong received. – *vb.* **revenging, revenged** – *adj.* **revengeful.**

revenue (**re** vě nū) *n.* money from property or shares; money raised by the government from taxes, etc.

●*Revere, Paul* (1735-1818) was a patriot and hero of the AMERICAN WAR OF INDEPENDENCE. He is most famous for his night ride on 18 April 1775 to warn the MINUTEMEN of Lexington and Concord, Massachusetts that British troops were coming.

revere (ri **vēr**) *vb.* **revering, revered** to feel or show great affection and respect for. **reverence** (**re** vě rěns) *n.* great respect. **reverent** *adj.* showing or feeling great respect.

reverse (ri **vûrs**) *vb.* **reversing, reversed 1** to move in an opposite or backwards direction: *Richard reversed his car into a wall.* **2** to put into an opposite or contrary, position, state, order, etc. **3** to change a policy, decision, etc. to the exact opposite. – *n.* **1** the opposite or contrary of something: *Rachel did the reverse of what her Mum told her to do.* **2** an act of changing to an opposite or contrary position, direction, state, etc. **3** the side of a coin, medal, note, etc. with a secondary design on: *the reverse side of a penny.*

Paul Revere in fact made two famous 'rides'. The first ride was to warn the revolutionaries to hide their arms.

Rhinoceros comes from the Greek *rhin-* meaning 'nose' and *keras* meaning 'horn', forming the word meaning 'nose-horn'.

review (ri **vū**) *n.* **1** an act of examining or revising, or the state of being examined or revised. **2** a general survey: *Here is a review of what happened.* **3** a survey of the past and past events: *the newspaper's annual review of the year.* **4** a critical report on a book, play, film, etc. – *vb.* **reviewing, reviewed 1** to examine. **2** to look back on events in the past. **3** to write a critical report on a book, play, etc. **4** to inspect troops, ships, etc. officially.
reviewer *n.* a person who writes critical reviews of books or plays.

revise (ri **vīz**) *vb.* **revising, revised 1** to examine again in order to correct faults, etc.: *I revised the text of my history of the modern world.* **2** to change an opinion, etc.: *Roger has revised his views on smoking now that he has given up.*
revision (ri **vi** zhǒn) *n.* the act of revising.

revive (ri **vīv**) *vb.* **reviving, revived 1** to come or bring back to consciousness, strength, health, etc.: *Ron quickly revived from his fall.* **2** to come or bring back to use, to notice, etc.: *The theatre group revived an old play.*
revival *n.* the act of reviving.

revoke (ri **vōk**) *vb.* **revoking, revoked** to cancel or make a will, etc. no longer valid.

revolt (ri **vōlt**) *vb.* **revolting, revolted 1** to rebel against a government, authority, etc. **2** to feel disgust, loathing, horror, or revulsion: *Richard's unkindness to his mother revolted us.* – *n.* a rebellion against authority. – *adj.* **revolted.**
revolting *adj.* causing a feeling of disgust.

revolution (re vǒ **lōō** shǒn) *n.* **1** the usually violent overthrow of a government by the governed. **2** a far-reaching change: *the computer revolution.* **3** a complete circle or turn round an axis. **4** a planet's orbit.
revolutionary *adj.* **1** of or like a revolution. **2** completely new or different.
revolutionize or **revolutionise** *vb.* **revolutionizing, revolutionized** to cause great or fundamental changes in.

● **Revolution, American.** See **American War of Independence.**

revolve (ri **volv**) *vb.* **revolving, revolved 1** to move or turn in a circle around a central point; to rotate. **2** to have as a centre or focus. – *adj.* **revolvable.** – *n.* & *adj.* **revolving.**
revolver *n.* a pistol with a revolving cylinder which holds several bullets.

revulsion (ri **vul** shǒn) *n.* **1** a feeling of complete disgust or distaste. **2** a sudden and often violent change of feeling.

reward (ri **wörd**) *n.* something given or received in return for work done, a service rendered, good behaviour, etc. – *vb.* **rewarding, rewarded.**
rewarding *adj.* giving personal satisfaction.

rheumatism (**rōō** må ti zěm) *n.* a disease marked by painful swelling of the joints.

● **Rhine** the main waterway of EUROPE, rising in the Swiss Alps and emptying into the sea near Rotterdam, Holland.

rhinoceros (rī **nos** ě rǒs) *n.* **rhinoceros** or **rhinoceroses** a large thick-skinned plant-eating animal with one or two horns on its nose, found in AFRICA and ASIA.

The rhinoceros is one of the heaviest of all land animals and may weigh over 3 tonnes. Africa has two species – black and white, but both are really grey! Egrets often follow rhinos to eat insects stirred up by their huge feet. They sometimes perch on the rhino's back.

● **Rhode Island**. See Supplement, **USA**.

rhododendron (rō dŏ **den** drŏn) *n.* an evergreen shrub with large colourful flowers.

rhubarb (**rōō** bärb) *n.* a large-leaved garden plant with reddish stalks which can be cooked.

rhyme (rīm) *n.* a word which has the same sound as another: *'Beef' is a rhyme for 'leaf'*. **3** a short poem, verse, or jingle written in rhyme. – *vb.* **rhyming, rhymed** to have the same final sounds and so form rhymes.

rhythm (ri Thĕm) *n.* the regular arrangement of stress, notes of different lengths, and pauses in a piece of music.
rhythmic or **rhythmical** *adj.* of or with rhythm. – *adv.* **rhythmically**.

rib (rib) *n.* any one of the slightly flexible bones which curve round from the spine, forming the chest wall and protecting the heart and lungs.

ribbon (ri bŏn) *n.* **1** a long narrow strip of material used for decorating clothes, tying hair and parcels, etc. **2** any ribbon-like strip: *a typewriter ribbon*.

rice (rīs) *n.* is one of the most important cereal crops in the world. It is grown mainly in ASIA.

Young shoots of rice are planted in flooded fields called paddies. Young rice has long narrow leaves and fine clusters of flowers that turn into the grain that we eat.

rich (rich) *adj.* **1** having a lot of money, property, or possessions. **2** costly and elaborate: *She always wears such rich clothes*. **3** high in value or quality: *a rich harvest*. **4** (of a soil, a region, etc.) productive, fertile. **5** (of colours) vivid and deep. – *n.* **richness**.
riches *n.* (*plural*) wealth.

● **Richelieu, Cardinal** (1585-1642) was an influential French statesman.

People do not usually notice an earthquake until its strength reaches 4 on the **Richter Scale**: (1) Felt only by seismographs. (2) Feeble: just noticeable. (3) Slight: similar to a heavy lorry passing. (4) Moderate: loose objects rock. (5) Quite strong: noticed even when you are asleep. (6) Strong: trees rock. (7) Very strong: walls crack. (8) Destructive: weak buildings collapse. (9) Houses collapse. (10) Disastrous: ground cracks. (11) Very disastrous: few buildings remain. (12) Catastrophic: ground rises and falls in waves.

Earthquakes can be terribly destructive, and be the cause of huge casualties from collapsing buildings. In an earthquake in 1906 much of San Francisco burned down as the gas mains broke and caught fire (above).

● **Richter, Charles F.** (1900-85) the American inventor of a scale for measuring the strength of earthquakes.

rickshaw or **ricksha** (**rik** shö) *n.* a small, two-wheeled, hooded carriage drawn either by a person on foot, or attached to a bicycle.

rid (rid) *vb.* **ridding, rid** to free or clear from something unwanted.

ridden. See **ride**.

riddle (ri dĕl) *n.* a short humorous puzzle, often in the form of a question, which describes an object, person, etc. in a mysterious way.

ride (rīd) *vb.* **riding, rode** (rōd), **ridden** (ri dĕn) **1** to sit on and control a bicycle, horse, etc. **2** to travel or be carried in a car, train, etc. or on a bicycle, horse, etc. – *n.* a journey on horseback or by vehicle.
rider *n.* a person who rides.

ridge (rij) *n.* **1** a strip of ground raised either side of a ploughed furrow. **2** any long, narrow, raised area on an otherwise flat surface.

ridicule (ri di kūl) *n.* language, laughter, behaviour, etc. which makes someone or something appear foolish; mockery: *Jane held him up to ridicule*. – *vb.* **ridiculing, ridiculed**.
ridiculous (ri dik ū lŭs) *adj.* silly or absurd.

rife (rīf) *adj.* very common.

rifle (rī fĕl) *n.* a gun fired from the shoulder.

RHYMING PAIRS
Have you noticed what a lot of rhyming expressions we use? Here are some examples: argy-bargy, brain-drain, easy-peasy, hi-fi, hoity-toity, namby-pamby, tit-bit, nitwit, nitty gritty, bigwig, no-go, pow-wow, hanky panky, high and dry, wear and tear, hotch potch, silly billy, wheeler-dealer, fair and square.

rig (rig) *vb.* **rigging, rigged 1** to fit a ship with ropes, sails, and rigging. **2** to control or manipulate for dishonest purposes, for personal profit, or advantage. – *n.* **1** the arrangement of sails, ropes, and masts on a ship. **2** an oil-rig. **3** gear or equipment, especially that used for a specific task.

rigging *n.* the system of ropes, wires, etc. which support a ship's masts and sails.

right (rīt) *adj.* **1** of or on the side of someone or something which is towards the east when the front is facing north. **2** (of a river bank) on the right hand of a person going downstream. **3** correct; true. **4** suitable; appropriate: *They are right for one another.* **5** in a correct, proper, satisfactory, or healthy condition: *Can you put things right?* – *adv.* **1** exactly or precisely. **2** immediately; without delay: *He'll be right over.* **3** completely; all the way: *Run right round the field.* **4** straight; directly: *They went right to the top.* **5** to or on the right side. – *n.* **1** (often in *plural*) a power, privilege, etc. that a person may claim legally or morally. **2** (often in *plural*) a just or legal claim to something: *mineral rights.* **3** the right side, part, or direction. **4** (in *plural*) the legal permission to print, publish, film, etc. a book, usually sold to a company by the author or by another company. – **right away** immediately; at once.

right angle *n.* an angle of 90°, formed by two lines which are perpendicular to each other.

rigid (**ri** jid) *adj.* **1** completely stiff and inflexible. **2** not able to be moved. **3** (of a person) strictly sticking to ideas, opinions, and rules: *she's a rigid disciplinarian.* – *n.* **rigidity** or **rigidness**.

rim (rim) *n.* **1** a raised and often curved edge or border: *the rim of a cup.* **2** the outer circular edge of a wheel to which the tyre is attached.

rind (rīnd) *n.* a thick, outer layer or covering as on cheese or bacon, or the peel of fruit.

ring¹ (ring) *n.* **1** a small circle of gold, silver, or some other metal, worn on the finger. **2** any object, mark, or figure which is circular in shape. **3** a group of people or things arranged in a circle. **4** an enclosed and usually circular area for competitions or exhibitions, especially at a circus, showjumping, etc.

ringleader *n.* the leader of a group of people who are causing trouble.

ring² (ring) *vb.* **ringing, rang** (rang), **rung** (rung) **1** to make a sound, especially a bell-like sound. **2** to telephone. **3** to ring a bell as a summons: *We rang the doorbell.* – *n.* **1** the act or sound of ringing. **2** the act of ringing a bell. **3** the clear resonant sound of a bell, or a similarly resonant sound. **4** (*British*) a telephone call. – *adj.* **ringing**. – *vb.* **ring back** to telephone someone who telephoned earlier.

rink (ringk) *n.* **1** an area of ice. **2** or an area of smooth floor for ice skating, roller skating, etc.

rinse (rins) *vb.* **rinsing, rinsed** to wash soap, detergent, etc. out of clothes, hair, dishes, etc. with clean water.

● **Rio de Janeiro** is Brazil's main seaport and a major commercial and cultural centre.

● **Rio Grande** a river that forms the entire boundary between Texas, USA and Mexico.

riot (**rī** o̊t) *n.* a noisy disturbance by a large group of people. – *vb.* **rioting, rioted** to take part in a riot. – *n.* **rioter**.

riotous *adj.* **1** likely to start, or like, a riot. **2** noisy, and wild. – *n.* **riotousness**.

rip (rip) *vb.* **ripping, ripped 1** to tear or come apart violently or roughly. **2** to remove quickly and violently: *Rita ripped pages out of the book.* – *n.* a rough tear or split. – *vb.* **rip off** (*colloquial*) to cheat or steal from.

ripe (rīp) *adj.* fully matured and ready to be picked and eaten: *ripe fruit.* – *n.* **ripeness**.

ripen *vb.* **ripening, ripened** to make or become ripe or riper.

ripple (**ri** pe̊l) *n.* a slight wave or series of slight waves on the surface of water. – *vb.* **rippling, rippled**.

● **Rip van Winkle** is a character in stories by the American writer, Washington Irving (1783-1859).

Rip Van Winkle returns to his village to learn that 20 years have passed since he fell asleep. During those years his wife has died, his children grown up, and the colonists won the War of Revolution against the British.

rise (rīz) *vb.* **rising, rose** (rōz), **risen** (ri zĕn) **1** to get or stand up, especially from a sitting, kneeling, or lying position. **2** to get up from bed, especially after a night's sleep. **3** to move upwards; to ascend: *The hot air balloon rose in the sky.* **4** to increase in size, amount, volume, strength, degree, intensity, etc.: *The sound at the football match rose with excitement.* **5** (of the Sun, Moon, planets, etc.) to appear above the horizon. **6** to rebel: *The mob rose against the dictator.* – *n.* **1** an act of rising. **2** an increase in size, amount, volume, strength, status, rank, etc. **3** (*British*) a salary increase.

risk (risk) *n.* the chance or possibility of suffering loss, injury, damage, or failure. – *vb.* **risking, risked** to expose to danger or risk: *We risk getting fat by eating too much.* – *adv.* **riskily**. – *adj.* **risky, riskier, riskiest**.

ritual (ri choo ål) *n.* the set order or words used in a religious ceremony. – *adj.*

rival (rī vål) *n.* a person or group of people that tries to compete with another for the same goal or in the same field. – *adj.* being a rival. – *vb.* **rivalling, rivalled** to be in competition with someone.

river (ri vĕr) *n.* a large natural stream that usually flows along a definite course.

rivet (ri vĕt) *n.* a metal bolt for fastening plates of metal together.

riveting *adj.* fascinating; enthralling.

road (rōd) *n.* an open, usually specially surfaced or paved way, for people, vehicles, or animals to travel on from one place to another.

roam (rōm) *vb.* **roaming, roamed** to wander about without purpose.

roar (rör) *vb.* **roaring, roared** to give a loud growling cry: *Lions roar.*

roast (rōst) *vb.* **roasting, roasted** to cook by exposure to dry heat, especially in an oven: *Tim is roasting a chicken.*

On the inner curve of a meander the river deposits sand and silt.

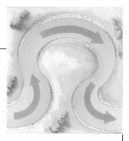

The neck of the loop may greatly narrow as the loop develops.

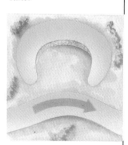

The old channel may be cut off to form an oxbow lake.

Rivers have helped to shape the landscape. They have provided means of transport from the sea to inland areas. And rivers have supplied food, and water for drinking and irrigation. Some rivers start life as springs, others are fed by melting glaciers. Most rivers come from rain and snow that falls on uplands.

A river flowing quickly down a steep slope of hard rocks cuts a deep gorge.

When a river flows slowly over soft rock, the valley is worn back and widened into a V shape.

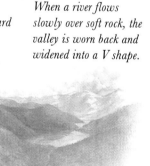

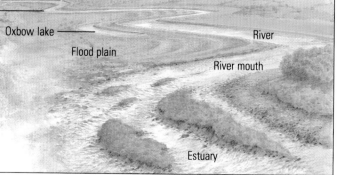

Glacier

Meltwater

Waterfall

Rapids

Stream

Tributary stream

Meander

Oxbow lake

Flood plain

River

River mouth

Estuary

LONGEST RIVERS

Nile (Africa) 6670km	Zaire (Africa) 4667km
Amazon (South America) 6437km	Amur (Asia) 4506km
Mississippi-Missouri (N. Am.) 6212km	Lena (Russia) 4269km
Yangtze (China) 5520km	Yenisey (Russia) 4506km
Ob-Irtysh (Russia) 5151km	Mekong (Asia) 4184km
Huang Ho (China) 4845km	Niger (Africa) 4000km

An 18th-century stagecoach being held up by highwaymen at gunpoint and its passengers robbed of their money and possessions.

rob (rob) *vb.* **robbing, robbed** to steal something from a person or place, especially by force or threats. – *n.* **robber**.
robbery *n.* **robberies** the act of robbing.
robe (rōb) *n.* **1** (often in *plural*) a long loose garment, especially one worn for special ceremonies as a mark of office.

● **Robespierre** (rōbz pē ār), **Maximilien de** (1758-94) was a French revolutionary leader who started the 'Reign of Terror', the most violent period of the FRENCH REVOLUTION.

robin (ro bin) *n.* **1** (also **robin redbreast**) a small brown European thrush with a red breast. **2** a North American thrush with an orange-red breast.

● **Robin Hood** was a legendary English outlaw of the 1100s who robbed the rich to give to the poor.

robot (rō bot) *n.* an automatic machine programmed to perform specific tasks. The word robot comes from the Czech for 'forced labour'. Robots can be used in industry to do jobs that are dangerous or repetitive.

robust (rō **bust**) *adj.* strong and healthy; with a strong constitution. – *n.* **robustness**.

rock¹ (rok) *n.* **1** the hard mineral matter which forms part of the Earth's crust. **2** a mass of this mineral matter forming a cliff, peak, reef, etc. **3** a large stone or boulder. **4** (*US*) a stone.
rock bottom *n.* the lowest level possible.
rocky *adj.* **rockier, rockiest 1** full of rocks. **2** full of problems.

rock² (rok) *vb.* **rocking, rocked 1** to sway gently backwards and forwards or from side to side: *Rock the baby to sleep.* **2** to shake violently. – *n.* **1** a rocking movement. **2** (also **rock music**) a form of popular music developed in the mid-1950s, a mixture of black rhythm and blues music and country and western.

● **Rockefeller** is the name of an American family noted for its activities in business, politics, and philanthropy.

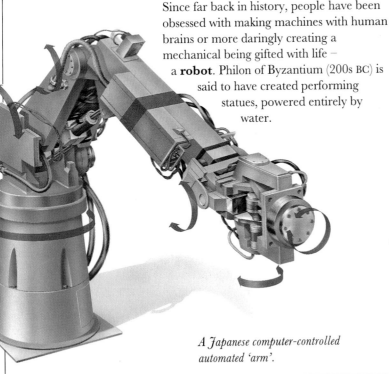

Since far back in history, people have been obsessed with making machines with human brains or more daringly creating a mechanical being gifted with life – a **robot**. Philon of Byzantium (200s BC) is said to have created performing statues, powered entirely by water.

A Japanese computer-controlled automated 'arm'.

Lunakhods, unmanned Soviet Moon cars, were controlled from Earth by radio and travelled the Moon's surface collecting information.

In the Czech play R.U.R. mechanical men do all the work of the world. Few robots in fact look like such machines.

rocket (**ro** kit) *n.* **1** a self-propelling, cylindrical projectile which is driven forwards and upwards by the gas it expels from burning fuel, for example one forming the basis of a jet engine. **2** such a device used as a firework or distress signal. **3** anything which is propelled by such a device, for example a spacecraft.

●**Rockwell, Norman** (1894-1978) was an American painter of realistic detail, famed for the covers he painted for the newspaper, the *Saturday Evening Post.*

●**Rocky Mountains** This mountain system stretches over 4500 km along the west side of NORTH AMERICA. The highest peak is Mount Elbert (4300 metres above sea level).

rod (rod) *n.* **1** a long slender stick or bar of wood, metal, etc.: *a curtain rod.* **2** a stick used to beat people as a punishment. **3** a fishing-rod.

rode. See **ride**.

rodent (**rō** dĕnt) *n.* any of the group of small mammals with strong sharp teeth for gnawing, including mice and squirrels.

rodeo (rō **dā** ō) or (**rō** di ō) *n.* **rodeos** a show or contest of cowboy skills.

●**Rodgers, Richard** (1902-79) was an American composer of musicals including: *Oklahoma!* and *South Pacific* which he wrote with Oscar HAMMERSTEIN.

●**Rodin** (**rō** dan), **Auguste** (1840-1917) was a French sculptor of *The Kiss* and *The Thinker.*

roe¹ (rō) *n.* the eggs of a fish.

roe² (rō) *n.* (also **roe deer**) a small deer found in Europe and Asia.

role or **rôle** (rōl) *n.* **1** an actor's part in a play, film, etc. **2** a part played in life, business, etc.

roll (rōl) *n.* **1** anything flat, such as paper, fabric, etc., which is rolled up to form a cylinder or tube: *a roll of kitchen paper.* **2** a small piece of bread for one person. **3** an official list of names, for example of school pupils, members of a club, etc. **4** an act of rolling. **5** a swaying or rolling movement: *the roll of a boat.* **6** a long low prolonged sound: *a roll of thunder.* – *vb.*

rolling, rolled 1 to move by turning over and over, as if on an axis, and often in a specified direction: *We rolled the logs into position.* **2** to move on wheels, rollers, etc., or in a vehicle with wheels: *Roy rolled his bike into the shed.* **3** (of a person or animal, etc. lying down) to turn with a rolling movement to face in another direction: *The kittens rolled on the bed.* **4** to pronounce with a trill: *The Scots roll their 'r's.* – **be rolling in** (*colloquial*) to have large amounts of money. – *vb.* **roll up 1** to form into a roll. **2** (*colloquial*) to arrive.

roller *n.* **1** any of a number of cylindrical objects or machines used for flattening, crushing, spreading, printing, applying paint, etc. **2** a small cylinder on which hair is rolled for curling. **3** a long heavy sea wave.

Rodin's bronze statue, The Thinker.

rollercoaster *n.* a raised railway with sharp curves and steep inclines, ridden on for excitement, and usually found at funfairs.

●**Rolling Stones** a British rock group, formed in 1962.

ROM (rom) see **Computer terms.**

Roman (**rō** mån) *adj.* **1** of, or related to, modern or ancient Rome. **2 roman** (of printing type) written in ordinary upright letters (as opposed to italics). – *n.* an inhabitant of ROME.

Roman Catholic *adj.* of the Christian Church which recognizes the Pope as its head. – *n.* a member of this Church. – *n.* **Roman Catholicism** (kå **thol** i si zĕm).

Roman numeral *n.* any of the figures used to represent numbers in the system developed by the ancient Romans, for example I (= 1), V (= 5), X (= 10), etc.

romance (rō **mans**) *n.* **1** a love affair. **2** a sentimental account, especially in writing or on film, of a love affair. – *adj.* **Romance** of, or relating to, the languages which have developed from Latin.

A roller skate consists of either a series of wheels attached to a frame which can be fitted over a shoe, or a shoe with wheels attached to the sole. Inside the wheels of a roller skate are ball bearings. These help the wheels move round smoothly, reducing friction and wear.

The **Roman Empire** was founded by emperor Augustus in 27 BC and lasted for nearly 500 years. Until about AD 200 the empire was prosperous and peaceful. A network of roads linked all parts of the empire helping trade and defence. Towns had fine public buildings and in the countryside farming was efficient.

The empire had a common coinage.

According to tradition Rome was founded by Romulus and Remus in 753 BC. The twins were abandoned as babies but were found by a she-wolf who raised them.

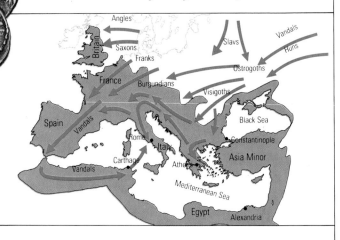

From about AD 200 the empire was under constant attack from invading tribes. Rome was finally overrun by Alaric, leader of the Visigoths, in AD 410.

The Roman army conquered a vast area. An ordinary Roman soldier carried a sword, a dagger, and a rectangular shield.

The Romans built long straight roads which enabled their armies to travel quickly.

The arch of Constantine, built in AD 312.

Everyday objects such as oil lamps were hand crafted.

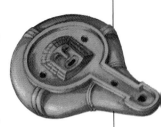

Rome's chariot-racing stadium, the Circus Maximus, could hold up to 250,000 spectators.

●**Roman Empire** Legend says that Rome was founded in 753 BC by the twins ROMULUS and Remus. From a cluster of villages along the river Tiber, Rome grew to be the centre of a mighty empire, covering most of Europe and the lands around the Mediterranean. The Romans first set up a republic, but were later ruled by emperors. The Romans were practical people – splendid builders, engineers, and lawmakers. They took most of their learning and culture from the Greeks. By AD 476 the empire had collapsed.

●**Romania**. See Supplement, **Countries**.

Romanian (roo **mān** i ån) or (rō **mān** i ån) *n.* **1** the official language of ROMANIA. **2** an inhabitant of or person from ROMANIA. – *adj.* of, or relating to, ROMANIA.

●**Romanov** is the name of the dynasty that ruled Russia from 1613 to 1917.

romantic (rō **man** tik) *adj.* **1** of, like, or feeling sentimental and idealized love. **2** dealing with or suggesting adventure, mystery, and sentimentalized love: *romantic fiction.*
Romany (**ro** må ni) or (**rō** må ni) *n.* **Romanies** **1** a gipsy. **2** the language spoken by gipsies. – *adj.* of the Romanies.

●**Rome** is today the capital of ITALY. It was once the centre of the ROMAN EMPIRE.

●**Romulus** (**rom** ū lůs) according to legend, was the founder of ROME. He and his twin brother, Remus, were suckled by a wolf after they had been abandoned as babies.

roof (roof) *n.* **roofs 1** the covering of a building or vehicle. **2** the top inner surface of an oven, refrigerator, the mouth, etc. – *vb.* **roofing, roofed** to cover with a roof.
roofing *n.* materials for building a roof.
rook (rook) *n.* a large crow-like bird.
room (room) *n.* **1** a part of a building which is separated from the rest of the building by having a ceiling, floor, and walls. **2** a space or area which is occupied by or is available to someone or something. **3** opportunity, scope: *There is room for improvement in his work.*
roomy *adj.* **roomer, roomiest** spacious. – *n.* **roominess**.

●**Roosevelt, Franklin Delano** (1882-1945) was elected to four terms as president of the United States, the longest any US president has served. With Winston CHURCHILL and Joseph STALIN he was one of the great Allied leaders in the Second WORLD WAR (1939-45).

roost (roost) *n.* a branch, perch, etc. on which birds rest at night. – *vb.* **roosting, roosted** (of birds) to settle on a roost, especially for sleep. **rooster** *n.* (especially *US*) a farmyard cock.
root[1] (root) *n.* **1** the underground part of a plant that absorbs water and nourishment from the soil. **2** the part of a tooth, hair, nail, etc. which attaches it to the body. **3** the basic cause, source, or origin of something: *We must get to the root of the problem.* **4** the basic element in a word which remains after all the affixes have been removed, and which may form the basis of a number of related words: *'Love' is the root of 'lovable' and 'loveliness'.* – *vb.* **rooting, rooted** to grow roots; to become established. **rooted** *adj.* firmly established.
root[2] (root) *vb.* **rooting, rooted** (especially of pigs) to dig up the ground with the snout in search of food.

Franklin D. Roosevelt became president in 1933. He steered the United States out of the deepest economic Depression and the costliest war in history (the Second World War of 1939-45).

Roots anchor a plant firmly in the soil and supply it with water and mineral salts. Plants such as grasses have a mass of fibrous roots. Roots can store food for such plants as carrots and beet. Potato tubers and corms are really underground stems, not roots. A tree's roots grow deep into the soil and can find water even in a drought.

rope (rōp) *n.* **1** strong thick cord made by twisting fibres together. **2** a number of objects, especially pearls or onions, strung together. – *vb.* **roping, roped** to tie with a rope.
rose[1] (rōz) *n.* **1** any of a family of shrubs with prickly stems and often sweet-smelling flowers. **2** a darkish pink colour. – *adj.* of or like roses.
rosy *adj.* **rosier, rosiest 1** rose-coloured; pink. **2** hopeful; optimistic; cheerful.
rose[2]. See **rise**.
Rosh Hashanah (rosh hå **shä** nå) *n.* the Jewish festival of New Year.

●**Rossini, Gioacchino** (1792-1868) was an Italian opera composer who wrote *The Barber of Seville*.

rot (rot) *vb.* **rotting, rotted** to decay. – *n.* decay; something which has decomposed.

rota (**rō** tå) *n.* (especially *British*) a list of duties that are to be done and the names of the people who are to do them.

rotary (**rō** tå ri) *adj.* turning on an axis.

rotate (**rō** tāt) *vb.* **rotating, rotated 1** to turn on an axis like a wheel. **2** to arrange in an ordered sequence.
  rotation *n.* **1** an act of rotating. **2** one complete turn around an axis. **3** (also **crop rotation**) the growing of different crops on a field, usually in an ordered sequence.

●**Rothko, Mark** (1903-70) was a Latvian-born American abstract painter.

rotor (**rō** tŏr) *n.* a system of blades which rotate at high speed to provide the force to lift and propel a helicopter.

rotten (**ro** tĕn) *adj.* **1** having gone bad, decayed: *I can't possibly eat these apples, they're rotten.* **2** (*colloquial*) miserably unwell: *I've got a cold and I'm feeling rotten.* **3** (*colloquial*) unsatisfactory.

●**Rotterdam** is Europe's busiest port and a major manufacturing city in the Netherlands.

Rottweiler (**rot** vīl ĕr) *n.* a large powerfully built black and tan dog.

rough (ruf) *adj.* **1** (of a surface) not smooth, even, or regular. **2** (of ground) covered with stones, tall grass, bushes, etc. **3** harsh or grating: *a rough voice.* **4** (of a person's character, behaviour, etc.) noisy, coarse, or violent. **5** stormy: *rough winds.* **6** requiring hard work or considerable physical effort, or involving great difficulty, tension, etc.: *Mum had a rough day at work.* – *n.* **roughness**. – *vb.* **roughing, roughed**: **rough it** (*colloquial*) to live without the usual comforts.
  roughage *n.* coarse bulky material in food, which helps digestion.
  roughen *vb.* **roughening, roughened** to make or become rough.

round (rownd) *adj.* **1** shaped like a circle or a ball. **2** not angular; curved and plump. **3** moving in or forming a circle. **4** (of numbers) complete and exact: *That makes a round dozen.* **5** (of a number) without a fraction. – *adv.* **1** in a circular direction or with a circular or revolving movement: *The wheels whirred round.* **2** on all sides so as to surround: *Gather round!* **3** in rotation, so as to return to the starting point. **4** from place to place: *Drive round for a while.* – *prep.* (also and *US* **around**) on all sides of so as to surround or enclose: *He pulled the blanket round him.* – *n.* **1** something round, and often flat, in shape. **2** a complete revolution round a circuit or path. **3** a sandwich, or set of sandwiches, made from two complete slices of bread. **4** the playing of all 18 holes on a golf course in a single session. **5** one of a recurring series of events, actions, etc.: *a round of talks.* – *vb.* **rounding, rounded 1** to make or become round. **2** to go round: *The car rounded the corner.* – *n.* **roundness**. – **round about 1** on all sides; in a ring surrounding. **2** approximately. – *vb.* **round on** to turn on in anger and attack, usually in speech. – *vb.* **round up 1** to raise a number so that it can be expressed as a round number: *Round 15.89 up to 16.* **2** to collect people, or things together.
  roundabout *n.* **1** a revolving platform, usually with seats, on which you can ride for pleasure. **2** (*British*) a circular road junction, usually with an island in the middle.
  rounded *adj.* curved

Round Table (rownd **tā** bĕl) *n.* the table of King Arthur, in legend. Its shape meant that no one sitting at it would have precedence. Today it has come to mean a meeting of people on equal terms: *a round table conference.*

Arthur and the knights of the Round Table. There are many romantic stories told about the British king, Arthur, his court at Camelot, and his knights of the Round Table.

route (rōōt) *n.* a particular group of roads followed to get to a place.

routine (rōō **tēn**) *n.* a regular or fixed way of doing things. – *adj.* unvarying; ordinary.

row[1] (rō) *n.* a number of people or things, such as theatre seats, numbers, etc. arranged in a line: *She planted three rows of beans.*

row[2] (rō) *vb.* **rowing, rowed** to move a boat through the water using oars. – *n.* **rower**. **rowing boat** *n.* (*British*) a small boat which is moved by oars.

row[3] (row) *n.* a noisy quarrel; a disturbance. – *vb.* **rowing, rowed** to quarrel noisily.

rowdy (**row** di) *adj.* **rowdier, rowdiest** noisy and rough. – *adv.* **rowdily**. – *n.* **rowdiness**.

royal (**roi** ål) *adj.* **1** of, or suitable for, a king or queen. **2** being a member of the king or queen's family.

The badge of the Royal Canadian Mounted Police.

●**Royal Canadian Mounted Police** (RCMP) the federal police force of CANADA. They are known as Mounties because they used to travel only on horseback.

rub (rub) *vb.* **rubbing, rubbed 1** to move your hand, an object, etc. back and forwards over a surface with pressure. **2** to move backwards and forwards over a surface with pressure and friction: *The dog rubbed its back against the tree.* **3** to apply ointment, lotion, polish, etc. **4** to clean, polish, dry, smooth, etc. – *n.* an act of rubbing. – *vb.* **rub out** to remove by rubbing; to erase, remove.

rubber (**ru** běr) *n.* **1** a strong elastic substance obtained from the latex of various trees or plants or produced synthetically. **2** (*British*) a small piece of rubber or plastic used for rubbing out pencil or ink marks on paper; an eraser. **3** (especially *US slang*) a condom. – *adj.* of or producing rubber. – *adj.* **rubbery**.

rubbish (**ru** bish) *n.* **1** waste material. **2** nonsense: *Don't talk rubbish.*

rubble (**ru** běl) *n.* broken stones, bricks, plaster, etc. from ruined or demolished buildings.

●**Rubens, Sir Peter Paul** (1577-1640) was a Flemish painter of large colourful pictures.

ruby (**rōō** bi) *n.* **rubies** a precious red stone. **ruby wedding** *n.* a fortieth wedding anniversary.

rucksack (**ruk** sak) *n.* a bag carried on the back by means of straps over the shoulders.

rudder (**ru** děr) *n.* a flat piece of wood, metal, etc. fixed vertically to a ship's stern or an aircraft's fin for steering.

ruddy (**ru** di) *adj.* **ruddier, ruddiest 1** having a healthy glowing complexion. **2** reddish.

rude (rōōd) *adj.* **1** impolite; showing bad manners. **2** roughly made: *They could only build a rude shelter.* **3** vulgar; indecent. – *n.* **rudeness**.

ruffian (**ru** fi ån) *n.* a violent lawless person.

ruffle (**ru** fěl) *vb.* **ruffling, ruffled 1** to make wrinkled or uneven; to spoil the smoothness of. **2** to make or become irritated. **3** (of a bird) to erect its feathers, usually in anger or display. – *n.* a frill worn either round the neck or wrists.

rug (rug) *n.* **1** a small carpet. **2** a thick blanket.

Rugby (**rug** bi) *n.* (also **Rugby football**) a form of football played with an oval ball which players may pick up and run with and may pass from hand to hand.

Ruffian has nothing to do with the word 'rough', but comes from the Italian word *ruffiano*, taken from an older word *roffia* which meaning 'beastly thing'.

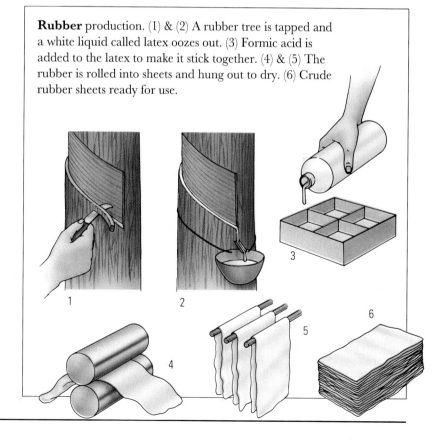

Rubber production. (1) & (2) A rubber tree is tapped and a white liquid called latex oozes out. (3) Formic acid is added to the latex to make it stick together. (4) & (5) The rubber is rolled into sheets and hung out to dry. (6) Crude rubber sheets ready for use.

From a ruin (of say, a castle) you can work out what it once looked like. For instance, fireplaces and holes for beams will show you where each floor was. The shape of some rooms will be shown by the remains of foundations.

rugged (**ru** gid) *adj.* **1** having a rough uneven surface; steep and rocky: *The Alps are a rugged range of mountains.* **2** (of the face) having features that are strongly marked and furrowed. **3** involving physical hardships: *a rugged life.* **4** (of equipment, a machine, etc.) strongly or sturdily built. – *n.* **ruggedness**.

●**Ruhr** This region in Germany in the Ruhr valley is noted for its industry and coal-mining.

ruin (**roo** in) *n.* **1** a broken, destroyed, decayed state: *The castle is a ruin.* **2** a complete loss of wealth, social position, power, etc.: *She faces financial ruin as a result of the depression.* – *vb.* **ruining, ruined** to cause ruin to; to destroy. – *adj.* **ruined**.

rule (rool) *n.* **1** a principle, order, or direction which controls some action, function, form, use, etc. **2** the period during which government or control is exercised. **3** a general principle or custom: *Make it a rule always to be punctual.* – *vb.* **ruling, ruled 1** to govern; to exercise authority. **2** to keep control of or restrain. – *vb.* **rule out** to leave out or not consider.
ruler *n.* **1** a person, for example a sovereign, who rules or governs. **2** (or **rule**) a strip of wood, metal, or plastic with straight edges marked off in units used for measuring.
ruling *n.* an official decision.
rum¹ (rum) *n.* a spirit made from sugar cane.
rum² (rum) *adj.* **rummer, rummest** (*British colloquial*) strange; odd; bizarre.
ruminant (**roo** mi nănt) *n.* any mammal which chews the cud, such as cattle, sheep and goats.
rummage (**ru** mij) *vb.* **rummaging, rummaged** to search thoroughly or turn things over untidily in. – *n.* a thorough search.

rumour (**roo** mŏr) *n.* information which is passed from person to person.
rump (rump) *n.* the rear part of an animal.
rumple (**rum** pĕl) *vb.* **rumpling, rumpled** to make untidy or wrinkled. – *n.*
run (run) *vb.* **running, ran** (ran), **run** (run) **1** (of a person or animal) to move on foot so quickly that both or all feet are off the ground together for an instant during each step. **2** to cover, accomplish, or perform by, or as if by, running: *Sarah often runs errands for her grandmother.* **3** to move quickly and easily on, or as if on, wheels. **4** (of water, etc.) to flow; to allow liquid to flow: *The river runs to the sea; Run cold water into the bath.* **5** to operate or work. **6** to organize or manage. **7** (especially *US*) to stand as a candidate. – *n.* **1** an act of running; the distance covered by running. **2** a rapid running movement: *The walkers broke into a run.* **3** a continuous and unbroken period or series of something: *She's recently had a run of bad luck.* **4** freedom to move about or come and go as you please: *You can have the run of the house.* **5** a route which is regularly travelled: *a coach on the London to Glasgow run.* – *vb.* **run after** to chase. – *vb.* **run away 1** to escape or flee. **2** (of a horse) to gallop off uncontrollably. **3** to steal: *The thieves ran away with a video.* – *vb.* **run down 1** (of a clock, battery, etc.) to stop working because of a gradual loss of power. **2** to knock to the ground: *The bike ran down the*

RUN RUNS RIOT

There are an almost innumerable number of ways that we can use the little verb 'run'. Like 'get' and 'pop' it is very useful.

to tend towards: *run to fat.*

to be an inherent or recurring part of: *Blue eyes run in the family.*

to be affected by or subjected to: *run a high temperature* or *run risks.*

to spread quickly: *The colour in his shirt ran* or *The rumour ran through the office.*

to move or pass quickly: *Run your eyes over the report* or *Excitement ran through the audience.*

to continue or extend in a specified direction, time, or distance: *The play ran for ten years* or *This road runs south.*

to continue to have legal force: *Their lease still has a year to run.*

to accumulate: *He's run up debts at the bank.*

to get past or through: *run a blockade.*

Runs to a lot of examples!

boys. **3** to speak badly of, usually without good reason. – *vb.* **run into 1** (*colloquial*) to meet unexpectedly. **2** to crash into or collide with. **3** to suffer from: *Their plans ran into difficulties.* – *vb.* **run out 1** (of a supply) to come to an end; to be used up. **2** to use up: *The project has run out of money.* – *vb.* **run over 1** (of a vehicle or driver) to knock down and drive over, and injure or kill. **2** to overflow. **3** to repeat or glance over quickly, especially for practice.

runner *n.* **1** a person or thing that runs. **2** a groove or strip along which a drawer, sliding door, etc. slides.

runner-up *n.* **runners-up** a competitor who finishes in second place.

runway *n.* a wide hard surface from which aircraft take off and on which they land.

rung¹ (rung) *n.* a step on a ladder.

rung². See **ring²**.

● **Runyon, Damon** (1884-1946) was an American short-story writer, notably of life in New York City's underworld.

rural (r**ōō** răl) *adj.* of the countryside.

rush¹ (rush) *vb.* **rushing, rushed** to hurry or go quickly. – *n.* **1** a sudden quick movement, usually towards a single goal: *a gold rush.* **2** a sudden general movement. **3** haste; hurry: *He was in a dreadful rush.* – *adj.*

rush² (rush) *n.* a tall grass-like plant which grows in or near water.

● **Rushdie, Salman** (1947-) is a British novelist, born in Bombay, author of *Midnight's Children* and *The Satanic Verses.*

rusk (rusk) *n.* a slice of bread which has been rebaked until it is crisp.

● **Russia** is a republic which until 1991 formed three-quarters of the former Union of Soviet Socialist Republics. Even without the other 14 republics, Russia is still by far the largest country in the world: it is nearly twice as big as Canada. Russia stretches from St Petersburg (formerly Leningrad) on the Baltic Sea to Vladivostok on the Sea of Japan. Russia has a great variety of scenery and climate – Arctic wastes, vast forests, grassy plains, and high mountains. Many different crops can be grown and a large number of minerals are mined for the many industries. Until 1917 the country was ruled by Tsars.

Then Bolshevik communists under LENIN seized power and the USSR was ruled as a strict communist state. In 1985 Mikhail Gorbachev became president and introduced reforms. See also Supplement, **Countries**.

Russian (**ru** shăn) *n.* **1** a person born in or living in Russia or (*loosely*) the other former Soviet republics. **2** the language of Russia.

rust (rust) *n.* **1** a reddish-brown brittle coating which forms on iron caused by the action of oxygen and moisture. **2** the colour of rust, usually a reddish-brown. **3** a fungus causing a plant disease. – *vb.* **rusting, rusted** to become coated with rust.

rusty *adj.* **rustier, rustiest 1** covered with or affected by rust. **2** (of a skill, knowledge of a subject, etc.) not as good as it used to be.

rustic (**rus** tik) *adj.* of or living in the country.

rustle (**ru** sĕl) *vb.* **rustling, rustled** to make a soft whispering sound as of dry leaves. – *vb.* **rustle up** to arrange or prepare quickly: *After the match Mark rustled up a snack.*

rustler (**rus** lĕr) *n.* (especially *US*) a person who steals cattle or horses.

rut (rut) *n.* a deep track made by wheels.

● **Ruth, George Herman 'Babe'** (1895-1948) was an American professional baseball player.

● **Rutherford, Ernest** (1871-1937) was a New Zealand scientist who helped lay the foundations of modern nuclear physics.

ruthless (r**ōō**th lĕs) *adj.* without pity. – *n.* **ruthlessness**.

● **Rwanda**. See Supplement, **Countries**.

rye (rī) *n.* a cereal which produces a grain used for making bread and whiskey.

Rust is the visible evidence of a chemical reaction known as oxidation. Oxygen in the air takes electrons from the atoms in the metal. This produces the signs of rust. Salt water speeds rusting.

Rusted metal

S s

●**Saarinen, Eero** (1910-61) was a Finnish-born American architect.

Sabbath (**sa** båth) *n.* a day of the week set aside for religious worship and rest, Saturday among the Jews and Sunday among Christians.

sable (**sā** běl) *n.* a small flesh-eating mammal of northern Europe and Asia.

sabotage (**sa** bŏ täzh) *n.* deliberate damage or destruction, especially carried out for military or political reasons.

sabre (**sā** běr) *n.* a curved single-edged sword.

●**Sacagawea** (1787-1812) was a guide and interpreter from the Shoshone tribe of Native Americans. She guided the explorers Lewis and Clark.

sack¹ (sak) *n.* **1** a large bag, especially of coarse cloth or paper. **2** (*colloquial*) dismissal from employment: *Bob was given the sack.* – *vb.* **sacking, sacked** (*colloquial*) to dismiss from employment.

sack² (sak) *vb.* **sacking, sacked** to plunder.

sacred (**sā** krid) *adj.* **1** devoted to God or a god and therefore regarded with solemn respect. **2** connected with religion: *sacred music.*

sacrifice (**sak** ri fĩs) *n.* **1** an offering made to God or a god. **2** any thing, especially something valuable, given up or given away for the sake of another thing or person. – *vb.* **sacrificing, sacrificed.**

sad (sad) *adj.* **sadder, saddest 1** feeling unhappy. **2** causing unhappiness: *sad news.* – *n.* **sadness.**

sadden *vb.* **saddening, saddened** to make or become sad: *The cat's death saddened Sam.*

saddle (**sa** děl) *n.* **1** a horse-rider's seat, usually made of leather, fitting on the horse's back. **2** a fixed seat on a bicycle or motorcycle. – *vb.* **saddling, saddled 1** to put a saddle on a horse. **2** to burden: *saddled with problems.*

When she was a little girl Sacagawea was captured by the Hidatsa tribe of Native Americans and sold to a French Canadian fur trader. She later proved invaluable as a guide on the Lewis and Clark expedition across the American continent.

safe (sāf) *adj.* **1** free from danger or harm. **2** giving protection from harm; secure: *a safe place.* **3** not dangerous: *It's safe to go out.* – *n.* a sturdily constructed metal cabinet in which valuables can be locked away.

safety *n.* the condition of being safe.

sag (sag) *vb.* **sagging, sagged 1** to sink or bend downwards. **2** to hang loosely.

saga (**sä** gå) *n.* **1** a medieval Scandinavian tale of legendary heroes and events. **2** any long detailed piece of fiction depicting successive generations of the same family.

sage¹ (sāj) *n.* a plant with aromatic leaves.
sage² (sāj) *adj.* wise; prudent.
Sagittarius (sa ji **tār** i ŭs). See **zodiac**.

● **Sahara** the world's biggest hot desert, in North Africa. About a third is covered by sand.

said. See **say**.

sail (sāl) *n.* **1** a sheet of canvas spread to catch the wind and make a ship move. **2** a trip in a boat or ship. **3** any of a windmill's revolving arms. – *vb.* **sailing, sailed 1** to travel by boat or ship: *sail the Pacific.* **2** to control a boat or ship. **3** to depart by boat or ship: *We sail at noon.* **4** to move smoothly and swiftly.
sailor *n.* any member of a ship's crew.

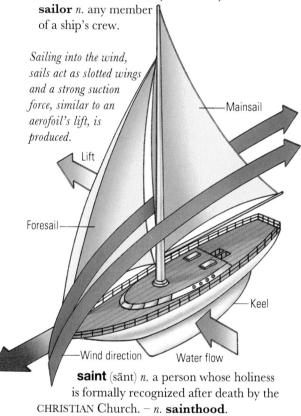

Sailing into the wind, sails act as slotted wings and a strong suction force, similar to an aerofoil's lift, is produced.

Mainsail

Lift

Foresail

Keel

Wind direction

Water flow

saint (sānt) *n.* a person whose holiness is formally recognized after death by the CHRISTIAN Church. – *n.* **sainthood**.

● **St Kitts-Nevis**. See Supplement, **Countries**.

● The **St Lawrence Seaway** connects the GREAT LAKES with the ATLANTIC Ocean and forms part of the UNITED STATES-Canadian border.

● **St Lucia**. See Supplement, **Countries**.

● **St Petersburg**, a city and port in north-west Russia founded by Peter the Great in 1703.

● **St Vincent and the Grenadines**. See Supplement, **Countries**.

salaam (så **läm**) *n.* a word used as a greeting in Eastern countries, especially by Muslims.
salad (sa låd) *n.* a cold dish of usually raw vegetables, usually served with a dressing.

● **Saladin** (1138-93) was an Arab soldier who repelled the Third Crusade.

salamander (sa lå man dẽr) *n.* a lizard-like amphibious creature.
salary (sa lå ri) *n.* **salaries** a fixed regular payment for work: *a salary of £15,000 a year.*
sale (sāl) *n.* **1** the act or practice of selling; the selling of an item: *the sale of a bicycle.* **2** an item sold. **3** a period during which goods are offered at reduced prices: *the January sales.*

● **Salinger, Jerome David** (1919-) is an American novelist: *The Catcher in the Rye.*

saliva (så **lī** vå) *n.* the watery liquid produced by glands in the mouth to aid digestion.

● **Salk, Jonas** (1914-) developed a vaccine that prevents the crippling disease, poliomyelitis.

salmon (sa mŏn) *n.* **salmon** or **salmons 1** a large silvery marine fish that lays its eggs in fresh water. **2** any of various related fishes.
salt (sölt) *n.* **1** (also **common salt**) sodium chloride, a white crystalline substance found as a mineral (**rock-salt**) or in solution in sea water (**sea-salt**), used to season and preserve food. **2** a chemical compound in which one or more hydrogen atoms have been replaced by a metal atom or atoms. – *vb.* **salting, salted** to season or preserve food with salt. – *adj.* **1** preserved with salt: *salt pork.* **2** containing salt: *salt water.* – *adj.* **salted**.
salty *adj.* **saltier, saltiest** containing salt or tasting of salt. – *n.* **saltiness**.

● **Salt Lake City** is the capital of Utah, USA. It was founded in 1847 as the world capital of the MORMON religion.

salute (så **lōōt**) *vb.* **saluting, saluted 1** to pay formal respect to with a set gesture, especially with the right arm or a weapon. **2** to greet with a show of friendship.

A fire salamander. There are over 300 species of these amphibians. They are sometimes mistaken for lizards. Unlike lizards they have rounded heads, moist skins without scales, and no claws on their toes.

Salary is from the Latin *salarium*, in turn from the word *sal* meaning 'salt'. This is because a salary was originally money given to Roman soldiers to buy salt.

salvage (**sal** vij) *vb.* **salvaging, salvaged** to rescue from damage or loss, for example in a fire or shipwreck: *The Smiths managed to salvage their valuable pictures from the fire.*

salvation (sal **vā** shŏn) *n.* **1** the act of saving a person or thing from harm. **2** a person or thing that saves another from harm: *The fact that we have a car phone was our salvation when we broke down.* **3** liberation from the influence of sin.
Salvation Army *n.* a Christian organization, with a semi-military structure of ranks, aiming to help the poor and spread Christianity. It was founded in England in 1865 by the METHODIST minister William Booth.

salve (salv) *n.* ointment to heal or soothe. – *vb.* **salving, salved** to ease: *salve your conscience.*

same (sām) *adj.* **1** exactly alike or similar: *All the puppies look the same.* **2** not different. **3** unchanged or unchanging: *Sam is wearing the same shirt as yesterday.* **4** previously mentioned; the actual one in question: *Do you mean this same man?* – *pron.* the same person or thing, or the one previously mentioned: *She drank lemonade, and I drank the same.* – *n.* **sameness**. – **all** or **just the same** nevertheless.

samovar (**sa** mŏ vär) *n.* a Russian tea urn.

sample (**säm** pĕl) *n.* a part that shows what the whole looks like: *This piece of cloth is a sample of my dress material.* – *vb.* **sampling, sampled** to take or try as a sample: *Sample the soup.*

samurai (**sa** moo rī) or (**sa** mū rī) *n.* **samurai** a member of an aristocratic class of Japanese warriors between the 11th and 19th centuries.

sanction (**sangk** shŏn) *vb.* **sanctioning, sanctioned** to authorize or confirm formally.

sanctuary (**sangk** choo å ri) *n.* **sanctuaries** **1** a holy place, for example a church or temple. **2** a nature reserve in which the animals or plants are protected by law.

sand (sand) *n.* a grainy substance forming beaches and deserts, consisting of rock powdered by the action of the sea or wind.
sandstone *n.* a type of rock formed from compressed sand, used in building.
sandstorm *n.* a strong wind sweeping along clouds of sand.
sandy *adj.* **sandier, sandiest** **1** containing sand. **2** a pale yellowish-brown.

sandal (**san** dål) *n.* a shoe with straps for holding the sole on the foot.

sandwich (**san** wij) or (**san** wich) *n.* a snack consisting of two or more slices of bread or a roll with a filling of cheese, meat, etc. – *vb.* **sandwiching, sandwiched** to squeeze in between two other things: *I just managed to sandwich a driving lesson into my busy schedule.*

sane (sān) *adj.* **1** not mad. **2** sensible.

●**San Francisco** is one of the most colourful cities in the UNITED STATES and is its chief PACIFIC port. It is well known for its Golden Gate Bridge and cable cars. It was nearly destroyed by an earthquake in 1906.

Samurai in battle, equipped with the newly introduced firearm. Meaning 'one who serves', the samurai warrior of Japan gloried in warfare, in self-discipline, and toughness. To avoid capture in battle he would disembowel himself.

sang. See **sing**.

sanitation (sa ni **tā** shŏn) *n.* standards of public hygiene; having to do with health.

sank. See **sink**.

Sanskrit (**san** skrit) *n.* a language of ancient India.

● **São Tomé e Príncipe**. See Supplement, **Countries**.

sap¹ (sap) *n.* the juice in the stems of plants.
sapling *n.* a young tree.

sap² (sap) *vb.* **sapping, sapped** to tire, weaken: *The long cross country run has sapped her energy.*

sapphire (**sa** fīr) *n.* a precious stone of a transparent dark blue colour.

sarcasm (**sär** ka zěm) *n.* bitter, usually ironical remarks expressing scorn or contempt: *"I am sure you'll be glad to hear that you've failed your exams," he said with sarcasm.*
sarcastic (sär **kas** tik) *adj.* containing or tending to use sarcasm. – *adv.* **sarcastically**.

sardine (sär **dēn**) *n.* a small fish that is tinned.

● **Sargent, John Singer** (1856-1925) was an American portrait painter.

sari (**sä** rē) *n.* **saris** (also **saree**) a traditional garment of HINDU women, a single long piece of fabric wound round the body.

● **Sartre, Jean-Paul** (1905-80) was a French philosopher and writer.

sash¹ (sash) *n.* a broad band of cloth worn round the waist or over one shoulder.

sash² (sash) *n.* either of two glazed frames for a window that slides up and down.

● **Saskatchewan** is one of CANADA's three 'Prairie Provinces', which are major producers of wheat and oil.

Satan (**sā** tǎn) *n.* the Devil.

satellite (**sa** tě līt) *n.* **1** a heavenly body that orbits a larger planet or star, as the Earth does the Sun. **2** an artificial device set in orbit around the Earth, for example as an aid to global television transmission.

satellite dish *n.* a dish-shaped aerial for receiving television programmes via satellite.

satin (**sa** tin) *n.* a fabric with a shiny finish.

satire (**sa** tīr) *n.* a variety of humour aiming at mockery or ridicule, often using sarcasm. – *adj.* **satirical** (să **tir** i kǎl).

satisfy (**sa** tis fī) *vb.* **satisfies, satisfying, satisfied 1** to fulfil the needs or desires of; to meet the requirements of: *Sally was not satisfied with the picture she'd painted, so she did it again.* **2** to remove the doubts of; to convince: *Stephen was satisfied of Tom's ability to do the job.* – *adj.* **satisfied**. – *adj.* **satisfying**.
satisfaction *n.* the state or feeling of being satisfied: *It gives me great satisfaction to read.*
satisfactory *adj.* adequate; acceptable. – *adv.* **satisfactorily**.

saturate *vb.* **saturating, saturated** to soak or fill completely: *The sponge is saturated with water.* – *adj.* **saturated**. – *n.* **saturation**.

Saturday (**sa** tŭr dā) *n.* the seventh day of the week. It is named after Saturn, a Roman god.

Most Hindu women wear a sari. They place the loose end over the head or shoulder.

Saturn¹. See **Myths and Legends**.

● **Saturn²** is the second largest of the planets.

sauce (sös) *n.* any seasoned liquid that food is cooked or served in.

saucer (**sö** sěr) *n.* a small shallow round dish for placing under a tea or coffee cup.

● **Saudi Arabia**. See Supplement, **Countries**.

saunter (**sön** těr) *vb.* **sauntering, sauntered** to walk at a leisurely pace; to stroll.

sausage (**so** sij) *n.* minced and seasoned meat enclosed in a tube-shaped casing.

Fresh sausages may be fried or boiled. There are also smoked sausages and dry sausages such as salami. The Frankfurter or hot dog, named after Frankfurt, Germany, is a cooked sausage and probably the most famous of all sausages.

savage (**sa** vij) *adj.* **1** untamed; uncivilized: *a savage animal.* **2** ferocious.

savanna or **savannah** (så **van** å) *n.* a grassy plain of tropical or subtropical areas.

The savanna is home to many species of grazing animals. Each species feeds differently so they do not compete with each other.

save (sāv) *vb.* **saving, saved 1** to rescue from danger, harm, loss, or failure: *The firefighters saved the children from burning to death.* **2** to set aside for future use; to set money aside for future use: *Sol is saving up to buy a computer.* **3** to use economically so as to avoid waste: *You must save water in a drought.* **4** to cause to escape possible inconvenience; to spare: *That will save you the trouble of making the trip.* – *n.* **1** an act of saving a ball or shot, or preventing a goal. **2** an instruction for a computer to store data.

saving *n.* **1** an economy made. **2** (in *plural*) money saved up: *Have you any savings?*

savour (**sā** vŏr) *vb.* **savouring, savoured 1** to taste or smell with relish. **2** to take pleasure in.

savoury *adj.* not sweet.

saw¹. See **see¹**.

saw² (sö) *n.* a tool with a toothed metal blade for cutting, hand-operated or power-driven. – *vb.* **sawing, sawed, sawn** to cut with a saw: *Sue sawed seven sticks.*

The chainsaw has a never-ending blade in the shape of a chain loop bearing teeth. A small engine (electric or petrol driven) turns the drive cog and makes the chain move.

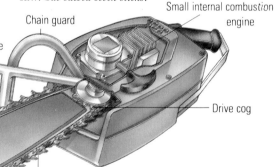

Chain guard

Chain guide

Small internal combustion engine

Drive cog

Chain with cutting teeth

sawdust *n.* tiny bits of wood produced when wood is sawn.

sawmill *n.* a factory in which timber is cut.

Saxon (**sak** sŏn) *n.* a member of a Germanic people that conquered much of Britain in the 5th and 6th centuries.

say (sā) *vb.* **saying, said** (sed) **1** to utter or pronounce. **2** to express in words: *Say what you mean.* **3** to state as an opinion: *I say we should refuse.* **4** to suppose: *Say he doesn't come, what do we do then?* **5** to judge or decide: *It's difficult to say which is best.* **6** to argue in favour of or against: *There's a lot to be said for it.* **7** to communicate: *She talked for ages but didn't actually say much.* **8** to indicate: *The clock says ten o'clock.* – *n.* **1** a chance to express an opinion: *You've had your say.* **2** the right to an opinion: *We had no say in the matter.* – **go without saying** to be obvious. – **there's no saying** it is impossible to guess or judge.

saying *n.* a proverb or expression.

scab (skab) *n.* a crust of dried blood formed over a healing wound.

scaffold (**ska** fōld) *n.* a framework of metal poles and planks used when building repair or construction is carried out.

scald (sköld) *vb.* **scalding, scalded** to injure with hot liquid or steam.

scale¹ (skāl) *n.* **1** a series of markings or divisions at regular known intervals, for use in measuring; a system of such markings or divisions. **2** the relationship between actual size and size as represented on a model or drawing. **3** a complete sequence of notes in music. – *vb.* **scaling, scaled 1** to climb: *scale a mountain.* **2** to change the size of something, making it larger (**scale up**) or smaller (**scale down**).

scale² (skāl) *n.* any of the small thin plates that cover the skin of fish and reptiles. – *vb.* **scaling, scaled** to remove scales from fish.

scalene (**skā** lēn) *adj.* (of a triangle) having each side a different length.

scales (skāls) *n.* (*plural*) an instrument for weighing. – **tip the scales 1** to be the decisive factor. **2** to have your weight measured at: *He tips the scales at 14 stones.*

scallop (**sko** lŏp) or (**ska** lŏp) *n.* an edible shellfish that has a pair of hinged shells.

scalp (skalp) *n.* the skin on your head.

scalpel (**skal** pĕl) *n.* a small surgical knife.

scamper (**skam** pĕr) *vb.* **scampering, scampered** to run quickly taking short steps.

scan (skan) *vb.* **scanning, scanned 1** to read through or examine carefully. **2** to look over quickly. **3** to produce an image of an internal part of the body using any of various electronic devices. **4** to search an area using radar. **5** (of a poem) to conform to a pattern of rhythm.

A patient having a body scan. The X-ray pictures are computerized into 'slice' images

scandal (**skan** dål) *n.* widespread public outrage; an event or fact causing this. **scandalous** *adj.* disgraceful.

Scandinavian (skan di **nāv** i ån) *adj.* of, or relating to, Scandinavia, the countries of SWEDEN, NORWAY, and DENMARK collectively, sometimes also including FINLAND and ICELAND. – *n.* a native or inhabitant of Scandinavia.

scar (skär) *n.* a mark left on the skin after a wound has healed. **2** a blemish. – *vb.* **scarring, scarred** to be marked with a scar.

scarce (skārs) *adj.* **1** not often found; rare. **2** in short supply: *Coal was scarce during the miners' strike.*
scarcely *adv.* **1** only just. **2** hardly ever. **3** not at all: *That was scarcely a reason to hit him.*

scare (skār) *vb.* **scaring, scared 1** to frighten or become afraid. **2** to startle. **3** to drive away by frightening. – *n.* **1** a fright. **2** a sudden feeling of alarm: *a bomb scare.*

scarf (skärf) *n.* **scarfs** or **scarves** a strip or square of fabric worn around the neck.

scarlet (**skär** lit) *n.* a bright red colour.

scatter (**ska** tẻr) *vb.* **scattering, scattered 1** to throw haphazardly: *Sam scattered grass seed on the lawn.* **2** to rush off in different directions.

scavenge (**ska** vinj) *vb.* **scavenging, scavenged** to search among waste.

scene (sēn) *n.* **1** the setting in which a real or imaginary event takes place. **2** a unit of action in a play or film. **3** a landscape, situation, etc. as seen by someone: *A delightful scene met their eyes.* – **behind the scenes** unknown to, or out of sight of, the public.
scenery (**sēn** ẻ ri) *n.* **1** landscape: *The New England scenery in autumn is quite beautiful.* **2** the items making up a stage or film set.

scent (sent) *n.* **1** the distinctive smell of a person, animal, or plant. **2** a trail of this left behind: *dogs on the scent.* **3** perfume.

sceptic (**skep** tik) *n.* a person who believes that nothing can be known with certainty. – *adj.* **sceptical.** – *n.* **scepticism** (**skep** ti si zẻm).

sceptre (**sep** tẻr) *n.* a ceremonial rod carried by a monarch as a symbol of supreme authority.

schedule (**shed** ūl) *n.* **1** a list of activities or events planned to take place at specific times. **2** a timetable; a scheme. – *vb.* **scheduling, scheduled** to plan to happen at a specific time.

Ultrasound scanners are used in the treatment of heart or kidney disease.

scheme (skēm) *n.* **1** a plan of action. **2** a system or programme: *a pension scheme.* **3** a careful arrangement of different parts: *a colour scheme.* – *vb.* **scheming, schemed** to plan or act secretly. – *n.* **schemer.**

scholar (**sko** lår) *n.* **1** a learned person. **2** a person who studies; a pupil or student.

school[1] (skōōl) *n.* **1** a place where a formal general education is given. **2** a place offering formal instruction in a particular subject: *My brother is doing a fashion course at art school.*

school[2] (skōōl) *n.* a group of fish, whales, etc.

schooner (**skōō** nẻr) *n.* **1** a fast sailing-ship with two or more masts. **2** a large sherry glass.

●**Schubert, Franz** (1797-1828) was an Austrian composer, notably of songs.

PRONUNCIATION GUIDE	
fat a	all ö
fate ā	foot oo
fast ä	moon ōō
among å	boy oi
met e	house ow
mean ē	demon ỏ
silent ẻ	thing th
loch hh	this Th
fin i	but u
line ī	mute ū
quick kw	fur û
got o	brochure ů
note ō	vision zh

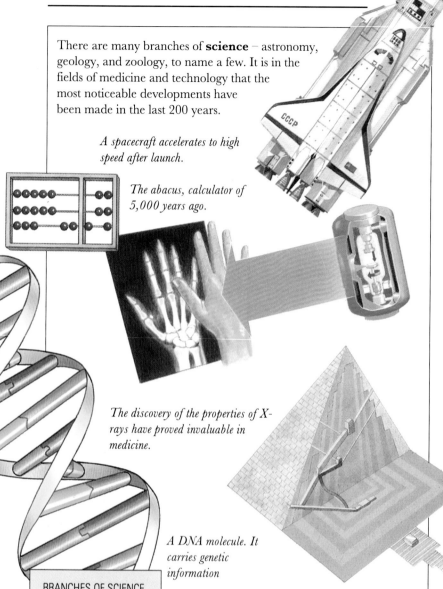

There are many branches of **science** – astronomy, geology, and zoology, to name a few. It is in the fields of medicine and technology that the most noticeable developments have been made in the last 200 years.

A spacecraft accelerates to high speed after launch.

The abacus, calculator of 5,000 years ago.

The discovery of the properties of X-rays have proved invaluable in medicine.

A DNA molecule. It carries genetic information

The Egyptian pyramid-builders of 5,000 years ago used geometry in their constructions.

BRANCHES OF SCIENCE
Science *Study of*
aerodynamics
  properties of flowing air
anatomy
  structure of the body
anthropology
  origins of human beings
linguistics
  languages
metallurgy
  metals
oceanography
  waves, tides, ocean life
palaeontology
  plant and animal fossils
psychology
  working of the brain

science (sī ĕns) *n.* **1** the formal study of the natural world, through observation and experiment. **2** any area of knowledge obtained using, or arranged according to, formal principles: *political science.*
  science fiction *n.* fiction presenting a view of life in the future, incorporating space travel.
  scientific (sī ĕn **tif** ik) *adj.* of, relating to, or used in science. – *adv.* **scientifically.**
  scientist *n.* a student of or expert in science.
sci fi (**sī** fī) *n.* (*colloquial*) science fiction.
scintillate (**sin** til āte) *vb.* **scintillating, scintillated** to sparkle.

scissors (si zŏrz) *n.* (*plural*) a cutting tool with two long blades joined in the middle.
scoff[1] (skof) *vb.* **scoffing, scoffed** to express scorn or contempt; to jeer. – *adj.* **scoffing.**
scoff[2] (skof) *vb.* **scoffing, scoffed** (*colloquial*) to eat rapidly and greedily.
scold (skōld) *vb.* **scolding, scolded** to rebuke.
scone (skon) or (skōn) *n.* a small flat cake, usually halved and spread with butter and jam.
scoop (sko͞op) *vb.* **scooping, scooped** to lift or dig with a sweeping circular movement. – *n.* **1** a spoon-like implement for handling or serving food. **2** a shovel-like part of a mechanical digger.
scooter *n.* (**sko͞ot** ĕr) **1** a child's toy vehicle consisting of a board on two wheels, pushed along the ground with one foot. **2** (also **motor-scooter**) a small-engined motorcycle.
scope (skōp) *n.* the range of topics dealt with.
scorch (skörch) *vb.* **scorching, scorched** to burn slightly on the surface. – *n.* a mark made by scorching. – *adj.* **scorching.**
score (skör) *vb.* **scoring, scored** **1** to achieve a point, etc. in games: *Sasha scored 120 with three darts.* **2** to keep a record of points gained during a game. **3** to make cuts or scratches in the surface of. – *n.* **1** a number of points, etc. scored. **2** a scratch or shallow cut. **3** a set of twenty: *three score.* **4** a written copy of music.
  scorer *n.* a person who keeps a written record of the score during a game.
scorn (skörn) *n.* mocking contempt. – *vb.* **scorning, scorned.** – *adj.* **scornful.**
Scorpio (skör pi ō) *n.* See **zodiac.**
  scorpion (skör pi ŏn) *n.* a desert creature with a spider-like body, four pairs of legs, pincers, and with a poisonous sting.

Scorpions will not sting humans unless provoked. The main danger is their coming into houses and getting into clothing.

Scot (skot) *n.* a native of SCOTLAND.
Scotch (skoch) *adj.* (of things; not now of people) Scottish. – *n.* Scotch whisky.

● **Scotland** (*Alba* in Gaelic) is one of the countries comprising the United Kingdom (the crowns of Scotland and England were united when James the Sixth of Scotland became James the First of

Great Britain). The parliaments united in 1707. The country has three main regions: the highlands in the north, the fertile central lowlands, and the southern uplands. Glasgow is the largest city; EDINBURGH is the capital.

● **Scotland Yard** in London is the national base of the Criminal Investigation Department (CID).

Scots (skots) *adj.* (especially of law and language) Scottish. − *n.* any of the dialects related to English used in Lowland Scotland. **Scots pine** *n.* the only native British pine.

● **Scott, Robert Falcon** (1868-1912) was a British explorer of the ANTARCTIC.

● **Scott, Walter** (1771-1832) was a Scottish poet and novelist, author of the *Waverley* novels.

Scottish (**sko** tish) *adj.* of SCOTLAND.

scoundrel (**skown** drĕl) *n.* a rogue or villain.

scour¹ (skowr) *vb.* **scouring, scoured** to clean by hard rubbing.

scour² (skowr) *vb.* **scouring, scoured** to make an exhaustive search of an area, etc.: *We scoured the house looking for the kitten.*

scout (skowt) *n.* **1** a person or group sent out to observe the enemy and bring back information. **2** a member of the Scout Association, a worldwide youth organisation. − *vb.* **scouting, scouted** to make a search: *We're scouting about for new premises.*

scowl (skowl) *vb.* **scowling, scowled** to wrinkle the brow in displeasure or anger.

scramble (**skram** bĕl) *vb.* **scrambling, scrambled 1** to crawl or climb using hands and feet, especially frantically: *We scrambled to safety behind the boulders.* **2** to cook eggs whisked up with milk.

scrap¹ (skrap) *n.* **1** a small piece; a fragment. **2** waste material; waste metal for recycling or re-using. **3** (in *plural*) leftover pieces of food. − *vb.* **scrapping, scrapped** to discard or give up as useless.

scrap² (skrap) *n.* (*colloquial*) a fight or quarrel.

scrape (skrāp) *vb.* **scraping, scraped 1** to push or drag something along a hard or rough surface. **2** to remove something from a surface with a grazing action: *Please can you scrape the mud off your boots?* **3** to damage by such contact: *Max scraped his elbow.* − *n.* **1** an

instance, or the action, of dragging or grazing. **2** a part damaged or cleaned by scraping.

scratch (skrach) *vb.* **scratching, scratched 1** to rub or drag a sharp or pointed object across a surface, causing damage or making marks. **2** to rub the skin lightly with the fingernails, for example to relieve itching. − *n.* **1** a mark made by scratching. **2** an act of scratching. **3** a superficial wound or minor injury.

scrawl (skröl) *vb.* **scrawling, scrawled** to write or draw untidily or hurriedly.

scream (skrēm) *vb.* **screaming, screamed** to cry out in a loud high-pitched voice, e.g. in fear, pain, or anger.

screech (skrēch) *n.* a harsh shrill cry, voice, or noise. − *vb.* **screeching, screeched**.

screen (skrēn) *n.* **1** a movable hinged panel or panels, used to partition part of a room off for privacy or used for protection against strong heat or light. **2** the part of a television set on which the images are formed. **3** a white surface on to which films or slides are projected. − *vb.* **screening, screened 1** to separate with a screen. **2** to show at the cinema or on television. **3** to subject to an examination, for example to test trustworthiness.

screw (skrōō) *n.* **1** a type of nail with a spiral ridge down its length and a slot in its head, driven into place using a twisting action with a special tool. **2** (*slang*) a prison officer. − *vb.* **screwing, screwed** to twist a screw into place: *Screw the lid on to the jar.* − **have a screw loose** (*colloquial*) to be slightly mad or crazy. **screwdriver** *n.* a tool used to twist a screw.

scribble (**skri** bĕl) *vb.* **scribbling, scribbled** to write quickly or untidily.

script (skript) *n.* **1** the printed text, or the spoken dialogue, of a play, film, or broadcast. **2** a system of characters used for writing: *Chinese script.* **3** handwriting.

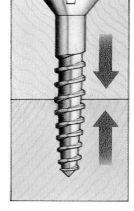

The screw is one of the six simple machines, acting like a long thin wedge that has been wrapped around a cylinder. When you turn the screw, the action of the wedge forces the two pieces of wood together.

Scrap metals, glass, paper, and organic waste can be recycled, thus enabling us to use smaller amounts of limited resources.

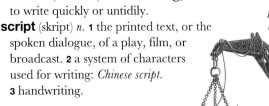

scripture (**skrip** chŭr) *n.* the sacred writings of a religion. – *adj.* **scriptural**.

scroll (skrōl) *n.* **1** a roll of paper or parchment written on. **2** a decorative spiral shape, for example in stonework or handwriting. – *vb.* **scrolling, scrolled** to move the displayed text on a computer screen up or down.

scrub[1] (skrub) *vb.* **scrubbing, scrubbed** to rub hard, especially with a brush, to remove dirt. – *n.* an act of scrubbing.

scrub[2] (skrub) *n.* land covered with low-growing bushes and shrubs. – *n.* **scrubland**.

scruff (skruf) *n.* the back of the neck; the nape.

scruffy (skruf i) *adj.* **scruffier,**

The aqualung or scuba (self-contained underwater breathing apparatus) has a 'demand' valve that regulates the exact amount of air needed by a diver to breathe.

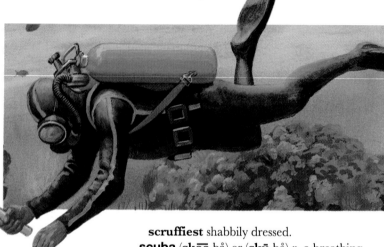

scruffiest shabbily dressed.

scuba (**skōō** bå) or (**skū** bå) *n.* a breathing device for underwater divers.

scuffle (**sku** fĕl) *n.* & *vb.* **scuffling, scuffled** (to take part in) a confused fight.

sculpt (skulpt) *vb.* **sculpting, sculpted** to create a solid model in clay, etc.

sculptor *n.* a person who practises sculpture.

sculpture *n.* **1** the art of carving or modelling with clay, wood, stone, plaster, etc. **2** a work or works of art produced in this way.

scum (skum) *n.* dirt or waste matter floating on the surface of a liquid.

scurf (skûrf) *n.* dandruff.

scythe (sīdh) *n.* a tool with a handle and a long curved blade, for cutting crops or grass.

Like many hand tools, the scythe dates back to prehistoric times. This Roman scythe was used for cutting corn.

sea (sē) *n.* **1** the great mass of salt water that covers most of the Earth's surface. **2** any named part of this, usually smaller than an ocean. **3** an area of this with reference to its calmness or turbulence: *choppy seas.* **4** a vast expanse or crowd: *a sea of worshippers.* – **all at sea** completely disorganized or at a loss.

seaboard *n.* a coast.

seafaring *adj.* travelling by or working at sea.

seagull. See **gull**[1].

sea horse *n.* a small fish with a curling tail and a horse-like head.

sea level *n.* the average level of the sea's surface, from which land height is measured.

sea-lion *n.* a Pacific seal with large ears.

seashore *n.* land next to the sea.

sea urchin *n.* a sea creature with a small rounded body protected by a hard spiky shell.

seaweed *n.* any plant growing in the sea or among rocks on the seashore.

seaworthy *adj.* (of a ship) fit to be sailed.

seal[1] (sēl) *n.* **1** a device, for example a strip of plastic or metal, that keeps something closed. **2** a piece of rubber or other material serving to keep a joint airtight or watertight. **3** a piece of wax or other material attached to a document and stamped with an official mark: *the royal seal.* – *vb.* **sealing, sealed 1** to make securely closed, airtight, or watertight with a seal: *The plumber sealed up the pipes.* **2** to stamp with a seal. – *vb.* **seal off** to isolate an area, preventing entry.

seal[2] (sēl) *n.* any of several types of fish-eating sea mammal, with flippers.

seam (sēm) *n.* **1** a join between edges, especially one sewn or welded. **2** a layer of coal or ore in the earth.

search (sûrch) *vb.* **searching, searched** to carry out a thorough exploration to try to find something. – *n.* an act of searching.

searchlight *n.* a pivoting exterior light with a powerful beam.

season (**sē** zŏn) *n.* **1** any of the four major periods – spring, summer, autumn, and winter – into which the year is divided according to differences in weather patterns, etc. **2** a period of the year during which a particular sport or activity is carried out or which has a particular characteristic: *fishing season; holiday season; rainy season; our busy season.* – *vb.* **seasoning, seasoned** to flavour food by adding salt, etc.

seasonal *adj.* available, happening, or taking place only at certain times of the year.

●As the Earth travels around the Sun, first one Pole and then the other leans towards the Sun. When the NORTH POLE tips towards the Sun, it is summer in the northern half and winter in the southern half. Six months later it is the SOUTH POLE's turn to lean towards the Sun.

seat (sēt) *n.* **1** a thing designed for sitting on, for example a chair or bench. **2** a place for sitting, for example in a cinema or theatre, often reserved. **3** an established centre: *Universities are seats of learning.*

● **Seattle** is an important port and the largest city in the state of Washington, USA.

second¹ (se kȯnd) *adj.* **1** next after the first, in order of sequence or importance: *We live in the second house on the right.* **2** alternate: *They come every second week.* **3** additional; supplementary: *Have a second go.* **4** subordinate; inferior: *His designs are second to none.* – *n.* a person or thing next in sequence after the first. – *adv.* in second place: *George came second in the race.*
 second cousin *n.* the child of a parent's cousin.
 second-rate *adj.* inferior; substandard.
second² (se kȯnd) *n.* a 60th of a minute.
secondary (se kȯn då ri) *adj.* of lesser importance than the primary concern.
secret (sē krėt) *adj.* **1** hidden from or undisclosed to others, or to all but a few. **2** whose activities are unknown to or unobserved by others: *a secret army.* – *n.* a piece of information not to be revealed to others.
 secrecy *n.* the ability or tendency to keep information secret.
 secretive *adj.* fond of secrecy: *Simon was secretive about where he had been last night.*
secretary (sek rė tå ri) *n.* **secretaries** a person employed to perform administrative or clerical tasks; the member of a club or society responsible for its correspondence and records.
 – *adj.* **secretarial** (se krė **tār** i ȧl).
section (sek shȯn) *n.* any of the parts into which a thing can be divided, or from which it is constructed.
secular (se kū lȧr) *adj.* not religious.
secure (si **kūr**) *adj.* **1** free from danger; providing freedom from danger: *Put your key in a secure place, not under the doormat.* **2** free from trouble or worry. **3** firmly fixed or attached. – *vb.* **securing, secured 1** to fasten or attach firmly. **2** to get or get possession of.
 security *n.* **securities 1** the state of being secure. **2** freedom from the possibility of future financial difficulty. **3** something given as a guarantee, e.g. of repayment of a loan.
sediment (se di mėnt) *n.* solid matter that settles at the bottom of a liquid.

see¹ (sē) *vb.* **seeing, saw** (sö), **seen 1** to look at with the eyes: *I saw three ships sailing by.* **2** to have the power of vision: *I can see well with these spectacles.* **3** to watch: *Shall we go and see a play?* **4** to understand: *I don't see what you mean.* **5** to find out: *Wait and see.* **6** to meet up with; to be in the company of: *I haven't seen her for ages.* **7** to speak to or consult: *The angry customer asked to see the manager.* – *vb.* **see about** to attend to the matter of. – *vb.* **see into** to investigate; to look into. – *vb.* **see out 1** to escort out. **2** to stay until the end of. **3** to outlive. – *vb.* **see through 1** to be able to see what is behind or under something. **2** to recognize a lie, trick, etc.
see² (sē) *n.* the post of bishop.
seed (sēd) *n.* **seeds** or **seed 1** the fruit of a plant from which a new plant grows. **2** source or origin: *What were the seeds of the idea?* – *vb.* **seeding, seeded 1** to plant seeds. **2** to remove seeds from a fruit. **3** in sport, to rank a player in a tournament according to his or her likelihood of winning.

The coconut is the hard-shelled seed or fruit of the coconut palm. It is a seed that is spread by being carried along on water.

At the centre of a **seed** is a tiny embryo of a new plant. Around this there is a stock of food for the embryo, enclosed by a hard, protective outside. Seeds spread in many ways.

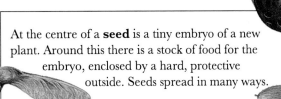

The maple's winged seeds fly through the air.

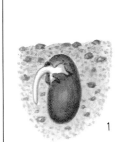

The seeds of the thistle and the dandelion are scattered by the wind.

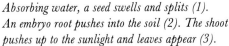

The burdock seed (above) has tiny hooks that cling to animals.

Acorns and blackberries (above) are dispersed by being stored or eaten by animals.

Absorbing water, a seed swells and splits (1). An embryo root pushes into the soil (2). The shoot pushes up to the sunlight and leaves appear (3).

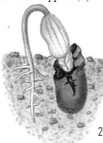
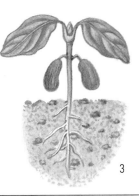

1   2   3

●**Seeger, Pete** (1919-) is an American song-writer, known for his protest songs *We shall Overcome, Where have all the Flowers Gone?*, etc.

seek (sēk) *vb.* **seeking, sought** (söt) **1** to look for. **2** to try to get or achieve. **3** to try or endeavour: *Martha is always seeking to please.* **4** to ask for: *Wendy sought his advice.*

seem (sēm) *vb.* **seeming, seemed 1** to appear; to give the impression of being. **2** to be apparent: *There seems no good reason for refusing.*

seen. See **see**[1].

seep (sēp) *vb.* **seeping, seeped** (of a liquid) to escape slowly through a narrow opening.

segment (seg mĕnt) *n.* **1** a part, section, or portion: *Would you like a segment of orange?* **2** a part of a circle or sphere separated off by an intersecting line. – (seg **ment**) *vb.* **segmenting, segmented**.

●**Segovia, Andrés** (1894-1987) was a Spanish classical guitar player.

segregate (seg rĕ gāt) *vb.* **segregating, segregated** to separate from others or from each other: *The fans were segregated.* – *adj.* **segregated** – *n.* **segregation**.

●**Seine** a river in northern FRANCE which flows through Paris to the NORTH Sea.

seismograph (sīz mŏ gräf) *n.* an instrument that measures and records the force of earth-quakes.

During an earthquake seismic waves travel through the Earth. These waves are recorded on a seismograph. The word seismic comes from Greek and means 'shaking'.

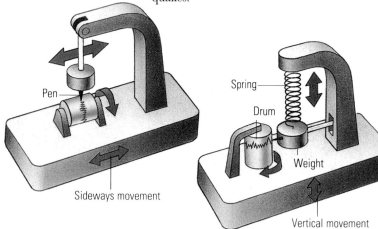

Pen — Sideways movement

Spring — Drum — Weight — Vertical movement

seize (sēz) *vb.* **seizing, seized 1** to take or grab suddenly: *Sue seized my hand.* **2** to overcome: *Paul was seized by panic.*

seldom (sel dŏm) *adv.* rarely.

select (sĕ lekt) *vb.* **selecting, selected** to choose from among several: *Simon selected the green apples instead of the red ones.* – *adj.* picked out in preference to others.

selection *n.* **1** the act or process of selecting or being selected. **2** a thing or set of things selected. **3** a range from which to choose.

self (self) *n.* **selves** (selvz) **1** personality, or a particular aspect of it. **2** a person as a whole, a combination of characteristics of appearance and behaviour: *He isn't his usual happy self.* – *pron.* (*colloquial*) myself, yourself, himself, or herself.

selfish *adj.* tending to be concerned only with personal welfare.

self- (self-) *in compounds* **1** of, by, for, in, to, or in relation to yourself: *self-doubt; self-inflicted.* **2** acting automatically: *This door is self-closing.*

self-confidence (self kon fi dĕns) *n.* total absence of shyness. – *adj.* **self-confident**.

self-conscious (self kon shŭs) *adj.* ill at ease in company as a result of feeling observed by others.

self-pity (self pi ti) *n.* excessive grumbling or moaning about your own misfortunes.

self-respect (self ri spekt) *n.* concern for your dignity and reputation.

self-satisfied (self sat is fĭd) *adj.* smug.

self-supporting (self sŭ pör ting) *adj.* earning enough money to meet all your own expenses.

sell (sel) *vb.* **selling, sold** (sōld) **1** to give in exchange for money: *Sam sold his bike for £15.* **2** to have available for buying: *This shop sells video equipment.* **3** to be in demand: *Compact discs sell well.* – *n.* **seller**. – **sell down the river** (*colloquial*) to betray. – *vb.* **sell off** to sell remaining goods quickly and cheaply.

semaphore (se mă för) *n.* a system of signalling with flags.

semen (sē mĕn) *n.* a thick whitish liquid containing sperm, ejaculated by the penis.

semi- (se mi-) *prefix* **1** half: *semiquaver.* **2** partly: *semiconscious.*

semicircle (se mi sûr kĕl) *n.* one half of a circle.

semicolon (se mi kō lon) *n.* a punctuation mark (;) indicating a pause stronger than that marked by a comma (,).

seminary (se mi nă ri) *n.* **seminaries** a college for the training of members of the clergy.

senate (se nåt) *n.* a law-making body, especially the upper chamber of the national assembly in the UNITED STATES.

senator *n.* a member of a senate.

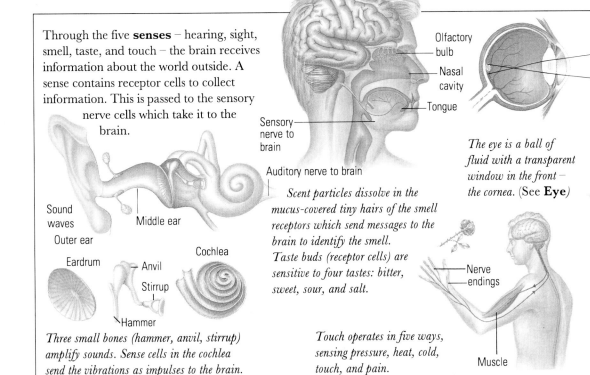

Through the five **senses** – hearing, sight, smell, taste, and touch – the brain receives information about the world outside. A sense contains receptor cells to collect information. This is passed to the sensory nerve cells which take it to the brain.

Sensory nerve to brain

Auditory nerve to brain

Sound waves

Outer ear

Middle ear

Eardrum

Anvil

Stirrup

Hammer

Cochlea

Three small bones (hammer, anvil, stirrup) amplify sounds. Sense cells in the cochlea send the vibrations as impulses to the brain.

Olfactory bulb

Nasal cavity

Tongue

Scent particles dissolve in the mucus-covered tiny hairs of the smell receptors which send messages to the brain to identify the smell. Taste buds (receptor cells) are sensitive to four tastes: bitter, sweet, sour, and salt.

Touch operates in five ways, sensing pressure, heat, cold, touch, and pain.

Nerve endings

Muscle

The eye is a ball of fluid with a transparent window in the front – the cornea. (See **Eye***)*

Nucleus

Cell body

Axon

Muscle

A typical nerve cell (often called a neuron) has a cell body with short fibres called dendrites branching from it. These dendrites send electrical impulses (messages) to the cell body. A long fibre, or axon, carries messages away from the cell body.

● The United States Senate, one of the two houses of CONGRESS, has 100 members, two from each state. They serve six-year terms.

send (send) *vb.* **sending, sent 1** to cause or order to go or be conveyed or transmitted: *Stephen sent the children to their bedroom.* **2** to cause to become in a state of: *My joke sent him into fits of laughter.* – *n.* **sender.** – *vb.* **send away for** to order goods by post. – *vb.* **send for 1** to ask or order to come; to summon. **2** to order to be brought or delivered. – *vb.* **send off 1** to dispatch by post. **2** to dismiss, especially from the field of play in sport.

● **Senegal.** See Supplement, **Countries**.

senior (sēn yǒr) *adj.* **1** higher in rank or authority than. **2** (*US*) of final-year college or university students. – *n.* **seniority**.

sensation (sen sā shǒn) *n.* **1** awareness, by means of the nervous system, being able to hear, touch, smell, and taste. **2** a physical feeling: *I had a burning sensation in my mouth.* **3** an emotion or general feeling.

sensational *adj.* **1** causing widespread excitement, or shock. **2** (*colloquial*) marvellous: *What a sensational hat!*

sense (sens) *n.* **1** any of the five powers – hearing, taste, sight, smell, and touch – used to perceive the physical world or the condition of the body. **2** an awareness or appreciation of some specified thing: *Tim's businesses always fail because he has such bad business sense.* **3** (often in plural) soundness of mind: *Guy has lost his senses.* **4** wisdom; practical worth: *There's no sense in doing it now.* – *vb.* **sensing, sensed 1** to perceive using any of the five senses. **2** to be aware of by means other than the five senses.

sensible (sen så běl) *adj.* showing good judgement: *What a sensible plan!* – *adv.* **sensibly**.

sensitive (sen si tiv) *adj.* **1** responding readily, strongly, or painfully. **2** able to feel or respond to. **3** easily upset or offended. **4** about which there is much strong feeling or difference of opinion: *Some people prefer to avoid discussing sensitive issues.* – *n.* **sensitivity**.

sentence (sen těns) *n.* **1** a sequence of words forming a complete grammatical structure, when written beginning with a capital letter and ending with a full stop. **2** a punishment determined by a court or judge. – *vb.* **sentencing, sentenced** to announce the punishment to be given to: *The judge sentenced him to prison.*

sentiment (**sen** ti mĕnt) *n.* an emotion, especially when expressed.

sentimental (sen ti **men** tăl) *adj.* **1** easily feeling and expressing tender emotions, especially love, friendship, and pity. **2** closely associated with fond memories of the past: *My mother cherishes these objects of sentimental value.* – *n.* **sentimentality** (sen ti men **tal** i ti).

sentry (**sen** tri) *n.* **sentries** a soldier or other person on guard to control entry or passage.

sepal (**sē** păl) *n.* a group of leaf-like parts protecting an unopened flower bud.

separate (**se** på rāt) *vb.* **separating, separated 1** to set, take, keep, or force apart: *A river separates the two counties.* **2** to move apart; to become detached; to cease to be or live together: *After mother's death, we separated and went our own ways.* – (**se** på råt) *adj.* distinctly different; unrelated: *That's a separate issue.*

separation *n.* the act of separating or the state or process of being separated.

September (sep **tem** bĕr) *n.* the ninth month of the year. September has 30 days.

sequel (**sē** kwĕl) *n.* a book, film, or play that continues an earlier story.

sequence (**sē** kwĕns) *n.* a series of things following each other in a particular order.

sequoia (si **kwoi** å) *n.* either of two types of giant Californian coniferous tree.

● **Serbia** with Montenegro forms part of Yugoslavia. See Supplement, **Countries**.

serene (sĕ **rēn**) *adj.* (of a person) calm. – *n.* **serenity** (sĕ **ren** i ti).

sergeant (**sär** jănt) *n.* an officer above the rank of corporal in the armed forces.

serial (**sēr** i ăl) *n.* a story published or broadcast in regular instalments.

serial killer *n.* a person committing a succession of murders.

series (**sēr** ēz) *n.* **series** a number of similar, related, or identical things arranged or produced one after the other.

serif (**se** rif) *n.* a short decorative line on the end of a printed letter, as in E as opposed to the sanserif (= without serifs) E.

serious (**sē** ri ŭs) *adj.* **1** solemn; not light-hearted or flippant. **2** dealing with important issues: *My father likes to read a serious newspaper.* **3** severe: *a serious accident.* – *n.* **seriousness**.

sermon (**sûr** mŏn) *n.* a public speech forming part of a church service.

serpent (**sûr** pĕnt) *n.* a snake.

servant (**sûr** vănt) *n.* a person employed by another to do household work.

serve (sûrv) *vb.* **serving, served 1** to work for the benefit of: *He served the community well.* **2** to carry out duties as a member: *They serve on a committee.* **3** to act as a member of the armed forces: *Simon served in the marines.* **4** to give assistance to customers; to provide to customers. **5** to respond to the needs or demands of someone: *These shoes have served me well.* **6** to bring or present food or drink. **7** to provide specified facilities to: *There are buses serving the entire city.*

service (**sûr** vis) *n.* **1** (often in *plural*) work performed for or on behalf of others; use or usefulness; a favour, or any act with beneficial results: *Your services are no longer required.* **2** an organization working to serve or benefit others in some way: *the civil service.* **3** assistance given to customers. **4** a facility provided: *The bus company runs a great service.* **5** a religious ceremony: *the marriage service.* **6** a complete set of crockery: *a dinner service.* **7** a periodic check of the workings of a vehicle. **8** an act of putting the ball into play in racket sports. **9** (often in *plural*) any of the armed forces.

service station *n.* a petrol station providing facilities for motorists, e.g. car washing.

The abbot is shown here entering the choir to celebrate solemn sung High Mass, one of the most important services in an abbey's day. Leading the procession is the thurifer, carrying a censer, followed by a cross-bearer and two acolytes with candles.

S S

Serifs were developed by Roman stonecutters who carved letters in stone. They found it difficult to end wide strokes without ugly, blunt lines. So they added a graceful decoration to the tops and bottoms of many letters

Pyramids of Egypt

Tomb of Mausolus at Halicarnassus, Turkey

Colossus at Rhodes

Pharos (lighthouse), Alexandria, Egypt

Temple of Artemis at Ephesus

Statue of Zeus at Olympia

Hanging Gardens of Babylon

serviette (sûr vi **et**) *n.* a table napkin.

session (**se** shŏn) *n.* a meeting of a court, council, or parliament; a period during which such meetings are regularly held.

set[1] (set) *vb.* **setting, set 1** to put into a certain position or condition: *set free; set fire to.* **2** to become solid or motionless: *The cement hasn't set.* **3** to fix, establish, or settle: *Sasha set a new record in the high jump.* **4** to put into a state of readiness: *Set the table.* **5** to adjust to the correct reading: *Can you set the clock?* **6** to fix a broken bone in its normal position, for healing. **7** to place on or against a background, or in surroundings: *The story is set in France.* **8** to stir, provoke, or force into activity: *I set her to work.* − *n.* **1** form; shape: *the set of his jaw.* **2** the scenery and props used to create a particular location in filming. − *adj.* **1** fixed; allowing no variations: *The restaurant had a set menu.* **2** never changing: *He's so set in his ways.* − *vb.* **set back 1** to delay or hinder the progress of. **2** to cause to return to an earlier and less advanced stage: *These changes will set the health service back decades.* (*n.* **setback**) − *vb.* **set in** to become firmly established: *Winter has set in.* − *vb.* **set off 1** to start out on a journey. **2** to provoke into action or behaviour of a particular kind; to cause: *The sad film set her off crying.*

set[2] (set) *n.* **1** a group of related or similar things regarded as a complete unit: *a set of books.* **2** a complete collection of pieces needed for a particular activity: *a chess set; a train set.* **3** one of the major divisions of a match in some sports, for example tennis. **4** an instrument for receiving broadcasts.

set[3] or **sett** (set) *n.* a badger's burrow.

settle (**se** tĕl) *vb.* **settling, settled 1** to make or become firmly or satisfactorily positioned or established. **2** to come to an agreement: *Let's settle on a date.* **3** to come lightly to rest: *The butterfly settled on the flower.* **4** to become calm or disciplined after a period of noisy excitement or upheaval: *Please settle down.* **5** to establish a permanent home or colony in: *The Pilgrim Fathers settled on the east coast of America.* **6** to pay off: *Settle up with her.* **7** to sink to the bottom of something; to sink lower: *The leaves settled at the bottom of the pond.*

settlement *n.* **1** the act of settling. **2** a community of recently settled people. **3** an agreement, especially ending a dispute.

settler *n.* a person who settles in a country that is being newly populated.

seven (**se** vĕn) *n.* the number or figure 7. − *n., adj.,* & *adv.* **seventh**.

● **Seven Deadly Sins** sins that medieval theologians believed led to the damnation of a person's soul. They are pride, covetousness, lust, envy, gluttony, anger, and sloth.

● **Seven Hills of Rome** the hills on which ancient Rome was built: *the Palatine, Capitoline, Quirinal, Caelian, Aventine, Esquiline, and Viminal.*

seventeen (se vĕn **tēn**) *n.* the number or figure 17. − *n., adj.,* & *adv.* **seventeenth**.

seventy (**se** vĕn ti) *n.* **seventies** the number or figure 70. − *n., adj.,* & *adv.* **seventieth**.

seventies *n.* (*plural*) the period of time between the seventieth and eightieth years of a century or your seventieth and eightieth birthdays.

● **Seven Wonders of the World** seven outstanding objects which were built in ancient times. Only one Wonder, the pyramids, exists today.

sever (**se** vĕr) *vb.* **severing, severed** to cut off physically: *severed limbs*. – *n.* **severance**.

several (**sev** rǎl) *adj.* more than a few, but not a great number.

severe (si **vēr**) *adj.* **1** extreme and difficult to endure; marked by extreme conditions: *We had severe weather last winter*. **2** very strict towards others. **3** austere. **4** grave. – *adv.* **severely**. – *n.* **severity** (si **ver** i ti).

sew (sō) *vb.* **sewing, sewn** or **sewed** to stitch, attach, or repair fabric with thread, by hand with a needle or by machine.

sewage (**sōō** ij) *n.* waste matter carried away in drains.

sewer (**sōō** ĕr) *n.* an underground pipe for carrying away sewage from drains and water from road surfaces; a main drain.

sex (seks) *n.* either of the two groups – male and female – into which animals and plants are divided.

sexism *n.* contempt shown for a particular sex, usually by men of women, based on prejudice or stereotype. – *n.* & *adj.* **sexist**.
sexual *adj.* concerned with or suggestive of sex or love-making. – *n.* **sexuality**.

sextant (**sek** stǎnt) *n.* an instrument like a small telescope, used for measuring distance.

● **Seychelles**. See Supplement, **Countries**.

shabby (**sha** bi) *adj.* **shabbier, shabbiest** (especially of clothes or furnishings) old and worn. – *adv.* **shabbily**. – *n.* **shabbiness**.

shack (shak) *n.* a roughly built hut.

shade (shād) *n.* **1** an area from which sunlight has been partially blocked. **2** the state of appearing comparatively unimpressive: *His painting puts mine in the shade*. **3** any device used as a shield from direct light; a lampshade. **4** any of a number of varieties of a colour: *different shades of brown*. – *vb.* **shading, shaded** to block out sunlight from.

shadow (**sha** dō) *n.* a dark shape on a surface, produced when an object stands between the surface and a source of light.

shadowy *adj.* dark and not clearly visible.

shaft (shäft) *n.* **1** the long straight handle of a tool or weapon. **2** any long straight part, a revolving rod that transmits motion in vehicle engines. **3** a vertical passageway, especially one through which a lift moves.

4 the projecting parts of a cart to which a horse, etc. is fastened.

shaggy (**sha** gi) *adj.* **shaggier, shaggiest** covered with rough and untidy hair.

shake (shāk) *vb.* **shaking, shook** (shook), **shaken** (**shā** kĕn) **1** to move with quick to-and-fro or up-and-down movements: *The branches shook in the gales*. **2** to mix in this way. **3** to wave violently and threateningly. **4** to tremble, totter, or shiver: *She shook with terror*. **5** to cause intense shock: *His revelations shook the nation*. **6** to cause to waver; to weaken: *That incident shook my confidence*. – *n.* an act or the action of shaking. – **shake the head** to move the head from side to side as a sign of rejection or disagreement.

shaky *adj.* **shakier, shakiest** **1** trembling, as with weakness or illness. **2** (*colloquial*) not solid. – *adv.* **shakily**. – *n.* **shakiness**.

A sextant, by means of mirrors and a telescope, measures the angle between a star and the horizon. From this the position of a ship or aircraft can be determined.

● **Shakespeare, William** (1564-1616) is the greatest English dramatist. He wrote comedies (e.g. *As You Like It*), tragedies (e.g. *Macbeth* and *Hamlet*), English histories (e.g. *Richard III*), and classical histories (e.g. *Antony and Cleopatra*).

Shakespearean or **Shakespearian** (shǎk **spēr** i ǎn) *adj.* of, or relating to, SHAKESPEARE.

shale (shāl) *n.* soft rock formed from compressed clay, splitting easily into layers.

shall (shal) *vb.* (*auxiliary*) expressing **1** the future tense of other verbs, especially when the subject is *I* or *we*: *We shall see you tomorrow*. **2** determination, intention, certainty, and obligation, especially when the subject is *you, he, she, it*, or *they*: *They shall succeed; You shall have what you want; He shall become king; You shall not kill*. **3** a question implying future action, often with the sense of an offer or suggestion, especially when the subject is *I* or *we*: *What shall we do? Shall I give you a hand?*

shallow (**sha** lō) *adj.* having little depth.

shalom (sha **lōm**) or (sha **lom**) *n.* & *interjection* a Jewish greeting or farewell.

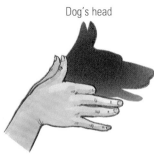

Dog's head

Chicken's head

Flying bird

Rabbit's head

Shadow play. You can use your hands to make different animal shapes.

shame (shåm) *n.* **1** an embarrassing or degrading sense of guilt, foolishness, or failure as a result of having done something wrong. **2** disgrace or loss of reputation. **3** a regrettable or disappointing event or situation: *It's a shame you can't come.* – *vb.* **shaming, shamed** to provoke by inspiring feelings of shame: *They shamed him into telling the truth.*

shameful *adj.* bringing or deserving shame.

shameless *adj.* showing no shame.

shampoo (sham p$\overline{oo}$) *n.* **shampoos** a soapy liquid for washing the hair and scalp. – *vb.* **shampoos, shampooing, shampooed.**

shamrock (sham rok) *n.* a plant whose leaves have three rounded leaflets, e.g. clover, used as the national emblem of Ireland.

shandy (shan di) *n.* **shandies** a mixture of beer and lemonade or ginger beer.

shan't (shänt) shall not.

shanty¹ (shan ti) *n.* **shanties** a roughly built hut.

shanty² (shan ti) *n.* **shanties** a song formerly sung by sailors working in unison.

shape (shāp) *n.* **1** the outline or form of anything: *round, square, or triangular in shape.* **2** a person's body or figure. **3** condition generally: *Her car is in bad shape.* – *vb.* **shaping, shaped 1** to give a particular form to; to fashion: *She shaped the clay into a pot.* **2** to influence: *These events shaped history.* – *vb.* **shape up** to progress or develop well.

shapeless *adj.* having no regular shape.

shard (shärd) or **sherd** (shûrd) *n.* a fragment of pottery, especially on an archaeological site.

share (shār) *n.* **1** a portion given to or contributed by each of several people or groups. **2** any of the units into which the total wealth of a business company is divided. – *vb.* **sharing, shared 1** to have joint use of, with another or others: *We share the same office.* **2** to divide into portions.

shareholder *n.* a person who owns shares in a company.

shark (shärk) *n.* **1** a large flesh-eating fish. **2** (*colloquial*) a ruthless or dishonest person.

● Sharks are sometimes called the 'tigers of the sea'. Some sharks, such as the dogfish, are small. The huge whale shark, the biggest of all fishes, is harmless, eating only tiny plankton. The most feared shark is the great white shark, which sometimes attacks swimmers.

sharp (shärp) *adj.* **1** having a thin edge that can cut or a point that can pierce. **2** having a bitter taste. **3** severely felt: *sharp pain.* **4** sudden and acute: *Watch out for the sharp bend.* – *adv.* **1** punctually; on the dot. **2** suddenly: *The bus pulled up sharp.* – *n.* **sharpness.**

sharpen *vb.* **sharpening, sharpened** to make or grow sharp. – *n.* **sharpener.**

shatter (sha těr) *vb.* **shattering, shattered** to break into tiny pieces, usually suddenly or forcefully. – *adj.* **shattered.** – *adj.* **shattering.**

shave (shāv) *vb.* **shaving, shaved 1** to cut off hair from the face or other part of the body with a razor or shaver. **2** to remove thin slivers from the surface of wood with a bladed tool.

shawl (shöl) *n.* a large piece of fabric used as a loose covering for the head or shoulders.

she (shē) *pron.* the female person or animal named before or understood from the context.

shear (shēr) *vb.* **shearing, sheared, shorn** (shörn) **1** to clip or cut off with a large pair of clippers. **2** to cut the fleece off a sheep. – *n.* (in *plural*) a two-bladed cutting-tool like a large pair of scissors; clippers. – *n.* **shearer.**

shed¹ (shed) *n.* an outbuilding of any size, for working in or for storage or shelter.

shed² (shed) *vb.* **shedding, shed 1** to release or cause to flow: *shed tears.* **2** to get rid of: *The tree shed its leaves.*

sheep (shēp) *n.* **sheep** an animal of the goat family, reared for its meat and its wool.

sheepish *adj.* embarrassed because of having done something wrong or foolish.

sheer (shēr) *adj.* **1** complete; absolute; nothing but: *Your plan is sheer madness.* **2** (of a cliff, etc.) very steep.

sheet (shēt) *n.* **1** a large broad piece of fabric, especially for covering a bed. **2** any large broad expanse: *a sheet of glass.* **3** a piece of paper.

sheikh or **sheik** (shāk) or (shēk) *n.* a Muslim leader. – *n.* **sheikhdom** or **sheikdom.**

PRONUNCIATION GUIDE	
fat a	all ö
fate ā	foot oo
fast ä	moon $\overline{oo}$
among å	boy oi
met e	house ow
mean ē	demon ȯ
silent ė	thing th
loch hh	this Th
fin i	but u
line ī	mute ū
quick kw	fur û
got o	brochure ů
note ō	vision zh

Sharks mostly hunt alone, but the smell and taste of blood is enough to bring them together as a pack, in a 'feeding frenzy', when they will attack anything, including each other.

shelf (shelf) *n.* **shelves** (shelvz) a flat board for laying things on, fixed to a wall or as part of a cupboard, etc.

shell (shel) *n.* **1** the hard protective outer covering of numerous organisms, for example an egg, a nut, or a mollusc. **2** the empty covering of a mollusc. **3** any hard outer case: *the shell of a ship.* **4** a round of ammunition for a large-bore gun. – *vb.* **shelling, shelled 1** to remove the shell from. **2** to bombard with (for example mortar) shells. – *n.* **shelling**.

shellfish *n.* any of numerous sea creatures with an outer shell, for example mussels.

she'll (shēl) she will; she shall.

● **Shelley, Percy Bysshe** (1792-1822) was an English ROMANTIC poet.

shelter (shel těr) *n.* **1** protection against weather or danger. **2** a place or structure giving this. – *vb.* **sheltering, sheltered**.

● **Shepard, Alan** (1923-) was the first United States astronaut to be launched into space, on 5 May 1961.

shepherd (shep ěrd) *n.* a person who looks after sheep.

sheriff (she rif) *n.* the chief police officer in a United States county.

● **Sherman, William** (1820-91) was a leading Union Army general in the American Civil War.

Sherpa (shûr på) *n.* a member of an Eastern Tibetan people living high in the HIMALAYAS.

shield (shēld) *n.* **1** a piece of armour carried to block an attack with a weapon. **2** a protective plate or screen. – *vb.* **shielding, shielded** to protect from harm or danger.

shift (shift) *vb.* **shifting, shifted 1** to change the position or direction of: *The wind shifted to the south.* **2** to transfer, switch, or re-direct: *Why does he always shift the blame on to someone else?* **3** to remove or dislodge. – *n.* **1** a change or change of position. **2** the group of workers taking turns with other workers on duty.

shifty *adj.* **shiftier, shiftiest** sly.

shilling (shi ling) *n.* a former British coin worth one-twentieth of £1.

shimmer (shi měr) *vb.* **shimmering, shimmered** to shine quiveringly.

shin (shin) *n.* the bony front part of the leg below the knee.

shine (shīn) *vb.* **shining, shone** (shon) or (sense 3) **shined 1** to reflect light. **2** to direct the light from: *Anthony shone the torch in my face.* **3** to make bright and gleaming by polishing: *He shined the tables.* **4** to be outstandingly impressive.

shiny *adj.* **shinier, shiniest** reflecting light.

Sea**shells** are the skeletons of animals we call molluscs. Unlike humans and other mammals, molluscs and a number of other animals such as insects and crabs have outer skeletons which protect their soft bodies from other animals. There are five major groups of mollusc.

Philippine Nerite, a shell of estuary waters.

A pearl is made when a piece of grit irritates the soft tissue of a mollusc's mantle. The animal covers it with shell lining to protect itself, and this forms into a pearl.

Textile cone – one of over 500 species. All cone shells inject poison into their victims. The sting of some large species can kill a human.

Tusk shells burrow in sand.

Scallops are two part (bivalve) shells which live on the sea bed.

Triton's trumpet is a snail-like gastropod. There are about 80,000 types of gastropod. Many are found on rocks or stones.

Queen conch. The conch is a family of sea snails whose shells have been used as trumpets. They live in shallow tropical waters and feed on seaweed.

The largest seashell in the world – the Giant Clam, the biggest being 109 cm wide and weighing 263 kg.

shingle¹ (**shing** gĕl) *n.* small pebbles on a seashore.

shingle² (**shing** gĕl) *n.* a roof-tile.

Shinto (**shin** tō) *n.* the principal religion of JAPAN.

ship (ship) *n.* **1** any large boat intended for sea travel. **2** (*colloquial*) a spaceship or airship. – *vb.* **shipping, shipped** to send or transport by ship. – **when your ship comes in** when you become rich.

Supertankers are not only the biggest ships, but the biggest vehicles of any kind. This oil supertanker is 379 metres long and 62 metres wide.

●Today most ships are cargo vessels, such as tankers which carry liquids like oil or wine, or container ships, refrigerator ships, and bulk carriers which transport wheat, coal, etc. Planes have replaced most passenger ships but there are still many ferries, which take people and cars over small stretches of water.

shipping *n.* ships as traffic.

shipshape *adj.* in good order; neat and tidy.

shipwreck *n.* **1** the accidental sinking or destruction of a ship. **2** the remains of a sunken or destroyed ship. – *vb.* **shipwrecking, shipwrecked**.

shipyard *n.* a place where ships are built.

-ship (-ship) *suffix* **1** rank, position, or status: *lordship*. **2** a period of office: *during his chairmanship*. **3** a state or condition: *friendship*. **4** a type of skill: *craftsmanship*. **5** a group of individuals: *membership*.

shire (shīr) *n.* a county.

shirk (shûrk) *vb.* **shirking, shirked** to avoid doing work. – *n.* **shirker**.

shirt (shûrt) *n.* a long- or short-sleeved garment for the upper body, usually with a collar, especially worn by men. – **keep your shirt on** (*slang*) to control your temper.

shiver (**shi** vêr) *vb.* **shivering, shivered** to quiver or tremble with cold or fear. – *n.* an act of shivering. – *adj.* **shivery**.

shoal¹ (shōl) *n.* a large number of fish.

shoal² (shōl) *n.* an area of shallow water.

shock (shok) *n.* **1** a strong emotional disturbance, especially a feeling of extreme surprise, outrage, or disgust: *Her decision to leave the country was a great shock to her parents*. **2** a convulsion caused by the passage of electricity through the body. **3** a heavy jarring blow or impact. – *vb.* **shocking, shocked 1** to cause to feel extreme surprise, outrage, etc.

shocking *adj.* outrageous, or disgusting.

shoe (shōō) *n.* **1** a shaped outer covering for the foot, usually finishing below the ankle. **2** a horseshoe.

shone. See **shine**.

shook. See **shake**.

shoot (shōōt) *vb.* **shooting, shot** (shot) **1** to fire a gun or other weapon, or bullets, arrows, or other missiles. **2** to hit, wound, or kill with a weapon or missile. **3** in sport, to strike the ball, etc. at goal. **4** to film or take photographs. – *n.* **1** an act of shooting. **2** a new plant growth.

shooting star *n.* a meteor.

shop (shop) *n.* **1** a place where goods or services are sold: *a bookshop*. **2** a place in which work of a particular kind is carried out: *a machine shop*. – *vb.* **shopping, shopped** to visit a shop in order to buy goods. – *n.* **shopper**. – **talk shop** (*colloquial*) to talk about your work.

shopping centre *n.* an area containing a large number of shops often under one roof.

shore¹ (shōr) *n.* land bordering on a sea or lake.

shore² (shōr) *n.* a prop. – *vb.* **shoring, shored** to support with props.

short (shört) *adj.* **1** not long: *Simone's hair is short*. **2** of little height. **3** brief; concise: *a short journey; a short meeting*. **4** (of a temper) easily lost. **5** rudely abrupt; curt. **6** not having enough of; deficient: *We're short of glasses for the party*. – *adv.* abruptly: *She stopped short*. – *n.* **shortness**. – **short and sweet** (*colloquial*) agreeably brief.

shortage *n.* a lack or deficiency.

short circuit *n.* a cut in an electrical circuit caused by a fault.

IN SHORT...
...a synonym is not always an exact equivalent of another word. Little can mean small – for example 'a small boy' or 'a little boy'. But 'Little Larry fights for his life' or 'The little old lady who chased off a burglar' cannot be replaced by 'small Larry' or 'small old lady' The 'little' here is suggesting defence-lessness or weakness rather than actual height. In little...

shortcoming *n.* a fault or defect.

shorten *vb.* **shortening, shortened** to make or become shorter: *She shortened her skirt.*

shorthand *n.* a method of rapid writing.

short-handed *adj.* having fewer helpers than usual.

shorthorn *n.* a breed of cattle with short horns.

shortlist *n.* a selection of the best candidates from the total number submitted.

shortly *adv.* soon.

shorts *n.* (*plural*) short trousers.

short-sighted *adj.* **1** seeing clearly only things that are near. **2** showing a lack of foresight: *To give up your training is short-sighted.* – *n.* **short-sightedness**.

shot¹ (shot) *n.* **1** an act of firing a gun; the sound of a gun being fired. **2** small metal pellets fired from a shotgun. **3** an act of shooting or playing a stroke in sport. **4** a single scene in a film; a photograph. **5** (*colloquial*) an attempt: *Have a shot at driving.* **6** (*colloquial*) an injection. – **like a shot** without hesitating. – **a shot in the dark** a wild guess.

shot-put *n.* an athletics event in which a heavy metal ball is thrown from the shoulder as far as possible. – *n.* **shot-putter**.

shot². See **shoot**.

should (shood) *vb.* (*auxiliary*) expressing **1** obligation; ought to: *You should brush your teeth regularly.* **2** likelihood or probability: *He should have left by now.* **3** condition: *if I should die before you.* **4** (with *1st person pronouns*) a past tense of *shall* in reported speech: *I told them I should be back soon.* **5** statements in clauses with *that*, following expressions of feeling or mood: *It seems odd that we should both have had the same idea.* **6** (with *1st person pronouns*) doubt or polite indirectness in statements: *I should imagine he's left. I should think I'll get the job.*

shoulder (shōl děr) *n.* **1** the part of the body between the neck and upper arm. **2** the part of a garment covering this. **3** (in *plural*) the person as a bearer of burdens: *He has a lot of responsibility on his shoulders.* – *vb.* **shouldering, shouldered** to bear a responsibility. – **straight from the shoulder** (*colloquial*) frankly and forcefully. – **rub shoulders with** (*colloquial*) to meet or associate with. – **a shoulder to cry on** a person to tell your troubles to.

shoulder blade *n.* the broad flat triangular bone behind either shoulder.

shout (showt) *n.* a loud cry or call. – *vb.* **shouting, shouted** to utter a loud cry or call.

shove (shuv) *vb.* **shoving, shoved** to push or thrust with force.

shovel (**shu** věl) *n.* a deep-sided spade-like tool for lifting. – *vb.* **shovelling, shovelled** to lift or carry with a shovel.

show (shō) *vb.* **showing, showed, shown** or **showed 1** to be or become visible or noticeable: *Her elbow showed through the hole in her shirt.* **2** to present or give to be viewed: *We showed our tickets.* **3** to display or exhibit. **4** to prove, indicate, or reveal: *Show me how it's done.* **5** to teach by demonstrating: *The art teacher showed me how to draw.* **6** to lead, guide, or escort: *The hotel porter showed you to your room.* **7** to give: *Show him some respect.* – *n.* **1** an entertainment or spectacle of any kind: *the Chelsea Flower Show.* **2** an exhibition. **3** a pretence: *It was merely a show of friendship.* **4** a display of true feeling: *no show of emotion.* – *vb.*

show off 1 to display proudly, inviting admiration. **2** to display to good effect: *The cream rug shows off the red carpet nicely.*

showing *n.* **1** an act of exhibiting or displaying. **2** a screening of a cinema film.

show business *n.* the entertainment industry.

shower (**show** ěr) *n.* **1** a sudden but brief fall of rain, snow, or hail. **2** a cubicle fitted with a device producing a stream of water for bathing under. – *vb.* **showering, showered 1** to bathe under a shower. **2** to rain in showers.

shown. See **show**.

shrank. See **shrink**.

shred (shred) *n.* a thin strip cut or ripped off. – *vb.* **shredding, shredded** or **shred** to reduce to shreds by ripping.

shrew (shroo) *n.* a small mouse-like animal with a long pointed snout.

Shrews are related to moles. They spend most of their time above ground. They are intensely active, and must eat three times their own weight every day.

Pygmy shrew

Common shrew

shrewd (shrōōd) *adj.* having good judgement.

shriek (shrēk) *vb.* **shrieking, shrieked** to utter a piercing scream. – *n.* such a scream.

shrill (shril) *adj.* high-pitched and piercing.

shrimp (shrimp) *n.* a small shellfish, smaller than a prawn.

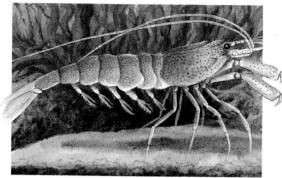

The common shrimp is abundant in coastal waters. By day it buries itself in sand or mud, coming out after dark to walk and feed on the sea bottom.

shrink (shringk) *vb.* **shrinking, shrank** (shrangk), **shrunk** (shrungk) or (especially as *adj.*) **shrunken** (shrung kĕn) **1** to make or become smaller: *My socks have shrunk in the wash.* **2** to move away in horror.

shrub (shrub) *n.* a bushy plant like a small tree.

shrug (shrug) *vb.* **shrugging, shrugged** to raise the shoulders briefly to show doubt or indifference. – *n.* an act of shrugging.

shrunk, shrunken. See **shrink.**

shuffle (shu fĕl) *vb.* **shuffling, shuffled 1** to move your feet with short quick sliding movements. **2** to rearrange or mix up roughly or carelessly: *She shuffled the papers.*

shun (shun) *vb.* **shunning, shunned** to avoid.

shut (shut) *vb.* **shutting, shut 1** to place or move so as to close an opening: *The door shut.* **2** not to allow access to: *The office shuts at weekends.* – *adj.* not open; closed.

shutter *n.* **1** a movable cover for a window. **2** a device in a camera that opens and closes, exposing the film to light.

shuttle (shu tĕl) *n.* **1** in weaving, the device carrying the horizontal thread (the **weft**) backwards and forwards between the vertical threads (the **warp**). **2** an aircraft, train, or bus running frequently between two places.

shuttlecock *n.* a cone of feathers, or a plastic imitation, used in badminton.

shy (shī) *adj.* **shyer, shyest** or **shier, shiest 1** embarrassed or unnerved by the company or attention of others. **2** easily scared; timid.

Siamese (sī ă mēz) *adj.* of Siam (now Thailand), its people, or their language; Thai.

sibling (sib ling) *n.* a brother or sister.

sick (sik) *adj.* **1** vomiting; feeling the desire to vomit. **2** ill; unwell. **3** relating to ill health: *sick pay.* **4** (also **sick and tired**) thoroughly weary or fed up: *We are sick of hearing your excuses.*

sicken *vb.* **sickening; sickened 1** to cause to feel like vomiting. **2** to show symptoms: *I think I'm sickening for the flu.* – *adj.* **sickening.**

sickly *adj.* **sicklier, sickliest** often ill.

sickness *n.* **1** an illness; **2** vomiting.

sickle (si kĕl) *n.* a tool with a short handle and a curved blade for cutting grain.

side (sīd) *n.* **1** any of the flat or flattish surfaces that form the shape of something; any of these surfaces other than the top and bottom; any of these surfaces other than the front, back, top, or bottom: *A cube has six sides. A barn has four sides. There are no windows in the sides of the house, just at the front and back.* **2** an edge or border: *We found the puppy sitting at the side of the road.* **3** either of the parts or areas produced when the whole is divided up the middle: *the right side of your body.* **4** either of the broad surfaces of a flat object: *the two sides of a coin.* **5** any of the lines forming a geometric figure: *A triangle has three sides.* **6** any of the groups or teams in a conflict or competition: *Which side do you want to win?* – *adj.* **1** located at the side: *We were asked to use the side entrance.* **2** subsidiary: *side road.*

side effect *n.* an unexpected and usually undesirable effect, especially of a drug.

The traditional shuttlecock comprises a hemispeherical cork base to which are fastened 16 goose feathers.

For thousands of years farmers harvested corn by hand with a sickle or scythe. This illustration is of a medieval harvest scene.

sidetrack *vb.* **sidetracking, sidetracked** to divert the attention of someone away from something already begun.

sidewalk *n.* (*US*) a pavement.

sideways *adv.* & *adj.* **1** from, to, or towards one side. **2** with one side foremost: *The car slid sideways into the wall.*

siege (sēj) *n.* an attempt to capture a fort or town by surrounding it with troops and forcing surrender. – **lay siege to** to subject to a siege.

● **Sierra Leone**. See Supplement, **Countries**.

● **Sierra Nevada** a North American mountain range, running through eastern California.

siesta (sē **es** tå) *n.* an afternoon sleep.

sieve (siv) *n.* a utensil with a meshed or perforated bottom, used to separate solids from liquids or large particles from smaller ones. – *vb.* **sieving, sieved** to strain or separate with a sieve.

sift (sift) *vb.* **sifting, sifted 1** to pass through a sieve. **2** to separate out as if by passing through a sieve.

sigh (sī) *vb.* **sighing, sighed** to release a long deep breath, especially indicating sadness, longing, or relief. – *n.*

sight (sīt) *n.* **1** the power of seeing; vision. **2** a thing seen. **3** your field of vision: *Christina caught sight of the helicopter.* **4** (usually in *plural*) a thing that is particularly interesting to see: *We're seeing the sights of the town.* **5** a device on a firearm through which you look to take aim.
– *vb.* **sighting, sighted** to get a look at.
– **a sight for sore eyes** a very welcome sight.

sighted *adj.* having the power of sight.

sign (sīn) *n.* **1** a printed mark with a meaning; a symbol: *a multiplication sign.* **2** an indication: *There are signs of improvement.* **3** a board or panel displaying information for public view. **4** a signal: *He gave me the sign to enter by waving his hat.* **5** a sign of the zodiac. – *vb.* **signing, signed** to write a signature on.

signal (**sig** nål) *n.* a message in the form of a gesture, light, sound, etc., conveying information. – *vb.* **signalling, signalled**.

signature (**sig** nå chůr) *n.* your name written by yourself as a formal mark of authorization, acceptance, etc.

significance (sig **nif** i kåns) *n.* meaning: *What is the significance of a red ribbon?*

significant *adj.* **1** important; worth noting: *a significant drop in temperature.* **2** having some meaning; indicating something.

Sikh (sēk) *n.* a follower of a religion founded in 16th-century INDIA, worshipping one god.

silence (**sī** lěns) *n.* absence of sound. – *vb.* **silencing, silenced** to cause someone to stop speaking or stop making a noise.

silent *adj.* **1** free from noise. **2** not speaking.

silhouette (si lōō et) *n.* **1** a dark shape seen against a light background. **2** an outline drawing of a person, especially a portrait in profile, usually filled in with black.

silicon (**si** li kŏn) *n.* an element (symbol **Si**), a non-metallic component of the mineral silica.

silicon chip *n.* a minute piece of silicon on which electronic microcircuits are formed.

silk (silk) *n.* a fine soft fibre produced by the silkworm; fabric made from such fibres.

silky *adj.* **silkier, silkiest** soft like silk.

sill (sil) *n.* a ledge of wood, stone, or metal forming the bottom of a window or door.

silly (**si** li) *adj.* **sillier, silliest** not sensible; foolish; frivolous. – *adv.* **sillily**. – *n.* **silliness**.

silt (silt) *n.* fine sand and mud deposited by flowing water. – *vb.* **silting, silted** to become blocked by silt: *The estuary is silting up.*

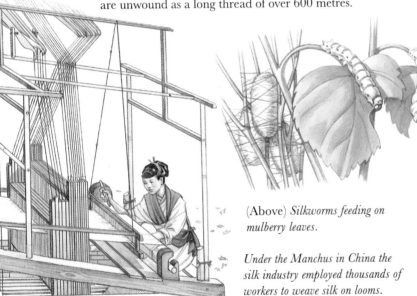

Silk is made from the cocoon of one kind of moth. Silkworms (caterpillars) are fed on mulberry leaves for about four weeks. They then spin their cocoons and start to turn into moths. The cocoons are unwound as a long thread of over 600 metres.

(*Above*) *Silkworms feeding on mulberry leaves.*

Under the Manchus in China the silk industry employed thousands of workers to weave silk on looms.

An ancient Greek silver coin – the owl, which symbolized the owl-eyed goddess of Athens, Athena.

Silver can be found as lumps of metal in the ground, but most silver is extracted from ores.

silver (**sil** vĕr) *n.* **1** an element (symbol **Ag**), a precious shiny grey metal widely used in making jewellery and coins. **2** coins made of this metal. **3** cutlery made of (or coated with) this metal. – *adj.* **1** of a whitish-grey colour. **2** (of a wedding or other anniversary) 25th. **silvery** *adj.* having the colour of silver.

similar (**si** mi lăr) *adj.* alike; of the same kind, but not identical: *The two makes of car look very similar.* – *n.* **similarity** (si mi **la** ri ti).

simile (**si** mi li) *n.* any phrase in which a thing is described by being likened to something, usually using 'as' or 'like', as in 'eyes sparkling like diamonds'.

simmer (**si** mĕr) *vb.* **simmering, simmered** to cook gently at just below boiling point.

simple (**sim** pĕl) *adj.* **1** easy; not difficult; straightforward; not complex or complicated. **2** plain or basic; not elaborate or luxurious. **3** down-to-earth; unpretentious. **4** (often *ironic*) foolish; gullible; lacking intelligence: *How could you be so simple!* – *n.* **simplicity** (sim **plis** i ti).

simply *adv.* **1** in a straightforward, uncomplicated way. **2** just: *Your accusation is simply not true.* **3** absolutely: *The party was simply marvellous.* **4** merely: *I simply wanted to help.*

simplify (**sim** pli fī) *vb.* **simplifies, simplifying, simplified** to make less complicated or easier to understand. – *n.* **simplification**.

simplistic (sim **plis** tik) *adj.* unrealistically straightforward or uncomplicated.

simultaneous (si mŭl **tān** i ŭs) *adj.* happening, or done, at exactly the same time: *simultaneous translation.*

sin (sin) *n.* an act that breaks religious law or teaching. – *vb.* **sinning, sinned** to commit a sin. – *adj.* **sinful**. – *n.* **sinner**.

since (sins) *conj.* **1** during or throughout the period between now and some earlier stated time: *I've been here since midday.* **2** as; because.

– *prep.* during or throughout the period between now and some earlier stated time.

sincere (sin **sĕr**) *adj.* genuine; not pretended or affected. – *n.* **sincerity** (sin **se** ri ti).

sinew (**sin** ū) *n.* a strong fibrous tissue joining a muscle to a bone; a tendon.

sing (sing) *vb.* **singing, sang** (sang), **sung** (sung) **1** to make sounds in a musical rhythmic fashion. **2** to make a sound like a musical voice; to hum, ring, or whistle: *Can you hear the kettle singing on the stove?* – *n.* **singer**. – *n.* **singing**. – *vb.* **sing out** to shout or call out.

● **Singapore**. See Supplement, **Countries**.

singe (sinj) *vb.* **singeing, singed** to scorch.

single (**sing** gĕl) *adj.* **1** of which there is only one; solitary. **2** unmarried. **3** for use by one person only: *a single room.* – *vb.* **singling, singled** to pick from among others. **single-minded** *adj.* determinedly pursuing a single aim. – *n.* **single-mindedness**. **singly** *adv.* one at a time; individually.

singular (**sing** gū lăr) *adj.* **1** single; unique. **2** extraordinary; exceptional: *It's a singular sound to hear cuckoos in winter.* **3** strange; odd. **4** in grammar, referring to one person, thing, etc.

sinister (**si** ni stĕr) *adj.* suggesting or threatening evil: *The castle felt sinister.*

sink (singk) *vb.* **sinking, sank** (sangk), **sunk** (sungk) or (especially as *adj.*) **sunken** (**sung** kĕn) **1** to fall below the surface of water: *The boat sank in the storm.* **2** to collapse downwardly or inwardly; to fall because of a collapsing base or foundation. **3** to produce the sensation of a downward collapse within the body: *My heart sank at the news.* **4** to embed: *Sally sank the pole into the ground.* **5** (of the sun) to disappear slowly below the horizon. – *n.* a basin with taps and drainage. – *vb.* **sink in** to be fully understood.

● **Sinn Fein** (shin **fān**) meaning 'we ourselves' is a nationalist political party in Ireland.

sinus (**sī** nŭs) *n.* air-filled hollows in the bones of the skull, connected with the nose.

● **Sioux** a Great Plains tribe of NATIVE AMERICANS who live mainly in what are now Minnesota, South Dakota, and Nebraska.

sip (sip) *vb.* **sipping, sipped** to drink in very small mouthfuls: *I sipped my tea as it was too hot.*

PRONUNCIATION GUIDE	
fat a	all ö
fate ā	foot oo
fast ä	moon ōō
among å	boy oi
met e	house ow
mean ē	demon ŏ
silent ĕ	thing th
loch hh	this Th
fin i	but u
line ī	mute ū
quick kw	fur û
got o	brochure ŭ
note ō	vision zh

siphon or **syphon** (sī fŏn) *n.* a bent pipe through which, by atmospheric pressure, a liquid is drawn from one container into a second container placed at a lower level. – *vb.* **siphoning, siphoned** or **syphoning, syphoned**.

A straw in a carton of juice acting as a siphon. If the end of the straw dips below the level of the juice in the carton, the juice will flow.

sir (sûr) *n.* a term of politeness used in addressing a man.

siren (sīr ĕn) *n.* a device that gives out a loud wailing noise, usually as a warning signal.

sister (sis tĕr) *n.* **1** a female child of the same parents as another. **2** a nun.
sister-in-law *n.* **sisters-in-law** the sister of your husband or wife.

sit (sit) *vb.* **sitting, sat** (sat) **1** to rest the body on the buttocks; (of a bird) to perch or lie. **2** to lie, rest, or hang: *The cup sitting on the shelf is an antique.* **3** to be a member, taking regular part in meetings: *Our headmaster sits on several committees.* **4** to take an examination. – **be sitting pretty** (*colloquial*) to be in a very advantageous position. – *vb.* **sit down 1** to adopt a sitting position. **2** to give in or submit meekly.

site (sīt) *n.* **1** the place where something was, is, or is to be situated. **2** an area set aside for a specific activity: *camping site.*

● **Sitting Bull** (*died* 1890) was a NATIVE AMERICAN chief of the Dakota SIOUX who led the SIOUX in a war against the UNITED STATES army in which George CUSTER was killed at the Battle of Little Bighorn in 1876.

Sitting Bull fought fiercely against the wagon trains that crossed the lands of the Indians.

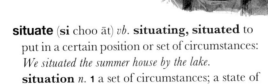

situate (si choo āt) *vb.* **situating, situated** to put in a certain position or set of circumstances: *We situated the summer house by the lake.*
situation *n.* **1** a set of circumstances; a state of affairs. **2** a position or location. **3** a job.

six (siks) *n.* **1** the number or figure 6. **2** in cricket, a hit scoring 6 runs. – *adj., n., & adv.* **sixth**.
– **at sixes and sevens** in a state of total disorder or confusion.

sixteen (sik stēn) *n.* the number or figure 16. – *adj., n., & adv.* **sixteenth**.

sixty (sik sti) *n.* **sixties** the number or figure 60. – *adj., n., & adv.* **sixtieth**.
sixties *n.* (*plural*) the period of time between the sixtieth and seventieth years of a century or your sixtieth and seventieth birthday.

size (sīz) *n.* **1** length, breadth, height, or volume, or a combination of all or any of these. **2** largeness: *I was astonished by its size.*

sizzle (si zĕl) *vb.* **sizzling, sizzled** to make a hissing sound when, or as if when, frying in hot fat: *The bacon is sizzling in the pan.*

skate (skāt) *n.* a boot with a device fitted to the sole for gliding smoothly over surfaces, either a steel blade for use on ice (**ice-skate**) or a set of small wheels for use on wooden and other surfaces (**roller-skate**). – *vb.* **skating, skated** to move around on skates. – *n.* **skater**. – *n.* **skating**.
skateboard *n.* a narrow shaped board mounted on sets of small wheels, for riding on in a standing or crouching position.

skeleton (ske lĕ tŏn) *n.* the framework of bones supporting a human or animal body. – *adj.* **skeletal**.

● There are more than 200 bones in the human skeleton. These include the bone of the spine, skull, ribs, pelvis, breastbone, and limbs. Joints are places where bones meet. Some joints, like those in the skull, do not move. Others, like those in the shoulders and hips, help us to move about. Muscles across the joints tighten, or contract, to move the bones.

sketch (skech) *n.* **1** a rough drawing quickly done. **2** any of several short pieces of comedy presented as a programme. – *vb.* **sketching, sketched** to do a rough drawing.
sketchy *adj.* **sketchier, sketchiest** lacking detail; not complete or substantial.

ski (skē) *n.* **skis 1** a long narrow strip of wood, metal, or plastic, upturned at the front, for gliding over snow, attached to each of a pair of boots or to a vehicle. **2** (also **water-ski**) a similar object worn on each foot for gliding over water. – *vb.* **skis, skiing, skied** or **ski'd** to move on skis. – *n.* **skier**. – *n.* **skiing**.

skid (skid) *vb.* **skidding, skidded** to slide out of control: *The lorry skidded over the ice.*

skill (skil) *n.* **1** expertness; dexterity. **2** a talent or accomplishment: *I admire Sally's skill as a dentist.* – *adj.* **skilled**.
skilful *adj.* having or showing skill.

skim (skim) *vb.* **skimming, skimmed 1** to remove floating matter from the surface of a liquid. **2** to read superficially: *I skim through the headlines.* **3** to glide lightly over a surface: *Harry loves skimming stones on the sea.*

skin (skin) *n.* **1** the tissue forming the outer covering on the bodies of humans and animals. **2** the outer covering of some fruits and vegetables. **3** an animal hide, with or without fur or hair attached. – *vb.* **skinning, skinned 1** to strip the skin from. **2** to injure by scraping the skin from: *Sam skinned his knee when he slipped.* – **by the skin of your teeth** very

skipping-rope. **3** to omit: *I skip the boring bits in a book.* – *n.* a skipping movement.

skipping rope *n.* a rope twirled in a circular motion by the person skipping or by two other people each holding an end, for jumping over as exercise or as a children's game.

skip² (skip) *n.* a large metal container for rubbish from building work, etc.

skipper (ski pěr) *n.* the captain of a ship, aircraft, or team.

skirt (skûrt) *n.* a woman's garment that hangs from the waist. – *vb.* **skirting, skirted 1** to border. **2** to pass along or around the edge of.

FIND THE SKIPPER
Skipper is from the Dutch *schipper*, from the word *schip* 'ship'. The English 'equip' is from the same source. In early France the word for 'boarding ship' was taken from the Dutch, becoming eskip or esquip. The 's' was dropped, forming the word 'equip' which has, over the years, changed its meaning.

Skin helps to keep out harmful germs and stops us from getting too hot or too cold. The outer layer, called the epidermis, is constantly being rubbed away and replaced from beneath. The dermis beneath is thicker and contains nerves, blood vessels, hair roots, and sweat glands.

Fingerprints are unique. No two people have the same pattern of loops and whorls on their skin. Use a magnifying glass to compare your fingerprint pattern with those of your friends.

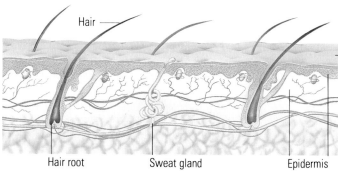
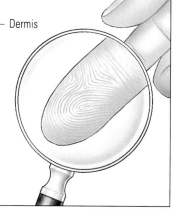

Hair — Dermis — Hair root — Sweat gland — Epidermis

The skin contains sweat glands which carry moisture and waste material to the surface. Hair roots and little muscles cause 'goose flesh' and make our hair 'stand on end'.

narrowly; only just. – **get under someone's skin** (*colloquial*) **1** to greatly annoy and upset someone. **2** to become a consuming passion with someone.

skin-deep *adj.* superficial.

skin-diving *n.* underwater swimming with no wet suit and only simple breathing and other equipment. – *n.* **skin-diver.**

skinflint *n.* a person who is very mean and niggardly.

skinhead *n.* a youth with closely cropped hair, tight jeans and heavy boots.

skinny *adj.* **skinnier, skinniest** very thin.

skip¹ (skip) *vb.* **skipping, skipped 1** to go along with light springing or hopping steps on alternate feet. **2** to make jumps over a

skittle (ski těl) *n.* any of several bottle-shaped targets, usually made of wood, at which a ball is aimed in the game of **skittles.**

skua (skū å) *n.* a large gull-like bird.

skull (skul) *n.* the head's framework of bone.

The human skull (far right) has 22 bones. Eight of these bones form the cranium which encloses the brain. The other 14 bones form the face and jaw. Only the jaw bone moves. (Right) A hyena's skull showing its stabbing canine teeth.

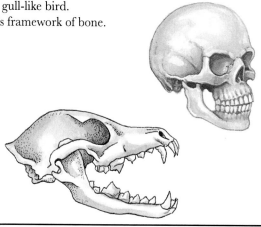

Like all members of the weasel family the skunk has a musk gland at the base of its tail. It can squirt a foul-smelling liquid a distance of 3.7 metres to drive off even the most intrepid attacker.

skunk (skungk) *n.* a North American animal with a black and white coat, which defends itself by squirting out an unpleasant-smelling liquid.

sky (skī) *n.* **skies** (often in *plural*) the vast area of space visible above the Earth, in which the Sun, Moon and stars can be seen; the heavens.

sky-diving *n.* free-falling from an aircraft, often involving performing manoeuvres in mid-air, with a long delay before the parachute is opened. – *n.* **sky-diver**.

skylight *n.* a small window in a roof.

skyline *n.* the outline of buildings, hills, and trees seen against the sky.

skyscraper *n.* an extremely tall building.

● The first skyscraper was built in 1884 in Chicago, USA. For many years the world's tallest building was the Empire State Building, New York which is 102 storeys high. Now there are two taller ones – the Sears Tower in Chicago and the World Trade Center in New York, both 110 storeys.

slab (slab) *n.* a thick flat rectangular piece, slice.

slack (slak) *adj.* **1** loose; not pulled or stretched tight. **2** not careful or diligent: *Your work is full of errors; you've become slack.* **3** not busy: *Business is slack.* – *vb.* **slacking, slacked** (also **slacken, slackening, slackened**) **1** to become slower; to slow your working pace through tiredness or laziness. **2** to make or become looser: *Slacken your belt.* **3** to become less busy.

slain. See **slay**.

slam (slam) *vb.* **slamming, slammed** to shut loudly and with violence: *Don't slam the door.*

slander (slän dẽr) *n.* a false spoken (not written) statement about a person, intended to damage his or her reputation.

slang (slang) *n.* words and phrases used informally, not usually in writing or polite speech.

slant (slänt) *vb.* **slanting, slanted 1** to be at an angle, not horizontal or vertical; to slope: *The picture slants to the right.* **2** to present in a biased way: *Propaganda is slanted information.* – *n.* a sloping position, surface, or line.

slap (slap) *n.* a blow with the palm of the hand or anything flat. – **a slap in the face** (*colloquial*) an insult or rebuff. – **a slap on the back** (*colloquial*) congratulations.

slapdash *adj.* careless and hurried: *Your writing is untidy and slapdash.*

slat (slat) *n.* a thin strip of wood or metal. – *adj.* **slatted**: *a slatted door.*

slate[1] (slāt) *n.* a fine-grained, usually dull grey rock splitting easily into thin layers, used for roofing tiles, etc.

slate[2] (slāt) *vb.* **slating, slated** to criticize harshly: *The critics all disliked the play and slated it.* – *adj.* **slating**.

slaughter (slö tẽr) *n.* **1** the killing of animals for food. **2** cruel and violent murder. – *vb.* **slaughtering, slaughtered** to kill animals for food.

Slav (släv) *n.* a member of any of various Central and Eastern European peoples speaking Slavonic languages such as Russian.

slave (släv) *n.* **1** a person owned by and acting as servant to another, with no personal freedom. **2** a person who works extremely hard for another. – *vb.* **slaving, slaved** to work hard: *Sean slaved away for hours at digging the garden.*

slavery (slā vẽ ri) *n.* **1** the state of being a slave. **2** the practice of owning slaves.

A slave market in the Yemen in 1237. Slaves were mostly brought from Africa and from central Asia. The Koran forbade people from making other Muslims slaves.

PRONUNCIATION GUIDE	
fat **a**	all **ö**
fate **ā**	foot **oo**
fast **ä**	moon **ōō**
among **å**	boy **oi**
met **e**	house **ow**
mean **ē**	demon **ŏ**
silent **ĕ**	thing **th**
loch **hh**	this **Th**
fin **i**	but **u**
line **ī**	mute **ū**
quick **kw**	fur **û**
got **o**	brochure **ů**
note **ō**	vision **zh**

slay (slā) *vb.* **slaying, slew** (sloo), **slain** (slān) to kill: *St George slew the dragon.*

sled (sled) *n.* a sledge.

sledge (slej) *n.* a vehicle with ski-like runners for travelling over snow, drawn by horses or dogs.

sledgehammer (**slej** ha mer) *n.* a large heavy hammer swung with both arms.

sleek (slēk) *adj. (*of hair, fur, etc.) smooth, soft, and glossy: *a sleek new car.*

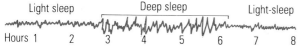

Light sleep — Deep sleep — Light-sleep

Hours 1 2 3 4 5 6 7 8

Periods of light and deep sleep can be measured from the electrical waves given off by the brain during sleep. Dreams occur during light sleep.

sleep (slēp) *n.* **1** rest in a state of near unconsciousness, with the eyes closed. **2** a period of such rest. – *vb.* **sleeping, slept** (slept) to rest in a state of sleep.

sleeping-bag *n.* a large quilted sack for sleeping in when camping, etc.

sleepy *adj.* **sleepier, sleepiest 1** feeling the desire to sleep; drowsy. **2** suggesting sleep or drowsiness: *sleepy music.* – *adv.* **sleepily.**

sleet (slēt) *n.* rain mixed with snow or hail.

sleeve (slēv) *n.* the part of a garment that covers the arm. – **up your sleeve** held secretly in reserve, for possible later use.

sleigh (slā) *n.* a large horse-drawn sledge.

slender (**slen** der) *adj.* **1** attractively slim. **2** narrow; slight: *They won by a slender margin.*

slept. See **sleep**.

slew. See **slay**.

slice (slīs) *n.* a thin broad piece, or a wedge, cut off: *a slice of cake.* – *vb.* **slicing, sliced 1** to cut up into slices. **2** to cut as, or as if as, a slice: *He sliced a piece off his finger.*

slick (slik) *adj.* **1** dishonestly or slyly clever: *Her sales talk was just too slick.* **2** superficially smart or efficient: *slick organization.* – *n.* (also **oil slick**) a wide layer of spilled oil floating on the surface of water.

slide (slīd) *vb.* **sliding, slid** (slid) **1** to move or run smoothly along a surface. **2** to move or place softly and unobtrusively: *I slid the letter into his pocket.* **3** to slip. – *n.* **1** an act or instance of sliding. **2** a structure for children to play on with a narrow sloping part to slide down.

slight (slīt) *adj.* **1** small in extent, importance, or seriousness: *We have a slight difference of opinion.* **2** slender. **3** lacking solidity; flimsy. – *vb.*

slighting, slighted to insult by ignoring or dismissing abruptly; to snub. – *adv.* **slightly.**

slim (slim) *adj.* **slimmer, slimmest** attractively thin; slender. – *vb.* **slimming, slimmed** to make yourself slim, especially by diet.

slime (slīm) *n.* a thin unpleasantly slippery or mud-like substance.

sling (sling) *n.* **1** a cloth hoop supporting an injured arm, one end hanging round the neck and the arm passed through the other end. **2** a weapon for launching stones.

slingshot *n.* (especially *US*) a catapult.

slip¹ (slip) *vb.* **slipping, slipped 1** to lose your footing and slide accidentally. **2** to slide, move, or drop accidentally: *The soap slipped through my hands.* **3** to place quietly or secretively: *Lucy slipped the envelope into her pocket.* **4** to pull free from smoothly and swiftly; to escape suddenly from: *The dog slipped its lead. The name has slipped my mind.* **5** to make a slight mistake inadvertently. – *n.* **1** an instance of losing your footing and sliding accidentally. **2** (also **slip-up**) a slight and inadvertent mistake: *a slip of the tongue.* – **let slip 1** to reveal in speech accidentally. **2** to fail to take advantage of an opportunity, etc.

slipped disc *n.* a dislocation of the layer of cartilage between any of the vertebrae.

slipper *n.* a soft loose laceless indoor shoe.

slippery *adj.* so smooth as to cause slipping.

slipshod *adj.* untidy or carelessly done.

slipstream *n.* a stream of air driven back by a moving vehicle, especially an aircraft.

slip² (slip) *n.* a small strip or piece of paper.

slit (slit) *n.* a long narrow cut or opening. – *vb.* **slitting, slitted** to cut a slit in.

sliver (**sli** ver) *n.* a splinter.

slogan (**slō** gan) *n.* a phrase used to identify a group or organization; a motto: *"Workers of the world unite".*

slope (slōp) *n.* **1** a position or direction that is neither level nor upright; an upward or downward slant. **2** a slanting surface; an incline; the side of a hill or mountain. – *vb.* **sloping, sloped** to rise or fall at an angle.

slot (slot) *n.* a narrow opening into which something is fitted or inserted.

sloth (slōth) *n.* **1** a long-haired slow-moving tree-dwelling mammal of South America. **2** laziness. – *adj.* **slothful.**

slouch (slowch) *vb.* **slouching, slouched** to sit, stand, or walk with a drooping posture.

The sloth spends most of its life hanging upside down from branches, using its long curved claws as hooks. There are two main types of sloth: the two-toed and the three-toed.

Smart was once used only in the sense of a sharp stinging pain. In the 12th century it also came to mean 'brisk' and later still 'clever'. The meaning of 'well-dressed' dates from the 18th century.

Slovak *n.* (**slō** vak) the people or language of SLOVAKIA.

● **Slovakia**. See Supplement, **Countries**.

● **Slovenia**. See Supplement, **Countries**.

slovenly *adj.* (**sluv** ĕn li) messy.

slow (slō) *adj.* **1** having little speed or pace; not moving fast or quickly. **2** taking a long time, or longer than usual. **3** (of a watch or clock) showing a time earlier than the correct time. **4** not quickly or easily learning: *a slow pupil.* – *adv.* in a slow manner. – *vb.* **slowing, slowed** to reduce speed, or rate of progress: *Slow down at the traffic lights.* – *n.* **slowness. slow-worm** *n.* a small legless lizard.

slug (slug) *n.* a land mollusc like a snail but with no shell.

sluggish *adj.* unenergetic; lazy.

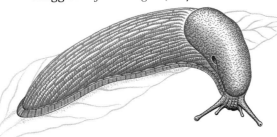

Slugs have two pairs of tentacles with eyes at the tips of the longer ones. A coating of thick, sticky slime helps to prevent desiccation (drying up). Slugs are most active at night or after a daytime rainshower.

sluice (slōōs) *n.* **1** a channel or drain for water. **2** an act of washing down or rinsing. – *vb.* **sluicing, sluiced.**

slum (slum) *n.* a run-down, dirty house.

slump (slump) *vb.* **slumping, slumped 1** to drop or sink suddenly and heavily, for example with tiredness: *Jake slumped into an armchair.* **2** (of trade, etc.) to decline suddenly.

slung. See **sling**.

slush (slush) *n.* half-melted snow.

sly (slī) *adj.* **slyer, slyest** or **slier, sliest 1** clever; cunning. **2** secretively deceitful.

smack (smak) *vb.* **smacking, smacked** to hit loudly and heavily: *Her head smacked against the wall.* – *n.* **1** the sound of smacking. **2** a loud enthusiastic kiss. – *adv.* (*colloquial*) precisely: *The dart landed smack in the middle.*

small (smöl) *adj.* **1** little in size or quantity. **2** little in extent, importance, or worth; not great. **3** humble: *small beginnings.* **4** young: *a small child.* – *n.* **smallness.**

smallpox *n.* a highly contagious disease characterized by fever and a severe rash of large blisters.

● There have been no new outbreaks of smallpox in the world for several years. It has been wiped out.

Lady Mary Wortley Montagu who pioneered an early form of vaccination against the killer disease smallpox. The next step was taken by Edward Jenner in 1796.

small print *n.* the perhaps unattractive details of a contract often printed very small.

small talk *n.* polite trivial conversation.

smart (smärt) *adj.* **1** neat and well-dressed. **2** clever; astute; shrewd. **3** expensive and sophisticated: *We're staying in a smart hotel.* **4** brisk: *He always walks at a smart pace.* – *vb.* **smarting, smarted** to feel or be the cause of a sharp stinging pain: *My hand smarts from the smack.* – *n.* a sharp stinging pain.

smash (smash) *vb.* **smashing, smashed 1** to break violently into pieces; to destroy or be destroyed in this way: *Sarah smashed the glass on the floor in temper.* **2** to strike with violence: *The angry farmer smashed his fist down on the table.* – *n.* **1** an act, or the sound, of smashing. **2** a powerful overhead stroke in racket sports. **smashing** *adj.* (*colloquial*) excellent; splendid.

smear (smēr) *vb.* **smearing, smeared 1** to spread something sticky or oily thickly over a surface. **2** to smudge. – *n.* **1** a greasy mark or patch. **2** a damaging criticism.

smell (smel) *n.* **1** the sense by which you become aware of the odour of things, located in the nose. **2** odour or scent: *I love the smell of new-mown hay.* – *vb.* **smelling, smelled** or **smelt 1** to be aware of, or take in, the odour of. **2** to give off an odour of: *Susan smells of onions.* – *vb.* **smell out** to track down, uncover.

● Some animals use smell to find food and to avoid enemies, and to recognize their own home territory. The human sense of smell is weak but it can still identify more than 10,000 different odours.

smelly *adj.* **smellier, smelliest** (*colloquial*) unpleasant-smelling. – *n.* **smelliness.**

smile (smīl) *vb.* **smiling, smiled** to turn up the corners of the mouth, as an expression of pleasure or amusement. – *adj.* **smiling.**

smith (smith) *n.* (especially *in compounds*) **1** a person who makes articles in a particular metal: *silversmith*. **2** a blacksmith.

smog (smog) *n.* fog mixed with smoke.

smoke (smōk) *n.* **1** the gases and fine particles given off by something burning. **2** visible fumes or vapours. − *vb.* **smoking, smoked 1** to give off smoke or visible fumes or vapours: *The chimney is smoking.* **2** to draw in and puff out the smoke from burning tobacco. **3** to preserve or flavour food by the action of smoke. − *adj.* **smoked**.
− **go up in smoke** to be completely destroyed by fire. − **the Smoke** (*colloquial*) the nearby big city; a country's capital city.

smokestack *n.* a tall industrial chimney.

smoky *adj.* **smokier, smokiest 1** giving out too much smoke. **2** filled with (especially tobacco) smoke. **3** having a smoked flavour.

smooth (smōōTh) *adj.* **1** having an even regular surface; not rough, coarse, bumpy, or wavy: *The sheets are smooth.* **2** free from problems or difficulties: *We had a smooth journey.* − *vb.* **smoothing, smoothed** to make smooth: *She smoothed the wrinkles in her blouse.* − *n.* **smoothness**.

smother (smu Thẻr) *vb.* **smothering, smothered 1** to kill with or die from lack of air, especially with an obstruction over the mouth and nose; to suffocate. **2** to extinguish a fire by cutting off the air supply, for example by throwing a blanket over it. **3** to cover with a thick layer: *My brother smothers his toast with jam.*

smoulder (smōl dẻr) *vb.* **smouldering, smouldered** to burn slowly or without flame.

smudge (smuj) *n.* a mark or blot spread by rubbing. − *vb.* **smudging, smudged**.

smuggle (smu gẻl) *vb.* **smuggling, smuggled** to take goods into or out of a country secretly and illegally, for example to avoid paying duty. − *n.* **smuggler**.

snack (snak) *n.* a light meal quickly taken.

snag (snag) *n.* a problem or drawback.

snail (snail) *n.* a slow-crawling soft-bodied legless creature with a spiral shell into which the whole body can be coiled.

snake (snāk) *n.* a legless crawling reptile with a long narrow body. Some species have a poisonous bite.

Photochemical smog is the result of chemical reactions caused by the action of sunlight on nitrogen oxides and unburnt fuel from car exhausts.

snap (snap) *vb.* **snapping, snapped 1** to break suddenly and cleanly with a sharp cracking noise: *He snapped the stick over his knee.* **2** to move quickly and forcefully with a sharp sound: *The lid snapped shut.* **3** to make a biting or grasping movement: *The alligator snapped the piece of meat.* **4** to speak abruptly with anger or impatience.
− *n.* **1** the act or sound of snapping. **2** a fastening that closes with a snapping sound. **3** (also **cold snap**) a sudden brief period of cold weather. **4** a card game. − *adj.* made without long consideration: *a snap decision*.

snappy *adj.* **snappier, snappiest 1** irritable. **2** smart and fashionable: *a snappy dresser*. **3** lively: *at a snappy tempo*. − *adv.* **snappily**.

snare (snār) *n.* an animal trap, especially one with a noose to catch the animal's foot.

snarl[1] (snärl) *vb.* **snarling, snarled 1** (of an animal) to growl angrily, showing the teeth. **2** to speak aggressively in anger.

snarl[2] (snärl) *n.* a knotted or tangled mass. − *vb.* **snarling, snarled** to make or become knotted, tangled, confused, or congested.

snatch (snach) *vb.* **snatching, snatched 1** to seize or grab suddenly. **2** to make a sudden grabbing movement. **3** to pull suddenly and forcefully: *She snatched her hand away.* − *n.* **1** an act of snatching. **2** a fragment overheard or remembered: *Nanna could only remember a few snatches of the old song.*

sneak (snēk) *vb.* **sneaking, sneaked 1** to move or go quietly and secretly, avoiding notice. **2** (*colloquial*) to tell tales: *He sneaked on a schoolmate.*

sneakers *n.* sports shoes.

sneaky *adj.* **sneakier, sneakiest** done or operating with secretive unfairness or dishonesty. − *adv.* sneakily.

sneer (snēr) *vb.* **sneering, sneered** to show scorn or contempt for, especially by drawing the top lip up at one side.

sneeze (snēz) *vb.* **sneezing, sneezed** to blow air out through the nose suddenly, violently, and involuntarily, especially because of irritation in the nostrils.

In Europe, the 18th century was the heyday of smuggling. Goods such as wine and spirits were secretly and illegally imported to avoid paying taxes or to get round trade bans between countries at war.

sniff (snif) *vb.* **sniffing, sniffed 1** to draw in air through the nose in short sharp bursts, for example when crying. **2** to smell at in this way.

snigger (**sni** gĕr) *vb.* **sniggering, sniggered** to laugh quietly in a foolish or mocking way.

snip (snip) *vb.* **snipping, snipped** to cut, especially with a single quick action with scissors. – *n.* **1** an act of snipping. **2** a small piece snipped off.

snipe (snīp) *n.* **1** a marshland wading-bird with a long straight bill. **2** criticism.

snippet (**sni** pit) *n.* a scrap, e.g. of information.

snob (snob) *n.* someone who places too high a value on wealth or social status, admiring those higher up the social ladder and despising those lower down. – *n.* **snobbery**. – *adj.* **snobbish**.

snooker (**snoo** kĕr) *n.* a game played on a billiard table using cues and coloured balls.

snooze (snooz) *vb.* **snoozing, snoozed** to sleep lightly; to doze. – *n.* a nap.

snore (snör) *vb.* **snoring, snored** to breathe with a snorting sound while sleeping.

snorkel (**snör** kĕl) *n.* a tube through which air from above the surface of water can be drawn into the mouth while a person is swimming just below the surface.

snort (snört) *vb.* **snorting, snorted** (especially of animals) to force air noisily out through the nostrils. – *n.* the sound of snorting.

snout (snowt) *n.* the projecting nose and mouth parts of certain animals, e.g. the pig.

snow (snō) *n.* **1** frozen water vapour falling to the ground in soft white flakes. **2** a fall of this:

heavy snows. – *vb.* **snowing, snowed** to fall to Earth as snow. – *adj.* **snowy, snowier, snowiest**. – **snowed under** overwhelmed: *We have been snowed under with work.*

snowdrop *n.* a small white flower growing from a bulb in early spring.

snowflake *n.* a feathery crystal of snow.

snowline *n.* the height on a mountain above which there is a permanent layer of snow.

snowmobile (**snō** mŏ bēl) *n.* a vehicle, on skis, for travelling on snow.

snowplough *n.* a vehicle or train fitted with a large shovel-like device for clearing snow from roads or tracks.

● **Snowden** is the highest mountain in WALES.

snub (snub) *vb.* **snubbing, snubbed** to insult someone by openly ignoring them. – *adj.* short and turned up at the end: *a snub nose.*

snug (snug) *adj.* **snugger, snuggest 1** enjoying or providing warmth, comfort, and shelter: *Snug as a bug in a rug.* **2** comfortably close-fitting: *a snug jersey.* – *adv.* **snugly**.

snuggle *vb.* **snuggling, snuggled** to settle into a position of warmth and comfort.

so (sō) *adv.* **1** to such an extent: *This chocolate is so expensive that nobody buys it.* **2** to this, that, or the same extent; as: *This one is lovely, but that one is not so nice.* **3** very: *She is so talented!* **4** also; likewise: *She's my friend and so are you.* **5** used to

Snowshoes were first used by the Native Americans. They distribute the wearer's weight over a broad area.

In very cold air water vapour can condense directly into ice crystals. These crystals may cling together to form **snow**flakes. Seen under a microscope, snow crystals are all six-sided. They all have wonderfully different shapes such as stars, needles, pyramids, and prisms.

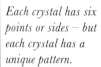

Each crystal has six points or sides – but each crystal has a unique pattern.

A snowmobile is a motorized sledge that is designed to move easily and swiftly across snow or ice.

Polar bears and seals live in the snow-covered Arctic. Northern forests with snow-clad mountains are home to such animals as beavers and moose.

avoid repeating a previous statement: *You've to take your medicine because I said so.* – *conj.* **1** therefore: *He insulted me, so I hit him.* **2** (often **so that**) in order that: *Lend me the book, so I can read it.* – *interjection* used to express discovery: *So, that's what you've been doing!* – **just so** neatly, precisely, or perfectly: *Her hair is always arranged just so.*

so-and-so *n.* (*colloquial*) **1** a person whose name you cannot remember. **2** used in place of a vulgar word: *You crafty little so-and-so!*

soak (sōk) *vb.* **soaking, soaked 1** to stand in a liquid for some time: *You must leave dried apricots to soak overnight.* **2** to drench. **3** to absorb: *Sponges soak up water.* – *adj.* **soaked**. – *n.* & *adj.* **soaking**.

soap (sōp) *n.* a mixture of oils or fats, in the form of a liquid, powder, or solid block, used with water to remove dirt.

soapbox *n.* an improvised platform for public speech-making.

soap opera *n.* a radio or television series dealing with the daily life and troubles of a regular group of characters, originally applied to those sponsored in the United States by soap manufacturing companies.

soar (sōr) *vb.* **soaring, soared** to fly or glide high into the air.

sob (sob) *vb.* **sobbing, sobbed** to cry uncontrollably with gulps for breath.

sob-story *n.* **sob-stories** (*colloquial*) a story of personal misfortune told in order to gain sympathy.

sober (sō bĕr) *adj.* **1** not at all drunk. **2** serious or solemn; not frivolous.

soccer (so kĕr) *n.* a form of football played between teams of eleven players with a round ball, in which the players attempt to kick or head the ball into the opposing team's goal.

sociable (sō shå bĕl) *adj.* friendly; fond of the company of others.

social (sō shǎl) *adj.* **1** of or for the welfare of people or society as a whole: *social policies*. **2** living with others; not solitary: *Ants are social creatures*.

socialism *n.* the economic system in which a nation's wealth – its land, industries, and transport systems – belongs to the people as a whole rather than being owned by private individuals. – *n.* & *adj.* **socialist**.

society (sŏ sī ĕ ti) *n.* **societies 1** all human beings as a whole, or a group of them such as

one nation, considered as a single community. **2** an organized group or association.

sock (sok) *n.* a fabric covering for the foot and ankle, sometimes reaching to the knee, worn inside a shoe or boot. – **pull your socks up** (*colloquial*) to make an effort to do better.

socket (so kit) *n.* a specially-shaped hole or set of holes into which something is fitted: *an electrical socket*.

● **Socrates** (**sok** rå tēz) (470-399 BC) was a Greek philosopher who asked endless questions in the search for truth.

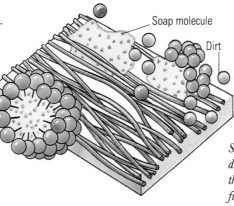

Soap and detergent molecules dislodge dirt particles by sticking to them, and squeezing them out of the fibres.

soda (sō då) *n.* **1** a common name given to various compounds of sodium in everyday use, e.g. sodium carbonate (**washing soda**) or sodium bicarbonate (**baking soda**). **2** soda water. **3** (*US*) a fizzy soft drink of any kind.

sodium (sō di ŭm) *n.* an element (symbol **Na**), a bluish-white metal of which many compounds exist as everyday substances, including common salt (**sodium chloride**).

sofa (sō få) *n.* an upholstered seat with a back and arms, for two or more people.

soft (soft) *adj.* **1** easily yielding or changing shape when pressed; pliable: *Clay is soft.* **2** (of fabric, etc.) having a smooth surface producing little or no friction. **3** quiet: *a soft voice.* **4** of little brightness: *soft colours.* **5** kind or sympathetic, especially excessively so. **6** lacking strength of character; easily influenced.

softball *n.* a game similar to baseball, played with a larger, softer ball.

soft drink *n.* a non-alcoholic drink.

soften (so fĕn) *vb.* **softening, softened** to make or become soft or softer. – *n.* **softener**.

soft-soap *vb.* **soft-soaping, soft-soaped** (*colloquial*) to speak flatteringly to, especially in order to persuade or deceive.

soft spot *n.* a fondness: *have a soft spot for.*

software *n.* computer programs, and the floppy disks, tapes, etc. on which information is recorded.

softwood *n.* wood from conifers.

soggy (**so** gi) *adj.* **soggier, soggiest** thoroughly wet; saturated: *The pitch is soggy.*

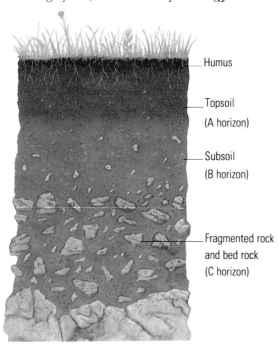

Humus

Topsoil
(A horizon)

Subsoil
(B horizon)

Fragmented rock and bed rock
(C horizon)

Soil forms in layers called 'horizons'. Horizon A is rich in decomposed plants and animal matter. The B horizon is mainly mineral particles.

soil¹ (soil) *n.* the upper layer of the Earth's land surface, in which plants grow.

soil² (soil) *vb.* **soiling, soiled** to dirty or stain: *They soiled their shirts playing rugby.*

solar (**sō** lår) *adj.* of, or relating to, the Sun.

solar system *n.* the system of planets, etc. that radiate around our Sun.

sold (sōld). See **sell**.

solder (**sōl** der) *n.* an alloy melted over the join between two metals, to form a seal.

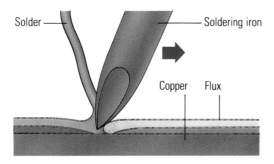

Solder

Soldering iron

Copper   Flux

soldier (**sōl** jěr) *n.* a member of a fighting force, especially a national army.

sole¹ (sōl) *n.* the underside of the foot or of a shoe or boot.

sole² (sōl) *n.* **sole** or **soles** a small edible flat-bodied fish.

sole³ (sōl) *adj.* **1** only. **2** exclusive: *This magazine has sole rights to the story.*

solely *adv.* **1** alone: *He is solely to blame.* **2** excluding all else: *It's done solely for profit.*

solemn (**so** lêm) *adj.* earnest and serious: *a solemn occasion; solemn music.* – *n.* **solemnity.**

solicitor (så **lis** i tŏr) *n.* a lawyer who prepares legal documents and gives legal advice.

solid (**so** lid) *adj.* **1** in a form other than a liquid or a gas, and resisting changes in shape. **2** of the same nature or material throughout; pure: *a solid oak table.* **3** firmly constructed or attached: *It's a solid piece of furniture that will last for years.* **4** difficult to undermine or destroy; sound: *We found solid support for the scheme.* – *n.* a substance that is neither liquid nor gas.

solidify *vb.* **solidifies, solidifying, solidified** to make or become solid.

solitary (**so** li tå ri) *adj.* **1** single; lone. **2** preferring to be alone; not social.

solo (**sō** lō) *n.* **solos** a piece of music for a single voice or instrument. – *adv.* alone: *Can you fly solo?* – *n.* **soloist.**

● **Solomon Islands**. See Supplement, **Countries**.

soluble (**sol** ū běl) *adj.* **1** capable of being dissolved. **2** capable of being solved.

solution (så **lo͞o** shŏn) *n.* **1** an answer to a problem or puzzle. **2** a liquid which has a solid or gas dissolved in it.

solve (solv) *vb.* **solving, solved** to discover the answer to a puzzle or a way out of a problem.

● **Somali Republic**. See Supplement, **Countries**.

sombre (**som** běr) *adj.* **1** sad and serious; grave: *a sombre occasion.* **2** dark and gloomy.

sombrero (som **brā** rō) *n.* **sombreros** a straw hat with a wide brim, popular in Mexico.

Solder is an alloy of tin and lead and is used in joining metals in plumbing and electrical circuits. The solder melts more easily than the metals to be joined. Flux is used to remove any oxide from the metals.

some (sum) *adj.* **1** denoting an unknown or unspecified amount or number of. **2** of unknown or unspecified nature or identity: *He's had some problem with the engine.* **3** quite a lot of: *I've been waiting for some time.* **4** at least a little: *Try to feel some excitement.* – *pron.* **1** certain unspecified things or people: *Some say he should resign.* **2** an unspecified amount or number: *Give him some, too.* – *adv.* to an unspecified extent: *Play some more.*

somehow *adv.* **1** in a way not yet known: *We'll find the answer somehow.* **2** for a reason not easy to explain: *It just happened somehow.*

something *pron.* **1** a thing not known or not stated: *Take something to eat.* **2** an amount or number not known or not stated: *Something short of a thousand people marched on the rally.*

sometime *adv.* at an unknown time in the future or the past: *I'll see you again sometime.*

sometimes *adv.* occasionally.

somewhat *adv.* rather; a little.

somewhere *adv.* in or to some place or degree, or at some point, not known or not specified: *We must go somewhere tonight for a change.*

-some (-sum) *suffix* **1** causing or producing: *troublesome.* **2** inviting: *cuddlesome.* **3** tending to: *quarrelsome.*

somersault (**sum** ĕr sölt) – *vb.* **somersaulting, somersaulted** to turn head over heels.

● **Somme** a river in northern FRANCE and scene of terrible fighting in the First WORLD WAR.

son (sun) *n.* a male child.
son-in-law *n.* **sons-in-law** the husband of your daughter.

sonar (**sō** när) *n.* **1** a system of underwater navigation and missile targeting in which the echoes from projected sound waves indicate the presence of objects. **2** an echo-sounding navigation technique used by bats, etc.

sonata (sō **nä** tå) *n.* a piece of music, in three or more movements, for a solo instrument.

song (song) *n.* **1** a set of words to be sung. **2** the musical call of certain birds.

sonic (**so** nik) *adj.* using sound.
sonic boom *n.* a loud explosive noise heard when the shock wave produced by an aircraft travelling faster than the speed of sound reaches the ground.

sonnet (**so** nit) *n.* a poem with fourteen lines and a regular rhyming pattern.

soon (sōōn) *adv.* **1** in a short time from now or from a stated time: *Soon it will be summer.* **2** quickly; with little delay. **3** willingly: *I would sooner pay the fine than go to prison.*

soot (soot) *n.* a black powder produced when coal or wood is burned.

soothe (sōōTh) *vb.* **soothing, soothed 1** to bring relief from a pain, etc. **2** to comfort or calm. – *adj.* **soothing**.

● **Sophocles** (5th century BC) was one of the greatest of the ancient Greek playwrights.

soprano (sŏ **prä** nō) *n.* **sopranos** a singing voice of the highest pitch for a woman.

sore (sör) *adj.* **1** painful when touched; tender. **2** (especially *US*) angry or resentful. – *n.* a diseased spot or area, an ulcer or boil.

sorrow (**so** rō) *n.* grief or deep sadness because of your own or someone else's loss or disappointment. – *vb.* **sorrowing, sorrowed** – *adj.* **sorrowful**.

sorry (**so** ri) *adj.* **sorrier, sorriest 1** feeling regret or shame: *She was sorry for being so naughty.* **2** feeling pity or sympathy: *We feel sorry for your bad luck.* **3** pitifully bad: *The house is in a sorry state.* – *interjection* used as an apology.

Sonar is a system that uses sound and echoes to detect objects in deep water. The word sonar is made from SOund Navigation And Ranging. (Ranging means measuring distance.) In nature, sonar is used by some animals, such as whales, to detect the animals they eat. Passive sonar means listening for sounds – submarines pick up the noise of a ship's engines. Active sonar works by sending bursts of sound and picking up the echoes that bounce back.

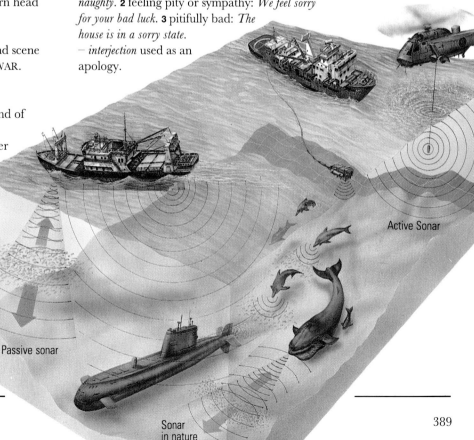

Active Sonar

Passive sonar

Sonar in nature

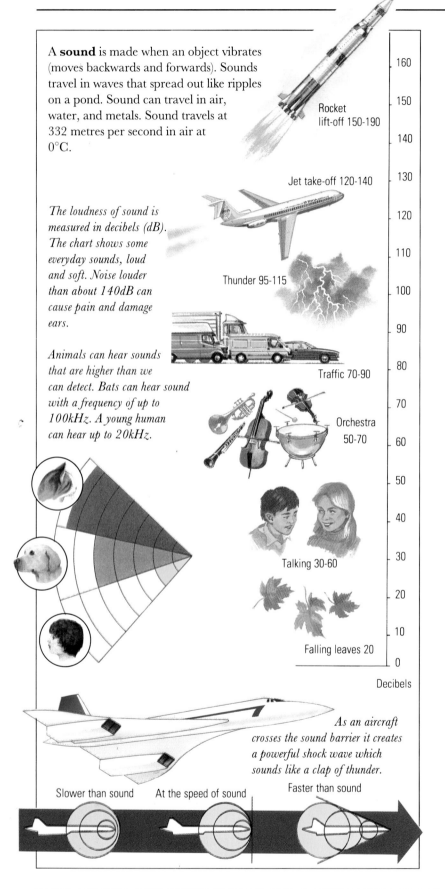

A **sound** is made when an object vibrates (moves backwards and forwards). Sounds travel in waves that spread out like ripples on a pond. Sound can travel in air, water, and metals. Sound travels at 332 metres per second in air at 0°C.

The loudness of sound is measured in decibels (dB). The chart shows some everyday sounds, loud and soft. Noise louder than about 140dB can cause pain and damage ears.

Animals can hear sounds that are higher than we can detect. Bats can hear sound with a frequency of up to 100kHz. A young human can hear up to 20kHz.

Rocket lift-off 150-190

Jet take-off 120-140

Thunder 95-115

Traffic 70-90

Orchestra 50-70

Talking 30-60

Falling leaves 20

160
150
140
130
120
110
100
90
80
70
60
50
40
30
20
10
0

Decibels

As an aircraft crosses the sound barrier it creates a powerful shock wave which sounds like a clap of thunder.

Slower than sound   At the speed of sound   Faster than sound

sort (sört) *n.* a kind, type, or class: *Carrots and swedes are different sorts of root vegetable.* – *vb.* **sorting, sorted 1** to arrange into different groups according to type or kind. **2** (*colloquial*) to put right. – **a sort of** something like a: *It's a sort of bottle with a tube attached.* – **sort of** (*colloquial*) rather; in a way; to a certain extent: *Ed was feeling sort of embarrassed.*

sought. See **seek**.

soul (sōl) *n.* **1** the non-physical part of a person, with personality, emotions, and intellect, widely believed to survive in some form after the death of the body. **2** ordinary human feelings of sympathy: *This is an act of cruelty committed by brutes with no soul.*

soul music *n.* a jazzier, more mainstream type of blues music, typically emotional in tone, usually dealing with love.

sound[1] (sownd) *n.* **1** vibrations in the air carrying information to the brain by the sense of hearing. **2** a thing heard; a noise. **3** quality of sound: *The guitar has a nice sound.* – *vb.* **sounding, sounded 1** to cause or make a sound: *The foghorn sounded.* **2** to pronounce: *Hannah doesn't sound her h's.*

sound barrier *n.* increased air resistance met by an aircraft at around the speed of sound, requiring a huge increase in power for a small increase in speed.

soundtrack *n.* a band of magnetic tape along the edge of a cinematographic film, on which the sound is recorded.

sound[2] (sownd) *adj.* **1** not damaged or injured; in good condition; healthy: *The horse is sound after its fall.* **2** sensible; well-founded: *Ann always gives sound advice.* **3** thorough: *Tom gave the rug a sound beating.* **4** (of sleep) deep and undisturbed. – *adv.* deeply: *sound asleep.*

soup (sōōp) *n.* a liquid food made by stewing meat, vegetables, or grains. – **in the soup** (*slang*) in trouble or difficulty.

sour (sowr) *adj.* **1** having an acid taste or smell, similar to that of lemon juice or vinegar. **2** sullen; miserable: *a sour-faced old man.*

source (sörs) *n.* **1** the place, thing, person, or circumstance from which anything begins; origin: *A dictionary is a wonderful source of information.* **2** where a river begins: *We followed the river back to its source.*

south (sowth) *n.* the direction to the right of a person facing the rising Sun in the northern hemisphere, directly opposite north, or any part of the Earth. – *adv.* towards the south.

– *adj.* **1** of, facing, or lying in the south; on the side or in the part nearest the south. **2** (of wind) blowing from the south.

southbound *adj.* travelling south.

south-east and **south-west** *n.* the direction midway between south and east or south and west. – *adv.* in this direction. – *adj.* of, facing, or lying in the south-east or south-west. – *adj.* **south-eastern** and **south-western**.

southerly *adj.* & *adv.* south.

southern *adj.* south; of the south.

southerner *n.* a native or inhabitant of a southern region or country.

the South Pole *n.* the southernmost point of the Earth's axis of rotation, in ANTARCTICA. The first person to journey to the pole was the Norwegian explorer, Roald AMUNDSEN, in December 1911.

southward *adj.* travelling towards the south. – *adv.* (also **southwards**) towards the south.

● **South Africa** is a country in southern AFRICA. Most of the country is a region of flat-topped hills. South Africa is rich in minerals, is industrialized, and produces many crops. Almost three-quarters of the people are black Africans to whom in recent years democratic rights have been extended. Modern South Africa came into being in 1910 when the four provinces, Cape Province, Orange Free State, Natal, and Transvaal were united.

● **South America** is the fourth largest continent. Some people there are American Indians, but many are descendants of people from Europe, especially Spain and, in Brazil, Portugal, and from Africa, and Asia. South America is rich in natural resources such as silver in Peru, tin in Bolivia, copper in Chile, and oil in Venezuela. The vast grasslands of Argentina, Uruguay, and Paraguay provide food for millions of sheep and cattle, yet most South Americans are poor.

● **South Carolina**. See Supplement, **USA**.

● **South Dakota**. See Supplement, **USA**.

souvenir (soō vĕ **nēr**) *n.* a thing bought, kept, or given as a reminder of a place, person, or occasion; a memento.

sovereign (**sov** rin) *n.* **1** a supreme ruler or head, especially a monarch. **2** a former British gold coin worth £1.

Soviet (**sō** vi ĕt) *n.* a native or inhabitant of the former SOVIET UNION.

● **Soviet Union** the common name of the former USSR (Union of Soviet Socialist Republics). See **Russia**.

sow[1] (sō) *vb.* **sowing, sowed, sown** or **sowed** to plant seed; to plant land with crops of a particular kind: *The farmer sowed her fields with barley.*

sow[2] (sow) *n.* an adult female pig.

soya bean (**so** yå bēn) *n.* an Asian bean eaten as a vegetable and used as a source of oil and flour (meal).

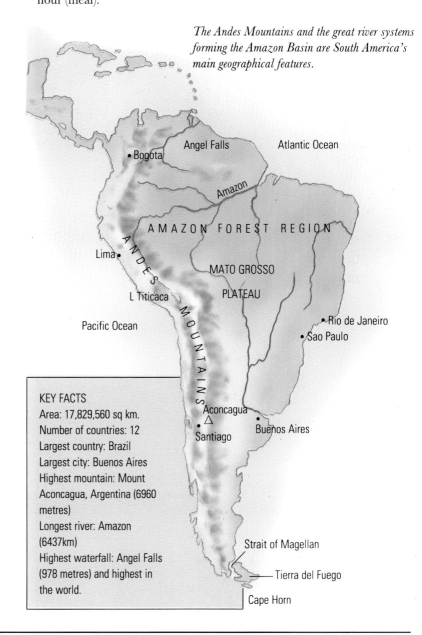

The Andes Mountains and the great river systems forming the Amazon Basin are South America's main geographical features.

KEY FACTS
Area: 17,829,560 sq km.
Number of countries: 12
Largest country: Brazil
Largest city: Buenos Aires
Highest mountain: Mount Aconcagua, Argentina (6960 metres)
Longest river: Amazon (6437km)
Highest waterfall: Angel Falls (978 metres) and highest in the world.

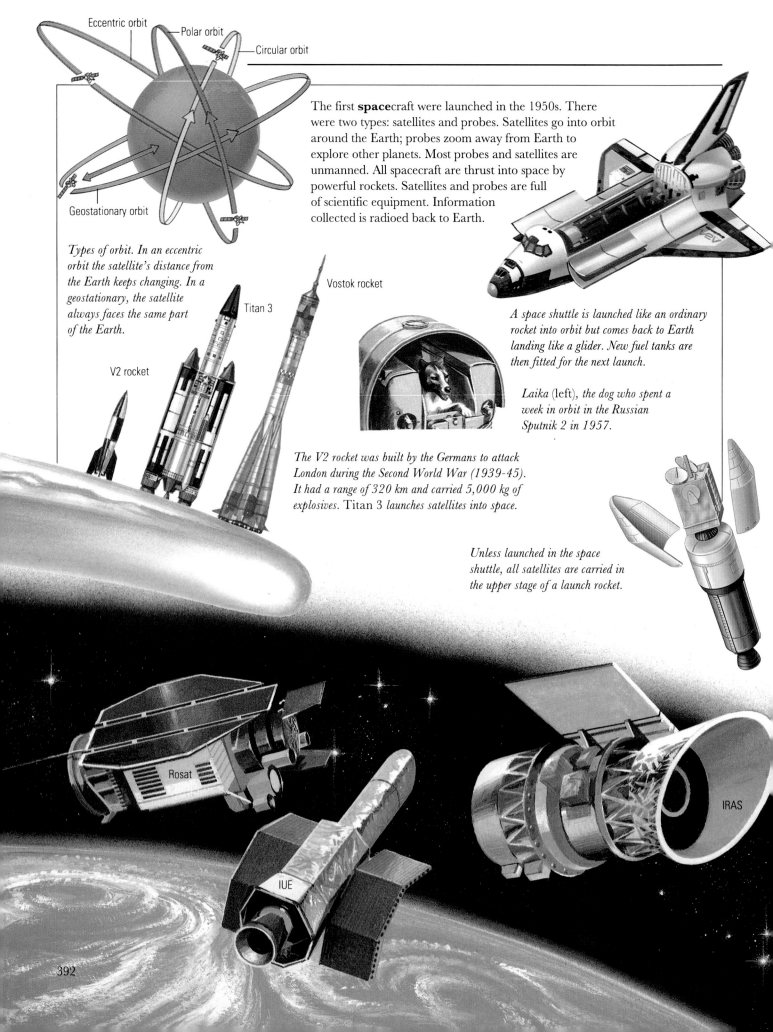

Eccentric orbit

Polar orbit

Circular orbit

Geostationary orbit

Types of orbit. In an eccentric orbit the satellite's distance from the Earth keeps changing. In a geostationary, the satellite always faces the same part of the Earth.

The first **space**craft were launched in the 1950s. There were two types: satellites and probes. Satellites go into orbit around the Earth; probes zoom away from Earth to explore other planets. Most probes and satellites are unmanned. All spacecraft are thrust into space by powerful rockets. Satellites and probes are full of scientific equipment. Information collected is radioed back to Earth.

A space shuttle is launched like an ordinary rocket into orbit but comes back to Earth landing like a glider. New fuel tanks are then fitted for the next launch.

V2 rocket

Titan 3

Vostok rocket

Laika (left)*, the dog who spent a week in orbit in the Russian Sputnik 2 in 1957.*

The V2 rocket was built by the Germans to attack London during the Second World War (1939-45). It had a range of 320 km and carried 5,000 kg of explosives. Titan 3 *launches satellites into space.*

Unless launched in the space shuttle, all satellites are carried in the upper stage of a launch rocket.

Rosat

IUE

IRAS

space (spās) *n.* **1** the limitless area in which all physical things exist. **2** a portion of this; room: *Is there enough space in the garden for a pool?* **3** an interval of distance; a gap: *There's little space between the houses.* **4** an empty place: *a space at our table.* **5** a period of time: *It all happened within the space of ten minutes.* **6** (also **outer space**) the region beyond the Earth, in which other planets and stars are located; the universe. – (in *compounds*), for use or travel in the region beyond the Earth: *spacesuit; spaceship.* – *vb.* **spacing, spaced** to arrange with intervals of distance or time between each one.

the space age *n.* the present period in history, in which travel in space has become possible.

space shuttle *n.* an aircraft-like space vehicle designed to make repeated journeys into space.

spacious (spā shůs) *adj.* extending over a large area. – *n.* **spaciousness**.

spade[1] (spād) *n.* a long-handled digging tool with a broad metal blade for digging the earth. – **call a spade a spade** to speak plainly.

spadework *n.* boring preparatory work.

spade[2] (spād) *n.* a playing-card that carries an emblem like a black blade.

spaghetti (spå **get** i) *n.* pasta in the form of long thin string-like strands.

● **Spain** in south-western Europe, beyond the Pyrenees, is covered mostly by high plains and mountains. Many Spaniards work as farmers or by fishing. The main industrial areas are around Bilbao and Barcelona. Spain was once occupied by Moors. Spain also had a huge empire which it lost in the 1800s. Spain is a monarchy. Madrid is the capital city. See also Supplement, **Countries**.

span (span) *n.* **1** the length between the supports of a bridge or arch. **2** (often in *compounds*) length from end to end in distance or time: *the wingspan of an aircraft; the timespan of the war.* – *vb.* **spanning, spanned** to extend across or over: *The bridge spans the river.*

spangle (spang gěl) *n.* a small piece of glittering material, especially a sequin.

Spaniard (span yård) *n.* a native of Spain.

spaniel (span yěl) *n.* a breed of dog with long drooping ears and a silky coat.

Spanish (span ish) *n.* **1** (*plural*) the people of Spain. **2** their language, also spoken in the southern United States and Central and South America. – *adj.* of the people and language.

spank (spangk) *vb.* **spanking, spanked** to strike or slap with the flat of the hand usually as a punishment.

spanner (spa někr) *n.* a tool for turning a nut or bolt, a lever with a shaped end. – **throw a spanner in the works** to upset a plan or system.

spare (spār) *adj.* **1** held in reserve as a replacement: *a spare tyre.* **2** available for use; unoccupied: *There's a spare seat next to me.* **3** lean; thin. – *vb.* **sparing, spared 1** to afford to give or give away: *Can you spare a minute?* **2** to be merciful, to refrain from harming: *Spare his life.*

sparing *adj.* economical or frugal.

spark (spärk) *n.* **1** a tiny red-hot glowing particle thrown off by burning material: *A spark flew from the match.* **2** an electric flash as produced by a spark plug in a car engine to explode a mixture of air and petrol.

spark plug *n.* an electrical device in a vehicle engine that produces a spark to ignite the air and petrol mixture.

sparkle (spär kěl) *vb.* **sparkling, sparkled 1** to give off sparks. **2** to shine with tiny points of bright light. **3** to be lively or witty. – *adj.* **sparkling**.

sparrow (spa rō) *n.* any of a family of small brown or grey birds similar to finches.

sparse (spärs) *adj.* thinly dotted about.

spartan (spär tån) *adj.* austere; basic: *She has little money and so leads a spartan life.*

AXAF

Many orbiting satellites send us valuable information. Rosat is recording X-ray sources from dim stars. The International Ultraviolet Explorer studies stellar ultraviolet light. IRAS stands for Infra-Red Astronomy Satellite. AXAS is the Advanced X-ray Astrophysics Facility.

PRONUNCIATION GUIDE	
fat a	all ö
fate ā	foot oo
fast ä	moon ōō
among å	boy oi
met e	house ow
mean ē	demon ô
silent ě	thing th
loch hh	this Th
fin i	but u
line ī	mute ū
quick kw	fur û
got o	brochure ů
note ō	vision zh

spasm (spa zěm) *n.* a sudden uncontrollable jerk caused by a contraction of the muscles.

spat. See **spit**[1].

spatula (spat ū lå) *n.* a tool with a broad flat flexible blade used for spreading.

spawn (spön) *n.* the eggs of frogs, fish, and molluscs, laid in water in a soft transparent jelly-like mass. – *vb.* **spawning, spawned**.

speak (spēk) *vb.* **speaking, spoke** (spōk), **spoken** (spō kěn) **1** to utter; to talk. **2** to talk to someone or each other: *They haven't spoken for years*. **3** to be able to communicate in a particular language: *He speaks French*. – **speak your mind** to say boldly what you think.

spear (spēr) *n.* a weapon consisting of a long pole with a sharp point, for throwing from the shoulder.

special (spe shål) *adj.* **1** distinct from, especially better than, others of the same kind; exceptional: *Birthdays are special days*. **2** designed for a particular purpose: *There is a special tool for cutting tiles*.
specialize or **specialise** *vb.* **specializing, specialized** to devote all your efforts to one particular activity, field of study, etc. – *n.* **specialization**. – *adj.* **specialized**. – *n.* **specialist**.

speciality (spe shi al i ti) *n.* **specialities** (also, especially *US*, **specialty** (spe shål ti), **specialties**) a thing specialized in: *Seafood is the restaurant's speciality*.

species (spē shēz) *n.* **species 1** a group of closely related plants or animals able to breed together; a subdivision of a genus. **2** a type.

specify (spe si fï) *vb.* **specifies, specifying, specified** to refer to or identify precisely: *Please specify exactly what you want*.

specimen (spe si měn) *n.* a sample or example of something, especially an object studied or put in a collection.

speck (spek) *n.* a small spot, stain, or particle. **speckled** *adj.* marked with small dots.

spectacle (spek tå kěl) *n.* **1** a thing seen; a sight, especially impressive, wonderful, or ridiculous: *The Lords Mayor's Show is a wonderful spectacle*. **2** (in *plural*) a pair of lenses held in a frame over the eyes, used to correct faulty eyesight; glasses.

spectacular (spek tak ū lår) *adj.* impressively striking to see or watch. – *n.* a spectacular show or display.

spectator (spek tā tör) *n.* a person who watches an event or incident.

spectrum (spek trům) *n.* **spectra** or **spectrums** the range of colours – red, orange, yellow, green, blue, indigo, and violet – that make up white light, separately visible when the light is passed through a prism.

Fastest car: *the British* Thrust 2 *set the world land speed record in 1983. Using an aircraft jet engine, it reached nearly 1,020 km/h.*

Thrust 2

Fastest plane: *The world record was set in 1976 when the USA's SR-71A, nicknamed* Blackbird, *reached 3,530 km/h.*

SR-71A Blackbird

speculate (spek ū lāt) *vb.* **speculating, speculated 1** to make guesses. **2** to buy, e.g. stocks and shares, in the hope of making profitable sales. – *n.* **speculation**. – *n.* **speculator**.

speech (spēch) *n.* **1** the ability to speak. **2** a talk.
speechless *adj.* temporarily unable to speak, because of surprise, shock, etc.

speed (spēd) *n.* **1** rate of movement or action. **2** quickness; rapidity: *with speed*. – *vb.*

Fastest boat: *in 1977 Ken Warby roared to 556 km/h in his jet-powered hydroplane,* Spirit of Australia.

Spirit of Australia

The black widow spider is one of the few spiders that are poisonous to humans.

speeding, sped (sped) **1** to move quickly: *The train was speeding down the line.* **2** to drive at a speed higher than the legal limit.

spell¹ (spel) *vb.* **spelling, spelt** (spelt) or **spelled** to write or name the letters of words in their correct order: *Can you spell 'accommodate'?*
spelling *n.* a way a word is spelt.

spell² (spel) *n.* a set of words believed to have magical power: *The fairy cast a spell over him.*

spelt. See **spell¹**.

spend (spend) *vb.* **spending, spent** (spent) to use up or pay out money: *Dad spent £50 on a new hat!* **2** to use or devote time or energy.

spent (spent). See **spend**. – *adj.* used up; exhausted.

sperm (spûrm) *n.* **1** fertilizing cells contained in semen. **2** semen.
sperm whale *n.* a whale with a large head that contains oil for which it is hunted.

sphere (sfēr) *n.* **1** a round solid figure with a surface on which all points are an equal distance from the centre; a globe or ball. **2** a field of activity: *the sphere of sport.*
spherical (**sfe** ri kål) *adj.* sphere-shaped.

sphinx (sfingks) *n.* in Greek mythology, a monster with the head of a woman and the body of a lioness, that killed travellers who could not solve the riddles it set.

spice (spīs) *n.* any of various strong-smelling vegetable substances used to flavour food, for example pepper, ginger, and nutmeg. – *adj.*
spicy, spicier, spiciest.

spider (**spī** děr) *n.* an eight-legged creature, many varieties of which spin silky webs to catch insects for food.

● When a spider catches something, it stuns or kills it with a poisonous bite. In most cases spiders do not harm humans. There are about 30,000 different kinds of spider. The comb-footed spider is no bigger than a pinhead; some bird-eating spiders of America can be 25 cm across.

spike (spīk) *n.* a pointed piece of metal, for example one of several on railings.

spill (spil) *vb.* **spilling, spilt** (spilt) or **spilled** to (cause to) run or flow out from a container, especially accidentally: *The baby spilt her milk over the high chair.* – *n.* an act of spilling. – **spill the beans** (*colloquial*) to give away information, especially a secret.

spilt. See **spill**.

spin (spin) *vb.* **spinning, spun** (spun) **1** to rotate repeatedly, especially quickly: *The wheels of the bike spin.* **2** to draw out and twist fibres, etc. into thread. – *n.* **1** an act of spinning or a spinning motion. **2** rotation in a ball thrown or struck. – *vb.* **spin a yarn** to tell a story, especially a long improbable one.
spin-off *n.* a thing developed from an earlier product or idea, for example a television series derived from a successful film.

spinach (**spin** ich) *n.* a dark green leafy vegetable.

spine (spīn) *n.* **1** the back-bone. **2** a projecting thorn-like growth on a plant or animal.
spinal *adj.* of, or relating to, the spine.
spinal column *n.* the spine. It is made up of a number of small bones called vertebrae. A child has 33 vertebrae, but as it grows older some of the vertebrae grow together, so that an adult has only 26.
spinal cord *n.* a cord-like mass of nerve tissue running along the spine and connecting the brain to nerves in all parts of the body.
spine-chilling *adj.* (*colloquial*) frightening.

Before refrigeration or canning, spices were often used to disguise food that was not quite fresh. Cloves (1) are the dried flower buds of a plant native to south-east Asia. Nutmeg (2) is the dried kernel of a fruit that looks like an apricot. Mace (3) comes from the outer covering of the nutmeg. Pepper (4) is a common spice widely used as a seasoning.

Most spires are tall and pointed and made of stone or of timber covered with slates.

spiral (spī rål) *n.* the pattern made by a line winding downwards from a point in near-circles of the same or ever-increasing size, as if round a cylinder or cone: *A corkscrew is a spiral.* – *adj.* of the shape of a spiral: *a spiral staircase.*

spire (spīr) *n.* a tall structure tapering upwards to a point, especially on a church.

spirit (spi rit) *n.* **1** the force within a person that is or provides the will to live: *Sad news broke his spirit.* **2** (usually in *plural*) emotional state; mood: *The children were in high spirits.* **3** a distilled alcoholic liquid for drinking, e.g. whisky.

spirited *adj.* full of courage or liveliness; a mood or attitude: *high-spirited; public-spirited.*

spiritual (spi ri choo ål) *adj.* **1** of, or relating to, the spirit or soul, rather than to the body. **2** religious: *a spiritual leader.* – *n.* a religious folk song developed by black people in the southern UNITED STATES.

spit (spit) *vb.* **spitting, spat** (spat) **1** to throw out saliva from the mouth, often as a gesture of contempt. **2** to force food out of the mouth. – *n.* saliva spat from the mouth.

spite (spīt) *n.* the desire to hurt or offend. – *adj.* **spiteful**. – *n.* **spitefulness**.

splash (splash) *vb.* **splashing, splashed** to cause large drops of a liquid to be thrown about: *Sheilagh splashed cold water over her face.* – *n.* a sound of splashing. – *vb.* **splash out** to spend a lot of money.

splashdown *n.* a landing at sea of the crew capsule of a space rocket. – *vb.* **splash down**.

splendid (splen did) *adj.* **1** magnificent: *a splendid palace.* **2** very good. – *adv.* **splendidly**.

splinter (splin těr) *n.* a thin sharp piece broken off a hard substance, for example wood or glass. – *vb.* **splintering, splintered** to break into splinters: *The cup broke and splintered.*

split (split) *vb.* **splitting, split 1** to (cause to) break apart or into pieces: *Nancy split the plank in two with an axe.* **2** to divide up into separate smaller amounts or groups: *Split up into pairs.* – *n.* **1** a lengthways break or crack. **2** a separation or division through disagreement. – **split hairs** to make, or argue about trivial distinctions.

split infinitive *n.* an infinitive with an adverb between 'to' and the verb, as in *to boldly go*, considered grammatically incorrect by some.

spoil (spoil) *vb.* **spoiling, spoilt** (spoilt) or **spoiled 1** to ruin, or make useless or valueless: *The rain has spoiled our game.* **2** to make selfish and unable to accept hardship by consistently giving in to all demands or wishes: *a spoilt child.* **3** (of food) to become unfit to eat.

spoke[1]. See **speak**.

spoke[2] (spōk) *n.* a rod or bar attaching the rim of a wheel to its centre.

spoken (spō kěn). See **speak**. – *adj.* expressed in speech: *Tapes can record the spoken word.*

sponge (spunj) *n.* **1** a simple sea creature with a body that has many holes. **2** a piece of the springy skeleton of such a creature, or a man-made substitute, used in washing and cleaning. – *vb.* **sponging, sponged** to wash or clean with a sponge and water.

spongy *adj.* **spongier, spongiest** soft and springy like a sponge.

Sponges are some of the earliest and simplest forms of living things. There are about 5,000 species.

sponsor (spon sŏr) *n.* a person or organization that finances an event or broadcast in return for advertising. – *vb.* **sponsoring, sponsored** to act as a sponsor for: *A sportswear company sponsored the match.* – *n.* **sponsorship**.

spontaneous (spon tān i ŭs) *adj.* unplanned; occurring naturally or by itself: *Her warm welcome was spontaneous.* – *n.* **spontaneity** (spon tå nā i ti) or (spon·tå nē i ti).

spool (spōōl) *n.* a small cylinder on which thread, film, tape, etc. is wound; a reel.

spoon (spōōn) *n.* a utensil with a handle and a shallow bowl-like part, for eating, serving, or stirring food. – *vb.* **spooning, spooned**.

spoonerism (spōōn ěr i zěm) *n.* an accidental, and often comic, slip in speech which reverses the positions of the first sounds of a pair of words, as in *shoving leopard* for *loving shepherd*.

spore (spōr) *n.* a cell produced by many plants that can grow into a new plant alone: *Mosses grow from spores.*

sport (spört) *n.* **1** any activity or competition designed to test physical skills: *Football and baseball are sports.* **2** good-humoured fun: *They did it in sport.*

> **sporting** *adj.* of, or relating to, sport: *sporting achievements.* – *adv.* **sportingly.**
>
> **sports car** *n.* a small fast car.

spot (spot) *n.* **1** a small mark or stain: *There's a red spot on your nose.* **2** a drop or small amount of liquid: *ink spots.* **3** a place: *What a lovely spot for a picnic!* – *vb.* **spotting, spotted 1** to mark with spots. **2** to see; to catch sight of. – **in a tight spot** (*colloquial*) in trouble or difficulty.

> **spotless** *adj.* absolutely clean; unblemished.
>
> **spotlight** *n.* a lamp casting a concentrated circle of light on a small area, especially of a theatre stage.
>
> **spotty** *adj.* **spottier, spottiest** marked with spots: *a spotty face.* – *n.* **spottiness.**

spout (spowt) *n.* **1** a tube or lip through which liquid is poured. **2** a jet or stream of liquid, for example from a fountain or the blowhole of a whale. – *vb.* **spouting, spouted 1** to flow out in a jet or stream: *Water spouted from the pipe.* **2** to speak or say, especially at length.

sprain (språn) *vb.* **spraining, sprained** to injure the muscles of by a sudden twisting. – *n.* such an injury, causing swelling.

sprang. See **spring.**

sprawl (spröl) *vb.* **sprawling, sprawled** to sit, lie, or fall lazily with the arms and legs spread out wide.

spray (språ) *n.* **1** a fine mist of small flying drops of liquid. **2** a device for dispensing a liquid as a mist; an atomiser or aerosol: *a hairspray.* – *vb.* **spraying, sprayed.**

spread (spred) *vb.* **spreading, spread 1** to apply in a smooth coating over a surface: *She spread butter on the bread.* **2** to (cause to) extend or scatter, often more widely or more thinly: *Spread the cards on the table.* **3** to open or unfold.

> **spreadsheet** *n.* a computer program displaying different batches of figures simultaneously.

sprig (sprig) *n.* a twig: *a sprig of heather.*

spring (spring) *vb.* **springing, sprang** (sprang), **sprung** (sprung) **1** to leap with a sudden quick launching action. **2** to move suddenly and swiftly by elastic force. **3** to appear or come into being suddenly: *Three new buildings have sprung up in this part of town recently.* – *n.* **1** a device that expands and contracts freely, returning to its original shape when released: *My mattress has good springs.* **2** a natural outflow of water from the ground. **3** the season between winter and summer. **4** a leap.

> **springbok** *n.* a South African antelope renowned for its high springing leaps.
>
> **springy** *adj.* **springier, springiest** readily springing back into its original shape when released; elastic.

sprinkle (**spring** kẻl) *vb.* **sprinkling, sprinkled** to scatter in tiny drops or particles.

sprint (sprint) *n.* a race at high speed over a short distance. – *vb.* **sprinting, sprinted** to run at full speed. – *n.* **sprinter.**

sprout (sprowt) *vb.* **sprouting, sprouted** to develop a new growth, for example of leaves. – *n.* **1** a shoot or bud. **2** a Brussels sprout.

spruce (sproōs) *n.* an evergreen tree.

sprung. See **spring.**

spud (spud) *n.* (*colloquial*) a potato.

spun. See **spin.**

spurn (spûrn) *vb.* **spurning, spurned** to reject.

spurt (spûrt) *vb.* **spurting, spurted** to flow out in a sudden sharp jet.

spy (spī) *n.* **spies 1** a person employed by a government to gather information secretly about political enemies. **2** a person observing others in secret. – *vb.* **spies, spying, spied 1** to work as a spy. **2** to catch sight of; to spot.

squad (skwod) *n.* a small group of soldiers.

squalor (skwo lòr) *n.* filth; dirt.

squander (skwon dèr) *vb.* **squandering, squandered** to use up or spend wastefully: *Jim squandered £10 on cheap, worthless toys.*

square (skwār) *n.* **1** a two-dimensional figure with four sides of equal length and four right angles. **2** an open space in a town, shaped vaguely like this. – *adj.* **1** square-shaped.

Dampers stop springs bouncing back too quickly after the spring has been compressed by the vehicle going over a bump. The oil in the cylinder slows down the spring's 'bounce back'.

In most road vehicles the suspension system and its shock absorbers of springs and dampers is hidden inside. This off-road buggy reveals all. Without shock absorbers to swallow up bumps and jolts road travel would be very uncomfortable.

PRONUNCIATION GUIDE

fat **a**	all **ö**
fate **ā**	foot **oo**
fast **ä**	moon **ōō**
among **å**	boy **oi**
met **e**	house **ow**
mean **ē**	demon **ồ**
silent **ẻ**	thing **th**
loch **hh**	this **Th**
fin **i**	but **u**
line **ī**	mute **ū**
quick **kw**	fur **û**
got **o**	brochure **ů**
note **ō**	vision **zh**

The squid sucks water into its body and then squirts it out through a narrow tube. The force of the jet can propel the squid through the water at enormous speeds. The squid's tentacles are covered with suckers which hold the prey firmly while the squid bites it.

2 measured in length and breadth; of an area equal to a square whose sides are the stated length: *One room is three metres square.* – *vb.* **squaring, squared** to multiply a number by itself.

square dance *n.* a popular American folk dance performed by couples in a square formation.

square root *n.* the number which, when multiplied by itself, gives the number in question: *The square root of sixteen is four.*

squaw (skwö) *n.* a NATIVE AMERICAN name for a woman or wife.

squawk (skwök) *n. & vb.* **squawking, squawked** (to utter) a loud croaky cry, like that of a parrot.

squash (skwosh) *vb.* **squashing, squashed 1** to crush or flatten by pressing or squeezing. **2** to force your body into a confined space. – *n.* **1** a drink made by diluting a concentrated fruit syrup. **2** a crushed or crowded state. **3** (also **squash rackets**) a game for two players on a walled indoor court.

squat (skwot) *vb.* **squatting, squatted 1** to be sitting in a low position with the knees fully bent and the weight on the soles of the feet. **2** to occupy an empty building without legal right. – *adj.* short and broad or fat.

squeak (skwēk) *n.* a short high-pitched cry like that of a mouse or a rusty gate. – *vb.* **squeaking, squeaked** to make a squeak: *My shoes squeak.*

squeal (skwēl) *n.* a long high-pitched cry or yelp, like that of a pig or a child in pain. – *vb.* **squealing, squealed**.

squeeze (skwēz) *vb.* **squeezing, squeezed 1** to grasp or embrace tightly: *Sally squeezed my hand to show she loves me.* **2** to press forcefully, especially from at least two sides: *We squeezed the box to see if it was empty.* **3** to press or crush so as to extract juice, etc. – *n.* **1** an act of squeezing. **2** a crowded or crushed state: *It's a bit of a squeeze with four on the sofa.*

squid (skwid) *n.* **squid** or **squids** a sea creature with a long body and ten tentacles.

squint (skwint) *vb.* **squinting, squinted** to look with eyes half-closed; to peer.

squirm (skwûrm) *vb.* **squirming, squirmed** to wriggle.

squirrel (**skwi** rẻl) *n.* a tree-dwelling rodent with a large bushy tail and grey or reddish-brown fur.

● **Sri Lanka**. See Supplement, **Countries**.

stab (stab) *vb.* **stabbing, stabbed 1** to wound or pierce with a pointed instrument. **2** to make a quick thrusting movement with something sharp. – *n.* **1** an act of stabbing. **2** (*colloquial*) a try: *Have a stab at doing this.*

stable¹ (stā běl) *adj.* **1** firmly balanced or fixed; not likely to wobble or fall: *The shelves are stable.* **2** firmly established; not likely to be abolished: *a stable government.* – *n.* **stability**.

stable² (stā běl) *n.* a building for horses.

stack (stak) *n.* a large neat pile of hay, etc: *a stack of books.* – *vb.* **stacking, stacked 1** to arrange in stacks. **2** to arrange aircraft waiting to land into a queue in which each circles the airport at a different altitude.

stadium (stā di ům) *n.* **stadiums** or **stadia** a large open air sports ground with rows of seats.

staff (stäf) *n.* **1** the employees working in an organization. **2** (**staffs** or **staves** (stāvz)) a stick or rod carried in the hand.

stag (stag) *n.* an adult male deer.

stage (stāj) *n.* **1** a platform in the theatre on which a performance takes place. **2** any of several distinct and successive periods. **3** the theatre as a profession: *She has devoted her life to the stage.* – *vb.* **staging, staged 1** to present a performance of a play. **2** to organize an event.

stagger (sta gẻr) *vb.* **staggering, staggered 1** to walk or move unsteadily. **2** to cause extreme shock or surprise to: *The bad news staggered her.* **3** to arrange so as to begin at different times: *The rally had a staggered start.*

stagnant (**stag** nånt) *adj.* (of water) dirty and foul-smelling because of not flowing.

stain (stān) *vb.* **staining, stained 1** to make or become marked or discoloured: *She stained the carpet when she spilt the coffee.* **2** to change the colour of wood, etc. by applying a dye.

stair (stār) *n.* a series of steps connecting the floors of a building.

staircase or **stairway** *n.* a set of stairs.

stake¹ (stāk) *n.* a stick or post, usually with one end pointed, knocked into the ground as a support, for example for a young tree or a fence. – *vb.* **staking, staked**.

stake² (stāk) *n.* **1** a sum of money risked in betting. **2** an interest, especially financial: *They have a stake in the project's success.*

stalactite (sta låk tīt) *n.* an icicle-like mass of limestone attached to the roof of a cave, etc.

stalagmite (sta låg mīt) *n.* a spiky mass of limestone sticking up from the floor of a cave.

stale (stāl) *adj.* (of food) not fresh, and therefore dry and tasteless: *This cake tastes stale.*

stalk¹ (stök) *n.* the principal stem of a plant.

stalk² (stök) *vb.* **stalking, stalked** to hunt, follow, or approach quietly. – *n.* **stalker**.

stall¹ (stöl) *n.* **1** a space for a single animal in a cowshed, stable, etc. **2** a platform or stand on which goods for sale are displayed. **3** (in *plural*) the seats on the ground floor of a theatre.

stall² (stöl) *vb.* **stalling, stalled 1** to delay. **2** to do something in order to delay something else. **3** to stop a car engine by mistake.

stallion (stal yŏn) *n.* an adult male horse.

stamen (stā měn) *n.* a small stalk-like pollen-bearing part on the inside of a flower.

stamina (sta mi nå) *n.* energy needed to endure prolonged physical or mental exertion.

stamp (stamp) *vb.* **stamping, stamped 1** to bring the foot down with force: *The horse stamped its hoof on the road.* **2** to imprint with a mark or design: *You must stamp the date on the incoming mail.* **3** to stick a postage stamp on. – *n.* (also **postage stamp**) a small piece of gummed paper with the official mark of a nation's postal system, stuck to mail to show that postage has been paid. – *vb.* **stamp out 1** to put out a fire by stamping on it. **2** to put an end to.

stand (stand) *vb.* **standing, stood** (stood) **1** to be in, or move into, an upright position on the feet or a base. **2** to place or be placed: *Sue stood the grandfather clock in the corner. Our house stands in a valley.* **3** to be a particular height: *The tower stands 300 feet tall.* **4** to tolerate or put up with: *I can't stand him.* **5** to be a symbol or representation of: *If Y equals oranges, what does*

X stand for? – *n.* **1** a base on which something is supported: *a cake-stand.* **2** a stall displaying goods or services for sale. **3** a structure with sitting or standing accommodation for spectators. **4** a rack on which coats, hats, umbrellas, etc. may be hung. **5** a firm attitude or opinion: *The council is taking a stand against further building.* – *vb.* **stand by 1** to be in a state of readiness to act (*n.* **standby**). **2** to give support in time of difficulty: *Steve stood by Sarah when she had her breakdown.* **3** to look on without taking the expected action: *They stood by and watched her fail.*

standstill *n.* a complete stop; no progress.

The British 'penny black' of 1840, the first stamp on which the postage was prepaid, and a US 'local' stamp.

standard (stan dård) *n.* **1** an accepted model against which others are compared, measured, or judged. **2** (often in *plural*) a principle of behaviour. **3** a flag or other emblem, especially one carried on a pole. – *adj.* of the normal or accepted kind, without variations or additions.

stank. See **stink**.

stanza (stan zå) *n.* a verse in poetry.

As water drips into a limestone cave, lime deposits may come out of solution to form a rocky 'icicle'. These icicles are called stalactites if they hang from the ceiling or stalagmites if they build up from the ground.

STAMP TERMS
commemorative a stamp issued to celebrate an event.
mint an unused stamp in perfect condition.
perforation the row of holes punched in a sheet of stamps.
philately the study and collection of stamps.
postmark a mark stamped on mail to cancel the stamp.

Red Giant

Main sequence star
(such as the Sun)

Blue Giant

White dwarf

Red dwarf

Black hole

Neutron

Our Sun shines with a yellow light. The hottest stars shine with a white-blue light. They are known as blue giants. The cool stars are known as red dwarfs. There are also relatively cool red giants and dim white dwarfs. In a white dwarf the atoms are crushed tightly together. A neutron is a dead star made from solid nuclei of atoms, the densest material in the universe. A black hole is a massive neutron star.

star (stär) *n.* **1** any of the innumerable bodies in the night sky that appear as points of light. **2** a figure with five or more radiating points. **3** a celebrity, especially from the sporting or entertainment world: *a film star. – vb.*
starring, starred to feature or appear as a principal performer.
starfish *n.* a sea creature with a flat body and usually five radiating arms.
starlight *n.* the light from the stars. *– adj.* **starlit**.
Star of David *n.* the symbol of Judaism, a six-pointed star formed by overlapping two equilateral triangles.
starry *adj.* **starrier, starriest** **1** filled or decorated with stars. **2** shining brightly.
the Stars and Stripes *n.* the national flag of the United States.
starboard (stär börd) *n.* the right side of a ship or aircraft, as viewed when facing forwards.
starch (stärch) *n.* a carbohydrate stored in plants in the form of tiny white granules, used in solution with water as a fabric stiffener.
stare (stār) *vb.* **staring, stared** to look with a fixed gaze. *– n.* an act of staring; a fixed gaze.
starling (stär ling) *n.* a small bird with dark glossy speckled feathers and a short tail.
start (stärt) *vb.* **starting, started** **1** to begin; to bring or come into being. **2** to set or be set in motion, or put or be put into a working state: *Can you start the engine?* **3** to be at first: *She started her career in the company as a lorry driver.*

4 to initiate or get going; to cause or set off.
5 to begin a journey: *To get to the station you must start from the bridge. – n.* **1** the first or early part. **2** a beginning, origin, or cause. **3** the time or place at which something starts.
startle (stär těl) *vb.* **startling, startled** to give a sudden fright to; to surprise. *– adj.* **startling**.
starve (stärv) *vb.* **starving, starved** to (cause to) suffer extreme ill-health, or die, through lack of food. *– n.* **starvation**.
state (stāt) *n.* **1** the condition, e.g. of health, appearance, or emotions, in which a person or thing exists at a particular time. **2** a nation. **3** (*colloquial*) an emotional condition: *She was in a state of collapse. – adj.* of, relating to, or controlled or financed by the State. *– vb.* **stating, stated** to express clearly.
state of the art *n.* the current advancement achieved by the most up-to-date technology or thinking in a particular field.
station (stā shŏn) *n.* **1** a stopping-place for passenger trains or buses, with facilities for refuelling, ticket-purchasing, etc. **2** a local head-quarters: *a police station.* **3** a building equipped for some particular purpose: *a power station.* **4** a radio or television channel.
stationary (stā shŏ nå ri) *adj.* not moving.
stationery (stā shŏ ně ri) *n.* paper, envelopes, pens, and other writing materials.
statistics (stå tis tiks) *n.* (*singular*) the science dealing with the classification, and interpretation of numerical information. *– adj.* **statistical**.
statue (sta chōō) *n.* a sculpted, moulded, or cast figure, especially of a person or animal.
stay (stā) *vb.* **staying, stayed** **1** to remain in the same place or condition, without moving or changing: *The dog stayed in her basket all day.* **2** to reside temporarily, for example as a guest: *We're staying in a hotel on the sea front. – n.* a period of temporary residence; a visit.

The Statue of Liberty, which was given to the United States by France in 1886, stands on Liberty Island in New York Bay. Two spiral staircases wind up inside it.

steady (ste di) *adj.*
steadier, steadiest
1 firmly fixed or balanced; not tottering or wobbling. **2** regular; constant; unvarying: *The horse canters at a steady pace.* – *vb.* **steadies, steadying, steadied** to make or become steady. – *adv.* **steadily**. – *n.* **steadiness**.

steak (stāk) *n.* a thick slice of beef (or fish).

steal (steal) *vb.* **stealing, stole** (stōl), **stolen** (stō lĕn) **1** to take away another person's property without permission, especially secretly. **2** to go about quietly so as not to be noticed: *She stole out of the room when everyone was watching TV.*

steam (stēm) *n.* **1** the gas into which water is converted by boiling, invisible but generally becoming visible as a white mist of fine water vapour. **2** this gas as a source of mechanical power: *steam-driven.* – *vb.* **steaming, steamed 1** to give off steam. **2** to cook or otherwise treat with steam: *steamed fish.* – *adj.* powered by steam. – **let off steam** to release anger or energy.

● Steam will fill 1700 times more space than the water it comes from. So if you squash steam into a small container it presses hard against the sides. If one side is free to move, the steam pressure will push it outwards. In the 1700s onwards British inventors such as Thomas Newcomen and James Watt began to use this fact to build engines powered by steam.

steel (stēl) *n.* a tough metal alloy of iron and carbon, with numerous industrial uses.

steep¹ (stēp) *adj.* rising or sloping sharply: *a steep hill.* – *n.* **steepness**.

steep² (stēp) *vb.* **steeping, steeped** to soak.

steeple (stē pĕl) *n.* a tower with a spire.

steer¹ (stēr) *vb.* **steering, steered** to guide or control the direction of a vehicle or vessel.

steer² (stēr) *n.* a young bull reared for beef.

stellar (ste lăr) *adj.* of or like stars.

stem¹ (stem) *n.* **1** the central part of a plant, growing upward from the root. **2** any long slender part. – *vb.* **stemming, stemmed** to originate or spring.

stem² (stem) *vb.* **stemming, stemmed** to stop the flow of something: *Stem the flood water!*

stench (stench) *n.* a very unpleasant smell.

step (step) *n.* **1** a single movement of the foot in walking or running. **2** one of a pattern in dancing. **3** (often in *plural*) a single often outdoor stair, or any stair-like support used to climb up or down. **4** a single action or measure taken in proceeding towards an end: *What steps should be taken to control the noise?* – *vb.* **stepping, stepped** to move by taking steps, quietly or carefully. – **step by step** gradually. – *vb.* **step down** to resign from a position of authority.

step- (step-) *prefix* indicating a relationship not by blood but through a second or later marriage or partnership, for example, **stepchild, stepfather**.

steppe (step) *n.* a vast dry grassy plain.

stereo- (ste ri ō-) or (stēr i ō-) three-dimensional.

stereophonic (ste ri ō **fon** ik) or (stēr i ō **fon** ik) *adj.* (of sound) recorded so as to be reproduced with different elements fed through two or more loudspeakers, creating the effect of live sound.

The iron used in steel making is mined as iron ore. The ore is smelted in a furnace. It is then made into cast iron and poured into moulds to make engine blocks, etc.; or the ore is mixed with small amounts of carbon to form steel.

stereotype (ste ri ō **tīp**) or (stēr i ō **tīp**) *n.* an over-generalized idea, impression, or point of view allowing for no individuality or variation: *Not all Scots wear kilts, eat haggis, and are mean. That's a stereotype.* – *vb.* **stereotyping, stereotyped** to think of in an over-generalized way. – *adj.* **stereotyped**.

sterile (ste rīl) *adj.* **1** biologically incapable of producing offspring, fruit, or seeds. **2** made free of germs. – *n.* **sterility** (stĕ ril i ti).

sterilize or **sterilise** (ste ri līz) *vb.* **sterilizing, sterilized** to make sterile. – *n.* **sterilization**.

sterling (**stûr** ling) *n.* British money.

stern[1] (stûrn) *adj.* strict; authoritarian; harsh.

stern[2] (stûrn) *n.* the rear of a ship or boat.

stethoscope (**ste** thŏ skōp) *n.* an instrument for listening to sounds made inside the body.

stetson (**stet** sŏn) *n.* a broad-brimmed hat with a high crown, worn especially by cowboys.

● **Stevenson, Robert Louis** (1850-94) was the Scottish author of adventure stories such as *Treasure Island* and *Kidnapped*.

stew (stū) *vb.* **stewing, stewed** to cook by long simmering.

steward (**stū** ård) and **stewardess** *n.* an attendant on a passenger ship or aircraft.

stick[1] (stik) *n.* **1** a twig or thin branch. **2** any long thin piece of wood shaped for a particular purpose, e.g. striking the ball in hockey, or playing a percussion instrument. — **get hold of the wrong end of the stick** to misunderstand a situation.

stick insect *n.* a tropical insect with a long twig-like body and legs.

stick[2] (stik) *vb.* **sticking, stuck** (stuk) **1** to push or thrust especially something pointed: *Your elbow is sticking through your sleeve.* **2** to fasten by piercing with a pin or other sharp object: *Stick it up with drawing-pins.* **3** to fix, or be or stay fixed, with an adhesive: *Can you stick this broken plate with glue?* **4** to remain: *It's an episode that sticks in my mind.* **5** to be unable to move: *We're stuck in a traffic jam.* **6** not to stray from: *Stick to the point!* — *vb.* **stick at** to continue doggedly with.

sticker *n.* an adhesive label.

sticky *adj.* **stickier, stickiest 1** able or likely to stick: *sticky toffee.* **2** (of weather) humid; muggy. — *n.* **stickiness**.

stiff (stif) *adj.* **1** not easily bent or folded; rigid: *Cardboard is stiff.* **2** lacking suppleness; not moving or bending easily: *Sam's arm is stiff from playing too much tennis.* **3** (of punishment, etc.) harsh; severe. **4** (of a task, etc.) difficult.

stiffen *vb.* **stiffening, stiffened** to make or become stiff or stiffer.

stifle (**stī** fĕl) *vb.* **stifling, stifled** to have difficulty in breathing, because of heat and lack of air.

stifling *adj.* unpleasantly hot or airless.

stigma (**stig** må) *n.* **stigmas** the part of a flower that receives pollen.

stile (stīl) *n.* a step for climbing over a fence.

The bodies of some stick insects are so twig-like that they are almost impossible to see as they sit on trees or bushes. There are about 2,000 species of the insect.

still (stil) *adj.* **1** motionless; inactive: *There's not a breath of wind; the air is still.* **2** quiet and calm; tranquil: *The sea is still tonight.* — *adv.* **1** continuing as before, now, or at some future time: *Phil is still my best friend.* **2** up to the present time, or the time in question; yet: *I still haven't finished my homework.* **3** even then; nevertheless: *Although it was raining, they still went out.* **4** quietly and without movement: *Please try to sit still.* — *n.* **1** stillness; tranquillity. **2** a photograph used for publicity purposes. — *n.* **stillness**.

stimulate (**stim** ū lāt) *vb.* **stimulating, stimulated 1** to excite or arouse the senses of. **2** to create interest and enthusiasm in someone. — *adj.* **stimulating**. — *n.* **stimulation**.

stimulus (**stim** ū lŭs) *n.* **stimuli** (**stim** ū lī) a thing that stimulates; an incentive: *Anne's winning the swimming prize was a stimulus to Steve to do better.*

sting (sting) *n.* **1** a sharp part of some plants or animals that can pierce skin and inject poison: *a bee sting.* **2** the poison injected or wound inflicted: *I had a nasty sting when I sat on that nettle.* — *vb.* **stinging, stung** (stung) **1** to pierce, poison, or wound with a sting. **2** to produce a sharp tingling pain. — *adj.* **stinging**.

stink (stingk) *n.* a strong and unpleasant smell. — *vb.* **stinking, stank** (stangk) or **stunk** (stungk), **stunk 1** to give off a stink. **2** to be bad or unpleasant: *I think the whole idea stinks.*

stir (stûr) *vb.* **stirring, stirred 1** to mix a liquid or semi-liquid substance by moving it around with circular strokes with a spoon or other utensil: *Stir the sauce until it is smooth.* **2** to arouse the emotions of; to move: *The rebels stirred up the crowd.* — *n.* **1** an act of stirring a liquid, etc.: *Give it a good stir.* **2** a commotion: *His remarks caused quite a stir.*

stirrup (**sti** rŭp) *n.* either of a pair of metal loops hanging on straps from a horse's saddle to support the rider's foot.

stitch (stich) *n.* **1** a single link of thread or yarn in sewing, knitting. **2** a sharp ache in the side. **3** (*colloquial*) the least scrap of clothing: *without a stitch on.* — *vb.* **stitching, stitched**. — **in stitches** (*colloquial*) helpless with laughter.

stoat (stōt) *n.* a small mammal of the weasel family, called an ermine in its white winter fur.

stock (stok) *n.* **1** the total goods stored in a warehouse, etc. **2** a supply kept in reserve: *I always keep a stock of candles in case there's a power cut.* **3** equipment or raw material in use: *rolling* *stock.* **4** liquid in which meat or vegetables have been cooked, used as a base for a soup. **5** farm animals; livestock. – *adj.* of a standard type, size, etc., constantly in demand and always kept in stock. – *vb.* **stocking, stocked** to keep a stock of for sale. – **out of stock** not available in a shop, etc.

stocking (sto king) *n.* a covering for the legs.

stole. See **steal**.

stolen. See **steal**.

stomach (stu måk) *n.* the bag-like organ of the body into which food passes when swallowed, and where digestion starts.

stone (stōn) *n.* **1** the hard solid mineral substance of which rocks are made. **2** a piece of rock. **3** (also **gemstone**) a shaped and polished piece of a precious mineral. **4** the hard seed in various fruits: *a peach stone* – *vb.* **stoning, stoned 1** to pelt with stones.

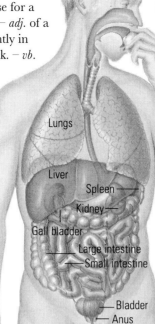

Lungs
Liver
Spleen
Kidney
Gall bladder
Large intestine
Small intestine
Bladder
Anus

In your stomach, juices moisten and start digesting food. Stomach muscles churn the mixture, then force it into the small intestine.

A Stone Age fish spear and flint arrowhead.

2 to remove the stone from fruit.

the Stone Age *n.* the earliest period in human history, during which primitive tools and weapons were made of stone.

●**Stonehenge** is a prehistoric temple on Salisbury Plain in southern England. The main part is a great circle of huge standing stones.

stood. See **stand**.

stool (stōol) *n.* a seat without a back.

stoop¹ (stōop) *vb.* **stooping, stooped** to bend from the waist: *She stooped to avoid the low beams.*

stoop² (stōop) *n.* (*US*) a veranda.

stop (stop) *vb.* **stopping, stopped 1** to bring or come to rest, a standstill, or an end; to cease moving, operating, or progressing: *Sally stopped the car at the lights.* **2** to prevent. **3** to block, plug, or close: *Dirt was stopping the drain.* – *n.* **1** an act of stopping. **2** a place stopped at, for example, a bus stop. **3** a full stop.

stopgap *n.* a temporary substitute.

stoppage *n.* an act of stopping or the state of being stopped.

stopwatch *n.* a watch fitted with a device that can instantly stop the hands, used for timing races, etc.

store (stör) *n.* **storing, stored 1** a supply kept in reserve: *Dad keeps a store of tinned food in his shed.* **2** a shop, especially when large and one of a chain. – *vb.* **1** to put aside for future use. **2** to build up a reserve supply of. **3** to put into a computer's memory.

storey (stör i) *n.* **storeys** a level, floor, or tier of a building.

storm (störm) *n.* **1** an outbreak of violent weather, with severe winds. **2** a violent show of feeling. – *vb.* **storming, stormed** to go or come loudly and angrily: *Simon stormed out.*

story (stör i) *n.* **stories 1** a written or spoken description of real or imaginary events. **2** a news article. **3** (*colloquial*) a lie.

stout (stowt) *adj.* **1** rather fat: *a stout man.* **2** robust: *stout boots.* **3** a heavy dark beer.

stove (stōv) *n.* a domestic cooker.

stowaway (stō å wā) *n.* someone who hides on a ship, etc. to avoid paying the fare.

straggle (stra gĕl) *vb.* **straggling, straggled 1** to grow or spread untidily. **2** to lag behind or stray from the main group. – *n.* **straggler**.

straight (strāt) *adj.* **1** not curved, bent, curly, or wavy: *There are four straight lines in a square.* **2** without deviations or detours; direct: *Follow the straight path.* **3** frank; open; direct: *My straight answer is 'No'.*

straighten *vb.* **straightening, straightened** to make or become straight.

strain¹ (strān) *vb.* **straining, strained 1** to injure or weaken a part of one's body through over-exertion: *He strained a muscle in his leg through jogging too much.* **2** to make violent efforts. **3** to pour into a sieve or colander.

strainer *n.* a sieve or colander.

PRONUNCIATION GUIDE	
fat **a**	all **ŏ**
fate **ā**	foot **oo**
fast **ä**	moon **ōō**
among **å**	boy **oi**
met **e**	house **ow**
mean **ē**	demon **ŏ**
silent **ĕ**	thing **th**
loch **hh**	this **Th**
fin **i**	but **u**
line **ī**	mute **ū**
quick **kw**	fur **û**
got **o**	brochure **ů**
note **ō**	vision **zh**

strain² (strān) *n.* a breed of animals or plants.

strait (strāt) *n.* **1** (often in *plural*) a narrow strip of sea between two land masses. **2** (in *plural*) difficulty; hardship: *The company is in dire straits.*

strand¹ (strand) *vb.* **stranding, stranded** to leave in a helpless position.

strand² (strand) *n.* a single thread or fibre.

strange (strānj) *adj.* **1** not known or experienced before; unfamiliar or alien: *Tibet is a strange country to us.* **2** not usual; odd. **3** ill at ease: *I have a strange feeling you don't like me.* – *n.* **strangeness.**

stranger *n.* a person whom you do not know.

strangle (strang gĕl) *vb.* **strangling, strangled** to kill by squeezing the throat with the hands, a cord, etc. – *n.* **strangler.**

strap (strap) *n.* a narrow strip of leather or fabric by which a thing is carried, or fastened.

strategy (strat ĕ ji) *n.* **strategies** a long-term plan for future success or development.

stratum (strä tŭm) or (strā tŭm) *n.* **strata** a layer of sedimentary rock.

●**Strauss** (strows), **Johann** (1825-99) was an Austrian composer, famous for his waltzes.

●**Strauss** (strows), **Richard** (1864-1949) was a German composer of operas.

●**Stravinsky, Igor** (1882-1971) was a Russian-born American composer, famous for his ballets *Petrushka* and *The Rite of Spring.*

straw (strö) *n.* **1** the dried cut stalks of corn and similar crops. **2** a thin hollow tube for sucking up a drink.

strawberry (strö bĕ ri) *n.* **strawberries** a small juicy red fruit of a low-growing plant.

stray (strā) *vb.* **straying, strayed** to wander away: *The ramblers strayed from the footpath.* – *n.* a lost or homeless pet or child. – *adj.* random.

streak (strēk) *n.* **1** a long irregular stripe or band. **2** an element or characteristic: *a cowardly streak.* – *vb.* **streaking, streaked** to dash. – *adj.* **streaked.**

stream (strēm) *n.* **1** a very narrow river. **2** a continuously moving line or mass: *a stream of cars.* – *vb.* **streaming, streamed 1** to flow or move continuously. **2** to trail: *Her long hair streamed in the wind.*

streamlined *adj.* (of a vehicle, aircraft, or vessel) shaped so as to move smoothly with minimum resistance to air or water.

street (strēt) *n.* a public road, especially one in a town with pavements and buildings at the side.

streetwise *adj.* (*colloquial*) experienced in, and able to survive, ruthless urban life.

strength (strength) *n.* **1** the quality or degree of being physically or mentally strong: *Sue has great strength of character.* **2** the ability to withstand pressure or force: *Has the rope got enough strength?*

strengthen *vb.* **strengthening, strengthened** to make or become stronger.

strenuous (stren ū ŭs) *adj.* requiring, or performed with, great effort or energy.

stress (stres) *n.* **1** mental or emotional pressure; acute anxiety: *The worry of keeping her deadline has been the cause of great stress.* **2** physical pressure or tension. **3** emphasis on a particular syllable or word: *The stress in 'particular' is on the second syllable 'tic'.* – *vb.* **stressing, stressed.**

stretch (strech) *vb.* **stretching, stretched 1** to make or become longer or wider by pulling or drawing out: *Sonia stretched the elastic band until it broke.* **2** to extend in space or time: *The Atlantic stretches from Ireland to America.* **3** to straighten and extend fully your body, for example when waking or reaching. – *n.* **1** an act of stretching, especially the body. **2** a period of time; a spell.

stretcher *n.* a moveable bed for carrying a sick or wounded person. – *n.* **stretcher-bearer.**

strict (strikt) *adj.* **1** demanding obedience or close observance of rules; severe. **2** that must be obeyed: *The rules are strict but fair.* – *adv.* **strictly.** – *n.* **strictness.**

stride (strīd) *n.* **1** a single long step in walking. **2** (usually in *plural*) a measure of progress or development: *We have made great strides.* – *vb.* **striding, strode** (strōd), **stridden** (stri dĕn).

strife (strīf) *n.* bitter conflict or fighting.

strike (strīk) *vb.* **striking, struck** (struk) **1** to hit; to give a blow to; to come or bring into heavy contact with: *Her head struck the doorframe.* **2** to make a particular impression on: *It strikes me as a great idea.* **3** to occur to. **4** to ignite through friction: *strike a match.* **5** (of a clock) to announce the time with a chime. **6** to happen suddenly: *Disaster struck.* **7** to find a source of: *We've struck oil.* **8** to stop working as part of a collective protest against an employer. – *n.* **1** an act of hitting or dealing a blow. **2** a usually collective refusal to work, as a protest against an employer.

PRONUNCIATION GUIDE	
fat a	all ö
fate ā	foot oo
fast ä	moon ōō
among å	boy oi
met e	house ow
mean ē	demon ŏ
silent ĕ	thing th
loch hh	this Th
fin i	but u
line ī	mute ū
quick kw	fur û
got o	brochure ŭ
note ō	vision zh

string (string) *n.* **1** thin cord. **2** any of a set of stretched wire, catgut, nylon vibrated to produce sound in musical instruments.

strip (strip) *n.* a long narrow piece of anything: *a strip of paper.* – *vb.* **stripping, stripped 1** to remove by peeling or pulling off: *Strip off the old paint.* **2** to take your clothes off.

    strip cartoon *n.* a sequence of drawings, e.g. in a newspaper, telling an adventure story.

stripe (strīp) *n.* a band of colour: *The Irish flag has stripes of green, white, and orange.*

strive (strīv) *vb.* **striving, strove** (strōv), **striven** (stri věn) to try hard; to struggle.

strode. See **stride**.

stroke (strōk) *n.* **1** an act of striking: *a stroke of the bat.* **2** a single movement with a pen, paintbrush, etc. **3** a gentle caress or other touching movement. **4** a sudden loss of consciousness caused by the bursting or blocking of a blood vessel in the brain. – *vb.* **stroking, stroked** to caress: *Di stroked her dog.*

stroll (strōl) *vb.* **strolling, strolled** to walk in a slow leisurely way.

strong (strong) *adj.* **1** exerting great force or power: *Elephants are very strong.* **2** able to withstand rough treatment; robust. **3** firmly held or boldly expressed: *Sam has strong views on politics.* **4** (of light, etc.) intense.

    strong point *n.* a thing in which a person excels.

strove. See **strive**.

struck. See **strike**.

structure (struk chŭr) *n.* **1** the way in which the parts of a thing are arranged or organized. **2** a thing built from many smaller parts.

struggle (stru gěl) *vb.* **struggling, struggled** to move the body around violently in an attempt to get free. – *n.* **1** an act of struggling. **2** a contest: *a struggle for power.*

strum (strum) *vb.* **strumming, strummed** to play a stringed musical instrument with sweeps of the fingers.

strung. See **string**.

● **Stuarts** The House of Stuart was a royal family that ruled Scotland from 1371 to 1603 and England and Scotland from 1603 to 1715.

stub (stub) *n.* a short piece, of a cigarette or a pencil, etc., left after the rest has been used up. – *vb.* **stubbing, stubbed** to bump your toe against a hard surface.

stubble (stu běl) *n.* **1** the mass of short stalks left in the ground after a crop has been harvested. **2** a short growth of beard.

stubborn (stu bŏrn) *adj.* obstinate. – *n.* **stubbornness**.

stuck. See **stick²**.

student (stū děnt) *n.* a person following a formal course of study.

The Stuart King James VI of Scotland became James I of England when the two crowns united in 1603. The first Union flag (above) was created in 1606 by combining the crosses of St George and St Andrew, the national flags of England and Scotland. With the union with Ireland in 1800 the saltire of St Patrick was added.

The **structure** of something is the way it is put together. We see evidence of structure all around us. Things that are well constructed are efficient and last.

Scientists study the molecular structure of, for example, the crystals of an element.

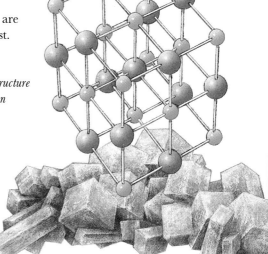

The structure of a building such as a skyscraper – involving many people such as architects, builders, and civil engineers – is complex.

The sophisticated structure of an artifical limb requires careful and painstaking design.

Stupid is from the Latin word *stupidus*, taken from the verb *stupere* meaning 'to be amazed'. At one time the word meant 'stunned with surprise', but took on its present meaning in the 16th century.

studio (**stū** di ō) *n.* **studios 1** the workroom of an artist or photographer. **2** a room for recording and broadcasting.

study (**stu** di) *vb.* **studies, studying, studied 1** to learn about a subject by giving time and attention to it. **2** to look at or examine closely, or think about carefully: *Study the facts before deciding.* – *n.* a private room where quiet work or study is carried out.

stuff (stuf) *n.* **1** any material, substance, or equipment. **2** luggage; belongings: *That's my stuff.* **3** matter; essence: *the very stuff of life.* – *vb.* **stuffing, stuffed 1** to fill the hollow or hollowed-out part of, for example a chicken or pepper, with a seasoned mixture of other foods (**stuffing**). **2** to fill to capacity. **3** to cram or thrust in: *Stephen stuffed his shirts into the case.*

stumble (**stum** bĕl) *vb.* **stumbling, stumbled** to lose your balance; to trip. – *n.* an act of stumbling.

stumbling-block *n.* an obstacle or difficulty.

stump (stump) *n.* **1** the part of a felled or fallen tree left in the ground. **2** the short part of anything left after the larger part has been removed: *the stump of a tooth.* – *vb.* **stumping, stumped** to baffle or perplex: *I'm stumped for an answer to your question.*

stun (stun) *vb.* **stunning, stunned** to make unconscious by a blow to the head.

stung. See **sting**.

stunt[1] (stunt) *vb.* **stunting, stunted** to prevent the full growth of: *Lack of sun stunted the plants.*

stunt[2] (stunt) *n.* a daring act or spectacular event: *an acrobatic stunt.*

stupid (**stū** pid) *adj.* having a lack of common sense. – *n.* **stupidity**.

sturdy (**stûr** di) *adj.* **sturdier, sturdiest** strongly built; robust: *a sturdy tree.*

stutter (**stu** tĕr) *n.* a stammer. – *vb.* **stuttering, stuttered**.

●**Stuyvesant, Peter** (1592-1672) was governor of the Dutch colony of New Netherland from 1646 to 1664 when he was forced to surrender the colony to the British.

Peter Stuyvesant was an unpopular governor of the colony of New Netherland. When the British captured it in 1664, the colonists readily surrendered.

sty[1] (stī) *n.* **sties** a pen in which pigs are kept.

sty[2] or **stye** (stī) *n.* **sties** or **styes** a tiny swelling on the eyelid, at the base of the lash.

style (stīl) *n.* **1** a manner or way of doing something, e.g. writing, speaking, painting, or designing buildings. **2** a striking elegance: *She dresses with style.* **3** a small stalk-like part on the inside of a flower. – *adj.* **stylish**.

●**Styx** in Greek mythology, was a river in the Underworld (Hades) across which the souls of the dead were ferried by Charon.

sub- (sub-) *prefix* **1** under or below: *submarine.* **2** secondary; lower in rank or importance: *subdivision; subsoil,* etc. **3** less than: *subhuman.* **4** a part or division of: *subcommittee.*

subaqua (sub **ak** wå) *adj.* of, for, or for use in underwater activities.

subject (**sub** jikt) *n.* **1** a matter or topic under discussion or consideration: *Sandra is the subject of everyone's interest.* **2** an area of learning that forms a course of study: *Geography is Simon's favourite subject.* **3** a person under the ultimate rule of a monarch or government: *a British subject.* **4** in grammar, a word or phrase referring to the person or thing that performs the action of a verb, as in '*He* dropped it' and '*It* was dropped by him'. – *adj.* **1** showing a tendency; prone: *She's subject to backache.* **2** dependent: *We're all subject to the law.* – (sůb **jekt**) *vb.* **subjecting, subjected 1** to cause to undergo or experience: *"I won't subject you to any pain," said the dentist.* **2** to bring under the control. – *n.* **subjection**.

submarine (**sub** må rēn) *n.* a vessel, especially military, able to travel underwater. – *adj.* under the surface of the sea: *Ann is studying submarine animals such as whales.*

submerge (sůb **mûrj**) *vb.* **submerging, submerged** to plunge or sink under the surface of water or other liquid; to overwhelm: *Sue is submerged with work.* – *n.* **submersion**.

submit (sůb **mit**) *vb.* **submitting, submitted 1** to give in, especially to the wishes or control of another person: *We submitted to their decision.* **2** to present for consideration by others.

submissive *adj.* meek; obedient.

subscribe (sůb **skrīb**) *vb.* **subscribing, subscribed** to pay money, for example a membership fee. – *n.* **subscriber**.

subscription (sůb **skrip** shŏn) *n.* a payment made when subscribing to a magazine, club.

subside (sŭb sīd) *vb.* **subsiding, subsided**
1 (of land, buildings, etc.) to sink to a lower level; to settle. **2** to die down: *His fury subsided.*
– *n.* **subsidence** (sŭb sīd ĕns) or (**sub** si dĕns).

substance (**sub** stăns) *n.* **1** the matter or material that a thing is made of; anything that can be seen or touched. **2** a particular kind of matter: *a sticky substance.* **3** the essence or basic meaning of something.

substantial (sŭb **stan** shăl) *adj.* **1** large in amount, or importance. **2** solidly built.

substitute (**sub** sti tūt) *n.* a person or thing that takes the place of, or is used instead of, another: *Saccharin is a substitute for sugar.*

subtle (**su** tĕl) *adj.* **1** not straightforwardly or obviously stated or displayed. **2** (of flavours, etc.) extremely faint or delicate.

subtract (sŭb **trakt**) *vb.* **subtracting, subtracted** to take one number or quantity from another; to deduct. – *n.* **subtraction.**

suburb (**sub** ûrb) *n.* (often in *plural*) a district, especially residential, on the edge of a town.
suburban (sŭ **bûr** băn) *adj.* of or in a suburb.

subway (**sub** wā) *n.* **1** a passage under a road or railway, especially for pedestrians, also for pipes, etc. **2** (*US*) an underground railway.

succeed (sŭk **sēd**) *vb.* **succeeding, succeeded 1** to achieve an aim or purpose: *Sabina succeeded in learning Czech.* **2** to develop or turn out as planned. **3** to come next after.

success (sŭk **ses**) *n.* **1** the state of having succeeded; a favourable development or outcome: *The play was a huge success.* **2** the attainment of fame, power, or wealth. – *adj.*
successful. – *adv.* **successfully.**
succession *n.* a series of people or things coming one after the other.

such (such) *adj.* **1** of that kind, or the same or a similar kind: *You can't reason with such a person.*
2 so great: *I'm not such a fool as to believe that.*
– *adv.* extremely: *It was such a lovely present.*

suck (suk) *vb.* **sucking, sucked 1** to draw liquid into the mouth. **2** to hold in the mouth and draw the flavour from a sweet, etc.

suckle (**su** kĕl) *vb.* **suckling, suckled** to suck milk from a breast or udder.

● **Sudan.** See Supplement, **Countries.**

sudden (**su** dĕn) *adj.* happening quickly or unexpectedly. – *n.* **suddenness.**

sue (sū) *vb.* **suing, sued** to take legal proceedings against a person or company.

● **Suez Canal** This is the world's longest canal (160 km) and links Port Said (pronounced sīd) on the Mediterranean and Suez on the Red Sea. The canal was begun in 1859 by the French engineer, Ferdinand de Lesseps.

Submersibles like this Deepstar IV *can sink to depths of 1,200 metres and are used in underwater exploration, surveying wrecks, laying pipelines, etc.*

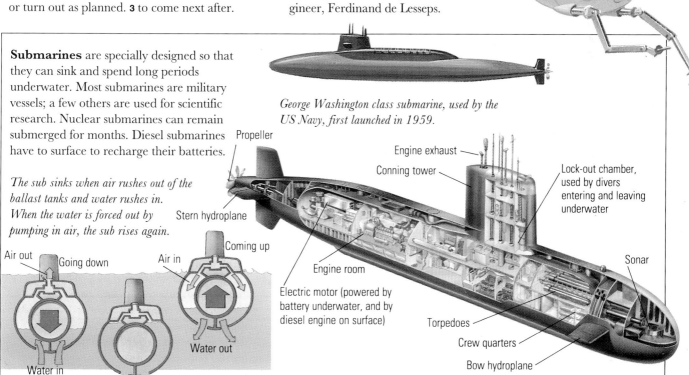

Submarines are specially designed so that they can sink and spend long periods underwater. Most submarines are military vessels; a few others are used for scientific research. Nuclear submarines can remain submerged for months. Diesel submarines have to surface to recharge their batteries.

The sub sinks when air rushes out of the ballast tanks and water rushes in. When the water is forced out by pumping in air, the sub rises again.

George Washington class submarine, used by the US Navy, first launched in 1959.

Air out — Going down
Air in — Coming up
Water in
Water out

Propeller
Stern hydroplane
Engine exhaust
Conning tower
Lock-out chamber, used by divers entering and leaving underwater
Engine room
Electric motor (powered by battery underwater, and by diesel engine on surface)
Torpedoes
Crew quarters
Bow hydroplane
Sonar

suffer (su fĕr) *vb.* **suffering, suffered 1** to undergo or endure physical or mental pain or other unpleasantness. **2** to deteriorate as a result of something. – *n.* **sufferer**. – *n.* **suffering**.

sufficient (sŭ **fi** shĕnt) *adj.* enough; adequate.

suffix (su fiks) *n.* a word ending to mark a grammatical inflection or form a derivative, for example the -*tude* in *certitude*.

suffocate (su fŏ kāt) *vb.* **suffocating, suffocated** to kill with or die from lack of air. – *adj.* **suffocating**. – *n.* **suffocation**.

sugar (shoo går) *n.* a sweet-tasting substance found in sugar-cane and other plants, refined into white or brown crystals. – *vb.* **sugaring, sugared**.

suggest (sŭ **jest**) *vb.* **suggesting, suggested 1** to put forward as a possibility. **2** to make someone think of; to create an impression of. **suggestion** *n.* **1** a thing suggested; a proposal or recommendation. **2** a hint or trace.

suicide (soo i sīd) *n.* the act of killing yourself deliberately. – *adj.* **suicidal**.

suit (soot) *n.* **1** a jacket with trousers or a skirt, made from the same material. **2** any of the four groups into which a pack of playing cards is divided. **3** a legal action taken against someone. – *vb.* **suiting, suited 1** to be acceptable to or what is required by: *What time would suit you to see me?* **2** to be in harmony with or attractive to: *That scarf suits you.* – **suit yourself** to do what you want to do, without considering others. **suitable** *adj.* that suits; appropriate or agreeable; convenient. – *n.* **suitability**.

suite (swēt) *n.* **1** a set of rooms. **2** a matching set of furniture.

sulk (sulk) *vb.* **sulking, sulked** to be silent out of bad temper.

sullen (su lĕn) *adj.* silently and stubbornly angry.

sulphur (sul fŭr) *n.* an element (symbol **S**), a yellow brittle non-metallic mineral that burns with a blue flame and a choking smell.

sultry (sul tri) *adj.* **sultrier, sultriest** (of weather) hot and humid. – *adv.* **sultrily**.

sum (sum) *n.* **1** the amount produced when numbers or quantities are added together: *The sum of three and three is six.* **2** an amount of money.

summary (su må ri) *n.* **summaries** a short account outlining the main points.

summer (su mĕr) *n.* the warmest season of the year, between spring and autumn.

summit (su mit) *n.* the highest point; peak.

summon (su mŏn) *vb.* **summoning, summoned** to order a person to come or appear, for example in a court of law.

sun (sun) *n.* **Sun** the star that is the source of light, heat, and gravitational pull for all the planets in the Earth's planetary system.
sunflower *n.* a large tall-stemmed flower with yellow petals and edible seeds.
sunlight *n.* light from the sun. – *adj.* **sunlit**.
sunrise *n.* the Sun's appearance above the horizon in the east in the morning.
sunset *n.* the Sun's disappearance below the horizon in the west in the evening.

Sunday (sun di) *n.* the first day of the week and for most Christians the day of worship. – **a month of Sundays** a very long time.

sung. See **sing**.

sunk. See **sink**.

sunken (sung kĕn). See **sink**. – *adj.* at a lower level than the surrounding area: *a sunken pond.*

super- (soo pĕr-) *prefix* **1** great or extreme in size or degree: *supertanker*. **2** above or beyond: *supernatural*. **3** outstanding: *superhero*.

superb (soo pûrb) *adj.* **1** (*colloquial*) outstandingly excellent. **2** magnificent.

superficial (soo pĕr fi shål) *adj.* **1** of, on, or near the surface: *a superficial cut.* **2** not thorough or in-depth – *n.* **superficiality** (soo pĕr fish i **al** i ti). – *adv.* **superficially**.

superior (soo pĕr i ŏr) *adj.* **1** higher in rank or position. **2** better in a particular way; of high quality: *Sue's woodwork is far superior to Jane's.* **3** arrogant: *She laughed at our efforts in a superior way.* – *n.* a person of higher rank or position. – *n.* **superiority** (soo pĕr i **o** ri ti).

superlative (soo pûr lå tiv) *adj.* (of an adjective or adverb) expressing the highest degree of a particular quality, for example *nicest* and *most beautiful*.

supersede (soo pĕr sēd) *vb.* **superseding, superseded** to take the place of: *Word processors have largely superseded typewriters.*

supersonic (soo pĕr son ik) *adj.* capable of travelling faster than the speed of sound.

superstition (soo pĕr sti shŏn) *n.* belief in a mysterious influence that certain objects, actions, or occurrences have on events, people's lives, etc. – *adj.* **superstitious**.

supervise (soo pĕr vīz) *vb.* **supervising, supervised** to be in overall charge of; to oversee: *The editor supervises my work.* – *n.* **supervision**. – *n.* **supervisor**.

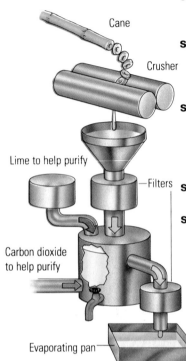

Cane

Crusher

Lime to help purify

Filters

Carbon dioxide to help purify

Evaporating pan

Making sugar from sugar cane: the stems of the canes are crushed and the juice filtered and purified. The sugar solution is evaporated to produce sugar crystals. Sugar beet is treated in a similar way.

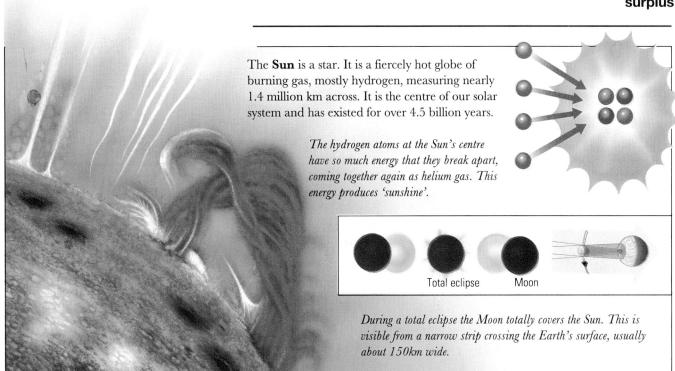

The **Sun** is a star. It is a fiercely hot globe of burning gas, mostly hydrogen, measuring nearly 1.4 million km across. It is the centre of our solar system and has existed for over 4.5 billion years.

The hydrogen atoms at the Sun's centre have so much energy that they break apart, coming together again as helium gas. This energy produces 'sunshine'.

Total eclipse   Moon

During a total eclipse the Moon totally covers the Sun. This is visible from a narrow strip crossing the Earth's surface, usually about 150km wide.

supper (**su** pĕr) *n.* a light evening meal.

supple (**su** pĕl) *adj.* bending easily; flexible: *An acrobat's body has to be supple.* – *n.* **suppleness**.

supplement (**su** plĕ mĕnt) *n.* a thing added to make something complete or to make up a deficiency: *Simon takes vitamins as a supplement to his diet.* – (**su** plĕ ment) *vb.* **supplementing, supplemented** to add to.

supply (sŭ **plī**) *vb.* **supplies, supplying, supplied** to provide or make available: *The shop supplies us with fresh vegetables.* – *n.* **supplies 1** an amount supplied regularly. **2** a stock. – *n.* **supplier**.

support (sŭ **pört**) *vb.* **supporting, supported 1** to keep upright or in place; to bear the weight of: *The pillars support the roof.* **2** to give active encouragement to: *We totally support your views on equal rights for all.* **3** to provide with the means necessary for living or existing: *He supports his four children alone.* – *n.* the act of supporting or the state of being supported.

suppose (sŭ **pōz**) *vb.* **supposing, supposed 1** to consider likely or probable: *We suppose you are the right person for the job.* **2** to treat as a fact for the sake of argument: *Let us suppose he's out.*

supreme (soo **prēm**) *adj.* **1** of highest rank, power, or importance. **2** best.

sure (shör) or (shoor) *adj.* **1** confident beyond doubt in your belief or knowledge; convinced: *Are you sure you want to go abroad?* **2** guaranteed or certain: *It will be a sure winner.* – *n.* **sureness**.

surely *adv.* **1** without doubt; certainly. **2** (in questions and exclamations) it must be that: *Surely you're not leaving already!*

surf (sûrf) *n.* the foam produced on the surface of the sea by breaking waves.

surface (**sûr** fĭs) *n.* **1** the outer side of anything: *The surface of the table is polished.* **2** external appearance, rather than underlying reality: *On the surface the plan seems good.* – *adj.* at, on, or relating to a surface. – *vb.* **surfacing, surfaced** to rise to the surface of a liquid: *The diver surfaced in the middle of the lake.*

surge (sûrj) *n.* **1** a sudden sharp increase: *There was a surge of interest in chess following the world championships.* **2** a rising and falling of the sea.

surgeon (**sûr** jŏn) *n.* a doctor specializing in surgery.

surgery (**sûr** jĕ ri) *n.* **surgeries 1** the treatment of disease or injury by cutting into the patient's body to operate directly on, or remove, the affected part. **2** the place where a community doctor or dentist carries out treatment.

●**Surinam**. See Supplement, **Countries**.

surname (**sûr** nām) *n.* a family name.

surpass (sŭr **päs**) *vb.* **surpassing, surpassed** to be better than: *Bob's exam results surpassed all our expectations.*

surplus (**sûr** plŭs) *n.* an amount more than is required or used. – *adj.* extra.

surprise (sûr **prīz**) *n.* something sudden or unexpected: *Your visit is a complete surprise.* – *vb.* **surprising, surprised** to cause surprise. – *adj.* **surprised**. – *adj.* **surprising**.

surrender (sǔ **ren** děr) *vb.* **surrendering, surrendered** to admit defeat by giving yourself up to an enemy; to give in. – *n.*

surround (sǔ **rownd**) *vb.* **surrounding, surrounded** to be on all sides; to encircle: *The sea surrounds the island.* – *adj.* **surrounding**. **surroundings** *n.* (*plural*) environment; the places and things round about.

survey (sûr **vā**) *vb.* **surveys, surveying, surveyed 1** to look at or examine in detail: *We need to survey the plans.* **2** to measure land heights and distances for the purposes of drawing a detailed map. – (**sûr** vā) *n.* **surveys**.

survive (sûr **vīv**) *vb.* **surviving, survived** to remain alive or undamaged in spite of; to come through: *The old barn survived the storm.* – *n.* **survival**. – *adj.* **surviving**. – *n.* **survivor**.

suspect (sǔ **spekt**) *vb.* **suspecting, suspected 1** to consider likely: *We suspect you are wrong.* **2** to think a person possibly guilty of a crime or other wrongdoing. – (**su** spekt) *n.* a person suspected of committing a crime, etc.

suspend (sǔ **spend**) *vb.* **suspending, suspended 1** to hang or hang up: *The hammock was suspended from the two trees.* **2** to delay or postpone: *The meeting is suspended until next week.*

suspense (sǔ **spens**) *n.* a state of anxiety or excited uncertainty. – *adj.* **suspenseful**.

suspension (sǔ **spen** shǒn) *n.* **1** the act of suspending or the state of being suspended. **2** a mixture of solid particles in a liquid or gas.

suspicion (sǔ **spi** shǒn) *n.* **1** the feeling of suspecting. **2** an act of suspecting; a belief or opinion based on slender evidence. – **under suspicion** suspected of a crime. **suspicious** *adj.* arousing suspicion.

swallow¹ (swo **lō**) *vb.* **swallowing, swallowed 1** to allow to pass down the throat to the stomach: *Sal swallowed the nasty medicine.* **2** to stifle or repress: *Simon swallowed his pride.* – *n.* an act of swallowing: *a quick swallow.*

swallow² (swo **lō**) *n.* an insect-eating bird with long pointed wings and a forked tail.

swam. See **swim**.

Leaves fall into the water of shallow lakes; a layer of peat accumulates to form a swamp.

swamp (swomp) *n.* permanently wet, spongy ground, especially overgrown or forested. – *vb.* **swamping, swamped** to overwhelm or inundate: *Stan is swamped with work.*

swan (swon) *n.* a large water-bird with a long curving neck.

swarm (swörm) *n.* a large group of bees flying off in search of a new home.

swat (swot) *vb.* **swatting, swatted** to crush, especially a fly, with a heavy slapping blow.

sway (swā) *vb.* **swaying, swayed** to cause to swing from side to side, especially slowly and smoothly: *The trees sway in the wind.*

● **Swaziland**. See Supplement, **Countries**.

swear (swār) *vb.* **swearing, swore** (swör), **sworn** (swörn) **1** to use vulgar language. **2** to promise solemnly, as if by taking an oath.

sweat (swet) *n.* the salty moisture that the body gives off through the skin's pores; perspiration. – *vb.* **sweating, sweated** or **sweat**.

Swede (swēd) *n.* a native or citizen of SWEDEN. **Swedish** *n.* the language of SWEDEN. – *adj.* of, or relating to, SWEDEN, its people, etc.

swede (swēd) *n.* a large turnip with yellow flesh.

Swallows return from South Africa to the same nesting site in Europe each year. Their nests are built against buildings.

●**Sweden** is a mountainous country in north-west Europe. Manufacturing, mining, and forestry are the main sources of the country's prosperity. The capital is Stockholm. See also Supplement, **Countries**.

sweep (swēp) *vb.* **sweeping, swept** (swept) **1** to clean or remove dirt, dust, etc. with a brush or broom: *He swept the room.* **2** to take, carry, or push suddenly and with irresistible force: *The crowd was swept behind the railings.* – *n.* **1** an act of sweeping. **2** a sweeping movement, etc.

sweet (swēt) *adj.* **1** tasting like sugar; not sour, salty, or bitter: *Honey is sweet.* **2** pleasing to any of the senses, especially smell and hearing: *It smells sweet.* **3** charming: *Aren't the kittens sweet?* – *n.* any small sugar-based confection. – *n.* **sweetness**.

sweetcorn *n.* kernels of a variety of maize.

sweeten *vb.* **sweetening, sweetened** to make food sweet or sweeter.

sweet tooth *n.* a fondness for sweet foods.

swell (swel) *vb.* **swelling, swelled, swollen** (swō len) or **swelled** **1** to make or become bigger through injury, infection, or filling with liquid or air: *Your eye is swollen as a result of the punch.* **2** to increase in number, size, etc.

swept. See **sweep**.

swerve (swûrv) *vb.* **swerving, swerved** to turn or move aside suddenly and sharply: *We swerved to avoid running over the rabbit.*

swift (swift) *adj.* **1** fast-moving. **2** done quickly. – *n.* a small fast-flying bird similar to the swallow. – *adv.* **swiftly**. – *n.* **swiftness**.

●**Swift, Jonathan** (1667-1745) was an Irish writer, poet, and churchman. His most famous book is *Gulliver's Travels.*

swim (swim) *vb.* **swimming, swam** (swam), **swum** (swum) **1** to move through water by moving the arms and legs or (in animals) other parts of the body. **2** to cross a stretch of water in this way. **3** to be flooded or awash: *The cellar is swimming with water after the flood.* – *n.* a spell of swimming. – *n.* **swimmer**.

swindle (swin del) *vb.* **swindling, swindled** to cheat or trick: *She swindled me out of £10.*

swine (swīn) *n.* **swine** a pig.

swing (swing) *vb.* **swinging, swung** (swung) **1** to (cause to) open, close, or move to and fro: *The door is swinging on its hinges.* **2** to undergo a sudden sharp change or changes: *Public opinion is swinging against the government.* – *n.* **1** an act, manner, or spell of swinging: *a swing of the axe; the swing of a golf club.* **2** a seat suspended from a frame or branch, for a child to swing on. – **in full swing** at the height of liveliness.

Swiss (swis) *adj.* of, or relating to, SWITZERLAND or its people. – *n.* a native or citizen of SWITZERLAND.

switch (swich) *n.* a button, knob, or lever that makes or breaks an electrical circuit, turning an appliance on or off. – *vb.* **switching, switched 1** to turn an appliance on or off by means of a switch. **2** to exchange one thing or person for another, especially quickly and without notice: *Sam switched the dirty cup for the clean one.*

●**Switzerland**. See Supplement, **Countries**.

swollen. See **swell**.

swoop (swōōp) *vb.* **swooping, swooped** to fly down with a fast sweeping movement: *An eagle swoops on its prey.* – *n.* an act of swooping.

swop. See **swap**.

sword (sörd) *n.* a hand weapon with a long blade.

Greek kopi (curved sword)

Roman sword

A 15th-century cut and thrust sword

sword dance *n.* in Scotland, a dance performed over an arrangement of swords laid on the ground.

swordfish *n.* a large sea-fish with a very long and pointed upper jaw used as a weapon.

swore. See **swear**.

sworn (swörn). See **swear**. – *adj.* bound as if by an oath: *The brothers are in fact sworn enemies.*

swot (swot) (*colloquial*) *vb.* **swotting, swotted** to study hard and seriously.

swum. See **swim**.

swung. See **swing**.

The handle of a sword is called a hilt. Sword blades may have one or two cutting edges and some are curved. Very narrow swords are called rapiers. Today swords are used mainly in the sport of fencing or on military ceremonial occasions.

● **Sydney** is the largest city in AUSTRALIA and the capital of New South Wales. It is famous for its steel-arch bridge and opera house.

Australia's most famous building – the Sydney Opera House – under construction. The sail-like roofs were particularly difficult to erect. The building was completed in 1973.

syllable (**si** lå bĕl) *n.* any of the parts, consisting of one or more sounds and usually including a vowel, that a word can be divided into: *The word 'telephone' has three syllables, 'te', 'le', and 'phone'.*

symbol (**sim** bŏl) *n.* a thing that represents or stands for another: *The dove is a symbol of peace. Red is the symbol of danger.*
symbolic (sim **bol** ik) *adj.* relating to symbols.
symbolize or **symbolise** *vb.* **symbolizing, symbolized** to be a symbol of; to stand for.

symmetry (**si** mĕ tri) *n.* **symmetries** exact similarity between two parts or halves, as if one were a mirror image of the other. – *adj.* **symmetrical** (si **met** ri kål). – *adv.* **symmetrically.**

sympathetic (sim på **thet** ik) *adj.* **1** acting or done out of sympathy. **2** in keeping with your mood or feelings: *Her ideas are sympathetic to mine.* – *adv.* **sympathetically.**

sympathy (**sim** på thi) *n.* **sympathies 1** a deep and genuine understanding of the sadness or suffering of others. **2** loyal or approving support or agreement: *The hospital porters are on strike in sympathy with the nurses.*
sympathize or **sympathise** *vb.* **sympathizing, sympathized** to feel or express sympathy.

symphony (**sim** fŏ ni) *n.* **symphonies** a long musical work in several parts, or movements, played by a full orchestra.

symptom (**simp** tŏm) *n.* an indication of the presence of illness: *A fever and rash are symptoms of chickenpox.*

synagogue (**si** nå gog) *n.* a Jewish place of worship.

synecdoche (si **nek** dŏ ki) *n.* a figure of speech in which a part of something is used to denote the whole thing, or the whole to denote a part, as *wiser heads* meaning *wiser people.*

synod (**si** nŏd) *n.* a council of the Church.

synonym (**si** nŏ nim) *n.* a word having the same, or very nearly the same, meaning as another: *'Anger' and 'fury' are synonyms.*
synonymous (si **non** i mŭs) *adj.* having the same meaning: *'Little' and 'small' are synonymous.*

synopsis (si **nop** sis) *n.* **synopses** (si **nop** sēz) a brief outline, e.g. of the plot of a book.

syntax (**sin** taks) *n.* the positioning of words in a sentence and their relationship to each other.

synthetic (sin **thet** ik) *adj.* created artificially by combining chemical substances.

● **Syria**. See Supplement, **Countries**.

syringe (si **rinj**) *n.* a medical instrument for injecting or drawing off liquid, consisting of a hollow cylinder with a plunger inside and a thin hollow needle attached. – *vb.* **syringing, syringed** to inject using a syringe.

syrup (**si** rŭp) *n.* the thick sweet sticky concentrated juice of various plants, for example the sugar-cane and the maple.

system (**sis** tĕm) *n.* **1** a set of interconnected or interrelated parts forming a complex whole: *the transport system; the human digestive system.* **2** a way of working; a method. **3** society, or the network of institutions that control it: *You can't beat the system.*
systematic (si stĕ **mat** ik) *adj.* **1** making use of a method. **2** methodical. – *adv.* **systematically.**

Tt

tab (tab) *n.* a small flap or strip of material attached to an article for hanging it up, etc.

tabernacle (**ta** běr na kěl) *n.* a place of worship for various religious groups.

table (**tā** běl) *n.* **1** a piece of furniture consisting of a flat surface supported by legs. **2** a group of figures, etc. arranged in columns and rows.

table tennis *n.* a game based on tennis which is played indoors on a table with small bats and a light hollow ball.

An elaborately carved and gilded French 16th-century table with an onyx top.

A nest of red and gold lacquered French tables of 1860. The set of tables of different sizes are designed to fit one over the other.

tablet (**tab** lit) *n.* **1** a small solid measured amount of a medicine; a pill. **2** a piece of soap.

tabloid (**tab** loid) *n.* a newspaper with small pages and many photographs.

tack (tak) *n.* **1** a short nail with a sharp point and a broad flat head. **2** a long loose stitch used to hold material together while it is being sewn properly. **3** saddle, bridle, etc. for a horse.

tackle (**ta** kěl) *n.* **1** in sport, the act of trying to get the ball away from a player on the opposing team. **2** the equipment needed for a particular sport or occupation. – *vb.* **tackling, tackled 1** to try to solve a problem. **2** in sport, to try to get the ball from a player.

tact (takt) *n.* the ability to deal with difficult situations so as to avoid offending or upsetting other people. – *adj.* **tactful**.

tactics (**tak** tiks) *n.* (*singular*) the method used to achieve an end or aim.

tadpole (**tad** pōl) *n.* the larva of the frog or toad, with a rounded body and long tail.

tag (tag) *n.* a piece of material, etc. that carries information about the object to which it is attached: *She looked at the price tag to see how much the coat cost.*

tail (tāl) *n.* **1** the part of an animal's, bird's, or fish's body that sticks out from the lower end of the back. **2** the last or rear part: *the tail of the storm.* **3** (in *plural*) the reverse side of a coin, usually the side which does not bear a portrait. – *vb.* **tailing, tailed** to follow closely: *The police car tailed the burglars for many kilometres.*

tailor (**tā** lŏr) *n.* a person who makes clothes to measure, especially for men.

taint (tānt) *vb.* **tainting, tainted** to affect or spoil by pollution or contamination.

● **Tajikistan**. See Supplement, **Countries**.

PRONUNCIATION GUIDE

fat **a**	all **ö**
fate **ā**	foot **oo**
fast **ä**	moon **ōō**
among **å**	boy **oi**
met **e**	house **ow**
mean **ē**	demon **ỏ**
silent **ẻ**	thing **th**
loch **hh**	this **Th**
fin **i**	but **u**
line **ī**	mute **ū**
quick **kw**	fur **û**
got **o**	brochure **ů**
note **ō**	vision **zh**

take (tāk) *vb.* **taking, took** (took), **taken 1** to reach out for and grasp, lift, pull, etc.: *She took the book down from the shelf.* **2** to move, carry, or lead to another place: *They took him some grapes.* **3** to accept as true or valid: *I'll have to take her word for it.* **4** to commit yourself to: *He took her side in the argument.* **5** to need or require: *This job will take all day to finish.* **6** to use as a means of transport: *He took the bus.* **7** to remove or borrow without permission: *He took her coat by mistake.* **8** to eat or drink: *Do you take sugar in coffee?* – *adj.* **taken.** – *vb.* **take after** to be like a parent or relation in appearance or character. – *vb.* **take down** to make a written note or record of. – *vb.* **take off 1** to remove. **2** (of an aircraft) to leave the ground. – *vb.* **take on 1** to agree to do; to undertake. **2** to give employment to someone. **3** to challenge or compete against an opponent. – *vb.* **take over** to assume control of something.

takeaway *n.* a cooked meal prepared and bought in a restaurant but taken away and eaten somewhere else.

takeover *n.* the act of taking control of something, especially a company.

takings *n.* (in *plural*) the amount of money taken at a concert, in a shop, etc.

tale (tāl) *n.* a story.

talent (ta lềnt) *n.* a natural skill or ability, especially for art, music, etc. – *adj.* **talented.**

talk (tök) *vb.* **talking, talked** to express ideas, feelings, and thoughts to someone in words; to have a conversation or discussion about something. – *n.* **1** a conversation or discussion. **2** (often in *plural*) a formal discussion or series of negotiations. – *n.* **talker.** – *vb.* **talk back** to answer rudely. – *vb.* **talk over** to discuss.

talkative *adj.* talking a lot.

tall (töl) *adj.* **1** of above average height. **2** having a stated height: *one metre tall.* – *n.* **tallness.**

tallow (ta lō) *n.* hard fat from sheep and cattle used to make candles, soap, etc.

Talmud (tal mood) *n.* the books containing the ancient Jewish law. – *adj.* **Talmudic.**

talon (ta lỏn) *n.* a hooked claw of a bird of prey.

tame (tām) *adj.* (of animals) used to living or working with people; not wild or dangerous. – *vb.* **taming, tamed 1** to make an animal used to living or working with people. **2** to subdue. – *n.* **tameness.** – *n.* **tamer.**

tamper (tam pểr) *vb.* **tampering, tampered** to interfere or meddle with.

tan (tan) *n.* **1** the brown colour of the skin after exposure to the sun's ultraviolet rays. **2** a tawny brown colour. – *adj.* tawny brown in colour. – *vb.* **tanning, tanned 1** to become brown in the sun. **2** to convert animal hides into leather.

tandem (tan dểm) *n.* a type of cycle for two people, with two seats and two sets of pedals.

tangerine (tan jẻ rēn) *n.* a variety of orange with a loose reddish-orange skin and flesh.

tangible (tan jả bểl) *adj.* **1** able to be felt by touch. **2** real or definite: *tangible evidence.*

tangle (tang gểl) *n.* **1** an untidy, confused, or knotted state, for example of hair. **2** a confused state or situation. – *vb.* **tangling, tangled.**

tank (tangk) *n.* **1** a large container for holding, storing, or transporting liquids or gas. **2** a heavy military vehicle armed with guns.

tanker *n.* a ship, lorry, or aircraft which transports large amounts of liquid, often fuel.

Tanks were first used in the First World War (from 1916), but their full potential was not realized until the success of the German tank-borne invasion of France in the Second World War.

The French NC2 (1931) had a special suspension. The British Vickers Medium Mark II (below) was one of the most successful tanks built between the two World Wars. It carried a crew of five.

The Americans developed the M-60 tank in the 1950s when they were faced with the Russian-built tanks of the North Korean army.

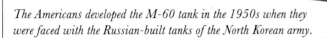

tantrum (**tan** trŭm) *n.* a fit of bad temper.

● **Tanzania**. See Supplement, **Countries**.

taoiseach (**tē** shăhh) *n.* the prime minister of the Republic of Ireland.

Taoism (**tow** i zĕm) or (**dow** i zĕm) *n.* a Chinese philosophical and religious system based on the teachings of Lao-Tzu (*c.* 6th century BC). – *n.* & *adj.* **Taoist**.

A statue of a Taoist founder, Lao-Tzu, riding an ox.

tap¹ (tap) *n.* **1** the sound made by a quick or light touch, knock, or blow. **2** tap-dancing. – *vb.* **tapping, tapped** to knock lightly.
tap-dance *n.* a dance performed wearing shoes with metal on the soles and toes so that the dancer's steps can be heard clearly.

tap² (tap) *n.* a device attached to a pipe that can be turned to control the flow of liquid or gas. – *vb.* **tapping, tapped** to let out liquid from a vessel by opening a tap.

tape (tāp) *n.* **1** a narrow strip of woven cloth used for tying, fastening, etc. **2** a ribbon of thin plastic or metal used for recording sounds or images: *She put the videotape in the video machine.* **3** a ribbon of thin paper or plastic with a sticky surface, used for fastening, sticking, etc. – *vb.* **taping, taped 1** to tie or seal with tape. **2** to record sounds or images on magnetic tape.
tape measure *n.* a length of plastic or cloth marked with cm and m, for measuring.
tape-record *vb.* **tape-recording, tape-recorded** to record sounds on magnetic tape.

tape-recorder *n.* a machine which records sounds on magnetic tape and reproduces them when required.

taper (**tā** pĕr) *n.* a long thin candle. – *vb.* **tapering, tapered** to make or become gradually narrower towards one end.

tapestry (**ta** pis trĭ) *n.* **tapestries** a thick woven cloth with an ornamental design on it.

tapir (**tā** pir) or (**tā** pēr) *n.* **tapir** or **tapirs** a large hoofed mammal with a snout, found in SOUTH AMERICA and Malaysia.

tar (tär) *n.* a thick dark sticky liquid obtained by distilling matter such as wood, peat, or coal.

● **Taranaki** is a province on North Island, NEW ZEALAND.

tarantula (tă **ran** tū lă) *n.* any of several large hairy spiders, some of which are poisonous.

target (**tär** git) *n.* an object aimed at in shooting practice or competitions, especially a flat round board marked with circles and with a bull's-eye in the centre.

tariff (**ta** rif) *n.* a list of prices or charges: *The price of a single room was listed in the hotel tariff.*

tarnish (**tär** nish) *vb.* **tarnishing, tarnished** (of metal) to become dull and discoloured.

tarpaulin (tär **pŏ** lin) *n.* a sheet of heavy canvas which has been made waterproof.

tart (tärt) *n.* a pie with pastry underneath the filling but not on top of it.

tartan (**tär** tăn) *n.* a distinctive checked pattern, especially one of the very many designs associated with the different Scottish clans.

task (täsk) *n.* a piece of work to be done, especially one which is unpleasant or difficult.

tassel (**ta** sĕl) *n.* a decoration, on a cushion, consisting of a hanging bunch of threads.

taste (tāst) *vb.* **tasting, tasted 1** to discover the flavour of food or drink by taking a small amount of it into your mouth. **2** to be aware of or recognize the flavour of: *I can taste nutmeg in this cake.* – *n.* **1** the sense by which flavours are distinguished by the tongue and nose. **2** a first, usually brief experience of something.
tasty *adj.* **tastier, tastiest** having a good flavour. – *adv.* **tastily**. – *n.* **tastiness**.

tatter (**ta** tĕr) *n.* (usually in *plural*) a torn, ragged shred of cloth, especially of clothing.
tattered *adj.* ragged or torn.

tattoo¹ (tă **too**) *vb.* **tattooing, tattooed** to mark designs or pictures on the body by pricking the skin and putting in coloured dyes.

Tarantula is the name given to the large spiders variously called bird spiders or monkey spiders. The original tarantula was the wolf spider, found near the town of Taranto, in southern Italy.

tattoo² (tå tōō) *n.* **tattoos** an outdoor military entertainment with military bands, etc.

taunt (tönt) *vb.* **taunting, taunted** to tease and say unpleasant things to someone in a cruel and hurtful way.

Taurus (tö rŭs) *n.* See **zodiac**.

taut (töt) *adj.* pulled or stretched tight.

tautology (tö **tol** ŏ ji) *n.* **tautologies** the use of words which only repeat the meaning found in other words already used, as in *All of a sudden she suddenly remembered*. Commonly used tautological expressions include: *added bonus; end result; true facts; free gift; past history*.

tavern (**ta** věrn) *n.* an inn.

tawdry (tö dri) *adj.* **tawdrier, tawdriest** cheap and showy and of poor quality.

tawny (tö ni) *n.* & *adj.* **tawnier, tawniest** (of) a yellowish-brown colour.

tax (taks) *n.* a contribution towards a country's expenses paid to the government from people's salaries, property, and from the sale of goods and services. – *vb.* **taxing, taxed** to impose a tax on a person, goods, etc. – *adj.* **taxable**.

taxi (**tak** si) *n.* **taxis** (also **taxicab**) a car which may be hired together with its driver to carry passengers on usually short journeys.

●**Tchaikovsky, Peter Ilyich** (1840-93) was a Russian composer, perhaps most famous for his ballet music: *Swan Lake* and *The Nutcracker*.

tea (tē) *n.* **1** an evergreen shrub or tree grown in Asia, especially India and China. **2** the dried leaves of this plant used to make a hot drink by pouring on boiling water.

teach (tēch) *vb.* **teaching, taught** (töt) **1** to give knowledge to; to instruct in a skill or help to learn. **2** to give lessons in a subject.

teacher *n.* a person who teaches, especially professionally in a school.

teaching *n.* **1** the work or profession of a teacher. **2** (often in *plural*) that which is taught.

teak (tēk) *n.* a large tree with very hard wood, which grows in India, Malaysia, etc.

team (tēm) *n.* **1** a group of people forming one side in a game. **2** a group of people working together. – *vb.* **teaming, teamed** to form or make into a team for some common action.

tear¹ (tēr) *n.* a drop of clear salty liquid that moistens and washes the eye and eyelid and is often shed as a result of emotion.

tear² (tār) *vb.* **tearing, tore** (tör), **torn** (törn) **1** to pull or rip apart by force; to make a hole, etc. by ripping. **2** to force or persuade to leave: *She enjoyed the show so much she could hardly tear herself away.* – *n.* a hole or other damage caused by tearing.

tease (tēz) *vb.* **teasing, teased** to laugh at or make fun of unkindly.

technical (**tek** ni kǎl) *adj.* **1** having knowledge of or specializing in a practical skill, especially one that is useful to industry. **2** showing great practical skill: *She plays with technical brilliance.*

technique (tek **nēk**) *n.* **1** skill in the practical aspects of an art: *She has a beautiful voice but poor technique.* **2** the method of doing something.

technology (tek **nol** ŏ ji) *n.* **technologies** the study of science which has a practical value, especially in industry. – *adj.* **technological** (tek nŏ **loj** i kǎl).

teddy (**te** di) *n.* **teddies** (also **teddy bear**) a child's stuffed toy bear.

tedious (**tē** di ŭs) *adj.* boring and monotonous.

teem¹ (tēm) *vb.* **teeming, teemed** to be full of; to be present in large numbers.

teem² (tēm) *vb.* **teeming, teemed** (of water, especially rain) to pour in torrents.

teen (tēn) *n.* **1** (in *plural*) the years of a person's life between the ages of 13 and 19. **2** (in *plural*) the numbers from 13 to 19.

teenager *n.* a person aged between 13 and 19.

telecommunications (te li kŏ mū ni **kā** shŏnz) *n.* (*singular*) the technology of sending information or messages over a distance by telephone, television cable, etc.

telegraph (**te** li gräf) *n.* a system of sending messages or information through electrical impulses along a wire. – *vb.* **telegraphing, telegraphed**.

telephone (**te** li fōn) *n.* an instrument which allows a person to speak to someone in a different place by transmitting sound in the form of electrical signals. – *vb.* **telephoning, telephoned**.

telescope (**te** li skōp) *n.* a tube-shaped instrument with a combination of lenses and mirrors inside that make distant objects seem closer and larger.

television (**te** li vi zhǒn) or (te li **vi** zhǒn) *n.* **1** the sending of pictures and sound in the form of radio waves to be reproduced on a screen in a person's home, etc. **2** (also **television set**) an apparatus with a screen and speakers which is able to receive radio waves and reproduce them in the form of pictures and sounds.

Most tea today is grown in China, northern India, and Sri Lanka. The tea plant is pruned to keep it small and bushy so that all its energy goes into making new leaves. Unpruned it could reach ten metres high.

Some of the major technological changes of the last 150 years have been in **telecommunications** – the long distance communication by telephone, telegraph, radio, television, and telex. The electric telegraph was developed in the 1850s; the first electric telephone was made by Alexander Bell in 1876; and in 1926 John Logie Baird demonstrated his television set. Today most telephone systems and cable TV use optical fibres to carry signals in the form of light rays fired along each fibre by a laser.

Telecommunications 18th-century style. After 1794 coded messages could be sent by the semaphore telegraph invented by the French engineer, Claude Chappe. Moveable metal arms on top of towers sent coded messages great distances.

(Above) *An early telephone; it carried a weak electrical wave over long distances.*

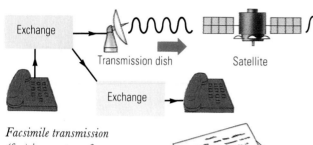

Exchange → Transmission dish → Satellite → Receiver dish → Exchange

Exchange

Like radio and television, telephones, except for short distances, employ radio waves and use aerials (dishes) to send and receive signals to and from satellites over great distances.

A modern telephone, using radio waves.

Facsimile transmission (fax) is a system of sending exact copies of letters and documents in a matter of seconds along telephone lines. The document is scanned and the image converted into electrical signals. At the other end another fax machine decodes the signals and prints out a copy of the original document.

In television broadcasting, pictures are converted into electrical signals by cameras and sounds are converted into signals by microphones. The signals are sent to transmitting aerials. Receiving aerials pick up the signals and feed them to television sets which change the signals back into pictures and sound.

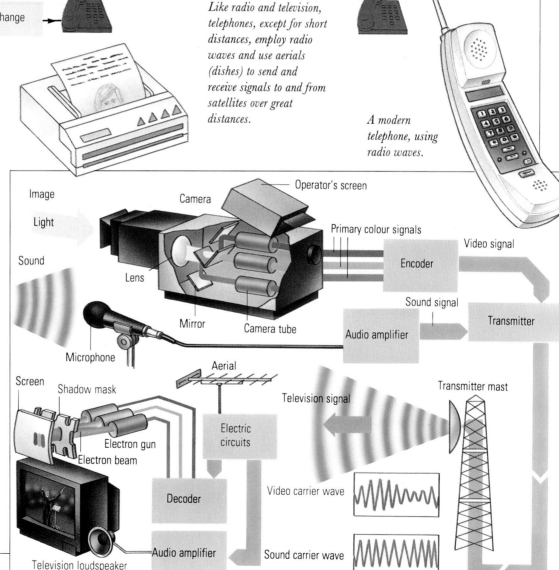

Image
Light
Sound

Camera
Operator's screen
Lens
Mirror
Camera tube
Microphone

Primary colour signals
Encoder
Video signal
Sound signal
Audio amplifier
Transmitter

Screen
Shadow mask
Electron gun
Electron beam
Decoder
Audio amplifier
Television loudspeaker

Aerial
Electric circuits

Television signal
Transmitter mast

Video carrier wave

Sound carrier wave

● **Telford, Thomas** (1757-1834) was a Scottish engineer who built numerous roads and bridges.

tell (tel) *vb.* **telling, told** (tōld) **1** to give information to someone in speech or writing: *He told her about his plans.* **2** to order: *She told him to leave.* **3** to distinguish: *I can't tell Brie from Camembert.*

telling *adj.* having a great or marked effect.

temper (tem pẻr) *n.* **1** a characteristic state of mind; mood or humour: *She has an even temper.* **2** a state of uncontrolled anger.

temperament (tem pẻ rå mẻnt) *n.* a person's natural character which governs the way he or she behaves and thinks.

temperamental (tem pẻ rå **men** tål) *adj.* given to extreme changes of mood.

temperate (tem pẻ råt) *adj.* moderate and self-restrained in behaviour.

temperature (tem prå chůr) *n.* **1** the degree of hotness, for example of air or water as measured by a thermometer. **2** the level of body heat in a person: *The doctor took his temperature.*

tempest (tem pist) *n.* a violent storm.

temple[1] (tem pẻl) *n.* a building used for worship by people in various religions.

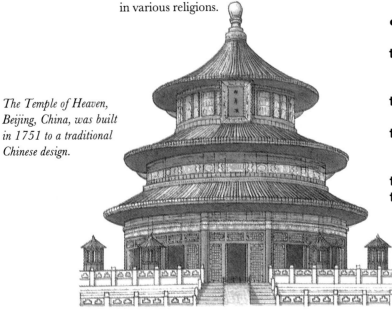

The Temple of Heaven, Beijing, China, was built in 1751 to a traditional Chinese design.

temple[2] (tem pẻl) *n.* either of the flat parts of the head at the side of the forehead.

tempo (tem pō) *n.* **tempos** or **tempi** (tem pē) the speed at which a piece of music is played.

temporary (tem pỏ rå ri) *adj.* lasting, used, etc. for a limited period of time only.

tempt (tempt) *vb.* **tempting, tempted 1** to persuade someone to do something, especially something wrong. **2** to be strongly inclined to do something: *I was tempted to buy the dress.*

temptation *n.* **1** the state of being tempted. **2** something that tempts.

ten (ten) *n.* the number or figure 10.

tenth *n.* **1** one of ten equal parts. **2** the last of ten; the next after the ninth.

tenant (te nånt) *n.* a person who pays rent to another for the use of property or land.

tend[1] (tend) *vb.* **tending, tended** to take care of; to look after: *She tended her plants carefully.*

tend[2] (tend) *vb.* **tending, tended** to be likely or inclined to: *I tend to fall asleep after lunch.*

tendency *n.* **tendencies** a likelihood of acting or thinking in a particular way: *She has a tendency to talk too much.*

tender (ten dẻr) *adj.* **1** (of meat) easily chewed or cut. **2** easily damaged; sensitive: *She has a tender heart.* **3** sore and easily hurt: *Her foot was tender for days after the horse trod on it.*

tendon (ten dỏn) *n.* a cord of strong tissue that joins a muscle to a bone.

tenement (ten ẻ mẻnt) *n.* (especially in Scotland) a large building divided into several individual, self-contained flats or apartments.

● **Tennessee**. See Supplement, **USA**.

tennis (te nis) *n.* a game in which two players or two pairs of players use rackets to hit a light ball across a net on a rectangular court.

tenor (te nôr) *n.* the highest natural adult male singing voice.

tense[1] (tens) *n.* the form of a verb that shows whether the time of its action is in the past, present, or future.

tense[2] (tens) *adj.* feeling worried or nervous.

tent (tent) *n.* a shelter made of material supported by poles or a frame and fastened to the ground with ropes and pegs, that can be taken down and carried from place to place.

tentacle (ten tå kẻl) *n.* a long thin flexible organ used by an animal to feel, grasp, and feed: *An octopus has eight tentacles.*

tepee or **teepee** (tē pē) *n.* a NATIVE AMERICAN tent formed of skins stretched over a cone-shaped frame of poles.

● **Teresa, Mother** (1910-) was born in Macedonia and gave up her life in a convent in INDIA to help the poor in the slums of Calcutta.

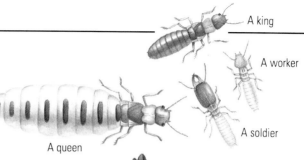

A king

A worker

A soldier

A queen

term (tûrm) *n.* **1** a word or expression, especially one used with a precise meaning in a specialized field: *That is a scientific term.* **2** (in *plural*) a particular way of describing something: *She criticized him in no uncertain terms.* **3** (in *plural*) a relationship between people or countries: *They are on good terms.* **4** one of the divisions into which the school year is divided.

terminal (tûr mi nål) *adj.* **1** (of an illness) causing death; fatal. **2** forming or occurring at the end or boundary of something. – *n.* **1** an arrival and departure building at an airport. **2** a device consisting usually of a keyboard and screen, which allows a user to use a distant computer.

terminus (tûr mi nůs) *n.* **termini** (tûr mi nī) or **terminuses** the end of a railway line or bus route, usually with a station.

termite (tûr mīt) *n.* a pale-coloured ant-like insect which feeds on wood, found mainly in the tropics.

tern (tûrn) *n.* any of several sea-birds which have long wings and a forked tail.

terrace (te ris) *n.* **1** a series of raised level banks of earth, like large steps on the side of a hill, used for growing crops. **2** a row of identical and connected houses.

terrapin (te rå pin) *n.* any of several North American freshwater turtles.

terrible (te rå běl) *adj.* **1** (colloquial) very bad: *He is a terrible singer.* **2** (colloquial) very great; extreme: *She is a terrible gossip.* **3** causing fear.

terrier (te ri ěr) *n.* any of several breeds of small dog bred to hunt animals in burrows.

terrific (tě **rif** ik) *adj.* (colloquial) marvellous.

terrify (te ri fī) *vb.* **terrifies, terrifying, terrified** to make very frightened; to fill with terror. – *adj.* **terrified**. – *adj.* **terrifying**.

territory (te ri tǒ ri) *n.* **territories 1** an area of land under the control of a ruler, government, or state. **2** an area which a bird or animal defends against others of the same species.

terror (te rǒr) *n.* very great fear or dread.
terrorism *n.* the systematic and organized use of violence to attempt to force a government to accept certain demands. – *n.* & *adj.* **terrorist**.

terse (tûrs) *adj.* (of language) brief and abrupt.

test (test) *n.* an examination or trial of a person's or thing's qualities, abilities, etc.: *Marathon-running is a test of endurance.* – *vb.* **testing, tested** to examine someone or something, abilities, qualities, etc.

testament (tes tå měnt) *n.* **1** a will.

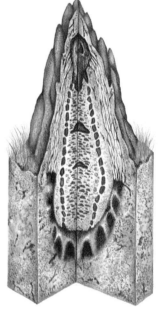

These towers of mud are termites' nests. Inside are many tunnels where the termites live. Each colony has a king and queen. Thousands of small white workers dig the tunnels and find food and water. There are also soldier termites. They have huge heads and jaws to defend the nest from enemies. New males and females periodically swarm from the nests to mate and form new nests.

2 Testament either of the two main divisions of the Bible, the **Old Testament** or the **New Testament**.

testicle (tes ti kěl) *n.* either of the two glands in the male body which produce sperm.

testify (tes ti fī) *vb.* **testifies, testifying, testified** to give evidence in court.

testimony (tes ti mǒ ni) *n.* **testimonies** a statement made under oath.

tether (te Ther) *n.* a rope or chain for tying an animal to a post. – *vb.* **tethering, tethered**.

● **Texas**. See Supplement, **USA**.

text (tekst) *n.* the main body of printed words in a book rather than the pictures, etc.
textbook *n.* a book containing information on a certain subject, intended for students.

textile (tek stīl) *n.* any cloth or fabric.

texture (teks chŭr) *n.* the way the surface of a material or substance feels when touched.

● **Thailand**. See Supplement, **Countries**.

● **Thames** a river in southern ENGLAND, flowing through London into the English Channel.

Terracotta is Italian, and literally means 'cooked earth'. The English use of the word to describe brownish-orange unglazed pottery dates from the 18th century.

than (Than) or (Thǎn) *conj.* **1** used to introduce the second part of a comparison: *She is older than he is.* **2** used to introduce the second of two alternatives: *I would rather swim than play football.*

thank (thangk) *vb.* **thanking, thanked 1** to express gratitude to: *She thanked him for his help.* **2** to hold responsible for: *You have only yourself to thank for your failure.* – *n.* (in *plural*) an expression of gratitude.

thanksgiving *n.* **1** a formal act of giving thanks, especially to God. **2** (**Thanksgiving**, also **Thanksgiving Day**) a public holiday occurring on the fourth Thursday in November in the UNITED STATES and the second Monday in October in CANADA.

● The first Thanksgiving Day was celebrated in America by the PILGRIM FATHERS in 1621, the year after they had settled there to follow their religious beliefs in peace.

Wampanoag Native Americans joined the Pilgrims for the first Thanksgiving in 1621. Without their advice on farming and fishing, the Plymouth settlement may well not have survived.

that (That) *adj.* **those** (Thōz) indicating the thing, person, or idea already mentioned or understood: *I would like that cake, please.* – (Thǎt) *relative pron.* used instead of **which, who,** or **whom** to introduce a relative clause: *He punished all the children that were late.* – *conj.* used to introduce a clause showing reason, purpose, consequence, a result, or expressing a wish or desire: *She spoke so quickly that no one could understand.*

thatch (thach) *n.* a roof covering of straw and reeds. – *vb.* **thatching, thatched.**

thaw (thö) *vb.* **thawing, thawed 1** (of snow or ice) to melt. **2** (of anything frozen) to defrost.

the (Thě) or (Thē) the definite article, used to refer to a particular person or thing, or group of people or things.

theatre (thē ǎ těr) *n.* **1** a building specially designed for the performance of plays, operas, etc. **2** (*British*) a specially equipped room in a hospital where surgery is performed.

theft (theft) *n.* stealing: *she was arrested for theft.*

their (Thār) *adj.* of, or belonging to, them: *They watched their son win the race.*

theirs *pron.* a person or thing that belongs to them: *That car is theirs.*

them (Them) or (Thěm) *pron.* people or things already mentioned or spoken about: *I love my grandparents – I want to see them.*

themselves *pron.* **1** the reflexive form of **them** and **they**: *They helped themselves.* **2** used for emphasis: *They did it themselves.*

theme (thēm) *n.* the subject of a discussion, speech, or piece of writing.

theme park *n.* a large amusement park in which all of the rides and attractions are based on a particular theme, such as outer space.

then (Then) *adv.* **1** at that time. **2** soon or immediately after that: *She looked at him, then turned away.* **3** in that case; that being so: *If you're tired, then you should rest.*

theology (thē **ol** ǒ ji) *n.* **theologies** the study of God and religion. – *adj.* **theological.**

theory (thē ǒ ri) *n.* **theories 1** a series of ideas and general principles which explain some aspect: *We learned about the theory of relativity.* **2** an idea which has not yet been proved.

therapy (the rǎ pi) *n.* **therapies** the treatment of illness without using drugs or surgery. – *n.* **therapist.**

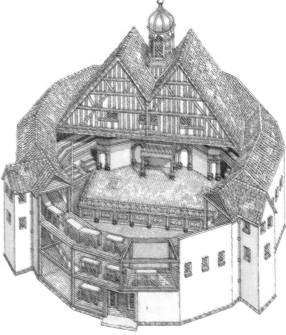

The Globe, one of London's first public theatres. Here many of Shakespeare's plays were performed.

there (Thār) *adv.* **1** at, in, or to a place or position. **2** used to begin a sentence: *There are no mistakes in this.* – *n.* that place or point.
therefore *adv.* for that reason.
thermometer (thěr **mom** i těr) *n.* an instrument for measuring temperature.

Many thermostats contain a coiled bimetallic strip made of two different metals welded together which expand and contract at different rates causing the strip to bend. Here a tube of mercury is used to complete the circuit between the contacts. The circuit is broken when the tube tips the mercury away.

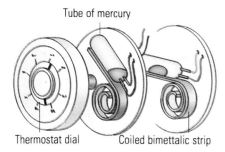

Tube of mercury

Thermostat dial — Coiled bimettalic strip

thermostat (**thûr** mō stat) *n.* an apparatus which automatically controls temperature.
thesaurus (thi **sö** rǔs) *n.* **thesauruses** or **thesauri** (thi **sö** rī) a book which lists words in groups together according to their meaning.
they (Thā) *pron.* the people, animals, or things already spoken about or being indicated: *We visited my grandparents – they looked very well.*
they'll **1** they will. **2** they shall.
they're they are.
they've they have.
thick (thik) *adj.* **1** having a large distance between opposite sides. **2** having a certain distance between opposite sides: *The rope is three centimetres thick.* **3** (of liquids) containing a lot of solid matter: *She made a delicious thick soup.* **4** grouped close together; dense: *He has lovely thick hair.*
thickness *n.* **1** the state or degree of being thick. **2** a layer.
thicket (**thik** it) *n.* a dense mass of bushes.
thief (thēf) *n.* **thieves** (thēvz) a person who steals things.
thieve *vb.* **thieving, thieved** to steal.
thigh (thī) *n.* the fleshy part of the leg between the knee and hip.
thimble (**thim** běl) *n.* a small metal or plastic cap worn on the finger to protect it and push the needle when sewing.

Minimum thermometer — Metal index — Maximum thermometer

Mercury

Alcohol

A maximum thermometer contains mercury. As the temperature rises, the mercury expands and pushes a metal index up the tube, which remains there. An index in the minimum thermometer (containing alcohol) records the lowest temperature.

thin (thin) *adj.* **thinner, thinnest**
1 having a short distance between opposite sides. **2** having a small thickness; narrow or fine. **3** (of people or animals) not fat; lean. **4** (of liquids) containing very little solid matter.
thing (thing) *n.* **1** any object, rather than an animal or a human being, especially one that cannot move. **2** an event, affair, or circumstance: *Things are getting out of hand.* **3** an obsession or interest: *She has a thing about horses.*
think (thingk) *vb.* **thinking, thought** (thöt) **1** to have ideas in the mind about a subject, person, etc. **2** to consider, judge, or believe: *People once thought the world was flat.* **3** to consider: *We must think of the children first.*
think tank *n.* (*colloquial*) a group of experts who research into an area to find solutions to problems and think up new ideas.
third (thûrd) *adj.* **1** coming next after second in time, place, or order; last of three. **2** being one of three equal parts. – *n.* one of three parts.
the Third World *n.* a term sometimes used to describe the poorer countries of AFRICA, ASIA, and LATIN AMERICA.
thirst (thûrst) *n.* the need to drink something.
thirsty *adj.* **thirstier, thirstiest** **1** needing or wanting to drink. **2** causing thirst: *Digging is thirsty work.* – *adv.* **thirstily**. – *n.* **thirstiness**.
thirteen (thûr **tēn**) *n.* the number or figure 13. – *n., adj.,* & *adv.* **thirteenth**.
thirty (**thûr** ti) *n.* **thirties** the number or figure 30. – *n., adj.,* & *adv.* **thirtieth**.
this (This) *pron.* **these** (Thēz) **1** a person, animal, thing, or idea already mentioned or about to be mentioned: *This is my house.* **2** the present time or place. – *adj.* the person, animal, thing, or idea which is nearby, especially closer than something else: *Do you want this book or that one?*
thistle (**thi** sěl) *n.* any of several plants with prickly purple flowers.

●**Thomas, Dylan** (1914-53) was a Welsh poet, perhaps best known for his play *Under Milkwood*.

Thesaurus is from a Greek word meaning 'treasury', and was used in the early 19th century to describe a treasury of knowledge or words.

The spear thistle – one of several varieties of this vigorous plant. To gardeners the thistle is a troublesome weed. To the Scots it is their national emblem.

● **Thomas, Saint**, also called 'doubting Thomas', was one of the twelve apostles of Jesus.

thong (thong) *n.* a narrow strip of leather, e.g. used to fasten something.

thorax (thö raks) *n.* **thoraxes** or **thoraces** (thö rå sēz) or (thö **rā** sēz) the part of the body between the head and abdomen, in humans the chest, and in insects the middle section that bears the wings and legs.

● **Thoreau, Henry David** (1817-62) was an American writer and philosopher.

A threshing machine of 1860. It would have been powered by a steam engine standing on the edge of the field.

thorn (thörn) *n.* a hard, sharp point sticking out from the stem or branch of certain plants. **thorny** *adj.* **thornier, thorniest** full of or covered with thorns.; difficult; causing trouble.

thorough (thu rů) *adj.* **1** (of a person) extremely careful and attending to every detail. **2** carried out with great care and great attention to detail: *She gave the spoon a thorough clean.* **thoroughbred** *n.* an animal, especially a horse, bred from the best specimens.

thoroughfare *n.* a public road or street.

though (Thō) *conj.* **1** despite the fact that: *She ate her pudding even though she was full.* **2** if: *He looked as though he would cry.* **3** and yet; but: *I like the new car, though not as much as the old one.* – *adv.* however; nevertheless.

thought (thöt). See **think**. – *n.* **1** an idea or opinion. **2** careful consideration: *I must give some thought to the problem.* **thoughtful** *adj.* **1** appearing to be thinking deeply; reflective. **2** showing careful or serious thought: *He wrote a thoughtful review of the book.* **3** thinking of other people; considerate: *She is very thoughtful; she brought me some flowers.* **thoughtless** *adj.* inconsiderate.

thousand (thow zånd) *n.* **thousands** or (after another number) **thousand** the number or figure 1000. – *n. & adj.* **thousandth**.

thrash (thrash) *vb.* **thrashing, thrashed 1** to beat soundly. **2** to defeat thoroughly. – *vb.* **thrash out** to discuss a problem.

thread (thred) *n.* **1** a fine strand of silk, cotton, or wool. **2** the spiral ridge round a screw or on the lid of a container. – *vb.* **threading, threaded** to pass a thread through the eye of a needle.

threat (thret) *n.* **1** a warning that someone is going to hurt or punish someone. **2** a sign that something unpleasant is about to happen. **threaten** *vb.* **threatening, threatened 1** to make a threat to. **2** to seem likely to happen: *A storm was threatening.* – *adj.* **threatening**.

three (thrē) *n.* the number or figure 3. **three-dimensional** *adj.* having or appearing to have three dimensions: height, width, depth.

thresh (thresh) *vb.* **threshing, threshed** to beat stalks of corn in order to extract the grain.

threshold (thresh hōld) *n.* **1** any doorway or entrance. **2** a starting-point: *He is on the threshold of a new career.*

thrift (thrift) *n.* **1** careful spending or management of money. **2** a wild plant with narrow bluish-green leaves and pink flowers. **thrifty** *adj.* **thriftier, thriftiest** economical.

thrill (thril) *vb.* **thrilling, thrilled** to feel a sudden strong sensation of excitement, emotion, or pleasure. – *adj.* **thrilling**.

thrive (thrīv) *vb.* **thriving, throve** (thrōv) or **thrived 1** to grow strong and healthy. **2** to prosper and be successful. – *adj.* **thriving**.

throat (thrōt) *n.* **1** the top part of the passage which leads from the mouth and nose to the stomach. **2** the front part of the neck.

throb (throb) *vb.* **throbbing, throbbed** to beat or vibrate with a strong, regular rhythm.

thrombosis (throm **bō** sis) *n.* **thromboses** (throm **bō** sēz) a clot in a blood vessel which prevents the flow of blood around the body.

throne (thrōn) *n.* the ceremonial chair of a king, queen, or bishop, used on official occasions.

throng (throng) *n.* a large crowd of people. – *vb.* **thronging, thronged** to crowd or fill.

through (throō) *prep.* **1** going from one side of something to the other: *A road ran through the village.* **2** from the beginning to the end of; during: *We stayed in France through the summer.* **3** (especially *US*) up to and including: *He worked Tuesday through Thursday.* **4** because of: *He lost* his job through stupidity. **5** by: *They are related through marriage.* – *adv.* **1** into and out of; from one side to the other. **2** from the beginning to the end. **3** completely: *soaked through.*

throw (thrō) *vb.* **throwing, threw** (throō), **thrown 1** to hurl through the air with force, especially with a rapid forward movement of the hand and arm. **2** to put someone into a certain condition, especially suddenly: *My words threw them into confusion.* **3** to put clothes on quickly and carelessly. – *n.* **1** an act of throwing. **2** the distance something is thrown.

thrush (thrush) *n.* any of several songbirds with brown feathers and a spotted chest.

thrust (thrust) *vb.* **thrusting, thrust** to push suddenly and violently.

thumb (thum) *n.* the short thick finger on the side of the hand.

thunder (**thun** děr) *n.* **1** a deep rumbling or loud cracking sound heard after a flash of lightning. **2** any loud deep rumbling noise.

Thursday (**thûrz** di) *n.* the day between Wednesday and Friday.

thus (Thus) *adv.* **1** in the way or manner shown: *You must tie the knot thus.* **2** to this amount, distance, etc.: *You have come thus far.* **3** therefore: *He didn't finish: thus he must start again.*

thyme (tīm) *n.* any of several herbs and shrubs.

●**Tibet** is a country in central ASIA which was taken over by CHINA in 1959.

Tibetan (ti **bet** ǎn) *n.* **1** an inhabitant of TIBET. **2** the main language of TIBET. – *adj.* of, or relating to, TIBET, its people, language, etc.

tick¹ (tik) *n.* **1** a regular tapping or clicking sound, such as that made by a watch or clock. **2** a small mark used to show that something is correct or to mark off items on a list. – *vb.* **ticking, ticked 1** (of, e.g. a clock) to make a regular clicking sound. **2** to mark with a written tick. – *vb.* **tick off** (*colloquial*) to scold.

tick² (tik) *n.* any of several bloodsucking insects living on the skin of some animals.

ticket (**ti** kit) *n.* a printed piece of paper or card which shows that the holder has paid money for a fare or for admission.

tickle (**ti** kěl) *vb.* **tickling, tickled** to touch a part of the body lightly in order to produce a tingling sensation and laughter.

tiddler (**tid** lěr) *n.* (*British colloquial*) a small fish.

tide (tīd) *n.* the regular rise and fall in the level of the sea.

tidal *adj.* depending on or affected by tides.

tidal wave *n.* an enormous wave that causes great destruction if it touches land.

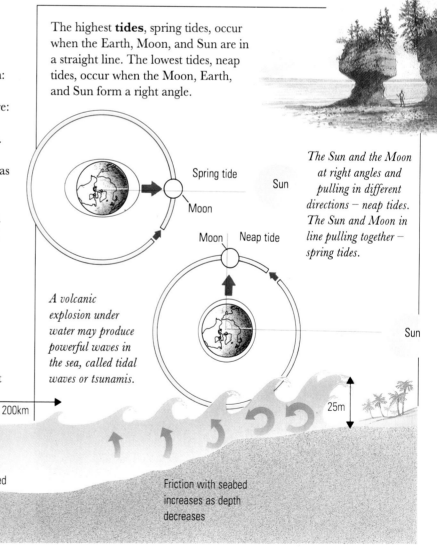

The Bay of Fundy, Canada boasts the world's greatest spring tidal range – 14.5m between high and low tides.

The highest **tides**, spring tides, occur when the Earth, Moon, and Sun are in a straight line. The lowest tides, neap tides, occur when the Moon, Earth, and Sun form a right angle.

Spring tide

Sun

Moon

Moon Neap tide

Sun

The Sun and the Moon at right angles and pulling in different directions – neap tides. The Sun and Moon in line pulling together – spring tides.

A volcanic explosion under water may produce powerful waves in the sea, called tidal waves or tsunamis.

200km

25m

Volcanic eruption

Seabed

Friction with seabed increases as depth decreases

tidy (**tī** di) *adj.* **tidier, tidiest 1** neat and in good order. **2** methodical. – *vb.* **tidies, tidying, tidied** to make neat. – *adv.* **tidily.** – *n.* **tidiness.**

tie (tī) *vb.* **tying, tied 1** to fasten with a string, ribbon, rope, etc. using a bow or knot. **2** to have the same score or final position as another competitor in a contest. – *n.* **1** a narrow strip of material worn round the neck under a shirt collar and tied in a knot or bow at the front. **2** a link or bond: *There are strong ties of friendship between the two countries.* **3** a competition in which the result is an equal final score or position for each competitor.

tier (tēr) *n.* any series of levels placed one above the other, for example of seats in a theatre.

tiger (**tī** gẽr) *n.* a very large wild cat with a striped tawny coat, found in ASIA.

The tiger is the largest member of the cat family. Males have been found up to 3.2 m in length.

tight (tīt) *adj.* **1** fitting very closely: *These shoes rub because they are too tight.* **2** stretched so as not to be loose; tense; taut. **3** fixed or held firmly in place: *His hood was tied with a tight knot.* **4** strictly and carefully controlled: *She keeps a tight rein on her emotions.* **5** (of a contest or match) closely or evenly fought. **6** (of a schedule or timetable, etc.) not allowing much time.

tighten *vb.* **tightening, tightened** to make or become tighter.

tight-fisted *adj.* ungenerous with money.

tight-knit *adj.* closely organized or united.

tightrope *n.* a tightly-stretched rope or wire on which acrobats balance.

tights *n. (plural)* a close-fitting garment covering the feet, legs, and body to the waist, worn by women, dancers, acrobats, etc.

tigress (**tī** grẽs) *n.* a female tiger.

tile (tīl) *n.* a flat thin slab of clay, cork, or linoleum, used to cover roofs, floors, walls, etc. – *vb.* **tiling, tiled** to cover with tiles.

till[1] (til) *prep.* up to the time of: *Wait till tomorrow.* – *conj.* up to the time when: *Go on till you reach the station.*

till[2] (til) *n.* a container or drawer in a shop in which money taken from customers is put.

till[3] (til) *vb.* **tilling, tilled** to prepare land for growing of crops.

tiller (**ti** lẽr) *n.* the lever used to turn the rudder of a boat.

tilt (tilt) *vb.* **tilting, tilted** to slope; to put in a slanting position. – *n.* a slant; a sloping position or angle. – **at full tilt** at full speed or with full force.

timber (**tim** bẽr) *n.* wood, especially prepared for building or making furniture.

timbered *adj.* built completely or partly of wood.

timbre (**tam** bẽr) or (**tim** bẽr) *n.* the particular quality and characteristics of a sound produced by a musical instrument or voice.

time (tīm) *n.* **1** the continuous passing of minutes, days, years, etc. **2** a particular point in time expressed in hours and minutes, or days, months, and years: *The time is ten o'clock.* **3** (often in *plural*) a point or period which is marked by some event or some particular characteristic: *She was very thin at the time of her marriage.* **4** the period required or available for some particular activity: *How much time do we need to rehearse?* **5** one of a number or series of occasions: *I have been to Spain three times.* **6** (in *plural*) expressing multiplication: *Three times two is six.* – *vb.* **timing, timed 1** to measure the time taken by an event, journey, etc. **2** to arrange or choose a time for. – **at times** occasionally. – **behind the times** out-of-date; old-fashioned. – **for the time being** meanwhile; for the moment. – **from time to time** occasionally; sometimes. – **have no time for** to have no interest in or patience with. – **in good time** early. – **in no time** very quickly. – **take your time** to not hurry.

timebomb *n.* a bomb that has been set to explode at a particular time.

time-honoured *adj.* respected and upheld because of being a custom or tradition.

timeless *adj.* not belonging to or typical of any particular time or date; ageless; eternal.

timely *adj.* coming at a suitable moment. – *n.* **timeliness.**

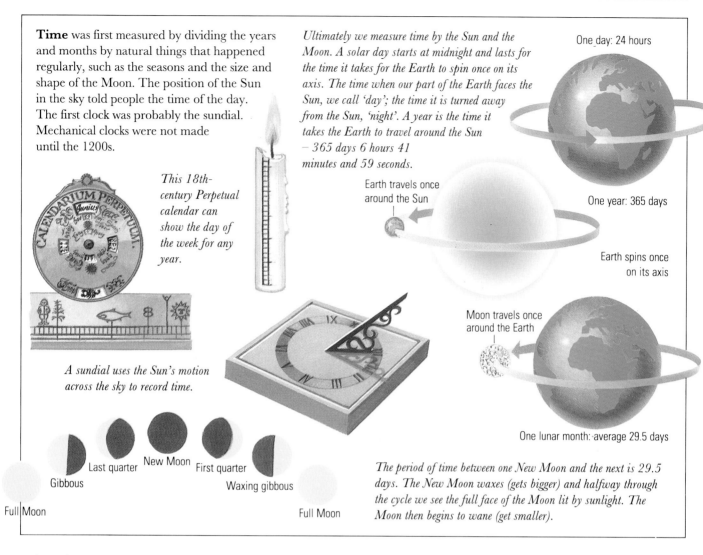

Time was first measured by dividing the years and months by natural things that happened regularly, such as the seasons and the size and shape of the Moon. The position of the Sun in the sky told people the time of the day. The first clock was probably the sundial. Mechanical clocks were not made until the 1200s.

This 18th-century Perpetual calendar can show the day of the week for any year.

A sundial uses the Sun's motion across the sky to record time.

Ultimately we measure time by the Sun and the Moon. A solar day starts at midnight and lasts for the time it takes for the Earth to spin once on its axis. The time when our part of the Earth faces the Sun, we call 'day'; the time it is turned away from the Sun, 'night'. A year is the time it takes the Earth to travel around the Sun – 365 days 6 hours 41 minutes and 59 seconds.

One day: 24 hours

Earth travels once around the Sun

One year: 365 days

Earth spins once on its axis

Moon travels once around the Earth

One lunar month: average 29.5 days

Gibbous
Last quarter
New Moon
First quarter
Waxing gibbous
Full Moon
Full Moon

The period of time between one New Moon and the next is 29.5 days. The New Moon waxes (gets bigger) and halfway through the cycle we see the full face of the Moon lit by sunlight. The Moon then begins to wane (get smaller).

timepiece *n.* a watch or clock.

timer *n.* a device like a clock which switches an appliance on or off at pre-set times.

timetable *n.* **1** a list of the departure and arrival times of trains, coaches, buses, etc. **2** a plan showing the order of events, especially of classes in a school.

timing *n.* the skill of co-ordinating actions and events to achieve the best possible effect.

timid (**ti** mid) *adj.* nervous; shy. – *n.* **timidity**.

tin (tin) *n.* **1** a soft silvery-white metallic element (symbol **Sn**), which is used in alloys. **2** a metal container for storing food. – *adj.* made of tin.

tinfoil *n.* very thin paper-like sheets made of metal, used especially for wrapping food.

tinge (tinj) *n.* a trace or hint of a colour.

tingle (**ting** gĕl) *vb.* **tingling, tingled** to feel a prickling or slightly stinging sensation.

tinker (**ting** kĕr) *n.* someone who travels from place to place to place mending pots, pans, and other household items. – *vb.* **tinkering, tinkered** to fiddle with machinery, etc.

tinkle (**ting** kĕl) *vb.* **tinkling, tinkled** to make a sound like the ringing of small bells.

tinsel (**tin** sĕl) *n.* a long strip of glittering coloured metal threads used as a decoration, especially at CHRISTMAS.

tint (tint) *n.* a variety of a colour, especially one made softer by adding white. – *vb.* **tinting, tinted** to colour slightly.

tiny (**tī** ni) *adj.* **tinier, tiniest** very small.

tip[1] (tip) *n.* the end of something long and thin: *She pointed with the tip of her finger.*

tip[2] (tip) *vb.* **tipping, tipped 1** to lean or slant. **2** to remove or empty something from its container by overturning or upsetting it: *She tipped out the contents of her purse.* – *n.* a place for tipping rubbish, coal, etc.

PRONUNCIATION GUIDE	
fat a	all ö
fate ā	foot oo
fast ä	moon o͞o
among å	boy oi
met e	house ow
mean ē	demon ȯ
silent ê	thing th
loch hh	this Th
fin i	but u
line ī	mute ū
quick kw	fur û
got o	brochure ǔ
note ō	vision zh

tip³ (tip) *n.* **1** a gift of money given to a waiter, taxi driver, etc. in return for service. **2** a helpful hint. – *vb.* **tipping, tipped** to give a tip to.

tiptoe (**tip** tō) *vb.* **tiptoing, tiptoed** to walk quietly on the tips of the toes. – *n.* the tips of the toes. – *adv.* on the tips of the toes.

tire (tīr) *vb.* **tiring, tired** **1** to make or become weary and in need of rest: *The walk tired her out.* **2** to lose patience with; to become bored with.
tired *adj.* **1** exhausted. **2** lacking freshness: *The lettuce looked old and tired.*
tireless *adj.* never becoming weary.

tissue (**ti** sho͞o) *n.* **1** a group of cells with a similar structure and particular function in an animal or plant: *They transplanted some muscle tissue.* **2** a piece of thin soft paper used as a handkerchief or as toilet paper.

tit (tit) *n.* any of several small songbirds.

● **Titanic** the British ocean liner which struck an iceberg and sank on its maiden voyage to the UNITED STATES in 1912.

titanium (ti **tān** i ům) *n.* a white metallic element (symbol **Ti**), used to make strong, light alloys.

Titanium being extracted from the rich sands on the Australian coast.

● **Titans** in Greek mythology, were the sons and daughters of the very first gods, Uranus (sky) and Gaea (Earth).

title (**tī** têl) *n.* **1** the name of a book, play, work of art, piece of music, etc. **2** a word used before a person's name to show rank, occupation.

titter (**ti** têr) (*colloquial*) *vb.* **tittering, tittered** to giggle or snigger. – *n.* a giggle or snigger.

to (to͞o) or (tǒ) *prep.* **1** towards; in the direction of; with the destination of: *I am going to America.* **2** used to express an aim or purpose: *You must boil the fruit to a pulp.* **3** used to express addition:

Add one to ten. **4** before the hour of: *The time is ten minutes to three.* – *adv.* **1** into a nearly closed position: *He pulled the window to.* **2** back into consciousness: *He came to a few minutes later.*

toad (tōd) *n.* an amphibian with a dry warty skin, related to the frog but larger.
toadstool *n.* a kind of fungus with round umbrella-like tops.

A toad darts out its long sticky tongue to capture a meal. Most toads and frogs eat insects and other small creatures.

toast (tōst) *vb.* **toasting, toasted** to make brown by putting it near direct heat, for example under a grill.

tobacco (tǒ **bak** ō) *n.* **tobaccos** or **tobaccoes** **1** any of several American plants with large leaves. **2** the leaves of these plants which are dried and can be smoked in a pipe or made into cigarettes, etc.

toboggan (tǒ **bog** ån) *n.* a long, light sledge which curves up at the front, used for riding over snow and ice.

today (tǒ **dā**) *n.* **1** this day. **2** the present time. – *adv.* on or during this day: *We're going shopping today.*

toe (tō) *n.* **1** any of the five finger-like parts at the end of the foot. **2** the front part of a shoe or sock, covering the toes.

toffee (**to** fi) *n.* a sticky sweet made by boiling sugar and butter.

tofu (**tō** fo͞o) *n.* a type of food made from soya beans, with a creamy colour.

toga (**tō** gå) *n.* a loose garment worn draped around the body by men of ancient Rome.

together (tǒ **ge** Thêr) *adv.* **1** with someone or something else; in company: *It is nicer to travel together.* **2** at the same time: *We arrived together.*

●Togo. See Supplement, **Countries**.

toil (toil) *vb.* **toiling, toiled** to work long and hard; to labour.

toilet (**toi** lit) *n.* a bowl-like receptacle for the body's waste matter, with a water supply for washing this into a drain.

token (**tō** kĕn) *n.* **1** anything serving as a reminder or souvenir. **2** a voucher worth a stated amount of money which can be exchanged for goods of the same value.

●Tokyo is the capital of JAPAN. It is one of the biggest cities in the world. Almost every kind of work goes on in this enormous city. It contains a number of beautiful buildings, including the Imperial Palace, and many ancient temples.

tolerate (**to** lĕ rāt) *vb.* **tolerating, tolerated** to endure or put up with.

tolerance *n.* **1** the ability to be fair towards other people's religious or political beliefs or opinions. **2** the ability to resist or endure pain or hardship. – *adj.* **tolerant**. – *n.* **toleration**.

toll¹ (tōl) *vb.* **tolling, tolled** to ring a bell with slow measured strokes.

toll² (tōl) *n.* a tax paid for the use of some bridges and roads.

●Tolstoy, Count Leo (1828-1910) was a Russian nobleman and considered to be one of the world's greatest writers. His finest works are *War and Peace* and *Anna Karenina*.

tomahawk (**to** må hök) *n.* a small axe used as a weapon by Native Americans.

tomato (tŏ **mä** tō) *n.* **tomatoes** a round red juicy fruit eaten as a vegetable in salads.

tomb (tōōm) *n.* a chamber for a dead body, either below or above ground; a grave.

tomcat (**tom** kat) *n.* a male cat.

tomorrow (tŏ mo rō) *n.* **1** the day after today. **2** the future: *The cars of tomorrow will use a different fuel.*

ton (tun) *n.* **1** (*British*) a unit of weight equal to 2240 lb (approximately 1016.05 kg). **2** (*US*) a unit of weight equal to 2000 lb (approximately 907.2 kg).

tone (tōn) *n.* **1** the quality of a musical or vocal sound. **2** the character of the voice expressing a particular feeling, mood, etc.: *He could tell from the tone of her voice that she was angry.*

Tonga. See Supplement, **Countries**.

tongs (tongz) *n.* (*plural*) a tool consisting of two arms joined by a hinge, for lifting objects.

tongue (tung) *n.* **1** the fleshy muscular organ attached to the floor of the mouth, used for eating, licking, tasting and, in people, speaking. **2** a particular language.

tongue-twister *n.* a phrase or sentence that is difficult to say quickly, usually because it contains a series of similar sounds, e.g. *She sells sea shells on the sea shore.*

tonight (tŏ **nīt**) *n.* the night of this present day.

tonne (tun) *n.* (also **metric ton**) a unit of weight equal to 1000 kg (2204.6 lb).

tonsil (**ton** sil) *n.* either of two oval lumps of tissue at the back of the throat.

too (tōō) *adv.* **1** more than is required, desirable, or suitable: *I have too many things to do.* **2** as well; also: *I enjoy swimming and I like cycling too.*

took. See **take**.

tool (tōōl) *n.* any hand-held instrument used for cutting, digging, etc., e.g. a spade or hammer.

tooth (tōōth) *n.* **teeth** (tēth) **1** any of the hard enamel-coated objects set in the mouth and used for biting and chewing. **2** anything like a tooth in shape, such as the points on a comb or on a zip. – **in the teeth of** against.

The tomb of Karl Marx is in London. Marx was probably the most influential of all modern political thinkers. His Das Kapital *formed the basis of modern Communism.*

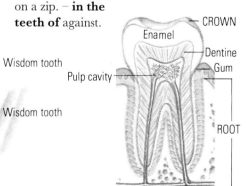

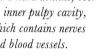

Children have 20 milk (first) teeth. These gradually fall out to be replaced by 32 adult teeth (far left).

A tooth has three main layers (left). The outside is made of hard enamel, to resist wear; underneath lies a hard dentine, over an inner pulpy cavity, which contains nerves and blood vessels.

● An animal's teeth are adapted to its diet. Gnawing creatures such as rats have sharp, pointed teeth, whereas grazing creatures such as horses have flat grinding teeth. Beavers use their teeth to fell trees.

top¹ (top) *n.* **1** the highest part, point, or level of anything. **2** the person or thing having the most important rank or position: *He is top of the class.* **3** a lid for covering the top of something: *Put the top back on the jam, please.* – *adj.* being the highest or most important: *She stopped on the top step.* – *vb.* **topping, topped 1** to cover or form the top of something: *She topped the cake with cream.* **2** to be better than; to reach the top of: *The song topped the charts for one week only.*
top-secret *adj.* very secret.

top² (top) *n.* a wooden or metal toy which spins on a pointed base.

topic (**to** pik) *n.* a subject or theme.

topography (tŏ **pog** rǎ fi) *n.* **topographies** the natural and man-made features on the surface of land, such as rivers, mountains, valleys, bridges, and railway lines.

topple (**to** pĕl) *vb.* **toppling, toppled 1** to fall over. **2** to overthrow: *The rebels toppled the government and took power into their own hands.*

Torah (**tō** rǎ) *n.* (*Judaism*) **1** the first five books of the OLD TESTAMENT. **2** the scroll on which this is written, used in a synagogue.

torch (tŏrch) *n.* **1** (*British*) a small light carried in the hand and powered by electric batteries. **2** a burning piece of wood or bundle of cloth, etc.

torment (**tŏr** ment) *n.* very great pain, suffering, or anxiety. – (tŏr **ment**) *vb.* **tormenting, tormented** to cause great pain, suffering, or anxiety to.

In 1493 Torquemada became Inquisitor-General and organized a campaign of imprisonment and torture against Arabs, Jews, and people with Protestant beliefs. Heretics were burnt at the stake.

torn. See **tear²**.

tornado (tŏr **nā** dō) *n.* **tornadoes** a violent destructive storm accompanied by whirlwinds.

● **Toronto** is a Native American word meaning 'a place of meeting' and is the name of the capital of Ontario province in CANADA.

● **Torquemada, Tomas de** (1420-98) was a Dominican friar who organized the Spanish Inquisition to persecute non-Catholics.

torrent (**to** rĕnt) *n.* a great rushing stream or downpour of water, lava, etc. – *adj.* **torrential**.

torso (**tŏr** sō) *n.* **torsos** the main part of the human body, without the arms, legs, and head.

tortoise (**tŏr** tŏs) *n.* a slow-moving reptile with a hard, bony or leathery shell that lives in fresh water and on land.

The now rare desert tortoise lives in the American deserts. It feeds mainly on cacti, storing water from the plant in its body.

torture (**tŏr** chŭr) *n.* severe pain or mental suffering deliberately caused in order to punish someone or to persuade them to give information. – *vb.* **torturing, tortured** to cause great suffering.

Tory (**tō** ri) *n.* **Tories** a member or supporter of the British Conservative Party. – *n.* **Toryism**.

toss (tos) *vb.* **tossing, tossed 1** to throw up into the air lightly and carelessly. **2** to move restlessly or from side to side repeatedly: *She tossed sleeplessly all night.* **3** to jerk the head, especially as a sign of impatience or anger. **4** to throw a coin into the air and guess which side will land facing up.

total (**tō** tǎl) *adj.* whole; complete. – *n.* the whole or complete amount, for example of various things added together. – *vb.* **totalling, totalled** to amount to. – *adv.* **totally**.

An early and intricate woodcarving by Maoris of New Zealand for a type of totem pole.

totem (tō tĕm) *n.* an object used as the badge of a tribe or an individual person among NATIVE AMERICANS.

toucan (tōō kăn) *n.* a tropical American bird with a huge orange beak.

touch (tuch) *vb.* **touching, touched 1** to bring something into contact with something else so as to feel: *He touched her cheek gently.* **2** (of something) to come into contact with something else: *The branch touched the window.* **3** to be in contact with something else without overlapping. – *n.* **1** an act of touching or the sensation of being touched. **2** the sense by which you feel objects through contact with the hands, feet, skin, lips, etc. **3** the particular qualities of an object as felt through contact with the skin: *She loved the silky touch of the fabric against her skin.* – **touch and go** of a very uncertain outcome. – *vb.* **touch down** (of aircraft or spacecraft) to land.

touching *adj.* causing pity or sympathy.

touchline *n.* in football, rugby, etc., either of the two lines marking the side boundaries of the pitch.

tough (tuf) *adj.* **1** strong and long-lasting; not easily cut, broken, torn, or worn out. **2** (of food) difficult to chew. **3** (of people and animals) strong and fit and able to endure hardship. **4** difficult to deal with or overcome.

toughen *vb.* **toughening, toughened** to make or become tough or tougher.

tour (tōōr) *n.* a long journey stopping at various places along the route. – *vb.* **touring, toured**.

tourism *n.* the industry providing services for tourists, e.g. accommodation.

tourist *n.* a person who travels for pleasure.

tournament (tōōr nă mĕnt) *n.* a competition, for example in tennis or chess, between many players for a championship.

tourniquet (tōōr ni kā) *n.* a bandage that is tied tightly round a limb to stop the flow of blood.

tow (tō) *vb.* **towing, towed** to pull a vehicle behind another vehicle.

towpath *n.* a path beside a canal or river formerly used by horses towing barges.

towards (tŏ **wördz**) or **toward** (tŏ **wörd**) *prep.* **1** in the direction of: *She turned towards him.* **2** in relation to; about: *She has a strange attitude towards the new manager.* **3** as a contribution to: *I donated £1000 towards the cost of a new school.* **4** near: *We sat towards the back of the hall.*

towel (**tow** ĕl) *n.* a piece of thick soft cloth or paper for drying yourself, washed dishes, etc. – *vb.* **towelling, towelled**.

tower (**tow** ĕr) *n.* a tall narrow structure often forming part of a larger lower building such as a church. – *vb.* **towering, towered** to reach a great height or rise high above: *The skyscraper towers above all the other buildings in the city.*

towering *adj.* reaching a great height.

town (town) *n.* a place with buildings and streets larger than a village.

toxic (**tok** sik) *adj.* poisonous.

toy (toi) *n.* an object made for a child to play with. – *adj.* made to be played with: *a toy car.*

trace (trās) *n.* **1** a mark or sign that some person, animal, or thing has been in that place. **2** a very small amount of something that can only just be detected. – *vb.* **tracing, traced 1** to track and discover by following clues or a trail. **2** to make a copy of a drawing, design, etc. by covering it with a sheet of transparent paper and drawing over the visible lines.

trachea (tră **kē** ă) or (**trā** ki ă) *n.* **tracheae** (tră **kē** ē) or (**trā** ki ē) or **tracheas** the windpipe.

track (trak) *n.* **1** a mark or trail left by the passing of a person, animal, or thing, especially a footprint. **2** a rough path, especially one made by feet. **3** a specially prepared course for racing. **4** the rails along which a train runs. – *vb.* **tracking, tracked 1** to follow the marks, footprints, etc. left by a person or animal. **2** to follow and plot the course of a spacecraft, satellite, etc. by radar.

track event *n.* in athletics, a race.

tract (trakt) *n.* **1** a large area of land. **2** a system in the body with a particular function, such as the digestive tract. **3** a short essay or book.

traction (**trak** shŏn) *n.* **1** the action of pulling or the force used in pulling. **2** a medical treatment using a series of pulleys and weights to pull on a muscle or limb, to correct some condition.

tractor (**trak** tŏr) *n.* a vehicle with two large rear wheels, for pulling farm machinery, etc.

The Canadian National Tower in Toronto is taller than any skyscraper at 553 metres.

trade (trād) *n.* the buying and selling of goods or services between people or countries. – *vb.* **trading, traded** to buy and sell.
trademark *n.* a name, word, or symbol shown on all of the goods made or sold by a particular company or individual.
trade, or **trades**, **union** *n.* an organization of workers or employees formed to protect their interests and generally try to improve working conditions and pay. – *n.* **trade unionism**.
tradition (trå di shŏn) *n.* the handing down of beliefs, customs, etc. from generation to generation. – *adj.* **traditional**.

● **Trafalgar** off the south coast of SPAIN, was the scene in 1805 of a great victory for the British fleet under NELSON over the Spanish and French fleets.

traffic (tra fik) *n.* the vehicles, ships, aircraft, etc. that move along a particular route.
tragedy (tra jĕ di) *n.* **tragedies 1** a serious drama, film, opera, etc. in which the main character or characters are eventually destroyed through a combination of events and circumstances. **2** a catastrophe.
tragic (tra jik) *adj.* sad; very distressing.
trail (trāl) *vb.* **trailing, trailed 1** to drag loosely behind you as you move: *They trailed the fishing line behind the boat.* **2** to move along slowly and wearily. **3** to fall behind a competitor in a race or contest. – *n.* a series of marks, footprints, etc. left by a passing person, animal, or thing.
trailer *n.* a vehicle for towing behind a car.
train (trān) *n.* a string of carriages or wagons pulled by a railway engine. – *vb.* **training, trained 1** to teach a person or animal to do something. **2** to prepare for performance in a sport by instruction, practice, exercise, diet, etc.: *He is training for the marathon.* – *adj.* **trained**. – *n.* **training**.

Today trains are particulary useful for carrying heavy freight long distances and for taking commuters to and from their jobs in city centres. The illustration shows an American Union Pacific freight train.

trainer *n.* **1** a person who trains racehorses, athletes, sportsmen and -women, etc. **2** (*British*) a soft running shoe with a thick sole.
trait (trā) or (trāt) *n.* a distinguishing feature or quality, especially of a person's character.
traitor (trā tŏr) *n.* a person who betrays his or her country, or a friend's trust.
tram (tram) *n.* an electrically-powered passenger vehicle which runs on rails laid in the streets.
tramp (tramp) *vb.* **tramping, tramped 1** to walk with firm heavy footsteps. **2** to make a journey on foot: *We tramped over the hills.* – *n.* a person who travels from place to place on foot, and who lives by begging and doing odd jobs.
trample (tram pĕl) *vb.* **trampling, trampled** to tread heavily or roughly; to tread on: *There was cigarette ash trampled into the carpet.*
trampoline (tram pŏ lēn) *n.* a piece of tough canvas attached to a framework by cords or rope and stretched tight, for acrobats, gymnasts, children, etc. to jump on.
tranquil (trang kwil) *adj.* quiet; peaceful; undisturbed. – *n.* **tranquillity**.
trans- (trans-) or (tranz-) *prefix* **1** across; beyond; on the other side of: *transatlantic.* **2** into another state or place: *transform.*
transfer (tran sfûr) *vb.* **transferring, transferred** to move from one place, person, or group to another.
transform (trans förm) *vb.* **transforming, transformed** to change completely and often dramatically: *The good news transformed her mood from gloom to elation.* – *n.* **transformation**.
transistor (tran zis tŏr) *n.* **1** a small electrical device in radios and televisions which performs serveral functions including amplification. **2** (in full **transistor radio**) a small portable radio.
translate (trans lāt) *vb.* **translating, translated** to put speech or written text into another language. – *n.* **translator**.
translation *n.* speech or written text that has been put into one language from another.
translucent (trans lōō sĕnt) *adj.* allowing some light to pass through; semi-transparent.
transmission (tranz mi shŏn) *n.* something broadcast, especially on radio or television.
transmit (tranz mit) *vb.* **transmitting, transmitted 1** to pass or hand something on: *The disease is transmitted through dirty water.* **2** to broadcast a radio or television programme.
transmitter *n.* an apparatus for transmitting radio or television signals.

transparent (trans **pa** rĕnt) *adj.* able to be seen through; clear.

transplant (trans **plänt**) *vb.* **transplanting, transplanted** to transfer an organ, skin, etc. from one person or part of the body to another. – (**trans** plänt) *n.* anything which has been transplanted.

transport (tran **spört**) *vb.* **transporting, transported** to carry goods, passengers, etc. from one place to another. – (**trans** pört) *n.* **1** a system of moving people, goods, etc. from place to place: *He runs a transport business.* **2** a means of getting from place to place: *My car's broken down so I've no transport at the moment.*
transportation *n.* the act of transporting.

● **Transvaal** is a province in SOUTH AFRICA, containing the world's richest goldmines.

trap (trap) *n.* a device or hole, usually with bait attached, for catching animals. – *vb.*
trapping, trapped to catch an animal in a trap.
trapdoor *n.* a small opening in a floor.

trapeze (trǎ **pēz**) *n.* a swing-like apparatus on which gymnasts or acrobats perform tricks.

trash (trash) *n.* (especially *US*) rubbish.
trashcan *n.* (*US*) a dustbin.

travel (**tra** vĕl) *vb.* **travelling, travelled 1** to journey, especially abroad or far from home. **2** to move: *Light travels in a straight line.*

trawl (tröl) *n.* (in full **trawl-net**) a large bag-shaped net used to catch fish in the sea. – *vb.*
trawling, trawled to search the sea for fish.
trawler *n.* a fishing-boat used in trawling.

tray (trā) *n.* a flat piece of wood, metal, plastic, etc. for carrying dishes, crockery, etc.

treacherous (**tre** chĕ rŭs) *adj.* **1** not able to be trusted. **2** having hidden dangers: *The river looks calm but its fast current is treacherous.*

tread (tred) *vb.* **treading, trod** (trod), **trodden** or **trod 1** to walk or step on. **2** to crush or press into the ground; to trample: *Don't tread dirt into the carpet.* – *n.* **1** a manner or the sound of walking: *He has a heavy tread.* **2** an act of treading. **3** the thick, grooved, and patterned surface of a tyre that grips the road.

treason (**trē** zŏn) *n.* (also **high treason**) disloyalty to or betrayal of your country.

treasure (**tre** zhŭr) *n.* **1** a collection of gold, silver, precious stones, and jewels, etc. which have often been hidden for a period of time. **2** any thing of great value. – *vb.* **treasuring,**

treasured to value greatly.
treasurer *n.* the person who is in charge of the money and accounts in an organization.
treasury *n.* **treasuries** a place where treasure is stored.

treat (trēt) *vb.* **treating, treated 1** to behave towards a person or thing in a certain manner: *She treated him badly.* **2** to care for a person with an illness or injury: *The doctor treated the accident victims for shock.*
treatment *n.* **1** the medical care given to a patient. **2** the manner of dealing with something: *I like the artist's treatment of the sky.*

treaty (**trē** ṭi) *n.* **treaties** a formal agreement between states or governments.

treble (**tre** bĕl) *n.* **1** anything which is three times as much or as many. **2** in music, a soprano, especially a boy with a soprano voice; a part written for this voice. – *vb.*
trebling, trebled to make or become three times as much.

tree (trē) *n.* a tall woody plant with a trunk and branches on its upper part.

Trees are the largest and oldest living things. The biggest is the giant redwood of the sequoia family. These trees come from North America and can grow up to 100 metres tall.

Bonsai is the ancient Japanese art of growing miniature trees. Grown in pots, the trees are constantly pruned and shaped.

trellis (**tre** lis) *n.* a frame of narrow wooden strips used to support climbing plants.

tremble (**trem** bĕl) *vb.* **trembling, trembled** to shake, for example with cold, fear, weakness, etc. – *n.* a trembling movement; a shudder or tremor. – *adj.* **trembling.**

tremendous (trĕ **men** dŭs) *adj.* enormous.

tremor (**tre** mŏr) *n.* a shaking or quivering.

trench (trench) *n.* a long narrow ditch dug in the ground.

trend (trend) *n.* **1** a general tendency. **2** the current general movement in style.

trendy *adj.* **trendier, trendiest** (*British colloquial*) following the latest fashions.

trespass (**tres** pås) *vb.* **trespassing, trespassed** to enter someone else's property without permission to do so. – *n.* the act of entering someone else's property without permission. – *n.* **trespasser**.

tri- (trī-) *prefix* three or three times.

trial (**trī** ål) *n.* **1** a legal process by which a person accused of a crime is judged by a judge or jury in a court of law. **2** an experiment.

triangle (**trī** ang gěl) *n.* **1** a shape with three sides and three angles. **2** a musical percussion instrument shaped like a triangle.

triangular (trī **ang** gū lår) *adj.* in the shape of a triangle.

tribe (trīb) *n.* a group of families or communities with the same customs, language, leader, etc., who often share the same area of land.

tributary (**trib** ū tå ri) *n.* **tributaries** a stream or river that flows into a larger river or lake.

tribute (**trib** ūt) *n.* something given or said as an expression of praise, thanks, admiration, or affection: *The bridegroom paid tribute to everyone who had helped to organize the wedding.*

trick (trik) *n.* **1** a mischievous act or plan; a prank or joke. **2** a clever or skilful act or feat which astonishes, puzzles, or amuses: *The magician astonished everyone with his tricks.* – *adj.* intended to deceive or give a certain illusion: *She specializes in trick photography.* – *vb.* **tricking, tricked** to cheat or deceive: *She tricked him out of his money.*

tricky *adj.* **trickier, trickiest** needing skill and care. – *adv.* **trickily**. – *n.* **trickiness**.

trickle (**tri** kěl) *vb.* **trickling, trickled** to flow in a thin slow stream or drops.

tricolour (**tri** kǒ lǒr) *n.* a three-coloured flag.

tricycle (**trī** si kěl) *n.* a cycle with three wheels.

trident (**trī** děnt) *n.* a spear with three prongs, especially as carried by a sea god, such as Neptune or Britannia, or a Roman gladiator.

triennial (trī **en** i ål) *adj.* happening once every three years.

trifle (**trī** fěl) *n.* **1** anything of very little value. **2** a dessert made of sponge-cake soaked in sherry and spread with jam and fruit, topped with custard and whipped cream.

trigger (**tri** gěr) *n.* **1** a small lever which is squeezed to fire a gun. **2** anything which starts a train of actions or reactions.

trilobite (**trī** lō bīt) *n.* any of various extinct sea animals, now found as FOSSILS.

trim (trim) *vb.* **trimming, trimmed 1** to make neat and tidy, especially by clipping: *The hedge looked better after being trimmed.* **2** to make less by cutting: *It is important to trim costs.*

● **Trinidad and Tobago**. See Supplement, **Countries**.

trinity (**trin** i ti) *n.* **trinities** a group of three.

trinket (**tring** kit) *n.* a cheap piece of jewellery.

trio (**trē** ō) *n.* **trios 1** a group of three. **2** a piece of music composed for a group of three instruments, players, or singers.

trip (trip) *vb.* **tripping, tripped** to stumble or fall over. – *n.* **1** a short journey, usually to a place and back again. **2** a stumble.

triple (**tri** pěl) *adj.* made up of three parts or things. – *vb.* **tripling, tripled** to make or become three times as great, much, or many.

triplet (**trip** lit) *n.* one of 3 children or animals born to the same mother at the same time.

tripod (**trī** pod) *n.* a stand with three legs for supporting a camera or telescope.

trireme (**trī** rēm) *n.* an ancient Greek warship with three banks of rowers on each side.

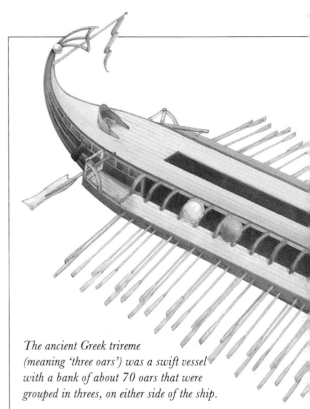

The ancient Greek trireme (meaning 'three oars') was a swift vessel with a bank of about 70 oars that were grouped in threes, on either side of the ship.

triumph (**trī** umf) *n.* a great or notable victory, success, or achievement. – *vb.* **triumphing, triumphed** to win a victory or be successful. **triumphal** *adj.* of or celebrating a triumph. **triumphant** *adj.* feeling great joy at a victory.

trivia (**tri** vi å) *n.* (*plural*) unimportant details. **trivial** *adj.* of very little importance. – *n.* **triviality** (tri vi **al** i ti), **trivialities**.

trod, trodden. See **tread**.

trolley (**tro** li) *n.* **trolleys** (especially *British*) a small basket on wheels used for carrying luggage, shopping, etc.

trombone (trom **bōn**) *n.* a brass wind instrument, with a U-shaped slide used to alter the pitch of the notes. – *n.* **trombonist**.

troop (trōop) *n.* (in *plural*) soldiers.

trophy (**trō** fi) *n.* **trophies** a cup, medal, etc. awarded as a prize for victory in a contest.

tropic (**tro** pik) *n.* **1** either of two imaginary circles running round the Earth at 23°27′ north (the **Tropic of Cancer**) or 23°27′ south (the **Tropic of Capricorn**) of the equator. **2** (in *plural*) the part of the Earth lying between these two circles, noted for its hot, dry weather. – *adj.* **tropical.**

trot (trot) *vb.* **trotting, trotted 1** (of a horse) to move at a steady medium pace. **2** to move or proceed at a steady fairly brisk pace.

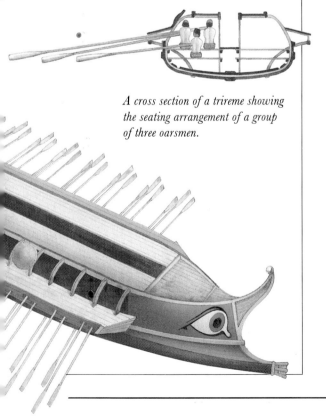

A cross section of a trireme showing the seating arrangement of a group of three oarsmen.

trouble (tru **běl**) *n.* **1** something which causes distress, worry, concern, or annoyance. **2** a problem or difficulty: *Your trouble is that you're too generous.* – *vb.* **troubling, troubled** to feel distress, worry, concern, anger, or sadness. **troubleshooter** *n.* a person who is employed to find and solve problems.

trough (trof) *n.* **1** a long narrow open container for holding water or feed for animals. **2** a long, narrow area of low atmospheric pressure.

trousers (**trow** zěrz) *n.* (*plural*) a piece of clothing for the lower part of the body, reaching from the waist and covering each leg separately down to the ankle.

trout (trowt) *n.* **trout** or **trouts** any of several freshwater fish of the salmon family.

trowel (**trow** ěl) *n.* **1** a small hand-held tool with a flat blade, used for spreading mortar, etc. **2** a garden tool like a small spade.

● **Troy** was an ancient city in Asia Minor which, according to Greek mythology, was besieged for ten years.

truant (**trōo** ånt) *n.* someone who stays away from school or work without good reason or without permission.

truce (trōos) *n.* an agreement to stop fighting.

truck (truk) *n.* **1** (*British*) an open railway wagon for carrying goods. **2** (especially *US*) a large motor vehicle for transporting goods; a lorry.

trudge (truj) *vb.* **trudging, trudged** to walk with slow heavy weary steps.

Triumphal arches date back to Roman times and usually were built to commemorate a great victory. The Arc de Triomphe in Paris (here clad in protective boards during the 1870 siege of the city) was ordered to be built by Napoleon in 1806 to commemorate his great victory over the Austrians and Russians at Austerlitz. It was completed in 1836.

Truant once had the meaning 'idle rogue', but in the 16th century took on the meaning of a pupil absent from school. It is related to the Welsh word *truan* meaning 'wretched'.

true (trōō) *adj.* **1** agreeing with fact or reality; not false or wrong: *This is a true story.* **2** accurate or exact: *A photograph doesn't give a true idea of the size of the building.*

truly *adv.* really; genuinely; honestly: *I truly believe it to be for the best.*

trumpet (**trum** pit) *n.* **1** a brass instrument with a powerful, high, clear tone. **2** anything like this in shape, such as the flower of a daffodil. **3** the loud cry of an elephant.

trunk (trungk) *n.* **1** the main stem of a tree without the branches and roots. **2** a person's or animal's body without the head, arms, and legs. **3** a large box or chest for storing or transporting clothes and other items. **4** (*US*) the boot of a car. **5** the long nose of an elephant.

trust (trust) *n.* **1** belief or confidence in the goodness, character, and ability of someone or something. **2** charge or care: *The child was placed in my trust.* – *adj.* held in trust. – *vb.* **trusting, trusted 1** to have confidence or faith in; to depend on: *I trust her to be able to cope.* **2** to allow someone to use something in the belief that they will behave responsibly: *I wouldn't trust him with your new car.*

make an effort to do something. **2** to test or to experiment with something: *We tried out a new flavour of ice cream but we didn't like it.* – *n.* **tries 1** an attempt or effort. **2** in rugby, a scoring touch-down.

trying *adj.* causing strain or anxiety.

tsar or **czar** (zär) or (tsär) *n.* (also **tzar**) the title given to the emperors of Russia until 1917. **tsarina** or **czarina** (zä **rēn** å) or (tsä **rēn** å) *n.* (also **tzarina**) the title given to a female tsar or to the wife or widow of a tsar.

tub (tub) *n.* **1** a small barrel. **2** a small, round container for holding cream, ice cream, yoghurt, etc.

tuba (**tū** bå) *n.* a large brass musical instrument with a low-pitched tone.

tubby (**tu** bi) *adj.* **tubbier, tubbiest** (*colloquial*) plump; short and fat. – *n.* **tubbiness**.

tube (tūb) *n.* **1** a long hollow pipe used for carrying liquids. **2** (*British*) (a train running on) the underground railway in London.

tuber (**tū** běr) *n.* a short fleshy stem found underground, such as the potato.

tuberculosis (tū bûr kū **lō** sis) *n.* a serious infectious disease that affects the lungs.

A slave family finds shelter on the journey north along the 'Underground Railroad'. It was not a real railroad, but the people who worked for it – notably Harriet Tubman – used railroad terms to describe the system. As many as 100,000 slaves may have been helped to freedom by the Railroad.

trustworthy *adj.* able to be trusted or depended on. – *n.* **trust-worthiness**.

trusty *adj.* able to be trusted or relied on: *My trusty old car never fails me.*

truth (trōōth) *n.* **truths** (trōōThz) **1** the state of being true, genuine, or factual. **2** something that is established or generally accepted as true. – *adj.* **truthful**.

try (trī) *vb.* **tries, trying, tried 1** to attempt or

● **Tubman, Harriet** (1820-1913) was one of the black Americans who risked their lives to organize the 'underground railroad' which helped slaves escape captivity from the southern states in the 1850s.

tuck (tuk) *vb.* **tucking, tucked** to push or fold the outer edges of something together or into something, to make secure or tidy: *You must tuck your shirt in.*

Two of the leading monarchs of the House of Tudor: Henry VIII, who broke all ties with the pope and the Catholic Church, and Elizabeth I under whom England became powerful and prosperous.

Tudor (tū dŏr) *adj.* of the royal family which ruled ENGLAND from 1485, when HENRY the Seventh came to the throne, until the death of ELIZABETH THE FIRST in 1603, or of this period in English history.

Tuesday (tūz di) *n.* the day of the week between Monday and Wednesday.

tufa (tū fă) *n.* a rock formed from calcium carbonate deposited by springs rich in this mineral.

tuft (tuft) *n.* a small bunch or clump of grass, hair, feathers, wool, etc. attached or growing together at the base. – *adj.* **tufted.** *adj.* **tufty, tuftier, tuftiest.**

tug (tug) *vb.* **tugging, tugged 1** to pull sharply and strongly: *She tugged at the door until it opened.* **2** to tow a ship with a tugboat. – *n.* **1** a strong sharp pull. **2** (in full **tugboat**) a small boat with a very powerful engine for towing larger ships and barges.

tug of war *n.* **1** a contest in which two people or teams pull at opposite ends of a rope, trying to pull their opponents over a centre line. **2** any struggle between two opposing sides.

tuition (tū i shŏn) *n.* teaching, often in small groups in a college or university.

tulip (tū lip) *n.* a plant of the lily family grown from a bulb with a brightly-coloured flower.

tumble (tum bĕl) *vb.* **tumbling, tumbled 1** to fall helplessly or clumsily. **2** to perform as an acrobat, especially turning somersaults. **3** to understand or realize suddenly: *Only then did I tumble to her intentions.* – *n.* a fall.

tumble-drier or **-dryer** *n.* a machine for drying washing with a drum which tosses the clothes around while blowing hot air into them. – *vb.* **tumble-dry, tumble-dries, tumble-drying, tumble-dried.**

tumbler *n.* **1** a large drinking glass without a stem or handle. **2** an acrobat.

tumour (tū mŏr) *n.* a dangerous mass of tissue in the body formed by a new growth of cells.

tuna (tū nă) *n.* **tuna** or **tunas** a large sea-fish of the mackerel family caught for food.

tundra (tun dră) *n.* a vast flat Arctic plain with permanently frozen subsoil, and sparse vegetation.

tune (tūn) *n.* a pleasing succession of musical notes; a melody. – *vb.* **tuning, tuned 1** to adjust a musical instrument to the correct pitch. **2** to adjust a radio to pick up signals from a required frequency for a particular programme: *She likes to tune in to the Archers.* – **change your tune** to change your attitude or opinions. – **in tune 1** (of a musical instrument or voice) producing the correct pitch: *She sings beautifully in tune.* **2** having the same pitch as other instruments or voices: *The two guitars aren't in tune.*

tuneful *adj.* **1** having a pleasant tune; melodious. **2** full of music. – *n.* **tunefulness.**

tunic (tū nik) *n.* a close-fitting belted jacket with a high collar worn as part of a soldier's or policeman's uniform.

● **Tunisia.** See Supplement, **Countries.**

tunnel (tu nĕl) *n.* **1** a man-made underground passage for pedestrians, vehicles, trains, etc. **2** an underground passage dug by an animal such as a mole. – *vb.* **tunnelling, tunnelled.**

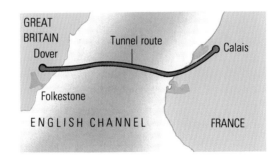

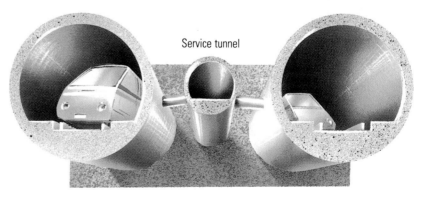

Service tunnel

The word tulip comes from a Turkish word, *tulbend*, meaning turban which the opened bloom was thought to resemble. Other Turkish words that have taken root in English are *divan* (a kind of couch), *kiosk* (a small shop), *kismet* (fate), and *yoghurt*.

The Eurotunnel linking Great Britain with France is nearly 50 km long. It is in fact three tunnels – two railway and one service. The rail tunnels measure 7.5 metres across. The service tunnel, which is nearly 5 metres across, is used by workers to carry out repairs and it is also an emergency escape route. Trains carry cars and passengers across the Channel in about 35 minutes.

Kemal Atatürk was elected the first president of the modern republic of Turkey in 1923. His name 'Atatürk' means 'Father of Turks'.

turban (tûr bǎn) *n.* a man's headdress consisting of a long piece of cloth wound round the head, worn especially by MUSLIMS.

turbine (tûr bīn) *n.* a motor in which a wheel or drum with blades is driven by a flow of water, steam, gas, etc. to produce power.

turbo- (tûr bō-) *prefix* driven by a turbine.

tureen (tū rēn) or (tǔ rēn) *n.* a deep dish with a cover, from which soup is served.

turf (tûrf) *n.* **turfs** or **turves** (tûrvz) the surface of the soil consisting of grass and matted roots.

● **Turin** is a city on the River Po in northern ITALY and is the home of the Italian car industry.

Turk (tûrk) *n.* a person from the modern state of Turkey or the former Ottoman Empire.
Turkish *adj.* of Turkey, its people, language, etc. – *n.* the official language of Turkey.
Turkish bath *n.* a type of bath in which the bather first sits in a hot room filled with steam.
Turkish delight *n.* a sticky jelly-like sweet.

● **Turkey**. See Supplement, **Countries**.

turkey (tûr ki) *n.* **turkeys** a large farmyard bird of the pheasant family, valued as food.

● **Turkmenistan**. See Supplement, **Countries**.

turmoil (tûr moil) *n.* wild confusion, agitation, or disorder: *His mind was in a turmoil.*

turn (tûrn) *vb.* **turning, turned 1** to move or go round in a circle. **2** to change position so that a different side or part comes to the top or front: *She turned the pages slowly.* **3** to change direction or take a new direction: *Turn left at the corner.* **4** to direct, aim, or point: *He turned his thoughts to supper.* **5** to become or change into: *They have turned the book into a film.* **6** to move or swing around a point: *A gate turns on its hinge.* – *n.* **1** an act of turning; a rotation: *He gave the wheel a turn.* **2** a change of direction or position: *At the crossroads take a turn to the right.* **3** a change in nature, character, condition, etc.: *Her condition took a turn for the worse.* **4** an opportunity that comes to each of several people in succession: *It's her turn to bat.* – *vb.* **turn down** to refuse. – *vb.* **turn out 1** to send away. **2** to make or produce. **3** to happen or prove to be: *She turned out to be right.* – *vb.* **turn up 1** to be found

unexpectedly. **2** to shorten a garment by folding part up and stitching it in place.

turnpike *n.* (especially *US*) a motorway on which a toll is paid.

turnstile *n.* a revolving gate with metal arms which allows only one person to pass through at a time, usually after paying a fee.

● **Turner, J.M.W.** (1775-1851) was one of England's greatest painters, famous for his dazzling effects with light, water, and weather.

turnip (tûr nip) *n.* a plant of the cabbage family with a large round white or yellowish root.

turquoise (tûr kwoiz) or (tûr kwäz) *n.* **1** a light greenish-blue gemstone. **2** its colour.

turret (tu rit) *n.* a small tower on a castle or other building.

turtle (tûr těl) *n.* any of several marine or freshwater tortoise-like reptiles, with a hard shell and flippers for swimming.

tusk (tusk) *n.* one of a pair of long curved pointed teeth which project from the mouth of certain animals e.g. the elephant. – *adj.* **tusked**.

The gold mask that covered the face of the mummy of the Egyptian boy-king Tutankhamen. He was buried surrounded by treasure and beautiful furniture.

● **Tutankhamen** was a pharaoh of ancient EGYPT whose tomb was discovered in 1922 by the British archaeologist, Howard Carter.

tutor (tū tǒr) *n.* **1** a university or college teacher. **2** a private teacher. – *vb.* **tutoring, tutored**.

TWINNED BUT TIRED

Clichés are words or phrases that have been used too often and so have become tired, and hackneyed. Here are some clichés using 'twinned' words:
by leaps and bounds,
to pick and choose,
tooth and nail,
trials and tribulations,
slow but sure,
fast and furious.

●**Twain, Mark** (1835-1910) was an American story-teller and humorist. His best known novels are *The Adventures of Tom Sawyer* and *The Adventures of Huckleberry Finn.*

tweed (twēd) *n.* a thick rough woollen cloth made originally in SCOTLAND.

tweezers (twē zěrz) *n.* (*plural*) a small pair of pincers for pulling out individual hairs, etc.

twelfth (twelfth) *n.* **1** one of twelve equal parts. **2** the last of twelve; the next after the eleventh. **Twelfth Night** *n.* the evening before the twelfth day after Christmas (5 January) or the evening of the day itself (6 January).

twelve (twelv) *n.* the number or figure 12. **twelvefold** *adj.* **1** twelve times as much or as many. **2** divided into twelve parts. – *adv.* by twelve times as much.

twenty (**twen** ti) *n.* **twenties** the number or figure 20. – *pron.* 20 people or things. – *n., adj., & adv.* **twentieth.**

twice (twīs) *adv.* **1** two times; on two occasions: *I've only seen him twice.* **2** double in amount: *I would like twice as much.*

twig (twig) *n.* a small branch of a tree, bush, etc.

twilight (**twī** līt) *n.* the faint light in the sky when the sun is just below the horizon immediately after sunset.

twin (twin) *n.* either of two people or animals born to the same mother at the same time.

twine (twīn) *n.* strong string.

twinge (twinj) *n.* a sudden sharp pain.

twinkle (**twing** kěl) *vb.* **twinkling, twinkled 1** (of a star, etc.) to shine with a bright flickering light. **2** (of the eyes) to shine or sparkle with amusement or mischief.

twirl (twûrl) *vb.* **twirling, twirled** to turn, spin.

twist (twist) *vb.* **twisting, twisted 1** to wind or turn round: *He twisted round in his seat.* **2** to follow a winding course: *The road twisted through the mountains.* **3** to wrench out of the correct shape or position with a sharp turning movement: *He twisted his ankle.* – *n.* **1** the act of twisting. **2** a turn or coil; a bend. **3** a sharp turning movement which pulls something out of shape. – *adj.* **twisted.**

twitch (twich) *vb.* **twitching, twitched 1** to move jerkily. **2** to pull sharply or jerkily.

twitter (**twi** těr) *n.* a light repeated chirping sound made by small birds.

two (tōō) *n.* the number or figure 2. – *pron.* two people or things. **two-faced** *adj.* deceitful and hypocritical.

tycoon (tī **kōōn**) *n.* a rich and powerful businessman or businesswoman.

type (tīp) *n.* **1** a class or group of people, animals, or things which share similar characteristics; a kind or variety: *Trains, cars, and aircraft are all types of vehicle.* **2** (*colloquial*) a person, especially of a specified kind: *He is a quiet type of person.* – *vb.* **typing, typed** to write words, text, etc. using a typewriter or word processor. – *n.* **typing.**

typewriter *n.* a machine with a keyboard that prints letters.

typist *n.* a person who types.

typhoid (**tī** foid) *n.* (in full **typhoid fever**) a dangerous infectious disease, caused by a bacterium in food or drinking water.

typhoon (tī **fōōn**) *n.* a violent storm occurring in the China Sea and western Pacific area.

typical (**ti** pi kål) *adj.* being a characteristic or representative example showing the usual characteristics of behaviour, attitude, etc.: *A hostile reaction is typical of him.* – *adv.* **typically.**

tyrannosaur (ti **ran** ȯ sör) or **tyrannosaurus** *n.* a large flesh-eating dinosaur with two large hind legs for walking on and smaller front legs.

With its powerful legs and razor-like jaws, Tyrannosaurus must have been a terrifyingly efficient killer. It measured over 12 metres – about the length of three cars. It had tiny arms with only two claws – used perhaps for picking its teeth!

tyrant (**tī** rånt) *n.* a cruel and unjust ruler.

tyre (tīr) *n.* a thick rubber air-filled or hollow ring placed over a wheel.

PRONUNCIATION GUIDE	
fat a	all ö
fate ā	foot oo
fast ä	moon ōō
among å	boy oi
met e	house ow
mean ē	demon ȯ
silent ė	thing th
loch hh	this Th
fin i	but u
line ī	mute ū
quick kw	fur û
got o	brochure ů
note ō	vision zh

U u

U-boat (ū bōt) *n.* a German submarine, especially of the First and Second World Wars.

udder (u děr) *n.* the bag-like milk-producing organ of a cow, sheep, or goat.

● **Uganda**. See Supplement, **Countries**.

ugly (**ug** li) *adj.* **uglier, ugliest 1** unpleasant to look at. **2** threatening danger or violence.

● **Ukraine**. See Supplement, **Countries**.

ulcer (**ul** sěr) *n.* a slow-healing internal or external wound. – *adj.* **ulcerous**.

● **Ulster** is the name of a former kingdom of IRELAND. Six of its nine counties have, since 1921, formed NORTHERN IRELAND.

ultimate (**ul** ti mǎt) *adj.* **1** last or final. **2** most important; greatest possible. **3** fundamental. **ultimately** *adv.* in the end; finally.

ultra- (**ul** trǎ-) *prefix* **1** beyond in place, range, or limit: *ultra-microscopic*. **2** extremely: *ultra-conservative*.

Ulysses. See **Myths and Legends**.

umbrella (um **bre** lǎ) *n.* a device carried to give shelter against rain, etc., consisting of a fabric canopy on a folding framework.

umpire (**um** pīr) *n.* a person supervising play in various sports, for example cricket and tennis.

un- (un-) *prefix* **1** not, or the opposite of: *unacceptable*; *unattractive*. **2** the reversal of a process: *unplug*; *unhook*. **3** a release from, or depriving of: *uncage*; *unthrone*. If the meaning of the main word is known then the sense of the word with the added prefix should usually be clear, for example *unable, unclear, uncommon,* *unemployed, unfair, unhappy, unhealthy, unimportant, unkind, untrue, unwell,* etc.

unanimous (ū **nan** i mǔs) *adj.* all in complete agreement: *The decision was unanimous*.

unbecoming (un bi **kum** ing) *adj.* not suited to the wearer.

uncanny (un **kan** i) *adj.* **uncannier, uncanniest** strange or mysterious: *There was an uncanny sound in the cave*.

uncertain (un **sûr** tin) *adj.* **1** not sure, certain, or confident. **2** not definitely known or decided: *Una is uncertain whether she can come.* – *n.* **uncertainty**.

uncle (**ung** kěl) *n.* the brother or brother-in-law of a father or mother; the husband of an aunt. **Uncle Sam** *n.* the United States.

uncomfortable (un **kum** fŏr tǎ běl) *adj.* **1** not comfortable: *The mattress is hard and uncomfortable*. **2** awkward: *Ursula feels uncomfortable with grown-ups*.

unconscious (un **kon** shǔs) *adj.* **1** without consciousness; senseless. **2** not aware.

unconstitutional (un kon sti **tū** shǒn ǎl) *adj.* not allowed by or consistent with a nation's constitution. – *adv.* **unconstitutionally**.

uncouth (un **kōōth**) *adj.* coarse in behaviour.

undecided (un di **sīd** id) *adj.* not having decided; not able to decide.

under (**un** děr) *prep.* **1** below or beneath; on the downward-facing surface of. **2** at the foot of. **3** less than: *It costs under £3*. **4** lower in rank than. **5** during the reign or administration of: *Under George the Third the American colonies rebelled.* – *adv.* in or to a lower place: *The swimmer went under again*.

under- (**un** děr-) *in compounds* **1** beneath or below: *underfoot*. **2** too little in quantity or degree; insufficient: *The workers complained* *because they were underpaid.* **3** lower in rank or importance: *under-secretary.* **4** less than: *underbid.* **5** less or lower than expectations or potential: *underdeveloped.* When the meaning of the main word is known the sense of the prefixed word should be clear, for example *underfed, undersized, underweight,* etc.

undercarriage (**un** dĕr ka rij) *n.* the landing-gear of an aircraft.

undergo (un dĕr **gō**) *vb.* **undergoes, undergoing, underwent** (un dĕr **went**), **undergone** (un dĕr **gon**) to endure, experience, or suffer.

undergraduate (un dĕr **gra** joo åt) *n.* a student who has not taken a degree.

underground (**un** dĕr grownd) *n.* **1** a place or area below ground level. **2** a system of electric trains running in tunnels below ground: *We'll go to the museum on the underground.* – (un dĕr **grownd**) *adj.* existing or operating below the surface of the ground.

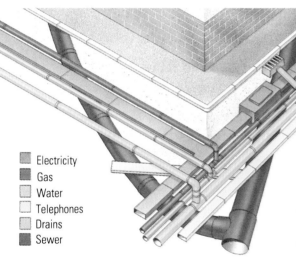

- Electricity
- Gas
- Water
- Telephones
- Drains
- Sewer

The underground world of city streets is a maze of drains, sewers, pipes, and cables. These are the city's lifelines – bringing gas, water, and electricity and taking away waste from kitchens and bathrooms.

undergrowth (**un** dĕr grōth) *n.* a thick growth of shrubs and bushes among trees.

undermine (un dĕr **mīn**) *vb.* **undermining, undermined 1** to dig or wear away the base or foundation of. **2** to weaken or destroy: *Ulrich is trying to undermine my confidence.*

underneath (un dĕr **nēth**) *prep. & adv.* beneath or below; under: *I like to sit underneath the trees.*

underpass (**un** dĕr päs) *n.* a tunnel under a road or railway; a subway.

underprivileged (un dĕr **priv** i lijd) *adj.* not having the basic living standards and rights enjoyed by most people in society.

understand (un dĕr **stand**) *vb.* **understanding, understood** (un dĕr **stood**) **1** to grasp with the mind the meaning, nature, or explanation: *Some people find Spanish easy to understand.* **2** to know, believe, or infer, from information received. – *adj.* **understandable.** – *adv.* **understandably.**

understood. See **understand.**

undertake (un dĕr **tāk**) *vb.* **undertaking, undertook** (un dĕr **took**), **undertaken** (un dĕr **tā** kĕn) **1** to accept a duty or task. **2** to promise or agree: *Uriah undertook to look after us.*

undertaker (**un** dĕr tā kĕr) *n.* a person whose job is organizing funerals.

underwear (**un** dĕr wār) *n.* clothes worn under shirts, trousers, dresses, and skirts.

underwent. See **undergo.**

undo (un **doo**) *vb.* **undoes** (un **duz**), **undoing, undid** (un **did**), **undone** (un **dun**) to open, unfasten, or untie: *I can't undo my shoelaces.*

undoubted (un **dow** tid) *adj.* clear; evident.

undress (un **dres**) *vb.* **undressing, undressed** to take your clothes off.

undue (un **dū**) *adj.* unjustifiably great; excessive: *They gave her undue praise.* – *adv.* **unduly.**

uneasy (un **ē** zi) *adj.* **uneasier, uneasiest** nervous, anxious, or unsettled; ill at ease.

unequal (un **ē** kwål) *adj.* **1** not equal in quantity, value, or rank. **2** not evenly matched.

uneven (un **ē** vĕn) *adj.* **1** not smooth or flat; bumpy: *This croquet lawn is uneven.* **2** (of a contest) with sides poorly matched; unequal.

unfair (un **fār**) *adj.* not fair or just.

unfold (un **fōld**) *vb.* **unfolding, unfolded** to open out the folds of; to spread out.

unhappy (un **ha** pi) *adj.* **unhappier, unhappiest** sad; in low spirits. – *adv.* **unhappily.** – *n.* **unhappiness.**

uni- (**ū** ni-) *prefix* one; a single: *unilateral.*

unicorn (**ū** ni körn) *n.* a mythical animal like a white horse with a long horn on its forehead.

uniform (**ū** ni förm) *n.* distinctive clothing worn by members of a particular organization or profession: *Mark wears his nurse's uniform at work.* – *adj.* not changing or varying in form or nature: *The books are of a uniform size.*

Perhaps of all uniforms military uniforms are the most colourful. At one time both dress and field uniforms were bright and coloured – and conspicuous. In order to be less noticeable and less a target for firearms, armies adopted khaki-coloured field and service uniforms, following the British army lead during the South African Boer War (1899-1902).

The countries of the United Kingdom of Great Britain and Northern Ireland. Southern Ireland (now the Republic of Ireland) became independent of Great Britain after the Anglo-Irish Treaty of 1921.

unify (ū ni fī) *vb.* **unifies, unifying, unified** to bring together to form a single unit or whole.

union (ūn yŏn) *n.* **1** the act of uniting or the state of being united. **2** an association of people or groups united in a common, especially political, purpose. **3** a trade union.

Union Jack *n.* (also **union flag**) the national flag of the UNITED KINGDOM, combining the crosses of St GEORGE, St ANDREW, and St PATRICK.

unique (ū nēk) *adj.* **1** being the only one of its kind; having no equal. **2** found solely in or belonging solely to. – *n.* **uniqueness**.

unit (ū nit) *n.* **1** a single item or element regarded as the smallest subdivision of a whole. **2** a set of mechanical or electrical parts, or a group of workers, that is part of a larger construction or organization.

unite (ū nīt) *vb.* **uniting, united 1** to make or become a single unit or whole. **2** to bring or come together in a common purpose or belief: *We must unite to win our cause.* – *adj.* **united**.

● **United Arab Emirates**. See Supplement.

● **United Kingdom**. The full title is the United Kingdom of Great Britain and Northern Ireland. (Great Britain consists of England, Scotland, and Wales.) The Channel Islands and the Isle of Man are dependencies of the British Crown. The UK's longest rivers are the Severn and the Thames on which London, the capital, stands. The south of the country is flat with rolling hills in parts. The north of the country, especially the Highlands of Scotland, is mountainous. The country has a moist temperate climate. Some 91 per cent of the population lives in towns, though farming is highly efficient. Industry is varied and the country is rich in natural gas and oil. In 1973 the UK joined the European Community. See separate entries: **England, Ireland, Scotland, Wales**.

● **United Nations** Most countries belong to the United Nations. Each member country sends delegates to regular meetings of the General Assembly in New York City. The UN works largely through 14 agencies. The Food and Agricultural Organization helps countries to grow more food. The World Health Organization fights disease. The International Monetary Fund lends countries money.

The United Nations aims to maintain international peace and to solve problems through international co-operation.

● **United States of America** 48 of the US states are in the same part of North America. The other two are Alaska in the north and the Pacific islands of Hawaii. The US mainland stretches from the Atlantic Ocean to the Pacific. Long mountain ranges run down the Pacific coast. Inland are flat-topped mountains and basins. In this region is the GRAND CANYON. Farther east beyond the Rocky Mountains are the great plains where the Mississippi River flows.

The first Americans were the native 'Indians'. Europeans started colonies in the 1500s, bringing black slaves from Africa. In 1776, 13 colonies rebelled against British rule and set up a republic. George WASHINGTON became its first president. Today the United States is the world's richest and most powerful nation and the world's largest producer of cars and chemicals. It produces more farm produce than any other country and is almost self-supporting in gas, oil, and coal. See also Supplement, **Countries**.

Key Facts
Capital: Washington, D.C.
Area: 9,399,320 sq. km (3,615,123 sq. mi.)
Population: 256,600,000
Largest city: New York City
Highest point: Mount McKinley, Alaska, 6194m (20,320 feet).

universe (ū ni vûrs) *n.* everything that exists everywhere, on Earth and in space.
universal *adj.* **1** of the universe. **2** of, relating to, or affecting the whole world or all people.

university (ū ni vûr si ti) *n.* **universities** a place of higher education with the authority to award degrees.

unleaded (un led id) *adj.* (of petrol) with a low lead content in order to reduce environmental pollution from exhaust fumes.

unleavened (un **lev** ênd) *adj.* (of bread) made without yeast.

unless (ŭn **les**) *conj.* if not; except if.

unlike (un **līk**) *prep.* **1** different from. **2** not typical or characteristic of: *It's unlike you to go for a walk.* – *adj.* different; dissimilar.

unlikely *adj.* **1** probably untrue. **2** not expected or likely to. **3** not obviously suitable: *an unlikely choice of partner.* – *n.* **unlikelihood**.

unload (un **lōd**) *vb.* **unloading, unloaded 1** to remove cargo from a vehicle: *Jo unloaded the van.* **2** to remove the ammunition from a gun.

unmistakable or **unmistakeable** (un mi **stāk** å bêl) *adj.* too easily recognizable to be mistaken for anything or anyone else: *Her voice is unmistakable.* – *adv.* **unmistakably** or **unmistakeably**.

unnatural (un **na** chů rål) *adj.* **1** different from the way things usually happen in nature. **2** insincere. – *adv.* **unnaturally**.

unpopular (un **pop** ū lår) *adj.* generally disliked: *Someone who tells lies is unpopular.* – *n.* **unpopularity** (un pop ū **la** ri ti).

unruly (un **rōō** li) *adj.* **unrulier, unruliest** disorderly: *an unruly mob.* – *n.* **unruliness**.

unsavoury (un **sā** vô ri) *adj.* unpleasant.

unscathed (un **skāThd**) *adj.* not harmed.

unskilled (un **skild**) *adj.* not having or requiring any special skill or training: *Washing dishes is unskilled work.*

unsophisticated (un sô **fis** ti kā tid) *adj.* **1** simple. **2** not experienced in life.

untie (un **tī**) *vb.* **untying, untied 1** to undo from a tied state. **2** to set free: *Untie the dog.*

until (ŭn **til**) *prep.* and *conj.* **1** up to the time of. **2** as far as: *I slept until Edinburgh.* **3** (with a negative) before: *The dentist can't give you an appointment until next week.*

untold (un **tōld**) *adj.* **1** not told. **2** too severe to be described: *The storm did untold damage.*

up (up) *prep.* at or to a higher position on, or a position farther along: *They climbed up the stairs.* – *adv.* **1** at or to a higher position or level: *Turn up the volume.* **2** in or to a more erect position: *Jake stood up.* **3** fully or completely: *All the food was eaten up.* **4** into the state of being gathered together: *I saved up for it.* **5** out of bed: *Anthony got up.* **6** to or towards: *The teacher walked up to him.* – *adj.* **1** placed in, or moving or directed to, a higher position: *Take the up escalator.* **2** out of bed: *He's not up yet.* **3** (of the sun) above the horizon.

upheaval *n.* a violent change or disturbance.

upkeep *n.* the cost of keeping something in good order or condition.

upright *adj.* **1** standing straight up; erect or vertical. **2** honest, good, moral: *John is an upright and sincere person.*

uprising *n.* a rebellion or revolt.

upshot *n.* the final outcome or ultimate effect: *What was the upshot of your meeting?*

upside-down or **upside down** *adj.* & *adv.* with the top part at the bottom.

upstairs *adj.* & *adv.* on or to an upper floor: *She ran to an upstairs room.* – *n.* an upper floor.

upstream *adv.* towards the source of a river.

upward *adv.* (also **upwards**) to or towards a higher place, a more important position: *The steps led upwards.* – *adj.* moving or directed upwards. – *adv.* **upwardly**.

upon (ŭ **pon**) *prep.* on or on to.

upper (**u** pêr) *adj.* **1** higher; situated above. **2** high or higher in rank or status.

upper-case *adj.* (of a printed letter) capital.

uproar (**up** rör) *n.* a noisy and angry protest.

upset (up **set**) *vb.* **upsetting, upset 1** to cause to be emotionally distressed: *We were upset to hear your sad news.* **2** to ruin or spoil plans. **3** to disturb the proper function of: *an upset stomach.* **4** to knock over: *The cat upset the milk.* – (**up** set) *n.* a disturbance, e.g. of plans.

● **Ur** was an ancient city in Mesopotamia.

KEY TO STATES
1 Alabama
2 Alaska
3 Arizona
4 Arkansas
5 California
6 Colorado
7 Connecticut
8 Delaware
9 Florida
10 Georgia
11 Hawaii
12 Idaho
13 Illinois
14 Indiana
15 Iowa
16 Kansas
17 Kentucky
18 Louisiana
19 Maine
20 Maryland
21 Massachusetts
22 Michigan
23 Minnesota
24 Mississippi
25 Missouri
26 Montana
27 Nebraska
28 Nevada
29 New Hampshire
30 New Jersey
31 New Mexico
32 New York
33 North Carolina
34 North Dakota
35 Ohio
36 Oklahoma
37 Oregon
38 Pennsylvania
39 Rhode Island
40 South Carolina
41 South Dakota
42 Tennessee
43 Texas
44 Utah
45 Vermont
46 Virginia
47 Washington
48 West Virginia
49 Wisconsin
50 Wyoming

●**Ural Mountains** (ū rǎl) This range of mountains in Russia forms a natural boundary between Europe and Asia.

uranium (ū **rān** i ům) *n.* an element (symbol **U**), a silvery radioactive metal.

●**Uranus** is one of our Sun's planets. It is 19 times farther away from the Sun than Earth is. One of its years lasts 84 of ours.

urban (ûr bǎn) *adj.* of, or relating to, a town or city; not rural.

Urdu (o͞or do͞o) *adj. & n.* (of or relating to) the official language of PAKISTAN.

urge (ûrj) *vb.* **urging, urged 1** to persuade forcefully; to beg or entreat. **2** to recommend earnestly: *I urge you to leave before it's too late.* **3** to drive onwards. – *n.* a strong desire or impulse.

urgent (ûr jěnt) *adj.* needing immediate attention: *an urgent message.* – *n.* **urgency**.

urine (ū rin) *n.* the yellow liquid mixture of waste protein and salts produced by the kidneys and discharged from the body via the bladder.

urn (ûrn) *n.* **1** a vase with a rounded body and a small narrow neck. **2** a large metal cylinder with a tap for serving tea or coffee.

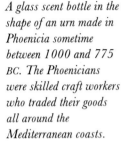

A glass scent bottle in the shape of an urn made in Phoenicia sometime between 1000 and 775 BC. The Phoenicians were skilled craft workers who traded their goods all around the Mediterranean coasts.

●**Uruguay**. See Supplement, **Countries**.

us (us) *pron.* the speaker or writer together with another person or other people; the object form of **we**: *He saw us at the game today* .

use¹ (ūz) *vb.* **using, used 1** to put to a particular purpose: *You use scissors to cut cloth.* **2** to consume; to take as a fuel. – *adj.* **usable**. – *n.* **user**. – **used to** accustomed to: *She's not used to exercising.* – *vb.* **used** (*auxiliary*) was or were formerly: *They used to be friends. She never used to be so grumpy.*
used *adj.* not new; second-hand.
user-friendly *adj.* designed to be easy or pleasant to use.

use² (ūs) *n.* **1** the act of using. **2** the state of being used: *This room is not in use.* **3** a practical purpose a thing can be put to: *What use are these old shirts?* **4** the quality of serving a practical purpose: *It's no use complaining.* **5** the length of time for which a thing is serviceable: *It should give you plenty of use.*
useful *adj.* serving a helpful purpose or various purposes. – *n.* **usefulness**.

●**USSR** (**Union of Soviet Socialist Republics**). See **Commonwealth of Independent States** and **Russia**.

usual (ūzh oo ǎl) *adj.* done or happening most often; customary: *He did the work with his usual enthusiasm.* – *adv.* **usually**.

●**Utah**. See Supplement, **USA**.

utensil (ū **ten** sil) *n.* an implement or container, especially for everyday use: *cooking utensils.*
uterus (ū tě rǔs) *n.* **uteri** (ū tě rī) the womb.

Utopia, *by the English scholar and politician, Sir Thomas More, was published in 1516. It describes an ideal land where everything is shared and everyone is educated.*

utility (ū **til** i ti) *n.* **utilities** usefulness.
utopia (ū tōp i ǎ) *n.* any imaginary place or situation of ideal perfection. – *adj.* **utopian**.
utter¹ (u těr) *vb.* **uttering, uttered** to express as speech or a sound; to speak.
utter² (u těr) *adj.* complete; total; absolute: *What an utter fool she is!* – *adv.* **utterly**.
U-turn (ū tûrn) *n.* a manoeuvre in which a vehicle is turned to face the other way in a single continuous movement.

●**Uzbekistan**. See Supplement, **Countries**.

V v

vacant (vā kånt) *adj.* empty or unoccupied.
vacation (vā **kā** shǒn) *n.* a holiday.
vaccine (vak sēn) *n.* a substance containing usually dead bacteria or viruses, injected into the blood to stimulate the production of antibodies and give immunity to a specific disease. – *n.* **vaccination**.
vacuum (vak ū ům) or (vak ūm) *n.* **vacuums** a space from which all matter, air or other gas, has been removed.

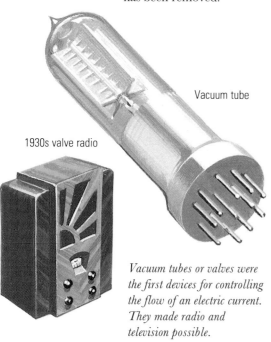

1930s valve radio

Vacuum tube

Vacuum tubes or valves were the first devices for controlling the flow of an electric current. They made radio and television possible.

vacuum cleaner *n.* an electrically powered machine that lifts dust and dirt by suction.
vagina (vå **jī** nå) *n.* the passage connecting the external female sex organs to the womb.
vague (vāg) *adj.* indistinct, imprecise, unclear: *I have only a vague recollection of what he looks like.*

vain (vān) *adj.* having too much pride in your own appearance; conceited. – *n.* **vanity**. – **in vain** with no success.
valentine (va lěn tīn) *n.* a message of love sent, usually anonymously, on 14 February, St *Valentine*'s Day.

●**Valentino, Rudolph** (1895-1926) an Italian-born American film star of the silent screen.

Valhalla (val **hal** å) *n.* in Scandinavian mythology, the place where the souls of slain heroes live in eternal bliss.
valiant (**val** i ånt) *adj.* brave; heroic.
valid (**va** lid) *adj.* **1** based on truth or sound reasoning. **2** (of a ticket, passport, etc.) legally acceptable for use.
valley (**va** li) *n.* **valleys** an area of low flat land between hills or mountains, often with a river running through.
valuable (**val** ū běl) *adj.* of considerable value or usefulness.
value (**val** ū) *n.* **1** worth in money terms: *That painting has great value.* **2** the quality of being useful: *A knowledge of Russian is of great value today.* – *vb.* **valuing, valued** to esteem.
valve (valv) *n.* a device that controls the flow of a liquid or gas in a pipe by opening and closing an aperture.
van (van) *n.* a covered road vehicle for transporting goods.

●**Vancouver** in British Columbia, is CANADA's third largest city and chief Pacific port.

vandal (**van** dål) *n.* a person who purposely and pointlessly damages public property. – *n.* **vandalism**.

The letter *V*, like all the letters, has a long history. The earliest alphabets were taken and adapted by the Greeks. The Greek *beta*, when combined with the first letter, *aleph*, gives us the word alphabet.

The Greeks passed on their letters to the Romans who developed the alphabet we use today, although they used only capital letters. Small letters developed in the AD 700s.

An early form of the letter V, used in the Middle East over 3000 years ago.

This letter was taken by the Greeks and became upsilon.

Over the years different versions of the letter V have been developed.

●**Vanderbilt** One of the most important families in the history of American business, finance, and transport. Their fortune was founded by Cornelius (1794-1877) in shipping and railways.

vane (vān) *n.* a weathervane, a device that shows the wind direction.

●**Van Gogh, Vincent** (1853-90) was a Dutch painter who specialized in colourful landscapes and portraits with a simple form.

vanilla (vå **nil** å) *n.* a flavouring substance obtained from the pod of a Mexican orchid.

vanish (**va** nish) *vb.* **vanishing, vanished** to disappear.

The Vatican, government headquarters of the Roman Catholic Church, is the world's smallest independent state, covering 44 hectares. It is dominated by the basilica of St Peter's, the largest Christian church in the world. The Vatican publishes its own daily newspaper and has its own postal and broadcasting services.

●**Vanuatu**. See Supplement, **Countries**.

vapour (**vā** pŏr) *n.* tiny droplets of moisture rising as a cloud or mist from a liquid or solid: *Smoke and steam are vapour.*

variable (**vār** i å bĕl) *adj.* not steady or regular; changeable: *variable weather.*

variation *n.* **1** a thing that varies from a standard. **2** the extent to which a thing varies from a standard: *The variation in temperature between winter and summer is 40°C.*

variety (vå **rī** ĕ ti) *n.* **varieties** any of various types of the same thing; a kind or sort: *They sell a variety of goods.*

various (**vā** ri ŭs) *adj.* several different: *She has worked for various companies.*

varnish (**vär** nish) *n.* a liquid containing resin, painted on to a surface, especially wood, to give a hard glossy finish.

vary (**vār** i) *vb.* **varies, varying, varied 1** to change, especially according to different circumstances: *Veronica's moods vary according to how nice her boss is to her.* **2** to make more diverse: *Vanessa varies her diet each week.*

vase (väz) *n.* a container for flowers.

vast (väst) *adj.* great in size, extent, or amount.

vat (vat) *n.* a large barrel or tank for storing or holding liquids, especially alcoholic drinks.

●**Vatican City** in Rome, is the POPE's official residence and the headquarters of the Roman CATHOLIC CHURCH. It is also the world's smallest independent state.

vault¹ (vŏlt) *n.* an arched roof, e.g. in a church.

vault² (vŏlt) *vb.* **vaulting, vaulted** to leap over, especially assisted by a pole.

veal (vēl) *n.* the flesh of a calf, used as food.

vegetable (**vej** tå bĕl) *n.* any part of a plant used for food, for example the tuber, root, leaves, or fruit of numerous plants used in salads or to accompany meat.

vegetarian (vej ĕ **tār** i ån) *n.* a person who does not eat meat or fish.

vegetation (vej ĕ **tā** shŏn) *n.* all the plants growing in one place: *Rain forests have thick vegetation.*

vehicle (**vē** i kĕl) *n.* anything, especially self-propelling, that is used for transporting people or things: *Trains and planes are vehicles.*

Parts of plants that are eaten as vegetables include tubers (potatoes), bulbs (onions), roots (carrots), leaves (spinach), and flower clusters (cauliflower). We also eat the seeds of plants (peas).

veil (vāl) *n.* **1** a covering for a woman's head or face, forming part of traditional dress in some religions. **2** a fine netting covering for a woman's head: *a bride's veil.*

vein (vān) *n.* any of the vessels or tubes that carry BLOOD back to the HEART.

●**Velázquez, Diego Rodríguez de Silva** (1599-1660) was the court painter to Philip the Fourth of SPAIN. He is best known for his painting the *Rokeby Venus.*

velocity (vi **los** i ti) *n.* **velocities 1** rate of motion in a particular direction. **2** speed.

velvet (**vel** vit) *n.* a fabric with a short soft closely woven pile on one side. – *adj.* **velvety**.

Venetian (vě **nē** shǎn) *adj.* of, or relating to, VENICE, a city in ITALY.

●**Venezuela**. See Supplement, **Countries**.

●**Venice** is a beautiful city in north-eastern ITALY built on islands in a lagoon of the Adriatic Sea. Venice was once the most important centre of trade between EUROPE and ASIA.

venom (**ve** nŏm) *n.* a poisonous liquid that some creatures, e.g. scorpions, inject in a bite or sting. – *adj.* **venomous**.

vent (vent) *n.* an opening allowing air, gas, or liquid into or out of a confined space: *Vents in the cellar allow fumes to escape.*

ventilate (**ven** ti lāt) *vb.* **ventilating, ventilated** to allow fresh air to circulate throughout. – *n.* **ventilation**.

ventriloquism (ven **tril** ŏ kwi zěm) *n.* the art of speaking in a way that makes the sound appear to come from elsewhere, for example a dummy's mouth. – *n.* **ventriloquist**.

venture (**ven** chǔr) *vb.* **venturing, ventured** to dare: *Chris ventured to criticize the chairman.*

●**Venus** is the the brightest planet in the solar system and is named after the Roman goddess of beauty and love. Venus takes only 225 days to orbit the Sun but Venus itself spins so slowly that one day on Venus lasts 243 days on Earth.

veranda or **verandah** (vě **ran** dǎ) *n.* a sheltered terrace attached to a house.

verb (vûrb) *n.* a class of words that represent an action, experience, occurrence, or state; *do, feel, happen,* and *remain* are all verbs.

●**Verdi, Giuseppe** (1813-1901) was the Italian composer of operas: *Rigoletto* and *La Traviata.*

verdict (**vûr** dikt) *n.* **1** the decision arrived at by the jury in a court of law. **2** any decision.

verge (vûrj) *n.* **1** a limit, boundary, or border. **2** a point or stage immediately beyond or after which something lies or occurs: *I was on the verge of striking him.*

●**Vermont**. See Supplement, **USA**.

●**Versailles** is a town just outside Paris, famous for its palace, begun by Louis the Fourteenth in 1661. The great expense and luxury at this palace was one of the causes of the FRENCH REVOLUTION.

versatile (**vûr** sǎ tīl) *adj.* **1** adapting easily to different tasks. **2** having numerous uses or abilities. – *n.* **versatility** (vûr sǎ **til** i ti).

verse (vûrs) *n.* poetry, as opposed to prose.

version (**vûr** shǒn) *n.* any of several types or forms in which a thing exists or is available, for example a particular translation of a book, or one person's account of an incident: *the King James version of the Bible.*

This figure of Aphrodite, the Greek goddess of love, is generally known as the Venus de Milo (Venus is the Roman name for Aphrodite). It was sculpted in 130 BC by Alexandros of Antioch.

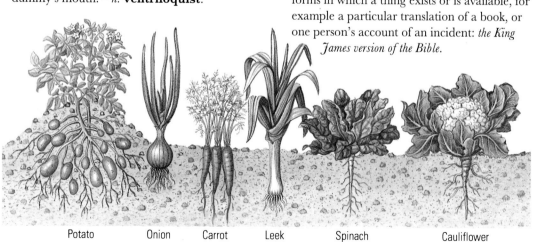

Potato · Onion · Carrot · Leek · Spinach · Cauliflower

versus (**vûr** sŭs) *prep.* in a contest against. It is often shortened to *v.* when referring to football matches: *Scotland v. France.*

vertebra (**vûr** tĕ brå) *n.* **vertebrae** (**vûr** tĕ brē) any of the segments of bone that form the spine. – *adj.* **vertebral.**

vertebrate (**vûr** tĕ brĕt) *adj.* having a spine. – *n.* any creature that has a spine. The main groups of vertebrates are: bony FISH, AMPHIBIANS, REPTILES, BIRDS, and MAMMALS.

vertical (**vûr** ti kål) *adj.* perpendicular; upright.

vertigo (**vûr** ti gō) *n.* dizziness.

very (**ve** ri) *adv.* to a great extent: *very kind.*

●**Vespucci, Amerigo** (1451-1512) was an Italian explorer who claimed to be the first to sight America and after whom the continent is named.

vessel (**ve** sĕl) *n.* **1** a container, especially for liquid. **2** a ship or large boat.

vest (vest) *n.* an undershirt.

●**Vesuvius** is one of the world's most famous volcanoes. It rises above the Bay of Naples, Italy. In AD 79 it erupted violently and buried the Roman cities of Pompeii and Herculaneum.

vet (vet) *n.* a veterinary surgeon. – *vb.* **vetting, vetted** to examine or investigate.

veteran (**vet** ĕ rån) *n.* a person with many years of experience in a particular activity.

veterinary (**vet** ĕ rin å ri) or (**vet** in å ri) *adj.* concerned with diseases of animals.

veterinary surgeon or **veterinarian** (vet ĕ ri **nār** i ån) *n.* a person who treats animals.

veto (**vē** tō) *n.* **vetoes** the right to reject a proposal or forbid an action, e.g. in a law-making assembly.

via (**vī** å) or (**vē** å) *prep.* by way of or by means of; through: *We went home via my school.*

viaduct (**vī** å dukt) *n.* a bridge-like structure that carries a road or railway across a valley.

vibrate (**vī brāt**) *vb.* **vibrating, vibrated** to move back and forth rapidly. – *n.* **vibration.**

vicar (**vi** kår) *n.* the minister of a parish.

vice[1] (**vīs**) *n.* a tool for gripping.

vice[2] (**vīs**) *n.* a habit or activity considered immoral or evil, e.g. cruelty to children.

vice- (**vīs-**) *prefix* next in rank to, and acting as deputy for: *vice-admiral; vice-president.*

vice versa (**vī** si) or (**vīs vûr** så) *adv.* with elements reversed; the other way round.

vicinity (vi **sin** i ti) *n.* **vicinities** a neighbourhood.

vicious (**vi** shŭs) *adj.* violent or ferocious.

victim (**vik** tim) *n.* a person or animal subjected to death, suffering, ill-treatment, or trickery.

victor (**vik** tŏr) *n.* the winner in a contest.

●**Victoria** is the name of an Australian state. Its capital is Melbourne.

●**Victoria, Queen** (1819-1901) became queen in 1837 and ruled Britain for 64 years, longer than any other monarch. During her reign the nation grew richer and the empire larger than it had ever been before.

Victorian (vik **tör** i ån) *adj.* of, or relating to, Queen *Victoria* or the period of her reign (1837-1901).

victory (**vik** tŏ ri) *n.* **victories** success against an opponent in a war or contest.

victorious (vik **tör** i ŭs) *adj.* **1** winning a war or contest. **2** marking or representing a victory.

video (**vid** i ō) *adj.* of, or relating to, the recording or broadcasting of visual, especially televised, images on magnetic tape. – *n.* **videos 1** a videocassette or videocassette recorder. **2** a film or programme pre-recorded on videocassette. – *vb.* **videos, videoing, videoed** to make a videocassette recording of.

video camera *n.* a camera recording moving images and sound on to videotape.

videocassette *n.* a cassette containing videotape.

videotape *n.* magnetic tape on which visual images and sound can be recorded.

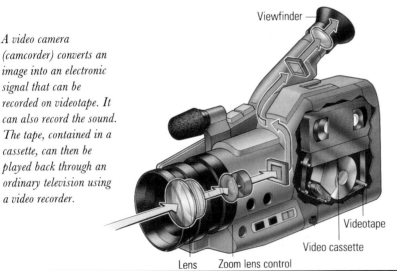

A video camera (camcorder) converts an image into an electronic signal that can be recorded on videotape. It can also record the sound. The tape, contained in a cassette, can then be played back through an ordinary television using a video recorder.

Viewfinder

Videotape

Video cassette

Lens   Zoom lens control

vie (vī) *vb.* **vies, vying, vied** to compete.

● **Vienna** is the capital of Austria and until 1918 was the home of the powerful HABSBURG family.

● **Vietnam**. See Supplement, **Countries**.

view (vū) *n.* **1** an act or opportunity of seeing without obstruction: *We have a good view of the stage.* **2** something, especially a landscape, seen from a particular point: *There is a magnificent view from the summit.* – *vb.* **viewing, viewed 1** to see or look at. **2** to examine: *They viewed the house before buying it.* – **in view of** taking account of; because of. – **on view** displayed for all to see or inspect.

vigour (vi gŏr) *n.* great strength and energy of body or mind. – *adj.* **vigorous**.

Viking (vī king) *n.* any of the Danes, Norwegians, and Swedes who raided by sea, and settled in, much of northern EUROPE between the 8th and 11th centuries.

village (vi lij) *n.* a cluster of houses and shops smaller than a town. – *n.* **villager**.

villain (vi lăn) *n.* a violent or wicked person.

vine (vīn) *n.* a plant that produces grapes.

vinegar (vin i găr) *n.* a sour liquid made by fermenting beer, wine, or cider, used for flavouring or for pickling food.

vineyard (vin yård) *n.* a plantation of vines.

viola (vī ō lå) *n.* a musical instrument similar to, but larger than, the violin.

violate (vī ŏ lāt) *vb.* **violating, violated** to disregard or break a law or a promise. – *n.* **violation**. – *n.* **violator**.

violent (vī ŏ lĕnt) *adj.* marked by or using great physical force: *a violent explosion.* **violence** *n.* violent behaviour.

violet (vī ŏ lit) *n.* **1** a flowering plant with large purple or blue petals. **2** a bluish-purple colour.

violin (vī ŏ **lin**) *n.* a four-stringed musical instrument played with a bow.

viper (vī pĕr) *n.* any of a family of poisonous snakes, including the common viper or adder.

virgin (vûr jin) *n.* a person who has never had sexual intercourse.

● **Virginia**. See Supplement, **USA**.

Virgo (vûr gō) *n.* See **Zodiac**.

virtue (vûr choo) *n.* a quality regarded as morally good: *Patience is a virtue.* – *adj.* **virtuous**.

From the late 700s until about 1100 **Vikings** ventured from their Scandinavian homelands in their lightweight, flat-bottomed ships in search of treasure and farmland. They plundered and in places they settled. They colonized Iceland and Greenland and even reached America.

Thor, the Viking god of thunder and war. Thursday is named after him.

Swords were highly valued by the Vikings and were often richly decorated with gold and silver.

virus (vī rŭs) *n.* **1** any of numerous types of micro-organism, smaller than bacteria, that can cause disease. **2** a piece of computer information inserted into a program to destroy or disrupt data.

visible (vi zi bĕl) *adj.* able to be seen: *The ship was visible on the horizon.* – *n.* **visibility**.

vision (vi zhŏn) *n.* **1** the ability to see. **2** an image conjured up vividly in the imagination.

visit (vi zit) *vb.* **visiting, visited** to go or come to see a person or place. – *n.* a call or stay. – *n.* **visitor**.

visor (vī zŏr) *n.* the movable part of a helmet.

visual (vi zhoo ăl) *adj.* of, relating to, or received through sight or vision: *a visual handicap.* – *adv.* **visually**.

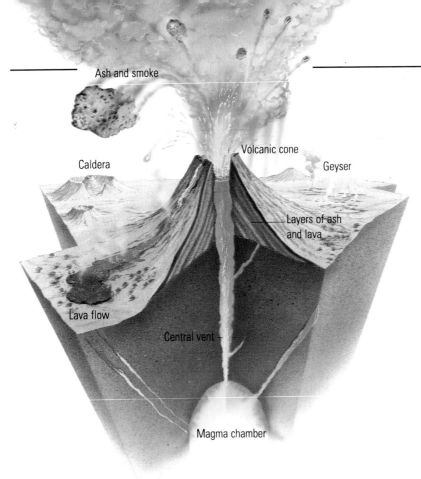

Ash and smoke

Volcanic cone

Caldera

Geyser

Layers of ash
and lava

Lava flow

Central vent

Magma chamber

A typical 'central' kind of volcano has a crater and cone of solidified lava and ash. The activity takes places in the central vent through which the material erupts.

vital (**vī** tǎl) *adj.* **1** of, relating to, or essential for life: *Oxygen is vital for all life.* **2** essential.
  vitality (vī **tal** i ti) *n.* liveliness and energy.
vitamin (**vit** ǎ min) *n.* any of a group of substances essential for healthy life, present in small quantities in various natural foods, and referred to by the letters A, B, C, D, E, etc.
vivacious (vi **vā** shǔs) *adj.* having an attractively lively personality.

●**Vivaldi, Antonio** (1678-1741) was the Italian composer who wrote *The Four Seasons.*

vivid (**vi** vid) *adj.* (of colour) very bright.
vivisection (vi vi **sek** shǒn) *n.* the performance of surgical experiments on live animals for medical research.
vixen (**vik** sěn) *n.* a female fox.
vocabulary (vǒ **kab** ū lǎ ri) *n.* **vocabularies** the words of a particular language.
vocal (**vō** kǎl) *adj.* of, relating to, or produced by the voice.
  vocal cords *n.* (*plural*) folds in the membrane lining the larynx, vibrated by the breath to produce sound.
voice (vois) *n.* **1** the ability to speak using the mouth and vocal chords; the power of speech: *Abdul lost his voice.* **2** a way of speaking or

VITAMINS	
Vitamin	Used for
A	Fighting disease
B	Healthy appetite; skin and nerves
C	Healthy blood; help against colds
D	Strong bones
E	We don't know!
K	Clotting blood

singing peculiar to each individual.
  voice-over *n.* the voice of an unseen narrator in a film or television advertisement.
void (void) *adj.* not valid or legally binding: *The judge declared the contract null and void.*
volcano (vol **kā** nō) *n.* **volcanoes** an opening in the Earth's crust, through which molten rock, ash, and gases erupt periodically.
vole (vōl) *n.* a small mouse-like rodent.

●**Volga** the longest river in EUROPE flows from near St Petersburg, Russia, to the Caspian Sea.

volt (vōlt) *n.* the standard unit for measuring the force of an electric current.
voltage (**vōl** tij) or (**vol** tij) *n.* electrical force measured in volts.
volume (**vol** ūm) *n.* **1** the amount of space occupied by an object, gas, or liquid. **2** loudness of sound; the control that adjusts it on a radio, hi-fi system, etc. **3** a book.
voluntary (**vo** lǔn tǎ ri) *adj.* **1** done, given, taken, etc. by choice, not by accident or compulsion. **2** (of work) unpaid: *Vera does voluntary work at the nursery.* – *adv.* **voluntarily** (**vo** lǔn tǎ ri li) or (vo lǔn **ta** ri li).
volunteer (vo lǔn **tēr**) *vb.* **volunteering, volunteered** to offer help or services willingly, without being persuaded or forced.
vomit (**vo** mit) *vb.* **vomiting, vomited** to be sick. – *n.* matter vomited from the stomach.
vote (vōt) *n.* a formal indication of choice or opinion, for example in an election or debate. – *vb.* **voting, voted 1** to cast a vote for or against. **2** to decide, state, grant, or bring about by casting votes. – *n.* **voter**.
voucher (**vow** chěr) *n.* a ticket exchangeable for goods or services; a token: *a gift voucher.*
vow (vow) *n.* a solemn promise. – *vb.* **vowing, vowed** to promise or declare solemnly.
vowel (**vow** ěl) *n.* any speech-sound representing the letters *a, e, i, o, u,* and in some words *y.*
voyage (**voi** ij) *n.* a long journey to a distant place, especially by sea or in space: *Columbus made four voyages to America.* – *vb.* **voyaging, voyaged** to travel. – *n.* **voyager**.
vulgar (**vul** gǎr) *adj.* showing a lack of manners or taste. – *n.* **vulgarity**.
vulnerable (**vul** ně rǎ běl) *adj.* **1** easily hurt. **2** unprotected against attack, e.g. with weapons or criticism. – *n.* **vulnerability**.
vulture (**vul** chǔr) *n.* a large bird of prey which feeds chiefly on dead animals.

W w

wad (wod) *n.* **1** a thick mass of soft material used for packing, etc. **2** a bundle of banknotes, etc.

waddle (**wo** dĕl) *vb.* **waddling, waddled** to sway from side to side when walking.

wade (wād) *vb.* **wading, waded 1** to walk through deep water. **2** to make your way laboriously through: *He is wading through legal documents.*

wader *n.* any long-legged bird that wades in shallow waters in search of food.

wafer (wā fĕr) *n.* a light finely layered kind of biscuit.

wag (wag) *vb.* **wagging, wagged 1** to wave to and fro vigorously; (of a dog) to wave its tail. **2** (of tongues, chins) to move busily in chatter.

wage (wāj) *vb.* **waging, waged** to fight: *In the Second World War the Allies waged war against Germany.* – *n.* payment for working.

● **Wagner, Richard** (1813-83) was the German composer of operas: *The Ring of the Nibelung.*

wagon or **waggon** (**wa** gŏn) *n.* a four-wheeled vehicle for carrying loads, often pulled by a horse or tractor.

waist (wāst) *n.* the narrow part of the human body between the ribs and hips.

wait (wāt) *vb.* **waiting, waited 1** to delay action, or remain in a certain place, in expectation of something: *We must wait for the bus.* **2** (of a task, etc.) to remain temporarily undealt with: *The ironing can wait.* **3** to serve people with food at a restaurant, etc.

waiter or **waitress** *n.* a man or woman who serves people with food at a restaurant, etc.

wake (wāk) *vb.* **waking, woke** (wōk), **woken** (wō kĕn) to rouse or be roused from sleep.

waken (wā kĕn) *vb.* **wakening, wakened** to rouse or be roused from sleep.

● **Wales** (*Cymru* in Welsh) is one the countries that make up the UNITED KINGDOM. Although united with England in 1536, the Welsh people have retained their own culture and some 20 per cent of the people speak Welsh, a Celtic language. The capital is Cardiff.

Settlers travelling westward across North America took all their possessions with them in huge wagons drawn by oxen or mules.

The letter *W*, like all the letters, has a long history. The earliest alphabets were taken and adapted by the Greeks. The Greek *beta*, when combined with the first letter, *aleph*, gives us the word alphabet.

The Greeks passed on their letters to the Romans who developed the alphabet we use today, although they used only capital letters. Small letters developed in the AD 700s.

An early form of the letter W, used in the Middle East over 3000 years ago.

This letter was taken by the Greeks and became phi.

Over the years different versions of the letter W have been developed.

PRONUNCIATION GUIDE

fat **a**	all **ö**
fate **ā**	foot **oo**
fast **ä**	moon **o͞o**
among **å**	boy **oi**
met **e**	house **ow**
mean **ē**	demon **o̊**
silent **e̊**	thing **th**
loch **hh**	this **Th**
fin **i**	but **u**
line **ī**	mute **ū**
quick **kw**	fur **û**
got **o**	brochure **ů**
note **ō**	vision **zh**

Walruses lie on beaches and ice floes, diving to great depths to catch clams from the seabed with their long curving tusks. Apart from humans their only enemies are polar bears and killer whales.

● **Walesa, Lech** (1943-) was a Polish trade-union leader and since 1990 has been president of Poland.

walk (wök) *vb.* **walking, walked 1** to go in some direction on foot, by putting one foot in front of the other on the ground. **2** to take a dog out for exercise. – *n.* **1** the motion, or pace, of walking: *She slowed to a walk.* **2** an outing or journey on foot, especially for exercise: *They went for a walk in the hills.*

wall (wöl) *n.* **1** a solid vertical brick or stone structure that surrounds or divides an area of land. **2** the side of a building or room. – *vb.* **walling, walled** to surround with a wall: *He has a beautiful walled garden.*

wallpaper *n.* paper used to decorate the interior walls of houses, etc.

wallet (**wo** lit) *n.* a flat folding case for holding banknotes, etc.

wallow (**wo** lō) *vb.* **wallowing, wallowed 1** to lie or roll about in water, mud, etc. **2** to indulge excessively in self-pity.

Wall Street (**wöl** strēt) *n.* a street in New York, USA, where the large banks are situated.

walnut (**wöl** nut) *n.* an edible nut with a hard wrinkled shell.

walrus (**wöl** růs) *n.* **walruses** or **walrus** a large sea mammal with a whiskery muzzle and large downward-pointing tusks.

waltz (wöls), (wols), (wölts), or (wolts) *n.* **1** a ballroom dance in triple time. **2** a piece of music for this dance.

wand (wond) *n.* a rod used by magicians.

wander (**won** de̊r) *vb.* **wandering, wandered 1** to walk about, heading for no particular destination. **2** to stray, e.g. from the right path, or from the point of an argument. – *n.* a ramble or stroll. – *n.* **wanderer**.

want (wont) *vb.* **wanting, wanted** to feel a desire for; to wish to do something, someone to do something, etc.: *She doesn't want you to leave.* – *n.* a need or requirement; a lack: *She shows a want of discretion.*

wanted *adj.* being sought by the police on suspicion of having committed a crime, etc.

war (wör) *n.* **1** an openly acknowledged state of armed conflict, especially between nations: *The Germans declared war on the French.* **2** any long-continued struggle or campaign: *We are fighting a war against drug-dealing.*

warhead *n.* the front part of a missile containing the explosives.

warlike *adj.* fond of fighting; aggressive.

ward (wörd) *n.* any of the rooms in a hospital with beds for patients.

warden (**wör** de̊n) *n.* **1** a person in charge of a hostel, student residence, old people's home, etc. **2** an official responsible for maintaining law and order: *She works as a traffic warden.*

warder (**wör** de̊r) *n.* a prison officer.

wardrobe (**wör** drōb) *n.* **1** a cupboard in which to hang clothes. **2** your collection of garments: *my winter wardrobe.*

-wards (-wördz) *suffix* (also **-ward**) in the direction of; towards: *westwards; backwards.*

ware (wār) *n.* manufactured goods of a specified material (*glassware, silverware*), or type of use (*kitchenware*).

warehouse *n.* a building for storing goods.

● **Warhol, Andy** (**wör** hōl) (1926-87) was an American artist, famous for his 'pop art'.

warm (wörm) *adj.* **1** comfortably or pleasantly hot. **2** (of clothes) providing and keeping in heat: *She put on a warm pair of socks.* **3** kind-hearted and affectionate. **4** enthusiastic; whole-hearted: *They gave him warm support.* – *vb.* **warming, warmed** to heat gently.

warm-blooded *adj.* (of animals, etc.) having a relatively high blood temperature that remains constant.

warmth *n.* the condition of being warm; moderate, pleasant, or comfortable heat.

warn (wörn) *vb.* **warning, warned 1** to make someone aware of possible danger. **2** to advise strongly: *I warned them to book early.*

warning *n.* something that is said or happens that warns someone. – *adj.* intended to warn.

warrant (**wo** rånt) *vb.* **warranting, warranted** to justify: *The circumstances are suspicious enough to warrant a full investigation.*

warren (**wo** re̊n) *n.* an underground maze of interconnecting tunnels linking rabbit burrows.

warrior (**wo** ri o̊r) *n.* a skilled fighting man, especially of earlier times.

● **Wars of the Roses** the name given to the civil wars in which the Houses of York (symbolized by the white rose) and Lancaster (the red rose) fought for the throne of ENGLAND between 1455 and 1487.

● **Warsaw** is the capital of POLAND.

wart (wört) *n.* a small hard growth of horny
skin, for example on the hands or face.

wary (wā ri) *adj.* **warier, wariest** cautious and
distrustful. – *adv.* **warily**. – *n.* **wariness**.

was. See **be**.

wash (wösh) *vb.* **washing, washed** to clean
with water and soap or detergent. – *n.* the
process of washing or being washed. – *vb.*
wash your hands of to abandon
responsibility for.

washer *n.* **1** a machine for washing: *We've just
bought a dishwasher.* **2** a flat ring of rubber or
metal for keeping a joint tight.

washout *n.* **1** *(colloquial)* a failure or flop. **2** a
rained-off event, for example a match.

● **Washington D.C.** is the capital of the UNITED
STATES. It is named after the first president
George WASHINGTON who chose the site on
the Potomac River on the border between
Maryland and Virginia. It stands on a piece of
land called the District of Columbia (D.C.).
Washington is the seat of the Congress and
Supreme Court. It also contains the WHITE
HOUSE, the official residence of the president.

● **Washington, George** (1732-99) was the first
president (1789-97) of the UNITED STATES.
He led the victorious colonists during the
AMERICAN WAR OF INDEPENDENCE. He is
buried at Mount Vernon.

*In 1787 George Washington chaired a series of
meetings held in Philadelphia to discuss a draft
Constitution among delegates of the
13 new states that made up the
newly formed United States of
America.*

● **Washington State**. See Supplement, **USA**.

wasp (wosp) *n.* a stinging insect with black and
yellow stripes.

waspish *adj.* sharp-tongued.

waste (wāst) *vb.* **wasting, wasted 1** to use or
spend extravagantly. **2** to fail to make the best
of an opportunity, etc. **3** to throw away
unused. – *adj.* **1** rejected as useless. **2** (of
ground) lying unused, uninhabited, or
uncultivated. – *n.* **1** failure to take
advantage of something: *Giving up the
piano would be a waste of talent.* **2** rubbish.

wastage *n.* the amount lost through
wasting.

wasteful *adj.* causing waste; extravagant.

wasteland *n.* a desolate and barren region.

wastepaper basket or **bin** *n.* a container for
waste paper and office or household waste.

wastepipe *n.* a pipe carrying waste material
or waste water from a sink, etc.

watch (woch) *vb.* **watching, watched 1** to
look at someone or something moving, doing
something, etc. with close attention. **2** to guard,
look after, or keep an eye on. **3** to keep track
of, follow, or monitor: *We must watch
developments in the Middle East.* – *n.* **1** a small
instrument for telling the time, usually worn
strapped to the wrist or in the waistcoat
pocket. **2** the activity or duty of watching or
guarding: *You must keep watch.* – *vb.* **keep a
watch on** to keep under observation. – *vb.*
watch out 1 to be careful. **2** to be on guard
against; to look out for. – *vb.* **watch over** to
guard, look after.

watchdog *n.* **1** a dog kept to guard premises,
etc. **2** a group of people that guards against
unacceptable standards, behaviour, etc.

watchful *adj.*
alert, vigilant,
and wary.

*Many kinds of wasp dig
nest-tunnels in the
ground. Potter wasps
make beautiful nests out
of clay. They lay an egg
in each pot and fill it
with food for the
developing grub.*

Water

Water is the most common substance on Earth. Seven-tenths of the Earth's surface is covered with water. Without water, life as we know it would be impossible. Life, scientists say, started in water and the bodies of all living things are mainly water. Besides supporting life, water helps to shape the land by wearing away valleys and depositing material elsewhere. Water exists in three forms: it is normally a liquid; at 0° it freezes into solid ice; at 100° Celsius it turns into steam.

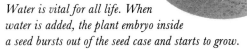

Water is vital for all life. When water is added, the plant embryo inside a seed bursts out of the seed case and starts to grow.

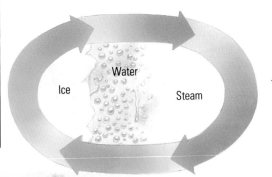

Water exists in three states. Ice takes a lot of energy to melt to water, just as water does to become vapour. This latent heat is given out again when vapour condenses to water.

Water power was used in medieval water wheels to drive hammers for iron working.

Animals around a waterhole in central Africa – again water is vital for all life.

Water has the amazing property of expanding when it freezes solid while all other liquids slowly contract as they cool. A frozen water pipe may split because of this; and when the ice melts you will have a leak.

Most of the world's water (below left) is found in the oceans. Of the 3 per cent of the rest of the water some 77 per cent is frozen in the ice caps and glaciers of the Arctic and Antarctic.

Fresh water 3%

Sea water 97%

Groundwater 22%

Ice sheets and glaciers 77%

Water vapour 0.05%
Moisture in soil 0.2%
Rivers and lakes 0.35%
Salt water lakes and inland seas 0.4%

WATERFALLS
The world's longest unbroken falls of water.

Angel Falls, Venezuela 978m

Yosemite Falls, USA 739m

Mardalsfossen, Norway 655m

Tugela, Africa 614m

If soft rock over which a river flows is eroded enough for its face to be vertical, the river will cascade over as a waterfall.

water (wo tẽr) *n.* a colourless, transparent, tasteless, and odourless liquid that is a compound of hydrogen and oxygen, falls as rain, and forms seas, lakes, and rivers. – *vb.* **watering, watered 1** to wet, soak, or sprinkle with water. **2** to irrigate land. **3** (of the mouth) to produce saliva in response to the expectation of food. **4** (of the eyes) to fill with tears, e.g. when irritated. – **hold water** to prove sound; to be valid. – **in deep water** in trouble, danger, or difficulty. – **make your mouth water** to increase your appetite for something. – **pass water** to urinate. – **throw cold water on** (*colloquial*) to be discouraging or unenthusiastic about. – *adj.* **water down 1** to dilute or thin with water. **2** to reduce the impact of something; to tone down. – **water under the bridge** experiences that are past and done with.

water buffalo *n.* **buffalo** or **buffaloes** the common domestic buffalo of India and South Asia, with backward-curving horns.

watercolour *n.* **1** a paint thinned with water, not oil. **2** a painting done in such paint. – *n.* **water-colourist.**

waterfall *n.* a place in a river or stream where the water drops a considerable height down steep rocks, over a precipice, etc.; a cascade.

● The most famous waterfalls are Niagara, between the United States and Canada, and the Victoria Falls in the Zambezi River, Africa. The highest waterfall in the world is Angel Falls in Venezuela. It is 978 metres high.

waterfowl *n.* a bird living on or near water, especially a swimming bird such as a duck.

waterhole *n.* a pond, pool, or spring in a desert area, where animals can drink.

water lily *n.* **lilies** a floating plant with large flat circular leaves.

waterlogged *adj.* completely full of water.

water melon *n.* a melon native to AFRICA, with dark green coarse skin and red flesh.

waterproof *adj.* treated or coated so as to resist water.

watershed *n.* **1** the high land separating two river basins. **2** a crucial point after which events take a different turn.

watertight *adj.* so well sealed as to be impenetrable by water.

waterway *n.* a channel, e.g. a canal or river, used by ships or smaller boats.

watery *adj.* **1** of, or consisting of, water: *It sank to the watery depths.* **2** over-diluted; weak or thin.

● **Waterloo**, near Brussels, Belgium, was the scene of a battle fought in 1815 by British and Prussian forces under the Duke of Wellington and Field Marshall Blücher against the French under NAPOLEON. The French were defeated.

● **Watson, Dr** is a doctor and the assistant of Sherlock HOLMES in the detective stories of Sir Arthur Conan DOYLE.

watt (wot) *n.* a unit of power.

● **Watt, James** (1736-1819) was a Scottish engineer who greatly improved the steam engine.

wave (wāv) *vb.* **waving, waved 1** to move your hand to and fro in greeting, farewell, or as a signal: *She waved to her father.* **2** to direct with a gesture of the hand: *He waved the waiter away.* – *n.* **1** any of a series of ridges moving across the sea. **2** the form in which heat, light, sound, etc. travel through air. **3** the circles of disturbance moving outwards from the site of a shock such as an earthquake.

wavy *adj.* **wavier, waviest 1** (of hair) falling in waves. **2** (of a line or outline) curving alternately upward and downward.

waver (wā věr) *vb.* **wavering, wavered** to falter, weaken, etc.; to hesitate.

wax[1] (waks) *n.* any of various fatty substances, typically shiny and easily moulded, used to make candles and polishes.

wax[2] (waks) *vb.* **waxing, waxed** (of the Moon) to appear larger as more of its surface is illuminated by the Sun.

way (wā) *n.* **1** a route providing access somewhere: *This is the way in.* **2** a direction: *This is a one-way street.* **3** position: *That picture is the wrong way up.* **4** a distance in space or time: *My birthday is a long way off.* **5** a distinctive manner or style: *She has a funny way of walking.* **6** a method: *I'll show you an easy way to cook fish.* **7** a mental approach, attitude, or opinion: *There are different ways of looking at it.* – **by the way** let me mention while I remember.

-ways (-wāz) *combined form* direction or manner: *lengthways, edgeways.*

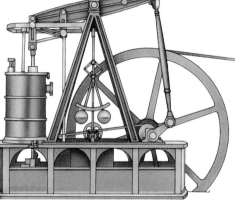

James Watt made steam engines that were far more efficient than other steam engines of his time. The 'Age of Steam' was largely due to him.

The weasel family includes the stoat, the common weasel, the American mink, the polecat (the ferret when domesticated), the pine marten, and the bear-like wolverine.

weak (wēk) *adj.* **1** lacking physical strength: *Her voice was weak.* **2** liable to give way or fail: *He is the weak link.*

weaken *vb.* **weakening, weakened 1** to become weaker. **2** to give way to pressure.

weakling *n.* a physically weak person.

weakness *n.* the condition of being weak.

wealth (welth) *n.* **1** the possession of riches and property. **2** abundance of resources: *The country has a huge mineral wealth.*

wealthy *adj.* **wealthier, wealthiest** possessing riches and property; rich.

wean (wēn) *vb.* **weaning, weaned** to accustom a baby to taking food other than milk.

weapon (we pȯn) *n.* **1** a device used to kill or injure people in a war or fight. **2** something someone can use to get the better of others: *Patience is our best weapon.* – *n.* **weaponry**.

wear (wār) *vb.* **wearing, wore** (wȯr), **worn** (wȯrn) **1** to be dressed in: *She was wearing a red skirt.* **2** to have your hair, beard, etc. cut a certain length or in a certain style: *He wears his hair long.* **3** to have a certain expression. **4** (of a carpet or garment) to become thin or threadbare through use. – *n.* **1** clothes suitable for a certain purpose, person, occasion, etc.: *We were looking for the menswear department.* **2** the amount or type of use that clothing, carpeting, etc. gets: *This carpet is subjected to heavy wear.* – *adj.* **wearable**. – *n.* **wearer**. – *vb.* **wear away** to become thin or disappear completely through rubbing, weathering, etc. – *vb.* **wear off** (of a feeling, pain, etc.) to become less intense; to disappear gradually. – *vb.* **wear out 1** to become thin and weak through use. **2** to tire utterly; to exhaust.

weary (wēr i) *adj.* **wearier, weariest 1** tired out; exhausted. **2** tired; fed up. – *adv.* **wearily**. – *n.* **weariness**.

weasel (wē zėl) *n.* a small slender short-legged reddish-brown animal that feeds on frogs, mice, etc.

weather (we Thėr) *n.* the atmospheric conditions in any area at any time, with regard to Sun, cloud, temperature, wind, rain, etc. – *vb.* **weathering, weathered** to be exposed to the effects of wind, Sun, rain, etc.; to alter in colour, etc. through such exposure.

weathervane *n.* a revolving arrow that turns to point in the direction of the wind.

weave¹ (wēv) *vb.* **weaving, wove** (wōv), **woven** (wō vėn) to make cloth on a loom, passing threads under and over each other.

weave² (wēv) *vb.* **weaving, weaved** to move to and fro or wind in and out.

web (web) *n.* **1** a network of slender threads constructed by a spider to trap insects. **2** a piece of skin connecting the toes of a swimming bird or animal. – *adj.* **webbed**.

● **Webster, Noah** (1758-1843) compiled the first American dictionary in 1806. His *American Dictionary of the English Language,* published in 1828, had 70,000 entries. Webster simplified American spelling and eliminated many silent letters that remain in British English.

we'd (wēd) we would or we should.

wedding (wed ing) *n.* a marriage ceremony.

wedge (wej) *n.* a piece of solid wood, metal, or other material, with a thick edge tapering to a thin edge, driven into wood to split it, or used to hold something in place, e.g. a door.

Wednesday (wed ėnz di) or (wenz di) *n.* the day between Tuesday and Thursday.

weed (wēd) *n.* a wild plant growing among cultivated plants or elsewhere where unwanted.

week (wēk) *n.* a period of seven consecutive days, usually beginning on Sunday.

weekend *n.* the non-working period from Friday evening to Sunday night.

weigh (wā) *vb.* **weighing, weighed 1** to measure how heavy something is. **2** to have a certain weight: *The books weigh eight kilos.*

weight (wāt) *n.* **1** the heaviness of something; the amount anything weighs. **2** a piece of metal of a standard weight, against which to measure the weight of other objects. **3** a heavy load.

weightless *adj.* (of astronauts in space) not subject to Earth's gravity, so able to float free. – *n.* **weightlessness**.

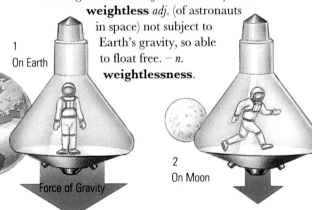

1 On Earth
Force of Gravity
2 On Moon

weir (wēr) *n.* a shallow dam constructed across a river to control its flow.

weird (wērd) *adj.* strange or bizarre.

welcome (wel kŏm) *vb.* **welcoming, welcomed 1** to receive a guest, visitor, etc. with a warm greeting and kind hospitality. **2** to invite and encourage: *The museum welcomes children.* – *interjection* an expression of pleasure on receiving someone: *Welcome home!* – *n.* the act of welcoming.

weld (weld) *vb.* **welding, welded** to join pieces of metal or plastic by first heating the edges to soften them then letting them harden together. – *n.* a joint made by welding. – *n.* **welder**.

welfare (wel fãr) *n.* the health, comfort, happiness, and general wellbeing of a person, group, etc.

well[1] (wel) *adv.* **better** (be tĕr), **best** (best) *adv.* **1** competently; skilfully: *She plays well.* **2** satisfactorily: *All went well.* **3** kindly: *I was well treated.* **4** thoroughly; properly; carefully; fully: *Make sure you wash it well.* **5** intimately: *I don't know her well.* **6** by a long way: *It's well past midnight.* – *adj.* **better** (be tĕr), **best** (best) **1** healthy. **2** advisable: *It would be as well to check.* – **as well 1** too; in addition. **2** (also **just as well**) for all the difference it makes: *I may as well tell you.* – **well off** wealthy.

well-balanced *adj.* sane, sensible, and stable.

well[2] (wel) *n.* a hole bored into the ground to give access to a supply of water, oil, or gas.

we'll (wēl) we will or we shall.

● **Wellington** is the capital of NEW ZEALAND.

● **Wellington, Duke of** (1769-1852) was a British soldier and statesman. He led British troops victoriously against NAPOLEON and was prime minister between 1828 and 1830.

Astronauts become weightless as they escape Earth's gravity. On the Moon, where gravity is weak, an astronaut would weigh less.

In Space

wellington (we ling tŏn) *n.* a waterproof boot.

Welsh (welsh) *adj.* **1** of, or belonging to, Wales. **2** of, or in, the language of Wales. – *n.* **1** the language of Wales. **2** the people of Wales.

went. See **go**.

wept. See **weep**.

were. See **be**.

we're (wēr) we are.

weren't (wûrnt) were not.

Gas welding uses heat from a gas torch to join two metal parts which then melt and mix. As they cool, the parts fuse together.

● **Wesley brothers** John (1703-91) was an English religious leader who founded METHODISM; Charles (1707-88) wrote over 6,000 hymns, many of which are still popular.

● **Wessex**, the kingdom of the west SAXONS, was the most powerful of the Anglo-Saxon kingdoms by the 10th century. It remains a historic region of ENGLAND.

west (west) *n.* the direction in which the Sun sets, or any part of the Earth, a country, town, etc. lying in that direction. – *adj.* **1** in the west; on the side that is on or nearer the west. **2** (of a wind) blowing from the west. – *adv.* toward the west. – **the West** the countries of EUROPE and NORTH AMERICA, in contrast to those of ASIA.

westerly *adj.* (of a wind) coming from the west.

western *adj.* of the west or the West. – *n.* a film about cowboys in the west of the USA.

West Indian *n.* & *adj.* a native or inhabitant of the West Indies, an island chain separating the Caribbean Sea from the ATLANTIC.

● **Western Australia** is the largest Australian state. Its capital is Perth.

● **Western Samoa**. See Supplement, **Countries**.

● **Westinghouse, George** (1846-1914) was an American inventor and businessman.

● **Westminster** is a borough in London containing Westminster Abbey, Buckingham Palace, and the Houses of Parliament.

● **West Virginia**. See Supplement, **USA**.

Welsh is from the Old English word *waelisc* meaning 'foreign'. It is the second part of the name 'Cornwall'. The word 'walnut' means literally 'foreign nut'.

PRONUNCIATION GUIDE	
fat **a**	all **ŏ**
fate **ā**	foot **oo**
fast **ä**	moon **ōō**
among **å**	boy **oi**
met **e**	house **ow**
mean **ē**	demon **ŏ**
silent **ĕ**	thing **th**
loch **hh**	this **Th**
fin **i**	but **u**
line **ī**	mute **ū**
quick **kw**	fur **û**
got **o**	brochure **ů**
note **ō**	vision **zh**

wet (wet) *adj.* **wetter, wettest 1** covered or soaked in water, rain, or other liquid. **2** (of weather) rainy. **3** (of paint, etc.) not yet dried. – *n.* **1** moisture. **2** rainy weather; rain. – *vb.* **wetting, wet** or **wetted** to make wet.

we've (wēv) we have.

whale (wāl) *n.* any of several huge sea mammals that breathe air through an opening on top of the head. – *vb.* **whaling, whaled** to hunt whales. – *n.* **whaling**.

The blue whale is by far the largest animal. The elephant is the largest land animal and the giraffe the tallest, while the ostrich is the largest bird.

● There are two groups of whale: toothed whales like the dolphin mostly catch fish; baleen whales include the blue whale, the largest mammal that has ever lived. Baleen whales catch shrimplike creatures with a 'sieve' of a horny substance called baleen or whalebone.

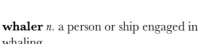

whaler *n.* a person or ship engaged in whaling.

wharf (wörf) *n.* **wharfs** or **wharves** (wörvz) a place for loading and unloading vessels.

what (wot) **1** used in requesting information about a thing or person: *What street are we in?* **2** used in exclamations: *What lies she tells! What awful clothes!* – **what about ...? 1** do you want to do something? **2** what is your opinion of ...? **3** aren't you forgetting ...? – **what ... for?** why? – **what if ...?** what will happen if ...? – **what ... like?** used in requesting a description: *What does it look like?*

whatever *relative pron.* & *relative adj.* any things or quantity that: *Take whatever money you need.* – *pron.* & *adj.* no matter what: *I must finish, whatever else I do.* – *adj.* at all: *It has nothing whatever to do with you.* – *pron.* an emphatic form of **what**: *Whatever shall I do?*

wheat (wēt) *n.* any of a variety of grasses, or their grain, providing flour for bread, etc.

wheel (wēl) *n.* **1** a circular object rotating on an axle, on which a vehicle moves along the ground. **2** a steering-wheel, spinning-wheel, or water wheel.

wheelbarrow *n.* a hand-pushed cart with a wheel in front and two legs at the rear.

whelk (welk) *n.* a shellfish with a spiral shell.

when (wen) *adv.* at what time?; during what period?; how soon?: *When does the plane arrive?* – *conj.* **1** at the time, or during the period, that: *She locks the door when she goes to bed.* **2** as soon as: *I'll come when I've finished.* **3** but just then: *I was about to leave when the telephone rang.* **4** at which time; for at that time: *Ring tomorrow, when I'll have more information.*

whenever *conj.* **1** at every time that: *He gets furious whenever he fails to get his way.* **2** if ever; no matter when: *I'll be here whenever you need me.*

where (wār) *adv.* **1** in, at, or to which place?; in what direction?: *Where is she going?* **2** in what respect?: *He showed me where I'd gone wrong.* – *pron.* what place?: *Where have you come from?* – *conj.* or *relative pron.* **1** in, at, or to the place that: *We visited the village where I was born.* **2** the respect in which: *That's where you're wrong.*

whereabouts *adv.* roughly where?

wherever *relative pron.* in, at, or to every place that: *She takes it wherever she goes.* – *conj.* in, at, or to whatever place: *They were welcomed wherever they went.* – *adv.* **1** no matter where: *I won't lose touch, wherever I go.* **2** an emphatic form of **where**: *Wherever can they be?*

whether (we Ther) *conj.* **1** used to introduce an indirect question: *I asked whether it was raining.* **2** used to introduce alternative possibilities: *I was uncertain whether or not he liked her.*

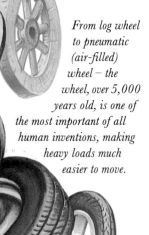

From log wheel to pneumatic (air-filled) wheel – the wheel, over 5,000 years old, is one of the most important of all human inventions, making heavy loads much easier to move.

which (wich) *adj.* or *pron.* used in requesting information about a thing or person from a known set or group: *Which twin did you mean?* – *relative pron.* **1** used to introduce a clause: *These are all animals which hibernate.* **2** used to add a commenting clause: *She parked her car, which usually sat out in the street, in the garage.*
whichever *relative pron.* & *relative adj.* **1** the one(s) that; any that: *Take whichever coat fits better.* **2** according to which: *You can see the doctor at 10.00 or 10.30, whichever is more convenient.* – *adj.* & *pron.* no matter which: *We'll be late, whichever way we go.*

whiff (wif) *n.* a slight smell.

while (wīl) *conj.* **1** at the same time as: *She worked while I gardened.* **2** for as long as; for the whole time that: *He guards us while we sleep.* **3** during the time that: *It happened while we were abroad.* – *n.* a space of time: *She came in after a while.*

whim (wim) *n.* a sudden fanciful idea.

whimper (**wim** pĕr) *vb.* **whimpering, whimpered** to cry feebly.

whine (wīn) *vb.* **whining, whined** to complain.

whip (wip) *n.* a thin piece of leather or cord attached to a handle, for hitting animals or people. – *vb.* **whipping, whipped**.

whirl (wûrl) *vb.* **whirling, whirled** to spin rapidly.
whirlpool *n.* a fast-circling current that can draw ships, etc. down into its centre.
whirlwind *n.* a violently spiralling column of air. – *adj.* rapid: *It was a whirlwind courtship.*

whisk (wisk) *vb.* **whisking, whisked 1** to brush or sweep lightly: *She whisked the crumbs off the table.* **2** to transport rapidly: *He was whisked into hospital.* **3** to beat egg-whites, etc. till stiff.

whisker (**wis** kĕr) *n.* any of the long coarse hairs around the mouth of a cat, mouse, etc.

whisky (**wis** ki) *n.* **whiskies** an alcoholic spirit distilled from a fermented mixture of cereal grains, for example barley, wheat, or rye.

whisper (**wis** pĕr) *vb.* **whispering, whispered** to speak quietly so that other people cannot hear you.

whistle (**wi** sĕl) *n.* **1** a shrill sound produced through pursed lips or through the teeth. **2** any of many devices producing a similar sound, e.g. one on a kettle. – *vb.* **whistling, whistled**.

● **Whistler, James** (1834-1903) was an American painter who lived in Paris and London. His best known painting is *The Artist's Mother*.

white (wīt) *adj.* of the colour of snow, milk, salt, etc. – *n.* **1** white colour. **2** (also **egg-white**) the clear fluid surrounding the yolk of an egg. – *n.* **whiteness**. – *adj.* **whitish**.
white blood cell *n.* one of the colourless cells that protect the body against disease.

● **White House** the official residence of the president of the United States since 1900. It is situated in WASHINGTON D.C.. It contains the president's office as well as his living quarters.

● **Whitman, Walt** (1819-92) was an American poet whose 'free verse' caused a sensation. He is best known for his *Leaves of Grass*.

● **Whitney, Eli** (1765-1825) was the American inventor of the cotton gin, a machine that quickly removed the seeds from cotton.

● **Whitsun** (**wit** sŭn). See **feasts**.

● **Whittington, Richard** (**Dick**) (1358-1423) an English merchant and three times mayor of London. He was the subject of legends.

whittle (**wi** tĕl) *vb.* **whittling, whittled 1** to cut or carve a stick, piece of wood, etc. **2** to reduce, by cutting something out repeatedly: *They whittled down the guest list.*

who (hōō) *pron.* what person or people?: *Who did you give it to?* – *relative pron.* used to introduce a clause **1** that: *I saw the boy who gave you the frog.* **2** used to add a commenting clause: *Bellini, who was born almost 200 years ago, was a great composer.*
whoever *relative pron.* any person or people that: *Whoever is appointed must face this challenge.* – *pron.* no matter who: *Whoever calls, I'm out.*

who'd (hōōd) **1** who would. **2** who had.

whole (hōl) *n.* all of something. – *adj.* **1** all of; no less than: *I'd like to eat the whole cake.* **2** in one piece: *I swallowed it whole.* **3** unbroken: *There are only two cups left whole.* – *n.* **wholeness**.
wholemeal *adj.* (of flour) made from the entire wheat grain.
wholesale *n.* the sale of goods in large quantities to a shopkeeper.
wholesome *adj.* attractively healthy.
wholly *adv.* completely; altogether.

whom (hōōm) the object form of **who**: *To whom am I speaking?*

Eli Whitney's cotton gin was used to remove seeds and impurities from cotton fibres. It was worked by hand.

Wife comes from an Old English word meaning 'woman'.

who's (hooz) **1** who is. **2** who has.

whose (hooz) *pron. & adj.* belonging to which person or people: *Whose is this jacket?* – *relative pron. & relative adj.* used to introduce a clause of whom or which: *I am talking about the children whose parents are divorced.*

why (wī) *adv.* for what reason: *Why do you ask?* – *relative pron.* for, or because of, which: *There is no reason why I should get involved.*

wick (wik) *n.* the string running up through a candle, that burns when lit.

wicked (wi kid) *adj.* **1** evil; sinful. **2** mischievous. – *n.* **wickedness**.

wicker (wi ker) *adj.* (of a basket, etc.) made of interwoven twigs, canes, etc.

wide (wīd) *adj.* **1** large in extent from side to side. **2** (of a range, selection, etc.) covering a great variety. **3** general, as opposed to particular: *We must consider the wider implications.* – *adv.* **1** over an extensive area: *I have been travelling far and wide.* **2** to the fullest extent: *She stood with legs wide apart.* – **wide awake** fully awake or alert.

widen *vb.* **widening, widened** to make wider.

widespread *adj.* extending over a wide area: *There is widespread flooding.*

widow (wi dō) *n.* a woman whose husband is dead and who has not remarried.

widower *n.* a man whose wife is dead and who has not remarried.

width (width) *n.* extent from side to side.

wife (wīf) *n.* **wives** (wīvz) the woman to whom a man is married; a married woman.

wig (wig) *n.* a false head of hair.

wigwam (wig wam) *n.* a domed tent made by Native Americans.

●**Wilberforce, William** (1759-1833) was an English reformer who campaigned against slavery and the slave trade.

wild (wīld) *adj.* **1** (of animals) untamed; not dependent on humans. **2** (of plants) growing in a natural, uncultivated state. **3** (of country) desolate and rugged. **4** unrestrained; uncontrolled; frantically excited: *The spectators went wild.* **5** (of weather) stormy: *It was a wild night.* – *n.* a wild animal's or plant's natural environment: *The zoo returned the cub to the wild.*

wildlife *n.* wild animals, birds, and plants.

Wigs today are worn mainly by actors, legal officials in some countries, and some bald people. Wigs have been found on Egyptian mummies and were worn by the Persians, Greeks, and Romans. Wig wearing by men and women became fashionable in 17th-century France. Above are shown a French officer's campaign wig of 1670 and the wig of a wealthy Spanish lady of the 1650s.

●**Wilde, Oscar** (1854-1900) was an Irish poet, dramatist, and wit. His most famous works include *The Importance of Being Earnest* and *Lady Windermere's Fan.*

●**Wilder, Thornton** (1897-1975) was an American playwright and novelist.

wilderness (wil der nes) *n.* an uncultivated or uninhabited region.

will¹ (wil) *vb.* (*auxiliary*) used **1** to form a future tense: *He will arrive soon.* **2** to express intention or determination: *We will not give in.* **3** to make requests: *Please will you shut the door?* **4** to express commands: *You will apologise to your mother immediately!* **5** to indicate willingness: *Any of our branches will exchange the goods.* **6** to make an invitation: *Will you have a coffee?*

will² (wil) *n.* **1** the determination to succeed; desire: *She has lost the will to live.* **2** a document containing instructions for the disposal of your possessions and money after your death.

●**William** is the name of two kings of England and two of Great Britain. William the First 'the Conqueror' (1066-87) and William the Second (1087-1100); and William the Third of Orange (1689-1702) and William the Fourth (1830-37).

●**Williams, Tennessee** (1911-83) was an American dramatist whose plays include *A Streetcar Named Desire* and *Cat on a Hot Tin Roof.*

willing (wil ing) *adj.* eager and co-operative.

willow (wi lō) *n.* a tree with flexible branches.

wilt (wilt) *vb.* **wilting, wilted 1** (of flowers) to droop or wither, for example from heat.

wily (wī li) *adj.* **wilier, wiliest** cunning.

●**Wimbledon** in London is the site of annual international tennis championships.

wimp (wimp) *n.* someone who is weak-willed.

win (win) *vb.* **winning, won** (wun) **1** to come first in a contest, war, election, etc. **2** to obtain by struggle or effort: *The firm won a large contract.* – *n.* a victory. – *n.* **winner**.

wince (wins) *vb.* **wincing, winced** to shrink back or grimace, e.g. in pain.

winch (winch) *n.* a drum-shaped roller round which a rope or chain is wound for hoisting or hauling heavy loads. – *vb.* **winching, winched** to hoist with a winch.

wind¹ (wind) *n.* **1** a current of air moving across the Earth's surface. **2** your breath or breath supply: *She was panting and short of wind.* – *vb.* **winding, winded** to deprive of breath temporarily: *She was winded by her fall.*

wind instrument *n.* a musical instrument such as a clarinet, flute, or trumpet, played by blowing air through it.

windmill *n.* a mill for grinding grain, or a machine for pumping water or generating electricity, operated by wind-driven sails.

windpipe *n.* the passage running from the back of the throat to the lungs, through which air passes in and out of the body.

windscreen *n.* the front window of a motor vehicle.

windsurfing *n.* a sport that combines elements of sailing and surfing, using a board equipped with a sail.

windy *adj.* **windier, windiest** exposed to, or affected by, strong wind.

wind² (wīnd) *vb.* **winding, wound** (wownd) **1** to wrap or coil around something. **2** to move along a path with many twists and turns: *The town is full of winding lanes.* **3** to tighten the spring of a clock, watch, or other clockwork device by turning a knob or key.

Window means 'wind's eye' for, besides letting in light, windows let in air. For centuries the windows of ordinary European houses had no glass in them.

window (**win** dō) *n.* an opening in a wall, usually covered with glass.

wine (wīn) *n.* an alcoholic drink made from the fermented juice of grapes, or one made from other fruits, plants, etc.

wing (wing) *n.* **1** the parts of the body on a bird, insect, or bat that are adapted for flying. **2** the structures projecting from either side of an aircraft body. **3** (in *plural*) the area at each side of a stage, where performers wait to enter.

wink (wingk) *vb.* **winking, winked** to shut an eye briefly, often as a signal to someone.

forty winks *n.* (*plural*; *colloquial*) a short sleep.

●**Winnipeg** is the capital of Manitoba province, and the name of Canada's third largest lake.

winter (**win** tĕr) *n.* the coldest season of the year, coming between autumn and spring. – *adj.* of, or belonging to, winter.

winter sports *n.* (*plural*) sports held on snow or ice, e.g. skiing and tobogganing.

An 18th-century fantail windmill. The small fantail attached to the main sail kept the main sail turned towards the wind.

wipe (wīp) *vb.* **wiping, wiped** **1** to clean or dry with a cloth, on a mat, etc. **2** to remove by wiping. **3** to rub material off a tape.

wire (wīr) *n.* **1** metal drawn out into a narrow flexible thread, used for making fences, etc. **2** a length of this, usually wrapped in insulating material, used for carrying an electric current.

wiring *n.* a circuit or system of electrical wires.

wiry *adj.* **wirier, wiriest** **1** of slight build, but strong and agile. **2** (of hair) coarse and wavy.

●**Wisconsin**. See Supplement, **USA**.

wisdom (**wiz** dŏm) *n.* **1** the ability to make sensible judgements and decisions, especially on the basis of experience, prudence, and common sense. **2** learning; knowledge.

wise (wīz) *adj.* **1** having or showing wisdom; prudent; sensible. **2** learned. – **be wise to** (*colloquial*) to be aware of.

-wise (-wīz) *suffix* **1** denoting direction or manner: *lengthwise*; *clockwise*; *likewise*; *otherwise*. **2** as regards: *money-wise*; *business-wise*.

wish (wish) *vb.* **wishing, wished** **1** to want; to desire: *I wish I'd known.* **2** to long vainly for: *I've often wished for a quieter life.*

wit (wit) *n.* **1** humour; the ability to express yourself amusingly. **2** a person with this ability. **3** (in *plural*) common sense. – **at your wits' end** (*colloquial*) reduced to despair.

PRONUNCIATION GUIDE	
fat a	all ŏ
fate ā	foot oo
fast ä	moon ōō
among å	boy oi
met e	house ow
mean ē	demon ŏ
silent ė	thing th
loch hh	this Th
fin i	but u
line ī	mute ū
quick kw	fur û
got o	brochure ů
note ō	vision zh

witch (wich) *n.* a person, especially a woman, supposed to have magical powers.

witchcraft *n.* magic or sorcery of the kind practised by witches.

with (wiTh) *prep.* **1** in the company of; partnering or co-operating: *I danced with him.* **2** by means of; using: *They raised it with a crowbar.* **3** used after verbs of covering, providing, etc.: *The pit was filled with rubbish; They are equipped with firearms.* **4** as a result of: *She was shaking with fear.* **5** at the same time or rate as: *Discretion comes with age.* **6** used in describing: *They saw a man with a limp.*

withdraw (wiTh **drŏ**) *vb.* **withdrawing, withdrew** (wiTh **drōō**), **withdrawn 1** to move somewhere else more secluded: *She withdrew into her bedroom.* **2** (of troops) to move back; to retreat. **3** to pull in or back: *She withdrew her hand from his.*

withdrawn *adj.* shy or reserved.

wither (wi Thĕr) *vb.* **withering, withered 1** (of plants) to dry up and die. **2** to fade and disappear: *Love that never withers.*

within (wiTh **in**) *prep.* inside; enclosed by: *This must stay within these four walls.*

without (wiTh **owt**) *prep.* **1** not having the company of: *She went home without him.* **2** deprived of: *I can't live without her.* **3** not having: *There was a blue sky without a cloud.* **4** not giving, showing, etc.: *He obeyed without a murmur.*

withstand (wiTh **stand**) *vb.* **withstanding, withstood** (wiTh **stood**) to resist: *The wall can withstand the fiercest of storms.*

witness (wit nĕs) *n.* **1** someone who sees and can give a direct account of an event, occurrence, etc. **2** a person who gives evidence in a court of law.

witty (wit i) *adj.* **wittier, wittiest** able to express yourself cleverly and amusingly.

wizard (wi zård) *n.* a man supposed to have magic powers; a magician or sorcerer.

wobble (wo bĕl) *vb.* **wobbling, wobbled** to rock, sway, or shake unsteadily.

woe (wō) *n.* grief; misery.

wok (wok) *n.* a large bowl-shaped metal pan used in Chinese cookery.

woke, woken. See **wake**.

wolf (woolf) *n.* **wolves** (woolvz) a wild animal of the dog family, that hunts in packs. – **cry wolf** to give a false alarm.

● **Wolfe, James** (1727-59) was a general who fought against the French in North America in the Seven Years' War. He won the Battle of Quebec in which both he and the French commander, Montcalm, were killed. As a result of the victory CANADA became a British possession.

General James Wolfe's capture in 1759 of Quebec, the capital of New France (present-day Canada), ensured that Britain gained all of France's lands in North America.

woman (woo mån) *n.* **women** (wi min) **1** an adult human female. **2** women generally.

women's liberation *n.* a movement, started by women, aimed at freeing them from the disadvantages they suffer in a male-dominated society.

● At the beginning of this century women did not have the right to vote, so they were powerless to get changes through parliament or congress. In 1903 Mrs Emmeline Pankhurst and her daughter Christabel started the Women's Social and Political Union in Britain. In the

In 1893 New Zealand became the world's first country to give women equal voting rights. In the USA and Britain the struggle for suffrage (the right to vote) continued for many more years. Women demonstrated in the streets and publicized injustices through poster campaigns.

United States a women's rights convention was organized as early as 1848 by Lucretia Mott and Elizabeth Cady Stanton. It was not until 1928 that the voting laws for women became the same as those for men in Britain. In America women received the right to vote in 1920. Most people now accept that women should be judged as individuals, just as men are. Still much remains to be done before complete equality is reached.

womb (wōōm) *n.* the uterus, the organ in female mammals in which the baby develops.

wombat (**wom** bat) *n.* an Australian marsupial.

won. See **win**.

wonder (**wun** dĕr) *n.* **1** the state of mind produced by something extraordinary, new, or unexpected; amazement; awe. **2** a marvel. – *adj.* notable for accomplishing marvels: *It is a wonder drug.* – *vb.* **wondering, wondered 1** to be curious: *I often wondered about her background.* **2** to be surprised: *I shouldn't wonder if she won.* **3** to be uncertain: *I wonder whether to go.*

wonderful *adj.* **1** extraordinary. **2** excellent.

won't (wōnt) will not.

wood (wood) *n.* **1** the material which forms the trunk and branches of trees; this used in building, for making furniture, etc., or as a fuel. **2** (in *singular* or *plural*) an expanse of growing trees. – *adj.* made of, or using, wood.

● Wood is one of the most useful materials that we use. It can be sawn, carved, and worked into all kinds of shapes. There are two types of wood: softwood and hardwood. Softwood comes mostly from conifers. Much of it is turned into pulp for making paper and plastics. Hardwood comes from broad-leaved trees and is used for furniture and construction work.

woodcutter *n.* a person who fells trees and chops wood.

wooden *adj.* **1** made of wood. **2** (of an actor, performance, etc.) lacking liveliness and expression; stiff.

woodpecker *n.* a bird with a strong, sharp beak with which it bores into tree bark searching for insects to eat.

woodwind *n.* any of the orchestral wind instruments including the flute, oboe, clarinet, and bassoon.

woodwork *n.* the art of making things out of wood; carpentry.

wool (wool) *n.* **1** the soft wavy hair of sheep and certain other animals. **2** this spun into yarn for knitting or weaving. – *adj.* made of wool.

woollen *adj.* **1** made of wool. **2** producing, or dealing in, goods made of wool: *The town has many woollen manufacturers.* – *n.* (often in *plural*) a woollen, especially knitted, piece of clothing.

● **Woolf, Virginia** (1882-1941) was an English novelist, author of *Mrs Dalloway, To the Lighthouse*, and *The Waves*.

word (wûrd) *n.* **1** the smallest unit of spoken or written language that can stand alone. **2** a brief conversation on a particular matter: *I'd like a word with you.* **3** news or notice: *She sent word she'd arrive tomorrow.* – *vb.*

wording, worded to express in carefully chosen words: *She worded her refusal tactfully.* – **have words** (*colloquial*) to quarrel.

word processor *n.* an electronic machine with a screen, into which text can be entered by a keyboard and organized, stored, updated, and printed out. – *n.* **word-processing**.

● **Wordsworth, William** (1770-1850) was an English Romantic poet.

wore. See **wear**.

work (wûrk) *n.* **1** physical or mental effort made in order to achieve or make something; labour, study, research, etc. **2** employment: *He is out of work.* **3** your place of employment. **4** the product of mental or physical labour: *This is a splendid piece of work.* **5** a literary, artistic, musical, or dramatic composition or creation: *We are studying the complete works of Milton.* **6** (in *plural*) building or repair operations: *There were traffic jams because of the roadworks.* **7** (in *plural*; *colloquial*)

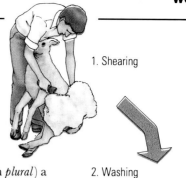

1. Shearing

2. Washing

3. Squeezing

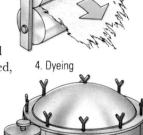

4. Dyeing

5. Carding

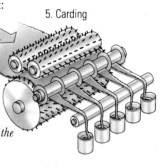

6. Roving

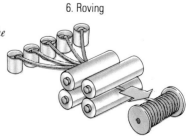

The fleece is clipped with electric shears and washed to remove grease and dirt (1&2). The wool is then squeezed to remove water and dyed (3&4). The wool is 'carded' through wire-toothed rollers to produce loose ropes called 'slivers' (5). A number of slivers are rolled (roving) into a thin rope which will be used to spin yarn (6).

the operating parts of a watch or machine. – *adj.* relating to, suitable for work: *I'm wearing my work clothes.* – *vb.* **working, worked** **1** to do work; to toil, labour, or study. **2** to be employed; to have a job; to perform the tasks and duties involved in a job: *He works a nine-hour day.* **3** to operate properly: *Does this radio work?* – *vb.* **work off** to get rid of energy or a feeling by energetic activity.

worker *n.* **1** a person who works. **2** amongst social insects such as bees or ants, a female that does the work of the colony.

workforce *n.* the number of workers engaged in a particular industry, factory, etc.

workload *n.* the amount of work expected of a person or machine.

work station *n.* a person's seat at a computer terminal.

world (wûrld) *n.* **1** the Earth; the planet we inhabit. **2** the people inhabiting the Earth; humankind: *We must tell the world.* **3** human affairs: *They discussed the present state.* **4** **World** the people of a particular region or period, and their culture: *the Third World.* – *adj.* of, relating to, or important throughout, the whole world: *I took part in the world championships.* – **the best of both worlds** the benefits of both alternatives with the drawbacks of neither.

worldly *adj.* **worldlier, worldliest** relating to this world; material, not spiritual or eternal: *They left behind all their worldly possessions when they fled the country.*

● **World War, First** (1914-18) between the Allied Powers (Britain, France, Russia, and later the United States) and the Central Powers (Germany, Austria-Hungary, and Turkey) was caused by territorial rivalries. It became bogged down in unremitting trench warfare with enormous loss of life. In this futile costly war the Allied Powers eventually won. Indirect consequences were the break up of the Austro-Hungarian empire, and revolution in Russia.

● **World War, Second** (1939-45) was between the Allies (led by Britain, France, Russia, and later the United States) and the Axis Powers (HITLER's Germany, MUSSOLINI's Italy, and Japan). The immediate causes were HITLER's invasion of Poland (1939) and the Japanese attack on Pearl Harbor (1941). The Allied Invasion of France in 1944 led to the liberation of Europe and Germany's defeat. The dropping of two atomic bombs on Japan in 1945 ended the war in the east.

worm (wûrm) *n.* **1** a long slender animal without backbone or limbs, found in soil; an earthworm. **2** the larva of any of various insects; a grub.

worn (wörn). See **wear**. – *adj.* **1** looking old and weary. **2** thin and threadbare through long use.

A gas mask. Gas was one of the new horrors of warfare.

For four years, fighting in the First World War centred around two lines of trenches stretching across western Europe – the Western Front. There was no decisive battle. Conditions in the dirty, waterlogged trenches became increasingly intolerable.

worry (wu ri) *vb.* **worries, worrying, worried** 1 to be anxious. 2 to cause anxiety to. 3 to bother. – *n.* **worries** 1 a state of anxiety. 2 a cause of anxiety. – *adj.* **worried about.** – *n.* **worrier.**

worse (wûrs) *adj.* (*comparative* of **bad**) 1 more bad: *To be blind or deaf – which is worse?* 2 more grave, serious, or acute. – *n.* something worse: *Worse was to follow.* – *adv.* less well; more badly. **worsen** *vb.* **worsening, worsened** to grow worse.

worship (wûr ship) *vb.* **worshipping, worshipped** 1 to honour God or a god with praise, prayer, hymns, etc. 2 to love or admire, especially blindly; to idolize. – *n.* **worshipper.**

There are over 20,000 species of worm. They include segmented worms such as earthworms, marine worms (lugworms) and leeches, parasites such as the tapeworm or flatworms.

worst (wûrst) *adj.* (*superlative* of **bad**) 1 most bad, awful, unpleasant, etc. 2 most grave or severe. – *n.* the worst thing or possibility: *I hope the worst is over.* – *adv.* most severely; most badly: *That was the worst I've ever played.*

worth (wûrth) *n.* 1 value; importance; usefulness. 2 the quantity of anything that can be bought for a certain sum, accomplished in a certain time, etc.: *We lost a thousand pounds' worth of equipment and three days' worth of work.* – *adj.* having a value of: *This painting is worth several thousand pounds.*

worthless *adj.* of no value or merit.

worthwhile *adj.* worth the time, money, or energy spent; useful or rewarding.

People first worshipped life-giving mother goddesses. Early farmers worshipped and asked the help of nature gods, such as the Sun and Moon.

worthy (wûr Thi) *adj.* **worthier, worthiest** admirable; deserving: *I support several worthy causes.* – *adv.* **worthily.** – *n.* **worthiness.**

would (wood) *vb.* used as past tense of **will** 1 in reported speech: *She said she would leave at ten.* 2 to indicate willingness, readiness, or ability: *He was asked to help, but would not.* 3 to indicate habitual action: *He would always telephone at six.* 4 in making polite invitations, offers, or requests: *Would you like to go?*

would-be *adj.* hoping or pretending to be.

wouldn't (wood ênt) would not.

wound¹. See **wind²**.

wound² (woond) *n.* an injury to living animal or plant tissue, caused by a cut, blow, etc. – *vb.* **wounding, wounded.**

wove, woven. See **weave.**

wrap (rap) *vb.* **wrapping, wrapped** *vb.* 1 to fold or wind something around something else: *She wrapped the shawl round the baby.* 2 to cover something in something: *Wrap up this present.*

wrapper *n.* a cover round a packet, etc.

wrath (roth) *n.* anger; fury. – *adj.* **wrathful.**

wreak (rēk) *vb.* **wreaking, wreaked** (especially *old*) 1 to cause damage on a disastrous scale. 2 to take revenge on someone.

wreath (rēth) *n.* a ring-shaped garland of flowers and leaves placed on a grave, or hung up as a decoration.

wreck (rek) *n.* 1 the destruction of a ship at sea. 2 a hopelessly damaged ship; a crashed aircraft; a ruined vehicle. 3 (*colloquial*) someone in a bad state of fitness or mental health. – *vb.* **wrecking, wrecked** to break; to destroy.

wren (ren) *n.* a very small songbird with short wings and a tail that sticks up.

●**Wren, Christopher** (1632-1723) was an English architect who designed St Paul's Cathedral and 50 other churches after the Great Fire of London (1666).

wrench (rench) *vb.* **wrenching, wrenched** 1 to pull or twist violently: *He wrenched the shelf off the wall.* 2 to sprain an ankle, etc.

Worm has not always meant 'earthworm'. It was originally used to describe dragons and serpents.

wrestle (re sĕl) *vb.* **wrestling, wrestled 1** to fight by trying to grip and throw your opponent; to do this as a sport. **2** to struggle: *She wrestled with her conscience for many days.* – *n.* **wrestler**.

wrestling *n.* the sport in which each of two opponents tries to throw the other to the ground, without striking with the fist.

Wrestling, the oldest sport of all, goes back over 4,500 years. In Japan today, Sumo wrestlers (left) are national heroes.

wretched (re chid) *adj.* **1** miserable and unhappy. **2** poor: *They lived in a wretched hovel.*

wriggle (ri gĕl) *vb.* **wriggling, wriggled** to twist to and fro. – *n.* a wriggling action.

wright (rīt) *n. suffix* a maker or repairer: *a playwright, shipwright, wheelwright*, etc.

● **Wright Brothers** Orville (1871-1948) and Wilbur (1867-1912) were American inventors who built and flew the first person-carrying aeroplane in 1903.

● **Wright, Frank Lloyd** (1867-1959) was an American architect who pioneered the use of new materials (for example reinforced concrete).

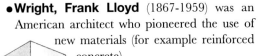

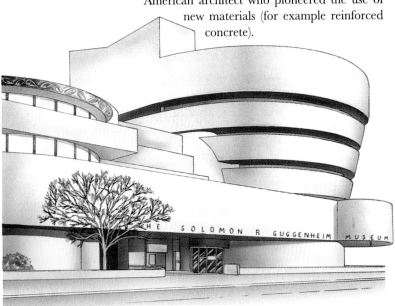

wring (ring) *vb.* **wringing, wrung** (rung) **1** to force liquid out of something by twisting or squeezing. **2** to break the neck of a bird by twisting. – **wringing wet** soaking wet.

wrinkle (ring kĕl) *n.* **1** a crease or line in the skin. **2** a slight crease in any surface. – *vb.* **wrinkling, wrinkled** to develop wrinkles.

wrist (rist) *n.* **1** the joint between the hand and arm. **2** the part of a sleeve covering this:

writ (rit) *n.* a legal document by which someone is required to do or stop doing something.

write (rīt) *vb.* **writing, wrote** (rōt), **written** (ri tĕn) **1** to produce letters, symbols, numbers, words, sentences, etc. on a surface, usually using a pen or pencil. **2** to compose or create a book, music, newspaper articles, etc. **3** to make or fill in a document, form, etc.: *The doctor wrote a prescription.*

writer *n.* a person who writes, especially as a living; an author.

writing *n.* **1** written or printed words. **2** handwriting. **3** the art or activity of writing books, poetry, etc.

wrong (rong) *adj.* **1** not correct. **2** mistaken: *I was quite wrong about her motives.* **3** not appropriate or suitable: *I'm always saying the wrong thing.* **4** not good; not sensible: *It's wrong to waste the good weather.* **5** bad: *It's wrong to tell lies.* **6** defective or faulty: *There is something wrong with the radio.* **7** causing trouble, pain, etc.: *She wouldn't cry unless something was wrong with her.* – *n.* **1** whatever is not right or just: *I know right from wrong.* **2** any injury done to someone else: *He did her wrong.*

wrongdoer *n.* a person guilty of an illegal act. – *n.* **wrongdoing**.

wrote. See **write**.

wrung. See **wring**.

wry (rī) *adj.* **wryer, wryest** or **wrier, wriest 1** slightly mocking or bitter; ironic. **2** (of a facial expression) with the features twisted into a grimace in reaction to a bitter taste, etc.

● **Wycliffe, John** (1328-84) was a religious reformer who began the first translation of the Bible into English.

● **Wyoming**. See Supplement, **USA**.

The Guggenheim Museum in New York, completed in 1960, is perhaps Frank Lloyd Wright's best known building. Inside a spiral ramp runs from the ground floor to the ceiling.

X x

X (eks) *symbol* **1** (especially in mathematics; also **x**) an unknown quantity. **2** the Roman numeral for ten. **3** a mark used to symbolize a kiss, to indicate an error, etc.

● **Xavier, Saint Francis** (1506-52) was a Spanish missionary who helped to found the JESUITS. He is called 'the Apostle of the Indies' because of his missionary journeys to India, China, the East Indies, and Japan. His feast day is 3 December.

xenophobia (zen ồ fōb i å) *n.* intense fear or dislike of foreigners or strangers.

Xerxes, king of Persia, failed to conquer Greece. In 480 BC from a hillside overlooking the Bay of Salamis he watched the swift Greek triremes crush his fleet.

Xerox (zē roks) *n.* a type of photographic process used for copying documents.

● **Xerxes the First** (**the Great**) (519-465 BC) was a king of Persia who won a victory over Greece at Thermopylae but his fleet was later defeated at Salamis.

Xhosa (kō så) *n.* **1** a member of a group of Bantu-speaking people of southern Africa. **2** the Bantu language of the Xhosa, recognizable by the use of click sounds.

Xmas (**kris** mås) or (**eks** mås) *n. (colloquial)* short for **Christmas**.

X-ray (**eks** rā) *n.* **1** (usually in *plural*) an electromagnetic ray which can pass through most substances except metal and bone, producing an image on photographic film. The image shows the outline of the objects through which the X-ray does not pass, e.g. the bones of a hand. **2** a photograph taken using X-rays. – *vb.* **X-raying, X-rayed** to take a photograph using X-rays.

● X-rays were discovered by accident in 1895 by William Roentgen while he was passing electricity through gas.

xylophone (**zī** lồ fŏn) *n.* a musical instrument consisting of a series of wooden, or sometimes metal, bars of different lengths, played by being struck by wooden hammers. Xylophone takes its name from two Greek words, *xylo* meaning 'wood' and *phonos* meaning 'sound'. – *n.* **xylophonist**.

The letter *X*, like all the letters, has a long history. The earliest alphabets were taken and adapted by the Greeks. The Greek *beta*, when combined with the first letter, *aleph*, gives us the word alphabet.

The Greeks passed on their letters to the Romans who developed the alphabet we use today, although they used only capital letters. Small letters developed in the AD 700s.

An early form of the letter X, used in the Middle East over 3000 years ago.

This letter was taken by the Greeks and became xi.

Over the years different versions of the letter X have been developed.

Y y

yacht (yot) *n.* a boat or small ship, usually with sails, often with an engine, built and used for racing or cruising. – *n.* **yachting**.

yak (yak) *n.* **yaks** or **yak** a type of long-haired ox found in Tibet.

yam (yam) *n.* **1** a large edible potato-like root. **2** (especially *southern US*) a sweet potato.

yap (yap) *vb.* **yapping, yapped** (of a puppy or small dog) to give a high-pitched bark.

yard¹ (yärd) *n.* **1** a unit of length equal to 3 feet (0.9144m).
  yardstick *n.* a standard for comparison.

yard² (yärd) *n.* **1** an area of enclosed ground near a building; enclosed ground used for a special purpose: *a shipyard.* **2** (*US*) a garden.

yarn (yärn) *n.* thread spun from wool, cotton.

yashmak (**yash** mak) *n.* a veil worn by MUSLIM women, covering the face below the eyes.

yawn (yön) *vb.* **yawning, yawned** to open the mouth wide and take a deep breath when tired or bored. – *n.* an act of yawning.

year (yēr) *n.* **1** the period of time the

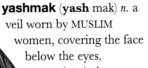

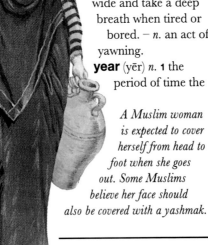

A Muslim woman is expected to cover herself from head to foot when she goes out. Some Muslims believe her face should also be covered with a yashmak.

Earth takes to go once round the Sun, about 365 days; the equivalent time for any other planet. **2** the period from 1 January to 31 December – 365 days, except in a leap year, when it is 366 days.
  yearly *adj.* happening every year; once a year.

yearn (yûrn) *vb.* **yearning, yearned** to feel a great desire. – *n.* **yearning**.

yeast (yēst) *n.* a substance which causes fermentation, used to make dough rise in bread-making, etc.

yell (yel) *n.* a loud shout or cry. – *vb.* **yelling, yelled** to shout.

Old Faithful in Yellowstone National Park, a geyser that spouts a plume of hot water 45 m high every hour.

yellow (ye lō) *adj.* **1** of the colour of gold, egg-yolk, a lemon, etc.: *Yellow is a primary colour.* – *n.* the colour of gold, butter, egg-yolk, etc.

● **Yellow River** (China). See **Huang Ho**.

● **Yellowstone National Park** was established in 1872 and is the oldest and largest park in the United States. It lies in Wyoming, Idaho, and Montana. It has about 10,000 hot springs. The most famous of these is Old Faithful, a geyser that erupts once an hour.

● **Yeltsin, Boris** (1931-) was elected president of RUSSIA in 1991.

●**Yemen Republic**. See Supplement, **Countries**.

yen (yen) *n.* **yen** the standard unit of Japanese currency.

yesterday (**yes** tẽr di) *n. & adv.* **1** the day before today. **2** the recent past.

yet (yet) *adv.* **1** up till now or then; by now or by that time: *He had not yet arrived.* **2** at this time; now; as early as this: *You can't leave yet.* **3** at some time in the future; before the matter is finished; still: *She may yet make a success of it.*

yeti (**ye** ti) *n.* the abominable snowman, an ape-like creature supposed to live in the Himalayas.

yew (ū) *n.* (also **yew tree**) an evergreen tree with dark needle-like leaves and red berries.

Yiddish (**yid** ish) *n.* a language spoken by many Jews, based on medieval German. It gets its name from the German word *Jüdisch*, which means Jewish.

yield (yēld) *vb.* **yielding, yielded 1** to produce or supply as a crop or natural product: *Cows yield milk.* **2** to surrender.

yob (yob) *n.* (*slang*; also **yobbo** (**yo** bō), **yobbos** or **yobboes**) a lout or hooligan.

yoga (**yō** gå) *n.* **1** a system of HINDU philosophy showing how to free the soul from reincarnation and reunite it with God. **2** a system of physical and mental discipline.

yoghurt, yogurt, or **yoghourt** (**yog** ůrt) or (**yōg** ůrt) *n.* a type of semi-liquid food made from fermented milk.

yoke (yōk) *n.* **1** a wooden frame placed over the necks of oxen to hold them together when they are pulling a plough, cart, etc. **2** something oppressive; a great burden: *the yoke of slavery.* – *vb.* **yoking, yoked** to join or unite.

yolk (yōk) *n.* the yellow part of an egg.

Yom Kippur (yom **ki** půr) or (yōm ki **pōōr**) *n.* the Day of Atonement, an annual JEWISH religious festival devoted to repentance for past sins and celebrated with fasting and prayer.

yonder (**yon** dẽr) *n. & adv.* (situated) over there.

you (ū) *pron.* **1** the person or persons, etc. spoken or written to. **2** any or every person: *You don't often see that nowadays.*

you'd (ūd) **1** you would. **2** you had.

you'll (ūl) **1** you will. **2** you shall.

young (yung) *adj.* in the first part of life, growth, etc.; not old. – *n.* (*plural*) young animals or birds: *Some birds feed their young on insects.*

●**Young, Brigham** (1801-77) was the American religious leader of the MORMONS, who led his followers to settle in Salt Lake City.

your (ūr) or (yör) *adj.* belonging to you: *This is your scarf, I think.*
  yours *pron.* something belonging to you: *Is this scarf mine or is it yours?*
  yourself *pron.* **yourselves 1** the reflexive form of **you**. **2** used for emphasis: *You must do what you yourself think best.*

Yoga is intended to remove all distractions that may prevent a person from reaching a physical and mental state to live a life of the spirit. The physical training gets more and more difficult and its aim is to bring the body under complete control.

you're (ūr) or (yör) you are.

youth (ūth) *n.* **1** the early part of life, between childhood and adulthood. **2** a boy or young man. **3** (*plural*) young people in general.
  youthful *adj.* young, especially in maner or appearance. – *n.* **youthfulness**.
  youth hostel *n.* a place for young people, especially hikers, on holiday, where cheap and simple accommodation is provided.

yo-yo (**yō** yō) *n.* **yo-yos** a toy consisting of a reel which spins up and down on a string.

●**Yugoslavia** is a country in south-eastern Europe (in the Balkans) and until 1992 consisted of six federal republics: Serbia, Croatia, Slovenia, Montenegro, Bosnia-Hercegovina, and Macedonia. Today it comprises Serbia and Montenegro. See also Supplement, **Countries**.

●**Yukon Territory** is a region of north-western CANADA, on the border with Alaska.

Yule (ūl) *n.* Christmas.

yuppie or **yuppy** (**yu** pi) *n.* **yuppies** (*colloquial*) an ambitious young professional person.

PRONUNCIATION GUIDE	
fat a	all ö
fate ā	foot oo
fast ä	moon o͞o
among å	boy oi
met e	house ow
mean ē	demon ỏ
silent ẽ	thing th
loch hh	this Th
fin i	but u
line ī	mute ū
quick kw	fur û
got o	brochure ů
note ō	vision zh

YE OLDE TEA SHOPPE Strictly speaking it is quite incorrect to pronounce the Ye in 'Ye Olde Tea Shoppe' as *yee*. The y represents a discarded Anglo-Saxon letter called *thorn* which looked a bit like Y. (It survives in modern Icelandic.) The letter has been replaced by *th*. So we should really say 'The Olde Tea Shoppe'!

Z z

● **Zaire**. See Supplement, **Countries**.

● **Zaire River** in Central AFRICA, formerly called
the Congo. It is Africa's second longest river,
after the NILE.

● **Zambia**. See Supplement, **Countries**.

zany (**zā** ni) *adj.* **zanier, zaniest** amusingly
crazy; wildly mad in a funny kind of way.

*Modern Zimbabwe is named after the
African walled city of Great Zimbabwe
which was built between the 11th and
14th centuries. Nobody knows who
built it or why it was built, but the
city seems to have been a centre of
religion and the gold trade.*

zap *vb.* (zap) **1** to destroy
suddenly. **2** to change TV
channels etc. frequently
using a remote control device.

zeal (zēl) *n.* great enthusiasm.
  zealous *adj.* enthusiastic; keen.
zebra (**ze** brå) or (**zē** brå) *n.* **zebras** or **zebra** a
  black-and-white striped animal of the horse
  family, found wild in Africa.
  zebra crossing *n.* (*British*) a pedestrian
  crossing marked by black and white stripes.
zenith (**ze** nith) *n.* the highest point in the sky.
zero (**zēr** ō) *n.* **zeros** the number or figure 0.
zest (zest) *n.* **1** keen enjoyment; enthusiasm. **2** in
  cooking, the peel of an orange or lemon.
Zeus. See **Myths and Legends**.
ziggurat (**zig** oo rat) *n.* a pyramid-like temple
  in ancient MESOPOTAMIA.

zigzag (zig **zag**) *n.* one of two or more sharp
bends to right and left in a path, etc. – *adj.*
having sharp bends to right and left. – *vb.*
zigzagging, zigzagged to move in a zigzag
path or manner.

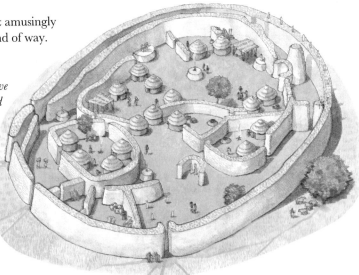

● **Zimbabwe**. See Supplement, **Countries**.

zinc (zingk) *n.* a bluish-white metallic element
(symbol **Zn**) used in brass.
zinnia (**zin** i å) *n.* an originally tropical
American plant cultivated for its showy
flowers.
Zion (**zī** on) *n.* **1** the hill on which part of
Jerusalem stands, often taken as representing
Jerusalem itself. **2** the JEWISH people.
zip (zip) *n.* (also **zip fastener** &, especially *US*,

zipper) a device for fastening clothes, bags, etc., in which two rows of metal or nylon teeth fit into each other when a sliding tab is pulled along them.

zip code *n.* in the UNITED STATES, a postal code with a five-figure number.

zither (**zi** Ther) *n.* a stringed musical instrument which is played by plucking while resting on a table or on the player's knees.

zloty (**zlot** i) *n.* **zloty** or **zlotys** the principal money currency of Poland. The words means 'golden'.

zodiac (**zō** di ak) *n.* an imaginary belt across the sky through which the Sun, Moon, and planets appear to move, divided into twelve equal parts called the **signs of the zodiac**. Each sign is named after a CONSTELLATION which used to lie in it (although the signs and constellations now no longer match up) and corresponds in astrology to a different part of the year and to a particular human character-type.

● **Zola, Emile** (1840-1902) was a French novelist who intervened in the DREYFUS affair with *J'Accuse*, an open letter to the President of France.

zombie or **zombi** (**zom** bi) *n.* a corpse brought to life again by magic.

zone (zōn) *n.* an area or region of a country, town, etc., especially one marked out for a special purpose or by a particular feature. – *vb.* **zoning, zoned** to divide into zones; to mark as a zone. – *adj.* **zonal**.

zoo (zōō) *n.* a place where wild animals are kept for the public to see, and for study, breeding, etc.

zoology (zōō ol o̊ ji) or (zō ol o̊ ji) *n.* the scientific study of animals. – *n.* **zoologist**.

zoom (zōōm) *vb.* **zooming, zoomed 1** to move very quickly, making a loud low-pitched buzzing noise. **2** to move very quickly: *The aircraft zoomed past us.* – *n.* the act or sound of zooming. – *vb.* **zoom in** to direct a camera towards someone or something using a zoom lens to make the person or thing appear to come closer.

● **Zulu** a member of the Bantu people of AFRICA, noted for their massive physique.

● **Zürich** is the largest city in SWITZERLAND and famous for its banking and finance houses.

The first people to study the **zodiac**, over 4,000 years ago, were the astronomers of ancient Babylon. They divided it into 12 sections with a group of stars in each section.

Thousands of years ago people divided the stars into groups or constellations. Few of these patterns resemble what they are supposed to be, although with a bit of imagination Leo can look quite lion-like!

The Egyptian mummy case (above) shows Nut, sky goddess, surrounded by signs of the zodiac, many of which are still in use.

1 Capricorn (Goat) 22 Dec. – 19 Jan.
2 Aquarius (Water carrier) 20 Jan. – 18 Feb.
3 Pisces (Fish) 19 Feb. – 20 March
4 Aries (Ram) 21 March – 19 April
5 Taurus (Bull) 20 April – 20 May
6 Gemini (Twins) 21 May – 21 June

7 Cancer (Crab) 22 June – 22 July
8 Leo (Lion) 23 July –22 Aug.
9 Virgo (Virgin) 23 Aug. – 22 Sept.
10 Libra (Scales) 23 Sept.– 23 Oct.
11 Scorpio (Scorpion) 24 Oct. – 21 Nov.
12 Sagittarius (Archer) 22 Nov. – 21 Dec.

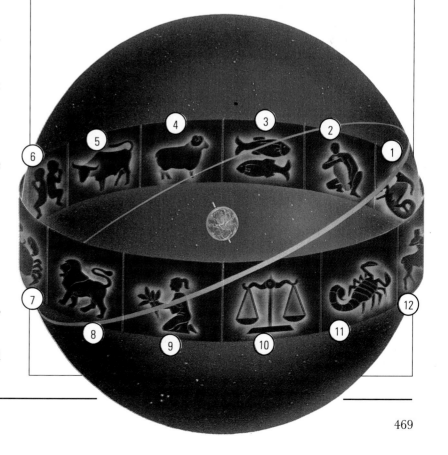

SUPPLEMENT

COUNTRIES OF THE WORLD

Country	Adjective	Capital	Currency	Language
Afghanistan	Afghan	Kabul	Afghani	Pushtu
Albania	Albanian	Tirane	Lek	Albanian
Algeria	Algerian	Algiers	Dinar	Arabic
Andorra	Andorran	Andorra La Vella	Franc/Peseta	Catalan
Angola	Angolan	Luanda	Kwanza	Portuguese
Antigua & Barbuda	Antiguan/Barbudan	St John's	Dollar	English
Argentina	Argentinian or Argentine	Buenos Aires	Peso	Spanish
Armenia	Armenian	Yerevan	Rouble	Armenian
Australia	Australian	Canberra	Dollar	English
Austria	Austrian	Vienna	Schilling	German
Azerbaijan		Baku	Manat	Azerbaijani
Bahamas	Bahamian	Nassau	Dollar	English
Bahrain	Bahraini	Manamah	Dinar	Arabic/English
Bangladesh	Bangladeshi	Dhaka	Taka	Bengali
Barbados	Barbadian	Bridgetown	Dollar	English
Belarus	Belarussian	Minsk	Rouble	Belorussian
Belgium	Belgian	Brussels	Franc	Dutch/French
Belize	Belizian	Belmopan	Dollar	English
Benin	Beninese	Porto Novo	Franc	French
Bhutan	Bhutanese	Thimphu	Ngultrum	Dzongkha
Bolivia	Bolivian	La Paz	Boliviano	Spanish
Bosnia & Hercegovina	Bosnian	Sarajevo	Dinar	Serbo-Croat
Botswana	Botswanan	Gaborone	Pula	English/Setswana
Brazil	Brazilian	Brasilia	Cruzado	Portuguese
Brunei	Bruneian	Bandar Seri	Dollar	Malay Begawan
Bulgaria	Bulgarian	Sofia	Lev	Bulgarian
Burkina Faso	Burkinese	Ouagadougou	Franc	French
Burundi	Burundian	Bujumbura	Franc	French/Kirundi
Cambodia	Cambodian	Phnom Penh	Riel	Khmer
Cameroon	Cameroonian	Yaoundé	Franc	English/French
Canada	Canadian	Ottawa	Dollar	English/French
Cape Verde	Cape Verdean	Praia	Escudo	Portuguese
Central African Republic		Bangui	Franc	French
Chad	Chadian	N'Djamena	Franc	French
Chile	Chilean	Santiago	Peso	Spanish
China	Chinese	Beijing	Yuan	Chinese
Colombia	Colombian	Bogotá	Peso	Spanish
Comoros	Comoran	Moroni	Franc	French/Arabic
Congo	Congolese	Brazzaville	Franc	French

Country	Adjective	Capital	Currency	Language
Costa Rica	Costa Rican	San José	Colon	Spanish
Côte d'Ivoire		Abidjan	Franc	French
Croatia	Croatian	Zagreb	Dinar	Serbo-Croatian
Cuba	Cuban	Havana	Peso	Spanish
Cyprus	Cypriot	Nicosia	Pound	Greek/Turkish
Czech Republic	Czech	Prague	Koruna	Czech
Denmark	Danish	Copenhagen	Krone	Danish
Djibouti	Djiboutian	Djibouti	Franc	French/Arabic
Dominica	Dominican	Roseau	Dollar	English
Dominican Republic	Dominican	Santo Domingo	Peso	Spanish
Ecuador	Ecuadorean	Quito	Sucre	Spanish
Egypt	Egyptian	Cairo	Pound	Arabic
El Salvador	Salvadorean	San Salvador	Colon	Spanish
Equatorial Guinea	Guinean	Malabo	Franc	Spanish
Eritrea	Eritrean	Asmera		
Estonia	Estonian	Tallinn	Kroon	Estonian
Ethiopia	Ethiopian	Addis Ababa	Birr	Amharic
Fiji	Fijian	Suva	Dollar	English
Finland	Finnish	Helsinki	Markka	Finnish/Swedish
France	French	Paris	Franc	French
Gabon	Gabonese	Libreville	Franc	French
Gambia, The	Gambian	Banjul	Dalasi	English
Georgia	Georgian	Tbilisi	Lary	Georgian
Germany	German	Berlin	Mark	German
Ghana	Ghanaian	Accra	Cedi	English
Greece	Greek	Athens	Drachma	Greek
Grenada	Grenadian	St George's	Dollar	English
Guatemala	Guatemalan	Guatemala City	Quetzal	Spanish
Guinea	Guinean	Conakry	Franc	French
Guinea-Bissau	Guinean	Bissau	Peso	Portuguese
Guyana	Guyanese	Georgetown	Dollar	English
Haiti	Haitian	Port-au-Prince	Gourde	French
Honduras	Honduran	Tegucigalpa	Lempira	Spanish
Hungary	Hungarian	Budapest	Forint	Hungarian
Iceland	Icelandic	Reykjavik	Krona	Icelandic
India	Indian	New Delhi	Rupee	Hindi/English
Indonesia	Indonesian	Jakarta	Rupiah	Bahasa
Iran	Iranian	Tehran	Rial	Farsi (Persian)
Iraq	Iraqi	Baghdad	Dinar	Arabic
Ireland, Republic of	Irish	Dublin	Pound (Punt)	English/Gaelic
Israel	Israeli	Jerusalem	Shekel	Hebrew/Arabic
Italy	Italian	Rome	Lira	Italian
Ivory Coast see Côte d'Ivoire				
Jamaica	Jamaican	Kingston	Dollar	English
Japan	Japanese	Tokyo	Yen	Japanese
Jordan	Jordanian	Amman	Dinar	Arabic
Kazakhstan	Kazakh	Almaty	Tenge	Kazakh
Kenya	Kenyan	Nairobi	Shilling	English/Swahili
Kiribati	Kiribati	Tarawa	Dollar	English
Korea, North	Korean	Pyongyang	Won	Korean
Korea, South	Korean	Seoul	Won	Korean

Country	Adjective	Capital	Currency	Language
Kuwait	Kuwaiti	Kuwait	Dinar	Arabic
Kyrgyzstan		Bishkek	Som	Kyrgyz
Laos	Laotian	Vientiane	Kip	Lao
Latvia	Latvian	Riga	Lat	Latvian
Lebanon	Lebanese	Beirut	Pound	Arabic
Lesotho	Lesuthan	Maseru	Loti	English/Sesotho
Liberia	Liberian	Monrovia	Dollar	English
Libya	Libyan	Tripoli	Dinar	Arabic
Liechtenstein	Liechtenstein	Vaduz	Franc	German
Lithuania	Lithuanian	Vilnius	Litas	Lithuanian
Luxembourg	Luxembourger	Luxembourg	Franc	French/German
Macedonia	Macedonian	Skopje	Denar	Macedonian
Madagascar	Madagascan	Antananarivo	Franc	French/Malagasy
Malawi	Malawian	Lilongwe	Kwacha	English/Chichewa
Malaysia	Malaysian	Kuala Lumpur	Ringgit	Malay
Maldives	Maldivian	Male	Rufiyaa	Divehi
Mali	Malian	Bamako	Franc	French
Malta	Maltese	Valletta	Lira	English
Marshall Is.		Majuro	US Dollar	English
Mauritania	Mauritanian	Nouakchott	Ouguiya	Arabic/French
Mauritius	Mauritian	Port Louis	Rupee	English
Mexico	Mexican	Mexico City	Peso	Spanish
Micronesia	Micronesian	Palikir	US Dollar	English
Moldova	Moldavian	Chisinau	Leu	Romanian
Monaco	Monegasque	Monaco	Franc	French
Mongolia	Mongolian	Ulan Bator	Tugrik	Mongolian
Morocco	Moroccan	Rabat	Dirham	Arabic
Mozambique	Mozambican	Maputo	Metical	Portuguese
Myanmar	Burmese	Yangon	Kyat	Burmese
Namibia	Namibian	Windhoek	Rand	English
Nauru	Nauruan	Yaren	Dollar	English/Nauruan
Nepal	Nepalese	Kathmandu	Rupee	Nepali
Netherlands	Dutch	Amsterdam	Guilder	Dutch
New Zealand	New Zealand	Wellington	Dollar	English
Nicaragua	Nicaraguan	Managua	Cordoba	Spanish
Niger	Nigerien	Niamey	Franc	French
Nigeria	Nigerian	Abuja	Naira	English
Norway	Norwegian	Oslo	Krone	Norwegian
Oman	Omani	Muscat	Rial	Arabic
Pakistan	Pakistani	Islamabad	Rupee	Urdu
Panama	Panamanian	Panama City	Balboa	Spanish
Papua New Guinea	Papua New Guinean	Port Moresby	Kina	English
Paraguay	Paraguayan	Asunción	Guarani	Spanish
Peru	Peruvian	Lima	Sol	Spanish
Philippines	Filipino	Manila	Peso	English/Filipino
Poland	Polish	Warsaw	Zloty	Polish
Portugal	Portuguese	Lisbon	Escudo	Portuguese
Qatar	Qatari	Doha	Riyal	Arabic
Romania	Romanian	Bucharest	Leu	Romanian
Russia	Russian	Moscow	Rouble	Russian
Rwanda	Rwandan	Kigali	Franc	French/Kinyarwanda

Country	Adjective	Capital	Currency	Language
St Christopher (Kitts) & Nevis	Kittsian/Nevisian	Basseterre	Dollar	English
St Lucia	St Lucian	Castries	Dollar	English
St Vincent & the Grenadines	St Vincentian	Kingstown	Dollar	English
San Marino	San Marinese	San Marino	Lira	Italian
São Tomé and Príncipe	São Toméan	São Tomé	Dobra	Portuguese
Saudi Arabia	Saudi Arabian	Riyadh	Riyal	Arabic
Senegal	Senegalese	Dakar	Franc	French
Seychelles	Seychellois	Victoria	Rupee	English/French
Sierra Leone	Sierra Leonean	Freetown	Leone	English
Singapore	Singaporean	Singapore	Dollar	Malay/Tamil/Chinese
Slovakia	Slovakian	Bratislava	Koruna	Slovak
Slovenia	Slovenian	Ljubljana	Tolar	Slovenian
Solomon Islands	Solomon Islander	Honiara	Dollar	English
Somalia	Somali	Mogadishu	Shilling	Somali
South Africa	South African	Pretoria & Capetown	Rand	Afrikaans/English
Spain	Spanish	Madrid	Peseta	Spanish
Sri Lanka	Sri Lankan	Colombo	Rupee	Sinhalese/Tamil
Sudan	Sudanese	Khartoum	Dinar	Arabic
Suriname	Surinamese	Paramaribo	Guilder	Dutch
Swaziland	Swazi	Mbabane	Lilangeni	English/Swazi
Sweden	Swedish	Stockholm	Krona	Swedish
Switzerland	Swiss	Berne	Franc	French/German/Italian
Syria	Syrian	Damascus	Pound	Arabic
Taiwan	Taiwanese	Taipei	Dollar	Chinese
Tajikistan	Tajikistan	Dushanbe	Rouble	Tajik
Tanzania	Tanzanian	Dar es Salaam	Shilling	Swahili/English
Thailand	Thai	Bangkok	Baht	Thai
Togo	Togolese	Lomé	Franc	French
Tonga	Tongan	Nuku'alofa	Pa'anga	Tongan/English
Trinidad & Tobago	Trinidadian/Tobagian	Port of Spain	Dollar	English
Tunisia	Tunisian	Tunis	Dinar	Arabic
Turkey	Turkish	Ankara	Lira	Turkish
Turkmenistan	Turkmen	Ashgabat	Manat	Turkmen
Tuvalu	Tuvaluan	Fongafale	Dollar	Tuvaluan/English
Uganda	Ugandan	Kampala	Shilling	English
Ukraine	Ukrainian	Kiev	Karbovanets	Ukrainian
United Arab Emirates	Emirian	Abu Dhabi	Dirham	Arabic
United Kingdom	British	London	Pound	English/Welsh
United States	American	Washington DC	Dollar	English
Uruguay	Uruguyan	Montevideo	Peso	Spanish
Uzbekistan	Uzbek	Tashkent	Som	Uzbek
Vanuatu	Vanuatuan	Port Vila	Vatu	Bislama/English/French
Vatican City			Lira	Latin/Italian
Venezuela	Venezuelan	Caracas	Bolivar	Spanish
Vietnam	Vietnamese	Hanoi	Dong	Vietnamese
Western Samoa	Samoan	Apia	Tala	Samoan/English
Yemen	Yemeni	Sana'a	Rial	Arabic
Yugoslavia (Serbia & Montenegro)	Yugoslavian	Belgrade	Dinar	Serbo-Croat
Zaire	Zairean	Kinshasa	Zaire	French
Zambia	Zambian	Lusaka	Kwacha	English
Zimbabwe	Zimbabwean	Harare	Dollar	English

COUNTIES OF THE UNITED KINGDOM AND THE REPUBLIC OF IRELAND

England	
County	*County Town*
1. Avon	Bristol
2. Bedfordshire (Beds.)	Bedford
3. Berkshire (Berks.)	Reading
4. Buckinghamshire (Bucks.)	Aylesbury
5. Cambridgeshire (Cambs.)	Cambridge
6. Cheshire (Ches.)	Chester
7. Cleveland	Middlesbrough
8. Cornwall (Corn.)	Truro
9. Cumbria	Carlisle
10. Derbyshire (Derbys.)	Matlock
11. Devon	Exeter
12. Dorset	Dorchester

13. Durham (Dur.)	Durham	57. Grampian	Aberdeen
14. East Sussex	Lewes	58. Highland	Inverness
15. Essex	Chelmsford	59. Lothian	Edinburgh
16. Gloucestershire (Glos.)	Gloucester	60. Strathclyde	Glasgow
17. Greater London	London	61. Tayside	Dundee
18. Greater Manchester	Manchester	*Islands*	
19. Hampshire (Hants.)	Winchester	62. Orkney	Kirkwall
20. Hereford & Worcester	Worcester	63. Shetland	Lerwick
21. Hertfordshire (Herts.)	Hertford	64. Western Isles	Stornoway
22. Humberside	Kingston-upon-Hull		
23. Isle of Wight (IOW)	Newport		
24. Kent	Maidstone	**Wales**	
25. Lancashire (Lancs.)	Preston	65. Clwyd	Mold
26. Leicestershire (Leics.)	Leicester	66. Dyfed	Carmarthen
27. Lincolnshire (Lincs.)	Lincoln	67. Gwent	Cwmbran
28. Merseyside	Liverpool	68. Gwynedd	Caernarfon
29. Norfolk	Norwich	69. Mid Glamorgan	Cardiff (Caerdedd)
30. Northamptonshire (Northants.)	Northampton	70. Powys	Llandrindod
31. North Yorkshire	Northallerton	71. South Glamorgan	Cardiff (Caerdedd)
32. Northumberland	Morpeth	72. West Glamorgan	Swansea (Aber Tawe)
33. Nottinghamshire (Notts.)	Nottingham		
34. Oxfordshire (Oxon.)	Oxford		
35. Shropshire	Shrewsbury	**Republic of Ireland**	
36. Somerset (Som.)	Taunton	*Provinces*	*Counties*
37. South Yorkshire	Barnsley	73. Connacht	Galway
38. Staffordshire (Staffs.)	Stafford		Leitrim
39. Suffolk	Ipswich		Mayo
40. Surrey	Kingston-upon-Thames		Roscommon
41. Tyne and Wear	Newcastle-upon-Tyne		Sligo
42. Warwickshire (War.)	Warwick	74. Leinster	Carlow
43. West Midlands	Birmingham		Dublin
44. West Sussex	Chichester		Kildare
45. West Yorkshire	Wakefield		Kilkenny
46. Wiltshire (Wilts.)	Trowbridge		Laoighis
			Longford
			Louth
Northern Ireland			Meath
47. Antrim	Belfast		Offaly
48. Armagh	Armagh		Westmeath
49. Down	Downpatrick		Wexford
50. Fermanagh (Ferm.)	Enniskillen		Wicklow
51. Derry	Londonderry	75. Munster	Clare
52. Tyrone	Omagh		Cork
			Kerry
			Limerick
Scotland			Tipperary
Regions			Waterford
53. Borders	Newton St Boswells	76. Ulster	Cavan
54. Central	Stirling		Donegal
55. Dumfries & Galloway	Dumfries		Monaghan
56. Fife	Glenrothes		

US STATES

State	Abbreviation	Capital	Bird	Flower
Alabama	AL	Montgomery	Yellowhammer	Camellia
Alaska	AK	Juneau	Willow ptarmigan	Forget-me-not
Arizona	AZ	Phoenix	Cactus wren	Saguaro
Arkansas	AR	Little Rock	Mockingbird	Apple blossom
California	CA	Sacramento	Valley quail	Golden poppy
Colorado	CO	Denver	Lark bunting	Rocky Mountain columbine
Connecticut +	CT	Hartford	Robin	Mountain laurel
Delaware +	DE	Dover	Blue hen chicken	Peach blossom
Florida	FL	Tallahassee	Mockingbird	Orange blossom
Georgia +	GA	Atlanta	Brown thrasher	Cherokee rose
Hawaii	HI	Honolulu	Hawaiian goose	Hibiscus
Idaho	ID	Boise	Mountain bluebird	Mock orange
Illinois	IL	Springfield	Cardinal	Native violet
Indiana	IN	Indianapolis	Cardinal	Peony
Iowa	IA	Des Moines	Eastern goldfinch	Wild rose
Kansas	KS	Topeka	Western meadow lark	Sunflower
Kentucky	KY	Frankfort	Kentucky cardinal	Goldenrod
Louisiana	LA	Baton Rouge	Brown pelican	Magnolia
Maine	ME	Augusta	Chikadee	White pine cone and tassel
Maryland +	MD	Annapolis	Baltimore oriole	Black-eyed Susan
Massachusetts +	MA	Boston	Chicadee	Mayflower
Michigan	MI	Lansing	Robin	Apple blossom
Minnesota	MN	St Paul	Common loon	Pink and white lady's slipper
Mississippi	MS	Jackson	Mockingbird	Magnolia
Missouri	MO	Jefferson City	Bluebird	Hawthorn
Montana	MT	Helena	Western meadowlark	Bitterroot
Nebraska	NE	Lincoln	Western meadowlark	Goldenrod
Nevada	NV	Carson City	Mountain bluebird*	Sagebrush*
New Hampshire +	NH	Concord	Purple finch	Purple lilac
New Jersey +	NJ	Trenton	Eastern goldfinch	Purple violet
New Mexico	NM	Santa Fe	Roadrunner	Yucca
New York +	NY	Albany	Bluebird	Rose
North Carolina +	NC	Raleigh	Cardinal	Flowering dogwood
North Dakota	ND	Bismarck	Western meadowlark	Wild prairie rose
Ohio	OH	Columbus	Cardinal	Scarlet carnation
Oklahoma	OK	Oklahoma City	Scissor-tailed flycatcher	Mistletoe
Oregon	OR	Salem	Western meadowlark	Oregon grape
Pennsylvania +	PA	Harrisburg	Ruffed grouse	Mountain laurel
Rhode Island +	RI	Providence	Rhode Island Red	Violet
South Carolina +	SC	Columbia	Carolina wren	Carolina jessamine
South Dakota	SD	Pierre	Ring-necked pheasant	American pasque flower
Tennessee	TN	Nashville	Mocking bird	Iris
Texas	TX	Austin	Mocking bird	Blue bonnet
Utah	UT	Salt Lake City	Seagull	Sego lily
Vermont	VT	Montpelier	Hermit thrush	Red clover
Virginia +	VA	Richmond	Cardinal	Flowering dog-wood
Washington	WA	Olympia	Willow goldfinch	Coast rhododendron
West Virginia	WV	Charleston	Cardinal	Rhododendron
Wisconsin	WI	Madison	Robin	Wood violet
Wyoming	WY	Cheyenne	Meadowlark	Indian paintbrush

+ One of the 13 original states   * Unofficial

PRESIDENTS OF THE UNITED STATES

	In office	Party
1. George Washington (1732-1799)	1789-97	Federalist
2. John Adams (1735-1826)	1797-1801	Federalist
3. Thomas Jefferson (1743-1826)	1801-09	Democratic-Republican
4. James Madison (1751-1836)	1809-17	Democratic-Republican
5. James Monroe (1758-1831)	1817-25	Democratic-Republican
6. John Quincy Adams (1767-1848)	1825-29	Democratic-Republican
7. Andrew Jackson (1767-1845)	1829-37	Democrat
8. Martin Van Buren (1782-1862)	1837-41	Democrat
9. William Henry Harrison (1773-1841)	1841	Whig
10. John Tyler (1790-1862)	1841-45	Whig
11. James Knox Polk (1795-1849)	1845-49	Democrat
12. Zachary Taylor (1784-1850)	1849-50	Whig
13. Millard Fillmore (1800-74)	1850-53	Whig
14. Franklin Pierce (1804-69)	1853-57	Democrat
15. James Buchanan (1791-1868)	1857-61	Democrat
16. Abraham Lincoln+ (1809-65)	1861-65	Republican
17. Andrew Johnson (1808-75)	1865-69	National Union
18. Ulysses Simpson Grant (1822-85)	1869-77	Republican
19. Rutherford B. Hayes (1822-93)	1877-81	Republican
20. James Abram Garfield+ (1831-81)	1881	Republican
21. Chester Alan Arthur (1829-86)	1881-85	Republican
22. Grover Cleveland (1837-1908)	1885-89	Democrat
23. Benjamin Harrison (1833-1901)	1889-93	Republican
24. Grover Cleveland (1837-1908)	1893-97	Democrat
25. William McKinley+ (1843-1901)	1897-1901	Republican
26. Theodore Roosevelt (1858-1919)	1901-09	Republican
27. William Howard Taft (1857-1930)	1909-13	Republican
28. Woodrow Wilson (1856-1924)	1913-21	Democrat
29. Warren Gamaliel Harding (1865-1923)	1921-23	Republican
30. Calvin Coolidge (1872-1933)	1923-29	Republican
31. Herbert Clark Hoover (1874-1964)	1929-33	Republican
32. Franklin Delano Roosevelt (1882-1945)	1933-45	Democrat
33. Harry S. Truman (1884-1972)	1945-53	Democrat
34. Dwight David Eisenhower (1890-1969)	1953-61	Republican
35. John Fitzgerald Kennedy+ (1917-63)	1961-63	Democrat
36. Lyndon Baines Johnson (1908-73)	1963-69	Democrat
37. Richard Milhous Nixon (1913-94)	1969-74	Republican
38. Gerald Rudolph Ford (1913-)	1974-77	Republican
39. James Earl Carter (1924-)	1977-81	Democrat
40. Ronald Wilson Reagan (1911-)	1981-89	Republican
41. George H.W. Bush (1924-)	1989-93	Republican
42. William Jefferson Clinton (1946-)	1993 -	Democrat

+ Assassinated in office

RULERS OF ENGLAND, SCOTLAND AND GREAT BRITAIN

Saxon	Ruled
Egbert	827-839
Ethelwulf	839-858
Ethelbald	858-860
Ethelbert	860-866
Ethelred	866-871
Alfred the Great	871-899
Edward the Elder	899-924
Athelstan	924-939
Edmund	939-946
Edred	946-955
Edwy	955-959
Edgar	959-975
Edward the Martyr	975-978
Ethelred the Unready	978-1016
Edmund Ironside	1016

Danes	
Canute	1016-35
Harold I Harefoot	1035-40
Hardicanute	1040-42

Saxon	
Edward the Confessor	1042-66
Harold II	1066

House of Normandy	
William I the Conqueror	1066-87
William II	1087-1100
Henry I	1100-35
Stephen I	1135-54

House of Plantagenet	
Henry II	1154-89
Richard I	1189-99
John	1199-1216
Henry III	1216-72
Edward I	1272-1307
Edward II	1307-27
Edward III	1327-77
Richard II	1377-99

House of Lancaster	
Henry IV	1399-1413
Henry V	1413-22
Henry VI	1422-61

House of York	
Edward IV	1461-83
Edward V	1483
Richard III	1483-85

House of Tudor	
Henry VII	1485-1509
Henry VIII	1509-47
Edward VI	1547-53
Mary I	1553-58
Elizabeth I	1558-1603

House of Stuart	
Rulers of Scotland	
Robert II	1371-90
Robert III	1390-1406
James I	1406-37
James II	1437-60
James III	1460-88
James IV	1488-1513
James V	1513-42
Mary	1542-67
James VI	1567-1625
Rulers of Great Britain	
James I (VI of Scotland)	1603-25
Charles I	1625-49
(Commonwealth	1649-60)
Charles II	1660-85
James II (VII)	1685-88
William III 1689-1702 jointly with Mary II	1689-94
Anne	1702-14

House of Hanover	
George I	1714-27
George II	1727-60
George III	1760-1820
George IV	1820-30
William IV	1830-37
Victoria	1837-1901
Edward VII	1901-10

House of Windsor	
George V	1910-36
Edward VIII	1936
George VI	1936-52
Elizabeth II	1952-

PRIME MINISTERS

United Kingdom (since 1900)

Arthur James Balfour *Conservative*	1902-05
Henry Campbell Bannerman *Liberal*	1905-08
Herbert Henry Asquith *Liberal*	1908-15
Herbert Henry Asquith *Coalition*	1915-16
David Lloyd George *Coalition*	1916-22
Andrew Bonar Law *Conservative*	1922-23
Stanley Baldwin *Conservative*	1923-24
James Ramsay MacDonald *Labour*	1924
Stanley Baldwin *Conservative*	1924-29
James Ramsay MacDonald *Labour*	1929-31
James Ramsay MacDonald *National*	1931-35
Stanley Baldwin *National*	1935-37
Arthur Neville Chamberlain *National*	1937-40
Winston Churchill *Coalition*	1940-45
Clement Attlee *Labour*	1945-51
Winston Churchill *Conservative*	1951-55
Anthony Eden *Conservative*	1955-57
Harold Macmillan *Conservative*	1957-63
Alec Douglas-Home *Conservative*	1963-64
Harold Wilson *Labour*	1964-70
Edward Heath *Conservative*	1970-74
Harold Wilson *Labour*	1974-76
James Callaghan *Labour*	1976-79
Margaret Thatcher *Conservative*	1979-90
John Major *Conservative*	1990-

Canada (since 1900)

Sir Robert L. Borden	1911-20
Arthur Meighen	1920-21
W.L. Mackenzie King	1921-30
R.B. Bennett	1930-35
W.L. Mackenzie King	1935-48
Louis St Laurent	1948-57
John G. Diefenbaker	1957-63
Lester B. Pearson	1963-68
Pierre Trudeau	1968-79
Charles (Joe) Clark	1979-1980
Pierre Trudeau	1980-84
John Turner	1984
Brian Mulroney	1984-1993
Kim Campbell	1993
Jean Chrétien	1993-

Australia (since 1900)

Edmund Barton	1901-03
Alfred Deakin	1903-04
John C. Watson	1904
George Houston Reid	1904-05
Alfred Deakin	1905-08
Andrew Fisher	1908-09
Alfred Deakin	1909-10
Andrew Fisher	1910-13
Joseph Cook	1913-14
Andrew Fisher	1914-15
William M. Hughes	1915-23
Stanley M. Bruce	1923-29
James H. Scullin	1929-31
Joseph A. Lyons	1932-39
Robert Gordon Menzies	1939-41
Arthur William Fadden	1941
John Curtin	1941-45
Joseph Chiefley	1945-49
Robert Gordon Menzies	1949-66
Harold Edward Holt	1966-67
John Grey Gorton	1968-71
William McMahon	1971-72
Edward Gough Whitlam	1972-75
John Malcolm Fraser	1975-83
Robert James Hawke	1983-91
Paul Keating	1991-

New Zealand (since 1900)

William Hall Jones	1906
Joseph George Ward	1906-12
Thomas Mackenzie	1912
William Ferguson Massey	1912-25
Francis Henry Dillon Bell	1925
Joseph Gordon Coates	1925-28
Joseph George Ward	1928-30
George William Forbes	1930-35
Michael J. Savage	1935-40
Peter Fraser	1940-49
Sidney J. Holland	1949-57
Keith J. Holyoake	1957
Walter Nash	1957-60
Keith J. Holyoake	1960-72
Sir John Marshall	1972
Norman Kirk	1972-74
Wallace Rowling	1974-75
Robert Muldoon	1975-84
David Lange	1984-89
Geoffrey Palmer	1989-90
Mike Moore	1990
Jim Bolger	1990-

We should like to thank the following artists who have contributed to **Chambers Children's Illustrated Dictionary**:

Jonathan Adams 37,390, 433, 440 **Graham Allen** 320 **Hemesh Alles** 90, 109, 176, 195, 292, 325, 361, 439, 451 **Marion Appleton** 31, 67, 90, 49, 169, 217, 224, 227, 228, 263, 265, 290, 291, 311, 340, 351, 352, 353, 357, 405, 415, 417, 427, 446, 447, 469 **Craig Austin** 193, 213, 307, 314, 373, 341 **Noel Bateman** 280 **Bampton & Thornton** 148 **Sue Barclay** 436 **Owain Bell** 101, 274 **Richard Bonson** 81, 103, 122, 166, 234, 246, 301, 349, 353, 361, 395, 423 **J. Bowgins** 302 **Trevor Boyer** 303 **Maggie Brand** 178 **Peter Bull** 89, 310, 304 **Norma Burgin** 242 **John Butler** 148, 248, 290 **Vanessa Card** 70, 88, 120, 128, 204, 215, 218, 228, 254, 270, 382 **Tony Chance** 175, 263 **Jim Channel** 308 **Kuo Kang Chen** 47, 216, 244, 364, 380, 381, 390, 405, 454 **Jeanne Colville** 245, 277 **Stephen Conlin** 11, 210, 267 **David Cook** 86 **Richard Coombes** 398 **Joanne Cowne** 262, 269 **Peter Dennis** 102, 350, 356, 372, 385, 452 **Richard Draper** 129, 202, 252, 401, 409 **J. Dugdale** 76 **Dave Etchell** 12, 129, 219, 249, 323 **James Field** 263 **Michael Fisher** 32, 75, 87, 297, 321, 400, 412, 429, 444, 466 **Eugene Fleury** 18, 27, 35, 39, 73, 90, 154, 155, 207, 228, 280, 441 **Chris Foley** 185 **Wayne Ford** 150 **Werner Forman** 216 **Chris Forsey** 32, 116, 140, 165, 229, 242, 243, 273, 278, 318, 394, 423, 447, 448, 449, 464, 466 **John Francis** 192 **Mark Franklin** 93, 96, 101, 105, 145, 162, 219, 247, 279, 338, 344, 388, 421, 417, 457 **Oliver Frey** 447 **Terence Gabbey** 31, 37, 65, 87, 195, 207, 229, 258, 261, 264, 378, 428, 429, 452, 463 **Garden Studio** 285 **John Gillatt** 219 **Simon Girling Associates** 64 **Matthew Gore** 383, 440, 474 **Jeremy Gower** 40, 99, 122, 235, 238, 253, 282, 329, 330, 332, 355, 390, 408 **Peter Gregory** 267, 275 **Sally Gregory** 273 **Ray Grinaway** 28, 36, 94, 113, 181, 343, 410, 419 **Alan Hardcastle** 282 **Nick Harris** 273 **Allen Harris** 161, 331 **R. Hayward** 120, 133, 240 **Nick Hewetson** 67, 109, 198, 207, 224, 296 **David Holmes** 69, 251 **Richard Hook** 114, 235, 332, 339 **Lisa Horstman** 367 **Simon Huson** 295 **André Hrydziusko** 111, 260, 262 **Ian Jackson** 150, 277, 452 **John James** 24, 46, 90, 224, 241, 275, 311, 345, 420, 434 **Ron Jobson** 151, 245, 276, 324, 364, 365, 454 **Kevin Jones Associates** 108 **Peter Jones** 97 **Felicity Kayes** 220 **Roger Kent** 113, 118, 173, 237, 349, 362 **S. Kent** 305 **Peter Kestervan** 352, 462 **Deborah Kindred** 228, 239, 263, 269, 311, 352, 354, 468 **Steve Kirk** 327, 437 **Mike Lacy** 252 **Adrian Lascom** 236 **S. Latibeaudiere** 368 **Christopher Lenthall** 229, 291, 352, 460 **D.Lewis** 344 **Jason Lewis** 259, 420, 442, 459 **Linden Artists** 209 **J. Lloyd** 452 **Bernard Long** 87, 382 **Mike Long** 154 **Chris Lyon** 145, 151, 218, 224, 291, 344 **Andrew Macdonald** 39, 313 **Louis Mackay** 200, 211, 342 **Kevin Maddison** 26, 40, 46, 84, 87, 109, 216, 233, 261, 291, 305, 316, 352, 377, 442 **Mainline Design** 64, 76, 96, 101, 104, 105, 145, 181, 184, 186, 188, 213, 293, 333, 338, 349, 350, 351, 400, 409, 439, 464, 469 **Alan Male** 177, 221, 462 **Maltings Partnership** 12, 14, 19, 23, 26, 29, 30, 31, 34, 37, 43, 44, 49, 53, 56, 57, 58, 59, 60, 62, 63, 70, 74, 75, 83, 84, 89, 92, 94, 97, 101, 103, 104, 105, 105, 110, 111, 112, 115, 121, 126, 134, 135, 144, 154, 164, 173, 183, 185, 188, 190, 194, 196, 201, 211, 226, 233, 236, 244, 256, 271, 284, 291, 296, 307, 317, 334, 371, 378, 385, 413, 426, 452, 467 **Janos Marffy** 74, 87, 120, 231, 263, 425 **John Marshall** 261 **Josephine Martin** 24, 115, 126, 142, 153, 174, 283, 312, 319, 379 **David McHallister** 305 **Angus McBride** 65, 167 **Doreen McGuiness** 347 **Brian McIntyre** 246 **Eva Melhuish** 328 **David More** 172 **Stefan Morris** 399 **Tony Morris** 314 **Edward Mortelmans** 435 **William Olliver** 187, 450 **Denys Orender** 15 **Chris Orr** 218, 418 **Liz Pepperell** 240 **Melvyn Pickering** 218, 318 **Malcolm Porter** 70, 158 **Portram Artists** 20 **Sebastian Quigley** 334, 430, 435 **Elizabeth Rice** 122, 445 **Paul Richardson** 369, 427, 463 **John Ridyard** 459 **Bernard Robinson** 54, 303, 424 **Eric Robson** 25, 28, 42, 69, 139, 255, 383, 396, 456 **Michael Roffe** 36, 44, 88, 93, 224, 231, 324, 350, 362, 390, 392, 417, 443 **David Russell** 37, 392 **David Salariya** 323 **John Scorey** 446 **Rodney Shackell** 305 **Nick Shewling** 304 **Rob Shone** 272, 318, 422, 445 **Mark Stacey** 318, 363 **Roger Stewart** 304 **Mike Taylor** 169, 377, 410 **Guy Smith** 238, 358, 364, 386, 387, 432, 470, 474, 477, 478, 479 **Simon Tegg** 407 **Temple Art Agency** 78 **G. Thompson** 416 **G. Thurston** 129 **Guy Troughton** 187, 198, 376 **Tudor Art** 202 **Brian Watson** 178 **Ross Watton** 321, 326 **Rosie Watts** 27 **Tracy Wayte** 419 **Philip Weare** 322, 359, 381, 426 **David Wright** 48, 58, 229, 268, 282, 309, 364, 428